CRITICAL SURVEY OF POETRY

Second Revised Edition

Volume 6

E. J. Pratt - Wallace Stevens

Editor, Second Revised Edition
Philip K. Jason
United States Naval Academy

Editor, First Edition, English and Foreign Language Series
Frank N. Magill

SALEM PRESS, INC.
Pasadena, California   Hackensack, New Jersey

∞ The paper used in these volumes conforms to the American National Standard for Permanence of Paper for Printed Library Materials, Z39.48-1992(R1997).

Library of Congress Cataloging-in-Publication Data

Critical survey of poetry / Philip K. Jason, editor.—2nd rev. ed.

p. cm.

Combined ed. of: Critical survey of poetry: foreign language series, originally published 1984, Critical survey of poetry: supplement, originally published 1987, and Critical survey of poetry: English language series, rev. ed. published 1992. With new material. Includes bibliographical references and index.

ISBN 1-58765-071-1 (set : alk. paper) — ISBN 1-58765-077-0 (v. 6 : alk. paper) —

1. Poetry—History and criticism—Dictionaries. 2. Poetry—Bio-bibliography. 3. Poets—Biography—Dictionaries. I. Jason, Philip K., 1941 - .

PN1021 .C7 2002
809.1′003—dc21 2002008536

Third Printing

PRINTED IN THE UNITED STATES OF AMERICA

CONTENTS

COMPLETE LIST OF CONTENTS

VOLUME 1

VOLUME 2

VOLUME 3

VOLUME 4

VOLUME 5

VOLUME 6

VOLUME 7

VOLUME 8

CRITICISM AND THEORY

POETRY AROUND THE WORLD

RESEARCH TOOLS

INDEXES

CRITICAL SURVEY
OF
POETRY

E. J. Pratt

Born: Western Bay, Newfoundland; February 4, 1882
Died: Toronto, Ontario, Canada; April 26, 1964

Principal poetry

Rachel: A Sea Story of Newfoundland in Verse, 1917
Newfoundland Verse, 1923
The Witches' Brew, 1925
Titans, 1926
The Iron Door: An Ode, 1927
The Roosevelt and the Antinoe, 1930
Many Moods, 1932
The Titanic, 1935
The Fable of the Goats and Other Poems, 1937
Brébeuf and His Brethren, 1940
Dunkirk, 1941
Still Life and Other Verse, 1943
Collected Poems, 1944
They Are Returning, 1945
Behind the Log, 1947
Ten Selected Poems, 1947
Towards the Last Spike, 1952
Magic in Everything, 1955
The Collected Poems of E. J. Pratt, 1958
Here the Tides Flow, 1962

Other literary forms

E. J. Pratt's career as a poet began with an unpublished verse drama, *Clay*. The play is weak in many ways, but as a whole it shows Pratt's early interest in dramatic intensity, a characteristic of his later poetry. *Clay* reveals the poet's increasing ability to control monologue and dialogue within a larger literary structure. Other literary efforts include two short stories ("'Hooked': A Rocky Mountain Experience," 1914, and "Golfomania," 1924), critical articles, reviews, and introductions to books (most notably, Herman Melville's 1929 edition of *Moby Dick*, and Thomas Hardy's 1937 edition of *Under the Greenwood Tree*). Two other works of significance are his published thesis, *Studies in Pauline Eschatology and Its Background* (1917) and his religious verses and hymns, included in Denzil D. Ridout's *United to Serve* (1927).

Achievements

To define E. J. Pratt's accomplishment is problematic: He is the best-known and most respected of all Canadian poets, yet he is an isolated and a solitary figure. His achievement is based on compelling and moving lyric and narrative verse, but his poetic masters cannot be easily traced and his poetic disciples cannot be found. Pratt avoided formulating a strict poetic creed, and he refused to follow the rules of any poetic school; thus he cannot be conveniently categorized or explained. Pratt's artistic vision is indisputably broad, warm, humanistic, and universal. Courage in the face of a hostile natural environment, fidelity to the values that cultivate and civilize, compassion for those not always able to endure the trials of simple existence—these compose the core of Pratt's preoccupation as a poet. His success in making these concerns concrete, particular, and forceful twice won him the Governor General's Award, Canada's most coveted prize for literature.

Part of Pratt's success rests in his conviction that poetry is public writing, not private exposé or confession. By using plain language and traditional end-rhyme, as well as disarmingly simple plots or events (subtly enhancing all of these through wit, irony, and contemporary themes), Pratt created a poetry that caught the attention and earned the admiration of both the general reader and the scholar. If anything, his career marks the culmination of the poetry and poetic craft which preceded him—that of Bliss Carman, Charles G. D. Roberts, F. R. Scott, and Archibald Lampman; it also led the way to the acceptance of modernism, though Pratt stops just short of being Canada's first indisputable modernist.

Pratt's most significant contributions to Canadian literature lie in the concreteness and precision of his "impersonal" lyrics and his fast-paced, economical, direct narratives. His lyrics resemble small sculptures; the visual and emotional impact of feeling arrested in words durable as stone attracts the reader's eye. The representative images of love or hope or loss or fear captured in these poems are never clever, abstruse, academic, or strained. Pratt was the first Canadian poet to present an image and then refrain from commenting, explaining, moralizing, or philosophizing for the reader—tendencies which often characterized the poets who preceded him.

In the narratives, Pratt's contribution is even more significant. In poems such as *The Titanic* and *Brébeuf and His Brethren*, he gave shape to and refined the "documentary" narrative in verse, a form no longer popular. Pratt can be viewed as the last practitioner of direct narratives in Canadian writing. Second, Pratt was the last Canadian who did not fall under the spell of modernism *à la* T. S. Eliot or Ezra Pound. Pratt wrestled with a poetic form which he himself termed *extravaganza*. The form is based on wit, comedy, hyperbole, and discontinuity, and the narratives of this type may represent the first literary form of significance created by a Canadian.

Biography

Edwin John Pratt was born in Newfoundland, the son of John Pratt, a Methodist missionary from Yorkshire, and of Fanny Knight, a sea-captain's daughter. Pratt spent his first twenty-three years in Newfoundland, and his early life in the outport villages marked him: The sea can be felt in his rhythms and the coastal shore perceived in his imagery. In 1901, he was graduated from the Methodist College in St. John's. For nearly six years, Pratt was a probationer in the Methodist ministry who taught and preached in various villages. In 1907, he elected to go to Toronto to study philosophy at Victoria College. He soon earned his M.A. degree, then decided to complete a B.A. in divinity. In 1917, having again changed his field of study, he received his Ph.D. in psychology. Pratt married Viola Whitney in 1918; two years later she gave birth to their only child, Mildred Claire. Also in 1920, Pratt shifted careers again: This time he became a professor of English at Victoria College, a position he retained until his retirement in 1954, when the title Professor Emeritus was conferred upon him. Pratt died ten years later. In academic terms, then, this poet's training was unusually long and varied; its effects can be seen in his poetry. Pratt's early life in Newfoundland taught him to love poetry that was as direct and immediate as a ballad of the sea, and his later years of education in philosophy, divinity, psychology, and literature supplied his characteristic themes. Pratt's language is clear and plain, not regional; his themes are universal, not private.

Analysis

The poetry of E. J. Pratt falls into three categories: the shorter lyrics, the documentary-like narratives, and the *extravaganzas*. The division in form, however, does not suggest a division in outlook. Pratt is almost always concerned with the clash between the human, as individual or group, and the amoral strength and power of the natural world. As a man, Pratt admired courage, civilization, and compassion; as a poet, he celebrated their purpose, function, and value. He saw man inhabiting a world where there are no answers about the rightness of values, but he also perceived that no man can live without them. Pratt did not preach or lecture his readers, nor did he argue with them; rather, he showed his readers the paradoxes and ironies which result when a morally sensitive being inhabits an essentially amoral world.

The theme is examined most easily in Pratt's lyrics. The short poems are often elusive and complex, rich in meaning and powerful in impact. Many of the poems, moreover, begin in Pratt's own experience, but by the time he has finished with them, they are purified of the narrowly private and personal. Once Pratt has finished with a lyric, it stands open for all readers of all ages.

"Erosion"

A poem such as "Erosion" is typical of Pratt's artistry and technical mastery. When Pratt was a young boy in a Newfoundland fishing village, his father, a minister, would often, as the most trying of his duties, have to announce to a woman the death at sea of her husband or son. The shock recorded in the woman's face etched itself on the poet's mind immediately, but it took him nearly thirty years to record the experience properly in verse.

The final version of the poem is only eight lines long, and Pratt omits everything that would detract from his central idea—the impact of the sea's force upon the woman's life. Pratt dismisses his father's presence, his own presence, and the announcement of death. In their place, the poet stresses the passage of time. The first stanza of the poem portrays the sea's unending effort to "trace" features into a cliff. The features in the stone, as all those who have walked along a shoreline know, have a disconcertingly "human" look. In Pratt's poem, then, the sea has, for more than a thousand years, attempted to humanize nature (the cliff) by giving it a face.

The second stanza of the poem stresses that the woman looking at the sea-carving changes dramatically in the mere hour of watching the power and strength of a storm at sea. Possibly her son or husband is in a ship caught in that storm, but the poet deliberately avoids commenting on that point. It is enough to know that the sea has failed to complete the face in the cliff, and that the woman's face, in an hour, has turned to granite. The result, the poem suggests, is that the face of the cliff and the face of the woman resemble each other. The complex response that the short poem elicits, then, is that the sea may be humanizing the cliff, but that it is dehumanizing the woman, for she takes on a more elemental, stonelike appearance.

The poem, then, records the irony of an amoral world that appears to humanize, but, in fact, dehumanizes. The poem, however, is multileveled. Throughout the eight lines, the sea is compared to an artist who traces and sculpts his forms with diligence and care. To attribute artistic qualities to the sea outlines its creative, rather than its destructive, power. The reader who puzzles over this positive feature is on the way to an understanding of Pratt's complexity, despite the seeming simplicity. A second reading of this elusive poem suggests that the woman may be merely overawed by the sea's power, magnificence, and force. Recalcitrant nature, insensitive to the movements and powers surrounding it, requires centuries to change; the woman is transformed in her moment of insight. The rock passively undergoes its metamorphosis as the sea carves its pattern upon it. The permanence, durability, and strength of the cliff rest upon its impassive and insensible state.

The woman, in sharp contrast, observes the storm at sea and undergoes a metamorphosis springing from the inner source of being, the emotions. Unlike the cliff, which is acted upon by an outside force, the woman actively responds to what she sees. Her sensibility, in other words, sets her apart from nature. Furthermore, her ability to feel is similar to that of the sea, yet stronger; what the sea can do in a thousand years, her emotions can do in an hour. At the same time, the sculpture of the cliff resembles the sculpture on her face, a parallelism that suggests the truly complex, ambiguous, and ironic tone of the poem. The essential quality which distinguishes a human being from nature (the ability to feel) is precisely the characteristic that underscores the resemblance to it, since both must suffer physical "erosion." Ironically, the inner ability to respond affirms that human sensitivity, perception, and insight are both magnificent and frightening—in a word, awesome. Loneliness, fear, isolation, and loss are felt by all humans, and Pratt points out the irony of all human experience—the very ability to *feel* emotions can both ennoble and destroy.

"The Shark" and "From Stone to Steel"

In numerous other poems, Pratt constantly reinvigorates his theme by illustrating how man can be both elevated and demeaned by the qualities he cherishes most. In "The Shark," a speaker sees this "tubular" creature as the symbol of man's need to inhabit a world filled by creatures wholly other than man, for they are "cold-blooded." The very ability to perceive differences isolates man and adds to his fear and loneliness. In "From Stone to Steel," Pratt sees man's inherent urge to offer sacrifices as the supreme example both of man's noblest virtue and of his most ignominious vice. On one hand, the sacrifice indicates a belief in something or someone higher than man, thereby leading humans to the grace of the temple. On the other hand, the urge to sacrifice may be abused, leading man to tyranny and barbarism, for man can also force others to *become* sacrificed.

Documentary realism: "The Ice-Floes"

In the lyrics, no emotion presented by Pratt is simple or clear-cut. In fact, he delights in tracing the complexities of emotions that all humans feel and experience, but can never explain or understand. When a reader turns to the longer narratives, he is again astounded by Pratt's mastery of a direct, clear story which, on careful reading, demands all of a reader's intelligence, sensibility, and emotion. The most notable of these narratives are "The Ice-Floes," *The Titanic*, *The Roosevelt and the Antinoe*, and *Brébeuf and His Brethren*. All of the narratives listed here share the quality of "documentary" realism. Pratt carefully researched and studied the materials for these poems, and one of their features is historical accuracy. The poems are, however, profound studies of human emotion. In each work, furthermore, Pratt concentrates on the interest of a community in crisis.

"The Ice-Floes" centers upon the Newfoundland seal-hunt. A group of hunters form the focus, although the events are recorded through one spokesman. The narrative concentrates on the dangers undertaken by the men in order that they may survive in a hostile environment. The very courage, determination, and relentlessness that they display, however, makes them the victims of the elements they are attempting to overcome. Staying too late and too long on the ice floes, wholly immersed in the challenge of their hunt, they become trapped by a sudden, violent storm. Like the seals they hunt, the men have become the victims of a force they cannot master. Their dogged endurance and determination has betrayed them.

The Titanic and The Roosevelt and the Antinoe

In *The Titanic* and *The Roosevelt and the Antinoe*, Pratt again explores the need for courage, fidelity, and compassion. In *The Titanic*, he ruthlessly documents the sleep of human reason. The ship's machinery is believed to be infallible. The illusion that man can rival God by creating an unsinkable ship leads to hubris. The intelligence which can design the ocean liner fails to recognize that no human creation is perfect. The delusion holds to the end; man has created the very force that takes him to death at sea. In *The Roosevelt and the Antinoe*, the form of presentation is reversed. The captain of the ship perceives that success is based on the unpredictable toss of a wave and that no resource known to man can foretell the result. Without the courage to try, without the conviction that nature is fundamentally indifferent, Pratt's captain learns to understand, no human achievement is possible.

Brébeuf and His Brethren

The final poem of interest in Pratt's series of documentary narratives is *Brébeuf and His Brethren*. The poem is acknowledged as his masterpiece in this vein. It presents the lives of the martyrs who brought the Christian faith to Canada and who eventually died at the hands of the Indians. The climax of the poem is crucial to an understanding of the whole. Brébeuf is violently tortured by the Indians, who celebrate his murder with a mock baptism and communion. Dying, Brébeuf must endure the abuse of the very religious rites that he has taught the Indians. The rituals which are to cleanse, ennoble, and enlighten the spirit merely allow the Indians to indulge in barbarism and brutality, culminating in cannibalism. The poem, then, echoes the ambiguous sacrifices of "From Stone to Steel" and indicates Pratt's ever-increasing sense of irony in human experience and action.

In the atomic age, far removed from the pioneers and early settlers, an age wherein the products of intelligence have given man reason to fear even the best in himself, Pratt is not foreign or incomprehensible or old-fashioned. The documentary narratives may appear traditional, but their philosophical outlook is extremely modern.

Extravaganzas: The Witches' Brew

One further strand of Pratt's development should be discussed here, his extravaganzas: *The Witches' Brew*, *Titans* ("The Cachalot" and "The Great Feud"), *The Fable of the Goats*, and *Towards the Last Spike*. All of these works are characterized by wit, irony, and humor. Each is based on some kind of trial, and, by the end of every one of them, the reader's ability to master ambiguities, inconsistencies, and paradoxes is fully tested as well. In the extravaganzas, Pratt vigorously displays that no intuition or perception or theory about reality is adequate to explain the world that man inhabits. In *The Witches' Brew*, a tour de force about an alcoholic orgy among sea creatures who are visited by an incongruous assemblage of theorizers about reality—from John Calvin to Immanuel Kant—no one, including the narrator, can explain the behavior of Tom, the rakish cat from Zanzibar. The cat is partly a creature of evolution and partly a creature derived from some magic spark, but once drunk he is brutal, callous, and dangerous. *The Witches' Brew* is a black comedy centering upon man's inexplicable beginnings and his intrinsic irrationality. No one in the poem, least of all Tom, can understand why he does the things he does, and not one of the wise shades can provide an answer.

In many ways the narrative is amusing, but it is equally terrifying, for Tom murders all of his kin in the course of the poem. At each turn of events, moreover, the reader questions why the cat should be compelled to destroy every warm-blooded creature in sight. Pratt seems to be drawing upon his eclectic education to dismiss theories of Christianity, science, philosophy, and evolution. The world, Pratt's extravaganzas insist, will not conform to the expectations, wishes, theories, or desires of man or creature.

Such a vision, however, should not be read as pessimism. For Pratt, the acknowledgment of human reason is central because the admission compels men to rely on compassion, understanding, and mercy, rather than on theory or abstraction. Alexander Pope once expressed this notion by declaring that "a little knowledge is a dangerous thing"; Pratt would modify the line this way: The illusion that the quantity of knowledge can replace its quality is even more dangerous than the knowing of nothing at all.

Towards the Last Spike

In *Towards the Last Spike*, Pratt's last major narrative, he redevelops his *extravaganza* by muting its outrageousness. He now blends *extravaganza* and narrative to examine the history of the Canadian transcontinental railway. The final product is Pratt's most daring experiment, and, if it fails, it fails only in the sense that Pound's *Cantos* (1925-1972) dealing with John Adams may be said to have failed. The deliberate fragmentation, the mixture of history and invention, and the blend of the actual and the literary often tax the reader beyond endurance.

The poem is necessary, however, for a complete understanding of Pratt's aims as a poet. In *Towards the Last Spike*, Pratt wished to unify the various strands of his writing. The poem dramatizes what man can achieve with courage, compassion, and fidelity to the values that advance the ambitions of a culture. Pratt chooses for subject matter the forging of a railway line which, both metaphorically and literally, made a physical reality of a nation previously only dreamed of and talked about. It is, above all, a positive vision, although the poem is neither naïvely optimistic nor overly idealistic about human success in a world that is fundamentally *other* than sentient man. The universe cannot be conquered, controlled, or explained in Pratt's poetic vision, but man can be dignified by his actions. *Towards the Last Spike*, in a huge "Panorama," records Pratt's belief that man does not simply exist in a monstrous world, but that he is a being burdened with the awesome task of using his vision, courage, and endurance to accomplish the dreams with which he is, for some inexplicable reason, born. This constant determination to face the test is, for E. J. Pratt, man's central claim to dignity.

Other major works

short fiction: "'Hooked': A Rocky Mountain Experience," 1914; "Golfomania," 1924.

nonfiction: *Studies in Pauline Eschatology and Its Background*, 1917; "Introduction," in *Moby Dick*, 1929; "Introduction," in *Under the Greenwood Tree*, 1937.

Bibliography

Djwa, Sandra. *E. J. Pratt: The Evolutionary Vision*. Vancouver: Copp Clark, 1974. An authoritative and insightful study of Pratt and a must for scholars of his work. Particularly noteworthy is how Djwa delineates Pratt's views on the roles of fate and free will in determining human action. Especially informative is the section on how Pratt adapts his many sources for *The Titanic*.

Gingell, Susan. *E. J. Pratt on His Life and Poetry*. Toronto: University of Toronto Press, 1983. A valuable resource of Pratt's evaluation of his life and work from the mid-1920's to the 1950's. This volume provides much understanding about Pratt and his creative process. Included are two interviews Pratt gave on Canadian television in the 1950's. Gingell's introduction explores the nature of Pratt's commentaries on his work and appraises their value in terms of their literary and social context.

McAuliffe, Angela T. C. *Between the Temple and the Cave*. Ithaca, N.Y.: McGill-Queen's University Press, 2000. A critical study of Pratt's poetry with a focus on its religious aspects. Includes bibliographical references and index.

Pitt, David G. *E. J. Pratt: The Truant Years, 1882-1927*. Toronto: University of Toronto Press, 1984. The first volume in a full-length biography of Pratt, highly recommended for Pratt scholars and general readers alike. It is meticulously researched and contains plenty of biographical details to enhance understanding of Pratt's poems.

_______. *E. J. Pratt: The Master Years, 1927-1964*. Toronto: University of Toronto Press, 1987. The second volume in Pitt's biography, equally accessible to both scholar and general reader.

Vinson, James. *Great Writers of the English Language: Poets*. New York: St. Martin's Press, 1979. The entry on Pratt acknowledges that he is regarded as Canada's "pre-eminent narrative poet." Cites *Brébeuf and His Brethren* as his finest long narrative, an example of his ability to establish dramatic coherency in his verse. Notes also Pratt's preoccupation with primeval themes of conflict in his poems.

Wilson, Milton. *E. J. Pratt*. Toronto: McClelland and Stewart, 1969. A concise but comprehensive literary criticism of Pratt's works, emphasizing his strength as a narrative poet. Discusses his shorter, more lyrical poems, his longer narratives, as well as the sea poems and *Brébeuf and His Brethren*.

Ed Jewinski;
bibliography updated by the editors

Jacques Prévert

Born: Neuilly-sur-Seine, France; February 4, 1900
Died: Omonville-la-Petite, France; April 11, 1977

Principal poetry

Paroles, 1945
Histoires, 1946 (with André Verdet)
Poèmes, 1946
Contes pour enfants pas sages, 1947
La Pluie et le beau temps, 1955
Selections from "Paroles," 1958 (Lawrence Ferlinghetti, translator)
Fatras, 1966
Prévert, 1967
Arbres, 1976
Words for All Seasons, 1979
Soleil de nuit, 1980
Blood and Feathers: Selected Poems of Jacques Prévert, 1988 (includes selections from *Paroles*, *Spectacle*, *Soleil de nuit*, and more)

Other literary forms

Outside France, Jacques Prévert is best known as a screenwriter; among his credits are a number of films that have become classics of the French cinema. His first screenplay was written for his brother, Pierre Prévert, the director of *L'Affaire est dans le sac* (1932). The success of his dialogue in Jean Renoir's *Le Crime de Monsieur Lange* (1935) led to more such scripts, marked by Prévert's sparkling wit and poetic repartee. His long collaboration with director Marcel Carné (born 1909) produced eight major films by 1950, including such masterpieces as *Jenny* (1936), *Drôle de drame* (1937), and *Les Enfants du paradis* (1945; *Children of Paradise*, 1968). Many film historians credit Carné's success to Prévert's scripts, although it must be pointed out that the highly successful *Le Jour se lève* (1939) was simply adapted by Prévert from an existing script, and that Prévert also adapted the unsuccessful 1956 version of *Notre Dame de Paris*. Carné regards Prévert as "the one and only poet of the French cinema," one whose contribution "reflects the soul of the people."

Prévert's cabaret-style songs and stage pieces for the group Octobre are often overlooked in his oeuvre. Although they predate his major film successes and seem minor in comparison, these verses contain the seeds of both Prévert's screen dialogue and his later poetry. Most screenwriters of Prévert's time came to the new art burdened with preconceptions from the theater or literature, but Prévert himself simply wrote scenarios that he thought would appeal to moviegoers, and he succeeded. Many of his scripts have been published and today provide texts for students writing screenplays.

Prévert also produced several charming books for children, including *Le Petit Lion* (1947) and *Des bêtes . . .* (1950). In 1953, he wrote lyrics for Christiane Verger's *Tour de chant* and *L'Opéra de la lune*. His translation into French of the medieval *Carmina burana*, set to the music of Carl Orff, was published in 1965 and achieved high critical esteem. In the United States, Prévert is known as the lyricist of such popular songs as "Les Feuilles mortes" ("Autumn Leaves") and "Ne me quitte pas" ("Don't Leave Me").

Achievements

Despite his sweeping success, Jacques Prévert received no major literary awards. For his work as a filmmaker, he received the Grand Prix from Société des Auteurs et Compositeurs Dramatiques in 1973 and the Grand Prix National from *Cinéma* in 1975.

Jacques Prévert

The appellation "the most popular poet" (in this case, of postwar France) carries a stigma in the world of poetry, where popularity is not usually a mark of quality. The French writer Guy Jacob good-naturedly referred to Prévert's "easy-going muse," who had "lent him in place of a lyre a barrel-organ." His apparent simplicity of expression, his concern with the emotions and things of everyday life, his singsong rhythms and insistent rhymes combined to create a poetry at once accessible and self-explanatory. Prévert restored the popular validity of poetry to a literature that had been rarefied and intellectualized by movements such as Surrealism, Dadaism, and Symbolism. He refused to permit poetry to remain the means of expression of the privileged, helping himself freely to the argot of the streets for his verses.

Free of allegiance to any literary clique, Prévert reinforced the very idea of individuality at a time when the historical and political developments of World War II had necessitated conformity. A Marxist without theoretical pretensions and an anarchist at heart, he mocked pomposity and unmasked exploitation wherever he found them, all the while maintaining an aloof attitude toward partisan politics. His poetry demonstrates the charm, wit, and humanistic goals of popular poetry as well as its limitations.

Biography

The son of working-class parents, Jacques Prévert was born February 4, 1900, in Neuilly-sur-Seine. At the age of fifteen, having completed his primary education—a process he obviously did not enjoy—he left school and began to earn his living. He once, in a radio interview, confessed that, had the label "juvenile delinquent" been part of the vocabulary of the early twentieth century, it would have been applied to him.

Despite his distaste for school, Prévert read a great deal and was particularly interested in the authors of the Enlightenment and their ideas about the natural rights of man, as well as such distinctions as natural evil as opposed to human evil. Nevertheless, he quickly developed a distrust of great intellectual constructs and philosophical debate. His friendship with the Surrealist painter Yves Tanguy began in the regiment in which they both served in 1920, as part of the occupation army of Thessaloníki, Greece. There he also made the acquaintance of Marcel Duhamel, who would later become a film director. The three young men went to Paris upon their demobilization and established what they jokingly called a phalanstery (after the Fourierist communes known by that name) in the no longer extant rue de Château. Raymond Queneau, who thirty years later would write critical works on Prévert, soon joined them, and their house became a gathering point for the young writers and artists of the Surrealist movement.

A shared passion for the cinema prompted them to attend films daily, sometimes three or four in a single day. Prévert and his friends, including his brother, Pierre, later attested the significant impact of these cinematic experiences upon their later work. Prévert fondly recalled long walks in the middle of the night through the streets of Paris, from which he returned to the rue de Château full of life, and impatient with the intellectual turmoil of the Surrealists. His disdainful attitude toward the dogmatism of the movement ultimately led to his being excluded by its leader, André Breton.

Prévert circulated his poems in handwritten form, a habit that led to the existence of numerous textual variations. Between 1930 and 1936, three long poems appeared in reviews. "Souvenirs de famille, ou l'Ange garde-chiourme," published in *Bifur* in 1930, appealed to an extremely refined literary audience. In 1931, the magazine *Commerce* at first hesitated to publish "Tentative de description d'un diner de têtes à Paris-France" ("An Endeavor to Describe a Dinner of Heads at Paris, France"), but it conceded at the insistence of St.-John Perse. The third poem, "La Crosse en l'air," appeared in *Soutes* in 1936, a Communist tract more dedicated to politics than to literature. Such beginnings reflect the diversity of Prévert's appeal as well as his difficulty in getting his poetry published.

In 1933, with the theater group Octobre, Prévert visited Moscow to perform on the occasion of the International Olympiad of Theater. In 1938, he spent a year in the United States, returning home in time to be called up in the French mobilization in 1939. An attack of appendicitis prevented his military service in the war.

After the war, the Hungarian-born composer Joseph Kosma, who had worked on films with the Prévert-Carné team, began to set Prévert's verses to music, and the songs were every bit as popular as Prévert's volumes of poetry, which had also begun to appear after the war. Prévert carried his celebrity quite modestly and was regarded as a man of the people. He was, for example, a figure of interest for the most popular magazines in France, which celebrated him in interviews and profiles.

Other artistic inclinations found expression in Prévert's collages. He enjoyed two exhibitions, one in Paris in 1957 and one in 1963 in Antibes on the Riviera. In 1977, Prévert died after a long illness and was buried in a quiet, simple ceremony in his village of Omon-la-Petite near the English Channel.

Analysis

The poetry of Jacques Prévert is pervaded by an innocence that allows him to cultivate a world in which animals, plants, and objects speak or are metamorphosed at will. There is in his verse no development of a self-contained world of fable or faerie with symbolic weight; rather, the Surrealist influence manifests itself in vignettes or episodes within individual poems. Prévert brought an unaccustomedly cheerful mien to Surrealism, employing its devices not to frighten or to dwell on the victimization of men but to portray the imagination as an escape route from the dreariness of life's minor burdens.

In his less childlike or innocent verses, Prévert expresses outraged indignation at social and political injustice and is capable of piercing the affectations of those whom he considers unworthy of respect. There is a remarkable consistency of tone and outlook throughout Prévert's work, and whether one draws examples from early volumes or later ones, one finds an unchanging *Weltanschauung*. In part, this consistency can be attributed to Prévert's comparatively late success at a time when stylistic experiment was behind him.

Poems about children

From Prévert's poems about children to his antiwar utterances, there persists a naïveté that seems to challenge the values of the adult world and its rationalizations of man's inhumanity to man. Children, according to Prévert, are blessed with an innocence and a capacity to dream that can be corrupted only by growing up. One of his oft-cited poems from *Paroles*, "Page d'écriture," depicts a math lesson during which a child, seeing a lyrebird fly by, asks it for help. The bird's help is forthcoming but causes something of an insurrection in the classroom before the entire scenario is metamorphosed in the final lines into a scene from nature.

In "En sortant de l'école" (from *Histoires*), Prévert portrays the gentle fantasies of a group of children, who, upon coming out of school, discover a train with a gilded wagon to take them through the world, where the sea promenades with all of her seashells. From the same volume comes "Jour de fête," a heartfelt expression of the disappointment of a child who wants to celebrate a holiday dedicated to the frog, an animal that is not only a friend but that also sings to him nightly. The adults, who cannot comprehend this liaison, will not let the child go out in the rain. In the opening line, Prévert captures the parents' inhibiting concern: "Ou va-tu mon enfant avec ces fleurs/Sous la pluie/ Il pleut il mouille/ Aujourd'hui c'est la fête à la grenouille" ("Where are you going my child with these flowers/ in the rain/ it's raining it's pouring/ Today is a holiday in honor of the frog"). The difference between the child's world and the world of adults is expressed in another way in "Arbres" (from *Arbres*), in which a child understands when trees "speak tree"; only later, when he learns to speak "arboriculture," does he not understand the voice of the trees, the song of the wind. The dreamworld of the child is that of the poet. In "Dehors" (from *La Pluie et le beau temps*), Prévert describes a child who, dreaming, follows his dream smiling, for the dream is hilarious and almost alive. In "Encore une fois sur le fleuve" (from *Histoires*), Prévert advises: "alors fais comme moi . . ./ parle seulement des choses heureuses/ des choses merveilleuses rêvées et arrivées . . ." ("Then do as I . . . / speak only of happy things/ of marvelous things dreamed and come to pass . . .").

ANIMALS

Some of Prévert's most charming poems are addressed, in fact, to children by way of amusing descriptions of animals. *Contes pour enfants pas sages* contains a dialogue between Tom Thumb and an ostrich who rescues him; the latter complains that the child's mother sports ostrich feathers in her hat and that his father, upon seeing an ostrich egg, thinks: "That would make a great omelette!" Another dialogue, "L'Opéra des girafes," is written as an opera. A dromedary, antelopes, elephants, a horse on an island, a young lion in a cage, and a good-natured donkey are all subjects of brief fables, unburdened by any higher mythology. Throughout, Prévert's sympathies lie with the beasts, who are maltreated or misunderstood by humans.

The bird achieves a special status in Prévert's poems—sometimes representing liberation, as in "Quartier libre" ("Free Sector," from *Paroles*), sometimes as a symbol of sorrow, as in "Les Oiseaux du souci" ("Birds of Sorrow"), where the first line, "Pluie des plumes, plume de pluie" ("Rain of feathers, feather of rain"), reflects the indifference of the lonely poet in an atmosphere of despair and boredom to some birds who are trying to console him. One of Prévert's best-known poems, featuring a consummate demonstration of his technique of repetition, is "Chanson de l'oiseleur," a poem of thirteen brief lines, the first twelve of which begin with the words "L'Oiseau," followed by descriptive characteristics. In the thirteenth and final line, the bird becomes a woman's heart beating its wings pathetically in her hard, white breast.

In "Au hasard des oiseaux" (from *Paroles*), the poet opens by regretting that he learned to love the birds too late, then continues with a diatribe against a certain Monsieur Glacis, who is ironically portrayed as having fought courageously in the war against young Paul, a character described as poor, handsome, and decent, who later becomes old Paul, rich, aged, honorable, and stingy but masquerading as philanthropic and pious. Prévert adds that Paul had a servant who led an exemplary life, because she never quarreled with her master or mentioned the unmentionable question of wages. The poem concludes by contrasting again the bestial nature of man with the humane nature of the birds: "La lumière des oiseaux" (the light of the birds), in the final line, carries the implication of enlightenment.

JUSTICE AND PACIFISM

Prévert's sense of justice finds metaphoric expression in "Les Prodiges de la liberté" (from *Histoires*), which opens with the pathetic picture of the paw of a white fox caught in the teeth of a trap in the snow. The fox holds between its teeth a rabbit, still alive. Prévert seems to be able to reconcile himself to the natural order but continually objects to the evil that originates with humankind. For example, in the poem "La Pêche à la baleine" ("Whaling," from *Paroles*), a father is astounded that his son does not want to go whaling with him. "Why," asks the son, "should I hunt a beast who has done nothing to me, Papa?"

Prévert's antiwar sentiments were perhaps best formulated in "Barbara" (from *Paroles*), in which a tender and tragic tone is established in his comparison between the fate of a young girl and that of the city of Brest. The individual experiences pain in the loss of life, love, hope, and happiness, while the collective loss is shown in the destruction of the town, the ruins, and the fire raining down on one and all.

In 1952, Prévert took up his pen against the colonial war in "Entendez-vous gens du Viet-Nam" (from *La Pluie et le beau temps*), in which he denounces the French use of sophisticated tactics against the unarmed peasants. He notes that with the arrival of Admiral Thierry d'Argenlieu came a recrudescence of terror and suffering.

"Familiale"

One of Prévert's best-known pacifist poems is "Familiale" (from *Paroles*), which is characteristic of his ability to paint in a brief scene a moral dilemma:

> La mère fait du tricot
> Le fils fait la guerre
> Elle trouveça tout naturel la mère
> Et le père qu'est-ce qu'il fait le père?
> Il fait des affaires. . . .
> (A mother makes a sweater,
> a son makes war,
> which she finds quite natural,
> but the father—what is he doing?
> Business.)

The rhymes and the singsong rhythm lend the poem the aspect of a children's chant, but the content grows grim after the innocent opening of a mother knitting. The reduction of each life to its most typical activity shows the isolation in which people play out their roles, unconscious of the interdependence of their activities.

Love

Prévert championed love as passionately as he railed against war. Human happiness recognizes its most profound expression in love, and Prévert's contribution to erotic poetry has the simplicity of the classical Greek lyric poets. "Fiesta" (from *Histoires*) describes a seduction over empty glasses and a shattered bottle; the bed is wide open and the door closed; the poet is drunk and his lover is likewise drunk but lively and naked in his arms. The image of a woman "naked from head to toe" occurs frequently in Prévert's poems, but his physical descriptions rarely go further. In "Les Chiens ont soif" (from *Fatras*), the poet describes two lovers he has seen naked and entwined; he then assumes the point of view of the man: "He looks at her and knows without saying it that there is nothing more . . . indispensable, more simple and more inexplicable than love on a bed, than love on this earth."

The lighter side or more ephemeral aspect of love does not escape Prévert's wit. A character in *Fatras* exclaims how happy she is because her lover has said that he loves her, but she is even happier because she is still free, since he did not say he would love her forever. The lover in "Les Chansons les plus courtes . . ." (from *Histoires*) complains of the bird in his head repeating the refrain "I love you" so insistently that he will have to kill him the next morning. In "Le Lézard" (from *Histoires*), the poet declares: "The lizard of love has fled once again and left his tail between my fingers and that's all right/ I wanted to keep something for myself."

Many critics find the mechanics of Prévert's poetry too obtrusive, arguing that his rhymes and his wordplay, the adroit twists with which he frequently concluded his poems, lack the depth and resonance of great poetry. That he was a genuinely popular poet, however, is denied by none. The natural quality of his verse had an appeal that revived the spirit of France after World War II, and his can be called a poetry of recovery.

Other major works

SCREENPLAYS: *L'Affaire est dans le sac*, 1932; *Le Crime de Monsieur Lange*, 1935; *Jenny*, 1936 (with Marcel Carné); *Drôle de drame*, 1937 (with Carné); *Le Jour se lève*, 1939; *Les Visiteurs du soir*, 1942 (with Carné and Pierre Laroche); *Les Enfants du paradis*, 1945 (with Carné; *Children of Paradise*, 1968); *Notre Dame de Paris*, 1956.

CHILDREN'S LITERATURE: *Le Petit Lion*, 1947; *Des bêtes . . .* , 1950; *Bim, le petit âne*, 1952 (*Bim, the Little Donkey*, 1973).

TRANSLATION: *Carmina burana*, 1965.

MISCELLANEOUS: *Spectacle*, 1949, 1951 (includes poetry, plays, and prose); *L'Opéra de la lune*, 1953 (song lyrics); *Tour de chant*, 1953 (songs for piano and voice).

Bibliography

Baker, William E. *Jacques Prévert*. New York: Twayne, 1967. One of the single best overviews in English, fair and balanced in assessment and limited only by its date. Prevert's work is discussed as "anti-poetry," as the poetry of plain talk, and as an expression of both romanticism and stark political views. A good annotated bibliography in both French and English is included.

Bertelé, René. *Images de Jacques Prévert*. Paris: Filipacchi, 1974. Examines Prévert's imagery. In French.

Blakeway, Claire. *Jacques Prévert: Popular French Theatre and Cinema*. Cranbury, N.J.: Associated

University Presses, 1990. Although the focus is on Prévert's work in cinema and theater, especially his collaborations with Marcel Carné, the discussions of politics and Surrealism apply also to the poetry. Of special interest are the abundant black and white photographs.

Fay, Eliot. "The Poetry of Jacques Prévert." *The Emory University Quarterly* 3, no. 4 (December, 1947): 231-227. Without penetrating deeply into Prévert's thought or fully savoring the poet's irony, Fay's readings are nevertheless important as the first to appear in learned American journals. This article provides general interpretations of *Paroles* along with an awareness of Prévert's potential appeal to English-speaking readers.

Greet, Anne. *Jacques Prevert's Word Games*. University of California Publications in Modern Philology 89. Berkeley: University of California Press, 1968. A brief examination of Prévert's wordplay. Bibliographical footnotes.

Quéval, Jean. *Jacques Prévert*. Paris: Mercure de France, 1955. One of the few biographies of Prévert, this is the standard. In French.

Rachline, Michel. *Jacques Prévert: Drôle de Vie*. Paris: Éditions Ramsay, 1981. For French readers, a lively examination of the entire career, with emphasis on the ways in which the writings express the life experiences and philosophy of the poet.

Karen Jaehne;
bibliography updated by Allene Phy-Olsen

F. T. Prince

Born: Kimberley, South Africa; September 13, 1912

Principal poetry

Poems, 1938
Soldiers Bathing and Other Poems, 1954
The Stolen Heart, 1957
The Doors of Stone: Poems, 1938-1962, 1963
Memoirs in Oxford, 1970
Drypoints of the Hasidim, 1975
Afterword on Rupert Brooke, 1976
Collected Poems, 1979 (includes *A Last Attachment*)
The Yüan Chên Variations, 1981
Later On, 1983
Walks in Rome, 1987
Collected Poems, 1935-1992, 1993

Other literary forms

F. T. Prince has written widely in addition to his poetry. Among his more important publications are *The Italian Element in Milton's Verse* (1954), *William Shakespeare: The Poems* (1963), and *The Study of Form and the Renewal of Poetry* (1964).

Achievements

Equally distinguished as poet and scholar, F. T. Prince brings to all of his work a formidable and wide-ranging intellect, an informed compassion, and a remarkable eloquence. In addition, his poetry demonstrates that he has a perfect ear. Never involved in "movements" in the politics of literature, he has sometimes seemed a lonely figure, yet other poets have always been aware of his quality and importance, and his dedication to his craft has been a signal influence on younger writers at times when contemporary work has seemed to have lost its way. A consummate craftsman, at home in free or fixed forms, he is almost unique in being able to place all of his learning at the service of his poetry.

His work has been recognized by the award of honorary doctorates in literature from both the University of Southampton and New York University. In 1982, he won the E. M. Forster award from the American Academy and Institute of Arts and Letters.

Biography

Frank Templeton Prince was born in Kimberley, Cape Province, South Africa, where his father, Henry Prince, was a prosperous businessman in the diamond trade. His mother, Margaret Hetherington Prince, had been a teacher. Both parents were English. Prince was a sensitive and studious child. He already possessed keen powers of observation and an eye for detail which led to an early interest in painting. His mother's influence and the stories and poems she read to Prince and his sister encouraged the boy to write, and he was a poet from the age of fifteen.

After a short period in which he trained as an architect, Prince went to England in 1931 and entered Balliol College, Oxford. He took a first-class honors degree in English in 1934. It is apparent that the move to Oxford was both important and inevitable, since the poet's sensibility and culture were, almost from the start, strongly European. He went up to Oxford already fluent in French and deeply read in French poetry. He supported this by reading Dante in Italian and by making several visits to Italy. He found the whole period of the Renaissance, and in particular its art, highly congenial.

A meeting with T. S. Eliot in 1934 probably led to the later inclusion of Prince's first collection, *Poems*, in the Faber and Faber poetry list in 1938. Eliot recognized Prince's ability as well by printing the younger poet's "An Epistle to a Patron" in the *Criterion*, which Eliot edited.

During 1934-1935, Prince was a visiting fellow at Princeton University, but he returned to London to work

F. T. Prince

at the Royal Institute of International Affairs, an unlikely office for so apolitical a man. He was, however, writing, and a meeting with William Butler Yeats in 1937, when Prince traveled to Dublin to meet the great man, suggests that poetry held pride of place in his mind.

There is no acknowledgment in Prince's work at this point that Europe was on the point of war, but the poet was soon to be personally involved. He was commissioned into the Intelligence Corps of the British army in 1940, and sent to Bletchley Park. This was the Government Communications Centre, hardly a typical army environment. Men were allowed to wear civilian clothes, discipline was relaxed, and among the creative people involved there, many were not of the type to worry unduly about military correctness. The poet Vernon Watkins served there, as did the composer Daniel Jones, a friend of Dylan Thomas. Prince was at Bletchley Park until March, 1943, when he was posted to Cairo. Before leaving, he married Elizabeth Bush. There are two daughters of the marriage.

His time in Egypt, which lasted until 1944, gave Prince the experience which resulted in the writing of his best-known poem, "Soldiers Bathing." On his return, Prince spent several months as an interpreter in Italian prisoner-of-war camps in England before his demobilization.

In 1946, Prince began his academic career, being appointed lecturer in English at the University of Southampton, at that time a small university in an interesting city, which must have been a pleasant appointment for Prince. In any event, he stayed there for nearly thirty years, becoming eventually professor of English and, between 1962 and 1965, dean of the faculty of arts. It was there, moreover, that he wrote the great bulk of his postwar poetry. He was a visiting fellow of All Souls College, Oxford, in 1968, and Clark Lecturer at Cambridge in 1972. From 1975 to 1978 he was a professor of English at the University of the West Indies, in Mona, Kingston, Jamaica. He then spent the next years as visiting professor at several institutions that included Amherst College, Washington University, and Sana'a University in North Yemen, Arab Republic. He was writer in residence at Hollins College in Virginia in the spring of 1984 and spent two summers teaching at Dalhousie University, Halifax in the mid-1980's.

During the 1980's his American admirers, among them John Ashbery, showed their respect for his work and assisted in its dissemination. Prince continues to have a permanent home in Southampton and, if he travels less frequently, continues to write.

Analysis

The *Collected Poems* of 1979 brought together all the early work from *Poems* and *Soldiers Bathing and Other Poems* which F. T. Prince wanted to retain. He also included the whole of *The Doors of Stone* and four long, late poems, *Memoirs in Oxford*, *Drypoints of the Hasidim*, *Afterword on Rupert Brooke*, and *A Last Attachment*. These poems may be safely considered the work by which Prince would wish to be judged.

"An Epistle to a Patron" and "To a Man on His Horse"

The first poem is "An Epistle to a Patron," so admired by Eliot. When one recalls that the great young poet of the day was W. H. Auden and that the most admired poetry then was political and very aware of the contemporary world, Prince's lines are startling.

> My lord, hearing lately of your opulence in promise
> and your house
> Busy with parasites, of your hands full of favours,
> your statutes
> Admirable as music, and no fear of your arms not
> prospering, I have
> Considered how to serve you . . .

The reader is at once in Renaissance Italy, a period much favored by Prince and one in which he is at home. Yet, although the poem is written in the first person, it must not be assumed that the voice is Prince's voice. Rather, the poem is a dramatic monologue. It is not in the manner of Robert Browning either, although it moves in an area Browning sometimes occupied. Its splendid opulence, its sonorous and bewitching periods, are not like Browning. Nor do they hide the slyness, the mockery behind the flattery with which this postulant addresses his hoped-for patron. Ben Jonson could have written it, but it is a strange invention for the late 1930's. And if Prince uses the first person voice, as he does often throughout his career, rarely does he speak as himself—then he is a more everyday speaker altogether—but rather as a real resident of those times and places into which his learning and his curiosity have led him. His manner is courtly and aristocratic. If he uses, as he does in the opening lines of "To a Man on His Horse," a poetic inversion, it is for the dance of the statement, because he wants the movement:

> Only the Arab stallion will I
> Envy you. Along the water
> You dance him with the morning on his flanks . . .

The early work is full of such lines, stately, strangely out of time, full, too, of references to painters such as Paolo Veronese or statesmen such as Edmund Burke. It is a paradox when one realizes that Prince's most famous poem, "Soldiers Bathing," is not at all like the rest of the early work, that it is written about ordinary men, poor, bare, forked animals of the twentieth century. It gave Prince an immediate fame and is known to many readers who know nothing else the poet has written.

"Soldiers Bathing"

"Soldiers Bathing" is a poem of sixty-six lines, organized in six irregular verse paragraphs. The lines are not of regular length, and they rhyme in couplets. In it, the poet, an army officer, watches his men as, forgetting momentarily the stress and mire of war, they swim and play in the sea. It is often a clumsy poem, the longer second line of some of the couplets occasionally dragging along without grace, the structure and movement absurdly prosaic for a poet of Prince's skill. Yet it is intensely moving. The extraordinary syntax of the last line of the first stanza, so written, surely, to accommodate the rhyme, has been noted by many critics, particularly by Vernon Scannell in *Not Without Glory*. "Their flesh worn by the trade of war, revives/ And my mind towards the meaning of it strives." It is also, however, full of marvelous compassion, as Prince, recalling Michelangelo's cartoon of soldiers bathing, is able to unite friend and foe, dead and living soldiers, through his insight into the continuing folly of wars. He does this through his knowledge of art, but his own comfort comes from his religion. Prince is a Catholic, and the reader's understanding of his poetry is incomplete without this knowledge. He arrives at a sad conclusion: "Because to love is frightening we prefer/ The freedom of our crimes." He began the poem under "a reddening sky"; he ends it "while in the west/ I watch a streak of blood that might have issued from Christ's breast." This is a typical movement in a poem by Prince, one in which the plain and dissimilar elements are united in an understanding brought about by the poet's belief.

The great popularity of that fine poem tended to overshadow a number of poems which might more surely have suggested the nature and direction of Prince's gift. There were, for example, some love poems of great beauty and passion. He was to develop this ability until, in July, 1963, an anonymous reviewer in *The Times Literary Supplement* could write of Prince that he is "one of the best love poets of the age, a lyricist of great charm and tenderness and emotion, counter-balanced by a subtlety of thought and metaphor which often reminds one of Donne. . . ." The reference to John Donne is felicitous, since there is an affinity in the work of these men, brought into even clearer focus by Prince's liking for and familiarity with the seventeenth century.

The Doors of Stone

The Doors of Stone, then, contains poems of all the categories noted so far: monologues such as "Campanella" and "Strafford," love poems such as the eighteen sections of "Strombotti," poems suggested, like "Coeur de Lion," by history. They demonstrate once again the curious, elusive quality of Prince's poetry; it possesses dignity, honesty, even directness, yet the poet himself remains aloof, often behind masks.

Memoirs in Oxford

Almost as a rebuff to that opinion. Prince's next book was a long autobiographical poem, *Memoirs in Oxford*. Written in a verse form suggested by the one Percy Bysshe Shelley used in *Peter Bell the Third* (1839), it is at once chatty, clever, and revealing. It is particularly helpful about the poet's early life. It is also a delightful and accomplished poem—and a very brave one. To write a long poem in these days is unusual; to abandon what seems to be one's natural gift for eloquence and adopt a different tone altogether in which to write a long poem might seem foolhardy. Yet it is a very successful poem, having the virtues of clarity, wit, and style as well as some of the attraction of a good novel.

Drypoints of the Hasidim

Prince's father was of partly Jewish extraction, which might account for his interest in those "Dark hollow faces under caps/ In days and lands of exile . . . and among unlettered tribes" which figured so strongly in his next long poem, *Drypoints of the Hasidim*. Hasidism was a popular Jewish religious movement of the eighteenth and nineteenth centuries, and Prince's poem is a long meditation on the beliefs of this movement. Despite its learning, it is extremely clear, like all of Prince's poetry. Rarely can there have been a poet so scholarly and knowledgeable whose verse is so accessible.

As if to emphasize his virtuosity, Prince's next work is a verse reconstruction of the life and times of Rupert Brooke, the young and handsome poet whose early death in World War I assured him of fame. Using the information provided by Christopher Hassall in his biography of Brooke, Prince wrote from his own standpoint of "the damned successful poet" and also added, years after his own war, a commentary on youth and love and the ironies of war. The texture of these lines is far removed from the great splendors of the young Frank Prince:

> But Bryn quite blatantly prefers
> Walking alone on Exmoor to the drawing-room
> With the Ranee, and she finds all the girls so odd . . .

It does, however, contain a real feeling of the times, despite occasional prosiness.

A Last Attachment

Prince has never been afraid of the long poem; even as a young man, he wrote pieces of unusual length for modern times. *A Last Attachment* is based on Laurence Sterne's *Journal to Eliza* (1904). Shorter than the two poems previously noted, it once again considers the recurring problems which are central to Prince's preoccupations: love, the onset of age, an inability to settle and be content, jealousy, the triumphs and failures of the creative and artistic life—all great problems, glanced at, too, in *The Yüan Chên Variations*. They are problems that no doubt beset Prince himself, but he has chosen with dignity and objectivity to consider them most often through a series of characters taken from literature or history or art, rather than use direct personal experience. He has written of them all with elegance and seriousness and with great skill and honesty. His poetry is sometimes said to be unfashionable, and so it is if the word means that he belongs to no group, is determined to be his own man. He has always commanded the respect of his fellow poets, and that, very probably, is a guarantee of his importance and his growing stature.

Collected Poems, 1935-1992

Prince converted to Catholicism in the 1930's and his poetry did not take on a doctrinal cast, even though the exotic aestheticism of his earliest poems cooled somewhat. The resulting seriousness and intensity benefits from this interesting mix of sensuous diction and moral gravity. For example, in "An Epistle to a Patron," the poet speaker addresses his "patron" as "A donor of laurel and of grapes, a font of profuse intoxicants." This kind of aesthetic paganism yields to the passionate religious feeling of "Soldiers Bathing":

I feel a strange delight that fills me full
Strange gratitude, as if evil itself, were beautiful
And kiss the wound in thought, while in the west
I watch a streak of red that might have issued from
 Christ's breast.

Although the modern reader will detect touches of late Pre-Raphaelite sensual religiosity in these lines, a second look will also evoke the tragic joy of Gerard Manley Hopkins at his most intense. As evident in many of the poems in this collection, the opposites of sense and spirit never cease to dance their all-consuming rhythms in Prince's verse.

Opposites are a dialectical challenge for Prince. They do not deconstruct into a deferred meaning that is food only for skeptical detachment. The voice of the Sibyl (from the myth involving Apollo and Sibyl of Cumae) is historicized in the monologue, "The Old Age of Michelangelo." The great artist speaks for Prince's own struggle with the opposites of desire and faith that have rages in unabated confrontation:

And now I have grown old
It is my own life, my long life I see
As a combat against nature, nature that is our enemy
Holding the soul a prisoner by the heel;
And my whole anxious life I see
As a combat with myself, that I do violence to myself
To bruise and beat and batter
And bring under
My own being,
Which is an infinite savage sea of love.

Prince also has his lighter vein and delights in the play of verse as well as its passion. In "The Doors of Stone," he experimented with an Italian stanza first introduced to English poetry by Sir Thomas Wyatt. These stanzas, "Strambotti," enable Prince to exercise his dialectical imagination in a poised, cerebral dance of witty argument and rhyme.

The collection also showcases Prince's cosmoppolitan life, perhaps most impressively in "Drypoints of the Hasidim," a later and long poem of more than four hundred lines. It is a measure of his devotion to religious experience that he, a devout Catholic, should have been drawn to the intense inwardness of Jewish mysticism.

Other major works

nonfiction: *The Italian Element in Milton's Verse*, 1954; *William Shakespeare: The Poems*, 1963; *The Study of Form and the Renewal of Poetry*, 1964.

translation: *Sir Thomas Wyatt*, 1961 (of Sergio Baldi's biography).

Bibliography

Davie, Donald. "Beyond the Here and Now." *The New York Times Book Review*, April 8, 1979, 13, 43. In reviewing *Collected Poems*, Davie notes that Prince has done nothing as fine as "Soldiers Bathing," considered one of the best poems to come out of World War II. He criticizes Prince for not "giving us what we ask for," although he concedes that *Collected Poems* will be well liked.

Levi, Peter. "F. T. Prince." *Agenda* 15 (Summer/Autumn, 1977): 147-149. An appreciative review of Prince, commending him for his craftsmanship. Levi calls him a distinguished poet and scholar, one who is both intelligent and curious. Reviews *Drypoints of the Hasidim* and discusses the iambic pentameter verse and the allusive stories that form a complete sequence of the history of Hasidism.

Nigam, Alka. *F. T. Prince: A Study of His Poetry*. Salzburg, Austria: Institut fur Anglistik and Amerikanstik, 1983. In the foreword, Prince himself praises Nigam for her "careful and sensitive" study of his poetry. In this full-length study, Nigam analyzes Prince's art and vision, including a historical background of his poetry and its place in twentieth century verse. Contains solid literary criticism. A must for Prince scholars.

Leslie Norris

Matthew Prior

Born: Wimborne, England; July 21, 1664
Died: Wimpole, England; September 18, 1721

Principal poetry

A Satyr on the Modern Translators, 1685
Satyr on the Poets: In Imitation of the Seventh Satyr of Juvenal, 1687
An English Ballad, 1695
Carmen Saeculare, For the Year 1700—To the King, 1700
Poems on Several Occasions, 1707, 1709
Solomon on the Vanity of the World, 1718
Lyric Poems, 1741

Other literary forms

Matthew Prior is primarily known for his poetry. His verse, however, ranges widely, from verse epistles and songs to prologues and epilogues for plays. Indeed, there is virtually no kind of poem that he did not attempt, with the exception of the epic. His age expected such versatility from a serious poet, and it regarded him as one of its best. Even if today's readers have relegated him to the second rank, they must acknowledge his virtuosity.

Achievements

Matthew Prior does not have the literary stature of his contemporaries Alexander Pope or John Dryden, but he is probably the foremost Augustan poet after them. Augustan poetry takes its name from the Rome of Caesar Augustus, patron of the arts, with whose values many English poets of the late seventeenth and eighteenth centuries felt a special kinship. One way for a poet to establish his ties with ancient Rome was to write the kinds of poetry that the Romans wrote; a hierarchy of such kinds or genres in art had existed since the Renaissance.

Prior wrote in all of them except epic poetry, which stood at the pinnacle of the hierarchy and was the form which Dryden and Pope so brilliantly exploited satirically. Prior's strength was in some of the lesser genres, including odes, pastorals, verse narratives, epigrams, satires, verse essays, elegies, and epitaphs. According to the British *Dictionary of National Biography*, Prior "is one of the neatest of English epigrammatists, and in occasional pieces and familiar verses has no rival in English." Samuel Johnson, the dominant literary figure of the later eighteenth century, wrote that Prior's "diligence has placed him amongst the most correct of the English poets; and he was one of the first that resolutely endeavored at correctness." Prior may not have possessed the force of Dryden or the penetrating vision of Pope, but he achieved an elegance seldom matched by poets of any age.

Biography

Matthew Prior, born July 21, 1664, was himself aware of his limitations as a poet. In his "Essay on Learning," he observes: "I had two Accidents in Youth which hindred me from being quite possest with the Muse." One was the accident of his education. He had been singularly fortunate, as the son of a laborer, to have been assisting in his uncle's tavern one day when Lord Dorset found him reading Horace and asked him to turn an ode into English. Impressed with the result, Dorset undertook to provide for Prior's subsequent education. Advantageous as this sponsorship proved, Prior lamented that he was "bred in a Colledge where prose was more in fashion than Verse . . . so that Poetry which by the bent of my Mind might have become the business of my Life, was by the Happyness of my Education only the Amusement of it." The other accident of youth was, likewise, a form of success in activities other than writing poetry. As secretary to the newly appointed ambassador to The Hague for King William in 1691, Prior showed such political and business aptitude that he found himself serving in various diplomatic roles over the next twenty-two years, including negotiator for the Treaty of Utrecht in 1711-1712, a treaty that would become popularly known—especially among Queen Anne's Whig opposition—as "Matt's Peace."

When the queen died in 1714 and the Whigs assumed power, Prior found himself under house arrest. His friends came to his financial rescue after his release in 1716, and Lord Harley helped Prior purchase Down Hall, whose condition he joked about in one of his last poems: "Oh! now a low, ruined white shed I descern/ Until'd, and unglaz'd, I believe 'tis a barn." After some rebuilding under the direction of the architect James Gibbs, however, Prior was able to spend his last years, like Horace on his Sabine Farm, in rural retirement. Prior died while visiting Lord Harley in 1721, equally famous for his political career as for his poetic one. Even if he was not the foremost poet of his age, Prior is to be admired as a late Renaissance embodiment of the "universal man," a statesman and a poet.

Matthew Prior (Hulton Archive)

Analysis

Matthew Prior's political and poetical interests served each other well when special events called for panegyrical poems. Much of Prior's early poetry is of this kind. His first published poem was an ode, "On the Coronation of the Most August Monarch K. James II, and Queen Mary. The 23rd. of April, 1685." Prior writes that he cannot prevent his fancy from imagining the king, rowing up the Thames with his company, to be crowned. Prior compares the impending arrival with Jason's when he bore the golden fleece back to Greece, with the rising of the sun, with a Roman triumph, and with the first coming of Christ. The urge to draw such analogies was typical of Augustan poets, but to do so in praise of the king was to risk seeming self-serving, if not obsequious. Indeed, many writers of birthday odes to the king or queen were exactly that. Prior avoids the trap by framing his praise as a flight of fancy, as a prompting of his soul which he cannot restrain as he anticipates the event.

Prior's poems of praise do not always take the stricter poetic forms that the term "ode" may imply. His 565-line poem to the king, *Carmen Saeculare, For the Year 1700. To the King*, is in rhymed quatrains, or linked pairs of couplets. In 1695, he wrote a ballad to celebrate the English recapture of Namur from France, a poem that mocks a French "victory" poem of 1692, stanza by stanza.

Perhaps the best example of Prior's ability to carry off a difficult task with elegance is his poem "To a Child of Quality of Five Years Old: The Author suppos'd Forty." To write a poem praising the child of a nobleman (the earl of Jersey) is to risk sentimentality, if not fulsomeness. Prior amuses his readers by amusing himself with the idea that an age difference will always separate this girl from him. He can lament her indifference now, as if he were a Petrarchan lover, and at the same time describe the reality of seeing his verses used to curl her doll's hair. His regrets are not wholly contrived since, trapped by old age, Prior will indeed "be past making love,/ When she begins to comprehend it." Unlike the occasional poems, of little interest today, this lyrical ode reveals Prior's ability to bring freshness to a potentially tedious subject and to execute a difficult task with grace.

Cloe poems

Prior wrote numerous love poems which in their use of artificial diction, their shepherds and shepherdesses, and their imaginary, timeless, deity-inhabited landscape of Arcadia, are pastoral. In the last of a sequence of poems about Cloe, his mistress in these poems, he calls their dispute a "Pastoral War"; she is no milkmaid, however, and Prior's pastorals are personal lyrics as well as exercises within this conventional genre. Prior implies his regard for Cloe in traditional ways: Cupid mistakes Venus for Cloe and shoots his mother, or Venus mistakes a picture of Cloe for one of herself. In "Cloe Hunting," Apollo mistakes her for his sister Cynthia, only to be chided by Cupid.

In later poems to Cloe, however, the pastoral setting becomes less important, while the relation between Prior and Cloe becomes less convention-bound and more psychologically interesting. In "A Lover's Anger," Prior begins peevishly to chide Cloe for being two hours late. Cloe protests that a rosebud has fallen into her dress and invites him to look at the mark it has made on her breast. Prior looks and immediately forgets what he had been about to say, having been drawn from the world of watches and missed appointments into her innocent paradise, where one need worry only about love and, occasionally, a falling rosebud. Clearly, however, the pastoral condition is a temporary and imaginary refuge from the real world, which also exists in the poem.

In "Cloe Jealous," Prior's beloved is no longer content to believe in the "pastoral" world that idealized their relationship. Although at first Cloe pretends to weep for "Two poor stragling Sheep," she quickly reveals that she really worries that she is losing her beauty. Prior's "Answer to Cloe Jealous, in the same Stile. The Author sick" avoids her concerns as he describes himself as a dying shepherd, never more to torment her with jealousy. "A Better Answer," he decides, is to treat her as an equal, to flatter her into accepting his infidelities as mere "Art," whereas his "Nature" is to love Cloe best. "I court others in Verse; but I love Thee in Prose," he adds, neglecting to point out that this very answer is another set of verse fabrications. This is one of Prior's most delightful poems, and one that pushes the Cloe series of love lyrics beyond the ordinary limits of its convention; "A Better Answer" both assumes and undercuts the pastoral tradition, while, at the same time, the poem reasserts it.

Ribald tales

Prior is perhaps less successful as a storyteller than he is as a lyricist. The best-told of his ribald tales is "Hans Carvel," the Rabelaisian story of a man who, "Impotent and Old,/ Married a Lass of LONDON Mould." Hans contracts with Satan (in the shape of a lawyer) to restrain his wife's social activities. In solving his problem, Hans finds that the devilish joke is on him, in an ending that Samuel Johnson accurately describes as "not over-decent." By contrast, "Henry and Emma: A Poem, Upon the Model of the Nut-brown Maid," is a moral tale. Most readers agree that the testing of Emma by Henry, who pretends to be leaving for a life of exile to see whether she will accompany him, makes both characters unsympathetic. The possibility exists that Prior meant the poem to be an ironic adaptation, a mocking of the fidelity endorsed in the original, but the evidence for this reading is thin. In either case, Johnson's charge that the dialogue is "dull and tedious" cannot be refuted.

Epigrams and epitaphs

There can be little disputing Prior's excellence as a writer of epigrams, or short verses with a surprising turn or insight. His best known epigram he calls "A True Maid": "No, no; for my Virginity,/ When I lose that, says ROSE, I'll dye:/ Behind the Elmes, last night, cry'd DICK/ Rose, were You not extreamly Sick?" An epigram of unknown date pushes a philosophical commonplace to a very unphilosophical conclusion: "RISE not till Noon, if Life be but a Dream,/ As Greek and Roman Poets have Exprest:/ Add good Example to so grave a Theme,/ For he who Sleeps the longest lives the best." Epigrams have been described as having a sting in the tail, and Prior's sting is sharp enough to lead one to wonder whether he had a natural bent for satire that his political interests led him to restrict.

Satires

Prior did write some satires on nonpolitical subjects. One of his earliest poems is *A Satyr on the Modern Translators*, on John Dryden in particular for his translation of Ovid's *Epistles* (1681-1683). In a letter, Prior objects: "Our Laureate might in good manners have left the version of Latin authors to those who had the happiness to understand them." Imitations of the

Roman literati, on the other hand, were not an abuse of their work but rather an almost obligatory exercise. For example, Prior wrote *Satyr on the Poets: In Imitation of the Seventh Satyr of Juvenal*. Perhaps Prior's most original piece is "Alma: Or, The Progress of the Mind," which he wrote while under arrest in 1715-1716. Johnson found the poem in need of a design, while others have argued that Pyrrhonism unifies it. Satire, however, is traditionally loose in its structure, and "Alma" is surely a satire on intellectual systems. The poem's main speaker is Matt, a system-builder. The poem was inspired by *Hudibras* (Part I, 1663; Part II, 1664; Part III, 1678) Prior says, and Matt's less learned companion, Dick, like Ralpho or Don Quixote's Sancho Panza, is not readily impressed by Matt's ethereal notions. The soul or mind, poetically termed "Alma," Matt explains, sits in judgment over the testimony of the senses. He goes on to develop a theory that the mind enters the toes at birth, makes its way to the midsection by adulthood, and causes the enmity and senility of later age when it rises from the seat of action to the head, from which it escapes—ever upward—at death. Dick questions Matt, usually to be put in his place, but Dick does have the last say in the last stanza, where he rejects this sort of wisdom in favor of folly—and calls for a bottle of wine. When one considers the satire of Prior's friend Jonathan Swift in *The Mechanical Operation of the Spirit* (1710), one senses the limits of Prior's explorations as a satirist. Nevertheless, "Alma" is original enough to be of considerable historical interest.

Solomon on the Vanity of the World

The poem that Prior believed he would be remembered for is *Solomon on the Vanity of the World*, his longest poem, in which Solomon examines knowledge, pleasure, and power, in turn, as sources of human happiness. Not surprisingly, since texts from Ecclesiastes precede each section, Solomon concludes that all human endeavor is vain. Before he submits to the will of his Creator, however, Solomon reflects at length, and even at their best the reflections are disappointing. Book II, for example, opens with the building of a palace and garden, as grand as wealth can provide. There is no ironic edge to the description, which might have made Solomon's folly more evident; instead, the expensive undertaking sounds very magnificent and Solomon's sudden change of attitude—"I came, beheld, admir'd, reflected, griev'd"—seems unmotivated. Everyone has experienced a sense of "the Work perfected, the Joy was past," but one hopes for more than commonplaces, or at least for more pleasure in the weaving of a fabric on which the commonplaces can be stitched, in a poem of 2,652 lines.

"Jinny the Just"

Epitaphs are meant for tombstones, and Prior composed them throughout his career, from his "An Epitaph on True, her Majesty's Dog," in 1693, to a surprisingly long one for his own tomb in the Poets' Corner of Westminster Abbey. Elegies are about loss, and when they are about a specific death they become occasional poems. One of Prior's best poems is his verse portrait "Jinny the Just," about a recently deceased serving woman whom he describes as "the best Wench in the Nation." She is "just" in that she is naturally moderate, "between the Coquette, and the Prude." In one stanza (of thirty-five), Prior seems to capture the essence of a lifetime: "While she read and accounted and pay'd and abated/ Eat and Drank, play'd and work't, laught and cry'd, lov'd and hated/ As answer'd the End of her being created." Jinny actually existed, though her identity has never been discovered. She is assumed to have been Prior's mistress for a time, and Prior's lifelong preference for women of the lower classes seemed evidence, to his friends, of Prior's own humble origins. Prior never married.

Other major works

SHORT FICTION: *Dialogues of the Dead*, 1721.

MISCELLANEOUS: *The Literary Works of Matthew Prior*, 1959 (H. Bunker Wright and Monroe K. Spears, editors).

Bibliography

Eves, Charles K. *Matthew Prior: Poet and Diplomatist*. New York: Columbia University Press, 1939. Prior's uncommonly rich life will probably always be more interesting than his poetry, and Eves's biography remains the best modern treatment of that life. Well written and still useful, especially when combined with Frances Mayhew Rippy's Twayne entry.

Gildenhuys, Faith. "Convention and Consciousness in Prior's Love Lyrics." *Studies in English Literature, 1500-1900* 35, no. 3 (Summer, 1995): 437. The poetry of Prior was part of the growing eighteenth century interest in women as subjects rather than simply objects of male passion. The amorous lyrics of Prior and their popularity are examined.

Kline, Richard B. "Tory Prior and Whig Steele: A Measure of Success?" *Studies in English Literature* 9 (Summer, 1969): 427-437. Any evaluation of Prior's poetry must recognize the intensely active role that politics played in his life and work. By pairing Prior with the redoubtable Whig Sir Richard Steele, Kline provides a nice sense of the complex political climate of the late seventeenth and early eighteenth centuries.

Rippy, Frances Mayhew. *Matthew Prior.* New York: Twayne, 1986. This is the single best assessment of Prior's life and work, and, given the paucity of critical materials, an invaluable source book. Follows the Twayne format in providing a biography, critical evaluations of the major works, and an attempt to "contextualize" Prior. Includes a chronology and a bibliography.

Sitter, John. "About Wit: Locke, Addison, Prior, and the Order of Things." *Rhetorics of Order/Ordering of Rhetorics in English Neoclassical Literature*, edited by J. Douglas Canfield and J. Paul Hunter. Newark: University of Delaware Press, 1989. A very nice attempt to place Prior within the early neoclassical tradition—a tradition influenced as much by the empiricist philosophy of Locke as by the "classics."

Spears, Monroe K. "Some Ethical Aspects of Matthew Prior's Poetry." *Studies in Philology* 45 (October, 1948): 606-629. This is one of three essays on Prior published by Spears in 1948. ("Matthew Prior's Attitude Toward Natural Science" appeared in *Publications of the Modern Language Society* 63, June: 485-507, and "Matthew Prior's Religion" in *Philological Quarterly* 27, April: 159-180). Taken together, these provide an excellent context within which to read Prior's work.

Thorson, James L. "Matthew Prior's 'An Epitaph.'" *The Explicator* 51, no. 2 (Winter, 1993): 84. Prior's "An Epitaph" is discussed. Prior's theme, that retiring to the country in not an ideal but, to a thoughtful person, a sentence of mental and moral death, is beautifully exemplified.

James R. Aubrey;
bibliography updated by the editors

Sextus Propertius

Born: Assisi(?), Umbria; c. 57-48 B.C.E.
Died: Place unknown; c. 16 B.C.E.-2 C.E.

Principal poetry

Monobiblos, wr. c. 30 or 29 B.C.E.
Elegies, after 16 B.C.E. (first printed version, 1472; English translation, 1854)
Propertius Elegies: Book I, 1961, *Book II*, 1967, *Book III*, 1966, *Book IV*, 1965 (W. A. Camps, editor)

Other literary forms

Sextus Propertius is known primarily for his poetry.

Achievements

An extremely popular poet in Augustan Rome, Sextus Propertius brought to perfection the love elegy form which flourished briefly in Rome in the late first century B.C.E. Clearly influenced by the poetry of Catullus and the elegies of such contemporary poets as Calvus and Gallus, whose works are now lost, Propertius claimed in his poetry to have imitated the style of the Alexandrian poets Callimachus and Philetas. Like the other Latin love elegists whose works have survived, Propertius made the elegiac meter, previously used especially for epigrams and reflective themes, into a meter of love. The Latin love elegist focuses his poetry on his devotion to a single woman and depicts the love affair in its various stages but not necessarily chronologically. Propertius's poetry, centered on a woman he called Cynthia, reveals his ability to handle well the conventional themes and forms of the genre, including the theme of the *exclusus amator*, or "locked-out lover," and forms such as the birthday poem, the ecphrastic poem, which describes a piece of artwork, and the love letter (elegy 3 in the fourth book may have provided the model for Ovid's *Heroides*). Preeminently, however, Propertius is admired for his ability to combine the personal love theme with a whole range of elements from Greek mythology and Roman religion and politics in a sophisticated and original way.

Propertius's influence on Ovid is evident especially from book 4, elegy 3, and book 4, elegy 5. Propertius was mentioned favorably or imitated by later Latin writers, including Lucan, Juvenal, and Martial. In the late Silver Age, a revival of interest in Propertius was evident, especially in the poetry of Claudian (late fourth century C.E.). Propertius was known but not popular in the Middle Ages, during which period his fellow elegist, Ovid, was preferred. Petrarch was the first Renaissance humanist to show an interest in Propertius and even imitated the Roman elegist in his sonnets. In the eighteenth century, Johann Wolfgang von Goethe's *Römische Elegien* (1793; *Roman Elegies*) was also influenced by Propertius. It has been in the twentieth century, however, that Propertius has made the strongest impact, especially on the poetry of Ezra Pound, whose *Homage to Sextus Propertius* (1917) is partly free translation and partly poetic creation in its own right, and whose *Literary Essays* (1954) provide a significant modern interpretation of the Latin elegist.

BIOGRAPHY

Sextus Propertius wrote in the period just after the tumultuous series of civil wars that followed the assassination of Julius Caesar in 44 B.C.E. Both Propertius's life and his poetry were deeply affected by the social and political changes which resulted from the near anarchy lasting from 44 B.C.E. until the defeat of Mark Anthony by Octavian, the future Augustus, at Actium in 31 B.C.E. In the early years of the *Pax Augustana*, Octavian's near-paranoid dread of opposition to his autocratic rule, as well as a general fear of the return of civil war, encouraged intensely propagandistic literature, evident in the poetry of both Vergil and Horace. It was a period of contradictions when Augustus strove vainly, through legislation, to encourage a return to old Roman values and virtues centered on marriage and the family, while, at the same time, Roman society experienced major social upheavals resulting from the political rise of the equestrian class and from the emancipation of women. The major themes of Latin love elegy, including allusions to contemporary political events and a yearning for the Golden Age of Rome's past, were clearly the result of the prevailing social and political mood, and the women about whom the Latin love elegists wrote, such as Propertius's Cynthia, were examples of the new breed of Roman women, socially independent and politically powerful.

What little is known about Propertius's life is derived from references in his own poetry, especially book 1, elegy 22, and book 4, elegy 1. There are almost no independent ancient references to the poet, and what information can be inferred from his poetry is often unreliable because of the difficulty in distinguishing between the historical Propertius and the persona projected in the poetry. Propertius was writing love elegies, not autobiography, and was therefore not bound by historical accuracy, even in references to his own life. Consequently, there is almost no aspect of his biography that is not disputed today.

Propertius was born sometime in the decade 57-48 B.C.E. into a well-to-do equestrian family of Umbria, in North Italy. Traditionally, he is said to have been from Assisi, but this is uncertain. Propertius's pride in his native Umbria and its Etruscan heritage is evident in his poetry (book 1, elegy 22; book 4, elegy 1; and book 4, elegy 2). His family supported the wrong side in the war between Octavian and Anthony, and their property was almost certainly confiscated by Octavian in 41-40 B.C.E. to pay his troops. While Propertius was still a child, his father died, and the boy was reared by his mother. Book 4, elegy 1, line 134, implies that Propertius was sent by his mother to study in Rome for a career as a lawyer; the many rhetorical features of Propertius's poetry, such as his fondness for methodically enumerating instances as proof, support such an inference.

While in Rome, Propertius apparently met the woman who so strongly affected his life and made him into a poet instead of a lawyer. She is called Cynthia in his poetry, but this is clearly a pseudonym in the tradition of ancient love poetry; Catullus's Lesbia was really named Clodia. Cynthia's pseudonym is poetically appropriate because of its associations with Apollo, the Greek god of inspiration, and with his sister Diana, the Roman goddess of the moon. Ancient sources say that Cynthia's real name was Hostia, but Propertius's poetic reference to Hostius, an epic poet of the late second century B.C.E., as Hostia's grandfather, is generally discounted today as poetic license. The image of Cynthia developed in Propertius's poetry is of a well-educated freedwoman, probably a high-class *meretrix*, or prostitute (although some still argue today that Cynthia was actually a respectable married woman). Propertius developed a relationship with Cynthia in his poetry that appears to have lasted, on and off, for approximately five years. Based on the evidence of book 4, elegy 7, Cynthia probably died in poverty about 18 B.C.E. and was buried at Tibur. Experts generally agree today that the poetic relationship between Propertius and Cynthia was based loosely upon actual events, although facts cannot be distinguished from poetic distortion in the *Elegies*.

J. P. Sullivan, in his book on Propertius, has used these meager biographical details concerning Propertius, as well as the attitude of the poet toward Cynthia in his *Elegies*, to advance the theory that Propertius's relationship with Cynthia can be explained by Sigmund Freud's theory of *Dirnenliebe*, or prostitute love. Propertius's loss of his father at an early age and his maternal upbringing suggest the Freudian description of men who are unable to dissociate their lofty maternal image from the general female image and are thus able to develop a passionate relationship only with a female who is the opposite of the maternal image, such as a prostitute. The general pattern of this passion exactly fits Propertius's relationship with Cynthia: the presence of an injured third party, either a husband or another lover; the love of a woman who is neither faithful nor chaste; a contradictory overestimation of the beloved, despite her sexual shortcomings; a false ideal of the lover's own fidelity; intense jealousy toward potential rivals; and the desire to "rescue" the beloved from her degradations. The close similarity between Propertius's feelings for Cynthia and Freud's theory of *Dirnenliebe* sheds great light on Propertius's characterization of his relationship with Cynthia and strongly suggests a kernel of personal experience and feeling lying behind the poetic screen.

It is generally assumed that after the appearance of his first book of *Elegies*, Propertius was invited to join the poetic circle of Maecenas, who was the patron of Vergil and Horace and the intimate friend of Augustus. Certainly, Maecenas is presented in book 2, elegy 1, and book 3, elegy 9, as suggesting historical/epic themes for Propertius, which the poet rejects in favor of love elegy. The unsuitability of elegiac themes to the political and social program of Augustus is something of which Propertius is acutely conscious in his poetry. Book 4, published after 16 B.C.E. and conspicuously different from the earlier books with its prominent aetiological poems and praise of Actium, is usually said to mark Propertius's final conversion to the propaganda poetry advocated by Maecenas and Augustus and demonstrated by Horace and Vergil; Sullivan, however, has argued convincingly that this is not the case at all, that the poems of book 4 are not sincere but rather deliberate parodies of propaganda poetry. Whatever the actual relationship between Propertius and Maecenas, it is clear that the poet moved in Maecenas's circle, at least after 30 B.C.E. Propertius gives evidence of his good relations with the imperial family in book 3, elegy 18, and book 4, elegy 11. He knew Vergil and appears to have been greatly influenced in book 3 by Horace's *Odes* (23 B.C.E., 13 B.C.E.). There is a strong suggestion in their poetry, however, that Horace and Propertius disliked each other, at least professionally. Curiously, Propertius and Tibullus, another contemporary love elegist, appear to have worked independently, with no allusions to each other's works. Ovid, however, shows a deep regard for Propertius and frequently imitates Propertius's work.

The later part of Propertius's life lies completely in shadows. The last datable reference to contemporary events in his poetry, the funeral of Cornelia, took place in 16 B.C.E. From a reference in Ovid's *Remedia amoris* (before 8 C.E.), it is certain that Propertius was dead by 2 C.E. Some critics argue that Propertius's poetic silence after 16 B.C.E. was caused by early death; others, by the dangerous political climate that led eventually to Ovid's banishment in 8 C.E. Some ancient evidence exists to suggest that Propertius married and produced an heir before his death. Propertius's trip to Greece about 20 B.C.E., mentioned by some critics, is completely hypothetical.

The personality of Propertius projected through his poetry is that of a young man whose unhappy childhood, scarred by the death of his father and the loss of his family farm, led to an only slightly veiled disillusionment with the totalitarian rule of Augustus, whose conception of poetry as a political tool Propertius rejected. Indeed, Propertius's infatuation with the love theme and with the creation of poetry for its own sake was clearly antithetical to Augustan tastes and may help to explain his poetic silence after 16 B.C.E.

ANALYSIS

The genre of Latin love elegy in which Sextus Propertius wrote was a rich amalgam of the early Greek lyric tradition of Archilochus and Sappho; of the intensely learned and form-conscious poetry of Hellenistic writers, especially Callimachus; and of the distinctly Roman contributions of the lyric poet Catullus and of the elegiac writers, such as Propertius himself. From the Greek lyricists, the Roman elegist inherited the "lyric," first-person voice which permits the vivid expression of moods and personal feelings, including love, for which the elegist is noted. Especially from the Hellenistic poets, the love elegy derived a fondness for mythic and geographical allusions, as well as a particular concern for artificial poetic expression, in selection of both form and word, of which Propertius became a master. To this Greek tradition, which provided the Roman poet with a well-established list of conventional themes and poetic forms, were added indigenous Latin themes, such as references to Roman institutions and to the Golden Age of Rome's past. In particular, the Romans brought to lyric and elegy a marked tendency toward autobiographical expression and a habit of writing poetry as if it were addressed to friends, which is not common in Greek. It is this autobiographical mode, permitting the poet to unify his poems around the real or imagined history of a love affair, which is the distinctive characteristic of the Latin love elegy.

ELEGIES

Propertius's poetry starts from this autobiographical form of expression and from the conventions of the Greek tradition but exhibits some particularly Propertian themes and characteristics. The *Elegies* of Propertius are distinctive especially for a unity of structure and theme not achieved by earlier love and elegiac poets; the poet shows, in the arrangement of his poems within each book, a new concern for balance and contrast of mood and structure between particular poems that intensify the overall unity based upon the love theme. Even within individual elegies, the poet is noted for his ability to combine sudden changes of mood and thought and complex structures to create an especially intense and unified poem (a feature unfortunately not always recognized by modern editors, who, overly conscious of Propertius's poor manuscript tradition, often tend to interpret a change of mood as a new poem).

Propertius was a poet of the city, of Rome, rather than of the bucolic landscape, like Tibullus. He was particularly fond of incorporating Roman religious themes into his elegies, especially metaphorically—for example, depicting the poet as priest and the love relationship between himself and Cynthia as a marriage rite. This Roman emphasis is extended, however, only indirectly to themes, especially military ones, from the glorious Roman past or from contemporary events. Despite apparently intense pressure from the Augustan political establishment to write poetry more acceptable to the regime, Propertius generally introduced such historical themes only in the form of a *recusatio*, the refusal to write on themes that the author finds unsuitable; in Propertius's case, *recusatio* is the love elegist's refusal to write on more historical subjects in lofty genres such as epic or tragedy. It has, in fact, been argued by Sullivan that in book 4 Propertius used the *recusatio*, perhaps more ironically and subtly, as a final rejection of approved Augustan themes in favor of love poetry. Finally, Propertius's conscious efforts to be a Roman Callimachus not only made him employ mythic allusions more than earlier love elegists but also made him a particularly skilled master of language who could control the multiple meanings of words rather than be controlled by them. This ability to manipulate words and their meanings, which Pound called *logopoeia*, lies at the core of Propertius's poetry and, perhaps, constitutes its crux, since it has often led to confusion and ambiguity in the reading of his *Elegies*.

BOOK 1, ELEGY 19

Book 1, elegy 19, is part of a series dealing with different aspects of separation from the beloved, either by geographic distance or by death. The conversational tone of book 1, elegy 19, contrasts with the soliloquy structure of book 1, elegy 17 and elegy 18; as book 1, elegy 19, begins, Propertius is in the middle of a discussion with Cynthia about death. In a colloquial tone marked by phrases such as "now I don't" and "but least perhaps," the poet begins to develop a reflection on death which is not unusual in Latin love elegy but which Propertius expresses in his distinctive style. Sudden thought transitions and mood changes are particularly noteworthy in this poem. Propertius moves in thought, from his undying love for Cynthia even after his own death, to his continued love for Cynthia after *her* death, to his fear that she will not be true and, finally, to the plea that they love each other while both are still alive. This rambling train of thought is unified not only by the themes of the poet's fidelity and Cynthia's faithlessness, which are basic to the relationship as developed in Propertius's *Elegies*, but also by a sequence of mood changes, which draws the poem together in a ring structure.

The poet's initial colloquial mood is maintained through the first six lines but changes in the center of the poem into a more formal tone marked by a combination of mythological allusions and the triple anaphora of "there." The solemn reference to the story of Protesilaus's love for Laodamia beyond the grave shows Propertius's tendency to incorporate mythological exempla of his love for Cynthia and "the chorus of beautiful heroines," possibly derived from traditional catalogs of dead mythological beauties such as in the *Aeneid* (c. 29-19 B.C.E.), and further develops Propertius's love for Cynthia in a formal and hyperbolic way. In the last section of the poem, the poet returns to the colloquial tone of the beginning with the use of a parenthetical statement and exclamation. The poem thus begins and ends on an informal note, in marked contrast to its grave subject matter and formal central section. This contrast is furthered on the level of vocabulary, where Propertius juxtaposes concrete and abstract terms throughout the poem, such as "fate" and "pyre" in the second line and "dust" and "love" in line six (repeated in line twenty-two). The vivid concrete words, such as "pyre" and "dust," invoke the Roman burial rite of cremation and provide further reinforcement of the formal, solemn tone of the poem. At the same time, Propertius's manipulation of words, his *logopoeia*, can be noted in the use of "dust" in lines six and twenty-two to refer not only to the physical remains of Propertius after death and to the Roman funeral rite, but also, metaphorically, to the psychological condition of Propertius when his love for Cynthia is forgotten (*oblito . . . amore*) and when Cynthia forgets the dead Propertius in line twenty-two. In either case, "dust" is an appropriate term to describe Propertius both physically and emotionally.

BOOK 2, ELEGY 6

The tight control of tone, structure, and vocabulary that Propertius demonstrates in book 1, elegy 19, can also be seen in book 2, elegy 6. Together with elegy 5 from the same book, elegy 6 is an exhortation to Cynthia to be true to Propertius, but, while the tone of book 2, elegy 5, is threatening and critical of Cynthia and is modeled, perhaps, on the harsh invective of Catullus in a similar situation, book 2, elegy 6, is a formal and polite warning to Cynthia against the dangers of promiscuity. The formality is established at the very beginning of the poem by the use of the favorite Hellenistic convention of the catalog. In lines one through six, Propertius presents a list of prostitutes culled from Greek comedy and implies a contrast with Cynthia by the words "thus," "so great," and "so." This contrast is only indirect and polite because the specific reference to Cynthia that the comparatives "thus," "so great," and "so" demand is not made by Propertius.

The catalog structure is continued in lines seven through fourteen, where Propertius lists all people whose closeness to Cynthia makes him jealous. The formal tone of both catalogs is tempered by the use of references from Greek comedy for humorous effect as well as by the exaggerated jealousy of Propertius for infants whom Cynthia kisses. In lines fifteen through twenty-six, Propertius turns to a third catalog, this one mythological, where Cynthia is given mythic examples of the dangers of masculine lust. Humor is added here, too, by the reference to the Centaurs breaking their wine jugs over Perithous's head. In the final exemplum, a reference to the Rape of the Sabine Women, the humorous tone is completely lost as Propertius's train of thought moves from the mild warnings to Cynthia against lust to a new theme of the deterioration of Roman morals that dominates the rest of the poem.

A reference to the long-past Golden Age of Roman virtue leads the poet into a tirade against contemporary painters, whose obscene works corrupt Roman morals.

Perhaps the reader is meant to imagine the setting of the elegy to be Cynthia's own house, where such paintings may be seen. The word order reinforces the contrast in morals with the juxtaposition of "chaste"/"base" and "ingenuous"/"corrupt." This passage on the painters' contribution to the baseness of contemporary Roman morals is framed by two references to a parallel deterioration of Roman religious sentiment in lines twenty-five to twenty-six and thirty-five to thirty-six. The second reference, describing empty Roman temples veiled with spiderwebs, is another example of Propertius's *logopoeia*, his conscious use of words in unusual contexts. "Veiled" suggests the Roman custom of worshiping with the head covered, but this pious act is distorted in context by the fact that the veil is a spiderweb. The veil becomes a vivid metaphoric statement of Rome's lost religious zeal. The yearnings that the poet expresses in these lines for a return to old Roman virtues and piety *appear* to agree with Augustan policy, but the solemnity and formality of this appeal for virtue is deliberately undermined in the following ways: Not only does the next elegy joyfully celebrate the repeal of one of the very marriage laws that Augustus had passed to improved Roman morals, but also book 2, elegy 6, lines thirty-eight through forty-three, shows that for Propertius the desire for virtue does not go beyond his own illicit relationship with Cynthia. The poet wants Cynthia to be faithful to him and lists two of love poetry's traditional impediments to love, a "guard" and the "closed door," which are useless barriers if the girl wishes otherwise.

Propertius's plea for Cynthia's exclusive love is climaxed in the last elegiac couplet of the poem with a promise of his own fidelity. This contrast between Propertius's and Cynthia's attitudes toward their relationship was also noted in book 1, elegy 19, and is a unifying theme of the *Elegies*. In lines forty-one and forty-two, Propertius promises to have no "wife" and no "girlfriend" except Cynthia. The application of the term "wife" to Cynthia is a final example of Propertius's *logopoeia* in this poem. The poet's earlier call for a return to Roman virtue, including a respect for marriage, is debased by his own reference to his mistress as his wife. Propertius does here to the Roman vocabulary of marriage what the obscene painter in the poem did to the innocent walls of Roman houses. Yet "wife" at the same time implies a sanctity of the marriage bond which Propertius is metaphorically and ironically applying with great effect to his relationship with Cynthia. For Propertius, Cynthia is both wife and religion.

Book 3, elegy 4

Both book 1, elegy 19, and book 2, elegy 6, were written as private conversations with Cynthia. Book 3, elegy 4, must be read in the context of the elegies that surround it, especially book 3, elegies 1 through 5, all of which are considered appropriate subject matter for Propertius's poetry. As a group, these five elegies firmly argue that Propertius can be nothing but a poet of love, specifically a poet-priest (*sacerdos*) who gets his inspiration from the Greek poets Callimachus and Philetas and from Cynthia herself. In book 3, elegy 4, too, Propertius sings as a priest-prophet who prays for and predicts the success of Augustus's campaign to avenge the defeat of Crassus by the Parthians. The disaster of Carrhae in 53 B.C.E., in which Crassus perished, haunted Augustan politics and poetry until the Roman military standards were quietly restored by the Parthians in 20 B.C.E. Book 3, elegy 4, begins with a patriotic fervor vividly at odds with the normally private tone of the Latin love elegy. In lines one through six, Propertius anticipates the actual victory and describes Parthia as already a Roman province; lines seven through ten constitute an exhortation to the armed forces to avenge Crassus's defeat; and lines eleven through twenty-two consist of a prayer to the gods that Augustus will celebrate a triumph in Rome for his defeat of Parthia and that Propertius will live to see it. The formal and public prayer form is here suddenly made quite personal, with the poet's reference to his own death and his eyewitness account of the future triumph.

The reader's attention to the public success of Augustus is distracted by the poet himself, who watches the triumphal procession while reclining on his lady's breast, and the poem ends with a significant *recusatio*, Propertius's rejection of personal military glory. The poet is content, rather, to cheer the victor from the sidelines. The love elegist's distaste for military success is particularly strong in Propertius, and the juxtaposition of public and private themes in book 3, elegy 4, shows that, for Propertius, the public world intrudes into his poetry only by way of contrast with his private world. This contrast, however, is a fertile one semantically, for, on another level of interpretation, Propertius is not rejecting the military world and its vocabulary but appropriating them for his own amorous theme. Is the victor in this poem Augustus on his chariot or Propertius in the arms of his mistress? Does the poet cheer in the last line because the Parthians have been defeated or because Cynthia has been won? Propertius has transformed a public poem into a very personal statement and has demonstrated once again his control over structure, tone, and diction.

The *Elegies* of Propertius thus function in a carefully delineated and controlled world centered on the poet's relationship with his mistress Cynthia. The love theme is not strong in every elegy; for example, the aetiological and historical poems of book 4 are usually said to represent Propertius's attempts to reconcile the elegiac form with Augustan demands for more acceptable themes. As Sullivan has shown, however, even these poems cannot be separated from the personal love tone that pervades the corpus and can be seen to operate in an ironic mode as the poet's ultimate *recusatio* of the public world in favor of the private world. Propertius's desire to apply Callimachean poetic principles to the love elegy made his poetry particularly dependent upon careful manipulation of structure and tone within and between elegies and upon a striking attempt to employ vocabulary in violently different semantic contexts.

Bibliography

Bailey, D. R. Shackleton. *Propertiana*. Amsterdam: Hakkert, 1967. Bailey provides critical notes on selected passages that have proven problematic. He takes into account particular scholars and editors, suggests alternate readings, and provides textual analysis.

Benediktson, D. Thomas. *Propertius: Modernist Poet of Antiquity*. Carbondale: Southern Illinois University Press, 1988. The anticlassical and "modernist" characteristics of Propertius's poems are explored through his use of interior monologue, imagist (vorticist) style, and the organizational device of ring composition.

Butrica, James L. *The Manuscript Tradition of Propertius*. Toronto: University of Toronto Press, 1984. This highly technical survey, catalog, and study of known Propertian manuscripts and incunabula is aimed at the serious student of the poet and provides a clear and detailed picture of the transmission of the poems.

Greene, Ellen. *The Erotics of Domination: Male Desire and the Mistress in Latin Love Poetry*. Baltimore: Johns Hopkins University Press, 1998. Chapter 3 is a feminist critique of gender roles and ideology in the *Monobiblos*. Greene sees Cynthia not as a true subject, but rather as being reduced to *materia*, an object of Propertius's male fantasy.

Günther, Hans Christian. *Quaestiones Propertianae*. New York: Brill, 1997. A comprehensive study dealing with the major critical problems of one of the most difficult authors of Latin literature. A systematic examination of the two major factors which have been assumed to be responsible for the state of the transmitted text of Propertius: dislocation and interpolation. Günther covers a large number of cases of verbal corruption and discusses problems of the manuscript tradition on the basis of the most recent research.

Hubbard, Margaret. *Propertius*. London: Duckworth, 1974. An introductory work for a general readership, though with insight of value to veteran readers. Hubbard moves through the poems, placing them in their historical and biographical contexts and comparing them technically and aesthetically with those of Propertius's contemporaries.

Janan, Micaela Wakil. *The Politics of Desire: Propertius IV*. Berkeley: University of California Press, 2001. Janan radically reassesses Propertius's last elegies, using contemporary psychoanalytic theory to illuminate these challenging texts. Janan finds that the upheaval of Rome's transformation to empire corresponds to the intellectually unsettled conditions of our own time, so that contemporary methodologies offer an uncannily suitable approach for understanding Propertius.

Sullivan, John P. *Propertius: A Critical Introduction*. New York: Cambridge University Press, 1974. An introduction aimed at a technically prepared audience. Sullivan sketches the development of his poems from books 1 to 4 in terms of his changing social and political world. He sees strong continuities in content, though he survived due to use of increasingly "subtler techniques of self expression."

Thomas J. Sienkewicz;
bibliography updated by Joseph P. Byrne

ALEXANDER PUSHKIN

Born: Moscow, Russia; June 6, 1799
Died: St. Petersburg, Russia; February 10, 1837

PRINCIPAL POETRY

Ruslan i Lyudmila, 1820 (*Ruslan and Liudmila*, 1936)
Gavriiliada, 1822 (*Gabriel: A Poem*, 1926)
Kavkazskiy plennik, 1822 (*The Prisoner of the Caucasus*, 1895)
Bratya razboyniki, 1824
Evgeny Onegin, 1825-1832, 1833 (*Eugene Onegin*, 1881)
Bakhchisaraiskiy fontan, 1827 (*The Fountain of Bakhchisarai*, 1849)
Graf Nulin, 1827 (*Count Nulin*, 1972)
Tsygany, 1827 (*The Gypsies*, 1957)
Poltava, 1829 (English translation, 1936)
Domik v Kolomne, 1833 (*The Little House at Kolomna*, 1977)
Skazka o mertvoy tsarevne, 1833 (*The Tale of the Dead Princess*, 1924)
Skazka o rybake ir rybke, 1833 (*The Tale of the Fisherman and the Fish*, 1926)
Skazka o tsare Saltane, 1833 (*The Tale of Tsar Saltan*, 1950)
Skazka o zolotom petushke, 1834 (*The Tale of the Golden Cockerel*, 1918)
Medniy vsadnik, 1837 (*The Bronze Horseman*, 1899)
Collected Narrative and Lyrical Poetry, 1984
Epigrams and Satirical Verse, 1984

OTHER LITERARY FORMS

Often considered the founder of modern Russian literature, Alexander Pushkin was a prolific writer, not only of poetry but also of plays, novels, and short stories. His *malenkiye tragedii*, or "little tragedies"—brief, dramatic episodes in blank verse—include *Skupoy rytsar* (wr. 1830, pr., pb. 1852; *The Covetous Knight*, 1925), *Kamyenny gost* (wr. 1830, pb. 1839; *The Stone Guest*, 1936), *Motsart i Salyeri* (pr., pb. 1832; *Mozart and Salieri*, 1920), and *Pir vo vryemya chumy* (pb. 1833; *The Feast in Time of the Plague*, 1925).

Boris Godunov (wr. 1824-1825, pb. 1831; English translation, 1918) is Pushkin's famous historical tragedy constructed on the Shakespearean ideal that plays should be written "for the people." A story set in late sixteenth century Russia—a period of social and political chaos—it deals with the relationship between the ruling classes and the masses; written for the people, it, not surprisingly, gained universal appeal.

Pushkin's most important prose work, *Kapitanskaya dochka* (1836; *The Captain's Daughter*, 1846), is a historical novel of the Pugachev Rebellion. *Pikovaya dama* (1834; *The Queen of Spades*, 1858) is another well-known prose work, which influenced Fyodor Dostoevski's novels.

With its emphasis on civic responsibility, Pushkin's works have been translated into most major languages. His letters have been collected and annotated in English by J. Thomas Shaw as *The Letters of Alexander Pushkin* (1963).

ACHIEVEMENTS

Alexander Pushkin was the first poet to write in a purely Russian style. Aleksandr Tvardovsky calls him "the soul of our people." Considered as one of Russia's greatest poets, if not the greatest, he does not hold the same place in foreign countries, because his greatest achievement is in his use of the Russian language, with a flavor impossible to capture in translation. Even today his verses are regarded as the most natural expression of Russian poetry. After a lengthy period of stiff classicism and excessive sentimentality in eighteenth century literature, as seen in Konstantine Batyushkov, Vasily Zhukovsky, and Nikolai Karamzin, Pushkin breathed freshness and spontaneity into Russian poetry. Zhukovsky, the acknowledged dean of Russian letters, recognized this new spirit when, after the publication of *Ruslan and Liudmila* in 1820, he gave Pushkin a portrait of himself with the inscription: "To the victorious pupil from the vanquished master on that most important day on which he completed *Ruslan and Liudmila*."

It was Pushkin who brought the Romantic spirit to Russia, although it is impossible to categorize him as a pure Romantic. Pushkin's Byronic heroes in *The Prisoner of the Caucasus* and Aleko in *The Gypsies* introduced a new type of character, proud, disillusioned, and in conflict with himself and society, which greatly appealed to the Russia of the 1820's. Pushkin also introduced a love for the primitive and the exotic, which he found especially in southern Russia, and a deep and personal appreciation of nature. In the Romantic spirit, Pushkin showed a fond appreciation of Russia's past, her heroes, her folklore, and her people, which Soviet critics see as *narodnost*.

Alexander Pushkin (Library of Congress)

Pushkin was also a realist who maintained a certain detached objectivity and distance, never quite penetrating beneath the surface of his heroes or completely identifying with them. He documents even his most Romantic poems. Pushkin's last post permitted him access to the imperial archives, a privilege that he deeply cherished. His interest in history led him to works on Peter the Great, on the Pugachev Rebellion, and into his own family history in *Arap Petra velikogo* (1828-1841; *Peter the Great's Negro*, 1896).

Although Pushkin was primarily a lyric poet, he was accomplished in all genres. *Eugene Onegin*, the only Russian novel in verse, lacks the richness of plot and social commentary which Honoré de Balzac, Leo Tolstoy, and Fyodor Dostoevski were later to develop, but it does contain humor, satire, and tender lyricism, all presented in poetry of incomparable assurance and grace. The work was acclaimed by the great nineteenth century critic Vissarion Belinsky as "an encyclopedia of Russian life."

Pushkin aimed at revitalizing the Russian theater and saw William Shakespeare as a better model than Jean Racine or Molière. Although his major play *Boris Godunov*, falls short of dramatic intensity in its failure to realize the tragic fate of the hero, it is a lyric masterpiece and a profound study of ambition and power. Never a success on the stage, Pushkin's play was the inspiration for operas by Modest Mussorgsky and Sergei Prokofiev. The "little tragedies" are models of concision and true classical concentration. Each highlights one main theme: covetousness (*The Covetous Knight*), envy (*Mozart and Salieri*), passion (*The Stone Guest*, on the Don Juan theme), and pleasure before death (*Feast in Time of the Plague*). These plays rank among Pushkin's finest achievements.

Pushkin's later years were devoted more to prose than to poetry, with the exception of *The Bronze Horseman*, the folktales in verse, and several lyric poems. Pushkin did for Russia what the Brothers Grimm did for Germany in folk literature. Although many of his sources were not specifically Russian, such as *The Tale of the Dead Princess*, Pushkin transformed them into authentic national pieces by his unaffected use of folk expressions, alliteration, and real feeling for the people. In all of his work, his effortless rhymes, easy and varied rhythms, natural speech, and true identification with the spirit of his time make him beloved by the Russian people and the father of all Russian literature.

BIOGRAPHY

Alexander (Aleksandr) Sergeyevich Pushkin was born in Moscow on June 6, 1799, the second of three children. His mother, Nadezhda Osipovna Hannibal, was of African descent through her grandfather, Abram Hannibal, who was immortalized by Pushkin in *Peter the Great's Negro*. His father, Sergei Lvovich, and his uncle, Vasily Lvovich, were both writers. His father frequently entertained literary friends and had an excellent library of French and Russian classics, in which Pushkin by the age of twelve had read widely but indiscriminately. Pushkin's childhood was marked by the lack of a close relationship with his parents, although he formed lasting ties with his maternal grandmother, Marya Alexeyevna, and his nurse, Arina Rodionovna, who was responsible for his love of folklore. The family could boast of very ancient aristocratic roots but suffered from a lack of money.

In 1811, Pushkin was accepted into the newly founded lycée at Tsarskoe Selo, designed by the czar to give a broad liberal education to aristocrats, especially those destined for administrative posts in the government. He remained there until his graduation in 1817, where he distinguished himself less by diligence than by natural ability, especially in French and Russian literature. Always of uneven temperament, he was not the most popular student in his class, but he did form lasting friendships with schoolmates Ivan Pushchin, Wilhelm Küchelbecker and Baron Anton Delvig; he also formed ties with such great literary figures as Zhukovsky and Karamizin, as well as bonds with the hussar officers, notably Pyotr Chaadayev. Pushkin began writing his earliest verses in French but soon turned to Russian.

After completing the lycée, Pushkin was appointed to the Ministry of Foreign Affairs in St. Petersburg. From 1817 to 1820, he led a dissipated life in the capital, much like that of Onegin in chapter 1 of *Eugene Onegin*. He became involved in liberal causes, though not as a member of the more revolutionary secret societies, and began to circulate his liberal verses. This alarmed the authorities, who proposed exile in Siberia, but because of the intercession of prominent personalities, among them Zhukovsky and the former principal of the lycée, Egor Englehardt, Pushkin was simply transferred to the south under the supervision of the paternal General I. N. Inzov.

Pushkin's first months in the south were spent traveling with the family of General Nikolai Raevsky through the Caucasus and the Crimea. Overwhelmed by the beauty of nature and the simplicity of the people, it was here that he wrote most of his so-called southern poems. The Raevskys introduced him to an appreciation of Lord Byron, which was reflected in his works of this period. Their daughters, especially Marya, were among Pushkin's many passions. Between 1820 and 1823, a productive literary period, he remained mostly in Kishinev. This peaceful existence was to end when Pushkin was transferred to Odessa under the stern General Vorontsov, whose wife Elisa became the object of Pushkin's attentions after Amalia Riznich. For this and other offenses, Pushkin was dismissed from the service in 1824 and sent to his mother's estate at Mikhailovskoe near Pskov. Here he was placed under the direct supervision of his father and the local authorities. He quarreled constantly with his family, so that all of them withdrew and left him alone from 1824 to 1826. He had few companions other than the aged nurse Arina Rodionovna. This enforced isolation proved very productive, for it was here that he composed a great deal of *Eugene Onegin* and wrote *Boris Godunov* and many short poems, and drew his inspiration for later *skazki* (tales).

The death of Alexander I in 1825 provoked the Decembrist Revolt on December 26 of the same year. Pushkin's sympathies were with the revolutionaries, but his exile fortunately prevented him from participating. He took the opportunity of the new czar's accession to the throne, however, to make a successful plea for liberation. After 1826, he was permitted to travel to Moscow and, with reservations, to the capital, although his supervisor, Count Benkendorf, was not amenable to his requests. The years between 1826 and 1830 were a period of maturing and searching; they were also rich in literary output, especially of lyric poetry and the "little tragedies."

In 1830, Pushkin became engaged to the Moscow beauty Natalia Nikolayevna Goncharova, whom he married in 1831. It was an unsuccessful match, though not a completely disastrous marriage. Pushkin's wife had no interest in literature and had social aspirations far beyond either her or her husband's means. Four children were born to them, but Natalia's dissipation and Pushkin's jealousy eventually led him to melancholy and resentment. Financial worries and lack of advancement added to his problems. When Baron Georges d'Anthès, a young Alsatian, began paying undue attention to Pushkin's wife and the entire affair became a public scandal, Pushkin challenged d'Anthès to a duel. Pushkin was mortally wounded, and died on February 10, 1837.

Analysis

Alexander Pushkin's first verses were written in the style of French classicism and sentimentalism. His models were Voltaire and Evariste Parny, Gavrila Derzhavin, Zhukovsky, and Batyushkov. He wrote light, voluptuous verses, occasional pieces, and epigrams. Even in his early works, of which the most important is *Ruslan and Liudmila*, he shows restrained eroticism, always tempered by his classical training, which led him from the very beginning into excellent craftsmanship, brevity, and simplicity.

Wit, humor, and satire

The lively wit, humor, and satire that were evident from the first continued to characterize Pushkin's work. *Ruslan and Liudmila* is a mock-epic, and the same strain appears in chapters 1 and 2 of *Eugene Onegin. Gabriel*, a parody on the Annunciation, which caused Pushkin a great deal of embarrassment with the authorities, has many witty passages, such as Satan's ensnarement of Adam and Eve by love. Pushkin achieves his humor by the use of parody, not hesitating to use it in dealing with the greatest authors such as Shakespeare and Voltaire, and with his friend and master Zhukovsky. Like Molière, however, he never really offends; his satire and dry irony produce a generally good-natured effect.

Political poems

Pushkin first became known in St. Petersburg as a writer of liberal verses, and this—coupled with charges of atheism—made him a constant target of the imperial censors. His famous "Vol'nost': Oda" ("Ode to Freedom") is severe on Napoleon and condemns the excesses of the French Revolution, yet it reminds monarchs that they must be subservient to the law. In "Derevnya" ("The Countryside"), he longs for the abolition of serfdom, yet looks to the czar for deliverance. Pushkin did not conceal his sympathy for the Decembrists, and in his famous "Vo glubine sibirskikh rud" ("Message to Siberia") he reminds the exiled revolutionaries that "freedom will once again shine, and brothers give you back your sword." His later poems address more general issues, and in 1831 during the Polish Uprising he speaks out clearly in favor of the czar "Klevetnikam Rossii" ("To the Slanderers of Russia"). Finally, *The Bronze Horseman* addresses the very complex theme of the individual in conflict with the state.

Heroines and love poetry

Pushkin knew many passions in his brief lifetime, and several women inspired both his life and poetry. Marya Raevskaya became the model for many of his heroines, from the Circassian girl in *The Prisoner of the Caucasus* to Marya in *Poltava*. Amalia Riznich, destined to die in Italy, reappears in "Dlya beregov otchizny dal'noy" ("Abandoning an Alien Country") in 1830. Elisa Vorontsova, the wife of Pushkin's stern superior in Odessa, was a powerful influence who haunted the poet long after his return to the north. The ring she gave him is immortalized in "Khrani menya, moy talisman" ("Talisman") and "The Burned Letter," where the ashes recall her memory. Anna Kern was the inspiration for the almost mystical "Ya pomnyu chudnoye mgnoven'ye" ("I Remember a Wonderful Moment"). Natalya Goncharova, while still Pushkin's fiancé, likewise assumes a spiritual role in "Madona" ("Madonna"). Pushkin's love poetry, while passionate, is also delicate and sensitive, and even the most voluptuous evocations concentrate on images such as those of eyes and feet.

Nature

In Romantic fashion, Pushkin was one of the first to introduce nature into his works. First inspired by the trip to the south, where the beauty of the Caucasus overwhelmed him, he sees freedom in the wide expanses and steep mountains. Later, on a second trip—as described in "Kavkazsky" ("The Caucasus")—he evokes the playful rivers, the low clouds and the silver-capped mountains. He feels that the sight of a monastery brings him to the neighborhood of Heaven. The north also has its charms, particularly the Russian winter. There are exquisite verses on winter in the fifth chapter of *Eugene Onegin*, and in his lyrics about the swirling snowstorm in "Zinniy Vecher" ("Winter Evening") or the winter road that symbolizes his sad journey through life. Both city and country come alive in the crisp cold of winter in the prologue to *The Bronze Horseman*.

Melancholy

Despite ever-recurring wit, irony, and gentle sensitivity, Pushkin's poetry is fundamentally melancholy and often tragic. This dichotomy corresponds to the division of his personality: dissipated yet deep. The southern poems all end tragically, his plays are all tragedies, and *Eugene Onegin* ends with the death of Lensky and the irremediable disappointment of Tatyana and Onegin. Pushkin frequently writes of the evil and demonic forces of nature (as in Tatyana's dream), of madness (Eugene in *The Bronze Horseman*), and of violence (in "Zhenikh," "The Bridegroom"). A melancholy vein permeates his lyrics as well. Like the Romantics, Pushkin speaks frequently of death, perhaps foreseeing his own. The hour of parting from a loved one, a frequent subject of his lyrics, foreshadows death. As early as 1823, in "Telega zhizni" ("The Wagon of Time"), he sees the old man as the one who calmly awaits eternal sleep. Pushkin's tragic vision is complicated by the absence of a Christian worldview with a belief in life after death. Unlike Dostoevski, Pushkin writes of unmitigated, not of redemptive, suffering. S. M. Frank, who does admit a spiritual dimension in Pushkin, compares his work to Mozart's music, which seems gay, but is in fact sad. Yet it is this very sadness which puts him in the tradition of Russian literature, anticipating Nikolai Gogol's "laughter through tears."

Ruslan and Liudmila

Pushkin's first major work, *Ruslan and Liudmila*, was published in 1820. It is now usually placed in a minor category, but it was important at the time as the first expression of the Russian spirit. Witty and ironic, the poem is written in the style of a mock-epic, much in the tradition of Ariosto's *Orlando furioso* (1516, 1521, 1532; English translation, 1591). It also echoes Voltaire, and the fourth canto parodies Zhukovsky's "Spyaschaya carevna" ("Twelve Sleeping Maidens"). In fact, the whole plot resembles Zhukovsky's projected "Vladimir." It consists of six cantos, a prologue added in 1828, and an epilogue. Pushkin began the poem in 1817 while still in school, and he was already in exile in the south when it was published.

Ruslan and Liudmila, in Walter Vickery's words, transports the reader to the "unreal and delightful poetic world of cheerful unconcern," returning to the legendary days of ancient Kiev, where Prince Vladimir is giving a wedding feast for his daughter Liudmila. The fortunate bridegroom Ruslan is about to enjoy the moment he has so voluptuously awaited when a clap of thunder resounds and his bride is snatched away from him by the dwarf enchanter Chernomor. Prince Vladimir promises half of his kingdom and Liudmila as a bride to the man who rescues her. Ruslan sets off with his three rivals, Ratmir, Rogdai, and Farlaf. Ratmir eventually chooses a pastoral life; Rogdai is slain, and Farlaf reappears at the moment when Ruslan is about to return with Liudmila. In true knightly fashion, Ruslan saves Kiev from an attack by the Pechenegs, kills his last rival, and marries the princess.

Pushkin's poem captures many exaggerated scenes from the *byliny* or heroic tales, such as the death of the giant head, and ends with a full-scale epic battle. It is a gentle mockery of chivalry, sorcery, and love. Critics from Zhukovsky to the Soviets hailed it as a true folk-epic in the spirit of *narodnost* (nationalism) although many of Pushkin's contemporaries were shocked at his unfaithfulness to classical antiquity and his trivial subject. The public, however, welcomed it, seeing in it a new inspiration for the times. The prologue, especially, captures the popular spirit with its learned cat on a green oak who recites a folktale when he turns to the left and a song when he moves to the right.

As in all of Pushkin's works, the language is the most important feature, offsetting the many flaws of Pushkin's still immature talent. His choice of vocabulary is very Russian, even popular, and his rhythms and rhymes are graceful and effortless. Henri Troyat refers to him as "a virtuoso of rime" and says that this talent alone announced possibilities for the future.

Eugene Onegin

Eugene Onegin, Pushkin's novel in verse, was begun in 1823 in Kishinev and completed in 1830. It is composed of eight cantos or chapters, as Pushkin preferred to call them. There are projects and fragments for two other parts, including Onegin's journey. Each chapter contains forty to fifty-four stanzas of fourteen lines each, in four-foot iambic, and with a special rhyme scheme called the "Onegin stanza": *AbAbCCddEffEgg* (small letters indicating masculine and capitals feminine rhymes). Pushkin did not return to this stanza form and it has rarely been used since. The novel itself resembles sentimental types such as Jean-Jacques Rousseau's *La Nouvelle Héloïse* (1761; *Julia: Or, The New Eloisa*, 1773) and Benjamin Constant's *Adolphe* (1815; English translation, 1816). It is also a type of *Bildungsroman* or the *éducation sentimentale* of Tatyana and Onegin. It is in reality a combination of several genres: novel, comic-epic, and above all poetry, for it is inseparable from the verse in which it is written.

The first two chapters, the product of Pushkin's youth, show the greatest absence of structure. They abound in digressions and poetic ruminations ranging from the ballet to women's feet. They introduce us to the hero Eugene Onegin, a St. Petersburg dandy, who spends his life in boredom until an inheritance brings him to an equally boring life in the provinces. Here he meets the dreamy poet Lensky, in love with a neighbor, Olga Larin. It is at this point that the tone of the poem changes, as Olga's older sister, Tatyana, immediately develops an intense passion for Onegin, and in her simplicity reveals her love for him in her famous letter. Onegin politely refuses her and continues his aimless existence, interrupted by a flirtation with Olga, thus provoking a duel with Lensky in which the poet is killed.

Years pass, and Tatyana is married against her will to an elderly and unattractive general. Onegin meets her in Moscow and falls passionately in love with her. He declares his love, but this time it is Tatyana in her mature serenity who informs him: "I love you . . . but I have become another's wife; I shall be true to him through life." Here the poem ends abruptly yet fittingly as Tatyana emerges as the tragic heroine in this tale of twice-rejected love.

The poem maintains an internal unity through the parallel between Onegin's rejection of Tatyana and her refusal of him. *Eugene Onegin* is, however, essentially a lyric poem about the tragic consequences of love rather than a pure novel with a solid substructure. Pushkin draws poetry out of a samovar, the wrinkled nanny who is modeled on Arina Rodionovna, and the broken-hearted resignation of Tatyana. The changing of the seasons indicates the passage of time as Pushkin sings of the beautiful Russian countryside. He likewise enters into his characters, and makes of Onegin a realistic hero and the first of a long line of "superfluous men" to appear in Mikhail Lermontov, Ivan Goncharov, and Ivan Turgenev. Tatyana is perfectly consistent as her youthful naïveté changes into a controlled maturity. She has often been described as the purest figure in the whole of Russian literature, and has become the prototype of Russian womanhood. Pushkin's contemporaries read his poem with enthusiasm, and today it is still one of the great classics of Russian literature. Foreign readers may know it better through Pyotr Ilich Tchaikovsky's opera; again, this results from the fact that it is essentially a poem, defying translation.

Poltava

Pushkin always showed a great deal of interest in Peter the Great, and refers to him in his lyric poetry, in longer poems, and in his prose (*Peter the Great's Negro*). It is in *Poltava* and *The Bronze Horseman* that he reaches his height. *Poltava*, written in three weeks in 1828, has an epic quality but also draws on the ballad, ode, and oral tradition. It recalls Sir Walter Scott's *Marmion* (1808), since it places historical characters in a Romantic background. Lord Byron in *Mazeppa* (1819), drew on the same sources but used instead an apocryphal account of the hero's youth.

The main focus of *Poltava* is the battle of 1709, in which the Russians under Peter the Great defeated the Swedes under Charles XII. Poltava was the turning point in the Russo-Swedish War. Against this historical backdrop is set the romance of the aged Ukrainian Cossack hetman Mazepa with the young and beautiful Marya, daughter of Kochubey, who refuses to allow the marriage. The two marry in spite of him, and Kochubey seeks revenge by revealing, to Peter, Mazepa's plan of revolt against him. His project miscarries, however, when Peter believes Mazepa's denials. Kochubey is taken prisoner by Mazepa and is about to be executed when Marya learns about her husband's treachery against her father. Arriving too late to save him, she leaves, returning to her husband only briefly as a madwoman before Mazepa's flight with Charles XII after leading an unsuccessful revolt against the victorious Peter.

Although Pushkin has interwoven much historical material into his tale, he has been charged with excessive melodrama by critics from Belinsky to the present day, who see in Mazepa a kind of Gothic villain. Pushkin is likewise charged with unsuccessfully fusing the historical and the Romantic, and more recently, by John Bayley, for the gap "between two kinds of romance, the modern melodrama and the traditional tragic ballad." Mazepa is one of Pushkin's few dark and villainous characters, but Marya has been acknowledged as truly *narodnaya* by Belinsky and contemporary Soviet critics. Peter is the all-pervading presence, larger than life, who symbolizes the growing importance of Russia.

THE BRONZE HORSEMAN

In *The Bronze Horseman*, Peter reappears in retrospect. Pushkin wrote *The Bronze Horseman* in 1833 partially in response to the Polish poet Adam Mickiewicz, who had attacked the Russian autocracy. It is composed of an introduction and two parts, 481 lines in all, and is rightly considered one of Pushkin's greatest masterpieces. It combines personal lyricism, political, social, and literary themes, and raises philosophical questions in paradoxical fashion. The title refers to the equestrian statue of Peter the Great by E. M. Falconet which still stands along the Neva River. The historical incident that inspired the poem was the devastating flood that struck St. Petersburg on November 7, 1824.

In the introduction, Peter the Great stands looking over the Neva, then a deserted swamp with a few ramshackle huts. He plans to build a city there, which will open a window to the West and terrify all of his enemies. A hundred years pass, and the young city is the pride of the north, a cold sparkling gem of granite and iron, the scene of royal balls, military reviews, and winter sports. Suddenly, the picture changes as Pushkin begins his sad tale. Eugene, a poor government clerk (whose last name is not important), is making plans to marry Parasha. That very night, the Neva whirls and swirls and rages like an angry beast; the next day Parasha's home is destroyed, and she is lost. Eugene visits the empty spot, and goes mad from the shock. Life continues as usual, but poor Eugene wanders through the city until one day he shakes his angry fist at the Bronze Horseman, who gallops after him down the streets of St. Petersburg. Later, a dilapidated house is washed up on one of the islands; near it Eugene's corpse is found.

Pushkin's poem shows complete mastery of technique. In lines starkly terse yet rich with onomatopoeic sounds, Pushkin conjures up the mighty flood, the proud emperor, and the defenseless Eugene. In the last scene, Peter and Eugene come face to face, and seemingly the emperor wins, yet Pushkin is far from being reconciled to the notion that individual destiny must be sacrificed to historical necessity. Indeed, Eugene is the first of a long line of downtrodden Russian heroes, such as Akakiy Akakyevich and Makar Devushkin, possessing dignity and daring to face authority. Peter is the human hero, contemplating greatness; he is also the impassive face of destiny. The poem itself poses the problem of Pushkin's own troubled existence as well as the ambiguous and cruel fate of all human beings.

OTHER MAJOR WORKS

LONG FICTION: *Arap Petra velikogo*, 1828-1841 (*Peter the Great's Negro*, 1896); *Kirdzhali*, 1834 (English translation, 1896); *Kapitanskaya dochka*, 1836 (*The Captain's Daughter*, 1846); *Dubrovsky*, 1841 (English translation, 1892); *Yegipetskiye nochi*, 1841 (*Egyptian Nights*, 1896); *Istoriya sela Goryukhina*, 1857 (*History of the Village of Goryukhino*, 1966).

SHORT FICTION: *Povesti Belkina*, 1831 (*Russian Romance*, 1875; better known as *The Tales of Belkin*, 1947); *Pikovaya dama*, 1834 (*The Queen of Spades*, 1858).

PLAYS: *Boris Godunov*, wr. 1824-1825, pb. 1831 (English translation, 1918); *Skupoy rytsar*, wr. 1830, pr., pb. 1852 (*The Covetous Knight*, 1925); *Kamyenny gost*, wr. 1830, pb. 1839 (*The Stone Guest*, 1936); *Motsart i Salyeri*, pr., pb. 1832 (*Mozart and Salieri*, 1920); *Pir vo vryemya chumy*, pb. 1833 (*The Feast in Time of the Plague*, 1925); *Stseny iz rytsarskikh vryemem*, wr. 1835, pr., pb. 1937; *Rusalka*, pb. 1837 (*The Water Nymph*, 1924); *Little Tragedies*, pb. 1946 (includes *The Covetous Knight*, *The Stone Guest*, *Mozart and Salieri*, and *The Feast in Time of the Plague*).

NONFICTION: *Istoriya Pugacheva*, 1834 (*The Pugachev Rebellion*, 1966); *Puteshestviye v Arzrum*, 1836 (*A Journey to Arzrum*, 1974); *Dnevnik, 1833-1835*, 1923; *Pisma*, 1926-1935 (3 volumes); *The Letters of Alexander Pushkin*, 1963 (3 volumes); *Pisma poslednikh let 1834-1837*, 1969.

MISCELLANEOUS: *The Captain's Daughter and Other Tales*, 1933; *The Works of Alexander Pushkin*, 1936; *The Poems, Prose, and Plays of Pushkin*, 1936; *Polnoye sobraniye sochineniy*, 1937-1959 (17 volumes); *The Complete Prose Tales of Alexander Pushkin*, 1966; *Pushkin Threefold*, 1972; *A. S. Pushkin bez tsenzury*, 1972; *Polnoye sobraniye sochineniy*, 1977-1979 (10 volumes); *Alexander Pushkin: Complete Prose Fiction*, 1983.

BIBLIOGRAPHY

Bethea, David M. *Realizing Metaphors: Alexander Pushkin and the Life of the Poet*. Madison: University of Wisconsin Press, 1998. Bethea illustrates the relation between the art and life of Pushkin and shows how he still speaks to our time. The Pushkin who emerges from Bethea's portrait is one who, long unknown to English-language readers, closely resembles the original both psychologically and artistically.

Evdokimova, Svetlana. *Pushkin's Historical Imagination*. New Haven, Conn.: Yale University Press, 1999. An examination of the range of Pushkin's fictional and nonfictional works on the subject of history. Evdokimova considers Pushkin's ideas on the relation between chance and necessity, the significance of great individuals, and historical truth.

Feinstein, Elaine. *Pushkin*. London: Weidenfeld & Nicolson, 1998. A chronicle of Pushkin's life that explores the paradoxes of his personality and reveals information surrounding his death. Feinstein has captured for the reader the essence of one of the most intriguing men ever to enter the pantheon of literary geniuses.

Ryfa, Juras T., ed. *Collected Essays in Honor of the Bicentennial of Alexander Pushkin's Birth*. Lewiston, N.Y.: Edwin Mellen Press, 2000. A collection of critical essays on the works of Pushkin. Includes bibliographical references and index.

Vitale, Serena. *Pushkin's Button*. Translated by Ann Goldstein and Jon Rothschild. New York: Farrar, Straus and Giroux, 1999. A cultural history and narrative of the last months of Pushkin's life before his fatal duel. Vitale brings to life the world of St. Petersburg in the 1830's using her own research with information gleaned from secondary literature and the memoirs and letters of Pushkin's contemporaries.

Irma M. Kashuba;
bibliography updated by the editors

Q

FRANCIS QUARLES

Born: Romford, Essex, England; baptized May 8, 1592

Died: London, England; September 8, 1644

PRINCIPAL POETRY

A Feast for Wormes Set Forth in a Poeme of the History of Jonah, 1620
Pentelogia: Or, The Quintessence of Meditation, 1620 (appended to *A Feast for Wormes*), 1626 (published as a separate chapbook)
Hadassa: Or, The History of Queene Ester, 1621
Job Militant, with Meditations Divine and Morall, 1624
Sions Elegies, Wept by Jeremie the Prophet, 1624
An Alphabet of Elegies upon the Much and Truly Lamented Death of . . . Doctor Ailmer, 1625
Sions Sonets Sung by Solomon the King, 1624
Argalus and Parthenia, 1629
The Historie of Samson, 1631
Divine Fancies: Digested into Epigrammes, Meditations, and Observations, 1632 (in four books)
Divine Poems, 1633
Emblemes: Divine and Moral, 1635 (in five books)
Hieroglyphikes of the Life of Man, 1638
Solomons Recantation, Entituled Ecclesiastes Paraphrased, 1645
The Shepheards Oracles: Delivered in Certain Eglogues, 1646
Hosanna: Or, Divine Poems on the Passion of Christ, 1647

OTHER LITERARY FORMS

In later life Francis Quarles published a pious work in prose called *Enchiridion, Containing Institutions Divine and Moral* (1640). This very popular collection of aphorisms on religious and ethical subjects was reissued in an expanded edition the year after its original publication. It is notable for its stylish phrasing and wordplay.

Always strongly royalist in his sympathies, Quarles produced several prose works of a political nature toward the end of his life, as the struggle between king and Commons became more pronounced. *Observations Concerning Princes and States upon Peace and Warre* (1642) may perhaps be grouped with such works; although it is essentially another collection of pious meditations, it had obvious political implications in such volatile times, similar to those of the poetry in *The Shepheards Oracles*. More explicitly polemical is *The Loyal Convert* (1644), a defense of the king's political and religious position. Of a like nature are *The Whipper Whipt* (1644) and *The New Distemper* (c. 1644). The three royalist polemics were republished under the collective title *The Profest Royalist in His Quarrell with the Times* (1645) shortly after the author's death.

Among Quarles's other posthumous publications are *Judgement and Mercy for Afflicted Soules: Or, Meditations, Soliloquies, and Prayers* (1646; an unauthorized and inaccurate edition of Part II of this work had been published in 1644 under the title *Barnabas and Boanerges: Or, Wine and Oyl for Afflicted Soules). Judgement and Mercy for Afflicted Soules* is a book of prose meditations which would today probably be classified as prose poems. Also among the posthumous works, and somewhat surprisingly, is a play—or rather an interlude or masque—called *The Virgin Widow: A Comedie* (1649, written in 1641 or 1642). This comedy in mixed prose and verse is less amusing than it might have been, overwhelmed as it is by its strong didactic purpose and allegorical framework.

ACHIEVEMENTS

Nowhere in literary history is the fickleness of fashion more clearly illustrated than in the case of Francis Quarles. As Horace Walpole, looking back on the earlier period from the vantage point of 1757, aptly observed in a letter to George Montagu, "Milton was forced to wait till the world had done admiring Quarles." In the century of William Shakespeare, John Donne, Ben Jonson, Robert Herrick, George Herbert, John Milton, Richard Crashaw, Andrew Marvell, Henry Vaughan, and John Dryden, Quarles was by far the most popular poet.

Francis Quarles (Hulton Archive)

The success of Quarles in his own day can be explained in relation to those very weaknesses that deny him an audience today and mark his productions as mere historical curiosities, for Quarles had a special genius for popularization. His objective throughout his career was to reach a wide audience with an uplifting message. In this objective—so unlike Milton's appeal to a "fit audience though few"—he succeeded as few authors have; yet his success is exactly analogous to the success of a contemporary poet such as Rod McKuen. The difference is only that the seventeenth century was profoundly moved by religious and political emotions, whereas in contemporary society it is romantic love alone that can fire the imagination of the general public.

Biography

Francis Quarles was a younger son of an old gentry family settled in Essex. He was born in 1592 at his father's manor of Stewards at Romford and baptized on May 8 of the same year. One of his sisters became by marriage an aunt of the poet Dryden. Quarles attended Christ's College, Cambridge, receiving the degree of B.A. in 1608 while still in his teens. Afterward he spent some time at Lincoln's Inn studying law, although there is no indication that he ever pursued the law as a profession. In 1613 he embarked on what promised to be a career as a courtier with an appointment as Cup-Bearer to Princess Elizabeth on her marriage to Frederick V, Elector of the Palatinate. Quarles accompanied the couple to Germany, but he had returned to England before the terrible reversal of their fortunes in 1620, when the armies of the emperor expelled them from Bohemia, where Frederick had served briefly as elective king.

Back in England, Quarles married Ursula Woodgate on May 28, 1618. He and his wife had eighteen children. The eldest son, John, grew up to become a minor poet in his own right. It was shortly after his marriage that Quarles began publishing poetry, and numerous volumes of his biblical paraphrases and other religious poems issued from the press in rapid succession.

As a result of a reputation for piety that grew as each new volume was published, Quarles was offered the post of private secretary to James Ussher, then Bishop of Meath, later Anglican Archbishop of Armagh and Primate of Ireland. Quarles and his whole family lived in Ussher's episcopal palace in Dublin. Ussher is remembered as the author of a biblical chronology cited by fundamentalists in their rejection of the theory of evolution, and he was helped in his historical researches by Quarles. Yet curiously it was during this period that Quarles published his first secular work, *Argalus and Parthenia*.

Retiring to Essex, Quarles spent several years preparing his next work for publication. This was *Emblemes*, the volume which brought him his greatest fame. It was an immediate and enormous success, which Quarles followed up a few years later by issuing another volume in a similar vein, *Hieroglyphikes of the Life of Man*. This was the last book of his poetry published during his lifetime; during the remaining years of his life, however, he did publish occasional elegies as chapbooks.

In 1639 Quarles was appointed to succeed the playwright Thomas Middleton in the largely ceremonial office of chronologer to the city of London. Taking up his residence in London, he thereafter devoted himself to prose composition. In addition to writing an extremely popular manual of piety, as the political situation worsened he also began writing polemical tracts in defense of the king's policies. With these he became politically suspect to the Parliamentarians despite the continued attraction his poetry had for the whole Puritan party. The Parliamentary army searched his library, and manuscripts are said to have been burned. If any of his manuscripts were destroyed at the time, they must have been of a political nature, since after his death in 1644 his widow published a number of works of various other sorts, including a play and religious works in both prose and verse.

Analysis

Francis Quarles was not an innovator. Most of his works are in genres that were already riding a wave of popularity when he wrote—in fact, genres that had just become popular. He had a special knack for seeing the basic principles governing such genres and for creating works that adhered to these aesthetic principles with stark simplicity and without deep-felt personal involvement of the sort that is now regarded as the hallmark of, for example, the Metaphysical poets, the poets among Quarles's fellows who have enjoyed the highest critical prestige among later generations. Of course, it is not to be doubted that Quarles had deeply felt religious and political beliefs, but the popular success he enjoyed in his own day was a direct consequence of his inability to express more than surface impressions and clichés—or, to put the most positive face on his achievement—of his willingness to circumscribe his literary compositions by those surface impressions and clichés that express the popular imagination. It was with considerable truth that in the second half of the seventeenth century an antiquary described Quarles as "the sometime darling of our plebeian judgment."

Emblem books

Quarles's popularization of the emblem is of great historical interest. The enormous sales of emblem books in the seventeenth century are at first hard to understand. Certainly the special attraction of such works for the Puritans was as an alternative to the images that their religious beliefs proscribed inside churches, and Quarles was phenomenally popular with this group despite his avowed royalism and his support of episcopacy. For other readers, emblems were expressions of the fashionable baroque sensibility.

Emblems are, indeed, more important to the history of poetry than the fleeting popularity of emblem books during the seventeenth century would suggest. The emblematic frame of mind was fundamental to the age, informing many of the works of its major poets, and especially those of such Metaphysicals as Herbert. In fact, to understand Metaphysical imagery it is necessary to know something of the emblem tradition. Quarles's abiding historical significance is as the exemplary writer of emblem books. It is, however, important to remember that the works of Quarles always illustrate and synthesize trends; they capitalize on rather than inaugurate fashions. Herbert wrote emblematically but not because he had read Quarles. It was Quarles who read—and in his way popularized—Herbert. Although Herbert was certainly influenced by emblem books, Quarles's own emblem books were not published until after Herbert's death.

Mottoes, images, and epigrams

The art of the emblem consists of the successful marshaling of three things: a motto or scriptural text, a picture, and a poem or epigram. Emblem books had been published in English before Quarles, but his were the first English emblem books to be based exclusively on biblical texts, even though similar Continental works had been circulating and their popularity with English audiences had, in fact, inspired Quarles to produce his works. The shift in popularity from secular to religious emblems at the end of the sixteenth century has been chronicled by Mario Praz.

The emblem poet chooses a motto; he commissions an engraving to provide a literalist illustration of the motto; but from the modern point of view he creates only the epigram commenting on the significance of the motto and making use of the imagery of the picture. In the case of *Emblemes* and *Hieroglyphikes of the Life of Man*, Quarles's contribution was, in fact, somewhat less. According to Gordon S. Haight, all but ten of the mottoes and illustrations in *Emblemes*, for example, were derived from two Continental emblem books, although the illustrations were redrawn and newly engraved—in somewhat less than inspired fashion. Quarles's poems in *Emblemes* are not, however, mere translations of the anonymous *Typus Mundi* (1629, *Image of the World*) and of Herman Hugo's *Pia Desideria* (1624, *Holy Cravings*). As Rosemary Freeman points out, the similarities between Quarles's emblem poems and those of his sources are for the most part only such as inevitably occur when two authors treat the same subject.

In fact, Quarles's poems tend to overwhelm his illustrations and take on a life beyond the scope of true emblems. The poor quality of the engravings aside, Pope's jibe in *The Dunciad* (1728-1743) that "the pictures for the page atone," that "Quarles is sav'd by beauties not his own," is thus somewhat wide of the mark. Poetry so interrelated with illustration could not, of course, retain its popularity when fashions in the visual arts changed.

Quarles nevertheless achieved some critical respectability in the nineteenth century as a result of his skillful metrics. Since then, fashions in content have changed. Indeed, the bizarre imagery of Quarles's emblem illustrations is probably more in tune with contemporary taste than are his religious values. The chief recommendation of Quarles's emblem poetry today is its metrical control and variety. Although the diction is sometimes questionable and the subject matter is usually conventional, at least in these emblem poems Quarles did not hobble himself even further by restricting his verse to the couplet.

Meditations

The poems of *Emblemes* chronicle the troubled relationship of Anima, the soul, and Divine Love, pictured throughout as the Infant Jesus. The poems of *Hieroglyphikes of the Life of Man*, a shorter volume utilizing a somewhat wider range of verse forms, belabor the image of a candle to illustrate the workings of God's grace.

The systematic practice of meditation was a popular pursuit in the seventeenth century, and works of devotion based on principles of meditation, as Helen C. White has shown, were popular reading matter in a way that transcended sectarian interests. In fact, the two standard guidebooks of meditative technique in Protestant England were by Roman Catholics. Quarles's works in the meditation genre are in the tradition of *The Spiritual Exercises* (1548) of St. Ignatius Loyola, which emphasize an initial composition of place (a descriptive setting of the scene), rather than in the tradition of St. Francis de Sales, whose recommendation of sensuous immediacy was so influential with the Metaphysical poets.

Often described by Quarles simply as biblical paraphrases, his meditations typically deal with material from the historical books of the Old Testament. As a result, while the meditations of Donne and Thomas Traherne can still be appreciated for their powerful personal involvement with salvation and while the meditative poems of Richard Crashaw can still overwhelm modern readers with their sensuousness, the meditations of Quarles now seem to be simply quaint—to be merely decorative distortions of the compelling simplicities of biblical chronicle. *A Feast for Wormes*, *Hadassa*, *Job Militant*, and *The Historie of Samson* are works in this vein. In *The Historie of Samson*, in particular, Quarles seems to miss the spiritual and even the dramatic point of the story (so effectively retold by Milton) when he devotes seven times as much space to the woman of Timnath as to the final destruction of the Philistines.

Leaving Old Testament material and turning to the Passion and Death of Christ for material in *Pentelogia* and *Hosanna*, Quarles is no more successful. He tends to moralize a scene rather than to evoke it, and his work is at best uneven, showing lapses of taste and diction as, indeed, Grosart—Quarles's warmest appreciator—admits. The purely analytic and contemplative sections that follow the explicit paraphrases in all the works of this group, however, contribute to meditative objectives in a more consistent way. Quarles usually writes in couplets, and the analytic sections in particular occasionally achieve some of the grace and lucidity of Alexander Pope.

Divine Fancies

In fact, the best of Quarles's work ostensibly in the meditative genre is in the *Divine Fancies*, a book which uses meditative technique very impressionistically. In the *Divine Fancies* Quarles moves into explicit epigram, a more congenial format for couplets since it is the nature of epigram to be pointed, biting, limited. The epigrams of *Divine Fancies* are also essentially argumentative rather than devotional and thus really not meditative in tone. They frequently summarize in a few terse lines some point of catechism, but they have no poetic resonance. In fact, despite W. K. Jordan's description of Quarles as an early advocate of a kind of religious toleration, these epigrams reveal a considerable narrowness of spirit on points of sectarian dispute, especially those concerning church discipline.

Pastoral works

Another popular form which Quarles adapted was the pastoral. Pastoral works are descriptions of the lives of shepherds by people who know a great deal about poetic technique but very little about sheep. The object is to create an idealized world beyond the distractions of this world. Secular pastoral does so chiefly to provide enjoyment; works in this genre are romances. Religious pastoral does so to promote understanding of spiritual realities. Quarles works in both genres.

Argalus and Parthenia, his secular pastoral, is a versification of Sir Philip Sidney's *Arcadia* (1590). While usefully circumscribing the wild richness of Sidney's interminable prose romance, Quarles unwisely chooses his favorite verse form, the couplet, for this work. Couplets easily become tedious in a long narrative work unless the constant rhymes can be given a satirical point, as in *The Rape of the Lock* (1712, 1714) by Alexander Pope or *Hudibras* (1663, 1664, 1678) by Samuel Butler, but, even though Quarles substitutes for Sidney's engaging gaiety a tone of cool detachment, he fails to take the further step into satire.

Quarles's chief religious pastoral is in *The Shepheards Oracles*. The eclogues—or dialogues—in this work are textbook illustrations of how religious pastoral works. The pastoral poet begins by taking literally Christ's image of himself as the Good Shepherd. Indeed, it is from this image that the conventional term *pastor* for priest is derived. The dialogues of *The Shepheards Oracles* concern a wide variety of subjects from the Nativity to the wars of religion. Roman Catholics and Dissenters come in for considerable abuse.

Two works very hard to classify are *Sions Elegies, Wept by Jeremie the Prophet* and *Sions Sonets Sung by Solomon the King*. Each is in form no more than a free translation of a book of the bible. The lament of the Prophet Jeremiah for the lost Jerusalem that Quarles presents in *Sions Elegies, Wept by Jeremie the Prophet* has more in common with traditional works of religious pastoral than with the elegiac poems that Quarles wrote about his contemporaries. Through Jeremiah, Quarles is asking his readers to contemplate religious truths. *Sions Sonets Sung by Solomon the King* is a free rendering of The Song of Solomon. Quarles carefully includes marginal glosses so that the reader will not lose sight of the religious allegory and think he is reading love poems.

Elegies

Quarles also wrote a number of elegies; his most famous work in the genre is his epitaph for the poet Michael Drayton (1631), which appears on Drayton's memorial in Westminster Abbey. Quarles's only substantial book of elegiac poetry is *An Alphabet of Elegies*. These twenty-two short poems and an epitaph commemorate Dr. Aylmer, Archdeacon of London. The twelve-line verse form is a kind of truncated sonnet with a sprightliness at odds with—or perhaps redeeming—the lugubrious content.

Archbishop Ussher is commemorated in one of the poems in *Divine Fancies*, and included in *The Shepheards Oracles* is an elegy for the great Protestant hero Gustavus II Adolphus, King of Sweden. Published as individual chapbooks in Quarles's later years were elegies commemorating Sir Julius Caesar (1636); Jonathan Wheeler (1637); Dr. Wilson of the Rolles (1638); Mildred, Lady Luckyn (1638); Sir Robert Quarles, the poet's brother (1639); Sir John Wostenholme (1640); and the countess of Cleveland and her sister Cicily Killigrew (1640). Interesting for its verse forms but not included in Grosart's standard edition is a chapbook called *Threnodes on the Lady Marshall . . . and . . . William Cheyne* (c. 1641); and recently Karl Joseph Höltgen has identified both an epitaph for Sir Charles Caesar and the inscription on the D'Oyley monument at Hambleden as being by Quarles.

Other major works

PLAY: *The Virgin Widow: A Comedie*, pb. 1649 (masque).

NONFICTION: *Enchiridion, Containing Institutions Divine and Moral*, 1640; *Observations Concerning Princes and States upon Peace and Warre*, 1642; *The Loyal Convert*, 1644; *The Whipper Whipt*, 1644; *The New Distemper*, c. 1644; *The Profest Royalist in His Quarrell with the Times*, 1645; *Judgement and Mercy for Afflicted Soules: Or, Meditations, Soliloquies, and Prayers*, 1646.

Bibliography

Diehl, Houston. "Into the Maze of Self: The Protestant Transformation of the Image of the Labarynth." *Journal of Medieval and Renaissance Studies* 16 (Fall, 1986): 281-301. Examines how Quarles's poetry was a major factor in the change of meaning of the maze in literature. Quarles used the emblem of the maze to mean the soul, or the interior life of the individual.

Gillmeister, Heiner. "Early English Games in the Poetry of Francis Quarles." In *Proceedings of the XI HISPA International Congress*, edited by J. A. Mangan. Glasgow: Jordanhill College of Education, 1986. Gillmeister explores Quarles's use of British games played in the Middle Ages to add metaphorical meaning and structure to his poetry.

Gosse, Edmund. *The Jacobean Poets*. New York: Charles Scribner's Sons, 1894. This is an old book that nevertheless gives good comprehensive coverage of twelve poets from the late sixteenth and early seventeenth centuries. The chapter on Quarles provides a short biography and discusses his major works.

Hassan, Masoodul. *Francis Quarles: A Study of His Life and Poetry*. Aligarh, India: Aligarh Muslim University, 1966. This volume is one of the few modern books on Quarles, and so is valuable to any student of his work. As the title suggests, Hassan provides a comprehensive biography interwoven with an analysis of Quarles's major works. Includes a bibliography.

Leach, Elsie. "The Popularity of Quarles's Emblems: Images of Misogyny." *Studies in Iconography* 9 (1983): 83-97. Feminist critic Leach describes the moral and divine imagery used by Quarles in his poetry in terms of how it supported the status quo of male domination over women. An interesting and unusual study of the Jacobean era poet. Valuable for serious Quarles scholars.

Wilcher, Robert. "Quarles, Waller, Marvell, and the Instruments of State." *Notes and Queries* 41, no. 1 (March, 1994): 79. The influence that poets Francis Quarles, Edmund Waller, and Andrew Marvell had on each other and exerted in the development of government is discussed.

Edmund Miller;
bibliography updated by the editors

Salvatore Quasimodo

Born: Modica, Sicily, Italy; August 20, 1901
Died: Naples, Italy; June 14, 1968

Principal poetry

Acque e terre, 1930
Oboe sommerso, 1932
Odore di eucalyptus e altri versi, 1932
Erato e Apollion, 1936
Poesie, 1938
Lirici greci, 1940 (translation of Greek lyric poets)
Ed è subito sera, 1942
Il fiore della georgiche, 1944 (partial translation of Vergil's *Georgics*)
Dall'Odissea, 1945 (translation of Homer's *Odyssey*)
Con il piede straniero sopra il cuore, 1946
Giorno dopo giorno, 1947
La vita non è un sogno, 1949
Il falso e vero verde, 1954
Poesie scelte, 1958 (translation of selected poems of E. E. Cummings)
La terra impareggiabile, 1958
Tutte le poesie, 1960
Dare e avere, 1966 (*To Give and to Have and Other Poems*, 1969; also as *Debit and Credit*, 1972)
Dall'Iliade, 1968 (translation from Homer's *Iliad*)
Donner à voir, 1970 (translation of Paul Éluard's book of the same title)

Other literary forms

Although outside his native country Salvatore Quasimodo's reputation rests primarily on his poetry, in Italy he achieved prominence for his many other literary activities as well. He wrote a number of important critical studies, and his librettos have been performed in opera theaters as well-known as those of Venice and Palermo. More important, however, is his work as a translator. One of the finest literary translators of his time, Quasimodo ranged from Homer to the twentieth century: His translations include classical Greek and Latin poetry, the Gospel of John, and writers as varied as William Shakespeare, Molière, Pablo Neruda, E. E. Cummings, Conrad Aiken, Tudor Arghezi, Yves Lecomte, and Paul Éluard.

ACHIEVEMENTS

Together with Giuseppe Ungaretti and Eugenio Montale, Salvatore Quasimodo unquestionably belongs to the select circle of world-renowned modern Italian poets. Of the three, however, Quasimodo was the first to win wide acclaim, perhaps because he was able to express most lucidly the anguish and the doubts of a poet in a time when the irrational seemed to gain steadily at the expense of the rational, when poetry had gradually turned inward, divorcing itself from its tormented historical and social context. The winner of several prestigious awards (the Etna-Taormina International Poetry Prize, which he shared in 1953 with Dylan Thomas, and the 1958 Viareggio Prize, among others), Quasimodo received in 1959 the prestigious Nobel Prize in Literature.

BIOGRAPHY

Born in Modica, Sicily, the son of Gaetano Quasimodo and Clotilde Ragusa, Salvatore Quasimodo, the second of four children, spent the first years of his life following his father, a humble stationmaster, as the family moved from one small Sicilian railroad station to another. In 1908, his father settled in Gela, where Quasimodo was able to attend grade school. In 1909, he again followed his father, this time to Messina, the Sicilian town which, along with Reggio Calabria, had just been hit by the terribly destructive earthquake of 1908. In 1916, after a few years spent near Palermo, Quasimodo returned with his family to Messina, where he and his older brother were enrolled in the local trade school.

At this time, Quasimodo's poetic vocation, nurtured by careful reading of the classics as well as the major contemporary Russian and French writers, began to surface. He published his first two lyrics, one in the journal *Humanitas* and the other, a Futurist poem, in *Italia futurista*. In 1917, together with his lifelong friends Giorgio La Pira and Salvatore Pugliatti, Quasimodo founded the *Nuovo giornale letterario*, which was in print from March to November of that year.

In 1919, Quasimodo left Messina for Rome in order to attend the engineering school of that city's university. He soon dropped out, however, and spent the next few years working at odd jobs and leading a rather bohemian life. In 1926, he succeeded in obtaining a position as a land surveyor with the government's Civil Engineering Department at Reggio Calabria, and thus was able once again to meet regularly with his friends among the Sicilian literati. At this point he began to write seriously; some of the poems included in *Acque e terre* (waters and lands) date from this period.

The year 1929 was a decisive one in Quasimodo's life. He was invited by his brother-in-law Elio Vittorini (later

Salvatore Quasimodo, Nobel laureate in literature for 1959.
(© The Nobel Foundation)

to become one of the leading literary figures of contemporary Italy) to go to Florence. There, he was introduced to an influential group of writers and poets, among them Eugenio Montale, and in 1930, he published his first collection of poems, *Acque e terre*, which met with favorable critical reviews. For work-related reasons, he was sent to Liguria in 1931, where he published the widely acclaimed *Oboe sommerso* (the sunken oboe) in 1932. That same year, he was awarded the Florentine Prize of the Antico Fattore, which had been given the year before to Eugenio Montale. Sent in 1934 to Valtellina (Lombardy) after a short stay in Sardinia, Quasimodo entered the Milanese intellectual milieu, and in 1935, his daughter, Orietta, was born out of wedlock.

In Milan in 1936, Quasimodo published another book, *Erato e Apollion* (Aerato and Apollyon), and in 1938 he finally quit his job as a land surveyor to begin working as an editor and assistant to Cesare Zavattini, then the editor of several Mondadori periodicals. In 1939, Quasimodo was made literary editor of the weekly magazine *Il tempo*. The same year, his son, Alessandro, was born. In 1940, Quasimodo published his controversial translation *Lirici greci* (Greek lyric poets), notable for its aggressively modern idiom, and the following year he was appointed professor of Italian literature at the Giuseppe Verdi Conservatory in Milan. In 1942, he published the most successful of his works: *Ed è subito sera*, the volume which marked his shift from the hermetic style of his early verse.

During the war years, without being overtly involved in the anti-fascist resistance movement, Quasimodo nevertheless took a firm stand against fascism, and in 1945, soon after the war, he joined the Italian Communist Party. That same year, he published his masterful translations of Sophocles and of the Gospel of John. Belonging also to this period are a number of critical essays and two collections of socially and ideologically oriented poems: *Con il piede straniero sopra il cuore* (with an invader's foot on your heart), published in 1946, and *Giorno dopo giorno* (day after day), published the following year. In 1948, following the death of his first wife, Bice Donetti, he married Maria Cumani, the mother of his son, Alessandro; he then began his career as a theater editor for the journal *Omnibus* and in the same capacity, shortly after, for the weekly *Il tempo*, while continuing to publish translations and another collection of poems titled *La vita non è un sogno* (life is not a dream), which appeared in 1949.

In 1950, Quasimodo received the San Babila Prize and, in 1953, with Dylan Thomas, the Etna-Taormina International Poetry Prize. In 1954, *Il falso e vero verde* (the true and the false green) was published; it was republished two years later with added translations and the famous speech, "Discorso sulla poesia" (speech on poetry), in which Quasimodo maintained the necessity for the true poet to express in his verses his ideological and social commitment. In 1958, after the publication of several other translations, he published yet another collection of poems, *La terra impareggiabile* (the incomparable land), but during a trip to Russia in that same year, he had a heart attack which forced him to remain there until the spring of 1959. His hospital expenses were covered by a subscription organized by Russian writers on his behalf. In 1959, Quasimodo attained world recognition on receiving the Nobel Prize in Literature "for his lyric poetry, which expresses with classic fire the tragic experience of life in our time." In Italy, however, this award prompted a negative reaction from critics who thought that Ungaretti and Montale were both more deserving of the honor.

Shortly after receiving the Nobel Prize, Quasimodo began to travel throughout Europe and the United States. In 1960, he separated from his second wife and published a collection of essays titled *Il poeta e il politico e altri saggi* (*The Poet and the Politician and Other Essays*, 1964), which includes the acceptance speech he had read in Stockholm. He was thereafter the recipient of several other honors and awards. In 1966, he published his last collection of poems, *To Give and to Have, and Other Poems*, which is virtually a balance sheet of his life, strongly overshadowed by the presentiment of death. In 1967, Oxford University bestowed an honorary degree upon him. He died in Naples the following year as a result of a cerebral hemorrhage suffered in Amalfi, where he had been invited to preside over a poetry competition.

Analysis

Salvatore Quasimodo lived and worked in a period which harbored innumerable contrasting poetic voices.

His courageous attempt to extricate himself from the arid, desolate sphere of an excessively introspective style pointed the way to a new poetry—a poetry which, without losing its lyric essence, aspires to a modern aesthetic in which civil ethics and poetic vision can coexist.

Unlike that of his two great contemporaries, Quasimodo's poetry can be divided into two sharply distinct periods. In his first phase, prior to World War II, Quasimodo wrote hermetic poetry characterized by highly compressed images, allusive language, and a pervasive existential anguish. In his second phase, Quasimodo became convinced that hermetic poetry had exhausted itself in excessively self-absorbed, contorted, and abstract imagery. He came to believe that the poet's moral duty was to be socially committed and to express the collective despair, sorrow, and frustration of his time, a position first made clear in the collection *Ed è subito sera* (and suddenly it's evening).

This second phase of Quasimodo's poetry—characterized by a more discursive style, the use of a plainer language, and, above all, a strong ideological and social content—need not be interpreted, however, as an unequivocal rejection of his hermetic past, but may rather be seen as an evolution (dictated, perhaps, by the historical situation) toward new themes and a more decisive social, political, and moral commitment. In his evolution from modernist hermeticism to a poetry of engagement, Quasimodo was able to capture and express with rare insight and sensitivity not only his own feelings and aspirations but also those of his era.

Acque e terre

Echoes of many poetic traditions, particularly of such poets as Giovanni Pascoli, Gabriele D'Annunzio, Filippo Marinetti, and Sergio Corazzini, are clearly detectable in Salvatore Quasimodo's first book of verses, *Acque e terre*. The gravitational presence of Ungaretti and Montale is even more noticeable in this volume. The recurrent theme of the poet's youth, evoked through the rediscovery of the ancient myths of Sicily, is a constant in Quasimodo's work. Quasimodo further intertwines an incisive imagery, boldly carved, and a personal use of antithesis employed on a conceptual as well as on a semantic level. It is through the analysis of opposites such as life/death and joy/sorrow that the reader gradually penetrates the existential inner world of the poet and the quasi-metaphysical anguish of the moral and historical wasteland of his age.

Ideology and social engagement

World War II brought about the externalization of the poet's feelings, a sort of psychological denouement along with a measure of objectivity induced by the mercilessly all-encompassing war years. Beginning with the poems of *Giorno dopo giorno*, Quasimodo made a conscious and coherent effort to overcome early unresolved dissonances and to present the reader with his own historical experience defined within the framework of a choral poetic. As Quasimodo moved toward a poetry of ideological and social engagement, he gradually rejected the poetics of memory, seen as a negation of life as exemplified in "Quasi un madrigale" ("Almost a Madrigal") from *La vita non è un sogno:* "I have no more memories, I do not want to remember;/ memory stems from death,/ life is endless." The final assimilation of opposites was dialectically assured by Quasimodo's realization of the necessity for a new ethical dimension; he was forced to abandon once and for all his poetic monologue in favor of a socially committed dialogue with his fellowman. In "Epitaffio per Bice Donetti" ("Epitaph for Bice Donetti"), from *La vita non è un sogno*, life and death are no longer antithetical and their synthesis is suggested by his discovery of a shared destiny: He is "one of many others" and thus finds his roots in the sorrowful plight common to all humankind.

Ed è subito sera

The collected verses of *Ed è subito sera* were the result of painstaking revision and selection of poems from Quasimodo's previous collections, from *Acque e terre* and *Oboe sommerso* to *Erato e Apollion*. With the addition of a number of new poems, *Ed è subito sera* constituted both the definitive statement of his past work and the assertion of a new aesthetic vision. With the new poems which concluded the collection, Quasimodo turned to longer, more discursive verse forms (especially the hendecasyllable) and to a less cryptic use of language. While these changes reflected to a certain extent the vogue for neorealism, Quasimodo's stylistic evolution was also influenced significantly by two other factors: first, the stylistic models that he encountered in translating the classics, and second, the urgency of speaking out against the ills of fascism and war, which necessitated the establishment of a new relationship with his readers.

From "I" to "we"

The twenty poems of *Con il piede straniero sopra il cuore*, eighteen of which were to be included the following year in *Giorno dopo giorno*, dramatically reaffirm the new poetic phase initiated in *Ed è subito sera*. Quasimodo's hermetic phase, with its inward focus on the self and on memory, is typified by the careful choice of a few nouns and adjectives in the poem "L'eucalyptus" ("The Eucalyptus") from *Oboe sommerso:* "In me un albero oscilla/ da assonnata riva,/ alata aria/ amare fronde esala" ("Within me sways a tree/ from sleeping shores/ winged air exhales/ my bitter fronds"). By contrast, in "Alle fronde dei salici"—published in 1947 in *Giorno dopo giorno* but written three years earlier, in the winter of 1944, during the harshest period of the German Occupation—Quasimodo is painfully aware that the time has come to break away from his hermetic past in order to speak with a new voice and of new themes: "E come potevamo noi contare/ con il piede straniero sopra il cuore,/ fra i morti abbandonati nelle piazze/ . . . Alle fronde dei salici, per voto/ anche le nostre cetre erano appese" ("And how could we sing/ with an invader's foot on your heart/ among the dead abandoned in the squares/ . . . To the branches of the willow, as a vow/ also our lyres were hung up"). The language is no longer rarefied and impenetrable; it is almost epic in tone, and the poet has switched from "I" to the choral "we." As Quasimodo himself said in a speech in 1953,

> something happened in the field of poetry about 1945, a dramatic destruction of the content inherited from an indifferent idealism and the poetic language flourishing up to that time. . . . All of a sudden the poet found himself thrust out of his own internal history; in war his individual intelligence was worth no more than the collective intelligence of the people. . . . The private (lyric) discourse . . . became choral. . . .

Quasimodo continued to develop in this direction; in *La vita non è un sogno*, certain poems are unusually long, and throughout the volume the poet actively seeks dialogue with his readers. *Il falso e vero verde* comprises fourteen poems and translations covering a wide variety of themes and levels of experience, moving from the medieval Lauds (honoring a fallen Resistance fighter) to a quasi-surrealistic search for roots. A progression of moods and subjects, from the Athenian Acropolis to the Sputnik, also prevails in the twenty-five poems of *La terra impareggiabile*. A dominant theme, however, is clearly identifiable in the first poem of the collection, "Visibile, Invisibile" ("Visible, Invisible"): The search for the great divide of time, for a dividing line between the present (visible) and the past or future (invisible), bears witness to Quasimodo's unrelenting quest for a poetic and ideological fusion of form and content.

To Give and to Have

The final stage, the "synthesis" of Quasimodo's dialectical probing into the self while reaching for universal truths, is contained in the twenty-three poems of *To Give and to Have* (also published under the title *Debit and Credit*). In this last book of poems—to which are appended the text of the libretto *Billy Budd* (1949), as well as translations from Homer's *Iliad* (c. 800 B.C.E.), from Boccaccio's *Bucolicum carmen* (1351-1366; *Olympia*), and from the Romanian poet Tudor Arghezi—Quasimodo makes his final statement on life and death, an absorbed and reflective pulling together of the threads of his total poetic experience. As the title implies, *To Give and to Have* is a sort of balance sheet of the poet's life, a summation, of his dialectic search.

Somberly reviewing his life and world, the poet softens the tones of his social and ideological commitment, looking again within the self, pondering his human adventure and his passage through time. The presentiment of death is everywhere, but in conjunction with calm acceptance: "I am not fearful before death/ just as I was not timid before life," he writes while lying in his hospital bed in Russia ("Varvàra Alexandrovna"). Acceptance, if not detachment, is again pervasive in "Il silenzio non m'inganna" ("The Silence Does Not Deceive Me"): "I write down words, analogies, and try/ to trace a possible link/ between my life and death. The present is outside."

Quasimodo's language, too, seems to have gained a new equilibrium in which meditative expression predominates. More accessible than his obscure and often strident early style, it is, at the same time, less discursive and more controlled than the language of the war years. The poet has taken stock of himself and appears reconciled to the idea of impending death, which he acknowledges in a kind of spiritual testament to his fellowman devoid of anguish and metaphysical anxieties.

Other major works

nonfiction: *Petrarca e il sentimento della solitudine*, 1945; *Il poeta e il politico e altri saggi*, 1960 (*The Poet and the Politician and Other Essays*, 1964); *Scritti sul teatro*, 1961; *Leonida di Taranto*, 1968.

translations: *Edipo re*, 1946 (of Sophocles' play); *Romeo e Giulietta*, 1948 (of William Shakespeare's play); *Le coefore*, 1949 (of Aeschylus's play *Choēphoroi*); *Macbeth*, 1952 (of Shakespeare's play); *Riccardo III*, 1952 (of Shakespeare's play); *Elettra*, 1954 (of Sophocles' play); *Il Tartufo*, 1957 (of Molière's play); *Otello*, 1959 (of Shakespeare's play); *Antonio e Cleopatra*, 1966 (of Shakespeare's play); *Erakle*, 1966 (of Euripides' play).

miscellaneous: *The Selected Writings of Salvatore Quasimodo*, 1960.

Bibliography

Beall, Chandler B. "Quasimodo and Modern Italian Poetry," *Northwest Review* 4 (1961): 41-48. A critical analysis of Quasimodo's work and the cultural background of twentieth century Italian poetry.

Bevan, Jack, trans. Introduction to *Complete Poems*, by Salvatore Quasimodo. New York: Schocken Books, 1984. Bevan is a longtime translator of Quasimodo's works, and his introduction casts useful light on the poet.

Hays, Gregory. "Le morte stagioni: Intertextuality in Quasimodo's *Lirici greci*." *Forum Italicum* 29, no. 1 (Spring, 1995): 26-43. A critical study of Quasimodo's translations of ancient Greek poetry.

Loriggio, Francesco. "Modernity and the Ambiguities of Exile: On the Poetry of Salvatore Quasimodo." *Rivista di Studi Italiani* 12, no. 1 (June, 1994): 101-120. A critical study of selected poetry by Quasimodo.

Williamson, Edward. Introduction and biographical notes to *Twentieth Century Italian Poetry*, edited by Levi R. Lind. Indianapolis, Ind.: Bobbs-Merrill, 1974. Williamson's introduction and notes offer some historical and biographical background to Quasimodo's life and work.

Roberto Severino;
bibliography updated by the editors

R

Miklós Radnóti

Miklós Glatter
Born: Budapest, Hungary; May 5, 1909
Died: Abda, Hungary; November 8(?), 1944

Principal poetry

Pogány köszöntő, 1930 (*Pagan Salute*, 1980)
Ujmódi pásztorok éneke, 1931 (*Song of Modern Shepherds*, 1980)
Lábadozó szél, 1933 (*Convalescent Wind*, 1980)
Ujhold, 1935 (*New Moon*, 1980)
Járkálj csak, halálraítélt!, 1936 (*Walk On, Condemned!*, 1980)
Meredek út, 1938 (*Steep Road*, 1980)
Tajtékos ég, 1946 (*Sky with Clouds*, 1980)
Bori notesz, 1970 (*Camp Notebook*, 2000)
Subway Stops, 1977
The Witness: Selected Poems by Miklós Radnóti, 1977
Radnóti Miklós müvei, 1978
Forced March, 1979
The Complete Poetry, 1980

Other literary forms

Miklós Radnóti excelled as a translator of classical and modern poetry from a number of Western languages into Hungarian. A collection of his translations appeared in 1943 under the title *Orpheus nyomában* (in the footsteps of Orpheus). Of his prose, *Ikrek hava* (1939; *The Month of Gemini*, 1979), a quasi autobiography, is most significant; also noteworthy is his doctoral dissertation on the Hungarian novelist and poet Margit Kaffka, *Kaffka Margit művészi fejlődése* (1934; the artistic development of Margit Kaffka).

Achievements

Miklós Radnóti received his doctoral degree in 1934 and was awarded the prestigious Baumgarten Prize only four years later. From this auspicious beginning, he began building his readership, so that by the height of his career few modern Hungarian poets had a wider reading public than Radnóti. Radnóti's forte was his ability to fuse elements from diverse poetic traditions, filling traditional forms with new, unexpected messages, especially the terrifying experiences resulting from the Nazi Occupation of Central and Eastern Europe. While, as a young man, he boldly experimented with free verse, his mature poetry is devoid of flamboyance, characterized instead by classical simplicity and dignity. His major contribution to Hungarian letters is that he served as an artistic, as well as a moral example for several generations of Hungarian artists, a poet speaking for his nation, representing his country's best humanist traditions amid war, privation, and persecution.

Biography

Miklós Radnóti (born Miklós Glatter) lived for only thirty-five years, and even his birth was darkened by tragedy: It cost the lives of his mother and twin brother. Radnóti's father soon remarried; Radnóti deeply loved his stepmother and the daughter born of the second marriage, yet grief and guilt feelings concerning the double tragedy of his birth influenced his entire creative life. The figure of his mother is a recurring image in Radnóti's poetry and prose.

Radnóti completed his elementary and high school education in Budapest. Then, following the suggestion of his guardian (his father, too, had died), he spent 1927 and 1928 in Liberec, Czechoslovakia, studying textile technology and working in an office. In the fall of 1930, he enrolled at Szeged University, majoring in Hungarian and French. By the time he received his doctorate in 1934, he had several volumes of poetry in print. It was during this period that he assumed the name "Radnóti," after Radnót, the town in northeastern Hungary where his father had been born.

During the late 1920's and at the beginning of the 1930's, Radnóti became involved with youth organizations that were culturally nurtured by ideas from the Left. During this period, he wrote "engaged" poetry, using a deliberately nonpoetical language which was meant to identify him with the working class. Since that identification lacked the reality of experience, it exhausted itself in language and remained unconvincing. During his first trip to Paris in 1931, Radnóti met a number of French writers and artists, who introduced him to the poetry of Guillaume Apollinaire, Blaise Cendrars, Paul Valéry, and Valery Larbaud. The progressive nature of this poetry liberated Radnóti from the confines of narrow social protest, and with his *Sturm und Drang* period behind him, he began to develop his mature style.

In 1935, Radnóti married his childhood sweetheart, Fanni Gyarmati, hoping to secure a teaching position in the Hungarian high school system. When this did not work out, he took temporary jobs, chiefly private tutoring, and accepted partial support from his wife's family.

As Hungary's political climate turned increasingly fascist, Radnóti shared the fate of those who had been persecuted for their Jewish origins. With the exception of brief periods of respite, he spent the years from 1940 until his death in various forced-labor camps, first in Hungary and later, after Hungary's occupation by the Nazis (March 19, 1944), working a copper mine in Bor, Yugoslavia. In the course of the Nazi retreat, Radnóti's company was also returned to Hungary, then moved west in the direction of the German (Austrian) border. Radnóti, however, died while still in Hungary, murdered by the soldiers guarding his group. He was among those who were shot after being forced to dig their own graves.

When Radnóti's body was exhumed on June 23, 1946, nearly two years after his death, a small, black notebook was found in which Radnóti had written ten poems. (These poems appear in the volume *Sky with Clouds*.) It is a measure of Radnóti's current standing in Hungarian poetry that a scholarly facsimile edition of this notebook, *Camp Notebook*, originally issued in 1970, had gone into multiple printings.

ANALYSIS

At the beginning of his career, Miklós Radnóti saw himself as a representative of a new literature, different in language and style from that of the previous generation of Hungarian poets. Together with fellow rebels, he attacked what he regarded as the tepid traditions of the past, boldly declaring himself one of the "modern shepherds." The title of his first volume, *Pagan Salute*, suggests the rebellious spirit of Radnóti's early work. The narrator of this first collection rejects the pacifying teachings of church and state and sings about the freedom of love and his desire for a natural life. The Romantic image of the shepherd placed in a pastoral landscape is one of the few happy, carefree images in all Radnóti's work.

"LAW"

Radnóti's youthful poems are characterized by social commentary, often obliquely expressed by means of images from nature. In "Law," for example, an allegory about the illegal Socialist movement after the Nazi victories of 1933, Radnóti advances his political views in the guise of a "nature poem." The wind "drops" passwords and whistles the secret signals of the conspirators. The political freeze is described as winter, and the new grass bares not the expected "blade" but a "dagger." The laws of nature are translated by Radnóti into the law of revolution, and in the last stanzas the poet confirms his ties with the underground movement and calls on others to follow his example. A tree dropping a "leaf," which by this point in the poem can be interpreted only as a political "leaflet" or flier, compels the reader to respond; thus, the poem becomes its own political leaflet.

LOVE POEMS

Radnóti's early work is also characterized by a strong erotic charge, although it is often unclear whether this represents a genuine expression of sexual desire or is merely another manifestation of the poet's urge to revolt against social conventions. Between 1933, however, and 1935, when he married Fanni Gyarmati, Radnóti's erotic/political poems changed dramatically. A new gravity and a mood approaching resignation accompanied his awareness of impending war; his manner became calmer and more controlled. His language, too, was simplified, so that a more personal, lyric voice could emerge.

The erotic flame of the sexual poems was replaced by a lyric glow, and the violent sexual images by intimate, tender descriptions of lovers. Radnóti became protective of married love, remaining silent about sexual relations. Indeed, Radnoti's love poems to Fanni recall in their classical simplicity the great love lyrics of Mihály Vörösmarty and Sándor Petőfi, the preeminent Hungarian poets of the nineteenth century.

"LIKE A BULL"

Finally, the transition from Radnóti's youthful, rebellious stance to his mature style can be traced in the poet's changing self-image. In "Like a Bull," written in 1933, the poet is represented by a young bull, a pointedly strong and masculine image chosen to reflect an unsentimental view of the cruelties of the world during troubled times. In other poems of this period, the narrators are young men who do not attempt to hide from their fate and who openly condemn the perpetrators of evil.

"War Diary"

Gradually, however, there is a transformation in the poet's self-image: He is reduced, as it were, to his pure function as a poet. This transformation begins with the cycle "War Diary," in which the poet envisions himself both as a corpse and as a disembodied spirit. The entire cycle of four poems is marked by a sense of distance, as if the poet had already died and was now observing life from the other side. The effect is not one of detachment but rather of extraordinary poignancy: The poet has stripped himself of all that is inessential, but not of his humanity. This cycle anticipates the poems which Radnóti wrote in Serbian concentration camps during the final days of his life; in one of these last poems, "Root," the poet writes: "I am now a root myself—/ it's with worms I make my home,/ there, I am building this poem." This image is a far cry from the bold, patriotic, young songster of Radnóti's early verse.

"I Cannot Know . . ."

Among Radnóti's images, there are a few which run throughout his oeuvre as recurring metaphors and symbols. He uses the figure of the pilot, for example, as an embodiment of the amorality chillingly evident in the war. The pilot becomes a symbol of all willing instruments in the service of inhumanity; his actions derive from a worldview in which *separation* leads to indifference. When sufficient distance is created between malefactor and victim, the wrongdoer ceases to feel any guilt concerning his crime. In the poem "I Cannot Know . . ." (written in 1944), Radnóti pits the humanist's values against those of the pilot. It is a poem about Hungary as seen, on the one hand, by a native son, the poet, and, on the other hand, by a pilot of a bomber from another country. The poet sees his "tiny land" on a human scale: "when a bush kneels, once in a while,/ at my feet, I know its name and can name its blossom;/ I know where people are headed on the road, as I know them." To the man in the plane, however, "it's a map, this country,/ he could not point to the home of Mihály Vörösmarty." The pilot sees only military targets—"army posts, factories"—while the poet sees "grasshoppers, oxen, towers, farms, gentle fields."

"Second Eclogue"

Radnóti treats the symbolic figure of the pilot with greater complexity in his "Second Eclogue," a poem in dialogue form which opens with the bragging of a dashing pilot. The pilot concludes his speech, the first of the poem's four parts, by asking the poet, "Have you written since yesterday?" The poet answers, "I have," and while he retains a touch of a child's wonder at the miracle of men being able to fly, he goes on to identify the differences between his permanent role as a humanitarian and the pilot's temporary role in social change. Listening to each other, they begin to perceive themselves better. The poet recognizes the strengths of his own position by measuring his moral courage against the daring stunts of the pilot. As the poet discovers with surprise his own courage, so in his second speech the pilot admits his fears. Indeed, he goes beyond this admission to acknowledge a far more troubling truth: He, who "lived like a man once," has become something inhuman, living only to destroy. Who will understand, he asks, that he was once human? Thus, he closes his second speech with a plea to the poet: "Will you write about me?" The poet's answer, which concludes the dialogue, is brief: "If I live. And there's anyone around to read it."

In this poem, written in 1941, Radnóti anticipated the conclusions drawn by survivors of the Holocaust: He penetrated and understood the psyche of the offender. He does not forgive. Rather, he draws a circle to connect the murderer and his victim, by which a sort of intimacy is established: In a terrible, absurd way, they alone share the crime.

"A Little Duck Bathes" and "Song"

Radnóti employed recurring images such as that of the pilot to add resonance to his verse, to create a rich texture of associations and layers of meaning. The same impulse lies behind his "quotation" of poetic forms and themes from a great diversity of sources, varying from Vergil to Hungarian folk culture, in which he establishes a fruitful tension with his models. "A Little Duck Bathes," for example, is based on one of the most popular Hungarian nursery rhymes. By reversing the structure of the first sentence, Radnóti establishes the dialectical tension by which the entire poem is structured: The unabashed eroticism of the text is counterpointed by the original meter of the nursery rhyme. The energy of the new poem derives from its conflict with its model. Similarly, Radnóti's poem "Song" is modeled on the "outlaw song," a readily identifiable type of Hungarian folk song. Dealing with the misery of the homeless refugee, the poor exile, and the defeated patriot, the outlaw song (derived in turn from the *kuruc* song) provides Radnóti with a vehicle for calling attention to historical precedents for the exile of poets *within* their homeland.

Radnóti's technique of complex "quotation" is supremely exemplified in his eclogues. Radnóti's eight poems written in this classical form constitute his literary testament. In them, he describes and responds to the devastating events of his time, deliberately choosing this traditionally bucolic genre to convey his tragic vision.

"Eighth Eclogue"

Radnóti's eclogues achieve their greatest evocative power precisely from this conflict between form and content, which forces the reader to assume a critical distance, to reflect on the implications of this violation of genre. In these poems, Radnóti meditates on the nature of poetry and on the poet's commitment to a better world. For Radnóti, to live meant to create, and even amid filth, indignities, and the fear of death, the concept of home appears in a literary metaphor, a land in which it is known what a hexameter is. The "Eighth Eclogue," the last of the series, combines biblical and classical traditions. Here, the poet conducts a dialogue with the biblical Nahum, a true prophet; Nahum encourages the poet by telling him that prophets and poets are closely related, suggesting that they should "take to the road" together. Thus, in his "Eighth Eclogue," Radnóti revived the messianic conception of the poet that was at the heart of the Romantic movement in Hungary.

Long before the actual forced march which ended in his death, Radnóti spiritually set out on the lonely road leading to the grave. By 1940, his imminent death had become a recurring image in his poems, frequently appearing in concluding lines. Here, Fanni alone can offer him comfort; her bodily closeness is his only haven. Her presence quiets his fears following nightmares about death ("Your Right Hand on My Nape"), and only her embrace can make the moment of death pass as if it were a dream ("In Your Arms").

"Forced March"

Although he had long been prepared for death, Radnóti paradoxically regained a hope for survival during the last bitter weeks of his life. The wish to live, to return to Fanni, to tell about the horrors, and to wait for a "wiser, handsome death" permeates several of the poems so aptly called the "hymns from Bor." Well aware that this hope was flimsy at best, based on desire more than on truth, Radnóti expressed its elusiveness in "Forced March."

The poem begins with a judgmental view of the poet, observed in the third person. His unreasonable behavior is exposed, his foolish agreement to his own torture is condemned. He is called upon to explain his decision to walk on, and his answer is shown up as a naïve, self-deceiving daydream. Halfway through the poem, however, a sudden transformation occurs, a shift from the third person to the first. Judgment turns into a confession of hope, the war-torn landscape is transmuted into an idyll of bygone days, dogged resistance into a cosmic, optimistic message. In a world from which reason has disappeared, anything, including superstition and magic, can serve as crutches. Thus, by the end of the poem, the two halves of the lyric ego merge, and harmony is reestablished—a new harmony in which primordial beliefs are accepted as truth, befitting a world devoid of civilization.

Each line of "Forced March" is broken by a caesura, marked by a blank space, so that the poem is divided into two jagged columns. The pounding rhythm of the verse re-creates the sound of the heavy footsteps with which the exhausted men dragged themselves on the road—a beautiful example of form functioning as message. "Forced March" impresses and moves the reader with its spontaneity, its simple vocabulary and familiar imagery, its emotional directness, and yet—characteristically of Radnóti—the texture of the poem is more complex than might at first appear, for woven into it are allusions to a medieval masterpiece, Walther von der Vogelweide's "Ouwe war sint verswunden alliu miniu jar?" ("Where Have All My Years Disappeared?")—a poem which Radnóti had translated. There, too, home can never again be what it once was; the people are gone, the farmhouse has collapsed, and what was once joyous has disappeared.

"Forced March" has a special place in Radnóti's oeuvre: It represents hope's triumph over despair. Above all, it shows the artist's triumph over his own fate. It proves that even during the last weeks of his tormented life, Radnóti was able to compose with precise poetic principles in mind, that he was in control of his material, playing secretly with literary and existential relationships and creating out of all this an enduring testament.

"Razglednicas"

Radnóti's last poems were four short pieces which chart his final steps toward death and, at the same time, signal his withdrawal from participation in life. These poems are collectively titled "Razglednicas," a word of Serbo-Croatian origin meaning picture postcards, and indeed they provide a terrifyingly precise pictorial description of the horrors which the poet experienced in the last month of his life. Separate as they stand in their unique message, the "Razglednicas" are by no means unrelated to the rest of Radnóti's poetry. They have a particularly close emotive and textual contact with his longer poems (such as "Forced March" and "Letter to My Wife") written during the same period, and together they render a final panorama of Radnóti's surroundings, depicting the devastation that man and nature suffer in a ravaging war.

Other major works

nonfiction: *Kaffka Margit művészi fejlődése*, 1934; *Ikrek hava*, 1939 (*The Month of Gemini*, 1979).

translation: *Orpheus nyomában*, 1943.

Bibliography

George, Emery Edward. *The Poetry of Miklós Radnóti*. New York: Karz-Cohl, 1986. A critical study of Radnóti's poetic works. Includes bibliographic references and an index.

Gömöri, George and Clive Wilmer, eds. *The Life and Poetry of Miklós Radnóti: Essays*. New York: Columbia University Press, 1999. A collection of biographical and critical essays on Radnóti. Includes bibliographical references.

Ozsváth, Zsuzsanna. *In the Footsteps of Orpheus: The Life and Times of Miklós Radnóti*. Bloomington: Indiana University Press, 2000. Considers the life and work of Miklós Radnóti and examines Radnóti's artistic development and premonitory poetry and illuminates the intellectual ambience in which he lived. Ultimately, it follows the poet's route into the forced labor camp and on the death march, exploring both the circumstances of his murder and the impact of the atrocities he suffered on his creative imagination.

Petty, Ryan. *Miklós Radnóti*. Austin, Tx.: Cold Mountain Press, 1974. A brief biography of Radnóti with bibliographic references.

M. D. Birnbaum;
bibliography updated by the editors

Carl Rakosi

Callman Rawley

Born: Berlin, Germany; November 6, 1903

Principal poetry

Two Poems, 1933
Selected Poems, 1941
Amulet, 1967
Ere-VOICE, 1971
Ex Cranium, Night, 1975
My Experiences in Parnassus, 1977
The Collected Poems of Carl Rakosi, 1986
Poems, 1923-1941, 1995
The Earth Suite, 1997

Other literary forms

Although Carl Rakosi is known principally for his poetry, he has published a collection of nonfiction writings, *The Collected Prose of Carl Rakosi* (1983).

Achievements

Carl Rakosi came to public attention fairly late. Between 1939 and 1965, he wrote no poetry. A young English poet who was doing research at the State University of New York at Buffalo contacted him and asked about his post-1941 work; it was this query that spurred him to begin writing once more. His *Selected Poems*, published by New Directions in 1941, had received little notice, but the growing audience for poetry in the 1960's welcomed *Amulet*, his second New Directions book. Since that time, New Directions, Black Sparrow Press, and the National Poetry Foundation at the University of Maine have kept his writing in print, and it has continued to spark the interest of critics and a new generation of poets and readers.

Rakosi won the National Endowment for the Arts award in 1969 and fellowships from the same institution in 1972 and 1979. He also won a Distinguished Service award from the National Poetry Association in 1988, and the Penn Award for *Poems, 1923-1941* in 1996. He was the honored guest at the International Objectivist Conference in France in 1990. His manuscripts and letters are split between the holdings of the University of Wisconsin in Madison and the Widener Library at Harvard.

Carl Rakosi (Courtesy of Carl Rakosi)

Biography

Carl Rakosi was born on November 6, 1903, to Hungarian nationals, Leopold Rakosi and Flora Steiner, who were at that time living in Berlin. The young Rakosi was brought to the United States in 1910; his father and stepmother reared him and his brother in various Midwestern cities—Chicago; Gary, Indiana; and Kenosha, Wisconsin.

Rakosi made many attempts to begin a career. After earning his B.A. in literature at the University of Wisconsin at Madison, he tried social work in Cleveland and New York City. He returned to Madison for an M.A. in educational psychology and then worked as the staff psychologist in the personnel department at Bloomingdale's for a time. He taught English at the University of Texas at Austin and made forays into law school (in Austin) and medical school (in Galveston). Having found neither law nor medicine congenial, he taught high school in Houston for two years. At the outset of the Depression, he tried social work again, returning to Chicago to work at the Cook County Bureau of Public Welfare. By now he had changed his name, to Callman Rawley. He served a two-year stint as a supervisor at the Federal Transit Bureau in New Orleans; then, following a period of working as a field supervisor for Tulane University, he started to work—in a pioneering role—as a family therapist at the Jewish Family Welfare Society in New York. At the same time, he pursued graduate studies at the University of Pennsylvania; in 1940 he received an M.A. in social work.

His professional course was now clear. After three years as a case supervisor at the Jewish Social Service Bureau in St. Louis, and two years as assistant director of the Jewish Children's Bureau in Cleveland, in 1945 he became executive director of the Jewish Family and Children's Service in Minneapolis. He continued in this post until 1968; between 1958 and 1968 he also had a private practice.

One notes in this chronology the marked absence of any job directly connected to writing. Rakosi's first spell as a poet had resulted in publication in the prestigious *Little Review*, alongside James Joyce's *Ulysses* (1922) in serial form; he had also been included in *An "Objectivists" Anthology* (1932), edited by Louis Zukofsky, which many years later came to be seen as a landmark event. The long hiatus that followed has been described thus by Rakosi himself:

> By 1939 writing was coming harder and slower to me as more of me became involved in social work and in reading and writing professional articles. . . . I wrote some sixty . . . and my evenings were swallowed up by the things that a man who is not a writer normally spends his time on in a big city: the theater, concerts, professional meetings, friends, girlfriends. . . . In addition, my Marxist thinking had made me lose respect for poetry itself. So there was nothing to hold me back from ending the problem by stopping to write. I did that. I also stopped reading poetry. I couldn't run the risk of being tempted.

In December, 1965, he received a letter from British poet Andrew Crozier asking what had become of his poetry since 1941. This letter prompted him to take up his pen once again.

The results were soon made available to the poetry-reading public in a series of books; the work was much anthologized, and Rakosi was asked to give readings at a number of distinguished venues. This Rip Van Winkle of poetry had reawakened to a different decade—one for which his gifts appeared to have been waiting.

His resume soon began to show many jobs related to his poetry and writing: From 1968 to 1975 he was writer in residence in Saratoga Springs, New York; he was writer in residence at the University of Wisconsin from 1969 to 1970; he served as a faculty member for the National Poetry Festival in 1973; and he was poet in residence for Michigan State University in 1974. Since 1986 he has been the senior editor of the literary magazine *Sagetrieb*, a critical journal located in Maine.

In 1939, Rakosi was married to Leah Jaffe. Their daughter, Barbara, was born in St. Louis in 1940, and a son, George, was born in Cleveland in 1943. The couple stayed together for half a century; Leah Jaffe Rakosi died in San Francisco in 1988. San Francisco continued to be his home in the 1990's and into the twenty-first century.

Analysis

Because of his early connection with Louis Zukofsky, Carl Rakosi is often spoken of as an Objectivist poet. When both poets were young, Zukofsky had been advised by Ezra Pound to start a literary movement, the better to draw attention to his own poetry. Pound told him that he need not look for complete agreement among the members of his movement, as long as certain views were held in common. Zukofsky took his mentor at his word. He contacted several poets of his generation (along with William Carlos Williams, who was some twenty years their senior) and published their work as the Objectivists Anthology, with an introduction by himself. This essay has long been puzzled over by students of American poetry.

Rakosi himself found Zukofsky's definition of Objectivism baffling. "It was so at odds," he says, "with any association I could make with the word "Objectivist," which has "object" in its belly." Rakosi has characterized Zukofsky's tone in the essay as "aloof" and "rebuffing," as if he were simultaneously presenting the poetry for inspection and arrogantly dismissing his readership. Zukofsky's explanation, according to Rakosi, fit only his own poetry. There was a fundamental gulf between Zukofsky and the three other poets most often named as Zukofsky's fellow Objectivists: Charles Reznikoff, George Oppen, and Rakosi. These three "were credited with a place in literary history for the wrong reason, because of a name."

Nevertheless, Rakosi came to like the label "Objectivist." Although Zukofsky's tortuous definition left him cold, the name "conveyed a meaning which was, in fact, my objective: to present objects in their most essential reality and to make of each poem an object, meaning by this the opposite of vagueness, loose bowels and streaming, sometimes screaming, consciousness." Even as Zukofsky spurned the term, Rakosi welded it to his own practice. He aimed to convert the subjective experience into an object "by feeling the experience sincerely; by setting boundaries to it and incorporating only those parts which belong together." The poem, he has said, should be like a sculpture; the reader should be able to come at it from any angle and find it "solid and coherent." Honesty and craftsmanship are the qualities needed for constructing such poems.

As is often the case when a poet supplies a definition of poetry, there is a certain amount of question-begging here. What guarantee can the poet give (even to himself) of his own sincerity and honesty? By what criteria does one decide which parts belong together? Will everyone who "views" (reads) the poem find it solid and coherent? If so, how does one account for readers' variation in taste? Yet Rakosi's aims become clearer when they are viewed in historical context and in the light of his actual practice.

Zukofsky launched his movement in 1930, some two decades after Ezra Pound and H. D. (Hilda Doolittle) had declared themselves Imagists in the process of renovating poetry by throwing out "bad habits dear to the poets of the Victorian age." Zukofsky was heavily influenced by Pound and by another inductee in the Imagist movement, William Carlos Williams. Given that Rakosi, Reznikoff, Oppen, and others anthologized under Zukofsky's editorship were also mindful of, and to some extent sympathetic with, the principles of Imagism, it is small wonder that there are several points of resemblance between Imagism and the Objectivists.

"A Retrospect"

The theoretical writing of Ezra Pound, however, had a lucidity of expression that frequently eluded Zukofsky. In "A Retrospect" Pound articulated the following principles for Imagism:

1. Direct treatment of the "thing" whether subject or objective
2. To use absolutely no word that does not contribute to the presentation.
3. As regarding rhythm: to compose in the sequence of the musical phrase, not in sequence of a metronome.

The result is well known: a radical reappraisal of poetic terms and practice; the birth within English-language poetry of "the modern"; "free" verse; a cessation of "moral tagging" or other explicit aid to the reader as to the poem's meaning; an endeavor to rescue the art from the muddyings to which it had been subjected when its practitioners sought to truck and higgle with the increasingly wide—and not necessarily deep—audience brought by universal education.

Rakosi's brief lyrics are rightfully classified as modernist for their terse, stripped-down qualities, which give the *impression* (and that is what counts) of sincerity and honesty. Yet they could hardly be called straightforward—and that is fortunate. They have far too much art to them. In fact, it is hard to take at face value Rakosi's oft-repeated assurances of his ingenuous nature, for his poems strike one as weapons of supreme irony. Ingenuousness is simply one of the more empowering poses available to such an artist, although on any given occasion he may be actually ingenuous. Reading Rakosi, it is hard to forget that for many years he worked as a psychotherapist, picking with care the words needed to lead his clients toward self-discovery. Not that he lied to them—quite the contrary: He had to stay with what was true. His role was to select, from all there was to talk about, that which he perceived as being of most use in the present. At any given moment much had to be suppressed; otherwise there would have been a blurring of outline, a loss of necessary definition and discovery.

"The Experiment with a Rat"

These are the considerations and requisite skills of the psychotherapist—and in Rakosi's poetry they are also the chief characteristics. Here is "The Experiment with a Rat":

> Every time I nudge that spring
> a bell rings
> and a man walks out of a cage
> assiduous and sharp
> like one of us
> and brings me cheese.
>
> How did he fall
> into my power?

One notes the absence of a rhyme scheme and regular rhythm, but one also notices subtle juxtapositions of sound, rhythms that are less obvious than the iambic but distinct nevertheless, Pound's "cadence of the musical phrase." The vocabulary is spare, and there are only two adjectives, segregated on their own line, as though to prevent their contaminating the rest of the poem. Most of the words are of Anglo-Saxon provenance, giving the Latinate "assiduous" a certain shock value. The tone is quiet, casual, even offhand. The reader may not at first grasp the radical nature of the point of view, for the casual air disarms attention. Suddenly one realizes how the tables have been turned—almost. While it is true that the laboratory assistant endures a trapped existence akin to that of the laboratory rat—a fact it could be salutary for the assistant to acknowledge—the slight exaggeration involved in equating rat and human being implies another truth. When one is actually trapped like the rat, one is quite capable of denying it by the kind of presumption evidenced in the final question.

"Family Portrait, Three Generations"

"Family Portrait, Three Generations" is similarly thought-provoking:

> all looking
> into the lens,
> eyes wide,
> straight ahead:
> holding:
>
> "We're plain,
> we're church goers,
> Who dares
> say anything
> against that?"

As if he were a combination of camera and tape recorder, the poet refrains from any direct comment upon the phenomena he presents "objectively." Because of this approach, the poem has the ring of truth. It is not easy to see how the poet has in fact rigged things—he has put words in the mouths of his subjects. Yet, after all, are these not exactly the right words? Surely this is what these good folk "say"—not in words, but in their demeanor, their bearing, their lives. Every reader has known someone like the family in the poem. Perhaps the reader has a bit of it in himself. Do not most human beings lead their lives principally in the eyes of others, afraid of censure, terrified of scandal?

Many of Rakosi's poems are equally disarming, apparently simple, certainly economical studies of American life. He sees Americans with remarkable clarity—piercing through a democrat's clothing to reveal the would-be emperor underneath. No doubt the dislocations of his own life—being virtually abandoned by his parents for most of his infancy, and coming to the United States at the age of seven and having to replace German and Hungarian with English—helped shape Rakosi into the careful observer who wrote these poems. Perhaps one should in fact identify a third dislocation and view his twenty-five-year poetic hiatus as a further estrangement that came to enhance his later work. He is certainly not one of the herd.

Rakosi had even held himself apart from the movement with which he has been so often associated, Objectivism. His eye is always cool; his poetry is elegant even when he chooses to write in the vernacular; in his poems great and trivial become the same (since nothing can manifest itself except in the everyday); the surfaces of his work never ruffle.

"Domination of Wallace Stevens"

In reading Rakosi one is reminded at times of that other master of elegance in American poetry, Wallace Stevens. In 1925, in fact, Rakosi wrote a six-part poem called "Domination of Wallace Stevens." It is a remarkable pastiche, and all the more noteworthy when one realizes that it was written by a young man of twenty-two. It begins, "Clear me with this master music/ when the coryphee skips on the oak floor/ and the clouds depress me like the lower keys." The reader soon encounters "Miss Ordway in a plush repose,/ counting the curves pitched in her portly mirrors/ by seven bored and pygmy globes." This is excellent fun, and by the poem's end the reader may well judge that Stevens had been dominated by young Carl Rakosi, and that the domination of the man twice his age had been shaken off. Yet like Jacob, who wrestled with the angel and limped thereafter, throughout his career Rakosi recurs to certain tones—one might call them "dictive gestures"—that set an echo of the other poet resonating between text and reader, as in "The Transmutation into English":

> And let them watch their examples,
> for in England the example of quintessence
> is *The Law Of England*
> *is the quintessence of reason.*
>
> They will try to sneak into heaven on that word.

Rakosi's sparer idiom, however, always reasserts itself quickly and most effectively. The Protestant Stevens and the Jewish Rakosi, the classic American and the recent immigrant, do make a strange couple, as Rakosi no doubt knows. It is a knowledge that he probably savors—for, after all, he can "do" Stevens, while Stevens never "did" Rakosi.

"VI Dirge" and "The Review"

Rakosi has said that of the four principal Objectivists, it was Reznikoff for whom he felt the greatest affinity. At times he has taken a leaf from the older poet's book and let document testify with no more interference than arrangement. Reznikoff's *Testimony* (1934) made use of court transcripts in this way; for Rakosi, notes to the welfare department at times said all there was to be said. "VI Dirge," for example, comes from the gathering called "American Nymphs":

> This is
> to let
> you know
> that my husband
> got his
> project cut off
> two weeks ago
> and I
> have not
> had any
> relief since.

Rakosi's work can be hilarious, kindly, and sarcastic all at once—and the masterful self-restraint the reader is induced to picture him exercising makes his terseness all the more amusing. The moment of deflation proves to be worth the wait, as in "The Review," which quotes a journalistic piece that pictures a famous American poet on a stage, gazing at an audience with "Olympian disdain." The quote is followed by Rakosi's eloquently brief comment: "Aw sheeit!" This final exclamation might only be an echo of what the Olympian figure himself muttered, looking out at an audience that was projecting—as the reviewer did—tragic and heroic qualities onto him. This kind of sympathy always hovers about Rakosi's satire, a constant possibility. When Faust puts a word wrong, Rakosi will hear him, but that angel will always save the poem from utter condemnation.

Later years

In the 1980's and 1990's Rakosi's work began to be included in the major poetry anthologies and taught in universities as the Objectivists as a group came to be recognized as an important part of the literary canon. Not only did the long careers of the Objectivists allow them to be important writers in both the modern and postmodern periods, but, in terms of influence studies, the Objectivists were quite literally deemed to be the inheritors of the legacy of Pound and Williams. It was a legacy that they would fundamentally call into question, even as they served as mentors themselves to many major contemporary poets. Although Rakosi preferred the friendship of poets to acclaim by literary scholars, he eventually found himself serving as the last surviving Objectivist for posterity.

Other major works

NONFICTION: *The Collected Prose of Carl Rakosi*, 1983.

MISCELLANEOUS: *The Old Poet's Tale*, 1999 (poetry and prose).

Bibliography

Bromige, David, et al. "The Royaumont Conference." *Poetry Flash,* November, 1989-June, 1990. A full account of the September, 1989, conference on the Objectivists held at the Abbeye Royaumont near Paris, with American and French poets as panelists and Carl Rakosi, the only surviving Objectivist poet, as featured speaker. Bromige's article, in the November, 1989, issue, discusses some of the conference's salient issues; one such issue, the matter of opacity in the poem, stirred up a controversy that was carried on in letters and articles from January through June, 1990. Rakosi contributed a revealing letter.

Heller, Michael D. *Conviction's Net of Branches*. Carbondale: Southern Illinois University Press, 1985. Discusses the Objectivists movement and examines Rakosi's varying styles.

Heller, Michael D., ed. *Carl Rakosi: Man and Poet*. Orono, Maine: National Poetry Foundation, 1993. Offers criticism and interpretation of Rakosi's work. Bibliography and index included.

Perloff, Marjorie. "Looking for the Real Carl Rakosi: Collected and Selecteds." *Journal of American Studies* 30 (August, 1996): 271-283. Perloff reviews *Poems, 1923-1941* and *The Collected Poems of Carl Rakosi*, both by Rakosi, as well as *Carl Rakosi: Man and Poet*, edited by Michael D. Heller.

Rakosi, Carl. *The Collected Prose of Carl Rakosi*. Edited by Burton Hatlen. Orono, Maine: National Poetry Foundation, 1983. These pieces shed much light on Rakosi's poetry. "Poetry, like metaphysics, craves to find something permanent behind changing appearances, some yet unknown form of a transcendent nature," Rakosi says in "Day Book." Hatlen, editor of the volume, supplies an afterword, "Carl Rakosi and the Re-invention of the Epigram." This essay touches also on other aspects of Rakosi's writing, beginning with a general survey of the work in its historical setting. His inevitable mention of Reznikoff, Zukofsky, and Oppen is thought-provoking: Hatlen postulates that these three poets share "a distinctively (but not exclusively) Jewish sense of speech as sacred event, of language as, not 'about' the world, but constitutive of it."

_______. Interview by L. S. Dembo. In *The Contemporary Writer*, by L. S. Dembo. Madison: University of Wisconsin Press, 1972. Rakosi and Dembo engage in an interesting, revealing discussion of such matters as Rakosi's Marxism, the influence of Wallace Stevens on his poetry, his views of Zukofsky and other of his contemporaries, and his compositional process. (He says that his first draft is generally "raw data" that has been somehow changed by "a mystery.")

Shoemaker, Steve. "Carl Rakosi Interview." *Sagetrieb* 11 (Winter, 1992): 93-132. Shoemaker interviews Rakosi.

David Bromige

Sir Walter Ralegh

Born: Hayes Barton, England; c. 1552
Died: London, England; October 29, 1618

Principal poetry

The Poems of Sir Walter Ralegh, with a Biographical and Critical Introduction, 1813
The Poems of Sir Walter Ralegh, 1962 (Agnes Latham, editor)

Other literary forms

Almost immediately after his execution in 1618, Sir Walter Ralegh's reputation as a patriotic and courageous opponent to James I developed, and as opposition to James and Charles I increased, many prose works were attributed to Ralegh from about 1625 through the end of the seventeenth century. Of those certainly written by Ralegh, there are two pamphlets, *A Report of the Fight About the Iles of Açores* (1591) and *The Discoverie of the Large, Rich and Bewtiful Empyre of Guiana* (1596), which express the aggressive buoyancy of Elizabethan imperialist designs on South America and of the control of trade to the New World. Ralegh's major work outside his poetry is the monumental, unfinished *The History of the World* (1614), dedicated to and yet containing scarcely disguised criticism of King James, who had him imprisoned between 1603 and 1616, and who (after Ralegh's hopeless expedition to Guiana to find El Dorado) had him executed. *The History of the World* was part therapy, part histrionic pique and, like most of Ralegh's career, significant far beyond its surface ambiguities and chronological contradictions. Torn between being an account of the "unjointed and scattered frame of our English affairs" and a universal history, it is a tribute as well to the dead Queen Elizabeth, "Her whom I must still honour in the dust," and an indictment of what Ralegh perceived as the corruption of the Jacobean court. For Ralegh, in *The History of the World* as much as in his poetry, the court was his stage, a place of "parts to play," in which survival depended on "fashioning of our selves according to the nature of the time wherein we live," and the power of which dominated his language and, in the most absolute sense, his life. Like his poems, *The History of the World* is a moving and (far beyond his knowledge) revealing document of the power of the court over the men and women who struggled within it.

Achievements

Sir Walter Ralegh's importance belies the slimness of his poetic output. The author of perhaps two dozen extant poems and a number of brief verse translations, the latter appearing in his *The History of the World*, Ralegh is nevertheless one of the most important of the Elizabethan courtly makers, articulating with fearful

Sir Walter Ralegh (Library of Congress)

clarity not merely the gaudy surface and fashions of the late Elizabethan age, but also much of the felt pressure of the court, his society's dominant social power, upon the lives and sensibilities of those caught in it. Ralegh described himself toward the end of his life as "a seafaring man, a Souldior and a Courtier," and his poetry articulates much of what drove him to those vocations. He knew, deeply and bitterly, that, as he puts it in *The History of the World*, there is nothing more to "becoming a wise man" than "to retire himself from Court." Yet the court was his stage and it was, he wrote, the "token of a worldly wise man, not to warre or contend in vaine against the nature of the times wherein he lived." The achievement of his poetry is that it gives reverberating expression to the struggles of those who lived in and were controlled by the Elizabethan court. Most of his poems look, on the surface, like delicate, even trivial, songs, complaints, and compliments typical of Petrarchanism; but they are rich, if often confused, responses to the complex and powerful set of discourses, symbolic formations, and systems of representation that constituted the Elizabethan court. They offer a unique insight into the interplay between the social text of Elizabethan society (the events that made Ralegh's history) and the literary text (the poems that he made of those events). He is, in many ways, the quintessential court poet of the Elizabethan period inasmuch as his poems are haunted by, determined by, and finally silenced by, the power of the court.

Biography

Although Ralegh is often spelled as Raleigh, Walter Ralegh signed his name once as Rawleyghe, in 1587, then signed it Rauley until 1583, and more or less spelled it consistently as Ralegh from 1584 until his death in 1618. He was the quintessential *arriviste*: Born in Devon, educated at Oxford, he rapidly became a court favorite, was knighted in 1584, but fell into disgrace when, after a bitter rivalry with the up-and-coming younger earl of Essex, he was imprisoned for seducing one of the queen's maids-of-honor, Elizabeth Throckmorton, whom he later married. He was increasingly unpopular for, among other things, his flamboyant lifestyle. When James came to the throne, Ralegh was sentenced to death for treason, although the sentence was reduced to imprisonment in the Tower of London. During his imprisonment, between 1603 and 1616, Ralegh became a close friend of the Prince of Wales, wrote extensively, and became a center of influence and even of counterestablishment power. He was released by James in 1616 and sent on an ill-fated expedition to Guiana, and on his return, executed—his death bewailed by as many people in 1618 as had desired it fourteen years earlier.

Analysis

If readers take him at his face value (or at the value of one of his many faces), Sir Walter Ralegh epitomized, accepted, and chose to live out the daring expansiveness and buoyancy of the Elizabethan court. He conceived of his own life as a poem, as a flamboyant epic gesture, and his poems were the manifestations of his public role and his political ambitions. However disguised in the garment of Petrarchan plaint, mournful song, lament for lost love, *carpe diem* or *ubi sunt* motif, Ralegh's poems are the articulation of the ruthless and sometimes blatant struggle for power that created and held together the court of Elizabeth. "Then must I needes advaunce my self by skyll,/ And lyve to serve, in hope of your goodwyll" he (possibly) wrote— and advancing himself with skill meant using the court as an arena of self-assertion, or (in another of the metaphors which disseminate contradictions throughout his work) as a new world to be conquered.

Ralegh's career as a poet and a courtier (the two are almost inseparable, literary and social text repeatedly writing and rewriting each other throughout his life) should not be simply seen as the daring, willful assertion of the gentleman adventurer who strode into the queen's favor with a graceful and opportune sweep of his cloak. That would be to take too much for granted at least some of his poems and the power in which, through them, Ralegh hoped to participate. Ralegh's poetry is put into play both by and in power; it demonstrates, probably more clearly than that of any other Elizabethan poet, the unconscious workings of power upon discourse, specifically upon the language which it controlled, selected, organized, and distributed through approved and determined procedures, delimiting as far as possible the emergence of oppositional forces and experiences. The Elizabethan court used poetry and poets alike as the means of stabilizing and controlling its members. To confirm its residual values, it tried to restrict poet and poem as far as possible to the dominant discourses of a colorful, adventurous world, but only at the cost of a frustrating, and, in Ralegh's case, despairing powerlessness.

Petrarchan lyrics

Much of Ralegh's poetry looks like typical Petrarchan love poetry—it can be, and no doubt was, to many members of its original audience, read as such. The surface of his verse presents the typical paraphernalia of the Petrarchan lyric—hope and despair, pleasure and fortune, fake love, frail beauty, fond shepherds, coy mistresses, deceitful time. The magnificent "As you came from the holy land," which is possibly by Ralegh, can be read as a superbly melancholy affirmation of love, one of the most moving love lyrics of the language. "Nature that washt her hands in milke" takes the reader through a witty blazon of the perfect mistress's charms, her outside made of "snow and silke," her "inside . . . only of wantonesse and witt." Like all Petrarchan mistresses, she has "a heart of stone" and so the lover is poised, in frustration, before his ideal. Then in the second half of the poem, Ralegh ruthlessly tears down all of the ideals he has built. What gives the poem its power is the unusually savage use of the Elizabethan commonplace of Time the destroyer, the thief—ravaging, lying, rusting, and annihilating. Time "turnes snow, and silke, and milke, to dust." What was to the lover the "food of joyes" is ceaselessly fed into the maw of death by time and remorsely turned into excreta; the moistness of the mistress's wantonness rendered dry and repulsive. Likewise, the reply to Christopher Marlowe's "The Passionate Shepherd" is an impressively terse expression of the *carpe diem* principle, creating an impassioned stoical voice through the stylistic conventions of the plain Elizabethan voice. Typically, Ralegh has superb control of mood, movement, voice modulation, and an appropriately direct rhetoric.

Gifted amateur

Ralegh's poems are those of the gifted amateur—seemingly casual compliment, occasional verse typically dropped, as the manuscript title of another poem has it, "into my Lady Laiton's pocket." Such a poem looks like one of the many erotic lyrics of the Renaissance which, as Michel Foucault has written, allowed men to overhear and will another to "speak the truth of" their sexuality. Ralegh's poetry, however, does more than introduce sexuality into discourse: Inevitably the language of erotic compliment and complaint is inseparable from the language of power. Despite their seemingly trivial, light, or occasional nature—epitaphs on Sir Philip Sidney's death, "A farewell to false love," dedicatory poems to works by George Gascoigne or Edmund Spenser, or poems directly or indirectly written to the queen—their significance reverberates far beyond their apparently replete surface configuration of stock metaphor and gracefully logical structure.

Ralegh's public roles

Ralegh's predominant public roles were those of a man who consciously identified entirely with what he perceived as the dominant forces of his society—and, like his poetry, Ralegh's life is like a palimpsest, requiring not only reading but also interpretation and demystification in depth. As Stephen Greenblatt has suggestively argued, "Ralegh" is in a way a curiously hollow creation, the production of many roles in the theater of the court. Greenblatt has argued that Ralegh saw his life as a work of art, and the court as a "great theater" in which the boldest author would be the most successful. His career from the late 1570's might suggest that his multiplicity reflects an inner hollowness as he shifts back and forth among the roles of courtier, politician, explorer, freethinker, poet, philosopher, lover, and husband.

In Ralegh's public career, two dominant discourses clash and contradict—one seeing all human activity as an assertion of the adaptability of the actor, the other a pessimistic view of life as an empty, futile, and unreal theater. While Ralegh adapted to different roles as his ambitions shifted, his very restlessness bespeaks the power of the court. Unlike Sir Philip Sidney, who was a courtier by birth and privilege, Ralegh became one because his identity and survival depended on it. His place in a world that was dangerous and unpredictable was never stable, and even its apparently fixed center, the queen, was unpredictable and arbitrary.

PROBLEMS OF ATTRIBUTION

Introducing Ralegh's role as a poet, it must be noted how the term "possibly" must be continually used to qualify assertions about the authorship of many of the poems attributed to him. Despite the confident assertions of some modern editors, Michael Rudick has shown that scholars do not in fact know whether many of the poems attributed to Ralegh in the manuscripts and miscellanies in which Elizabethan court poetry habitually circulated are in fact his; despite possessing more holograph material for Ralegh than for any other Elizabethan poets except Sir Thomas Wyatt and Robert Sidney, scholars can only speculate about the authorship of many of the best poems attributed to him. Even modern editors and biographers attribute poems to him on primarily sentimental grounds, but in one important sense, the lack of definitive attribution does not matter: Elizabethan court poetry often speaks with the voice of a collectivity, its authors *scriptors* or spokesmen for the values of a dominant class and its ideology. In short, the author's relationship to the languages that traverse him is much more complex than is allowed for by the sentimental nineteenth century biographical criticism that has held sway in Ralegh scholarship until very recently. In any court lyric, there is an illimitable series of pretexts, subtexts, and post-texts that call into question any concept of its "author" as a free, autonomous person. Ralegh's poems, like those of Sidney or Spenser, are sites of struggle, attempts by Ralegh (or whatever court poet may have "written" them) to write himself into the world. Hence there is a sense in which we should speak of "Ralegh" as the symptomatic court poet, rather than Ralegh the poet—or, perhaps, of "Ralegh" and "his" poems alike as texts, requiring always to be read against what they seem to articulate, often speaking out in their silences, in what they cannot or dare not say but nevertheless manage to express.

COURT IDEOLOGY

Some of the poems are, however, very explicit about their ideological source, even verging on propagandist art. "Praisd be Dianas faire and harmles light" is a poem (again possibly by Ralegh) which reifies the ideals of the court in a hymn of celebration, demanding in ways that other Elizabethan lyrics rarely do, allegiance to the magical, timeless world of the Elizabethan court, in which no challenge to the replete atmosphere can be admitted and in which the readers are permitted to share only so long as they acknowledge the beauty of the goddess whom the poem celebrates. The poem's atmosphere is incantatory, its movement designed like court music to inculcate unquestioning reverence and subordination. Only the subhuman (presumably any reader foolish, or treasonous, enough to dissent from its vision) are excluded from the charm and power that it celebrates: "A knowledge pure it is hir worth to kno,/ With Circes let them dwell that thinke not so."

George Puttenham mentions Ralegh's poetry approvingly as "most lofty, insolent and passionate," and by the mid-1580's, when he expressed his view, Ralegh already had the reputation of being a fine craftsman among the "crew of courtly makers, noblemen and gentlemen" of Elizabeth's court. In what another of Ralegh's contemporaries called the "*Terra infirma* of the Court," Ralegh used his verse as one of the many means of scrambling for position. His verse, in C. S. Lewis's words, is that of the quintessential adaptable courtly amateur, "blown this way and that (and sometimes lifted into real poetry)." He is the lover, poor in words but rich in affection; passions are likened to "floudes and streames"; the lover prays "in vayne" to "blinde fortune" but nevertheless resolves: "But love, farewell, thoughe fortune conquer thee,/ No fortune base nor frayle shall alter mee" ("In vayne my Eyes, in vayne yee waste your tears"). However apparently depoliticized these poems are, they are the product of the allurement and dominance of the court, their confidence less that of the poet himself than of the power of the structures in which he struggles to locate himself. His characteristic pose is that of the worshiper, devoted to the unapproachable mistress or, as the idealizing devotee with the queen as the unwavering star, the chaste goddess, the imperial embodiment of justice, the timeless principle around which the universe turns. In the way that Ben Jonson's masques were later to embody the ideology of the Jacobean court, so Ralegh's poems evoke the collective fantasy of the Elizabethan—a world that is harmonious and static, from which all change has been exorcized.

Hatfield poems

Aside from this miscellany (sometimes startlingly evocative, invariably competent and provoking), there are four closely connected and important poems, all undoubtedly Ralegh's, which were found in his own handwriting among the Cecil Papers in Hatfield House, north of London, the family home of Ralegh's great enemy Robert Cecil. They are "If Synthia be a Queene, a princes, and supreame," "My boddy in the walls captivated," "Sufficeth it to yow, my joyes interred"—the second of which is headed "The 11th: and last booke of the Ocean to Scinthia," and the fourth "The end of the bookes, of the Oceans love to Scinthia, and the beginninge of the 12 Boock, entreatinge of Sorrow." The existence of a poem, or poems, directly written to the queen and titled *Cynthia* seems to be mentioned by Spenser in *The Faerie Queene* (1590) and it is usually characterized as being parts of or related to the Hatfield poems. It is probably, however, that the third and fourth poems were written, or at least revised, during Ralegh's imprisonment in 1592.

"The 11th: and last booke of the Ocean to Scinthia"

"The 11th: and last booke of the Ocean to Scinthia," the most important of the group, appears to be a scarcely revised draft of an appeal, if not to the queen herself, at least to that part of Ralegh's mind occupied by her power. It lacks narrative links; its four-line stanzas are often imperfect, with repetitions and gaps which presumably would have been revised later. Its unfinished state, however, makes it not only a fascinating revelation of Ralegh's personal and poetic anguish, but in its very fragmentariness it is perhaps the clearest example in Elizabethan court poetry of the way the dynamics and contradictions of power speak through a text. "The 11th: and last booke of the Ocean to Scinthia" repeatedly deconstructs the philosophy to which it gives allegiance: Its incoherences, gaps, uncertainties, and repetitions both affirm and negate Elizabethan mythology. What in Ralegh's other poems is expressed as complete ideological closure is undermined by the fractures and symptomatic maladjustments of the text. Nowhere in Elizabethan poetry is a poem as obviously constitutive of ideological struggle.

The poem is addressed to a patently transparent Cynthia who has withdrawn her favor from the faithful lover. Ralegh projects himself as a despairing lover fearfully aware that his service has been swept into oblivion, simultaneously acknowledging that honors inevitably corrupt and that he cannot keep from pursuing them. The "love" that he has seemingly won includes favors that open doors not only to glory but also to ruin and death. Yet even knowing this, it is as if he cannot help himself "seeke new worlds, for golde, for prayse, for glory," with the tragic result that "Twelve yeares intire I wasted in this warr." The result of his "twelve yeares" dedication has been imprisonment and disgrace. Yet he is helpless before his own inability to abandon the glories of office. "Trew reason" shows power to be worthless, yet even while he knows that "all droopes, all dyes, all troden under dust" he knows also that the only stability in the world of power is the necessity of instability and emulation.

The Petrarchan motifs with which the successful courtier has played so effectively, almost on demand—the helpless lover wooing the unapproachable mistress who is the unattainable goal of desire—have suddenly and savagely been literalized. The role that Ralegh has played has exploded his habitual adaptability. He cannot protest that the game of the despairing lover is only a game; it has now become real. In 1592 he wrote to Cecil: "My heart was never broken till this day, that I hear the queen goes away so far off—whom I have followed so many years with so great love and desire, in so many journeys, and am now left behind her in a great prison alone." The letter is an obvious echo of the lines from Ralegh's adaption of the Walsingham ballad, "As you came from the holy land." The contradictions of Ralegh's life which the poem now voices had been repressed and silenced during his imprisonment, but now they are revealed as terrifyingly real. By marrying, Ralegh himself has ceased to play Elizabeth's game; he has thus found that the role of masochistic victim in which he cast himself for political advantage has been taken literally and he has become an outcast. "The 11th: and last booke of the Ocean to Scinthia" expresses the agony of a man whose choices and commitments have been built on the myth of a changeless past in an ever-moving power struggle. The very unfinished quality of Ralegh's fragment is the perfect formal expression of the disruptiveness that has overwhelmed him.

"The Lie"

It is fortunate that another key poem in this period is among the Hatfield manuscripts. "The Lie" is a release of explicit rage, a struggle to find form for deep frustration and venom, finding no alternative to renunciation and repulsion. It is a statement of deeply felt impotence, probably written after Ralegh's release from prison in 1592, but before he was restored to favor. Ralegh's poem is seemingly total in its rejection of the ideology by which he has lived: Natural law, universal harmony, love, and court artifice are all rejected in a mood of total condemnation. Yet Ralegh's poem is neither philosophically nihilistic nor politically radical: The force of his revulsion from the court does not allow for any alternative to it. What dies is the "I" of the poem, as he gives the lie to the world, and takes refuge in a savage *contemptus mundi*. "The Lie" is at once an explosion of frustration and beneath ideological confidence. In such poems the ideology is betrayed by writing itself; the poem constantly releases an anxiety for realities which challenge the surface harmonies and struggle unsuccessfully to be heard against the dominant language of the court poetic mode. What readers start to recognize as Ralegh's characteristic melancholic formulation of the persistence of "woe" or pain as the very mark of human self-consciousness is the special telltale sign of his texts as sites of struggle and repression. "The life expires, the woe remaines" is a refrain echoed by "Of all which past, the sorrow, only stays" ("Like truthless dreams") and by phrases in *The History of the World* such as "Of all our vain passions and affections past, the sorrow only abideth." Such recurring motifs impart more than a characteristic tone to Ralegh's verse. They point to the frustrated insurrection of subjugated experience struggling to find expression, knowing that there are no words permitted for it.

Legacy

Ralegh's poems, then, are haunted by what they try to exorcise: a fragility which arises from the repressed political uncertainties of court life in the 1580's and 1590's and which undermines his chosen role as the spokesman of a replete court ideology. Despite its confident surface, all of his verse is less a celebration of the queen's power than a conspiracy to remain within its protection. The Petrarchan clichés of "Like truthless dreams, so are my joys expired" and the Neoplatonic commonplaces of the "Walsingham" ballad become desperate pleas for favor, projections into lyric poems of political machinations. "Concept begotten by the eyes" also starts out as a stereotypical contrast between "desire" and "woe" and emerges as a poignant cry of radical insecurity and a powerless acknowledgment that the personality of the court poet and of Ralegh himself is a creation of the discourses he has uneasily inhabited and from which he now feels expelled. The Hatfield poems illustrate with wonderful clarity what all Elizabethan court poetry tries to repress: that however the poet asserts his autonomy, he is constituted through ideology, having no existence outside the social formation and the signifying practice legitimized by the power of the court. Ralegh, like every other poet who wrestled within the court, does not speak so much as he is spoken.

More than twenty years later, after a revival of fortunes under Elizabeth, arrest, imprisonment, release, and rearrest under James, Ralegh prematurely brought his history to an end. The work, written to justify God's providential control of time, articulates a view of history that radically undercuts its author's intentions. For Ralegh, history has no final eschatological goal, no ultimate consummation. It consists only of the continual vengeance of an angry God until "the long day of mankinde is drawing fast towards an evening, and the world's Tragedie and time neare at an end." A few years later, on the eve of his execution, Ralegh took up the last lines of the lyric written twenty-five years before on the ravages of time which he had felt all his life—

> Even such is tyme which takes in trust
> Our yowth, our Joyes, and all we have,
> And payes us butt with age and dust:
> When we have wandred all our wayes,
> Shutts up the storye of our dayes.

—and appends to it in two new lines the only hope of which he could conceive, a *deus ex machina* to rescue him, in a way that neither queen nor king had, from the grip of time's power: "And from which earth and grave and dust/ The Lord shall raise me up I trust." It is a cry of desperation, not a transformation of "the consuming disease of time" as he puts it in *The History of the World*. What is finally triumphant over Ralegh is the power of the world in which he courageously yet blindly struggled and of which his handful of poems are an extraordinarily moving acknowledgment and testament.

Other major works

NONFICTION: *A Report of the Fight About the Iles of Açores*, 1591; *The Discoverie of the Large, Rich and Bewtiful Empyre of Guiana*, 1596; *The History of the World*, 1614.

MISCELLANEOUS: *Works of Sir Walter Ralegh*, 1829 (8 volumes; Thomas Birch and William Oldys, editors); *Selected Prose and Poetry*, 1965 (Agnes Latham, editor).

Bibliography

Greenblatt, Stephen J. *Sir Walter Ralegh: The Renaissance Man and His Roles*. New Haven, Conn.: Yale University Press, 1973. Greenblatt discusses Ralegh's role-playing and theatrical nature as demonstrated in his court poetry and in *The History of the World*, both of which receive chapter-length treatments. He also provides the context for *The Discoverie of the Large, Rich and Bewtiful Empyre of Guiana*, which he regards as reflecting Ralegh's personal sorrow and the national myths of his age.

Lacey, Robert. *Sir Walter Ralegh*. London: Phoenix Press, 2000. Lacey's account reflects the multifaceted nature of his subject in the book's structure. There are some fifty chapters, divided into seven sections, each charting the ups and downs of Ralegh's uniquely checkered career. From country upstart to royal favorite, from privateer to traitor in the Tower, his life was never still.

Oakeshott, Walter. *The Queen and the Poet*. New York: Barnes & Noble Books, 1961. The first book to analyze in depth Ralegh's poetry, Oakeshott's study concerns his subject's relationship to Queen Elizabeth, the person his "occasional" poetry was designed to please or placate. Using passages from Edmund Spenser and William Shakespeare's *Love's Labour's Lost*, Oakeshott places the poems in their context. The second half of the book contains an edition of the poems associated with the queen, with the Cynthia poems receiving extensive explication.

Ralegh, Walter. *The Letters of Sir Walter Ralegh*. Edited by Agnes Latham and Joyce Youings. Exeter, England: University of Exeter Press, 1999. Brings together all that is known of Ralegh's correspondence, uncollected since 1868 and much expanded and refined. Students of history and literature will grasp at this book as it throws a beam across the life of one of the more attractive personalities of the late Tudor and early Jacobean periods.

Rowse, A. L. *Sir Walter Ralegh: His Family and Private Life*. New York: Harper and Brothers, 1962. The first truly significant biography of Ralegh, Rowse's book offers a new perspective, one gained from the recently discovered diary of Sir Arthur Throckmorton, Ralegh's brother-in-law, on Ralegh's life and writing. Rowse, an expert biographer knowledgeable about Renaissance England, has supplemented his text with many illustrations.

Stein, Arnold. *The House of Death: Messages from the English Renaissance*. Baltimore: The Johns Hopkins

University Press, 1986. In a chapter titled "Dying in Jest and Earnest: Ralegh," Stein discusses three Ralegh poems about death, "The Life of Man," a jest at the theatrical nature of life; "The Lie," a defiant defense against persecution; and "The Passionate Man's Pilgrimage," a comparison of Christian and secular justice.

Tennenhouse, Leonard. "Sir Walter Ralegh and the Literature of Clientage." In *Patronage in the Renaissance*, edited by Guy Fitch Lytle and Stephen Orgel. Princeton, N.J.: Princeton University Press, 1981. Tennenhouse examines Ralegh's lyric poetry, with its Petrarchan themes, in the light of their political significance: Political service becomes love, and reward becomes favor for the courtier/lover. Ralegh's *The History of the World* is likewise read in terms of the poet's own position at court, for Tennenhouse believes the history operates analogically, using the past to criticize the present.

Waller, Gary. *English Poetry of the Sixteenth Century.* London: Longman, 1986. Waller deconstructs Ralegh's poetry, which he claims demonstrates how power works on language. For Waller, Ralegh's poetry simultaneously pays homage to and criticizes the courtly arena where he must play different roles. "As You Come from the Holy Land" and one of the "Scinthia" poems, thus, become poems of tension and value.

Gary F. Waller;
bibliography updated by the editors

Dudley Randall

Born: Washington, D.C.; January 14, 1914
Died: Southfield, Michigan; August 5, 2000

Principal poetry

Poem Counterpoem, 1966 (with Margaret Danner)
Cities Burning, 1968
Love You, 1970
More to Remember: Poems of Four Decades, 1971
After the Killing, 1973
A Litany of Friends: Poems Selected and New, 1981, revised 1983

Other literary forms

Despite his primary interest in poetry, Dudley Randall wrote short stories, articles, and reviews. In the mid-1960's, he founded the Broadside Press, which thereafter consumed much of his energy, as he began to direct most of his writing toward poetry and critical articles. For the Broadside Press he edited, with Margaret G. Burroughs, *For Malcolm: Poems on the Life and the Death of Malcolm X* (1967), the press's second publication. His introductory essay succinctly foreshadowed the influence that Malcolm X was to have on many of the newly emerging black poets of the 1960's; it also helped to introduce many of the contributors to readers of black literature.

In 1969, aware that many current anthologies excluded or gave only limited representation to black poets, Randall edited and published *Black Poetry: A Supplement to Anthologies Which Exclude Black Poets*, which brought such omissions to the attention of larger publishing houses in the country. By 1971, a number of anthologies of African American poetry were in circulation, but many of them were seriously flawed by too-narrow criteria for selection. Randall's *The Black Poets* (1971) enjoyed wide distribution in an inexpensive paperback format and corrected many of the deficiencies of previous black poetry anthologies. Presenting a full range of African American poetry from folklore and spirituals to the Black Nationalist poets of the late 1960's, the anthology offered a substantial selection from each of its contributors and stressed the continuity of a rich oral tradition while delineating various periods in the history of black American poetry. It quickly became one of the most widely read and influential anthologies of its kind.

In his critical writings Randall came to be known as a moderating voice, maintaining respect for poets of earlier periods while accepting the new directions of black poetry since the 1960's. One important article, "The Black Aesthetic in the Thirties, Forties, and Fifties" (*The Black Aesthetic*, 1971), clearly establishes the vital role of such poets as Sterling Brown, Margaret Walker, Melvin B. Tolson, Robert Hayden, and

Gwendolyn Brooks, among others who wrote in the wake of the Harlem Renaissance. In providing an essential chapter in black literary history, Randall, here and in other essays, countered eloquently the tendency for young black poets in the 1960's to dismiss gifted, significant writers because they seemed too accommodationist. On the other hand, Randall's productive generosity in publishing and reviewing introduced a great variety of young black poets to literary America and provided an unparalleled availability of black poetry, in general, not only to the black community but also to the mainstream reading public.

Two additional literary forms must be mentioned in assessing Randall's career: interviews and translations. His insights into literary history, political developments, and his own methods of composition can be found in published interviews. While such interviews are frequently useful in understanding his own work, they are also immensely instructional in the field of African American poetry. Randall's translations from Russian, Latin, and French are also worthy of note. He published translations from major figures influential on his own poetic sensibilities, from an Alexander Pushkin to K. M. Simonov. Translating from the Latin, he has mastered the classical lyricism of Catullus. From Paul Verlaine, Randall assimilated the influence of the French Symbolists.

While he became well practiced in classical and European forms and techniques, Randall studied equally thoroughly the folk forms of the African American heritage. In these forms, he absorbed the patterns of dialect and commonsensible observation that informed much of the black poetry in the 1960's. Much of this poetry—including some of Randall's own—he made available on tape recordings, through Broadside Press. These tape recordings highlight the performance qualities of the black oral tradition. Randall himself was known as a gifted and effective reader of his own works.

ACHIEVEMENTS

Beyond his own poetry, it is as an editor and publisher that Dudley Randall's literary talents have been most significant. Randall's principal literary accomplishment is the founding of Broadside Press in September, 1965. With an initial investment of twelve dollars, he began by issuing a run of one broadside (a poem printed on a single sheet). These inexpensive broadsides could be folded and carried to be read on lunch breaks, on buses, or virtually anytime, anywhere. They could also be posted just about anywhere as well; thus, Randall's idea succeeded in bringing poetry to the ordinary citizens of the community: The venture was more educational than commercial. (This idea has since been imitated by small presses all over the country.) Within a few years, Broadside was publishing anthologies, volumes by new poets, criticism, and recordings. By example, other black writers also began to establish independent presses that specialized in reaching the black community with inexpensive editions of poetry, most notably Haki R. Madhubuti's Third World Press. One can fairly credit Randall, then, as one of the most influential black publishers of his time: His refusal to place commercial interests ahead of literary education has helped to inform a whole generation of the richness and diversity of black poetic traditions. In doing so, he has introduced new African American writers, and he has fostered an awareness of the reciprocity between black writers in the United States and Africa.

Randall's own poetry, however, has not been without acclaim in its own right. While the critical reception in reviews has been laudatory, however, thorough critical appraisal has been oddly sparse, at best. Despite the lack of proper critical assessment, Randall remains a significant member of the "post-renaissance" generation that followed the Harlem Renaissance. Along with Hayden and Brooks, he has assimilated into his poetry the variety of techniques and experimentation offered by modernism without extensive imitation of any of the modernists. Despite his lack of wide publication until the early 1960's, Randall has pursued poetry consistently with an openness to sources the world over as well as with a persistent study of the literary heritage of blacks. Fusing the eloquence and power of the classical lyric with the terseness and common sense of the oral tradition, yet remaining in the context of modernism, Randall's voice concentrates on the integrity of craft, music, and delight in his poetry. His rhythm is graceful without becoming strained, his tone compassionate without becoming sentimental. Randall's images are precise without becoming obscure and his diction is relevant without becoming contrived. His themes are universal without becoming clichéd. Even without widespread critical evaluation, Randall's work has not gone unnoticed. In 1962, he received the Tompkins Award from Wayne State University for both poetry and fiction, and in 1966, he received the same award for poetry. In recognition of his contributions to black literature, he received the Kuumba Liberation Award in 1973. He was awarded National Endowment for the Humanities fellowships in 1981 and 1986, and was named the first poet laureate of the city of Detroit in 1981. In 1996, Randall received a Lifetime Achievement Award from the National Endowment for the Arts.

BIOGRAPHY

Born in 1914 to Arthur and Ada Randall, Dudley Felker Randall spent his childhood in Washington, D.C., his birthplace, and East St. Louis. His father was responsible for the young Randall's awareness of political commitment; he frequently campaigned for blacks seeking political office, and he took Randall with him to hear such speakers as James Weldon Johnson and W. E. B. DuBois (although Randall reports that at the time he "preferred playing baseball"). Randall's public education continued when his family moved to Detroit. By this time, he was conscious not only of the political process, but also of black literature. Having first begun to write poetry at the early age of thirteen, Randall purchased a copy of Jean Toomer's *Cane* (1923) when he was sixteen; he was so impressed by Toomer's precise images and powerful symbolism that Toomer became—and remains—his favorite black poet. By 1930, the time of his graduation from the public school system, also at sixteen, Randall was well read in the major writers of the Harlem Renaissance.

After graduation in the midst of the Great Depression, Randall eventually found work as a foundry worker for the Ford Motor Company from 1932 to 1937. Sometime in 1933, he met the poet Robert Hayden, also living in Detroit, with whom he shared his poetry and discussed the major poets of the time. Their exchange of poems and ideas was to help him sharpen his skills and was to remain a mutually enriching friendship for many years. By 1938, Randall had taken a job with the U.S. Post Office as a letter carrier, work he was to continue until 1951, except for his service in the United States Army during World War II as a member of the signal corps in the South Pacific (1942-1946). After returning from military duty, Randall attended Wayne State University and was graduated in 1949. While still working for the post office, Randall also managed to complete work for a master's degree in library science from the University of Michigan in 1951.

Degree in hand, Randall began his career as a librarian by accepting an appointment with Lincoln University in Jefferson City, Missouri, where he remained until 1954. He was promoted to associate librarian when he moved to Baltimore to work for Morgan State College for the next two years. In 1956, he returned to Detroit, where he was to work for the Wayne County Federated Library System until 1969, first as a branch librarian and then as head of the reference and interloan department (1963-1969). Randall's introduction to several relatively unknown black poets from Detroit at a planning meeting for a special issue of *Negro History Bulletin* in 1962 led to his determination to see more work by new black poets become available; thus, he became the founding editor of the Broadside Press in 1965. His collaboration with Margaret Danner, who had founded Boone House, a Detroit cultural center, produced his first published book of poems, *Poem Counterpoem* from Broadside Press (its first publication as well).

With the publication of Randall's second book, *Cities Burning*, his reputation as a poet and publisher grew, and he doubled as poet in residence and reference librarian for the University of Detroit from 1969 to 1975. During this time, he also taught courses in black literature at the university, gave a number of readings, and was involved in conferences and seminars throughout the country. In 1966, Randall, with a delegation of black artists, visited Paris, Prague, and the Soviet Union, where he read his translations and his own poems to Russian audiences. In 1970, he visited West Africa, touring Ghana, Togo, and Dahomey, and meeting with African writers. After his retirement in 1975, Randall continued his involvement in writing conferences and readings, but he devoted the majority of his time to the Broadside Press and his own writing. Melba Boyd's well-received documentary film on Randall's life and work, *Black Unicorn*, was released in 1996. Randall died of congestive heart failure on August 5, 2000.

Analysis

Like fellow black writers of the "post-renaissance" school that followed the Harlem Renaissance, Dudley Randall embraces not only the concerns of modernism in discovering new modes of expression and technique, but also the increasing awareness of a black literary heritage that begins in slave songs and spirituals. While much of his earlier work experiments with classical forms, primarily the rhymed lyric and the sonnet, Randall also works in free verse and with the terseness of folk expression. He cherishes the freedom of the individual poet to explore ideas and forms central in his poetry. Although he is primarily lyrical in his tone, his work demonstrates sensitivity to the ordinary experiences of the working man, the political struggles of black Americans, and the sanctity of personal relationships. Cognizant of new developments and "trendy" fashions in poetry, Randall never allows himself the comforting isolation of an art-for-art's-sake poetics; instead, he insists on the integrity of the fundamental values of joy, music, and craft in his poetry while lyrically rendering common experiences in the form of new insights which are comprehensible for the majority of readers. He embodies, in short, that sometimes too-often-neglected maxim of Sir Philip Sidney's in *Defence of Poesie* (1595) that poetry ought "to teach and delight." That Randall achieves both while using an essentially modern black idiom ensures him of a significant place among his generation of poets.

Poem Counterpoem

The polarities of tension in Randall's poetry seem to be the necessity of personal love and social change. These themes underlie most of his poems, which sometimes focus on the one value while faintly suggesting the other but more often than not are characteristic of a tension between the two. In one early poem from his first book, *Poem Counterpoem*, Randall reflects on his youthful experience as a foundry worker while he visits an ailing coworker many years later in a hospital. In "George," the speaker recalls "the monstrous, lumpish cylinder blocks" that too often "clotted the line and plunged to the floor/ With force enough to tear your foot in two." George's response to the industrial hazards of the assembly line was to step calmly aside; working side by side with the older man in his younger days, the speaker looked to George as an example of quiet endurance, even though George, "goggled, with mask on [his] mouth and shoulders bright with sweat," was not particularly articulate in his guidance of the young Randall. George's "highest accolade," in fact, following the clean-up of "blocks clogged up" which came "thundering down like an avalanche," was the gnomic folk expression: "'You're not afraid of sweat. You're strong as a mule.'" As the speaker visits George in a "ward where old men wait to die," he realizes that George "cannot read the books" brought to him while he sits "among the senile wrecks,/ The psychopaths, the incontinent." In the transition from the first stanza (set in the past) to the second (set in the present), the long lines of the first (which suggest the rhythm of the assembly line) give way to a shorter line that underscores George's confinement. When George falls from his chair in the course of the visit, his visitor lifts him back into it "like a cylinder block" and assures him: "'You'll be here/ A long time yet, because you're strong as a mule.'"

While the poem relates little more than the memory of assembly line comradeship and the subsequent visit many years later, it suggests a great deal more than that. The sheer physical drudgery of the foundry site is apparent in both imagery and rhythm; George's quiet but resolute determination to survive the toll of accidents is also implicit, but he survives only to find himself relegated to little more than a warehouse for the aged. Juxtaposed, however, with the dismal irony of George's fate is Randall's emphasis on the personal bond of mutual respect between the two men. Just as George encouraged him, the younger man now offers the aging George the same encouragement that he once offered the young worker. George's persistence in overcoming his fear of death, however, is not enough to restore his dignity. The social conditions must change as well, and that will necessitate formal education; this, too, as Randall's own biography might suggest, has been an inadvertent gift from the older man. In stressing the personal bond between them and yet not losing sight of their common experience in the workplace, Randall celebrates the endurance of friendship while condemning the dehumanizing factors of the assembly line and the hospital. That all of this is expressed in one brief mirrored, metaphorical aphorism suggests that the simple eloquence of the poem itself is, like George, rich beneath its surface.

Cities Burning

Randall's second book, *Cities Burning*, focuses on the disintegrating cities during the urban riots and civil struggles of the 1960's. His observations on social change are not, however, solely the result of the 1960's, for several of these poems were written much earlier. "Roses and Revolution," for example, was written in 1948 and attests to Randall's exploration of the dual themes of personal love and social change long before that tumultuous decade. Hauntingly prophetic, Randall's apocalyptic poem speaks of "the lighted cities" that "were like tapers in the night." He sees "the Negro lying in the swamp with his face blown off" and "in northern cities with his manhood maligned." Men work but take "no joy in their work." As a result of the inner turmoil caused by prejudice and oppression, love becomes severely distorted; they greet "the hard-eyed whore with joyless excitement" and sleep "with wives and virgins in impotence." While the poem's speaker searches for meaningful value "in darkness/ and felt the pain of millions," he sees "dawn upon them like the sun," a vision of peace and beauty in which weapons are buried "at the bottom of the ocean/ like the bones of dinosaurs buried under the shale of eras." Here people "create for others the house, the poem, the game of athletic beauty." Having described the misery in the first stanza and the vision of deliverance in the second stanza, Randall proceeds to analyze its meaning in the third: "Its radiance would grow and be nourished suddenly/ burst into terrible and splendid bloom/ the blood-red flower of revolution."

As it is for many of the poems in this volume, the title of the collection is somewhat misleading with respect to "Roses and Revolution," for the city in *Cities Burning* is humankind and the fires are transforming agents. While acknowledging the violence and destruction as literal events, Randall also sees revolution occurring within the heart of man as well. The real revolution is "not for power or the accumulation of paper," greed for money, but for a blossoming of love that can occur when the black American no longer feels "the writhing/ of his viscera like that of the hare hunted down or the bear at bay." The symbolic rose no longer holds its power for transformation unless it is "blood-red" in its "terrible and splendid bloom," for Randall does not sentimentalize love at the expense of the political process.

In "Ballad of Birmingham," for example, Randall dramatically presents a dialogue between a black mother, who fears for her daughter's safety and forbids her to "march the streets of Birmingham/ to make our country free," and the girl herself, who is willing to risk the "clubs and hoses, guns and jails" in order to assert her rights. Obeying her mother, the daughter goes "to church instead" to "sing in the children's choir" rather than join the other children in the freedom march. The historical event on which the ballad is based was the bombing of a black church in Birmingham on September 15, 1963, when four teenage girls were murdered in a dynamite explosion while they were attending a Bible class. When the mother hears the explosion, she rushes to the scene of the violence; although she claws "through bits of glass and brick," she finds only a shoe: "O, here's the shoe my baby wore,/ but, baby, where are you?" Her protective reluctance to become involved in the Civil Rights struggle, although understandable, has failed to preserve her loving security for her daughter or even her daughter herself. Despite the elegiac ballad form, Randall's dramatic irony here is politically and personally potent: Love cannot hide from death in the pursuit of freedom; it must risk it.

Randall, however, is unwilling to endorse violence for its own sake—in revolution or in literature. In "The Rite" and in "Black Poet, White Critic," he addresses, respectively, both the young militant black poet who would annihilate the pioneers of the black literary tradition and the white critic who would deny that such a tradition even existed. The young poet in "The Rite" murders an older poet, whom he views as reactionary, but in sacrificing him to the new revolutionary program, the young poet ritually "drank his blood and ate his heart," thus drawing his revolutionary sustenance from his forebears without conscious knowledge of doing so. That the older writer provides continuing life for the younger one—and is conscious of that fact—not only endorses the persistence of the political struggle, but also establishes a political context for black literature that reaches back to protest elements in the slave songs. The struggle is nothing new to Randall's generation, or to those generations before him; yet the older poet is quite willing to offer his life in order to broaden the continuity of that protest. On the other hand, Randall challenges—in "Black Poet, White Critic"—the establishment critic who "advises/ not to write on controversial subjects/ like freedom or murder" to reexamine his own critical premises. The critic suggests "universal themes/ and timeless symbols/ like the white unicorn," to which Randall responds: "A *white* unicorn?" Refusing to deny his own heritage and experience as a black man, he realizes that the argument is bogus in any context: The timeless drama of Sophocles or William Shakespeare can hardly be said to ignore freedom and murder. Randall, then, implies that the critic who so blatantly misreads his own literary tradition fears not so much a lack of quality on the part of black poets as the fulfillment of that advice on "universal themes" and "timeless symbols" that would indict the critic's own racism and shoddy intellect as a result of that racism. Black poets might, indeed, write *too well*.

Love You, After the Killing, and A Litany of Friends

Randall's third volume of poems, *Love You*, consists entirely of lyric love poems, but unlike those in *Cities Burning*, these poems more frequently use open forms and free verse. While the previous volume is more likely to explore ideas, the poems in this one concentrate on feelings (although the poems in both volumes, of course, embrace both ideas and feelings). The emphasis in *Love You* shifts from the complexity of the political struggle to the complexity of interpersonal conflicts and seems to suggest that social change requires the resolution of such conflicts before its advances can be permanent. These poems, like those in *More to Remember: Poems of Four Decades*, are drawn from several decades, and they offer the intimate but not confessional experience of the classical lyricist. Along with his selected poems, those in *Love You* offer a full range of poetic device and subject matter, although the themes generally oscillate between the polarities of personal love and social change. In his 1973 volume, *After the Killing*, Randall moves to a lyrical form that is closer to free-verse folk expression than the lyric poems of his earlier work. The themes, however, remain generally the same, although he introduces an emphasis on Pan-African concerns, particularly in the section "African Suite," which is based in part on his travels to West Africa.

A stanza from "A Poet is not a Jukebox," from *A Litany of Friends* (1981), perhaps sums up Randall's position on the role of the poet as an artist above all, who will write of matters such as race and politics only as these subjects inspire him, not out of any requirement laid on him by his skin color:

> Telling a Black poet what he ought to write
> Is like some Commissar of Culture in Russia telling a poet
> He'd better write about the new steel furnaces in the
> Novobigorsk region
> Or the heroic feats of Soviet labor in digging the trans-
> Caucasus canal,
> Or the unprecedented achievements of workers in the
> sugar beet industry who exceeded their quota by 400
> percent (it was later discovered to be a typist's error).

Randall may be remembered as an outstanding publisher and editor who was also a poet, but he has written a sufficient number of moving poems to keep him in anthologies for many years to come. Some of his ballads, such as "Ballad of Birmingham," have been set to music and popularized in that fashion. His terse expression and probing voice in poems such as "Black Poet, White Critic" will remind readers that poetry can indeed teach much about what it means to be human without compromising the inherent delight in reading—and living.

Other major works

nonfiction: *Broadside Memories: Poets I Have Known*, 1975.

edited text: *For Malcolm: Poems on the Life and the Death of Malcolm X*, 1967 (with Margaret G. Burroughs); *Black Poetry: A Supplement to Anthologies Which Exclude Black Poets*, 1969; *The Black Poets*, 1971; *Homage to Hoyt Fuller*, 1984.

Bibliography

Melhem, D. H. "Dudley Randall: A Humanist View." *Black American Literature Forum* 17 (1983): 157-

167. This excellent article surveys Randall's poetry and includes a biographical overview of his life and career and brief analyses of significant poems. Melhem stresses that Randall is a humanist, a label the poet himself accepts. Includes notes that are somewhat useful in finding other sources on Randall, especially general surveys and interviews.

Randall, Dudley. "Black Publisher, Black Writer: An Answer." *Black World* 24 (March, 1975): 32-37. This article records Randall's own reflections about the world of black publishing houses and the pros and cons concerning a black writer's use of a black or white publisher. Although interesting, the article does not address Randall's profession as a poet. He does, however, make several general remarks concerning other black poets, and he does comment on the role of oral tradition in poetry.

_______. "Interviews: Dudley Randall." *Black Books Bulletin* 1 (Winter, 1972): 23-26. An informative but short article dealing mostly with Randall's involvement with Broadside Press. Includes some discussion of Randall's poetry and the earlier African American poets who have influenced him. Randall makes general comments about African American poetry which may shed some light on his own poems.

_______. "The Message Is in the Melody: An Interview with Dudley Randall." Interview by Leana Ampadu. *Callaloo* 22, no. 2 (Spring, 1999): 438-445. Randall discusses his family and work.

Redding, Saunders. "The Black Arts Movement in Negro Poetry." *The American Scholar* 42 (1973): 330-336. This article attempts to criticize the "increasing rigidity" of the Black Arts movement, with particular regard to the "new concept of the black and blackness." In contrast to those within this movement, Randall, though a publisher of many poets in the movement, exhibits an earlier, more humanistic tradition in touch with the American past.

Rowell, Charles H. "In Conversation with Dudley Randall." *Obsidian* 2, no. 1 (1976): 32-44. In this important interview focusing primarily on Randall's poetic career rather than his role as a publisher, the poet discusses his background and the influences on his life and work. Includes some useful discussion of Randall's indebtedness to the Harlem Renaissance, his views of poetry, and his process of composition. Randall also comments on his poems collected in *Cities Burning* and *After the Killing*, among others. Notes leading to other sources are included.

Thompson, Julius Eric. *Dudley Randall, Broadside Press, and the Black Arts Movement in Detroit, 1960-1995*. Jefferson, N.C.: McFarland, 1999. A history of the Broadside Press founded by Randall and his subsequent involvement in the Civil Rights movement. Through Randall and the Broadside Press, hundreds of black writers were given an outlet for their work and for their calls for equality and black identity.

Waters, Mark V. "Dudley Randall and the Liberation Aesthetic: Confronting the Politics of 'Blackness.'" *CLA Journal* 44, no. 1 (September, 2000): 111-139. A summary of Randall's efforts as both publisher and poet. The platform for black poetry of diverse style, language, and theme maintained by Randall helped counter the rising influence of radical and militant black poetry that threatened to engulf the larger array of black poetic expression under its own political agenda.

Michael Loudon,
updated by Leslie Ellen Jones

John Crowe Ransom

Born: Pulaski, Tennessee; April 30, 1888
Died: Gambier, Ohio; July 3, 1974

PRINCIPAL POETRY

Poems About God, 1919
Armageddon, 1923
Chills and Fever, 1924
Grace After Meat, 1924
Two Gentlemen in Bonds, 1927
Selected Poems, 1945, revised and enlarged 1963, 1969
Poems and Essays, 1955

Other literary forms

John Crowe Ransom published a substantial body of prose devoted to social and literary criticism. Mildred Brooks Peters, in the bibliography in her book, *John Crowe Ransom* (1968), lists 124 of his essays and articles and more than seventy signed book reviews. The essays and articles appeared in many journals, notably *The Kenyon Review*, the *Fugitive*, and *The Sewanee Review*. The social criticism is concentrated in a ten-year period from the late 1920's through the mid-1930's. Of particular interest in this category are his contributions to the agrarian manifesto *I'll Take My Stand: The South and the Agrarian Tradition, by Twelve Southerners* (1930) for which he wrote the introduction and the leading essay, "Reconstructed but Unregenerate." He was to write more than two dozen essays of social criticism in this period, including "The South Defends Its Heritage" (1929), "Modern with a Southern Accent" (1935), "The South Is a Bulwark" (1936), and "What Does the South Want," which was included in *Who Owns America? A Declaration of Independence* (1936; Herbert Agar and Allen Tate, editors).

The greater bulk of Ransom's prose is devoted to literary criticism, dating from his essays in the *Fugitive* and the *Literary Review* in the early 1920's. His three principal book-length collections are *God Without Thunder: An Unorthodox Defense of Orthodoxy* (1930), *The World's Body* (1938), and *The New Criticism* (1941). In the first, he established the terms for one of his most fundamental philosophical and critical concerns, the dangers inherent in the abstractions of scientific thought. Recapturing the "completeness of actual experience," in contrast to such abstractions, is possible, he held, only through art and religious myth. That line of thought was to be pursued through *The World's Body* in "Poetry: A Note in Ontology," and in *The New Criticism*, with its final essay, "Wanted: An Ontological Critic." The thesis central to Ransom's thought is that poetry constitutes a kind of knowledge, and that it is at least as valid as science as one index to the nature of reality.

Achievements

John Crowe Ransom's distinguished career as man of letters has three clearly definable categories. He was a poet, a literary and social critic, and a teacher and editor. While it is in terms of the first two categories that he is principally known to the world, the third might be seen as all-encompassing and thus as the major achievement. His roles as teacher and editor made him a central figure in the development of Fugitive poetry and the New Criticism, as well as, though to a somewhat lesser degree, Agrarianism.

John Crowe Ransom in 1966. (© Bettmann/Corbis)

Central to that all-encompassing achievement as teacher and editor was a philosophical quest that sent him in search of a cognitive process to counter the overwhelmingly pervasive abstractions of modern science. That quest, with its roots in nineteenth century Romanticism, was central to the Modernist period and to the development of the New Criticism. Ransom and his peers were trying to solve the century-old problem of the nature of the relationship between the imaginative re-creation of experience and the empirical and rational analysis of it. Thus for Ransom, as for Allen Tate, Cleanth Brooks, and Robert Penn Warren, poetry must be defined as a kind of knowledge, deserving a place in serious epistemological and ontological considerations at least equal to that afforded scientific knowledge. The development and application of that definition as a major premise of the New Criticism is one of Ransom's two historic achievements. The second is his poetry, and the consensus is that the best of his poetry will constitute Ransom's most enduring achievement.

In addition to his early scholarships, he received numerous awards and prizes, attesting the national recognition of his stature as perhaps the most influential scholar-critic of his generation. In 1947, he was awarded a life membership in the National Institute of Arts and Letters. In 1951, he received the Institute's Russell Loines Award for Poetry and the Bollingen Prize. He became an honorary consultant in American Literature for the Library of Congress in 1957, and *Selected Poems* (1963), won the 1964 National Book Award. He was elected to membership in the American Academy of Arts and Letters in 1966 and received the Academy's Emerson-Thoreau medal in 1968.

BIOGRAPHY

John Crowe Ransom was born in Pulaski, Tennessee, in 1888. His father was a Methodist minister and the family moved with such frequency that the children were taught at home, Ransom not entering public school until he was ten years old. The relationship thus established with his father in the role of teacher-critic became an enduring one, Ransom valuing critical exchanges over his work with his father throughout his lifetime. That early and enduring relationship can be seen as a kind of paradigm of the series of similar relationships that were to be central to Ransom's development well into his mature years. He thrived on discussion groups or circles, characterized by critical exchanges, such as those in which he participated as an undergraduate at Vanderbilt and Oxford, and especially, with his fellow Fugitives, Agrarians, and New Critics. The exchanges with his father when he was a boy foreshadow his exchanges in his maturity with Allen Tate.

Ransom's career was divided almost equally between his tenures at Vanderbilt and Kenyon College. After receiving his B.A. from Vanderbilt in 1909, he went as a Rhodes Scholar to Oxford, where he took a second B.A. in 1913. In 1914, he began his teaching career at Vanderbilt as an instructor. Except for his two years in the armed forces during World War I, and a leave of absence on a Guggenheim Fellowship in 1931, that tenure went uninterrupted until 1937, when he resigned to take a position at Kenyon College. While at Vanderbilt he, Donald Davidson, Allen Tate, and Robert Penn Warren, among others, participated in a discussion group which led between 1922 and 1925 to the publication of the poetry magazine the *Fugitive*. His association with that group continued into the 1930's, when their interests and writing shifted from poetry to social and then to literary criticism. Known as Fugitives in the 1920's, the group became known as the Agrarians around 1930, with their publication of *I'll Take My Stand*, and later, with considerably less cohesiveness, as the New Critics. Ransom left Vanderbilt to go to Kenyon College, where he founded both *The Kenyon Review*, which he edited until his retirement in 1958, and the Kenyon School of English.

After his retirement, Ransom taught on short-term appointments at Northwestern, Ohio State, and Vanderbilt. He continued to give public readings and to lecture occasionally until 1968, after which he accepted no invitations to do either outside Gambier.

Ransom and his wife Robb Reavill had three children. He died in his sleep at home in Gambier, Ohio, in the early morning hours of July 3, 1974.

ANALYSIS

Three salient features of John Crowe Ransom's poetry are his irony, the distinctive, highly mannered texture of his verse, and the relationship between the two. Ransom admired Robert Frost as poet, but his reservations about Frost derived from what he considered the relative thinness of Frost's poetic texture. Frost's colloquial style, Ransom objected, reduces the textural richness of the verse to the barest minimum. What it actually does is to lower the sensitivity to its textural character by making the verse look and sound like more or less ordinary speech. Frost's style is calculated to create the effect that there is no style at all. Ransom's style, in contrast, is highly mannered, calculated to call attention to itself through its texture. His use of the texture of that mannered style to mask the terrible ironies of existence is his principal achievement as a modern poet.

"Bells for John Whiteside's Daughter"

A particularly good example of one of Ransom's exercises in ironic masking is "Bells for John Whiteside's Daughter." The paraphrasable content of the poem, Ransom's "structure," is easily accounted for. Adults, presumably the family, are awaiting the beginning of the funeral of a very young girl who has died unexpectedly. As they wait, they remember how active the child was, with dramatic recollections of her playing at war and of her chasing geese across the lawn into the pond. The slightness of the subject in summary, though universal and poignant, provides a dramatic illustration of how much the structure of the poem depends for its transformation into art upon texture, that is, upon diction, imagery, metaphor, and meter.

One of Ransom's most distinctive touches throughout his poetry is his use of archaic diction. In "Bells for John Whiteside's Daughter" the word "bruited" is the only technically archaic word, but as such it stands at the center of a nexus filled out by "harried" and "brown study," and by the allusion to William Shakespeare's *Hamlet, Prince of Denmark* (c. 1600-1601) in line 7. What all four have in common is their Renaissance currency. In the *Oxford English Dictionary*, one finds the conjecture that "brown study" derives "originally from brown in sense of 'gloomy,' " and an example attributed to "Dice-Play 6" of 1532. The first example from the same source for "bruit" is from John Skelton for 1528, and the second example for "harry" is from John Palsgrave for 1530. Additional coherence for the nexus comes from the tonal appropriateness of both "bruit" and "harry" to the playing at war, and from the Shakespearean allusion to taking up arms, which comes out of the context not only of Hamlet's personal anguish, but also of a state troubled by rumors of war. Knowing this significantly deepens one's appreciation of the poem. It also contributes a great deal to one's understanding of what Ransom means by texture.

Other examples of noteworthy diction in the poem are "astonished," "tireless," "vexed," and "primly." "Tireless," the most explicitly ironic of the four, is at the center of the disparity between what should be—a young, vibrant body full of vitality and energy—and what is—a dead child. The ironic treatment of that disparity, a kind of masking which obscures the awful reality, comes into focus when the stilled heart is described as "tireless." Further, the word catches up in summation the flow of energy that begins with the first line of the poem and continues down through the fourth stanza. The adults in attendance are so accustomed to that energy that they are first, in stanza 1, "astonished" at the child's "brown study," and finally, in stanza 5, "vexed" at it. That is, they never really credit it for what it is. Startled at first, they continue to mask the untimely death with their vexation, a defense against grief. It is as if the child is to be blamed for dying, as if she is guilty of wanton misbehavior, and that, first having defied her elders, she now adds insult to injury by lying there before them "so primly propped." The apparent tonal and thematic rightness of that final phrase is such as to invite questions about the causes of its effectiveness, one of which is clearly the emphasis given by alliteration. There is, however, just as clearly, more to it than that, the more having to do in part with versification and meter.

The alliterative emphasis to the final descriptive passage is reinforced by its place at the very end of the poem, and by the accentual pattern of the whole of the line, which throws two of its three stresses onto the key syllables "prim" and "propped." The words "lying" and "primly," natural trochees, pick up the principal rhythmical character of the poem which derives from the recurrence throughout of alternate feminine endings. The falling rhythm of "body" and "study," and of the alternate lines of each of the verses, except the third, is concentrated in the last line, which ends with the counterpoint of a stressed masculine ending. Such intricate precision of phrasing and meter reinforces the impression that the concept of "primness" embodies the poem's tonal and thematic essence. Further, each of the stanzas is characterized by a similar though not identical precision. The first and last stanzas are most alike in that each is end-stopped. In contrast, the three central stanzas are open, running on from the second line of stanza two to the exclamation point at the end of stanza four. The middle, or third, stanza is unique metrically, being the only one of the five not characterized by alternate feminine endings. This uniqueness underscores its centrality and the three-part structure of the poem.

The beginning of the poem is clearly contained in the first stanza, as the end is in the last. The body of the poem is made up of the three middle stanzas, with its metrically unique center and its fairy-tale ascription of human language to geese who cry "Alas." The beginning and the end contain the adult responses to the child's behavior and death—astonishment, vexation, and an all-encompassing primness. Though the point of view is technically consistent throughout the poem—the editorial "we" of the adult audience—a transformation takes place in the body of the poem where the reader enters the child's world vicariously. It is a world of imaginary wars played out under orchard trees. The stick that is part of the regal image of the "Lady with rod," has probably been in hand all along as sword, as she did battle with her shadow, and as stick-horse to carry her on her harrying raids against the geese. At the very center of this truly remarkable poem, the adults' world and the child's world come together momentarily in the word "Alas." Talking geese scuttling before the queen of the realm are the essential stuff of fairyland. The one word they utter, however, unites them in their annoyance with the sternly vexed adults who, poignantly in retrospect, always have wanted before all else that the child be still and quiet. The child's perverse response to that most familiar of adult admonitions provides the savage irony of the poem which is masked by the intricate texture and thus contained, as if in a crucible at white-hot intensity, for all who would read.

As one of Ransom's very best poems, "Bells for John Whiteside's Daughter" is also representative of his most distinctive verse and of his ironic treatment of the ordinary but universal human dilemma: Death or dying, or moral choices that hinge upon the relationship between body and soul, constitute his principal subject matter. Other useful examples of both his themes and his considerable talents for the felicitous blending of the parts into the whole poem are "Janet Waking," "Piazza Piece," and "The Equilibrists."

"Janet Waking"

"Janet Waking" tells, not of a child's death, but of her painful first confrontation with it. Instead of geese, the poem has a pet chicken, "Old Chucky," who has died unexpectedly in the night, presumably from a bee sting. Janet, waking, finds the hen dead and will not be consoled or "instructed" in how "deep" is the "kingdom of death." As with "Bells for John Whiteside's Daughter," it is diction and phrasing which most clearly mark the poem with Ransom's distinctive touch. The "deeply morning" of stanza 1 parallels the "how . . . purply did the knot swell" of stanza 5. The colloquial use of "kept" at the end of the first stanza is balanced by the "crying her brown hen . . . to rise" of stanza 6. The one word which does most, however, to establish the poem's characteristic mannered quaintness is "transmogrifying." This strikingly unusual word, whose origins are unknown, comes at the very middle of the poem and carries, with its two meanings, the theme and counter-theme of the poem. One of the meanings of "transmogrify" is "to astonish utterly." That definition, the very word itself, and its adjectival modification of the bee in its act of stinging Chucky's "poor old bald head," all taken together are humorous in effect. Ransom treads a dangerously thin line in this poem with his nearly comic presentation of this most mundane of subjects—a pet chicken stung by a transmogrifying bee. This seems to have none of the sobering substance of his account of the death of a child, and the risk that Ransom takes is that the reader may be at best simply amused by the tale. The second meaning of "transmogrify," however, is "to transform," and it is with Chucky's "transformation" and its effect on Janet that Ransom is most concerned.

The impact of this transformation from life to death is the subject of the final two stanzas. The shift in tone from the nearly comic presentation of the pet hen's death of the first five stanzas is effected in part simply by the shift in focus from Chucky to Janet. The name "Chucky," so important in itself in establishing the earlier tone, is absent from the closing stanzas. Rather, readers focus on Janet in her grief, "kneeling" and "weeping fast." The textural contribution to that tonal shift, however, is so characteristically significant as to provide another very illustrative example of Ransom's distinctive style. The paraphrasable substance of the final stanzas, that Janet is heartbroken over the death of her hen, simply fails to account for the emotional intensity of the verse itself. A mature, rational judgment of that bare substance would put it into perspective as one of those childhood experiences that, sad enough for the moment, will very quickly be forgotten, or if remembered at all, fondly so. It is "texture," of course, that makes the difference between that rational perspective and the deeper impact which the poem makes upon the sensibility. Central to that texture, with its accompanying tonal shift, is Janet's admonition, "kneeling on the wet grass," to her hen (significantly not "chicken" nor "Chucky" here) to "rise and walk upon it." The immediate and compelling association is with Christ's walking on the water. The secondary, though equally compelling association, is with Christ's raising of Lazarus from the dead and of his own resurrection. In the middle of that allusion, offering substantial tonal support, is the biblical phrase "the daughters of men," from the sixth chapter of Genesis. In that textural context, the mature, rational perspective on the child's experience is replaced by the deeply sobering realization that her anguish and her plea are the universal, timeless manifestations of mortal man's basic dilemma.

The irony of "Janet Waking" depends upon the juxtaposition of the nearly comic account of bald old Chucky's demise with the sudden confrontation with the mystery of death. The "waking" of the title, like the word "transmogrify," carries the essential irony. Janet wakens literally at first to her breakfast with her family and to her concern for her pet. At the end of the poem there is a second wakening, this time to the beginning of the understanding of mortality. There is less masking here than in "Bells for John Whiteside's Daughter," where the adults hold vexation like a shield between themselves and the girl's death. Janet, in contrast, has nothing between her and raw grief save the ineffectual efforts at "instructing" her in "how deep/ Was the forgetful kingdom of death." That instruction comes from the "us" of line two, from the world of adults who are again attempting, as in "Bells for John Whiteside's Daughter," to soften the impact of the grimmest of realities. These adults, however, are closer to the fire, closer to the truth as Ransom himself perceived it about the "kingdom of death."

"Piazza Piece"

There is what might be considered a kind of realistic core to "Bells for John Whiteside's Daughter," and to an even greater degree to "Janet Waking." The occasion and circumstances of each are credible and filled out with particular and concrete details. In other poems, such as "Piazza Piece," and, more particularly, "The Equilibrists," Ransom moves in the direction of pure allegory. Although there are two "real" figures, a man and a woman, in "Piazza Piece," one of Ransom's finely turned sonnets, it is clear that they are not to be seen with the literal individuality of John Whiteside's daughter or of Janet. They represent types, *the* beautiful young woman and *the* old man, and ultimately symbols rather than individuals. For if the gentleman in the dust coat, a "grey man," is to have the "lovely lady soon," as he says he must, he is not to be taken literally as a suitor, but rather as the personification of death. His words come to her "dry and faint as in a dream," suggesting that her awareness of him is filtered up from the subconscious, an awareness that she resists and from which she turns away, waiting for her true love. In her choice, she represents all women and, indeed, all men. She has none of the individualized particularity of the children of the other two poems, and little, if any, of their poignance. This is not to suggest that "Piazza Piece" is not a very successful poem. It is. Rather, it is to illustrate the difference between Ransom's treatment of his central theme in it and in poems like "Bells for John Whiteside's Daughter" and "Janet Waking." In his notes to his revision of "Here Lies a Lady," a poem more like these two than the allegorical mode of the sonnet, Ransom describes the third stanza, which tells of the lady's death, as "almost unutterably painful." That intensity is muted in "Piazza Piece," where Ransom steps back from the experiential fire of his theme to assume a more philosophical posture.

"The Equilibrists"

The irony of "Piazza Piece" is dramatic irony, which depends upon a relatively high degree of aesthetic distance between reader and character. The reader is invited to consider the human dilemma rather than to feel the experience with the participants. In "The Equilibrists" Ransom moves even further away from the immediacy of Janet's awakening in one of his most allegorical poems. The lovers here have no individuality: no names, no physical characteristics at all save physical beauty, no distinguishing marks of character except for the universal counter-forces of desire and honor. They are, then, not a particular pair of lovers but all lovers, and they are ultimately to be seen, in the terms of the Epitaph, as even more abstract than that. Although there are two lovers throughout the poem, there is also the early implication that the two forces keeping them in that tortured equilibrium might be equated with a basic conflict in either one of them as human beings. That is, in stanza 2, the conflict is seen in terms of *one* head, presumably the woman's, a conflict between the tower, the skull where the gray doves are housed, and the lips, the "quaint orifice" which breathes heat upon the kiss. In the Epitaph, strangers are admonished to "tread light" out of respect for the grave of the equilibrists. Then comes the line, "Mouldered the lips and ashy *the* tall skull," (emphasis added). The conflict is "really" between any two lovers, but it is also really to be found in any one human being. The forces keeping the lovers in orbit are contained in each of them. The tortured equilibrium is between the conceptual reality of the head and the physical reality of the flesh, symbolized by the lips, synecdoche for the body's beauty, for passion and desire. Ransom has here reduced his most fundamental theme, the psychic tensions arising out of the dualism of body and soul, to its barest terms. The remarkable thing about the achievement is that he succeeded so well in fleshing out this allegorical skeleton with the substance of concrete and even sensual imagery; that, to use his terms for it, he found the appropriate and dramatic texture for one of his most abstract structures.

The concreteness of the texture of "The Equilibrists" is achieved primarily by means of allusion. The first three stanzas, with their jacinth, myrrh, and ivory, their "body's field, with the gaunt tower above," and their invitation to "bruise and break" the lilies, echo that most sensual of poems, *The Song of Solomon*. The sword imagery of the fourth and sixth stanzas call up one famous pair of tortured lovers, Tristan and Isolde, as the torments of Hell of stanza 12 call up that other, Dante's Paolo and Francesca. Thus, although the lovers of the poem have no individuality of their own, the particularity of their passion and their anguish is made vivid and dramatic by allusion to their famous predecessors. The overwhelming sweetness of the flesh that they know is chronicled by the singer of *The Song of Solomon*. Their anguished efforts to resolve the conflict between passion and desire is the substance of the romance of Tristan and Isolde. The tortured equilibrium, which is the best resolution they can achieve, is the resolution of the damned, of the great lovers who "lie in hell."

The allusive texture of the poem is complemented by distinctive metrics and characteristic diction. As he often does, Ransom establishes a counterpoint in his meter by varying line length and juxtaposing masculine and feminine endings within his otherwise quite regular verse. His cadence is thus characterized by a tension between a very modern improvisational movement and the formal restraints of seemingly very conventional quatrains. The striking diction is largely concentrated in stanza 9, with its "puddled," "devising," "gibbeted," and "descanting." "Saeculum," of stanza 10, "stuprate," of stanza 12, and the nice play on "tinder" of stanza 11, are all noteworthy. Yet the readers' attention must be focused on stanza 9 with its quantitative density of quaint diction, that most distinctive of Ransom's touches, and to the question to which it points: "Man, what would you have?" Substance and style come together here to bare the very heart of the poet by bringing into sharp focus his most fundamental concern and his most characteristic aesthetic mode; the intensity of the question is moderated, at least partially masked, by the quaintness of the diction.

Exploration of mortality

Ransom's most pervasive thematic concern is given philosophical and explicit expression in "The Equilibrists." In the body of his most intensely effective lyrical poetry, that concern is the underlying premise, implicit in the concretely experiential terms of death and dying. Resolve the question "Man, what would you have?" and there is no ironic tension in "Bells for John Whiteside's Daughter." Accept the resolution and there is no anguish in "Janet Waking"—nor in "Blue Girls," "Vision by Sweetwater," "Emily Hardcastle, Spinster," "Necrological," "Dead Boy," or "Here Lies a Lady," among others. The tensions and the anguish at the heart of Ransom's poetry derive from his preoccupation with mortality. That preoccupation gives rise to various dualistic patterns, body and soul, feeling and reason, youth and age, passion and honor, that must all be held, like the bridal couple in Keats's ode, in a state of suspended animation in the imagination. Grief for the death of a child *in time* passes. That same grief *in the imagination* is by definition beyond the ameliorative effects of time. Where Keats gives us the essence of poignance, Ransom gives us the fundamental anguish of mortal beings aware of their mortality. To contain the fierce heat of that essence, he devised the well-wrought urn of his highly mannered texture and style.

Other major works

NONFICTION: *I'll Take My Stand: The South and the Agrarian Tradition, by Twelve Southerners*, 1930; *God Without Thunder: An Unorthodox Defense of Orthodoxy*, 1930; *Topics for Freshman Writing*, 1935; *The World's Body*, 1938; *The New Criticism*, 1941; *American Poetry at Mid-century*, 1958 (with Delmore Schwartz and John Hall Wheelock); *Symposium on Formalist Criticism*, 1967 (with others); *Beating the Bushes: Selected Essays, 1941-1970*, 1972; *Selected Letters of John Crowe Ransom*, 1985 (Thomas Daniel Young and George Core, editors).

EDITED TEXTS: *Studies in Modern Criticism from the "Kenyon Review,"* 1951; *The Kenyon Critics*, 1967.

Bibliography

Abbott, Craig S. *John Crowe Ransom: A Descriptive Bibliography*. Troy, N.Y.: Whitston, 1999. Abbott utilized archives at Vanderbilt, Kenyon, and the University of Texas for a first-hand look at original documents, manuscripts, and first editions of Ransom's work. Abbott includes complete bibliographic information for each entry, as well as an extensive physical description. He also includes the history of each work from conception to publication, making the book interesting to read as well as an important research tool.

Gelpi, Albert. "Robert Frost and John Crowe Ransom." In *A Coherent Splendor: The American Poetic Renaissance, 1916-1950*. Cambridge, England: Cambridge University Press, 1987. Gelpi stresses Ransom's connection with Robert Frost; the two poets admired each other and Frost helped to promote Ransom's work. Ransom viewed his main task as restoring poetic diction. He sharply opposed idealism, stressed irony and paradox, and aimed at presenting a world stripped of illusion. Gelpi provides a very useful metrical analysis of "Janet Waking" enabling the reader to see how Ransom achieves his ironic mood. Gelpi also includes a discussion of Ransom's ideological views, as expressed in the *Fugitive*, the journal of the Southern Agrarians.

Malvasi, Mark G. *The Unregenerate South*. Baton Rouge: Louisiana State University Press, 1997. A critical study of the works of selected Agrarian writers of the southern United States, including Ransom. Bibliographical references, index.

Pearce, Roy Harvey. *The Continuity of American Poetry*. Middletown, Conn.: Wesleyan University Press, 1987. In an earlier edition (1961), this work became a standard survey of American poetry. Ransom was a pedagogical poet, using his verse to teach lessons about life. He thought that human sensibility operated within strict limits and attempted to inculcate this view through the irony of his poetic diction. Death is a frequent theme in Ransom's work. Pearce brings out very well the conflict in Ransom between insistence on realism and devotion to a particular vision of history and tradition.

Suchard, Alan, et al. "Crosscurrents of Modernism." In *Modern American Poetry, 1865-1950*. Amherst: University of Massachusetts Press, 1989. Suchard, although aware of Ransom's merits, is restrained in his enthusiasm. He sees Ransom as a poet of death. Although devoted to tradition, his poems in fact convey the breakdown of faith and the enigmatic nature of existence. His irony is often presented by the use of charming and old-fashioned forms, such as ballads, to express dark thoughts. Suchard claims that Ransom's devotion to New Criticism helped discourage innovation in American poetry.

Turco, Lewis P. *Visions and Revisions of American Poetry*. Fayetteville: University of Alabama Press, 1986. Turco sees Ransom as an agonist: a poet who spends most of his time elaborating a theory of poetry. Much of Ransom's work is thus embodied in essays as he wrote few poems. Of these, the best are "Bells for John Whiteside's Daughter" and "Blue Girls."

These poems date from the 1920's, and Ransom's return to poetry in the 1960's was unsuccessful. Turco calls Ransom an academic poet, a term he does not intend as praise.

Waggoner, Hyatt H. "Irony and Orthodoxy." In *American Poets: From the Puritans to the Present*. Baton Rouge: Louisiana State University Press, 1984. Waggoner notes Ransom's witty, elegant language but claims that this serves mainly to cover up the precarious balance of his poetry. He was torn between devotion to tradition and realism. A detailed analysis of "Antique Haunts" is given in order to illustrate Ransom's ambiguity. The poem is a defense of the Southern way of life, but Ransom's own perspective is deliberately elusive.

Wellek, René. "John Crowe Ransom." In *A History of Modern Criticism: American Criticism, 1900-1950*. Vol. 6. New Haven, Conn.: Yale University Press, 1986. The best analysis of Ransom's philosophy. Wellek claims that Ransom's key thought is the contingency of the world. Objects do not form a unified system but are separate. Pluralism thus becomes a key artistic value. The aim of poetry is mimesis: The particularity of things must be described. Wellek also clarifies Ransom's dichotomy between structure and texture.

Lloyd N. Dendinger;
bibliography updated by the editors

Henry Reed

Born: Birmingham, England; February 22, 1914
Died: London, England; December 8, 1986

Principal poetry

A Map of Verona: Poems, 1946
Collected Poems, 1991

Other literary forms

Most of Henry Reed's work was in genres other than poetry. His first publication was a critical study, *The Novel Since 1939* (1946), and he also translated Paride Rombi's *Perdu and His Father* (1954) and Dino Buzzati's *Larger than Life* (1962).

Mainly, however, Reed was a prolific creator of drama, especially radio plays. In particular, he enjoyed a fruitful literary relationship with the Italian language and the Italian playwright Ugo Betti, a number of whose works Reed translated and adapted for radio broadcast in London and for stage production in London and New York. His adaptations of Betti include *The Queen and the Rebels*, *The Burnt Flower-Bed*, and *Summertime*, all produced in London in 1955 and published as *Three Plays* (1956). Later adaptations of Betti were *Island of Goats*, produced in New York in 1955 and published as *Crime on Goat Island* (1955), and *Corruption in the Palace of Justice*, produced in New York in 1958. He also adapted Natalia Ginzburg's play *The Advertisement* (1968) for production in London in 1968 and in New York in 1974. Reed's most fruitful relationship, however, was with the British Broadcasting Corporation, for which he wrote or adapted some forty to fifty radio plays, including the previously mentioned works by Betti. Reed's writing for radio began with *Moby Dick: A Play for Radio from Herman Melville's Novel* (1947), brief lyric sections of which form the last part of Reed's collection *A Map of Verona: Poems*.

Achievements

In Britain, Henry Reed was perhaps better known for his radio plays and his adaptations of Ugo Betti than for his poetry, whereas in the United States he was known almost exclusively for his poetry—or, more specifically, for "Naming of Parts" and "Judging Distances," which originally appeared with a third poem ("Unarmed Combat") under the general title "Lessons of the War." Much anthologized for introductory literature courses, these two humorous lyrics emphasizing the futility of war have been read by possibly half the undergraduate population of the United States during the past two decades. During the period of the Vietnam War especially, the two poems struck a responsive chord in the hearts of American college students. These two fine poems deserve the circulation they have achieved, but unfortunately the rest of Reed's poetry is little known in this country. His other work is even less known, except possibly among scholars of drama and Italian.

For a first collection of poetry, *A Map of Verona: Poems* maintains a remarkably high quality throughout, though it does not entirely escape the unevenness typical of first collections. For the sake of completeness, and perhaps for its greater explicitness, the less-inspired third poem of the "Lessons of the War" group should be read. Among other poems which stand out, and which illustrate other aspects of Reed's poetic talent, are "A Map of Verona," "The Door and the Window," "The Builders," a group titled "Tintagel" ("Tristram," "Iseult Blaunchesmains," "King Mark," and "Iseult la Belle"), and a group titled "Triptych" ("Chrysothemis," "Antigone," and "Philoctetes"). Finally, admirers of T. S. Eliot, as well as other readers, should not miss Reed's wicked little parody, "Chard Whitlow/(Mr. Eliot's Sunday Evening Postscript)."

Perhaps time will smooth out some of the imbalances in Reed's reputation, but as a poet he will likely remain known as someone who strangely produced only one early collection and who is best known for his gently humorous antiwar sentiments. No doubt Reed himself could well appreciate the irony of this situation, since one of his favorite poetic subjects is the person transfixed in time by a single defining (and somewhat immobilizing) act. Reed's act of poetic self-definition, however, is certainly not the whole story of his writing career. He will probably also be known as something of a media pioneer, a writer who could switch smoothly from print to performance to electronic medium. These smooth transitions were forecast in the nature of his poetry.

Biography

Henry Reed was born and educated in Birmingham, a sprawling manufacturing center in the English Midlands. There is no evidence that this setting had much influence on his poetry, unless it encouraged a desire to travel to and write about sunnier climes. He attended the King Edward VI School in Birmingham and took an M.A. degree at the University of Birmingham.

The influence of his education is evident throughout Reed's poetry, which, like the poetry of so many young Britons from the universities, smacks somewhat of Survey of British Literature. For example, one can detect choes of Andrew Marvell, Alfred, Lord Tennyson, Matthew Arnold, Joseph Conrad, and Eliot. In addition, many of Reed's subjects are literary in inspiration. Seemingly, the weight of the great tradition bore down heavily on Reed, and reaction to this weight could have contributed to his move from poetry to radio plays.

Certainly another influence on Reed's writing career was his experience of World War II, when he served in the Royal Army and with the Foreign Office. His military training provided inspiration for the poems in the "Lessons of the War" series. In addition, the war brought him to London, where he subsequently formed the association with the BBC which defined his career. He died on December 8, 1986, in London.

Analysis

In "A Map of Verona," Henry Reed states that "maps are of place, not time," while in "Judging Distances" one reads that "maps are of time, not place." These two versions of reality are not as contradictory as they might appear, if one considers the source of each. The first version comes from Reed himself, while the second is the official army doctrine mechanically voiced by a training officer to a group of recruits. The first version acknowledges the inability of man's puny symbols to represent reality, while the second asserts the military's wishful thinking, its need to be in control, to pour reality into a uniform and make it stand up and salute. One cannot blame the military for trying, as indeed it must, but the futility of its efforts is laughable: In "Judging Distances" the military theory is demolished, appropriately enough, by a pair of lovers in the distance, who finish making love even as the training officer and woebegone recruits watch.

Like the military, though with somewhat more success, Reed in his poems is intent on creating maps of reality. In his poems, both place and time have important roles, as they intersect with human actions. Reed is interested in place for its own sake, but he is also interested in its effects on human actions. Even more, he is interested in how human actions reverberate in time—the anticipation of actions, how actions fade from memory, how the meaning of actions changes with time, how, on the other hand, actions define and transfix personalities. For Reed, reality is as fluid as the stream in his poem "Lives" that cannot be caged. To try as best he can to catch and bottle this reality, Reed concentrates on dramatic moments or their consequences, particularly their moral consequences. Supporting Reed's penchant for the dramatic is his gift of mimicry, for capturing the sound of the human voice, as amply demonstrated in his parodies of T. S. Eliot and of the training officer in the "Lessons of the War" poems. Thus, it should come as no surprise that, although Reed writes in a variety of forms, some of his best poems are dramatic monologues. It should also come as no surprise that he eventually changed to writing drama.

"A Map of Verona"

Perhaps the most important poem for understanding Reed's ontology, and a good poem in its own right, is "A Map of Verona." At first, it seems no more than a pleasant travel advertisement: For "a whole long winter season" Reed's thoughts have dwelt on an open map of Verona. His intention to visit Verona reminds him of a stay in another Italian city, "My youthful Naples." Naples is associated in his mind with "a practice in sorrow," with "a sketch in tenderness, lust, and sudden parting." No doubt at the time this experience, despite its air of youthful experimentation, was deeply moving; now, however, he can barely recall its "underground whispers of music." Reed does recall, though, that he once studied an open map of Naples with the same expectation with which he now studies the map of Verona, and his map-studies then were totally "useless," since "maps are of place, not time." Still, studying the map of Verona and hearing other travelers relate their tourist impressions of the city help to "calm" Reed's "winter of expectations." The city of Verona does indeed exist, and "one day" Reed will go there: "in tomorrow's cave the music/ Trembles and forms inside the musician's mind." Meanwhile, echoing the poem's epigraph from Arthur Rimbaud, Reed can only wonder "in what hour of beauty" and "in what good arms" he will attain "those regions and that city." Finally, he wonders "what good Arms shall take them away again."

On both a literal and a symbolic level, "A Map of Verona" suggests the nature of experience. Among other things, Reed seems to say that, for the most part, people's lives are suspended between remembrance and expectation. Then, when a big moment comes, people are often too youthful to appreciate it or too experienced to believe that it will last. Still, even though remembrance fades and expectation is uncertain, both enrich one's life. Indeed, their enriching context makes it possible for a person to know a big moment when it arrives. Then there is always the potential for the big, fulfilling moment to come, in whatever "hour of beauty" or in whatever "good arms." In "A Map of Verona," the city of Verona, a jewel of Western civilization and the home of Romeo and Juliet, symbolizes this fulfillment.

"Lessons of the War" poems

Reading "A Map of Verona" is good preparation for reading the "Lessons of the War" poems. Though vastly different in subject, the poems are not as different in theme as might appear; they merely approach much the same theme from different directions. Despite the tenuous nature of experience and the way so much of life hangs between memory and expectations, "A Map of Verona" asserts the potential for human fulfillment. If there is one sure way of cutting off that potential, and typically at an early age, it is war. The incongruity—indeed, insanity—of war is suggested in the "Lessons of the War" poems by the way time and place conspire against the military training going on. While a training officer tries to hammer home his dull lessons, springtime is bursting out all over: Flowers are blooming, bees are "assaulting and fumbling the flowers," and lovers are making love. While nature moves full speed ahead toward the fulfillment of life, the soldiers train to eliminate life and in so doing put their own lives on the line. How such lessons go against the grain is also rendered dramatically in the person of Reed's recruit, who has trouble paying attention and through whose mind the reader hears the training officer's words and the recruit's spoken and unspoken responses. His rather obsessional notions demonstrate the difficulty, in springtime, of turning a young man's fancy to thoughts of war.

Although the theme of these poems is sober, their predominant tone is not. Their tone is established by the humorous dramatic situation, especially as this situation is reflected in the diction. Each of the poems begins with a parody of the training officer that reveals his routine mentality, his jargonistic but otherwise limited vocabulary, and his limited knowledge. All of these provide marvelous openings for the clever young recruit, who responds to the officer's military litany by twisting it into poetic or profound—but always humorous—meanings. In "Naming of Parts," for example, the officer's breakdown on a rifle's parts gives the recruit a fertile field for sexual puns. This particular instance of contrasting diction, like the general contrast between the voice of the training officer and the voice of the recruit, reinforces the theme of the military's sterile, deadening influence.

"Tintagel" and "Triptych"

The "Lessons of the War" poems well illustrate Reed's talent for humor, but most of his poems are somber both in theme and tone. What does not change is Reed's eye for the dramatic situation. His sense of drama can be felt strongly in two groups of poems that consist mostly of dramatic monologues and that might be considered the peak of Reed's poetic achievement. These are the two groups titled "Tintagel" and "Triptych." "Tintagel" consists of four poems named after the principals in the Tristram story: "Tristram," "Iseult Blaunchesmains," "King Mark," and "Iseult la Belle." In a note, Reed indicates that these four characters "represent four aspects of a problem known (in one or more of these aspects) to most men and women." He depends on the reader's knowledge of the Tristram legend to fill in the details—that these characters represent four corners of a love quadrangle with one side missing: Iseult Blaunchesmains loves Tristram who loves Iseult la Belle who returns his love but is married to King Mark. Already the poems sound like the scenario of an Italian drama or opera, and as the four characters speak their loves and sorrows, either through their own voices or the voice of a sympathetic narrator, they sound more and more like Luigi Pirandello's six characters, doomed to repent their roles to eternity. They have, in effect, become archetypal characters transfixed in time by their self-defining actions. They are like some traumatized people in real life, locked into one searing emotional experience that repeats itself endlessly in their consciousness.

The three characters in "Triptych," all from Greek drama, have likewise defined their personalities for all time through their actions. Here, however, the characters are not equally condemned; indeed, Reed notes that the speakers in the three poems "represent a moral progression, culminating in a decision." The three poems are "Chrysothemis," "Antigone," and "Philoctetes." Chrysothemis and Philoctetes speak for themselves in dramatic monologues, but in the second poem two witnesses to Antigone's death react to it in a dialogue. Chrysothemis, the sister of Electra and Orestes, represents the onlooker who will not get involved no matter how many atrocities she witnesses; after the house of Atreus has decimated itself, she stays behind to care for the remaining children and the decaying house. The house symbolizes her moral state, though she tries to believe she is playing a useful role. The main speaker in "Antigone" is a chance onlooker who, though not involved in the action, is sensitive to its moral consequences, in particular to the way Antigone acts unhesitatingly on what she knows is right. Finally, the ostracized Philoctetes represents the person who wants to get involved and is rejected, but who overcomes his bitter suffering and sense of personal wrong to act decisively when the time comes: Even after years of intense frustration, he goes as straight to his mark as do his blessed arrows. The traumatized person is not necessarily transfixed in time; rebirth is possible.

These two groups of poems involving serious drama verge closer and closer to drama itself. The last group of five poems in *A Map of Verona: Poems* comes from an actual drama, Reed's radio version of *Moby Dick* for the BBC. In a note, Reed refers to these poems as "lyric interludes." The transition from poet to dramatist is complete. Very likely Reed's friends mourned the transition, but very likely William Shakespeare's friends did the same.

Other major works

TRANSLATIONS: *Perdu and His Father*, 1954 (of Paride Rombi's novel); *Larger than Life*, 1962 (of Dino Buzzati's novel).

NONFICTION: *The Novel Since 1939*, 1946.

PLAYS: *Moby Dick: A Play for Radio from Herman Melville's Novel*, pr., pb. 1947 (radio play);

Island of Goats, pr. 1955 (adaptation of Ugo Betti; also known as *Crime on Goat Island*); *The Queen and the Rebels*, pr. 1955 (adaptation of Betti); *The Burnt Flower-Bed*, pr. 1955 (adaptation of Betti); *Summertime*, pr. 1955 (adaptation of Betti); *Three Plays*, pb. 1956; *Corruption in the Palace of Justice*, pr. 1958 (adaptation of Betti); *The Advertisement*, pr. 1968 (adaptation of Natalia Ginzburg); *The Streets of Pompeii and Other Plays for Radio*, pb. 1971; *Hilda Tablet and Others: Four Pieces for Radio*, pb. 1971.

Bibliography

Drakakis, John, ed. *British Radio Drama*. Cambridge, England: Cambridge University Press, 1981. Contains an excellent chapter by Roger Savage which, although ultimately concerned with Reed's radio plays, gives exceptional biographical information and makes numerous references to the poetry. It embraces Reed's career and acknowledges his work as a poet, critic, translator, and dramatist. This introductory essay includes notes with references that are reviews of Reed's work and some articles not necessarily concerning him directly.

Gunter, Liz, and Jim Linebarger. "Tone and Voice in Henry Reed's 'Judging Distances.'" *Notes on Contemporary Literature* 18 (March, 1988): 9-10. Provides an informative analysis of the structure and theme of Reed's poetry. Useful information on Reed's poetic and technical devices.

O'Toole, Michael. "Henry Reed, and What Follows the 'Naming of Parts.'" In *Functions of Style*, edited by David Birch and Michael O'Toole. London: Pinter, 1988. Examines the stylistics of modern English. Central to an appreciation and understanding of Reed's poetic works. Includes a foreword by M. A. K. Halliday.

Taylor, John Russell. *Anger and After*. London: Methuen, 1962. Rev. ed. *The Angry Theatre: New British Drama*. New York: Hill & Wang, 1969. Although it focuses on British drama, Taylor's book places Reed in the cultural context of his time. A standard resource, important for students of twentieth century British arts and literature. Bibliography.

Harold Branam;
bibliography updated by the editors

Lizette Woodworth Reese

Born: Waverly, Maryland; January 9, 1856
Died: Baltimore, Maryland; December 17, 1935

Principal poetry

A Branch of May, 1887
A Handful of Lavender, 1891
A Quiet Road, 1896
A Wayside Lute, 1909
Spicewood, 1920
Wild Cherry, 1923
The Selected Poems of Lizette Woodworth Reese, 1926
Little Henrietta, 1927
White April and Other Poems, 1930
Pastures and Other Poems, 1933
The Old House in the Country, 1936

Other literary forms

Although primarily a poet, Lizette Woodworth Reese published at least fourteen short stories, which appeared in various literary magazines, including *Harper's*, *Lippincott's*, and *Outlook*. Five of these fictional pieces are reprinted in her semiautobiographical work *The York Road* (1931). In *A Victorian Village: Reminiscences of Other Days* (1929), Reese reminisces about her girlhood in and around Waverly, a hamlet on the outskirts of Baltimore. Reese's only other major work is the unfinished *Worleys* (1936), a fictional piece published after her death. She also wrote a few essays on teaching and published several magazine poems which were not included in any of her books.

Achievements

By the time Lizette Woodworth Reese retired at the age of sixty-five from her position as a public school English teacher, she had published only about half of her poems. Yet to come were the poems in *Wild Cherry*, the new work contained in *The Selected Poems of Lizette Woodworth Reese*, and the long elegy *Little Henrietta*. Also still to come was the somewhat belated recognition as a significant contributor to the mainstream of American lyricism. By 1924, Reese began receiving the awards and honors that she deserved. The College of William and Mary initiated Reese as an honorary member of Phi Beta Kappa. In 1925, the Tudor and Stuart Club at The Johns Hopkins University selected Reese for honorary membership.

The most public expression of recognition occurred on December 15, 1926, when the George H. Doran Company, publisher of *The Selected Poems of Lizette Woodworth Reese*, hosted a testimonial dinner for Reese at the Brevoort Hotel in New York. Many prominent literary figures of the day attended, including DuBose Heyward, Edwin Markham, Carl Van Doren, Elinor Wylie, William Rose Benét, and Robert Frost. Other honors followed: In 1930, Reese received the Percy Bysshe Shelley Memorial Award for achievement in poetry; in the same year, an honorary Doctor of Letters degree from Goucher College; and, in 1934, designation as National Honor Poet of Poetry Week.

Ultimately, Reese's place in American literary history may depend on the impetus that she gave to a modern, native lyricism. This impetus dates from the publication of her first book in 1887, more than twenty years before the flowering of the Imagist movement. Reese, who styled herself a "conventional traditionist" and spoke unflatteringly of the "precious imagists," was, nevertheless, a poet whose work is characterized by many of the qualities that the Imagists praised: simplicity, concentration, sharp sensory appeal, and, as Ezra Pound demanded, "direct treatment of the thing." David Perkins says in *A History of Modern Poetry* (1976) that Reese handled images "in a way that anticipates Imagist poetry," and other critics have noted the modern texture of her verse, lying under the traditional structure of rhymed quatrains and sonnets. Forgiving her lapses into "poetic" diction and inversions ("hath," "grasses green") and stock rhymes ("fall/all," "spring/thing"), one still detects a genuine voice, a voice that breaks with the genteel tradition to which Reese has been unfairly assigned.

Ironically, Reese has been to some extent the victim of the success of her famous sonnet "Tears." First published by *Scribner's Magazine* in 1899, and later included in *A Wayside Lute*, "Tears" has been anthologized so frequently that even a serious student of American poetry might conclude that Reese wrote one brilliant sonnet and little else of merit. H. L. Mencken said that "we have here a sonnet that no other American has ever approached." Such singular praise for "Tears" from Mencken and others (Padraic Colum said that he knew it by heart) tended to distinguish it as *the* Reese poem, identifying it in the public's mind in much the same way that William Ernest Henley and "Invictus" are inevitably linked.

Finally, Reese's achievement should be gauged in terms of her influence. In *American Poetry Since 1900* (1923), Louis Untermeyer considers Reese the "forerunner of Sara Teasdale, Edna St. Vincent Millay and the new generation to whom simplicity in song is a first essential." Influence is difficult to assess in precise terms, but one often hears echoes of Reese in the poetry of the younger lyricists. Teasdale and Wylie particularly admired Reese's work, and Wylie was a featured speaker at the Brevoort Testimonial.

Biography

Lizette Woodworth Reese and her twin sister, Louisa, were born, according to their mother, "in the worst storm of the winter" of 1856 at their maternal grandparents' house in Waverly, Maryland. Of Welsh descent on her father's side and German on her mother's, she early learned to love, as she recalls in one poem, the "Saxon tang" which "clung to our elders' speech." Her preference then for the Anglo-Saxon monosyllable came naturally to her reticent, yet vivid, lyrics which seem to blend what she called the "silent" tendency of her father's Welsh ancestry, while retaining the vivacity of her talkative, musically inclined mother, Louisa Gabler Reese.

Mrs. Reese and the young twins moved in with her parents during the Civil War while her husband, David Reese, served with the Confederate forces and her brother with the Union. In *A Victorian Village*, Reese recalls the Civil War days in the border state of Maryland: "Between the blue forces and the gray we were ground between two millstones of terror." Against this terror stood her sprightly, devoutly religious mother from whom the girl acquired a love of gardening and growing things—the lilac bushes, hawthorn trees, daffodils, and succory blossoms which the visual and olfactory imagery of her poetry constantly evokes.

As a well-read girl of seventeen with what she called the "gift of authority," Reese began teaching English at St. John's Parish School in Waverly. After two years, she transferred to the Baltimore district where she taught in three different high schools, eventually retiring in 1921 from Western High after a forty-five-year career. To honor her on the occasion of her retirement, Western High erected a bronze tablet inscribed with her celebrated sonnet "Tears."

Although she never married, lived all her life near or in Baltimore, and taught English for more than four decades, Reese was not a sheltered "schoolmarm." She was a founding member of "The Women's Literary Club of Baltimore" and enjoyed an active public life which included readings and lectures for civic and literary groups. She knew and corresponded with many members of literary society, especially Louise Imogen Guiney, Edmund Clarence Stedman, John Hall Wheelock, Untermeyer, and Mencken. Although Reese was a woman of literary affairs, the world of her poetry is the Maryland world of trees, flowers, and country lanes where she first learned, through her own sensory perception, the metaphorical equivalence between a mood and the natural stimuli which engender it.

ANALYSIS

Several critics have identified Lizette Woodworth Reese's major thematic concern, which she herself specifies in the imperative opening of her poem "To a Town Poet": "Snatch the departing mood;/ Make yours its emptying reed, and pipe us still/ Faith in the time. . . ." Reese follows her own advice as she explores in poem after poem the "departing mood," ranging from bittersweet recollections to the intense memory that redeems some part of an otherwise irrecoverable past. "To a Town Poet," Reese's manifesto for a native lyricism proclaims "faith in our common blood" and directs the poet's attention *toward* the "huddled trees," the "smoky ways," the "vendor, swart but free" and *away* from the period's sentimental, genteel verse with its stilted diction, classical allusions, and didactic guidance. Reese did not, however, mean a lyricism like Walt Whitman's free verse; she meant a lyricism in the traditional forms from which she herself rarely departed and to which some poets, such as Millay and Frost, turned during the modern lyric renaissance.

A fascination with mood—with the fine gradations of multiple sensations—certainly goes back to Reese's girlhood. Growing up with the terror of war, the young Lizette enjoyed the contentment that she found in the natural setting of her grandfather's farm, stories which she delightfully retells in *A Victorian Village*. She took additional comfort in the Victorian literature which she eagerly read—particularly Charles Dickens and Alfred, Lord Tennyson, her masters in the school of literary mood.

Considering her work in its historical and social milieu, one finds a poetry oblivious to the Gilded Age and its associated social problems. Reese was not indifferent to the issues of her time, but she did not consider her lyrics as a forum for any causes except those of emotion and beauty. Her subjects may vary from love to death to nature, but the theme almost always comes back to the belief that an appreciation of experience depends on isolating the "mood" associated with it and then crystallizing it through sensory appeals, especially the tactile, auditory, and olfactory imagery which further distinguishes her poetic voice.

METRICS

The key to a formal appreciation of Reese's work lies in the recognition of her poetic voice. This voice, heard throughout her eleven books of poetry, makes a unique contribution to the American impulse toward a modern lyric verse. Examining her prosody, diction, rhythms, and syntax, one soon discovers a repetitively expressive pattern, with artistic variations, that constitutes a talented poetic voice. An outstanding feature of this voice is her penchant for the Anglo-Saxon monosyllable. She wanted to write a lyric that was native both in locale and tongue, and, accordingly, she wanted to avoid the Latinate, polysyllabic words of which her genteel contemporaries were much too fond. In "Betrayed," the first poem in her first book, the word "perfect" is the only polysyllabic word, and she continued to favor spare and economical diction. This preference for the simple, native words permitted her to achieve a "classical" American idiom, an idiom less showy than Whitman's, less intense than Emily Dickinson's, yet vivid and evocative in its own quiet manner.

One metrical trait of Reese's voice is the substitution of a trochaic foot in the prevailing iambic meter, especially in the initial position where the trochee and the following iamb actually constitute a choriambus. The choriambus, such as "Blówn lĭke ă fláme" and "Héaped ĭn thĕ róads," then becomes a "long foot" that frames or freezes an image, particularly with an active verb in the dynamic stress position where it militates against the rhythmical stasis of imagery locked into what Paul Fussell, in *Poetic Meter and Poetic Form* (1965), calls "the pleasantly predictable, manageable world of the iambic."

Mood

In the first stage of Reese's long literary career are exemplified all the characteristic traits and tricks of her poetic voice. Her thematic concern with the "departing mood"—to an extent that theme and tone become one—consistently typifies the poems of the early period. Reese is not, however, merely a poet of mood like the poetasters who contributed sentimental verse to the ladies' magazines. She is, rather, a poet who locates the gentle irony where the woof of a pleasant image interlaces, and thus partly obscures and softens, the warp of hard reality. The bittersweet, the wistful, and the poignant form the emotional province of Reese's voice, but these emotions come from an artistic distance, from an awareness by the lyric persona that mood is not only crystallized feeling but also recaptured thought. Mood is then, for Reese's lyric speaker, a complex response to the sensory appeal of imagery, and the mood itself becomes the healthy equilibrium between the venting of emotion on the one hand and the containing of emotion on the other.

"In Time of Grief"

"In Time of Grief," from *A Quiet Road*, illustrates the essential method of Reese's early lyricism. The poem combines an array of images within its tight structure of three ballad-stanza quatrains. Noteworthy is the emphasis on olfactory imagery, for Reese knows that the sense of smell, as effectively as sight or sound, evokes memories and their associated feelings. The lyric speaker, referring to the box shrub along the "wall of stone," says that "Its odor through my house was blown/ Into the chamber there." Compatibly mixing her sensory impressions, she defines this "scent" in auditory and tactile terms: "As though one spoke a word half meant/ That left a sting behind." The brief resolution of the poem leaves the speaker uncertain about the abstract quality of "grief" but comforted in the knowledge of "how keen the box can be/ After a fall of rain." Thus Reese's lyric persona encounters an ironic variation: The "reality" of abstractions (grief, love, beauty, truth) is hardly separable from the masking, imagistic "appearance," because, unexpected and unsummoned, the departing mood may instantly return when the sensory conditions are right.

"Tears"

Published in 1909 on the threshold of the New Poetry, *A Wayside Lute* represents an advance in stylistic variations and dramatic vigor, even though Reese's standard themes of mood and memory, along with her poetic staples—the poplar trees, the color white, the month of April—remain the same. Unexpectedly, it is the Petrarchan sonnet "Tears"—a poem neither concerned with the departing mood nor informed by her usual images—which distinguishes this collection. In "Tears," Reese still relies on the heavy monosyllabic diction, the trochaic inversions, and the auditory imagery ("A call to battle," "The last echo," "The burst of music"), but she widens her poetic scope to ponder the brevity of life and, in the apostrophe that comprises the sestet, to ask the "Chieftains, and bards, and keepers of the sheep" to release her from a mood she can no longer tolerate: "Loose me from tears, and make me see aright/ How each hath back what once he stayed to weep." The understated effect of "stayed," suggesting only a pause, exercises the ironic control which prevents the poem from stumbling into sentimentality. In the climactic last line, the lyric speaker who wants an "intimation of immortality" cites two—one a bard and one a keeper of the sheep—who stayed to weep: "Homer his sight, David his little lad!" Here, in one memorable line, Reese sweeps up, and juxtaposes, two representatives from the great shaping forces of Western civilization: the Hellenic tradition of humanistic culture and the Judeo-Christian tradition of religious hope. The optimistic thread in each branch justifies the enlightening exclamation which closes the sestet—a lyric shout back to the "old, old dead" that the promise of immortality is implicit in the ironic brevity of life.

SPICEWOOD AND WILD CHERRY

In the third stage of her career, Reese reaches the height of her lyric voice, achieving her finest sustained yet tightly controlled lyricism. This control is evident in *Spicewood*, where half the poems are Petrarchan sonnets, each one containing six, rather than the prescribed five, rhymes in one of two patterns: either *abba*, *cddc*, *efg*, *efg*, or *abab*, *cdcd*, *efg*, *efg*. In poetic voice and imagery, these sonnets are typically Reese's, but they are plaintive notes of a speaker who is more introspective and less exuberant, and fully prone to sound the characteristically modern theme of alienation still comprehended in the resonance of mood and memory.

In this period, Reese elevates some of her favorite images to the eminence of symbol. The color white, for example, makes the transition from a descriptive to a symbolic term, becoming what Robert D. Rhode calls "a manifold symbol. . . . It is a spiritual force that inspires, tortures, and subdues." "In Vain," one of the finest lyrics in *Wild Cherry*, illustrates the new symbolic aura for the word "white." In the first three quatrains, the lyric speaker, remembering a lost lover, cries "for a world empty of you" but realizes that "Some small thing thereabout/ Would bring the same hurt back again." As usual, the speaker emphasizes the aching, inescapable mood which sensory impressions will inevitably provoke. In the climatic quatrain, struggling against the lovesick mood, the lyric "I" yearns for "the smell of yarrow flowers . . . set/ In a lost field." Then, reinforcing the olfactory imagery, the forsaken lover simply repeats the desire with the modifying color and conditions: "White yarrow flowers,/ Out in the August wet." There is no complete subject/verb relationship in the quatrain; it works its culminating effect strictly through the exposition of imagery. One should not incorrectly conclude that the flowers have an antecedent in "some small thing" that would remind the lyric "I" of the lost lover or that, in the opposite direction, they represent a remedy for heartache. The speaker simply ponders submission to the sensory assault of the strongly scented yarrow and its eye-catching whiteness—a whiteness meaning, on the sensory level, more than brilliance or color, and meaning, on the metaphorical level, more than "pristine" or "virginal," and pointing, ironically, toward the muted eroticism of a "lost field . . ./ Out in the August wet." Here, as in other notable lyrics from this period ("A Puritan Lady," "Fog," "Alien"), Reese invests the color white with a private symbolism that defines a complex mood and finally rounds, in "Reparation," to the philosophy that "what is fair is permanent." For Reese, the single word which best renders the essence of "fair"—not merely as synonym but as the natural stimulant of, and symbolic correlative for, mood and memory—is "white."

Readers of *The Selected Poems of Lizette Woodworth Reese* should be aware that the George H. Doran Company could not get permission from the Norman, Remington Company, the publishers of *Spicewood* and *Wild Cherry*, to reprint poems from these two volumes, thus precluding a proper estimation of Reese's talent by anyone who mistakenly believes that the book contains a representative "selection" of her best work.

LITTLE HENRIETTA

Little Henrietta, written in thirty-nine ten-line stanzas, excluding a three-couplet poem titled "Shelter" and "An Epitaph," is actually an elegy for a child whom the young Reese knew in Waverly. Uncharacteristically Reese does not employ regular rhyme, although there are occasional true and slant rhymes. With a sure sense of her own talent, Reese knew that the traditional elegiac mode offered her poetic voice a perfect medium with its flower symbolism, meditative mood, and expression of grief which submits to Christian consolation. A significant part of her achievement is in the poem's structural design: The first fifteen stanzas serve as an introductory narrative which details Henrietta's childhood and the impression which she made on her friends and elders, leading up to her death in stanza fifteen. The last twenty-four stanzas follow the general pattern of the pastoral elegy with a questioning invocation in stanza 16: "Have we not waked at time," the narrator asks, "And thought our eyes amiss?" The digression on the church, in stanzas 22-25, is not condemnatory, as in John Milton's "Lycidas," but the narrator feels the irony of the funeral that "left us naked by a churchyard wall." A neglected contribution to the elegiac genre in American literature, *Little Henrietta* ranks with "Tears" as Reese's major achievement.

Later years

The poems from Reese's last period, written after she had turned seventy, betray a weakening of her poetic voice. Although *White April* and *Pastures* contain poems which recapture the old lyric energy—"White April" and "Women" in the former volume, "A Country Doctor" and "Cynical Advice" in the latter—there is a tendency, avoided in her early work, toward didactic conclusions and moral sentiment.

Published posthumously in 1936, *The Old House in the Country* is a curious addition to the Reese canon. It is a rhymed, autobiographical poem in fifty-two ten-line stanzas, the structure used so successfully in *Little Henrietta*; yet, without the internal conventions of the elegy, this poem lacks unity, causing single stanzas to fragment into separate poems.

Reading Reese's work from this distance, one necessarily considers it on two levels: first, on the basic plane of its lyrical beauty—developed and extended by a poetic voice that maintains its typifying notes and themes throughout her work—and, second, on the plane of its influence, where Reese promoted by example a trend that hastened American lyricism away from a pseudoclassical gentility toward an image-conscious modernity.

Other major works

long fiction: *Worleys*, 1936.

nonfiction: *A Victorian Village: Reminiscences of Other Days*, 1929.

miscellaneous: *The York Road*, 1931 (stories, essays, and poetry).

Bibliography

Harris, R. P. "April Weather: The Poetry of Lizette Woodworth Reese." *The South Atlantic Quarterly* 29 (April, 1930): 200-207. This essay, appearing before Reese died in 1935, is an early and valuable recognition of her place in American lyric poetry. Surveying her career, Harris shows that, even during the period that Edmund Clarence Stedman called "a twilight interval" (1890-1910), Reese was publishing the "clear, natural lyrics" that anticipated the later works of Edna St. Vincent Millay and Sara Teasdale.

Hill, Phyllis. *Who Will Sing My Songs?* Hagerstown, Md.: Freline, 1988. As a "dialogue" between the author of the book and Reese, the text will appeal primarily to young readers who seek an introduction to her philosophy of life and her poetry. Contains some photographs of Reese, a brief bibliography, and a selection of her poems.

Kindilien, Carlin T. "The Village World of Lizette Woodworth Reese." *The South Atlantic Quarterly* 56 (January, 1957): 91-104. This essay begins with a biographical sketch of Reese, but then quite perceptively analyzes the distinguishing characteristics of her poetry: its simplicity of diction and imagery, its embrace of the natural world, and its spiritual aesthetic. Concludes with a pertinent comparison of Reese and Emily Dickinson.

Knight, Denise D. "Lizette Woodworth Reese." In *Nineteenth-Century American Women Writers*, edited by Denise D. Knight and Emmanuel S. Nelson. Westport, Conn.: Greenwood, 1997. A biographical sketch of Reese with a bibliography.

Morris, Lawrence S. "Some Flowers Down a Lane." *The New Republic* 48 (August 25, 1926): 23-24. A brief but sensitive review of *The Selected Poems of Lizette Woodworth Reese*, this essay touches on the characteristic themes and beauties of Reese's verse, particularly her fascination with mood, memory, and grief.

Rhode, Robert D. "Lizette W. Reese: 'Fair White Gospeler.'" *The Personalist* 31 (1950): 390-398. Using Reese as an example of the teacher-poet, Rhode illustrates how she writes within, but ultimately transcends, the didactic nature of the genteel tradition. Rhode acutely analyzes Reese's choice of "white" and "April" as symbolically important words that help her escape "the excesses of narcissistic romanticism on one hand, and of ethical nihilism on the other."

Scholnick, Robert J. "Lizette Woodworth Reese." *Legacy* 15, no. 2 (1998): 213-221. A short biographical study of Reese and her work.

Ronald K. Giles;
bibliography updated by the editors

Pierre Reverdy

Born: Narbonne, France; September 13, 1889
Died: Solesmes, France; June 17, 1960

Principal poetry

Poèmes en prose, 1915
Quelques poèmes, 1916
La Lucarne ovale, 1916
Les Ardoises du toit, 1918 (*Roof Slates*, 1981)
Les Jockeys camouflés, 1918
La Guitare endormie, 1919
Étoiles peintes, 1921
Cœur de chêne, 1921
Cravates de chanvre, 1922
Grande Nature, 1925
La Balle au bond, 1928
Sources du vent, 1929
Pierres blanches, 1930
Ferraille, 1937
Plein verre, 1940
Plupart du temps, 1915-1922, 1945
Le Chant des morts, 1948
Main d'œuvre: Poèmes, 1913-1949, 1949
Selected Poems, 1969
Roof Slates and Other Poems of Pierre Reverdy, 1981

Other literary forms

Pierre Reverdy worked extensively in other forms besides poetry. He wrote two novels and many stories and published collections of prose poems. Most of these are in a Surrealist vein, mixing experimentation in language with personal and unconscious reflection. As an editor of an avant-garde review, Reverdy also contributed important theoretical statements on cubism and avant-garde literary practice. Later in his career, he published several volumes of reminiscences, including sensitive reevaluations of the work of his near contemporaries, including Guillaume Apollinaire.

Achievements

Pierre Reverdy is one of the most central and influential writers in the tradition of twentieth century avant-garde poetry. Already well established in terms of both his work and his theoretical stance by the mid-1910's, Reverdy exerted considerable influence over the Dada and Surrealist movements, with which he was both officially and informally affiliated.

Reverdy's firm conviction was in a nonmimetic, nontraditional form of artistic expression. The art he championed and practiced would create a reality of its own rather than mirror a preexisting reality. In this way, the language of poetry would be cut loose from restraining conventions of meter, syntax, and punctuation in order to be able to explore the emotion generated by the poetic image.

In connection with the avant-garde artists of cubism, Dada, and Surrealism, Reverdy's formulations helped to break down the traditional models of artistic creation that then held firm sway in France. Reverdy's firm conviction was that artistic creation precedes aesthetic theory. All the concrete means at an artist's disposal constitute his aesthetic formation.

Along with Apollinaire, his slightly older contemporary, Reverdy became a central figure and example for a whole generation of French poets generally grouped under the Surrealist heading. His having been translated into English by a range of American poets from Kenneth Rexroth to John Ashbery shows the importance of his work to the modern and contemporary American tradition as well.

Biography

Pierre Reverdy was born on September 13, 1889, in Narbonne, France, a city in the Languedoc region. The son and grandson of sculptors and artisans in wood carving, he grew up with this practical skill in addition to his formal studies. The Languedoc region at the turn of the century was an especially volatile region, witnessing the last major peasant uprising in modern French history.

After completing his schooling in Narbonne and nearby Toulouse, Reverdy moved to Paris in 1910, where he lived on and off for the rest of his life. Although exempted from military service, he volunteered at the outbreak of World War I, saw combat service, and was discharged in 1916. By profession a typesetter, Reverdy also worked as the director of the review *Nord-Sud*, which he founded in 1917.

Reverdy worked during the years 1910 to 1926 in close contact with almost all the important artists of his time. He had especially close relationships with Pablo Picasso and Juan Gris, both of whom contributed illustrations to collections of his verse. As the editor of an influential review, he had close contact with and strong influence on the writers who were to form the Dada and Surrealist movements. Already an avant-garde poet and theorist of some prominence by the late 1910's, Reverdy was often invoked along with Apollinaire as one of the precursors of Surrealism. He collaborated with the early Surrealist efforts and continued his loose affiliation even after a formal break in 1926.

That year saw Reverdy's conversion to a mystic Catholicism. From then until his death in 1960, his life became more detached from the quotidian, and he spent much of his time at the Abbey of Solesmes, where he died.

Analysis

In an early statement on cubism, Pierre Reverdy declaimed that a new epoch was beginning, one in which "one creates works that, by detaching themselves from life, enter back into it because they have an existence of their own." In addition to attacking mimetic standards of reproduction, or representation of reality, he also called for a renunciation of punctuation and a freeing of syntax in the writing of poetry. Rather than being something fixed according to rules, for Reverdy, syntax was "a medium of literary creation." Changing the rules of literary expression carried with it a change in ideas of representation. For Reverdy, the poetic image was solely responsible to the discovery of emotional truth.

Pierre Reverdy

In the years 1915 to 1922, Reverdy produced many volumes of poetry. The avant-garde called for an overturning of literary conventions, and Reverdy contributed with his own explosion of creative activity. In addition to editing the influential review *Nord-Sud*, he used his experience as an engraver and typesetter to publish books, including his own. The list of artists who contributed the illustrations to these volumes of poetry by Reverdy reads like a Who's Who of the art world of the time: Juan Gris, Pablo Picasso, André Derain, Henri Matisse, Georges Braques, among others. Reverdy's work, along with that of Apollinaire, was cited as the guiding force for Surrealism by André Breton in his *Manifestes du surréalisme* (1962; *Manifestoes of Surrealism*, 1969).

Reverdy's early work achieves an extreme detachment from mimetic standards and literary conventions that allows for the images to stand forth as though seen shockingly for the first time. The last two lines from "Sur le Talus" (on the talus), published in 1918, show this extreme detachment: "L'eau monte comme une poussière/ Le silence ferme la nuit" (The water rises like dust/ Silence shuts the night). There can be no question here of establishing a realistic context for these images. Rather, one is cast back on the weight of emotion that they carry and which must thus guide their interpretation. Reflections off water may appear to rise in various settings, though perhaps particularly at twilight. The dust points to a particular kind of aridity that may be primarily an emotional state. The sudden transition from an (implied) twilight to an abrupt nightfall undercuts any kind of conventional emotional presentation. The quick cut is a measure perhaps of the individual's lack of control over external phenomena and, by extension, inner feelings as well.

"Carrefour"

Much of Reverdy's early work is based on just such an imagistic depiction of interior states, with a strong element of detachment from reality and a certain resulting confusion or overlapping. The force of emotion is clearly there, but to pin it down to a particular situation or persona proves difficult because any such certainty is constantly being undercut by the quick transitions between images. The complete suppression of punctuation as well as a certain freedom of syntax as one moves from line to line are clearly tools that Reverdy developed to increase the level of logical disjunction in his poetry. At times, however, this disjunction in the logical progression of word and image gives way to a resolution. The short poem "Carrefour" (crossroad) sets up a surreal image sequence:

De l'air
De la lumière
Un rayon sur le bord du verre
Ma main déçue n'attrape rien
(Air
Light
A ray on the edge of the glass
My disappointed hand holds nothing)

Here the elements are invoked, and then two images, one of an inanimate object and one the hand of the speaker. From this atmosphere of mystery and disjunction, the poem's conclusion moves to a fairly well-defined emotional statement:

Enfin tout seul j'aurai vécu
Jusqu'au dernier matin
Sans qu'un mot m'indiquât quel fut le bon chemin
(After all I will have lived all alone
Until the last morning
Without a single word that might have shown me
which was the right way)

Here, as in many of Reverdy's poems, the emotion evoked is a kind of diffused sadness. The solitary individual is probably meant to stand for an aspect of the human condition, alone in a confrontation with an unknown destiny.

It was Reverdy's fate to see actual military duty during World War I, and it may well be that the magnitude of human tragedy he witnessed at the front lines served to mute the youthful enthusiasm that pervades his earliest works. It may also be the case that Reverdy, while espousing radical measures in literary practice, still was caught in the kind of bittersweet ethos that characterizes *fin de siècle* writers generally.

"Guerre"

Whatever the case may be, there is no question that Reverdy wrote some of the most affecting war poems in the French language. One of the most direct is titled simply "Guerre" (war). Running through a series of disjointed, if coherent, images, Reverdy toward the end of the poem approaches direct statement, when the speaker says:

Et la figure attristée
Visage des visages
La mort passe sur le chemin
(And the saddened figure
Visage of visages
Death passes along the road)

Close to a medieval allegorizing of death, this figure also incorporates a fascination with the effect of the gaze. One's face is revealing of one's emotion because of the way one looks—the distillation of the phenomenon into a general characteristic is a strong term to describe death. If this image is strong, the poem's ending is more forceful still:

Mais quel autre poids que celui de ton corps
as-tu jeté dans la balance
Tout froid dans le fossé
Il dort sans plus rêver
(But what other weight than that of your body
have you thrown in the balance
All cold in the ditch
He sleeps no longer to dream)

Philosophers have questioned whether the idea of death is properly an idea, since strictly speaking it has no content. Caught between viewing another's death from the outside and facing one's own death, which one can never know, death is a supreme mystery of human existence. Reverdy in these lines seems to cross the line between the exterior, objective view of another's death and the unknowable, subjective experience of the individual. This is what he means by the emotion communicated through the poetic image.

Despite a continued tendency toward the surreal image in Reverdy's work, these poems in *Sources du vent* (sources of the wind) also represent the first major collection of poems after Reverdy's conversion to a mystic Catholicism in 1926. Increasingly, his poetry of the postconversion period tends toward an introjection of the conflicts raised through the poetic image. While a tone of lingering sadness had always been present from the earliest work, in these poems the atmosphere of sadness and loss moves to the center of the poet's concerns. Unlike the conservative Christian poets Charles Péguy and Paul Claudel, the content of the poems is never directly religious. Rather, a mood of quietism seems to become more prominent in the collections of poems after the conversion. A concurrent falling off in the level of production also takes place. After 1930, Reverdy publishes only two more individual collections of verse, along with two collected volumes and works in other forms. After 1949, for the last twelve years of his life, the heretofore prolific Reverdy apparently ceased to write altogether.

"Mémoire"

The poem "Mémoire" (memory) from *Pierres blanches* (white stones), shows this mood of increasing resignation in the face of worldly events. The poem invokes a "she," someone who has left or is going to leave, but then, in apparent reference to the title, says there will still be someone:

> Quand nous serons partis là-bas derrière
> Il y aura encore ici quelqu'un
> Pour nous attendre
> Et nous entendre
> (When we will have gone over there behind
> There will still be someone
> To wait for us
> And to understand us)

The positive mood of these lines, however, is undercut by the poem's ending: "Un seul ami/ L'ombre que nous avons laissée sous l'arbre et qui s'ennuie" ("A single friend/ The shadow we have left beneath a tree and who's getting bored"). The impersonality tending toward a universal statement that was present in Reverdy's early work here seems to work toward an effacement of the individual personality. If memory can be imaged as a bored shadow left beneath a tree, the significance of the individual seems tenuous at best. The emotion generated through the poetic image here seems to be one of sadness and extreme resignation.

The interpretation of a poet's work through biography must always be a hazy enterprise, all the more so in a poet such as Reverdy, whose life directly enters into his work not at all. In a general sense, then, the course of his poetic life and production might be said to mirror the course of French literary life generally. The enthusiasm of the avant-garde literary and artistic movements in Europe generally in the early years of the twentieth century saw a reaction in the post-World War I years toward an art that questioned societal assumptions. Dada and Surrealism can be seen in terms of this large movement, and Reverdy's work as an example. The coherence of the Surrealist movement in turn breaks down in the late 1920's and early 1930's with the split coming over what political allegiance the Surrealist artists should take, according to its leaders. Reverdy's personal religious convictions cause him to cease active involvement with the movement altogether. It is a measure of his status as a strong precursor to the movement that he is not attacked directly by the more politically motivated leaders of Surrealism.

"Main-Morte"

With the extreme politicization of the Surrealist movement in the late 1930's, even some of the most dedicated younger adherents to Surrealism cut their formal ties with the movement. René Char is an example. The young Yves Bonnefoy is an example of a poet with early leanings toward Surrealism who in the late 1940's moved more in the direction of a poetry expressive of essential philosophical and human truths. It might be possible, in like manner, to trace Reverdy's increasing distance from Surrealism as a movement to some kind of similar feelings that have been more openly expressed by his younger contemporaries. His collection *Plein Verre* (full glass) does indeed move more toward the mode of longer, contemplative poems, still in the atmosphere of sadness and resignation to life. The end of "Main-Morte" (dead-hand) shows this well:

> Entre l'aveu confus et le lien du mystère
> Les mots silencieux qui tendent leur filet
> Dans tous les coins de cette chambre noire

Où ton ombre ni moi n'aurons jamais dormi
(Between the confused vow and the tie of mystery
The silent words which offer their net
In every corner of this black room
Where your shadow nor I will have ever slept)

Even the highly suggestive early lyrics do not contain quite the level of hovering mystery and intricate emotional states offered in these lines. One may well wonder if the "you" invoked here even refers to a person or whether it might be a quasi-human interior presence such as that invoked in the later poems of Wallace Stevens (such as "Final Soliloquy of the Interior Paramour"). The weight of the images in the direction of silence lends to this whole utterance an aura of high seriousness.

"ENFIN"

The last poem of the same collection, titled "Enfin" (at last), also ends with a statement hinting at a highly serious attitude. The speaker states:

À travers la poitrine nue
Là
Ma clarière
Avec tout ce qui descend du ciel
Devenir un autre
À ras de terre
(By means of the naked breast
There
My clearing
Along with all that descends from the sky
To become an other
At earth level)

More and more in the later poems, a level of ethical statement seems to emerge. Whereas the early poems introduce strange and startling images in an apparently almost random fashion, the images here seem to be coordinated by an overall hierarchy of values, personal and religious. The naked breast at the beginning of this passage thus could refer to the lone individual, perhaps alone with his or her conscience. This is in contrast to something which descends from the sky, an almost unavoidably religious image. The wish "To become an other/ At earth level" might then be interpreted as the fervent desire of an extremely devoted individual to attain a higher level of piety here on earth.

LE CHANT DES MORTS

The extended sequence, *Le Chant des morts* (the song of the dead), composed in 1944-1948 and published in 1948 as part of the collected volume *Main d'oeuvre* (work made by hand), presents an extended meditation on the emotional inner scene of war-devastated France. Like he did in his earlier poems on World War I that drew on his direct experience of the horrors of war, Reverdy in this sequence utilizes a diction stripped bare of rhetoric, preferring instead the direct, poignant images of death and suffering. Death in these poems is both inescapable and horrible, or as he calls it: "la mort entêtée/ La mort vorace" ("stubborn death/ Voracious death"). As a strong countermovement to the implacable march of death, there is also a tenacious clinging to life. As the poet says: "C'est la faim/ C'est l'ardeur de vivre qui dirigent/ La peur de perdre" ("It is hunger/ It is the ardor to live that guide/ The fear of losing"). The poet of the inner conscience in these poems confronts the essential subject of his deepest meditations: the conscious adoption of his authentic attitude toward death.

The ultimate renunciation of poetry that characterizes the last years of Reverdy's life is preceded by an exploration of the subject most suited to representing death (remembering Sigmund Freud): that is, silence.

"ET MAINTENANT"

The poem that Reverdy seems to have chosen to come at the end of his collected poems, titled "Et Maintenant" (and now), ends with a poignant image of silence: "Tous les fils dénoués au delà des saisons reprennent leur tour et leur ton sur le fond sombre du silence" ("All the unknotted threads beyond the seasons regain their trace and their tone against the somber background of silence"). Reverdy here seems to hint at what lies beyond poetic expression in several senses. His entire ethos of poetic creation has been consistently based on an act of communication with the reader. Thus, the threads he refers to here could well represent the threads of intention and emotion that his readers follow in his poetry in order to achieve an experience of that emotion themselves, or to discover an analogous emotional experience in their own memory or personal background. He might also be hinting at those threads of intention and emotion that led beyond the limitations of individual life in a reunification with a divine creator. In the former interpretation, the background of silence would be that silence which precedes the poetic utterance or act of communication, as well as the silence after the act of communication or once the poet has ceased to write. In the religious interpretation, the background of silence would be that nothingness or nonbeing out of which the divine creation takes place and which, in turn, has the capability of incorporating silence or nonbeing into self, a religious attitude of a return to the creator even in the face of one's own personal death.

Legacy

Reverdy is a complex and fascinating figure in the history of French poetry in the first half of the twentieth century. He was a committed avant-garde artist in the years directly preceding, during, and following World War I; his outpouring of poetry and aesthetic statements made him one of the most significant precursors to the movements of Dada and Surrealism. Though his formal affiliation with the Surrealist movement was of brief duration, his example of using the poetic image to communicate emotion is central to everything for which Surrealism stood. The extreme respect shown to his work by other poets and artists confirms his importance as a creative innovator. Reverdy, in turn, paid respectful homage to his poet and artist contemporaries a stance that shows his ongoing intellectual commitment to the importance of art and literature in human terms, despite his personal isolation and quietism toward the end of his life. The poems from the end of his career that bear the weight of a continued meditation on death are a moving commentary on that from which language emerges and into which it returns: silence.

Other major works

long fiction: *Le Voleur de Talan*, 1917; *La Peau de l'homme*, 1926.

short fiction: *Risques et périls*, 1930.

nonfiction: *Self-defence*, 1919; *Le Gant de crin*, 1927; *Le Livre de mon bord*, 1948; *Note éternelle du présent*, 1975; *Nord-Sud, Self Defence, et autres écrits sur l'art et la poésie*, 1975; *Cette émotion appellée poésie: Écrits sur la poésie, 1932-1960*, 1975.

Bibliography

Greene, Robert W. *The Poetic Theory of Pierre Reverdy.* Berkeley, Calif.: University of California Press, 1967. An analysis of Reverdy's work in poetic theory.

Rizzuto, Anthony. *Style and Theme in Reverdy's "Les Ardoises du toit."* Tuscaloosa: University of Alabama Press, 1971. Rizzuto's critical study of one of Reverdy's poetic works. Includes bibliographic references.

Rothwell, Andrew. *Textual Spaces: The Poetry of Pierre Reverdy.* Atlanta, Ga.: Rodopi, 1989. A critical analysis of Reverdy's works. Includes bibliographic references.

Schroeder, Jean. *Pierre Reverdy.* Boston: Twayne, 1981. An introductory biography and critical study of selected works by Reverdy. Includes an index and bibliographic references.

Peter Baker;
bibliography updated by the editors

Kenneth Rexroth

Born: South Bend, Indiana; December 22, 1905
Died: Montecito, California; June 6, 1982

Principal poetry

A Prolegomenon to a Theodicy, 1932
In What Hour, 1940
The Phoenix and the Tortoise, 1944
The Signature of All Things, 1949
The Dragon and the Unicorn, 1952
The Art of Worldly Wisdom, 1953
Thou Shalt Not Kill, 1955
A Bestiary, 1955
In Defense of the Earth, 1956
Natural Numbers, 1963
The Homestead Called Damascus, 1963
The Collected Shorter Poems, 1966
The Collected Longer Poems, 1967
The Heart's Garden, the Garden's Heart, 1967
The Spark in the Tinder of Knowing, 1968

Sky Sea Birds Trees Earth House Beasts Flowers, 1971
New Poems, 1974
The Silver Swan, 1976
On Flower Wreath Hill, 1976
The Morning Star, 1979
Selected Poems, 1984
Sacramental Acts: The Love Poems of Kenneth Rexroth, 1997

OTHER LITERARY FORMS

In addition to more than thirty books of poetry, of which nearly half are translations from six languages, Kenneth Rexroth philosophically developed his erotic mysticism in verse drama, autobiographies, and critical essays. His four ritual plays of ecstatic transcendence in the midst of collapsing Classical Greek civilization, influenced by Japanese Nō and Greek tragedy, were collected in 1951 as *Beyond the Mountains*, premiered by the Living Theater in New York. Praised as one of Rexroth's most enduring achievements by poet William Carlos Williams, the classical scholar George Woodcock, and Japanese scholars Kodama Sanehide and Sakurai Emiko, *Beyond the Mountains* is distinguished by its faithfulness to both the Eastern and Western traditions that fed its subtle form, by its passionate characters who dramatize modern as well as ancient spiritual crises, and by its sensuously intellectual style.

In *An Autobiographical Novel* (1966, 1978) and *Excerpts from a Life* (1981), Rexroth's adventures are boldly narrated just as he spoke—with the uncanny power of epigrammatically characterizing everyone he met. Moreover, his religious, philosophical, and literary ideas are amplified in his wide-ranging essays, which have served to expand the audience for modern poetry. Most of his essays have been collected, and he also provided important introductory essays to his editions other writers.

ACHIEVEMENTS

Kenneth Rexroth's contributions to diverse literary and intellectual movements are suggested by Louis Zukofsky's inclusion of *A Prolegomenon to a Theodicy*, a long, cubist, philosophical revery, in *An "Objectivists Anthology"* (1932) and by Rexroth's membership in the Industrial Workers of the World, the John Reed Clubs, and the San Francisco "Libertarian Circle," among other revolutionary organizations, in which nonviolent, communitarian anarchism set an independent line in opposition to totalitarian communism and fascism as well as to the injustices of capitalistic democracy. His leadership in the Libertarian Circle was indispensable to the San Francisco Poetry Renaissance years before the Beat poets emerged in 1956, when Rexroth introduced poet Allen Ginsberg and others at the famous debut of Ginsberg's *Howl*. He helped to advance the work of such poets as Denise Levertov, Gary Snyder, Jerome Rothenberg, Shiraishi Kazuko, and many others, and his translations of women poets of China and Japan were deliberately feminist contributions.

Rexroth's work is read widely in Asia and Europe as well as in the United States. His international reputation has been aided by the popularity of his translations, his extensive travels and publication abroad, his collaboration with many writers in Europe and Asia, and the steady support of James Laughlin, whose New Directions published many of Rexroth's books. Rexroth's anthologies and editions of other writers extended his influence in England, and his reputation in Europe is reflected in his Akademische Austauschdienst Award from West Berlin which, with a Rockefeller grant, allowed him to travel around the world in 1967 on a poetry tour. Several tours of Asia, some of them sponsored by the United States Agency of International Communication, indicate the esteem with which he is held in that part of the world.

Rexroth received other honors as well: two California Silver Medal Awards (1941), two Guggenheim Fellowships (1948-1949), a Chapelbrook Award and a Eunice Teitjens Award from *Poetry* magazine (1957), a Longview Award (1963), a Shelley Memorial Award from the Poetry Society of America (1957), an Amy Lowell Fellowship (1958), a grant from the National Institute of Arts and Letters (1964), and a W. C. Williams Award from *Contact* magazine (1965). He contributed to many prestigious magazines and newspapers, conducted a program of poetry and comment on KPFA in San Francisco, and, despite his aversion to academic restrictions and his lack of any degrees, taught at San Francisco State College, the University of Wisconsin at Milwaukee, and the University of California at Santa Barbara, besides giving lectures and readings at many other universities around the world.

Biography

Born in South Bend in 1905, Kenneth Rexroth grew up in Indiana, Michigan, Ohio, and Illinois. His ancestors were scholars, peasants, and religious and political dissenters from Germany and Ireland, along with native and black Americans, and pioneers, all of whom enriched his unique personality. His parents were sophisticated travelers who took him on his first European tour when he was seven. After they died a few years later, he became independently active in Chicago as a precocious and revolutionary painter, poet, actor, and journalist—appearing as a character in James T. Farrell's *Studs Lonigan* (1934). After exploring Europe, Mexico, and the West Coast, he moved to San Francisco in 1927, where he made his home until moving to Santa Barbara in the late 1960's. Eastern and Western contemplative practices affected the visionary orientation of his poetry, painting, and philosophy. During World War II, he was a conscientious objector, working in a psychiatric hospital where he was severely injured by a patient. He also assisted interned and otherwise harassed Japanese Americans, and his friendships with Asians deepened his lifelong interest in Asian culture, especially Buddhism, which harmonizes in his work with an ecologically based sense of universal community.

He was married to Andrée Dutcher, an anarchist painter, from 1927 until her death in 1940; to Marie Kass, a nurse, from 1940 until their divorce in 1948; and to Marthe Larsen, a member of the "Libertarian Circle," from 1949 until their divorce in 1961. Two daughters, Mary and Katherine, were born to them in 1950 and 1954 respectively. In 1974, he married the poet Carol Tinker, and they spent a year in Kyoto before returning to their home in Montecito. Rexroth also toured Asia in 1967, 1972, 1978, and 1980. He died on June 6, 1982.

Analysis

Kenneth Rexroth wrote in the tradition of contemplative, mystical, visionary, philosophical, and prophetic poets such as William Butler Yeats, D. H. Lawrence, Walt Whitman, William Blake, Dante, Du Fu, Seami, and Sappho, all of whom influenced him. Rexroth was an eclectic student of many traditions from many cultures: Judeo-Christian, Classical Greek and Roman, Chinese, and Japanese. He was a modernist poet with a passionate commitment to tradition—to that which has lasted for centuries and is worth saving. His work as a whole, expository and autobiographical prose as well as passionate love lyrics, heartrending elegies, ferocious satires, and richly intellectual epic-reveries and dramas, must be read in the context of these diverse traditions. His style ranged from cubist innovations that ally him with Ezra Pound, Gertrude Stein, T. S. Eliot, and other revolutionists of the word, to the limpid simplicity he learned from Chinese and Japanese masters. This stylistic variety, however, is informed by an unwavering central vision of mystical love, universal responsibility, and spiritual realization.

The Collected Shorter Poems

The Collected Shorter Poems offers a brilliant diversity of styles and forms drawn from Rexroth's work over four decades. "Andromeda Chained to the Rock the Great Nebula in Her Heart" and other cubist poems share affinities with Gertrude Stein and Louis Zukofsky, as well as with African and Native American song. In a more direct style are exquisite lyrics of love and nature, such as "We Come Back"; fierce intellectual satires such as "Last Visit to the Swimming Pool Soviets" (with aspersions on the so-called chic Hollywood leftists); prophetic poems of revolutionary heroism and defeat, such as "From the Paris Commune to the Kronstadt Rebellion"; and Chinese translations.

"Yin and Yang," Rexroth's most liturgical poem of natural cycles, is an Easter vision of resurrecting birds, flowers, and constellations in which imagery and rhythms are perfectly balanced. In it, the moon, moving through constellations from Leo to Virgo, fertilizes the Virgin, and the ear of wheat symbolizes the creative process of nature as it did in the Eleusinian mysteries. As moonlight proclaims the climactic coming of spring, under the world the sun swims in Pisces, the double fish and the Chinese symbol of Yin and Yang, the harmonious interactions of darkness and light, coldness and heat, female and male. The regular prosody, supporting the orderly revelation of mythology, is a combination of accentual and syllabic patterns. All but three lines have nine syllables each, and most lines have three accents each, with a fundamentally dactyllic movement supporting the prophetic tone of this memorable poem.

"When We with Sappho," perhaps Rexroth's greatest love poem, begins with his first translation, done as a teenager and convincing him that he was a creative artist; there follows his sacramental lyric of erotic bliss, in which he and the woman he loves—also his muse—merge in a summer meadow into the immortal world of Sappho. As he speaks intimately, hypnotically repeating "summer," each body becomes a "nimbus" over the world, as they unite in thunder, before separating toward death.

"A Letter to William Carlos Williams" centers on the sacramental value of poetry as living speech, person to person (rather than as a text analyzed as an object). The style echoes the intimate ebb and flow of conversation with an old friend, whom he compares with St. Francis (whose flesh united with all lovers, including birds and animals) and Brother Juniper (a wise fool who laughed at indignities). Citing the quiet imagery of daily life in Williams's poetry, Rexroth praises Williams's stillness (like that of the Quaker George Fox and the peace of Jesus), and the poem concludes with a utopian vision of a beautiful Williams River, as a young woman of the future tells her children how it used to be the filthy Passaic, and how the poet Williams had embodied in his poetry a creative community of sacramental relationships.

Rexroth's most famous protest poem, "Thou Shalt Not Kill," has been recorded with jazz accompaniment. An elegy for Dylan Thomas, it mourns the destruction of many poets in this depersonalizing, violent century. Young men, Rexroth proclaims, are being murdered all over the world—such as Saints Stephen, Lawrence, and Sebastian—by the superego in uniform. The second section is reminiscent of "Lament for the Makaris," the elegy by the sixteenth century Scottish poet William Dunbar; in it Rexroth laments the impoverishment and deaths of many poets from Edward Arlington Robinson through Elinor Wylie and Countée Cullen to Ezra Pound. The third section, in a deepening tone, tells of many others struck down by the Moloch of the modern world. Accusations become lyrical in the last section, as nearly everyone is blamed for having a hand in the destruction of poetic vision—even writers such as T. S. Eliot and Ernest Hemingway who have enjoyed fame and power. The poem has been condemned by some critics but praised by others as a passionate call for prophetic vision.

The Collected Longer Poems

The Collected Longer Poems, which should be read as a whole work, reveals Rexroth's spiritual and artistic development as summarized in the introduction to the original publication of *The Phoenix and the Tortoise* in 1944—from despair and abandon in the face of the violent collapse of civilization, through erotic mysticism and sacramental marriage, to a sense of universal responsibility. *The Homestead Called Damascus*, the first of five long philosophical reveries in the collection, is a richly allusive work reminiscent of Marcel Proust and Wallace Stevens. The loose syllabic verse—generally nine syllables per line—allows Rexroth considerable freedom for discursive, philosophical reflections. In part I, the Damascan brothers, Thomas and Sebastian, whose names suggest the themes of skepticism and martyrdom that are interwoven throughout the poem, seek some kind of erotic-mystical escape from the decaying civilization symbolized by the mansion, the landscape, and the dreamy Renaissance girl, Leslie. In part II, Sebastian yearns for an earth goddess envisioned as a black stripper named Maxine, whereas Thomas seeks faith in the black wounds of Jesus. Part III elaborates the dilemma between erotic/heroic mysteries and the decadence of domestic bliss. Both alternatives paralyze the brothers, although they speculate about the "ambivalent vicarity" of each person symbolizing others. In the final part, Thomas settles for this philosophical notion, while Sebastian sinks into sterility. Although the poem suffers from some obscurity of characterization and theme, it is a work of serious speculation, resplendent with hallucinatory images, mythological puns, and metaphysical questioning.

A Prolegomenon to a Theodicy and The Dragon and the Unicorn

A Prolegomenon to a Theodicy, Rexroth's second long poem, is a search for transcendent perfection within the flux of experience, a search conducted by means of a cubist aesthetic in which he analyzes and recombines the elements of experience and language. He passes through a Dantean Hell before envisioning the Apocalypse in the most explicitly Christian imagery to be found in any of his poems. In his third long poem, *The Phoenix and the Tortoise*, whose title and theme of mystical love are derived from William Shakespeare's *The Phoenix and the Turtle*, Rexroth develops a religious, ecological viewpoint in which World War II and the injustices of all governments are anarchistically denounced, while value painfully emerges out of personal love. The style is clear, direct, often epigrammatically conveying a deeper faith in life than the previous two long poems. The fourth long poem, *The Dragon and the Unicorn*, is a postwar travel narrative in which Rexroth searches for the meaning of responsibility and its source in love as he proceeds across the United States and Europe. Witnessing the physical and spiritual effects of war and historical depersonalization, he condemns the collectivities of church, state, political parties, armies, and corporations for suppressing and destroying personality, and he celebrates the community of lovers that actually, miraculously, continues to exist.

The Heart's Garden, the Garden's Heart

The last long poem in the collection, *The Heart's Garden, the Garden's Heart*, extends this celebration of actuality. It is a masterpiece of poetic communion with the *tao* in Japan, rich in allusions to Asian poetry and Buddhist wisdom, and culminating, in a musical style that shines with the sensuous imagery of rural and urban Japan, in the most fully realized passages of illumination in all of his poetry. Hearing the music of waterfalls, he listens deep in his mind to transcendent music, overcoming the gap between actuality and Otherness. He does not seek visions, but rests in the innocent vision of actuality, which is also ultimate. Professor Kodama Sanehide of Doshisha Women's College in Kyoto has traced intricate allusions to Japanese poetry in this poem and others, leading him to conclude that of all American poets, Rexroth best understands Japanese culture. Certainly *The Heart's Garden, the Garden's Heart* is the most delightfully and wisely realized of his long poems.

Asian influences

Asian influences, apparent from the beginning of Rexroth's career, intensify in his later work, which includes several volumes of Chinese and Japanese translations, with women poets being singled out in three of them. Buddhist allusions radiate from *New Poems*, *On Flower Wreath Hill* (his sixth long reverie), *The Silver Swan*, and, most of all, *The Love Poems of Marichiko* (1978), a long sequence of Tantric ecstasy.

Rexroth has sometimes been criticized for being more concerned with philosophical speculation than with the subtleties of language, but these charges seem as superficial as the categorization of his work, by some early reviewers, as merely West Coast nature poetry; there is a vast range of linguistic and prosodic technique in his work. At one extreme is the cubist free verse of *A Prolegomenon to a Theodicy*, at the other extreme is the syllabic versification of much of his poetry of direct statement, influenced by Greek, Chinese, and Japanese traditions. Often nine syllables are a norm around which lines ranging from seven to ten syllables are skillfully arranged, the sounds falling into remarkable melodic patterns rare in modern poetry. Rexroth's vowel-patterns are especially distinctive, a technique absorbed from Japanese poetry. Sometimes jazz rhythms ("Travelers in Ere whom," for example), and ballad stanzas ("Songs for Marie's Lute-Book"), as well as a host of other styles, forms, and techniques are employed.

Finally, the many translations are of enormous value. They have not only introduced many readers to poetry in Chinese, Japanese, and European languages, but they also deserve to be read as enduring works of art in their own right. The translations are organically inseparable from Rexroth's other work, bringing to life voices that harmonize with his own, in a complex but coherent vision of worldwide community.

Other major works

PLAY: *Beyond the Mountains*, pb. 1951 (4 plays).

NONFICTION: *Bird in the Bush: Obvious Essays*, 1959; *Assays*, 1961; *An Autobiographical Novel*, 1966, 1978; *Classics Revisited*, 1968; *The Alternative Society: Essays from the Other World*, 1970; *With Eye and Ear*, 1970; *American Poetry in the Twentieth Century*, 1971; *The Elastic Retort*, 1973;

Communalism: From the Neolithic to 1900, 1975; *Excerpts from a Life*, 1981; *World Outside the Window: The Selected Essays of Kenneth Rexroth*, 1987; *More Classics Revisited*, 1989; *Kenneth Rexroth and James Laughlin: Selected Letters*, 1991.

TRANSLATIONS: *Fourteen Poems by O. V. de L. Milosz*, 1952, 1982; *Poems from the Japanese*, 1955, 1957, 1964; *One Hundred Poems from the French*, 1955, 1972; *One Hundred Poems from the Chinese*, 1956, 1965; *Thirty Spanish Poems of Love and Exile*, 1956; *Poems from the Greek Anthology*, 1962; *Pierre Reverdy Selected Poems*, 1969; *Love in the Turning Year: One Hundred More Poems from the Chinese*, 1970; *The Orchid Boat: Women Poets of China*, 1972 (with Ling Chung); *One Hundred More Poems from the Japanese*, 1974; *The Burning Heart: Women Poets of Japan*, 1977 (with Atsumi Ikuko); *Seasons of Sacred Lust: Selected Poems of Kazuko Shiraishi*, 1978; (with Carol Tinker, Atsumi Ikuko, John Solt, and Morita Yasuyo); *The Love Poems of Marichiko*, 1978; *Li Ch'ing Chao: Complete Poems*, 1979 (with Ling Chung).

MISCELLANEOUS: *The Kenneth Rexroth Reader*, 1972 (Eric Mottram, editor).

Bibliography

The Ark 14 (1980). This Festschrift honors Rexroth with entries by more than one hundred writers, critics, and friends. Includes brief tributes to the poet, essays (some especially helpful on the Japanese influences), drawings by Morris Graves, an introduction by the editor, and notes on the contributors.

Gibson, Morgan. *Kenneth Rexroth*. New York: Twayne, 1972. The first book-length study of Rexroth, this volume is a good introduction to his life and work. Chronological in approach, the book traces the step-by-step progression of Rexroth's career. Supplemented by a chronology, notes, a good select bibliography (including an annotated list of secondary sources), and an index.

_______. *Revolutionary Rexroth: Poet of East-West Wisdom*. Hamden, Conn.: Archon Books, 1986. This book expands *Kenneth Rexroth* (1972) in order to assess the poet's entire career. Benefiting from the close friendship with Rexroth, Gibson traces the evolution of themes and styles, and in separate chapters, analyzes the poems, plays, translations, and essays. Contains notes, a comprehensive bibliography (including an unannotated list of secondary sources), and an index.

Grisby, Gordon K. "The Presence of Reality: The Poetry of Kenneth Rexroth." *The Antioch Review* 31 (Fall, 1971): 405-422. Grisby links the directness and clarity of Rexroth's style to the nature of his vision. Influenced by Chinese poetry and the ideas of Martin Buber, Rexroth achieves a kind of wisdom. Many well-chosen examples from the poems illustrate the main themes of Rexroth's poetry.

Gutierrez, Donald. *The Holiness of the Real: The Short Verse of Kenneth Rexroth*. Madison, N.J.: Fairleigh Dickinson University Press, 1996. A critical study of selected poems by Rexroth. Includes bibliographical references and indexes. Divided into six chapters, the book provides a general introduction to Rexroth, covering his career, his position in American society, his prosody, influences on his verse, theorizing on his poetics, and discussion of why he has been ignored in academe. Four chapters deal with subjects in Rexroth's verse: nature, politics, love, and love-nature verse. The last chapter examines Rexroth as a literary and social critic-journalist.

_______. "Rexroth's 'Incarnation.'" *The Explicator* 53, no. 4 (Summer, 1995): 236. Rexroth's poem "Incarnation" consciously or subliminally startles and rivets the reader by offering a vision to a man coming down a mountain instead of going up it. Gutierrez explores how Rexroth renders sexual love in a context of nature so that nature ceases to be context.

Hamalian, Linda. *A Life of Kenneth Rexroth*. New York: W. W. Norton, 1991. The first book-length biography of Rexroth. Relies on extensive interviews with Rexroth and other key individuals. Illustrating both positive and negative qualities, this book corrects Rexroth's account in *An Autobiographical Novel* (1966).

Hartzell, James, and Richard Zumwinkle. *Kenneth Rexroth: A Checklist of His Published Writings*. Los Angeles: Friends of the University of California in Los Angeles Library, 1967. This bibliography, covering 1929 to 1965, illustrates the quantity and variety of Rexroth's writing. Most entries include brief descriptive but not evaluative annotations. The poems in Rexroth's collections are listed individually and in sequence. Ten illustrations give a good sense of the poet's personality. Contains a foreword by Lawrence Clark Powell.

Rexroth, Kenneth. "An Interview with Kenneth Rexroth." Interview by Cyrena N. Pondrom. *Contemporary Literature* 10 (Summer, 1969): 313-331. Reprinted in *The Contemporary Writer: Interviews with Sixteen Writers and Poets*, edited by L. S. Dembo and Cyrena N. Pondrom. Madison: University of Wisconsin Press, 1972. This thorough, excellent interview focuses on the mystical and philosophical ideas underlying Rexroth's poetry. Rexroth explains in detail the effects he tries to achieve in a poem. The influence of Asian culture, especially that of Buddhism, is abundantly illustrated.

Morgan Gibson;
bibliography updated by the editors

Alfonso Reyes

Born: Monterrey, Mexico; May 17, 1889
Died: Mexico City, Mexico; December 27, 1959

Principal poetry

Huellas, 1923
Ifigenia cruel, 1924
Pausa, 1926
Cinco casi sonetos, 1931
Romances del Rio de Enero, 1933
A la memoria de Ricardo Güiraldes, 1934
Golfo de Mexico, 1934 (*Gulf of Mexico*, 1949)
Yerbas del Tarahumara, 1934 (*Tarahumara Herbs*, 1949)
Infancia, 1935
Minuta, 1935
Otra voz, 1936
Cantata en la tumba de Federico García Lorca, 1937
Poema del Cid, 1938 (modern version of *Cantar de mío Cid*)
Villa de Unión, 1940
Algunos poemas, 1941
Romances y afines, 1945
La vega y el soto, 1946
Cortesía, 1948
Homero en Cuernavaca, 1949
Obra poética, 1952

Other literary forms

Alfonso Reyes was an essayist, short-story writer, and critic as well as a poet. Indeed, the bulk of the more than twenty volumes of his *Obras completas* (1955-1967; complete works)—an ongoing project undertaken by the Mexican Fondo de Cultura Económica to make accessible the seemingly inexhaustible archive of manuscripts and papers that he left behind—is criticism rather than poetry. Spanning cultures and disciplines, the breadth of his knowledge was truly astounding. His *Grata compañía* (1948; pleasing company), for example, includes essays on Robert Louis Stevenson, G. K. Chesterton, Marcel Proust, Jean-Jacques Rousseau, René Descartes, Jakob Burckhardt, José María Eça de Queiroz, Hermann Alexander Keyserling, Graça Aranha, Leopoldo Lugones, Miguel de Unamuno y Jugo, Antonio Caso, and Pedro Henríquez Ureña. In the fourteen issues of his personal newsletter, *Monterrey*, sent from Rio de Janeiro and Buenos Aires, he particularly liked to focus on the relationship of great European intellectual figures to the American experience: Johann Wolfgang von Goethe and the United States, Giuseppe Garibaldi and Cuba, Ramón del Valle-Inclán and Mexico, Luis de Góngora y Argote and New Spain, Paul Morand and Brazil, and so on.

Reyes's masterpiece, *Visión de Anáhuac* (1917; *Vision of Anáhuac*, 1950)—its title referring to the Aztec name for the Valley of Mexico, the site of the mighty Aztec capital, Tenochtitlán (today Mexico City)—written in Madrid in 1915, is a brilliant prose poem of some twenty-five pages depicting the Indian civilization on the eve of the Spanish conquest. *Cartones de Madrid* (1917; sketches of Madrid) is a collection of impressionistic essays. Reyes's essays are always lyric—even when they treat philosophical themes—and are

Alfonso Reyes (© Alberto Dallal)

often laced with humor. Some of his finest short stories, such as "La cena" (the dinner) and "La mano del comandante Aranda" ("Major Aranda's Hand"), blend a lyric realism with supernatural or fantastic elements, while others, such as "El testimonio de Juan Peña" (the testimony of Juan Peña) and "Silueta del indio Jesús" (silhouette of the Indian Jesus), treat indigenous themes. His best literary criticism is included in the essays of *La experiencia literaria* (1942; literary experience) and in "Sobre la estética de Góngora" (on the aesthetics of Góngora), an essay which contributed significantly to the modern reappraisal of the Baroque poet. In *El deslinde: Prolegómenos a la teoría literaria* (1944; the boundary line: prolegomenon to literary theory), he addressed a wide range of aesthetic questions, drawing on semantics, philology, and the philosophy of language.

Reyes was an avid translator. He rendered several of Chesterton's works, including a volume of his detective stories, *El candor de Padre Brown* (1921), into Spanish. He also translated *Olalla* (1922), by Stevenson, and *A Sentimental Journey* (1768), by Laurence Sterne (*Viaje sentimental por Francia e Italia*, 1919). Reyes's translation of the first nine books of the *Iliad* (c. 800 B.C.E.) as *La Ilíada de Homero* is considered the best available in Spanish, and he also produced a modern prose version of the *Cantar de mío Cid* (early thirteenth century) as *Poema del Cid*. He translated poems by Stéphane Mallarmé, José María de Hérédia, Robert Browning, Oliver Goldsmith, Dante, and Goethe, and, in conjunction with N. Tasin, a story by Anton Chekhov. Finally, Reyes produced Spanish versions of C. M. Bowra's *Ancient Greek Literature* (1933) as *Historia de la literatura griega* (1948), and Gilbert Murray's *Euripides and His Age* (1913) as *Eurípides y su época* (1949).

ACHIEVEMENTS

Alfonso Reyes strove indefatigably to draw the literature and culture of Latin America into the Latin cultural sphere of Spain, France, and Italy, and to effect a reconciliation between Spain and her former colonies. Indeed, his cosmopolitan spirit did much to internationalize a hitherto parochial Latin American literature. In his own country, he cast the light of Vergil and Goethe upon the Mexican landscape. Reyes assimilated a great deal from contemporary French writers such as André Gide, Paul Valéry, and Valéry Larbaud, and he maintained lifelong friendships and correspondences with the most influential Spanish intellectuals of his time—Unamuno, Valle-Inclán, José Ortega y Gasset, Juan Ramón Jiménez, and Ramón Gómez de la Serna. Reyes was able to disprove to the Spaniards by his own example the widely held opinion that Spanish-American writers were capable of nothing more inspired than exaggerated stylistic flourishes. As Mexican ambassador to Brazil, he worked to improve cultural relations between the Spanish-speaking countries and Brazil. He opened so many channels of communication with the outside world that Octavio Paz (quoting a phrase used in another context by Reyes himself) called him "the horseman of the air," and Xavier Villaurrutía dubbed him "the man of the roads."

Considering the unique nature of Reyes's literary contributions, he has neither direct antecedents nor direct successors in the Hispanic tradition, yet many have learned from his example. Octavio Paz has cited *La experiencia literaria* and *El deslinde* as works of particular value to him. Gabriela Mistral described *Vision of Anáhuac* as the best single piece of Latin American prose, and Valéry Larbaud and Juan José Domenchina have suggested that the work exercised an influence on the *Anabase* (1922; *Anabasis*, 1930) of Saint-John Perse.

In the realm of poetry, Reyes stands out as one of the first Latin American writers to incorporate into Spanish verse the casual tradition of the English lyric with its alternations of delicacy with diversion, seriousness with whimsy. As a critic working under the tutelage of Ramón Menéndez Pidal, Reyes wrote important analyses of past writers; in particular, he was instrumental in refurbishing the image of the seventeenth century poet, Góngora, a rediscovery of great importance to Spanish literature.

The University of California, the University of Michoácan, and the University of Mexico, as well as Tulane University, Havana University, Harvard University, and Princeton University, awarded honorary degrees to Reyes. He received the Premio Nacional de Ciencias y Artes (National Prize for Arts and Sciences) in 1945 and in 1957 was named president of the Mexican Academy after having been a member for nearly forty years.

Biography

Alfonso Reyes was born in Monterrey, Nuevo León, Mexico, the ninth of twelve children born to General Bernardo Reyes and Aurelia Ochoa, both of whom were from the environs of Guadalajara in the state of Jalisco. General Reyes (1850-1913), himself the author of an array of military manuals, brochures, and histories, was an enlightened and efficient governor of the state of Nuevo León and was largely responsible for the progressive spirit which obtains in Monterrey even today. Of his early years, Reyes wrote in "Sol de Monterrey" ("Monterrey Sun"), "I knew no shadow in my childhood,/ only the brilliance of the sun"; a sun that followed at his heels "like a Pekinese." Reyes entered the Escuela Nacional Preparatoria in Mexico City in 1905, and went on to the Escuela Nacional de Altos Estudios. Mexico at that time was in the tight grip of the dictator Porfirio Díaz, and although the positivist milieu that Díaz encouraged was not favorable to the study of the humanities, Reyes immersed himself in the study of the classics.

Reyes married Manela Mota in 1911, and their only child, Alfonso, was born in 1912. The following year, Reyes received a law degree from the University of Mexico. He became the youngest member of the Centennial Generation (which included Pedro Henríquez Ureña, Antonio Caso, and José Vasconcelos), a group dedicated to changing the official modes of thought in Mexico. Reyes also helped to found the Ateneo de la Juventud (Athenaeum of Youth), an institution for young intellectuals that flourished until 1940.

When Porfirio Díaz was ousted by Francisco Madero in 1910, Mexico was thrown into a welter of revolt and banditry. Before dawn on February 9, 1913, rebel troops tried to install as head of state General Bernardo Reyes, long viewed as a successor to the aging dictator Díaz. General Reyes was shot to death in street fighting at the Zocalo in Mexico City; seventeen years later, his son honored General Reyes—that "tower of a man"—in a prose elegy, "Oración del 9 de febrero de 1913" ("Prayer of the Ninth of February"), giving Reyes the opportunity to observe in himself a "presentiment of an obscure equivocation in the moral clockwork of our world." There is also a four-stanza poem on the same subject, "+9 de febrero de 1913," in which the poet asks, "Where are you, man of seven wounds,/ blood spurting at midday?" and proceeds to promise that "if I have continued to live since that day,/ it is because I carry you with me, where you are inviolable."

In August of that same year, Reyes went to Paris as second secretary of the Mexican Legation. The following year, he gravitated to Madrid, where he earned a meager living from journalism. He soon became associated with the famous Center of Historical Studies in Madrid, directed by Ramón Menéndez Pidal, and made valuable contributions to the *Revista de filología española*. He worked in the company of such scholars as Américo Castro, Federico de Onís, Tomás Navarro Tomás, Antonio Solalinde, all of whom Reyes called "the princes of Spanish philology" and into whose society he was readily admitted. Reminiscing years later about those days in Madrid, Reyes wrote that literature had been everywhere—in the air, in the cafés, and in the streets.

In 1927, Reyes returned to Mexico and became the Mexican ambassador to Argentina, where he remained until 1930, when he went to Rio de Janeiro as ambassador to Brazil. In 1939, he returned to Mexico to stay, after nearly twenty-five years of almost continuous diplomatic service. He proceeded to establish two great educational institutions: the group of scholars called El Colegio Nacional and the graduate school of the humanities, El Colegio de México. His home in Mexico City included a magnificent library that became for Reyes a sanctuary of the muses; the library was dubbed "Capilla Alfonsina" (Alfonsine Chapel) by his friend, Enrique Díez-Canedo, a Spanish poet.

At the age of seventy, Reyes succumbed to the last of a series of heart attacks and was buried in the Rotonda de los Hombres Ilustres in the Panteón Civil de Dolores in Mexico City. His wife was killed in an accident in 1965, and their granddaughter, Alicia Reyes, directs the Alfonsine Chapel, used as a research center and sponsored by the Mexican government.

Analysis

Like his contemporaries, the Argentine Ricardo Güiraldes, the Chilean Pedro Prado, and the Colombian José Eustasio Rivera, Alfonso Reyes was above all a writer of prose, yet at no time in his life did he cease to write poetry. He began to write verse at an early age, and his first poems appeared in print when he was sixteen. The poems reflect his love for ancient Greece and for the sculptures of Phidias and Praxiteles. Reyes's first book of verse, *Huellas* (footprints), containing pieces from the years 1906 to 1919, appeared in 1923. These poems reveal a Parnassian influence evident in the works of other Latin American poets of the time, yet they already showed some of Reyes's characteristic variety of subject matter, mood, and style. Later, he would make use of realism (especially in his descriptions of Mexico) and Surrealism in *Gulf of Mexico*.

There is something of the dilettante about Reyes the poet; chatting with or about his friends, musing over feminine beauty, worrying about death, reworking the *ubi sunt* commonplace, or simply delighting in intellectual silliness. "I prefer to be promiscuous/ in literature," Reyes wrote in the poem "Teoría prosaica" ("Prose Theory"), claiming further that he preferred the antiquated measurements of the *almud*, the *vara*, and the *cuarterón* to the metric system. Reyes kept his poetic sanity by alternating "the popular ballad/ of my neighbor/ with the rare quintessence/ of Góngora and Mallarmé."

Exhaustive vocabulary

A traveler and an explorer in different worlds, Reyes made use of everyday speech, the Greek chorus, the monologue of Mallarmé, the Spanish of the Golden Age, and names from the Tarahumara pharmacopoeia. Reyes exhausted all sources of Spanish vocabulary. In his poems, there are Latin expressions, Greek words, and obscure Arabisms not normally used in conversational language–*alcatraz* (cornucopia), *almirez* (brass mortar), *alquitara* (still)—yet none of these occurs in such profusion or within such complicated syntax as to overwhelm the reader. Reyes delighted in placenames, in words peculiar to certain countries that gave his work local color–*ñañigo* (member of a secret Cuban society of blacks), *tamanco* (Brazilian sandal)—and in chatty words–*corretón* (gadding about), *copetín* (little goblet). He frequently repeated synonymous or near-synonymous words in the same line, as if searching for maximum precision–*curuja, buho* (both meaning "owl"); *alfónsigo, pistacho* (both meaning "pistachio"); and *tierra, terrena, terruño* (all meaning "land").

Epithets

Reyes was also fond of epithets. His father is the "ruddy lion," Benito Juárez is the "master of the bow" whose arrows "fastened in the heavens' red meteors," and the American Hispanist Sylvanus Griswold Morley is the "California Quijote." Occasionally, Reyes embedded in his poetry significant lines from Dante or Mallarmé in the original Italian or French. Nothing was alien to Reyes, and the world that he inhabited is "our" world rather than "the" world. The statue of David in Florence is "my" David, the street in Rio de Janeiro where he lived is "my" rua de Laranjeiras, and his native city, Monterrey, was so much his that he marveled at why he had never attached its name to his own. He sometimes spoke of himself as Alfonso in his poems and especially delighted in words or neologisms that resembled his name, such as *alfónsigo* (pistachio), *alfonsecuente* (on the model of *consecuente*, coherent, or "Alfonso-coherent").

Hellenism

Reyes considered even the humblest subject matter worthy of poetry, and much of his charm stems from his ability to popularize intellectual material. He demonstrated his love of Greek mythology and Hellenism in his verse play, *Ifigenia cruel*, which is crafted in the simplest language. Here, he converted the Euripidean heroine into a formidable Amazon torn between her career as a sacrificial priestess and her desire for her home. Eventually, she opts for the former; as Barbara Bockus Aponte observes, the Iphigenia who prefers her liberty to the tradition of her home in Greece is the Reyes who left behind the strife of Mexico and abjured thoughts of vengeance in the search for his own freedom.

Reyes's Hellenism is evident as well in *Homero en Cuernavaca* (Homer in Cuernavaca), comprising thirty sonnets that are sometimes romantic but just as often satirical (as in "De Helena"). In these poems, as well as in *Ifigenia cruel*, the language is kept simple.

"Lamentación de Navidad" and "Jacob"

While the Bible did not inspire Reyes as much as did the *Iliad*, a biblical influence is nevertheless apparent in his poetry. His "Lamentación de Navidad" (Christmas lament) ends with a prayer that the poet be given works to accomplish or be made to fly like the seeds to settle eventually on fertile ground. He utilized the theme of Jacob wrestling with the angel (his "white enemy") in "Jacob," which Reyes narrates in the first person, and this poem, too, ends with a prayer that the angel win the match. Reyes used the same theme in his essay "Jacob o la idea de la poesía" (Jacob or the idea of poetry), in which he describes the artistic process as a struggle with "lo inefable" (the unutterable).

"Sopa"

Typical of Reyes's mixture of learning and playfulness are his poems titled *Minuta* (menu)—poems about such "unpoetic" subjects as soup, bread, salad, a plate of almonds. His two-stanza poem "Sopa" (soup), for example, is introduced by an epigraph from Saint Theresa ("between the soup pots walks the Lord"). In a simple four-line poem, Reyes honored the aperitif: "Exquisite collaboration/ of host and hostess;/ the ice of the visit is broken/ in the glass that brings good cheer." Elsewhere, Reyes reminded his readers that gastronomic concerns have always occupied an important place in Hispanic literary tradition, citing *La celestina* (1499; *The Spanish Bawd*, 1634), *Don Quixote de la Mancha* (1605, 1615; English translation, 1652), and *La lozana andaluza* (1528).

Reyes was clearly one of the most brilliant and versatile writers in modern Spanish, yet his great gifts never produced the masterpieces that his readers expected from him. His most lasting contribution to Latin American culture lies in his example as an international man of letters, a lover of literature, and a tireless cultural activist.

Other major works

long fiction: *Viaje sentimental por Francia e Italia*, 1919.

short fiction: *El plano oblicuo*, 1920; *El candor de Padre Brown*, 1921; *Olalla*, 1922; *Quince presencias*, 1955; *Alfonso Reyes: Prosa y Poesía*, 1977 (includes "Major Aranda's Hand," "Silueta del indio Jesús," and "El testimonio de Juan Peña").

nonfiction: *Cuestiones estéticas*, 1911; *Cartones de Madrid*, 1917; *Visión de Anáhuac*, 1917 (*Vision of Anáhuac*, 1950); *Retratos reales e imaginarios*, 1920; *Simpatías y diferencias*, 1921-1926; *Cuestiones gongorinas*, 1927; *Capítulos de literatura española*, 1939; *La crítica en la edad ateniense*, 1941; *La experiencia literaria*, 1942; *Ultima Thule*, 1942; *El deslinde: Prolegómenos a la teoría literaria*, 1944; *Grata compañía*, 1948; *Historia de la literatura griega*, 1948; *Eurípides y su época*, 1949; *The Position of America and Other Essays*, 1950 (includes *Vision of Anáhuac*); *Parentalia: Primer libro de recuerdos*, 1954; *Albores: segundo libro de recuerdos*, 1960; *Mexico in a Nutshell and Other Essays*, 1964.

translations: *Viaje sentimental por Francia e Italia*, 1919 (of Lawrence Sterne's *A Sentimental Journey*); *El candor de Padre Brown*, 1921 (of G. K. Chesterton's detective stories); *Olalla*, 1922 (of Robert Louis Stevenson's stories); *Historia de la literatura griega*, 1948 (of C. M. Bowra's *Ancient Greek Literature*); *Eurípides y su época*, 1949 (of Gilbert Murray's *Euripides and His Age*).

miscellaneous: *Obras completas*, 1955-1967.

Bibliography

Aponte, Barbara Bockus. *Alfonso Reyes and Spain*. Austin: University of Texas Press, 1972. The author explores the dialogues that Reyes maintained with Miguel de Unamuno y Jugo, Ramón del Valle-Inclán, José Ortega y Gasset, Juan Ramón Jimémez, and other Peninsular literary contemporaries. Their correspondence sheds light upon the lives and works of all these writers. Reyes relied upon this form of communication to maintain friendships and share ideas. As a member of the Mexican intellectual elite, Reyes recognized that his Spanish contacts were vital to his literary development.

Carter, Sheila. *The Literary Experience*. Mona, Jamaica: Savacou, 1985. A critical analysis of *El deslinde* with bibliographic references.

Robb, James W. *El estilo de Alfonso Reyes: Imagen y estructura*. Mexico City: Fondo de Cultura Económica, 1978. This thorough study of representative poetry and prose writings elaborates upon a 1975 study by Robb, *Prosa y poesía/ Alfonso Reyes*. The authority on Reyes's life and works analyzes a variety of styles and techniques and their evolution during a long and prolific writing career. The critic and biographer focuses on Reyes's early poems and essays. A chronological panorama of genres mastered by Reyes is elucidated in this authoritative study by Robb. In Spanish.

_______. *Estudios sobre Alfonso Reyes*. Bogotá: Ediciones El Dorado, 1976. Robb collects a variety of essays on Reyes. Topics include a discussion of similarities and differences between Jorge Luis Borges and Reyes, images of America through portrayals by Germán Arciniegas and Reyes, and his mastery of narrative style in essays and other prose works. These essays are not included in Robb's other studies. In Spanish.

_______. *Patterns of Image and Structure*. New York: AMS Press, 1969. Critical analysis of the essays of Alfonso Reyes.

Trend, J. B. *Alfonso Reyes*. Cambridge, England, 1952. A brief biography of Reyes.

Jack Shreve;
bibliography updated by Carole A. Champagne

Charles Reznikoff

Born: Brooklyn, New York; August 31, 1894
Died: New York, New York; January 22, 1976

Principal poetry

Rhythms, 1918
Rhythms II, 1919
Poems, 1920
Uriel Accosta: A Play and a Fourth Group of Verse, 1921
Jerusalem the Golden, 1934
Separate Way, 1936
Going To and Fro and Walking Up and Down, 1941
By the Waters of Manhattan: Selected Verse, 1962
Testimony: The United States, 1885-1890—Recitative, 1965
By the Well of Living and Seeing: New and Selected Poems, 1918-1973, 1974
Holocaust, 1975
Poems, 1918-1936: Volume I of the Complete Poems of Charles Reznikoff, 1976
Poems, 1937-1975: Volume II of the Complete Poems of Charles Reznikoff, 1977
Poems, 1918-1975: The Complete Poems of Charles Reznikoff, 1989
Testimony: The United States, 1885-1915—Recitative, 1978-1979 (2 volumes).

Other literary forms

In addition to poetry, Charles Reznikoff wrote fiction and verse drama and was active as a translator, historian, and editor. His novels include *By the Waters of Manhattan* (1930), a title Reznikoff also used for a later collection of his poetry, and *The Manner "Music"* (1977). The novels, as well as his historical work such as *Early History of a Sewing Machine Operator* (1936), are, like his poetry, sharply observed but detached, nearly autobiographical accounts and impressions of family and working life. Although thematically much of his fiction may be compared with the "proletarian" literature of the 1930's, its spareness and restraint give it a highly individual stamp. Reznikoff also wrote a historical novel, *The Lionhearted: A Story About the Jews in*

Medieval England (1944), which portrays the fate of English Jewry during the reign of Richard the Lionhearted.

Reznikoff's verse plays, such as *Uriel Accosta* (1921) and *Meriwether Lewis's: Three Plays* (1922), extend his interest in the individual in history along dramatic lines. The plays make use of choruslike recitations both to convey offstage occurrence and to develop character much in the manner of the classical theater.

Reznikoff was the editor of the collected papers of Louis Marshall and a translator of two volumes of Yiddish stories and history. Much of his work in law was in writing and editing for the legal encyclopedia *Corpus Juris*. His few prose comments on the art of writing poetry are contained in a slim volume of prose titled *First, There Is the Need* (1977).

Achievements

A rubric for Charles Reznikoff's career might well read: early, nearly precocious development; late recognition. Reznikoff, without ever seeking to be unique, was one of the twentieth century's most original writers virtually with the publication of his first work. His abandonment, as early as 1918, of the verse conventions of late nineteenth century poetry and his utilization of prose-like rhythms anticipate a kind of American plain song which is to be found in the work of the most diverse poets writing today. Reznikoff, in reinventing the image as an element of realist rather than symbolic notation, also made a significant contribution to the notion of imagery as the cornerstone of the modern poem.

His highly unconventional and imaginative use of historical materials sets him off from the vogues of confessional and psychological poetry, but only in his later years did literary critics begin to appreciate the unprecedented and original manner in which Reznikoff brought history, both contemporary and biblical, alive. In 1971, he was the recipient of the Morton Dauwen Zabel Award for Poetry from the National Institute of Arts and Letters.

Biography

Born in a Jewish ghetto in Brooklyn and ultimately to live most of his life in New York City, Charles Reznikoff drew, for all his writing, on the very circumstances and surroundings of his life. Like his near-contemporary, William Carlos Williams, the "local" was to be the source of all that was universal in his work. Reznikoff sought out his poems not only in the lives of those around him, in the newly immigrant populations seething in the New York streets, but also in the European and biblical histories, and even customs, which these immigrant groups had brought with them to the New World.

Graduating from a high school in Brooklyn, Reznikoff spent a year at the new School of Journalism of the University of Missouri but returned to New York to enter the New York University Law School, a decisive move for both his livelihood and his poetry. The influence of his legal training and his work in law were to affect his notions of poetry profoundly; his love of "the daylight meaning of words," as he put it in one of his autobiographical poems, stemmed from this education, and it was this sense of language that from the beginning Reznikoff developed into one of the most unique and moving bodies of contemporary poetry. Reznikoff actually practiced law only briefly; he worked a number of years for *Corpus Juris*, the legal encyclopedia, however, and maintained his interest in the law throughout his entire career.

Except for short sojourns elsewhere, Reznikoff lived and worked in New York City. One three-year period, however, was spent in Hollywood working for a film producer; this visit was the source of some of Reznikoff's wittiest verse and furnished the background for his novel *The Manner "Music."* On his return to New York from Hollywood, Reznikoff took up freelance writing, editing, and translating.

Reznikoff was one of the city's great walkers; late in his life, he would still stroll for miles on foot through the city's parks and streets. In this regard, he was close to the boulevardiers and *flâneurs* of nineteenth century Paris so aptly described by Walter Benjamin. Like them, he was attracted to the anonymity of the solitary walker, to the possibility of a simultaneous distance and engagement. Out of such walks, Reznikoff fashioned an extraordinary body of poetry, one which only now after his death is receiving adequate critical attention. From younger poets and from those poets around him, George Oppen, Louis Zukofsky, and William Carlos Williams, attention had been there from the beginning. Reznikoff had early discovered something new and of major importance in the writing of poetry and stayed with it, despite neglect, throughout his long and fruitful life.

Analysis

Of all the poets loosely gathered under the Objectivist label coined by Zukofsky for Harriet Monroe's *Poetry* magazine in 1931, none seems to have been quite as "objective" as Charles Reznikoff. In him, legal training and the moral imperative of the Jew as a historical witness combine with the Objectivist and Imagist principles, which guided such writers as William Carlos Williams and Louis Zukofsky, to produce a body of poetry distinguished by its clarity, judgment, and tact. This notion of witness or bystander, of someone who is at the scene of events but not of the events themselves, is implicit in all Reznikoff's work. Such titles as *By the Waters of Manhattan*, *Testimony*, *Separate Way*, *Going To and Fro and Walking Up and Down*, and *By the Well of Living and Seeing* are indicative of a poetic stance that was to be, as Reznikoff once put it, "content at the periphery of such wonder." This wonder was to embrace both the urban experience, in particular its relation to the life of newly immigrant Jews, but also to range across such topics as early Jewish history, legal proceedings in nineteenth and twentieth century America, and the Holocaust of European Jewry.

The urban environment

Reznikoff's stance is not so much concerned with a conventional sense of poetic distance or with irony per se as with precision of realization. The modern city, the source of much of Reznikoff's most memorable work, is for him a place one continually passes through, a locus of large anonymous forces encountered tangentially yet which overshadow and overwhelm the experience of the city inhabitant. The truths of the city are multiple, highly individualized, and—in Reznikoff—caught not as part of some grand design but as minor resistance to its forces. Victories and defeats occur not in the towers and offices of government but in street corner and kitchen tableaux in which individual fate is registered. Thus, in his work, the urban environment and the lives caught up in the vast workings of the city and of history tend to remain resolutely what they are, to resist being read analogically or symbolically. The poems hover on the edge of factual materiality with few gestures toward the literary. Yet their construction has a cleanliness and freshness found in few other contemporaries. One goes to Reznikoff's work not only for its poetic beauty and its surety of language but also for its historical testimony.

Imagism vs. image

Reznikoff began to publish his work in 1918, when the traditionalist devices of fixed meter and rhyme were already under attack from Ezra Pound's and T. S. Eliot's modernism. Yet Reznikoff was not to traffic in the obviously unconventional or extreme writing of the early twentieth century avant-grade. Even the Imagist movement, which certainly influenced Reznikoff and to which he pays homage, was refined and transmuted by him into something that would not be particularly recognizable to the founders of the movement. The "image" of the Imagists was something decidedly literary, something used for its allusive or symbolic effect, whereas in Reznikoff it becomes a construction, made out of observation and precise detail, concerned primarily to render a datum.

This "nonliterary" use of the image characterizes all Reznikoff's work. His poems strike the reader almost as a kind of low-key reportage, making use of proselike speech rhythms and barely discernible shifts in discourse from statement to simile or metaphor, as in this early example: "Suddenly we noticed we were in darkness/ So we went into the house and lit the lamp/ And sat around, dark spaces about a sun." This shorn-down language inhabits a number of linguistic realms at once; the datum and its meaning for the poet are so inextricably linked that the usual suspension of belief or accounting for poetic license no longer applies. The poetry has about it a "documentary" effect, one that is both tactful and powerful by virtue of its being stripped, it would seem, of any attempt by the poet to persuade.

Reznikoff's poetry can be likened to the photograph, something profoundly and intimately linked to the visible world, and yet, by virtue of the camera angle or constraint of the frame, necessarily and profoundly something selected. Like photographs, in which what is beyond the frame may be hinted at by that which is included, Reznikoff's poems, while framing actual particularities and occasions, resonate with a life of associations far beyond the frame of the image which the language constructs. This image, less metaphoric than informative, becomes a possibility for emotional response but not an occasion for dictating it. If through Reznikoff one sees or knows a certain life intimately, a history, custom or usage, it is because in his work the lyricist and the chronicler are joined with minimal rhetorical flourish.

Recitative

This poetic technique, which Reznikoff called "recitative," stresses the evidential or communicative aspect of language over the figurative; it unites all Reznikoff's work, from the early *Rhythms* published in 1918 up to and through the late volumes *Testimony* and *Holocaust*. This minimal use of poetic devices such as rhyme, metaphor, or exaggerated imagery results in a restrained tone that balances irony, sarcasm, and humor with emotional distance. It is particularly apt for the short two- or three-line poem (one of Reznikoff's trademarks) that combines a wise knowingness and bleak hilarity, as in: "Permit me to warn you/ against this automobile rushing to embrace you/ with outstretched fender." It also attains a meditative strength, as in: "Among the heaps of brick and plaster lies/ a girder, still itself among the rubbish." Here, the double reading of "still itself" transforms the poem from mere description to enigmatic philosophy.

Such surety of technique makes Reznikoff's poems radiate with both completeness of finish *and* mystery, as though their author, while knowing much, says little. Indeed, they sustain an aphoristic or epigrammatic tone, even in poems of great length and over a wide variety of subject matter.

In Reznikoff, this reticence has little to do with modesty. Rather, understatement becomes a device for achieving accurate registration, for giving subjects their due in the reader's mind by not imposing attitudes or judgments on experience. It is, in its way, a form of humility, a desire, as Reznikoff noted, that "we, whose lives are only a few words" meet in the thing seen not in the personality of the see-er.

Solitude of the moral witness

At the very center of Reznikoff's writing, concomitant with the objectivity of his technique, is the aloneness of the moral witness, of a deep and abiding solitude that moved C. P. Snow, in commenting on Reznikoff's work, to regard him as a lonely writer. In Reznikoff, this isolation is less a product of experience than of fundamental choice. As he says of his life in the poem "Autobiography: New York": "I am alone—and glad to be alone . . . I like the sound of the street—but I, apart and alone,/ beside an open window/ and behind a closed door." This desire for isolation, for witnessing as from a distance, can be traced back to the traditions embedded in Jewish religious and philosophical works which influenced him. In the Cabalistic tradition which informs Reznikoff's work, language, as Gershom Scholem notes, "reflects the fundamental spiritual nature of the world." The Cabalists, Scholem points out, "revel in objective description." This sacred attitude toward language is manifest in Reznikoff. As he says in one of his poems, "I have learned the Hebrew blessing before eating bread./ Is there no blessing before reading Hebrew?"

Coupled with this respect for language is the influence of Reznikoff's early legal training on his poetic style. As he relates of his law school days: "I found it delightful . . ./ to use words for their daylight meaning/ and not as prisms/ playing with the rainbows of connotation." Like Williams, Reznikoff seems to have thoroughly refused the artifice of high style in favor of the "daylight meaning" of words, to produce a style which is at once humane and communicative.

As Reznikoff's few prose comments on his poetry make clear, craft and technique stem for him from communicative and ethical concerns as opposed to literary ones, and it is this urge to communicate which is his primary motive. One finds in his work that nearly lost sense of the poet as reteller of tales as tribal historian. The poet, according to Reznikoff (perhaps in particular the Jewish poet of the People of the Book) stands always with history at his back. For such a poet, the work is not one of self-expression but of a desire to be an agency for those voices lost or denied in time, for individuals caught up in historical forces beyond their control.

Jews in Babylonia

This urge to reclaim in Reznikoff has deeper implications, however, as demonstrated in one of Reznikoff's longer historical poems, *Jews in Babylonia*, where a collagist technique initially yokes natural phenomena—the passing of seasons, growth of plants, and the behavior of animals—with simple actions of the biblical tradesmen: "Plane the wood into boards; chisel the stone." The rhythms here are stately and the imagery peaceful. As the poem continues, however, the harmony begins to come apart. Now there is "A beast with its load/ and a bit in its mouth" and "the horn gores/ the hoof kicks/ the teeth bite." The shift in tone becomes even more "unnatural": "The bread has become moldy/ and the dates blown down by the wind . . . the dead woman has forgotten her comb." The lines become a litany of ruin and decay which has both historical and metaphysical implications: "But where are the dead of the Flood . . . the dead of Nebuchadnezzar?" until finally the images express a kind of visionary chaos where "the hyena will turn into a bat/ and a bat will turn into a thorn," where what is seen is "the blood of his wounds/ and the tears of her eyes" and "the Angel of Death in time of war/ does not distinguish/ between the righteous and the wicked."

The effect of this technique is to create something that seems at once cinematic and apocalyptic, forcefully in keeping with the historical situation itself while at the same time suggesting both foreboding and prophecy. In this regard, Reznikoff's work is no simple addition or nostalgic reminder of the past but, like the songs and poems of the biblical prophets, a potential guide to personal and social action. As he says of his grandfather's lost poetry in "By the Well of Living and Seeing": "All the verse he wrote was lost—except for what/ still speaks through me/ as mine."

Testimony and Holocaust

It is in Reznikoff's most difficult and controversial works, *Testimony* and *Holocaust*, that his sense of historical urgency and the need to testify culminate. In these works, Reznikoff may be said to have created a new poetic form (or as some critics have claimed, absence of form) which is meant to do justice to the full weight of man's inhumanity to man. In these two works, legal records—American courtroom proceedings in *Testimony* and the Nuremberg war crimes trials and the accounts of victims and witnesses in the case of *Holocaust*—are unsparingly worked into verse form, shorn of poetic devices. The author's hand appears solely in the austere editing and lineation of the historical record. Here, the "poetic" by its very absence in the poetry seems to be both witness and prosecutor, a reminder to the reader not only of the events that have occurred but also the life, grace, and possibility denied by the events. The works curiously penetrate the reader's consciousness since, by leaving all the individual interpretation, they undermine, in their account of devastating cruelty and horror, the reader's conventional notions of civilization and culture.

Such penetration, accomplished in such a "hands off" manner, has the further effect of evoking and calling to account the reader's humanity. It is this effect which gives Reznikoff's "objectivity" such moral power. This wedding of artistic means and the procedures of the law courts gives to Reznikoff's work a unique contemporaneity, one which honors and respects the individual while in no way striving for egocentric novelty. This is a *communitas* at its most moving and profound. It can be said of Reznikoff that he is one of the few contemporary poets to have transformed literary artistry into a major historical vision.

Other major works

LONG FICTION: *By the Waters of Manhattan*, 1930; *The Lionhearted: A Story About the Jews in Medieval England*, 1944; *The Manner "Music,"* 1977

PLAYS: *Uriel Accosta: A Play and a Fourth Group of Verse*, pb. 1921; *Chatterton, The Black Death, and Meriwether Lewis: Three Plays*, pb. 1922; *Coral and Captive Israel: Two Plays*, pb. 1923.

NONFICTION: *Early History of a Sewing Machine Operator*, 1936; *First, There Is the Need*, 1977; *Selected Letters of Charles Reznikoff, 1917-1976*, 1997.

TRANSLATIONS: *Stories and Fantasies from the Jewish Past*, 1951 (of Emil Cohn); *Three Years in America, 1859-1862*, 1956 (of Israel Joseph Benjamin).

EDITED TEXT: *Louis Marshall, Champion of Liberty; Selected Papers and Addresses*, 1957 (2 volumes).

Bibliography

Fredman, Stephen. *A Menorah for Athena: Charles Reznikoff and the Jewish Dilemmas of Objectivist Poetry*. Chicago: University of Chicago Press, 2001.

An analysis of the poetry of Reznikoff and objectivity in literature. Includes bibliographical references and index.

Gefin, Laszlo K. *Ideogram: History of a Poetic Method.* Austin: University of Texas Press, 1982. Gefin cites Reznikoff as one of the poets who use the synthetical or ideogrammatic method in their poetry. He sees this composition as an "aesthetic form extending from a postlogical and even posthumanist consciousness." In the chapter titled "Sincerity and Objectification," Gefin remarks on the influence of Chinese poetry on Reznikoff and, at the same time, calls him the "Giacometti of poetry," because he pares down his words to bare essentials.

Heller, Michael. "Reznikoff's Modernity." *The American Book Review* 2 (July/August, 1980): 3. Reviews a number of Reznikoff's works in the light of modernism. States that this poet stands out in the continuity of his work rather than the more usual modernist discontinuity. Admires Reznikoff's restraint and his ability to allow readers to come to their own conclusions.

Hindus, Milton. *Charles Reznikoff: Man and Poet.* Orono, Maine: National Poetry Foundation, 1984. A full-length study, initially conceived to correct the relative obscurity and neglect dealt to Reznikoff. Half the volume is devoted to the author's personal accounts of Reznikoff's life; the latter half is a compilation of important critical essays on his poetry. Includes a section on his prose and concludes with a useful and thorough annotated bibliography of his works. Highly recommended for Reznikoff's scholars.

Lehman, David. Review of *Holocaust. Poetry* 128 (April, 1976): 37-45. In reviewing *Holocaust*, Lehman does not really classify Reznikoff as an Objectivist because of his "authentic and original voice." He cites his capacity for irony along with human sympathy, considered a rarity in American poets and praises Reznikoff for opening the "mouth of suffering" and making it "quiver with the voice of survival."

Reznikoff, Charles. *Family Chronicle.* New York: Markus Wiener, 1988. A fascinating background account of the Reznikoff family, from their origins in Russia to their immigration to America and establishment in New York. Contains three accounts of family members, including "Needle Trade," an autobiographical piece by Charles Reznikoff, and much useful information that illuminates the themes in his poetry.

_______. *Selected Letters of Charles Reznikoff, 1917-1976.* Edited by Milton Hindus. Santa Rosa, Calif.: Black Sparrow Press, 1997. A collection of letters which reveal some of the poet, but much more of the man. Includes an essay by Hindus on Reznikoff's life and work.

Michael Heller;
bibliography updated by the editors

Adrienne Rich

Born: Baltimore, Maryland; May 16, 1929

Principal poetry

A Change of World, 1951
The Diamond Cutters and Other Poems, 1955
Snapshots of a Daughter-in-Law, 1963
Necessities of Life, 1966
Selected Poems, 1967
Leaflets, 1969
The Will to Change, 1971
Diving into the Wreck, 1973
Poems: Selected and New, 1950-1974, 1975
Twenty-one Love Poems, 1975
The Dream of a Common Language, 1978
A Wild Patience Has Taken Me This Far, 1981
Sources, 1983
The Fact of a Doorframe: Poems Selected and New, 1950-1984, 1984
Your Native Land, Your Life, 1986
Time's Power: Poems, 1985-1988, 1989
An Atlas of the Difficult World: Poems, 1988-1991, 1991
Collected Early Poems, 1950-1970, 1993
Dark Fields of the Republic: Poems, 1991-1995, 1995

Selected Poems, 1950-1995, 1996
Midnight Salvage: Poems, 1995-1998, 1999
Fox: Poems, 1998-2000, 2001

Other literary forms

Adrienne Rich is known primarily for her poetry, but she has produced essays on writing and politics as well: *Of Woman Born: Motherhood as Experience and Institution* (1976) is an analysis of the changing meanings of childbirth and motherhood in Anglo-American culture, in which Rich draws upon personal experience as well as sources in mythology, sociology, economics, the history of medicine, and literature to develop her analysis. *On Lies, Secrets, and Silences: Selected Prose, 1966-1978* (1979) is a collection of essays on women writers (including Anne Bradstreet, Anne Sexton, Charlotte Brontë, and Emily Dickinson) and feminism. *Blood, Bread, and Poetry: Selected Prose, 1979-1985* (1986) followed with further essays on women writers and feminist criticism. *What Is Found There: Notebooks on Poetry and Politics* (1993) delivers just what the title promises. For several years Rich also coedited, with Michelle Cliff, the lesbian feminist journal *Sinister Wisdom*.

Achievements

Adrienne Rich's work has been at the vanguard of the women's movement in the United States. Her poems and essays explore her own experience and seek to develop a "common language" for women to communicate their values and perceptions. She has received numerous awards, including two Guggenheim fellowships, the National Institute of Arts and Letters award for poetry (1960), several prizes from *Poetry* magazine, the first annual Ruth Lilly Poetry Prize, the Shelley Memorial Award of the Poetry Society of America (1971), and the National Book Award for *Diving into the Wreck* in 1974. Other recognitions include the Lenore Marshall Poetry Prize, a MacArthur Fellowship, the Wallace Stevens Award, the Frost Medal and the Lifetime Achievement Award from the Lannan Foundation.

Biography

Adrienne Cecil Rich was born in 1929, into a white, middle-class Southern family. Her Jewish father, Arnold Rice Rich, taught medicine at The Johns Hopkins University. Her southern Protestant mother, Helen Jones Rich, was trained as a composer and concert pianist but gave up her career to devote herself to her husband and two daughters. She carried out their early education at home, until the girls began to attend school in fourth grade. Arnold Rich encouraged his daughter to read and to write poetry. From his library, she read the work of such writers as Matthew Arnold, William Blake, Thomas Carlyle, John Keats, Dante Gabriel Rossetti, and Alfred, Lord Tennyson. Rich was graduated from Radcliffe College in 1951, the year her first volume of poetry was published. She traveled in Europe and England on a Guggenheim Fellowship in 1952-1953.

Rich married Alfred H. Conrad in 1953 and in the next few years gave birth to three sons, David (1955), Paul (1957), and Jacob (1959). She lived with her family in Cambridge, Massachusetts, from 1953 to 1966, but spent 1961-1962 in the Netherlands on another Guggenheim Fellowship. In 1964, Rich began her involve-

Adrienne Rich (Library of Congress)

ment in the New Left, initiating a period of personal and political growth and crisis. In 1966, the family moved to New York, where Conrad taught at City College of New York. Rich also began to teach at City College, where she worked for the first time with disadvantaged students. In 1970, Rich ended her marriage, and latter the same year Conrad ended his life. Rich continued teaching at City College and then Rutgers University until 1979, when she moved to western Massachusetts. Poems of these years explore her lesbian relationships.

Rich eventually moved to northern California to continue her active career as poet, essayist, and sought-after speaker. Rich spent time in the 1980's and early 1990's at numerous California colleges and universities, acting as visiting professor and lecturer. Her stops included Scripps College, San Jose State University, and Stanford University. In 1992, she accepted the National Director of The National Writer's Voice Project. In the 1990's she joined several advisory boards, including the Boston Woman's Fund, National Writers Union, Sisterhood in Support of Sisters in South Africa, and New Jewish Agenda.

Analysis

Adrienne Rich's successive volumes of poetry chronicle a contemporary woman artist's odyssey. Her earliest work is a notable contribution to modern poetry. Her later work has broken new ground as she redefines and reimagines women's lives to create a female myth of self-discovery. In her life and work she has been struggling to break out of patriarchal social and literary conventions, to redefine herself and to create new traditions. W. H. Auden praised her first volume for its stylistic control, its skillful use of traditional themes such as isolation, and its assimilation of influences such as the work of Robert Frost and William Butler Yeats. He wrote: "The poems . . . in this book are neatly and modestly dressed, speak quietly but do not mumble, respect their elders but are not cowed by them, and do not tell fibs."

Since then, however, Rich has been reshaping poetic conventions to develop her own themes and to create her own voice, often a radical (and sometimes a jarring) one. Reviewer Helen Vendler termed *Diving into the Wreck* "dispatches from the battlefield." Central concerns of Rich's poetry include the uses of history and language, the relationship of the individual to society, and the individual's quest for identity and meaning. The home is often a site for the working out of these themes.

A Change of World

Auden chose Rich's first volume of poetry, *A Change of World*, for the Yale Younger Poets Award. Despite the title, the poems have to do with resisting change. Rich's early training at her father's hands reinforced her allegiance to a literary tradition of meticulous craft, of "beauty" and "perfection." Accordingly, these poems are objective, carefully crafted, and rhymed, with echoes of W. H. Auden, T. S. Eliot, and Robert Frost. A recurring image is that of the home as a refuge that is threatened by social instability ("The Uncle Speaks in the Drawing Room") or natural forces ("Storm Warnings"). The women in these poems remain at home, occupied with women's tasks such as embroidering ("Aunt Jennifer's Tigers"), weaving ("Mathilde in Normandy"), and caring for their families ("Eastport to Block Island"). A central theme of these poems is the use of art as a technique for ordering experience ("Aunt Jennifer's Tigers" and "At a Bach Concert"). "At a Bach Concert" is written in a musically complex form, a variant of the intricate *terza rima* stanza used by Dante. Rich's poem weaves together many strands of poetic technique (assonance, consonance, internal rhyme, off-rhyme, alliteration) and rhetorical devices (oxymoron and parallelism) into a rich textural harmony to develop the theme that formal structure is the poet's gift of love: "Form is the ultimate gift that love can offer—/ The vital union of necessity/ With all that we desire, all that we suffer."

The Diamond Cutters

The theme of artistic control and craft is repeated in Rich's second book, *The Diamond Cutters*. Written when Rich was traveling in Europe as the recipient of a Guggenheim Traveling Fellowship, this volume is a tourist's poetic diary. Landscape and scenery are prominent. The book blends two moods, nostalgia for a more beautiful past and ironic disillusionment with a present that falls short of perfection (as in "The Ideal Landscape," "Lucifer in the Train," or "The Strayed Village."

In a profound way, all the characters in this book are exiles, aliens, uneasy in the places they inhabit. The heroines of poems such as "Autumn Equinox," "The Prospect," and "The Perennial Answer" are dissatisfied with their lives, but unable to change. They hold on to history and to the social structures it has produced, refusing to question present conditions. Suppressed anger and unacknowledged tensions lie just beneath the surface of all the poems; the book's tone is passive, flat. Eight years passed before Rich's next book appeared. Its stylistic and thematic changes reflect changes in her outlook.

SNAPSHOTS OF A DAUGHTER-IN-LAW

In her next two books, *Snapshots of a Daughter-in-Law* and *Necessities of Life*, Rich begins to move away from conventional poetic forms, to develop her own style, and to deal more directly with personal experience. Her attitudes toward literary tradition, history, and the home have changed markedly. She questions traditional attitudes toward home and family. As she found the patriarchal definitions of human relationships inadequate, her work became more personal and more urgent.

Snapshots of a Daughter-in-Law is written in a looser form than Rich's previous work. Language is simpler, texture less dense. The title poem is a series of vignettes of women's experiences. It fairly bristles with quotations drawn from Rich's wide-ranging reading. According to the poem, male authorities have always defined women in myths and literature. Thus, women lacked a literature of their own in which to define themselves. Rich wrote that she composed the poem "in fragments during children's naps, brief hours in a library, or at 3 A.M. after rising with a wakeful child." Because of these interruptions, she wrote the poem over a two-year period. In this poem, she wrote, "for the first time, directly about experiencing myself as a woman" rather than striving to be "universal." As the title indicates, these are static, fixed vignettes: The women are trapped, denied scope for action and choice.

Another poem in this volume, "The Roofwalker," speaks again of entrapment. The poem's speaker is a builder or architect who is no longer satisfied with the enclosure he has built. The role of the artist is here redefined. Whereas "At a Bach Concert" celebrated the need for objectivity, distance, and form, the speaker of "The Roofwalker" feels constrained by forms: "Was it worth while to lay—/ with infinite exertion—/ a roof I can't live under?" The poet begins to wonder whether her tools—rhyme, alliteration, meter, poetic conventions—are stifling her imagination.

The well-planned house that Rich rejects in "The Roofwalker" is the house of formalist poetry as well. She finds the measured stanzas, rhymed couplets, and blank verse rhythms of her earlier books too rigid for her present purposes. Writing a poem no longer means finding a form for a preconceived idea. Instead, each experience informs its own expression; the poem is not product, but process. The poet, like "The Roofwalker," must break out of the stultifying traditional structure. Like most of her contemporaries, she now writes in freer forms. Yet Rich never abandons rational structure or rootedness in social context as do some experimental writers.

NECESSITIES OF LIFE

Rich's next book, *Necessities of Life*, continues her movement toward a freer poetic line and toward subjectivity. Where she formerly spoke of history in terms of objects, products of tradition, she now identifies with historical persons (Antinous, Emily Dickinson, and others). A struggle between death and life, between winter and spring, is in process. Indoor-outdoor imagery carries the weight of these tensions. Poems of death and disappearance take place indoors; the expansive, life-enhancing experiences occur outdoors.

These poems are a retreat from the angry stance of "Snapshots of a Daughter-in-Law" and the daring escape of "The Roofwalker." Because at the time of *Necessities of Life* Rich feels oppressed by the human world, she turns to nature for sustenance. *Necessities of Life* establishes a deep relationship with the world of nature; it is one of the "bare essentials" that preserve the heroine in her difficulties. Through a bond with the vegetable and animal world, the world of warmth and light, the book is able to bring life to bear against death and darkness. Nature's cyclical pattern provides clues for survival. Plants move from winter's icy grip into spring's renewal by learning to exist on little. In order to achieve similar rebirth, humans must consciously will change and force themselves into action. This is the pattern of death and rebirth that structures the book.

Leaflets

Rich's first four books are built on linear oppositions. Balanced groups of stanzas articulate dichotomies between art and emotion, control and chaos, passivity and action, indoors and outdoors. Often characters must choose between alternatives. Tension between polarities becomes a controlling force, focusing the poems' energies. In her next books of poetry, Rich would modify the dualistic structure of the earlier books. At the end of *Leaflets* (1969), she introduces the ghazal, a series of two-line units that conflate many ideas. These poems are collagelike, offering multiple perspectives.

Prompted by her increasing social concern and the leftist political critique evolving in the middle and later 1960's, Rich turned from personal malaise to political struggle, from private meditation to public discourse. Her jarring tone reflects her anger and impatience with language. Rhythms are broken, speech is fragmented. The poems suggest hurried diary entries. Images of violence, guerrilla warfare, and global human suffering suggest an embattled society. Yet anger is close kin to hope: It asserts the wish to effect change. Therefore, alongside the destruction, symbols of fertility and rebirth appear. Rich writes of an old tradition dying and a new one struggling to be born. Fear of change dominated her earlier books, but the "will to change" is paramount here. The poems of this period describe Rich's heroines casting off traditional roles and preparing for journeys. The titles of the next three books represent steps in this process. *Leaflets* is a manifesto for public involvement, *The Will to Change* is the determination to move forward, and *Diving into the Wreck*, the first title to contain a verb, is the act itself.

The evolution of *Leaflets* epitomizes Rich's movement from the personal to the political. The first poem, "Orion," is written in regular six-line stanzas and built on a typical pattern of balanced contrast. Indoors and outdoors, feminine and masculine, stagnation and adventure are the poles. The poem is a monologue in which the speaker blames herself for her failures as a woman. In contrast, the last poem in the book, "Ghazals," is a series of unrhymed couplets arranged in a seemingly random conflation of ideas and images. "Ghazals" is a multivoiced political critique of contemporary America. The heroes and heroines of the book are revolutionaries, protesters, challengers of an old order: Frantz Fanon, Walt Whitman, Galileo, LeRio Jones (Amiri Baraka), Eldridge Cleaver, Dian Fossey. Turning her back on a political tradition that she now equates with death and destruction, Rich is saddened and estranged. Yet she not only wants to last until the new tradition begins but also will attempt to create that new tradition. To do so, she must substitute new ideas and modes of expression for the old, wishing "to choose words that even you/ would have to be changed by" ("Implosions"). Because the values and attitudes she wants to modify are so deeply entrenched in people's most fundamental assumptions, language itself must be reshaped to provide a vocabulary equal to her task of reconstruction. Consequently, language becomes a crucial issue.

Rich believes that "only where there is language is there world" ("The Demon Lover"). She fears, however, that the English language is "spoiled." If the poet is using the "oppressor's language," how may her words avoid contamination?

The Will to Change

Her powerful meditation on language and power "The Burning of Paper Instead of Children" (in *The Will to Change*) draws upon her classroom experience with disadvantaged students. Unlike the poet, whose privileged childhood opened the possibilities of language to her, the children of the ghetto find the worlds of literacy and power closed to them. Rich quotes a student whose grammatical awkwardness lends his description of poverty a pointed eloquence: "a child steal because he did not have money to buy it: to hear a mother say she do not have money to buy food for her children . . . it will make tears in your eyes." Because she mistrusts rhetoric, the poet closes her meditation with a prose passage of bald statement.

> I am in danger. You are in danger. The burning of a book arouses no sensation in me. I know it hurts to burn. There are flames of napalm in Catonsville, Maryland. I know it hurts to burn. The typewriter is overheated, my mouth is burning, I cannot touch you and this is the oppressor's language.

Her simple syntax affirms her identification with the disadvantaged student, the oppressed. In her refusal to use complex diction or traditional metrics she argues by implication for a rhetoric of honesty and simplicity.

Diving into the Wreck

Rich's poetry revises the heroic myth to reflect women's experiences. *Diving into the Wreck* presents questing female heroes for the first time in her work. On their quests, they reconnect with lost parts of themselves, discover their own power, and build commonality with other women. Women's lives are the central focus as Rich's project becomes that of giving voice to women's experience, developing a "common language" that will bring the "dark country" of women's lives into the common light of day. Yet Rich also claims another task for women: They must struggle to redeem an endangered society. She argues that patriarchy's exaggerated aggressiveness, competition, and repression of feeling have led Western civilization to the brink of extinction. The task of reconstruction must be taken up by women. Working for change, the women in this book seek to turn civilization from its destructive paths by persuasion, creation of new myths, or redirection of anger.

In order to understand and overcome patriarchy's suicidal impulses, Rich attempts to open a dialogue. Almost all the poems in *Diving into the Wreck* are cast as dialogue. Conversation is the book's central metaphor for poetry. The book begins with "Trying to Talk with a Man," a poem that deals with the dangers of an accelerating arms race but also has a deeper subject: the creation of a dialogue between men and women. Perceiving gender as a political issue, Rich calls upon men to join her in rethinking gender questions.

Yet the book comes to question the possibility of real communication. "Translations" examines the gulf between the languages spoken by women and men. In "Meditations for a Savage Child," the concluding poem, scientists cannot teach the child to speak.

Poems: Selected and New, 1950-1974

Poems: Selected and New, 1950-1974 includes early unpublished poems and several new ones. In the final poem of this book, "From an Old House in America," Rich uses the home image as a starting point for a reconsideration of U.S. history from a woman's point of view. She reimagines the lives of women, from immigrants to pioneers to the new generation of feminist activists. All are journeying. Simple and direct in language, written in stanzas of open couplets, the poem is a stream-of-consciousness meditation that builds in force as it imagines the unwritten history of North American women and reaches a profound celebration of sisterhood.

Thus, by the end of the book, the woman at home is transformed from the cautious door-closer of "Storm Warnings" (*A Change of World*) into the active participant in history and the questing adventurer eager to define herself by exploration and new experience.

The Dream of a Common Language

Transformation is the cornerstone of *The Dream of a Common Language* and *A Wild Patience Has Taken Me This Far.* The poet wishes to effect fundamental changes in social arrangements, in concepts of selfhood, in governmental politics, in the meanings of sexuality, and in language. To that end, transformation supplants her earlier idea of revolution.

The title *The Dream of a Common Language* suggests vision, community, and above all a language in which visions and shared experience may be conceived and expressed. Dream is the voice of the nocturnal, unconscious self breaking into daytime existence. The terrain Rich explores here is the unknown country of the self, discovered in dream, myth, vision, ritual. Like dreams, the poems telescope time and space to make new connections among past, present, and future, between home and world. "Common" signifies that which is communal, habitual, shared, widely used, ordinary. Rich sets great value on the common, choosing it over the extraordinary.

In *The Dream of a Common Language*, the poet affirms that poetry stems from "the drive/ to connect. The dream of a common language." The book's central section, "Twenty-One Love Poems," orchestrates the controlling themes of women's love, power, language, world. Images of light and dark, dream and reality, speech and silence, home and wanderer structure the sequence. There are in fact twenty-two poems, for Rich has included an unnumbered "Floating Poem." Drawing from the sonnet tradition, Rich breaks formal conventions by varying the poems' lengths and departing from strict rhyme and meter. The sequence records a particular lesbian relationship, its joyous beginnings, the difficulties encountered, and the termination of the affair. The poems ask questions about the meanings of self, language, and love between women, and about the possibilities of sustaining love in a hostile world. Rich insists upon grounding her explorations in the quotidian as well as the oneiric world. To be "at home" in the world requires coming to terms with the ugliness and brutality of the city, the pain and wounds, as well as the beauty of love and poetry. Deliberately, Rich situates the first sonnet of her sequence "in this city," with its "rainsoaked garbage."

Because she wishes to escape false romanticism, she seeks to connect the poems firmly to the world of daily life, to avoid sentimentality, and to speak honestly of her feelings. Because she wishes to transform the selfeffacing behavior that has typically characterized women in love, she stresses self-awareness and deliberate choice. Caves and circles—images of roundness, completeness, wholeness—are dominant. Like the homes of Rich's earlier work, they are enclosures; however, the meaning of encirclement has been transformed, for in her new vision the poet no longer escapes from the world in her narrow room but reaches out to include the world, to bring it within her protected circle.

Poem XXI, the final poem of the sequence, is a complex network of dreamlike associations, of ritual and archetypal memory. In the sonnet, Rich moves from dark into light, from the prehistoric into the present, from inanimate nature ("the color of stone") into purposeful consciousness ("more than stone"). She becomes by choice "a figure in the light." The clarity of intelligence--"a cleft of light"—shapes her purpose. In drawing the circle she deliberately chooses her place.

Particularly in the last three poems of the book there is a sacramental quality, as Rich affirms her fusion with a world of women working together throughout time. Weaving, cooking, caring for children, they are crafting beautiful and utilitarian objects such as ceramic vessels, quilts, and clothing. Through these tasks, they create mementos of their lives and carry out the work of making a world.

"Transcendental Etude" is a long meditative poem of great richness and power. It traces the course of birth, death, and rebirth through a creativity that heals splits in the natural world and within the self. The poem begins in the pastoral imagery of an August evening and ranges over the realms of nature and of human life. Rich's vision here transforms the poet's craft. As a poet, she need not be, as she had once feared, an egocentric artist seeking undying fame at the expense of those she loves. Instead, through participation in the life of the physical universe, she articulates the patterns of her own being, of life itself. Thus, Rich's new metaphor of the poet is at once the most daring and the most simple: The poet is a common woman.

Achieving a selfhood that encompasses both creative work and human relationships, egotism and altruism, Rich and her women heal their psychic split in the symbolic return to home, to the full self represented by the circle. The voyage into history, the unconsciousness, the mind is completed in the return.

Exploring women's shared pasts

The next group of books–*A Wild Patience Has Taken Me This Far, Sources, The Fact of a Doorframe, Your Native Land, Your Life*, and *Time's Power*—continue to develop the themes broached in *The Dream of a Common Language:* exploration of women's shared past, the struggle to be "at home" in a strife-torn world, the vision of transforming the self and the world. Here again the imagery is that of simple, ordinary objects important to women's lives: books, kettles, beets. Yet these books speak in a more muted voice, the voice of resolution, acceptance, accomplishment, with less anger.

A Wild Patience Has Taken Me This Far is to a large extent a dialogue with nineteenth century women writers and thinkers: the Brontës, Susan B. Anthony, Elizabeth Barrett Browning. "Culture and Anarchy" takes its title from Matthew Arnold's essay on nineteenth century culture. Arnold longed for a literate, elite, verbal culture; Rich, on the other hand, celebrates a world of women's work, both verbal and nonverbal. Here, growing and cooking vegetables, responding to nature's seasonal rhythms, the simple tasks of women's lives, form a valuable cultural matrix out of which arise the heroic actions of individual women.

Rich's poem is a quilting together of the words of historical women (derived from the diaries and letters of Emily Dickinson, Susan B. Anthony, Elizabeth Barrett Browning, and Jane Addams) and meditation on her own life and work. The women's voices here replace the quotations of male words in "Snapshots of a Daughter-in-Law." Again Rich telescopes time, bringing the earlier women into the circle of her life, joining them in their acts and visions.

In *Sources* Rich returns to her past and engages in a dialogue with her dead father and husband. She is trying to come to terms with her own life and to put the lives of the others into perspective. *Your Native Land, Your Life* and *Time's Power* continue to develop the persona of the poet as representative woman facing the issues of her country and time. Language and poetry and their relation to history remain foci of concern: in "North American Time" she writes

> Poetry never stood a chance
> of standing outside history.
> . . . .
> We move   but our words stand
> become responsible
> for more than we intended

In the ruefully ironic "Blue Rock" she writes

> Once when I wrote poems they did not change
> left overnight on the page
> . . . .
> But now I know what happens while I sleep
> and when I wake the poem has changed:
> the facts have dilated it, or cancelled it.

Time's Power is a book of dialogue, with the poet's mother, her lover, and a cast of historical figures. "Letters in the Family" is a series of imagined letters written by fictionalized historical persons, such as a friend of the Hungarian partisan Chana Senesh or a South African mother writing to her child. The book ends with "Turning," a poem of quest for knowledge. It articulates a question the poet-speaker asks as she tries to understand her ongoing quest: "So why am I out here, trying/ to read your name in the illegible air?"

MIDNIGHT SALVAGE

Rich subtly moves toward a quieter wisdom in *Midnight Salvage*, passing the torch and trying to impart to future readers and writers what she has learned and how she learned it. In doing so, she reminisces of her girlhood and her past selves' varied goals and causes, perhaps best captured in the title poem, an ambitious, eight-section piece that sorts through her history. Her experience with aging and illness brings forth the subject matter of physical torture. "Shattered Head" ranges from one body's devastation ("a life hauls itself uphill") to the betrayal of the many, and by the end of the poem, to the victims of torture or warfare ("who did this to us?"). Her work continues to be combative, yet in this volume, it is in a quiet, more indirect way.

FOX: POEMS, 1998-2000

Fox: Poems, 1998-2000 continues to meld Rich's art with conviction, her familiar attentions to social injustice and intense personal introspection still present. She praises, commemorates, and questions friends and public figures, while also probing what political action means. Her usual strident tone makes a small retreat here, however, and her voice is less edgy, a little more malleable, than in previous collections. As she declares in "Regardless," a poem about loving a man, "we'd love/ regardless of manifestoes I wrote or signed." Yet familiar themes are present, whether she is writing about war in the long, provocative poem "Veterans Day," female identiy in the searing title poem, or the violence witnessed by a woman in "Second Sight," and Rich continues to give voice to the most fundamental of feelings.

POETIC EVOLUTION

Rich's successive volumes of poetry reveal her development as poet and as woman. As she breaks out from restrictive traditions her voice is achieving power and authenticity. From a poet of isolation and withdrawal, of constraint and despair, she has become a seer of wide-ranging communal sympathy and great imaginative possibility. She is redefining in her life and poetry the meanings of language, poetry, love, power, and home. In her earlier life and work, she accepted patriarchal definitions. Consequently, she felt trapped in personal and poetic conventions: a marriage that curbed her creativity, an aesthetic that split form and feeling, a language that ignored her experience, a position of powerlessness.

At first she spoke in a derivative voice, the language of the "universal"; reluctant to speak as a woman, she echoed the tone of her male poetic ancestors. Because she hesitated to voice her own experience, her early poems are highly polished but avoid emotional depth. She grew to mistrust a language that seemed alien. The fragmented, provisional, stark poems of *Leaflets*, *The Will to Change*, and *Diving into the Wreck* record her groping toward a new language in which to voice her deepest concerns. In subsequent books, she wrote in a freer form, viewing poems as "speaking to their moment." This stance is particularly noticeable in such works of the 1990's as *An Atlas of the Difficult World*, with its powerhouse title poem, *Dark Fields of the Republic*, and *Midnight Salvage*. These volumes, produced almost on schedule every three or four years, also suggest less urgency and a more relaxed authority as a voice at once personal and representative. In *Fox: Poems, 1998-2000*, there seems to be a gradual falling off of intensity, a quieter wisdom, as Rich moves into her seventies.

Through the major phases of her career, the transformations of Rich's home imagery parallel her growth of poetic force and political awareness. In early poems the home was entrapping, because patriarchal voices defined women's roles. As Rich's women became more self-defining, the old relationships were abandoned or modified to fit the real needs of the persons involved. Achieving selfhood, Rich's female heroes came to seize control of their homes, their lives. Through metaphorical journeys exploring the world, women's history, and their own psychic heights and depths, they struggle for knowledge and self-mastery. Healing their tormenting self-division, they grow more "at home" in the world. They recognize and cherish their links to a women's tradition of great power and beauty and to the natural world. In this process the idea of home has acquired new significance: from frail shelter or painful trap it has grown to a gateway, the starting point for journeys of self-exploration, and the magic circle to which women return so that they may participate in the work of "making and remaking" the world.

Other major works

NONFICTION: *Of Woman Born: Motherhood as Experience and Institution*, 1976; *On Lies, Secrets, and Silence: Selected Prose, 1966-1978*, 1979; *Blood, Bread, and Poetry: Selected Prose, 1979-1985*, 1986; *What Is Found There: Notebooks on Poetry and Politics*, 1993; *Arts of the Possible: Essays and Conversations*, 2001.

EDITED TEXT: *The Best American Poetry: 1996*, 1996.

MISCELLANEOUS: *Adrienne Rich's Poetry and Prose: Poems, Prose, Reviews, and Criticism*, 1993 (Barbara Chartesworth Gelpi and Albert Gelpi, editors).

Bibliography

Altieri, Charles. "Self-Reflection as Action: The Recent Work of Adrienne Rich." In *Self and Sensibility in Contemporary American Poetry*. Cambridge, England: Cambridge University Press, 1984. This essay treats *The Dream of a Common Language* and *A Wild Patience Has Taken Me This Far*. Altieri examines the way in which Rich's poetry emphasizes "the connection between composition and constructing a responsible self."

Cooper, Jane Roberta, ed. *Reading Adrienne Rich: Review and Re-Visions, 1951-1981*. Ann Arbor: University of Michigan Press, 1984. A useful collection of reviews and critical studies of Rich's poetry and prose. It includes Auden's foreword to *A Change of World* and other significant essays. The aim is for breadth and balance.

Dickie, Margaret. *Stein, Bishop, and Rich: Lyrics of Love, War, and Place*. Chapel Hill: University of North Carolina Press, 1997. Examination of the poets Gertrude Stein, Elizabeth Bishop and Rich, with three of the book's nine chapters devoted to Rich. Bibliography, index.

Gelpi, Barbara Charlesworth, and Albert Gelpi, eds. *Adrienne Rich's Poetry and Prose*. New York: W. W. Norton, 1993. This volume in the Norton Critical Edition series presents a significant sampling of Rich's work, biographical materials, and a carefully representative selection of essays (sometimes excerpted) and reviews. It provides a chronology and a list of selected criticism for further study.

Juhasz, Suzanne. *Naked and Fiery Forms: Modern American Poetry by Women, a New Tradition*. New York: Harper & Row, 1976. An early study of the developing tradition of American poetry by women, which sets Rich's work into the context of an evolving feminist tradition. The book examines themes and imagery.

Keyes, Claire. *The Aesthetics of Power: The Poetry of*

Adrienne Rich. Athens: University of Georgia Press, 1986. Keyes discusses Rich as a feminist poet. Introduction provides a biographical and historical overview. Each of the ten chapters discusses one of Rich's books, from *A Change of World* through *A Wild Patience Has Taken Me This Far.*

Ratcliffe, Krista. *Anglo-American Feminist Challenges to the Rhetorical Traditions: Virginia Woolf, Mary Daly, Adrienne Rich*. Carbondale: Southern Illinois University Press, 1996. A feminist perspective on the rhetoric and literary devices of these three writers. Bibliography, index.

Templeton, Alice. *The Dream and the Dialogue: Adrienne Rich's Feminist Poetics*. Knoxville: University of Tennessee Press, 1994. Templeton finds each of Rich's volumes both responsive to and party to the dominant critical issues at the time of publication. Templeton's exploration of Rich's "feminist poetics" posits feminism as a way of reading literature, so that reading in itself becomes a political act.

Yorke, Liz. *Adrienne Rich: Passion, Politics, and the Body*. Newbury Park, Calif.: Sage Publications, 1998. This accessible introduction to Rich's work reviews the process and development of her ideas, tracing her place in the major debates within second-wave feminism. Yorke assesses Rich's contribution to feminism and outlines her ideas on motherhood, heterosexuality, lesbian identity, Jewish identity, and issues of racial and sexual otherness.

Karen F. Stein,
updated by Philip K. Jason and Sarah Hilbert

JAMES WHITCOMB RILEY

Born: Greenfield, Indiana; October 7, 1849
Died: Indianapolis, Indiana; July 22, 1916

PRINCIPAL POETRY

The Old Swimmin'-Hole, and 'Leven More Poems, 1883
Afterwhiles, 1887
Old-Fashioned Roses, 1888
Pipes o' Pan at Zekesbury, 1888
Rhymes of Childhood, 1891
Neighborly Poems, 1891
Green Fields and Running Brooks, 1892
Poems Here at Home, 1893
The Days Gone By and Other Poems, 1895
A Tinkle of Bells and Other Poems, 1895
A Child-World, 1896
Riley Love-Lyrics, 1899
Home-Folks, 1900
Riley Songs o' Cheer, 1905
Early Poems, 1914
The Complete Poetical Works of James Whitcomb Riley, 1937

OTHER LITERARY FORMS

Above all, James Whitcomb Riley was a poet; he did, however, try his hand (apparently with little success) at other literary forms. His second book, *The Boss Girl, a Christmas Story, and Other Sketches*, published in 1886, was a collection of prose pieces which went largely unnoticed. Reprinted in 1891 under the title of *Sketches in Prose and Occasional Verses*, it still attracted no appreciable attention. Other prose sketches were included in his *Pipes o' Pan at Zekesbury.* As Riley's commentator, Peter Revell (*James Whitcomb Riley*, 1970), points out, these "abortive" efforts at prose show Riley experimenting in an amateurish fashion with various forms of social and psychological realism. Riley also wrote one verse drama in three acts, *The Flying Islands of the Night* (pb. 1891), which his publisher, Bobbs-Merrill, advertised as "a weird and grotesque drama in verse." Apparently begun in the 1870's, *The Flying Islands of the Night* is a fantastic amalgam of fairy tales, Maurice Maeterlinck, and William Shakespeare. Although Riley was already an established, enormously popular writer by the time *The Flying Islands of the Night* was published, the drama was quite ignored. Finally, with humorist Bill Nye, Riley coauthored *Nye and Riley's Railway Guide* (1888).

ACHIEVEMENTS

Although his nickname, the Hoosier Poet, would suggest that he was writing for and about only Indianans,

James Whitcomb Riley was probably the most popular poet in the United States during the late 1880's, the 1890's, and throughout the early years of the twentieth century. In addition to several honorary degress at institutions of higher education, he received many significant honors: membership in the National Institute of Arts and Letters and the American Academy of Arts and Letters among them. Attesting to his great popularity were the public celebrations of his birthday, and in 1915 the National Committee of Education institutionalized this practice by directing that his birthday be observed by all public, private, and parochial schools in the United States.

His more than one thousand poems were eagerly purchased, read, and treasured not only by the rural midwesterners for whom he ostensibly wrote but also by the increasingly large numbers of Americans living in urban centers on the east and west coasts. Many of his poems were memorized by several generations of schoolchildren, and Riley so perfectly captured and expressed the pastoral myth of the American Eden that a number of his poems have become a permanent part of the collective American psyche.

Indeed, it would probably come as a surprise to many Americans that the now largely forgotten Riley was responsible for such familiar phrases and images as "When the frost is on the punkin," "Little Orphan Annie," and "the old swimmin'-hole." Although these fragments of Riley's work have endured and probably will continue to do so, it is nevertheless also true that, a century after his death, Riley is, for all intents and purposes, no longer read.

Part of the problem is that the very qualities of his verse that made him so beloved by the readers of several generations ago make him unappealing to contemporary readers. Horace Gregory and Marya Zaturenska are essentially correct in maintaining that Riley wrote poems "that would not depress his audiences, nor strike too deeply into the darkness of their fears and doubts. He had a great dread of the darker places of the soul, and of the sinister or complicated recesses of the mind" (*A History of American Poetry, 1900-1940*, 1946). Riley's brand of sanguine, superficial verse was ideally suited to a nation self-conscious about its new status as a world power and sufficiently prosperous, settled, and urbanized that it could afford to indulge in nostalgia about its "simple" rural origins. In fact, in the poems of "Sunny Jim," Riley tapped the same portion of the American mind that so enjoyed the best-selling novels of Riley's era: *Little Lord Fauntleroy* (1886), *Mrs. Wiggs of the Cabbage Patch* (1901), and *Rebecca of Sunnybrook Farm* (1903).

Riley's poems, be they of the "Hoosier" type (written in midwestern dialect) or of the "Lockerbie" type (in standard English), are of even less interest to critics than they are to modern readers. As Peter Revell has noted in the preface of his excellent study of Riley, the meanings of Riley's poems are readily apparent (although occasionally the dialect makes them a little difficult to decipher); he chose not to be "literary," studiously avoiding references to classical and contemporary writers and their works; he is not, except perhaps for the dialect, of any technical interest; and his work—so limited in sub-

James Whitcomb Riley (Hulton Archive)

ject, treatment, and style as to be virtually formulaic—shows little apparent development.

Even so, literary historians cannot afford to ignore Riley: His very popularity—not only among rural midwesterners but also with such well-established literary figures as Mark Twain, James Russell Lowell, Hamlin Garland, and Rudyard Kipling—attests that one cannot fully appreciate the American literary and social scene at the turn of the twentieth century without having some understanding of Riley's life and work.

Biography

James Whitcomb Riley was born on October 7, 1849 (some sources erroneously list the year as 1853), in the village of Greenfield in Hancock County, Indiana. Although is was small (it had a population of three hundred in 1844), Greenfield had some cultural pretensions, and in Riley's youth it saw the establishment of several schools, a library, and a dramatic society. This is important to bear in mind, for although Riley cultivated a public image as a sort of folksy cracker-barrel sage, he would scarcely qualify as one of the rural types whom he depicted so frequently in his verse and for whom he ostensibly wrote. Similarly, his father Reuben (or Reubin) Alexander Riley, far from being a farmer, was a prosperous attorney who had hoped that James (the third child of six, and the second son) would pursue a career in the law.

A Pennsylvanian of Dutch ancestry, Reuben had established himself as a leading citizen of Greenfield virtually from the town's founding. He edited Greenfield's local newspaper in 1847 and even became its first mayor in 1852. Politically astute and evidently ambitious, he named his second son for Governor James Whitcomb, under whom Reuben served as a member of the Indiana State Legislature beginning in 1844.

Not surprisingly, his father had little patience with James, a frail, sensitive boy who did rather poorly in school and who evinced no inclination toward any sort of professional or business career. The boy apparently was temperamentally much closer to his mother, Elizabeth Marine Riley, who enjoyed music and published her poems in local newspapers, and to Captain Lee O. Harris, a teacher who reportedly abandoned all efforts to teach arithmetic to young Riley and instead encouraged his interests in reading and acting—two skills which in the nineteenth century were frequently combined in the form of "declaiming": the memorization and dramatic recitation of passages of literature.

Captain Harris's encouragement proved fruitful in more ways than he could foresee, for through his reading Riley came to emulate such writers as Robert Burns and Charles Dickens, who shared with him an awareness of the literary potentialities of "humble" people; he apparently was especially impressed with *The Biglow Papers* (1848) of James Russell Lowell, a work that may well have inspired those attempts at the recording of Hoosier dialect which ultimately became his poetic trademark; and his talents in declaiming eventually led to his remarkably successful career as a poet/entertainer on the lecture circuit throughout the United States. Captain Harris, however, who was to become his lifelong friend, was unable to nurture in young Riley an appreciation for formal education, and at sixteen, he left school to engage in such inauspicious pursuits as clerking in a shoe store and selling Bibles.

In 1870, Riley's mother died, and in September of that year he published in the *Greenfield Commercial* "The Same Old Story Told Again," the first of several poems to be printed in local newspapers during this period of uncertainty about his future. At this time, his concerned father apprenticed him to a house and sign painter, an experience that provided a temporary outlet for young Riley's creativity and that led to his forming a partnership with two other youths. Collectively known as the Graphics, they traveled throughout Indiana, Illinois, and Ohio painting signs. The experience was an ideal one for the future Hoosier Poet, for it exposed him to the rural types and dialect that he would incorporate into his verse. So, too, with his experience as an assistant to a traveling vendor of patent medicines, for whom he painted signs and enlivened the "medical lectures" by playing his banjo and reciting dialect poems of his own composition.

It was during this period (approximately 1872-1875) that Riley seemed to be actively embarking on a career as a professional actor. He performed solo as a "humorist" throughout central Indiana, as well as with the Adelphian Society, the local dramatic club of Greenfield. In 1875, Riley's alarmed father managed to pressure him into studying law, but the son, now in his late twenties, could tolerate the law for only one year. By 1876 he was on the road again, this time with the Wizard Oil Company, another patent medicine business, and the peripatetic Riley came to realize that, with his success as a "recitationist," actor, and packager and seller of products (be they patent medicines or his own poems), he could make a career out of publishing and reciting poetry.

Back in Greenfield early in 1877, he became associated with the local paper as well as with the Anderson *Democrat*, the circulation of which Riley is credited with increasing sixfold by virtue of his commercial jingles, comic renderings of local news, and such regular features as the column he dubbed "The Rhyme-Wagon." Feeling more confident about his abilities as a writer, Riley began to make serious efforts to publish his poems in local newspapers, but his verses were not always well received. In a rather spiteful response to this cool reception, he decided in the summer of 1877 to prove his point that any poem would become successful and popular if the author were assumed to be "a genius known to fame" by perpetrating a literary hoax: He wrote a poem he titled "Leonainie," signed it with the initials E.A.P., concocted the story that this was a long-lost poem by Poe newly discovered on the flyleaf of a dictionary owned by a local gentleman, and arranged for it to be printed in the *Kokomo Dispatch*.

The hoax, which he apparently had envisioned as causing only a local flurry of excitement, generated a nationwide controversy, and Riley was exposed as a fraud within the month. Riley's discomfited editor dismissed him from his job on the Greenfield newspaper, and the incident would be a source of embarrassment for Riley for the rest of his life; it did, however, earn him some local fame and it led to a job with the *Indianapolis Journal*, under the editorship of Judge E. B. Martindale. The move proved to be a fortunate one, for his association with the *Indianapolis Journal* from 1877 to 1888 coincided with the period of his greatest creativity, and pleasant Indianapolis would be his home for the rest of his life.

By 1881, Riley's local reputation as a poet had grown to the point where he signed on with Redpath Lyceum Bureau Circuit, an association which led to his appearances as a poet/entertainer throughout the Midwest, and occasionally in Boston. In June of 1882, Riley published in the *Indianapolis Journal* the first of his poems ostensibly written by a local farmer, "Benj. F. Johnson, of Boone, the Hoosier Poet," a series which proved to be so successful that he felt ready to collect and publish them in book form in 1883. The first edition of *The Old Swimmin'-Hole, and 'Leven More Poems* was financed by George C. Hitt, the business manager of the *Indianapolis Journal*; but the second edition was brought out by Merrill, Meigs, & Co., and so began the mutually beneficial business relationship between Riley and the Indianapolis publishing house which has come to be known as Bobbs-Merrill. According to Revell, Bobbs-Merrill published some ninety titles by Riley; as of 1949, the number of Riley books sold by Bobbs-Merrill was well beyond three million, although the exact number can never be determined since the sales records prior to 1893 evidently were destroyed.

That phrase "ninety titles" is, however, rather misleading, for Riley tended simply to rearrange and reprint his old, tried-and-true poems, many of them having appeared originally in Indiana newspapers. He also would take a single, especially popular poem, have it lavishly illustrated, and sell it as a hardcover book. Indeed, part of Riley's enormous popularity may be attributed to his two illustrators, Will Vawter and Howard Chandler Christy. Christy in particular was adept at evoking the genteel atmosphere of the twilight of the Victorian era, his illustrations being attractively tinted. The bindings featured lettering in gold (see, for example, the lavish *When She Was About Sixteen*, published in 1911).

At the same time that Riley was consolidating his highly lucrative publishing arrangement with Bobbs-Merrill, he was also furthering the remarkably successful career as a poet/entertainer which he had begun in the 1870's and which had received such impetus from his association with Redpath beginning in 1881. His career on the lecture circuit should not be dismissed lightly, for it is clear that it not only made him wealthy, was a form of self-advertisement, and appealed to his strong innate sense of histrionics, but also helps to explain his great popularity and, moreover, was a major factor in the crystallization of the distinctive Riley poetic style. Evidently Riley, like Ralph Waldo Emerson, was a charismatic speaker: Having developed a striking stage presence, Riley could slip in and out of Hoosier dialect at will, and he had so perfectly rehearsed his comic commentaries on his own poems that they seemed to be the spontaneous remarks of an unusually witty, genial man of the soil. The Riley-the-poet whom thousands flocked to see and hear was in fact a character or persona created by Riley-the-actor, with every gesture, aside, and intonation meticulously prepared in advance. As Riley himself noted with surprising candor,

> In my readings I had an opportunity to study and find out for myself what the public wants, and afterward I would endeavor to use the knowledge gained in my writing. . . . While on the lecture platform I watched the effect that my readings had on the audience very closely and whenever anybody left the hall I knew that my recitation was at fault and tried to find out why. . . . Thus, I learned to judge and value my verses by their effect on the public.

The subject matter, the treatment, even the dialect in his poems had been established and polished by years of experience on the lecture circuit, and Louis Untermeyer is probably correct in maintaining that Riley is "patently the most artificial of those poets who claim to give us the stuff of the soil" (*A Critical Anthology: Modern American Poetry* [*and*] *Modern British Poetry*, 1936).

Artificial or not, Riley was so notoriously successful on the lecture circuit throughout the Midwest that in 1887 it was arranged for him to appear at a literary gala at New York City's Chickering Hall on behalf of the International Copyright League. Sharing the spotlight with such luminaries as Mark Twain, James Russell Lowell, George Washington Cable, William Dean Howells, Charles Dudley Warner, Frank Stockton, and Edward Eggleston, Riley was the least-known writer in attendance, and yet so overwhelming was the impression he made during his recitation on the first day of the two-day affair that he was asked to speak again. In Riley's official biographical sketch is the familiar comment by Lowell, reportedly made in the course of reintroducing Riley to the sophisticated New York audience on the triumphant second day of the conference, that in Riley's verse he had found "so much of high worth and tender quality that I deeply regret I had not long before made acquaintance with his work." Lowell went on to call him a "true poet," and such an enthusiastic response from one of the most noted literary figures of the day served only to enhance Riley's career as a lecturer, and he began to appear throughout the United States, often accompanied by fellow-poet Eugene Field or the humorist Edgar W. ("Bill") Nye.

Riley continued to publish volumes of poetry with singular regularity, and in 1891, he paid a triumphant visit to the British Isles, where he was honored with a dinner at the Savoy in London. In 1893, he began his residence on Lockerbie Street in Indianapolis, where he was a boarder in the pleasant brick home of Major Charles L. Holstein. He also acquired the "Old Homestead" in Greenfield, which became his summer residence (in his old age he wintered in Miami). Riley also received numerous honorary degrees, including an M.A. from Yale University (1902) and doctorates from the University of Philadelphia (1904) and Indiana University (1907). He was elected to membership in the National Institute of Arts and Letters in 1908 and to the American Academy of Arts and Letters in 1911. Probably the honors he most valued, however, were the public celebrations of his birthday.

In 1911, the schools of Indiana and New York City held commemorative programs in his honor on his birthday, and in 1915 the National Committee of Education directed that his birthday be observed by all public, private, and parochial schools in the United States. Upon his death from heat prostration in 1916 (he already had become a semi-invalid because of a series of paralytic strokes), Riley was so well known as a public figure in Indiana that thirty-five thousand people filed past his body lying in state at the capitol building in Indianapolis. His name had become a household word throughout the United States. His reputation as a poet declined dramatically after his death, perhaps because his poems needed the commanding presence of the genial Riley himself to compensate for their obvious deficiencies; but despite the fact that Riley is now virtually forgotten by the reading public, it is probably true that he will always hold a place in American literary history by virtue of his truly extraordinary popularity at the turn of the twentieth century.

Analysis

Ordinarily one would be ill-advised to attempt to offer a broad statement concerning 1,044 poems. In James Whitcomb Riley's case, however, his poetic undertakings were so limited in subject, treatment, and style that it is indeed possible to make generalizations about them. Most of his poems fall into one or more of the following categories: pastoralized treatments of life in rural America, sentimentalized renderings of the relationships between family members or friends, and equally sentimentalized evocations of childhood. As illustrations of these three categories, one might consider "When the Frost Is on the Punkin," "Knee-Deep in June," "Nothin' to Say," "The Old Man and Jim," "The Raggedy Man," "Little Orphant Annie," and "The Old Swimmin'-Hole."

"When the Frost Is on the Punkin"

In an age when many Americans have never seen frost on a pumpkin—or, for that matter, pumpkin not in a pie—it is rather remarkable that the title of Riley's "When the Frost Is on the Punkin" is still in circulation, even if the poem itself is largely forgotten. Clearly working within the venerable tradition of the harvest poem (John Keats's "To Autumn" is a sterling example), Riley has so generalized and so de-emotionalized the potentially rich subject of the country autumn that the poem is strikingly charmless. Predictably, the air is "appetizin'" and the morning is "crisp and sunny"; the obligatory rooster crows his obligatory "hallylooyer"; and the requisite apples are "poured around the celler-floor in red and yeller heaps," dutifully ready to be made into cider and applesauce. Vague catalogs of stock autumnal delights, however, together with the overdone repetition of "When the frost is on the punkin and the fodder's in the shock," and the patently sentimental conclusion that any "Angels wantin' boardin'" would be more than happy to live in the country at harvest-time, simply cannot salvage the poem. To a nation which was still essentially rural—or, more important, which perceived itself as such—the bland catalogs probably struck deep emotional chords; but to modern readers all that remains of one of Riley's most famous poems is the fundamentally meaningless title.

"Knee-Deep in June"

Not all Riley's poems feature the flurry of farm activity depicted in "When the Frost Is on the Punkin." The other side of Riley's brand of rural American life—the "mild Bohemianism" and "fatuousness" which Donald Pizer has cited as characteristic of Riley's verse (*American Thought and Writing: The 1890's*, 1972)—are perhaps nowhere more apparent than in "Knee-Deep in June," originally published in the *Indianapolis Journal* in 1885. Overlong at eight stanzas, it enjoins one to find an orchard and "Lay out there and try to see/ Jes' how lazy you kin be!—" Although the persona explains in the first stanza that he engages in this sort of activity (or lack thereof) only on "some afternoon[s]," it is nevertheless apparent that he could do this "stiddy fer a year er two," if not for eternity; and the overall impression that one receives from "Knee-Deep in June" is that the Puritan work ethic has been rejected wholesale. Quite typical of Riley's verse are the poem's vague renderings of the details of a country landscape ("Hear the old hen squawk, and squat/ Over ever' chick she's got"), the domestic metaphors (the shadows are "thick and soft/ As the kivvers on the bed/ Mother fixes in the loft/ Allus, when they's company!"), and the strained attempts at quaint humor ("Mr. Bluejay, full o' sass,/ In them baseball clothes o' his"). Even the reference to death is carefully sentimentalized to contribute to the aura of lassitude:

> Thinkin' of old chums 'at's dead,
> Maybe, smilin' back at you
> In betwixt the beautiful
> Clouds o' gold and white and blue!

In keeping with the theme of the poem, "Knee-Deep in June" is spread out in leisurely fashion over seven pages of the volume *Songs of Summer* and features three illustrations by Will Vawter, including a full-page picture of a man "Sprawl[ed] out len'thways on the grass."

"Nothin to Say"

The sentimentality so characteristic of "When the Frost Is on the Punkin" and "Knee-Deep in June" is also evident in the Riley poems which focus on interpersonal relationships rather than on farm life as such. "Nothin' to Say," which was accepted for publication by the *Century Illustrated Monthly Magazine* in 1883 but which did not appear until August of 1887, was an immensely popular poem in its day. It is a dramatic monologue in which a father speaks to his daughter, who has declared her intention of getting married on her next birthday. The girl's mother is dead, having left her baby daughter a "little Bible" with "yer name acrost the page" and some earrings; and, as might well be anticipated, the daughter, in looks and size, is much like the mother. To complete the mother/daughter analogy, the father notes that "It'll 'most seem like you was dead like her!"; but, faced with the inevitability of his child marrying and moving away, the helpless father "hain't got nothin' to say!"

"The Old Man and Jim"

A poem equally predictable and sentimental is "The Old Man and Jim," one of Riley's most successful platform pieces. The unidentified narrator records the relationship between an old farmer and his favorite son Jim, "the wildest boy he had." Constitutionally ill-suited to farming, Jim enlists in the army for three months at the outbreak of the Civil War and his father, who is "jes' wrapped up in him," sends him off to the service with the words "'Well, good-by, Jim:/ Take keer of yourse'f!'" Those parting words become the refrain of the poem, as Jim distinguishes himself in battle, reenlists, and dies of his wounds. A woeful tale, "The Old Man and Jim" must have had quite an impact when dramatically recited by Riley.

"The Raggedy Man"

Considerably less depressing is the sentimentalized rendering of the relationship between a hired man and children in "The Raggedy Man," one of the best known of the poems Riley wrote depicting child life. Published in the *Century Illustrated Monthly Magazine* in December, 1890, the poem obviously stirred much interest, for Riley felt compelled to explain that "The Raggedy Man was not a tramp, nor was he so ragged as people usually seem to think. He was just a farmer boy from some neighboring family." Perhaps this was literally so, but the poem is told from the point of view of a child, and as a result that farmer boy emerges as a sort of combination hired man and oversized playmate. In the first two stanzas, the Raggedy Man embodies the world of adult labor which is so alien to the child-persona, and in that respect he serves to represent the parental figures who are most prominent in any child's formative years. In the third stanza, the poem begins to slip into the more imaginative aspects of child life, as the Raggedy Man tells how he picked roasted apples from a tree. This playful motif continues in subsequent stanzas, as the child recounts how the Raggedy Man plays "horsey" with him, tells him about giants and elves, pretends to shoot escaped pigs with his hoe (the "Old Bear-shooter"), reveals that the child is actually a prince whose real father has "gone/ To git more money," and "steals" the child and hides him in a "cave" (actually the haymow).

This heavily folkloric rendering of child life in rural America comes to an abrupt end in the final stanza, wherein the Raggedy Man asks whether the child wishes to become "a rich merchunt" like his father. The child predictably responds "'I'm ist go' to be a nice Raggedy Man!'"; but however appropriately "cute" that answer may be, the fact remains that there is an undercurrent in "The Raggedy Man" which is at odds with the folksy, childlike atmosphere it superficially creates. There is a world of difference between the hired man in his insistently "raggedy" attire (that adjective appears some forty-seven times in the eighty-three-line poem) and the persona's father in his "fine clothes"—a difference which is most apparent in the simple fact that the father, although he owns a farm, must hire the Raggedy Man to handle the decidedly nonpastoral, physically demanding chores associated with farm life. In the America which had once proudly proclaimed itself to be a nation of farmer-citizens, there had arisen by Riley's era a dichotomy between the rural poor and those prosperous urbanites who were quite willing to pastoralize their country roots as long as others would (literally) handle the dirty work. It is difficult to believe that Riley, himself a wealthy urbanite who had enjoyed a comfortable early life, was unaware of the tension generated in the poem by the child's double emotional allegiance to his wealthy, oddly remote father and to the poor, hard-working, fun-loving hired man whom the father employs; but Riley, true to form, does not develop the social consciousness which glimmers so faintly in "The Raggedy Man," and the poem remains essentially an evocation of childhood.

"Little Orphant Annie"

An equally well-known rendering of child life is "Little Orphant Annie." Originally titled "The Elf Child" and published in the *Indianapolis Journal* in 1885, it proved to be so popular that Riley was able to sell the little poem (four eight-line stanzas) as the lavishly illustrated *Orphant Annie Book*. Annie (or "Allie," as she was originally named) was based on a real person, an orphan who had lived briefly with the Riley children (she apparently has nothing in common with the saucer-eyed comic strip heroine of the same name). In Riley's poem, she was to "earn her board-an'-keep" by doing housework for the persona's family, but she was of special interest to the children because of her knowledge of witches, "Gobble-uns," and "Black Things." She entertains the family's children with her stories of little boys and girls being carried off by these supernatural creatures as punishment for being ill-behaved:

> You better mind yer parunts an' yer teachers fond an' dear,
> An' churish them 'at loves you, an' dry the orphant's tear,
> An' he'p the pore an' needy ones 'at clusters all about,
> Er the Gobble-uns'll git you
> Ef you Don't
> Watch
> Out!

Peter Revell is correct in maintaining that the overt didacticism of "Little Orphant Annie" is atypical of Riley's verse, but he probably underestimates Riley's inclination to introduce such dark elements into "the usually sunny world of Hoosierdom." This element of darkness in Riley's poetry is especially apparent in one of his earliest efforts, "The Old Swimmin'-Hole."

"The Old Swimmin'-Hole"

Originally published in the *Indianapolis Journal* on June 17, 1882, and reprinted as the title poem in Riley's first book, "The Old Swimmin'-Hole" proved to be one of the best-loved poems of the 1880's and 1890's, and it is easy to see why. It draws upon that universal tendency to long for a happier, simpler, and ostensibly problem-free past, whether that past be personal or national. In Riley's poem, the highly sentimentalized past is embodied in the controlling image of the swimming-hole, something which would be alien to the experience of most modern readers, but which in Riley's day would be readily acceptable as the vivid symbol of a carefree, self-indulgent youth. Riley's persona—an "old man" from whom "old Time's tuck his toll"—seems to strike a precarious mental balance between smiling nostalgia and acute depression, something which is quite uncharacteristic of Riley's work. The persona recalls that the "gurgle" of the "baby-river" of his boyhood sounded "like the laugh of something we onc't ust to know/ Before we could remember anything but the eyes/ Of the angels lookin' out as we left Paradise." This is an atypically profound way for a Riley poem to begin, and it takes an even more atypical turn as the potentially rich Wordsworthian concept of a prenatal existence is dropped in favor of a Narcissistic interpretation of the attractions of the swimming-hole.

Perhaps sensing that he was moving rather too close to the psychological implications of the swimming-hole, Riley does not pursue the poetic possibilities of the water imagery and instead has the persona recall playing hooky to go swimming. Immediately, however, the element of depression which so striates this poem becomes overt. After a typically Rileyan catalog of vague country delights, the final stanza makes explicit the connection between the mind of the persona and the swimming-hole: "When I last saw the place,/ The scenes was all changed, like a change in my face," and his response to those twin facts is not at all what one would expect in a poem by Riley. "I wish in my sorrow I could strip to the soul,/ And dive off in my grave like the old swimmin'-hole." A Riley persona with suicidal tendencies? Incredible as this may sound, the words on the page, taken at face value, would certainly suggest that the persona is reacting to his aging and the changes in his environment less with cheery nostalgia than with desires for oblivion, even self-destruction.

Riley's contemporary readers evidently chose not to acknowledge the blatant darker aspects of "The Old Swimmin'-Hole," aspects which may reflect the carefully nonpublicized side of the poet (offstage, "Sunny Jim" Riley drank heavily and suffered from exhaustion and depression), or which may reflect the angst-ridden modern man living in a world of isolation and extraordinary change. Much as the speaker in Riley's "Griggsby's Station" yearns to return to "where we ust to be so happy and so pore," far from "the city! city! city!" where there is "none that neighbors with us, or we want to go and see," so too the persona in "The Old Swimmin'-Hole" longs to escape from the miseries of his adult life but realizes that there can be no turning back. Unquestionably there was a dark side to sunny Hoosierdom, but it was a side which neither Riley nor his millions of readers cared to probe. For better or for worse, he will go down in literary history as "Sunny Jim" Riley.

Other major works

SHORT FICTION: *The Boss Girl, a Christmas Story, and Other Sketches*, 1886.

PLAY: *The Flying Islands of the Night*, pb. 1891.

NONFICTION: *Love Letters of the Bachelor Poet, James Whitcomb Riley to Miss Elizabeth Kahle*, 1922; *Letters of James Whitcomb Riley*, 1930.

MISCELLANEOUS: *Nye and Riley's Railway Guide*, 1888; *The Poems and Prose Sketches of James Whitcomb Riley*, 1897-1914 (16 volumes; Homestead Edition); *The Poems and Prose Sketches of James Whitcomb Riley*, 1900-1916 (14 volumes; Greenfield Edition); *The Complete Works of James Whitcomb Riley*, 1913 (6 volumes).

Bibliography

Brooks, Van Wyck. *The Confident Years, 1885-1915*. New York: E. P. Dutton, 1952. Riley played an important role in the time covered here. In the Midwest, where later writers would describe darker visions, Riley and Lewis Wallace expressed "smiling aspects." More important writers than Riley himself had a great liking for Riley's writing, including Eugene Field and Theodore Dreiser. Supplemented by footnotes and an index.

Crowder, Richard. *Those Innocent Years: The Legacy and Inheritance of a Hero of the Victorian Era, James Whitcomb Riley*. Indianapolis: Bobbs-Merrill, 1957. Crowder asserts that the significance of Riley transcends his Indiana reputation. The author narrates the poet's career in eleven chapters. From the "westward movement" beginning in 1819, through recognition by 1885, to the "apotheosis" of his death at the age of sixty-seven, Riley is described not only as heroic but also godlike. "Authorities" are given, as is an index.

Kindilien, Carlin T. *American Poetry In the Eighteen Nineties*. Providence, R.I.: Brown University Press, 1956. This study is based on a special collection of verse in the Brown University library, but it is a complete and generous assessment of the works of the period. Riley's contributions are closely analyzed, particularly as they are made to the development of what Kindilien calls "sentimental humor." Contains notes and an index.

Nolan, Jeannette Covert, Horace Gregory, and James T. Farrell. *Poet of the People: An Evaluation of James Whitcomb Riley*. Bloomington: Indiana University Press, 1951. In three brief, appreciative essays, Riley's work is examined as a contribution to children's poetry, as an expression of Victorian values, and as a product of frontier culture in the Midwest. His work therefore compares, sometimes favorably, with the achievements of William Dean Howells and Mark Twain.

Revell, Peter. *James Whitcomb Riley*. New York: Twayne, 1970. The first three chapters examine Riley as a popular poet then review his background and early writing. Three chapters present Riley as a Victorian poet, children's poet, and Hoosier poet. The last three chapters focus on his pastorals, his humor, and the significance of his popularity. Complemented by a chronology, notes, a select bibliography, and an index.

Van Allen, Elizabeth J. *James Whitcomb Riley: A Life*. Bloomington: Indiana University Press, 1999. Legends and rumors either elevate Riley as a hero who gave Hoosiers pride of place, or denigrate him as a drunken author of Victorian doggerel. Van Allen sifts facts from fiction to paint the truest portrait of this controversial poet.

Williams, Thomas E. Q. *James Whitcomb Riley: The Poet as Flying Islands of the Night*. Greenfield, Ind.: Coiny, 1997. Williams's premise is that the poem "The Flying Islands of the Night" reveals the multifaceted personality of Riley. A valuable resource for anecdotes about Riley and his friends.

Ziff, Larzer. *The American 1890's: Life and Times of a Lost Generation*. New York: Viking Press, 1966. Riley plays a part in this book's story, although he is not considered very important in a decade that included William Dean Howells, Henry James, Mark Twain, and Stephen Crane, for example. Still, Riley did contribute to what Ziff calls "the midwestern imagination," which is examined closely in chapter 4 of the book. Includes notes and an index.

Alice Hall Petry;
bibliography updated by the editors

Rainer Maria Rilke

Born: Prague, Czechoslovakia; December 4, 1875
Died: Valmont, Switzerland; December 29, 1926

Principal poetry

Leben und Lieder, 1894
Larenopfer, 1896
Wegwarten, 1896
Traumgekrönt, 1897
Advent, 1898
Mir zur Feier, 1899
Das Buch der Bilder, 1902, 1906
Das Stundenbuch, 1905 (*The Book of Hours*, 1961)
Neue Gedichte, 1907-1908 (2 volumes; *New Poems*, 1964)
Requiem, 1909 (*Requiem and Other Poems*, 1935)
Die frühen Gedichte, 1909
Das Marienleben, 1913 (*The Life of the Virgin Mary*, 1951)
Duineser Elegien, 1923 (*Duinese Elegies*, 1930; better known as *Duino Elegies*)
Die Sonette an Orpheus, 1923 (*Sonnets to Orpheus*, 1936)
Vergers, suivi des Quatrains Valaisans, 1926
Les Fenêtres, 1927
Les Roses, 1927
Gesammelte Werke, 1927
Verse und Prosa aus dem Nachlass, 1929
Späte Gedichte, 1934 (*Late Poems*, 1938)
Poèmes français, 1935
Christus—Visionen, 1950 (wr. 1896-1898)
Aus dem Nachlass des Grafen C. W.: Ein Gedichtkreis, 1950
Poems, 1906 to 1926, 1957
Poems, 1965
Uncollected Poems, 1996

Other literary forms

The rich symbolic content and specific themes that characterize Rainer Maria Rilke's famous lyrics also inform his narrative prose. Recollections of his boyhood and youth are given romantic, fairy-tale coloring in *Vom lieben Gott und Anderes* (1900; republished as *Geschichten vom lieben Gott*, 1904; *Stories of God*, 1931, 1963), a cycle of short tales that replace traditional Christian perceptions of God with depictions of a finically careful artist. *Die Weise von Liebe und Tod des Cornets Christoph Rilke* (1906; *The Tale of the Love and Death of Cornet Christoph Rilke*, 1932), a terse yet beautifully written story, is more like an epic poem than a prose work, especially in its emphasis on the power of the individual word and its intensely rhythmic language. The psychologically intricate novel *Die Aufzeichnungen des Malte Laurids Brigge* (1910; *The Notebooks of Malte Laurids Brigge*, 1930; also known as *The Journal of My Other Self*) is one of Rilke's most profound creations. Written from the point of view of a young Danish nobleman living in exile in Paris, it offers in random sketches a peculiar summation of the central concerns of the author's literary art.

In the decade between 1894 and 1904, Rilke wrote more than twenty plays, many of which were lost and never published. The most important of his remaining theatrical works are either pessimistically Naturalistic or intense dramas of the soul. *Jetzt und in der Stunde unseres Absterbens* (pr., pb. 1896; *Now and in the Hour of Our Death*, 1979) and *Im Frühfrost* (pr., pb. 1897; *Early Frost*, 1979) reflect the influence of Rudolf Christoph Jenny in their materialistic determinism, while later pieces such as *Höhenluft* (wr. 1897, pr. 1969; *Air at High Altitude*, 1979) and *Ohne Gegenwart* (pb. 1898; *Not Present*, 1979) document a development in the direction of Symbolism, motivated especially by the dramatic theories of Maurice Maeterlinck. Rilke's best-remembered play is *Die weiss Fürstin* (pb. 1929; *The White Princess*, 1979), which in its lyric depth and power illustrates his view that drama and poetry have similar goals.

Apart from his writings in other genres, Rilke also produced a few works of nonfiction. Most notable among these are the biographical study *Auguste Rodin* (1903; English translation, 1919) and the descriptive lyric essays of *Worpswede* (1903). Much of his extensive correspondence has been collected and published. Especially important for what they reveal of his artistic personality and poetic process are volumes of letters exchanged with Lou Andreas-Salomé and Princess Marie von Thurn und Taxis.

Achievements

Commonly ranked alongside Hugo von Hofmannsthal and Stefan George as a giant of twentieth century German poetry, Rainer Maria Rilke is perhaps the most controversial of the three in point of critical and popular reception of his works. Although his substantial collections published soon after the turn of the century, especially *The Book of Hours* and *New Poems*, were greeted with uniformly favorable recognition, there is wide disagreement among critics concerning the literary value of both his early poems and those of his final, major creative period. A significant key to the divided viewpoints is his boldly daring, uniquely creative use of language in strange new relationships, his peculiar departures from traditional grammar and syntax, and his unusual forms of subjective and objective expression. The pure individuality of his poetic utterances often makes them difficult to understand and repels the reader who approaches Rilke's art with anything less than full and active concentration. As a result, the most problematic of Rilke's mature poems, especially the *Duino Elegies*, are regarded by some scholars as the most important German lyric creations of the first half of the twentieth century, whereas others dismiss them as lacking substance. Regardless of these disagreements, Rilke's influence on the development of German verse is unrivaled by that of any other German language poet of his time. His most lasting and important contribution remains the concept of the *Dinggedichte* introduced in *New Poems*.

Rainer Maria Rilke

Biography

The life of René Karl Wilhelm Johann Josef Maria Rilke can be described in its entirety as a productive, if not always successful, search for fulfillment in reaction to an inhibiting, psychologically destructive childhood. Critical elements of Rilke's early experience contributed to his development as a hypersensitive individual unsuited to the demands of practical existence. They include the rapid failure of his parents' marriage; the rape of his personality by a mother who dressed him in feminine clothing and reared him for a time as a replacement for a lost daughter; a partial education in military academies and a school of commerce to which he could never adapt; and a brief exposure to the university world in Prague. The young Rilke responded to a continuing feeling of being out of place by trying diligently to become part of active cultural and artistic circles. While still a student, he published his first lyric anthology, composed Naturalistic plays, contributed literary reviews to newspapers and journals, and founded his own periodical. He also participated in cultural organizations, lecture presentations, readings of drama and poetry, and similar activities.

When Rilke left the university in 1896, he went to Munich. An incurable restlessness dictated his lifestyle from that time forward. His serious evolution as a writer began under the influence of significant figures whom he encountered in Munich; friendships with Jacob Wassermann and Wilhelm von Scholz were especially productive. Wassermann acquainted him with the writings of Jens Peter Jacobsen, which Rilke soon learned to treasure. Still more important was the relationship that he formed with Lou Andreas-Salomé, whom he met in 1897. It was she who persuaded him to change his name from René to Rainer. After she became his mistress, she exposed him to contemporary philosophical trends and the ideas of the Italian Renaissance. He quickly followed her to Berlin and later traveled with her and her husband twice to Russia, where he was introduced to Leo Tolstoy and other authors. The vast Russian landscape and the Russian people impressed him as examples of original, elemental nature. From them, he drew ideas and perceptions that informed his verse long afterward.

Rilke's only attempt to establish a permanent family situation ended in failure. In 1902, he dissolved his household in the Worpswede artists' colony, left his wife, the sculptress Clara Westhoff, and their daughter, and moved to Paris, where he intended to write a book about Auguste Rodin. His friendship with the famous sculptor was extremely significant for the direction of his poetic development in the years between 1902 and the beginning of World War I. Rodin provided Rilke with an example of strict artistic discipline that had profound impact upon his maturation as a poet.

Even more critical to his literary growth during this time was Rilke's association with Impressionist painter Paul Cézanne, whose painting technique contributed much to the evolving visual orientation of Rilke's verse. Not only special individuals but also Paris itself, the French people, and even the French language indelibly marked Rilke's subsequent creations, giving them substance and eventually, during his final years, their very medium of expression.

The atmosphere of two other locales gave peculiar flavor to Rilke's most powerful, most complex masterworks. The first was Duino Castle near Trieste; the second, the Château de Muzot in Valais. After visiting North Africa and Egypt in 1910 and 1911, he went to Duino Castle at the invitation of Princess Marie von Thurn und Taxis. There, he wrote the first two of the *Duino Elegies* before moving on to Spain and then back to Germany. The war years, which he spent primarily in Munich, constituted an unproductive interlude that was inwardly devastating to him. He found it exceedingly difficult to begin writing again when hostilities ceased. Only after moving to Switzerland and his secluded refuge at the Château de Muzot did he find inner peace sufficient to complete his finest lyric cycles. He spent most of the remainder of his life in the Rhône Valley, where he died of leukemia.

Analysis

During the course of his development as a poet, the creative task became for Rainer Maria Rilke a process of objectification and externalization of his own inner world. Couched in language that is notable for its musicality and its frequently playful moods are the peculiarities of a unique spiritual life that emerged from special responses to outside stimuli. The melody of lyrics rich in alliteration, assonance, consonance, and rhyme provides a naturally flowing framework for the presentation of the poet's feelings and reflections. Especially typical components of his verse are encounters with sorrow and pain, powerful absorption in specific objects, a strange blending of the experiences of death and love, and an overwhelming sense of isolation.

The landscape of these revelations of self is transformed and varied in direct relationship to new outward contacts with people, things, and places. Russia, Paris, Duino, and Valais provide for different works, shaping influence and substance, timeless symbols and concrete reality, worldview and microcosmic conception. Taken in sequence, Rilke's cycles and poems document his endeavors to purify the portrayal of the scenes within him, to clarify obscurities and nail down uncertainties. By its very nature, this act of poetic refinement was deeply religious, reflecting a sincere humility in the face of creation's vast mysteries. Rilke's entire oeuvre proclaims a consciousness of an artistic calling that had its basis in an existential anxiety that was translated into joyful, almost rapturous affirmation of mortality.

Early poems

Rilke's earliest published poems, which appeared in the collections *Leben und Lieder* (life and songs),

Larenopfer (offering to the household gods), *Wegwarten* (watch posts), and *Traumgekrönt* (dream-crowned), are marked by a naïve simplicity and a degree of sentimentality that are absent from his more mature writings. Under the influence of Jens Peter Jacobsen, he created particularly sensitive lyrics centered on nature, as well as penetrating psychological portraits of people. Among his favorite subjects were women and children. Even in these youthful creations, there is already a strong emphasis on visual imagery, although the artistic focus of attention is frequently not the object that is described, but rather the spiritual stirrings that occur within the poet because of what he sees.

Mir zur Feier

In *Mir zur Feier* (celebrating me), Rilke began to move away from the lyric forms and approaches of his student years, adopting in the transition techniques that he later perfected in his first broadly successful cycle, *The Book of Hours*. The poems of *Mir zur Feier* present in precise detail their creator's innermost personal concerns, describing in tones of religious fervor his yearnings, prayers, and self-perceptions. Framed in language that is rich in texture yet soft in tone, the poems glorify things that cannot be comprehended through human volition. These verse productions represent a calculated justification of the poet's art as a means of celebrating that which can be revealed in its essence and fullness in no other manner.

Das Buch der Bilder

Das Buch der Bilder (the book of pictures), a collection written at about the same time as *The Book of Hours*, is in some respects poetically stronger. Under the influence of Rodin, Rilke made the transition from a poetry informed by blurred feeling to precise, objective, carefully formed verse characterized by the complete sacrifice of the poet's immanence to an emphasis upon things in themselves. The creations of *Das Buch der Bilder* reveal the writer's progress toward the establishment of a literary integration of visual impressions with sight-oriented components of language. The artistic process becomes a perfecting of the act of seeing, in which the poet organizes the elements of the visual image through subjective cognition of his external world. Although these lyrics do not attain to the plastic monumentality of Rilke's later writings, they are forerunners of the *Dinggedicht* (thing poem) that are collectively the most important product of Rilke's years in Paris.

The Book of Hours

The commemoration of self is a significant aspect of *The Book of Hours*, divided into three sections that were the product of diverse influences and experiences: Rilke's impressions of Russia and Paris, his love affair with Lou Andreas-Salomé, the dramatic writings of Maurice Maeterlinck and Henrik Ibsen, Friedrich Nietzsche's philosophical ideas, and the cultural legacy of the Italian Renaissance. The work as a whole portrays the author's movement toward an internalization of external phenomena in a poetic act of preservation and redemption. There is evident within the individual poems a new kind of friendly relationship between the poet and God's handiwork that surrounds him. Nevertheless, what is presented is definitely not a traditional Christian attitude toward life. These lyrics are the product of an aggressively demanding mind; in them, a strongly individual interpretation of the religious dimension of experience is advanced without equivocation. The thrust of *The Book of Hours* is to refine the notion that God is not static, a complete and perfect being, but rather a continually evolving artistic creation. Rilke insists that the reader accept this idea on faith, equating his poetic message with spiritual revelation. The result is a celebration of "this world" which the poet continued to elaborate and modify until his death.

The three parts of *The Book of Hours* are discrete sets of deeply intimate confessions that arose out of special relationships and encounters that shaped Rilke's artistic outlook. "Das Buch vom mönchischen Leben" ("Of the Monastic Life"), written in 1899, reflects the strong influence of the poet's attachment to Lou Andreas-Salomé and the cultural, historical, and philosophical ideas to which she introduced him. His ecstatic love for Lou and their visits to Russia are the key elements that give "Das Buch von der Pilgerschaft" ("Of Pilgrimage") its specific flavor, while "Das Buch von der Armut und vom Tod" ("Of Poverty and Death") was a product of Rilke's impressions during his first year in Paris. The individual poems of the three cycles are experiments in which Rilke tested various symbols and metaphors, metric and rhythmic possibilities, and rhyme schemes in documenting a deep worship of life as a sacred motivating force.

"Of the Monastic Life" is a series of prayerful outpourings of the spirit in which a young monk addresses God. In this context, prayer is an elemental religious act with two goals: self-discovery in the process of establishing and expanding personal modes of expression, and the "creation" of God and the growth of a sense of brotherhood with him in one's relationship to nature. The fictive prayer situations provide the setting for a portrayal of the innermost stirrings of the soul in an endless reaching outward to illuminate the divine. Melodic language and strength of visual image are brought together with rich imagination to reveal the lyricist's almost Franciscan sympathy with the world.

Specific items of the cycle "Of Pilgrimage" attain peaks of religious rapture in the glorification of the mystical union between man and woman, offered in newly intensified homage to Lou. Thematically, however, this portion of *The Book of Hours* focuses primarily on key aspects of the poet's Russian experience. It emphasizes especially the idea that the pious Russian people are the embodiment of humility and spirituality within a topographical frame that is the archetype of God's creation. Spatial relationships are particularly important as the vastness of the Russian countryside melts into the author's inner landscape. A few of the lyrics reveal an inclination toward things that need man, presenting them in impressionistic trappings that show a predilection for that which is most immediate and intricate.

"Of Poverty and Death," the final segment of *The Book of Hours*, anticipates the negative, sometimes melancholy tone of Rilke's later collections. Its substance is human misery presented in variations that expose in stark coloration the world of the homeless, the infirm, the abandoned, and the afraid. Christian motifs and themes are employed to accentuate Rilke's rejection of the Christian God, while rich images establish a substantial tie to "Of the Monastic Life" in the affirmation of God as an original poetic creation.

Dinggedichte

Rilke's most lasting legacy and most important contribution to German poesy is the *Dinggedicht* (thing poem), an originally conceived interpretation of inner experience generated in response to encounters with external objects and phenomena that the poet transformed into symbols for the elements of human life. With *New Poems*, in which he perfected this particular form, Rilke made a breakthrough that was immeasurably far-reaching in its implications for the expansion of German poetry's expressive domain.

A reflection of Rilke's attention to impulses from Rodin's sculpture and Cézanne's paintings, the *Dinggedicht* is the product of disciplined and thorough scrutinization of its model. Outwardly, it seeks to offer the character and intrinsic constitution of an object that is described for its own sake in painstakingly refined language. On another level, however, it documents the acquisition of external things for the poet's inner domain, thereby transforming the physical phenomenon into a precise and specifically calculated symbol for a portion of his re-creation of the world for himself. Some of the poems analyze people, buildings, natural and artificial scenes, plants, animals, and even motifs from mythology and the Bible; others are lyric translations of statues and paintings. Each provides a segment of Rilke's new interpretation and clarification of existence. Unlike the earlier forms, the *Dinggedicht* renounces the commitment to melodic sound relationships and connected imagery chains. The exacting identification of the poem's external object and its reduction to its fundamental nature permitted the poet to place it into an absolute domain of pure symbol.

New Poems

Rilke achieved his most representative mastery of the *Dinggedicht* in *New Poems*, a collection in which heavy stress is placed on negative moods in the explication of the view that God is the direction and not the object of love. In their extreme subtlety and refinement of language, their worldly elegance, and their moral and emotional engagement, the most representative poems of Rilke's Paris period form the center of his work as a whole. The *Dinggedichte* of *New Poems* are a detailed reflection of his view that his poetic task was the interpretation and clarification of existence for the purpose of healing the world. By accepting, recognizing, and loving things for themselves, the poet places himself in a position to trace animals, plants, works of art, human figures, and other objects back to their true nature and substance. Precise seeing and artistic transformation enable him to project in symbols the content and meaning both of his surroundings and of that which is within him.

Divided into two loosely chronological parts, the poems in *New Poems* examine in objectively plastic, precisely disciplined structures representative manifestations and individuals that belong to the world of nature and to man's most important cultural attainments, from the Bible to classical antiquity, from the Middle Ages to the Renaissance. Mystical inwardness is projected in carefully defined symbols that objectively externalize the events within the poet that are stimulated by the process of seeing. Gloom, absurdity, and disintegration are common moods in poems that question the possibility for everything, including man, to exist and thereby to become the subject of literature.

"THE PANTHER"

The symbolic portraits of *New Poems* focus on a broad variety of models. Among the most successful are those based on impressions from the Jardin des Plantes. "Der Panther" ("The Panther"), the earliest and most famous of the *Dinggedichte*, transforms its object into a symbol of heroic existence. By the very power of its seeing, the panther, like the poet, is able to create its own inner landscape, absorbing the visual impressions of external objects into itself, where it may modify, penetrate, or even destroy them. One of Rilke's most vivid depictions of rapport with an object, achieved in the act of intense observation, is given in "Archaïscher Torso Apollos" ("Archaic Torso of Apollo"), the first work in the second volume of *New Poems*. The headless statue becomes a kind of spiritual mirror that directs the onlooker's gaze back into the self, enabling him to recognize the need for change in his own life.

DUINO ELEGIES AND SONNETS TO ORPHEUS

An important consequence of Rilke's Paris experience was a reevaluation of his literary existence that led ultimately to a significant turning point in his career. The problem of an irreconcilable conflict between the demands of practicality and art was compounded by a philosophical crisis involving the tensions that he felt in his need to make a definitive break with Christianity and in his loathing of modern technology. Against this background, an encounter with Søren Kierkegaard's existential philosophy led eventually to Rilke's production of the mythologically exaggerated *Duino Elegies* and *Sonnets to Orpheus* as the peak of his literary endeavor. In these mature lyrics, the creative attitudes and symbolic devices of *New Poems* were refined and perfected. Rilke responded to many different stimuli—World War I, the works of Friedrich Gottlieb Klopstock, Johann Wolfgang von Goethe, and Heinrich von Kleist, Sigmund Freud's psychology, among others—in creating a culminating synthesis of his own poetic view of human life and destiny. Dactylic and iambic meters, free rhythms, questions, and exclamations provide the frame for bold images that pinpoint once again the fundamental directions of Rilke's work as a whole.

Between 1912 and 1922, Rilke created the ten Duino elegies in monumental celebration of man as the final, most extreme possibility of existence. The ultimate refinement of the delineation of his own calling focuses no longer on the artist as interpreter and clarifier of his surroundings, but rather ordains the poet as a prophet and savior whose task is to preserve everything that has being. He thus becomes the protagonist and representative of humanity in a new religion of life that is an expression of unchecked aestheticism. By saving the world from a collapse that seems unavoidable, the poet engages in an act of self-purification and follows the only possible course of personal redemption.

Taken together, the elegies offer a mural of Rilke's inner landscape. Internalization of travel experiences, the lonely scenery at Duino Castle, the flight of birds, mythological constructs, and other phenomena create a background of timeless "inner space" against which the author projects his coming to grips with the existential polarities of life and death. Progressing from lament to profound affirmation of mortality, the poems glorify the fulfillment of humanity's promise to maintain all things of value through a process of transformation that rescues external nature by placing it in the protected realm of the spirit. The power by which this is accomplished is love, supremely manifested by lovers, people who die young, heroes, children, and animals. By bringing together earth and space, life and death, all dimensions of reality and time into a single inward hierarchical unity, Rilke sought to ensure the continuation of man's outward existence.

In the first elegy, the poet states his view of the human condition: imperfection, the questionable status of man, the experience of transience, the pain of love. Upon this basis he builds a new mythology of life. Its center is the non-Christian angel who appears in the second elegy as a symbol for the absolute and unattainable, the norm from which man in his limitations deviates. In a valid transformation of psychoanalysis into images, Rilke pinpoints the threat that exists within man's self in the power of natural drives. Illumination of the brokenness, ambiguity, superficiality, and mechanical senselessness of human pursuits is followed in the sixth elegy by identification of the hero as a symbolic concept that contrasts with average life. The seventh poem of the cycle breaks away from the lament of human insufficiency, suddenly glorifying the here and now in hymnic language that moves to a confessional peak. Renewed expression of the idea that the difference between man and the natural creature cannot be resolved is followed by an attempt to show that life must be accepted and made fruitful despite its limitations. The culminating elegy creates a balance between mourning and celebration that unites the antithetical problems in a grand, affirmative vision of pain and death as the destiny of man and the only true evidence of his existence.

Late poems in French

The verse written in French after *Duino Elegies* and *Sonnets to Orpheus* was anticlimactic for Rilke's career. It lacks the depth and profundity of earlier works, although individual poems achieve lightness and sparkle in their reflection of a new rejoicing in mortal existence.

Other major works

long fiction: *Am Leben hin*, 1889; *Die Letzten*, 1902; *Die Weise von Liebe und Tod des Cornets Christoph Rilke*, 1906 (*The Tale of the Love and Death of Cornet Christoph Rilke*, 1932); *Die Aufzeichnungen des Malte Laurids Brigge*, 1910 (*The Notebooks of Malte Laurids Brigge*, 1930; also known as *The Journal of My Other Self*); *Ewald Tragy*, 1929 (English translation, 1958).

short fiction: *Zwei Prager Geschichten*, 1899; *Vom lieben Gott und Anderes*, 1900 (republished as *Geschichten vom lieben Gott*, 1904; *Stories of God*, 1931, 1963); *Erzählungen und Skizzen aus der Frühzeit*, 1928.

plays: *Murillo*, pb. 1895 (English translation, 1979); *Jetzt und in der Stunde unseres Absterbens*, pr., pb. 1896 (*Now and in the Hour of Our Death*, 1979); *Höhenluft*, wr. 1897, pr. 1969 (*Air at High Altitude*, 1979); *Im Frühfrost*, pr., pb. 1897 (*Early Frost*, 1979); *Vigilien*, wr. 1897 (*Vigils*, 1979); *Ohne Gegenwart*, pb. 1898 (*Not Present*, 1979); *Waisenkinder*, pb. 1901 (*Orphans*, 1979); *Das tägliche Leben*, pr. 1901 (*Everyday Life*, 1979); *Die weisse Fürstin*, pb. 1929 (*The White Princess*, 1979); *Nine Plays*, pb. 1979.

nonfiction: *Auguste Rodin*, 1903 (English translation, 1919); *Worpswede*, 1903; *Briefe an einen jungen Dichter*, 1929 (*Letters to a Young Poet*, 1934); *Wartime Letters of Rainer Maria Rilke, 1914-1921*, 1940; *Letters of Rainer Maria Rilke*, 1945-1948 (2 volumes); *Selected Letters of Rainer Maria Rilke, 1902-1926*, 1947; *Briefwechsel [zwischen] Rainer Maria Rilke und Marie von Thurn und Taxis*, 1951 (*The Letters of Rainer Maria Rilke and Princess Marie von Thurn und Taxis*, 1958); *Rainer Maria Rilke, Lou Andreas-Salomé: Briefwechsel*, 1952.

Bibliography

Bernstein, Michael Andre. *Five Portraits: Modernity and the Imagination in Twentieth-Century German Writing (Rethinking Theory)*. Edited by Gary Saul Morson. Evanston, Ill.: Northwestern University Press, 2000. Rilke is regarded by many as the most important and influential German-language poet since Johann Wolfgang von Goethe. This work presents his poetry in the context of the shift among German writers from Romanticism and aestheticism to twentieth century modernism.

Freedman, Ralph. *Life of a Poet: Rainer Maria Rilke*. New York: Farrar, Straus & Giroux, 1996. A helpful complement to Donald Prater's definitive biography, this work draws extensive parallels between Rilke's life and the content of his poetry. Also contains several photographs of Rilke and his family.

Kleinbard, David. *The Beginning of Terror: A Psychological Study of Rainer Maria Rilke's Life and Work*. New York: New York University Press, 1993. A critical rather than comprehensive biography, attempting a psychoanalysis of Rilke and his published writing. Examines issues such as Rilke's childhood, his relationships with his parents (both biological and surrogate), and his debilitating blood disorder and its effect on his work.

Prater, Donald. *A Ringing Glass: The Life of Rainer Maria Rilke*. Reprint. New York: Clarendon Press, 1993. The definitive biography of Rilke; it concentrates especially on his European travels and correspondence with friends. Also, the bibliography is highly helpful for those who need a comprehensive, expert guide to Rilke criticism. Illustrated.

Ryan, Judith. *Rilke, Modernism, and Poetic Tradition*. New York: Cambridge University Press, 1999. Although Rilke saw himself as a more or less self-created writer, who needed extended periods of solitude in which to work, Ryan shows him in his relationship to other writers and even painters in the European culture of his day. Traces his movement from the art-for-art's-sake school of writing into modernism.

Lowell A. Bangerter;
bibliography updated by Craig Payne

Arthur Rimbaud

Born: Charleville, France; October 20, 1854
Died: Marseilles, France; November 10, 1891

Principal poetry

Une Saison en enfer, 1873 (*A Season in Hell*, 1932)
Les Illuminations, 1886 (*Illuminations*, 1932)

Other literary forms

Arthur Rimbaud's impact on the literary world stems entirely from his poetry.

Achievements

Arthur Rimbaud's meteoric career has forever earned for him a place as the brilliant *enfant terrible* of French verse. Since his death, he has attracted more critical attention than any French poet save Stéphane Mallarmé. A revolutionary both in his life and in his art, Rimbaud exerted a radical influence on the scope and direction of French poetry. He has been credited with introducing *vers libre* (free verse), which would come to dominate modern poetry, and his systematic cultivation of dreams, hallucinations, and madness anticipated modern interest in the irrational side of the human mind. He became, for a time, the patron saint of André Breton and the Surrealists. Rimbaud's conception of the poetical "I" as "other" ("Je est un autre") has been acclaimed as an intuitive perception of the unconscious that predated its mapping by Sigmund Freud. Finally, Rimbaud was the first French literary figure to sound a distinctly feminist note in his writings, condemning the cultural repression of women and looking forward to a future day of liberation when they would assume their rightful place in society and art. Faithful to his own precept, "Il faut être absolument moderne" ("We must be absolutely modern"), he prefigured key trends in modern art and thought.

Biography

Jean-Nicolas-Arthur Rimbaud was born in the provincial town of Charleville on the Franco-Prussian border. His mother, Vitalie Cuif, was of peasant stock and a devout Jansenist; his father, Captain Frédéric Rimbaud, was an itinerant army officer who abandoned the family when Rimbaud was only six years old. A brilliant student, Rimbaud completed nine years of schooling in eight, earning numerous literary prizes in the course of his studies. His earliest attempts at verse were in Latin, followed by his first poem in French, "Les Étrennes des orphelins" ("The Orphans' New Year's Day Gifts"), published in January, 1870. Encouraged by his teacher, Georges Izambard, Rimbaud sent off three poems to the Parnassian poet Théodore de Banville, who, however, failed to express any interest.

The outbreak of the Franco-Prussian War in July, 1870, put an end to Rimbaud's formal schooling. Alienated by the hypocrisy of provincial society, which he satirized in various poems composed in the early months of 1870, he ran away from home three times: first to Paris, then to Belgium, and again to Paris. He was back in Charleville when the Paris Commune was declared on March 18, 1871. Although much critical attention has

Arthur Rimbaud (Library of Congress)

been devoted to Rimbaud's possible ties with the Commune, there is no clear evidence that he ever left Charleville during the crucial period of the Paris uprising. On May 15, Rimbaud composed his celebrated "Lettre du voyant" ("Seer Letter"), addressed to a friend, Paul Demeny. Rimbaud's break with traditional poetry was by this time already complete, and on August 15, he again wrote to Banville, enclosing a new poem, "Ce qu'on dit au poète à propos de fleurs" ("What One Says to the Poet in Regard to Flowers"), a vitriolic attack on Parnassian poetics. Shortly thereafter, Rimbaud also sent off eight new poems, in two installments, to Paul Verlaine, who responded with the famous phrase "Venez, chère grande âme, on vous appelle, on vous attend" ("Come, dear great soul, we call to you, we await you").

Rimbaud arrived in the capital with a copy of his newly composed poem, "Le Bateau ivre" ("The Drunken Boat"), which brought him some notoriety among the Parisian literary crowd. The young poet's obnoxious behavior soon alienated him, however, both from Verlaine's family and his fellow artists, and March, 1872, found him back in Charleville. Rimbaud returned to Paris in May and there began a series of escapades with Verlaine which some have characterized as simply youthful exuberance and others as an unhappy love affair. The pair fled first to Brussels, then to London, where a quarrel erupted. Verlaine returned to Brussels, where he was soon followed by Rimbaud.

In Brussels, events soon took a tragic turn. In a moment of drunken rage, Verlaine fired on Rimbaud, wounding him slightly in the hand. The incident might have ended there, but Verlaine later accosted Rimbaud in the street, and the frightened youth sought help from a passing policeman. The authorities intervened, and Verlaine was sentenced to two years in prison. Rimbaud returned to his mother's family farm at Roche, where he completed *A Season in Hell*, begun in April. In late 1873, Rimbaud again visited Paris, where he made the acquaintance of the young poet Germain Nouveau, with whom he traveled to London in the early months of 1874. Almost nothing is known of this second friendship beyond the fact that it ended with Nouveau's abrupt return to Paris in June of that year.

In 1875, Rimbaud embarked on a new series of travels which led him to Stuttgart, across the Swiss Alps on foot into Italy, and back to Charleville via Paris. After visiting Vienna in April, 1876, he enlisted in the Dutch colonial army on May 19 and set sail for Java. He deserted ship in Batavia (modern Djakarta) and returned to Charleville. In May, 1877, Rimbaud was in Bremen, where he attempted (in vain) to enlist in the American Marines. Subsequent travels the same year took him to Stockholm, Copenhagen, Marseilles, Rome, and back to Charleville. In early 1878, he visited Hamburg, returning during the summer to work on the family farm at Roche. In October, he again traversed Switzerland on foot, crossing the Alps into Italy. There he took the train to Genoa and embarked for Alexandria, later departing for Cyprus, where he worked as a foreman in a marble quarry. Stricken with typhoid, he returned to Charleville in May, 1879, once again spending the summer at Roche. In March, 1880, he was back in Cyprus, where he found work as a construction foreman. An intemperate climate and a salary dispute soon forced him to resign his position and to seek employment elsewhere.

Rimbaud spent the remaining eleven years of his life as the business agent of a French colonial trading company in the remote wilds of Abyssinia (modern-day Ethiopia) and Aden. At the end of this time, he had amassed, through agonizing labor and in the face of constant adversity, the modest sum of 150,000 francs (approximately thirty thousand dollars). In February, 1891, intense pain in his right knee forced him to return to France for medical treatment. Doctors in Marseilles diagnosed his illness as cancer and ordered the immediate amputation of the infected right leg. The cancer proved too widespread to check, however, and Rimbaud died in a state of delirium on November 10, 1891. According to a tradition spawned by his devout sister, Isabelle, who was with the poet in his final moments, Rimbaud returned to Catholicism on his deathbed. Since Isabelle is, however, known to have tampered with her brother's personal letters, critics have given little credence to her testimony.

Analysis

Arthur Rimbaud's early verse (of which he published only three short pieces in various academic bulletins) falls into two general categories. First, there is his satiric verse, exemplified by such poems as "Les Premières Communions" ("First Communions") and "Les Assis" ("The Seated Ones"), which attacks religious hypocrisy and the sterility of bourgeois society. Second, there is his erotic verse, typified by such poems as "Vénus anadyomène" ("Venus Emerging from the Waves") and "Le Coeur volé" ("The Stolen Heart"), which speaks of the trauma of sexual coming-of-age. A pastiche of traditional styles and forms, these initial works nevertheless evidence a brilliant gift for verbal expression and announce the theme of revolt which informs all Rimbaud's writings.

"Seer Letter"

On May 15, 1871, Rimbaud declared his emancipation from traditional poetics in his celebrated "Seer Letter," addressed to his friend Paul Demeny. This letter, Rimbaud's *ars poetica*, begins with a contemptuous denunciation of all previous poetry as nothing more than rhymed prose. Only Charles Baudelaire, "un vrai dieu" ("a true god"), is spared and, even then, only partially—he frequented a self-consciously artistic milieu, and he failed to find new forms of expression. Rimbaud then calls for a radically new conception of the poet's mission: "Car je est un autre" ("For I is an other"). It is the essential task of the poet to give voice to the repressed, unconscious "other" that lies concealed behind the mask of the rational, Cartesian "I"—the "other" which societal restrictions have condemned to silence. This can be accomplished only by "un long, immense et raisonn édérèglement de tous les sens" ("a long, immense and reasoned derangement of all the senses"). Unlike his Romantic predecessors and such Symbolist contemporaries as Mallarmé, who passively awaited the return of the muse, Rimbaud insists on the active role the poet must take: "Le Poète se fait voyant" ("The poet makes himself a seer"). The poet must actively cultivate dreams, hallucinations, and madness. In so doing, he becomes the great liberator of humanity, a Prometheus who steals fire from the gods, the spokesman for all those whom society has ostracized: "Il devient entre tous le grand malade, le grand criminel, le grand maudit—et le grand Savant!" ("He becomes, more than anyone, the great sick one, the great criminal, the great accursed one—and the great Learned One!"). Such a poet will be "un multiplicateur de progrès" whose genius, unrestrained by societal taboos and the limitations of rational thought, will lead humankind into a new golden age.

Throughout the remaining months of 1871 and the following year, Rimbaud endeavored to give form to this poetic vision in a new series of songs and verse which are best exemplified by two poems which critics have universally acclaimed as masterpieces: "Le Bateau ivre" ("The Drunken Boat") and "Voyelles" ("Vowels").

"The Drunken Boat"

Perhaps the best known of Rimbaud's works, "The Drunken Boat" was composed during the summer of

1871 and presented to Verlaine in September of that same year. Although the work borrows from a wide variety of sources (Victor Hugo, Baudelaire, Jules Verne, and Vicomte Chateaubriand, to name but a few), it remains a stunning and original tour de force—particularly for a young poet of sixteen. The poem, composed of twenty-five quatrains in classical Alexandrines and narrated in the first person, is a symbolic drama in three acts. In the first act (quatrains 1 through 4), set on a vast river in the New World, the boat recounts its escape from its haulers, who are massacred by screaming natives, and its subsequent descent toward the sea. There follows a brief, transitional interlude (quatrain 5) in which the boat passes through a ritual purification: Its wooden shell is permeated by the seawater which cleanses it of wine stains and vomit and bears off the boat's rudder and anchor.

The second and central act (quatrains 6 through 22) tells of the boat's intoxicating maritime adventures and its fantastic, hallucinatory vision of a transcendental reality which ordinary mortals have only glimpsed in passing. Yet, the boat's long and frenetic voyage of discovery ultimately begins to turn sour. After braving whirlpools, hurricanes, raging seas, and Leviathans from the deep, the boat unexpectedly declares its nostalgia for the ancient parapets of Europe.

In the third and final act (quatrains 23 through 25), the boat's delirious optimism turns to anguished despair. Its quest for the absolute has at length proved futile, and the boat now seeks dissolution in death. If it desires a return to European waters, it is to the cold, black puddle into which a sad, impoverished child releases a boat as frail as a May butterfly. At the same time, the boat realizes the impossibility of any turning back to its previous mode of existence. It can no longer follow in the wake of the merchant ships, nor bear the haughty pride of the military gunboats, nor swim beneath the horrible eyes of the prison ships that lie at anchor in the harbor.

"The Drunken Boat" reflects both Rimbaud's new conception of the poet as "seer" and the influence of the French Symbolists, such as Verlaine and Baudelaire, who sought to replace the effusive, personalized verse of the Romantics with a symbolic, impersonal mode of expression. Critics have generally equated the work's "protagonist," the boat, with the poet himself, reading the poem as a symbolic account of Rimbaud's own efforts to transcend reality through language. Most critics are also agreed that the poem's final two stanzas, while they suggest the advent of a new self-awareness, evince a disillusionment with the "seer" experiment and prefigure Rimbaud's later renunciation of poetry.

"Vowels"

Rimbaud's celebrated sonnet "Vowels," written in decasyllabic verse, dates from the same period as "The Drunken Boat" and was similarly presented to Verlaine in September, 1871. Another of Rimbaud's "seer" poems, the work postulates a mystic correspondence between vowels and colors: "A noir, E blanc, I rouge, U vert, O bleu" ("A black, E white, I red, U green, O blue"). The poem has its literary source in Baudelaire's famous sonnet "Correspondences," which had asserted an underlying connection between sounds, perfumes, and colors and had popularized the concept of synesthesia. Another probable source for the work has been found in an illustrated alphabet primer which Rimbaud may have read as a child and which has served to elucidate some of the sonnet's enigmatic imagery.

Perhaps the most ingenious interpretation of the poem is that of the critic Lucien Sausy, who argued that the work exploits correspondences not between sound and color (there are, in fact, few traces of such matching within the phonetic content of the poem) but rather between the visual form of the vowels themselves and the images to which the latter are linked: *A*, if inverted, thus suggests the delta-shaped body of a fly; *E* (written as a Greek epsilon in the manuscript), if turned on its side, suggests vapors, tents, and glaciers; and so on. (Sausy's interpretation, first advanced in *Les Nouvelles Littéraires*, September 2, 1933, is available in the notes to the Pléiade edition of Rimbaud's works.) As a counterbalance, however, one might mention Verlaine's explanation of the sonnet: "Rimbaud saw things that way and that's all there is to it."

A Season in Hell

By his own account, Rimbaud composed *A Season in Hell* during the period from April to August of 1873. Rimbaud supervised the book's publication, and it was printed in Brussels in the fall of 1873 in an edition of five hundred copies. Rimbaud was unable, however, to pay the printing costs, and this first edition, save for six author's copies which circulated among his friends, remained in the attic of a Brussels publishing house until discovered in 1901 by a Belgian bibliophile, who did not make his discovery public until 1914.

The text, which Rimbaud had originally intended to entitle "Livre païen" (pagan book) or "Livre nègre" (Negro book—the French adjective is pejorative), consists of nine prose poems and seven poems in verse, the latter all contained within the section "Délires II" ("Deliria II"). The work has been variously acclaimed by critics for its original and stunning verbal display, its fantastic, visionary imagery, and its prophetic pronouncements concerning Rimbaud's own future. As the title indicates, *A Season in Hell* is Rimbaud's poetic attempt to come to grips with his recent "dark night of the soul"—his unhappy adventure with Verlaine and his anguished experience as "seer." Viewed from the perspective of Rimbaud's own metaphysical dictum—"I is an other"—the work, narrated in the first person, recounts a confrontation between the rational, conscious "I" and the irrational, unconscious "other" which the poet had systematically worked to cultivate.

The text opens with a brief introductory section (untitled) in which the poet evokes with longing his lost state of childhood innocence. He recalls his frenzied flight from reason, his revolt against traditional concepts of beauty and morality, his pursuit of crime, and his cultivation of madness. He momentarily dreams of regaining his former state of innocence through a return to Christian charity but immediately rejects the latter as an empty illusion. Inescapably condemned to death and damnation, he dedicates his opus not to the traditional poetic Muse but rather to Satan. This introductory segment serves to announce the key themes which the body of the work will subsequently develop: the abandonment of the "seer" experiment, the nostalgia for the comfort afforded by traditional Christian values, and the attainment of a new self-awareness which, however, prevents any naïve return to the past.

"Bad Blood"

In the following prose poem, "Mauvais Sang" ("Bad Blood"), the poet attributes his failure to transcend the vulgar world or reality to some inherited defect which now condemns him to a life of manual toil. Nor does he envision any hope in the progress promised by Cartesian rationalism and the advent of science. The world may yet be headed toward total destruction. Disillusioned with Western civilization, he seeks imaginative shelter in what he perceives as the savage freedom of black African society. His amoral utopia is, however, destroyed by the arrival of the white colonialists, who impose their debilitating Christian ethics by force of arms. Momentarily seduced by Christianity, the poet ultimately rejects it as an infringement on human freedom and refuses to embark on a honeymoon with Jesus Christ as father-in-law. Rather than remain enslaved, he hurls himself to his death beneath the horses of the conquering Europeans.

"Night in Hell"

The conflict between Christianity and paganism is further developed in "Nuit de l'enfer" ("Night in Hell"). Here, the poet is engulfed in the fires of Hell, to which his parents have condemned him through baptism and catechism lessons. His suffering derives from his inability to choose between the absolute but terrible freedom offered by Satan and the serene but limited freedom promised by the Christian God. Hell, in short, is a state of eternal and lucid alienation.

"Deliria I"

"Délires I" ("Deliria I") introduces a "Vièrge folle" ("Foolish Virgin") who recounts her difficult life with "l'Époux infernal" ("The Infernal Spouse") who seduced her with the false promise of an amoral and transcendent Paradise. Numerous critics have found in this passage a mythic retelling of Verlaine's intellectual and erotic seduction by Rimbaud; other critics have preferred to read the passage as emblematic of the seduction of the poet's rational and moral self by his own irrational and amoral unconscious. In either case, the poem is a bitter indictment of Rimbaud's failed efforts to transform reality.

"Deliria II"

In "Délires II" ("Deliria II"), subtitled "L'Alchimie du verbe" ("Verbal Alchemy"), the poet looks back on what he now views as an act of folly: his attempt to transcend reality through the systematic cultivation of the irrational and the invention of a new language that would draw in all the human senses and give voice to everything in man that had previously been barred from expression. He gives as tangible examples of this enterprise six verse poems, the visionary imagery of which speaks symbolically of his hunger and thirst for the absolute, his frustration with past theology and future technology, and his fervent conviction that he has indeed found the mystic line of juncture between sea and sky, body and soul, the known and unknown. This metaphysical quest has ultimately failed, the poet says, for he has been damned by the rainbow—an ironic allusion to the rainbow sent by God to Noah as a sign of future redemption. As his dream-filled night draws to a close, and morning approaches, the poet awakes to hear the strains of the hymn "Christus venit" (Christ has come) resounding through the somber cities of the world. His career as "seer" has ended with the bleak dawn of reality.

"The Impossible," "Lightning," "Morning," and "Farewell"

The four remaining prose poems, all of them brief, further expand upon major themes in the work. In "L'Impossible" ("The Impossible"), the poet tells of his futile efforts to reconcile Christianity and Eastern mysticism and his ultimate rejection of both. In "Éclair" ("Lightning"), the poet finds momentary comfort in the dignity of work but cannot avoid perceiving the vanity of all human efforts in the face of death and dissolution. "Matin" ("Morning") announces the end of the poet's night in Hell. In spite of the limitations imposed by the human condition, he chooses life over death. Although all men are slaves, they should not curse life. In the final passage, "Adieu" ("Farewell"), the poet renounces his unsuccessful career as "seer" in favor of a newfound divine clarity, the anguished self-knowledge which his experience has brought him. There will be no turning back to the past for solace, nor any attempt to seek oblivion in the love of a woman. Man must be absolutely modern, the poet declares; for himself, he is content to possess the truth that man is both body and soul.

Illuminations

Illuminations was published in 1886, without Rimbaud's knowledge. Some years earlier, he had left a manuscript of the work with Verlaine, whence it passed through several hands before it was published in the Symbolist periodical *La Vogue*, appearing in book form (edited and with a preface by Verlaine) later in the same year.

Although a century has passed since the first appearance of *Illuminations*, a number of fundamental questions concerning the collection remain to be resolved, and perhaps will never be definitely resolved. First there is the matter of the title. The manuscript itself is untitled, and the only evidence for the title by which the collection is known is the statement of Paul Verlaine, a notoriously unreliable witness. In a letter written in 1878 to his brother-in-law, Charles de Sivry, Verlaine says: "Have re-read *Illuminations* (painted plates). . . ." Later, in the preface to the first edition of *Illuminations*, he adds that "the word [that is, "illuminations"] is English and means *gravures coloriées*, colored plates," claiming that this was the subtitle which Rimbaud had chosen for the work.

The question of the title and subtitle may seem a mere scholarly quibble, but it is more than that, for at issue is the significance which Rimbaud himself attached to the title and, by extension, the spirit in which he intended the work to be read. Some critics, accepting Verlaine's testimony without qualification, suggest that by "painted plates" or "colored plates," Rimbaud meant the cheap colored prints which had recently become widely available. The tone of the title, then, would be highly ironic. Other critics suggest that Verlaine garbled Rimbaud's meaning—that Rimbaud had in mind the illuminated manuscripts of the Middle Ages. Still others reject Verlaine's testimony on this matter as another of his fabrications, arguing that by "illuminations" Rimbaud meant moments of spiritual insight; some readers have seen in the title a reference to the occult doctrines of Illuminism.

Another important debate concerns the date of composition. It was long believed that *Illuminations* preceded *A Season in Hell*, but later this assumption was seriously challenged. Again, the question of dating may appear to be of interest only to specialists, but such is not the case. The conclusion to *A Season in Hell* has been widely regarded as Rimbaud's farewell to poetry. If, in fact, he wrote *Illuminations* after *A Season in Hell*, many existing critical interpretations are invalid or in need of substantial revision

This argument for dating *Illuminations* after *A Season in Hell* is primarily based on the pioneering research of Henri de Bouillane de Lacoste. Bouillane de Lacoste's graphological analysis of the manuscript, in conjunction with other, more subjective, arguments, has persuaded many scholars to accept Verlaine's once-rejected assertion that the work was written during the period from 1873 to 1875 in the course of Rimbaud's European travels. On the other hand, there are a number of reputable Rimbaud scholars who find Bouillane de Lacoste's analysis inconclusive at best and who thus retain the old chronology. In any case, one cannot know with certainty the date of composition of the individual poems themselves, nor is there any clear indication of the final order in which Rimbaud intended them to appear. The reason for Rimbaud's prolongation of his poetic career beyond his abdication from poetry in *A Season in Hell* seems destined to remain a mystery.

Illuminations is regarded by many critics as Rimbaud's most original work and his consummate contribution to French poetry. While it represents a continuation of the "seer" experiment conducted in his earlier verse, it also marks a radical departure from the narrative, anecdotal, and descriptive modes of expression to be found in his previous poetry and in that of his contemporaries. The poems in *Illuminations* are strikingly modern in that each forms a self-contained, self-referential unit which stands independent of the collection as a whole and remains detached from any clear point of reference in the world of reality. They do not purport to convey any didactic, moral, or philosophical message to the reader. Ephemeral and dreamlike, each emerges from the void as a spontaneous flow of images generated by free association. They are works in which the rational "I" allows the unconscious "other" to speak. As manifestations of the unconscious, they reveal an almost infinitely rich condensation of meaning which defies any linear attempts at interpretation. They thus elucidate Rimbaud's earlier remark in *A Season in Hell* that he "reserved all translation rights." They are, again in the poet's own words, "accessible to all meanings." If they are coherent, it is in the way dreams are coherent, and, like dreams, they speak from the hidden recesses of the mind. Hermetic in form, they lead down a different path from that charted by the Symbolist verse of Rimbaud's contemporary, Mallarmé: They reflect not an aesthetic obsession with the problematics of language but a perpetual striving to give voice to all that reason and social mores have condemned to silence.

Although *Illuminations* consists of a discontinuous series of pieces devoid of any central narrative plot, critics have drawn attention to a number of major recurring themes to be found within the text. Given the work's dreamlike qualities and its close affinity with the unconscious, it is not surprising that the theme most often cited by critics is that of childhood. Numerous passages in the work evoke the blissful innocence of childhood, Rimbaud's "paradise lost," irrevocably destroyed by the advent of civilization and Christianity. The theme is developed at particular length in the two prose poems "Enfance" ("Childhood") and "Après le déluge" ("After the Deluge"). In the first, the child-poet tells of his Satanic fall from a state of divine omniscience and absolute freedom into a subterranean prison where he is condemned to silence. In the second, which ironically alludes to the biblical story of the Flood and the promise of divine redemption, the poet sees the natural innocence of childhood as being progressively corrupted by the rise of civilization, and he ends by conjuring up new floods that will sweep away the repressive work of society.

A second and related major theme, exemplified by such prose poems as "Villes I" ("Cities I"), "Villes II" ("Cities II"), and "Métropolitain" ("Metropolitan"), is that of the city. Although modeled in part on the Paris and London of Rimbaud's own time, the cities in *Illuminations* are phantasmagoric, shimmering cities of the future which present a vision of technological wonder and bleak sterility. Promised utopias, they repeatedly and rapidly degenerate into vast urban wastelands which devour their pitiful human prey. In the end, they are bitterly renounced by their creator and verbally banished back to the void from which they emerged.

A third major theme is that of metamorphosis—a theme that is a logical outgrowth of Rimbaud's own assertion that "I is an other." For Rimbaud, as his "Seer Letter" makes clear, the seemingly stable Cartesian I is merely an illusion which masks the presence of a multiplicity of repressed others. Man has no central, defining essence. In *Illuminations*, the poet thus undergoes a continual series of metamorphoses. In "Parade," he appears as a procession of itinerant comedians; in "Antique," as the son of the pagan god Pan, at once animal, man, and woman; in "Bottom," as the character in William Shakespeare's *A Midsummer Night's Dream* (1595-1596) who seeks to appropriate all the other characters' roles; and finally, in "Being Beauteous," as the incarnation of beauty itself. There are no limits to man's being, Rimbaud suggests, if he will only realize the vast potential within him.

Other major works

miscellaneous: *Œuvres complètes*, 1948 (*Complete Works, Selected Letters*, 1966).

Bibliography

Ahearn, Edward J. *Rimbaud: Visions and Habitations*. Berkeley: University of California Press, 1983. Discusses the influence of Rimbaud's early life and surroundings on his brief poetic career, including the anticlerical and anticonventional guidance he received during his teen years, when he began writing poetry. Points out links between Rimbaud's poetic images and his actual physical environment.

Hackett, Cecil Arthur. *Rimbaud: A Critical Introduction*. New York: Cambridge University Press, 1981. A good introduction for those beginning to explore Rimbaud's poetry. Contains much poem-by-poem explication, as well as analyses of Rimbaud's overall poetic achievement and cultural influence.

Perloff, Marjorie. *The Poetics of Indeterminacy: Rimbaud to Cage*. Evanston, Ill.: Northwestern University Press, 2000. This work contains only one chapter on Rimbaud but is highly useful in placing him within his historical context. Discusses his influence on modernist poets such as Gertrude Stein, Ezra Pound, and William Carlos Williams, as a transitional force between Symbolism and modernism.

Robb, Graham. *Rimbaud: A Biography*. New York: Norton, 2000. Presents a "reconstruction of Rimbaud's life"; discusses the revolutionary impact his poetry has had on twentieth century writers and artists, especially since Rimbaud's admirers primarily arose after his early death. Examines the influence of Rimbaud's early family life, in particular his stormy relationship with his mother, and presents thoroughly his checkered career after his abandonment of poetry at the age of twenty-one.

Steinmetz, Jean-Luc. *Arthur Rimbaud: Presence of an Enigma*. Translated by Jon Graham. New York: Welcome Rain, 2001. A comprehensive biography, this work focuses on Rimbaud's numerous self-contradictions and extremes of behavior, particularly in his stormy relationship with the older poet Paul Verlaine. The author analyzes Rimbaud's poetry primarily in its relation to the poet's life.

James John Baran;
bibliography updated by Craig Payne

Yannis Ritsos

Born: Monemvasia, Greece; May, 14, 1909
Died: Athens, Greece; November 11, 1990

Principal poetry

Trakter, 1934
Pyramides, 1935
Epitaphios, 1936
To tragoudi tes adelphes mou, 1937
Dokimasia, 1943
Agrypnia, 1954
Romiosyne, 1954 (*Romiossini: The Story of the Greeks*, 1969)
e sonata tou selenophotos, 1956 (*The Moonlight Sonata*, 1975)
Poiemata A', 1961
Poiemata B', 1961
To nekro spiti, 1962 (*The Dead House*, 1974)
Martyries, A' seira, 1963
Poiemata G', 1964
Philoktetes, 1965 (English translation, 1975)
Martyries, B' seira, 1966
Orestes, 1966
Gestures and Other Poems, 1971
e Elene, 1972

Cheironomies, 1972
Petres, epanalepseis, kigklidoma, 1972
Tetarte diastase, 1972
Chartina, 1974
Selected Poems, 1974
E Kyra ton Ampelion, 1975 (*The Lady of the Vineyards*, 1978)
Ta epikairika, 1975
Poiemata D', 1975
Chronicle of Exile, 1977
The Fourth Dimension: Selected Poems of Yannis Ritsos, 1977
Gignesthai, 1977
To Makrino, 1977
Monemvasiotisses, 1978 (*The Women of Monemvasia*, 1987)
Phaidra, 1978
Ritsos in Parentheses, 1979
Scripture of the Blind, 1979
Diaphaneia, 1980
Oneiro kalokairinou mesemeriou, 1980
Subterranean Horses, 1980
Erotika, 1981 (*Erotica*, 1982)
Monovasia, 1982 (English translation, 1987)
Selected Poems, 1983
Exile and Return: Selected Poems, 1967-1974, 1985
Antapokriseis, 1987
Yannis Ritsos: Selected Poems, 1938-1988, 1989
Repetitions, Testimonies, Parentheses, 1991
Arga, poly arga mesa ste nychta, 1992 (*Late into the Night: The Last Poems of Yannis Ritsos*, 1995)
Yannis Ritsos: A Voice of Resilience and Hope in a World of Turmoil and Suffering, Selected Poems, 1938-1989, 2001

Other literary forms

Although known almost exclusively as a poet, Yannis Ritsos published prolifically as a journalist and translator, less prolifically as a critic and dramatist. His collected criticism, available in *Meletemata* (1974; studies), includes, in addition to essays on Vladimir Mayakovsky, Nazim Hikmet, Ilya Ehrenburg, and Paul Éluard, two invaluable commentaries on Ritsos's own work. Among his translations are Aleksandr Blok's *Dvendtsat* (1918), anthologies of Romanian, Czech, and Slovak poetry, and selected poems by Mayakovsky, Hikmet, and Ehrenburg.

Yannis Ritsos (Greek Press and Information Service)

Achievements

Ignored or banned for decades by the establishment, Yannis Ritsos gradually became recognized, and was nominated for the Nobel Prize three times, although, unlike his compatriots George Seferis and Odysseus Elytis, he never received that honor. He received many others, however, including the International Dimitrov Prize (Bulgaria, 1974), an honorary doctorate from the University of Thessaloniki (1975), the Alfred de Vigny Poetry Prize (France, 1975), two of Italy's International Prizes for Poetry (1976), the Lenin Peace Prize (1977), Italy's Mondello Prize (1978), and honorary doctorate from Greece's Salonica University (1975) and the University of Birmingham, England (1978). In addition to his prolific output (nearly one hundred volumes of poetry), Ritsos continues to enjoy a growing reputation as more of his work is translated into English; were he not a poet of modern Greek, a minority language, his work would be as important a part of the comparative literature curriculum in Anglo-American colleges as is that of his more thoroughly translated and celebrated compatriots, such as Seferis, Elytis, Constantine Cavafy, and Nikos Kazantzakis.

Perhaps more important than such recognition is the contribution Ritsos made to his homeland: More thoroughly than any other Greek writer, Ritsos amalgamated the two ideologies that divided his country, the communist and the bourgeois. Though he espoused Marxist Leninism early in his career and remained faithful to the party to the end, he nevertheless borrowed from Western literary movements, especially Surrealism, and struggled frankly with the Western attractions of individualism and subjectivism. All in all, because he presents a communist orientation expressed through techniques that have evolved in ways typical of noncommunist authors, he speaks for and to the entire Greek nation.

Ritsos proved himself a virtuoso in technique. His range was enormous: from the tiniest lyric to huge narrative compositions, from impenetrable surrealistic puzzles to occasional verse promulgating blunt political messages, from poetry of almost embarrassing sensuality to rarefied philosophical meditations. He is also greatly esteemed because of his personal integrity, demonstrated over years of persecution, exile, and imprisonment. As he said in 1970 when interrogated by the ruling junta: "A poet is the first citizen of his country and for this very reason it is the duty of the poet to be concerned about the politics of his country."

Biography

Yannis Ritsos was born into a wealthy landowning family of Monemvasia, but he did not have a happy childhood. His father's fortunes declined because of the land reforms under Eleftherios Venizelos in the early 1900's, and their wealth was obliterated by the Asia Minor campaigns between 1919 and 1922, when labor was unavailable for the harvests. In addition, Ritsos's father gambled compulsively, accelerating the family's decline. As if this were not enough, Ritsos's older brother and his mother died of tuberculosis when Ritsos was only twelve—a prelude to the hardships and suffering that would mark his adult life.

Upon his graduation from high school in the town of Gythion, Ritsos moved to Athens; the year was 1925, a time when that city was desperately trying to assimilate a million and a half refugees from Asia Minor. He managed to find work as a typist and then as a copyist of legal documents, but in 1926 he returned to Monemvasia after coughing blood. There he devoted himself to painting, music, and poetry, completing a group of poems that he called "Sto paleo mas spiti" (in our old house). He returned to Athens in 1927, but a new crisis in his health confined him to a tuberculosis sanatorium for three years, during which, while continuing to write poems, he also began to study Marxism. By 1930, he had committed himself to the communist cause. Transferred to a sanatorium in Crete, he found conditions there so abominable that he exposed the facility's managers in a series of newspaper articles; this led to the removal of all the patients, including Ritsos, to a better facility, where his disease came under temporary control.

Back in Athens, Ritsos directed the artistic activities of the Workers' Club, appearing in in-house theatricals and also on the stage of the Labor Union Theater. Meanwhile, his father was confined to an insane asylum. While eking out a living as actor, dancer, copy editor, and journalist, Ritsos published his first two collections, *Trakter* (tractor) and *Pyramides* (pyramids). His career took a leap forward when, in May of 1936, he composed his *Epitaphios* immediately after the slaughter of twelve tobacco workers by Thessaloniki police during a strike. Issued in ten thousand copies, this became the first of Ritsos's poems to be banned. The Metaxas dictatorship, when it came to power in August, publicly burned the 250 unsold copies at the Temple of Olympian Zeus.

In this same year, Ritsos composed *To tragoudi tes adelphes mou* (the song of my sister), after his sister Loula was committed to the same asylum that housed their father. This private dirge, balancing the public one for the slain strikers, so impressed Kostis Palamas, Greece's most influential poet at the time, that he hailed the young poet as his own successor. Ritsos suffered a brief recurrence of his tuberculosis, requiring another period in a sanatorium, after which he worked again as an actor, all the while publishing new collections of verse.

During the period of the Albanian Campaign, the German invasion, and the Axis Occupation of Greece (1940-1944), Ritsos—now confined to bed almost continuously—wrote without respite but was unable to publish freely. Among the works produced was a long novel burned during the second round of the Civil War (December, 1944) and another prose composition, never published, titled "Ariostos o prosechtikos aphegeitai stigmes tou biou tou kai tou ypnou tou" (careful Ariostos narrates moments from his life and his sleep).

After the second round of the Civil War, Ritsos fled to northern Greece with the defeated communist forces. While in Kozani, he wrote plays for the People's Theater of Macedonia. The Varkiza Accord (February 12, 1945) enabled him to return to Athens, where he regularly contributed poems, prose pieces, translations, and dance criticism to the periodical *Elefthera grammata*, as well as collaborating with the artistic branch of the communist youth movement. It was at this time that he began to write *Romiossini: The Story of the Greeks* and *The Lady of the Vineyards*, his twin tributes to the Greek Resistance.

In 1948, Ritsos was arrested because of his political activities and sent to various concentration camps on Greek islands. Under the worst of conditions, he nevertheless wrote about his privations, burying manuscripts and notes in bottles to hide them from the guards. Naturally, his work was banned. An international protest by figures such as Pablo Picasso, Louis Aragon, and Pablo Neruda led to his release in August, 1952. Free again in Athens, he joined the newly founded party, the EDA (United Democratic Left), wrote for the left-wing newspaper *Avgi*, married Falitsa Georgiadis in 1954, and became the father of a daughter in 1955. The following year, he visited the Soviet Union, traveling outside Greece for the first time. *Epitaphios* was reissued in a twentieth-anniversary edition, and *The Moonlight Sonata* brought him his first public recognition since Palamas's early enthusiasm, in the form of the State Prize for Poetry. This, in turn, led to international acclaim when Aragon published *The Moonlight Sonata* in *Les Lettres françaises*, accompanied by a flattering notice. In Greece, the publishing firm Kedros began to bring out all the work that could not be published earlier and planned for a multivolume collection of Ritsos's poems.

In 1960, the popular composer Mikis Theodorakis set eight sections of *Epitaphios* to music, making Ritsos a household name in Greece. In 1962, Ritsos traveled again, this time to Romania, Czechoslovakia, and East Germany, as a result of which he became acquainted with the Turkish poet Hikmet and his anthologies of Balkan poets. Despite a relapse of his tuberculosis, Ritsos composed prolifically during this period. In May, 1963, he journeyed to Thessaloniki to participate in the vigil for the parliamentary deputy Gregory Lambrakis, who had been mortally wounded by right-wing thugs. The following year, Ritsos himself stood for parliament as an EDA candidate. In 1966, he traveled to Cuba. Theodorakis set *Romiosyne* to music, again with immense popular success.

On April 21, 1967, the day of the Colonels' Coup, Ritsos was arrested and again sent into exile on various islands, his works once more under ban. Protests poured in from around the world, leading to his transfer to house arrest in his wife's home in Samos. A group of seventy-five members of the French Academy and other writers, including several Nobel laureates, nominated him for the Nobel Prize. Translations of his poetry multiplied, especially in France.

Offered a passport by the junta to attend a poetry festival in England in 1970—on the condition that he refrain from all criticism of the regime—Ritsos refused, but later in the same year, owing to his health, he was allowed to return to Athens to undergo an operation and to remain there. In 1971, he joined others in publishing in *Ta nea keimena* in defiance of the regime. After the relaxation of censorship in 1972, Ritsos's works written in exile came out in a flood of publication that increased after the junta's fall in 1974. Thereafter, Ritsos continued to write poetry, but largely of a different sort; in the absence of a police state and finally out of prison, his concerns turned to more lyric and personal works. He produced some of his best work in this mode—attesting to the difficulty of pigeonholing him as a political poet.

He died in Athens, Greece, on November 11, 1990, fatefully on Armistice Day as well as the eve of the Soviet Union's dissolution. Despite his communist politics, Greece's president Constantine Mitsotakis announced that this nationally mourned poet would be buried with full state honors.

Analysis

Greece produced at least three world-class poets in the mid-twentieth century: George Seferis, Odysseus Elytis, and Yannis Ritsos. The first two received the Nobel Prize and are bourgeois; Ritsos received the Lenin Prize and was a communist. Yet it would be entirely wrong to call him Greece's leading leftist poet or even a political poet. His range is so immense, his career so diverse, the traditions from which he draws so eclectic that these or any other labels distort his contribution. Though the leftist element is clearly present in Ritsos's work, he shares with bourgeois poets an interest in nature, in personal anguish, even in Christianity, and he participates as fully as they do in pan-European movements such as Surrealism and folklorism. In sum, Ritsos speaks not only to one camp but also to all humanity.

Epitaphios

On the other hand, it is clear that Ritsos found his first voice only because he had aligned himself with the political Left. It was communism that transformed him, in the decade 1926-1936, from an imitator of others in content and style to a unique singer of revolution. *Epitaphios* provided the breakthrough. A dirge gasped out by a simple mother over the body of her son, slain by police in a labor dispute, this poem modulates from the dirge itself to the mother's thirst for revenge and finally to her solidarity with the oppressed working class. Every aspect of the poem—not merely its content—is intended by the author to make it accessible to the common people and not only about them. Thus, it exploits diverse elements from their cultural storehouse, primarily their Greek Orthodox liturgy and their folk songs, melding a call to revolution with the Christian hope for Resurrection, and voicing all this through the tone, metrics, and imagery of the demotic ballads that were produced by anonymous folk poets throughout the centuries of Turkish rule. Ritsos did not do this self-consciously in order to erect a bulwark of tradition that would fortify national identity, but almost naïvely; the liturgy and the demotic ballads were friends with which he had grown up as a child. What he sought to avoid, and conversely to accomplish, is best expressed by his estimation of Hikmet in *Meletemata:* "His poetry is not just . . . 'folkloristic' (that is, extremely . . . 'aesthetic' on a so-called popular plane—hence nonpopular) . . . but essentially *popular* because of participation . . . in popular forces, which it expresses not in their static, standardized forms . . . but . . . in their dynamic motion."

To tragoudi tes adelphes mou

It is characteristic of Ritsos's own dynamic motion that the mode of *Epitaphios* was never to be repeated. The poet broadened his range immediately—owing to the external circumstances of Yannis Metaxas's censorship, which confined Ritsos to nonpolitical subjects—but even when he returned to political poetry after the dictator's death early in 1941, Ritsos did so in a different way, if only because he had liberated his technique in the meantime from the constraints of rhyme and strict stanzaic form. *To tragoudi tes adelphes mou* is the chief fruit of the Metaxas period. The first of many extended elegies about family members or others, chiefly women, overcome by misfortune, it matches *Epitaphios* in that it shows how pain can lead to illumination, here the lamenting poet's conviction that poetry itself—the very act of singing of his sister's insanity—will save both him and her:

> The poem has subdued me.
> The poem has granted me the victory. . . .
> I who could not
> save you from life
> will save you from death.

Poetry thus joins revolution as a wonder-working power for Ritsos, who in his espousal of an "aesthetic solution" joined hands with his bourgeois colleagues throughout Europe.

"Engraving"

In the many short poems written during this same period, Ritsos learned to escape the stridency still present in both *Epitaphios* and *To tragoudi tes adelphes mou*; he learned to distance himself from his material, to be laconic, to have poems "be," not merely "say." This he achieved chiefly through a painterly technique whereby motion, time, and sound were transfixed into immobility, space, and sight. Consider these lines:

> Lone chimes speak silence,
> memories in groups beneath the trees,
> cows sad in the dusk.
> Behind the young shepherds a cloud was bleating at the sunset.

In this Keatsian, cold pastoral, sound is frozen into a *composition*, time is spatialized. It is no wonder that the poem is titled "Engraving."

"The Burial of Orgaz"

Similar techniques are more difficult to apply to longer works, which cannot help but evolve in time. One of Ritsos's most successful works is an extended political poem written in September and October, 1942. Titled "The Burial of Orgaz," it employs El Greco's celebrated painting *Burial of the Conde de Orgaz* (1586-1588) as a static, two-tiered composition, holding in place the extraordinarily varied figures of the poet's political vision: on the earthly level, mutilated veterans of Albania, resisters executed by the Germans, innocent Athenians dying from famine; on the heavenly, in place of El Greco's John the Baptist kneeling at Christ's feet, robust workers building a new road—a Marxist paradise. Because of the painterly technique, the emotions are frozen into beauty; life is transformed into art. Later in his career—as in *Philoktetes*, for example—Ritsos was to achieve the same control over the mad flow of life's images by superimposing them on a myth rather than on a painting.

"The Burial of Orgaz" treats war tragically. It is ironic that Ritsos could treat it exultantly only after his side had met defeat in the second round of the Civil War and had then begun to suffer systematic persecution. Mortified at the discrediting of the Resistance by the Greek Right, he determined to apotheosize the heroes (communist or not) who had opposed the Axis throughout the Occupation period and to insist on their patriotism. In *Romiosyne*, written between 1945 and 1947 but obviously not publishable until much later, he therefore amalgamated his twentieth century heroes with the historical freedom fighters in the Greek War of Independence and the legendary stalwarts who had harassed the Turks in preceding centuries. Ending as it does with the hope of a peaceful, loving tomorrow, the resulting ode combines visionary transcendentalism, realism, and epic exaggeration into a blend that energetically celebrates—along with *The Lady of the Vineyards*, written at the same time—Greece's most difficult years.

In the internment camps: 1948-1952

The exultant tone disappeared from Ritsos's poetry during the four years (1948-1952) that he spent once more in internment camps. His aim was no longer either epic or transcendental; it was merely to encourage his fellow prisoners with simple verses which they could understand. There is an entire collection of these poems written in 1949 while he was on the infamous island of Makronesos, the "Makronesiotika," available in *Ta epikairika*.

Many more were composed on Agios Efstratios (Ai-Strati), the most celebrated being the "Letter to Joliot-Curie" of November, 1950, which was smuggled out of Greece at the time. It begins:

> Dear Joliot, I'm writing you from AiStrati.
> We're about three thousand here,
> simple people . . .
> with an onion, five olives and a stale crust of light in
> our sacks
> . . . people who have no other crime to their account
> except that we, like you, love
> freedom and peace.

To his credit, Ritsos later realized that the comrades did have other crimes to their account, but the circumstances of imprisonment made such self-criticism inappropriate for the moment. What is remarkable, as Pandeles Prevelakes remarks, is that Ritsos "not only maintained his intellectual identity, but also prodded his sensibility to adjust to the conditions of exile."

More important is the tender poem titled "Peace," written soon after Ritsos's release. Here, the title word is no longer a political slogan; it expresses the poet's genuine sense of tranquillity after four years of terror:

> Peace is the evening meal's aroma,
> when a car stopping outside in the street isn't fear,
> when a knock on the door means a friend. . . .

The peaceful decade: 1956-1966

The years 1956 to 1966 were Ritsos's most remarkable decade of artistic productivity and growth. The great outpouring of this period surely derived in part from unaccustomed happiness—this was the first outwardly peaceful decade of his life—but also, paradoxically, from a new, disagreeable condition to which his sensibility (along with that of all communists) had to adjust. Soviet premier Nikita Khrushchev denounced dictator Joseph Stalin in 1956, whereupon the Greek

Communist Party immediately denounced its Stalinist leader, Nikos Zachariades. Later in the same year, the Soviet Union—presumably a lover of freedom and peace—invaded Hungary. Ritsos, who had sung hymns to both Stalin and Zachariades, was forced to step back from his previous commitments and certainties, to view them with doubt or irony. "The first cries of admiration," he wrote in his introduction to his criticism on Mayakovsky, "have given way to a more silent self-communing. . . . We have learned how difficult it is not to abuse the power entrusted to us in the name of the supreme ideal, liberty. . . ." This new understanding, he continued, has led modern poets to a self-examination which is at the same time self-effacing and hesitant. Elsewhere, he spoke of his growing consciousness of all that is "vague, complicated, incomprehensible, inexplicable and directionless in life."

The Moonlight Sonata

The first fruit of this new awareness of the complexity of life was *The Moonlight Sonata*, a nonpolitical poem constituting for Ritsos a breakthrough fully as significant as the one achieved precisely twenty years earlier by the quintessentially political *Epitaphios*. The 1956 poem, though once again a kind of elegy for a suffering woman, avoids all stridency and authorial assertion by hiding its tragic elements behind a mask of ironic impassivity. At the same time, however, it allows the woman's anguished emotions to stir the *reader's* emotions. Ritsos accomplishes this by making the major voice not his own but the woman's and then by framing her dramatic monologue inside yet another nonauthorial voice, a narrator's, which questions and neutralizes the emotions of the first voice. As a result, the reader is never quite sure how to feel about the poem or how to interpret it; instead, both emotionally and mentally, the reader is ushered into all that is "vague, complicated, incomprehensible. . . ."

Philoktetes

Philoktetes carries this process still further. It retains the technique of dramatic monologue inside a narrative frame but adds to it an all-encompassing myth that fulfills the same kind of "painterly" purpose served earlier by El Greco's *Burial of the Conde de Orgaz*. At the same time, the myth connects Ritsos's version of the Philoctetes story and hence the Greek Civil War (which is clearly suggested) not only with Homer's Achaeans and Trojans but also with the Peloponnesian War, clearly suggested in Sophocles' version. If one notes as well that the poem employs the surrealistic and expressionistic techniques that Ritsos had been perfecting in short poems dating from the same period (collected as *Martyries, A' seira*; testimonies), it becomes clear that a work of such complexity is deliberately meant to make the reader feel uncomfortably suspended above nothing. That, in turn, is a perfect technical equivalent for the thrust of the poem, which dismisses every justification for Philoctetes' collaboration in the Trojan War yet affirms his need to stand by his comrades even though he knows their perfidy. The poem thus examines Ritsos's own dilemma as a Stalinist betrayed by Stalin, determined to bring his understanding and indulgence to the cause instead of merely defecting. It is a self-examination which is at the same time self-effacing and hesitant.

Junta years: 1967-1974

The poet's new stance was soon put to the test by imprisonment under the Colonels. Despite this provocation, Ritsos did not revert to the optimistic assurance displayed during earlier privations; the new poems of exile are exasperated, sardonic, even sometimes despairing. Bitten (like Philoctetes) by the snake of wisdom, he could never return to the propagandistic verse produced on Agios Efstratios. On the contrary, he felt the need to reaffirm the predominance of mystery. "The Disjunctive Conjunction 'Or,'" written in exile on June 18, 1969, says this loud and clear: "O that 'or,'" cries the poet, that "equivocal smile of an incommunicable . . . wisdom/ which . . . / [knows] full well that precision/ . . . does not exist (which is why the pompous style of certainty is so unforgivable . . .)./ Disjunctive 'or' . . ./ with you we manage the troubles of life and dream,/ the numerous shades and interpretations. . . ."

Later poems

With the demise of the Colonels' dictatorship in the mid-1970's, Ritsos's poetry understandably began to retreat from the subjects so compelling during his days in prisons and a police state. Still, he continued to grapple with mystery, asking basic questions but realizing that answers do not always follow:

So many dead
without death
so many living corpses.
You sit in a chair
counting your buttons.
Where do you belong?
What are you?
What are you doing?

The sardonic element is still present, but so is a certain spirit of indulgence or clemency—precisely what Philoctetes brought to Troy. Furthermore, a parodistic flavor entered many of Ritsos's poems, a kind of macabre humor that neutralizes the worst that life can offer. Ritsos thus stood above all that his compatriots had done to him, playing with his experience, turning it round beneath his philosophic gaze—a gaze annealed by hardship into resilience.

He also began to compose domestic, amatory, or occasional lyrics; some of best love poems appear in 1981's *Erotica*, for example. The epic, mythic, poems that mined Greece's past to question its national present receded. It was not until near the end of his life that Ritsos returned to myth, and then the expression was intensely personal. As one of his chief translators, Peter Green, notes:

> Ritsos saw 'the black double-oared boat with its dark boatman drawing near.' . . . Ritsos paid more, over a long lifetime, than most writers are ever called upon to do, but the legacy that he left is imperishable.

OTHER MAJOR WORKS

PLAYS: *Pera ap ton iskio ton kyparission*, pb. 1958, pr. 1959; *Mia gynaika plai sti thalassa*, pr., pb. 1959.

NONFICTION: *Meletemata*, 1974.

BIBLIOGRAPHY

Bien, Peter. *Three Generations of Greek Writers: Introductions to Cavafy, Kazantzakis, Ritsos*, 1983.

Friar, Kimon, ed. *Modern Greek Poetry*. New York: Simon and Schuster, 1973. Nearly eight hundred pages of modern Greek poetry, compiled by Friar, a major translator. The introduction, essay on translation, and notes provided by Friar offer students an excellent means of becoming familiar with modern Greek poetry and its issues and themes.

Green, Peter. Review of *Repetitions, Testimonies, Parentheses*. *New Republic* 205, no. 16 (October 14, 1991). This lengthy essay reviews not only Ritsos's late work but also his entire career. An excellent resource in English. Green is one of Ritsos's primary translators.

Keeley, Edmund. *Inventing Paradise: The Greek Journey, 1937-47*. New York: Farrar, Straus and Giroux, 1999. The eminent translator of modern Greek literature provides a discussion that casts light on the context for much Greek poetry during the turbulent middle of the twentieth century. Bibliography.

_______. *Modern Greek Poetry: Voice and Myth*. Princeton, N.J.: Princeton University Press, 1983. An essential guide for students of modern Greek poetry, by one of its most important scholars and translators. Bibliography, indexes.

_______. *On Translation: Reflections and Conversations*. Amsterdam: Harwood Academic Publishers, 2000. Keeley's comments in this brief monograph of just over one hundred pages offers non-Greek readers some insights into translations from modern Greek, important to any full understanding of Ritsos's poetry.

Peter Bien,
updated by Christina J. Moose

EDWIN ARLINGTON ROBINSON

Born: Head Tide, Maine; December 22, 1869
Died: New York, New York; April 6, 1935

PRINCIPAL POETRY

The Torrent and the Night Before, 1896
The Children of the Night, 1897
Captain Craig, 1902, 1915
The Town Down the River, 1910
The Man Against the Sky, 1916
Merlin, 1917

Lancelot, 1920
The Three Taverns, 1920
Avon's Harvest, 1921
Collected Poems, 1921, 1927, 1929, 1937
Roman Bartholow, 1923
The Man Who Died Twice, 1924
Dionysus in Doubt, 1925
Tristram, 1927
Sonnets, 1889-1927, 1928
Cavender's House, 1929
The Glory of the Nightingales, 1930
Matthias at the Door, 1931
Nicodemus, 1932
Talifer, 1933
Amaranth, 1934
King Jasper, 1935

Other literary forms

Early in his literary career, well before he gained prominence as a poet, Edwin Arlington Robinson wrote a number of short stories that he planned to incorporate in a volume titled *Scattered Lives*. The stories do not survive, nor does the novel he tried his hand at writing some years later, but the twenty-six pieces of extant prose were collected by Richard Cary in *Uncollected Poems and Prose of Edwin Arlington Robinson* (1975). Of interest primarily for what they reveal of the life of this most private man, these undistinguished prose pieces include essays, autobiographical sketches, introductions to books, and like matter.

It was in drama, particularly in the years 1906 to 1913, that Robinson hoped to make an impression as some of his New York friends had in their attempts to revitalize the theater. Robinson did not relinquish the hope that he could achieve moderate success with his plays until 1917, when he finally recognized that his very considerable skills as a poet were not compatible with those required for the theater. His two published plays—*Van Zorn* (1914) and *The Porcupine* (1915)—were ineffective. The former was produced, however, in February, 1917, by an amateur group that used the facilities of a Brooklyn YMCA. It had a run of seven days.

Robinson was a prolific letter writer. Some of his letters have been collected in three major editions: *Selected Letters of Edwin Arlington Robinson* (1940), compiled by Ridgely Torrence with the assistance of several of the poet's friends; *Untriangulated Stars: Letters of Edwin Arlington Robinson to Harry de Forest Smith, 1890-1905* (1947), edited by Denham Sutcliffe; and *Edwin Arlington Robinson's Letters to Edith Brower* (1968), edited by Richard Cary. The letters that interest the student of Robinson the most are those to Harry de Forest Smith, a close friend from Gardiner, Maine, to whom the poet, during a very difficult time in his life, expressed in an uncharacteristically open fashion his thoughts and feelings on a number of subjects, including his literary likes and dislikes, his own struggles as a writer, his years at Harvard, and his cultural growth.

Achievements

For some twenty years before he gained acknowledgment as a poet of major proportions, Edwin Arlington Robinson had been publishing some excellent poems, particularly in the form of lyrics with a dramatic base. Indeed, his special genius has always been ascribed to the shorter poem, even though he has thirteen book-length narrative poems to his credit, eleven of which were published individually as books between 1917 and 1935 and two of which—*The Man Who Died Twice* and *Tristram*—were awarded Pulitzer Prizes in the 1920's. In 1922, the first edition of his *Collected Poems* had earned Robinson his first Pulitzer Prize.

In the 1920's, when T. S. Eliot and Robert Frost were acknowledged literary masters, Robinson was hailed by some discerning critics as America's foremost poet. In addition to the three Pulitzer Prizes, he received honorary degrees by Yale University in 1922 and Bowdoin College in 1925, and he was awarded the Levinson Prize in 1923. At the close of the decade, the National Institute of Arts and Letters presented Robinson with a gold medal in recognition of his outstanding accomplishments. Chosen by the Literary Guild of America as a monthly selection, *Tristram* sold over 50,000 copies. Not without good reason, *Tristram* and most of the long blank verse narratives are not read much today; they are dull and wordy. Some, however, contain passages of exceptional power, notably *Lancelot* and *The Man Who Died Twice*—the latter being the most impressive of the long poems.

In many of his shorter poems and in a few of his middle-length narratives, such as "Ben Jonson Entertains a Man from Stratford" and "Rembrandt to Rembrandt," Robinson's use of language is consistently superior and often brilliant. For example, he infuses his infrequently used but nonetheless striking images drawn from the natural world with metaphorical or symbolic meanings that contribute greatly to an understanding of his themes. Whether in the shorter or the longer pieces, Robinson is, above all, a poet of rational content, one who believes that what the poem says is of the utmost importance. His themes are both serious and significant.

Robinson may properly be classified as a traditional poet since he wrote regularly in blank verse, used meter, rhyme, and patterned stanzas, and was attracted to the English sonnet, a form in which his triumphs are many and which he expanded to include nontraditional subject matter, such as prostitution, suicide, and euthanasia. His most accomplished poems, among the best of their kind in English, are relatively brief yet intense and penetrating studies of the residents of Tilbury Town, the imaginary community that Robinson created based on Gardiner, Maine. His themes reflect a full awareness of the painful lives that many must endure. In these superior shorter poems, these compelling character studies, Robinson addresses the need to try to understand one's fellow man and to have compassion for him.

BIOGRAPHY

By the standards of the biographer's world, the life of Edwin Arlington Robinson provides little that is exciting. Born on December 22, 1869, in Head Tide, Maine, the third son of Edward and Mary Palmer Robinson, he led a life characterized by a very low profile, even after he was acknowledged by a number of critics and scholars in the 1920's as America's most distinguished poet. He shunned the public attention that was his for the asking, preferring instead to write in relative seclusion and to associate with only a very few close friends. Occasionally, he consented to an interview, but he never gave lectures or public readings of his poetry, or engaged in any activity in which he would have been the center of attention.

Ten months after his birth, the Robinson family moved to Gardiner, Maine, where his father, who had made his fortune in the timber business, became a civic figure and was elected to the state legislature. Although his father saw little need for his sons to receive college educations, he consented to sending Dean, his first born, to Bowdoin to begin the study of medicine. After Robinson took an extra year of high school and did odd jobs around Gardiner for a period, expressing all the while his disinclination for the world of business (the route taken by Herman, the second born), he was finally permitted to enroll in Harvard in 1891 as a "special student," where he remained for two years. Robinson treasured these years, and although he was never fully accepted by the student literati, he did publish five poems in *The Harvard Advocate*.

The decade following his years at Harvard was beset by family tragedies and discouragement; his resolve to be a writer elicited but few rewards. He paid for the publication of his first book of poetry, *The Torrent and the Night Before*; a friend paid the cost of printing *The Children of the Night*, the second; and *Captain Craig*, the third, was first rejected by five publishers and accepted only on the condition that its expense would be underwritten by friends. Although these volumes contain a number of excellent poems, they received little critical attention. Robinson's fortunes changed in 1905, when Theodore Roosevelt was sent a copy of *The Children of the Night* by his son Kermit. Roosevelt found a sinecure for the poet—who was living in New York in an impoverished state, discouraged, and given to drinking—with the United States Customs Service, a position he was to hold until the Taft administration. It gave him the opportunity to write free from financial worry, a condition which had plagued him since the Panic of 1893 took the family fortune.

He spent the summer of 1911 at the MacDowell Colony in Peterborough, New Hampshire, a retreat for artists to which the poet would return each summer for the rest of his life for three months of uninterrupted writing. The rest of the year he spent in New York, with occasional trips, mostly to Boston, to see friends. Then in 1916, *The Man Against the Sky*, his fifth volume of poetry, was favorably received, and Robinson was recognized as a significant American poet. Toward the end of his life, Robinson devoted nearly all his creative efforts to the long narrative poem, publishing eight book-length poems between 1927 and his death in 1935.

Analysis

In response to a 1931 letter from Bess Dworsky, who was preparing a thesis on Edwin Arlington Robinson's "philosophy," the poet wrote: "I am rather sorry to learn that you are writing about my 'philosophy'—which is mostly a statement of my inability to accept a mechanistic interpretation of the universe and of life." Critics have called Robinson an idealist, a Platonist, a transcendentalist, a pantheist, and many combinations thereof. While it is indeed possible to identify in his poetry some elements of all the above, he was not an advocate of any philosophical system. He was most assuredly aware of the scientific and philosophical concepts that pressed toward a "mechanistic interpretation of the universe and of life," which he rejected in favor of a personal idealism that nonetheless accepted the reality of matter. As Chard Powers Smith argues in *Where the Light Falls: A Portrait of Edwin Arlington Robinson* (1965), "He never denied the material world. What he did was to face it, defy it, and deny its capacity to destroy him." Against the forces of materialism he posited a life of the mind, and, as Smith suggests, "He respected the unique inner integrity of all individuals and he never judged anyone, in life or in fiction [poetry], for he did not know what pressures they had been under."

Several comments that Robinson made serve to illustrate his purpose in writing poetry and provide us with external evidence that, coupled with the internal evidence of the poems themselves, identifies his major thematic concerns. In a letter to Harry de Forest Smith, dated May 13, 1896, Robinson said what he hoped his poems would do:

> If printed lines are good for anything, they are bound to be picked up some time; and then, if some poor devil of a man or woman feels any better or any stronger for anything that I have said, I shall have no fault to find with the scheme or anything in it.

Writing to Smith again in February 3, 1897, Robinson reaffirmed his position: "I also make free to say that many of my verses [were] written with a conscious hope that they might make some despairing devil a little stronger and a little better satisfied with things—not as they are, but as they are to be." Sixteen years later, in reply to William Stanley Braithwaite's inquiry about his central "message," Robinson is reputed to have answered in terms remarkably consistent with his statements made years earlier:

> I suppose that a part of it might be described as a faint hope of making a few of us understand our fellow creatures a little better, and to realize what a small difference there is, after all, between ourselves, as we are, and ourselves, not only as we might have been but would have been if our physical and temperamental make-up and our environment had been a little different.

While this response may sound as if Robinson had embraced the philosophical determinism of the naturalistic writers, Robinson was quick to correct that impression: "If a reader doesn't get from my books an impression that life is very much worth while, even though it may not seem always to be profitable or desirable, I can only say that he doesn't see what I am driving at."

From *The Torrent and the Night Before* to *Dionysus in Doubt*, the last volume to contain significant shorter poems, the dual concept of understanding and compassion, Robinson's major thematic concern, is strongly evident in such outstanding poems as "Luke Havergal," "The Clerks," "The Growth of 'Lorraine,'" "The Whip," "How Annandale Went Out," "Flammonde," "The Gift of God," "Veteran Sirens," "The Poor Relation," "En Passant," and "Eros Turannos." Very closely aligned to the motif of understanding and compassion is the belief exemplified in many of his poems, and most convincingly so in "Eros Turannos," that no one person is ever able to fully understand another person. Although this may seem incompatible with Robinson's preoccupation with understanding and compassion, it is not, for the poet believed that the very act of trying to understand is of extreme value in itself.

Imagery, irony, and obscurity

In terms of technique—other than the conventions of rhyme and meter—Robinson works consistently in three areas worth noting: image patterns, irony, and the deliberate withholding of information. Robinson is not the New England poet who celebrates or even writes about snow, lilacs, or the like. In fact, he is lean in his use of imagery from the natural world; however, when he does draw upon the natural world, his images are functional, not decorative, and they are often framed in a metaphorical or symbolic context. Wherever his images come from—colors, a visionary light, water, leaves, to name a few sources—they often serve in patterns as ordering devices to provide unity and to enhance meaning. They contribute to the complex texture of some of his best poems, such as "Luke Havergal," "For a Dead Lady," and "Eros Turannos."

Irony is one of Robinson's most consistently employed tools, and he uses it variously to achieve various ends. In "How Annandale Went Out," for example, irony is situational and understated; the doctor-speaker feels that it is absurd in the first place that he is on trial for a justified mercy killing, and he pleads his case almost casually. In "The House on the Hill" and "Eros Turannos," Robinson is overtly caustic in his attitude toward people who feel compelled to speculate on the circumstances and personalities of others without much in the way of verification. In "The Man Against the Sky," the concept of a mechanistic universe is soundly indicted, while in "Cassandra," sarcasm is leveled, not very subtly, at American materialism. In "New England" the irony is so complex that readers first thought the sonnet was an attack on the rigidity of the Puritan afterglow in New England, when the poem actually denounces those who have wrongly interpreted this region.

While poets such as T. S. Eliot, Ezra Pound, and Wallace Stevens provide what amount to acceptable puzzles in their poetry, Robinson was, for a period, the object of some scorn for his obscurity. Since he was not given to the esoteric, readers perhaps came to him expecting to find neat, rational answers in technically sound poems. Because his language is relatively uncomplicated, descending probably from the Puritan "plain style," readers were confounded and even angered at not being able to determine what some of his poems meant. These interpretive problems derive from Robinson's technique of deliberately withholding information in the poem in order to make the reader think, to reward him when he arrives at his own understanding.

"Eros Turannos"

The most accomplished of Robinson's shorter poems, "Eros Turannos" is the favorite of anthologists and the poem most representative of Robinson's major thematic concerns and techniques. Set in a village on the coast of Maine, it recounts the courtship of a man and woman, and then tries to explain what happened to the woman once the man died. The speaker of the poem takes deliberate pains to inform the reader that he is really failing to understand her situation because he actually does not know what, in fact, she is experiencing.

The poem consists of six stanzas of eight lines each, with an *ababcccb* rhyme scheme and a metrical pattern of iambic tetrameter for all lines except those ending with the *b* rhyme. These are indented in the text and are in iambic trimeter with one extra unaccented syllable at the end of the line. The title is Greek for "Love, the Tyrant."

At the outset of this poem, which is narrated in the present tense to give its dramatic situation a sense of immediacy, the reader learns that the woman is afraid of the man despite his "engaging mask," that she has just cause for discounting him as a potential husband, but that she is willing to disregard her fears and uncertainties about him because she is more afraid of the "downward years," of growing old alone. Her insecurity is not merely a product of her relationship with the man: Rather, it is a component of her personality—she is simply afraid of life.

As "Eros Turannos" progresses to the close of the third stanza, which marks the end of the first part of this little drama, the woman is depicted as being once capable of penetrating with her "blurred sagacity" beneath his mask to the "Judas that she found him"; however, she finally relinquishes all objections, at whatever cost to her, and agrees to the union. So far, the reader may feel that the woman deserves pity, and the man, scorn; but in typical Robinson fashion, the situation is not that simple, for just as the woman has deliberately deceived herself into believing that marrying a man she fears and cannot trust is a lesser evil than growing old alone, so too has he been deceived into marriage by the prospect of living rather comfortably with her in a setting replete with tradition that "Beguiles and reassures him." Robinson adopts the stance that there are inevitably two sides to every story, and he is most reluctant to pass judgments. There are some exceptions, of course, such as the despicable Aaron Stark in the sonnet of that name. By and large, however, if judgment is to be passed, the reader must do so from whatever understanding he comes to in the poems. Almost always, the reader learns to have compassion once he understands the situations confronting the characters, their personal inadequacies or hells—or understands at least to the best of his ability.

The first three stanzas thus establish and resolve, for a time, the problems facing the man and the woman by having them marry. The husband is absent in the second part of the poem, the last three stanzas, and the wife is living alone. From the way she is described in the first four lines of the fourth stanza, it is evident that a considerable time has passed and that she is either in or rapidly approaching old age. In addition, she is suffering from a collapse of her mental faculties. The "pounding wave" repeats the same song: her husband's dirge. The word "illusion" refers to the speaker's conception of the manner in which the wife had viewed her husband who now is dead. Her fears of living alone in the "downward years" have materialized. Hiding from the world, she has become an object of curiosity and idle speculation among the Tilbury Town folk.

At the beginning of the fifth stanza, the speaker, who, in Robinson's characteristic manner, identifies himself as a townsman by the use of "we," comments ironically on the inability of people to know other people and on the penchant "we" have for gossiping. Yet, just as the use of the words "veil" and "visions" reinforces the illusory nature of the wife's assessment of her husband, so do the townspeople fall prey to illusions; they are mistaken in their conception of the "home, where passion lived and died," in their conjectures about the man and woman who enacted the drama. The point that Robinson insists on making is a familiar one in his poetry.

The opening lines of the final stanza state that whatever the townspeople are saying can do the wife no harm, for she has striven with a "god" and is oblivious to everything else. She made a lifelong commitment, not only to her husband, but to "Love, the Tyrant," as well, and she is living with—suffering—the consequences. Exactly "what the God has given" to her is unknown, but in his effort to approximate what he thinks it might be, the speaker formulates three similes. Since he is uncertain, he uses the words "though" and "or" to qualify his perceptions. Although critics uniformly admire the striking images that close the poem, they avoid commentary on what the images mean, preferring instead vaguely to call attention to their symbolic significance. Confusing as these images may be, they represent to the speaker his conception of the woman's mental death, which is what she finally received from the "god," "Love, the Tyrant," once her husband died. When waves break (the first image), they are finished, through, dead; the "changed familiar tree" (the second image) is a tree in autumn, its leaves going or gone, and a symbolic representation of death or impending death; and, lastly, the blind who are driven down "the stairway to the sea" suggest the "downward years" of the first stanza and serve as the concluding representation of death. Blindly driven by "Love, the Tyrant," the wife is being driven to death, just as the blind would drown were they forced into the sea. Words referring to vision and sight form a basic image pattern that unifies the poem and underscores the thematic concern: stanza (1) *mask*; (2) *blurred, sees, looks*; (3) *sees, dimmed*; (4) *illusion*; (5) *veil, vision, seen*; (6) *blind*. While not explicitly related to the motif, a second pattern of imagery also helps to unify the poem. Since the physical setting is a harbor community, water and nautical imagery is found in the infinitives "to sound" and "to secure," and in the mention of "foamless weirs," "sense of ocean," "pounding wave," "waves breaking," and "like a stairway to the sea." Finally, in keeping with the time of year in the second part of the poem, Robinson refers to the autumnal images of a "falling leaf" and "a changed familiar tree." Robinson is at his best in "Eros Turannos," a moving lyric unified through patterns of imagery, through the consistent use of the present tense, and through a logically balanced structure dividing the poem into cause and effect. It is through the speaker's struggles to understand the wife that the reader comes to an understanding of and compassion for her.

"The Whip"

In both "The Whip" and "How Annandale Went Out," as in "Eros Turannos," Robinson withholds from the reader an easy understanding of the central issues of the poems, thus forcing the reader to a scrupulous reading. When the reader does become aware of the circumstances behind the actions of the characters, he understands and feels compassion for them. Both poems, but especially "The Whip," have been the subject of considerable critical attention.

"The Whip," a forty-line poem in five stanzas of eight iambic trimeter lines with an *ababbcbc* rhyme scheme, is narrated by a Tilbury Townsman who has no obvious connection with the characters whose recent drama, which led to a suicide, he is trying to fathom. The setting is apparently a funeral home. The victim is in an open coffin and the speaker quizzically addresses him.

In the first stanza the speaker reveals that the suicide victim had been married to a woman who treated him tyranically and ruined him. During their marriage he constantly doubted her fidelity and became a cynic. As the poem progresses through the second and third stanzas, the speaker comments that the wife indeed had taken a lover and left. As a result, the husband chose death by drowning. Yet the speaker, recognizing that "the gall we drink/ Is not the mead we cry for," feels that the husband's plight did not justify his suicide. It was not "a thing to die for."

The specifics surrounding the suicide begin to take shape in the fourth stanza as the speaker, still bewildered by the situation, notices a blue mark "like a welt" on the husband's face; and in the final stanza the speaker and the reader come to understanding at the same time. The "chase" referred to in the fifth stanza involved the husband on a horse pursuing the wife and her lover, who were either on one horse or on separate ones. As they were crossing a river, the wife struck her husband in the face with her riding crop; hence the title, "The Whip." He fell off his horse and chose to drown. Earlier in the poem, knowing only that the husband committed suicide, the speaker asks, "Then, shall I call you blind?" He ends the poem with "Still, shall I call you blind?"—a question rhetorically posed, for the speaker has come to the realization that the husband's suicide came at a moment of emotional and physical frenzy. This knowledge finally becoming clear to him, his attitude undergoes a change.

"The Whip" is a little masterpiece of mystery and subsequent revelation. It is a testimony to Robinson's skill that he manages to have both the speaker and the reader simultaneously come to the realization of what actually happened. One of many in his repertoire of shorter poems devoted to the subject of suicide (others include "Luke Havergal," "Richard Cory," "The Growth of 'Lorraine,'" and "The Mill"), its thematic concerns are typically Robinson's: the interdependence of understanding and compassion, and the difficulty of knowing another person. Robinson wants us to understand the factors that lead to suicide and to have compassion for the victims. It should be remembered that, in Robinson's time, suicide was looked upon much more harshly and with much less understanding of the causal factors than it is today.

"How Annandale Went Out"

"How Annandale Went Out" is an English sonnet in which Robinson once again deliberately withholds information in order to make the impact of the poem more powerfully felt. It is also one of his sonnets that expands the range of the form by dealing with euthanasia, hardly the stuff of which sonnets were made prior to the twentieth century.

The doctor-speaker of the sonnet, which is entirely enclosed in quotation marks, is presenting the court with his reasons, however obliquely stated, for committing euthanasia in the case of Annandale, a man whose illness or injury, never identified, had reduced him from a man to a thing. The doctor refers to him in the octet as "it," "apparatus," and "wreck," terms which initially misdirect the reader but which establish the doctor's frame of mind. The doctor calls himself "Liar, physician, hypocrite, and friend," and, in the sestet, asks the court to bear in mind that he knew Annandale before misfortune reduced him to a "ruin." In addition, he asks the court to remember the "worst you know of me" and to consider his position with "a slight kind of engine," which probably refers to a hypodermic needle, the instrument with which he committed the mercy killing. He closes by saying, "You wouldn't hang me? I thought not."

This poem works so well because of the doctor's view that the entire situation of the trial is nothing less than ironic. "It is absurd," he seems to be saying, "that, given the circumstances, I should do anything other than put an end to the terrible suffering of my friend. This trial mocks the very humanitarian impulse in man." The power of the poem resides in the doctor's method of presentation. His ironic indictments, coupled with the very serious nature of the situation, generate tension; and by not identifying the source of Annandale's suffering, Robinson places the focus clearly on the doctor.

Arthurian poems

It is possible that Robinson's frustrations in not being able to write successful plays or fiction led him to expend the effort that he did on his long blank verse narrative poems. They may have satisfied his need to tell a story, to dramatize at length what he so nicely accomplished in his shorter poems. The longer works, like the shorter poems, are full of troubled characters from all walks of life. In detailed observation that often is tediousand conversations that are often lifeless, Robinson presents characters on the verge of or just after a trauma. Wallace L. Anderson observes in *Edwin Arlington Robinson: A Critical Introduction* (1967) that "most of the poem[s] [are] concerned with . . . efforts to find out why. . . . It is necessary, in other words, for the characters to understand each other and themselves. Robinson's concern in the long poems is essentially the same as in the short ones."

Since they are based, however loosely at times, on the myths that constitute the Arthurian legends, *Merlin*, *Lancelot*, and *Tristram* must necessarily deal with formed characters, events, and eventualities; yet the characters are troubled, they court and reach disaster, and they must gain understanding.

Yvor Winters, in *Edwin Arlington Robinson* (1946), remarks of Lancelot in the poem of that name: "[He] is not free, because of the Light; that is, because he has acquired understanding which he before had lacked, and of understanding one cannot divest oneself." With some exceptions understandably made for the Arthurian poems, Robinson's characters, whether in the longer poems or in the superior shorter ones, are often the maimed, the outcast, and the forgotten of society. While many are able to endure their situations stoically, others cannot and, as a result, choose antisocial behavior. For all, the poet has compassion, and he asks that of his readers, too.

Other major works

plays: *Van Zorn*, pb. 1914; *The Porcupine*, pb. 1915.

nonfiction: *Selected Letters of Edwin Arlington Robinson*, 1940; *Untriangulated Stars: Letters of Edwin Arlington Robinson to Harry de Forest Smith, 1890-1905*, 1947; *Edwin Arlington Robinson's Letters to Edith Brower*, 1968.

miscellaneous: *Uncollected Poems and Prose of Edwin Arlington Robinson*, 1975.

Bibliography

Barnard, Ellsworth. *Edwin Arlington Robinson: A Critical Study*. New York: Macmillan, 1952. This study is a labor of love. It is thorough and meticulous, provides a perceptive and helpful analysis of Robinson's poetic style, and is especially valuable on the long poems. Includes chapters on the development of Robinson's thought.

Bloom, Harold, ed. *Edwin Arlington Robinson*. New York: Chelsea House Publishers, 1988. A collection of nine critical essays discussing the American poet, arranged in chronological order of their original publication.

Boswell, Jeanetta. *Edwin Arlington Robinson and the Critics: A Bibliography of Secondary Sources with Selective Annotations*. Metuchen, N.J.: Scarecrow Press, 1988. This bibliography updates Nancy Joyner's *E. A. Robinson: A Reference Guide* (1978) and lists only materials published before 1983. The 1,383 items are arranged alphabetically by author. Includes ample annotations, a useful subject index, and a short introduction on Robinson's scholarship.

Burton, David Henry. *Edwin Arlington Robinson: Stages in a New England Poet's Search*. Lewiston, N.Y.: Edwin Mellen Press, 1987. A narrative of Robinson's life by an established historian and biographer. Includes an index and bibliography.

Fussell, Edwin Sill. *Edwin Arlington Robinson: The Literary Background of a Traditional Poet*. Berkeley: University of California Press, 1954. This study examines closely the influences under which Robinson produced his lyric and narrative poetry (Edgar Allan Poe, Henry Wadsworth Longfellow, Ralph

Waldo Emerson, and Henry David Thoreau, and others). Helpful on the sonnets and in its analysis of Robinson's diction. Shows Robinson to be a traditional poet, "content with the old-fashioned way to be new."

Hagedorn, Hermann. *Edwin Arlington Robinson: A Biography.* New York: Macmillan, 1938. This early account of the poet's life remains the best. Written by a close friend out of vivid recollections, it is extremely readable, tender, and affectionate. Especially useful on the poet's boyhood, on his friendship with Robert Frost, and on *Tristram.* Includes several anecdotes.

Kaplan, Estelle. *Philosophy in the Poetry of Edwin Arlington Robinson.* New York: Columbia University Press, 1940. This extended analysis of Robinson's thought is a must for any serious student of the poet. Includes a bibliography and an index.

Neff, Emery E. *Edwin Arlington Robinson.* New York: W. Sloane, 1948. This critical study accords Robinson, together with Robert Frost, the foremost place in poetry in the first half of the century. Provides a close analysis of Robinson's American themes, and is thorough on the Arthurian poems. One of the values of this study is in the portraits of the poet's friends. More biographical than critical.

Smith, Chard Powers. *Where the Light Falls: A Portrait of Edwin Arlington Robinson.* New York: Macmillan, 1965. The best of a number of personal reminiscences. Provides an affectionate and vivid picture of the poet's character and personality. Notes and bibliographical references fill 17 of the 420 pages.

Winters, Yvor. *Edwin Arlington Robinson.* Norfolk, Conn.: New Directions, 1946. One of Robinson's best critics and the most persistent of the poet's admirers, Winters sorts out the essential in Robinson. Cites eleven poems that "can be equaled . . . in the work of only four or five English and American poets of the past century and a half." Helpful on the shorter poems; Winters does not like the long poems. This volume is a stimulating work of biography and criticism. Contains four pages of bibliography.

Ronald Moran;
bibliography updated by the editors

John Wilmot, earl of Rochester

Born: Ditchley, Oxfordshire, England; April 10, 1647
Died: Woodstock, Oxfordshire, England; July 26, 1680

Principal poetry

"A Satire Against Mankind," 1675
Poems on Several Occasions by the Right Honourable the E. of R., 1680 (attribution questionable)
The Complete Poems of John Wilmot, Earl of Rochester, 1968 (David Vieth, editor)

Other literary forms

The first complete, unexpurgated edition of John Wilmot, earl of Rochester's letters appeared in 1980 as *The Letters of John Wilmot, Earl of Rochester,* edited by Jeremy Treglown. It includes more than one hundred very readable letters to his wife, to his mistress, and to his close friend, the courtier Henry Savile. Rochester's most sustained prose work is the broadside "Alexander Bendo's Bill," which satirized mountebanks and compared them to politicians, the quacks of state affairs. One version of this piece appears in Vivian de Sola Pinto's *Enthusiast in Wit: A Portrait of John Wilmot Earl of Rochester 1647-1680* (1962). There is also proof of Rochester's interest in drama—a scene for Sir Robert Howard's unfinished play *The Conquest of China*, and in 1678 a lengthy adaptation of John Fletcher's tragedy *Valentinian*, called in manuscript *Lucina's Rape*. Rochester did not live to complete the alteration, but in February, 1684, his play was given a magnificent production at the King's Theatre in London.

Achievements

John Wilmot, earl of Rochester is the one major poet among the literary courtiers of the Restoration. His standing as a poet still suffers from his reputation as a heartless rake. This view can no longer be taken seriously, since even in those of his love songs which express intense passion and cheerful irresponsibility there is also a powerful current of fidelity. Rochester's devotion to his friends was only exceeded by the sincere intensity of thought and sentiment of the lyrics that he addressed to his wife. He embodied the Restoration definition of wit, not only having the capacity for a clever turn of phrase but also possessing a fierce intelligence. In his satires, he becomes a poet of skepticism, morally indignant, drawn to heterodoxy and paradox, but continually searching for the eternal truths promised by religion and for the assurances of love, friendship, and power.

John Wilmot, earl of Rochester (Hulton Archive)

Although his importance must be decided on the basis of a rather small canon (about seventy-five poems, a hundred letters, and an adaptation of a play), he has maintained a vocal group of admirers. The poet Andrew Marvell thought him the "best English satyrist," Voltaire called him a "Man of Genius with a shining imagination," and Alfred, Lord Tennyson respected the "almost terrible force" of his "A Satire Against Mankind." In the twentieth century Rochester has been described as a traditional Augustan more akin to Jonathan Swift and Alexander Pope than to John Dryden, a destructive nihilist, and a Christian pilgrim journeying not toward a goal but in search of one. The diversity of these viewpoints is exceeded only by their relative narrowness or exaggeration.

The most plausible contemporary view finds Rochester a mature product of the Restoration; his work illuminates the cultural, literary, and intellectual climate of that period. Since the 1968 publication of Vieth's new critical edition of the complete poems, a Rochester revival has been in progress. Numerous books and articles and a concordance to the poems have followed, and in 1980, a major part of *Tennessee Studies in Literature* was dedicated to the poet. Rochester remains the finest lyrical poet of the Restoration, the last important Metaphysical poet, and an influential satiric poet who helped make possible the achievements of the Augustan satirists.

BIOGRAPHY

John Wilmot was born in Ditchley, Oxfordshire, England, on April 10, 1647. He was the son of Henry, Viscount Wilmot, a distinguished Cavalier general, who had fought for Charles I and was made earl of Rochester by him. Later his father would effect the escape of Charles II from England to exile in France. Anne St. John, his mother, was the daughter of Sir John St. John, a Wiltshire knight and prominent Puritan.

John Wilmot inherited the earldom of Rochester and Adderbury Manor at the age of eleven. A handsome and precocious youth, he entered Wadham College, Oxford, at thirteen, where he was exposed to the most advanced scientific and philosophical thinking of the time: "the real centre of the English Enlightenment." His earliest poetry was written there in celebration of Charles II on his return in May, 1660; these few lines reminded the king of his debt to Wilmot's father. He richly rewarded the son, conferring a master's degree on the boy, granting him a pension of five hundred pounds a year, and arranging for his Grand Tour complete with a learned Scottish physician and virtuoso as his tutor.

After touring France and Italy, he returned to England in the winter of 1664 and joined the court of Charles II, immediately gaining notoriety for wit, profanity, and debauchery. Soon Rochester became the informal leader of a fashionable group of literary wits known as "the merry gang," which included the playwright Sir George Etherege; John Sheffield, earl of Mulgrave; Charles Sackville, earl of Dorset; the poet Sir Charles Sedley; and Rochester's closest friend, Henry Savile.

Influenced by the writings of Thomas Hobbes, Rochester interpreted his materialist philosophy as a defense of sensuality and began an active revolt against both Cavalier romanticism and Puritan idealism. Although critics now agree that his reputation as a frantic rake and libertine was largely undeserved, the early lyrics and songs of this period display a determined hedonism and thorough enjoyment of the high-spirited frolic of the Whitehall Palace. In *Royal Charles: Charles II and the Restoration* (1979), Antonia Fraser describes the famous Cornelis Huysmans portrait of Rochester as "a young man of almost insolent sensuality, wide lips curling with devilment," but with "something of the Angel yet undefaced in him." This indiscriminate life of pleasure soon proved unsatisfactory, and thereafter Rochester pursued a less insecure style of living.

In 1665 he met the beautiful young heiress Elizabeth Malet, and with the encouragement of the king he asked her to marry him. When she refused, he abducted her; he was subsequently caught and imprisoned in the Tower. Soon released, he joined the Navy and fought in the Dutch War of 1665 and 1666. His valorous conduct in battle helped to restore him to the favor of the king, and, in 1667, he continued his success by marrying Malet. More honors descended on the twenty-one-year-old Rochester: The king appointed him a Gentleman of the Badchamber with a salary of one thousand pounds, commissioned him captain in the horse guards, and arranged his summons to a seat in the House of Lords.

By all accounts, Rochester and his wife enjoyed a happy marriage, and four children resulted. Monogamy, however, suffered numerous assaults; the custom of keeping a mistress was followed by most Restoration aristocrats, and Rochester was no different in this regard. Elizabeth Barry, who became the greatest actress of the age, bore a daughter in 1677 and regarded Rochester as the father both of her child and of her career.

The decade of the 1670's marks the real development of Rochester as a poet. Always an impressive conversationalist, he began writing realistic and energetic satires of court life. The outspoken quality of his criticism alienated many of its victims—especially the king, who had him banished from court more than once. This reaction did not deter him from writing more fierce lampoons and from actively supporting the theater. Dryden thanked Rochester for his help with the Epistle Dedicatory to *Marriage à la Mode* (1673). Within two years, however, Rochester attacked Dryden in his satire "An Allusion to Horace" (1675). This work served as a dividing line between the factions of Whig and Tory writers.

The last four years of Rochester's life were characteristically dramatic; the evidence delineates the final stages of his long syphilitic illness and a remarkable spiritual conversion only a few weeks before his death. In the winter of 1679 to 1680, he shocked friends by his sincere interest in meeting Gilbert Burnet, a Scottish clergyman, to discuss the principles of Christianity. Although Rochester had maintained a rigid skepticism throughout his life, these conversations, with the knowledge of imminent death, triggered a sensational repentance. Declaring that religion had brought him the sense of "felicity and glory" that he had missed pursuing worldly pleasures, Rochester died on July 26, 1680, at Woodstock. He was thirty-three, and his death would release a mass of contradictory comment from biographers proclaiming him either an edifying example of conversion or a debauched pornographer with, in Pope's phrase, "a very bad turn of mind." The one truth that can be acknowledged by the evidence is that he possessed "the greatest poetic gift of all the noble Wits."

ANALYSIS

The reputation of John Wilmot, earl of Rochester as a poet has suffered from the overly dramatic legends about his life. Whatever past judgments have been made of his work seem unfairly colored by a considerable amount of untruthful scandal. Although modern biographers tend to rehabilitate such men completely and to give less perfidious definitions to the term "libertine," there is little to be gained here by denying the truth of his professed hedonism and his actual debauchery. Unwilling to allow his biography to overwhelm his work, two contemporary critics, David Vieth and Dustin Griffin, have affirmed the undeniable wit and power of his verses. Appreciation of the value of the early satires, the songs, and "A Satire Against Mankind" develops from first agreeing that Rochester is a product of his own time. Although this work, particularly the late satires, was influential for the Augustans and even shared some of their values, one should view Rochester's poems as mirroring the Restoration milieu socially, intellectually, and stylistically.

The major themes of Rochester's poetry derive from his evaluation of love, friendship, and courtly life. In each of these areas, he weighs man's promise for achieving the ideal against his predilection for evil and folly. As a skeptic, he is not under the mystical spell of religion; his poems reveal a man in search of certainties in the face of an awareness that such serenity is, for him, remote and unrealizable.

As literature of the Restoration, the poems reveal aristocratic attitudes of the past under severe stress from the philosophies of the Enlightenment. Rochester's knowledge of René Descartes, Thomas Hobbes, and John Locke allows him to suspend an automatic acceptance of traditional value systems and instead to question, analyze, and debate issues concerning the human condition.

Griffin, in *Satires Against Man: The Poems of Rochester* (1973), finds that one constant motif of his work was a rational humanist morality. Rather than trusting society or religion to establish laws for the restraint of man, Rochester depends on pleasure and pain and on following "nature" as the way to govern conduct. His tendency toward skepticism causes him to doubt whether morals can guide man to right conduct; in typical Restoration fashion, Rochester insists upon the immediacy of experience both with regard to sensual desires and in more abstract concerns: belief, conduct, and literary convention. Immediacy suggests security, a safe haven from the "ugly cheat" of life. If traditional moral and religious restraints are held in contempt, as they were at court, Rochester has only to rely on sensual contentment. Inevitably, his poems reflect his dissatisfaction with such experience; in fact, his constant theme is the disproportion between our desires and the means for satisfying them. While remaining a sensualist, he never reflects satisfaction in the poetry, because he never loses sight of the ultimate futility of the human condition. His poetry describes the suffering, anger, frustration, and failure of man, and does so with energy and clarity. In failing to achieve security, Rochester's analysis also reveals the zest of man's restless, acquisitive, and competitive nature, while affirming his admiration of personal goodness, of freedom from pretension and greed.

Textual notes

During Rochester's lifetime, his lyrics, songs, lampoons, and satires were circulated in manuscript copies among the court of Charles II. A few of his writings were printed as broadsides or in miscellanies; his great "A Satire Against Mankind" was printed as a folio broadside in 1675. The textual issue of whether a reliable contemporary edition of his poetry exists is a complicated one. In the late summer of 1680, a book professing to be the *Poems on Several Occasions by the Right Honourable the E. of R.* was published under the ostensible imprint of a nonexistent Antwerp printer. In an effort to capitalize on his name and popular reputation as a wild courtier, sixty-one poems were offered, of which many were pornographic and more than a third were not even written by Rochester. Nevertheless, the book was extremely popular and numerous editions were produced to satisfy public demand. In his book *Attribution in Restoration Poetry: A Study of Rochester's "Poems" of 1680* (1963), David Vieth explains that the earliest of these editions was based on a responsible manuscript miscellany copy text, and that despite the shortcomings of *Poems on Several Occasions*, it is the most important edition of Rochester published prior to the twentieth century. Since 1926, many editors have struggled with the Rochester text. The difficulties arose over an unusually problematical canon, the varying authority of texts from which the poems came down to readers, and the obscene nature of some of the genuine poems. In 1968, the definitive critical edition was published: David Vieth's *The Complete Poems of John Wilmot, Earl of Rochester.* In solving the aforementioned difficulties, Vieth found seventy-five authentic poems, eight other poems possibly written by Rochester, and nearly two hundred spurious poems.

PRENTICE WORK: "A SONG: MY DEAR MISTRESS HAS A HEART"

Rochester's poems fall into four chronological categories: prentice work (1665-1671), early maturity (1672-1673), tragic maturity (1674-1675), and disillusionment and death (1676-1680). Representative of Rochester's prentice work is the early poem "A Song: My dear Mistress has a heart" (exact date unknown), a self-consciously conventional poem incorporating characteristics of the courtly love tradition. As in many of his other songs, Rochester explores the complexities of man's sexual nature while entertaining rather than instructing the reader. In two eight-line stanzas of ballad measures, the poet employs the familiar figures and concepts of Restoration lyrics—the enslaving mistress whose "resistless Art" has captured the poet's heart. While recognizing "her Constancy's weak," he is powerless to escape her "Killing pleasures and Wounding Blisses" and must only trust that this poem will convince her of his deepest regard. Without varying from the sophisticated pattern, Rochester writes a tender, graceful love lyric. What seems missing is the poet's individual voice, which would bring this artificial form to life with the sheer intensity of his wit.

"FAIR CHLORIS IN A PIGSTY LAY"

Another early poem, "Fair Chloris in a pigsty lay" (exact date unknown), marks him as an authentic poetic voice with its sudden, often brutal, wit that shocks the reader, demanding his notice. Rochester's Chloris is not the conventional dreaming shepherdess of the pastoral; she is a swineherdess of the most lustful and crude sort. Surrounded by her murmuring pigs while she sleeps, Chloris dreams of a "love-convicted swain" who calls her to a cave to rescue a trapped pig, only to throw himself lustfully upon her. Instead of a self-abasing lover pleading with his mistress, Rochester reverses the persona as Chloris finds herself the object of a crude rape. The poem's final stanza undercuts the brutality yet retains the indecency, as Chloris wakes, realizing that it was only a dream. Her innocence is preserved, although she has enjoyed the secret pleasure of a fantasy lover. While maintaining a humorous and playful tone, Rochester adds a final unexpected twist of eroticism which lifts this song above the conventionality of the earlier one. Such a mocking tone foreshadows the poems of his mature period; the "innocent" Chloris becomes the voracious Corinna of "A Ramble in St. James's Park"

EARLY MATURITY: "A RAMBLE IN ST. JAMES'S PARK"

The poems of 1672-1673, the period of Rochester's early maturity, reveal his accomplishment as a lyricist and his virtuosity as a satirist. Vieth believes that the satires of 1674 display the zenith of Rochester's achievement, but "A Ramble in St. James's Park" is a triumph. The poem is a comprehensive Juvenalian satire on sexual relations in the *beau monde*, displaying the speaker as one who ridicules the corruption in himself and in his fellow revelers. The speaker describes an after-dinner walk in the park in search of love. In the park, once a place of elegance and now a scene of dissipation, he unexpectedly "beheld Corinna pass," who is his mistress and should acknowledge him, but instead "proud disdain she cast on me." Watching further, he sees her leave in a coach with three "confounded asses." Bitterly disillusioned, not by her lust but by her passive and treacherous submission to fools, he curses her for a "fall to so much infamy." The speaker, who had considered himself morally superior to his companions, now concludes with an ironic self-satire, an attack on the pastoral for idealizing such settings, and a lampoon against indiscriminate lust.

The villain is not the libertine speaker but Corinna, who offends all humanity by engaging in sex unfeelingly. Honest lustful passion remains a justifiable principle, while unfeeling sex with affected fools is a far worse sin than mere lust. Rochester shows his displeasure with Restoration men and women who respond to unnatural longings and reject those desires born of natural reason. The material is vigorous and often violent in tone, impatient with the sham of Cavalier and Restoration conventions in love poetry. The best of Rochester's bawdy satires, it is motivated not by its profane qualities but in part by a prejudice against the debasement of sex.

TRAGIC MATURITY: SATIRE

In the period of his tragic maturity, Rochester found his vehicle as a poetic stylist by controlling the heroic couplet for formal verse satire. The influence of the Roman satirists Horace and Juvenal provided some impetus for Rochester; his best model, however, was Horace's disciple, Nicolas Boileau-Despréaux, the first major seventeenth century satirist to attempt a re-creation of classical forms. "Timon" and "A Satire Against Mankind" transcend Boileau-Despréaux with their economy of phrase, skillful use of narrative and descriptive styles from one victim's portrait to another, and the command displayed between the realization of the speaker and the various dramatic scenes. John Harold Wilson, in *The Court Wits of the Restoration* (1948), argues that Rochester was roused in the 1670's "to a true misanthropy by the contrast between man's promise and his performance . . . he made war on mankind at large." In these poems, the complacency of humankind provokes an outrage unmatched at any other point in his career.

"Timon"

"Timon" has as its principal speaker a man named Timon, who resembles Rochester in character, interests, and social status. The reference to William Shakespeare's misanthropic Timon of Athens is obvious, although the name may also allude to his honesty in the face of a corrupted humanity. The account begins with an unwilling visit to a dinner party where an insistent host—a total stranger "who just my name had got"—promises that the other guests will be his friends Sedley, Savile, and Buckhurst. Not surprisingly, these assurances remain unfulfilled. Timon's company consists of four fools, "Halfwit and Huff, Kickum and Dingboy." The hostess appears, an ancient flirt, and presides over a tedious banquet complete with displays of corrupted taste in food and poetry. Inevitably, rough verbal antics culminate in bouts of plate-hurling and Timon's own relieved escape into the night.

Rochester establishes the thematic unity of the poem by implying that Timon's social and intellectual standards have been violated by the attitudes and actions of the host, his wife, and the four "hectors." In the earlier model for the poem, the Horatian speaker was a paragon of good sense and propriety. Rochester's Timon flaunts a delighted malice before the rest of the human race and does so in the bawdiest terms. Detailing the physical characteristics of the hostess, Timon develops a vicious portrait; the entire description, however, includes the most damning evidence—the victim's conversation, which displays her foolishness, affectation, and crudity. The speaker's character also comes under scrutiny; his curious interest in the dinner conversation and his obsession with sex create a disturbing uncertainty in the poem. Rochester may have meant to mock Timon for having agreed to attend the dinner party; his skeptical nature should have warned him against finding true companions. Also, the speaker's sexual crudity, although strikingly overt, is at least without affectation. As in the earlier "A Ramble in St. James's Park," the rake admits his belief in sexual freedom, his appreciation for honest, generous lust. Ultimately he finds frustration and humiliation. The same theme which appeared in the earlier work is alluded to in "Timon"; sensual experience is ultimately a failure. Timon realizes the accuracy of this attitude in his comments on the host's wife: "Fit to give love . . . But age, beauty's incurable disease, had left her more desire than power to please." Timon's faults cannot be ignored, but in contrast to the affected hosts and boorish guests he gains the reader's trust.

"A Satire Against Mankind"

Rochester's most impressive poem is his "A Satire Against Mankind." It is a discourse in which the speaker offers the paradoxical thesis that it is better to be an animal than a man; however, Rochester is more concerned with emphasizing the loathsomeness of being human than the virtues of being an animal. He attacks Reason itself, the pure rationality that he had formerly worshiped.

The poem reflects the skepticism of the age, and the recurrent motif in Rochester's work of a division between the actual and the ideal. The philosophy of cynicism goes back to classical sources, to Epicurus and the Skeptics. It seems that Rochester adopted their arguments in order to counter particular schools of rationalistic thought such as the vain and strident Christian rationalism of the Cambridge Platonists, the godlike reasoning eminence of the university Schoolmen, and the anti-Aristotelian rationalism of the Anglicans. The exaltation of man, the thesis that God is pure reason, the continual optimism about man's capacities for perceiving the meaning of the cosmos and God's laws through reason—all of these notions were ridiculed by him.

Rochester's immediate, most influential source was Thomas Hobbes, whose materialist-sensationalist philosophy was the basis for his view of human motivation. Every man is an enemy to every other man in his desire for gain, for safety, and for glory. This continual desire for security, for certainty, is characteristic of the libertine, who disdains convention and orthodoxy as paths to power. The rake instead exploits other people's weaknesses, thus gaining mastery over their lives. Those conventional figures of the community who might censure him are hypocrites who have disavowed their true desires for gain and glory. All those virtues that man professes to follow in the name of social order are merely rationalizations of his fear and desire for security, and Rochester improves on Hobbes, believing that man only converts this fear into more "respectable" passions. Rochester exhibits a bitter, relentless cynicism about human possibility; even the rake's mastery proves to be a painful failure.

The poem is a formal verse satire in which the satirist contemplates a particular topic and anticipates the imaginary response of someone else to his thoughts. This structure of the satire has caused much debate among critics who believe that the poem is a philosophical discourse on epistemology and ethics. Other scholars make a good case for the view that the poem is a unified polemic against human pride: pride in reason, learning, and "accomplishment." Griffin accepts both viewpoints while offering his analysis of the work as primarily a four-part discourse, with a speaker presenting and defending the paradox that it is better to be an animal than a man.

The first part of the poem states the thesis, suggesting that all men are equally ridiculous, and proposes a distinction between wits and fools. This difference proves a false one. The second part raises the imagined objections of the satirist's opponent, who offers a distinction between wit and reason which only reveals the ambiguous, confused nature of the opponent's argument. The third part develops the satirist's response to these objections, analyzing first reason and then humankind's "wisdom" and "nature." He seems willing to accept the middle ground between pure instinct and pure reason "which distinguishes by sense." The paradoxical quality of the poem is again asserted as the satirist turns from this compromise to attack all humankind once more. Instinct, although preferable to right reason, remains unattainable since all men are "knaves." The fourth part functions as the epilogue in which the satirist recapitulates his argument and in so doing reformulates his paradox. Significantly, Rochester adds here that all men are slaves, as well as knaves, only some are worse in these respects than others. The final line—"Man differs more from man, than man from beast"—sharpens the total satiric effect of the poem. Animals, after this exacting analysis, still remain closer to the ideal of godlike man ("meek humble man of honest sense") than the rabble (wits, fools, cowards, knaves, and the poet). The beasts are a better reflection of man's moral ideals than is man himself.

"A Satire Against Mankind" remains an impressive effort and an example of the best Rochester was capable of during his mature period. Its effects are beautifully judged, as is its destructive critique of human pretension; however, Rochester's own predicament as a man and as an artist persists with no real hope or secure possibility for a better world.

Disillusionment and death: "An Epistolary Essay"

The sixteen poems of Rochester's final period, the period of disillusionment and death, reflect a decline in the quantity and quality of his work. The most effective poem of this group is "An Epistolary Essay from M. G. to O. B. upon their Mutual Poems" (1679). Serving as a companion piece to "A Very Heroical Epistle in Answer to Ephelia" (1675), this informal critical essay expresses the views on love and poetry of a bold libertine persona, M. G. (John Sheffield, earl of Mulgrave). The speaker writes to a friend, O. B. (John Dryden), in praise of the latter's poems and in defense of his own violations of the traditional canons of good writing. Furthermore, after having lampooned in "A Satire Against Mankind" the idea that rational man partakes of the divine, Rochester here attacks the idea that poetry has a divine source. By employing this approach, he criticizes conventional wisdom, putting the burden of writing well on the poet's egotism instead of on divine will. The argument concludes with the notion that a poet is his own best critic and must rely on his own self-judgment. The arrogance of the piece marks Rochester's strength as a poet but his weakness as a man.

Confident about his own artistic strengths, he had nothing but contempt for the rabble of hacks and critics. His work possesses the poetic virtues of vigor and force; although often unconventional and strikingly obscene, his poems grow out of a literary tradition both Classical and English. Although the spectacle of humankind provoked in him a Juvenalian outrage and profound disgust, he also revealed his admiration for personal goodness, for a man of Christlike humility and piety. The doubt that such a person existed would plague him his entire life; yet he continued the quest without abject despair. His complex emotional response to the literary, intellectual, and social milieu of the Restoration found an outlet in his poetry. Whether he projects rejection and nihilism or envisions an ideal which proves unreachable, Rochester remains one of the most original and notable poets of the age.

Other major works

play: *Lucina's Rape*, pr. 1684 (adaptation of John Fletcher's tragedy *Valentinian*).

nonfiction: *The Letters of John Wilmot, Earl of Rochester*, 1980 (Jeremy Treglown, editor).

Bibliography

Combe, Kirk. *A Martyr for Sin: Rochester's Critique of Polity, Sexuality, and Society*. Newark: University of Delaware Press, 1998. Combe offers a way of looking at the poetry of Rochester that does not ignore his politicality. Using the theories of Michel Foucault and others, the author analyzes Rochester's writings within their contemporary civil and cultural context.

Farley-Hills, David. *Rochester: The Critical Heritage*. London: Routledge & Kegan Paul, 1972. This collection of critical essays on Rochester's work includes comments by his contemporaries and by writers such as John Dryden, Alexander Pope, and Jonathan Swift. Only essays as recent as the early part of the twentieth century are included, and modern reassessments of Rochester are lacking. Even so, this volume offers valuable background material and fascinating insights into Rochester's position in literary history, as he has gone in and out of acceptability.

Fisher, Nicholas, ed. *That Second Bottle: Essays on John Wilmot, Earl of Rochester*. New York: St. Martin's Press, 2000. Explores the full range and variety of the poet's work. In three sections the essays offer complementary but contrasting interpretations of love and friendship in Rochester's poems and letters; multidisciplinary essays surveying the extent to which Rochester's love lyrics inspired composers up to a century after his death and the satiric significance of the famous "monkey portrait" of the poet in the National Portrait Gallery; and Rochester's contribution to the Restoration theater.

Griffin, Dustin H. *Satires Against Man: The Poems of Rochester*. Berkeley: University of California Press, 1973. This work offers a discussion primarily of Rochester's satires, with an interesting chapter on "The Pains of Sex" in Rochester's works. A good part of the book focuses on Rochester's "A Satire Against Mankind," offering extensive background on the poem as well as an in-depth examination of the poem itself. Includes a discussion of Rochester's relation to other satirists such as Alexander Pope and Jonathan Swift.

Pinto, Vivian de Sola. *Enthusiast in Wit: A Portrait of John Wilmot, Earl of Rochester*. London: Routledge & Kegan Paul, 1962. This biography is an updated, expanded version of Pinto's *Rochester, Portrait of a Restoration Poet* which was first published in 1935. Pinto offers a full biography of Rochester, with abundant detail on the poet's youth, riotous and colorful life in and out of exile at the court of Charles II, and dramatic deathbed conversion. The social, intellectual, and literary currents of Rochester's day are also treated in depth.

Rochester, John Wilmot, earl of. *The Letters of John Wilmot, Earl of Rochester*. Edited by Jeremy Treglown. Oxford: Basil Blackwell, 1980. This well-annotated, thorough edition of Rochester's letters affords unique insight into Rochester's life and work. Both sides of the correspondence are included in many cases, and a concise biographical introduction provides a brief but sound overview of Rochester's life.

Treglown, Jeremy, ed. *The Spirit of Wit: Reconsiderations of Rochester*. Oxford: Basil Blackwell, 1982. This collection of modern essays offers various views of the poet and his work. The essays examine topics such as Rochester's link with the Metaphysical poets, Rochester as a poet of "lyrical realism," and Rochester's attitude toward women. His life and poetry are discussed in the light of the intellectual, social, and political currents of his day.

Vieth, David. *Attribution in Restoration Poetry: A Study of Rochester's "Poems" of 1680*. New Haven, Conn.: Yale University Press, 1963. This extensive study, more than five hundred pages in length, considers early texts and ascriptions. Appendices list additional poems in the Yale manuscript. Bibliographical notes.

Paul J. deGrategno;
bibliography updated by the editors

Theodore Roethke

Born: Saginaw, Michigan; May 25, 1908
Died: Seattle, Washington; August 1, 1963

Principal poetry

Open House, 1941
The Lost Son and Other Poems, 1948
Praise to the End!, 1951
The Waking: Poems, 1933-1953, 1953
Words for the Wind, 1958
I Am! Says the Lamb, 1961
Sequence, Sometimes Metaphysical, 1963
The Far Field, 1964
The Collected Poems of Theodore Roethke, 1966

Other literary forms

Theodore Roethke devoted most of his energy to his poetry. Ralph J. Mills, however, has filled one small volume, *On the Poet and His Craft: Selected Prose of Theodore Roethke* (1965), with Roethke's essays and reviews. He has also edited *The Selected Letters of Theodore Roethke* (1968). In *Straw for the Fire: From the Notebooks of Theodore Roethke, 1943-1963* (1972), David Wagoner has selected and edited revealing passages from Roethke's 277 working notebooks and 8,306 loose sheets. All three of these books are very useful in understanding Roethke's difficult poetry, for the poet speaks about his own work as well as about poetry in general.

Achievements

Critics often consider Theodore Roethke and Robert Lowell to be the most important poets of the post World War II generation. Although Roethke's achievement with traditional forms, such as the difficult villanelle, is impressive, he will be remembered primarily for his longer poems, the series of "sequences" in which he broke new ground by forging a unique poetic voice that conveys the intensity and complexity of his emotional, psychological, and spiritual struggles. Roethke created a new style in which one finds a kind of "psychic short hand," to borrow the poet's phrase. With the telescoping and distortion of images, the striking juxtaposition of the commonplace and the bizarre, he evokes a variety of states of consciousness under great stress, including those of the child, the mentally ill, and the mystic. Influenced by William Wordsworth, Walt Whitman, and William Butler Yeats, he explores the depths of the psyche and captures the associative movement of the mind.

Roethke received many honors and awards throughout his career, including two Guggenheim Fellowships (1945, 1950), the Tietjens Prize (1947), the *Poetry* Magazine Award (1951), the Levinson Prize (1951), the American Academy of Arts and Letters Award (1952), and the Shelley Memorial Award (1961). Yet he did not receive widespread recognition until the publication of *The Waking: Poems, 1933-1953*, which won the Pulitzer Prize for poetry in 1953. The last decade of the poet's life was a period in which he received his most prestigious awards and attracted the attention that he so much desired. *Words for the Wind*, new poems, together with a selection of poems from previous volumes, won the National Book Award and the Bollingen Prize in *Poetry* as well as five other awards. *The Far Field* brought him a second National Book Award. Roethke's reputation has been steadily increasing since 1953. His poems have been translated into many foreign languages and there have been a number of critical books and many articles published on his work.

Biography

Theodore Huebner Roethke was born in Saginaw, Michigan, on May 25, 1908, to Otto Roethke and Helen Huebner Roethke. With his brother Charles, Otto Roethke owned an enormous greenhouse consisting of several buildings enclosing 250 thousand square feet under glass. The young Roethke was fascinated by his father's gigantic plant kingdom, and the greenhouse world would later become a literary storehouse of poetic images for the adult poet. In his fifteenth year, however, his ordered life was shattered. After his father and Charles quarreled, the greenhouse was sold. Charles committed suicide several months later, and shortly after that, Otto died of cancer, suffering greatly before his death. Otto's strong influence on his son can be seen in the poetry.

The first member of his family to attend college, Roethke was graduated from the University of Michigan at Ann Arbor in 1929. He spent one term at the University of Michigan Law School and then in 1930 transferred to the graduate school, where he studied English for two terms. Then he did graduate work at Harvard and decided to abandon career possibilities in law and advertising in order to become a poet.

In 1931, *The New Republic* and *The Sewanne Review* published Roethke's poems. After teaching English at Lafayette College, Pennsylvania, from 1931 to 1935, he accepted a position at Michigan State College in East Lansing. During the 1935 fall term, he suffered his first attack of a manic-depressive disorder that was to haunt him for the rest of his life. These mental breakdowns typically lasted from one to six months.

When Michigan State College failed to renew his contract, he accepted a position at Pennsylvania State College from 1936 to 1943 and again for one year in 1948. In 1941, his first volume of poetry, *Open House*, received praise from the critics. Because of his mental illness, he was not drafted during World War II but taught from 1943 to 1946 at Bennington College, Vermont. In 1947 he accepted an associate professorship at the University of Washington in Seattle and was promoted to professor the next year. The University of Washington was to be his academic affiliation for the remainder of his life; here he wrote his best poetry, taught courses on "The Writing of Verse" and "Types of Contemporary Poetry," and attracted many fine students, a number of whom became poets themselves.

In 1953 Roethke married a former student, Beatrice Heath O'Connell, and published *The Waking: Poems, 1933-1953*, which brought him the critical attention that he had been eagerly awaiting. During the next decade, he published several more volumes and his reputation grew. He died of a heart attack in 1963.

Analysis

Theodore Roethke can be best understood as a poet in the tradition of nineteenth century English and American Romanticism. His early poetry of the 1940's and 1950's has some significant similarities to that of the English Romantic poets, especially William Wordsworth and John Keats, while his later poetry, especially "North American Sequence," owes a large debt to Walt Whitman. In general, one can see a number of essential Romantic characteristics in his poetry. Although he often objectifies his feelings in concrete images, he also directly expresses emotion. Feeling over analytical reason, spontaneity over logic, exuberance over calculated thinking can be seen throughout his verse; dancing, singing, and jubilant exclaiming are ubiquitous.

Roethke's subject is that of the Romantics—the exploration of the mind or "imagination." While his voyage into the depths of his own mind is, at times, terrifying, it has positive consequences. The imagination's repeated attempts to affirm itself in the face of threatening reality is a constant ritual and a source of tension in Roethke's work. Often the imagination can transform the external world, at least momentarily, and the poet feels redeemed.

Nature functions in Roethke's poetry in a particularly Romantic fashion. He writes of nature not to achieve an objective perception of it or a lyrical description of its beauty, but as a way to attain a more profound awareness, a "vernal wisdom." Nature takes a variety of forms in his poetry; it mirrors the emotional vicissitudes of the poet. It may be vindictive or affirmative to the point that the poet merges momentarily with it. He does make clear, however, that dissolving one's identity and merging with nature is an uncommon experience, for man has a keen awareness of his separateness that is very difficult to ignore. In "Moss Gathering," the poet as a young boy sorrowfully realizes his separateness from the primordial order of nature when he digs up a loose carpet of green moss.

While Roethke is an affirmative poet who sees the process of becoming as ultimately joyful, there is a

Keatsian ambivalence in his work. The beautiful and the grotesque, the joyful and the painful are inextricably related. Even "Dinky," one of his "Poems for Children," has a macabre quality fused with its lightheartedness.

Finally, not only Roethke's sensibility but also his style is Romantic. While his style displays a number of Romantic characteristics, such as spontaneity, direct expression of emotion, and intuitive perceptions, the most important characteristic is its meditative quality. As in the important works of Wordsworth and Keats, Roethke's poetry progresses associatively, according to the discursive movement of the mind, not according to the dictates of logic. In short, his best work mirrors the meanderings of the imagination, or to paraphrase him, the goal is to capture the movement of the mind itself.

Influence of Wordsworth

Roethke has many attributes in common with Wordsworth, who wrote meditative poetry in which the interaction between the mind and the natural world is the central preoccupation. Both poets reveal an aspiring quality in their work; both use simple language; both rely on recollections of childhood as a source of their poetry and a key to their perception of the mystery of the human condition. In *The Prelude* (1850) Wordsworth similarly explains his strange experiences—"that calm delight/ Which, if I err not, surely must belong/ To those first born affinities that fit/ Our new existence to existing things" (see Book I, 11, lines 543-557). Sometimes both poets seem to be expressing animism: "Every flower/ Enjoys the air it breathes" (Wordsworth's "Lines Written in Early Spring," 11, lines 10-11). This Wordsworthian image of natural phenomenon "breathing" appears often in Roethke's poetry. In fact, he takes the idea to its logical conclusion—stones breathing. Yet it is unlikely that either poet really believed that nature and inanimate objects were endowed with sentient life. Both were realistic poets who depended heavily on precise observation. Significantly, Roethke seems to have borrowed Wordsworth's notion of the importance of the "eye close on the object," or as Wordsworth wrote in the Preface to *Lyrical Ballads* (1800), "I have at all times endeavored to look steadily at my subjects."

The mind enmeshed in nature can be seen in the poetry of Keats and Roethke, and both poets describe the mind in similar metaphoric fashion. Roethke writes of "The leafy mind, that long was tightly furled,/ Will turn its private substance into green,/ And young shoots spread upon our inner world" (*Collected Poems*, p. 11); Keats of "some untrodden region of my mind/ Where branchéd thoughts, new grown with pleasant pain . . ." ("Ode to Psyche," 11, lines 51-52). Keats's oxymoronic last phrase suggests the contraries of existence that both Roethke and Keats wrestle with throughout their work. Mutability is a painful reality that is finally accepted and affirmed. Life is viewed as process.

"The Visitant"

"The Visitant" (*Collected Poems*) is Roethke's "La Belle Dame sans Merci," although here the awakened speaker is not so "alone and palely loitering" as Keats's knight; he is also more easily reconciled to his situation than Keats's knight, and the evanescent tone and the delicate evocation of the landscape is in direct contrast to the stark images of Keats's poem. Nevertheless, despite the difference in style in these two poems, there are significant stylistic affinities between the authors. Both use sensuous, suggestive imagery that conveys the complex vicissitudes of the emotions. In their works one sees subtle shifts of feeling and emotionally charged language that works toward a strong identification with external reality.

Influence of Whitman

In Roethke's later poetry Whitman is a strong influence, and he acknowledges this fact in both his poetry and his letters. He borrows Whitman's techniques, especially his cataloging and his free-verse style, his "loose line," in Roethke's phrase. In his long poems, such as "North American Sequence," one finds Whitman's playfulness, irony, and comic relief; like Whitman, Roethke realized that these qualities are necessary in a long work in which it is impossible to maintain a single tone.

Roethke was also influenced by Whitman's mysticism. In "North American Sequence" there is the Whitmanesque desire to achieve a becoming that is not self-conscious—in which the poet tries to dissolve his self, to merge with the landscape. Both poets try to absorb and absolve the self and provide the necessary harmony that the world can never provide. There is the need in both poets to be free from the body by extending it throughout the landscape.

One must be careful, however, not to overstate Whitman's influence. While Whitman's catalogs are often mundane lists, Roethke's are not; rather, he seems to be borrowing nature's rhythm and applying it to the human realm. In general, Roethke does not have that tone of massive innocence that dominates Whitman's poetry. Roethke harmonizes the landscape, makes it part of him, but there is the feeling that it can be done for him alone.

Open House

Roethke's poetry developed from his early conventional verse with its regular meter and rhyme to the later innovative poetry with its associative, free-verse style. In his first collection, *Open House*, there are abstract, rhetorical poems as well as sensuous, pictorial ones. The poems of this volume are traditional in form and content, and Roethke does not speak with a unique voice, as he does in his subsequent work. "The Prayer" is a typical early poem with its closed couplets, regular rhythm, and slightly ribald humor. "The Premonition" has lucid images that take on symbolic power: "Hair on a narrow wrist bone" suggests a father's mortality. Minute observation of detail in "Interlude" also takes on symbolic significance. "Mid-Country Blow" shows the power of the imagination that can so dominate the senses that the poet still hears the "sound of the sea" even after his eye has proved his vision false. The poem is reminiscent of many of William Carlos Williams's poems, in which a banal scene is transformed into a vivid experience of near revelation. "The Bat" portrays a deliberate correspondence between the man and the animal realms; "When mice with wings can wear a human face" suggests a mysterious horror in which man participates. In contrast, D. H. Lawrence's poem by the same name emphasizes man's separateness from the demonic bat's universe.

"Idyll" can be taken as the representative poem of the first volume. The gulf between complacency and minatory reality is evoked by the contrast of the sleeping town and the encroaching unnamed "terror." The poem is divided into three stanzas with a rhyme scheme that creates a sense of regularity broken only in the final line. The "we" of the poem is meant to draw the reader into the work, while the present tense emphasizes the immediacy of the poem's situation. The slow rhythm conveys the sense of the inexorable encroaching darkness.

The first stanza depicts a scene in which something is "amiss." A child's tricycle inexplicably "runs crazily," evoking a mood of innocence being menaced. The second line describes the representative man of the sleeping town. He is completely self-absorbed, a stumbling drunk who talks to himself. In stanza two the darkness envelops the "well-groomed suburban town." "Creeps" suggests a bestial presence that the town, "indifferent to dog howls" and "the nestling's last peep," refuses to acknowledge. Like a drunk of the first stanza, the people of the town exist in a self-satisfied state. The final stanza evokes a surrealistic scene—the world is dissolving in "the black revolving shadow" as a far-off train "blows its echoing whistle once." The "unmindful" people go to sleep in their houses precariously located at the "edge of a meadow." The failure of rhyme and the monosyllabic finality of "guns" in the last line emphasize the disconcerting contrast between the complacent town and threatening external reality.

Greenhouse poems

The Lost Son and Other Poems breaks new ground with the "greenhouse poems" and the longer associative poems that form the last section of the volume. These longer associative poems become part of a sequence in the next volume, *Praise to the End!* The title of this later volume is taken from an obscure passage of Wordsworth's *The Prelude* (I, lines 340-350) and provides an important clue to Roethke's basic intention in his volumes of poetry of 1948 and 1951. Wordsworth suggests in this passage of *The Prelude* that the mind can order into a meaningful whole disparate, painful experiences of the past. Like Wordsworth, Roethke believes that the individual can create his identity only after he has plumbed the depths of his psyche, even though this interior journey might be terrifying and could at times lead one perilously close to madness. In this sequence, which focuses upon the psychological development of the child and the spiritual regeneration of the adult, Roethke uses a unique style similar to that of the shorter greenhouse poems.

"Root Cellar" is a representative greenhouse poem and clearly reveals Roethke's method. The "poem" evokes the paradoxical situation in which the remarkable vitality of natural life seems threatening to the self. The fecund realm of this strange plant life is not a human one; no human could exist in this thriving subterranean world. The cellar represents both womb and tomb, fecundity and destruction. The alliteration in the first three lines stresses the contrary pulls of the life force (evoked by the vitality of the bulbs breaking out of their boxes) and the death wish (evoked by the darkness). The ambivalent nature of the scene is further emphasized by the description of the growing plants in sexual imagery that has negative connotations: "Hunting for chinks in the dark" and "lolling obscenely." As the poet closely observes the procreative forces of nature, he becomes keenly aware of the noxious odor that accompanies vital growth. The sixth line—"And what a congress of stinks!—" divides the poem. Next follows an accumulation of details, stressing the richness and rankness of the plants. Life is seen as an irreversible bursting forth; even the dirt appears to be breathing at the end.

In short, the self feels attracted to and threatened by this subterranean world. The greenhouse poems remind one of some of D. H. Lawrence's poems in which he is seeking his primeval self, his deepest being that remains submerged in the primitive regions of nature. The problem for both Roethke and Lawrence is that while man wants to recapture the primal mystery, he feels alienated from his spiritual and physical origins.

THE WAKING

The Waking: Poems, 1933-1953 contains a selection from Roethke's previous volumes as well as new poems, some of which owe a large debt to Yeats, as Roethke himself admits. The title poem, however, does not reveal Yeats's influence; with its series of paradoxes and its Wordsworthian exuberance, it might be considered a metaphysical-romantic hybrid. This much-anthologized poem is not only one of the most difficult in Roethke's canon but also one of his best.

The Waking is a villanelle and thus is divided into five tercets and a concluding quatrain; it systematically repeats lines one and three of the first tercet throughout the work. The lines are end-stopped, and the intricate rhyme scheme links the stanzas together. The rhyme scheme and the steady, lofty rhythm create a sense of inexorable movement.

The structure and rhythm of the poem perfectly fit the content. The first four stanzas alternate two paradoxical truths that the work expresses: "I learn by going where I have to go" and "I wake to sleep, and take my waking slow." In the final stanza these two paradoxes are repeated in the last two lines. Though seemingly the opposites of each other, both suggest an acceptance of the inevitable—more specifically, they suggest an acceptance of mortality amid the flux of everyday existence.

Roethke suggests that underlying the chaos of existence is a fundamental unity. The series of oppositions, paradoxes, and seemingly unrelated statements in the poem are deliberately utilized by the poet to demonstrate an underlying unity. The interwoven rhythm and the repetition link the dissimilar elements together. The intricate form of the poem itself, with its wide-ranging content, suggests that there is coherence in the flux of existence—if one would only allow oneself to become aware of it.

In this poem the self has come to terms with the human condition. In addition to conveying the tone of jubilant resignation, the repetition in the work emphasizes the poet's intense awareness and acceptance of identity. "I wake," "I feel," "I learn," "I hear" are the beginnings of lines. In the middle line of each of the first five stanzas, the poet unfailingly expresses acceptance. Although he feels the presence of death, he can affirm his situation.

Stanza four, the most obscure section of the poem, takes this feeling of affirmation to a mystical point. "Light takes the Tree; but who can tell us how?" The evocation of transcendence is followed by doubts about whether a human can attain it, and the answer to the question is as enigmatic as the original question that prompted it: "The lowly worm climbs up the winding stair." This response is ambiguous, suggesting the procreative power as well as mutability, affirmation as well as negation. While the lowest creature ascends to the heights (a spiral tree is a common image of the transcendent in Roethke), man paradoxically becomes aware of his transitory nature.

At the end of the work, the poet exhorts his reader to "take the lively air." The concluding rhyme (slow/go) breaks the rhythm and creates a sense of finality. The poet has accepted the fact that he will die, yet he realizes that his awareness of his imminent death has made him alive to the possibilities of existence and allowed him a glimpse of the eternal. The final note is one of celebration.

Words for the Wind

Words for the Wind is Roethke's best single volume. The best parts of the work are the largest section titled "Love Poems" and the final section, the sequence of five poems titled "Meditations of an Old Woman." These two sections reveal a new development in Roethke's poetry. "Meditations of an Old Woman" represents the poet's most impressive achievement in capturing the labyrinthine movement of the mind, but the length and complexity of the sequence allows only a few brief comments here on Roethke's remarkable innovations in this mode. The powerful, tormented sensibility evident in the sequence is expressed in a vivid and complex style characterized by subtle tonal changes, comparisons of past and present, recurring symbols, patterns of imagery, and repetition of key words, to name only the most important. The compression of imagery and the intense lyrical quality of the work resemble Keats's odes, while the meditative sequence as a whole has the expansiveness of Wallace Stevens's "variations on a motif."

There are a number of different kinds of love poems in *Words for the Wind*, and they represent an achievement in style of nearly the magnitude of "Meditations of an Old Woman." "The Dream" presents an odd mixture of the sensual and the ethereal. In "Words for the Wind" the poet sings of his communion with his lover. In fact, this title poem evokes an evanescent sensual love similar to that in Denise Levertov's "Our Bodies," although Roethke is much more ethereal than Levertov. In "The Sententious Man" the attitude toward the self and the world is ambivalent. Spiritual emptiness is a formidable threat in these poems, and much of the time there is no separation of the "kiss" and the "abyss." Feeling alienated, the self strives for communion and love.

Roethke vividly expresses the awareness of existential nothingness in "The Renewal": "I paw the dark, the shifting midnight air." Yet the lost self may be found again, for there is the possibility of rebirth in the morning when the poet experiences a mystical identification with the inanimate world: "I touched the stones, and they had my own skin." The constriction of the self is being overcome. "The whole motion of the soul lay bare," the poet says, after he sees the "rubblestones begin to stretch."

The Far Field and Sequence, Sometimes Metaphysical

In Roethke's final volume, *The Far Field*, he becomes very mystical. Total dissolution of the self is often the goal; it can be seen in the abstract poems of *Sequence, Sometimes Metaphysical*, in the love poems, in the "Mixed Sequence" poems, and in the "North American Sequence." In this latter volume Whitman's influence is particularly evident. Whitman sees death as rejuvenating, and sometimes he describes it erotically or maternally. Like Whitman, Roethke continually, almost ritualistically, discovers death and the beneficent quality inherent in nature. One loses his identity to the point that he is consumed—death is the final culmination of all growth.

Despite its power, the "North American Sequence" does not break new ground, for it is very similar in technique to "Meditations of an Old Woman." *Sequence, Sometimes Metaphysical* is a more original work. First published in 1963 in a limited edition of 330 copies by the Stone Wall Press (Iowa City, Iowa), it came to form the concluding section of *The Far Field*, Roethke's final work. It is an appropriate culmination of the poet's career, examining in an innovative style the recurring themes in his canon—the relationship of the imagination to reality; the possibility of transcendence and the mystical annihilation of consciousness; and the search for identity. "In a Dark Time," the most difficult and probably the best poem of the sequence, focuses upon these themes.

"In a Dark Time"

"In a Dark Time" bluntly asks Roethke's obsessive question: "Which I is *I*?" There is no simple answer. Stanza one suggests that the inner "eye" of the imagination paradoxically begins to see "in a dark time," as the despairing poet probes the primordial depths of the psyche. A series of metaphors of the poet's spiritual journey follows. He meets his "shadow," his other self, in the "deepening shade," the ever-darkening journey into the night regions of the soul. The poet exists in an in-between time—he exists between the extremes of the heron, a bird associated with the earth and the sea, and the wren, a bird of the air, as well as between the beasts of the hill and the serpents of the den.

Stanza two suggests that "madness" can be regarded as the spirit's visionary perception as well as the ultimate fragmentation of the psyche. The illogical events of an intrinsically meaningless world are at odds with the spirit's quest, and consequently the poet has known "the purity of pure despair." Here "pure" suggests completeness as well as visionary intensity. "Pinned against a sweating wall" stresses the acuteness of the poet's spiritual torment. Yet this torment, which is both visionary perception and disintegration of the imaginative mind, leaves the poet in confusion: Is he ascending to the ethereal heights or descending to the ignorant depths? He cannot be certain whether he is heading toward constriction in the depths or freedom on the heights, and thus he is left on the threshold.

In stanza three, Roethke states the method by which he works—"A steady storm of correspondences!" Connections between inner and outer worlds occur. "Storm," "A night flowing with birds, a ragged moon" suggest the difficult obstacles that the poet must overcome on his spiritual journey in which he hopes to create a new identity—it is a hope that can become a reality only by the eradication of the conscious ego. After the painful "Death of the self in a long tearless night," the supernatural emerges out of the everyday. The imagination has transformed mundane reality; in the light of the common day, midnight has come "again." Midnight is a magical time for Roethke, the brink of visionary transcendence; "again" suggests that this visionary state has occurred before—perhaps it refers to that time of spiritual unity in childhood when one does not feel estranged from nature.

In stanza four Roethke suggests that it is necessary to descend into the darkness to attain inner illumination. On the brink of transcendence as well as insanity, he cannot reach a transcendent realm and thus remains pondering his identity on the threshold, looking upward. Finally, the soul does complete its journey. Although the poet has fallen to the depths of despair, he now "climbs" out. The poet eradicates his excessively self-conscious ego and attains a heightened awareness in which his sense of estrangement from the external world is overcome.

SEEKING THE SELF AMID CHAOS

In the poetry of Roethke, the Romantic problem of the relationship of the self to external reality becomes an obsessive concern. The attempt to overcome the age-old Romantic dichotomy between the self and the world can be seen throughout his work, from the earliest poetry to the posthumous volume, *The Far Field*. Roethke searches for his true identity amid the chaos of modern life. The supposition behind this quest is that the mundane world is intrinsically meaningless, and therefore the poet must affirm reality by his imagination. The mind must endow the external world with meaning or the poet walks a never-ending tightrope over the abyss, always a step away from despair and madness.

For Roethke, the mind is the most efficacious defense against the cold multiplicity of the modern world because it can create order and because it fuses inner and outer worlds. When the mind achieves a complete identification with the external world, the tension between the self and the world dissipates. To achieve this identification is extremely difficult; but the heroic task of the modern poet, Roethke believed, is to make the attempt.

OTHER MAJOR WORKS

NONFICTION: *On the Poet and His Craft: Selected Prose of Theodore Roethke*, 1965 (Ralph J. Mills, Jr., editor); *The Selected Letters of Theodore Roethke*, 1968 (Mills, editor); *Straw for the Fire: From the Notebooks of Theodore Roethke, 1943-1963*, 1972 (David Wagoner, editor).

BIBLIOGRAPHY

Bloom, Harold, ed. *Modern Critical Views: Theodore Roethke*. New York: Chelsea House, 1988. A collection of critical essays on Roethke ranging from the early trailblazing work of Kenneth Burke to the views of Thomas Gardner and James Applewhite. Contains an index and a bibliography.

Bogen, Don. *Theodore Roethke and the Writing Process*. Athens: Ohio University Press, 1991. A critical study of Roethke's writing and an analysis of his philosophy. Includes bibliographical references and index.

Bowers, Neal. *Theodore Roethke: The Journey from I to Otherwise*. Columbia: University of Missouri Press,

1982. Emphasizes Roethke's use of his episodes of mental illness and other states of nonordinary reality as the source and subject of much of his best poetry. Augmented by an index and a bibliography.

Kalaidjian, Walter B. *Understanding Theodore Roethke*. Columbia: University of South Carolina Press, 1987. An introductory reading of Roethke's work with emphasis on the poet's concern with uniting humankind with nature and using unusual psychological states as gateways to new knowledge of the self and the world. Supplemented by an index and a thoroughly annotated bibliography of other criticism.

Kusch, Robert. *My Toughest Mentor: Theodore Roethke and William Carlos Williams (1940-1948)*. Lewisburg, Pa.: Bucknell University Press, 1999. A study of the correspondence between Roethke and Williams and the relationship they developed. Provides some biographical and historical background to the works of both authors. Includes bibliographical references and index.

Malkoff, Karl. *Theodore Roethke: An Introduction to the Poetry*. New York: Columbia University Press, 1966. Presents a psychoanalytic reading of the poet's work. As a result, many later critics often begin by agreeing or disagreeing with Malkoff, using his work as a benchmark from which to begin their own studies. Contains an index and a bibliography of works by and about Roethke.

Seager, Allan. *The Glass House: The Life of Theodore Roethke*. New York: McGraw-Hill, 1968. This is a full-length biography of Roethke, written by a scholar and novelist who was also a close friend of the poet.

Stiffler, Randall. *Theodore Roethke: The Poet and His Critics*. Chicago: American Library Association, 1986. Stiffler reviews and evaluates the critical reception of Roethke's works. Contains an index and a bibliography.

Wolff, George. *Theodore Roethke*. Boston: Twayne, 1981. One of the Twayne series of introductory guides to American authors, this book offers a good brief review of the poet's life and work. Contains an index and an extensive annotated bibliography.

Allan Chavkin;
bibliography updated by the editors

Edwin Rolfe

Born: Philadelphia, Pennsylvania; September 7, 1909
Died: Los Angeles, California; May 24, 1954

Principal poetry

To My Contemporaries, 1936
First Love and Other Poems, 1951
Permit Me Refuge, 1955
Collected Poems, 1993
Trees Became Torches: Selected Poems, 1995

Other literary forms

Although Edwin Rolfe published mainly poetry, he also wrote reviews, short stories, screenplays, and prose narratives. His articles appeared mostly in leftist periodicals and newspapers such as *New Masses* and *The Daily Worker*. His experiences during the Spanish Civil War (1936-1939) led to a history of the International Brigades titled *The Lincoln Battalion: The Story of the Americans Who Fought in Spain in the International Brigades*, published by Random House in 1939. His 1946 mystery novel, *The Glass Room*, written in collaboration with Lester Fuller, was translated into Portuguese and French. He also wrote the verse accompaniment for *Muscle Beach*, a satirical short film that won a prize at the Edinburgh Film Festival in 1948, and a prose treatment based on Dorothy Parker's short story "Big Blond."

Achievements

Among American poets, Edwin Rolfe produced the most sustained work about the Spanish Civil War and McCarthyism. Most of the war poems are included in his book *First Love and Other Poems*. Among them, "Elegia" was translated by Rolfe's friend José Rubia Barcia and was often recited by Spanish exiles in Mexico, Argentina, and Chile at their gatherings. Rolfe's prose narrative *The Lincoln Battalion* is one of the earliest factual histories of the International Brigades in Spain. This history remains perhaps the best contemporary account of the battalion.

Biography

Born Solomon Fishman to a working-class immigrant family in Philadelphia, Edwin Rolfe was significantly influenced by his Jewish-Russian parents. Bertha and Nathan Fishman, both committed socialists and labor organizers, taught young Solomon to take up responsibility to correct the institutional injustice faced by the underprivileged. The Fishmans moved to New York in 1915, where Rolfe attended New Utrecht High School and met Leo Hurwitz, later a pioneer in left-wing documentary filmmaking. Hurwitz, then the editor for the school magazine, was Rolfe's first mentor in writing.

Rolfe's passion for writing developed into a career goal after he joined the Young Communist League in 1925 and Mike Gold's Youth's Literary Workshop in 1926. Between 1926 and 1929, he wrote poems, short stories and reviews for *The Saturday Review* and *The Daily Worker*, but to support himself he also had to work as a restaurant dishwasher, a shoe store assistant, a subway construction worker, and a punch press operator. Financial struggles and the necessity to keep marginal jobs marked the rest of his writing career.

Dissatisfied with the rigid loyalty demanded by the Communist Party, he enrolled, with a scholarship, in the Experimental College at the University of Wisconsin in fall, 1929; however, his commitment to socialism and to writing brought him back, after three semesters, to New York's left-wing journalism. In 1936, with help from other writers, especially Archibald MacLeish, Rolfe published his first book of poetry, *To My Contemporaries*. This collection about the Depression years was widely and favorably reviewed. *The New Yorker* declared Rolfe, "if not the most flowery, perhaps the most readable and sincere of the poets of the Left."

The same year he married Mary Wolfe, also a leftist activist. In 1937, he volunteered to join the International Brigades to defend the Spanish Loyalist government in Spain's civil war. After training, he was assigned to work in Madrid, where he met Ernest Hemingway. At the time, Rolfe was working as a radio programmer, a political commissar, and an editor for the brigade magazine *Volunteer for Liberty*. Rolfe finally joined the infantry in the Ebro offensive against Franco, which included the largest battle of the war, before the American volunteers were repatriated in fall 1938. It would take him a decade to crystallize his wartime experiences into *First Love and Other Poems*, published in 1951.

Back in the United States, Rolfe again worked as an editor for newspapers and magazines. After he and Mary moved to Los Angeles in 1943, he worked for the film industry, writing screenplays and dubbing foreign films into English. His mystery novel *The Glass Room* was his first financial success, but he gave up turning the novel into a screenplay after Warner Brothers canceled the project because of his Communist affiliations. After the House Committee on Un-American Activities came to Los Angeles, Rolfe, blacklisted, had difficulty in finding jobs.

Personal health also became a concern. He was drafted into the U.S. Army but was discharged because of amoebic dysentery. He suffered several heart attacks, and in 1954 one claimed his life. His last collection, *Permit Me Refuge*, was published posthumously by *California Quarterly* in 1955.

ANALYSIS

In a letter written in July, 1951, to Albert Maltz, one of the Hollywood Ten (a group of screenwriters ostracized by the Communist scare of the Cold War 1950's, which culminated in the hearings of the House Committee on Un-American Activities), Edwin Rolfe expressed his eagerness to publish *First Love and Other Poems*: "I'd hate to let 1951 pass without a small stab in the direction of a soul-satisfying project." His "soul-satisfying stab" underlines his expectations for himself as a poet of the American Left. Rolfe's poetry addresses the definitive historical moments of the Great Depression of the 1930's, the Spanish Civil War (1936-1939), and the postwar inquisition of the 1950's known as McCarthyism. Still, as Gary Nelson suggests in his biographical essay of the poet, Rolfe's poems are "not merely a response to history or a record of one's passage through history but also a rhetorical intervention in history." In his poetic writing, Rolfe positions himself as both an eyewitness and a commentator on history—history as the lived experiences of human suffering and aspirations, and as a process of engagement and transformation.

TO MY CONTEMPORARIES

In Rolfe's first collection, dedicated to documentary filmmaker Leo Hurwitz, Rolfe declares his leftist poetics. The opening poem, "Credo," stands as his mission statement: He aims to "pierce" the "dreamplate" of empty political rhetoric that recurs every day in the speeches of professors and politicians and to seek "the wisdom and the strength and the togetherness/ of bodies phalanxed in a common cause." The task is a collective one and he urges, in the title poem, his fellow poets of the Left to join him:

> You, Funaroff, and Hayes, and the others:
> enter with me the farthest regions
> of space and time, the body moving
> across huge continents, the brain surveying
> the contours of the land, destroying
> the cancerous trees and men, restoring
> the spark to bodies overwhelmed
> by drudgery and dross and dust.

While poems like "Unit Meeting," "Homage to Karl Marx," and "These Men Are Revolution" define his political commitment with the images of group involvement—"These the world resolves/ into men moving, becoming revolution/ surely as blown seed takes root, flowers in sun"—Rolfe sees the compelling reason for such commitment, the misery of the Great Depression, in the images of individuals exploited and starving.

In "Asbestos," for example, the body of John the working-class everyman who builds "the granite tower" becomes its own deathbed.

> John's deathbed is a curious affair:
> the posts are made of bone, the spring of nerves,
> the mattress bleeding flesh. Infinite air,
> compressed from dizzy altitudes, now serves
>
> his skullface as a pillow. Overhead
> a vulture leers in solemn mockery,
> knowing that what John had never known: that dead
> workers are dead before they cease to be.

In "Season of Death," the narrator is stopped by a man asking for a light:

> . . . His open eyes
> stay fixed on mine. And cold rain falling
> trickles down his nose, his chin.
> "Buddy," I begin . . . and look more closely—
> and flee in horror from the corpse's grin.

This shift from realist to surrealist images is not a casual stylistic exercise in this collection. "Unit Meeting" adopts the sonnet form to celebrate Communist comradeship rather than romantic love. "Asbestos" is a ballad that laments the fate of the oppressed working class in the modern capitalist society. "Letter for One in Russia" uses the epistolary convention to embody the communal spirit of international socialism. It seems safe to say that Rolfe sees himself early in his career as a poet not only of revolutionary political ideas but also of revolutionary experiments in poetic form and rhetorical strategy.

First Love and Other Poems

Reflecting on his experiences in the Spanish Civil War, Rolfe articulates a double consciousness of history—the singularity of individual moments and their historicized values. In "City of Anguish," Madrid is a city in the aftermath of a bombing raid but also a casualty of the paralyzing violence of war:

> No man knows war or its meaning who has not
> stumbled from tree to tree, desperate for cover,
> or dug his face deep in earth, felt the ground pulse with
> the ear-breaking fall of death. No man knows war
> who never has crouched in his foxhole, hearing
> the bullets an inch from his head, nor the zoom of
> planes like a Ferris wheel strafing the trenches . . .

Rolfe returns to the memory of Madrid again in "Elegia," detailing familiar scenes in the city's daily life but also nostalgic for the solidarity and idealism shown by people from different countries fighting for a common cause. In a lover's incantation and lament, the personal longing honors the historical memory:

> Madrid Madrid Madrid Madrid
> I call your name endlessly, savor it like a lover.
> Ten irretrievable years have exploded like bombs
> since last I saw you, since last I slept
> in your arms. . . .

Not surprisingly, death is a recurring theme in this collection. Rolfe eulogizes the sacrifices of international volunteers in poems such as "Casualty," "Death by Water," and "May 22nd 1939." Rolfe's metaphoric language becomes more sophisticated than his early verse and intentionally ambiguous. In "Epitaph," an elegy for Arnold Reid, his college friend and fellow volunteer, Reid's blood nourishes "vineyards for miles around,/ olive groves slanted on hillocks, trees/ green with young almonds, purple with ripe figs." The "Seven feet by three" grave offers no rest. Reid's body, a self-growing seed, brings vitality to the land of Spain. The battlefield of death is also a field of rebirth.

Similarly, in "First Love," Rolfe's most anthologized poem, the memory of Spain, personified in a female grim reaper and bacchanalian votary—"the black-smoked girl approaching, her hands laden with grapes"—is one of love harvested through death.

PERMIT ME REFUGE

In Rolfe's McCarthy-era poems, his faith in human perfectibility within history is tested in the purging storm of the Communist witch-hunt that became an inquisition. These poems present a variety of voices and styles to convey the mixed emotions of anger, powerlessness, and critique. In "Political Prisoner 123456789," Rolfe decries the humiliating treatment of his friends among the Hollywood Ten during the inquisition in what appears to be an eyewitness report:

> His age, description given, his children named, his wife
> mentioned profanely, his private habits exposed;
> the walls of his few rooms torn wide for all to see,
> the walls of his life's efforts crumbling, broken—

In "A Hunter Went Killing: A Fable," swallows learn a painful lesson of distrust from the hunter: "Don't pity his weeping. Watch his hands." "Bal Masqué" dramatizes the HUAC committee surveillance in an imaginary "Gala Event":

> And we line up like living puppets
> carved in a crazed alchemist's dungeon
> and colored with his mad imaginings;
> line up like children awaiting the terror
> of the giant stranger's question, or those
> small dwellers in the morbid glen.

As the music starts, the dancers waltz under the "penetrating eye" of the big Band Leader, crossing and intermingling "between life and death." The surreal sense of terror is more explicit in the allegorical "All Ghoul's Night":

> Compounded of deceit
>   and avarice and horror,
> shrieking *I am the state*,
>   Ghoul unleashed his terror to the world,
>
> destroyed all loveliness.

Rolfe's critique also targets a culture of paranoia and political slavery. In "Dawn Song," he describes the conforming majority as "savages/ who dragged themselves to darkest holes to die." In an uncollected poem, "Little Ballad for Americans—1954," written one month before his death, he expresses his keen bitterness toward a society lost in suspicion and betrayal.

> Housewife, housewife, never trust your neighbor—
> A chance remark may boomerang to five years at hard
>   labor.
>
> Student, student, keep mouth shut and brain spry—
> Your best friend Dick Merriwell's employed by the F.B.I.

Yet Rolfe is still willing to see hope in few voices of resistance. In "Bon Voyage," the poem that closes *Permit Me Refuge*, he asks that such voices be heard:

> Permit me refuge in a region of your brain:
> carry and resurrect me, whatever path you take,
> as a ship creates its own unending wake
> or as rails define direction in a train.

At the core of Edwin's "lyric politics," to borrow Gary Nelson's term, are his social concerns rather than ideological debates. He remained loyal to his leftist politics, if not to his party. Writing himself into the cultural memory of American poetry and political visions, Edwin Rolfe consistently sees himself, his poetry, and the society he criticizes as both personally and collectively significant, and both are historical.

OTHER MAJOR WORKS

LONG FICTION: *The Glass Room*, 1946 (with Lester Fuller).

NONFICTION: *The Lincoln Battalion: The Story of the Americans Who Fought in Spain in the International Brigades*, 1939.

BIBLIOGRAPHY

Kalaidjian, Walter. "'Deeds Were Their Last Words': The Return of Edwin Rolfe." *College Literature* 24

(October 1997): 55-69. The essay examines Rolfe's poetic strategies and socialist politics, emphasizing him as a subversive voice in the post-war solipsism. It also uses the reception of Rolfe's poetry to discuss how academic valuation of his poems is influenced by the dominating critical tradition, American New Criticism.

Nelson, Cary. Introduction to *Collected Poems*, by Edwin Rolfe. Urbana: University of Illinois Press, 1993. Nelson's introduction to this comprehensive edition of Rolfe's poetical work, which includes Rolfe's three collections and more than thirty previously uncollected and unpublished poems, examines Rolfe's life and poetry, focusing on his political belief, subject matter, and poetic techniques.

_______. "What Happens When We Put the Left at the Center?" *American Literature* 6, no. 4 (December, 1994): 771-779. Citing marginalized left-wing writers such as Rolfe and Alvah Bessie as examples, Nelson sees the traditional canon as products of differential relations that determine who and what are at the center of the landscape of American modern poetry. Recovering the works of the previously repressed writers allows a reexamination of assumptions about the writers of the American Left.

Nelson, Cary, and Jefferson Hendrick. *Edwin Rolfe: A Biographical Essay and Guide to the Rolfe Archive at the University of Illinois at Urbana-Champaign.* Urbana: University of Illinois Press, 1990. The first book-length biography of Edwin Rolfe as a poet, journalist, and war veteran. Includes illustrations, letters, photographs from his childhood to 1952, a working bibliography of his prose and poetry, and a detailed register of his correspondence.

Chih-Ping Chen

Pierre de Ronsard

Born: Castle of la Possonnièrre, France; 1524
Died: Saint-Cosme, France; December 27, 1585

Principal poetry

L'Hymne de France, 1549
Odes, 1550
Les Amours, 1552
Cinquièsme Livre des odes, 1552
Le Bocage, 1554
Continuation des amours, 1555
Les Hymnes, 1555-1556
Nouvelle Continuation des amours, 1556
Discours des misères de ce temps, 1562
Résponce aux injures et calomnies de je ne sçay quels prédicans et ministres de Genève, 1563
La Franciade, 1572
Les Amours sur la mort de Marie, 1578
Sonnets pour Hélène, 1578 (*Sonnets for Helen*, 1932)
Les Derniers Vers, 1586
Songs and Sonnets, 1903
Salute to Ronsard, 1960

Other literary forms

In 1565, Pierre de Ronsard published his *Abbregé de l'art poëtique français* (brief treatise on French poetics), a theoretical work written in prose. In addition, he wrote a number of prose prefaces to his poetry (notably to the first volume of odes), and political or religious tracts.

Achievements

Pierre de Ronsard, the Prince of Poets, was both a great writer and a writer fully aware of his greatness. Although he and the poets around him did not, as they may have thought, create something out of nothing, they clearly did create new and often brilliant poetry. They demonstrate a fresh and sometimes naïve exhilaration in their poetic mission and boundless pride in their accomplishments.

Fascinated with classical culture, with the possibilities of the French language, and with his own abilities, Ronsard set out to emulate and to rival the Greek and Latin poets. At times, his pursuit of that goal led him into pedantry, with conspicuous and often heavy-handed references to classical antiquity and myth. When he was at his best, however, such references were a poetic *means*, not an end; they were a way of translating his vision into accessible form. Moreover, at his best (particularly in his love lyrics), he used such mate-

Pierre de Ronsard (Hulton Archive)

rial judiciously, occasionally dispensing with it altogether in order to let his persona speak in a direct poetic voice.

Ronsard himself published only a minor treatise on poetic art, but he almost certainly played a major role in formulating the theory propounded in Joachim Du Bellay's *Defence et illustration de la langue françoyse* (1549; *Defense and Illustration of the French Language*, 1939), the principal manifesto and manual of Ronsard's poetic circle. Moreover, implicit in his poetry itself there is a fully developed theory of poetic inspiration and composition. His contribution to the development of the French language and of French letters was considerable, as he put into practice many of the specific precepts of Du Bellay's work. Ronsard sought the creation of new and compound words, the acceptance of regional, technical, and archaic forms, and the Gallicizing of foreign words. Ironically, these very practices—his liberties with, and expansions of, the language—led in part to Ronsard's disfavor among the writers and theorists of the following two centuries, when he was most often considered a pedant and a corrupter of the language. Partly for those same reasons as well, but primarily because he is a great poet, he was rediscovered during the nineteenth century, and he has since been accorded a fair measure of the favor he had attained in his own day.

Ronsard was a remarkably prolific poet, the preeminent poet of his age, and one of the primary creators of French lyrics. If he was mistaken in his impression that France produced no notable lyric poets before his century, that error in no way diminishes his own achievement. Anthologists have unfortunately created for many modern readers a "homogenized" Ronsard, by ignoring much of his work and by repeatedly reproducing a few well-known love poems. His poetry is in fact extremely varied; it can be whimsical or introspective, lyrical or vigorous, occasionally even vicious. His vision, his command of tone and style, his realization and exploitation of the full poetic potential of the French language all give persuasive evidence that his designation as Prince of Poets, while not undisputed, is far more than idle praise.

Biography

Pierre de Ronsard was born of a noble family in the Vendômois region of France in 1524. At the age of twelve, he became a page for the dauphin François, only to have his master die a mere three days later. He then began to serve Madeleine de France (the new wife of James Stuart and daughter of François I). Ronsard accompanied her to Scotland, where she died almost immediately, in 1537. Three years later, a disease left Ronsard partially deaf and apparently destroyed his hopes for a diplomatic or other public career. It may have been this condition, as much as his exposure to the arts (an exposure provided both by his father and by his association with other Humanists and poets), that pushed him toward a career in letters.

Whatever the reason, Ronsard threw himself into Humanistic studies and into his early poetic efforts with single-minded energy and ambition. In 1547, he and the poet Du Bellay entered the College of Coqueret to study with the Humanist Jean Dorat. Along with others, Ronsard and Du Bellay constituted a poetic group designated as the Brigade, which (later, and with some changes in membership) was to be known as the Pléiade. In 1549, Du Bellay published his *Defense and Illustration of the French Language*; this composition, to which Ronsard certainly contributed, was an important manifesto which provided both a theoretical foundation for poetry in the vernacular and practical advice for the development of its resources. A year later, Ronsard published his first four books of *Odes*.

Ronsard's poetic beginnings immediately earned for him large numbers of admirers—but also a good many detractors, who in general criticized him for pedantry. Subsequently, he moved gradually toward simpler, more direct, and more accessible poetry. This movement is evident already in *Les Amours*. Within several years, his poetry and his success had silenced most of his critics, and he had earned not only praise and respect, but also the honor and financial benefits that accompanied royal approval: after the death of Mellin de Saint-Gellais in 1558, Ronsard became court poet to Charles IX.

In addition to being a court poet, Ronsard soon became a pamphleteer and polemicist as well, using his pen as a potent weapon in the wars of religion and frequently interspersing his diatribes against the Protestants with attacks against his own political or literary enemies. The year 1572 saw the publication—and failure—of Ronsard's epic, *La Franciade*. His disappointment and his loss of favor with the new king, Henri III (who preferred the poetry of Philippe Desportes), led Ronsard to retire from court life. In 1578, he published the remarkable *Sonnets for Helen*, and throughout this period he continued to write, as well as revising and editing his complete works. His health had deteriorated significantly, and he suffered from recurrent attacks of gout and a variety of other ailments. In 1585, he died at Saint-Cosme, at the age of sixty-one.

Analysis

More than any other single theme or idea, it is Pierre de Ronsard's awareness of the role of the poet and of his own mission and immortality that defines his literary production. The true poet, he says, is the recipient of divine inspiration, and the implication (or, frequently, the explicit contention) is that the preeminent example of the true poet was Ronsard. He boasts of raising poetry in France to the level of a sublime art; indeed, he was known as the first French lyric writer. These are themes that recur with a striking degree of regularity throughout his work, interrupted only once, in the early 1560's, when he briefly doubted his creative powers and referred to himself as "half a poet." His confidence and pride quickly returned, however, and in his *Résponce aux injures et calomnies de je ne sçay quels prédicans et ministres de Genève* (response to the insults and calumnies of certain pastors and ministers of Geneva), he likened himself to a poetic fountain, while other poets are mere streams who have their source in his work and his "grandeur." Others plagiarize him (he noted), and with good cause, since his work rivals Latin and Greek poetry.

For a poet who at every turn boasts of his originality, Ronsard may at times impress modern readers as strikingly derivative, as he mines classical myth and letters for images. He provides an explanation of his method, however, noting that myth hides truths—that is, clothes them in presentable literary form. Myth is for him a key to truth, and one approaches that truth by a kind of allegorical method, extrapolating from heroes and mythic events to contemporary characters and occurrences.

Ronsard would doubtless suggest that his method is far from being as mechanical as these remarks suggest; he is free to use or ignore myth or any other material; he can exploit it to reveal truth or simply to adorn his verse. In any case (he would insist), poetic inspiration obeys its own laws, which are independent of habitual or logical practices. The autonomy of poetic inspiration becomes, in fact, a major theme of Ronsard's theoretical and polemical work, and it is his inspiration, he says, that raises him above others. In the preface to the first book of *Odes*, he informs his rivals: "I follow an unknown path to arrive at immortality."

Love poems and Petrarchism

For most readers, Ronsard's reputation rests most solidly on the sonnets, songs, and other lyrics expressing the poet's love for Cassandre, Marie, Hélène, and others. Occasionally obscure or pedantic in these compositions (and especially in the earliest ones), he is more often direct, accessible, and lyrical. Yet, even within the collections of love poems themselves, there is a considerable amount of diversity, and from one of them to the next, Ronsard's evolution is obvious. He himself acknowledges that evolution (in the preface to the second book of love poems), noting that his style is not as elevated as it had earlier been. He has come to believe that love is best expressed not by cultivated high seriousness, but by an appealing lower style. He adds that he "want[s] to follow a gentler Muse . . ." and concludes that he is now writing to please no one but his lady.

The love lyrics are strongly influenced by Petrarchan images and conventions. The poet—or at least his persona—loves his lady, finds himself constantly fascinated and inspired by her, and also suffers from the love. His suffering, however, is suspect. He asserts that, with her unpitying heart, she makes him languish; his spirit is heavy and sad, and he suffers great pain with only brief respite. There is a curious absence of passion, however, in most of these assertions; one has the impression that he makes them because the conventions he is following require it. One more readily accepts as accurate the poet's image of a "sweet venom," and in general he seems to derive far more pleasure than pain from his love. If this is a somewhat atypical expression of Petrarchism, one soon finds an explicit rejection of one aspect of it. In the prologue to the Marie poems, Ronsard insists that Petrarch has no authority to impose rules on him. Of course, there is good reason for him to reject Petrarch's influence. The French poet is after all defending himself against a possible accusation of poetic infidelity, since, after devoting more than two hundred poems to Cassandre, he is now turning his attention and affection to Marie. In the process, he questions certain assumptions about Petrarch himself: "Either he received pleasure from his Laura, or else he was a fool to go on loving with nothing in return." Ronsard goes on to suggest, uncharitably, that women are frequently the reason for men's inconstancy: If a woman is cold and unyielding, it is not merely natural, but even advisable, for a man to turn elsewhere.

Ronsard's lyrics at this point in his career offer a very curious version of Petrarchism: Its demands include neither permanent fidelity to one woman nor excessive anguish or melancholy on the part of the lover. One can see in these departures from Petrarchan conventions not only a particular conception of love, but also an attempt by Ronsard to affirm his own poetic originality and to avoid being seen as a mere imitation or reflection of the renowned Italian writer.

In any event, the reader often has the impression that love and the lady are being "used" by the poet, for they permit him to experience and express inspiration and beauty more intensely. Petrarchism is, in a sense, turned on its head, the lady becoming a means rather than an end; in fact, there is something of a Neoplatonist substructure in Ronsard's work, as love becomes the means of apprehending truth.

In the first sonnet for Hélène, composed late in his life, Ronsard seems once again self-conscious about transferring his allegiance and love to a different woman, and he swears to Hélène that she alone pleases him and that she will be his last love. In the process, the poet insists that he *chose* to love her and that he is not doing so lightly. Ronsard appears to be deliberately rejecting the Petrarchan notion of fate and suggesting instead that love is more to be valued if the man freely chooses the object of his love, rather than having her chosen for him by fate or chance.

In the later poems, at any rate, Ronsard's suffering is either more deeply felt or at least more effectively expressed. Of the many poems that might be discussed in this regard, none is more remarkable than "Quand vous serez bien vieille" ("When You Are Old"). Ronsard pictures an aged Hélène, sitting in her room; he marvels at the fact that he immortalized her when she was still young and beautiful. This is in many ways a key poem; it describes a woman who owes her fame not simply to her beauty, but specifically to the poet whom her beauty inspired. Moreover, the woman is portrayed long after time has stolen that beauty, and Ronsard is uncompromising to the point of brutality when he contrasts himself, famous and at rest in death, with the lady, of whom he says: "You will be an old woman hunched over the hearth."

"Darling, Let Us Go"

This text recalls many of Ronsard's earlier poems (in the exploitation, for example, of the *carpe diem* topos), but the technique and tone are entirely new. This poem, like earlier ones, urges the woman to live for the moment: "Gather now the roses of life." The rose, one of Ronsard's ubiquitous images, sometimes evokes the season of love or the color of a lady's cheek; more frequently (as here), it symbolizes either the pleasures of love or youth and beauty itself. In one of his best-known poems, "Mignonne, allons voir si la rose" ("Darling, Let Us Go," a poem for Cassandre), he had earlier written: "Let us go and see if the rose which bloomed just this morning has not already lost its beauty," and he concludes with an insistent plea for her to live fully, before age tarnishes her beauty, as it has so quickly for the rose.

Certainly the poems resemble each other in the rose imagery, but in spite of the similarities, there is a striking contrast between the earlier and the later poem. In works such as "Darling, Let Us Go," the threat of lost youth is blunted by a profusion of warmly lyrical rhythms, rich rhymes, and rounded back vowels, all creating an impression of beauty and lushness rather than desperation. The emphasis is on the present rather than the future, on pleasure rather than on pain and old age. In "When You Are Old," on the other hand, the tenses project the lady into a future that holds no promise for her except old age and an autumnal melancholy relieved only by recollections of the way Ronsard had presented her. The vocabulary and sound system effectively translate her bleak future into realistic terms. The word *accroupie* (hunched over, or squatting), for example, is surprising and effective, both because of its meaning and because of its sound (in contrast to *Rose, déclose*, and other sonorous words in the earlier poem).

As this brief discussion suggests, Ronsard's later work retains many of his early themes and images, but there is a distinct evolution toward realism, urgency, and a measure of resignation. He has clearly entered a new stage of his poetic (and personal) life, characterized by his continuing belief in his own poetic destiny, but especially by a new emphasis on aging, death, and the passing of beauty and sensual love.

"When You Are Old" and "Hymn to Death"

In "When You Are Old," the woman is the victim of passing time, but Ronsard reserves his most realistic details for his own aging. Noting in one of his final poems that "I am nothing but bones, a virtual skeleton," he asserts: "I cannot look at my own arms without trembling in fear." As confident as he may remain about his enduring fame, he is, quite simply, terrified of aging, physical change, and death. This is in striking contrast with his views in 1555, when he had composed "Hymne de la mort" ("Hymn to Death"). There he had emphasized, quite dispassionately, that all men must die, and he had looked with some scorn upon those who, forgetting that they are children of God, fear death. His conclusion: Death is not to be feared, because after death the body feels nothing. Yet, thirty years later, in a radical but quite understandable change of attitude, he recoils in horror at the sight of his own emaciated body. Near the end of his life, biological inevitability comes to occupy more and more of the poet's attention, profoundly coloring his late poetry and his views of life and love.

Polemics

Ronsard is most often thought of as the poet of love, as a poet who sang of beauty, youth, springtime, and pleasure. In addition, however, he was both an author of occasional verse and a polemical writer. A mark of literary success was the approval of the court, and currying favor with a prince or lesser noble was a far more respectable literary enterprise in the sixteenth century than it would be considered today. Ronsard, apparently, was something of a master of the art of soliciting royal patronage. Modern readers are, however, more likely to be impressed by his polemical writings.

When religious tensions began to develop in France, Ronsard entered the debate, speaking at first in moderate tones, but as these tensions erupted into open conflict, he became as engagé—and at times as brutal—as any of his Protestant adversaries. He endured virulent abuse, and he responded in kind in his *Discours des misères de ce temps*—especially those of 1562-1563—and in various other works. Throughout these exchanges of diatribes, political and religious discussions were often mixed with violent personal attacks.

Résponce aux injures et calomnies de je ne sçay quels prédicans et ministres de Genève

Résponce aux injures et calomnies de je ne sçay quels prédicans et ministres de Genève is his answer to those who accused him of being an atheist, a priest, a syphilitic, and a poet of limited talent. Ronsard was stung by all these charges, but the last one must have been particularly painful for him. He defends himself against all four in masterly fashion, and some of his most eloquent passages are reserved for his proud, almost arrogant, assessment of his own poetic abilities and accomplishments and of his opponents' limitations. He asserts the primacy of inspiration and the freedom of the true poet to choose his path and set his own rules.

Thus, even when defending his faith and himself, even when he is engaged in an exchange of vicious diatribes (or perhaps especially at these times), Ronsard remains fully conscious of his poetic destiny. His awareness of his status is, indeed, one of the few constants in his work. A creature of the Renaissance and one of its prime creators, Ronsard exhibits all its characteristic energy, its confidence, and (until late in his life) its optimism. He indisputably represents an important step in the development of French poetry, as he and his circle expanded and polished its resources and advanced it through precept and example. Inevitably, he experienced poetic failures and personal reverses, but he had far more successes and satisfactions; on balance, his glory is well-deserved. Through it all, he, like many of his colleagues and contemporaries, entertained no doubt about the identity of the Prince of Poets.

Other major works

NONFICTION: *Abbregé de l'art poëtique français*, 1565.

MISCELLANEOUS: *Œuvres complètes*, 1914-1975 (20 volumes).

Bibliography

Bishop, Morris. *Ronsard: Prince of Poets*. New York: Oxford University Press, 1940. Classic, spirited, and readable introduction to Ronsard, his works, and his times for the general reader.

Campo, Roberto. *Ronsard's Contentious Sisters: The Paragon Between Poetry and Painting in the Works of Pierre de Ronsard*. Chapel Hill: University of North Carolina Press, 1998. Continues previous studies of the relationship of poetry and painting as expressed in Ronsard's poetry, especially of words to pictorial images in both narrative and portraits.

Cave, Terence, ed. *Ronsard the Poet*. London: Methuen, 1973. A thorough biography of the poet with a bibliography and index.

Fallon, Jean M. *Voice and Vision in Ronsard's "Les Sonnets pour Hélène."* New York: P. Lang, 1993. A historical and critical study of Ronsard's love poetry. Includes bibliographical references and index.

Ford, Philip. *Ronsard's Hymnes: A Literary and Iconographical Study*. Tempe, Ariz.: MRTS, 1997. An examination of the parallels between methods and form in the pictorial and plastic arts, and those in Ronsard's hymns.

Jones, Kenneth R. W. *Pierre de Ronsard*. New York: Twayne, 1970. A brief overview of Ronsard's life and the major collections of his work, offering a descriptive rather than critical analysis.

Leslie, Bruce R. *Ronsard's Successful Epic Venture: The Epyllion*. French Forum Monographs 11. Lexington, Ky.: French Forum, 1979. Exploration of the failure of *La Franciade* as epic, and the success of the lesser "Hymne d'Hyver," which Leslie sees as a type of short epic.

Quainton, Malcolm. *Ronsard's Ordered Chaos: Visions of Flux and Stability in the Poetry of Pierre de Ronsard*. Manchester, England: Manchester University Press, 1980. A study of the major themes in Ronsard's work: change, fortune, time, and death. Includes illustrations, bibliography, index.

Silver, Isidore. *The Intellectual Evolution of Ronsard*. 3 vols. St. Louis, Mo.: Washington University Press, 1969, 1973; Geneva: Droz, 1992. A massive study of the traditions and literary influences that shaped Ronsard's poetic works. Volume 1 covers the formative influences, volume 2 Ronsard's general theory of poetry, and volume 3 Ronsard's philosophic thought. Bibliographical references, indexes.

_______. *Ronsard and the Hellenic Renaissance in France*. 3 vols. Geneva: Droz, 1981, 1985, 1987. Places Ronsard's poetry in the context of the main currents in the French Renaissance, especially Greek philology and cultural studies. Examines such topics as Ronsard and the Greek epic and the Grecian lyre.

Stone, Donald. *Ronsard's Sonnet Cycles: A Study in Tone and Vision*. New Haven, Conn.: Yale University Press, 1966. An early application of New Criticism through textual explications. For general readers; refers to Ronsard's works in the original French.

Sturm-Maddox, Sara. *Ronsard, Petrarch, and the Amours*. Gainesville: University Press of Florida, 1999. A critical analysis of *Les Amours* and the influence of Petrarch on this and other poems by Ronsard. Includes bibliographical references and an index.

Norris J. Lacy;
bibliography updated by Joseph P. Byrne

Isaac Rosenberg

Born: Bristol, England; November 25, 1890
Died: near Arras, France; April 1, 1918

Principal poetry

Night and Day, 1912
Youth, 1915
Moses, 1916 (includes verse drama)
Poems, 1922 (Gordon Bottomley, editor)
The Collected Poems, 1949

Other literary forms

Isaac Rosenberg's *Moses* combines poetry with verse drama. His *Collected Works of Isaac Rosenberg* (1979) includes poetry, prose, letters, paintings, and drawings.

Achievements

Isaac Rosenberg was one of a group of young poets, including Rupert Brooke, Edward Thomas, and Wilfred Owen, whose lives were tragically cut short by World War I. Rosenberg's early poems were slight; it is as a war poet that his reputation was established, largely through the efforts of his mentor, Gordon Bottomley. What makes him unusual among British poets in general, and war poets in particular, is his Jewish perspective. That aspect coupled with his working-class background sets his poetry apart from the Georgian tones of Thomas or Brooke, or the upper-class tones of Siegfried Sassoon or Robert Graves.

Biography

Isaac Rosenberg was the son of Barnett Rosenberg and Hacha Davidov. His father was a Lithuanian Jew whose impoverished family had emigrated from Russia to Bristol, England, shortly before Rosenberg's birth. Soon after, they moved to the East End of London, which was then the center of the Jewish immigrant community, a community that existed as a tightly knit group until the 1960's, and from which such Jewish writers emerged as the dramatists Bernard Kops and Arnold Wesker.

His father opened his own butcher shop; when that failed, he became an itinerant peddler. The family lived in constant poverty. However, there was a cohesiveness and a religious atmosphere. After an elementary school education, Isaac Rosenberg showed some artistic promise, and in 1907 he began attending evening classes at Birkbeck College, an affiliated college of the University of London, set up especially to help poor students. In 1908 he won the Mason Prize for his nude studies and several other awards. To earn a living he became apprenticed to an engraver.

A few people noticed his talent and sponsored him at the Slade, London's most prestigious art school, which he entered in 1911. There he was influenced by such British artists as the Pre-Rapaelites, particularly Dante Gabriel Rossetti, and also by William Blake and the modernist Roger Fry. While continuing to study at the Slade, he struck out as an artist, setting up a studio in 1912 in Hampstead Road. He had also been writing some poetry, some of which he sent to Laurence Binyon, an established Georgian poet who worked at the British Museum. He also sent some to the *English Review*. From both he received encouragement and decided to publish these poems at his own expense in a twenty-four-page pamphlet.

The next year he met Edward Marsh, editor of *Georgian Poetry* and an influential literary figure in London. Marsh purchased some of his paintings and encouraged him to go on writing, introducing him to other poets such as the modernists T. E. Hulme and Ezra Pound. He was still undecided as to whether he was better as a painter or as a poet.

At this point, Rosenberg's health deteriorated, and he sailed to South Africa to stay with one of his sisters. He remained there during 1914, returning to England in March, 1915. Marsh bought three more of his paintings, and Rosenberg published another volume of verse, again at his own expense. However, with the war on, the literary and artistic scene in London had broken up, and there were no immediate prospects or contacts for him. In the light of this he decided, reluctantly, to enlist, though feeling no particular patriotism.

He was not in good health, rather underweight and undersized. Nevertheless, he was accepted by the army, joining the "Bantams" of the 12th Suffolk Regiment, later transferring to the King's Own Royal Lancasters. After initial training he was despatched to the Somme battle area of northern France in June, 1916. During this time, he wrote a play, *Moses*, and then several other dramatic pieces based loosely on Jewish mythology.

He continued to write poetry, also, now influenced by his experience of war. By 1916 there were few illusions left about the nature of modern warfare. Rosenberg was able to embrace what he saw and sought some positive response to it. Apart from ten days of leave in September, 1917, and a few short spells in the hospital, he served continuously on or just behind the front lines until his death. He was killed shortly before the end of the war while riding dispatches at night. His body was never recovered. His war poems were first collected and published in 1922 by Gordon Bottomley.

Analysis

Such is the lateness in poetic development in Isaac Rosenberg's short life that the majority of his output could be termed "early." His earliest dated poem is from 1905, but the so-called trench poems, on which his reputation solely depends, did not begin until 1916, when he enlisted and was posted to France. Thus the earlier poems span eleven years, with the best gathered into the 1912 and 1915 collections. The total number of poems gathered by his editors, including all the unpublished ones, is 154, of which only 10 percent represent the war poems themselves.

Even though he did have friendships with several Imagist poets—Imagism being the first flowering of modern poetry—his early poetry, unlike his painting, seems typically Georgian. This movement, spanning the first fifteen years of the twentieth century, is best typified as Romantic in a suburban, restrained way, with the emphasis on nature as recreation and pretty images, being nostalgic in tone and with harmonious versification. Some critics have seen the influence of the Pre-Raphaelite painter-poet Dante Gabriel Rossetti, though the most obvious echoing is that of John Keats, another London city poet, whose poetry is full of woods, light, and shade and heightened sensory perceptions, with nature as escape for the trapped urban spirit.

"Night and Day"

The long opening poem of the 1912 collection is titled "Night and Day" and apostrophizes the stars as he walks out of the city into the woods. The poet feels himself "set aside," seeking symbolic meaning in nature. Keats's "Sleep and Poetry" forms an obvious comparison. Echoes also sound of E. M. Forster's character Leonard Bast in his novel *Howards End* (1910). Other poems in the volume talk of "Desire" with an interesting religious reference; others show sympathy for the common people, a sympathy Rosenberg was to demonstrate later in his war poems.

Youth

Youth, the 1915 volume, shows in some of its lyrics somewhat more focus and control, but the emotions stay at a very generalized level. "God Made Blind" is more like a poem by Thomas Hardy, England's most senior poet at the time. "The Dead Heroes" shows an entirely conventional view of patriotism at this stage.

"On Receiving News of the War"

The uncollected "On Receiving News of the War," written from Cape Town, South Africa, shows a much less conventional and more genuine response. He writes, "God's blood is shed/ He mourns from His lone place/ His children dead." There is no heroism here, only divine pity. In 1915 he sent some of these poems to Lascelles Abercrombie, one of the most popular of the Georgians, whom Rosenberg considered "our best living poet." Abercrombie found the poems to possess a "vivid and original impulse," though noting he had not yet found his true voice.

Moses

Rosenberg was also attracted to dramatic verse. In 1916 he had published *Moses*, which consisted of a small number of poems added to a fragment of what was presumably intended to be a larger dramatic work on the Israelite leader Moses. He took considerable license with the biblical story, placing Moses at the moment he was still a prince of Egypt, but just beginning to find his identity as a Hebrew. The speech rhythms and dramatic ideas show much more poetic talent than anything done before, but there is still too much verbiage to be truly dramatic.

Some of the other poems in the volume are much bolder in their conceptual range than anything before. "God" makes a defiant Promethean statement. "Chagrin" uses the image of Absalom hanging by his hair, linking this to Christ hanging on the cross, quite a new sort of poem. "Marching" is the first soldier poem, with taut strong rhythms. The language is much richer and more imagistic. In the volume as a whole, there is for the first time some awareness of modernism, as there had been for some time in his painting.

The Lilith theme

While enlisted, Rosenberg also experimented with another Jewish myth, that of Lilith, mixing it strangely with unicorn myths and even a "Rape of the Sabine Women" theme. In his unpublished papers there were a number of versions of this, titled variously "The Unicorn" or "The Amulet." As he works through various drafts, the blank verse becomes more dramatic, but his own imagination is revealed as mythic rather than dramatic, and there is no overall conceptual grasp of dramatic ideas or structure. Most of the verse consists of soliloquies or long monologues. Yet when it is considered that most of it was done under the most appalling physical conditions, it shows considerable commitment on the poet's part.

Trench poems

Once under the pressure of fighting in France, Rosenberg's poetic talents crystallized quickly. Flowery sentiments and unfocused images, typical also of Keats's early style, were, as with Keats himself, left behind, and a genuine unsentimental human sympathy was revealed. "The Dying Soldier" sets the tone: it is lyrical, almost balladic, but it focuses on the pathos of the actual death, not the stark horrors of the overall scene. "In War" shows a great advance in poetic technique: The controlled stanza form displays a control of tone and emotion, taking the reader from an almost anaesthetized calm to a sudden panic of realizing it was his brother they were burying. This movement from something "out there" to "right here" becomes typical of these war poems.

Several themes and poetic ideas are revealed. One is the "titan." "Girl to a Soldier on Leave" uses this image for the infantry soldier: Romantic love cannot really be sustained in the face of trench experience. Some new mode of tragedy is being forged. In "Soldier: Twentieth Century" for the first time a political comment is made. The modern soldier is a "great new Titan." In the past, soldiers were fodder to keep tyrants in power. Now it is time they woke up from sleeping "like Circe's swine" and rebelling.

The second theme is a Jewish one: the burning of Solomon's Temple. "Destruction of Jerusalem by the Babylonian Hordes" is too anachronistic to be fully effective. The theme is reworked in "The Burning of the Temple." The poet asks if Solomon is angry at the burning of his glorious temple, to which the answer is, apparently not. If "God" is read for "Solomon" and the human body for the "Temple," then a powerful statement emerges: God's anger can be only ambiguously discerned.

The third theme is humorous. "The Immortals" is mock heroic, leading the reader to believe the soldier is fighting a heroic battle. In fact, he is fighting lice, which are immortal. Similarly, "Louse Hunting" depicts the real enemy in its "supreme littleness." In fact, Rosenberg has very little conception of the "enemy." For example, "Break of Day in the Trenches" shows a poet who strikes no poses, makes no gestures, with all his sensitivities intact after two years of continuous warfare. Others were driven insane. It is a gentle, sad, slightly ironic poem that shows Rosenberg as a human being rather than a soldier. In fact, death on the battlefields is described as "murder," hardly a military perception.

The poem is an address to a rat, which like lice, were all too common in the trenches. However, the rat is not treated as vermin here. Rosenberg apostrophizes it for making no distinction between friend and foe, crossing indiscriminantly between the two sides. The rat is "sardonic"; it "inwardly grins" as it sees fine young men from both sides being killed randomly and haphazardly, "sprawled in the bowels of the earth."

"Dead Man's Dump"

Among the best war poems ever written are two by Rosenberg, "Returning We Hear the Larks," with its sense of precarious joy still possible for the human spirit, and "Dead Man's Dump." This poem is about the quintessential war dilemma: seeing individuals, living and worthy of life, even if on the point of dying, as against seeing the mass of impersonal lifeless corpses that are fit only for throwing into the ground and burying. Rosenberg seems to be on some sort of burial fatigue, jolting along in a mule-drawn cart somewhere in no-man's-land. All around "The air is loud with death," and corpses of friend and foe alike lay scattered around. Sometimes the cart jolts over them, crushing their bones. They come across one corpse of a man who has just died. The dead soldier must have heard them coming, for he tried to cry aloud. However, by the time the cart gets to him, he is dead, and "our wheels grazed his dead face."

The poet writes as a human being: There is pity but no sentimentality. Rosenberg's visual imagination is most clearly seen in his images of the corpses, their former strength and spirit seen against their present contorted lifelessness, especially in relationship to the earth, which is sensed as a living entity, to whose embrace the living return in a haphazard, random way. His imagination is also engaged in motion and motionlessness: Verbs are particularly vivid: "lurched," "sprawled," "crunched," "huddled," "go crying," and "breaking," "crying," "torturing," "break," "broke," "quivering," "rushing" in the climactic ending. These verbs are so violent they push away the poet's natural inclination to pity: "The drowning soul was sunk too deep/ For human tenderness." He writes of a soldier whose "brains splattered on/A stretcher-bearer's face."

This is a much more sustained poem than many of the other war poems. It is in free verse, divided into irregular stanzas, twelve in all, with occasional rhymes and half-rhymes. It is modern in its versification, unlike that of fellow war poets Brooke, Owen, and Sassoon, who tried, not always successfully, to adapt forms of the gentle, restrained Georgian versification to the horrendous scenes and emotions they were describing. Rosenberg's images and rhythmic structures create drama and movement much more fluidly, and the climax of the poem is as powerful as anything else in World War I poetry. Clearly, Rosenberg could have become a great poet had he lived. The very control of the poem, written in conditions of chaos and horror, suggests the triumph of the human spirit.

Other major works

MISCELLANEOUS: *The Collected Works of Isaac Rosenberg: Poetry, Prose, Letters, and Some Drawings*, 1937 (Bottomley and Denys Harding, editors); *The Collected Works of Isaac Rosenberg: Poetry, Prose, Letters, Paintings, and Drawings*, 1979 (Ian Parsons, editor).

Bibliography

Cohen, Joseph. *Journey to the Trenches: The Life of Isaac Rosenberg, 1890-1918*. London: Robson, 1975. Three biographies of Rosenberg were published in 1975, their combined effect being to bring him to public notice as a significant war poet. Cohen's account is the most sympathetic to his Jewish roots and background.

Desmond, Graham. *The Truth of War: Owen, Blunden, Rosenberg*. Manchester, England: Carcanet Press, 1984. A thoughtful approach to three contrasting World War I poets. A good bibliography with good commentaries on all of Rosenberg's trench poems.

Giddings, Robert. *The War Poets: The Lives and Writings of the 1914-18 War Poets*. London: Bloomsbury, 1988. A popular biographical approach, enacting Rosenberg's life and experience in the context of his contemporaries.

Liddiard, Jean. *Isaac Rosenberg: The Half-Used Life*. London: Gollancz, 1975. The second of the 1975 biographies, and probably the most straightforward one. A good approach to the poems.

Roberts, David. *Essential Poetry of the First World War in Context*. Burgess Hill, England: Saxon, 1996. Several critical books have tried to bring a historicist approach to Rosenberg and the other war poets, trying to reconstruct the overall social and political context out of which the poetry was generated. Roberts deals more with the poetic material than some others. Full bibliography.

Wilson, Jean Moorcroft. *Isaac Rosenberg, Poet and Painter: A Biography*. London: Cecil Woolf, 1975. The third of the 1975 biographies, this time tracing the growth of Rosenberg's artistic ideas and the interplay between poetry and painting.

David Barratt

Christina Rossetti

Born: London, England; December 5, 1830
Died: London, England; December 29, 1894

Principal poetry

Verses, 1847
Goblin Market and Other Poems, 1862
The Prince's Progress and Other Poems, 1866
Sing-Song, 1872, 1893
A Pageant and Other Poems, 1881
Verses, 1893
New Poems, 1896

Other literary forms

Commonplace and Other Short Stories (1870) suggests that Christina Rossetti may have once had the notion of becoming a novelist. Unlike other female poets of the period, she wrote a great deal in prose, both secular and religious. "Commonplace," the title story, is not usually considered to be the best of these prose pieces. That honor is reserved for "The Lost Titian," the plot of which revolves around two friends' competitive praise for another friend's painting. In the end, all three discover one another's vanities. "Vanna's Twins" is a touching story of childhood and demonstrates Rossetti's power in delineating character among lower-middle-class Italians. *Speaking Likenesses* (1874), a series of stories told to some girls by their aunt as they pass the time sewing, stands in the shadows of Lewis Carroll's and Jean Ingelow's works of the same period.

Annus Domini (1874) is a devotional prose work, the first of several, which includes a prayer for each day of the year. These pieces were influenced by *The Book of Common Prayer*. Other devotional works include *Seek and Find*, 1879; *Called to Be Saints*, 1881; *Letter and Spirit*, 1882; *Time Flies*, 1885; *The Face of the Deep*, 1892; and *Maude*, 1897.

Achievements

Soon after the publication of *Goblin Market and Other Poems*, *The British Quarterly Review*, a highly respected literary journal of the day, commented that all the poems were "marked by beauty and tenderness. They are frequently quaint, and sometimes a little capricious." Christina Rossetti was praised in her time for the clarity and sweetness of her diction, for her realistic imagery, and for the purity of her faith. She was widely read in the nineteenth century, but not often imitated. The latter is true perhaps because she did not introduce innovative techniques or subject matter. She is not read widely today, either, and is usually treated as a minor poet of the Victorian period, being eclipsed by her brother Dante Gabriel Rossetti and his fellow Pre-Raphaelite writers. Perhaps the simplicity of Christina Rossetti's faith seems remote and unrealistic to many contemporary readers, but this fact should not diminish her artistic contributions. Andrew Lang, in *The Cosmopolitan Magazine*, June, 1895, left this judgment: "For the quality of conscious art and for music and colour of words in regular composition, Miss Rossetti is unmatched."

Biography

Christina Georgina Rossetti was born on December 5, 1830, the youngest of four children. Her father, Gabriele, an Italian political refugee, was himself a poet and musician. Her mother, of half-Italian parentage, wrote a popular book on Dante, and her older brother, Dante Gabriel, became a noted poet and a leader of the Pre-Raphaelite Brotherhood.

Because of financial problems, the Rossettis moved from Portland Place to Mornington Crescent in 1851 in order for Mrs. Rossetti and Christina to open a small day school for children, thus providing a financial base for the family. By 1854, William Rossetti, Christina's brother, then a clerk in a revenue office, rented a house on Albany Street, where the family lived together. After Mr. Rossetti died in that year, Mrs. Rossetti and the children lived on there until 1867, and it was only because of William's marriage to Lucy Brown in 1874 that Mrs. Rossetti and Christina moved to Torrington Square.

Christina was not a world traveler, but her few experiences abroad did affect her poetry. She went abroad but twice, once in 1861 and again in 1865, and it was the Italian journey that is reflected in so much of her writing. She wrote some poetry in Italian, but her love for Italy can be seen in much of her English work. One excellent example is "Vanna's Twins," the story of an Italian family living in England.

Her first book, published in 1847 when she was seventeen, was a collection of poems privately printed by her grandfather Gaetena Polidori, himself a writer. The volume titled *Verses* contained sixty-six pages of poems written by Rossetti between the ages of twelve and sixteen. The longest piece in the volume was "The Dead City," a poem which exhibits both immature technique and masterful poetic potential. Immersed in a Poe-like atmosphere, the motif is that of a traveler in a dark wood, having passed from a stage of light. She finds herself in a deserted city resplendent with an ornate palace. A sumptuous banquet is ready, but the guests have turned to stone. The poem anticipates Robert Browning, Matthew Arnold, and T. S. Eliot in its wasteland motif and echoes Keats's sensualism.

Christina Rossetti (Hulton Archive)

By 1850, Christina had become a tangential member of the Pre-Raphaelite Brotherhood, of which her brother Dante was the center, and she published various poems in the Brotherhood's magazine *The Germ*. Although Christina loved her brother dearly and respected the other members of the group, she felt that they were too concerned with morally questionable subjects to engage herself directly in the work. It was, ironically, through the Pre-Raphaelites that she met a young man named James Collison, to whom she was greatly attracted and whom, had it not been for his Catholicism, she might well have married.

In 1862, after having gained much attention through the poems in *The Germ*, Rossetti published a volume titled *Goblin Market and Other Poems*. The work was greeted with general acclaim, her only critics being metric purists such as John Ruskin. She brought out another volume in 1866, *The Prince's Progress and Other Poems*, which established her as England's greatest living woman poet, since Elizabeth Barrett Browning had died in 1861.

Although Christina was sickly in her youth, it was in 1871 that she became seriously ill with Dr. Graves's disease, which brought many periods of depression. Now she adopted the role of recluse. During these years of severe illness, she experienced several unpleasant events: Her sister Maria died of cancer in 1876; in 1877 she and her mother began the miserable nursing of Dante Gabriel through five years of psychotic depression; and in 1886 her mother died. In the midst of all this suffering, Rossetti continued to write. Her third volume of poetry, *A Pageant and Other Poems*, was published in 1881 and praised highly by Algernon Swinburne, the only remaining member of the old Pre-Raphaelite coterie. She continued to enjoy the admiration of younger writers such as Theodore Watts-Dunton and Edmund Gosse.

Between 1879 and 1892 she published five volumes of spiritual meditations.

In May, 1892, Christina submitted to an operation for cancer, another Rossetti to be the victim of that disease. The operation was not successful; the cancer reappeared in a few months. After considerable suffering she died on December 29, 1894.

Analysis

Christina Rossetti, often thought of as a religious poet, actually became the major woman poet of mid-Victorian England. Her only true competitor, Elizabeth Barrett Browning, died a few months before Rossetti's *Goblin Market and Other Poems* appeared in 1862. "Goblin Market," the introductory poem of the volume, has remained her most famous work, and illustrates her mastery of the lyric.

"Goblin Market"

Because much of her lyric poetry is oriented toward children, "Goblin Market" is often classified as a children's poem. Even though the characters in the poem are young girls and goblins with fairy-tale associations, the poem is actually an allegory of temptation and redemption meant for adult reading. Rossetti's common theme of the need for renunciation is prevalent, though in the disguise of whimsical child's play. The poem produces a grotesque comic effect, supported by irregular meter and cumulative cataloging. The tempting fruit of the goblins, described in Rossetti's typical sensual manner as "sweet to tongue and sound to eye," causes Laura to succumb, desiring more, only to discover that her pleasure is terminated.

Lizzie acts as the savior. Like Christ, she goes into the grove of the men selling their wares and offers to buy some, only to discover that they really want her, not her penny. Although she suffers much physical abuse, the evil people are "worn out by her resistance," and she returns home jubilant with her penny in hand, able to comfort Laura with the assurance that one can find happiness without the temptations of pleasure. Later, when both girls have married, they are able to relate to their daughters in didactic fashion how one can avoid the pitfalls of the evil world.

Rossetti's strong visual imagination aligns her with the Pre-Raphaelites' interest in painting. Although she did not paint, Christina had a painter's eye: The love of colors, particularly gold, rose, violet, blue, and green, and the delight in decorative detail inform all her lyrics. Her eye often sees unexpected analogies. In "Goblin Market," for example, she compares Laura's arched neck to a swan and a lily, both natural phenomena, but also to a vessel being launched, a rather startling comparison somewhat in the vein of the seventeenth century metaphysical conceits. In fact, several critics have alluded to her love for seventeenth century poets, especially George Herbert and Henry Vaughan.

"The Prince's Progress"

In addition to her lyrics, Rossetti wrote a great deal of narrative verse, characteristically on the theme of lost or frustrated love. Most of these love-narratives are romantic and otherworldly; when Rossetti does attempt realism, especially in describing marital love, her images are pale and flat. One of the longer narratives, "The Prince's Progress," developed out of a lyric of 1861; Rossetti expanded it at her brother's suggestion to provide a title poem for her next volume of poetry. Much like the tale of Edmund Spenser's Red Cross Knight, this poem is the story of a princess waiting to be rescued by a prince.

The prince waits in his palace for a full month before leaving to meet his bride. When he finally hears the call, prompted by allegorical voices which represent fleeting time, he discovers that the journey will not be easy. It will be another Pilgrim's Progress. His first delay is the typical temptation of a beautiful maiden who keeps him as Dido detained Aeneas. Following his release, the prince finds himself in a nineteenth century wasteland with a blight lurking in the darkening air, "a land of neither life nor death." Here he discovers a cave with an old hermit who gives him the "Elixir of Life," but the elixir is insufficient. When he eventually leaves the cave, he is again diverted by self-indulgence, and when he finally arrives at his bride's door, he finds that she is dead, her body being prepared for burial. The poem is an interesting narrative in the vein of medieval romances, but it is obviously allegorical. The prince is admonished by the narrator, "You waited on the road too long, you trifled at the gate." The poem is permeated with ironies and allegorical symbolism proclaiming the vices of procrastination.

"From House to Home"

"From House to Home" is another long narrative, allegorical in character, with lost love at the center. It tells of a variety of states of being. In the first of these states, the narrator is living in an earthly paradise: a castle of transparent glass set against a background of stately trees and pastures full of swift squirrels, singing birds, and leaping lambs. The young lady is called away by a male "angel." Day and night she seeks for him to no avail—he has vanished. Eventually she has a vision of a marvelously beautiful woman who is suffering the usual tribulations of a pilgrim on an allegorical journey. The martyred woman stands on ground with budding flowers, but every flower has a thorn and galls her feet. Cruel laughter and clapping hands remind the reader of the ways of danger and rebuke in life. The martyred one can be read here as both the archetypal man or woman in search of love and the Christian Church attempting to extend its love to others.

Two of the narratives reveal sides of Rossetti's personality that most of her poetry does not demonstrate. One of these, "A Royal Princess," suggests political interests. The poem is about an imagined political situation. A highborn heroine is sympathetic toward the suffering masses who threaten a revolt against the kingdom, and she determines to descend from her secluded, protected palace to help them.

"The Lowest Room"

In "The Lowest Room," a poem that Dante Gabriel Rossetti did not like, there is an evident implication that, bound by society's rules, women *must* be passive and *must* play given roles in life. Again, there are two sisters in the poem, but unlike those in other works, only the ideal sister is here rewarded with husband and child. The ideal one is described in feminine language; the other one, less attractive, dreams of Homer's soldiers. Masculine voluptuousness affects her. In projecting such a contrast, Rossetti implies that women in her society are told how to dress, how to act, and how to be successful. There is little room for individuality. The final acceptance of this less attractive female, the speaker of the poem, places her in the role of the typical passive woman waiting for her turn without being able to help in creating it.

"The Iniquity of the Fathers, upon the Children" and "Maiden Song"

Another narrative which takes a critical view of social conventions is "The Iniquity of the Fathers, upon the Children," in which a lady who has a child out of wedlock is tormented by the community. The only justice, the narrator concludes, is that all are "equal in the grave." On the other hand, Rossetti's narrative style can show a fairy-tale naïveté, as in "Maiden Song," a tale of three sisters, Meggan, May, and Margaret, all of whom desire husbands. The first two take the first man who comes along, afraid they will be like Margaret sitting at home singing and spinning. Margaret's patience, however, is amply rewarded; she wins the king of the entire country for her husband.

Devotional poems

Rossetti's strong religious faith supported her during continuing illnesses and she began to give most of her attention to writing devotional material. Her first poetry had shown her strong family affection and her religious feelings, particularly the sentiment of renunciation. The later poems (such as "A Novice," "A Martyr," and "I Have Fought a Good Fight") continue to focus on renunciation. The first is a flight from the world into the calm of the cloister; the latter two praise the eager laying down of life for the glory of God. Actually, religious ardor colors most of Rossetti's thoughts and results in much oversimplified verse echoing common platitudes about devotion. A poem such as "Whitsun Eve," however, illustrates poetic maturity, blending the love of God and the love of the beauty of creation. All that is pure in nature is pressed into the service of the one shining lamb.

Dualism: clashing opposites

An interesting aspect of Rossetti's style is her use of the Victorian motif of two voices, so prominently associated with Alfred, Lord Tennyson's poetry. The Victorian world attempted to synthesize the Romantic values of the early nineteenth century with the classical theories of order and restraint more prominently displayed in the eighteenth century. From this attempt came a strong clash of values and great personal frustration. Adding to this problem was the growth of the industrial world and the increase in scientific knowledge. Rossetti's dualism establishes the concept of a universe based on a conflict of opposites, as in "Life and Death," "Twice," "Today and Tomorrow," and "Two Parted."

"Two Parted" deals with one true lover and one betrayer. Ironically, the betrayer in this case is the woman. "Today and Tomorrow" creates a dichotomy of living life to the fullest on the one hand and wishing to die on the other. "Life and Death" begins with a negative statement about life's bitterness, juxtaposing the good things of life with the unpleasant. "Twice" uses the counterpoint of the narrator's offering her heart while the male suggests that her heart is not ripe. In the narrative poems this technique is carried out through the use of two opposing characters. Lizzie and Laura of "Goblin Market" illustrate the dualistic motif; in "Maiden Song" the conflict is between two plain sisters and the beautiful Margaret. This dualism is also apparent in Rossetti's religious poems, where there appears to be a confrontation between different views of salvation or different moral attitudes. A great number of traditional opposites are used here—time and eternity, earthly misery and heavenly bliss—demonstrating the torment of a trapped soul longing for escape. One such poem, "This near-at-hand," stresses the antithesis of heaven and earth.

The religious poems often describe a destructive end that results from the speaker's being torn between duty and desire. Sometimes the choice appears to have been made in error, and when it is, it seems to have arisen from weakness or beguilement. So choice itself becomes destructive; there is no solution; life is an absurdity. Even when the speaker is not caught in a personal dilemma, the poem repeats the impression that the world, as Matthew Arnold suggests in "Dover Beach," is a place of uncertainty, a virtual wasteland, a "darkling plain" where ignorant armies fight by night.

In the midst of all this dualism, the reader is left with the impression that Rossetti is earnestly searching for unity but cannot find it. In the secular love poems she goes so far as to suggest that perhaps as ghosts, removed from the flesh, lovers could achieve such a unity. In the religious poems her solution is, of course, union with God through Christ in death. Needless to say, much of her poetry reflects the struggle in her own life to find some solution to the paradox, irony, and bifurcation that life in general repeatedly offers. Rossetti's poetry reveals a dual personality: one side reflecting Pre-Raphaelite traits of fictional effects and sensual imagery, often set in a dream world; the other reflecting the assurances of her orthodox faith.

Other major works

SHORT FICTION: *Commonplace and Other Short Stories*, 1870; *Speaking Likenesses*, 1874.

NONFICTION: *Annus Domini*, 1874; *Seek and Find*, 1879; *Called to Be Saints*, 1881; *Letter and Spirit*, 1882; *Time Flies*, 1885; *The Face of the Deep*, 1892; *Maude*, 1897.

Bibliography

Chapman, Alison. *The Afterlife of Christina Rossetti*. New York: St. Martin's Press, 2000. Through an analysis of her work, the construction of Christina Rossetti by her brothers, and the history of her reception, Chapman asks if it is possible to study the poet and her work and avoid critical ventriloquy.

Charles, Edna Kotin. *Christina Rossetti: Critical Perspectives, 1862-1982*. Selinsgrove, Pa.: Susquehanna University Press, 1985. Charles shows how literary criticism has changed in the last 120 years, and how these changing attitudes have affected the way in which Rossetti's poems were perceived. Many nineteenth century reviewers concentrated on her religious poems, whereas modern critics focus on her works of fantasy. Suitable for graduate students and advanced undergraduates.

Harrison, Antony H. *Christina Rossetti in Context*. Chapel Hill: University of North Carolina Press, 1988. This is a skillful, well-informed study that links Rossetti's religious beliefs to her Pre-Raphaelite writing techniques and themes. Harrison namedrops the faddish terms used in current literary criticism, yet, his study is useful for any student of Rossetti. Includes a bibliography.

Jones, Kathleen. *Learning Not to Be First: The Life of Christina Rossetti*. Moreton-in-Marsh, Gloucestershire, England: Windrush, 1991. An illuminating biography of Christina Rossetti, both product and victim of the Victorian era's social and religious standards. Includes bibliography and index.

Kent, David A., ed. *The Achievement of Christina Rossetti: England, Scotland, and the Union*. New York:

Cornell University Press, 1988. This anthology contains fifteen essays that contribute to Rossetti's growing reputation as an important Victorian religious poet, and as an artist separate from the rest of her famous family. This book would be valuable to any academic library, although it is suitable primarily for advanced students of Rossetti.

Marsh, Jan. *Christina Rossetti: A Writer's Life*. New York: Viking Press, 1995. A biography that explains Rossetti's recurrent bouts of depression, traces her ties to London's literati, and discusses her place in the Pre-Raphaelite movement.

Mayberry, Katherine J. *Christina Rossetti and the Poetry of Discovery*. Baton Rouge: Louisiana State University Press, 1989. Mayberry maintains that Rossetti was a meticulous professional writer, and not merely a talented amateur. She argues that Rossetti wrote about her role as a woman, and therefore was an early feminist. This study can be used with Antony H. Harrison's book, *Christina Rossetti in Context*. Supplemented by an index and a bibliography.

Rosenblum, Dolores. *Christina Rossetti: The Poetry of Endurance*. Carbondale: Southern Illinois University Press, 1987. Rosenblum is the first to analyze thoroughly the text of Rossetti's poetry in the light of the new feminist criticism. She especially examines the significance of "Goblin Market," the themes of which are central to all Rossetti's works. This book is dense and technical and is appropriate only for advanced students of Rossetti.

John W. Crawford;
bibliography updated by the editors

Dante Gabriel Rossetti

Born: London, England; May 12, 1828
Died: Birchington, England; April 9, 1882

Principal poetry

Poems, 1870, 1881
Ballads and Sonnets, 1881
Collected Works, 1886
The Works of Dante Gabriel Rossetti, 1911 (William Michael Rossetti, editor)

Other literary forms

Dante Gabriel Rossetti published the prose sketch "Hand and Soul" in *The Germ* (1850). In 1863, he completed the biography of William Blake left unfinished at the death of Alexander Gilchrist. Four volumes of Rossetti's letters, edited by J. R. Wahl and Oswald Doughty (1965-1967) have been published; his correspondence with Jane Morris was edited by John Bryson and Janet Camp Troxell and published in 1976.

Achievements

Significant both as a poet and as a painter, Dante Gabriel Rossetti offers an opportunity to study the relationship between poetry and art. Among Victorian poets, Rossetti was excelled only by Alfred, Lord Tennyson and Robert Browning, although, unlike other major poets of the period, he published relatively few poems. His work is chiefly concerned with the exploration of individual moments of experience. As a consequence, he worked best at the level of the short lyric or compressed narrative, in which his highly crafted style often achieves remarkable intensity.

Biography

Rossetti, christened Gabriel Charles Dante Rossetti, was born in London, May 12, 1828. His father, Gabriele Rossetti, was an Italian political exile with pretensions as a poet, who had published an eccentric commentary on Dante Alighieri's *The Divine Comedy* (c. 1320) and supported himself teaching his native language. Rossetti's mother, Frances Polidori, although of Anglo-Italian background, was staunchly English in her severe moral standards and religious beliefs. The opposing views of life represented by his father and mother determined a conflict from which Rossetti was never able to free himself. Like his amiable, self-indulgent father in many ways, he was never able to exorcise the accusing voice of his mother's puritanism. He led the bohemian life of an artist, but felt guilty for doing so.

In 1845, Rossetti entered the Academy Schools of the Royal Academy of Art. There he associated himself with a group of young artists—notably, John Everett Millais and Holman Hunt—who were dissatisfied with the style and subject matter of Establishment painting, but eager to make names for themselves with the Establishment. Because the effects of light and naturalistic detail they sought were also to be found in late medieval art (prior to the painter Raphael), they called themselves the "Pre-Raphaelite Brotherhood" and began initialing their more daring paintings "P.R.B." In 1849-1850, the Brotherhood published a journal, *The Germ*, which included several poems by Rossetti, including "The Blessed Damozel" and the prose piece "Hand and Soul." Also in 1850, Rossetti publicly exhibited a painting for the first time, "*Ecce Ancilla Domine*!" Reviews of the painting—as well as of works exhibited simultaneously by Hunt and Millais—were hostile. Stunned, Rossetti determined never to exhibit his work again (a determination which, on the whole, he maintained). The art critic John Ruskin, however, defended the Pre-Raphaelites, first in a series of letters to *The Times*, then in a pamphlet "Pre-Raphaelitism," and subsequently became Rossetti's patron, although Rossetti's contempt for what he perceived as Ruskin's bourgeois dilettantism prevented them from ever becoming close friends.

Dante Gabriel Rossetti (Hulton Archive)

In 1850, Rossetti also met Elizabeth Siddal, a sixteen-year-old shop girl who began serving as a model for members of the P.R.B. By 1852, Rossetti and Elizabeth Siddal were informally engaged. Despite her beauty and the limited artistic ability she developed under his influence, they were poorly matched. It is characteristic of Rossetti that he nevertheless married her in 1860. Their child was stillborn in 1861, and the next year Elizabeth committed suicide.

During the 1850's, while the Brotherhood itself was dwindling away, the reputation of its individual members had begun to grow. Rossetti never became a popular artist (as did Millais), but he began to receive commissions for his work and to attract a circle of younger admirers—two of whom, Edward Burne-Jones and William Morris, joined him in painting "frescoes" on the interior walls of the Oxford Union Society in 1857. There, Rossetti met Jane Burden, the woman he loved off and on for the rest of his life. Burden married William Morris in 1859 but seems to have become Rossetti's mistress in the late 1860's.

Fanny Cornforth was the third woman in Rossetti's life. They met sometime in the late 1850's, and after the death of Elizabeth Siddal, she became Rossetti's "housekeeper." Fanny was illiterate and lowborn, but with a striking voluptuous beauty very different from that of Elizabeth or Jane. Generally detested by Rossetti's friends, she was probably Rossetti's most loving companion.

Remorseful at the death of his wife, Rossetti had buried the manuscript of his poems with her and given up verse until at least 1866, when his relationship with Jane Morris prompted him to return to writing love poetry. In 1869, the manuscript of his earlier work was exhumed and these poems, together with his more recent work, were published as *Poems* (1870). By that time, Rossetti had a fairly steady income from his paintings. In 1862, he had leased "Tudor House," 16 Cheyne Walk, the London home that was to become notorious for his eccentric hospitality and collection of exotic animals. Yet his life during these years was not happy. He had become morbidly sensitive to criticism, and with the unfavorable reviews of his poetry (notably, Robert Buchanan's essay "The Fleshly School of Poetry" in 1871), he began to suspect a conspiracy against him. In 1872, he attempted suicide, and the last decade of his life was characterized by poor health, desultory work, and indulgence in the mixture of whiskey and chloral that became his favorite narcotic. A year after the publication of his second collection of poems, *Ballads and Sonnets* (1881), he died at the seaside town of Birchington, where he had gone hoping to recover his health.

ANALYSIS

Dante Gabriel Rossetti's poetry is conventionally divided into three periods. The first ends in 1850, with the publication of some of his best early poems in *The Germ* and the beginning of his relationship with Elizabeth Siddal. The second ends with her death in 1862; most of the poems from this period, however, were written between 1850 and 1854. The third and last group of poems date from 1868, when Rossetti began writing again after several years of relative inactivity, until his death in 1882. Again, however, most of the poems from this period were written during its first five years.

While these three periods can be differentiated, the actual placement of individual poems is often problematic. Since Rossetti did not publish a book of original verse until 1870 and since he habitually revised his poetry over the years, a particular work might in fact belong to more than one period. "The Blessed Damozel," for example, was written in 1847 and published, first in *The Germ* in 1850; then, in revised form, in *The Oxford and Cambridge Magazine* (edited by William Morris) in 1856; next, with further revision, in the 1870 *Poems*; and, finally, revised yet again, in the 1881 *Poems*.

This habit of lifetime reworking and revision, which extended to certain paintings as well, evidences two characteristics of Rossetti's work—a meticulous craftsmanship that defines the poem as a labored artifact rather than the spontaneous expression of feeling; and an intense personal identification with his own writing, that explains both his reluctance to publish and his extreme vulnerability to criticism. These two characteristics are contradictory if one assumes that personal identification with a text is a function of its truth to prior experience. Rossetti's case, however, argues that identification is not a function of mimesis, but of the act of writing. He identified with his poetry because he himself had written it. To acknowledge a poem "complete" was for him equivalent to acknowledging the end of one of his own life-processes. To bury the manuscript of his poems with the body of Elizabeth Siddal was not simply to bury his own past or sacrifice its achievement; it was, in a real sense, to bury a part of himself alive with her.

This is not to say that personal experience is not the subject matter of Rossetti's poetry—it often is—but that readers should expect to reach that experience only through the mediation of highly wrought style, the presence of which becomes, in his best poems, an index to the intensity of feeling it conceals. His concern with style makes Rossetti a difficult poet. It is difficult to naturalize his poetry—to reduce it to day-to-day familiarity. He offers no personality for the reader to admire—or hate. Indeed, this absence of self is a central concern of his creative effort. Rossetti's poems do not merely hide the self behind the artifice of verse-making; they explore a fundamental opposition between language and feeling—the teasing ability of language almost to control reality and the disillusionment that necessarily follows from recognizing its failure to do so; the apparent communication embedded in a work of art turns out to be a denial of communication.

In its awareness of the limits of communication, Rossetti's poetry is contemporary. In its basic distrust of—and therefore fascination with—sexuality, it remains solidly Victorian. In its fondness for allegory and contrivance, it exemplifies the Pre-Raphaelite commitment to the Middle Ages. In its concern for the intense experience of the moment, it anticipates the poetics of the last years of the nineteenth century. Rossetti's numerous sonnets on paintings—a genre particularly successful in distancing the reader from the poet—echo similar poems by the French symbolists. His ballad narratives link him to William Wordsworth and Samuel Taylor Coleridge; his concern for the self-sufficient consciousness, with Percy Bysshe Shelley. Rossetti can be said, therefore, to exemplify aspects of many periods but to be typical of none. He is typical only, perhaps, of himself, but it is a self carefully concealed behind, not expressed in, his writing. The study of Rossetti leads to an understanding, not of his own personality or philosophy of life or of the age in which he lived, but of poetry itself—an understanding both of its strengths and of its liabilities. For this reason, his work remains a spur to the imagination.

"The Blessed Damozel"

"The Blessed Damozel," the most familiar of Rossetti's early poems, illustrates this pattern of imaginative effort and disillusionment. The "Damozel" leans out "From the gold bar of Heaven," looking down through space for her earthly lover. Space, however, is vast. The moon itself is no more than "a little feather/ Fluttering far down the gulf." Because she cannot see him, she speaks, imagining the reunion that will come "When round his head the aureole clings." Then "Will I ask of Christ the Lord . . . Only to live as once on earth/ With Love." Yet imagination is an unsatisfactory substitute for real love; despite a Dantesque vision of angels in flight, she "laid her face between her hands./ And wept."

The poem turns on the old notion that lovers separated by death can take comfort in the hope of meeting again in the world to come. Rossetti, however, reverses the perspective. It is the lover in heaven who longs for earth; it is the spiritual world that is tormented by desire for the physical—and remains, for all its beatitude, "warm." Moreover, the consolation of hope is, it turns out, no consolation. It merely leads to an intense awareness of loss—not only on the part of the "Damozel" but for the speaker of the poem as well. For the "Damozel" is a fiction, and the parenthetical first-person interjections ground the poem in the fantasy of the earthly lover himself. He claims to "see" "her smile" and "hear" "her tears," but the protestation emphasizes the wishfulness of his dream. If her imagined reunion leads her to "tears," his imagined "Damozel" leads him to a heightened sense of separation from her. The "Damozel" is, as his attempt to visualize her suggests, unknowable. Her death is a barrier he cannot overcome by the language of the poem. The sensuousness of his conception—the "fleshliness" of which Rossetti was later accused—is not a radical characterization of the afterlife, but an implicit mark of the inadequacy of the earthly imagination.

"The Blessed Damozel" specifies the opposition between language and feeling as an opposition between poetry and eros. The poet's vision attempts to overcome the separation of lovers. His text is an act of desire that confronts him with the fact of desire—hence, of an unfulfilled and perhaps unfulfillable need. The world of Rossetti's poetry is thus one in which desire—generally sexual—defines itself by coming up against its own furthest limit—the verge of satisfaction. It asks the reader to experience the pain of near but never complete realization. It offers a nightmare world, in which all apparent realities are disclosed as expressions of the poet's desire.

The theme of frustrated eros is directly related to the tension between his father's bohemianism and his mother's puritanical morality. It enabled Rossetti to express his erotic sensibility while at the same time punishing himself for its existence. The inadequacy of poetic language is thus a function of the guilt that, in his own life, blocked Rossetti's personal happiness.

"The Bride's Prelude"

"The Bride's Prelude," which was begun in 1848 and returned to later in the 1850's but never completed, illustrates the link between eros, guilt, and the failure of language. The poem, even in its fragmentary form, is Rossetti's longest narrative. It records the conversation between two sisters in an unspecified medieval setting: Aloÿse, the elder, whose wedding day it is, and Amelotte, the younger, who is helping her dress. Aloÿse is strangely silent; then, having knelt in prayer with her sister, she reveals the story of her past life. She had, years before, while her sister was being educated in a convent, fallen in love with a young man, a distant cousin who had yet to make a name for himself in the world, then staying with her powerful family. When her family lost a political struggle and was forced temporarily to flee its ancestral seat, the cousin had deserted them, leaving her with child. Discovering the situation, her father and brothers had reluctantly spared her life but, it would seem—the poem is deliberately vague—killed her illegitimate child. Now, circumstances have changed again; the family is back in power, the cousin has returned, and it is he—Urscelyn—whom she is about to marry. With this revelation, the poem ends. Rossetti wrote a prose summary of a missing conclusion, which his brother later published. Urscelyn, he explains, having become a skilled soldier of fortune and therefore of use to her family, wanting to ally himself with them once more, has offered to marry Aloÿse. Aloÿse, meanwhile, had fallen in love with and secretly betrothed herself to another man, whom Urscelyn, knowingly and treacherously, killed in a tournament. Thus, the enormity of marrying a man who had both betrayed her and murdered her lover is the message she wishes to convey to her sister. In conclusion, Rossetti states that "as the bridal procession appears, perhaps it might become apparent that the brothers mean to kill Urscelyn when he has married her."

The "perhaps" tells all. "The Bride's Prelude" is incomplete because Rossetti was unable to imagine an appropriate ending, and his prose summary is merely an evasion. The poem is also Aloÿse's story, and she, too, cannot bring her narrative to completion. Significantly, the text as it stands makes no mention of the second lover. Urscelyn's flight labels him a betrayer—but Aloÿse suggests that his motives were political and does not indicate that he knew she was pregnant. In other words, without Rossetti's prose summary, what seems to block Aloÿse's happiness is less the character of Urscelyn than her own sense of guilt. The conclusion that Rossetti claims he intended but could not bring himself to write would have radically altered the moral perspective of the poem. With it, Urscelyn is a clear-cut villain; Aloÿse, despite her youthful indiscretion, is a victim. Without the conclusion, "The Bride's Prelude" is a poem about Aloÿse's own reluctance to accept a happy ending to her years of suffering—to marry the man she had loved and from whom she has been separated by war and family pride. By telling her story to her sister, she confesses and thus overcomes the guilt that is the only obstacle to her happiness. Indeed, when in the closing line of the poem Aloÿse admits that her prayer has been to be able to "Show her what I hide," it appears that confession of the past, not complaint about the present, has been her leading motive. This purgation, however, is precisely what Rossetti does not grant her. She tells her story, but the poem breaks off before the consequences of the telling can be felt.

The ballad form of "The Bride's Prelude" is typical of Rossetti's narrative poetry. He was particularly fond of stanzaic patterns that include a slightly varying refrain. The mode was both satisfyingly medieval (and therefore Pre-Raphaelite) and conveniently disjunctive. Breaking narrative into a series of discrete, artificially defined units obviated the need for a coherent narrative personality. In poems such as "Sister Helen" and "Eden Bower," the repetition of the verse form replaces development of the speaker's point of view as a unifying device. Even in "The Burden of Ninevah," an uncharacteristically ironic "modern" poem of social comment, patterns of repetition qualify the immediacy of the first-person speaker.

"A Last Confession"

In Rossetti's two "modern" narratives, "A Last Confession" and "Jenny," he uses the more typically Victorian mode of dramatic monologue to achieve comparable distancing. Both are poems about erotic failure; in both, erotic failure is related to the failure of language to communicate.

"A Last Confession," which is given the setting "Regno Lombardo-Veneto, 1848," is unique in its treatment of the political issue—the Austrian occupation of Italy—with which Rossetti's father was identified. Its confessional mode is comparable to that of "The Bride's Prelude"; what it confesses, however, is not illicit passion but murder by a rejected lover. The speaker had adopted a little girl deserted by her parents, who, under the rigors of the Austrian regime, no longer had the bread with which to feed her. In time this foster fatherly love becomes sexual, but whether she responds in kind is uncertain. At length, they are separated and she appears to have taken up flirting with Austrians. On the way to meet with her for the last time, the speaker buys her the parting gift of a knife, such as "Our Lombard country-girls . . . Wear" to defend themselves against each other and the possibility of "a German lover." When she laughs at the gesture—another example of failed communication—he is enraged and plunges the knife into her heart. It is not certain that she is the "harlot" he believes she has become; the act of confession is a strategy aimed at exonerating the speaker, but since we have only his unreliable point of view, his words can never fully realize their intention. The priest who listens to him is allowed no response. The reader is left with an uneasy feeling that the speaker's words, instead of unburdening his conscience, merely reiterate the crime.

"Jenny"

The speaker of "Jenny" is a man who has gone home with a prostitute, who, instead of making love, falls asleep on his knee while he meditates on the meaning of her condition and consequently his own. Among the ironies of the poem is the fact that his audience is sleeping. His words, whatever their merit, go unheard. Moreover, Jenny, who might well have added a significant point of view to the discussion, is necessarily mute, so the speaker remains trapped in his own consciousness.

What the speaker thinks he has learned is easily summarized. He begins with an ironic assessment of "Lazy laughing languid Jenny,/ Fond of a kiss and fond of a guinea," and moves on to a more sympathetic recognition of the plight of a prostitute. She is, after all, not essentially different from other women; like them, she is a victim "of man's changeless sum/ Of lust": "Like a toad within a stone/ Seated while Time crumbles on;/ Which sits there since the earth was curs'd/ For Man's transgression at the first." Finally, he sees that even her love of money is merely a reflection of the economic forces at work throughout English society. Then, leaving a few gold coins in her hair, he kisses her sleeping form and departs in the morning light.

Yet even in acknowledging that his own irony is a sign of being "Ashamed of my own shame," the speaker fails to achieve enlightenment. He remains ignorant of his own role in the situation and never gives credit to Jenny for being more than an attractive automaton. He does not blame himself for creating prostitution (although this is not his first such visit); he blames an abstract male "lust," and thus alienates himself from his own desire. The subject of the poem may be somewhat daring, but its inability to come to terms with female sexuality not only betrays Rossetti's participation in a Victorian stereotype, but also, and more significantly, betrays his tendency to treat women as counters in a process of masculine self-discovery. To acknowledge the full humanity of Jenny would legitimatize sexual relations with her: She would no longer be a victim, but a willing partner. She remains asleep, and the speaker's meditation has no practical consequences. The language of the poem, instead of effecting, across social and economic barriers, a relationship with Jenny, further insulates the speaker from significant behavior. He will return to his book-lined room—the books are emphasized in the poem—confident in decent feeling, incapable of decent action.

"The Stream's Secret"

Rossetti's love poetry, in which the speaker is closely identified with or indistinguishable from the poet himself, contains his most painful accounts of the inadequacy of language. "The Stream's Secret," written in 1869, has been called at once his most revealing and his most concealing poem. Certainly it is a quintessential statement of the dilemma at the heart of his poetry. The speaker, who addresses the stream, exemplifies noncommunication. The stream's "secret" is, finally, that it can neither hear nor speak; that to confide in nature is to confide in a vacuum, not only denying oneself the possibility of a response, but also deluding oneself in the false hope that language is a medium of communication.

"The Stream's Secret" is also one of the most deliberately artful of Rossetti's poems, and its complex play with figures of speech makes it one of his most difficult. Rhetorical trope circles back on rhetorical trope, as in this typical stanza:

> Dark as thy blinded wave
> When brimming midnight floods the glen,—
> Bright as the laughter of thy runnels when
> The dawn yields all the light they crave;
> Even so these hours to wound and that to save
> Are sisters in Love's ken.

Midnight, compared metaphorically to the stream, is itself a means of characterizing the stream; with dawn, it provides a figurative characterization of the personified hours that are "sisters" to allegorized "Love." The reader is encompassed in a world defined by poetic devices. The speaker, in addressing the unanswering flow of water, attempts to anchor this continuum of language in concrete reality, but reality continues to elude him. The poet, who begins by asking when he and his love will be reunited and moves into an imaginary depiction of their reunion, is led, in the poem's final stanzas, to the recognition that Love, whom he first saw as a figure of passionate life, is synonymous with death, and that hope itself, as in "The Blessed Damozel," is a source of tears.

THE HOUSE OF LIFE

The lesson of "The Stream's Secret" is borne out in Rossetti's major work, the collection of sonnets he called *The House of Life*. Originally published as a group of sixteen sonnets in 1869, extended into a group of fifty "Sonnets and Songs, toward a work to be called 'The House of Life'" in *Poems* (1870); and finally published as a collection of 102 sonnets titled "The House of Life: A Sonnet-Sequence" in *Ballads and Sonnets* (1881), the precise status of the work remains a problem. As ordered, the collection follows a general pattern of youth to age, love to loss, hope to disillusionment. Whether this ordering represents an organic sequence or is merely an adequate solution to the problem of arranging a large group of related but independent poems written over many years remains the object of critical debate.

The very existence of this critical debate argues that, if there is an organic sequence, it is not self-evident. Moreover, if there is no easy way to put the poems together, that difficulty may be an essential feature of Rossetti's conception. The untitled 1880 sonnet that introduces the collection suggests that the sonnets were written with deliberate reference to the limitations of their medium. "A Sonnet," Rossetti proclaims, "is a moment's monument,— Memorial . . . To one dead deathless hour." Such a poem is not a gesture of communication, but one of memorialization or arbitrary symbolism. Its message, explicit in the poem's leading similes, is akin to the carving on a tomb or the engraving on a coin. Verbal meaning is thus subservient to a role for which verbal meaning may in fact be irrelevant. The workmanship of the artifact increases its value, but one may appreciate the form of an inscription without in fact "reading" its message.

The introductory sonnet does not suggest that readers should look only at the form and not consider the expressive content of the sonnets that follow. Rather, it defines the limited role of the poet's art in the reader's experience of his poetry. Like the figures on John Keats's Grecian urn, the sonnets of *The House of Life* come into passionate being only insofar as the reader invests them with sympathy or understanding. The passion he can expect to experience in responding to the work of art will not be that of the poet/artificer who has provided its material cause, but his or her own. For, like a monument "in ivory or in ebony," the sonnet is not a recapturing of the past but an acknowledgment of its loss, not the living voice of its maker but an obstacle between its maker and the reader of the poem; the poem is like a coin, not of real value, but the sign of goods and services in a potential act of human exchange.

The notion of "a moment's monument" also offers a rationale for the atomistic structure of the collection. Limited to the depiction of discrete events, the poet's format cannot link individual experiences into a total rendering of human life. The whole is inevitably less than the sum of its parts; the work in its entirety cannot overcome the poet's fragmented experience of love and love's loss. (In this respect, the form of *The House of Life* is comparable to the "Short swallow-flights" of Tennyson's *In Memoriam*, which deny the possibility of an integrated response to death, even when the ordering of the poem seems to provide one.)

Sonnet XIX ("Silent Noon") exemplifies the notion of "a moment's monument" and thus typifies the collection. Two lovers pause in a summer landscape, the painterly details of which compose "visible silence, still as the hourglass." Recognizing the special nature of such moments, the poem ends by disrupting the landscape with the imperative cry, "Clasp we to our hearts, for deathless dower,/ This close-companioned inarticulate hour/ When twofold silence was the song of Love." The ultimate experience of love is silence—the postcoital oblivion of "Nuptial Sleep" (the sonnet singled out for its "fleshliness" by Buchanan and so deleted from the 1881 version of the collection). Language itself is therefore necessarily at odds with such states of being. The poet's description of landscape replaces the description of feeling denied here by the nature of feeling. The closing lines of the poem, in which he addresses his feelings, acknowledge their loss. Articulated self-consciousness implies that the "Inarticulate hour" has passed. Time, like the sand in the hour-glass, only passes; it does not develop. Thus, the development of the poem—the formal demand of the sestet—disrupts the special experience of the time it seeks to "clasp."

To memorialize love as verse is thus to admit the loss of love—not only because there is no need to memorialize the living present, but also because language itself is a sign of loss. The laurel, as Rossetti admits, in a trope borrowed from Petrarch, is "Love's Last Gift" (Sonnet LIX), not the sign of continuing favor. If poetic language celebrates not the absent loved one but the poet's isolated self, why then write poetry? This question, which Rossetti poses implicitly in "The Stream's Secret," is central to *The House of Life*.

The four sonnets grouped under the heading "Willowwood" (XLIX-LII) suggest an answer when they identify erotic desire as a longing for submergence in self. The poet who leans over a well to kiss the image of Love which has become the image of his lover is a version of Narcissus, unable to resist the reflection of his own image. Fittingly, the imagery of the four sonnets is derived from the Wood of the Suicides in Dante's *Inferno* (Canto 13). To dwell in the "Willowwood" of unfulfillable desire is to deny wholeness of self and cultivate in its place a self-destructive illusion of personal emptiness. Art, which once confronted man with spiritual truths, has turned, as Rossetti argues in "St. Luke the Painter" (Sonnet LXXIV), "To soulless self-reflections of man's skill."

Thus, the earlier sonnets of sexual fulfillment and momentary happiness give way to poems of loss. Through memory, the poet attempts to idealize and thus recapture lost passion, but memory, as the introductory sonnet suggests, is itself a confirmation of hopelessness. At the same time, even this overreaching logic is impotent in the face of individual experiences. Moreover, the love poems of *The House of Life*, written with at least three very different women in mind, reflect a range of diverse experiences. No summary of the collection is adequate even as a summary.

Like Rossetti's poetic achievement as a whole, *The House of Life* is elusive and, largely for that reason, difficult. It offers a solipsistic world defined totally by the self, a world in which no external reality functions as a measure of the speaker's perceptions. Yet, for this very reason, it blocks the consciousness of the poet from the reader. The dreamer turns out to be the most elusive element in the dream.

OTHER MAJOR WORKS

NONFICTION: *Letters of Dante Gabriel Rossetti*, 1965-1967 (4 volumes; Oswald Doughty and J. R. Wahl, editors); *Dante Gabriel Rossetti and Jane Morris: Their Correspondence*, 1976 (John Bryson and Janet Camp Troxell, editors).

TRANSLATION: *The Early Italian Poets*, 1861 (revised as *Dante and His Circle*, 1874).)

BIBLIOGRAPHY

Ash, Russell. *Dante Gabriel Rossetti*. New York: Harry N. Abrams, 1995. A beautifully illustrated book that analyzes the life and career of Rossetti as poet and painter. Includes bibliographical references.

Boos, Florence Saunders. *The Poetry of Dante G. Rossetti: A Critical Reading and Source Study*. The Hague: Mouton, 1976. The laborious research behind this dissertation makes it valuable for the "sources and resemblances" in particular works Rossetti may have drawn upon directly, as well as for information it contains on traditional genres and styles influencing Rossetti more indirectly. Contains an extensive bibliography.

Howard, Ronnalie Roper. *The Dark Glass: Vision and Technique in the Poetry of Dante Gabriel Rossetti*. Athens: Ohio University Press, 1972. A somewhat pedestrian stroll through a selection of Rossetti's poems, examined in detail for their technique, developing vision, thematic strains of isolation, medievalism, and modernity.

Johnston, Robert D. *Dante Gabriel Rossetti*. New York: Twayne, 1969. Tracing the theme of love through various mythical incarnations of women in Rossetti's work, Johnston organizes his chapters according to genre: translations and prose, *The House of Life*, narrative poems, and last academic pieces. Includes a chronology and a bibliography.

McGann, Jerome J. *Dante Gabriel Rossetti and the Game That Must Be Lost*. New Haven, Conn.: Yale University Press, 2000. Reacting to sixty years of literary criticism that diminished and downplayed Rossetti's work, McGann asserts the enormity of

Rossetti's accomplishment as a central artistic and intellectual figure of his generation.

Rees, Joan. *The Poetry of Dante Gabriel Rossetti: Modes of Self-Expression*. Cambridge, England: Cambridge University Press, 1981. Largely a study in influence and context, this book examines Rossetti's originality in relation to his Italian predecessors Dante and Petrarch for their treatment of love in sonnet form, and to his Victorian contemporaries William Morris, Alfred, Lord Tennyson, and Robert Browning for their uses of medievalism and the dramatic monologue.

Riede, David G., ed. *Critical Essays on Dante Gabriel Rossetti*. New York: G. K. Hall, 1992. A collection of critical essays including very early responses and work done from the 1970's to 1991. The early essays provide the traditional assessment of Rossetti's work and later essays indicate the directions that Rossetti criticism is likely to take in the coming years. Includes bibliographical references and index.

Rossetti, Dante Gabriel. *The House of Life: A Sonnet-Sequence*. Edited by Paul Franklin Baum. Cambridge, Mass.: Harvard University Press, 1928. The lengthy introduction and exhaustive notes are indispensable to the serious study of Rossetti's masterpiece. Discusses the structure and composition of *The House of Life*. The appendices discuss the dating of the sonnets and their prosody.

Sonstroem, David. *Rossetti and the Fair Lady*. Middletown, Conn.: Wesleyan University Press, 1970. A brilliant discussion of the roles played by women in Rossetti's life, poetry, and painting. The women who were his mistresses and models in real life become the mythicized muses of his art, including the heavenly lady, the sinful woman, the victimized woman, and the femme fatale. Illustrated.

Vogel, Joseph F. *Dante Gabriel Rossetti's Versecraft*. Gainesville: University Presses of Florida, 1971. As the title suggests, this monograph's narrow focus is upon the strictly technical aspects of Rossetti's verse, with chapters on meter, stanzaic forms, rhyme, and other sound echoing. A final chapter is devoted to "The Blessed Damozel," its prosody and revisions.

Frederick Kirchhoff;
bibliography updated by the editors

Tadeusz Różewicz

Born: Radom, Poland; October 9, 1921

PRINCIPAL POETRY

Niepokój, 1947 (*Unease*, 1980)
Czerwona rękawiczka, 1948
Pięc poematów, 1950
Czas który idzie, 1951
Wiersze i obrazy, 1952
Równina, 1954
Srebrny kłos, 1955
Uśmiechy, 1955
Poemat otwarty, 1956
Poezje zebrane, 1957
Formy, 1958
Rozmowa z księciem, 1960
Przerwany egzamin, 1960
Głos anonima, 1961
Zielona róża, 1961 (*Green Rose*, 1982)
Nic w płaszczu Prospera, 1962
Niepokój: Wybór wierszy, 1945-1961, 1963
Twarz, 1964
Poezje wybrane, 1967
Wiersze i poematy, 1967
Twarz trzecia, 1968
Regio, 1969
Faces of Anxiety, 1969
Plaskorzezba, 1970
Poezje zebrane, 1971
Wiersze, 1974
Selected Poems, 1976
"The Survivor" and Other Poems, 1976
"Conversation with the Prince" and Other Poems, 1982
Na powierzchni poematu i w środku, 1983
Poezje, 1987
Poezja, 1988 (2 volumes)
Tadeusz Rózewicz's Bas-Relief and Other Poems, 1991
They Came to See a Poet, 1991 (originally as *Conversation with the Prince*)
Opowiadania, 1994
Slowo po slowie, 1994

Niepokój: Wybór wierszy z lat 1944-1994, 1995
Selected Poems, 1995
"Zawsze Fragment" and "Recycling," 1996
Nozyk profesora, 2001
Recycling, 2001

Other literary forms

Tadeusz Różewicz is known as a playwright as well as a poet, a leading figure in postwar absurdist theater. He has also published both short fiction and novels, as well as essays.

Achievements

After World War II, Tadeusz Różewicz became a spokesman for his generation, and the Polish people responded quickly to his work. In 1955, he received the government's Art Award First Category for *Równina* (the plain), and in 1959, the city of Cracow gave him its literary award. In 1962, the Polish Ministry of Culture and Art gave him its First Category Award, and in 1966, he again received the government's Art Award First Category, in recognition of his entire œuvre. In 1970, he received a special prize from the magazine *Odra*. He received the Prize of the Minister of Foreign Affairs (Poland), 1974 and 1987; the Austrian National Prize for European Literature, 1982; the Gold Wreath Prize for Poetry (Yugoslavia), 1987; the Władysław Reymont Literary Prize, 1999. He was awarded other honors as well: the Home Army Cross (London) in 1956; the Alfred Jurzykowski Foundation Award (New York), 1966; the Medal of the 30th Anniversary People's Poland, 1974; the Order of Banner of Labour, Second Class, 1977; and the Great Cross of Order Polonia Restituta, 1996. In 2000 he was awarded Poland's prestigious Nike Award for his book *Matka odchodzi* (1999; mother departs).

Biography

Tadeusz Różewicz's father, Wladysław, worked as a clerk in the courthouse in Radom, a city in southeastern Poland. His mother, Stefania, came from the village of Gelbardów. They had three sons, Tadeusz being the middle child, born on October 9, 1921. The poet began his schooling in Radom, where he wrote his first works for school publications. When the Germans occupied Poland, they forbade all but the most primitive education for Poles; Różewicz worked as a manual laborer and as a messenger for the city government while continuing his education in a special underground school.

In 1943 and 1944, he fought against the German occupation forces as a member of the Home Army (the underground forces directed by the Polish government-in-exile, in London). His own brother was murdered by the Gestapo in 1944. In an interview with James Hopkins for *The Guardian*'s May 19, 2001, issue, he recalled: "I saw people who were brought through the streets on carts . . . dead bodies, naked bodies." After the war, he passed a special examination and entered Jagellonian University in Cracow, where he studied art history. Faced with the horrors inflicted by the Germans during the war, Różewicz determined that he must find a way to "create [Polish] poetry after Auschwitz," since the innocent Romanticism of the nation's prewar poetry seemed incompatible with postwar realities.

Because of the special circumstances of his youth, Różewicz knew comparatively little of the world outside

Tadeusz Różewicz

Radom when he entered the university. He first saw the mountains of southern Poland, for example, when he was twenty-five years old. His first journey outside the country took place in 1948, when he went to Hungary, a trip that he subsequently described in a travelogue. His later journeys have included visits to China, Germany, and Italy, but his work, even when it concerns foreign places, retains its unique Polish perspective.

In 1949, Różewicz married and moved to Gliwice, where his son Kamil was born in 1950. A second son, Jan, was born in 1953. He made trips abroad, including to the United States. In 1968, Różewicz moved to Wrocław, which would become his home for more than three decades. In his interview with Hopkins, the eighty-year-old Różewicz commented sardonically:

> I don't like bad journalists, bad poets, bad painters, bad singers, and bad politicians; the latter inflict most harm. Next to the Germans.

Różewicz does not forget the past.

Analysis

The horrific events experienced by Tadeusz Różewicz during World War II have led to his terse poetics that seek the voices of common people, often through quotations, anecdotes, news reportage: an "art of collage," as Różewicz put it. As a result, his tone is a populist, democratic one—humane and never grandiose.

Accordingly, sparseness characterizes Tadeusz Różewicz's poems, if not his poetic output. Many of his poems are exceedingly short, and even his longer works are often marked by short lines and short stanzas. Różewicz is a master of the dramatic break in the line and between stanzas. He uses the broad, blank margins of the page for dramatic impact, as if he were forcing the words out into the surrounding silence, as if he did not fully trust the power of words to convey his meaning. The effect is that of a speaker who broods as he speaks, choosing his words with extreme care and, after they have been said, relapsing into a brooding silence. "I See the Mad" presents a complex drama in ten lines arranged into four stanzas. An English translation contains a total of only thirty-nine words, but the Polish original is even more concise: It has a mere twenty-nine.

Różewicz speaks in straightforward sentences with straightforward words. Ordinary, even mundane, verbs and nouns abound, sometimes in lists, as if the poet were insisting to himself that the words actually correspond to the reality he sees before him. When one considers that he spent his youth subjected to the terrors of the Nazi occupation, one can understand his sense of wonder that the ordinary objects of daily life do indeed exist before him, that an ordinary existence is still possible.

Though the speaker of a Różewicz poem may participate in the action or even cause it, his most important role is almost always that of an observer: He witnesses the events of the poem. When he comments upon them, he often does so with terse, sardonic irony. The speaker confronts the reader, causing him to ask himself how a normal life can be possible after such horrifying experiences and even causing him to question what constitutes a normal life.

"I See the Mad"

Różewicz presents his work to the reader in a double dramatic context: the drama that he describes in the work, and the drama reinforced by Różewicz's sparseness, of the poet speaking or writing his words. Many of his poems may be seen as miniature plays, the characters acting out various roles. In "I See the Mad," for example, he presents himself at sea in a small boat—a traditional metaphor for life as a journey, especially a journey through obstacles. These obstacles give the poem its unique Różewicz stamp. They consist of crazy people who believe they can walk on water; instead, they have fallen into it. As the poet sails through their struggling bodies, they try to save themselves by grasping his boat. In order to keep his craft afloat, he is forced to knock their hands away from the boat. In effect, he must condemn them to death by drowning.

Who are these people floundering about in the water? One thinks immediately of Christ walking across the water to His disciples and of Peter attempting to walk on the water to meet Him and sinking. Are those in the poem Christians who think that the laws of physics will be suspended for them? Or are they arrogant people who think that they can perform miracles, claiming for themselves the power of God? The poet does not say. He cannot know, for he has no time, in his role of besieged traveler, for philosophical inquiries. He must keep pushing the frantic hands off his boat.

In the second stanza, the poet states: "even now they tilt/ my uncertain boat." At first reading, the words "even now" might seem superfluous, but they put the poem in a strange, new perspective. The poem is written in the present tense: "I see," not "I saw." When the poet shows himself in his boat in the first stanza, he also stands, in a sense, outside the boat, reliving the experience as he writes or thinks about it. Thus, the two actions, writing or speaking the poem and knocking away the hands that threaten the poet's safety, merge into one, just as the two narrators and the two times, past and present, also merge. In the first stanza, the poet plays a leading role in the drama. In the second, he effectively stands outside the proscenium arch, commenting on the action—only to be pulled dramatically back into the experience.

In the third stanza, the poet is again trying to keep his little boat steady. As he pushes the hands off, he notes that they are stiff, perhaps a natural result of being in cold water. With the word "stiff," the poet jumps forward in time, as if he already sees the hands as stiff and dead because of his actions. Nevertheless, he has no choice. The poem ends with the poet continuing his journey into the future: "I knock off their stiff hands/ knock them off/ year in year out."

The poem may be seen as a surrealistic nightmare, the poet sailing through a sea of the dead and dying. It contains also, with an ironic twist, the Darwinian concept of the survival of the fittest: The poet, the survivor, describes himself as "cruelly alive," and the word "cruelly" vibrates in this context. In one sense, he must be cruel to push off the desperate hands that threaten to capsize his little boat. In another sense, he is "cruelly alive" because his own life force sustains him at a time when it would be easier for him to give up the struggle and simply let his boat be overturned.

The poet remains afloat because he knows a human being cannot walk on the water. He sees the world as it is, and this concept of recognizing the nature of reality plays a central role in Różewicz's work. One who knows the nature of the world is not guaranteed a happy or beautiful life, but at least he has a chance to survive.

Central, too, is the function of the speaker, who acts on at least four levels: Różewicz himself, in his personal life; Różewicz as a Polish Everyman, responding to the situations a Pole finds in the contemporary world; Różewicz as a twentieth century Everyman, witnessing and responding to the events of the twentieth century; and Różewicz as a universal Everyman, witnessing and responding to the problems humanity has faced throughout its history.

"I Screamed in the Night"

In "I Screamed in the Night," the dead confront the poet. They may be people he knew as a young fighter in the Polish underground army. (In one of his short stories, Różewicz tells of having to pass a trash can every day, into which were stuffed bodies of Polish partisans for whom the Nazis had forbidden burial.) In addition, Róż-ewicz, speaking as a generic Pole, refers to the many Polish dead who fought against the Germans and the Russians. He may also be thinking of the Poles killed during the time of Joseph Stalin. The poem, however, has even broader meanings. It also refers to all the dead in World War II and, indeed, to all people killed in all wars. History haunts the poet. He screams in the literal night, perhaps in dreams or nightmares, but the darkness also becomes symbolic, a moral darkness: "cold and dead/ a blade from the darkness/ went into my body." The poem seems to offer no consolation, no solution.

"The Prodigal Son"

Sometimes Różewicz gains even greater dramatic impact and depth of narration by speaking through a persona. In "The Prodigal Son," the poet questions the routines of daily life from the point of view of an outsider. In the biblical story, the prodigal son leaves home and wastes his inheritance in riotous living. Reduced to beggary, he returns home to ask for a position as one of his father's servants. His father, however, embraces him, clothes him, kisses him, and tells his servants, "Bring out the fatted calf and kill it, and let us eat and make merry; because this my son was dead, and has come to life again; he was lost, and is found." Różewicz adds still another dimension by basing his poem on a painting that depicts the biblical story—a painting by Hieronymus Bosch, a Flemish painter of the late Gothic period who is noted for his grotesque and amusing caricatures of people in strange situations.

The prodigal son appears first at the inn from which he set out on his travels. There, he broods on the experiences he has undergone since the door of the establishment closed behind him. In the poem, the door seems to act on its own, as if its closing and opening were a natural process. When the symbolic door of his childhood home closes behind him, the young man must go out into the world. He finds that the world is filled with incredibly cruel and grotesque monsters. Senseless suffering abounds. Thus, the late medieval world of Bosch, with its grotesque characters, overlaps the contemporary world caught in the convulsions of World War II:

> I saw life
> with a wolf's jaw
> a pig's snout
> under the hood
> of a monk
> the open guts of the world
> I saw war
> on earth and in heaven
> crucified people
> who redeemed nothing

When Różewicz's prodigal son returns, he finds no father to welcome him, clothe him, or feed him. His former friends at the inn do not even recognize him. When he pays for a beer at the inn, the waitress looks suspiciously at the money, which she suspects may be counterfeit. Then she studies his face, as if it, too, were somehow suspect. She may be the same pretty Maggie who closed the door after he went out, but so many years have passed that they do not recognize each other. Perhaps, as she studies his face, she thinks she may have seen him someplace before. Another former friend sits in a corner with his back turned.

The prodigal son then thinks of how, out in the world, he was sustained by illusions, by thoughts of the joyful reception awaiting him when he returned home. "I thought every house/ would extend a glad hand," he states, "every branch bird and stone/ come to my reception." Having come to recognize the reality of the outside world, he returns home to recognize reality there also, and he decides not to go to his father's house. Instead, without revealing his identity, he goes out the door of the inn once again, vowing this time never to return.

Here again, the speaker functions on four levels. Różewicz speaks about his personal experience of growing up and going out into the world. On a national level, the prodigal son may be seen as one of the Polish soldiers, many of whom fought as members of the British and French forces, returning home to Poland after the fall of Germany to find the terror of the Stalinist period. The prodigal son may also be twentieth century man, finding it impossible to return to the comfortable beliefs of previous centuries. Finally, he represents the universal experience of a young person coming of age to find both the world and his home different from what he has always imagined.

The poem is not, however, entirely pessimistic. The prodigal son comes to know the true nature of both the outside world and the home he left behind, and for Różewicz such knowledge is the first step toward wisdom. Stripped of illusions, the prodigal son returns to the world with a strange, bitter sense of personal freedom, and his decision may be seen as a mark of moral growth.

"Falling"

Much of Różewicz's art concerns such moral development, although he seldom lectures the reader as he does in "Falling," in which he laments the absence of standards in contemporary life. One might expect such a moralistic poem to focus on the absence of God and Heaven in the modern world, but instead it focuses on the absence of Hell, of lower depths to which a person might sink and from which he might rise. Różewicz looks back ironically to the good old days when there were such phenomena as fallen women and bankrupt businessmen. He quotes the *Confessions* (c. 397) of Saint Augustine but laments that such distinctions between good and evil now seem possible only in literature, in such works as Albert Camus's *La Chute* (1956; *The Fall*, 1957). Stavrogin, "the monster"—and Różewicz's use of quotation marks illustrates his point about modern moral judgments—asks in Fyodor Dostoevski's *Prestapleniye i nakazaniye* (1866; *Crime and Punishment*, 1886) if faith can really move mountains. His question cannot be answered in the affirmative.

More typical of contemporary literature, Różewicz observes, is Françoise Sagan's *Bonjour tristesse* (1954; English translation, 1955), in which moral heights and moral depths do not exist, the entrance to Hell having been changed to the entrance to the vagina. Różewicz cites the Italian film *Mondo Cane* (1961) as giving an unforgettably grotesque but true moral picture of contemporary life, while the Vatican Council, which should be concerned with setting standards, tables a motion to debate the relationship between the faithful and the laity because it cannot define the term "the faithful." He concludes that contemporary man, like Adam, is morally fallen, but because of the lack of standards he does not fall down but falls in all directions at once. Indeed, he says that "falling" is the wrong word.

"To the Heart"

If, however, traditional religious and social norms no longer apply, an individual may still make moral progress personally by recognizing the world as it is. In this sense, even such a short, brutal drama as "To the Heart" may be read in a moral context. The poem begins with two words that might serve as a motto for all Różewicz's poetry, "I saw." The poet witnesses, reports the action. In this case, he sees a specialist—a cook—killing a sheep, and by placing the cook in the broader category of specialist, he gives the cook's actions wider application. He watches as the cook places his hand in the sheep's mouth, pushes it down through the animal's throat, grasps the beating heart, and tears it out. At the end, the poet comments tersely, "Yes sir/ that was/ a specialist."

Here, man obviously violates the natural world, but the implications go deeper. The cook, after all, does his job, putting meat on the table of those who employ him. Would it make any difference if he killed a chicken or a cow? It certainly would to the poet, for because of their nature, sheep have become important symbols. They stand for meek people. Christ, the Good Shepherd, spoke of people as sheep, and He charged Peter to care for them. If on one level the poem may be read as an allegory of man's violation of nature, it may be seen on another as man's violation of his fellow man. The cook may be compared to the man in the boat of "I See the Mad" who must beat off the hands of drowning people to stay afloat. The brutal cook, however, seems to have none of the compassion of the man in the boat. Nevertheless, the poet, viewing the action, retains his sensibility. In fact, he develops a kind of X-ray vision and supersensitive touch. He *sees inside* the sheep. As the cook touches the animal's heart, the poet feels it beating. He sees the cook close his fist on it and feels the heart torn out.

The title "To the Heart" has two meanings: It implies the direction of the cook's arm as he shoves it down the sheep's throat, as well as the direction of the poem, which becomes a short moral lesson directed to the heart of the poet and the heart of the reader. The "heart" of the title, therefore, comes to stand not only for the sheep's heart but also for the organ that is the traditional symbol of human kindness and love. Kindness and love that do not take into account the brutalities of life will surely lead to disaster, however, as perhaps they did for those naïve souls who believed they could walk on water.

"I Am a Realist"

Once a person sees the world as it is, can there be further progress? Is the brutal, material world the only reality? In several poems, Różewicz hints at a spiritual world, one that can be discovered only through recognizing all the ills of the material one. In his poem "I Am a Realist," he enumerates details of daily life: His young son plays with a ladybug, his wife makes coffee and complains that her hair is falling out, while the poet takes an apple from the table and goes to work writing realistic poetry. The poem, however, takes a strange twist at the end. The poet, tired of his realistic details, complains: "I am a realist and a materialist/ only sometimes I'm tired/ I close my eyes."

"Remembrance from a Dream in 1963"

In "Remembrance from a Dream in 1963," the poet shows what can happen when his eyes are closed. He dreams of Leo Tolstoy lying in a bed, his face pulsing with light. Suddenly, the scene becomes dark, and the poet asks Tolstoy what should be done. Tolstoy answers, "Nothing." Then he begins to glow again, even to burn like the sun: "a gigantic radiant smile/ burst into flame."

Here, Różewicz receives his revelation, such as it is, from a noted realistic writer, Tolstoy. When the blazing light around the novelist goes out just before he speaks, the poet notices that Tolstoy's skin is rough and broken, "like the bark of an oak." (Even in recounting dreams and mystic revelations, Różewicz remains a realist, noting such specific details.) When the poet asks what should be done, the reader is tempted to ask in return, "About what?" Both Różewicz and Tolstoy, however, understand the question, which appears on the surface to concern the temporary darkness. Darkness, however, serves as a traditional symbol of loss of faith. Różewicz's question concerns eternal verities, truth and love, and their place in the universe. He may also be asking what should be done about his own doubts about the purpose of life.

Tolstoy's answer, coming as it does with a huge smile, might seem to be a kind of cruel joke. Nevertheless, Tolstoy shares Różewicz's concerns, whereas the "specialists" of the world do not. The answer he gives comes in two ways: in his words and in his actions. He may well be counseling Różewicz that one person's actions cannot change the nature of things and that Różewicz, having done what he can, must accept that fact. To a writer who performs his task well, there may come a kind of mystical peace, even an unexplained joy in life. (Indeed, despite the gloom in his life and in his art, Róż-ewicz in person can be at times uncommonly cheerful.)

"Alpha"

In this way, the writer's craft itself becomes an important symbol in Różewicz's work. In "Alpha," he pictures himself as a medieval monk illuminating a manuscript that recounts a particularly brutal history:

> my left hand
> illuminates
> a manuscript
> of the murdered the blinded the burned

Why the left hand? The poet may be left-handed, but "left," signifying unlucky or awkward, is much more important. The ancient Greek augurs believed that omens seen over the left shoulder predicted evil. The Roman soothsayers divided the heavens vertically into two segments. If the omen appeared in the left side, it was considered unfavorable. In the Polish language, moreover, as in English, to say that someone did something "left-handedly" means that it was done suddenly, without much consideration, and probably badly. A student who has written an assignment poorly may be said to have done it with his left hand. Thus, Różewicz presents himself both as a prophet of ill tidings and as a rather awkward writer—implying not necessarily that his writing is inferior to that of others, but rather that it cannot equal his vision of the world. Even song, he says, did not "escape whole," a phrase that could have two meanings: Even song did not escape untouched from the ravages of history, or even song did not escape his clumsy, left-handed efforts.

Nevertheless, despite what he considers the clumsiness of his words and the terrible message they convey, in the very act of writing he stumbles on a kind of revelation that another world exists after all, a world of the spirit which he can but suggest in his work.

> my left hand
> paints
> white as a unicorn
> an unreal letter
> from the other world

Różewicz, in spite of the brutalities and injustices of history, which he insists on confronting head-on, retains a consistently moral stance in his work. Man must, he insists, recognize life as it actually is, not as he would like it to be. Reflecting on his own life, on the tragic history of his nation, on the convulsions of the twentieth century, and on the history of the world, he retains his sensibility, his ability to feel as a human being in the midst of uncaring and unfeeling people. His persistence is rewarded when he catches glimpses from time to time of a possible world beyond the one in which he lives—glimpses that on rare occasions afford him inklings of joy.

Recycling

As he entered his eightieth decade, Różewicz's concerns extended into his first English collection of the new millennium, *Recycling*. The subject matter is topical, but the themes are the enduring ones in Różewicz's poems: Man's inhumanity to man, and the horrors of war. Here they are juxtaposed to the trivialities of late twentieth century Western culture. In the title poem, three sections counterpose aspects of the war to modern life: In "Fashion (1944-1994)" the fashion industry is contrasted with Nazi brutality against women; in "Gold"—a reference to Nazi gold and its inhumane origins—Różewicz satirizes revisionists who argue that the Holocaust is a fiction; and "Meat," using a collage of news clippings, plays off the 1990's fear of Mad Cow disease, at times through the use of lurid humor ("a cow in a shed started singing"). Recycling into the present, the past appears throughout this collection—as both threat and admonition.

Other major works

LONG FICTION: *Śmierć w starych dekoracjach*, 1970; *Echa leśne*, 1985.

SHORT FICTION: *Opadly liście z drzew*, 1955; *Przerwany egzamin*, 1960; *Wycieczka do muzeum*, 1966; *Opowiadania wybrane*, 1968; *Próba rekonstrukcji*, 1979; *Opowiadania*, 1994.

PLAYS: *Kartoteka*, pr., pb. 1960 (*The Card Index*, 1961); *Grupa Laokoona*, pb. 1961, pr. 1962; *Świadkowie albo nasza mała stabilizacja*, pb. 1962, pr. in German 1963, pr. in Polish 1964 (*The Witnesses*, 1970); *Akt przerywany*, pb. 1964, pr. in German 1965, pr. in Polish 1970 (*The Interrupted Act*, 1969); *Śmieszny staruszek*, pb. 1964, pr. 1965 (*The Funny Old Man*, 1970); *Spaghetti i miecz*, pb. 1964, pr. 1967; *Wyszedł z domu*, pb. 1964, pr. 1965 (*Gone Out*, 1969); *Utwory dramatyczne*, pb. 1966; *Przyrost naturalny: Biografia sztuki teatralnej*, pb. 1968, pr. 1979 (*Birth Rate: The Biography of a Play for the Theatre*, 1977); *Stara kobieta wysiaduje*, pb. 1968, pr. 1969 (*The Old Woman Broods*, 1970); *The Card Index and Other Plays*, pb. 1970; *Teatr niekonsekwencji*, pb. 1970; *The Witnesses and Other Plays*, pb. 1970; *Na czworakach*, pb. 1971, pr. 1972; *Pogrzeb po polsku*, pr. 1971, pb. 1972; *Sztuki teatralne*, pb. 1972; *Białe małżeństwo*, pb. 1974, pr. 1975 (*White Marriage*, 1977); *Odejscie Głodomora*, pb. 1976, pr. 1977 (based on Franz Kafka's story "The Hunger Artist"); *Do piachu*, pr., pb. 1979 (wr. 1955-1972); *"Mariage Blanc" and "The Hunger Artist Departs": Two Plays*, pb. 1983; *Teatr*, pb. 1988; *Dramaty wybrane*, pb. 1994.

NONFICTION: *Przygotowanie do wieczoru autorskiego*, 1971; *Nasz starszy brat*, 1992; *Forms in Relief and Other Works*, 1994; *Matka odchodzi*, 1999.

EDITED TEXT: *Kto jest ten dziwny nieznajomy*, 1964.

MISCELLANEOUS: *Poezja, dramat, proza*, 1973; *Proza*, 1973; *Reading the Apocalypse in Bed: Selected Plays and Short Pieces*, 1998; *Proza*, 1990 (2 volumes).

Bibliography

Baranczak, Stanislaw, and Clare Cavanagh, eds. and trans. *Polish Poetry of the Last Two Decades of Communist Rule: Spoiling Cannibals' Fun*. Foreword by Helen Vendler. Evanston, Ill.: Northwestern University Press, 1991. Baranczak's masterful translations offer a sampling of Cold-War-era poems from an oppressed people. Bibliography, index.

Contoski, Victor. Introduction to *Unease*, by Tadeusz Różewicz. St. Paul, Minn.: New Rivers Press, 1980. Contoski's introduction provides some biographical and historical background.

Czerniawski, Adam, ed. *The Mature Laurel: Essays on Modern Polish Poetry*. Chester Springs, Pa.: Dufour, 1991. More than three hundred pages addresses contemporary Polish poetry, placing Różewicz's work in context. Bibliography, index.

Filipowicz, Halina. *A Laboratory of Impure Forms: The Plays of Tadeusz Rózewicz*. New York: Greenwood Press, 1991. Although it focuses on his drama, this monograph offers important context for understanding Różewicz's writing in general. Bibliographical references, index.

Gömöri, Georg. *Magnetic Poles: Essays on Modern Polish and Comparative Literature*. London: Polish Cultural Foundation, 2000. A brief (163-page) overview of Polish literature today and its foundations. Bibliography, index of names.

Hirsch, Edward. "After the End of the World." *The American Poetry Review* 26, no. 2 (March/April, 1997): 9-12. Focusing on the works of Polish poets Zbigniew Herbert, Tadeusz Różewicz and Wisława Szymborska, Hirsch reveals how their post-World War II poetry is similarly haunted by guilt. He has found that the major poets of post-war Poland share a distrust of rhetoric, of false sentiments and words.

Sokoloski, Richard. Introduction to *Forms in Relief and Other Works: A Bilingual Edition*, by R. Ottawa: Legas, 1994. Offers useful insights into Różewicz's poetics.

_______. "Modern Polish Verse Structures: Reemergence of the Line in the Poetry of Tadeusz Różewicz." *Canadian Slavonic Papers* 37, nos. 3/4 (September, 1995): 431-453. The general evolution of verse forms in modern Polish poetry is reexamined in order to distinguish certain modifications formulated by Różewicz.

Victor Contoski,
updated by Christina J. Moose

Ruan Ji

Juan Chi
Born: Weishi, China; 210
Died: China; 263

Principal poetry

Poetry and Politics: The Life and Works of Juan Chi, A.D. 210-263, 1976 (includes translations of his *yonghuai* verses, *fu* rhyme-prose, and essays; Donald Holzman, translator)

Other literary forms

Several of Ruan Ji's rhyme-prose works—quasi-poetic compositions incorporating rhyme and rhythm—are lengthy effusions, extending to many hundreds of lines, and are celebrated for their novel profundity of thought in their treatment of such themes as "The Doves," "The Monkey," "Biography of the Great Man," and "Essay on Music." Other essays discuss philosophical issues in the Daoist tradition—critical interpretations of Laozi, Zhuangzi, and the *I Ching* (*Book of Changes*).

Achievements

Together with his senior, Cao Zhi (192-232), Ruan Ji stands at the head of a new era in Chinese poetics. His verse provides a link between the earlier epoch of Han and pre-Han forms, and the post-Han tradition of lyric poetry. His diction and imagery often recall the canonic odes (1000-600 B.C.E.), the mid- to late-Zhou (600-221 B.C.E.) philosophical writings, and the rhetoric of the southern *Sao* anthology; in his hands, the new pentameter form becomes an acceptable and established vehicle for the expression of political and social anguish. Furthermore, in the long tradition in which courtly pomposities too frequently usurped genuine thought, Ruan Ji's poetry is admired to this day for its complexity of Confucian and Daoist ideals, its passionate concern for contemporaneous worldly ills, and the poet's own moral dilemmas, all expressed in a deceptively artless diction (characteristics for which the poetry of Tao Qian, 365-427, is also greatly admired). Indeed, so perplexing and perilous was Ruan Ji's political situation that his necessarily allusive satire became enigmatic, and his contemporaries, as much as later scholars, admitted difficulty in penetrating his precise import. Nevertheless, his quasi-religious mysticism has exerted a perennial fascination upon scholar-poets, and Ruan Ji's verse is among the most commonly cited and imitated in the Chinese literary heritage.

Biography

Ruan Ji, a member of the Daoist-inspired Seven Sages of the Bamboo Grove, was the son of Ruan Yu, himself a member of the celebrated coterie of poets known as the Seven Masters of the Jienan Era (the terminal period of the Han Dynasty, 196-220). Ruan Ji was ten years old at the time of the Caowei usurpation of the Han throne, and the latter half of his life was dominated by the decline of the Cao monarchs and the eventual usurpation of their power by the Sima clan.

Cao Cao overthrew the Han, and in 220, his son Cao Pei acceded to the throne as the emperor of the Caowei regime. He was succeeded at his death in 226 by Cao Rui, who squandered his patronage and oppressed the people. No direct offspring survived his death in 239, and a child successor was enthroned under the regency of Cao Shuang and an elderly general, Sima Yi. At first outmaneuvered by Cao Shuang, Sima Yi engineered a coup in 249 during which Cao Shuang, his relatives, and his supporters were massacred, so that the "number of famous men in the empire was reduced by half." Sima Yi himself died in 251 and was succeeded by his son Sima Shi, who executed still more of the Cao and their clique and in 254 deposed the twenty-year-old Cao Fang in favor of Cao Mao, seven years Fang's junior. Cao Mao was assassinated by the Sima in 260; Ruan Ji died in 263; and in 265 the Sima extinguished the Caowei and established the Jin Dynasty.

Ruan Ji's personal and political dilemma lay in his sense of obligation to serve in public office, his distaste for the degeneracy of his liege lords, the Cao rulers, to whom he was bound in loyalty, and his antipathy toward the cruel ambition of the Sima usurpers, into whose service he had become trapped. Actually a devout Confucianist, he turned to Daoist mysticism—the quasi religion available to third century Chinese—and the unconventional *ziran* (unrestrained spontaneity in behavior) and *qingtan* (pure discussion—that is, metaphysical speculation, rather than practical, political affairs) much in vogue among the politically disappointed and disillusioned intellectuals of his time. Such pursuits were typified by the activities of his coterie, the Seven Sages of the Bamboo Grove, among whom Ruan Ji gained a reputation for his skill as a cittern player.

Ruan Ji seems from his youth to have tried to avoid involvement in public affairs, however much this may have tormented his conscience. An anecdote relates how, at an interview with a provincial governor, the young Ruan Ji remained silent throughout—to the admiration of the officer, who deemed him extraordinary and "unfathomable." He must have resisted other summons, because it was not until 239, after the death of Cao Rui, that he was finally drafted, and he joined the entourage of regent Sima Yi. Ruan Ji was never thereafter able to retire from Sima employ and could only watch with dismay and passive resistance while the Sima furthered their own fortunes against the legitimate Cao, whom they ostensibly served.

In 242, Ruan Ji reluctantly accepted another post in the central government, but only after the composition of a now-celebrated letter to his patron, begging to be relieved. In any case, he later pleaded illness and returned home. In the late 240's, Cao Shuang's faction enlisted him, but again he soon resigned on the pretext of illness. He refused yet another post with Cao Shuang on the same pretense and retired to the countryside. When Cao Shuang was killed by Sima Yi in 249, Ruan Ji's reputation for political foresight was much enhanced.

With Sima Yi's death in 251, Ruan Ji was retained by Sima Shi, while all of those who had been associated with Cao Shuang were executed. Three years later, upon the accession of Cao Mao, Ruan Ji was awarded an honorary knighthood, an official sinecure, and a substantive administrative position in the imperial secretariat—by then dominated by the Sima. Sima Shi died soon after Cao Mao's installation, and his son and successor, Sima Zhao, drafted Ruan Ji into his military headquarters.

The following year, in 256, Ruan Ji was promoted to the office from which he derived his sobriquet, *bubingxiaowei* (colonel of infantry, hence "Infantry Ruan"). The reason traditionally given for his acceptance of the post may be apocryphal: He is supposed to have been attracted by the skillful brewing and the quantity of fine wine boasted by the official kitchens. Tradition further relates that he became deeply intoxicated while on the job and abandoned his official duties. Greatly favoring him, nevertheless, Sima Zhao attempted to wed his own daughter to him, but Ruan Ji again remained drunk (for two months) so that no arrangements could be made. Stories are also told of how, in a grotesque sign of his displeasure, he would roll his eyes so that only the whites showed. He was finally granted a post in the countryside, away from the intrigues and perils of the capital; his descriptions of his new environment indicate his disgust with the general poverty of body and spirit among the population there.

The assassination of the puppet emperor Cao Mao in 260 brought Ruan Ji back into the center of politics, writing apparently in support of the Sima. Confucianist commentators, however, have taken pains to explain away his change of heart: It was his official responsibility to write such commendations, he was deliberately drunk at the time of writing, and other, satirical compositions from his pen at the time represent his true desire for non-involvement. He died in office at the age of fifty-three.

Analysis

The works of Ruan Ji were mentioned in a sixth century imperial catalog that mentions Ruan Ji's collected works in fourteen folios (including a table of contents in one folio). A century later, they are listed as ten folios, and by the eleventh century they are reduced to five. In the fourteenth century, however, they appear again as ten folios. Extant editions of his works include considerably fewer: about twenty essays and *fu* rhyme-prose, official letters, and poetry.

Ruan Ji eschewed the traditional *yuefu* (music bureau songs—that is, new lyrics set to old tunes and titles) that were in great vogue before, during, and after his time, but he espoused the pentameter verse form established during the preceding Han era (206 B.C.E.-220 C.E.). Indeed, his eighty-two enigmatic verses under the general designation *yonghuai shi* (poems singing of my emotions) are among the most assiduously studied and imitated poems in this genre. They vary from eight to twenty lines, the majority being of ten or twelve lines, in the traditional *abcbdb* rhyme scheme.

In view of the dominating political influences upon Ruan Ji and the oblique style in which he expressed his moral conflicts, commentaries on his work have, reasonably, followed two interests: line-by-line interpretation, whereby political targets are identified and his satiric references and allusions are explicated, and appreciation of the genuine personal torment he expressed in attractive poetic form. Near-contemporaneous texts reflect these attitudes. For example, the court poet Yan Yazhi (384-456) says: "During the administration of Sima Zhao, Ruan Ji was ever fearful of catastrophe, and thus composed his verses." Yan Yazhi notes, again:

> Ruan Ji personally served in a chaotic regime and was ever fearful of being slandered and encountering disaster. Thus he composed his verses; and so, whenever he sighed, saddened for his life, although his situation lay in satire and ridicule, yet his writings contain enigma and obscurity. A hundred generations hence it will be difficult to fathom his sentiments. Thus I roughly clarify the overall meaning and outline the remote resonances.

A generation later, Zhong Hong (died 518) completed one of the first and greatest canons of Chinese literary theory and criticism, the *Shipin* (classification of poets). Herein, Ruan Ji is included in the top rank of three classifications, Zhong Hong saying that his poetic heritage was the minor odes (a section of the Confucian *Canon of Poetry*, 1000-600 B.C.E., traditionally associated with political satire) and commenting:

> He made no effort at worm-whittling [that is, intricate, superfluous embellishment], yet his poems on expressing his emotions shape one's spirit, and inspire one's innermost thoughts. His words lie within ordinary sight and sound, but his sentiments lodge beyond universal bounds.

The necessity for obscure allegory and the obscurity itself are undisputed. In setting a scene, Ruan Ji typically makes reference, itself disguised, to a similar situation in ancient history, his allusions cleverly enhanced by synonymous location or other nomenclature. For example, he will "hitch up a carriage and go forth from the Wei capital." Here he exploits the fortuitous existence of an ancient state of Wei during the Zhou Dynasty (1100-221 B.C.E.), synonymous with his own regime. The "Wei capital" may then refer either to the ancient Daliang or to the Caowei metropolis at Loyang. Elsewhere, he will say, "In the past I wandered in Ta-liang" and, again, "I gaze back toward Ta-liang" for the same effect. Other references, revealing Ruan Ji's exceptional scholarship in a milieu in which vast erudition was a mere *modus vivendi*, recall in similarly recognizable and pertinent allegory scenes of splendor long since turned to dust, sounding the familiar theme of the transience of mortal glory and warning against the excesses of current rulers.

"THE DOVES"

The decline of society and political morality also features prominently in Ruan Ji's satire. Political aspirations, he suggests, were the cause of the pollution of original innocence. Ruan Ji's principal villains are not identified directly, but commentators have been in general agreement in their speculations. For example, the lines "Reckless extravagance bringing decline to worldly custom./ How could one say he'd make eternal his years!" refer to Cao Rui, while in "The Doves" (traditional symbols of honest government), Sima Yi is lampooned as a "ravening dog" which in a rage destroyed the "doves"—that is, Cao Shuang and his brother Cao Xi.

Court officers as a class are also pilloried for their hypocritical Confucianism. They are "perfumed herbs" that exist "East of Liang," blooming twice or thrice in a single morn ("morning" being an ancient pun on "court"—held in the early morn); their doubtful "achievements" and influence will disappear with the moment. In other complex imagery, the lush decay of a southern scene is to be understood as representing the decline of Cao Fang and his clique. At the conclusion of yet another tirade against the hypocrisies of court life—courtesies, decorum, frugality, and virtue in public, but venal petty-mindedness in private—Ruan Ji flatly avows that the posturing of his colleagues sickens him to the heart.

As much as such plaints fill the pages of Ruan Ji's verse, it is his own toil and suffering that attract the sympathy of the reader. His ideal was honorable public administration in the service of a legitimate, stable, and righteous sovereign—that is to say, the ideal of the sincere Confucian who sought to combine literary and scholarly pursuits with a career of public service. Ruan Ji was to live out his life, however, in fear of slander, entrapment, and disaster. Unable to achieve his Confucian ideal, he turned to an uneasy and conscience-stricken espousal of Daoist retreat, abandoning his public career for the safety and nourishment of his inner, eternal spirit.

"Monkey"

Much of the rhetoric of this plaint derives from the *Chuci* (songs of the South), an anthology ranging from the fourth to the first century B.C.E., in which the lengthy poem "Li Sao" mourns a career destroyed by sycophantic court rivals. Such slander had brought about the demise of many of Ruan Ji's more illustrious colleagues, whom he mourns, and thus he writes that he fears not the naked sword, but rather the words of some insinuating tongue. Like Qu Yuan (343?-290? B.C.E.) of the "Li Sao," Ruan Ji feels that his sincerity, probity, and steadfastness—"a tall pine that does not wither in the bitter adversity of winter"—are not appreciated, but indeed are the source of jealousy and backbiting. In his "Monkey" rhyme-prose, he sees himself as an amusing pet, in captive service; at the same time, the animal may represent the empty ritual, the monkey tricks, of the lesser courtiers. In famous Daoist parlance, the poet recognizes that it is the useful who perish while the useless live out their vain lives.

Mount Shouyang

Under such circumstances, even traditional Confucianism sanctioned retreat. Ruan Ji's lines frequently summon forth the spirit of Mount Shouyang; indeed, he composed a forty-six-line rhyme-prose on the subject at the time of Cao Fang's removal in November, 254. This location was associated with the brothers Bo Yi and Shu Qi, who secluded themselves and died of hunger rather than serve the new Zhou Dynasty at the fall of the Shang (twelfth century B.C.E.).

One may give credence to Ruan Ji's own indifference to wealth and glory acquired during shameful times as he "northward gazed toward Shouyang's peak, below which those men gathered brambles." In Ruan Ji's mind, the argument of even this celebrated precedent was attenuated by his own very real potential, amply demonstrated by the favor shown to him by both the Cao and the Sima rulers.

Life in retreat

In all events, even when a long-sought posting to the countryside did offer Ruan Ji relief from metropolitan involvements, he found nothing of the bucolic idyll for which he yearned. Rather, his works describing his observations there became veritable models for misanthropic rhetoric. His rhyme-proses on the locations Kangfu and Dongping (in a marshy region of the modern northeastern province of Shandong), a total of three hundred lines, report that only inedible vegetables grow in the cold, wet climate there, and the peasantry are dull clods, for whom no civilization is possible.

Thus, neither circumstances nor venue permitted Ruan Ji the opportunity for either Confucian loyal service or the innocent simplicity of Daoist eremitism. Within this failure lie the tensions and paradoxes of Ruan Ji's thought, which have continued to intrigue Chinese intellectuals. Ruan Ji reveals contempt and shame for the corrupted Confucianism of his day, and he pines for settled times when moral virtue such as his can shine forth in worthy employment. Turning to Daoist principles, he despises himself for his fearful retreat. In his works there appears only justification for temporary retirement, and none of the ridicule for Confucian precepts that marks the committed Daoist. The swift passage of time enters as a motif, defeating, says Ruan Ji, any strategy for patiently waiting out current alarms.

Daoist mysticism

In the end, Ruan Ji's philosophical preoccupations led him into a profound, if quasi-religious, Daoist mysticism—quasi-religious because the concept of divinity was foreign to the Chinese at that time. True freedom, writes Ruan Ji in some of the most difficult and obscure poetry in Chinese literature, lies in abandoning attachment to the world and its values, to the emotions which trap mortal man in the snares of passion, and eventually to the self, at which point utter tranquillity is attained. This mystical rapture had been expressed in the fourth century B.C.E. by the Daoist Zhuangzi and would reappear centuries later in the Chinese Buddhist ethic. In the third century, however, Ruan Ji's sincerity of belief, born of his disillusionment with the social world, led him to strikingly original formulations. His search for a transcendent immortal, again made ambiguous by his rational Confucian disbelief in immortality, led him to what amounted to a concept of God, described in a vast effusion about a "Great Man" who would exemplify the ideal of sage-like aloofness from the dusty world while yet being of the world, and of service to it.

In summary, Ruan Ji favored the pentameter lyric poetry and rhyme-prose genres of his time, and while he added nothing to the development of these forms, he endowed them with a distinctive political, social, philosophical, and religious content, whose complexity of scholarship, allusion, and allegory has by turns bewildered and awed his audiences. He enlivened poems of dark political enigma and unfathomable mystical experience with profoundly sincere personal concern, and to the present day he remains one of the most admired and beloved of Chinese poets.

BIBLIOGRAPHY

Cai, Zong-qi. *The Matrix of Lyric Transformation: Poetic Modes and Self-Presentation in Early Chinese Pentasyllabic Poetry.* Ann Arbor: Center for Chinese Studies, University of Michigan, 1996. Includes an insightful study of Ruan Ji in the course of lyric genre transformation and poetic expression of the self and cultural identity.

Han, Ch'uan-ta. *Juan Chi p'ing chuan.* Pei-ching shih: Pei-ching ta hsüeh ch'u pan she, 1997. Excellent resource in Chinese.

Holzman, Donald. *Chinese Literature in Transition from Antiquity to the Middle Ages.* Brookfield, Vt.: Ashgate, 1998. Covers roughly the period from 221 B.C.E. through 960 C.E., placing Ruan Ji in context. Generous bibliographic references.

_______. *Immortals, Festivals and Poetry in Medieval China: Studies in Social and Intellectual History.* Brookfield, Vt.: Ashgate, 1998. Excellent for understanding Ruan Ji's poetry in context. Includes bibliographical references and index.

_______. *Poetry and Politics: The Life and Works of Juan Chi, a.d. 210-263.* New York: Cambridge University Press, 1976. A full-length critical study of Ruan Ji's life and literary achievements. An extension of his *Juan Chi and His Life* in 1953.

Watson, Burton, trans. *Chuang Tsu: Basic Writings.* New York: Columbia University Press, 1964. An essential reading for understanding Ruan Ji's Daoist mysticism.

_______, ed. *The Columbia Book of Chinese Poetry.* New York: Columbia University Press, 1984. An excellent anthology. As no special collections of Ruan Ji's poems in English translation are available, this is a good place to locate his poems in English and discussions of the Chinese poetry of retreat.

Yu, Pauline. "The Poetry of Retreat." In *Masterworks of Asian Literature in Comparative Perspective*, edited by Barbara Stoler Miller. Armonk, N.Y.: M. E. Sharpe, 1994. A thoughtful discussion of Ruan Ji in the Chinese poetic tradition of the recluse, along with other poets such as Tao Qian and Xie Lingyun. Includes provocative comments on Ruan Ji's eighty-two "Poems Singing My Thoughts" and the conflict between his fidelity to Confucian principles of service and his interest in Daoist mysticism.

John Marney;
bibliography updated by Qingyun Wu

MURIEL RUKEYSER

Born: New York, New York; December 15, 1913
Died: New York, New York; February 12, 1980

PRINCIPAL POETRY

Theory of Flight, 1935
U.S. 1, 1938

A Turning Wind: Poems, 1939
Beast in View, 1944
The Green Wave, 1948
Elegies, 1949
Selected Poems, 1951
Body of Waking, 1958
Waterlily Fire: Poems, 1935-1962, 1962
The Speed of Darkness, 1968
Twenty-nine Poems, 1972
Breaking Open, 1973
The Gates: Poems, 1976
The Collected Poems of Muriel Rukeyser, 1978
Out of Silence: Selected Poems, 1992

OTHER LITERARY FORMS

In addition to her own poetry, Muriel Rukeyser published several volumes of translations (including work by the poets Octavio Paz and Gunnar Ekelöf), three biographies, two volumes of literary criticism, a number of book reviews, a novel, five juvenile books, and a play. She also worked on several documentary film scripts. The translations were exercises in writing during dry spells; the biographies, like her poetic sequence "Lives," combine her interests in the arts and sciences. The two volumes of literary criticism (along with her uncollected book reviews) are central to understanding her views concerning poetry and life.

ACHIEVEMENTS

With the publication of *Theory of Flight* in the Yale Series of Younger Poets in 1935, Muriel Rukeyser began a long and productive career as a poet and author. Her work also earned for her the first Harriet Monroe Poetry Award (1941), a Guggenheim Fellowship (1943), the Copernicus Award and Shelley Memorial Award (1976), an honorary D. Litt. from Rutgers, and membership in the National Institute of Arts and Letters. She also won the Swedish Academy Translation Award (1967) and the Anglo-Swedish Literary Foundation Award (1978) for her translations.

BIOGRAPHY

Muriel Rukeyser was born on December 15, 1913, in New York City, the daughter of Lawrence B. Rukeyser, a cofounder of Colonial Sand and Stone, and Myra Lyons, a former bookkeeper. Her childhood was a quiet one, her protected, affluent life a source of her insistence on experience and communication in her poetry. In *The Life of Poetry* (1949), she tells of recognizing the sheltered nature of her life: "A teacher asks: 'How many of you know any other road in the city except the road between home and school?' I do not put up my hand. These are moments at which one begins to see."

Rukeyser's adult life was as eventful as her childhood was sheltered. In 1933, at age nineteen, she was arrested and caught typhoid fever while attending the Scottsboro trials in Alabama; three years later, she investigated at firsthand the mining tragedy at Gauley Bridge, West Virginia; and in 1936, she was sent by *Life and Letters Today* to cover the Anti-Fascist Olympics in Barcelona as the Spanish Civil War broke out around her. These crusades dramatize her intense conviction on the sanctity of human life and her desire to experience life actively, and they all served as inspiration for her poetry, fulfilling her declaration in "Poem out of Childhood" to "Breathe-in experience, breathe-out poetry."

Throughout the remainder of a life filled with traveling and speaking for causes in which she intensely believed, Rukeyser never stopped learning, teaching, and writing; she declared that she would never protest without making something in the process. The wide range of knowledge in her poetry and criticism and the large volume of poetry and prose she published testify to this fact. She attended the Ethical Culture School and Fieldston School, Vassar College, Columbia University, and the Roosevelt School of Aviation in New York City, and she learned film editing with Helen Van Dongen. Besides conducting poetry workshops at a number of different institutions, she taught at the California Labor School and Sarah Lawrence College and later served as a member of the board of directors of the Teachers-Writers Collaborative in New York.

Rukeyser made her home in New York City, except for the nine years she spent in California and the time she was traveling. She moved to California in 1945 and shortly afterward married painter Glynn Collins (although the marriage was soon annulled). Three years later, she had an illegitimate son and was disowned by

Muriel Rukeyser (Library of Congress)

her family, experiences which figure prominently in her poetry after this date. She moved back to New York in 1954 to teach at Sarah Lawrence College.

Rukeyser left Sarah Lawrence College in 1967. Although in failing health, she continued to write and protest. For the Committee for Solidarity, she flew to Hanoi in 1972 to demonstrate for peace, and later that year she was jailed in Washington, D.C., for protesting the Vietnam War on the steps of the Capitol. In 1974, as president of the American center for PEN, a society that supports the rights of writers throughout the world, she flew to Korea to plead for the life of imprisoned poet Kim Chi-Ha. Rukeyser died in New York City on February 12, 1980.

Analysis

While Rukeyser has been linked to W. H. Auden, Stephen Spender, and other political poets, her work more clearly evolves from that of Ralph Waldo Emerson, Herman Melville, and Walt Whitman. From Emerson and the Transcendental tradition, she developed her organic theory of poetry, from Melville, her poetry of outrage. From Whitman, however, she obtained perhaps her most distinguishing characteristics: her belief in possibility, her long, rhythmic lines, her need to embrace humanity, and her expression of the power and beauty of sexuality. Her feminist views link her also with Denise Levertov and Adrienne Rich, while her experimentation with the poetic line and the visual appearance of the poem on the page remind one at times of May Swenson. Both the quality and quantity of her work and the integrity of her feminist and mythic vision suggest that she will come to be seen as a significant figure in modern American poetry.

Theory of Flight

"Look! Be: leap," Muriel Rukeyser writes in the preamble to the title poem of her first collection, *Theory of Flight*. These imperatives identify her emphasis on vision, her insistence on primary experience, and her belief in human potential. Focusing on this dictum, Rukeyser presents to her readers "the truths of outrage and the truths of possibility" in the world. To Rukeyser, poetry is a way to learn more about oneself and one's relations with others and to live more fully in an imperfect world.

The publication of *Theory of Flight* immediately marked Rukeyser as, in Stephen Vincent Benét's words, "a Left Winger and a revolutionary," an epithet she could never quite shake although the Marxists never fully accepted her for not becoming a Communist and for writing poems that tried to do more than simply support their cause. Indeed, Rukeyser did much more than write Marxist poems. She was a poet of liberty, recording "the truths of outrage" she saw around her, and a poet of love, writing "the truths of possibility" in intimate human relationships. With the conviction of Akiba (a Jewish teacher and martyr who fought to include the Song of Songs in the Bible and from whom, according to family tradition, Rukeyser's mother was descended), Rukeyser wrote with equal fervor about social and humane issues such as miners dying of silicosis, the rights of minorities, the lives of women and imprisoned poets, and about universals such as the need for love and communication among people and the sheer physical and emotional joy of loving.

U.S. I

Unlike many political poets, Rukeyser tried to do more than simply espouse: to protect, but also to build, to create. For Rukeyser, poetry's purpose is to sustain and heal, and the poet's responsibility is to recognize life as it is and encourage all people to their greatest potential through poetry.

Refusing to accept the negation of T. S. Eliot's *The Waste Land* (1922), Rukeyser uses images of technology and energy extensively in her early volumes to find, in a positive way, a place for the self in modern technological society, thus identifying herself with Hart Crane and with the poets of the Dynamo school. "Theory of Flight" centers on the airplane and the gyroscope. The dam and the power plant become the predominant symbols in "The Book of the Dead," in *U.S. 1*, her next collection.

U.S. 1 also contains a series of shorter, more lyrical poems titled "Night-Music." While these poems are still strongly social in content, they are more personal and are based on what Rukeyser refers to as "unverifiable fact" (as opposed to the documentary evidence in "Theory of Flight" and "The Book of the Dead"). This change foreshadows the shifting emphasis throughout her career on the sources of power about which she writes—from machinery to poetry to the self. It is this change in conception that allowed Rukeyser to grow poetically, to use fewer of the abstractions for which many critics have faulted her, and to use instead more personal and concrete images on which to anchor her message.

A Turning Wind

This movement is evident in *A Turning Wind.* She begins to see the power and the accompanying fear of poetry, and her poetic voice becomes increasingly personal, increasingly founded in personal experience. Poetry becomes the means, the language, and the result of looking for connections or, in Jungian terms, a kind of collective unconscious. Rukeyser notices, however, that poetry is feared precisely because of its power: "They fear it. They turn away, hand up palm out/ fending off moment of proof, the straight look, poem." The fear of poetry is a fear of disclosure to oneself of what is inside, and this fear is "an indication that we are cut off from our own reality." Therefore, Rukeyser continually urges her readers to use poetry to look within themselves for a common ground on which they can stand as human beings.

"Lives"

The poetic sequence "Lives" (which extends through subsequent volumes as well) identifies another of Rukeyser's growing interests—"ways of getting past impossibilities by changing phase." Poetry thus becomes a meeting place of different ideas and disciplines. It is a place where the self meets the self, diving to confront unchallenged emotions in the search for truth, and a place where the self can face the world with newly discovered self-knowledge. Using the resources they discover both inside and outside themselves, people can grow to understand themselves and the world better. The subjects of the "Lives" exemplify values and traditions Rukeyser believes are important to the search.

Rukeyser's growth as a person and as a poet, then, has been a growth of the self, realizing her capabilities and her potential and, in turn, the capabilities and potential of those around her. She becomes increasingly open in her later poems, discussing her failed marriage, her illegitimate son and subsequent disinheritance, her son's exile in Canada during the Vietnam War, and her feelings about age and death. Yet while these poems may seem confessional, she is not a confessional poet such as Robert Lowell or W. D. Snodgrass. The details of her life, she tells the reader, are events she must consider from various angles as she dives within herself as Adrienne Rich goes "Diving into the Wreck," looking for the essence of being. "The universe of poetry is the universe of emotional truth." Rukeyser writes in her critical work *The Life of Poetry*, and it is the "breaking open" of her preconceived emotions to discover emotional truth that allows her to become closer to the humanity around her. "One writes in order to feel," she continues. "That is the fundamental mover."

"Ajanta"

In "Ajanta," Rukeyser makes perhaps her first statement of inner emotional truth, according to poet-critic Virginia R. Terris. In this mythic journey within the self, Rukeyser realizes that self-knowledge is the prerequisite for all other kinds of knowledge. Yet behind her search for self-knowledge and expansion of the self into the world is her belief in the necessity of communication. The silence she experienced at home as a child had a profound effect on her, and in many early poems, such as "Effort at Speech Between Two People," communication is ultimately impossible. This same silence appears to be at the root of many of the world's problems, and Rukeyser's open outrage and inner searching are attempts to right the problem, to achieve communication. By the time she wrote "Ajanta," silence had become a positive force, allowing her the opportunity to concentrate on her journey within.

Artist and audience

Rukeyser has at times been criticized for combining disparate images within the same poem, as in "Waterlily Fire," from her collection by the same name, but this seems unjust. Far from being unrelated elements, her images grow, change, and develop throughout a poem and throughout her poetic canon. She puts the responsibility for making connections on the reader; she gives clues but does not take all the work out of the poem: "Both artist and audience create, and both do work on themselves in creating." Rukeyser is not an easy poet, and one cannot read her poetry passively. Yet she is a rewarding poet for those who take the time to look at and listen to what she is doing.

Poetic sequences

Another distinguishing mark of Rukeyser's poetry is the numerous poetic sequences (such as "Lives") which are connected by a common situation, theme, or character. "Waterlily Fire," for example, is a group of five poems about the burning of Claude Monet's *Waterlilies* at the Museum of Modern Art in New York City. "Elegies" is a collection of ten poems extending over three volumes. "Poem out of Childhood" is a cluster of fifteen poems, of which one is also a cluster of three, centered on Rukeyser's childhood—what she learns from it and how she uses it poetically.

Rukeyser's interest in poetic sequences grew from her training as a film editor:

> The work with film is a terribly good exercise for poetry . . . the concept of sequences, the cutting of sequences of varying length, the frame by frame composition, the use of a traveling image, traveling by the way the film is cut, shot, projected at a set speed, a sound track or a silent track, in conjunction with the visual track but can be brought into bad descriptive verbal things and brought into marvelous juxtapositions.

The sequence makes more apparent to readers the necessity of looking for connections among poems—recurring images, phrases, and sounds—than could separate poems.

The Speed of Darkness

In *The Speed of Darkness*, Rukeyser returns to her preoccupation with silence, expressing it structurally both in and as a subject. From her earliest poems, she used space within lines (often combined with a proliferation of colons) to act as a new type of punctuation—a metric rest—but in *The Speed of Darkness*, she places greater emphasis on the placement of the poem on the page to achieve this metric rest, for space on the page "can provide roughly for a relationship in emphasis through the eye's discernment of pattern."

Moving toward shorter lines

Rukeyser's verse has often been characterized as half poetry, half prose because of the long, sweeping, encompassing, Whitmanesque free-verse lines especially noticeable in her early poems. In *The Speed of Darkness* and later poems, however, she moves toward shorter lines and works with smaller units of meaning in order to compensate for breathing. At times, her arrangement of these poems ("The War Comes into My Room," "Mountain: One from Bryant," and "Rune," for example) approaches Swenson's iconographs in their experimentation with the visual and physical movement of the line.

Perhaps another reason for the new, shorter lines is that they are more suited for the introspective journeys of Rukeyser's later work than are the long, flowing, altruistic lines she used earlier. They also help her to control more effectively her penchant for verbosity and maintain the development of her images. Yet the length and conclusion of the later lines are not without precedent. Many of the most powerful passages in the early poems were journalistic or cinematic passages, not yet matured but still effective in their performance. "The Book of the Dead" is especially noteworthy in this respect, for it contains the seeds of the concrete image and colloquial diction fully realized later.

Diction

Rukeyser's diction also gives ample reason for labeling her poetry half prose. Yet as startling as it may be to encounter words such as "eugenically," "silicosis," and "cantillations" in her poems, these words make the reader pay attention. She also employs words and even sounds as physical, musical, and thematic ties within and among poems in the same way other poets use rhyme and in the same way she uses image sequences.

With the variety of line length and placement evident in Rukeyser's work, it is not surprising that her canon is characterized by a rich variety of styles. Her experiments with language, line length, and rhythm easily lend themselves to experiments with different verse styles, including but extending beyond elegies, sonnets, odes, rounds, and rondels.

"Letter, Unposted"

While she uses traditional as well as nontraditional verse patterns, she often treats even her most traditional subjects untraditionally. Because of her belief in the community of humankind, she has written many love poems, yet she approaches even the most personal subjects in an unexpected way. A notable example is "Letter, Unposted" from *Theory of Flight*, which is centered on the traditional theme of waiting for a lover. Yet it is distinguished from other such poems by the speaker's refusal to languish in love and to see nature languishing along with her. The letter remains unposted because the speaker cannot write all the traditional sentimental foolishness expected of her. Instead, as in even the bleakest situations about which Rukeyser writes, she sees the positive side: "But summer lives,/ and minds grow, and nerves are sensitized to power . . . and I receive them joyfully and live: but wait for you." The speaker rejoices in life rather than feeling sorry for herself.

Feminist outlook

Although a feminine consciousness is evident in every volume of Rukeyser's poetry, *The Speed of Darkness* also begins a new and more imperative feminist outlook. In the same way that she refused to be simply a Marxist poet, neither is she simply a feminist poet. Rukeyser sees with a feminist point of view, but rather than rejecting the masculine, she retains valuable past information and revisualizes history and myth with female vitality. For example, in "Myth," one learns that Oedipus was not as smart as he thought he was; he did not answer the Sphinx's riddle correctly after all: "You didn't say anything about woman.'/ 'When you say Man,' said Oedipus, 'you include women / too. Everyone knows that.' She said, 'That's what / you think.'" "Ms. Lot" adds another perspective to the biblical story of Lot and his wife, and in "Painters" (from *The Gates*) she envisions a woman among the primitive cave painters.

Other poems written throughout her career on more contemporary issues reveal the strength of women while upholding their nurturing role. The mother in "Absalom" (from "The Book of the Dead") will "give a mouth to my son" who died of silicosis, and Kim Chi-Ha's mother in "The Gates" is portrayed as a pitchfork, one of Rukeyser's few uses of simile or metaphor. She also refuses to let women take the easy way out as some have been trained to do: "More of a Corpse than a Woman" and "Gradus Ad Parnassum," for example, display the vapidity of the stereotypical passive rich woman.

Yet while women are strong in Rukeyser's verse, they are still human. Sex is one of the driving forces in her work, and she frequently expresses the joys of love and sex, especially in *Breaking Open*. Significant examples are the powerful eroticism of "Looking at Each Other," the honesty of "In Her Burning" and "Rondel," and the power of sexual renewal in "Welcome from War." Giving birth is also a powerful image in many of the poems.

"The Gates"

"The Gates," a fifteen-poem sequence organized around Rukeyser's trip to Korea to plead for the release of imprisoned poet Kim Chi-Ha, synthesizes her recurring images and messages in a final, powerful poetic statement. Like "Night-Music," this sequence is at once social commentary and personal discovery, but it takes a much stronger stance in demanding freedom of speech and assessing Rukeyser's own development as a poet in the light of Kim Chi-Ha's life.

Legacy

"Breathe-in experience, breathe-out poetry" begins "Poem out of Childhood," the first poem in Rukeyser's first collection. Muriel Rukeyser wrote a poetry developing organically from personal experience and self-discovery, a poetry bringing the anguish, miseries, and misfortunes of human beings around the world to her readers' attention, a poetry demonstrating her exhilaration with life and love. Readers cannot hide from reality in her poetry, nor can they hide from themselves. There is always the journey, but possibility always lies at its end: "the green tree perishes and green trees grow." Rukeyser's challenge to the world she left behind is found near the end of "Then" (in "The Gates"): "When I am dead, even then, / I will still love you, I will wait in these poems . . . I will still be making poems for you / out of silence." The silence and passivity against which she fought throughout her life will not triumph if her readers are alive to her words and to the world around them.

Other major works

LONG FICTION: *The Orgy*, 1965.

PLAY: *The Color of the Day: A Celebration for the Vassar Centennial, June 10, 1961*, pr., pb. 1961.

NONFICTION: *Willard Gibbs*, 1942; *The Life of Poetry*, 1949; *One Life*, 1957; *Poetry and the Unverifiable Fact: The Clark Lectures*, 1968; *The Traces of Thomas Hariot*, 1971.

CHILDREN'S LITERATURE: *Come Back, Paul*, 1955; *I Go Out*, 1961; *Bubbles, 1967; Mazes*, 1970; *More Night*, 1981.

TRANSLATIONS: *Selected Poems*, 1963 (of Octavio Paz's poems); *Sun Stone*, 1963 (of Paz's poems); *Selected Poems*, 1967 (of Gunnar Ekelöf's poems; with Lief Sjöberg); *Three Poems*, 1967 (of Ekelöf's poems); *Early Poems, 1935-1955*, 1973 (of Paz's poems); *Brecht's Uncle Eddie's Moustache*, 1974; *A Mölna Elegy*, 1984 (of Ekelöf's poem).

Bibliography

Ciardi, John. *Mid-Century American Poets*. New York: Twayne, 1950. Ciardi profiles fourteen American poets who were active at the midpoint of the twentieth century. His article on Rukeyser is short but comprehensive and offers a short biography and an analysis of her major work. A good overview that illustrates Rukeyser in the context of her contemporaries.

Herzog, Anne F., and Janet E. Kaufman, eds. *How Shall We Tell Each Other of the Poet? The Life and Writing of Muriel Rukeyser*. New York: St. Martin's Press, 1999. A collection of tributes and essays regarding Rukeyser by poets and literary scholars. Includes bibliographical references and an index.

Kertesz, Louise. *The Poetic Vision of Muriel Rukeyser*. Baton Rouge: Louisiana State University Press, 1980. Kertesz provides the first book-length critical evaluation of Rukeyser's work. This book is flawed in that much of Kertesz's analysis is abandoned in favor of an angry defense of Rukeyser's work against critics who misunderstood it. However, Kertesz puts Rukeyser in context of her time and place, and so provides a valuable study for all Rukeyser students.

Moss, Howard. *The Poet's Story*. New York: Macmillan, 1973. Collected short stories of twenty writers who are much better known for their poetry. Moss includes Rukeyser's short story "The Club," which is interesting for its demonstration of Rukeyser's versatility as a writer.

Kenneth E. Gadomski;
bibliography updated by the editors

Jalāl al-Dīn Rūmī

Born: Balkh (now in Afghanistan); c. September 30, 1207

Died: Konya, Asia Minor; December 17, 1273

Principal poetry

Dīvan-e Shams-e Tabrīz, 1244-1273 (*Selected Poems from the Dīvanī Shamsi Tabrīz*, 1898)
Mas̄navī-ye Maʿnavī, 1259-1273 (*The Mathnavī of Jalālu'ddīn Rūmī*, 1925-1940)
Mystical Poems of Rūmī, 1968
The Love Poems of Rumi, 1998

Other literary forms

Among Jalāl al-Dīn Rūmī's prose works, a collection of transcribed talks titled *Fīhi mā fīhi* (*Discourses of Rumi*, 1961) deserves special mention. While in its spiritual messages and reflections this book is no less dense and subtle than the *Mas̄navī-ye Maʿnavī*, its free and informal prose style—in its original Persian as well as in the English translation by A. J. Arberry (1961)—provides a suitable introduction to the poet's teachings.

A book of correspondences (*Maktubāt*) and a collection of seven sermons (*Majāles-e Sab'a*) are also attributed to Rūmī.

Achievements

Speaking of Jalāl al-Dīn Rūmī and his *The Mathnvī of Jalālu'ddīn Rūmī,* the well-known fourteenth century Persian Sufi poet Jami said, "He is not a prophet and yet he has given us a Holy Book." The British Orientalist R. A. Nicholson, after having devoted much of his life to the study and translation of Rūmī's works, wrote,

> Today the words I applied to the author of the *Mathnawi* thirty-five years ago, 'the greatest mystical poet of any age,' seems to me no more than just. Where else shall we find such panorama of universal existence unrolling itself through Time and Eternity?

The American author and psychoanalyst Erich Fromm praised Rūmī as "a man of profound insight into the nature of man."

These are but a few examples of countless tributes bestowed upon the venerated Persian poet, who is also well known for having laid the foundations of what came to be known as the Order of Whirling Dervishes. All the same, Rūmī himself made no claims to any poetic accomplishments. Of writing poetry, he once said, "I do it for the sake of these people who come to see me and hope that I'd gladden their hearts a little bit. So I recite a poem or two for them. Otherwise what do I care for poetry?" (*Discourses of Rumi*). This was no false modesty but the expression of the genuine feeling of a man who wanted, first and foremost, to unburden his listeners and readers of the sorrow that comes with ignorance and to awaken them to what Søren Kierkegaard called "possibility of life." In the long run, Rūmī's greatest achievement has been just that—at least in the case of those readers who have found him, in the words of the celebrated Urdu and Persian poet Muḥammad Iqbāl, an opener of the doors: "What do I need of logicians' long polemics or professors' tedious lectures/ When a couple of lines from Rūmī or Jami open the closed doors?"

A Rūmī revival seems to have started, even if on a small scale, in the United States, and poets such as Robert Bly, Jack Marshall, and W. S. Merwin have produced modern renditions of some of the Persian poet's works.

Biography

Jalāl al-Dīn Rūmī, also known as Maulānā (our master), was born on or near September 30, 1207, in the city of Balkh (in modern northern Afghanistan). When he was five years old and shortly before the onset of the Mongol invasion, his father, who was a religious scholar of renown, left his native land in the company of his family and, traveling westward, finally settled in Konya, a city of Asia Minor (modern Turkey). After his father's death, Jalāl al-Dīn Rūmī succeeded him as a religious leader and scholar and soon gathered a large following.

The arrival in Konya of the wandering dervish Shams al-Din of Tabriz was an event of radical consequence in Rūmī's life. The details of the meeting between the two are rather sketchy and at times contradictory. The account that seems to be more reliable than others belongs to the chronicler Dowlatshāhi and can be summarized as follows. One day, the peripatetic Shams—who, in search of a kindred soul, had arrived in Konya and had taken lodgings in the Caravansarai of Sugar Merchants—saw a man riding on a mule while his disciples followed him on foot. The man was Rūmī, who after the death of his father had become Konya's most distinguished religious scholar, enjoying a large following. Walking up to him, Shams said, "Tell me, what is the purpose of all the discipline and study of books and recitation of knowledge?" "To know the religious laws and precepts, of course," the scholar answered. "That is too superficial," the Sage of Tabriz countered. Taken aback, the man of learning asked, "What else is there beyond these?" "True knowledge is that which leads you to the real, to the source," Shams replied and quoted a line from the Sufi poet Sanā'i: "Ignorance is far superior to that knowledge which does not free you of you." So profound was the impact of the exchange that Rūmī dismounted his mule and right there and then decided to turn his back on a life of secondhand knowledge and academic disputation.

The details of what followed are scanty, veiled in hagiographical embellishments. What is certain is that the result of the communion that took place between the two was nothing short of life-changing for the thirty-seven-year-old Rūmī: Soon, the respectable professor of religious studies turned into a poet of love and wisdom, and he altogether abandoned sermons and the seminary.

Utterly perplexed by the change in their master, Rūmī's disciples directed their ire at the stranger from Tabriz and plotted against him. Shams fled to Damascus. Rūmī dispatched his son and passionate poems of entreaty, asking the dervish to return. Shams complied and returned to Konya, only to find his enemies' anger and jealousy surging anew. Finally sensing that a plot against his life was imminent, Shams disappeared, in about 1247, never to be seen again.

Shams's disappearance caused further upheaval in the poet's consciousness and released torrents of rapturous ghazals (lyrics), whose themes ranged from the sorrow of separation and the longing to be reunited with the ecstasy of the perception of the unity of love. Soon Rūmī was to realize that Shams was, like himself, a mind reflecting the Supreme. Mirrors have no "content," therefore no separate entities. "While there was you I turned around you/ Once I became you, around myself I turn."

Two of Rūmī's later disciples became, in succession, the recipients of a similar proffering of love. The second, Husāmuddin Chalabi, who asked the Master to compose the *The Mathnvī of Jalālu'ddīn Rūmī*, was the transcriber of most of that monumental work and, in a way, its very *raison d'être*.

Analysis

In one of the *ghazals* of *Dīvan-e Shams-e Tabrīz*, Jalāl al-Dīn Rūmī cries out,

I have had it with the canons of measure, meter, rhyme
and ghazal
May floods come and take them away
Paper-crowns deserving of poets' heads.
A mirror am I and not a man of letters
You read me if your ears become eyes.

The lines are indicative of how "the greatest mystical poet of any age" was at odds with the artifices of poetry and, in fact, with the entrapments of language itself. "I banish the word and thought/ And, free of those intruders, commune with thee." *Khāmush* (Persian for "silent") was the poetic pen name he used for many of his *ghazals*.

In a similar way, Rūmī the thinker was a persistent negator of philosophical speculations of every kind. In fact, a recurrent theme of some twenty-seven thousand couplets that make up his magnum opus, the *The Mathnvī of Jalālu'ddīn Rūmī,* is the inadequacy of logic and reason. "The feet of logicians are of wood," and wooden legs cannot be trusted. To be sure, he attests the necessity of clear thinking and reasoning, but in the same breath he points to the paralyzing limitations of "partial intelligence" (aql-e jozʿi) which, anchored in knowledge, is in conflict with the wholeness of life:

Partial intelligence is not the intelligence of discovery.
It yields skill, and no insight.
It is clear, but it is a thing.
Nothing it has never been.
Caught between losing and gaining it totters.
Total intelligence soars high and is safe—come what may.

The Mathnavī of Jalālu'ddīn Rūmī

As can be seen from this small sample, *The Mathnavī of Jalālu'ddīn Rūmī* is not an easy book to read. Even though it has been revered through the ages, few people have the patience to carry on a sustained reading of even two or three pages of it. In part, its difficulty can be attributed to the author's multifarious nature.

The Rūmī of the *The Mathnavī of Jalālu'ddīn Rūmī* is at once a serious spiritual teacher, a love-intoxicated poet, an entertaining raconteur, a learned man familiar with most of the current knowledge of his time, and a Menschen-kenner of profound psychological insights. To give an example of the interplay of all these facets would not be possible in a limited space. To illustrate the point, however, here is how, in the middle of a moral discourse, one word leads by association to another, and the poet continues:

Once again I have become a madman. . . . And I have
not a speck of reason left in me, see?
So don't expect ceremonies and polite words, for
Heaven's sake. Once again I have become a madman . . .
Otherwise, how do you account for this erratic
Babble, O sober ones?

On another occasion, when he is telling the story of Ayaz—the beautiful, pure-hearted, righteous serf of Sultan Mahmoud—the poet suddenly abandons the ongoing narrative. "O Ayaz! The tale of your anguish and ecstasy made me so weak./ I stop. *You* tell *my* story." In the course of another discourse, having used the analogy of the sun, the word reminds him of its synonym *Shams*, and that in turn unleashes feelings about the vanished "king of love" Shams al-Din of Tabriz.

Such stream-of-consciousness interruptions and interpolations, which are found throughout the *The Mathnavī of Jalālu'ddīn Rūmī*, are responsible for its difficulty and for its unparalleled richness and density, as well as its unique stylistic features. It should be mentioned, however, that in no way is Rūmī composing self-conscious literary work, much less giving discourses according to any design or for any motive such as self-expression. Rather, he creates as he goes along, with the utter freedom and felicity of love. When at the end of the sixth and final book of the *The Mathnavī of Jalālu'ddīn Rūmī* he stops, even the promptings of his son Bahā al-Din Valad are of no avail, because as the latter quotes his father, "The camel of my speech is now laid to rest and not until doomsday will it raise its head."

Like any book of and on truth, *The Mathnavī of Jalālu'ddīn Rūmī* is full of seemingly contradictory statements: "Don't strive after water, seek thirst/ Waters will then spring aplenty, head to toe"; "So long as you haven't died [to yourself] the agony of dying will go on"; "Let go of your ears, then be all ears!/ Abandon your consciousness, then be conscious!" Paradoxes of this kind are scattered through *The Mathnavī of Jalālu'ddīn Rūmī.* Paradoxical also is the fact that the poet is consistently absent from and ubiquitously present in the book. Often, it is difficult to tell whether it is the character in a story who is speaking or whether it is Rūmī with one of his innumerable interpolations or poetic flights.

Scattered throughout the book are stories, ranging from anecdotes a sentence or two in length (such as the story of the ugly Negrito who rejoiced because others, not himself, saw his face) to elaborate tales. Some of the longer stories (such as the moving "Umar and the Harp Player" and "The Prophet and the Gluttonous Arab") are literary masterpieces and, at the same time, moral allegories with "epiphanies" at once ripe and hard-hitting. Seldom are the stories governed by the conventional demands of artistic unity; rather, their form is determined by the spontaneity borne of love, which "like life comes, in timeless moments, afresh."

Dīvan-e Shams-e Tabrīz

If love is the creative propeller of *The Mathnavī of Jalālu'ddīn Rūmī*, it is for the most part, the substance and subject matter of *Dīvan-e Shams-e Tabrīz.* Except for a limited number of *rubāʿiyāt* (quatrains), the *Dīvan-e Shams-e Tabrīz* is a collection of *ghazals* of mixed chronology (grouped alphabetically according to the last letters of end-rhymes). The word *ghazal*, which etymologically is related to love, lovemaking, and courting, denotes a lyric consisting of between six and seventeen lines, the last line containing the poet's *takhallos* (pen name). (For his *takhallos*, in most of the *ghazals* of the *Dīvan-e Shams-e Tabrīz*, Rūmī uses Shams's name, a token of love's undoing of separateness.) Originally an amatory lyric of mainly aesthetic significance, the *ghazal* underwent a transformation of intent and import in the hands of such Sufi-inspired poets as Arāqi, Sanāʾi, and Attār, who found in the form a vehicle for the expression of the ineffable feelings of transcendent love.

It is, however, in the pages of Rūmī's *Dīvan-e Shams-e Tabrīz* that the *ghazal* achieves an ecstatic quality unexampled by any other Persian poet, not even by such masters as Hāfiz or Saʿdi (the two names well known to Western readers, thanks in part to the efforts of such luminaries as Johann Wolfgang von Goethe and Ralph Waldo Emerson). What distinguishes Rūmī's poems from those of other lyricists cannot be elaborated here. Suffice it to mention that at their best the poems of the *Dīvan-e Shams-e Tabrīz* throb with the raptures of a religious self-abandonment—religion not in the conventional sense of organized religion or of dogma, sect, or ritual but, in Rūmī's own words, a "religion beyond all religions" (the complete line is: "The lover's religion is beyond all religions"). It is primarily the religion of lovers and love that permeates the pages of the poem. Here, to try to define the nature of love—as sacred, profane, personal, universal, divine, mystical and so on—or to identify the object of the poet's love (Shams? God? an "earthly" beloved such as a woman?)—to try to circumscribe love with such distinctions would be the result of thought's projections about love, whereas, as Rūmī tries to drive home again and again, not only can thought not fathom the mystery of love, it is in fact an obstacle to it:

Thought says, I have measured; all sides end in walls.
Love says, I have travelled beyond these walls many times.
Thought says, Beware! Don't step! the unknown is full of thorns.
Love says, look better, you're the maker of those thorns . . .
Love saw a corner market and erected its little shop
Love saw many a variegated bazaar beyond . . .

By now it may be fairly clear why in many poems of the *Dīvan-e Shams-e Tabrīz* the poet speaks in praise of wine, of taverns and tavern dwellers.

SOUND AND SENSE

The importance of the auditory aspect of the Rūmī *ghazal*, and that which is responsible for the difficulty of translating it into English, cannot be overemphasized. The poet, who was the founder of the Order of Whirling Dervishes, is believed to have composed most of his lyrics during *samāᶜ* (sessions of listening to music, mostly of primitive instruments such as the reed in the case of the Masnav, or the drum and tambourine in the case of the *Dīvan-e Shams-e Tabrīz*; ambulatory dances were part of the latter). Often, the lyric so seems to ride on the tidal wave of ecstatic rhythms that the poet refuses to bother about words as carriers of meaning. In one of the poems of the *Dīvan-e Shams-e Tabrīz*, for example, the repetition of the refrain *tananāhā yāhou* spills over into an entire couplet and becomes nothing more than a nonsense cluster of prosodic syllables: "Tatatantan tatatantan tatatatan tatatan/ Tatatantan tatatantan tatatantan tatatan." It is important to point out that there is not the slightest indication of poetic mannerism in *ghazals* of this kind; rather, the interplay of the sound with the sense comes naturally, as if inevitably, creating rare spiritual lyrics of rhapsodic beauty.

As was mentioned earlier, the matrix of the poetry of Rūmī, in *The Mathnavī of Jalālu'ddīn Rūmī* and the *Dīvan-e Shams-e Tabrīz* alike, is love, and love does not permit the extraneousness of the word. "I think of rhymes and the beloved taunts/ Don't ever think of aught but seeing me!" It may now be understood why the author of two hefty volumes of poetry spoke so often and so rapturously of silence: With the lifting of the veil of words and their mental associations, the face of the Real is revealed in all its splendor, and "The pen [that] was running so swift and smooth/ Shatters when it comes to love, and stops."

OTHER MAJOR WORKS

NONFICTION: *Fīhi mā fīhi*, early thirteenth century (*Discourses of Rumi*, 1961).

MISCELLANEOUS: *A Rumi Anthology*, 2000.

BIBLIOGRAPHY

Barks, Coleman, John Moyne, et al. *The Essential Rūmī*. New York: HarperCollins, 1995. This verse translation, by a well-known and popular renderer of Rūmī, includes a biographical sketch of Rūmī, explanatory notes, and a few exotic recipes.

Iqbāl, Afzal. *The Life and Work of Jalaluddin Rumi*. Foreword by A. J. Arberry. New York: Oxford University Press, 1999. Begins with an overview of thirteenth century Persia and then addresses Rūmī's life, the appearance and then disappearance of Shams al-Din of Tabriz. Chapter titles include "The Age of Rumi," "The Period of Preparation," "The Romance of Revolution," "The Miracle of the Muse," "The Message of the *Mathnawi*," "The Poet as a Thinker." Supported by a Latin translation of the *Mathnavī*, a select bibliography, and index.

Keshavarz, Fatemeh. *Reading Mystical Lyric: The Case of Jalal al-Din Rumi*. Columbia: University of South Carolina Press, 1998. Keshaverez examines Rūmī's literary contribution as a mystical poet by "observing the poems in action." She analyzes the literary enactment of love rather than a mere portrayal of love. Includes notes on transliteration, dating, historiography; biographical analysis; analysis of tropes, rhyme, imagery, and the "poetics of silence"; bibliography; index.

Khalili, Nader E. *Rumi: Fountain of Fire*. Carl Earth Press, 1994. A translation of seventy-five poems from the original Persian texts into English. Khalili aspires to show that Rūmī's poetry has direct relevance to everyday practical life because he gains inspiration from Rūmī in his own career as an architect.

Lewis, Franklin D. *Rumi, Past and Present, East and West: The Life, Teachings, and Poetry of Jalâl al-Din Rumi*. Oxford: Oneworld, 2000. A comprehensive (384-page) analysis that goes beyond biography to address Rūmī's times, teachers, and influences, with reference to many sources in their original languages. As the publisher states, "From the establishment of the Whirling Dervishes to Rūmī's phenomenal popularity in the West, every theme of importance is covered." Bibliography, index.

Moyne, John A. *Rumi and the Sufi Tradition: Essays on the Mowlavi Order and Mysticism*. Binghamton, N.Y.: Global Publications, IGCS, Binghamton University, 1998. The well-known translator of Rūmī offers this brief monograph analyzing the mystical roots and expression of Rūmī in the context of Sufism. Glossary, bibliographical references.

Nicholson, Reynold A. *The Mathnawi of Jalalu'ddin Rumi*. 1st Pakistani ed. Lahore, Pakistan: Islamic Book Service, 1989. An edited translation, with critical notes, of the oldest manuscripts available.

Schimmel, Annemarie. *The Triumphal Sun: A Study of the Works of Jalaloddin Rumi*. Albany: State University of New York Press, 1993. Schimmel's study connects Eastern and Western literary traditions through Rūmī's poetry.

Whinfield, E. H. *Teachings of Rumi: The "Mathnavi."* New York: E. P. Dutton, 1975. Whinfield intersperses a synopsis of stories, then translations of verses, and commentary. Although this mode of presentation lacks any correspondence with the original poetic style, the text is helpful as an overview of the stories included in the *Mathnavī*.

Massud Farzan;
bibliography updated by Mabel Khawaja

S

Umberto Saba

Born: Trieste; March 9, 1883
Died: Gorizia, Italy; August 25, 1957

Principal poetry

Poesie, 1911 (originally published as *Il mio primo libro di poesie*, 1903)
Coi miei occhi: Il mio secondo libro di versi, 1912
Il canzoniere, 1900-1921, 1921
Figure e canti, 1926
Tre composizioni, 1933
Parole, 1934
Ultime cose, 1944
Il canzoniere, 1900-1945, 1945
Il Mediterranee, 1946
Il canzoniere, 1900-1947, 1948
Uccelli, 1950
Quasi un racconto, 1951
Il canzoniere, 1961, revised 1965
Umberto Saba: Thirty-one Poems, 1978
The Dark of the Sun: Selected Poems of Umberto Saba, 1994

Other literary forms

Although remembered primarily for his poetry, particularly as assembled in the monumental editions of *Il canzoniere*, Umberto Saba also wrote several significant prose works, most of which were collected by Saba's daughter Linuccia in *Prose* (1964). *Scorciatoie e raccontini* (1946; short cuts and vignettes) consists mainly of terse reflections on poetry and meditations on politics and postwar society. The collection *Ricordi—racconti, 1910-1947* (1956; remembrances—stories) contains stories and sketches, some directly autobiographical. Saba's prose style is usually rich and complex, though not particularly experimental. Like his poems, the prose works are reflective and benefit from a careful rereading. The pieces in *Scorciatoie e raccontini* are "shortcuts" because they cut through the twisting paths of conventional, logical thought to arrive at a conclusion which is often startling in its revelation and insight. In *Storia e cronistoria del canzoniere* (1948; history and chronicle of the *canzoniere*), Saba turns his critical eye to his own works, explaining the biographical background of the poems in *Il canzoniere* and giving interpretations. This self-criticism not only recalls the commentary of Dante Alighieri on his own poems in the *La vita nuova* (c. 1292; *The New Life*) but also exemplifies the influence of Sigmund Freud and psychoanalysis on Saba's thought and technique. The incomplete novel *Ernesto*, published posthumously in 1975, is on the surface Saba's least typical work; set in Trieste and vividly capturing the dialect of that Mediterranean city, *Ernesto* depicts the love of a young boy for an older man. Still, while more realistic and explicit than Saba's other works, *Ernesto* develops the same themes—art, love, change, and loss—with an equal complexity and subtlety.

Achievements

Often considered one of the three great Italian poets of the twentieth century, along with Giuseppe Ungaretti and Eugenio Montale, Umberto Saba is also one of the most important poets to combine traditional verse forms with a modern restraint and to treat universal themes with an analytical and self-conscious approach typical of the twentieth century.

The clarity and reflectiveness of Saba's earlier poems reveal the influence of the nineteenth century poet Giacomo Leopardi, and the calm, melancholy atmosphere of many of Saba's poems has its roots in the poetry of the *crepuscolari* (twilight) poets such as Guido Gozzano and Sergio Corazzini, who described everyday objects and settings with a wistful nostalgia. Saba's later poems break more definitely with traditional meter and line length, reflecting the terse, ragged rhythms of Ungaretti.

Saba won several prizes and honors, including the Premio Viareggio in 1946 for *Scorciatoie e raccontini*, the Premio dell'Accademia dei Lincei in 1951, and the honorary degree in letters from the University of Rome in 1953; critics have generally appreciated Saba's works, particularly since the 1960's. While Saba's poeti-

Umberto Saba

cal works have been generally well received and studied in Italy, however, his place in modern world literature has not yet been established, perhaps in large part because of a scarcity of translations. As critics continue to construct an account of Saba's biography and his rich inner life, his significance should become increasingly apparent.

Biography

The life of Umberto Saba is reflected throughout his work, and this relationship is most evident in Saba's structuring of *Il canzoniere* around the three periods of his development—youth, maturity, and old age; for Saba, all literature is in a sense autobiographical. Still, the richness and complexity of the poems and prose works give no indication of the relatively simple life of the poet.

Saba was born Umberto Poli on March 9, 1883, in Trieste, then part of the Austro-Hungarian Empire. His father, Ugo Edoardo Poli, was the son of the contessa Teresa Arrivabene; Saba's mother, Felicita Rachele Coen, was the daughter of Jewish parents who had a fairly successful business in the ghetto of Trieste. The marriage did not last long, and Ugo Poli, who had converted to Judaism, abandoned his wife as soon as Umberto was born. Saba refers to his parental background in sonnets 2 and 3 from the chapter "Autobiografia" in *Il canzoniere*. In the second, "Quando nacqui mia madre ne piangeva" (when I was born my mother cried), Saba describes both his and his mother's sorrow at being abandoned by his father. The speaker's happy memories of his relatives in the ghetto shopping for him and his mother are tempered by his loneliness: "But I soon became an expert at melancholy;/ the only son with a distant father." The third sonnet, "Mio Padre è stato per me 'l'assassino'" (my father has been for me "the assassin"), recounts the meeting between Saba and his father when Saba was twenty, a meeting which surprises the speaker, for he realizes that he has much in common with his father, the man whom he had hated for so long: "His face had my azure stare,/ a smile, amid suffering, sweet and sly." The speaker remembers his mother's warning not to be like his father and then understands for himself what she meant, that "they were two races in an ancient strife." With this awareness, the poet also sees in himself the unreconciled opposition of two forces, Jewish and Christian, old and new, victim and assassin.

As a boy, Saba was sent to stay with a nursemaid, Giuseppina Sabaz, from whom he derived his pseudonym and whom he recalls as Peppa in the chapter "Il piccolo Berto" (little Berto) in *Il canzoniere*. In "Il figlio della Peppa" (the son of Peppa), Saba remembers the paradise of his stay with Peppa, who had found in Berto a replacement for her dead son. The speaker sees this time with his Catholic nurse as lighter and happier than the time with his mother; after three years, as Saba remembers, his mother took him away from Peppa.

Saba had formal schooling beyond high school, attending the Ginnasio Dante Alighieri in Trieste. Wanting to be a sailor, he took courses at a nautical academy but was not graduated, for his mother made him take a position as a clerk in a commercial firm. In 1902, he left this job, traveling in Northern Italy and reading widely such poets as Leopardi, Giosuè Carducci, and Giovanni Pascoli, major influences on Saba's first volume of poetry, which was originally published in a private edition as *Il mio primo libro di poesie* (my first book of poetry) in 1903 and republished in 1911 as *Poesie*.

In 1908, Saba was drafted into the infantry and was stationed at Salerno, an experience that he depicts in *Il canzoniere* in "Versi militari" (military verses) and an experience which gave him for the first time a sense of comradeship with others. The same year, after finishing his service, he married the seamstress Carolina Wölfler, the "Lina" of his love poetry, whom he had met in 1907. The couple settled near Trieste and had a daughter, Linuccia. Saba returned to the army during World War I as an airfield inspector but did not see combat. After the war, Saba opened an antiquarian bookstore in Trieste, which served as his chief source of income and which furnished a meeting place for numerous writers and artists; from his bookstore, Saba published the first edition of *Il canzoniere* in 1921.

Much of the rest of Saba's life was relatively uneventful, and he published little between the years 1934 and 1945. Just before World War II, the growing anti-Semitic atmosphere pressured Saba into fleeing to France; later, he returned to Italy, staying incognito in Rome and in Florence. After the Liberation, Saba returned to Trieste and published in 1944 the volume *Ultime cose* (last things). The title is somewhat misleading, though, for in 1945 Saba published the first definitive gathering and reworking of his poems in *Il canzoniere*. After this edition, Saba continued writing poetry and prose, including some of his most famous works, such as "Ulisse" ("Ulysses"). In 1956, Saba was confined to a clinic in Gorizia; his wife died in November, and nine months later, on August 25, 1957, Saba himself died.

Analysis

Although overshadowed by the monumental achievements of Ungaretti and Montale, Saba has, since just before his death in 1957, begun to acquire the critical acclaim that his life's work in poetry and prose deserves. As critics begin to evaluate the subtle innovations of Saba's style and the depth of his thematic development, Saba's position as a major early modern poet should become increasingly secure.

Il canzoniere

The connection between Umberto Saba's life and his poetry is nowhere more evident than in his organization of the 1945 edition of *Il canzoniere*, the collection and revision of all of his previous poems. *Il canzoniere* consists of chronologically arranged chapters (some of which had been published separately) and is divided into three sections or volumes, each of which corresponds to a phase of Saba's life—adolescence and youth (from 1900 to 1920), maturity (from 1921 to 1932), and old age (in the 1961 edition, this includes additional poems from 1933 to 1954). These three sections also correspond to stages of Saba's poetic development, although certain themes and techniques persist throughout his career. The most salient characteristics of Saba's poetry are his preoccupation with retrospection, his treatment of modern themes in traditional meter and form but with concrete, everyday language, and his development of the theme of love as a unifying force in a chaotic world.

The first section of *Il canzoniere* contains some very early verse, much of which is less interesting and innovative than later poems, but the section also contains several of Saba's best-known lyrics, including "A mia moglie" ("To My Wife") and "La capra" ("The Goat"). This section contains the chapters "Versi militari" (written during Saba's experience as an infantryman in 1908) and "Casa e campagna" (home and countryside), from which come "To My Wife" and "The Goat," "Trieste e una donna" (Trieste and a lady), which treats Saba's love for his wife Lina and for his native city, and "L'amorosa spina" (the amorous thorn), thirteen poems which analyze Saba's passion for Chiarretta, a young assistant in his bookstore.

The second volume of *Il canzoniere* begins with a group of poems based on the failed love for Chiarretta, "Preludio e canzonette" (prelude and songs), but these poems, written a year or two after the affair, are more sober and reflective. In fact, the majority of the second volume is retrospective, including the fifteen sonnets which make up "Autobiografia"—poems describing events and perceptions from the poet's birth to the opening of his bookstore and the development of his poetic career. The last section, "Il piccolo Berto," is dedicated to Edoardo Weiss, an Italian psychoanalyst who introduced Saba to Freudian psychology and to an analysis of Saba's past. These poems concentrate on Saba's relationship with his mother and the various mother figures of his childhood.

The third volume begins with "Parole" ("Words"), which, written after Saba's experience with psychoanalysis, marks a new direction in his poetic diction and form. The dense, often elliptical poems in this chapter recall the hermetic style of Eugenio Montale, but Saba's sparse style often suggests a richness of emotion rather than a dryness; the purifying of language and avoidance of traditional forms and rhymes, as well as the minimalization of narrative, allow the reader to concentrate on and appreciate anew the sharpness of the images and the resonance of the sounds. The chapter "Mediterranee" (Mediterranean) contains Saba's most famous poem and perhaps his most successful synthesis of form and content—the poem "Ulysses," which parallels the wandering of the Greek hero with the poet's sense of his own age and homelessness.

The evolution of a poetic idiom should not obscure the unchanging features of Saba's artistry. Since *Il canzoniere* itself is not only a collection but also a reworking of previous poems, this anthology presents the reader with a consistent, retrospective view of the poet's career. This retrospection is clear, for example, in the inclusion of the autobiographical poems of "Il piccolo Berto" in the second volume—the volume of Saba's middle age; these poems of childhood reflect not so much the child's perspective as that of the adult looking backward and seeking to understand or assimilate the past.

Trite rhymes and everyday words

To an extent, the poet's use of traditional versification parallels his concern for the past. The poem "Amai" ("I Loved"), from "Mediterranee," shows that Saba views poetic tradition not as a series of principles to be slavishly venerated or as a confining set of prescriptions but as a source of inspiration for innovation: "I loved the trite words that no one/ dared to use. I was enchanted by the rhyme 'flower—love' [*fiore-amore*],/ the oldest and most difficult in the world." The trite rhymes and everyday words are the most difficult because they have been used for so long, and yet, the poet implies, these words and forms have a beauty and a truthfulness that endures. The innovative use of tradition provides the poet with a common ground for communicating truth to the reader, and at the same time it requires that the poet find a new and personal way of perceiving and shaping this truth.

Suffering and love

For Saba, in fact, the role of the poet is to perceive the world—the world of the everyday—as it is, not as custom or habit deforms it, and to convey this childlike rediscovery to the reader. Since, however, the poet is also aware of the individual's ability to overlook or forget this primal joy and to fall prey to despair, he does not represent this rediscovery as a panacea for human suffering. This suffering, in fact, becomes as integral a part of the poem as is the joy, and in many of Saba's poems, the speaker's confrontation with pain is more significant than his apprehension of happiness. This awareness links the speaker with others who have suffered; it is the highest form of love. The poem "The Goat" illustrates this perception. At first, the speaker is intrigued by a tethered goat, as if for a joke, but then the speaker hears in the goat's bleating the eternal nature of suffering and sees in the goat's Semitic face "the complaint of every other being at every other evil."

This love—the yearning that binds all living beings—is perhaps the central theme of Saba's poetry. Love may be erotic, as in the love poems to Lina; or it may be filial, as in the poem "A mia figlia" ("To My Daughter"); it may be a love of one's city or society, as in "Città vecchia" ("Old Town") and other poems in "Trieste e una donna," or the poem "Ulysses"; or it may be a longing for the past, whether the past of childhood or the tradition of poetry.

One of Saba's most frequent attempts to make contact through love is to find a sense of community with his fellow humans. In "Old Town," the speaker discovers in the humblest, most squalid section of Trieste a kinship, a feeling of belonging, since in this section one finds the most characteristically human people (the most human because they suffer most). Still, as the poem "Il borgo" (the hamlet) shows, Saba does not expect this love to bring universal happiness or harmony. The poet laments the fact that his goal to become one with the ordinary people can never be fully realized, since the poet, in his very yearning to unite with the people, places himself on a higher level, an unchanging intellectual unable to become part of a changing society.

The poet finds more success in his amatory relationships, especially that with Lina. The poem "La brama" (hunger, desire) reveals the influence of Freudian psychoanalysis. Desire, or the libido, impels people, often with painful or destructive results, yet it is still a positive and necessary force in the world; in fact, *eros* is the quintessential motive for human beings.

Another source of inspiration for Saba is the animal world, as in the poem "The Goat." In his most famous love poem, "To My Wife," Saba combines both the erotic and the animal, comparing his wife to various animals—a hen, a heifer, a dog, a rabbit, a swallow, an ant. The simple joy that Lina gives Saba parallels the beauty and contentment of the domestic and wild animals; unlike poets in the courtly love tradition, elevating the beloved above the physical world, the poet elevates the potential for human love by appreciating fully the bond between the animal and the human world. In an earlier poem to his wife, "A Lina" ("To Lina"), Saba describes how the hooting of an owl reminds him of his sorrows with Lina, sorrows that he had wanted to forget. The animal world, then, often acts as a stimulus, a reminder of the need to go beyond one's narrow view of the world.

The experience of fatherhood, described in "To My Daughter," provided Saba with another opportunity for going outside himself, as well as a way of understanding the natural process of growth and change: "I don't love you because you bloom again from my stock,/ but because you are so vulnerable/ and love has given you to me.

"WINTER NOON" AND "ASHES"

In his later poetry, Saba contemplates the processes of change and aging with a sense of resignation, but not with despair or cynicism. The early poem "Mezzogiorno d'inverno" ("Winter Noon"), published in 1920, hints at such a mood. The speaker describes a sudden fit of sadness amid a great happiness. The source of this melancholy is not a beautiful girl passing by but a turquoise balloon floating in the azure sky, the loss of which must be causing a boy to grieve. The boy's pain is in contrast, however, to the beauty of the balloon, subtly contrasted against the sky, passing gracefully over the city of Trieste. In the later poem "Ceneri" ("Ashes"), from "Words," the poet strips away all unessential adornment and rhetoric from his description of an approaching death: "your bright/ flames engulf me as/ from care to care I near the sill/ of sleep." The speaker feels no anxiety, but instead sees death as a natural stage: "And to sleep,/ with those impassioned and tender bonds/ that bind the baby and the mother, and with you, ashes, I merge." The tone is reserved but not pessimistic: "Mute/ I leave the shadows for the immense empire."

"ULYSSES"

The poem that sums up Saba's poetic development is his "Ulysses," a compendium of his themes and a hallmark of the use of restrained, concrete language to convey a deep understanding of the eternal themes of isolation and community, love and loss. Actually, the second poem of this title, the "Ulysses" of "Mediterranee," conveys the poet's sense of age and decline, his feeling of displacement from his society, his love for his home, and his sadness after the events of World War II. Assuming the persona of the wanderer Ulysses (as many have noted, the Ulysses of canto 26 of Dante's *Inferno* c. 1320, the Ulysses who, imprisoned in Hell, had left behind home and family to sail in search of further knowledge of the world), Saba describes vividly and with nostalgia his past experiences and his present loneliness and sorrow. "In my youth I sailed/ along the Dalmatian coast. Islets/ emerged from the waves' surface, where rarely/ a bird intent on prey alit,/ algae-covered, skidding, sparkling in the sun like emeralds." The speaker recalls his present exile, in an allusion to Ulysses' tricking of Polyphemus: "Today my kingdom/ is No-man's land." In his old age, the speaker has become a no-man, cut off from the comforts of home; the harbor lights are for others now. "Again to the open sea/ I am impelled by my unconquered spirit/ and the sorrowful love of life." The journey of Ulysses and his indomitable spirit echo Saba's lifelong devotion to his artistry, his sense of never reaching a final destination, of never making a human contact free of pain, of feeling more sharply the sense of isolation caused by the very wish to know others, and yet at the same time of feeling the joy in recapturing through memory and poetry the bright images of the world.

OTHER MAJOR WORKS

LONG FICTION: *Ernesto*, 1975.

NONFICTION: *Scorciatoie e raccontini*, 1946; *Storia e cronistoria del canzoniere*, 1948; *Prose*, 1964.

MISCELLANEOUS: *Ricordi—racconti, 1910-1947*, 1956; *The Stories and Recollections of Umberto Saba*, 1993.

Bibliography

Cary, Joseph. *Three Modern Italian Poets: Saba, Ungaretti, Montale.* 2d ed. Chicago: University of Chicago Press, 1993. Focusing on three recent Italian poets Umberto Saba, Giuseppe Ungaretti, and Eugenio Montale, Cary presents striking biographical portraits as he facilitates our understanding of their poetry and guides us through the first decades of twentieth century Italy.

Renzi, Lorenzo. "A Reading of Saba's 'A mia moglie.'" *Modern Language Review.* 68 (1973): 77-83. A critical reading of one of Saba's poems.

Singh, G. "The Poetry of Umberto Saba." *Italian Studies* 23 (1968): 114-137. A critical analysis of Saba's poetic works.

Steven L. Hale;
bibliography updated by the editors

Nelly Sachs

Born: Berlin, Germany; December 10, 1891
Died: Stockholm, Sweden; May 12, 1970

Principal poetry

In den Wohnungen des Todes, 1946
Sternverdunkelung, 1949
Und niemand weiss weiter, 1957
Flucht und Verwandlung, 1959
Fahrt ins Staublose, 1961
Noch feiert Tod das Leben, 1961
Glühende Rätsel, 1964 (parts 1 and 2 of the cycle), 1965 (part 3, in *Späte Gedichte*), 1966 (part 4, in the annual *Jahresring*)
Späte Gedichte, 1965
Die Suchende, 1966
O the Chimneys, 1967
The Seeker and Other Poems, 1970
Teile dich Nacht, 1971

Other literary forms

Nelly Sachs published the short play, or "scenic poem," *Eli: Ein Mysterienspiel vom Leiden Israels* (1951; *Eli: A Mystery Play of the Sufferings of Israel*, 1967). Her fiction is collected in *Legenden und Erzählungen* (1921) and her correspondence with Paul Celan in *Paul Celan, Nelly Sachs: Correspondence* (1995).

Achievements

Nelly Sachs arrived at her characteristic poetic style late in life. She was heavily influenced by the German Romantic poets and did not consider her lyric poetry of the years prior to 1943 to be representative of her mature work, excluding those poems from the collection of 1961. Her first published book, a small volume of legends and tales published in 1921, was heavily indebted in style and content to the Swedish novelist Selma Lagerlöf. In the 1920's and 1930's, Sachs published lyric poetry in such respected newspapers and journals as the *Vossische Zeitung* of Berlin, the *Berliner Tageblatt*, and *Der Morgen*, the journal of the Jewish cultural federation.

Sachs's stylistic breakthrough came with the traumatic experience of her flight from Germany and exile in Sweden. The play *Eli* was written in 1943 but published privately in Sweden in 1951; it was first broadcast on Süddeutsche Rundfunk (South German Radio) in 1958, and had its theater premiere in 1962 in Dortmund. Acceptance of her poetry in West Germany was equally slow, partly because her main theme (Jewish suffering during World War II) stirred painful memories. In the late 1950's and 1960's, however, she was hailed as modern Germany's greatest woman poet and received numerous literary prizes. She was accepted for membership in several academies. In 1958, she received the poetry prize of the Swedish broadcasting system and in 1959, the Kulturpreis der Deutschen Industrie. The town of Meersburg in West Germany awarded her the Annette Droste Prize for women poets in 1960, and the city of Dortmund founded the Nelly Sachs Prize in 1961 and presented her with its first award. In the same year, friends and admirers published the first volume of a festschrift, followed by the second volume, *Nelly Sachs zu Ehren*, on the occasion of her seventy-fifth birthday in 1966. On October 17, 1965, she received the Peace Prize of the German Book Trade Association, and on December 10, 1966, she was awarded the Nobel Prize in Literature. Berlin, the city where she was born and in

Nelly Sachs, Nobel laureate in literature for 1966. (© The Nobel Foundation)

which she had lived for nearly half a century, made her an honorary citizen in 1967. The city of Dortmund, Germany, and the Royal Library in Stockholm, Sweden, have valuable collections of her letters and transcriptions of her early poems in their Nelly Sachs Archive.

BIOGRAPHY

Leonie (Nelly) Sachs was born in Berlin on December 10, 1891, the only child of William Sachs, an inventor, technical engineer, and manufacturer, and his wife, Margarete (né Karger). The family lived in very comfortable financial circumstances, and Sachs was educated in accordance with the custom for daughters of the upper-middle class. Although both of her parents were of Jewish ancestry, Sachs's family had few ties with the Jewish community and did not practice their religion. Sachs attended public schools from 1897 to 1900, but for reasons of poor health was removed and received private instruction until 1903. She then attended a private secondary school for daughters of wealthy and titled families and finished her education in 1908 without any formal professional training. In the summer of that year, she fell in love with a man whose name she never revealed. That experience, which ended unhappily, escalated into a crisis, making Sachs consider suicide. The man was later killed in one of Germany's concentration camps.

For the next twenty-five years, even after the death of her father in 1930, Sachs led a sheltered and not particularly noteworthy existence. She produced some poetry, read extensively, and did watercolors, some of which have been preserved in the Nelly Sachs Archive in Stockholm. In 1906, Sachs received Lagerlöf's novel *Gösta Berling* (1891) as a birthday present. Her admiration for the writer resulted in a correspondence between the two, and Sachs sent Lagerlöf many of her own literary experiments. Through the intervention of Lagerlöf and the brother of the reigning Swedish king, Sachs and her mother received permission to emigrate to Sweden in 1939. Shortly after Lagerlöf's death in 1940, Sachs received orders from German authorities to appear for deportation to a work camp. Leaving all their possessions behind, Sachs and her mother fled Germany, arriving in Stockholm on May 16, 1940. They took up residence in a small apartment in the industrial harbor area, where Sachs remained until her death in 1970.

The imagery in Sachs's later lyric poetry draws to a large extent on influences from her youth. Her father's extensive collection of rocks, gems, and fossils was a source of inspiration to her, and she continued his hobby with a collection of her own in Stockholm; not unexpectedly, the use of the stones as a cipher is very prevalent in her work "Chor der Steine" ("Chorus of the Stones"). From her father's library she was also familiar with the work of Maria Sibylla Merian, a seventeenth century entomologist and graphic artist who specialized in the study of butterflies. Sachs's poem "Schmetterling" ("Butterfly") exemplifies her metaphoric use of this and other insects in her work. In 1959, Sachs wrote that of all childhood influences upon her later works, her father's musical talent was paramount. When he played the piano during evenings after work, she frequently danced for hours to the strains of his music. In addition to her early lyric poems, which she characterized as "dance and music poems," the motif of the dance is also important in her later work.

In 1960, Sachs returned to Germany for the first time since her exile in order to receive the Annette Droste Prize. Not wishing to spend a night in Germany, she stayed instead in Zurich, traveling the short distance to Meersburg only in order to accept the honor. Hearing the German language spoken again proved to be so traumatic, however, that she experienced a "memory trip to hell." In Zurich, she met Paul Celan, another exiled poet, who invited her to his home in Paris. The meeting resulted in a continuing correspondence, but Celan was in the midst of a personal crisis as well and the relationship may have contributed to Sachs's difficulties. After her return to Stockholm, Sachs suffered a mental breakdown and was hospitalized with severe delusions of persecution. Although she worked feverishly during the next decade, she continued to suffer periodic attacks in which she imagined herself persecuted and threatened with death. Her cycle *Noch feiert Tod das Leben* (death still celebrates life) was written while she recovered in the hospital. Celan attempted to aid her recovery through an intensive, supportive correspondence which was also, however, an attempt at self-healing, inasmuch as he suffered from a similar ailment. Their poetry, beginning with Sachs's *Noch feiert Tod das Leben* and Celan's *Die Niemandsrose* (1963), shows their continuing "dialogue in poems." In the spring of 1970, Sachs became mortally ill and thus was not informed when Celan was reported missing early in April of that year. He was later found—an apparent suicide by drowning; his funeral services took place in the Cimetière Parisien near Orly, France, on the same day in May on which Sachs died in a Stockholm hospital.

Analysis

It is difficult to speak of development in Nelly Sachs's poetic works, inasmuch as she was well beyond fifty years old when she produced her first significant poems. It is true that she had published lyric poetry before the 1940's, but this early work has little in common with that of her mature years. Most of the poems from the 1920's and 1930's are thematically quite distinct from the later work, devoted to musicians such as Johann Sebastian Bach, Wolfgang Amadeus Mozart, Jean-Philippe Rameau, and Luigi Boccherini or dealing poetically with certain animals, such as deer, lambs, and nightingales. The Nelly Sachs archives in Dortmund and in Stockholm have copies of a substantial number of these early efforts.

In den Wohnungen des Todes

In contrast, the work of Sachs's last twenty-five years concerns itself largely with existential problems, particularly with topics related to the Holocaust and rooted in personal experiences of flight, exile, and the death of friends. Her first collection of poems, *In den Wohnungen des Todes* (in the habitations of death), refers in its title to the Nazi death camps and is dedicated to those who perished there. It is a mistake, however, to perceive her work solely in the context of these historical events. Her topic is on a larger scale—the cycle of life itself: birth, death, rebirth—and Sachs develops various metaphors and ciphers to express the agony and the hope of this cycle.

Sternverdunkelung

While it is desirable to interpret Sachs's work separately from the context of specific historical events, it is almost impossible to analyze an individual poem without relying on information gained from a broader knowledge of her work. This difficulty is the result of her frequent use of ciphers, poetic images that can be "decoded" only by reference to other poems in which the same images occur. Such a cipher in Sachs's work is the stone. Its properties are chiefly those of inert matter: lack of emotion, or lifelessness. The cipher may depict human callousness, death, or desolation in different contexts, and it is related to similar poetic images such as sand and dust—decayed rock—which signify the mortal human condition.

The poem "Sinai" from the collection *Sternverdunkelung* (eclipse of the stars) contains entirely negative images of the stone. Sachs compares the ancient times of Moses, in which humanity was still in intimate contact with the divine and thus vibrantly alive, with the present state of lifelessness; there are only "petrified eyes of the lovers" with "their putrefied happiness." Recounting Moses's descent from Mount Sinai, Sachs asks: "Where is still a descendent/ from those who trembled? Oh, may he glow/ in the crowd of amnesiacs/ of the petrified!" The eyes of the lovers turned to stone signify the death both of sensibility and of sensuousness, and the inability to recreate or reproduce. It is ultimately a death of humankind. The call is for one perhaps still alive among the multitude of those dead in mind and body.

In "Chassidische Schriften" ("Hasidic Scriptures," from *Sternverdunkelung*), Sachs writes: "And the heart of stones,/ filled with drifting sand,/ is the place where midnights are stored." "Drifting sand" is sand blown skyward by the wind; thus, while it is inert matter, it has lost this inertia momentarily on the wings of the wind. The dead has come to life. Midnight, on the other hand, represents the end of one day and the dawning of the next, a time of rebirth. Sachs contends that the stone, dead as it is, is imbued with the desire for rebirth and transubstantiation. Another possibility for the stone to attain a semblance of life is offered in "Golem Tod!" ("Golem Death!" from *Sternverdunkelung*). There, "The stone sleeps itself green with moss." The suggestion that the stone is merely sleeping, not dead, and that it is capable of producing living matter (moss) is also an affirmation of the possibility of renewal of life after death.

"Melusine, If Your Well Had Not" and "Chorus of the Stones"

Scarcely less negative is the stone cipher in the poem "Wenn nicht dein Brunnen, Melusine" ("Melusine, If Your Well Had Not"), from *Und niemand weiss weiter:* If it were not for the possibility of transformation and escape, "we should long have passed away/ in the petrified resurrection/ of an Easter Island." Easter Island's petrified statues are merely reminders of an extinct civilization, not a resurrection from the dead. Still, the poem indicates that transformation is possible (the symbol for it is Melusine). In the poem "Chorus of the Stones," from *In den Wohnungen des Todes*, stones are, like the statues of Easter Island, venerable objects depicting the history of humankind. The stone is symbolic of all that has died, but it carries memories within it and thus is not entirely devoid of life. The last lines of the poem even offer the hope that the stone is only "sleeping," that it may come to life again: "Our conglomeration is transfused by breath./ It solidified in secret/ but may awaken at a kiss."

Three ideas in "Chorus of the Stones" suggest that death is not the final answer to life: The lifeless entity (the stone) contains memories; it is imbued with breath, a necessary element of life; and it may be awakened by an act of love. Transformation, resurrection, and transfiguration are therefore within the realm of possibility. Such a flight from lifelessness to a new beginning is nevertheless fraught with difficulties.

"Halleluja"

The most dramatic depiction of the rebirth of the dead is to be found in Sachs's poem "Halleluja" ("Hallelujah"), from the volume *Flucht und Verwandlung* (flight and metamorphosis). The poem describes a mountain rising from the sea by volcanic action. The rock is portrayed as a beloved child, the crowning glory of its mother, the ocean, as it thrusts forth from the womb to the light of day. While still embedded in the sea, the rock showed signs of sustaining life. As in "Golem Death!" with its stone covered with moss, this rock has been nurturing life. For the sea algae, birth of the rock means death, which the "winged longing" of the rock will bring about; although one form of life dies, another takes its place. These poems therefore encompass the cycle of life and death of living and inert matter on Earth.

"Fleeing" and "Butterfly"

In tracing the cipher of the stone, it is evident that the nihilism of the earlier cycles has given way to a guarded optimism in the later ones. A more traditional image of transfiguration is that of the butterfly. Its life cycle includes the apparent death of the homely caterpillar and its re-emergence from the cocoon as a beautiful winged creature, and thus it is readily adaptable as a symbol of the soul's resurrection after physical death. Sachs uses the image of the butterfly within this tradition. The poem "In der Flucht" ("Fleeing," from the volume *Flucht und Verwandlung*) compares the flight of the Jews from their persecutors with the never-ending process of transformation, mutation, and metamorphosis. There is no rest and no end (no "Amen") for that which is considered mortal (sand, dust), for it experiences endless metamorphoses. The butterfly, itself a symbol of metamorphosis, will reenter the life-giving element at its death and complete the cycle of life.

In "Butterfly," from *Sternverdunkelung*, the butterfly is depicted as a mortal creature (one made of "dust") which nevertheless mirrors the beauty of a world beyond: "What lovely hereafter/ is painted in your dust." The butterfly is a messenger of hope for those who are dying, because it is aware through its own metamorphosis that death is only sleep. The butterfly is the symbol of farewell, just as it was the symbol of the last greeting before sleep.

"She Dances" and "Dancer"

More obscure than the image of the butterfly are Sachs's ciphers of music and dance. The dancer appears to be able to defy gravity in graceful and effortless leaps and spins. A new image of man is created in the dance—that of emancipation from earthly limitations and acceptance into the sphere of the incorporeal. On this premise, Sachs bases her depiction of the dancer as a re-creator, savior, and emancipator from material limitations. In the poem "Sie tanzt" ("She Dances," from *Noch feiert Tod das Leben*), the dancer rescues her lover from the dead. This act of rescue is not meant to save him from physical death, for he is no longer alive; metamorphosis is her aim. This she achieves, paradoxically, by her own death: "Aber plötzlich/ am Genick/ Schlaf beünt Sie hinüber" ("But suddenly/ at the neck/ sleep bends her over"). In German, the word "over" (*hinüber*) signifies "to the other side" and thus clearly suggests death; this connotation is underscored by the image of her bending at the neck (hanging) and by the word "sleep," which Sachs frequently uses as a synonym for physical, but not spiritual, death. In the act of dancing, the dancer has liberated both the dead lover and herself. The metamorphosis has released her from life and has rescued him from death. They are united in the spiritual realm. In *Flucht und Verwandlung*, a somewhat different form of creation is discussed in the poem "Tänzerin" ("Dancer"). Here the dancer becomes the vessel for the hope of the future, and Sachs depicts with physiological clarity the birth canal for a messianic prophecy: "In the branches of your limbs/ the premonitions/ build their twittering nests." The dancer's body becomes the maternal, life-giving promise of the future.

In the poem "She Dances," the beginning and the end of life are shown to coincide at the point of metamorphosis, the dancer being the agent. The medium for transfiguration is music. The poem "O-A-O-A," in *Glühende Rätsel* (glowing enigmas), describes the rhythmic "sea of vowels" as the Alpha and Omega. Music is the means of metamorphosis: "Du aber die Tasten niederdrücktest/ in ihre Gräber aus Musik/ und Tanz die verlorene Sternschunuppe/ einen Flügel erfand für dein Leiden" ("But you pressed down the keys/ into their graves of music/ and dance the lost meteor/ invented a wing for your anguish"). The English word "keys" is ambiguous, but the German *Tasten* refers solely to the keys of a piano in this context. The graves are made of music, the transforming factor, and are being played like the keys of a piano, while dance provides the wings for the flight from the corporeal.

"In the Blue Distance"

Finally, in the poem "In der blauen Ferne" ("In the Blue Distance," from *Und niemand weiss weiter*), the pregnant last lines combine the ciphers of stone, dust, dance, and music in the depiction of metamorphosis: "the stone transforms its dust/ dancing into music." The lifeless element needs no mediator here but performs the ritual of transubstantiation into music (release from corporeal existence) by "dancing" as "dust"—an action functionally identical to that of the drifting sand in the poem "Hasidic Scriptures."

It has frequently been assumed that Nelly Sachs is chiefly a chronicler of Jewish destiny during World War II, a recorder of death and despair. This narrow view does not do justice to her work. Sachs's poetry has many aspects of faith, hope, and love, and need not be relegated to a specific historical event or ethnic orientation. Sachs writes about the concerns of every human being—birth, life, love, spiritual renewal, and the possibility of an existence beyond physical death. To diminish the scope of her appeal is to misunderstand her message and to misinterpret her work.

Other major works

short fiction: *Legenden und Erzählungen*, 1921.

plays: *Eli: Ein Mysterienspiel vom Leiden Israels*, pb. 1951 (*Eli: A Mystery Play of the Sufferings of Israel*, 1967); *Zeichen im Sand: Die szenischen Dichtungen*, pb. 1962.

nonfiction: *Paul Celan, Nelly Sachs: Correspondence*, 1995.

Bibliography

Bahti, Timothy, and Marilyn Sibley Fries, eds. *Jewish Writers, German Literature: The Uneasy Examples of Nelly Sachs and Walter Benjamin*. Ann Arbor:

University of Michigan Press, 1995. Biographical and critical essays of Sachs's and Benjamin's lives and works. Includes bibliographical references and an index.

Bosmajian, Hamida. *Metaphors of Evil: Contemporary German Literature and the Shadow of Nazism*. Iowa City: University of Iowa Press, 1979. A historical and critical study of responses to the Holocaust in poetry and prose. Includes bibliographical references and index.

Bower, Kathrin M. *Ethics and Remembrance in the Poetry of Nelly Sachs and Rose Ausländer.* Rochester, N.Y.: Camden House, 2000. Critical interpretation of the works of Sachs and Ausländer with particular attention to their recollections of the Holocaust. Includes bibliographical references and index.

Rudnick, Ursula. *Post-Shoa Religious Metaphors: The Image of God in the Poetry of Nelly Sachs*. New York: P. Lang, 1995. A biography of the poet and an in-depth interpretation of seven poems. Rudnick traces the biblical and mystical Jewish tradition which grounds Sachs's work. Includes bibliographical references.

Sachs, Nelly. *Paul Celan, Nelly Sachs: Correspondence*. Translated by Christopher Clark. Edited by Barbara Wiedemann. Riverdale-on-Hudson, N.Y.: Sheep Meadow Press, 1995. A collection of letters by two poets living outside Europe and tormented by guilt that they had escaped the Holocaust. Includes bibliographical references and index.

Helene M. Kastinger Riley;
bibliography updated by the editors

THOMAS SACKVILLE

Born: Buckhurst, England; 1536
Died: London, England; April 19, 1608

PRINCIPAL POETRY

"Induction" and "The Complaint of Henry, Duke of Buckingham," in *A Mirror for Magistrates*, 1563 (second edition)

OTHER LITERARY FORMS

Thomas Sackville's other contribution to English literature was the play performed first before a select audience at the Inner Temple (where Sackville was a young student of the law) on January 6, 1561, and then before Queen Elizabeth on January 18, "with grett tryumphe" according to one observer. The title pages of two of the three editions printed in the sixteenth century describe the drama as the joint work of two fellow students, Sackville and Thomas Norton, yet the extent of Norton's contribution is disputed. Because the play was the first in England to use the elements of dramatic blank verse, the regular form of tragedy, and a subject from English chronicle history, its importance in literary history is assured. Moreover, the play is characteristic of the concerns of Sackville's two poems and of his long public life: In language, structure, and theme it focuses on the political evils caused by an insecure succession. Both Norton and Sackville were involved in parliamentary debate on the issue of Queen Elizabeth's reluctance to marry, which was for the majority of the years of her reign a topic of deep national concern.

One other work of Sackville is known, a prefatory sonnet commending Thomas Hoby's 1561 translation of Baldassare Castiglione's *Il Cortegiano* (1528; *The Courtier*). A recent survey of the evidence (by Allan H. Orrick in *Notes and Queries*, January, 1956) has concluded that there is no substance to the tradition that Sackville wrote a number of sonnets and other short poems now lost. Sackville had completed his few writings in belles letters by early 1561, when he was twenty-five or twenty-six years old and had already embarked upon his entirely absorbing, important career. In addition to his literary writings there have survived interesting letters and documents concerning public affairs.

ACHIEVEMENTS

Sackville's literary contemporaries, among them Joshua Sylvester, Thomas Campion, and George Turberville, praised his poetry highly. (Turberville would not himself try, he claimed, to compete with Sackville in the high style of epic.) In a dedicatory sonnet to *The Faerie Queene* (1590-1596), Edmund Spenser acknowledged that Sackville was "much more fit (were leasure to the same)" than he to write Elizabeth's praises.

Again, among the portraits of the courtiers of his day in Spenser's *Colin Clouts Come Home Againe* (1595), that of Aetion was probably meant to represent Sackville: "A gentler shepherd may no where be found:/ Whose *Muse* full of high thoughts invention,/ Doth like himselfe heroically sound." Certainly Sackville's high birth and important career encouraged such commendations. As Spenser's lines suggest, Sackville's contemporaries also recognized that his literary achievement mirrored that of his life.

A Mirror for Magistrates, a composite work which records the fall from power of figures in English history, made an important statement on matters of national import, first bringing into prominence the great Tudor investigation of issues of responsible government seen against a background of problems of recent history, familiar to today's readers in the history plays of William Shakespeare. Sackville's contribution has been recognized as outstanding by readers from his day to the present. Indeed, a false tradition soon developed making Sackville responsible for the planning and inception of the whole project. Sackville's "Complaint of Henry, Duke of Buckingham" and especially the artful "Induction" were recognized as first achieving a poetic style appropriate for a national epic. Indeed, Sackville was an important influence upon Spenser in *The Faerie Queene*.

Thomas Sackville (Hulton Archive)

Sackville has thus held an honored if minor position in literary history. His reputation was enhanced by the view (until recently the common one) that between Geoffrey Chaucer and Spenser, English poetry experienced an uninspired, dull period—lightened only by Sackville himself. This judgment is now seen as exaggerated. Still, it points to Sackville's early, transitional achievement in approaching the "golden" style of the New Poetry of the high Elizabethan era.

Biography

Thomas Sackville, Baron Buckhurst and the first Earl of Dorset, was born in 1536 into a noble family. One ancestor had come to England with William the Conqueror, and a more recent ancestor was also a forebear of Queen Elizabeth. Sackville received, in all probability, a thorough and progressive education—for his father was a friend of the humanist educational reformer Roger Ascham, tutor to Queen Elizabeth and author of *The Scholemaster* (1570, which Ascham in fact wrote at Sackville's father's request for the poet's son). He attended Oxford University and then the Inner Temple, one of the Inns of Court, where, as a law student, he produced *The Tragedie of Gorboduc* in 1561. Sometime between 1554 and 1559, when the first edition of *A Mirror for Magistrates* came out, Sackville had completed his two pieces for that work, although they were not included until the second edition, 1563. The poet's writings were encouraged by his humanistic studies in letters, complemented by an exposure at one of the Inns of Court to affairs and important personages. His travels to Rome and France (1563-1566), during which Sackville was given the first of many diplomatic assignments by the Queen, then filled out the traditional education of an Elizabethan gentleman.

In his formal education and travels, as in his writings, Sackville always aimed at a public career. In 1558 he first sat as a member of parliament, at twenty-two years of age. On his father's death in 1566, he undertook the management of a vast estate, had already begun a family, and was well embarked on his long career as an ambassador, statesman, and government official. A member of the Privy Council, he sat as Commissioner in a number of trials of national importance. He was perhaps Queen Elizabeth's ambassador to Mary, Queen of Scots, bearing to her the news of her sentence of death; tradition reports that his diplomatic skill and gentle character served him well in this assignment. In 1589 he became a member of the Order of the Garter, and two years later was appointed Chancellor of the University of Oxford. He succeeded Burleigh in 1599 as Lord High Treasurer of England, sat as Lord High Steward at the trial for treason of the Earl of Essex, and was appointed Lord High Treasurer for life upon the accession of James I in 1603. Aging and in progressively worsening health, Sackville remained in active service, dying suddenly at seventy-one or seventy-two years of age while sitting in session at the council table.

His life is not that of the prodigal Elizabethan courtier so much as of the dedicated and active man of public affairs. As the most recent commentator on the poet, Normand Berlin, points out, in Sackville "we have an interesting example of a man's life that imitated art." It is of great interest to the poet's youthful writings on the fall of princes that Sackville's subsequent career so often touched upon the fall of the great from political favor (and from life). He himself suffered an undeserved brief period of disfavor after failing to resolve an impossible political tangle associated with the Earl of Leicester's governorship of The Netherlands in 1587. In all these affairs Sackville showed depth of moral wisdom, devotion to his country, and an amiable but upright character. He fulfills to perfection the Renaissance humanistic dictum—indeed, it is the underlying thesis of Ascham's *The Scholemaster*—that practical training in letters and oratory would prepare a young "governor" for wise services to the realm.

ANALYSIS

Thomas Sackville's contributions to *A Mirror for Magistrates* shows a typical Elizabethan compound of classical, medieval, and "native" elements: Renaissance English literature owes its characteristic variety and vigor to a mixing of sources and styles. Deriving from medieval traditions are the complaint form of tragedy (in which the ghost of a fallen "prince" tells his life story), an interest in the vicissitudes of Fortune, imitations from Dante Alighieri, and use of dream-vision conventions. At the same time, Sackville turns to the classics, notably to Vergil, for the descent into hell as well as for much imagery and many details, and he evokes an atmosphere of classical myth and ancient history through allusion and example. He also employs artful figures of rhetoric in a manner newly stylish in contemporary Tudor letters and uses such "native" elements as archaic diction and syntax to further the effect of synthesis among diverse literary elements. The result is a dignified and serious mixing of richly traditional elements.

In the sentiments and atmosphere of his two pieces, Sackville evokes the brooding, melancholic air of Elizabethan tragedy, anticipating later Elizabethan achievements in drama. (In his exaggerated expression of extreme emotionality he works, however, quite in the earlier, mid-Tudor literary style.) He includes themes and images which become popular in Elizabethan drama and lyric, praising sleep, likening life to a play, and stressing that murder will not long remain hidden. Although such conceptions have roots in medieval and classical traditions, Sackville has gathered them into one poem where they work together with cumulative effect. Finally, Sackville's evocation of an atmosphere of woe and lamentation goes beyond the mere presenting of misery to anticipate the great Elizabethan treatments of mutability, which culminated in the mature works of Spenser.

A MIRROR FOR MAGISTRATES

A Mirror for Magistrates was planned as a continuation of John Lydgate's *The Falle of Princis* (1494, which itself followed the model of Giovanni Boccaccio's *De casibus virorum illustrium, 1355-1374*). Sometime after 1550 a group of collaborators headed by William Baldwin undertook to write a series of tragic episodes, selecting from the English historical chronicles those figures and episodes which would fit their design. A running prose commentary discusses each verse tragedy and links them together. Mentioning the authors of many of the pieces and here and there revealing the intentions of the compilers, this commentary evokes a real as well as literary world. The authors included well-known men respected as writers in their time, public figures who had survived the many political shifts of sixteenth century

England—in a word, these were men who knew by experience the political reality of the tales they told. A first version was partly printed in 1555 but was suppressed by Queen Mary's Chancellor Stephen Gardiner on suspicion of containing seditious references to contemporary conditions. Publication was made possible upon the accession of Elizabeth, in a first edition, in 1559, covering the period from Richard II to Edward IV and a second edition, 1563, presenting new tragedies primarily concerning Richard III.

Today's readers find *A Mirror for Magistrates* dull, didactic, and emotionally exaggerated. It was very popular in its time, however, going through a good number of editions and receiving successive versions and later imitations. Its analysis of recent political history brought to contemporary readers the latest thoughts on public issues; in addition, it provided some opportunity for the grim sport of seeking allusions to public controversies. The collection played a significant role in furthering the Tudor interpretation of history which has come to be called the Tudor Myth: A long period of destruction and disorder in the Wars of the Roses was England's punishment for violating the divinely sanctioned order when Henry IV deposed the rightful King, Richard II; a happy resolution was recently allowed in the accession of the great Tudor rulers.

Two central convictions underlie this reading of English history. First, the ruler of "magistrate" was believed to be the vice-regent of God, governing by divine right yet still accountable to God. Second, history was seen as a means of teaching political wisdom, presenting a "mirror" which shows (in Lily B. Campbell's words) "the pattern of conduct which had brought happiness or unhappiness to nations and to men in the past." In adopting these views, the authors of *A Mirror for Magistrates* played down the medieval vision of the capricious falseness of this world's glories, seeking instead to reveal the workings of divine justice in the affairs of men. Sackville thus presents his Duke of Buckingham as vulnerable to the uncertain charms of Fortune *because* of his own moral blindness and as being justly punished for his unscrupulous ambition.

The story of Sackville's contribution to *A Mirror for Magistrates* is obscure in many details, which were not entirely clarified with the discovery, by Marguerite Hearsey in 1929, of an early manuscript in the author's holograph. Generally, however, the introductory statements by Baldwin give a clear picture. When the first version was suppressed, Sackville proposed a more acceptable selection to which some new tragedies would be added which he would write himself, the whole to be prefaced by his "Induction" (introduction). This plan was not carried through, yet in the second edition (where it belonged chronologically) his "Complaint of Henry, Duke of Buckingham," was accompanied by the "Induction" because its literary excellence demanded inclusion.

"Induction"

Sackville chose the rhyme royal stanza of pentameter lines rhyming *ababbcc*, common in the late Middle Ages for serious verse, for both "Induction" and "Complaint of Henry, Duke of Buckingham." Although his strong iambics tend toward a thumping monotony, the effect is no more intrusive than in other mid-Tudor poets. Sackville also uses much alliteration; in Berlin's estimate, nine of ten lines use this device of repetition. Although such old-fashioned poetic techniques have been criticized, they actually support Sackville's overall intentions in both poems by helping to create a verbal texture of strong, heavy strokes in which opposition or contrast predominate. His is not a poetry of subtle effects. When the narrator of "Induction" sorrows to see "The sturdy trees so shattered with the showers,/ The fieldes so fade that floorisht so beforne," a stark and fundamental contrast is asserted. The language and imagery highlight significant polarities—summer and winter, day and night, joy and sorrow. The meters, figures, and diction preferred by mid-Tudor writers here work together to evoke bold, contrastive meanings.

"Induction" sets an appropriate mood for tragedy in the opening description of a harsh winter scene. This seasonal description and the hellish personifications which follow are picturesque, in the sense of using detail and image to evoke a mood rather than to suggest a full allegory or to state meanings directly. The harsh setting and images present a pervasive context for tragedy. By the tenth stanza the external details of winter are reflected in the narrator's inner thoughts about human failings; immediately such thoughts find externalization in trenchant personifications. First the figure of Sorrow conducts the narrator to the porch of hell, where, one by one, are met figures such as Remorse of Conscience, Dread, Misery, Revenge, Age, and Death. Again, the detailed descriptions of each figure contribute to the poem's melancholic atmosphere, but in their cumulative import the visions suggest that unhappiness, deserved or undeserved, is inescapable in the human condition. Sackville keeps his narrator posed between revulsion and sympathy: He fears and yet feels pity for Famine, "how she her armes would teare/ And with her teeth gnashe on the bones in vayne." In such ways the tragic visions impel emotional participation by the reader.

The portraits of Sleep and Old Age from this section of "Induction" have been much praised. Sackville's description of Old Age (lines 295-336) takes a detail or two from the mysterious old man of Chaucer's Pardoner's Tale; but it also borrows directly or indirectly from many classical and medieval sources. Typically, Sackville adapts and combines traditional materials, forming his own mixture and emphasis. In fact, the entire procession of figures in the middle section of the poem derives from a much briefer listing of personifications in Vergil's *Aeneid* (c. 29-19 B.C.E., Book VI). Sackville has expanded Vergil's suggestive, brief jottings into full portraits by calling upon many traditional literary images and concepts.

Increasingly, the poem dwells on the presence of change and loss in human affairs. At the end of the procession of figures, the narrator and Sorrow meet Death and then War. The latter presents his shield, in which may be seen historical instances of the destruction of cities and realms, culminating in a vision of vanquished Troy (lines 435-476). The poem has progressed from a view of individual sorrows to the universal principle of mutability seen on the scale of the destruction of civilizations. Moving across Acheron into deepest hell, Sorrow and the narrator enter a realm of intensified gloom and lamentation where the shades of the tragic dead, ghosts of "Prynces of renowne," tell their tales. In this way "Induction" leads up to the tragic narrative told by the Duke of Buckingham.

Sackville's "Induction" is, in Berlin's words, "essentially a mood piece that is brilliant in its evocation of atmosphere, vivid in its imagery, concrete in its description, effective in its fusion of sense and sound, and unified in concept and performance." Generally, the personifications as well as the historical figures are presented as tragic victims of misfortune or of irresistible forces of change. In "Complaint of Henry, Duke of Buckingham," however, there occurs a significant shift to a focus on the individual's responsibility for his own sufferings.

"Complaint of Henry, Duke of Buckingham"

As "Complaint of Henry, Duke of Buckingham" opens, the speaker Buckingham admits that his own choices led to his destruction, resulting from his opportunistic association with the villainous Richard of Gloucester. From the beginning the poem establishes a didactic manner which seeks to analyze errors of judgment and excesses of ambition. Buckingham's story centers on the gigantic figure of Richard III, according to the Tudor interpretation an arch-villain whose fierce reign constituted the final purgation of a sick England before God permitted the happy rule of the present Tudors. (Modern historians have shown that Richard III was much less evil and his opponents much less wholesome than in the Tudor Myth.)

In supporting Richard, the ambitious Buckingham takes advantage of "the state unstedfast howe it stood." He shares in murders, little thinking that blood will ask for "blud agayne." At this point Sackville interrupts the narrative with the first of five interludes, each an interpolated didactic meditation on a theme befitting the stage reached in the narrative. These interludes help to slow the pace of the narrative, lending a dignity which Elizabethans thought proper to epic subjects; in addition, they help Sackville to generalize from Buckingham's experiences to universal patterns. The first interlude discussed the folly of political murder, which is shown by many examples to lead to a chain of successive murders such as Shakespeare dramatizes in *Macbeth* (1606).

Buckingham resumes his narrative (line 169) to tell of a second wave of murders leading to Richard's coronation and of Buckingham becoming Richard's "chyefest Pyer." Hoping to ensure their final security, they kill Richard's two nephews (the notorious murder of the princes in the tower). With this act the chain of murders takes on destructive force, both psychological and social. First the conspirators experience the torments of inner fears, expounded upon in a brief second interlude (lines 211-238). When the narrative resumes, it reveals destructive external effects as well. Richard rules by fear, not love, violating the great Elizabethan commonplace that the people will lend assent to a benign rule: In the hearts of Richard's lieges there "lurkes aye/ A secrete hate that hopeth for a daye." The Tudor political theory of the divine right of kings stressed that kings are bound by morality and law. God allows rebellion against tyrants, and brings them war, guilty fear, and untimely death. A third interlude expounds this theme with gruesome historical instances (lines 267-329).

Thus far, Buckingham has described his immorality and errors of judgment objectively, allowing Sackville to survey Tudor political ideas relating to power, ambition, and tyranny. This objective tone weakens as Buckingham now turns from Richard, who has become too cruel even for him and who, moreover, has clearly revealed that Buckingham is next in line for destruction. Although Richard III remains the exaggerated villain of Tudor tradition, Buckingham takes on a certain depth of interest and evokes increasing sympathy. From this point in the narrative, Sackville allows a gradual return to the rhetoric of lamentation so prevalent in "Induction." Buckingham now blames not his moral flaws but fatal errors of overconfidence. He trusts, first, in the strength of his assembled soldiers, who desert him. (In lines 421-494 a fourth interlude expounds upon the folly of trusting the "fyckle fayth" of the mob.) Then, Buckingham places his final confidence in a disloyal friend, Humfrey Banastair, who betrays him to Richard and to death.

Buckingham now breaks off his narration to fall into a faint from grief. His distress over the falsity of a trusted friend will seem less excessive if it is remembered that treason is the arch crime in Dante's *La divina commedia* (c. 1320, *The Divine Comedy*), punished in deepest hell. Although today's readers will find the concluding sections of the poem, which elaborate upon this theme, exaggerated in their emotional extremes, it is suggestive to note to what degree Sackville has transformed Buckingham into a mistreated and sympathetic figure for the reader's contemplation. The last of the interludes is spoken by Sackville's narrator, for Buckingham remains in a distressed faint, with one brief awakening, from lines 540 to 617. This interlude picks up again the descriptive imagery and lyric movement of "Induction," painting an often-praised picture of the calm of deepest midnight, where the "golden stars" whirl in correct cosmic order and each creature is "nestled in his restyng place." Against this orderly security is shown the despairing unrest of Buckingham, who becomes a figure of genuine terror, emphatically teaching the lesson of the end to which lives such as his will lead, as well as an object for pity. Capping off this impression of desperation, Buckingham concludes with his notorious curse against the progeny of Banastair.

Finally, shaking off his episode of crazed cursing, Buckingham returns to his former objective tone in the poem's concluding six stanzas. He offers himself as a direct mirror to kings, showing that he "who reckles rules, right soone may hap to rue."

In "Induction" and "Complaint of Henry, Duke of Buckingham," Sackville achieves two very different ends. The introductory poem evokes a poetic atmosphere for tragic narrative, creating myth through imagery and description. The story of Buckingham is, in contrast, historical and dramatic, presenting and then analyzing Buckingham's actions in a context of serious thought on political themes. The poems together show both the range and the potential of poetry in the mid-Tudor period of English literature. Although Sackville's techniques and themes are seldom subtle, they make up for this lack with a consistency of effect and a concentration on bold contrasts and strong moral certainties. Recent studies of Sackville have found him to be as much a poet of his own time as an innovator anticipating the coming triumphs of later Elizabethan verse. It remains true, however, that he realized as did few of his contemporaries what his medium could accomplish, treating important themes with dignity, consistency, and poetic interest.

Other major works

PLAY: *Gorboduc*, pr. 1561 (authorized edition pb. 1570; also as *The Tragedy of Ferrex and Porrex*; with Thomas Norton).

Bibliography

Berlin, Normand. *Thomas Sackville*. New York: Twayne, 1974. This book closely examines Sackville's poems, the play *The Tragedie of Gorboduc*, and assesses his place in literary history. Includes a chronology, a biographical chapter, a discussion of Sackville's part in *A Mirror for Magistrates*, critical commentaries, sources, and an evaluation of Sackville's work and his historical significance. An annotated bibliography contains many references.

Campbell, Lily B., ed. *Mirrour for Magistrates*. Cambridge, England: Cambridge University Press, 1946. This is the definitive edition of this important compendium of tragical narratives from the sixteenth century. Includes Sackville's "Induction" and "Complaint of Henry, Duke of Buckingham." A sixty-page introduction discusses the content and background of the book and comments on Sackville's contribution.

Davie, Donald. "Sixteenth Century Poetry and the Common Reader: The Case of Thomas Sackville." *Essays in Criticism* 4 (April, 1954): 117-127. Primarily a discussion of Sackville's syntax and an exploration of his rhetorical style, this article also discusses other Sackville criticism. An interesting perspective on the poet's rhetoric in relation to the Elizabethan popular tradition.

Sackville, Thomas. *The Complaint of Henry, Duke of Buckingham*. Edited by Marguerite Hearsey. New Haven, Conn.: Yale University Press, 1936. A fine edition that includes the "Induction" and the unfinished "Epilogue." An informative introduction is included.

Swart, John B. *Thomas Sackville: A Study in Sixteenth-Century Poetry*. Folcroft, Pa.: Folcroft Library Editions, 1976. Primarily a literary history rather than a critical study, this book gives a good appraisal of Sackville. A biographical chapter is followed by chapters on sixteenth century poetry in general and how to approach it, Sackville's technique, and an assessment of his work. A bibliography is appended.

Vanhoutte, Jacqueline. "Community, Authority, and the Motherland in Sackville and Norton's *Gorboduc*." *Studies in English Literature, 1500-1900* 40, no. 2 (Spring, 2000): 227-239. Thomas Sackville and Thomas Norton's *Gorboduc* urges Elizabeth I to accept parliamentary advice by marrying, providing an heir, and ensuring the stability of England. Vanhoutte argues that the play renders this advice emotionally legitimate by advancing the claims of what it calls the "mother land," and in the process, the play questions dynastic notions of community.

Zim, Rivakah. "Dialogue and Discretion: Thomas Sackville, Catherine de Medici and the Anjou Marriage Proposal 1571." *The Historical Journal* 40, no. 2 (June, 1997): 287-310. Sackville's previously unpublished letters of his secret interview with Catherine de Medici concerning the 1571 Anjou marriage proposal exploit the actuality of dramatic dialogue beyond the normal use of diplomatic correspondence.

_______. "'Sacvyles Olde Age': A Newly Discovered Poem by Thomas Sackville, Lord Buckhurst, Earl of Dorset." *The Review of English Studies* 40, no. 157 (February, 1989): 1. "Sacvyles Olde Age," the "newly discovered" poem, seems to have been written later than Sackville's other known works.

Richard J. Panofsky;
bibliography updated by the editors

Saʿdi

Born: Shiraz, Persia; c. 1200
Died: Shiraz, Persia; c. 1291

Principal poetry

Bustan, 1257 (*The Orchard*, 1882)
Gulistan, 1258 (*The Rose Garden*, 1806)
Ghazals, thirteenth century
Khabisat, thirteenth century
Qasidas, thirteenth century
Rubáiyát, thirteenth century
Kolliyat Saʿdi, 1963

Other literary forms

Saʿdi wrote a number of prose tracts of minor significance, and *The Rose Garden* and the *Khabisat* are part prose. The prose of *The Rose Garden* has long been considered a model of Persian writing, while three scandalous mock-homilies in the *Khabisat* exhibit another side of Sa'di.

Achievements

One of Persia's great poets, sometimes called the greatest, Sa'di is venerated as almost a saint in his homeland, where his works are read alongside the Koran and where he is fondly referred to as Shaykh Sa'di or, for short, the Shaykh. Sa'di is also the best-known Persian poet in the West, except possibly for Omar Khayyám, whose one work (*Rubáiyát*, c. twelfth century; *The Rubáiyát of Omar Khayyám*, 1859) hardly compares with Sa'di's extensive and varied output. The English-speaking world became acquainted with Sa'di before it did with Omar Khayyám: Persian was the official language of India when the British arrived, and British officials used Sa'di's *The Rose Garden* as a language text. *The Rose Garden* was translated repeatedly into English during the nineteenth century—in expurgated versions still read as accurate texts (the Victorians were especially shocked by Sa'di's casual acceptance of pederasty, a common, albeit illegal, practice in the Persia of his day). Unfortunately, Sa'di has not found his own Edward FitzGerald, the superb English translator of the 1859 edition of Omar Khayyám. The best English translation of Sa'di now available is Edward Rehatsek's version of *The Rose Garden*, published in a limited edition for the Kama Shastra Society in 1888 and reissued in 1965.

As a battered survivor of difficult times, when the Muslim world was beset by Mongols on one side and Crusaders on the other (not to mention rulers at home), Sa'di still has some wisdom to offer the modern world. Sa'di's politics of survival is not the same pious wisdom he offered the Victorians, and his expedient advice might not be altogether pleasing. The literary historian Edward G. Browne called *The Rose Garden* "one of the most Machiavellian works in the Persian language" (whether he was admiring or condemning is not clear). Yet a survivor who came out singing, as Sa'di did, has something worth hearing on how to retain one's humanity through it all. Sa'di's humanity reverberates most strongly in *The Orchard* and *The Rose Garden*—even if, in translation, the singing is rather faint.

Biography

There are numerous entertaining stories about Sa'di's life, many from his own works, but their accuracy is uncertain. A few miraculous stories are obviously saints' legends, while others have a suspiciously legendary cast, such as the symmetrical division of his life into thirty years of study, thirty years of travel, and thirty years of writing (some versions stretch this last period out to forty, fifty, or sixty years). In the preface to *The Rose Garden*, Sa'di says that he took stock of his wasted life and settled down around the age of fifty, but he also says that his fame as a writer was already widespread. The unembellished truth about Sa'di is hard to establish, but what follows is a compendium of generally accepted information.

Sa'di's real name was apparently Mosharrif od-Din bin Moslih od-Din Abdullah, Sa'di being a *takhallus* (pen name) adopted from the Atabeg rulers of Fars Province, Sa'd bin Zangi, his son Abu Bakr bin Sa'd, and his grandson Sa'd bin Abu Bakr. Effusive flattery of rulers then was commonplace, even necessary for survival, since, as *The Orchard* and *The Rose Garden* show, these rulers were as capricious as they were powerful. Sa'di also perhaps had reason to feel genuine gratitude. Apparently Sa'di's father, a minor court official, died when Sa'di was a child, and Sa'd bin Zangi supported Sa'di's education, first at Shiraz and then at the Nizamiya College in Baghdad. According to *The Orchard*, Sa'di also held a fellowship at the Nizamiya College which required him to slave away at instructing. Possibly it was such an existence which encouraged him to become a mendicant dervish and trust his fortunes to the open road, although the invasion of the Mongol hordes in the 1220's might have influenced his decision to travel.

During his wanderings, Sa'di traveled to North Africa, Ethiopia, Palestine, Syria, Armenia, Arabia, India, and throughout the provinces of Persia. His adventures and the resulting lore are documented in *The Orchard* and *The Rose Garden*. In Palestine, he was captured by the Crusaders and put to work fortifying Tripoli (now in Lebanon). He was ransomed by an Aleppo friend, whose shrewish daughter he married (it proved to be a bad trade). Later Sa'di also married a woman in Arabia, who bore him a child who died. He made several pilgrimages to Mecca (the legendary number is fourteen).

In the early 1250's, Saʿdi returned to Shiraz to settle down alone, impelled by a sense of urgency: His own life was slipping away, and the eastern Muslim world was crumbling under another Mongol invasion. Before either event occurred, Saʿdi wanted to write what he knew, so in relative seclusion at Shiraz, he sat down to compose *The Orchard* and *The Rose Garden*. Shiraz was somewhat safe from the Mongol invasion, since the Fars rulers had made peace by bowing down and kissing the feet of the invaders. Baghdad, the political and cultural center of the eastern Muslim world, had no such luck; in 1258, the Mongols overran the city, slaughtering a million and a half inhabitants. Saʿdi wrote a famous lament on the occasion. At approximately the same time, he brought out *The Orchard* and *The Rose Garden*.

Analysis

In his best-known writings, *The Orchard* and *The Rose Garden*, Saʿdi is clearly working within a long and distinguished tradition, an Eastern tradition of didactic literature wherein the poet is also a teacher. Drawing on both literary and folk sources, and forming a symbiotic relationship with religion, this tradition usually brings forth a conventional product. Such is not the case with Saʿdi. He is entertaining because he is able to draw on an additional source, his own nomadic experiences that he somehow survived. Thus, Saʿdi is able to infuse his conventional wisdom with lively examples. At the same time, there is this danger involved: The examples set up a tension with the conventional wisdom, sometimes undercutting it and resulting not in morality but in expediency. The same result can be observed in his language and tone, which occasionally verge on parody, Saʿdi getting carried away and letting a devilish streak emerge.

In his writing as well as in his travels, Saʿdi liked to live dangerously. He obviously managed to satisfy the conventional expectations of his contemporaries, but for the modern reader the tension between the pious and the politic Saʿdi forms the main attraction of his work.

The Orchard

Written in epic meter throughout, *The Orchard* is divided into ten sections. Each section illustrates a particular public or private virtue—for example, good government, generosity, humility, resignation, contentment, gratitude—through a collection of brief stories, mostly exempla but occasionally parables and fables. Otherwise disconnected, the stories do provide a variety of content, including the author's own purported experiences.

In the few stories where he figures, Saʿdi does not hesitate to make himself a hero. For example, at a dinner put on by a *cadi* (a Muslim judge), Saʿdi is forced to sit among the inferior guests because of his impoverished appearance. In the legal disputations that follow, Saʿdi dominates, and the *cadi* takes off his fine turban, offers it to Saʿdi, and invites Saʿdi to sit among the lawyers and other guests of honor. Saʿdi turns down both offers and leaves, telling the *cadi* that it is what one has inside one's head rather than what one wears on it that matters. There is a further irony, directed at himself, in Saʿdi's references to the *cadi*'s big head, for Saʿdi was not modest about his own gifts; in the tag on a story advocating reticence (one of his favorite virtues), he advises the reader either to speak like Saʿdi or to remain silent.

Yet even Saʿdi opens his mouth once too often in another story set in India. In the midst of a temple crowd worshiping an idol, Saʿdi comments to a friend concerning the crowd's naïve superstition. The friend, however, proves to be a true believer himself, and he angrily denounces Saʿdi to the assembly. The crowd falls upon Saʿdi, and he saves himself only through fast talking and dissimulation. Pleading that he is an ignorant foreigner, he asks to be initiated into the true meaning of the worship. The chief Brahmin forces him to spend the night weeping, praying, and kissing the statue. In the morning, the statue rewards him and other worshipers by raising its hand. Several days later, when he is trusted, Saʿdi goes into the temple, slips behind the scenes, and discovers the chief Brahmin working the levers which operate the statue's hands. Saʿdi then kills the Brahmin by throwing him down a well and dropping a rock onto his head. The moral is: Once one exposes a villain, one must destroy him; if not, he will destroy you.

Similar advice is available for dealing with one's enemies. The general drift of Saʿdi's urgings is to remain quiet and not to make enemies, especially of people with power or wagging tongues. If, despite all one's caution, an enemy arises, one should take the first good opportunity to dash out his brains; such dealings improve not only one's predicament but also one's disposition. Saʿdi does warn, however, against lowering oneself to the level of one's enemy. Lastly, if a dangerous enemy is too powerful to handle, one should flee.

A number of Saʿdi's stories contain not only irony but also what would today be called black humor. The fortunes of a rich man and a beggar are reversed; a doctor who predicts a patient's imminent death dies himself instead, and the patient lives to a ripe old age; a haughty prince is ungrateful to a physician who cures him, so the physician returns him to his former state. In a cat fable, a discontented cat learns contentment by leaving home and becoming a target for archers. The wages of gluttony are illustrated by a fat man who climbs a date tree, falls out, and dies. A sultan, who feels pity for a shivering night watchman standing in the rain and snow, promises to send his fur coat out to the watchman. The sultan returns inside to the warm arms of his favorite harem girl and promptly forgets his promise. Repentance is demonstrated by the story of a man who rejoices over the death of his enemy—until he tears open the enemy's grave and sees the decaying corpse.

Aside from Saʿdi's slightly warped wisdom, part of the appeal of *The Orchard* is the apparently random juxtaposition of stories, offering not only variety but also contrast. Irony and black humor alternate with heavy moralizing. Stories of pleasant comedy about a polite but stingy host, for example, or about a newly groomed warrior who gets ashes dumped on his head and reflects that he deserved the fire, alternate with stories of sorrow or tragedy—for example, about a strong warrior whose will is broken, or about the death of Saʿdi's child. If the mood of one story does not satisfy, the reader may go on to the next. If Saʿdi seems to be laying on the conventional wisdom too heavily, then he is probably preparing a surprise. The random juxtaposition of material gives *The Orchard* the rough, unplotted texture of experience itself. Thus, there is wisdom embodied in the form as well as the content of *The Orchard*.

The Rose Garden

The Rose Garden is the same type of work as *The Orchard* and is organized along the same lines, with collections of anecdotes supposedly illustrating certain virtues or topics. There are eight chapters in all. A number of the headings overlap those in *The Orchard*, and, as in *The Orchard*, some of the stories do not particularly fit their headings. There, however, similarities of form end. *The Rose Garden* is written partly in prose, partly in verse of various kinds, mostly in Persian but containing passages of Arabic (including quotations from the Koran). *The Rose Garden* has a larger element of conventional lore, often displayed in striking comparisons, and is more heavily interlarded with commentary, usually taking the form of a pungent verse or two. The final chapter consists not of anecdotes but entirely of maxims and admonitions. If *The Orchard* offers an entertaining variety of content, *The Rose Garden* offers a delightful hodgepodge of content and form.

Some of the content recalls *The Orchard*. There is a long chapter on the behavior of kings, another long chapter on the behavior of dervishes, and contentment and silence are again treated. The morality likewise resembles that of *The Orchard*. For example, Saʿdi gives some familiar advice on revenge: One should take it at the first good opportunity, even if that means biding one's time for a while. In chapter 1, a brutal soldier hits a dervish on the head with a rock. The pious dervish saves the rock until the soldier falls out of favor with the king and is imprisoned in a well, then throws the rock down onto the soldier's head. The first story of *The Rose Garden* endorses well-intentioned lying; other stories warn against trusting one's friends too much.

In general, however, the tone of *The Rose Garden* is lighter than that of *The Orchard, The Rose Garden* containing more humor. An example is the story of Saʿdi's capture by the Crusaders. A friend from Aleppo ransoms Saʿdi for ten dinars, then pays Saʿdi a dowry of a hundred dinars to marry his daughter. Later, the woman turns shrewish and spitefully reminds Saʿdi of his rescue by her father. Saʿdi replies that, yes, it cost her father ten dinars to free him from the Crusaders but one hundred dinars to bind him to her. Besides male-female relationships, another source of humor is the bad voices of singers and muezzins. One muezzin who performs his office gratis is paid to go elsewhere, and a singing dervish cures Saʿdi of the frivolous desire to attend dervish parties. Aphorisms, epigrams, and folk sayings are still another source of humor; the following saying is typical: When the scorpion was asked why he did not come out in winter, he replied, "What renown do I have in summer that I should also come out in winter?"

A number of stories contain a combination of humor and irony, particularly a group stressing the relativity of everything. A boy afraid of being aboard a ship learns to love it after he is thrown into the ocean; after seeing a man without feet, Saʿdi feels happier about not having shoes; he also concludes it is better to beg than to have your hand cut off for stealing. A long story about a young man who sets off to make his fortune, but runs into numerous misfortunes, is reminiscent of the discontented cat fable in *The Orchard*; the young man returns home much more contented.

There is nothing funny, however, about many of the stories in *The Rose Garden*, including those in which Saʿdi's attempts at humor are askew, as in his bigotry toward Jews and blacks. Such bigotry is a reminder that Saʿdi lived in a harsh age when people could be, and often were, disposed of as objects. This attitude appears in a number of stories, as in the one in which a drunken king, whose advances were refused by a Chinese slave girl, turns her over to a black slave to ravish (after which the king wants to kill them both). In a time when the Mongols could raze the city of Baghdad and butcher its million and a half inhabitants, it is not surprising that Saʿdi should occasionally share such an attitude. What is surprising is that he should so often rise above it. While the Christians were mounting crusades to tame the infidels, Saʿdi, in *The Orchard* and *The Rose Garden*, was helping his age and subsequent ages define once again what it means to be human.

Bibliography

Barks, Coleman. *The Hand of Poetry: Five Mystic Poets of Persia*. New Lebanon, N.Y.: Omega, 1993. Translations of Sufi poetry, including lectures on Persian literature by Inayat Khan.

Ernst, Carl W. *The Shambhala Guide to Sufism*. Boston: Shambhala, 1997. A reference guide to classical and modern Sufi poetry and Sufism. Includes a summary of Saʿdi's work on the morals of the dervishes from *The Rose Garden* to show the various characteristics of an Islamic mystic in the classical sense. Glossary.

Motaghed, Ehsan. *What Says Saadi*. Tehran, Iran: 1986. An eighty-six page book collecting translated quotations and explanations that shed light on Saʿdi's philosophical themes embedded in his poetry.

Yohannan, John D. *The Poet Saʿdi: A Persian Humanist*. Lanham, Md.: University Press of America, 1987. A critical appraisal of Saʿdi as a Sufi poet, reminding the reader to avoid reading Saʿdi's narrative tales as didactic Aesopian fables because that would strip them of the multifaceted complexities of Sufi poetry. Bibliography, index.

Harold Branam;
bibliography updated by Mabel Khawaja

David St. John

Born: Fresno, California; July 24, 1949

Principal poetry

Hush, 1976
The Olive Grove, 1980
The Shore, 1980
The Man in the Yellow Gloves: A Poem, 1984
No Heaven, 1985
The Orange Piano, 1987
Terraces of Rain: An Italian Sketchbook, 1991
Study for the World's Body: New and Selected Poems, 1994
In the Pines: Lost Poems, 1972-1997, 1998
The Red Leaves of Night, 1999

Other literary forms

In addition to his own poetry, St. John has contributed to the translation of *God's Shadow: Prison Poems* (1976), by the Iranian poet Reza Baraheni. In 1995, St. John recorded one of his own poems, *Black Poppy*. His essays and interviews are published in *Where the Angels Come Toward Us: Selected Essays, Reviews, and Interviews* (1995). This volume is valuable because it contains six important interviews with St. John spanning the years from 1976 to 1994, in which he talks of his own poetry extensively and explains his poetic principles.

Achievements

In his relatively brief career, St. John has received considerable attention and numerous awards. His poems have appeared in more than three dozen anthologies and textbooks. His prose, which includes profiles of other writers, reviews, and critical essays, has been included in nearly twenty essay collections. In 1975, he received the Discovery prize from *The Nation*, and for his first poetry collection, *Hush*, he won the Great Lakes College Association New Writers award (1976). The National Endowment for the Arts awarded him fellowships in 1976, 1984, and again in 1994-1995. The American Academy of Arts and Letters awarded him a Rome Fellowship in 1984. He won a John Simon Guggenheim Fellowship for a year in 1978 and received a grant from the Ingram Merrill Foundation. His second poetry collection, *The Shore*, won the James D. Phelan Prize in 1980. Four years later, St. John was awarded a Prix de Rome fellowship in literature. *Study for the World's Body* was nominated for the National Book Award in Poetry, and two other volumes, *In the Pines* and *The Red Leaves of Night*, were nominated for the Los Angeles Times Book Prize in Poetry in 1999. St. John also contributes both poetry and critical essays regularly to a number of major periodicals, including *The New Yorker*, *Antaeus*, *Georgia Review*, *The New Republic*, and *Poetry*.

Biography

David St. John was born in Fresno, California, in 1949, into a family of accomplished individuals. His early years were strongly influenced by members of his family. His grandfather was an English professor and academic dean, and his father coached basketball and track and was a highly skilled tennis player. An uncle also played professional tennis. David himself was raised to be a tennis player, playing competitively from the age of seven until he was fifteen. He considers this training to have been excellent preparation for a career as a writer because it required him to be solitary and taught him tremendous self-discipline and psychological adroitness. At home, his father would read to David from the classics. The boy's favorite text was the opening of Vergil's *Aeneid* (c. 19 B.C.E.), but he also loved Robert Louis Stevenson's *Treasure Island* (1881-1882) and other modern fiction.

Another important aspect of St. John's early years was his interest in music. From the age of eight, he received piano lessons and began reading the jazz magazine *Downbeat*. In junior high and high school, his interest in folk music in the 1960's led to his playing in rock bands. He later admitted that these bands were not very good, but the experience gave him excellent training in combining music with language and performing.

St. John began his higher education at California State University, Fresno in 1967, earning a bachelor of arts degree in 1972. He enrolled at the University of Iowa in Iowa City and received a masters of fine arts degree from that institution in 1974. A paternal aunt who was a painter had already introduced the young David to the visual arts, but he discovered that his talents lay not in painting but in literature. Nevertheless, he spent much of his time in college among painters and sculptors, who taught him to see the visual arts for their materiality and physicality and made him want to incorporate the density and plasticity of sculpture and painting into the language of poetry. In these formative years he also became interested in film.

St. John married Bonnie Bedford in 1968 and with her had a son; they were divorced in 1974. From 1975 to 1977, St. John taught as an assistant professor of English at Oberlin College in Ohio, then transferred to The Johns Hopkins University in Baltimore, Maryland, in

David St. John (Bruno Jarret)

1977, teaching in writing seminars there for the next ten years. During this period, St. John served as assistant poetry editor for *The Iowa Review* (1974-1975) and associate editor for *Field* (1975-1977). He served as an editor for *Seneca Review* from 1977 to 1981 and began as poetry editor-at-large for the *Antioch Review* in 1981, in which capacity he would serve until 1995.

In 1987, St. John accepted a professorship in English at the University of Southern California, Los Angeles, where he also would serve as Director of Creative Writing. In 1990 he was married again, this time to poet Molly Bendall, and three years later they had a daughter, Vivienne. As the child grew, St. John would read Old English poems and ballads to her, in this way returning to one of his favorite literary genres, which would influence his own poetry later. Molly broadened his musical interest, which by now included classical music and jazz, by introducing him to the music of other nations. He particularly enjoyed the work of Indian musician Jai Uttal. He and his family moved into a house in Venice, California. This area, whose former residents included members of the pop-rock band The Eagles and rock musician Jim Morrison of The Doors, proved to be well suited to St. John's musical and literary tastes and pursuits. Venice retained much of the culture of the 1960's and 1970's and provided a compatible atmosphere in which St. John could both relax and write.

St. John has also been a visiting scholar at the Getty Research Institute for the History of Art and the Humanities. His contributions to literary magazines have been unstinting, and he is popular as the subject of interviews because he is articulate and his knowledge of contemporary poetry and literary history is extensive as well.

Analysis

Hush

In his first collection of poems, *Hush*, St. John established himself as a master of the musical line and vivid image. He uses details to create both mood and scenic clarity. More often than not, he imbues his imagery with shadows that suggest sadness, as in these lines from "For Georg Trakl":

> Your face,
> so pale now it is blue.
> And in the icy, dead moons
> of your eyes, the things you
> loved are trembling; all
> utterly blue . . .

Most of the poems depict relationships between men and women, with the woman as the focus. In one poem, the woman is the bearer of the poet's child; in another, she beckons from a hotel terrace. "For Lerida" offers a snapshot of a woman with "bruises, shadowed pink/ with make-up, around her eyes." Throughout the book, intimacy or fulfillment with a woman is seldom achieved. The focus is mainly on loss and separation, but the sadness of thc poems is held in check by the way St. John entwines images of beauty with fluid rhythms and a graceful of style. One critic noted that St. John speaks so often of absences that he makes them an actual presence in the poems. In the title poem "Hush," St. John himself illustrates the point in the poem's final line, speaking of his son: "The dark watermark of your absence, a hush." The sincerity of such lines and obvious effort to capture something ineffable in the experience are compelling elements in all of St. John's poems.

The Shore

In *The Shore*, the opposition between what the reader feels and understands and what the poet means to say and do becomes the subject of many of the poems, albeit metaphorically. The opposition between men and women, for example, may be viewed as a metaphor of the reader-poet opposition. In the descriptions of natural scenery, people, or situations, an opposition is implicit between what the poet sees and what he wishes to see. The image of the shore, which gives the book its title, implies this opposition, sea and land, which are, paradoxically, unified by the image. "Blue Waves" epitomizes many of the features that recur throughout this volume of poems, the focus on the female and her relationship with the speaker. The woman remains a vague, idealized presence:

> the red falls
> Of your hair rocking . . . framed by an
> open window. . . .

Again, St. John speaks of the woman's leaving. The poem concludes with the speaker imagining himself looking back "To these mornings, islands—/ The balance of the promise with what lasts." The irony here is that these mornings are marked by factory smokestacks, the sound of diesels, and the realization that the woman "left a husband,/ And I a son."

In other poems, the speaker looks ahead to a time when he will reflect nostalgically on the present time, which is fraught with tension and possible separation. In "Hotel Sierra," for example, he says:

> Next week, as you step out
> Of the darkroom with the glossy proofs . . . we
> Will have become only a few gestures
> Placed out of time.

In many of the poems, moments such as these entwine a woman, a place, a time, and the whole nexus is filled with longing, loneliness, and lost love.

No Heaven

The poems in *No Heaven* show a mastery of the narrative that surfaces in the previous volumes only occasionally. In other ways, too, St. John shows the full maturity of his talents, alternating short and longer lines, letting the poem's subject determine stanzaic structure, breaking lines in two and dropping the second part to the next line, and sometimes abandoning the use of commas, periods, and other end marks altogether, even at the end of the poem. The effect of such techniques is to suggest that the poem is unconfined, like thought itself.

The book's centerpiece is a narrative poem that fills seven pages, "The Man in the Yellow Gloves," which St. John also published separately in a limited edition. The poem recounts the story of a man whose hands are so disfigured by an accidental fire that he hides them with a pair of gloves. The gloves and hands together symbolize the union of the injured man and his grandfather, who owned a similar pair of gloves. Thus, the accident fosters a generational bond. The gloves also bond the speaker to the landscape:

> I have only to take off one glove
> Or another to stare down into the landscape
> Of each scorched stitched hand. . . .

Symbolically, he drapes the past over the present, both hiding it and beautifying it.

Terraces of Rain

This volume represents a departure in St. John's development as a poet in that many of the poems focus on art and Italian settings. The book is even designed like a sketchbook, wider than it is tall, and comes with colored drawings. Though many of the poems are about paintings, many are word portraits of people and depict the male and female together. The terrain of these poems is as much physical and sexual as it is artistic and geographical. The forms shift from terza rima to the villanelle to rhymed couplets, but much of St. John's creative energy, as before, is devoted to describing the women he encounters. This is a travelogue of tempting encounters, of temptresses and temporary relationships, of vivid but fleeting impressions, richly textured and expansive in their imagery, as in the description of a painting: "An angel whose scalloped, florid wings opened/ With a peacock's iridescence. . . ."

Study for the World's Body and In the Pines

St. John's next two volumes cover approximately the same poetic territory, with the exception that *Study for the World's Body* adds ten new poems and a nine-page poem that consists of parallel poems placed side by side on each page, each balancing and opposing the other in subject and style. The sequence of poems throughout both books exhibits St. John's mastery of image, rhythm, narrative, and portraiture, all with verbal fluency and highly skilled use of complex grammatical forms. One of the principal images of this collection of poems is that of the dance, which is a metaphor of life's journey.

"Slow Dance" develops the image through long, sinuous lines that describe various motions people make with their feet, bodies, clothing. St. John paces the music of his lines with pauses and syllables:

> . . . & we begin
> Once more to move: Place to place. Hand
> To smoother & more lovely hand. A slow dance. To get
> along.

The poet's persona is that of a young man mooning about the streets of a city thinking of his absent lover; his imagination has become securely fixed on a romantic, idealized beauty that is found in women, music, and the landscape. If physical love is passing, as many of the poems suggest, the mind's power to see beauty and feel love is the spirit's salvation.

The Red Leaves of Night

The tone as well as the subject of this volume is reflected in some titles, "Nocturnes and Aubades," "Rhapsody," "Fleurs Mystiques," "Mystic Eyes," "Prayer to Ondine," and "Solitude." Sorrow and yearning give the poems an elegiac cast, but the gloom is never so dark that it obscures the brilliant portraits, landscapes, or settings. St. John has dropped virtually all punctuation marks, using capitals only at the beginnings of the lines and occasionally elsewhere, using line length again to regulate the flow of thought and emotion. His affection for the landscape has been apparent from his first collection, and here his eye for the character of a place is everywhere evident. He constructs his images with a sharp focus, as in "Red Wheat: Montana":

> The magnificent hair . . .
> The blank of curls . . .
> A ragged field of red wheat clipped & bundles at harvest . . .

Such details imbue the subject with the evocative power of nature and impart some of the woman's allure to the natural landscape; both are thereby enriched. It is obvious that St. John loves language, but music is also essential to his vision and his art: "It became my passion to explain everything / With music . . . ," he says in the opening of one poem ("Music"). This volume, like the ones before it, proves that he has succeeded.

Other major works

nonfiction: *Where the Angels Come Toward Us: Selected Essays, Reviews, and Interviews*, 1995.

translation: *God's Shadow: Prison Poems*, 1976 (with others; of Reza Baraheni's poetry).

Bibliography

Plumly, Stanley. "Of Lyricism, Verbal Energy, the Sonnet, and Gallows Humor." *The Washington Post Book World*, November 2, 1980, pp. 10-13. In his review of St. John's *The Shore*, Plumly singles out some perceived defects in several poems but in the end gives the collection high praise.

Publishers Weekly. Review of *Study for the World's Body: New and Selected Poems*. 241 (June 27, 1994): 66-67. Studies the use of imagery and rhythmic lines and their relation to the metaphor of dance in several of St. John's poems, turning then to poems in which narrative, language, and imagination play a major role.

Roberts, Katrina. "David St. John's *Study for the World's Body*." *Agni Reviews* 41 (1995): 206-211. Roberts discusses St. John's style and the cohesive elements in this collection, such as his elegiac tone and psychological realism.

Shoaf, Diann Blakely. Review of *Terraces of Rain*. *Southern Humanities Review* 27 (Winter, 1993): 93-96. Shoaf comments on St. John's narrative skills, his Italian subjects in this collection, and his technical mastery.

Stitt, Peter. "Poets Witty and Elegiac." *The New York Times Book Review* 90 (September 1, 1985): 11. Reviewing *No Heaven*, Stitt discusses St. John's subjects and themes and his psychological poems.

Tillinghast, Richard. Review of *Study for the World's Body*. *Poetry* 166 (August, 1995): 290-292. Tillinghast looks at St. John's poems as expressions of a romantic rhapsody, comparing them to the lyrics found in songs written by rock musicians.

Bernard E. Morris

Pedro Salinas

Born: Madrid, Spain; November 27, 1891
Died: Boston, Massachusetts; December 4, 1951

Principal poetry

Presagios, 1923
Seguro azar, 1929 (*Certain Chance*, 2000)
Fábula y signo, 1931
La voz a tí debida, 1933 (*My Voice Because of You*, 1976)
Razón de amor, 1936
Largo lamento, 1936-1938
Lost Angel and Other Poems, 1938
Truth of Two and Other Poems, 1940
El contemplado, 1946 (*The Sea of San Juan: A Contemplation*, 1950)

Todo más claro y otros poemas, 1949
Confianza, 1955
Poesías completas, 1971
To Live in Pronouns, 1974

OTHER LITERARY FORMS

Although Pedro Salinas's reputation is based primarily upon his poetry, which forms the bulk of his work, he also wrote literary criticism, essays, translations, short stories, a novel, and plays. Through his literary criticism and essays, he contributed significantly to an understanding of the process of literary creation and to the appreciation of particular Spanish authors. His critical masterpiece, *Reality and the Poet in Spanish Poetry* (1940), contains six essays which focus on six different Spanish poets from medieval times to the nineteenth century. Salinas attempts to capture and comprehend the main theme of each author's work by assessing his attitudes toward reality. The variety and scope of Salinas's interpretations are also evident in his celebrated studies of the *Modernista* poet Rubén Darío and the medieval poet Jorge Manrique, and in the two published collections of his articles: *Literatura española: Siglo XX* (1941, 1949; twentieth century Spanish literature) and *Ensayos de literatura hispánica: Del "Cantar de mío Cid" a García Lorca* (1958; essays in Hispanic literature: from "Poem of the Cid" to García Lorca).

In contrast to his poetry and literary criticism, which he wrote and published throughout his creative years, Salinas's narrative prose represents the work of two distinct periods: his early beginnings as a writer and his final years. The early works are extremely lyric and impressionistic, almost like poems in prose, and they contain the same themes ever prominent in his poetry: love, illusion, fate, the poet. The later short stories represent a marked development in Salinas's narrative art. Each possesses a complex plot in which he combines lyricism, mystery, irony, humor, and criticism of the modern world. Salinas's only novel, *La bomba increíble* (1950; the incredible bomb), develops his concern about the ominous contemporary possibility: the destruction of the world by the atomic bomb. This allegorical satire of modern life ends, however, with the triumph of love.

Pedro Salinas

Salinas's plays (two three-act plays and twelve one-act plays) are the fruit of his mature years. With respect to their content, they, like the narratives, are for the most part an extension of his poetic work. Of particular significance are the themes of communication, love, brotherhood, illusion versus reality, human happiness, the poetic imagination, and the dehumanization of modern humankind.

ACHIEVEMENTS

Pedro Salinas, the eldest member of the celebrated *generación del 27*, or Generation of '27, was a leader in its vigorous revival of Spain's poetic past. He and his contemporaries successfully renewed appreciation of Spain's lyric tradition and fused this wealthy heritage with contemporary literary trends: The result was a second golden age of poetry in Spain. Although the Spanish Civil War (1936-1939) led to the disruption and displacement of the Generation of '27, Salinas flourished in exile and continued to stimulate interest in Spanish literature—not only as a poet but also as a teacher and critic.

Biography

Jorge Guillén, poet, critic, and intimate friend of Pedro Salinas, divided Salinas's sixty years into thirty years of preparation and thirty years of production. The early years Salinas spent in Madrid, obtaining his primary education from the Colegio Hispano-Francés, his secondary education at the Instituto San Isidro, and his licentiate degree in romance philology from the University of Madrid (1913). He then left for Paris and the Sorbonne, where from 1914 to 1917 he taught Spanish literature and completed his doctoral dissertation on the illustrators of Miguel Cervantes' *Don Quixote de la Mancha* (1605, 1615). While in Paris, he married Margarita Bonmatí; they later had two children. During the years in Paris, Salinas came into contact with many of the prominent writers and literary trends of the time. These modern influences, in combination with an attachment to the Spanish literary tradition, are evident in his poetry and in that of the other members of the Generation of '27.

Salinas was the oldest of this group of poets, whose prominent members include Rafael Alberti, Vicente Aleixandre, Dámaso Alonso, Manuel Altolaguirre, Luis Cernuda, Jorge Guillén, Federico García Lorca, and Emilio Prados. The Generation of '27 (sometimes referred to as the Generation of 1927—the year of the three-hundredth anniversary of the death of Golden Age poet Luis de Góngora y Argote) was responsible for rehabilitating the reputation of Góngora, for many years considered a writer of mostly obscure and frivolously ornate poetry. The revival of Góngora was indicative of the renewed appreciation of Spain's literary past which, fused with a variety of vanguardist currents—Symbolism, *Modernismo*, Creationism, pure poetry, Surrealism—characterized the works of Salinas and his contemporaries.

After his return from Paris, Salinas accepted a post as professor of Spanish literature at the University of Seville, where he taught for eight years. During that time, he published his first volume of verse, *Presagios*, translated Marcel Proust's *Á la recherche du temps perdu* (1913-1927; *Remembrance of Things Past*), contributed to numerous magazines, and published two critical editions and his early prose sketches. Also, he spent one year as a lecturer on Spanish literature at Cambridge University.

Salinas then moved to Madrid and worked as a researcher in Spain's Center for Historical Studies. There, in the country's literary center, he thrived on closer associations with his contemporaries. He taught at the University of Madrid and in 1933 founded the International Summer University of Santander. All the while, his reputation as a poet was growing. By 1936, he had published his famous love poetry along with numerous scholarly studies.

In 1936, after the outbreak of the Spanish Civil War, Salinas taught at Wellesley College as a visiting professor. Thus began his permanent exile from his native land and the period of his most prolific creative output. During the last fifteen years of his life, Salinas produced two more volumes of poetry, his finest literary criticism, his plays, a novel, and short stories. In 1940, he was appointed Turnbull Professor of Hispanic Literature at The Johns Hopkins University in Baltimore, Maryland, a position he held until his death. He spent summers at Middlebury College in Vermont and lectured at universities throughout the United States and South America.

Salinas was a very cosmopolitan man, stimulated by all sorts of intellectual currents. At the same time, he felt an attachment to classical tradition and culture and, in his later years, a strong nostalgia for his native Spain. He was an extremely cordial man, who was devoted to his family, loved by his students, and involved in close friendships, yet he was also a profoundly private person, who attempted to penetrate the varied experiences of life through literary creation. A deeply spiritual orientation is evident in all his works, but particularly in his poetry, the most profound expression of his concern with the nature of reality, the creative process, love, and existence in the modern world.

Analysis

Pedro Salinas's nine volumes of poetry can be divided into three groups, with each group representing a stage in his poetic development. In *Presagios* (presages), *Certain Chance*, and *Fábula y signo* (fable and sign), the poet reflects seriously on his inner and outer world, preoccupied with the creative process and with the deceptive nature of reality. The second period is his love cycle, for which he is best known: *My Voice Be-*

cause of You, *Razón de amor* (love's reason), and *Largo lamento*. The final three volumes make up the poetic production of Salinas in exile. *The Sea of San Juan: A Contemplation*, composed during the two especially happy years he spent in Puerto Rico, is a love-filled portrayal of the Caribbean Sea. *Todo más claro y otros poemas* (all more clear and other poems) combines the poet's positive reflections on the art of poetry with his anguish over the ravages of war, uncontrolled technology, and other aspects of modern life. *Confianza* (confidences) continues these themes, but here Salinas also communicates his hope and confidence in the future. Although differences of style and focus can be seen in the three phases, they overlap considerably, and there is no doubt that the poetry of Salinas forms an integral whole, in a voice that intensifies from *Presagios* to *Confianza*.

The poems of the first stage show Salinas's early attempts to come to terms with the act of creating poetry. The poet must face material reality, internalize it, and somehow transform it into a purer, more external reality. In the poem "Suelo" ("Soil"), for example, the soil or ground represents external reality. In a simple chain of connections, Salinas links it with artistic creation and with a newer, more permanent vision: "on the soil the feet are planted," "on the feet the body erect," "on the body the head firm," "in the lee of the forehead, pure idea," "in the pure idea, the tomorrow, the key—tomorrow—eternal." Yet the process is far from simple. Faced with the blank page, the poet finds it difficult to incorporate into a lyric experience his interior harmony and that which he perceives around him. The poem "Cuartilla" ("Sheet of Paper") illustrates this difficulty and also provides a representative example of Salinas's early style.

"Sheet of Paper"

In "Sheet of Paper," Salinas likens the writing down of one's first word to a battle. The pen is the "point of steel," "against the white." In addition to this most obvious metaphor, the poem contains a wealth of other metaphors and images which suggest whiteness and conflict and reveal the mixture of traditional and modern influences that inspired Salinas and his generation. The vocabulary is very much that of *Modernismo*, with its many indications of coldness, whiteness, flight, and opulence: "winter," "marble," "snows," "feathers," "tall columns," "flights of doves," "wings," "snowflakes," "ermines." The intertwining of metaphors and images, of paradoxical and opposing elements is reminiscent of Baroque poetry: "Light as feathers, illusive tall columns uphold roofs of white clouds"; "The snowflakes begin sudden attacks, noiseless skirmishes, snows, ermines, opposed." The "doves" are the thoughts of the poet, who stands on a border between his inner and outer worlds: "Flights of doves uncertain between white above and below, hesitant, withhold the whiteness of their wings." Finally, the pen conquers, and the word emerges, likened to "sun and dawn." The poet is engaged in a constant pursuit of clarity; the goal of poetry is to penetrate, harmonize, and illuminate internal and external reality.

"Here"

In the course of his pursuit, the poet sometimes rejoices in his discoveries. The poem "Aquí" ("Here") communicates his acceptance, exaltation, and idealization of external reality and manifests themes that will dominate his later poetry: love and the sea. The poet is completely content: "I would remain in all/ as I am, where I am;/ calm in the calm water,/ silent, deeply submerged/ in love without light." Here, he claims to require no illumination, and never to need to retreat inward: "Never shall I go from you/ in a ship with wind singing/ at the sail." Nevertheless, the poet does withdraw, because so often he beholds the illusive and deceptive nature of reality. In the poem "Pregunta más allá" ("Further Question"), the love theme is again present, and the poet questions both his loved one and himself: "Why do I ask where you are,/ if I am not blind,/ if you are not absent?" He is afraid to trust appearances, and his comparison of her body, which terminates in a voice, with a flame which rises in smoke, "in the air, impalpable," is ultimately a metaphor for what he fears will be the fate of their relationship. The skepticism, the dialogue form, the simple, almost conversational language, the images of smoke and fire, and similar opposing elements—light/shadow, clear sky/mist—reappear with intensified force in the final two stages of Salinas's poetic production.

The love cycle

Salinas's love trilogy is generally considered to be his best poetry. *My Voice Because of You* traces the history of a love relationship from its first stages to fulfillment, to separation, to a recovery of the experience by means of the poet's internalization of his past happiness. In *Razón de amor*, the poet continues to reflect upon past love. In his emotional meditations, he resolves the conflicts concerning love's illusive nature and proclaims love a permanent, redemptive reality for human existence. In *Largo lamento*, as the title suggests, some of the poet's bitterness returns. The poems of this volume foreshadow the disenchantment and preoccupation with the fragility of life that Salinas expresses in *Todo más claro y otros poemas*. Each poem of the love cycle forms an independent unit and at the same time is a part of the trilogy in its entirety.

Critics disagree on whether the poems are addressed to a real or an imaginary woman. She is never named, and all information about her is conveyed through the poet's internal consciousness. She remains quite vague, but the experiences of the poet in the love relationship are extremely vivid and deeply moving.

My Voice Because of You

One of the most beautiful poems in *My Voice Because of You* is "¡Sí, todo con exceso!" ("Yes, Too Much of Everything"), in which the poet communicates his ecstasy in the plenitude of love. A central metaphor and its numerous variations give the poem its structure: love compared with numbers. Salinas's predilection for paradox is evident in his juxtaposition of the "oneness" of love with love's infinity and freedom from all limits. There are images of ascension—"to mount up," "our slender joys . . . aloft to their height"—yet the lovers surrender "to a great uncertain depth" from which the culminating expression of love's infinity emerges: "This is nothing yet./ Look deeply at yourselves. There's more." The language is simple, often prosaic, antipoetic: "from dozens to hundreds," "from hundreds to thousands," "writing tablets, pens, machines," "ciphers," "calculations." Nevertheless, the result is poetry: "everything to multiply/ caress by caress/ embrace by wild passion." "Light" and "sea" are again present in this immeasurable experience—"too much light, life and sea/ Everything in plural,/ plural lights, lives and seas"—but gone are the more complicated metaphors and imagery of his earlier works. Salinas employs more wordplay, internal rhythm, and short phrases, but his work still possesses elegance and still makes use of traditional Spanish meters in varied combinations, in unrhymed verses, that echo Spanish Golden Age poets.

In "No quiero que te vayas" ("Sorrow, I Do Not Wish You"), the poet engages in a dialogue with his pain and desires to hold onto it as the "last form of loving." A profoundly emotional piece, the poem describes how the poet tries to cope with separation from his beloved. There are no metaphors in this poem; its tension and profundity are bound in clear, conceptual speech containing opposing elements. The poet's sorrow is the proof that his beloved once loved him: "Your truth assures me/ that nothing was untrue." He can thus live in "that crumbled reality which/ hides itself and insists/ that it never existed." In later poems, he no longer feels such anguish, but he clings to the sorrow. For example, in "¿Serás, amor?" ("Will You Be, Love?"), Salinas writes, "From the beginning, to live is to separate." He asks that love be "a long good-bye which never ends," because, for him, love is the most authentic reality: "And that the most certain, the sure is good-bye."

Eventually, the poet-protagonist reestablishes harmony in his soul. In "Pensar en ti esta noche" ("To Think of You Tonight"), he feels love rooted not only within him but also in all nature. The poem begins with his characteristic use of paradox: "To think of you tonight/ was not to think of you." Love in this poem relates to his earlier themes: It serves as a link between inner and outer reality ("An agreement of world and being"), and as a lyric inspiration ("the canticle singing for you in my heart"). The poet beholds love everywhere and believes that its omnipresence transcends even death (". . . in a love changed to stars, to quest, to the world,/ saved now from the fear/ of the corpse which remains if we forget"). This optimism prevails in the final stage of Salinas's poetic and spiritual development.

The Sea of San Juan

Salinas's last three volumes of poetry are quite different from one another in tone and content, but all reveal the poet's continued probing of the relationships between his inner and outer worlds. In *The Sea of San Juan*, Salinas speaks to the sea in what amounts to one long dialogue. The initial poem is labeled "El contempledo: Tema" ("Theme"), and it is followed by fourteen "Variaciones" ("Variations"). The poet rejoices in his beloved sea. Just as he finds spiritual harmony and permanence in love, so, too, he discovers the sea to be a symbol of everlasting beauty, life, and inspiration. The language and style are much like that found in his love poetry.

One of the central metaphors of this volume is that of the sea as the poet's light. In the fifth variation, "Pareja muy desigual" ("Pair So Unequal"), he completely surrenders to the sea's radiance "as a blindman to the hand" of his guide. The sea gives more to the poet than the poet can ever return with his glance. If the poet can hold its clarity in his eyes, "the past will never vanish." Through the sea, however, the poet recognizes his own temporality. In the fourteenth variation, "Salvación por la luz" ("Salvation Through the Light"), the poet writes, "Now, here, facing you, . . ./ I learn what I am: I am but a moment/ of that long gaze which eyes you." This does not disturb the poet, because he feels a bond with his "former brothers . . . blinded by death," who once contemplated the sea as he does now. He believes himself to be renewing their sight. Contemplation brings salvation: "perhaps your eternity,/ turned to light, will enter us through our eyes."

Todo más claro y otros poemas

The eyes of contemporary man, however, are focused elsewhere. In many of the poems of *Todo más claro y otros poemas*, Salinas denounces the destructive and dehumanizing aspects of modern life. One of the strongest expressions of Salinas's horror is his 1944 "Cero" ("Zero"), in which he prophetically envisioned nuclear holocaust (which occurred just months later in Hiroshima). This, his longest poem, depicts the annihilation of a city by a bomb dropped from a plane. The eyes of the poet overflow with tears: "Invitation to weeping. This is a plaintive cry,/ eyes, crying endlessly." With bitter irony, he narrates how the insensitive pilot, upon seeing the white clouds of destruction, is reminded of tufts of wool, of his playful childhood romps with little lambs in fields of clover. Salinas goes on to contrast what might have flowered had it not been for the tragic effects of misguided technology. His images are haunting, and they display the poet's high level of culture and continued immersion in literary tradition. After the nothingness, or "zero," falls upon everything, the poet gropes in the rubble for his dead. He finds "total shipwreck" in the sea of destruction. The desolation is overwhelming, but the poet keeps on searching. Even in this darkest of visions, the poet, in the closing stanza, finds a glimmer of hope: "I am the shadow searching the rubbish dump."

Confianza

Salinas's final volume of verse, *Confianza*, is a reaffirmation of his faith in life. His serenity returns; in "La nube que trae un viento" ("The Cloud That Bears Wind"), for example, he sings to a harmony he believes must exist: "The cloud that bears wind, the words that bring pain,/ other words cleanse those, another wind carries away." He finds this harmony in nature as seen in poems "Pájaro y radio" ("Bird and Radio"), "Nube en la mano" ("Cloud in Hand"), "¿Qué pájaros?" ("What Birds?"), and "En un trino" ("In the Trill of a Bird"). He also finds harmony in love with "Presente simple" ("Simple Present"), in art with "La estatua" ("The Statue"), and in his creation of poetry with "Ver lo que veo" ("Seeing What I See") and "Confianza" ("Confidence").

Reality and the Poet

Critics have followed Salinas's own guidance in *Reality and the Poet in Spanish Poetry* and have tried to determine the author's vision of the world by establishing his basic attitude toward reality. Their opinions differ greatly. He has been viewed as one who wavers between acceptance of reality and nothingness, as an escapist, a romantic idealist in search of the absolute, a kind of Neoplatonist, and a mystic. Those critics who point to Salinas's varying perspectives on reality are probably more correct. His works represent a synthesis of several possible attitudes toward reality: exaltation, idealization, escape, revolt, and acceptance. Yet, if one attitude can be said to prevail, it is Salinas's basic acceptance of reality. Although certain volumes convey the desire of the poet to look beyond his circumstances from a variety of perspectives, a fundamental acceptance of life is the ground note of Salinas's oeuvre.

Other major works

long fiction: *La bomba increíble*, 1950.

nonfiction: *Reality and the Poet in Spanish Poetry*, 1940; *Literatura española: Siglo XX*, 1941, rev. ed. 1949; *Jorge Manrique: O, Tradición y originalidad*, 1947; *La poesía de Rubén Darío*, 1948; *Ensayos de literatura hispánica: Del "Cantar de mío Cid" a García Lorca*, 1958.

Bibliography

Allen, Rupert C. *Symbolic Experience: A Study of Poems by Pedro Salinas*. Tuscaloosa: University of Alabama Press, 1982. A critical interpretation of selected poems by Salinas. Includes an index and bibliography.

Crispin, John. *Pedro Salinas*. New York: Twayne, 1974. An introductory biography and critical study of selected works by Salinas. Includes bibliographic references.

Newman, Jean Cross. *Pedro Salinas and His Circumstance*. San Juan, P.R.: Inter American University Press, 1983. A biography of Salinas offering a historical and cultural background of his life and works.

Shaughnessy, Lorna. *The Developing Poetic Philosophy of Pedro Salinas: A Study in Twentieth Century Spanish Poetry*. Lewiston, N.Y.: Mellen University Press, 1995. A critical analysis of the philosophy evident in Salinas's poetry. Includes bibliographical references and an index.

Stixrude, David. *The Early Poetry of Pedro Salinas*. Princeton, N.J.: Princeton University Press, 1967. A critical study of Salinas's early works. Includes bibliographic references.

Susan G. Polansky;
bibliography updated by the editors

Sonia Sanchez

Born: Birmingham, Alabama; September 9, 1934

Principal poetry

Homecoming, 1969
We a BaddDDD People, 1970
A Blues Book for Blue Black Magical Women, 1973
Love Poems, 1973
I've Been a Woman: New and Selected Poems, 1978
Homegirls and Handgrenades, 1984
Under a Soprano Sky, 1987
Wounded in the House of a Friend, 1995
Does Your House Have Lions?, 1997
Like the Singing Coming off the Drums: Love Poems, 1998
Shake Loose My Skin: New and Selected Poems, 1999

Other literary forms

Principally a poet, Sonia Sanchez has also included prose in her collections of poetry, most notably in *Homegirls and Handgrenades*. Interspersed through the four sections of poems, she includes autobiographical narratives. Other distinguished works are dramatic plays: *The Bronx Is Next* (pb. 1968, pr. 1970), *Sister Son/ji* (pb. 1969, pr. 1972), *Uh, Huh; But How Do It Free Us?* (pb. 1974, pr. 1975), *Malcolm Man/Don't Live Here No Mo'* (pr. 1979), and *Black Cats Back and Uneasy Landings* (pr. 1995). In addition, she has published speeches in *Crisis in Culture: Two Speeches by Sonia Sanchez* (1983) and stories and poems for children.

Achievements

A political activist of the 1960's Civil Rights movement, Sonia Sanchez has been recognized for her considerable poetic talents. Called "a lion in literature's forest" by poet Maya Angelou, Sanchez has authored many books. From her critically acclaimed *Homegirls and Handgrenades*, winner of the American Book Award, to her academic recognition as director of the women's studies program at Temple University, Sanchez has earned worldwide accolades for her art, which was born out of her political activism. As part of her major role in the Black Arts movement of the 1960's, she began teaching the first black studies curriculum in the United States at San Francisco State College in 1969 with fellow Black Arts movement members Askia Toure and Amiri Baraka.

A recipient of a National Endowment for the Arts Award and the Peace and Freedom Award from the Women's International League for Peace and Freedom in 1988-1989, Sanchez represents the best in American literature. In her works, she has described the struggles of people of color and other global themes, earning recognition for both her work and those humanistic ideals. Her 1997 work *Does Your House Have Lions?* was nominated for both the National Book Critics' Circle Award and the National Association for the Advancement of Colored People (NAACP) Image Award. In

2001, she was awarded the Frost Medal for distinguished lifetime service to American poetry. Sharing her poetry in Africa, Cuba, China, Norway, and Nicaragua, she has also traveled to more than five hundred U.S. universities and colleges, lecturing and providing poetry readings.

Biography

On September 9, 1934, Wilsonia Benita Driver—who later took the name Sonia Sanchez—was born to Wilson and Lena Driver in Birmingham, Alabama. A drummer in a jazz band, her father lost his wife when she and the twins she was carrying all died in childbirth. This family tragedy, occurring only a year after Sanchez's birth, resulted in tremendous upheaval for her and her older sister. Often cared for by her paternal grandmother, Sanchez grew attached to "Mama," the woman whom she credits with teaching her to read at age four and encouraging her great love of language. Describing how she used to fall to the floor laughing at her grandmother's words, Sanchez states: "I used to take the words and mull them over my tongue and give them back to her." When her grandmother died, Sanchez, at age six started to stutter. Her stuttering left her shy and somewhat isolated, but it also left her alone to write poetry, sometimes hiding it under the family's old, standing bath tub, which she was responsible for cleaning once a week.

When Sanchez was nine, her father moved the family to New York City. Living with her father and stepmother, she struggled with her shyness and stuttering. Being conscious of the rhythm of the black dialect spoken in the city streets, but not permitted in her parents' home, she absorbed a vernacular that became an important influence on her poetry. Her poetry also gave her an outlet for her dismay at family changes—including three different stepmothers—and an often-distant father.

Earning a B.A. (1955) in political science from Hunter College in Manhattan, she studied writing at New York University. After living in New York City for almost three decades, she finally decided to move to Philadelphia in 1976. She became the director of the women's studies program at Temple University in Philadelphia after teaching there beginning in 1977. A popular professor, she has won acclaim for teaching, including the Lindback Award for distinguished teaching and four honorary degrees, including a 1998 honorary doctor of humane letters from Temple and the Robert Frost Medal in poetry in 2001.

Analysis

Innovative in her use of language to convey provocative themes, Sonia Sanchez explores the various forms language takes. Using street language to lyrical haiku, she confronts and takes the reader on a metaphoric journey through both black and white America. Her political activism born in the 1960's is fused into her poetic voice and vision, as she stated in a 1999 interview: "All poets, all writers, are political." She further contends that her work has been built on her desire to change the world "for the better." Influenced by Malcolm X, a political activist along with Sanchez in Harlem, she asserts that she learned a great deal from this African American leader about language, presentation, and keeping the audience's attention. Moreover, she uses her poetry to share her vision of the world, both past and present. Integrating important figures in African American history such as Malcolm X and Martin Luther King, Jr., into her poetry, she dramatizes significant periods for her readers, both young and old, black and white.

Sanchez's poetic voice is always revealing and instructive. Elemental to her work is the articulate, engaging voice of the teacher, who with humor and technique labors to guide her students toward understanding and even revelation.

Homegirls and Handgrenades

Critically acclaimed, this significant Sanchez collection is divided into four sections: "The Power of Love," "Blues Is Bullets," "Beyond the Fallout," and "Grenades Are Not Free." The thematic opposites of rage and love, cynicism and compassion, and pain and joy coalesce in this volume.

The varying rhythmic style of the poems reflects the forms language takes in articulating diverse, sometimes conflicting, views. For example, the language of the street often labeled by Sanchez as "black English," spoken by her stepmother and her beloved grandmother, is used to describe "Poems Written After Reading Wright's

'American Hunger'": "such a simple need/ amid yo/easy desire."

In four of the poems she uses haiku, a Japanese lyric form that represents a single, concentrated image in seventeen syllables and arranged in three unrhymed lines of, traditionally, five, seven, and five syllables. Aptly named "Haiku," each poem conveys a single impression of a scene in motion: "your love was a port/ of call where many ships docked/ until morning came." In the section "Beyond the Fallout," the haiku exhibits raw anger: "I see you blackboy/ bent toward destruction watching/ for death with tight eyes."

The visionary quality of Sanchez's poem is articulated in poetic language that projects versatility because American life cannot be reflected in one homogenous voice. Sanchez uses the English vernacular to apprehend the complexity of human existence, as she states in a 1985 interview with Herbert Leibowitz: "Playing with words, as I used to, was like going outside and running and jumping over walls." As she explains further in the same interview, "A lot of my poetry expresses what it means to let people taste and feel sweetness and power running together, hate and love running together, beauty and ugliness also running together."

WE A BADDDDD PEOPLE

In the 1970 collection *We a BaddDDD People*, her political voice resonates in her poems as a way of protesting about how she could grow up in a country that did not "tell me about black history" and yet "ma[d]e me feel so inferior." In many ways her poetry becomes a way of answering those questions for herself. The discovery is certainly thematically addressed in the poem "Questions" and in the section titled "Survival." Depicting the political unrest of the period of the late 1960's, the collection has been criticized for being unoriginal in its political diatribe. However, the importance of the work in posing the political and personal questions of black existence for the poet and her readers is articulated in the following lines from "QUESTIONS": "we suicidal/ or something/ or are we all bugalooers/ of death:/ our own???" and "why they closing down/ prisons as they close off/ our blk/ minds."

The structure of the poems often represents the urgency of the poetic voice. For example, lines are fractured and split off by slashes and spaces. In "right on: wite america," the first stanza uses virgules and abbreviations:

starting july 4th is
bring in yr/guns/down/to
yr/nearest/po/lice/station/

The troubled tone of the collection, reinforcing the structure, is loud and vociferous, as in "words for our children (from their many parents)":

we are the
        screeeeeamers/
                        seaaaarcherrrs/
                                    weepeeers

Although the tone is often soul searching, the thrust of the poetry strives metaphorically to force change.

More than featuring poems of political dissent, the collection reaffirms the need for poetry, the desire to chant or even shout out one's thoughts, as exhibited in "a/coltrane/poem":

stretchen the mind
                till it bursts past the con/fines of
solo/en melodies

and concluding with the need to listen:

                        showen us life/
                                    liven.
a love supreme.
            for each
        other
    if we just
  lisssssssSSSTEN.

DOES YOUR HOUSE HAVE LIONS?

A deeply personal collection of poems that describe her brother's battle with AIDS, *Does Your House Have Lions?* captures the conflict and ultimate reconciliation among the voices identified in the sections as sister's voice, brother's voice, father's voice, and family voices/ ancestors' voices. The journey unfolds in a rime royal pattern, a stanza form consisting of seven five-stress lines in iambic pentameter with a specific rhyme pattern (*ababbcc*). This unique form of English verse, first used by Geoffrey Chaucer, initiates and ties the metaphoric thread of the poems between each of the sections, linking the voices together through time—the present (the sister's, the brother's, and then the father's) with the past, as represented by the ancestral voices.

Sanchez described the process of creating the work: "I envisioned the last section as father, sister, and brother in counterpoint, but the ancestors insisted on being included." Invoking African words and phrases, the poetry embraces a timeless quality and an ancestral continuity. In brother's voice, history provides the landscape for a personal, painful journey: "came the summer of nineteen sixty/ harlem luxuriating in Malcolm's voice/ became Big Red beautiful became a city/ of magnificent Black Birds steel eyes moist/ as he insinuated his words of sweet choice." With this, the protagonist's voice describes his connection: "then I began to think me alive with form and history/ then I made my former life an accessory." The question of how to create such a life in "a country of men/ where dollars pump their veins" appears unanswerable.

In father's voice, the persona attaches significance to his background as a "southern Negro man playing music," not prepared for the struggles of a young widower attracted to "this ruby-colored girl." Leaving son, daughter, and mother, he becomes an "absentee father" and carefree nightclub owner. Now, at seventy-eight, the voice radiates regret: "i sing a dirge of lost black southern manhood/ this harlem man begging pardon." In reference to this particular section, Sanchez asserts that in assuming the father's voice, she was trying "to reexamine him [her father] and his movement with women" and his relationship with his own children. Also, she learned through doing this how he felt about the loss of his first wife—the only woman he ever loved—and included the following in one of the poems: "this love . . . died in childbirth" and he "never called her name again, wrapped my heart in gauze."

In "family voices/ancestors' voices," the final section, the merging of diverse points of view is reflected in the dialogues between the personas. Challenging the reader, this final section unifies the personal theme with the universal one: the struggles and accomplishments of family. It becomes one family's history crystallized with past familial histories. Integrating the African word *nyata*, meaning how much, in the following, the ancestors' male voice asks, "*nyata?* how much for the walking air?"

Ultimately, the brother's voice finds comfort in the language of the ancestors: "I come ancestor" is his reply to their voices. Moreover, Sanchez declares that "we must at some point understand our history. . . . We must open our eyes to our ancestors to help us live and stay alive."

OTHER MAJOR WORKS

PLAYS: *The Bronx Is Next*, pb. 1968, pr.1971; *Sister Son/ji*, pb. 1969, pr. 1972; *Uh, Huh; But How Do It Free Us?*, pb. 1974, pr. 1975; *Malcolm Man/Don't Live Here No Mo'*, pr. 1979; *I'm Black When I'm Singing, I'm Blue When I Ain't*, pr. 1982; *Black Cats Back and Uneasy Landings*, pr. 1995.

NONFICTION: *Crisis in Culture: Two Speeches by Sonia Sanchez*, 1983.

CHILDREN'S LITERATURE: *It's a New Day: Poems for Young Brothas and Sistuhs*, 1971; *The Adventures of Fat Head, Small Head, and Square Head*, 1973; *A Sound Investment and Other Stories*, 1979.

EDITED TEXT: *We Be Word Sorcerers: Twenty-five Stories by Black Americans*, 1973.

BIBLIOGRAPHY

De Lancey, Frenzella Elaine. "Refusing to Be Boxed In: Sonia Sanchez's Transformation of the Haiku Form." In *Language and Literature in the African American Imagination*, edited by Carol Aisha Blackshire-Belay. Westport, Conn.: Greenwood Press, 1992. Focuses on Sanchez's use and adaptations of the haiku form.

Jennings, Regina B. "The Blue/Black Poetics of Sonia Sanchez." In *Language and Literature in the African American Imagination*, edited by Carol Aisha Blackshire-Belay. Westport, Conn.: Greenwood Press, 1992. Offers insight into critical views of Sanchez's use of language and culture.

Joyce, Joyce A. *Ijala: Sonia Sanchez and the African Poetic Tradition*. Chicago: Third World Press, 1996. A comprehensive look at Sanchez's body of work, covering almost thirty years, and its primary influences.

Reich, David. "As Poets, as Activists." *World*, May/June, 1999, 1-11. In a revealing interview, Sanchez describes the process of writing *Does Your House*

Have Lions? as well as other significant familial experiences. Details personal and historical events that influenced her poetry. Provides both personal and literary philosophy.

Sanchez, Sonia. "Exploding Myths: An Interview with Sonia Sanchez." Interview by Herbert Leibowitz. *Parnassus*, Spring/Summer/Fall/Winter (1985): 357-368. Points to important themes chronicled in *Homegirls and Handgrenades*. Links poetic analysis to poetic intent and purpose. Furnishes an examination of the award-winning collection.

Cynthia S. Becerra

Carl Sandburg

Born: Galesburg, Illinois; January 6, 1878
Died: Flat Rock, North Carolina; July 22, 1967

Principal poetry

Chicago Poems, 1916
Cornhuskers, 1918
Smoke and Steel, 1920
Slabs of the Sunburnt West, 1922
Selected Poems of Carl Sandburg, 1926
Good Morning, America, 1928
Early Moon, 1930
The People, Yes, 1936
Home Front Memo, 1943 (verse and prose)
Chicago Poems: Poems of the Midwest, 1946
Complete Poems, 1950
Wind Song, 1960
Harvest Poems, 1910-1960, 1960
Honey and Salt, 1963
Breathing Tokens, 1978 (Margaret Sandburg, editor)
Ever the Winds of Chance, 1983 (Margaret Sandburg and George Hendrick, editors)

Other literary forms

Besides his poetry, Carl Sandburg wrote a multivolume biography of Abraham Lincoln, composed children's stories, collected American folk songs, and worked for many years as a journalist.

Achievements

In "Notes for a Preface" to his *Complete Poems*, Carl Sandburg remarked,

> At fifty I had published a two-volume biography and *The American Songbag*, and there was puzzlement as to whether I was a poet, a biographer, a wandering troubadour with a guitar, a midwest Hans Christian Andersen, or a historian of current events whose newspaper reporting was gathered into a book *The Chicago Race Riots*.

That puzzlement has persisted since Sandburg's death in the critical reevaluations of his career. Sandburg was by turns journalist, poet, biographer, folklorist, and children's writer, and this is what makes it so difficult to assess his reputation. Was he a great poet, as Gay Wilson Allen has asked, or was he primarily a journalist and biographer? Somehow Sandburg's stature seems greater than the quality of his individual works. Certainly he was a great communicator—as writer, poet, folk singer, and entertainer—whose poetry reached out to millions of Americans, and certainly he was, like his hero, Lincoln, a great spokesman for the common man. Sandburg had a particular genius for reaching out to ordinary people and touching their lives through his poetry and song. In his public performances, one felt the power of a dynamic personality, which helped to establish the popularity of his poems.

During his lifetime, Sandburg published seven major volumes of poetry, and at his death he left enough uncollected verse for an additional posthumous volume, *Breathing Tokens*, which was edited by his daughter Margaret. Contained in these volumes are more than a thousand free verse poems. In *The People, Yes*, he compiled a record of American folk wisdom, humor, and truisms which Willard Thorpe called "one of the great American books." Besides his six-volume Lincoln biography, he completed biographies of his brother-in-law, the photographer Edward Steichen, and of Mary Todd Lincoln. His delightful children's books, the most popular of which remains *Rootabaga Stories* (1922), were read and admired by many adults, including the architect Frank Lloyd Wright. For many years Sandburg was a regular columnist for the *Chicago Daily News*. In 1928, he was named Harvard Phi Beta Kappa poet, and twice he won the Pulitzer Prize: in 1940, in history, for his *Abraham Lincoln: The War Years* (1939) and in 1951, in poetry, for his *Complete Poems*. Yet for many Americans he is best recalled as the genial, white-haired folk singer and poet, the embodiment of folksy Americana.

Even though Sandburg was perhaps justly called "America's best loved poet" during his lifetime, his reputation has steadily declined since his death in 1967. Most of all he has suffered from critical neglect, and his poetry has been largely dismissed for its sameness and lack of development, its lack of poetic structure, and Sandburg's lack of control over his material. At least one critic has found merit in Sandburg's last volume, *Honey and Salt*, but the consensus now seems to be that his poetry has been overvalued. It may well be that he will be remembered most for his Lincoln biography, but that judgment waits upon a full assessment of Sandburg's poetic career.

Chronologically, Sandburg belongs with Vachel Lindsay and Edgar Lee Masters as one of the poets of the "Chicago Renaissance." Like these other writers, he was one of the "sons of Walt Whitman." Early in his career, he adopted a style of loose, rhapsodic free verse, massive detail, a line pattern of parallelism and coordination, and the idiom and cadences of ordinary American speech. At his best, he is a verse reporter—a lyrical poet of the marketplace and the factory. His *Chicago Poems* are *vers libre* sketches of the city and its inhabitants in their various moods, but his poetry is often little more than sociological description in the service of liberal ideology. More than the others of his generation, Sandburg was the poet of labor and the common man. Along with Whitman and Lincoln he held a mystical faith in "the American people." He shares Whitman's principle of inclusiveness and his "cosmic affirmations" but lacks Whitman's innate sense of organic form that gave shape to his effusions. Sandburg's Imagist techniques were noted by Amy Lowell, and some of his poems, notably "Fog," may owe something to haiku, but Sandburg never developed a consistent critical theory, and his occasional pronouncements about his work or about the nature of poetry (as in *Good Morning, America*) are for the most part unenlightening.

Sandburg was thirty-six before he enjoyed any prominence as a poet, and much of the credit for discovering and promoting his work must go to Harriet Monroe, the editor of *Poetry: A Magazine of Verse*, which she published out of Chicago beginning in 1912. Through her magazine, she promoted the poetic innovations of the Imagists and the free verse experimentations of Ezra Pound, William Carlos Williams, Marianne Moore, and others. She recognized and encouraged the new American poetic talent of her generation, but she was especially partial to the poets of the "Chicago School." Sandburg must certainly be counted as her protégé, even though he soon found a wider audience. In 1914, Sandburg won the Levinson Poetry Prize. Although he began as a poet, Sandburg lacked the discipline and control to master fully the art of verse. The prose poem was his natural medium, and the biography of Lincoln was a natural subject for a prairie poet reared in Illinois. Through his biography, Sandburg wished "to restore Lincoln to the common people to whom he belongs." In *Abraham Lincoln: The War Years*, his epic portrait of Lincoln virtually becomes a history of the entire Civil War era, a vast accretion of factual material which presents Lincoln the man in the context of his times. Sensitive to criticism that *Abraham Lincoln: The Prairie Years* (1926) had been too "mythic" and free in its interpretations, Sandburg was determined in *The War Years* to stick close to the historical record. Even Lincoln's major contemporaries—Ulysses S. Grant, Robert E. Lee, Jefferson Davis, and others—receive full biographical treatment. Allen Nevins praised Sandburg's historical biography for its "pictorial vividness" and "cumulative force."

Perhaps Sandburg's greatest poetry appears in the final chapters of volume four of *The War Years*, in which he describes the impact of Lincoln's death on the nation in passages of lyrical free verse that rival in their power and eloquence Whitman's great elegy, "When Lilacs Last in the Dooryard Bloom'd." With characteristic humor, Sandburg observed of his work, "Among the biographers I am a first-rate poet, and among poets a good biographer; among singers I'm a good collector of songs and among song-collectors a nice judge of pipes."

BIOGRAPHY

Carl Sandburg was born on January 6, 1878, in Galesburg, Illinois, the second of five children in the

Carl Sandburg (Library of Congress)

the commemoration of the Lincoln-Douglas debate at Knox College, the pageant of General Grant's funeral procession, the excitement of the Blaine-Cleveland Presidential campaign, and the tension during the railroad strike of 1888. In his childhood autobiography, Always the Young Strangers (1953), Sandburg recalls playing baseball in cow pastures, walking along dusty roads to the county fair, carrying water for the elephants at the circus, and swimming in the forbidden brickyard pond. He enjoyed a typical if not always carefree Midwestern boyhood.

With seven children to be fed on his father's fourteen-cent hourly wage, Sandburg knew the pinch of childhood poverty, although his parents managed to provide the family with basic necessities. His elder sister Mary graduated from high school, but his family could not afford the same for Carl, so he left school at thirteen, after completing the eighth grade. From then on, his education came through practical experience. He would have continued in school but the extra income was needed at home. Sandburg wanted to learn a trade, but there were no openings for apprentices; as a teenager, he worked variously as a porter, newspaper boy, bootblack, bottle-washer, delivery boy, milkman, ice cutter, housepainter, and at other odd jobs. From these early job experiences came much of Sandburg's sympathy for labor and his identification with the common man. When he was nineteen, Sandburg spent a summer hoboing his way across the Midwest in boxcars, stopping in small farm towns to work for a meal or a place to sleep. He reached Denver before returning to Galesburg in the fall of 1897.

When the news of the sinking of the battleship *Maine* arrived on February 15, 1898, Sandburg enlisted as an infantryman in Company C of the Sixth Illinois Regiment of the State Militia. The men trained in Virginia and were on their way to Cuba when yellow fever broke out, and they were diverted to Puerto Rico. Along the way, Sandburg carried two books in his knapsack—

family of August and Clara Sandburg, Swedish immigrants of peasant stock. August Sandburg was a blacksmith's helper with the Chicago, Burlington and Quincy Railroad, and his wife kept house with the children and later took in boarders. The two had met in Illinois while Clara was working as a hotel chambermaid, and August had come to town as a section hand with the railroad. Carl had an older sister, Mary, a younger brother, Martin, and two younger sisters, Esther and Martha. Two other younger brothers died of diphtheria.

The Sandburgs were a thrifty, hardworking family, regular in their Lutheran Church attendance and conservative in politics. The elder Sandburg worked sixty hours a week at the railroad shops and spent his remaining time at home with his family. He had a reputation as a sober, dependable worker. Although both Carl's parents could read, they were not bookish and did not encourage their children's education. August Sandburg was scornful of books other than his Swedish Bible, and he never learned to read or speak English very well. His wife Clara had a better command of English and could sympathize with her son's interest in reading.

Sandburg's memories of Galesburg were of the close-knit, immigrant, working-class neighborhoods, an infantry drill regulation manual and a dictionary. From the army he sent back dispatches to the *Galesburg Evening Mail*. After his company had spent a month in Puerto Rico with intense heat, poor rations, and mosquitoes, Spain surrendered and the troops were mustered out in New York. By September, Sandburg was back in Galesburg with $122 in discharge pay. He decided to enroll in Lombard College as a special student.

Lombard was a small Universalist liberal arts college with a curriculum flexible enough that Sandburg could concentrate on humanities courses and avoid those he disliked, such as mathematics. Word came to him after his first year that he had been chosen for an appointment to West Point. Although Sandburg readily passed the physical examination, he failed in mathematics and grammar, so he continued at Lombard and became active in basketball, debating, drama, the college newspaper, and the yearbook. A professor there, Philip Green Wright, encouraged Sandburg's writing interests and later arranged privately to publish several of his early poetry volumes. Although he apparently enjoyed college life, Sandburg was never graduated from Lombard; in the spring of his senior year the call of the road proved irresistible, and he left school to wander again as a hobo. This time he worked his way across the country selling stereoscopic slides and absorbing the language and folklore of the people. The next four years found him restless and unwilling to settle down to any steady employment. Once, he was arrested for vagrancy in Pennsylvania and spent ten days in jail. After his release he continued west to Chicago, where he lectured and helped edit a lyceum paper.

In 1908, Sandburg met an organizer for the Social-Democratic Party in Wisconsin, who offered him a job in Milwaukee. At a party rally there, he met a young high school teacher, Lillian ("Paula") Steichen, who was home for the holidays. A shared ardent idealism and belief in socialism attracted them to each other, and by the spring of 1908, they were engaged. They married on June 15, 1908, and settled near Milwaukee. Sandburg continued to work as a party organizer and met Emil Seidel, Socialist candidate for mayor of Milwaukee. After his election, Seidel asked Sandburg to serve as his private secretary. This Sandburg did for two years before returning to newspaper work on the *Milwaukee Leader*. Meanwhile, his first daughter, Margaret, had been born in 1911, and his modest salary at the *Milwaukee Leader* no longer sufficed.

A Chicago newspaper strike in 1913 shut down the major dailies and temporarily expanded the readership of the small socialist tabloid, the *Chicago Daily World*. Sandburg was offered a job with a raise in salary and moved his family to Chicago, but when the strike ended, he lost his position. Several newspaper jobs later, he found a secure place with the *Chicago Daily News*, where he served as a special correspondent and columnist for the next fifteen years.

Meanwhile, Sandburg was writing verses at night and assembling notes for what was to become his monumental Lincoln biography. On a hunch, he submitted some of his "Chicago Poems" to *Poetry* magazine, where they were published in the March, 1914, issue and won the Levinson Poetry Prize that same year. *Poetry* editor Harriet Monroe was at first disconcerted by the boldness of the opening lines of "Chicago," but she recognized their strength and championed their free verse. At the age of thirty-six, recognition had finally come to Sandburg for his poetry. The money from the Levinson prize went to pay the hospital bills for the birth of Sandburg's second daughter, Janet, but he was still not earning enough from his poetry to support his family without his newspaper work. He remained active in the socialist movement and, along with Jack London, contributed much of the copy for the *International Socialist Review* in 1915; he became disillusioned with the socialist position on World War I, however, and eventually left the party, even though he remained liberal in his politics.

A publisher's representative for Holt, Alfred Harcourt, was so impressed with Sandburg's verse in *Poetry* that he asked to examine additional poems and persuaded his firm to publish them as the *Chicago Poems* in 1916. This began a long and cordial relationship between Sandburg and Harcourt, who later founded his own publishing firm. In 1918, Sandburg was sent to New York to cover a labor convention and while there discovered he had been chosen to travel to Sweden as a special war correspondent. His knowledge of Swedish served him well there, and he was glad of the opportunity to learn more about his cultural roots. He spent the remainder of the war in Stockholm, and while he was abroad, Holt brought out his second volume of poetry, *Cornhuskers*.

Sandburg returned to the United States a seasoned reporter and a poet with a growing reputation. In 1920, Cornell College in Iowa invited him to read from his poetry, and Sandburg made his first of many visits there, entertaining the audience with a public reading and then taking out his guitar to sing folk songs for the rest of the evening. This combination of poetry recitation and folk song fest came to be the standard Sandburg repertory on his tours and won for him many admirers. Also in 1920, his third daughter, Helga, was born, and a third poetry volume, *Smoke and Steel*, was published. *Slabs of the Sunburnt West*, another collection of verse, followed in 1922, along with *Rootabaga Stories*, a collection of children's stories that Sandburg had originally written for his daughters.

By 1923, Sandburg was deeply involved in a project that would occupy much of his time for almost the next twenty years—his multivolume Lincoln biography. The plans for the book originally grew from a conversation with Alfred Harcourt about a proposed children's biography of Lincoln, although Sandburg had been interested in Lincoln since childhood and had for some years been storing up anecdotes, stories, books, articles, and clippings about him. As the manuscript progressed, it rapidly outgrew its juvenile format and Sandburg continued it as a full-scale adult biography, written in clear, concise language. The two-volume *Abraham Lincoln: The Prairie Years* met with such immediate success that Sandburg was inspired to continue his biographical portrait in the four-volume *Abraham Lincoln: The War Years*, which won for him the Pulitzer Prize for history in 1940. These same years had seen him publish a fifth volume of poetry, *Good Morning, America*, and *The People, Yes*, a compilation of American folk sayings, proverbs, clichés, and commonplaces.

More than anything else, Sandburg earned critical acclaim for his Lincoln biography, hailed as the "greatest biography by one American of another." Literary awards and honorary degrees were bestowed upon him, including Litt. D.'s from Yale and Harvard. In 1945, the Sandburgs moved from Michigan to "Connemara," a picturesque mountain farm in Flat Rock, North Carolina, where Mrs. Sandburg continued to raise her prize-winning goats. The 1950's saw Sandburg reap the harvest of his long and successful career. He was honored by the states of Illinois and North Carolina and asked to give a joint address before both houses of Congress on February 12, 1959, the 150th anniversary of Lincoln's birth. In 1952, he was awarded The Frost Medal for distinguished lifetime service to American Poetry.

During the last few years of his life, Sandburg spent more and more of his time at "Connemara," surrounded by his family and his grandchildren, who called him "Buppong." He died at the age of eighty-nine on July 22, 1967, after a brief illness. After his death, tributes came from throughout the country, including a message from President Lyndon Johnson, who spoke for all Americans when he said that Sandburg "gave us the truest and most enduring vision of our own greatness."

Analysis

In his famous essay "The American Scholar," Ralph Waldo Emerson foresaw the conditions from which American poetry would emerge when he remarked that "I embrace the common, I explore and sit at the feet of the familiar, the low." The American poet would have to sing of "the shop, the plough, and the ledger." His subject matter would come from the world of trade and commerce and his language would be that of the common man. The democratic muse would be prosaic; there would be no sublime flights of poesy. Still, it would take a vigorous poetic imagination and a clear sense of poetic form to refine this ore to the pure metal of poetry. Otherwise the poet might well be overwhelmed by his material and slip imperceptibly from poetry to prose, from singing to talking. This is the problem with much of Carl Sandburg's verse, and it is intensified by his indifference to poetic craftsmanship and form.

Distaste for formal poetry

Sandburg makes clear his distaste for formal poetry in his "Notes for a Preface" to his *Complete Poems*. Instead, he is interested in the raw material for poetry, in the unpolished utterances and colloquial speech of Midwest American life. In this same preface, he lists eight poetic precursors—chants, psalms, gnomic utterances, contemplations, proverbs, epitaphs, litanies, and incidents of intensely concentrated action or utterance which form a vital tradition in the history of poetry. This list closely resembles the folk material he selected and edited for *The People, Yes*, and it suggests in many ways the limitations of Sandburg's poetics. He is the poet of names and places, of trades and occupations—of unreflected experience and undifferentiated fact. Without the discipline of poetic form, however, Sandburg's material proves refractory even by the loose standards of *vers libre*. Robert Frost, a poetic rival, once remarked apropos of Sandburg that "writing free verse is like playing tennis with the net down." The amorphous character and mechanical reiterations in so much of Sandburg's verse point to precisely this lack of the shaping imagination that Frost believed to be essential to the poetic vision.

Chicago Poems

In *Chicago Poems*, for example, which many critics believe to be the best of his early volumes, the vigorous lines of the opening apostrophe to the city itself are followed by a casual assemblage of character sketches, place descriptions, fleeting impressions, and renderings of urban life. Occasionally the sheer emotional power of a poem will register, as with the grief of "Mag," the frustration of "Mamie," or the anger of "To a Contemporary Bunkshooter," but most of the verses never transcend their prosiness. "Poetry," Sandburg once said, "is the achievement of the synthesis of hyacinths and biscuits," but too often he presents only the latter—the prosaic and commonplace—rather than lyrical compression or poetic eloquence.

Notable exceptions can be found in the sustained metaphor of "Fog" or the lyrical delicacy of "Nocturne in a Deserted Brickyard," but for the most part, Sandburg rejects the overrefinement of the genteel tradition by employing the coarse, vigorous language of the common people to present a frank, honest portrayal of his city in all its various moods. Poems such as "They Will Say" express a compassionate regard for the conditions of the working class, though other selections such as "Dynamiter" can be polemically one-sided. As Gay Wilson Allen, the most perceptive Sandburg critic, has observed, "A prominent theme in *Chicago Poems* is the longing of ordinary people for the beauty and happiness they have never known." The poem "Style" shows Sandburg aware of the stylistic deficiencies of his verse, but he insists that, for better or for worse, they are his own.

Cornhuskers and Smoke and Steel

In *Cornhuskers* and *Smoke and Steel*, Sandburg continued to explore the poetry of the Midwest, rural and urban. *Cornhuskers* includes a wider range of material than his first volume, and many of the poems reveal a new lyricism. Some of the most memorable titles evoke seasonal moods of the prairie landscape—"Prairie," "Prairie Water by Night," "Laughing Corn," "Falltime," and "Autumn Movement." Perhaps the most accomplished poem, "Prairie," shows Sandburg experimenting with variable lines and sprung rhythm. "Fire-Logs" offers a romantic treatment of a Lincoln legend and "Southern Pacific" comments ironically on the fate of a railroad baron.

Smoke and Steel extends the material of the previous volume, but on a less optimistic note. The title poem celebrates America's industrial prowess, but other selections reveal Sandburg's awareness of the darker side of American life in the 1920's—in the cynicism of "The Lawyers Know Too Much" and "Liars" and the gangland violence of "Killers" and "Hoodlums." Even with the inclusion of poems to his wife and daughters, *Smoke and Steel* is a less affirmative volume than Sandburg's earlier work.

Slabs of the Sunburnt West

By the time *Slabs of the Sunburnt West* was published, Sandburg had reworked the same material too often. Too many of the poems in this short volume are frankly repetitive of his earlier efforts, or else derivative of Walt Whitman in their vague inclusiveness and generalized evocations of "the people."

Good Morning, America and The People, Yes

With *Good Morning, America* and *The People, Yes*, Sandburg introduced a new direction in his work by reverting to the raw material of poetry in the slang and lingo of the people. Henceforth, as a poet of the people, he would take his material directly from them. In *Good Morning, America*, he offers something of an *ars poetica* in "Tentative (First Model) Definitions of Poetry," a collection of thirty-eight whimsical definitions of poetry. The problem with these definitions is that they seem to deny the role of poetic artistry by implying that poetry can be "found" virtually anywhere and that it consists of virtually anything that strikes the poet's fancy. At this point perhaps more folklorist than poet, Sandburg seems satisfied merely to collect and compile the words of the people rather than to exert artistic selection and control over his material. *The People, Yes* may have value as a collection of verbal portraits of the American people, but whether it is poetry in any traditional sense is debatable.

COMPLETE POEMS AND HARVEST POEMS

Two subsequent collections, *Complete Poems* and *Harvest Poems, 1910-1960*, each included new material and evinced a deepening of Sandburg's poetic talents. During the 1940's, he experimented with a new form of dramatized poetry or recitation—designed to be read publicly with musical accompaniment. Several of these occasional poems—"Mr. Longfellow and his Boy" and "The Long Shadow of Lincoln: A Litany"—are notable for the new note of somber dignity in his free verse. Sandburg read his Lincoln litany as the Phi Beta Kappa poem at the College of William and Mary in 1944 and used the occasion to draw an implicit parallel between Lincoln's struggle during the Civil War and the nation's efforts during World War II. This same patriotic note was struck in his moving elegy on Franklin Delano Roosevelt, "When Death Came April Twelve 1945."

HONEY AND SALT AND BREATHING TOKENS

Sandburg published one additional volume of poems during his lifetime, *Honey and Salt*, which appeared when he was eighty-five. This volume demonstrates the steady mastery and control of his craft that critics had sought in his earlier work. The verses are less strident and ideological, more quiet and reflective in their wisdom. Several notable poems, including "Honey and Salt," "Foxgloves," and "Timesweep," indicate the range of his achievement in what may be his finest volume. Additional poems of merit appeared in the posthumous volume *Breathing Tokens*, which suggests that William Carlos Williams and others may have been too quick to dismiss Sandburg's poetic achievement on the basis of the *Complete Poems*. Perhaps that achievement must now be reassessed. His two fine collections of children's poems, *Early Moon* and *Wind Song*, also deserve critical attention.

CRITICAL RECEPTION

A major objection among Sandburg's critics has been his lack of development. Detractors point to the formulaic nature of his poems and their lack of intellectual content or complexity. They comment on his neglect of prosody and his disdain for the traditional poetic devices that make poetry a "heightened and intensified use of language." They also comment that Sandburg did not master the major poetic forms—the elegy, the ballad, the sonnet, or the lyric. The neglect of form in favor of expression is certainly a trait common to much of modern poetry, however, and one must ask, finally, whether Sandburg is any more deficient in this respect than his contemporaries.

OTHER MAJOR WORKS

LONG FICTION: *Remembrance Rock*, 1948.

NONFICTION: *The Chicago Race Riots*, 1919; *Abraham Lincoln: The Prairie Years*, 1926 (2 volumes); *Steichen the Photographer*, 1929; *Mary Lincoln: Wife and Widow*, 1932 (with Paul M. Angle); *A Lincoln and Whitman Miscellany*, 1938; *Abraham Lincoln: The War Years*, 1939 (4 volumes); *Storm over the Land: A Profile of the Civil War*, 1942; *The Photographs of Abraham Lincoln*, 1944; *Lincoln Collector: The Story of Oliver R. Barrett's Great Private Collection*, 1949; *Always the Young Strangers*, 1953; *Abraham Lincoln: The Prairie Years and the War Years*, 1954; *The Sandburg Range*, 1957; "Address Before a Joint Session of Congress, February 12, 1959," 1959; *The Letters of Carl Sandburg*, 1968 (Herbert Mitgang, editor).

CHILDREN'S LITERATURE: *Rootabaga Stories*, 1922; *Rootabaga Pigeons*, 1923; *Abe Lincoln Grows Up*, 1928; *Potato Face*, 1930; *Prairie-Town Boy*, 1955; *The Wedding Procession of the Rag Doll and the Broom Handle and Who Was In It*, 1967.

EDITED TEXTS: *The American Songbag*, 1927; *The New American Songbag*, 1950.

BIBLIOGRAPHY

Allen, Gay Wilson. *Carl Sandburg*. Minneapolis: University of Minnesota Press, 1972. In this brief but informative pamphlet, Allen explains how Sandburg changed the course of American literature, despite the critical controversies about his work. Sandburg's major success, according to Allen, was his role as the voice and conscience of his generation. Allen justifies his critical study of Sandburg's life and career based on this role. Contains a bibliography.

Crowder, Richard. *Carl Sandburg*. New York: Twayne, 1964. This insightful work aims to give details of Sandburg's life that are relevant to his writing. Summarizes the prose and verse content of his major works, reviews the critics' reception of each major work, analyzes the themes and craftsmanship in each volume, and appraises Sandburg's achievement in American letters. Includes a bibliography.

Durnell, Hazel. *The America of Carl Sandburg*. Washington, D.C.: University Press of Washington, D.C., 1965. Durnell gives a chronological survey of Sandburg's life and achievement, discusses aspects of American life in his writing, examines Sandburg's place in American literature, and ends with a section on Sandburg and his critics. Includes a bibliography and photographs.

Golden, Harry Lewis. *Carl Sandburg*. Cleveland: World Publishing, 1961. Golden claims not to have written the definitive biography of Sandburg, but merely a brief sketch of the first half of the twentieth century using Sandburg as a reference point. Focuses on the five aspects of Sandburg's career that distinguished him: poetry, history, biography, fiction, and music.

Hallwas, John E., and Dennis J. Reader, eds. *The Vision of This Land: Studies of Vachel Lindsay, Edgar Lee Masters, and Carl Sandburg*. Macomb: Western Illinois University Press, 1976. The editors of this work view all the three authors discussed as having stood outside the main currents of twentieth century poetry. The section on Sandburg examines the poet's motives and methods, asserting the priority of populist traditions rather than intellectual values in his work. Sandburg is depicted as the preserver of traditions and ideals, rather than the breaker of new literary ground. Includes photographs and a bibliography.

Niven, Penelope. *Carl Sandburg*. New York: Charles Scribner's Sons, 1991. Niven utilizes more than 50,000 papers in the Sandburg Collection in Connemara, North Carolina, to chronicle Sandburg's life from his birth into his maturity and fame. Includes sixteen pages of photographs.

Yannella, Philip. *The Other Carl Sandburg*. Jackson: University Press of Mississippi, 1996. Yannella focuses on the articles Sandburg wrote during World War I for the *International Socialist Review* and uses this material to argue that the young Sandburg was a political opportunist and a far left radical.

Andrew J. Angyal;
bibliography updated by the editors

Sappho

Born: Eresus, Lesbos, Asia Minor; c. 630 B.C.E.
Died: Mytilene, Lesbos, Asia Minor; c. 580 B.C.E.

Principal poetry

Poetarum Lesbiorum Fragmenta, 1955
Sappho: A New Translation, 1958
Lyra Graeca, volume 1, 1958
Sappho: Poems and Fragments, 1965
The Poems of Sappho, 1966
The Sappho Companion, 2000 (Margaret Reynolds, editor)

Other literary forms

Sappho is known only for her poetry.

Achievements

One of the most admired poets of the ancient world, Sappho was widely popular not only during her lifetime but also for centuries after. Although she wrote nine books of poetry, very little of the corpus remains. Except for a very few phrases on vase paintings or papyri, Sappho's poetry has been preserved primarily in small bits that happened to be quoted by other writers. There are some 170 of these fragments extant, and although there may be among them one or two complete poems, most of the fragments consist of only a few lines or a few words. For Sappho's poem fragments, the numerical system of Edgar Lobel and Denys Page, *Poetarum Lesbiorum Fragmenta*, is used.

These fragments indicate that Sappho's poems were largely lyrical, intended to be sung and accompanied by music and perhaps dance. Although in form her poetry was thus traditional, in content it differed significantly from the larger body of Greek verse, which was written primarily by men. Whereas other Greek poets were mainly concerned with larger and more public issues and with such traditional masculine concerns as war and heroism, Sappho's poems are personal, concerned with the emotions and individual experiences of herself and her friends. In exploring and describing the world of passion, in particular, Sappho departed from conventional poetic themes. Perhaps that is one of the reasons that her poetry was so popular in the ancient world.

Sappho's work has continued to be popular, however, not only because of the timelessness of her subject matter but also because of the exactness of her imagery and the intensity of her expression. Although her style is simple, direct, and conversational, her poems are powerful in creating an impression or evoking an emotion. Her world is therefore not the larger world of politics or warfare, but the smaller world of personal feeling; nevertheless, in depicting the outer limits of that world—the extremes of jealousy as well as tenderness, the depths of sorrow as well as the heights of ecstasy—Sappho's poetry sets a standard to which all later writers of lyrics must aspire.

In addition to being well-known for her subject matter, Sappho has come to be associated with a particular metrical form. Although she was probably not the inventor of Sapphic meter, it has been so named because of her frequent use of it. In Sapphic meter, the stanza consists of three lines, each of which contains five feet—two trochees, a dactyl, and two more trochees—with a concluding fourth line of one dactyl and one trochee. The first line of the "Ode to Aphrodite" in the original Greek illustrates this meter. This ode is thought to have been accompanied by music written in the Mixolydian mode, a musical mode with which Sappho is also associated. Plutarch, in fact, claims that this mode, which is said to arouse the passions more than any other, was invented by Sappho.

Sappho's enduring reputation is based, however, upon the fragments of her poetry that remain. Although those fragments themselves indicate her poetry's worth, there is in addition the testimony of other writers regarding the greatness of her accomplishment. She was praised and revered by a long line of ancients, including Solon, Plato, Aristotle, Horace, Catullus, Ovid, and Plutarch. Proving that imitation is the highest form of praise, some later poets actually incorporated her verse into their own compositions; Catullus's Poem 51, for example, is a slight reworking of a poem by Sappho. Plutarch, who, like Catullus, admired this particular ode, described it as being "mixed with fire," a metaphor which could accurately be applied to the entire body of Sappho's poetry which remains.

Biography

There are few details about Sappho's life which can be stated with certainty; the only evidence is what other writers said about her, and there is no way of knowing whether what they said is true. She is thought to have been of an aristocratic family of the island of Lesbos and to have had three brothers and a daughter named Cleis; dates of her birth and death, however, are not known. Athenaeus, writing around 200 C.E., claimed that Sappho was a contemporary of Alyattes, who reigned in Lydia from 610 to 560 B.C.E.; Eusebius, who was writing in the

Sappho

late third and early fourth centuries C.E., refers to Sappho (also known as Psappho) in his chronicle for the year 604 B.C.E. Other writers indicate that Sappho lived at the time of another poet of Lesbos, Alcaeus, who seems to have been born around 620 B.C.E. It seems safe, therefore, to conclude that Sappho was born sometime during the last quarter of the seventh century and lived into the first half of the sixth century B.C.E.

Sometime between 604 and 592 B.C.E., Sappho seems to have been sent into exile in Sicily by Pittacus, who was then a democratic ruler of Mytilene on Lesbos; an inscription on the Parian marbles of the third century B.C.E. provides confirmation. Although it seems likely that such an exile would have been for political reasons, there are no clear references in any of the fragments of Sappho's poems to indicate that she was specifically concerned with political matters; in fact, based upon those fragments, her poetry appears to have been very much apolitical.

Whether Sappho was married is also uncertain; some say that she had a husband named Cercylas, but others believe this report to be a creation of the Greek comic poets. More suspect is the story that Sappho committed suicide by leaping from the Leucadian Cliff when rejected by a sailor named Phaon. To begin with, this story did not surface until more than two hundred years after her death, but more significant is the fact that Phaon has been found to be a vegetable deity associated with Aphrodite, and a god to whom Sappho wrote hymns. These hymns are thought to have provided the basis for this apocryphal account of her death.

There are, however, some assumptions which can be drawn from Sappho's own words. Her poetry indicates that she was the leader of a group of young women who appear to have studied music, poetry, and dance and who seem to have worshiped Aphrodite and the Muses. As the daughter of an aristocratic family, Sappho would probably not have conducted a formal school, but was more likely the informal leader of a circle of girls and young women. Scholars know from other references in her poetry that there were several such groups on Lesbos, with leaders who were rivals of Sappho.

Many of Sappho's poems also concern her romantic relationships with various women of her group, a fact which has evoked various responses throughout history, ranging from vilification to denial. Her reputation seems to have been first darkened in the fourth century B.C.E., long after her death, when she was the subject of a number of comic and burlesque plays; it is believed that many of the unsavory stories that came to be associated with Sappho were generated during this period. A serious and most unfortunate effect of this created and perhaps inaccurate reputation was that much of Sappho's work was later deliberately destroyed, particularly by Christians whose moral sensibilities were offended by some of the stories which circulated in the second, fourth, and eleventh centuries C.E. Sappho's reputation was also reworked by later scholars who admired her poetry but who were discomfited by her love for women; among their efforts to dissociate Sappho from her sexuality was the widely circulated story that there were in fact two Sapphos, one the licentious and immoral woman to whom all the unsavory tales applied, and the other a faultless and asexual woman who wrote sublime poetry. Most scholars today believe that there was only one Sappho, but they also believe that most of the stories told about her were untrue.

Thus, because of the legendary tales that have come to be associated with Sappho, and because of the lack of reliable historical evidence, there is little knowledge about her life which is certain. It seems reasonable to assume that she lived on Lesbos, that she was a poet, and that she valued personal relationships, about which she wrote. Both during her lifetime and after, she was much admired; statues were erected in her honor, coins were minted bearing her likeness, and she is said to have been given a heroine's funeral. Beyond these small pieces of information, scholars must turn to the fragments of her poetry for knowledge and understanding.

Analysis

Since Sappho's poetry is largely personal, it concerns her immediate world: her dedication to Aphrodite, her love of nature and art, and her relationships with lovers, friends, and family. Her poetry reflects her enjoyment of beauty in the natural world and the close connection that existed between that world and the lives of herself and her friends. Their worship of Aphrodite, their festive songs and dances, are all celebrated with flowers from the fields and with branches from the trees.

Her poetry also reflects her love of art, whether in the form of poetry, the music of the lyre, or the graceful movement of a maiden in a dance. Since these interests are, however, always presented through the perspective of a personal response, a chief defining characteristic of Sappho's poetry is that it is highly emotional.

"ODE TO APHRODITE"

Most of the extant fragments of Sappho's poetry were quoted by later writers to illustrate some point of dialect, rhetoric, grammar, or poetic style, and those writers usually quoted only that portion of Sappho's poem which was pertinent to their point. It is fortunate, then, that Dionysius of Halicarnassus, a Greek writer of treatises who lived in Rome around 30 B.C.E., quoted in its entirety Sappho's "Ode to Aphrodite," to illustrate "the smooth mode of composition." This poem, the longest of several by Sappho honoring Aphrodite, appears to be the most substantial complete work of Sappho which remains.

The ode contains the usual components of a celebration prayer to Aphrodite: the Invocation, the Sanction, and the Entreaty. The Invocation to the goddess consists of a series of epithets, "Dapple-throned Aphrodite,/ eternal daughter of God,/ snare-knitter"; the Sanction asks the goddess's generosity and assistance and reminds her of past favors she has granted; and the Entreaty urgently appeals to the goddess for aid in the present situation. Sappho employs this traditional form in a fresh way, however, not only by her use of vivid metaphors and lyrical language, but also by using the Sanction to reveal something of the goddess's character as well as something of Sappho's own psychology.

As Sappho employs it, the Sanction is a narrative passage within which both she and the goddess move back and forth in time. After describing a past occasion when the goddess came to Earth in a carriage pulled by sparrows, Sappho then recounts the goddess's questioning of her at that time. Using in her narrative the past tense and the indirect question, Sappho recalls the goddess's remarks: "You asked, What ailed me now that/ made me call you again?" Abruptly, then, Sappho places the goddess's gentle chiding within the present context; the poem shifts to direct discourse as the goddess questions Sappho directly: "Whom has/ Persuasion to bring round now/ to your love? Who, Sappho, is/ unfair to you?" This mix of the two temporal perspectives links and blends the present with the past, emphasizing not only Sappho's recurring states of anxiety over new love, but also illuminating the special and friendly relationship between the poet and the goddess: Aphrodite has obviously assisted Sappho before in similar matters of the heart. Continuing to reveal Sappho's character, the goddess reminds her that they are beginning a now-familiar pattern: A bemused Aphrodite recalls, "If she [the desired lover] won't accept gifts, she/ will one day give them; and if/ she won't love you—she soon will/ love." Sappho, manipulating the tradition of the Sanction for new purposes of self-mockery and character revelation, thus discloses her love for the courting period, as well as the shift in attitudes which will inevitably occur between her and her new lover. After the goddess's assurance that the sought-after lover will very shortly be seeking Sappho, the reader is then returned to the poem's outer frame, the prayer, as Sappho begs the goddess to help at once, to "Come now! Relieve this intolerable pain!"

Within the form of a traditional prayer honoring Aphrodite, the poem thus presents a delightful variety of tone. It discloses not only the intensity of Sappho's passion for the desired lover, but also her wry recognition that this intensity will be limited by time and by her own nature. The poem similarly indicates not only the immensity of the goddess's power but also her gentle amusement at the joys and woes of her followers; although Sappho's present sufferings in love will soon be in the past, a pattern underscored by the poem's movement between present and past time, there is every reason to believe that the goddess will assist Sappho once again in achieving the lover who will end her present suffering. In revealing not only something of the character of Aphrodite but also something of the character of Sappho, the poem thus transcends the limitations of its genre: It is a prayer, to be sure, and a narrative, but it is also a charmingly refreshing analysis of the poet's own psychology.

"ODE TO ANACTORIA"

Although there are a few other fragments of poems honoring Aphrodite, the largest number of Sappho's fragments which remain are concerned with love, a subject which occupied much of Sappho's attention. One love poem which may, like the "Ode to Aphrodite," be nearly complete, is the large fragment sometimes called the "Ode to Anactoria," although the poem may have been written for Atthis or even for some other woman whom Sappho loved. An unknown writer who has been labeled "Longinus," in a Greek work believed to date from the first or second century C.E., quoted this fragment to illustrate Sappho's mastery in depicting physical sensations. Extraordinary in its exquisitely precise delineation of the extremes of passion, the poem is also notable for the contrast between the control of its first section and the revealed intensity of its latter section, with the resulting alternations in tone as the speaker sits in the presence of two people, the woman she loves and the man who is evidently enjoying that woman's attentions.

Concisely and with control, the poem beings:

> He is a god in my eyes—
> the man who is allowed
> to sit beside you—he
> who listens intimately
> to the sweet murmur of
> your voice, the enticing
> laughter that makes my own
> heart beat fast.

This calm and steady beginning establishes an outer mood of control, an atmosphere of containment and casual social interplay; the poem turns, however, upon the word "laughter," and the rest of the fragment describes, rapidly and with great intensity, the physical symptoms of the poet's great passion. All her senses are affected: Her "tongue is broken," and she sees nothing; she hears only her "own ears drumming" as she drips with sweat; and, as "trembling shakes" her body, she turns "paler than dry grass." In one of Sappho's most superb lines, she declares that "a thin flame runs under/ my skin." Then, ending this rapid and graphic description of the physical results of intense emotion, the poet remarks, in a powerfully reserved manner, that "At such times/ death isn't far from me."

Scholars have long debated the cause of Sappho's passion, arguing whether it is love or jealousy or both; scholars have also quarreled over the identity of the woman and the relationship between the woman and the man who sits beside her. Such discussions are, however, ultimately irrelevant; the poet's salient point is her own overpowering feeling for the woman to whom she is listening, a feeling which prevents Sappho from exercising over her body any control; it is the physical manifestations of that feeling, the effects upon the body of great passion, which Sappho is recording. Within the poem, the effects of that passion are heightened by the contrast which turns upon the word "laughter"; just as the poem is divided between the controlled description of the outer situation and the blaze of feelings within the poet, so Sappho and the man are divided in their response to the woman's laughter; he "listens intimately," calmly, while Sappho experiences a whole cascade of violent physical and emotional reactions.

Sappho's description in this poem of the effects of passion has not been surpassed, although a number of later poets, including Catullus, have imitated, translated, or adopted her ideas. None, however, has been able to convey such intensity of feeling with the economy and precision of Sappho. It seems safe to say that there are few who would dispute Longinus's claim that this poem illustrates "the perfection of the Sublime in poetry."

16 L.-P.

In addition to considering the physical effects of love on the individual, Sappho also analyzes love's nature and power. One such poem, 16 L.-P., which refers directly to Anactoria, appears on a papyrus of the second century. The poem begins with a paratactic trope, a common device which presents the theme as the culmination of a series of comparisons:

> Some say a cavalry corps,
> some infantry, some, again,
> will maintain that the swift cars
> of our fleet are the finest
> sight on dark earth; but I say
> that whatever one loves, is.

More than illustrating normal differences of opinion, this means of introducing the theme establishes, as well, a decided difference between male and female values: Sappho seems clearly to imply that while men would see the ideal of beauty to be things having to do with war, she sees the ideal of beauty to be the thing beloved—in this case, the absent Anactoria.

Sappho then reinforces her contention that the beloved is the world's most beautiful sight by a reference to Helen, who had her pick of the world's men; in contrast to what one would expect, however, Helen was obliged, because of love, to choose "one who laid Troy's honor in ruin," one who "warped" her "to his will," one who caused her even to forget the "love due her own blood, her own/ child." Sappho uses the story of Helen to illustrate love's power to make insignificant all ordinary considerations and constraints. Yet Sappho clearly intends no judgment against Helen; the purpose of her allusion is simply to demonstrate the power of love and, by analogy, Sappho's love for her beloved.

Only then, after establishing by example and comparisons the supremacy and strength of love, does Sappho reveal in an apostrophe the name of her beloved. Addressing Anactoria and expressing her fear that Anactoria will forget her, Sappho confesses that the sound of her footstep, or the sight of her bright face, would be dearer "than glitter/ of Lydian horse or armoured/ tread of mainland infantry." In an intricate linking of end and beginning by means of metaphor and comparisons, the poem thus moves full circle, back to its starting place; the final sentence of the fragment reinforces the idea contained in the opening sentence as it simultaneously contrasts the tread of the infantry with the delightful sound of Anactoria's footstep, and the glitter of armor with the bright shine of Anactoria's face. In such ways Sappho clearly exposes the conflicting value systems which underlie her poems and those of her male contemporaries.

Several other fragments of varying size also treat the power of love, among them a particularly felicitous line quoted by Maximus of Tyre around 150 C.E.: "As a whirlwind/ swoops on an oak/ Love shakes my heart." An overpowering natural phenomenon, love is presented here as an elemental force which completely overcomes the lover, both physically and emotionally. As the wind physically surrounds the oak, so does love overpower the lover physically as well as emotionally. Love, a force which cannot be denied, is thus depicted as a violent physical and emotional assault, to which one may well respond with mixed feelings.

Sappho explores the ambiguity of the lover's response to love's violent assault in another fragment, quoted by Hephaestion around 150 C.E.: "Irresistible/ and bittersweet/ that loosener/ of limbs, Love/ reptile-like/ strikes me down." Again, love is depicted as an absolute power and as a violent force—in this instance as a reptile which, attacking a passive victim, creates in her a weakened state. That state is not, however, altogether unpleasant, as is indicated by the exquisite sensuality of the adjectival phrase describing love as "that loosener of limbs." Love's duality—its violence and its sweetness—and the lover's ambiguity of response—as the victim of assault and as reveler in love's sensuality—are further underscored by the oxymoronic adjective "bittersweet," an epithet for love which Sappho may have been the first to use.

94 L.-P.

In addition to analyzing the nature and effects of love, Sappho writes of love's termination, of separation, loss, and grief. One such fragment, 94 L.-P., found in a seventh century manuscript in very poor condition, contains many lacunae and uncertain readings. Nevertheless, enough of the poem remains to prove that Sappho was defining the state of bereavement and the effectiveness of memory in alleviating that state. In the course of exploring these themes, however, the poem presents an enchanting account of the life led by Sappho and the members of her group as they worshiped Aphrodite, celebrated the beauty of nature, and gloried in one another.

Like the "Ode to Aphrodite," the poem uses a frame of present time to contain an account of past time; in this poem, however, the past time frames an even earlier period, so that three time periods are represented. Beginning in her present situation, Sappho, alone, reveals her emotional state at the loss of her beloved: "Frankly I wish I were dead." Attempting then to console herself, Sappho recalls the occasion of their parting; at that time, in contrast to the present situation, Sappho controlled her grief in order to comfort her lover, who was overcome by weeping. On that occasion, Sappho urged her beloved to remember their former happiness and to comfort herself with the memory of their love. At this point in the past, the poem then removes to its third temporal setting, that idyllic period when the two were actually together. In a passage of great lyrical beauty, Sappho recalls the details of their life:

think
of our gifts of Aphrodite
and all the loveliness that we shared
all the violet tiaras
braided rosebuds, dill and
crocus twined around your young neck
myrrh poured on your head
and on soft mats girls with
all that they most wished for beside them
while no voices changed
choruses without ours
no woodlot bloomed in spring without song.

In re-creating, at the moment of their farewell, this earlier time of delight in love, nature, and each other, Sappho consoles her beloved by reminding her that the joys they shared are preserved in memories and that those memories can provide solace. At the same time, from her position in the outer frame of the poem—the present context—Sappho attempts to comfort herself by the same means.

Although the poem, on one hand, asserts the consolation that memory can offer, it testifies as well to memory's limitations. Even though Sappho has shared the joyful events of which she reminds her beloved, the poem indicates all too clearly that memory's ability to ease grief is restricted. As Sappho tersely and flatly demonstrates by her opening statement, in no way can memory truly compensate for the beloved's absence. Still, the enchantment of those memories remains, and even though they cannot totally eliminate the pain of parting, they can provide some surcease by powerfully evoking the time when the lovers' joy in nature and in their love created for them an existence truly idyllic.

In addition to these personal poems, private accounts of her own and her friends' feelings and activities, Sappho also wrote some poems of a more public nature. Notable among these "public" poems are a number of fragments from her epithalamiums, or wedding songs. Some of these are congratulatory pieces honoring bride or groom, some appear to have been part of good-humored songs of mockery or wedding jest, and some seem to have been serious considerations of what marriage meant, especially for a woman. Of the latter, particularly worthy of comment are two fragments thought by some to be part of a single poem concerning the loss of maidenhood. As is true of other poems by Sappho, opinion is divided as to the poem's ultimate meaning, some believing that it alludes to an ungentle lover who does not properly appreciate the maiden whose virginity he destroys, and others believing that the poem refers generally to the destruction of innocence and the loss of girlhood joys that marriage necessitates.

The fragments employ two similes, the first comparing the blushing girl to

a quince-apple
ripening on a top
branch in a tree top
not once noticed by
harvesters or if
not unnoticed, not reached.

The location of the apple high in the tree permits it to ripen without disturbance, perhaps as a girl's careful upbringing or superior social standing might shield her from importunate suitors. The second fragment compares the loss of the virginal state to

a hyacinth in
the mountains, trampled by shepherds until
only a purple stain
remains on the ground.

Through the powerful image of the delicate hyacinth roughly trod into the earth, the poem clearly delineates the destructive power of love and marriage.

112 L.-P.

That image is countered, however, in another fragment from an epithalamium, 112 L.-P., which rejoices in marriage and celebrates the groom's winning of the girl he desires. The bride is described as "charming to look at,/ with eyes as soft as/ honey, and a face/ that Love has lighted/ with his own beauty." Sappho, clearly indicating her own opinion as to which is the lucky partner in the marriage, reminds the groom, "Aphrodite has surely/ outdone herself in/ doing honor to you!" Such songs were thought to have been written for the weddings of Sappho's friends, and would have been accompanied by music and dance.

Sappho's legacy is meager in size, consisting of one or two poems which may be complete, together with a number of shorter fragments that tantalize by their incompleteness even as they enchant with what they do provide. These few pieces clearly manifest the enormous poetic talent that Sappho possessed: a genius for capturing a mood, for portraying an experience, and for depicting an emotion. While her poetry is personal in dealing with her own responses to life, it is, paradoxically, also universal; the feelings she describes, even though they are her own, are shared by all human beings who ever love, lose, or grieve, or who experience jealousy, anger, or regret. One of the first poets to explore the range and depth of the human heart, Sappho well deserves Plato's epithet for her, "the tenth Muse."

BIBLIOGRAPHY

Campbell, David A. *Greek Lyric I: Sappho, Alcaeus*. Cambridge, Mass.: Harvard University Press, 1982. Conservative edition of the Greek text, with rigorously literal translations on facing pages. Supersedes the 1928 Loeb Library edition by J. M. Edmonds.

DeJean, Joan. *Fictions of Sappho, 1547-1937*. Chicago: University of Chicago Press, 1987. Penetrating survey of attitudes to Sappho as reflected in various countries and determined by varying mores and manners.

DuBois, Page. *Sappho Is Burning*. Chicago: University of Chicago Press, 1995. The title is taken from part of David A. Campbell's translation of Sappho's fragment 48, in which the poet's "heart" is "burning with desire." DuBois assumes and examines an aesthetics of fragmentation and veers to a strained "postmodern" appreciation of the poet.

Greene, Ellen, ed. *Reading Sappho* and *Re-reading Sappho*. Berkeley: University of California Press, 1996. A two-volume collection of important essays and articles (by writers such as Mary Lefkowitz, Holt N. Parker, and Jack Winkler) in elucidation of Sappho's poetry.

Prins, Yopie. *Victorian Sappho*. Princeton, N.J.: Princeton University Press, 1999. Superb study of the presentations of Sappho in nineteenth century English literature. Exposes the imperfections of editions by Dr. Henry Wharton and "Michael Field" (pseudonym of Katherine Bradley and Edith Cooper). Cogent chapter on Sappho and Swinburne in "Swinburne's Sapphic Sublime."

Rayor, Diane. *Sappho's Lyre: Archaic Lyric and Women Poets of Ancient Greece*. Berkeley: University of California Press, 1991. In most respects, this is the best available translation of Sappho. Includes fragments of nine women poets besides Sappho, along with poems and fragments of seven male lyric poets.

Snyder, Jane MacIntosh. *The Woman and the Lyre: Women Writers in Classical Greece and Rome*. Carbondale: Southern Illinois University Press, 1989. Informative introduction to Sappho and eight female lyric poets of classical antiquity, with representative translations.

Evelyn S. Newlyn;
bibliography updated by Roy Arthur Swanson

MAY SARTON

Born: Wondelgem, Belgium; May 3, 1912
Died: York, Maine; July 16, 1995

PRINCIPAL POETRY

Encounter in April, 1937
Inner Landscape, 1939
The Lion and the Rose, 1948
The Land of Silence and Other Poems, 1953
In Time Like Air, 1958
Cloud, Stone, Sun, Vine: Poems, Selected and New, 1961
A Private Mythology, 1966
As Does New Hampshire and Other Poems, 1967
A Grain of Mustard Seed: New Poems, 1971
A Durable Fire: New Poems, 1972
Collected Poems, 1930-1973, 1974
Selected Poems of May Sarton, 1978 (Serena Sue Hilsinger and Lois Byrnes, editors)
Halfway to Silence, 1980
Letters from Maine, 1984
The Silence Now: New and Uncollected Earlier Poems, 1988
Collected Poems, 1930-1993, 1993
Coming into Eighty, 1994

Other literary forms

Although May Sarton considered herself to be first of all a poet, she is also well known for her fiction and her journals and autobiographical writings. Her first novel, *The Single Hound* (1938), received critical acclaim for its sensitive portrayal of the relationship between a troubled young writer and the elderly woman who serves as his mentor. Alluding to Emily Dickinson's image of the soul attended by "a single hound—/ Its own identity," this novel's title suggests a central theme of Sarton's fiction: the struggle of a vulnerable individual, often an artist, for creative autonomy and self-knowledge.

Important subsequent novels include *Faithful Are the Wounds* (1955), a work based loosely on the events surrounding the suicide of the Harvard English professor and author F. O. Matthiessen; *The Small Room* (1961), an exploration of teacher-student relationships in a New England women's college; and *Mrs. Stevens Hears the Mermaids Singing* (1965), a fictional rendering of Sarton's poetic theory through the reminiscences of the poet-protagonist Hilary Stevens. Three later novels treat with sensitivity the problems of aging: *Kinds of Love* (1970), *As We Are Now* (1973), and *A Reckoning* (1978). Sarton continued to publish novels until 1989, with the last being *The Education of Harriet Hatfield*.

Sarton also contributed significantly to the genre of women's autobiography. In *I Knew a Phoenix* (1959) she focuses on her relationship with her parents, her early education, and her theatrical endeavors and travels during the 1930's. A sequel, *Plant Dreaming Deep* (1968), tells of Sarton's later life, specifically her purchase of the country house in New Hampshire that for years provided a "life-restoring silence" that nourished her art. *Journal of a Solitude* (1973), one of Sarton's best-known works, explores further the importance of solitude for the writer who would "break through . . . to the matrix itself," thus coming to terms with her art and herself. Subsequent journals, *The House by the Sea* (1977) and *Recovering* (1980), deal with the poet's move to the coastal home in Maine, and with her struggle toward "valuing myself again" after professional disillusionment and a bout with breast cancer. *At Seventy* (1984), *After the Stroke* (1988), and *At Eighty-two* (1996) attest her determination to continue writing daily and living fully despite the exigencies of aging and ill health.

In addition to her novels and journals, Sarton published *A World of Light: Portraits and Celebrations* (1976), vignettes which profile, among others, the writers Louise Bogan and Elizabeth Bowen. Sarton's articles on writing and on rural life appeared in a variety of periodicals, including *The Writer*, *The Christian Science Monitor*, and *Family Circle*.

Achievements

May Sarton was among the most prolific and versatile of modern American writers. During a career that spanned more than six decades, she published many novels, volumes of poetry, works of nonfiction, and children's books. With the exception of the period during World War II, she produced virtually a book a year. Much of Sarton's popular acclaim came through her novels and journals, which inspired hundreds of letters from readers moved by her painstaking accounts of her

May Sarton (© Gabriel Amadeus Cooney, courtesy of W. W. Norton and Company)

solitary existence or by her frank treatment of aging—of friendship, sexuality, and anger among the elderly; of dying with dignity.

She received many grants and fellowships throughout her career, including a Guggenheim Fellowship in poetry (1954), a Phi Beta Kappa Visiting Scholarship (1959-1960), a Danforth Visiting Lectureship (1960-1961), and a National Foundation of the Arts and Humanities grant (1967). Honorary degrees flowed from more than a dozen American colleges and universities, as did numerous prizes and awards: the New England Poetry Club Golden Rose (1945), the Bland Memorial Prize awarded by *Poetry* magazine (1945), the Reynolds Prize from the American Poetry Society (1953), the Johns Hopkins University's Poetry Festival Award (1961), the Emily Clark Balch Prize (1966), the Sarah Josepha Hale Award (1972), the Alexandrine Medal from the College of St. Catherine (1975), a Ministry to Women Award from the Unitarian Universalist Women's Federation (1982), an American Book Award for prose from the Before Columbus Foundation (1985), a Maryann Hartman Award from the University of Maine (1986), a lifetime achievement award from the Women's Building/West Hollywood Connexxus Women's Center (1987), and the Northeast Author Award from the Northeast Booksellers' Association (1990).

Although Sarton has been labeled—sometimes pejoratively—an "old-fashioned" poet, a "sentimental" novelist, and a "lesbian writer," her work is far richer and more varied than such categorizations would suggest. Universal themes pervade her writing: the power of friendship and passionate love, the unique bond between parent and child, the quest for identity and inner order, the responsibility of art and the artist in modern society, the conflicts of the elderly. Sarton is also concerned with the unique dilemma of the female artist, who struggles to be both woman and writer in a male-oriented society. Her exploration of the woman poet's relationship to her creativity, found primarily in *Mrs. Stevens Hears the Mermaids Singing* and in her poems and journals, is perhaps Sarton's most significant literary contribution.

BIOGRAPHY

Eleanor May Sarton was born to Eleanor Mabel Elwes and George Sarton, who had met in Ghent, Belgium, during the early 1900's, while she was an art student and he a promising young scientist-scholar. In 1910 they married, and in 1912 their only daughter, May, was born, during the same spring that George Sarton founded the scientific journal *Isis*. That her father connected his daughter's birth with that of his publication is evident from her account in *I Knew a Phoenix* of the dedication of one of George Sarton's scientific works to his wife: "Eleanor Mabel, mother of those strange twins, May and Isis."

At the outbreak of World War I, Sarton's father decided that he could no longer work in Belgium; thus the family emigrated first to England and in 1916 to Cambridge, Massachusetts, where George was aided financially by the Carnegie Institute and was hired to teach half a course at Harvard University. In Cambridge he wrote his best-known work, the monumental *Introduction to the History of Science* (1928), and Mabel gained a modest reputation as a designer of furniture and clothing. In *Plant Dreaming Deep*, May Sarton has acknowledged her appreciation for "the rich gifts I was given by a scholar father and an artist mother, each strong in his own right."

From 1917 to 1926, Sarton attended Shady Hill School in Cambridge, an unorthodox institution whose founder, Agnes Hocking, contributed greatly to Sarton's love of learning and books. A year at the Institut Belge de Culture Française in Belgium provided Sarton with another important teacher and role model, Marie Closset, who encouraged her students to pay "enlightened homage" to the great literary masters. After graduating from the Cambridge High and Latin School in 1929, Sarton was apprenticed to Eva Le Gallienne's Civic Repertory Theatre in New York, where she remained from 1930 to 1936. During that time she founded and directed the Apprentice Theatre in the New School for Social Research and headed the Associated Actors Theater in Hartford, Connecticut. When her interest in the theater waned, Sarton traveled to England, where she met Virginia Woolf, Elizabeth Bowen, Julian Huxley, and S. S. Koteliansky, who became a lifelong friend. She also returned to a volume of poetry she had begun years earlier, and in 1937 *Encounter in April* was published.

Beginning in the early 1940's Sarton was a teacher as well as a writer. In 1945 she served as poet in residence at Southern Illinois University; from 1950 to 1953 she was Briggs-Copeland Instructor in Composition at Harvard; and from 1960 to 1964 she taught writing at Wellesley College. In the early 1960's Sarton bought the country home in New Hampshire whose serenity inspired *Plant Dreaming Deep*, *Journal of a Solitude*, and numerous volumes of poetry, particularly *As Does New Hampshire*, a collection of poems on nature and solitude dedicated to her neighbors in the village of Nelson.

Sarton taught, lectured, and gave readings of her poems widely and frequently at colleges and universities throughout the United States. She died in York, Maine, on July 16, 1995.

Analysis

"We have to make myths of our lives," May Sarton says in *Plant Dreaming Deep*. "It is the only way to live them without despair." Of the many modern American women poets who are also mythmakers, Sarton speaks often and most urgently about what it means to be a woman and a writer and about the female muse as a primary source of poetic inspiration. In the fourth "Autumn Sonnet" from *A Durable Fire*, she describes the crucial relationship between the woman poet and her muse, that elusive force whose function is "to help me tame the wildness in my blood,/ To bring the struggling poet safely home."

As "sister of the mirage and echo," Sarton's muse parallels in some respects the quasi-erotic, mystical woman invoked by Robert Graves in *The White Goddess* (1948), "she whom I desired above all things to know." For Sarton as for Graves, the muse is also a demoniac "shadow," a crucial Medusa-self against whom the poet must struggle and yet through whom she is able ultimately to transform her "wildness" into vital creative energy. For Sarton as for Hilary Stevens, the central character in *Mrs. Stevens Hears the Mermaids Singing*, the muse "destroys as well as gives life, does not nourish, pierces, forces one to discard, renew, be born again. Joy and agony are pivoted in her presence."

Sarton was a poet who never failed life. Her fierce and complex explorations of the creative process, her stunning homages to various female muses, and her rich encounters with both her darkest and most joyful selves continue to inspire those who read her work. Engaged fully with the paradoxes of writing and aging, living and dying, she offered through her work "a house of gathering," a poetic legacy of determined voice and powerful vision. Its rules are deceptively simple: "Work, love, be silent./ Speak."

Sarton's feminine aesthetic

To understand Sarton's theory of the muse and its importance to her poetry, one must first examine her view of female creativity, a view that centers on the antithesis between being an artist and being a woman. "I was broken in two/ by sheer definition," she exclaims in "Birthday on the Acropolis," and though she is reacting here to the "pitiless clarity" of the stark Greek light and landscape, the statement describes as well the conflict she experiences in attempting to reconcile her femininity with her art. Like other women writers from Emily Dickinson to Virginia Woolf to Adrienne Rich, Sarton struggles to overcome what Suzanne Juhasz in *Naked and Fiery Forms* (1976) has called the woman poet's "double bind": how to survive as both woman and poet in a culture that considers the two contradictory. As Juhasz and other critics have noted, the result of such a struggle is often psychic fragmentation, a feeling of self versus self. For Sarton, this quest to name and claim an autonomous creative identity is further complicated by her acceptance of the patriarchal definition of woman as "other"—as beloved rather than lover, object rather than subject;—in short, as inherently "other than" an active creator. She thus aligns herself with a perspective both Jungian and ahistorical in assuming an archetypal "feminine" that must be innately separate from the active "masculine" principle.

This assumption has enormous implications for her poetics, which posits an inevitable dichotomy between the "feminine" and the "artistic" sensibilities. The creative woman, Sarton suggests in *Mrs. Stevens Hears the Mermaids Singing*, is plagued by a "psychic tension" that compels her to strive for balance and wholeness. Although every person experiences such tension to a degree, it is manifested most intensely in the artist, who goes mad if he is unable to fulfill the need for balance. If the artist is a woman, however, she writes "at the expense of herself as a woman." The woman writer, Sarton concludes, is by definition "aberrant." Yet Sarton views such aberrance not as a liability but as an asset, a source of the woman writer's unique creative power. In this respect she takes issue with Sandra M. Gilbert and Susan Gubar, who argue in *The Madwoman in the Attic* (1979) that the woman who writes typically considers her gender a "painful obstacle" to be overcome and thus experiences an "anxiety of authorship." According to Sarton's schema, in contrast, the woman writer's aberrance serves as a source of wholeness rather than schizophrenia, a constructive rather than a destructive force, for it catapults her not toward neurosis but toward health. Anxiety is especially acute in the creative woman, Sarton acknowledges, as are frustration, fragmentation, and rage; but these feelings of being "rent in two" are precisely the raw material from which female art is sculpted, the female self validated.

Once her aberrance is accepted as a given, Sarton believes, the woman writer can set about the process of self-discovery that lies at the root of meaningful art, especially of poetry. For Sarton, the inspiration for such discovery comes from the muse, that crucial force that "throws the artist back upon herself," thereby facilitating an essential psychic exchange. In some respects, Sarton's muse resembles the classic, passive inspirational source of the male poet, the traditional female lover: She is mysterious, she cannot be pinned down, she "goes her way." As an alternate self to the woman poet, however, she also represents a vital, active aspect of the poetic process, a potent and often demoniac force against which the poet is constantly pitted. Like Plato, Sarton believes that creative energy is often a product of irrationality, "frenzy," and that the primary source of this tumult is the "Honeyed muse."

"My Sisters, O My Sisters"

Paralleling and complementing Sarton's theory of female creativity is her poetry itself—more than half a century's worth, written from the 1930's to 1995. In several poems about the act of writing, she explores the ambivalence and power that inform the woman poet's struggle for creative identity. Other poems refine and elaborate her view of the muse: as lover, "sister of the mirage and echo"; as demon, she of the "cold Medusa eyes"; and as mother, the core of life and art, "the never-ending/ the perfect tree." The scope and nature of the female poetic process, for example, provide the theme of "My Sisters, O My Sisters," an early poem in four parts.

In the first section, the poet discusses the difficulties the woman artist faces in her movement from silence to speech. As "strange monsters," a breed apart, Sarton alleges, women writers must set aside traditional female passivity, "the treasures of our silence," in order to uncover the "curious devouring pleasure" of creativity. Such sacrifices are often problematical, the poet admits, and she offers a catalog of "aberrant" women writers to support her argument: George Sand, who "loved too much"; Madame de Staël, "too powerful for men"; Madame de Sevigny, "too sensitive." Yet only through the self-imposed renunciation of traditional roles, she suggests, have authentic and autonomous female voices emerged: Emily Dickinson, who renounced society so that her art might flourish; Sappho, whose writing fed on "the extremity of spirit and flesh." The contemporary woman writer, Sarton continues, has much to learn from her forebears' attempts to break out of the prison of silence.

In the second stanza Sarton defines "that great sanity, that sun, the feminine power" as a revaluation of qualities typically associated with woman: fecundity, nurture, love. These "riches," which have heretofore sustained men and children, the poet continues, "these great powers/ which are ours alone," must now be used by women to fertilize their own creativity. As a model of the precarious balance for which women must strive, Sarton offers two biblical foremothers: Eve, the purveyor of female speech and knowledge; and Mary, giver of love and maternal nurture. The poet's complex task is to assimilate and affirm both branches of this full-bodied tree.

In the final section, Sarton submits female creativity, woman's solitary art, as a means of "re-joining the source" and thus attaining balance and clarity of vision. Taking to task herself and other women who have "asked so little of ourselves and men/ And let the Furies have their way," the poet calls upon her fellow women writers to claim as their own the "holy fountain" of creative imagination, transforming it into a wellspring of feminine song. Only by appropriating the "masculine" power of creation, the poet suggests, can women "come home to this earth," giving birth from its inner recesses to themselves as artists and as women, "fully human." "That great sanity . . . feminine power" will become a reality, Sarton concludes, when women "match men's greatness" with their own great works of art.

"Poets and the Rain"

Although "My Sisters, O My Sisters" is Sarton's most overtly feminist poem, other works also describe the woman poet's efforts to assert a vital, autonomous voice. This struggle provides the underlying dialectic of "Poets and the Rain," which addresses the problem of poetic stasis and subsequent rejuvenation. In the first stanza the poet-persona is debilitated by the rain, which reflects her own inertia and despair; she speaks not as an active creator but as a passive receptacle for the words of others. "I will lie here alone and live your griefs," she declares. "I will receive you, passive and devout." Yet as she offers such disclaimers, the poet hears her own creative instincts stirring, faint but intelligible. Plagued by the "strange tides" running through her head, she distinguishes three voices, each of which presents her with a different vision of life and art. The first "singer" is an old man who "looks out and taunts the world, sick of mankind," in a voice "shriller than all the rest." In an interesting reversal of a stereotype, Sarton associates shrillness not with a hysterical "feminine" voice but with a "masculine" cry of pessimism and derision. Although part of her sympathizes with this doomsday prophet, she ultimately rejects the model that he offers. She will "dream a hunting song to make the old hawk scream," but she is not sufficiently moved by the old man's "bird-scream" to adopt such a voice herself.

Contrasted to this male voice are two female speakers whose visions, when combined, posit a more balanced and optimistic stance. The first woman represents the traditional female voice, that of nurturer, comforter, inspirer. Touched by the love that this woman's song exudes, the poet is inspired to "weave" her own "simple song"—to become, that is, herself a voice of feminine wisdom and maternal love. Despite the strong appeal of this choice, however, it is not enough for the creative woman: The singer is "frustrate"; her purity and nest-building are essentially passive postures. Despite her connection with the traditional female arts, or perhaps because of it, this woman's song is too simple and static a model for the poet.

The speaker is most moved by the "blurred" yet potent voice of a "great girl, the violent and strong," who asks "deep questions in her difficult song." This description recalls Denise Levertov's celebration in "In Mind" of a "turbulent moon-ridden girl . . . who knows strange songs"; or Louise Bogan's "The Dream," in which a "strong creature . . . another woman" leaps and shouts until her passive counterpart is prodded into life-saving speech and action. In Sarton's poem, the girl's "deep questions" and "difficult song," her fierce commitment to her art and her beliefs, offer the questing poet her most inspirational model. Although she realizes the difficulties inherent in such a vision, the persona determines that her voice, like the great girl's, will emerge from an emotional and intellectual complex, a "labyrinth of mind." At last, "rapt with delight," the poet recites her poem, "leaves of a tree/ Whose roots are hidden deep in mystery."

"Journey Toward Poetry"

The special danger inherent in the woman poet's effort to "speak aloud" is also the subject of "Journey Toward Poetry." The poet's ordering of her imaginative experience, Sarton suggests, is analogous to a dangerous journey across foreign yet somehow familiar terrain, a haunting interior journey which produces ultimately for the chary traveler the ideal word or image or perspective. For Sarton, such a poetic voyage usually begins in anger, chaos, and concentrated violence. An array of intense and disturbingly surrealistic images accompanies the "beautiful mad exploration" that is poetry: hills winding and unwinding on a spool, rivers running away from their beds, geraniums bursting open to reveal "huge blood-red cathedrals," "marble graveyards" falling into the sea. One is reminded of William Butler Yeats's "blood-dimmed tide": "the center cannot hold," Sarton implies, when the imagination runs unchecked.

Yet the center does hold. Once the poet's errant imagination is stayed, her inner landscapes soften, become more pastoral. From disorder, to paraphrase Wallace Stevens, emerges a violent order, a silent stillness "where time not motion changes light to shadow." "Journey Toward Poetry" thus serves as Sarton's metaphoric depiction of the poetic process, fraught with danger for any poet, but intensely so for the woman. Beginning in rage or anxiety, at "white heat," the poet's mad racing ultimately gives way to that fruitful ripening of image and idea that inform the "birth of creation."

Out of the stillness and solitude that inevitably follow the poet-terrorist's "mad exploration," the "composed imagination" transfigures the ordinary into the extraordinary.

"These Images Remain"

For Sarton, such transfigurations are inspired by a female muse who appears in one of three manifestations: the erotic, the demoniac, or the maternal. In her maternal guise, the muse is sometimes a human lover-visitant, sometimes a goddess or mythological figure. One recurring muse-figure is Aphrodite, Greek goddess of love and sexuality who is also linked to ancient Eastern mother-goddesses, such as Ishtar, Isis, and Astarte. Because her powers are both matriarchal and sexual, Sarton often envisages Aphrodite as a primordial goddess of fecundity, "one who holds the earth between her knees." Such a goddess informs "These Images Remain," an early sonnet sequence in which the poet confronts the sexual tension at the heart of the poet-muse relationship. As the epitome of female beauty and eroticism, Aphrodite inspires Sarton to acknowledge her own creative capacity; thus she acts as both muse and mirror for the poet. Yet the "silent consummation" between poet and muse is as precarious as quicksand, Sarton suggests in the fifth sonnet; any union with Aphrodite must be transitory. The poet imagines herself as a sculptor whose creation grows "out of deprivation . . . a self-denying rage," evoked by the longing which accompanies any interaction with the muse. Never will the muse be possessed, the poet realizes, but it is the effort to possess that results in the "masculine and violent joy of pure creation," in the sculptor's lasting images, "great and severe."

"The Return of Aphrodite"

In "The Return of Aphrodite," Sarton describes another encounter with the erotic muse, here a "guiltless" goddess who advances "tranquil and transparent,/ To lay on mortal flesh her sacred mantle." The notion of transparency is central to Sarton's view of the muse as an extension of the self, a Medusa through whose eyes one can gaze upon one's mirror image. Unlike the poet's confrontations with Medusa, however, her exchange with Aphrodite is depicted in images of joy and tranquillity. The imagery also is richly erotic: As the mortal poet receives the goddess's "sacred mantle," the "green waves part," only to recede at once after the consummation, leaving in their wake a faint "stain" of light.

"A Divorce of Lovers"

The muse for Sarton also appears as a demoniac force with which the poet must reckon. Especially in poems about the demise of a relationship and the subsequent loss of creative energy, the muse appears as a fury who must be acknowledged and conquered. In the fourth sonnet of "A Divorce of Lovers," for example, Sarton accuses her lover of "chasing out the furies and the plagues of passion" rather than confronting them. In awe of these demons, the poet is nevertheless aware of the need for such "ghosts." When angels and furies "fly so near," she continues, "they come to force Fate at a crucial pass." This forcing of Fate, in turn, opens up an essential dialogue with the self that ultimately allows the poet to transform her violence and rage into creative energy.

"The Godhead as Lynx"

In some poems, Sarton replaces angels and furies with animals, powerful forces that must be accepted and assimilated rather than denied or tamed. In "The Godhead as Lynx," for example, the poet gleans nourishment from the power of the beautiful yet cold mother-lynx, "Kyrie Eleison." The poet images herself as a child transfixed and transfigured by the "absolute attention" that informs the lynx's "golden gaze." Sarton often uses the metaphor of face-to-face confrontation to dramatize the dialogue between poet and muse; here the speaker, though only a child, challenges the lynx by meeting her "obsidian eyes." Rather than fearing confrontation and dreading its aftermath, the speaker undertakes such an experience on her own terms. She abandons her pride and rage before the lynx, a necessary gesture, Sarton implies, if the child is to rejoin the mother, the human to encounter the divine.

Sarton goes on to envision the lynx as a "prehuman" maternal goddess into whose womb the poet-daughter is tempted to crawl. Like ancient goddesses, however, the lynx is linked with both creation and destruction. Despite the strong appeal of her "essential fur," her maternal comfort, she lacks compassion; she is cruel, "lightning to cut down the lamb,/ A beauty that devours without qualm." In her dual guise as beneficent and demoniac, therefore, the lynx evokes in the poet an ambivalent response: She is both appealing and frightening, and thus the tension with which the speaker approaches the powerful creature can be used for good or for ill. Through her encounter with the godhead as lynx, the poet's own strength is unleashed. She is forced to grow, at times to groan, but always to think in ways heretofore unknown.

"The Muse as Medusa"

The demoniac muse whom Sarton most often invokes is Medusa, the mythological "monster" whose hair writhed with serpents, whose glance turned men to stone. Because Medusa could be viewed only indirectly and because of the mystery and danger associated with her powers, she symbolizes the woman poet's struggle *with* herself *for* herself, thus serving as both a source and a manifestation of female creativity. In "The Muse as Medusa" Sarton describes an encounter with this fury, meeting Medusa as she has met the lynx: one-on-one, "straight in the cold eye, cold." Despite her "nakedness" and vulnerability, the poet challenges the Medusa myth by transforming the legendary monster from a debilitating force to a source of creative rejuvenation. Medusa's stony gaze does not destroy; it transfigures, by "clothing" the naked speaker in the warm, protective garment of thought. "Forget the image," Sarton exults, for this Medusa renews through the paradoxical vitality of her silent presence. "Your silence is my ocean," the poet tells Medusa, "and even now it seems with life."

Yet Medusa herself is not the power responsible for such teeming life; this motion continues in spite of, rather than because of, her presence. Medusa, after all, "chose/ To abdicate by total lack of motion," and abdicating is something the speaker refuses to do. Instead, Sarton creates a fluid seascape of which Medusa is merely a part, her destructive fury put to use. In remaking Medusa in her own image, the poet acknowledges a vital female creativity and affirms the demoniac part of herself. Medusa's face is *her* face, Sarton realizes; the monster's rage emerges from the poet's own "secret, self-enclosed, and ravaged place." As the poem ends, the poet thanks Medusa for her powerful "gift."

"An Invocation to Kali"

In one of her most provocative poems about female inspiration, "An Invocation to Kali," Sarton depicts the muse as both demon and mother, affirming the close connections that she perceives among demoniac rage, maternal love, and female creativity. The poem opens with an epigraph from Joseph Campbell's *The Masks of God* (1959), a description of "the Black Goddess Kali, the terrible one of so many names." As an aspect of the woman's creative self, Kali is both inspiring and threatening. Her dual powers intrigue the poet, arousing her envy and admiration; yet an identification with Kali also evokes shame, anger, and fear—that peculiar blend of self-love and self-loathing of one who is both trapped and freed by her art. In Section One, Sarton sets forth this poem's central issue: how best to cope with the demands of the "Black Goddess." A "voracious animal," the Kali within is a violent force whose "brute power" arouses in the poet both apprehension and guilt. Ambivalent toward this potent but demoniac force, the poet recognizes and fears its potential for debilitation and entrapment: "I am the cage where/ Poetry paces and roars." What then to do with Kali? the poet wonders. Is she to be murdered or lived with?

Part Two suggests the futility of any effort to kill the goddess; the anguish and rage which this "terrible one" promulgates is too awesome to be negated easily. Instead, the poet asserts, Kali "must have her hour." If the demon is denied, Sarton suggests, she will continue to inflict her bloody reign, but if she is faced "open-eyed," her explosive rage will be revealed for what it is: an emotion essential if creativity is to flourish. For every act of creation, Sarton insists, is preceded by destruction; "every creation is born out of the dark." Unless Kali does her "sovereign work," the poet continues, "the living child will be stillborn."

In the third and fourth sections, Sarton expands the image of Kali as a metaphor for the extreme social violence that has plagued Western culture, especially during the twentieth century. "The Concentration Camps" is packed with gruesome images depicting the tragic results of humanity's efforts to deny its furies, to pretend that violence and existential "dis-ease" do not exist. "Have we managed to fade them out like God?" the poet asks of Hitler's most poignant victims, children. In "turning away" from the "stench of bones," people have "tried to smother" fires that need desperately to burn, as vital reminders of what happens when violence is repressed and then unleashed. All are guilty, Sarton's indictment implies; refusing to meet demons is both a cultural and an individual sickness.

In Sarton's view, the solution to this widespread ailment is "to reckon with Kali for better or worse," to accept her violence as an essential purging force. Thus the poet turns to the goddess's sacred altar, offering her final invocation to this "terrible one." "Help us to bring darkness into the light," she begs, to see anger and pain in a new way, as "the balance-wheel for our vulnerable, aching love." Only by confronting the Kali within, she believes, can the poet become a "gardener of the spirit," thereby claiming the goddess's "awesome power" as her own.

"Of the Muse"

Whether she appears as an erotic, a demoniac, or a maternal force, the female muse serves for Sarton as a key image by which to depict the woman poet's struggle for voice and autonomy. The intense encounter with the muse forces the poet to come to terms with her own power of creativity. This confrontation, in turn, leads the poet closer to the balanced, integrated state which Sarton posits as an ideal. In "Of the Muse," the final poem of *Halfway to Silence*, Sarton offers a powerful and moving assessment of her creative philosophy. Poetry comes not from lies, she insists, but from a "crude honesty" which makes the poet "a great, cracked,/ Wide-open door/ Into nowhere." When young, she continues, the muse was beyond her comprehension, but now she is grateful for her as one is grateful for light. This poem suggests a new direction for Sarton in its emphasis on the link between poetry and honesty, an area of particular concern to many contemporary feminist theorists and women poets.

Women and writers have often been praised for lying, Adrienne Rich declares in *On Lies, Secrets, and Silence* (1979). Yet the unconscious, like the body, struggles for truth, Rich continues, and "the complexity and fecundity of poetry comes from the same struggle." Rich's statement might well be Sarton's, so accurately does it describe the theory implicit in "Of the Muse." Fighting to fulfill its desire for truth, Sarton suggests, along with Rich, the woman's poet's "fecund and complex" unconscious is awakened to vital insights and potent speech through her dialogue with that self who is also the muse. Once "misunderstood" as something to be subdued and conquered, the muse is now recognized by the aging poet as a force most closely analogous to light. "We do not thank the light," Sarton explains, "but rejoice in what we see/ Because of it." What she sees is the "crude" but honest power of poetry, its transformative potential. Through the muse, the poet concludes "all things are made new."

Letters from Maine

Letters from Maine continues this emphasis on the female muse by celebrating love and creative inspiration in old age. In the title work, a sequence of ten sonnet-like poems, Sarton pays homage to a "November muse" who brings her wisdom, clarity, and laughter. Although the poet and her lover-muse eventually separate, the force of her inspiration remains despite the poet's sense of loss: "everything stops but the poem." To encounter the muse as an aging woman poet seems to Sarton a special but difficult gift. In Poem Six she recalls a Nootka Indian legend about a "Primal Spirit," an old woman whom she greets, "deep inside myself," whenever she feels bereft: "Under the words you are my silence." The last poem in the sequence reveals Sarton's struggle to write against all odds, even when the muse appears as Medusa, playing "cruel games." Despite frequent obstacles, the poet expresses confidence in the reliability of her art.

The interwoven themes of creativity and aging recur in two poignant poems near the end of *Letters from Maine*, "Letters to Myself." In the first, Sarton acknowledges a "terrible fear, the fear of feeling" which besets her as she strives to write. Although the poet recognizes her capacity for self-healing, she relies as well on "the dark angel and silent charm," her muse, to lead her from despair to hope. Through poetry, Sarton asserts in the second poem, one encounters one's deepest self and thereby is changed. Such transformations anticipate the final transformation caused by death itself. The poem ends with a statement of the poet's complex goal: "to sustain tension, yet discover poise,/ For this Magnificat of severe joys."

The Silence Now

The Silence Now contains new and uncollected earlier poems, several of which reveal an ongoing concern with the perils and pleasures of silence, a theme central to Sarton's work and that of many other modern women poets. The title poem claims that silence is immense, a realization that motivates the poet to question what it signifies: "At the bottom of the silence what lies in wait?" Sarton responds to her own question by evoking images of transience from the natural world—dying daffodils, irises almost open, clouds moving rapidly as the sky clears. Such visionary, silent encounters with the world of nature, "moments of pure joy," move the poet as deeply as does the practice of her art.

Two poems about her mother suggest the powerful influence this inspirational figure had on her poet-daughter. In "Dream" Sarton finds herself "inside my mother's death," unable to breathe and struggling to break out of the imprisoning tomb. Despite her horror, she realizes that she could never emerge from the tomb without her mother, for their lives are entangled, "twice-born mystery/ where the roots intertwine." Sarton recognizes the complexity of mother-daughter symbiosis and, finally, experiences it as liberating; when the speaker awakens, she is free.

"August Third" commemorates Sarton's mother on her birthday, as the aging poet recalls her elderly parent's "inexhaustible flame." Mabel Sarton certainly experienced fatigue, her daughter declares, but she knew how to push it aside in order to tend lilies in the early morning. In this poem's moving final stanzas Sarton calls upon her mother for life energy and sustenance: "Mother, be with me." Sarton realizes that she is now older than her mother was when she died, an awareness that somehow gives her strength to greet a new day. From her maternal muse the poet has learned a vital lesson, "never to fail life."

Coming into Eighty

Sarton's final collection, *Coming into Eighty* was published only a year before her death and is a meditation on the meaning of old age, unaccustomed limitations, and anticipations of mortality. The everyday activities of the old person, taken for granted by those of younger generations, are highlighted and dramatized here, in curt lines that imitate the conservation of energy and snippets of memory typical of old age: "These days," she informs us, "Everything is an effort, . . . /An adventure." The poems therefore capture the nexus between the sublime and the mundane—the "effort" and the "adventure," or the "Muse" that, like her cat, "Mews." The poet becomes enthralled by even the most common daily sensations, "Alive to every stir of a leaf," which in turn reinforce her own, still living, state. These are the experiences, sharply focused, that move her, and us, on a "slowing ship," a "last mysterious voyage," toward a final destination.

Other major works

Long fiction: *The Single Hound*, 1938; *The Bridge of Years*, 1946; *Shadow of a Man*, 1950; *A Shower of Summer Days*, 1952; *Faithful Are the Wounds*, 1955; *The Fur Person: The Story of a Cat*, 1957; *The Birth of a Grandfather*, 1957; *The Small Room*, 1961; *Joanna and Ulysses*, 1963; *Mrs. Stevens Hears the Mermaids Singing*, 1965; *Miss Pickthorn and Mr. Hare: A Fable*, 1966; *The Poet and the Donkey*, 1969; *Kinds of Love*, 1970; *As We Are Now*, 1973; *Crucial Conversations*, 1975; *A Reckoning*, 1978; *Anger*, 1982; *The Magnificent Spinster*, 1985; *The Education of Harriet Hatfield*, 1989.

Play: *The Underground River*, pb. 1947.

Nonfiction: *I Knew a Phoenix: Sketches for an Autobiography*, 1959; *Plant Dreaming Deep*, 1968; *Journal of a Solitude*, 1973; *A World of Light: Portraits and Celebrations*, 1976; *The House by the Sea*, 1977; *Recovering: A Journal*, 1980; *Writings on Writing*, 1980; *May Sarton: A Self-Portrait*, 1982; *At Seventy: A Journal*, 1984; *Honey in the Hive: Judith Matlack, 1898-1982*, 1988; *After the Stroke: A Journal*, 1988; *Endgame: A Journal of the Seventy-ninth Year*, 1992; *Encore: A Journal of the Eightieth Year*, 1993; *At Eighty-two*, 1996; *Dear Juliette: Letters of May Sarton to Juliette Huxley*, 1999.

Children's literature: *Punch's Secret*, 1974; *A Walk Through the Woods*, 1976.

Miscellaneous: *Sarton Selected: An Anthology of the Journals, Novels, and Poems of May Sarton*, 1991 (Bradford Dudley Daziel, editor); *May Sarton: Among the Usual Days*, 1993 (Susan Sherman, editor); *From May Sarton's Well*, 1994 (Edith Royce Schade, editor).

Bibliography

De Shazer, Mary K. *Inspiring Women: Reimagining the Muse*. Elmsford, N.Y.: Pergamon Press, 1986.

Analyzes contemporary American women poets' sources of creative inspiration, their female muses, a subject much discussed by May Sarton. It includes a substantial chapter on Sarton's poetry and poetic muses, a close reading of *Mrs. Stevens Hears the Mermaids Singing*, and an assessment of Sarton's working relationship with poet Louise Bogan.

Drake, William. *The First Wave: Women and Poets in America, 1915-1945*. New York: Macmillan, 1987. Drake considers the lives and accomplishments of more than twenty-five modernist poets. Sarton is examined in the last chapter as a member of this generation yet as a poet who speaks to and with a new generation as well. Useful as background material.

Evans, Elizabeth. *May Sarton, Revisited*. Boston: Twayne, 1989. Updates the 1973 Twayne series volume on Sarton by Agnes Sibley, *May Sarton*. A revaluation of Sarton's lifetime achievement, it offers a useful biographical chapter followed by careful analytical chapters on her work in four genres. Evans focuses on Sarton as a writer who speaks for and about women and as one who considers poetry her primary genre, despite the popular appeal of her novels and journals. Includes a chronology of Sarton's life and accomplishments.

Hunting, Constance, ed. *May Sarton: Woman and Poet*. Orono, Maine: National Poetry Foundation, 1982. Twenty-four strong articles on Sarton's novels, journals, and poetry comprise this collection. Includes an important essay by Carolyn Heilbrun on Sarton's journals and memoirs, as well as Mary Lydon's analysis of French influences on Sarton's writing style. Contains a useful bibliography by Lenora P. Blouin of Sarton criticism through 1981.

Kallet, Marilyn, ed. *A House of Gathering: Poets on May Sarton's Poetry*. Knoxville: University of Tennessee Press, 1993. Written in honor of Sarton's eightieth birthday, these essays, along with Kallet's introduction, assess Sarton as a poet and woman writer. Bibliographical references, index.

Peters, Margot. *May Sarton: A Biography*. New York: Knopf, 1997. An authorized biography of the novelist, poet, and feminist. Peters was granted unprecedented access to personal papers and diaries, and she gives us a compelling look at the woman who influenced a legion of readers with rich and intimate writings. Includes bibliographical references and index.

Sarton, May. *May Sarton: Selected Letters*. Edited by Susan Sherman. New York: Norton, 1997. A collection of correspondence which offers invaluable insight into Sarton's life and work. Includes an index.

Swartzlander, Susan, and Marilyn R. Mumford, eds. *Critical Essays on May Sarton*. Ann Arbor: University of Michigan Press, 1992. Contains sixteen essays that analyze both the texts and contexts of Sarton's writing. Informed by feminist literary criticism, these essays link Sarton to an explicitly female tradition and address such topics as issues of female identity in her aesthetic philosophy, her "lesbian consciousness," and patterns of reader response to her work. Nancy Weyant's survey of Sarton criticism since 1981 updates Lenora P. Blouin's earlier bibliography. The volume also includes Elizabeth Evans's critical edition of fifteen unpublished letters from Sarton to Louise Bogan. An essential source.

Tillinghast, Richard. Review of *Coming into Eighty*. *Poetry* 166, no. 5 (August, 1995). A brief review of Sarton's last collection, as well as a eulogy to the poet.

Mary de Shazer,
updated by Christina J. Moose

SIEGFRIED SASSOON

Born: Brenchley, Kent, England; September 8, 1886
Died: Heytesbury, England; September 1, 1967

PRINCIPAL POETRY

The Daffodil Murderer, 1913
The Old Huntsman and Other Poems, 1917
Counter-Attack and Other Poems, 1918
War Poems, 1919
Picture Show, 1920
Recreations, 1923
Selected Poems, 1925
Satirical Poems, 1926

The Heart's Journey, 1927
Poems of Pinchbeck Lyre, 1931
The Road to Ruin, 1933
Vigils, 1935
Rhymed Ruminations, 1940
Poems Newly Selected, 1916-1935, 1940
Collected Poems, 1947
Common Chords, 1950
Emblems of Experience, 1951
The Tasking, 1954
Sequences, 1956
Lenten Illuminations and Sight Sufficient, 1958
The Path to Peace, 1960
Collected Poems, 1908-1956, 1961
An Octave, 1966

OTHER LITERARY FORMS

Siegfried Sassoon is nearly as well known for his prose works as for his poetry. During the twenty years from 1926 to 1945, he spent most of his time working on the two trilogies that form the bulk of his work in prose. The first of these was the three-volume fictionalized autobiography published in 1937 as *The Memoirs of George Sherston*. It begins in *Memoirs of a Fox-Hunting Man* (1928), by recounting the life of a well-to-do young country squire in Georgian England up to his first experiences as an officer in World War I. The second volume, *Memoirs of an Infantry Officer* (1930), and the third, *Sherston's Progress* (1936), describe the young man's war experiences. In the later trilogy, Sassoon discarded the thinly disguised fiction of the Sherston novels and wrote direct autobiography, with a nostalgic look back at his pleasant pastoral life in prewar England in *The Old Century and Seven More Years* (1938) and *The Weald of Youth* (1942). In *Siegfried's Journey 1916-1920* (1945), Sassoon looks again at his own experiences during and immediately following the war. These autobiographical works are invaluable to the student of Sassoon's poetry because of the context they provide, particularly for the war poems.

Siegfried Sassoon (Hulton Archive)

Two other significant prose works should be mentioned. The first is Sassoon's *Lecture on Poetry*, delivered at the University of Bristol on March 16, 1939, in which Sassoon delineated what he considered to be the elements of good poetry. The second work is Sassoon's critical biography of the poet George Meredith, titled simply *Meredith* (1948), which also suggests some of Sassoon's views on poetry.

ACHIEVEMENTS

According to Bernard Bergonzi, Siegfried Sassoon was the only soldier-poet to be widely read during the war itself. This gave Sassoon a unique opportunity to influence other war poets, which he did. Though his war poetry has been criticized for being mere description, for appealing to the senses only and not the imagination, for being uncontrolled emotion without artistic restraint, there can be no doubt than Sassoon's poetry represented a complete break with the war poetry of the past in tone, technique, and subject matter. With uncompromising realism and scathing satire Sassoon portrayed the sufferings of the front-line soldier and the incompetency of the staff for the express purposes of convincing his readers to protest continuation of the war. His *Counter-Attack and Other Poems* volume was nearly suppressed because of poems such as "The General," which broke the prohibition against criticizing those in charge of the war effort.

Unquestionably, Sassoon's realistic subject matter and diction influenced other poets, most notably his friend Wilfred Owen, whose poetry was posthumously published by Sassoon in 1920; but Sassoon failed to influence later poetry because, as John Johnston notes, his war poetry was all negative—he provided no constructive replacement for the myths he had destroyed. Nor did Sassoon influence the 1930's because, according to Michael Thorpe, he was still a prisoner of war, and through his autobiographies he retreated from the political struggle of W. H. Auden and Stephen Spender and others into his own earlier years.

When in the 1950's Sassoon finally did have something positive to offer, no one was willing to listen. He was no longer well known or critically acknowledged. Certainly his future reputation will rest on the war poems; but in his religious poems of the 1950's, Sassoon did achieve a style of simple expression, compact brevity, and concrete imagery with a universally appealing theme, and this should be noted as a remarkable though largely unrecognized achievement.

BIOGRAPHY

Siegfried Lorraine Sassoon was born in the Kentish weald in 1886, the second of three sons of Alfred Ezra Sassoon and Theresa Georgina Thornycroft. His father was descended from a long line of wealthy Jewish merchants and bankers who, after wandering through Spain, Persia, and India, had come to settle in England. The family was proud of its orthodoxy, and Siegfried's father was the first to marry outside the faith. Siegfried's mother, in contrast, was an artist, the close relative of three well-known sculptors, and a member of the landed gentry. The marriage was a failure, and Alfred Sassoon left when Siegfried was five, leaving the younger Sassoon to be reared by his mother as an Anglican.

Siegfried had no formal schooling as a child, though from the ages of nine to fourteen he learned from private tutors and a German governess. In 1902 he attended Marlborough, and in 1905 he entered Clare College, Cambridge. Sassoon's temperament was not disciplined enough for scholarly pursuits; he began by reading law, switched to history, and ultimately left Cambridge without a degree. He returned to Kent where, on an inherited income of five hundred pounds a year, he was able to devote his energies to fox-hunting, racing, and writing poetry. Sassoon loved the pastoral beauty of the Kentish downs and attempted to portray it in a number of dreamy, sentimental lyrics. Between the ages of nineteen and twenty-six, Sassoon had nine volumes of poetry privately published, before he enjoyed a mild success with *The Daffodil Murderer* in 1913. The poem was chiefly intended as a parody of John Masefield's *The Everlasting Mercy*, but Sassoon's poem had a strong human appeal of its own. By this time Sassoon had been befriended by Edward Marsh, the editor of *Georgian Poetry*. Marsh encouraged Sassoon's literary endeavors and persuaded him to come to London in May, 1914, where Sassoon began to move in the literary world and to meet such notable authors as Rupert Brooke. Sassoon, however, felt unhappy and lacked a sense of purpose, and when he enlisted in the army on August 3, 1914 (two days before England entered the war), it was to escape a sterile existence.

Sassoon's early life had been extremely sheltered, even pampered, and it was a very immature twenty-eight-year-old who went to war, totally unprepared for what he would find. After convalescence from injuries received in a fall during cavalry training, he accepted a commission and went through training as an infantry officer. Thus he did not arrive in France until November, 1915, where he became transport officer for the First Battalion of the Royal Welch Fusiliers. Here he met and befriended the poet Robert Graves. In *Goodbye to All That* (1929), Graves describes his first meeting with Sassoon, and relates how, when he showed Sassoon his first book of poems, *Over the Brazier* (1916), Sassoon, whose early war poems were idealistic, had frowned and said that war should not be written about in such a realistic way. Graves, who had been in France six months, remarked that Sassoon had not yet been in the trenches.

Graves already knew what Sassoon would soon discover, indeed what all the British troops in France were coming to feel: growing disillusionment at the frustration and the staggering casualties of trench warfare. There were 420,000 British casualties in the Somme offensive beginning on July 1, 1916—an offensive that gained virtually nothing. The Somme was Sassoon's most bitter experience in the trenches; after it, he would never write the old kind of poetry again.

In spite of his pacifist leanings, Sassoon distinguished himself in the war. Called "Mad Jack" by his troops, Sassoon was awarded the Military Cross and recommended for the Distinguished Service Order for his exploits in battle: After a raid at Mametz, he took it upon himself to bring back the wounded; in the Somme in early July he single-handedly occupied a whole section of an enemy trench, after which he was found in the trench, alone, reading a book of poetry. Ill with gastric fever in late July, he was sent home for three months, where he worked on poems to be included in *The Old Huntsman and Other Poems*.

While in England, Sassoon met Lady Ottoline Morrell and her liberal husband Philip, at whose home he spoke with such pacifists as Bertrand Russell, listened to open criticism of the war, and heard of Germany's peace overtures and the impure motives of members of parliament who wanted the war to continue.

Sassoon returned to active service in France in February, 1917, but in April he was wounded in the battle of Arras and sent home again. Haunted by nightmares of violence and by what the pacifists were saying, Sassoon resolved to protest the war on a grand scale. In July, in a remarkable move, risking public disgrace and military court-martial, Sassoon refused to return to active duty, and wrote a formal declaration of protest to his commanding officer, which was reproduced in the press and which Russell arranged to have mentioned in the House of Commons. In his letter, Sassoon charged that the war was being deliberately prolonged by the politicians for ignoble purposes, even though there was a chance for a negotiated settlement with Germany, thus leading the men at the front line to be slaughtered needlessly. Sassoon hoped to be court-martialed, so that his protest would have propaganda value. To his dismay, however, the official reaction was largely to minimize the letter. In a moment of despair, Sassoon flung his Military Cross into the Mersey River and vowed to continue his protest.

At that point, Graves stepped in. Graves agreed with Sassoon's letter, but considered the gesture futile and feared for Sassoon's personal welfare. Graves arranged to have Sassoon appear before a medical board and, chiefly on Graves's testimony, Sassoon was found to be suffering from shell shock. The incident was closed, and Sassoon was sent to Craiglockhart hospital in Edinburgh, where Dr. W. H. R. Rivers became his counselor and friend, and where in August he met the brilliant young poet Wilfred Owen. Owen knew and idolized Sassoon as the author of *The Old Huntsman and Other Poems* (which had appeared in May), and Sassoon's encouragement and insistence upon realism had greatly influenced him. At Craiglockhart, during the autumn of 1917, Sassoon composed many of the poems of *Counter-Attack and Other Poems*, which was published the following year.

Owen returned to active duty in November, and Sassoon, feeling that he was betraying his troops at the front by staying away in comfort, returned to duty a few weeks later. He went first to Ireland, then to Egypt, where he became a Captain, then back to France in May. On July 15, Sassoon, returning from an attack on a German machine gun, was wounded in the head by one of his own sentries. He was sent to a London hospital, where he spent the rest of the war.

After the war, Sassoon retreated from the active life, becoming more and more contemplative (he had always been introspective and solitary) until he acquired a reputation as a virtual hermit. Immediately after the war, he joined the Labor Party, and became editor of the literary pages of the *Daily Herald*, where he published satirical pieces with a socialist point of view. His satire of the 1920's, however, was uneasy and awkward, stemming from the fact that the issues of the day were not as clear-cut as the right and wrong about the war had been. Besides, he was not really sure of himself, feeling a need to explore his past life and find some meaning in it. Still, as the 1930's grew darker, Sassoon wrote poems warning of the horror of chemical and biological warfare. No one seemed to want to listen, however, and Sassoon, disillusioned, forsook "political" poetry completely. In part, the autobiographies that he worked on in those years were a rejection of the modern world and an idealization of the past. In part, too, they were an effort to look inside himself, and that same urge characterizes most of his later poetry, which is concerned with his personal spiritual struggle and development.

Thus the incidents of Sassoon's later life were nearly all spiritual. Only a few isolated events are of interest: In 1933, he finally married; he had a son, George, but Sassoon kept his personal relationships private, never mentioning them in his poetry. During World War II, Sassoon's home was requisitioned for evacuees, and, later, fifteen hundred American troops were quartered on his large estate. After the war, Sassoon remained very solitary, and appears to have cultivated his image as the "hermit of Heytesbury." When his volumes of poetry in the 1950's appeared, they were largely ignored by critics and public alike. The fiery war poet had outlived his reputation, but he had reached a great personal plateau: On August 14, 1957, Sassoon was received into the Catholic Church at Downside Abbey. His last poems, appearing in a privately published collection, *An Octave*, on his eightieth birthday (a year before his death), display a serene and quiet faith.

Analysis

In 1939, Siegfried Sassoon delineated his views on poetry in a lecture given at Bristol College. While what he said was not profound or revolutionary, it did indicate the kind of poetry Sassoon liked and tried to write, at least at that time. First, Sassoon said, poetry should stem from inspiration, but that inspiration needs to be tempered by control and discipline—by art. Second, the best poetry is simple and direct—Sassoon disliked the tendency toward complexity initiated by T. S. Eliot and Ezra Pound. Third, Sassoon held the Romantic view that poetry should express true feeling, should speak the language of the heart. Fourth, poetry should contain strong *visual* imagery, the best of which is drawn from nature. Finally, the subject matter of the best poetry is not political (again, he was reacting against the avowedly political poetry of Auden and his associates), but is rather personal, and this examination of self led Sassoon to write spiritual poetry.

A review of Sassoon's poetry will reveal, however, that even in his best poems he did not always follow all of these precepts, and that in his worst poems he seldom followed any. Sassoon's worst poems are most certainly his earliest ones. Sassoon's prewar lyric verses are lush and wordy, in weak imitation of A. C. Swinburne and the Pre-Raphaelites, but full of anachronisms and redundancies. Some, such as "Haunted" and "Goblin Revel," are purely escapist; Lewis Thorpe suggests that Sassoon was looking for escape from his own too-comfortable world. The best thing about these early poems is their interest in nature—an interest that Sassoon never lost and that provided him with concrete images in later pieces. The best poems that Sassoon wrote before the war, *The Daffodil Murderer* and "The Old Huntsman," abandon the poetic diction for a colloquial style, and "The Old Huntsman" reveals a strong kinship with nature.

The war poetry

Sassoon's early, idealistic war poetry is characterized by an abstract diction and generalized imagery. He was writing in the "happy warrior" style after the manner of Rupert Brooke's famous sonnet sequence, and was even able to write of his brother's death early in the war as a "victory" and his ghost's head as "laureled." Perhaps the best example of these early poems is "Absolution," written before Sassoon had actually experienced the war. Sassoon romanticizes war, speaking of the glorious sacrifice of young comrades in arms who go off to battle as "the happy legion," asserting that "fighting for our freedom, we are free." The poem is full of such abstractions, but no concrete images. Its language is often archaic ("Time's but a golden wind"), and it is the sort of thing that Sassoon soon put behind him.

Edward Marsh, after reading some of Sassoon's earlier poetry, had told him to write with his eye directly on the object. As Sassoon began to experience the horrors of trench warfare, he did exactly that. His poems became increasingly concrete, visual, and realistic, his language became increasingly colloquial, and his tone became more and more bitter as the war went on. Early in 1916, he wrote "Golgotha," "The Redeemer," and "A Working Party," in which he tried to present realistically the sufferings of the common soldier. Such realistic depiction of the front lines characterized one of two main types of war poetry that Sassoon was to write in the next few years. The best example of sheer naturalistic description is "Counter-Attack," the title poem of Sassoon's most popular and most scathing volume of poetry. "Counter-Attack" begins with a description of the troops who, having taken an enemy trench, begin to deepen it with shovels. They uncover a pile of dead bodies and rotting body parts—"naked sodden buttocks, mats of hair,/ Bulged, clotted heads."

"Repression of War Experience"

The horror of this description is without parallel, but where Sassoon really excels is in his realistic portrayal of the psychological effects of the war. Perhaps his best poem in this vein is "Repression of War Experience" (from *Counter-Attack and Other Poems*). The poem, in the form of an interior monologue, explores a mind verging on hysteria, trying to distract itself and maintain control while even the simplest, most serene events—a moth fluttering too close to a candle flame—bring nightmarish thoughts of violence into the persona's mind. In the garden he hears ghosts, and as he sits in the silence he can hear only the guns. In the end, his control breaks down; he wants to rush out "and screech at them to stop—I'm going crazy;/ I'm going stark, staring mad because of the guns."

"They"

Sassoon was not merely presenting realistic details; he was being deliberately didactic, trying to use his poetry to incite a public outcry against the war. When home on leave he had been appalled by the jingoistic ignorance and complacency on the home front. Sassoon's second main type of war poetry made a satirical attack on these civilians, on those who conducted the war, and on the irresponsible press that spread the lying propaganda. Justly the most famous of these poems is "They" (*The Old Huntsman and Other Poems*), in which Sassoon demolishes the cherished civilian notion that the war was divinely ordained and that the British were fighting on God's side. Sassoon presents a pompous Bishop declaring that, since the "boys" will have fought "Anti-Christ," none will return "the same" as he was. The irony of this statement is made clear when the "boys" return quite changed: blind, legless, syphilitic. The Bishop can only remark, "The ways of God are strange." "They" caused a great outcry in England by ruthlessly attacking the Church for forsaking the moral leadership it should have provided.

"They" also illustrates Sassoon's favorite technique in satire: concentration of his ironic force in the last line of the poem. This kind of "knock-out punch" may be seen most vividly in the poem "The One-Legged Man" (from *The Old Huntsman and Other Poems*), which describes a soldier, discharged from the war, watching the natural beauty of the world in autumn and considering the bright, comfortable years ahead. The poem ends with the man's crushingly ironic thought, "Thank God they had to amputate!"

Certainly there are flaws in Sassoon's war poetry. Some of the verses are nothing more than bitter invectives designed merely to attack a part of his audience, such as "Glory of Women," "Blighters," and "Fight to the Finish." Even the best poems often lack the discipline and order that Sassoon himself later advanced as one main criterion of poetry. Further, Sassoon almost never got beyond his feelings about immediate experiences to form theoretical or profound notions about the broader aspects of the war. Sassoon himself realized this lack when in 1920 he brought out his slain friend Wilfred Owen's war poetry, which converted war experiences into something having universal meaning.

"The Dug Out"

The war poetry, however, has a number of virtues as well. It uses simple, direct, and clear expression that comes, as Sassoon advocated, from the heart. Further, it uses vivid pictures to express the inexpressible horror of the trenches. "The Dug Out" (*Picture Show*) is an example of Sassoon's war poetry at its best. In its eight lines, Sassoon draws a clear picture of a youth sleeping in an awkward and unnatural position. The simple, colloquial language focuses on the emotional state of the speaker, and much is suggested by what is left unsaid. The speaker's nerves are such that he can no longer bear the sight of the young sleeper because, as he cries in the final lines, "You are too young to fall asleep for ever;/ And when you sleep you remind me of the dead." Arthur Lane compares such poems, in which the ironic effect is achieved through the dramatic situation more than through imagery, to those in the *Satires of Circumstance* (1914) of Sassoon's idol, Thomas Hardy, suggesting an influence at work.

"Everyone Sang"

Perhaps the culmination of Sassoon's attempt to transcend his war experience is the much-admired lyric "Everyone Sang" (from *Picture Show*). It is a joyous lyric expressing a mood of relief and exultation, through the imagery of song and of singing birds. Sassoon seems to have been expressing his own relief at having survived:

"horror/ Drifted away." Lane calls these lines "pure poetry" of "visionary power," comparing them to William Wordsworth and William Blake. He might have also mentioned Henry Vaughan, Sassoon's other idol, whose path toward poetry of a very personal spirituality Sassoon was soon to follow.

"LINES WRITTEN IN ANTICIPATION . . ."

Unquestionably, it is for his war poetry that Sassoon is chiefly admired. Still, he lived for nearly fifty years after the armistice, and what he wrote in that time cannot be disregarded. He first flirted with socialism after the war; "Everyone Sang" may be intended to laud the coming utopian society. Then he attempted satiric poetry during the 1920's, which must be regarded as a failure. His targets varied from the upper classes to political corruption and newspapers, but the poetry is not from the heart; the satire is too loud and not really convincing. Michael Thorpe points out the wordiness of Sassoon's style in these satires, together with the length of his sentences. One blatant example is "Lines Written in Anticipation of a London Paper Attaining a Guaranteed Circulation of Ten Million Daily." Even the title is verbose, but note the wordy redundancy of the lines:

> Were it not wiser, were it not more candid,
> More courteous, more consistent with good sense,
> If I were to include all, all who are banded
> Together in achievement so immense?

RELIGIOUS SEARCHING AND SPIRITUALITY

Though he soon abandoned the satiric mode, Sassoon did maintain what Joseph Cohen calls the role of prophet that he had assumed in the war years, by continually warning, through *The Road to Ruin* and *Rhymed Ruminations*, of the coming disaster of World War II; but his total despair for the modern world is expressed in "Litany of the Lost" (1945), wherein, with the ominous line "Deliver us from ourselves," Sassoon bid farewell to the poetry of social commentary. By now he was more interested in his spiritual quest.

Next to his war poems, Sassoon's poems of religious searching are his most effective. The quest begins with "The Traveller to His Soul" (1933), in which Sassoon asks, as the "problem which concerns me most," the question "Have I got a soul?" He spends over twenty years trying to answer the question. His work, beginning with *The Heart's Journey* and *Vigils*, is concerned with exploration of self and uncertainty about the self's place in the universe, with increasing questioning about what lies behind creation. With *Rhymed Ruminations*, Sassoon ends the 1930's on a note of uneasiness and uncertainty.

SEQUENCES

The questions are answered in the three volumes *Common Chords*, *Emblems of Experience*, and *The Tasking*, which were combined to make the book *Sequences*. In the poem "Redemption" (from *Common Chords*), Sassoon yearns for a vision of the eternal, which he recognizes as existing beyond his senses. Sassoon's lines recall Vaughan's mystical visions when he asks for "O but one ray/ from that all-hallowing and eternal day." In *The Tasking*, Sassoon reached what Thorpe calls a spiritual certainty, and his best poems in that volume succeed more clearly than the war poems in satisfying Sassoon's own poetic criteria as expressed in 1939. In "Another Spring," Sassoon speaks in simple, direct, and compact language about feelings of the heart—an old man's emotions upon witnessing what may be his last spring. The natural imagery is concrete and visual as well as auditory, concentrating upon "some crinkled primrose leaves" and "a noise of nesting rooks." Though the final three lines of the poem add a hint of didacticism, the poem succeeds by leaving much unsaid about the eternal rebirth of nature and its implications for the old man and the force behind the regenerative cycle of nature. It is a fine poem, like many in *The Tasking*, with a simple, packed style that makes these poems better as art, though doomed to be less familiar than the war poems.

OTHER MAJOR WORKS

LONG FICTION: *The Memoirs of George Sherston*, 1937 (comprising *Memoirs of a Fox-Hunting Man*, 1928; *Memoirs of an Infantry Officer*, 1930; and *Sherston's Progress*, 1936).

NONFICTION: *The Old Century and Seven More Years*, 1938; *Lecture on Poetry*, 1939; *The Weald of Youth*, 1942; *Siegfried's Journey, 1916-1920*, 1945; *Meredith*, 1948; *Siegfried Sassoon Diaries, 1920-1922*, 1981; *Siegfried Sassoon Diaries, 1915-1918*, 1983; *Siegfried Sassoon Diaries, 1923-1925*, 1985.

Bibliography

Caesar, Adrian. *Taking It Like a Man: Suffering, Sexuality, and the War Poets: Brooke, Sassoon, Owen, Graves*. New York: Manchester University Press, 1993. Caesar explores how four British poets reconciled their ideologies inherited from Christianity, imperialism, and Romanticism with their experiences of World War I.

Campbell, Patrick. *Siegfried Sassoon: A Study of the War Poetry*. Jefferson, N.C.: McFarland, 1999. Through primary documents and research, Campbell provides critical analyses of Sassoon's war poetry. Includes bibliographical references and an index.

Hart-Davis, Rupert, ed. *Siegfried Sassoon Diaries, 1915-1918*. London: Faber & Faber, 1983. This compilation of Sassoon's diaries offers a rare insight into his mind as he went through the terrors of World War I, reporting on it through his poetry. Contains good background information and is supplemented by an adequate index.

Lane, Arthur E. *An Adequate Response: The War Poetry of Wilfred Owen and Siegfried Sassoon*. Detroit: Wayne State University Press, 1972. Lane highlights the use of satire and parody as he analyzes Sassoon's war verse. Contends that Sassoon and others, when faced with the horrors of trench warfare, were charged with creating a new mode of expression since the traditional modes proved inadequate.

Mallon, Thomas. "The Great War and Sassoon's Memory." In *Modernism Revisited*, edited by Robert Kiely. Cambridge, Mass.: Harvard University Press, 1983. Attempts to isolate the effect that World War I had on Sassoon's mind and memory, thus distancing him from life. Mallon's studies concentrate on Sassoon's "twice" written memoirs of his early life.

Moeyes, Paul. *Siegfried Sassoon: Scorched Glory, A Critical Study*. New York: St. Martin's Press, 1997. Moeyes draws on Sassoon's edited diaries and letters to explore Sassoon's assertion that his poetry was his real autobiography. Includes bibliography and an index.

Spear, Hilda D. "An Unrecognized War Poem by Siegfried Sassoon." *Four Decades of Poetry: 1890-1930* 1 (1976): 141-142. In this brief article, Spear takes a detailed look at two poems by Sassoon, "Haunted" and "The Death Bed." She plots similarities throughout, showing that even though normally separated, they were in fact both taken from Sassoon's war experiences.

Thorpe, Michael. *Siegfried Sassoon: A Critical Study*. London: Oxford University Press, 1967. Thorpe's book follows the life and works of Sassoon, concentrating on his overall work, not merely his "war poetry," with particular attention being paid to his basic underlying framework of ideas. An index and a bibliography augment the text.

Wilson, Jean Moorcroft. *Siegfried Sassoon: The Making of a War Poet, A Biography*. New York: Routledge, 1999. Details Sassoon's early life, covering the years from his birth through 1918, and in doing so, closely examines his struggle to come to terms with his homosexuality.

Jay Ruud;
bibliography updated by the editors

Friedrich Schiller

Born: Marbach, Germany; November 10, 1759
Died: Weimar, Germany; May 9, 1805

Principal poetry

Anthologie auf das Jahr 1782, 1782
Xenien, 1796 (with Johann Wolfgang von Goethe)
Gedichte, 1800, 1803
The Poems of Schiller, 1851
The Ballads and Shorter Poems of Fredrick v. Schiller, 1901

Other literary forms

Although Friedrich Schiller wrote poetry throughout most of his life, the bulk of his œuvre belongs to other genres. He became especially famous for his powerful dramatic works. Among the most important of his ten major plays are *Die Räuber* (1781; *The Robbers*, 1792), *Don Carlos* (1787; English translation, 1798), *Maria Stuart* (1800; *Mary Stuart*, 1801), and *Wilhelm Tell* (1804; *William Tell*, 1841). During the early part of his career, his writings brought him little income, and poverty forced him to turn to fiction for a broader audience. *Der Verbrecher aus verlorener Ehre* (1786, 1802; *The Criminal in Consequence of Lost Reputation*, 1841) and the serialized novel *Der Geisterseher* (1789; *The Ghost-Seer: Or, The Apparitionist*, 1795) were among the most successful of these endeavors. While a professor of history at the University of Jena, he wrote a number of historical books and essays, and during the early 1790's, he published a variety of theoretical and philosophical studies on aesthetics, ethics, and literature. His "Über die ästhetische Erziehung des Menschen" ("On the Aesthetic Education of Man") and "Über naive und sentimentalische Dichtung" ("On Naïve and Sentimental Poetry") are among the most significant treatises on literature and art written in Germany during the second half of the eighteenth century. His extensive correspondence with Johann Wolfgang von Goethe is the high point in the several volumes of his letters that have been collected and published since his death.

Friedrich Schiller (Library of Congress)

ACHIEVEMENTS

Although most of Friedrich Schiller's verse was written for a highly intellectual audience, it also enjoyed popular success. His "thought poems" laid the groundwork for the ensuing development of the poetry of ideas and brought him rightful recognition as Germany's most important eighteenth century composer of philosophical lyrics. On the other hand, his didactic purpose and his capacity for evoking moods akin to those of folk literature, especially in his ballads, made Schiller also a poet of the common people.

Schiller's poems and other writings were quickly recognized for their quality by the German literary establishment and were published in the significant periodicals of the time. Supported by Christoph Martin Wieland and Johann Gottfried Herder, Schiller became an important force among the artistic giants in Weimar, even prior to his friendship with Goethe. During the decade of their poetic collaboration, Schiller joined Goethe in shaping literary attitudes, approaches, and forms that influenced German poets and determined the nature of German letters from that time onward.

Even in his own time, however, some of Schiller's poetic works were highly controversial. The "Epigram War" that he and Goethe waged against their critics was evidence that his works were not universally well received. During the years after his death, Schiller's reputation in critical circles waned in direct relationship to the increased advocacy of realism and, eventually, Naturalism. Near the turn of the century, a Schiller renaissance began on two levels. Writers such as Stefan George and Hugo von Hofmannsthal, who advocated a return to classical literary values, praised Schiller for his poetic models of idealism and beauty. Among the common people, such poems as "Das Lied von der Glocke" ("The Song of the Bell") were memorized in school, exposing a new generation of German youth to Schiller's thought. Although he was overshadowed by Goethe in pure poetic endowment, Schiller's impact on the whole of German literature is such that the renowned Thomas Mann called his works the "apotheosis of art."

BIOGRAPHY

The early life of Johann Christoph Friedrich von Schiller was shaped by two powerful influences: the Swabian Pietism of his origins, and the "benevolent" despotism of Karl Eugen, Duke of Württemberg. After serving as a lieutenant in Bavarian, French, and Swabian regiments, Schiller's father was rewarded with an appointment as superintendent of the duke's gardens and plantations. While Schiller's parents had planned for him to enter the ministry, those intentions were frustrated when the duke insisted that he be enrolled in a military academy at Stuttgart in 1773. After a brief and inconclusive period of legal studies at the academy, Schiller left the institution to become a medical officer in Karl Eugen's army. His dislike of the school's restrictions contributed substantially to the attacks on tyranny prevalent in his early writings.

Schiller's first poem was published in a Swabian literary magazine in 1776, and others appeared there and elsewhere during the remainder of his school years. Two months after his graduation, he rented a room from a widow, Luise Vischer, whom critics long regarded as the model for his Laura odes. While still in Stuttgart, Schiller wrote his first play, *The Robbers*. It premiered in Mannheim in January, 1782, and Schiller traveled, without the duke's permission, to attend the opening performance. Following Schiller's second secret theater visit to Mannheim, Karl Eugen placed him under two weeks' arrest and forbade him to write. The arrival of the Russian czar in Stuttgart took Karl Eugen's attention away from Schiller, and the latter fled to Mannheim.

Existence in Mannheim was a constant struggle for the young Schiller. His literary efforts brought him little monetary profit, and he survived only through the help of his friends. When the manager of the Mannheim theater refused to renew his contract as house dramatist, Schiller published a literary journal in an effort to straighten out his fiscal affairs. The emotional strain caused by his precarious economic condition and his unsuccessful encounters with women during those years is reflected in the poetry that he wrote after leaving Stuttgart. Not until he was rescued from financial disaster by Gottfried Körner and other admirers in 1784 did Schiller's personal life gain stability sufficient to foster the harmonious mastery of thought and form that typifies his more mature lyric creations. The friendship with Körner was a direct stimulus for the famous poem "An die Freude" ("Ode to Joy"), which Beethoven used for the choral movement of his Ninth Symphony.

A major turning point in Schiller's life came in 1787, after he had spent two relatively carefree years in Körner's household in Dresden. Disappointed by an unrewarding relationship with Henriette von Arnim, Schiller left Dresden for Weimar. There, he renewed an acquaintance with Charlotte von Kalb, the unhappy wife of an army major. Her friendship had created emotional problems for him in Mannheim, but she now introduced him into philosophical circles in Jena that influenced his life for years. In Weimar, he also made contact with Wieland and Herder, whose favor gave him access to the court.

In 1788, Schiller met Johann Wolfgang von Goethe for the first time. Although no close relationship developed at the time, Goethe soon recommended him for a professorship in history at the University of Jena. The stable situation provided by an annual income allowed Schiller to marry Charlotte von Lengefeld in 1790. His professional involvement in the years that followed reduced his poetic activity but moved him to concern himself more extensively with the philosophy of Immanuel Kant. His philosophical studies ultimately had a major impact on his creative work. In Jena, during the winter of 1790-1791, Schiller experienced the first attacks of the tuberculosis that eventually caused his death.

The most artistically productive period of Schiller's life began in the summer of 1794 when Goethe agreed to collaborate with him in the editing of a new journal. The intimate friendship that arose between the two authors provided them with mutual stimulus and gave rise to timeless masterworks of poetry and drama. Friendly competition between them in 1797 and 1798 yielded some of the most famous ballads in German literature. Also in 1797, the last of Schiller's historical writings was completed, winning for him membership in the Swedish Academy of Sciences. During the final years of his life, Schiller was feverishly active, writing the best of his mature plays, adapting works by William Shakespeare, Louis Picard, Gotthold Lessing, and Goethe, traveling, and gathering new dramatic materials in defiance of the malady that slowly destroyed him. Newly completed lines for "Demetrius," an unfinished play that might have become his greatest masterpiece, were found lying on his desk on the day he died.

ANALYSIS

In his essay "On Naïve and Sentimental Poetry," written soon after he began collaborating with Goethe, Friedrich Schiller outlined and clarified the characteristics of two kinds of poetic art, attempting to defend his own creative approach in the careful justification of "sentimental" literature. In contrast to the naïve poet, whose work is an expression of nature, Schiller's modern lyricist is a reflective creator who seeks to regain in his poetry a natural state that has been lost. The naïve poet moves the reader through an artistic presentation of sensual reality, while the sentimental poet achieves his effect in the successful development of ideas. Throughout Schiller's literary career, the conceptual tension between "naïve" and "sentimental," couched variously in the polarities of nature and culture, real and ideal, ancient and modern, and substance and form, remained the key to his poetic endeavor. Each new poem represented a concerted effort to create through art a harmonious resolution of the perpetual conflict between these fundamental aspects of man's existence.

ANTHOLOGIE AUF DAS JAHR 1782

The poetry of Schiller's youth is especially interesting for its clear illumination of the broad spectrum of eighteenth century literary forces that molded his attitudes. In the *Anthologie auf das Jahr 1782*, which was published to counteract what Schiller saw as the smarmy bent of other Swabian collections of the time, there are poems that reflect such diverse influences as the pathos of Friedrich Klopstock's odes, the Anacreontic tendencies of the early Enlightenment, Gottfried August Bürger's massive realism, Albrecht von Haller's philosophical lyrics, the political tendentiousness of Christian Friedrich Daniel Schubart, Christoph Wieland's Rococo style, and the purposeful tastelessness of *Sturm und Drang*. Although personal encounters provided immediate stimuli for some of the works, the calculated refinement of perceptions through the process of reflection sets the philosophical tone of Schiller's verse from the outset.

The naïve/sentimental dichotomy is visible in two characteristic forms in Schiller's early poetry. "Der Eroberer" ("The Conqueror") exemplifies Schiller's juxtaposition of political and divine order in the concept of the "noble criminal," an almost mythical figure who goes beyond the limits of conventional morality. The conquering tyrant emerges as the adversary of God and the destroyer of moral order. In the Laura odes, however, which are central to the lyrics of Schiller's youth, the focus of poetic tension is the tortuous conflict between love's physical and spiritual dimensions. By 1780, in direct response to the writings of Adam Ferguson and under the mediated influence of Francis Hutcheson and the philosopher, Lord Shaftesbury, Schiller had developed a personal metaphysics in which love is the binding force that holds the world together. The Laura odes and poems such as "Der Triumph der Liebe" ("The Triumph of Love") constitute the major literary treatments of those ideas.

A TRANSITIONAL PERIOD

The years immediately following the publication of the *Anthologie auf das Jahr 1782* were a transitional period in Schiller's growth as a lyric poet. In the lines of "Der Kampf" ("The Struggle") and "Resignation," the poet broadened the basic themes of his earlier works. While exploring in depth the conflict between man's right to joy and the reality of a tear-filled existence, he questioned the validity of God's justice in forcing man to choose between earthly pleasure and spiritual peace. Some of the lyrics written between 1782 and 1788 examine the possibility of achieving a harmony between the polar forces that act upon man; other poems conclude with terrible finality that the only alternatives, pleasure in this world or hope of peace in the world to come, are mutually exclusive. Only the famous "Ode to Joy," which praises the harmony between God and a glorified world in a profound affirmation of earthly existence, forms a distinct anomaly in the otherwise troubled reflection that typifies the verse produced during this period of Schiller's life.

The major poetic works of Schiller's mature years, beginning with the first version of "Die Götter Griechenlands" ("The Gods of Greece"), written in 1788, and ending with "Das Siegesfest" ("The Victory Celebration"), composed in 1803, offer a more calmly ordered, evenly balanced, and formally perfected presentation of the fundamental Schillerian dichotomies than can be found in the emotionally charged poems of the early 1780's. With increasing emphasis on natural order as an answer to the problems of civilized society, Schiller attempts to resolve the tension between the ideal and the real. Instead of seeking to establish an internal harmony between the spiritual and physical elements of man's being, he tries in the later poems to move his reader to accept an external creation of the desired metaphysical unity in art. The appropriate models for the new synthesis were to be found in the artistic and literary legacy of the ancients. Schiller's most powerful philosophical poems present the search for a golden age of accord between rational man and nature and the need to regain that state through reflection.

From the epigram to ballad to thought poem

It is important to understand that these writings are not simply versified philosophy. In Schiller's eyes, the poet differs from the philosopher in not being required to prove his assertions. Instead, the poet employs a variety of devices to convey his message on several levels of perception, at once teaching and moving the reader through his own personal enthusiasm. To achieve his purpose, Schiller masterfully cultivated a variety of poetic forms, ranging from the epigram to the ballad to the highly stylized "thought poem."

As a consciously developed form, the epigram is a special phenomenon of the collaboration between Schiller and Goethe. It is a particularly powerful genre for Schiller. His epigrams are basically of two kinds: satirical and purely philosophical. The sharply barbed satirical poems focus on poets, thinkers, and critics of his time, especially those who attacked Schiller and Goethe, as well as the literary movements and specific currents of thought that they represented. Epigrams in the other group, primarily the "Votivtafeln" ("Votive Inscriptions"), are more general in focus and didactic in purpose.

Schiller's ballads, which are also important documents of his friendship with Goethe, represent more clearly than the epigrams the general tendency of classical German poetry to seek and establish the harmony between the ideal and the real. In that regard, they are especially clear illustrations of Schiller's aesthetics. Many of them follow a pattern established in 1795 in "Das verschleierte Bild zu Sais" ("The Veiled Image at Sais") and are best described as lyrically narrated parables that resolve the poet's metaphysical conflicts by appealing to the natural nobility of the human soul. A second type of ballad, exemplified by "Die Kraniche des Ibykus" ("The Cranes of Ibycus"), addresses itself to art's ethical and moral purposes, employing the elements of legend to achieve its goals. The ballads are the most readable of Schiller's lyric works, simply because they benefit from his mastery of drama.

Among the poems of Schiller's final creative period are some of the most extraordinarily beautiful "thought poems" in German. While stressing the inherent interdependency of ethics and aesthetics, Schiller dealt with basic existential questions such as suffering, death, transience, the quest for truth, and the perception of the absolute. In poems such as the lovely "Nänie" ("Nenia"), written in 1796, he arrived at a final answer to questions posed in his early lyrics, replacing hopelessness and resignation with the achievement in art of a timeless unity of humanity's real and ideal dimensions.

The Laura odes

In 1781, Schiller published "Die Entzückung an Laura" ("Rapture, to Laura") in Gotthold Stäudlin's *Schwäbischer Musenalmanach auf das Jahr 1782* (Swabian almanac of the muses for the year 1782). It was the first of six poems that have since become known as the Laura odes. The other five, including "Phantasie an Laura" ("Fantasy, to Laura"), "Laura am Klavier" ("Laura at the Piano"), "Vorwurf an Laura" ("Reproach, to Laura"), "Das Geheimnis der Reminiscenz" ("The Mystery of Reminiscence"), and "Melancholie an Laura" ("Melancholy, to Laura") appeared for the first time in Schiller's *Anthologie auf das Jahr 1782*. As a group, these poems present Schiller's metaphysics of love. They are a product of creative reflection rather than intimate experience. When Schiller left the military academy, he had in fact had few encounters with women, and all his early works reveal a lack of realistic perception of the opposite sex.

"Rapture, to Laura" sets the tone for the odes in its portrayal of love as a force that links the real world with the cosmic realm of absolutes. Schiller employs well-developed images of sight and sound as the outward manifestations of love, with visual contacts playing an especially important role in the communication of feeling. The gaze and what the poet can see in the eyes of his imagined Laura transform him, granting him the ability to move from his own reality into the ideal domain symbolized by the young woman. The last stanza of the poem defines her glances and the love that they represent as a clearly comprehended creative influence that has the power to vivify even inanimate stone.

The external tension between the physical and the spiritual receives special emphasis in the lyric structure of "Fantasy, to Laura," in which bodily and mental activities are juxtaposed in alternate stanzas and lines. As in all the Laura odes, the two realms are bonded together through the force of love, without which the world would disintegrate into mechanical chaos. This poem, however, emphasizes the unresolved parallelism between sexual love, presented in the literary formulations of *Sturm und Drang*, and the philosophical love of Enlightenment thought, causing the concept of love as such to remain somewhat ambiguous.

In "Laura at the Piano," Schiller developed a more precise representation of love as a metaphysical phenomenon. Consistent with his ultimate goal of natural harmony, love appears not so much as a personal experience with the feminine, but as a manifestation of the creative power of the masculine through which man masters all the cosmos. The dual character of love thus comes to symbolize the opposed forces of chaos and creation that mold the universe. A key to Schiller's message in "Laura at the Piano" lies once more in Laura's ability, through her very presence, to move her lover into a unified transcendent realm. The scope of this act is divine, and her being emerges as a subtle "proof" for the existence of God.

The notion of conflicting polarities is so basic to the Laura poems that even love has its own antagonist: death. Schiller's manner of coming to grips with the latter accords the odes a distinct kinship with his early elegies, including "Elegie auf den Tod eines Jünglings" ("Elegy to the Death of a Young Man") and "Trauer-Ode" ("Ode of Mourning"). In "Melancholy, to Laura," the death motif receives its most powerful illumination in the baroque imagery of the beloved's decay. Laura is presented here as a symbol for the entirety of earthly existence, which rests on "mouldering bones." Even her beauty is not immune to the ravages of death. In the struggle between the optimism of love and the finality of death, death triumphs, devaluating mortality as it ends all human striving for happiness. This conclusion anticipates the pessimistic mood of the famous poem "Resignation." Although not specifically dedicated to Laura, "Resignation" may be regarded as the thematic culmination of the ideas presented in the odes, a culmination that is encapsulated in a single stanza of the lengthy poem. There, in harshly vivid imagery, the poet tears his Laura bleeding from his heart and gives her to the relentless judge, eternity, in payment for the hope of peace beyond the grave.

Perhaps the most interesting symbol of death in "Resignation" appears in the poem's second stanza in the silent god who extinguishes the poet's torch. He is a precursor of more carefully refined images that Schiller based on models from Greek and Roman antiquity and employed in the powerful philosophical lyrics of his classical period. This personification of death signals a transition that occurred in the poet's creative orientation during the mid-1780's. By the time the first version of "The Gods of Greece" was printed in Wieland's periodical *Der teutsche Merkur*, Schiller had abandoned his metaphysics of love in favor of a poetic search for man's lost golden age. The characteristics of this new approach are a juxtapostion of the ancient and modern worlds, renewal of classical aesthetic and ethical values, and an appeal for the creation of a unity of sensual and spiritual experience in art.

"The Gods of Greece"

The two variants of "The Gods of Greece," published in 1788 and 1793, respectively, have in common their focus on the concept of beauty. In the first version, Schiller presented a justification of sensual beauty, couching his arguments in a defense of ancient polytheism against modern monotheism and rationalism. The Christian God in his roles of avenger, judge, and rational defender of truth is too strict for the natural world. For that reason, Schiller advocated return to an order of existence based on feeling. From the notion that the Greek gods symbolize divine perfection in things earthly, a kind of theophany informs the world created by the poem, although the second rendering places heavier emphasis on the timelessness of beauty.

The carefully nurtured inner tension of "The Gods of Greece" derives from its dual nature. It is at once a lament for the loss of man's earlier existence in nature and a song of praise for the potential immanence of the ideal within the real. In the past for which the poet longs, a closer harmony existed between the physical and spiritual realms, because the gods were more human and man was more divine. When the old gods were driven away by reason, however, they took with them everything of beauty and majesty, leaving the world colorless, empty, and devoid of spirit. The final lines of the respective versions offer two different resolutions of the problem. In the first, the poet issues a simple plea for the return of the mild goddess, beauty. The final form of the poem places the responsibility for beauty's timeless preservation squarely in the lap of the creative artist. Next to Goethe's drama *Iphigenie auf Tauris* (1787; *Iphigenia in Tauris*), "The Gods of Greece" in its two versions is the most important document of Germanized Greek mythology in classical German literature.

Ballads

Most of Schiller's poems reflect the instructional orientation of his literary work as a whole. Early in his career, Schiller forcefully acknowledged the author's responsibility to move his reader toward personal, moral, and ethical improvement. The ballads that he wrote after 1795 are among the most successful didactic lyrics in all German literature. They are masterful combinations of simplicity and clarity with vivid, engaging sensual imagery. The parabolic ballads, among them "Der Taucher" ("The Diver"), "Der Handschuh" ("The Glove"), "Der Kampf mit dem Drachen" ("The Battle with the Dragon"), and "Die Bürgschaft" ("The Pledge"), reveal the inherent nobility of the human soul when tested in circumstances that threaten life itself. Each presents a variation on the problem of the individual's response to extraordinary challenge or temptation, laying bare the inner motivations for action and glorifying the deed that is based on ideal and principle rather than on material gain. In "The Diver," the implications and consequences of free will are central to the story of a young man who retrieves from the sea a golden chalice, its own reward for the daredevil act, then perishes in a second venture, when the prize is the king's lovely daughter. "The Battle with the Dragon" explores the dilemma of choice between noble intent and obedience. A heroic knight defies the command of his order's leader and slays a terrible monster that has ravaged the countryside. He then meekly accepts expulsion from the order as the penalty for disobedience, thereby redeeming himself. Friendship as a moral force is the primary focus of "The Pledge," Schiller's rendering of the famous Greek legend of Damon and Pythias.

Typically, the verse parables have a two-part structure that pairs an obviously rash, foolish, and dangerous act with a reasoned deed of noble sacrifice through which the central figure ascends to a higher moral plane. In the popular ballad "The Glove," the Knight Delorges is asked by Kunigunde to retrieve her glove from the arena, where she has purposely dropped it among bloodthirsty beasts of prey. Delorges demonstrates his stature as a man, not when he faces the tiger to obtain the glove, but when he subsequently rejects Kunigunde's favors. It is not physical courage but the spiritual act of overcoming self that provides the measure of personal worth in this and similar ballads.

"The Cranes of Ibycus"

Like the parable poems, "The Cranes of Ibycus" is a dramatic, didactic short story in verse form. Its orientation, however, differs markedly from that of the works which stress the importance of heroic self-mastery. In its examination and defense of art as an active moral force in society, "The Cranes of Ibycus" forms a bridge between the ballads and Schiller's more abstract philosophical lyrics, while providing a concise vindication of his own approach to the drama. The ballad describes the murder of Ibycus by two men. A flock of cranes flying overhead witnesses the crime and later reappears over an outdoor theater where the criminals sit watching a play. Caught up in the mood of the drama, the criminals forget themselves and respond to the sight of the cranes, thereby revealing themselves to the crowd. More than a simple examination of problems of guilt and atonement, the lyric work juxtaposes audience reaction to stage events with the behavior of the villain-spectators to shatter the border between theater and reality. The scene is transformed into a tribunal which has the power to bring criminals to justice, thereby influencing events in the external world.

"The Song of the Bell"

Schiller's most famous ballad, "The Song of the Bell," is also the most ambitious of his poetic works. In some 425 lines of verse, the poet projects the broad spectrum of man's mortal existence against the background of the magnificent bell's creation. Alternating stanzas of varying length parallel the process of casting the bell with characteristic events of life. Birth and death, joy and tragedy, accomplishment and destruction—all find their symbolic counterparts in the steps taken by the artisans to produce a flawless artifact. The imagery is vividly real, earthy, and natural, presenting the everyday world in a practical frame with which the reader readily identifies. At the same time, the stylized presentation successfully underscores the possibility of harmony between man's physical environment and the ideal domain of the mind.

In many respects, "The Song of the Bell" represents the culmination of Schiller's poetic art. The effective integration of the poem's two threads of description and discussion is a clear realization of the creative unity that he sought to achieve in all his literary works. In his classical ballads, Schiller at last achieved the resolution of tensions caused by the opposing forces that play upon man as he searches for personal meaning. Like "The Cranes of Ibycus," "The Song of the Bell" assigns to art an ultimate responsibility for man's attainment of peace through productive interactions between his absolute and his temporal essence. The finished bell's very name, Concordia, symbolizes the final accord of material and spiritual values that was for Schiller the goal of both literature and life.

OTHER MAJOR WORKS

LONG FICTION: *Der Verbrecher aus verlorener Ehre*, 1786 (as *Der Verbrecher aus Infamie*), 1802 (*The Criminal, in Consequence of Lost Reputation*, 1841); *Der Geisterseher*, 1789 (*The Ghost-Seer: Or, The Apparitionist*, 1795).

PLAYS: *Die Räuber*, pb. 1781 (*The Robbers*, 1792); *Die Verschwörung des Fiesko zu Genua*, pr., pb. 1783 (*Fiesco: Or, The Genoese Conspiracy*, 1796); *Kabale und Liebe*, pr., pb. 1784 (*Cabal and Love*, 1795); *Don Carlos, Infant von Spanien*, pr., pb. 1787 (*Don Carlos, Infante of Spain*, 1798); *Wallensteins Lager*, pr. 1798 (*The Camp of Wallenstein*, 1846); *Die Piccolomini*, pr. 1799 (*The Piccolominis*, 1800); *Wallensteins Tod*, pr. 1799 (*The Death of Wallenstein*, 1800); *Wallenstein*, pr. 1799, pb. 1800 (trilogy includes *The Camp of Wallenstein*, *The Piccolominis*, and *The Death of Wallenstein*); *Maria Stuart*, pr. 1800 (*Mary Stuart*, 1801); *Die Jungfrau von Orleans*, pr. 1801 (*The Maid of Orleans*, 1835); *Die Braut von Messina: Oder, Die feindlichen Brüder*, pr., pb. 1803 (*The Bride of Messina*, 1837); *Wilhelm Tell*, pr., pb. 1804 (*William Tell*, 1841); *Historical Dramas*, pb. 1847; *Early Dramas and Romances*, pb. 1849; *Dramatic Works*, pb. 1851.

NONFICTION: *Die Schaubühne als eine moralische Anstalt betrachtet*, 1784 (*The Theater as a Moral Institution*, 1845); *Historischer Kalender für Damen*, 1790, 1791; *Geschichte des dreissigjährigen Krieges*, 1791-1793 (3 vols.; *History of the Thirty Years War*, 1799); *Über den Grund des Vergnügens an tragischen Gegenständen*, 1792 (*On the Pleasure in Tragic Subjects*, 1845); *Über das Pathetische*, 1793 (*On the Pathetic*, 1845); *Über Anmut und Würde*, 1793 (*On Grace and Dignity*, 1875); *Briefe über die ästhetische Erziehung des Menschen*, 1795 (*On the Aesthetic Education of Man*, 1845); *Über naïve und sentimentalische Dichtung*, 1795 (*On Naïve and Sentimental Poetry*, 1845); *Über das Erhabene*, 1801 (*On the Sublime*, 1845); *Briefwechsel Zwischen Schiller und Goethe*, 1829 (*The Correspondence Between Schiller and Goethe*, 1845); *Aesthetical and Philosophical Essays*, 1845; *Schillers Briefwechsel mit Körner von 1784 bis zum Tode Schillers*, 1847 (*Schiller's Correspondence with Körner*, 1849).

MISCELLANEOUS: *Sämmtliche Werke*, 1812-1815 (12 volumes); *Complete Works in English*, 1870).

BIBLIOGRAPHY

Carlyle, Thomas. *The Life of Friedrich Schiller.* Reprint of 1825 edition with new introduction by Jeffrey L. Sammons. Columbia, S.C.: Camden House, 1992. A biography of Schiller by a contemporary historian and essayist. An excellent resource on Schiller's life and work. Includes bibliographical references and index.

Goethe, Johann Wolfgang von. *Correspondence Between Goethe and Schiller (1794-1805).* Translated by Liselotte Dieckmann. New York: P. Lang, 1994. A collection of letters that offers insight into the lives and works of Goethe and Schiller. Includes bibliographical references and index.

Kostka, Edmund. *Schiller in Italy: Schiller's Reception in Italy: Nineteenth and Twentieth Centuries*. New York: P. Lang, 1997. Kostka's comprehensive study expands and deepens our understanding of the German-Italian relationship during the past two centuries. The impact of Schiller's work on Italian poets, critics, musicians, and conspirators is evaluated against the history of the military upheaval in Europe.

Martinson, Steven D. *Harmonious Tensions: The Writings of Friedrich Schiller.* Newark: University of Delaware Press, 1996. A critical interpretation of selected writing by Schiller. Includes bibliographical references and index.

Reed, T. J. *Schiller.* New York: Oxford University Press, 1991. An introductory biographical study of Schiller and his work. Includes bibliographical references and an index.

Lowell A. Bangerter;
bibliography updated by the editors

Gjertrud Schnackenberg

Born: Tacoma, Washington; August 27, 1953

Principal poetry

Portraits and Elegies, 1982, revised 1986
The Lamplit Answer, 1985
A Gilded Lapse of Time, 1992
The Throne of Labdacus, 2000
Supernatural Love: Poems, 1976-1992, 2000

Other literary forms

In addition to her poetry, Gjertrud Schnackenberg has produced two nonpoetic works of note: a study on T. S. Eliot's "Marina" published in the *Yale Review* in 1989 and a 1990 essay on the Epistle of St. Paul to the Colossians, part of a collection of essays written by contemporary poets on the New Testament.

Achievements

Even before she graduated from Mount Holyoke College summa cum laude in 1975, Gjertrud Schnackenberg had begun winning recognition for her writing. In 1973 and 1974 she was presented the Glascock Award for poetry, a considerable accomplishment, since earlier winners had included Sylvia Plath, Robert Lowell, and James Merrill. In 1982, the year of publication of her first book, Schnackenberg received the Lavan Younger Poets Award from the Academy of American Poets. That same year the American Academy and Institute of Arts and Letters presented her with the Rome Prize in Literature. With this and an Amy Lowell Traveling Prize for 1984-1985, she was able to spend two years in Italy, absorbing the classical heritage that would figure so prominently in her writings. During this period Schnackenberg became closely connected with the poetic movement known as New Formalism, which brought greater attention to traditional devices such as regular rhythm and meter and the use of rhyme schemes (often elaborate) and literary allusions, especially to the "great tradition" of Western culture.

For Schnackenberg, honors and awards continued. Mount Holyoke awarded her an honorary doctorate in 1985. Radcliffe College's Bunting Institute presented her with a poetry fellowship, as did the Ingram Merrill Foundation. The National Endowment for the Arts awarded her a grant in 1986-1987, and she was the recipient of a Guggenheim Fellowship in 1987-1988.

Biography

Gjertrud Cecelia Schnackenberg, the daughter of Walter Charles and Doris Strom Schnackenberg, was born in Tacoma, Washington, on August 27, 1953. The Schnackenberg family is of Norwegian ancestry and Lutheran heritage. Gjertrud was raised in the Lutheran Church and throughout her literary career has shown a great familiarity with and affinity for the beliefs and language of Christianity. She has also made extensive use of historical personages and events, especially from classical Greece and Rome; her father was a professor of Russian and medieval history at Pacific Lutheran University in Tacoma.

Walter Schnackenberg died in 1973, and his passing had a profound impact on his daughter, who has fashioned a number of poems from her memories of him. Among these are "Bavaria," about their trip to Europe in 1962, "The Lamplit Answer," the title poem of her sec-

Gjertrud Schnackenberg (© Shyla Irving)

ond volume, and "Laughing with One Eye," a series of exquisitely wrought elegies composed in 1977 and one of Schnackenberg's most important early works.

Schnackenberg had begun writing poetry when she was nineteen and a student at Mount Holyoke, the year before her father died. She graduated from Mount Holyoke in 1975 and soon won a series of prestigious fellowships and awards. Her first book, the slim volume *Portraits and Elegies*, was published in 1982. This was followed three years later in 1985 with *The Lamplit Answer.*

On October 5, 1987, she married Robert Nozick, a noted professor of philosophy at Harvard. After the appearance of *The Lamplit Answer*, Schnackenberg published little poetry and only a few essays until 1992. In June, 1992, she published "The Gilded Lapse of Time" in *The New Yorker*; later that year, a book of verse with the same title appeared. She then added another volume of new work, *The Throne of Labdacus* (2000) and a collection of her earlier verse, *Supernatural Love: Poems, 1976-1992* (2000).

Analysis

One of the most important aspects of Gjertrud Schnackenberg's career has been her role as a leading voice of the New Formalism movement, which developed in the 1980's. Writers such as Schnackenberg, Dana Gioia, and Timothy Steele, all born around 1950, made their literary debuts about that time and, both individually and as a group, reacted against the loosely organized, free-verse, and often highly emotional poetry that had been the legacy of the Beats and the writers of the 1960's and 1970's. In its place the New Formalists advocated a return to traditional poetic forms that ranged from the relatively simple sonnet to the intricately patterned and rhymed villanelle. For many of these writers a self-conscious, ironic stance was also part of their poetics. However, Schnackenberg used her formalism to control and shape a content of strong, often intense personal emotions which are often a fundamental part of her poems.

Portraits and Elegies

Schnackenberg's first collection, the poetry chapbook *Portraits and Elegies*, consists of three parts: "Laughing with One Eye," a section of twelve poems which are memories of the poet's father; "Darwin in 1881," a portrait of the British naturalist the year before his death; and "19 Hadley Street," another section of individual poems, this time sixteen in all, about the legacy and inhabitants of a Massachusetts house from the present time back to the early eighteenth century. The section's chronology moves backward against the flow of time, the same way in which historians, such as the poet's dead father, discover the past.

The poems in *Portraits and Elegies* are marked by a careful handling of form and rhyme and an apt choice of appropriate words, especially those which evoke the past, either personally for the poet or universally for humanity. At times the two intersect, as in the poem "'There are no dead,'" which uses the Bayeux Tapestry and its story as a symbolic link between present and past, living and dead, William the Conqueror and Walter Charles Schnackenberg:

> There William of Normandy remounts his horse
> A fourth time, four times desperate to drive
> Off rumors of his death. His sword is drawn,

He swivels and lifts his visor up and roars,
Look at me well! For I am still alive!
Your glasses, lying on the desk, look on.

The Lamplit Answer

By the time her second volume of poetry was published, Schnackenberg's sense of loss for her dead father had been transformed into a more general contemplation of the passage of time and the persistence of human memory. To express this complex relationship she developed a poetic form that used characterization, description, and setting in an almost novelistic fashion.

"The Kremlin of Smoke," a sequence of eight poems about the Polish composer and pianist Frédéric Chopin, is one outstanding example of this technique. In these short, lyrical pieces Schnackenberg alternates between the "present" (Chopin's life as an émigré in Paris) and his "past" (memories, perhaps idealized, of his childhood in Warsaw). A second and even more technically impressive example is the long poem "Imaginary Prisons," which retells the Sleeping Beauty story. "Supernatural Love," the poem which concludes the book, brings Schnackenberg back to her own personal recollection of her father as he bends over a large dictionary to find for her the etymology of "carnation," connected in her child's mind with the "incarnation" of Christ. In her memories of that event her father's search for "the lamplit answer" gives the poem and the book their title and underlying meaning.

A Gilded Lapse of Time

After a period of relative silence, Schnackenberg published *A Gilded Lapse of Time* in 1992. It was her most intricate and ambitious work to that point and combined lyrical intensity with a sweeping vision of the artistic, religious, and historic legacy of the classical world and the Renaissance. With its longer lines, increasingly complex sentences and more selective and extensive vocabulary, the work marks a turning point in Schnackenberg's development as a writer.

The book is divided into three parts. The first, "A Gilded Lapse of Time," looks back on the intellectual and artistic tradition Schnackenberg and other modern poets have inherited; in her case this inheritance is not only cultural but personal, since it recalls European trips she made both as a younger poet and as a child with her father. The poems in this section refer to the golden legacies of the past, especially the legacy of poets such as Dante Alighieri, who becomes a sort of patron saint for the author who seeks to link art and religion.

"The Crux of Radiance," the central portion of the book, is a lengthy meditation on the often uneasy melding of the classical world, in particular imperial Rome, and Christianity. In Schnackenberg's handling, the truths of Greek and Roman mythology half foreshadow, half combat, the revelation that flows like an unstoppable tide from Palestine toward Byzantium, Athens, and ultimately Rome itself. While the new religion grows, the older empire fades, and, as the unnamed "empress" in "The Dream of Constantine" realizes, the new faith will supplant the old. In the poem, the empress in her hand mirror sees

the void at the heart of power

Where senators don't speak Latin anymore,
Where barbarian horses clatter the cavalry stairs—
But when she turns around to look, Rome isn't there,

The final section of the work, "A Monument in Utopia," brings the reader into the twentieth century, noted for its brutalities and inhumanity, especially in those false "utopias" such as Joseph Stalin's Soviet Union, where poets such as Osip Mandelstam, the central character of this section, were caught up in the bureaucratic machinery of indifferent and almost universal cruelty. Yet, these poems seem to suggest that despite the barbarity of the modern world, the past remains and can be recaptured to show people something of their common humanity.

The Throne of Labdacus

In Greek mythology, Labdacus was king of Thebes. More important, he was the father of Laius, who married Jocasta; together, the couple produced a son. Unfortunately, Apollo's oracle had declared that this son would one day murder his father and marry his mother. To avoid this fate, Laius ordered the newborn baby exposed on the mountainside to die; but the order was disobeyed and so the story of Oedipus began. That is the story which lies behind Schnackenberg's poem, presented in sparse but telling details and an economy of language and lyrics, but it is not the poem itself. Schnackenberg refrains from retelling the Oedipus legend.

Instead, she transports us to the premiere of Sophocles' *Oedipus Tyrannus* (429 B.C.E.) where, present in the audience (or above it, or somewhere), is the god Apollo. Apollo is there because he is the god of poetry and also the god of prophecy. Therefore, he is the god who has condemned (or at least, confirmed) Oedipus to his destiny and also ensured that his fate would be forever remembered, even celebrated. In a sense, out of the bleakest human tragedy imaginable comes the greatest artistic triumph possible.

That relationship between art and life is at the heart of *The Throne of Labdacus* and, indeed, at the heart of Schnackenberg's entire body of work. Where do art and memory, so closely linked in preservation of ourselves and our loved ones, disconnect themselves from life and loss, so intimately tied to human existence and the pain of loss and separation? In a personal and universal sense (which is, ultimately, one of Schnackenberg's greatest artistic strengths), is the death of Walter Charles Schnackenberg different from the death of Laius—or are both merely the deaths of fathers? Those are some of the questions which *The Throne of Labdacus* poses in its spare, haunting poetry, in language and images that summon up the history of civilization.

SUPERNATURAL LOVE: POEMS, 1976-1992

This volume, published at the same time as *The Throne of Labdacus*, brings together Schnackenberg's first three books, *Portraits and Elegies*, *The Lamplit Answer*, and *The Gilded Lapse of Time*. As such, it sums up what might be called the initial and secondary phases of her literary career, putting on display her earlier, more formalized and stylized works (the first two volumes) and her more expansive, less tightly disciplined period found in *The Gilded Lapse of Time*.

What is most notable in this collection is Schnackenberg's growth and development over a relatively short period, and how much her career has steadily fulfilled its early promise. The technical mastery and confidence of her first two volumes have been put to use in approaching broader, more ambitious, and more universal themes. She has taken the discipline of the New Formalists into areas of personal, even Romantic subject matter, but without losing the clarity of vision or steadiness of tone that helps a poem transcend its moment and reach for a place within a tradition that stretches back to Sophocles, and perhaps to Apollo himself.

BIBLIOGRAPHY

Cohen, Rosetta. "Magnifying Lens." *The Nation* 241 (December 7, 1985): 621-623. An essay review which focuses on Schnackenberg's "talent for creating small, intricate worlds," which are, paradoxically enough, novelistic in their ultimate impact. She emphasizes Schnackenberg's ability to establish a sense of place, character, and action with slight, even minimal efforts and likens this to authors such as Henry James and Ivan Turgenev. Her explication of "The Kremlin of Smoke" is outstanding in its depth and sympathy.

Gilbert, Sandra. Review of *The Lamplit Answer*, by Gjertrud Schnackenberg. *Poetry* 147, no. 3 (December, 1985): 165-167. An unflattering and unpleasant review that attacks Schnackenberg for the supposed failings of being relatively young at the time and of taking poetry seriously. Gilbert scolds Schnackenberg for showing "a bizarre intellectual nostalgia for those 1950's in which she was born and I grew up." Even worse for the reviewer is that she senses "the vaguely obnoxious presence of this poet as Poet" in the collection.

Gregerson, Linda. Review of *Portraits and Elegies*, by Gjertrud Schnackenberg. *Poetry* 145, no.1 (October, 1984): 40-42. A generous and appreciative review of Schnackenberg's first volume of verse with a keen understanding of its blend of the personal and the formal. "Within her carefully plotted sequences, Schnackenberg's breadth of sympathy accommodates some welcome variations of form and tone." Gregerson makes early note of Schnackenberg's use of what she calls "so much full rhyme," which became such a distinctive part of her work.

Mendelsohn, Daniel. "Breaking Out." *The New York Review of Books* 48, no. 5 (March 29, 2001): 38-40. A perceptive overview of Schnackenberg's work and accomplishments. Mendelsohn places Schnackenberg's poetry within a context of classical literature, as her frequent use of Greek and Roman allusions and references requires. He presents a convincing argument that Schnackenberg uses classical literature to present "the immanence of the divine in human history, the meaning of moral responsibility, the nature and limits of art itself."

Warren, Rosanne. "Visitations." *New Republic* 209 (September 13, 1996): 37-41. Warren examines the intricacies and interwoven themes of Schnackenberg's poetry and concludes that the complexity of form echoes the multiplicity of meaning and feeling. "In the magnitude and the intricacy of its design, *A Gilded Lapse of Time* may be compared to the art of the tapestry." Warren applauds Schnackenberg for taking the lyric of personal anecdote and setting in the light of more general life and history.

Michael Witkoski

James Schuyler

Born: Chicago, Illinois; November 9, 1923
Died: New York, New York; April 12, 1991

Principal poetry

Salute, 1960
May 24th or So, 1966
Freely Espousing, 1969
A Sun Cab, 1972
The Crystal Lithium, 1972
Hymn to Life, 1974
Song, 1976
The Fireproof Floors of Witley Court: English Songs and Dances, 1976
The Home Book: Prose and Poems, 1951-1970, 1977 (Trevor Winkfield, editor)
The Morning of the Poem, 1980
A Few Days, 1985
Selected Poems, 1988
Collected Poems, 1993

Other literary forms

James Schuyler wrote (or cowrote) three novels. Beginning with *Alfred and Guinevere* (1958), the novels deal with the upper middle class and show a good ear for the comic trivialities of ordinary conversation, whether of children and adolescents, sophisticated young adults, or middle-aged couples. They also demonstrate, with their precision in naming, Schuyler's connoisseur's eye for furniture, design, and objects used or displayed in the household. The satiric *A Nest of Ninnies* (1969), cowritten with John Ashbery, lacks the plot and fully developed characters of *What's for Dinner?* (1978), his most substantial novel, giving rich evidence of true command of the form as it traces an alcoholic's recovery in a mental hospital, her husband's simultaneous affair with a widowed friend, and the progress of several other patients on short-term stays in the hospital.

Three of Schuyler's plays have been produced: the one-act pieces *Presenting Jane* (1952) and *Shopping and Waiting* (1953), and *Unpacking the Black Trunk*, another collaboration with a fellow poet (Kenward Elmslie), produced off-Broadway in 1965. He wrote the libretto ("mostly collage from newspapers," he says) for *A Picnic Cantata* (1954), for which the writer Paul Bowles composed the music (for two pianos, percussion, and four women's voices); it was recorded by Columbia Records.

Like fellow New York poets Ashbery and Frank O'Hara, he also wrote art criticism—particularly for *Art News*, where he served for a time as associate editor.

Achievements

James Schuyler was a keen observer of the most intimate details of the world around him and of the sensations they evoked in him. His poetry captures those detailed impressions and sensations, however ephemeral they may be. This very ephemerality is the singular distinction of his world, particularly in his presentation of nature. The individual poem lives not so much as a perfected piece of art, frozen under glass; rather, it shimmers with movement and conveys a sense of being nearly as ephemeral as the impressions it records. Sometimes, of course, the impressions and mood are so fleeting as to leave the reader with virtually nothing but random actions and details—or even only words. This is the danger of Schuyler's method—one which its great propounder, Frank O'Hara, did not always steer clear of himself. Thus, some poems read as little more than notebook jottings.

Yet the method is also responsible for the brilliance of his two long poems, "Hymn to Life" and "The Morning of the Poem" (the title poem of the volume for which he was awarded the Pulitzer Prize in 1981). These poems ramble, it is true, down the streams of Schuyler's consciousness, across several weeks' time, from place to place, subject to subject, mood to mood. Yet each attains a remarkable unity through the skill and exactness with which Schuyler has captured his own voice, developed over the course of a rather short career (barely two decades of serious publishing), in order to penetrate and reveal his own mental and emotional states. His highly individual, warmly personal, frankly intimate voice is characterized by unforced humor, gentle self-deprecation, eagerness, equivocation, wonder, doubt, fascination. This is the voice, as well, of a series of simple and tender love poems, joyful and physical without being actually erotic, addressing another man with the greatest ease and naturalness imaginable. Schuyler's achievements in evoking the processes of nature, love, and mind are praiseworthy, for producing not only such thought-provoking and appealing major works as the two long poems but also many shorter ones that are sure to enchant readers over the years. Schuyler won several awards other than the Pulitzer Prize, including the Frank O'Hara Prize from *Poetry* in 1969; he received grants including a National Endowment for the Arts grant and an Academy of American Poets fellowship.

James Schuyler (© Thomas Victor)

BIOGRAPHY

Born in Chicago to a family with extensive roots in America, James Schuyler grew up in Washington, D.C., Buffalo, and East Aurora, New York, the family seat to which he returned. He attended Bethany College in West Virginia, served in the Navy in World War II, and worked for Voice of America in New York City before traveling to Italy, where he attended the University of Florence and lived in W. H. Auden's house in Ischia, typing some of the elder poet's manuscripts (as he notes in his obituary poem, "Wystan Auden"). After he returned to New York in the early 1950's, he became involved in art and poetry circles and took a curatorial position in the Department of Circulating Exhibitions at the Museum of Modern Art, organizing a number of shows. He also served as associate editor of *Art News*, for which Frank O'Hara and John Ashbery also worked; together, and with a number of other young poets, they changed the poetry scene in New York and became a major force in contemporary American poetry. Close friends as well as colleagues, they often have referred to one another in their books and poems and sometimes collaborated. Painters and musicians are included in this group; various artist friends of Schuyler are not only mentioned in his poems but have contributed cover illustrations for several of his books. Schuyler suffered personal traumas in the 1970's, and his recovery from a nervous breakdown is recorded in poems in *The Morning of the Poem*; he also sustained severe burns after falling asleep while smoking in bed. Nevertheless, in the late 1970's he began reading publicly for the first time. Schuyler died in New York City in 1991 after suffering a stroke.

ANALYSIS

James Schuyler was a master of subtle changes—in growing things, in weather, in time of day or year, in moods and thoughts. These he conveyed appropriately, without big effects, sudden bursts of insight, or harsh contrasts. Rather, his poems have the shimmering magical quality of familiar scenes and objects rendered in watercolor landscapes or still lifes, but they are anything but still: Even his most quiet and peaceful scenes contain movement, however nearly imperceptible. Such constant, inevitable movement is the manifestation of life for Schuyler, and through his poetry the reader too gains a more intense appreciation for the many wonders and delights of even the smallest details in this life, once a moment is taken to observe them.

In an interview, Schuyler once said that to him, "much of my poetry is as concerned with looking at things and trying to transcribe them as painting is. This is not generally true of poetry." Evidence of Schuyler's affinities to painting (which doubtless stem largely from his friendship with many painters as well as his own work in the art world) is abundant throughout his work, in his attention to color, light, texture, and other visual effects.

Besides being "very visual," his work also "seems to be especially musical," he goes on to say. Indeed, he counted important composers such as Virgil Thomson and Ned Rorem among his friends and wrote about music from Johannes Brahms and Sergei Rachmaninoff to Janis Joplin and Carly Simon. His is not the music of the conventional sonneteer, however, although he made an obligatory gesture or two in that direction. Rather, his poetry, almost without exception, ignores regular rhyme and meter in favor of free verse, appropriate for his emphasis on endless change. His styles of free verse change radically too, from lines of only two or three syllables in his self-styled "skinny poems," providing a slow, even, almost hesitant, occasionally fragmented pace appropriate for the meditative stance of some of these poems, to lines as long as each individual sentence unit requires (in "The Cenotaph"), to lines a page wide or more in the long poems. Line breaks are often capricious, but this very unpredictability allows him some splendid effects. For example, the minimally punctuated "Buttered Greens" has lines which make sense in one way, until the next line indicates that the last part of the preceding line is meant not as a completion of the preceding thought but as the beginning of a new statement: "inside all/ is not con-/ tent, yet/ the chance/ of it is/ there, free." A reader automatically assumes that "free" modifies "chance," but the next line suggests that it modifies the botanical noun: "there, free/ leaves fall." Often he abandons punctuation altogether, and a whole series of sensory impressions flows down or across the page as unmediated sensory input ("A Sun Cab"). Sentence fragments, composed of nouns, adjectives, and prepositional phrases, are frequent in many of these shorter poems, reminiscent of William Carlos Williams, whom Schuyler acknowledged as an early influence.

Yet musical aspects are present in occasional devices of structure and sound. Words or images are repeated, like leitmotifs; recurring themes and images are particularly important in the long poems, where depiction of rain or of sites in Washington, D.C., acts both as a cohesive device and as a counterpoint to other concerns in the poem. His free-verse lines often emulate the startling and open structures of much modern music. Finally, Schuyler does not neglect the traditional musical devices of sound; pleasing patterns of alliteration, assonance, consonance, and even exact rhyme (though usually internal and never long-sustained) appear casually in occasional poems such as "Song" and "Just Before Fall."

Most of his poems purport to do no more than map the stream of his consciousness, whether it consists chiefly of external impressions which engage his full attention or of thoughts and feelings and whatever sensory recollections they invoke. Sometimes it is a combination of the two—external impressions giving rise to memories, which are in turn interrupted by more sensory input from the present moment. Schuyler's is very much a poetry of the present. Nearly every poems begins directly in the present tense, often indicating the setting of place, time, weather; recollections of the past may intrude, described in the past tense as appropriate, but their appearance is strongly grounded in the immediacy of the present moment, rather than being a meditation on "remembrance of things past" or "emotion recollected in tranquillity" undertaken as an end in itself.

Time is certainly a central theme for Schuyler, but with an emphasis quite unlike that of most other poets. It passes as quickly (or slowly) for him as for another, but he does not bemoan its passing. He is not without regrets, but these are for friends who have died, lovers who have left: He accepts his move ahead into age, not with resignation but as merely another stage of life, for "Life will change and/ I am part of it and/ will change too."

Such an attitude informs his two longest poems, "Hymn to Life" and "The Morning of the Poem." Each embraces and celebrates change, the prevailing force in his work, the dominant characteristic of all life itself. In the earlier poem, Schuyler takes the reader with him along the paths of his mind and experiences, recording his various thoughts and sensory impressions as time moves on. It begins the day before spring (that is, in March), then moves imperceptibly into April and May. These shifts occur not with an abrupt, secretarial ripping-off of the old month's calendar page but with the gradualism of nature itself: This seventeen-page poem is not broken into sections as the time passes but reveals each new month's presence only in mid-line, appropriately for the subtle recognition of something new in the air, a change that has occurred while one was watching but was perhaps momentarily distracted, watching the many wonderful details all around, so exquisitely conveyed in this poem.

"Song"

Such unremarked changes, so lovingly dwelt on, are Schuyler's stock-in-trade, for the times *between* (parts of the year or the day) are his favorite poetic subjects. "Song," for example, concentrates on the hour of sunset. It begins: "The light lies layered in the trees" (with melodious alliteration and use of long vowel sounds). Then the sun sets, "not sharply or at once," but in "a stately progress down the sky." Other details around him, however, attract his attention: "Traffic sounds and/ bells resound . . . the grass is violent green." Several color sensations then yield to the sound of a car starting up, as the visual sense surrenders to darkness. Two short lines ("A horsefly vanishes./ A smoking cigarette.") capture the sense of increasing darkness: The normally quite visible insect is lost to sight while the glowing of the cigarette, normally not noticeable in daylight, appears, contrasting with the lack of light around it. Finally, the leaves merge, "discriminated barely/ in light no longer layered," because of the departure of the sun's light.

This poem, like so many others by Schuyler, simply presents a sequence of sensory images, vividly capturing the various components of a particular moment as it is experienced. Schuyler does not pretend to deal with the earth-shattering problems of humanity: That becomes editorial writing, he has said. Consequently, his poetry has often been regarded as trivial. Indeed, many of his poems do fail to register any significant impression. The comic criticism of himself that he quotes in "The Morning of the Poem"—"All he cares about are leaves and/ flowers and weather"—has validity, but not at all as a criticism. These subjects serve as indicators of his own understanding of life—its beauty, its transience, its variability, qualities that every human being must understand and accept to come fully to terms with existence as well as with such major human concerns as love and death.

These important concerns are not in the least absent from Schuyler's work. He often confronts death as he recalls or writes elegies for friend and fellow poet Frank O'Hara, other friends and lovers (Bill Aalto, his first lover, who died of leukemia after they had broken up), and musicians as diverse as Libby Holman, Janis Joplin, and Bruno Walter. Their deaths may be violent or gentle, but Schuyler accepts them with deepest serenity. He portrays love as "quiet/ ecstasy and sweet content." A lovely series in *Hymn to Life* records with utmost simplicity such joys as lying on the beach beside his lover or eagerly awaiting his return from a trip; later poems reveal with welcome understatement the pain of being without him, once the relationship has ended.

Love (and sex) and death, in addition to time and change (indeed, in conjunction with them, for the latter are ineluctably implicated with the former) form the major strands of the intricate but not at all impenetrable tapestry of Schuyler's longest poem, "The Morning of the Poem," which reads almost like a run-on, candid, and charmingly intimate conversational journal. Because it proceeds through sixty-one pages with no break other than a dot in the exact middle of the poem (separating an elegy from a grocery list), it would seem to be all of one piece. Schuyler maintains unity of place—that is, the East Aurora room where he sits at his typewriter—although his thoughts may range to New York City, New Brunswick, England, and Paris, and among similarly diverse subjects. Yet the reader discovers, moving through the poem, that these meditations occur not on a single morning or afternoon but over a nearly two-month span.

"The Morning of the Poem"

"The Morning of the Poem" takes Schuyler from the beginning of July to late August, when he leaves his rural family home in western New York to return to Manhattan. As he sits at his typewriter, thinking of his friend painting in New York (and addressing him, as if in a letter, throughout much of the poem), the weather, assorted deliveries, his aged mother's nagging, and many memories from various stages of the past (last night's dream, cruising another middle-aged man in the grocery store, boyhood and adolescent incidents, lovers and friends and a beloved dog now gone) impinge on his consciousness and accordingly enter the poem. Amid the many surrenders to thought and recollection, the recurring descriptions of the rainy weather, several lawn mowings, and a few passing references to the time of month give readers their bearings as to the progression of time—always to their surprise at its speed.

Schuyler has a vested interest in moving time rapidly—he is looking forward to rejoining his painter friend in New York. His recollections of the past enable time to pass more quickly for him, while the present-tense descriptions of the weather and activities around the house slow it down, reminding him only of the stretch of time still facing him. Yet this does not deny his ability to find pleasure even in the moments that drag on.

Schuyler keeps imagining his friend painting on his rooftop in New York and praises "the dedication of the artist" which characterizes him. Schuyler's question, "Whoever knows what a painter is thinking?" is echoed near the end of the poem, upon receipt of a postcard from composer Ned Rorem: "I wonder what it's like, being a composer?" He finds these other arts mysterious: painting involves colors whose names he can't remember; music demands "so much time" to write down "the little notes," whereas his own writing "goes by so fast:/ a couple of hours of concentration, then you're/ spent." Presented in counterpoint to these other artists, one introduced at the very beginning of the poem, the other at the end, James Schuyler as poet, seated at his typewriter, is seen by the reader to be every bit as dedicated, even when drinking limeade, or just lost in reverie—dedicated to the pursuit of self-knowledge, of an empathy with the life around him, natural and human. It has certainly demanded great effort to make this poem, composed presumably in countless sittings over two months, flow so smoothly and achieve a unity among the many subject of its meanderings.

A poetry of sheer stream of consciousness, of simple recording of sensory and mental experiences, would seem to be an easy achievement; many lesser poets have attempted it, but without the aura of mystery, celebration, wonder, and joy that Schuyler brings to such moments. He has no poetic program, no ambition to make his poems "more open," as "a clunkhead" suggests: rather, he wants "merely to say, to see and say, things/ as they are." It thus seems important to name things exactly, and he displays a splendidly precise vocabulary of nouns and verbs when describing his environment (climate, plant life, sea life, forest life, furnishings, art works). It is understandably frustrating, therefore, when he fails to remember certain names for things, as throughout "The Morning of the Poem." Yet specific names may not be so important when considered against appreciation for the things themselves and the experiences they create, as he tells his "dead best friend" in "The Morning of the Poem":

> this is not
> your poem, your poem I may
> Never write, too much, though it is there and
> needs only to be written down
> And one day will and if it isn't it doesn't matter:
> the truth, the absolute
> Of feeling, of knowing what you know, that is
> the poem . . .

To capture such "truth," such an "absolute of feeling" in words is, of course, far from easy. In "Hudson Ferry," Schuyler writes, with a kind of comic disgust, "You can't talk about the weather"—it's so easily susceptible to clichés. Yet Schuyler has paradoxically persisted, as "The Morning of the Poem" makes clear. How? He continues to remark that "You can't get at a sunset naming colors," so he uses other means: For example, noting the effects of the sunset in "Song," he is not afraid to use metaphors and similes—but characteristically with freshness and aptness: "An almost autumn sky, a swimming pool awash/ with cinnamon and gentian." Yet he also often mocks the poet's metaphorical and personifying tendencies and can undercut such poeticisms with a deft phrase, like the parenthesis that immediately follows the lines just quoted: "(The sky's the swimming pool, that is)," or the deflation of the grandiose apostrophe "O Day!" with the no less and possibly more appreciative "literal/ and unsymbolic/ day." As he writes in "The Cenotaph": "The hawkweed flowers are an idea about the color of fire./ The hawkweed are one thing and the fire is another." Thus he reminds the reader that the objects compared retain their own identities; it is the human mind that draws such parallels. For that very reason—that the human mind perceives things by making such comparisons—these poetic figures which indicate similarities must not be omitted from the writing of poetry; they are indispensable to the mind's process of perception. What he does seek to avoid poetically are the familiar standard associations: "fall/ equals melancholy, spring,/ get laid." "An Almanac" succeeds in this splendidly, tracing the passage of the seasons in an utterly fresh way—through nothing but discrete details of action, predominantly human, which indicate clearly the particular changes accompanying each new season, from fall to spring: "Shops take down their awnings . . . In cedar chests sheers and seersuckers displace flannels and wools."

Schuyler's poetry revels in the experience of any sort of weather, season, time of day, environment. He seems equally at home in city and country (though favoring the latter) and can paint a Manhattan street scene as luminously as a Long Island beach or a woodland walk in Vermont. The variety of the scenes he can enjoy and his ability to capture accurately the feel of such a range of experience richly display his appreciation for the fact of change—even in the breakup of love affairs, even in the losses of death. Toward the end of "The Morning of the Poem" he realizes "how this poem seems mostly about what I've lost," yet none of these losses has broken him. He does not elegize them with the typical "life must go on" resolution, for he knows very well that, *sub specie temporis*, there is nothing else life can do: "Life will change and/ I am part of it and/ will change too. So/ will you, and you. . . ." Death is merely another form of this change. The process of life contains "in repetition, change:/ a continuity, the what/ of which you are a part." There is no stability, as each season fades into the next, yet in each season is the promise of the future ones; as Schuyler writes in "Buttered Greens," our life means "leavings and/ the permanence/ of return."

When Schuyler in "The Morning of the Poem" receives a letter from a friend telling of her brother's dying while "the grandchildren and the dogs ran in and out as usual," Schuyler responds quoting the familiar litany, which is no less true: "'I the midst of life we are in death, in the/ Midst of death we are in life.'" This is the essence of Schuyler's attitude toward both life and death, including a healthy recognition of the passage of time and the inevitability of change ("This beauty that I see . . . it goes, it goes."). After he hears about a hurricane on Long Island, Schuyler asks himself in "The Morning of the Poem," "Why so much pleasure in wrack and/ ruin?" It may be the proof it gives of the ephemeral nature of all security and permanence. After all, "the scattered wrack" contains "(always) some cut-up surprise." Change gives no cause for fear or regret, Schuyler suggests through his wonderfully serene poetry; change in nature creates endless sequences of beauty, like the changing days in "Hymn to Life": "each so unique, each so alike." The seasons are predictable, yet full of unexpected variations: a cold, rainy July, a balmy November.

During the course of the marvelous abundance of "The Morning of the Poem," Schuyler, indulging in a favorite pastime, eating ("grapes, oysters/ And champagne"), remarks that "bliss is such a simple thing." So is most of Schuyler's poetry, yet it conveys a rich sense of the world around him and a healthy, joyous approach to existence.

Other major works

LONG FICTION: *Alfred and Guinevere*, 1958; *A Nest of Ninnies*, 1969 (with John Ashbery); *What's for Dinner?*, 1978.

PLAYS: *Presenting Jane*, pr. 1952; *Shopping and Waiting*, pr. 1953; *Unpacking the Black Trunk*, pr. 1964 (with Kenward Elmslie).

NONFICTION: *Two Journals: James Schuyler, Darragh Park*, 1995; *Diary of James Schuyler*, 1996.

Bibliography

Auslander, Philip. *The New York School Poets as Playwrights*. New York: Peter Lang, 1989. Although the focus of this volume is on plays, the chapter on Schuyler also examines his poetry, including his link to the New York School. An appreciative piece on Schuyler, discussing the imagery in his work, his numerous references to old things, and his thematic treatment of the past.

Kalstone, David. Review of *The Crystal Lithium. The New York Times Book Review* (November 5, 1972): 6. Review says volume contains the best poems Schuyler has ever written. Describes his work as having "the coveted directness, the openness to experience his plainest declarations." Praises Schuyler for being attuned to the way the awakened mind functions.

Malkoff, Karl. *Crowell's Handbook of Contemporary American Poetry*. New York: Thomas Y. Crowell, 1973. In the introduction, Malkoff discusses Schuyler's thoughts on the New York poets, of which he was one, and the influence of cubism and Surrealism on their work. Contains further discussion of Schuyler's "projective verse."

Schuyler, James. *The Diary of James Schuyler*. Edited by Nathan Kernan. Santa Rosa, Calif.: Black Sparrow Press, 1997. Schuyler's diary is a devastating account of his decline into mental illness and a narrative of his achievements. Includes bibliographical references.

Vinson, James, ed. *Contemporary Poets*. 3d ed. New York: St. Martin's Press, 1980. The entry on Schuyler, by Michael Andre, identifies his artistic leanings and his prolific writings. Calls *Salute* representative of his poems, which are "sensitive and perceptive." Notes that much of Schuyler's poetry describes what he sees and what he loves—and that is not New York.

Ward, Geoff. *Statutes of Liberty: The New York School of Poets*. 2d New York: Palgrave, 2001. An account of the key figures of the New York School including Schuyler. Ward provides up-to-date material on the group and its influence on postmodern poetics. Includes bibliographical references and index.

Scott Giantvalley;
bibliography updated by the editors

Delmore Schwartz

Born: Brooklyn, New York; December 8, 1913
Died: New York, New York; July 11, 1966

Principal poetry

In Dreams Begin Responsibilities, 1938 (includes poetry and prose)
Genesis, Book I, 1943
Vaudeville for a Princess and Other Poems, 1950
Summer Knowledge, 1959

Other literary forms

Although Delmore Schwartz thought of himself primarily as a poet, he wrote short stories, plays, and literary and film criticism as well. His masterful 1937 story, "In Dreams Begin Responsibilities," prefigures the major concerns of his later work and provides the title for his first collection of poetry in the following year. *The World Is a Wedding* (1948) contains this and most of the remainder of Schwartz's best stories. The later stories collected in *Successful Love, and Other Stories* (1961) are generally less noteworthy. Schwartz's retooling of William Shakespeare in *Coriolanus and His Mother*, which occupies a large part of *In Dreams Begin Responsibilities*, and the autobiographical *Shenandoah* (1941) are interesting, if not particularly stageworthy, contributions to verse drama. A good sampling of his essays on modern literature and its critics—T. S. Eliot, Ezra Pound, Edmund Wilson, Lionel Trilling—as well as occasional pieces on films such as *The Seven Year Itch* and *The Blackboard Jungle* reveals the characteristic interplay of his mind between high and popular culture, and may be found in the posthumous *Selected Essays of Delmore Schwartz* (1970). Schwartz's papers, recovered and presented to Yale University by his literary executor, Dwight Macdonald, mainly record the abandoned projects that littered Schwartz's career.

Achievements

Delmore Schwartz burst onto the New York literary scene when his best-known story, "In Dreams Begin Responsibilities," was published in the front of the first issue of the revised *Partisan Review* in Autumn, 1937.

Not yet twenty-four, Schwartz had passionately dramatized the adolescent trauma of the Jewish urban intellectual edging nervously into manhood in the 1930's. Vladimir Nabokov ranked "In Dreams Begin Responsibilities" among his half-dozen favorite modern stories. With the appearance of his first collection of poetry in 1938, Schwartz's reputation was firmly established. This volume, again titled *In Dreams Begin Responsibilities*, was praised by such luminaries as Allen Tate, John Crowe Ransom, W. H. Auden, and Wallace Stevens as the work of the ablest of the younger American poets. Schwartz's passionate rhetoric and unrelieved pessimism seemed perfectly to evoke the bleakness of the 1930's in poems that explored the tragic gap between human aspiration and fulfillment. Before the age of twenty-five Schwartz was bemoaning lost innocence and passing time and had fastened on his obsessive theme: the failure of life's hopes. Schwartz would embody his own poignant illustration of the life of shattered dreams; only rarely would his poetry approach the brilliance of his first collection.

Schwartz pinned his hopes for enduring fame on *Genesis*, an epic poem that expressed the "Spirit of America" through the life of Hershey Green, the poet's surrogate. Schwartz believed that the poem would confirm him as heir apparent to the modernist mantle of T. S. Eliot, one of his literary heroes. Despite some isolated passages of great brilliance, *Genesis*, too long, too diffuse, too remorselessly narcissistic, failed to embody its grandiose design. For some time, Schwartz continued the saga of Hershey Green, but with a mounting sense of futility; the proposed Books II and III of *Genesis* never appeared.

Vaudeville for a Princess and Other Poems, a grab bag of poems, comic prose, and literary burlesque, represents a further decline from Schwartz's earlier work. Often his own harshest critic, Schwartz admitted the collection's failure by including only three of its poems in *Summer Knowledge*. The first half of this volume consists of poems, many in revised versions, that appeared originally in 1938; the remainder is made up of new poems, the three from *Vaudeville for a Princess*, and a selection from *Genesis*. Nearly all Schwartz's enduring poetry is contained in this collection, for which he became the youngest poet ever to win the prestigious Bollingen Prize. Ironically, it marked the end of his poetic career. The remaining seven years of his life completed the paradigm of the tragic fate of the sensitive artist whose precipitous decline parallels his meteoric rise. Once the most precocious voice of his generation, Schwartz ended as the symbol of dazzling promise only sporadically fulfilled.

Biography

Delmore David Schwartz, who once confessed that his only subject was himself, owed his birth to a fluke, a fact which he never tired of recounting. In order to conceive, Rose Schwartz needed an operation which she financed by selling a French war bond, the gift of an overseas uncle. Since Harry Schwartz was unaware of Rose's ploy, Delmore's birth was the result of a deception which fascinated and repelled the poet for the rest of his life. Life with argumentative and histrionic parents is translated into the art of "In Dreams Begin Responsibilities," where the boy-narrator watches his parents' courtship unfold on the screen of an imaginary theater. When they decide, despite lingering doubts, to marry,

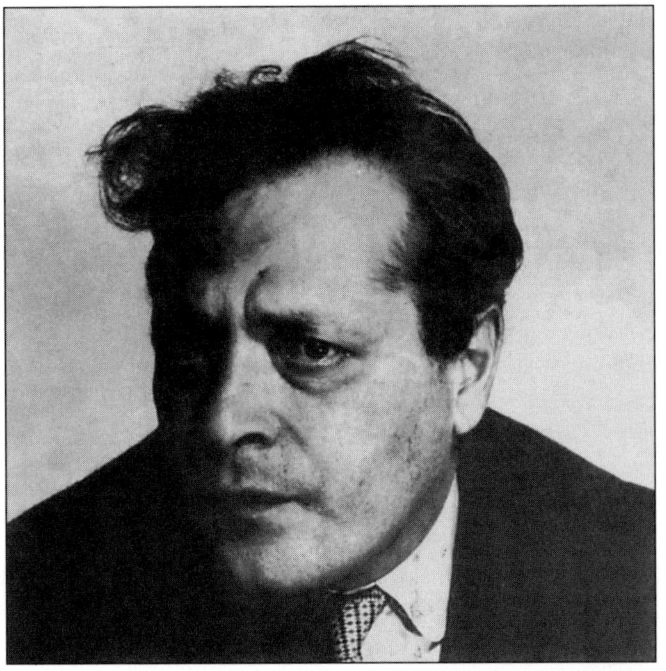
Delmore Schwartz (© Jane Lougee)

the boy leaps from his seat screaming at them to reconsider. Perhaps the most traumatic episode of Schwartz's childhood occurred one summer day in 1921 when Rose dragged him into a roadside café and found her husband with another woman, whom she denounced as a whore. Young Hershey Green in *Genesis* learns that this incident will critically influence his later life. Schwartz's father left home permanently in 1923 when Delmore was nine. Like his parents, Schwartz was to doubt the wisdom of marriage; both of his own marriages were conceived in uncertainty and terminated in divorce.

Brilliant but erratic, Schwartz decided early to become a poet, although he majored in philosophy, earning a B.A. degree from New York University in 1935. He started graduate study at Harvard but left in March, 1937, without taking a degree, returning to New York, where his criticism, poetry, and fiction soon began appearing in magazines. By the early 1940's, Schwartz's life had assumed the sort of pattern it would maintain thereafter, eddying between Cambridge, where he taught composition and advanced writing from 1940 to 1947, and New York, where he served as poetry editor of the *Partisan Review* from 1943 to 1955.

During his adolescence, Schwartz, the child of Jewish immigrants from Eastern Europe who could barely speak English, had lived simultaneously in Irving Howe's "world of our fathers" and the gleaming promised land of the aspiring New York literati. In one of Schwartz's finest stories, "America! America!," a promising young writer, Shenandoah Fish, listens to his mother's poignant tale of immigrant neighbors and gains a new appreciation of their lives that belies his initial contempt. Indeed the first and last names of Schwartz's hero reflect the odd mixture of the grandiose and mundane in his own. The tragedy of Schwartz's life was that the dialectical opposites so beautifully resolved in the fiction of "America! America!" and another fine story, "The Child Is the Meaning of This Life," could not be mediated in the real world. His inherent nobility and high purpose gave way to suspicions about wives, friends, and colleagues, resulting finally in paranoia. At Harvard, he envisioned a faculty cabal convened for the sole purpose of denying him tenure; his jealousy and insults finally alienated his most supportive colleague, Harry Levin. Back in New York, he reviled ancient enemies and steadfast friends alike, and the gloom of his last days was lightened only by friends such as Dwight Macdonald, Meyer Schapiro, and Saul Bellow, whose loyalty he could not destroy.

By then, however, Schwartz no longer cared. A boy wonder in 1938, he never surpassed and only rarely equaled his early achievements. By 1945, the failure of his first marriage, the lukewarm reception of *Genesis*, on which he had staked everything, and his heavy drinking had made him a "changed man" in the opinion of William Barrett, an old friend who renewed acquaintance with Schwartz upon returning from the war. Ironically, the onset of Schwartz's long decline coincided with his solidifying reputation as an American man of letters; by 1947 he was the most widely anthologized poet of his generation (which included Robert Lowell and John Berryman), one of the ablest critics of modern poetry and writing, and an editor of *Partisan Review*, the most respected intellectual journal of its day. Yet the only poetry he published during the remainder of his life was the slight *Vaudeville for a Princess*, 1950, and *Summer Knowledge*, 1959, the bulk of which was selected from his work prior to 1938.

By the 1950's, heavy drinking, sleeping pills, and massive doses of Dexedrine had, according to James Atlas, Schwartz's biographer, exacerbated his chronic insomnia, confirmed his manic-depressive mood cycles, and led to the "notorious paranoia that dominated his last years." After a painful three-year stint at Syracuse University in the mid-1960's, arranged by Meyer Schapiro with the help of recommendations from Robert Lowell and Saul Bellow, whose novel *Humboldt's Gift* (1975) brilliantly evokes Schwartz's last days, the poet returned to New York to die. Sporadically incarcerated in Bellevue, Schwartz finally succumbed to a heart attack in the seedy Manhattan hotel that was his last home, on July 11, 1966.

Analysis

Coming of age in the intellectual climate of New York in the 1930's, Delmore Schwartz could hardly have avoided the twin influences of Sigmund Freud and Karl Marx, whose ghosts meet to analyze the hero's motives in *Coriolanus and His Mother* (1938). Freud argues for Volumnia's primacy in the formation of Coriolanus's psyche, Marx for Rome's. Finally, mother and city merge into a symbol of the past which neither Coriolanus nor the poet can escape. The model is elaborated in one of his best essays, "The Two Audens," which appeared in the first issue of *The Kenyon Review* in 1939. In the essay, Schwartz defined the Marxist Auden, the poet of contemporary social concerns, and the Freudian Auden, who reported the "intuitions of psychic life." While Schwartz preferred Auden's latter persona, it is clearly the interplay between public (ego) and private (id) selves that fascinated him.

Yet it was Eliot who was Schwartz's "culture hero," the seer who discovered new forms and a new idiom for the modern world. Schwartz's ambition was to provide for the 1930's and 1940's the image of the times that Eliot had etched for an earlier generation. So long as Schwartz maintained a degree of Eliot's intellectual objectivity, his poetry, especially that of *In Dreams Begin Responsibilities*, brilliantly fulfilled his program, but he was compelled to treat the history of his times as inseparable from the history of himself. Thus *Genesis* is largely vitiated by Schwartz's obsession with the minutiae of Hershey Green's life, which is still bogged down in adolescence after two hundred pages of verse. James Atlas argues that Schwartz's background militated against the adoption of Eliot's poetic manner—authoritarian, aloof, detached—and that Arthur Rimbaud (whose *Une Saison en enfer*, 1873, he quirkily translated) and especially Charles Baudelaire provoked his rhetorical flights of grief and rage.

Baudelaire, Eliot, and another of his literary heroes, James Joyce, embody Schwartz's obsession with the social alienation of the poet, although Eliot was firmly ensconced in the literary establishment by the 1930's. The titles of such essays as "The Isolation of Modern Poetry," "The Vocation of the Poet in the Modern World," and "The Present State of Poetry" hint at the poet's marginality. Schwartz's alienation as a poet, deepened by his Jewishness, often took the form of a paranoia which he found increasingly difficult to suppress in his poetry.

Most of Schwartz's poetry is based on a varied but traditional iambic pentameter line which tends to lengthen and loosen in his later work. Images of snow—pacifying, concealing, obliterating—and light—dazzling, clarifying, transcending—permeate his poetry. No matter how they are structured and whatever imagery they employ, Schwartz's poems relentlessly explore his intertwined themes: the nature of the self, the alienation of the poet and Jew, the burden of the past, and the defeat of human aspirations. A discussion of his best poems most conveniently follows the order of their appearance in *Summer Knowledge*.

"The Ballad of the Children of the Czar"

"The Ballad of the Children of the Czar" imagines two events occurring simultaneously in 1916: The czar's children play with an erratically bouncing ball in their father's garden; six thousand miles away the two-year-old Schwartz eats a baked potato in his high chair. Simultaneity is reinforced by the mention of the poet's grandfather, who, after suffering in the czar's army, hid in a "wine-stinking barrel" for three days in Bucharest, and escaped to America where he "became a king himself." Yet the poem is no parable of freedom—quite the opposite. The czar's children cannot control the ball which rolls beyond the garden's iron gate; their frustrated howls are echoed by the infant Schwartz whose buttered potato slips from his hands. Next year the Russian Revolution will seal the fate of the czar's children, prefigured in the loss of their ball. A lost ball, a dropped potato: Man can neither arbitrate his happiness nor control his fate. Children of czars and immigrants alike are victims of inherited history which is at once irrecoverable and inescapable. Ironically, the very ubiquity of the past underlines man's fatal inability to change it. The poem recalls Aeneas bearing old Anchises on his back as they flee burning Troy; so must all children bear their fathers' weight, the burden of which they can never unload.

"In the Naked Bed, in Plato's Cave"

"In the Naked Bed, in Plato's Cave" expands Schwartz's discussion of the limits of human knowledge. Underlying the poem is Plato's parable of the cave where chained prisoners face a wall upon which they can see only shadows cast by firelight. So are all men chained, argues Plato, by their limited knowledge; they are doomed to take shadows for the reality that lies in the sunlight outside their cave. Schwartz, lying awake in bed, sees reflected headlights sliding along his wall, and hears the hammering of carpenters, the grinding of truck traffic, and finally the milkman striving up the stairs, his bottles chinking. Perplexed, still woozy from sleep, he greets the morning, which heralds the mystery of beginning again and again.

Schwartz takes over Plato's distinction between appearance and reality, but reverses the conclusions of the parable. An actual bedroom replaces the symbolic cave, and the intensity and immediacy of the narrator's impressions contrast with the shadowy and fragmentary perceptions of Plato's chained prisoners. Moreover, the narrator sidles between bed and window, between sleep and wakefulness; Plato's men are perpetual sleepers, condemned to watch an eternal shadow play. Yet the poem's conclusion points equally to human limitations, although in a different manner. The world in time—that is, the world apprehended by the speaker—*is* the real world. Schwartz has met Plato's dilemma, not by resolving its dualism but by denying its existence. "In the Naked Bed, in Plato's Cave" thus confirms the validity of human perception even as it fixes its boundaries.

"Far Rockaway"

"Far Rockaway" takes its title from the public beach where New Yorkers cast aside the "rigor of the weekday" with their shoes. The radiant seashore, the swaying light, the "passionate sun," and the glittering sea are positive images which, in the poem's first four stanzas, propose freedom not only from weekday care but perhaps from time itself. The fifth stanza, however, introduces "the novelist," a detached observer, an introspective man whose concern is "the cure of souls" first cited in the epigraph of the poem, where it is attributed to Henry James. In a series of rhetorical questions, the intruder reduces weekend joy to trivial escapism: a "cure" for the body but no surcease for the soul. Day's radiance yields to a "haunting, haunted moon." The lesson of the master, suitably opaque, may be that sensual abandonment, the summum bonum of the masses, is a delusion and is, in any case, impossible for the detached artist, forever on the boardwalk, never on the beach.

"Tired and Unhappy, You Think of Houses"

A variation on this theme occurs in "Tired and Unhappy, You Think of Houses," wherein another outsider imagines a cozy family scene which, for him, must remain a "banal dream." Turning away to the anonymity of the subway rush, he is "Caught in an anger exact as a machine!" Still another instance of the artist's social alienation is expressed dramatically in "Parlez-Vous Francais?" This time the scene is a barbershop, which, like the beach of "Far Rockaway" and the home of "Tired and Unhappy, You Think of Houses," embodies the communal values of everyday life. On the radio the voice of a demagogue Caesar, probably Hitler, seduces the recumbent men with extravagant promises calculated to appeal to their basest instincts. Enter the writer, "shy, pale, and quite abstracted," whose three-day beard and lack of tie define his separateness. He cries out—in French—that Caesar knows that most men lead lives of quiet desperation and can be deceived by dreams and lies which will inevitably lead them to war and death. Naturally the writer's rage is incomprehensible to the men, none of whom understands this "foreigner"; just as naturally his use of French deliberately underscores his estrangement. Whether the unheeded seer of "Parlez-Vous Francais?," the unnoticed observer of "Far Rockaway," or the wistful dreamer of "Tired and Unhappy, You Think of Houses," the artist remains divorced from quotidian life.

"Prothalamion"

"Prothalamion" announces Schwartz's forthcoming marriage. Its opening sections treat the subject with Spenserian reverence and dignity: "The feast of bondage and unity" is approached with "great piety"; the poet affirms his need for love and remembrance; the bride's beauty will engender the self-forgetfulness necessary for married life. There follows a catalog of events best forgotten: his mother's rage before her seven-year-old son when she trapped her husband "At dinner with his whore"; his terror at thirteen when "a little girl died," and he first confronted death.

Freud and Marx are invited to the wedding to "mark out the masks that face us there," since "No form is cruel as self-deception." Mozart shows up to reveal the "irreducible incorruptible good," presumably that arising from a life dedicated to high art. Then come jewelers, acrobats, florists, and finally Robinson Crusoe and Charlie Chaplin, as the poem explodes into joyous celebration.

These last two names, however, invoke the loneliness intrinsic to the human condition. The sublime vision of the wedding feast dissolves into something "fantastic and pitiful," as hopes and wishes yield to the "fear" that closes four of the stanza's eight lines. Even as he pledges to live with and care for his bride, the poet alludes to the heavy burden of his own mortality and of hers, which he must henceforth bear on his back. Moreover, the poet's unstable personality poses a threat to the marriage "because my circus self/ Divides its love a million times." Only a God conceived in the gathering darkness of the poet's fears can give the bride the understanding of the husband he wishes to be. The ending is ambiguous. Is the poet making a last desperate plea for the human understanding which will make life with another possible? Or, is he eschewing the lesson of Freud and Marx in embracing a final self-deception, one not so cruel as necessary for the survival of his marriage? The magic of the Spenserian moment is, in either case, long gone.

"The Heavy Bear Who Goes with Me"

Burdened with his past in "The Ballad of the Children of the Czar," with his affections in "Prothalamion," Schwartz is finally burdened with his very body in "The Heavy Bear Who Goes with Me." One of his finest and most anthologized pieces, this poem employs a beast fable to examine traditional philosophical dichotomies. Concerning the relationship between mind and body, "The Heavy Bear Who Goes with Me" immediately establishes its context by its epigraph—"The withness of the body"—originally attributed to the distinguished philosopher, Alfred North Whitehead, one of Schwartz's favorite Harvard professors. The bear—"clumsy," "lumbering," "brutish"—represents the grossness of the human body above which the aspiring spirit cannot ascend. "That inescapable animal" has accompanied the speaker from birth, distorting his gestures, thwarting his better impulses, and reducing his existence to a "scrimmage of appetite." The poem's brilliance results from Schwartz's manipulation of the bear metaphor: its honey-smeared face, its frenzied howling in the night, and its clownish showing-off evoke a primordial force as terrifying as it is grotesque.

"A Dog Named Ego, the Snowflakes as Kisses"

An equally brilliant companion piece immediately follows "The Heavy Bear Who Goes with Me" in *Summer Knowledge*. "A Dog Named Ego, the Snowflakes as Kisses" again explores the gulf between body and soul by means of an animal metaphor. This time the duality is expressed in Freudian rather than Platonic terms; the dog, unlike the bear, is inseparable from the self. Perhaps it is best to consider the dog as an aspect of the self, as its name suggests. Yet the narrator, the central ego of the poem, is the dog's master, at least in the sense that his walking the dog constitutes the poem's dramatic movement. Still another complication in the man-dog relationship is introduced by the speaker's description of the dog's actions. By observing the dog, he observes himself, and thereby dramatizes the human ego in the act of self-scrutiny.

Accompanying his master one chilly December evening, the dog Ego is distracted by falling snowflakes. While the man placidly accepts "the snowflakes as kisses," the dog, growing more and more excited, tries to swallow the snow, which continues "falling from some place half believed and unknown." The snow's kisses recall Schwartz's most haunting scene: waking to "the bleak winter morning of my 21st birthday, the windowsill shining with its lip of snow," which concludes "In Dreams Begin Responsibilities." In both contexts the snow—pure, beautiful, evanescent—promises a momentary vision of transcendence in its fleeting life between falling and melting.

Accompanied by such a dog, however, the hungering self destroys the object of its quest. Prey to his appetites embodied in the barking dog frantically devouring the snowflakes, the narrator helplessly witnesses the reversal of the master-dog relationship and his consequent enslavement by Ego. The drama of the lost self is played out in the dog's pursuit of the snowflakes, which now signify only illusion and obliteration. As night collapses around him, the speaker's double isolation—from self and heart's desire—is expressed in the repeated ending, "And left me no recourse, far from home."

"A Dog Named Ego, the Snowflakes as Kisses" contains Schwartz's most profound treatment of the self-alienation that results from thwarted aspiration. The poem implies, additionally, that this alienation lies at the root of the social estrangement portrayed in so many of his other poems. Whereas "The Heavy Bear Who Goes with Me" dramatizes Schwartz's dualism no less forcefully, "A Dog Named Ego, the Snowflakes as Kisses" is a subtler evocation of the interplay between the physical and spiritual. Taken together, the poems constitute Schwartz's most powerful essay on the endlessly fascinating topic of the divided self.

Summer Knowledge

The poems in *Summer Knowledge* reveal a mellower Schwartz. On the surface they represent an acceptance of the here and now heralded by an intensified use of light imagery and a new reliance on images drawn from nature. Schwartz describes his newly acquired "summer knowledge" as "supple recognition of the fullness and the fatness and the roundness of ripeness"; it might as easily be recognized as a surrender of the possibility of knowing. This shift from retrospective analysis to intuitive acceptance undermines the dialectical tension that rippled through Schwartz's youthful poems. More and more often his late poetry collapses into prosaic statement as its lines lengthen, its syntax relaxes, and its imagery diffuses. The quintessential poet of urban life and its discontents, Schwartz seems vaguely uncomfortable in his new role as celebrant of nature and its satisfactions. While the later work is more positive in its reconciliation of the self and the world and in its insistence on the primacy of the love equated with "summer knowledge," its forced earnestness and flaccid execution indicate the decline of Schwartz's power.

"Seurat's Sunday Afternoon Along the Seine"

Among the few later poems that bear comparison with Schwartz's early work, none is finer than "Seurat's Sunday Afternoon Along the Seine." This long poem, consisting of a meticulous description of Seurat's famous pointillist paiting *Un Dimanche d'été à la Grande Jatte* (called *A Sunday Afternoon on the Island of La Grand Jatte* in English), interspersed with narrative commentary, employs dazzling visual imagery to recreate the luminosity of George Seurat's greatest painting. Perhaps Schwartz was drawn to the painting by the intensity of its light, or he may have identified with Seurat, whose finest achievement came at twenty-five, when he hardly suspected—in the words of Schwartz's poem—"that in six years he will no longer be alive!" In any event, the poem's depiction of the communal enjoyment of the crowd recalls the weekend revelry of "Far Rockaway" but with a crucial difference. The radiant images of "Far Rockaway" were ironically conceived to expose carefree enjoyment as illusory escapism; reality was the province of the critically observant "novelist" strolling the boardwalk above the beach. In "Seurat's Sunday Afternoon Along the Seine," the shining sun fixes the Sunday people, "In glowing solidity, changeless, a gift, lifted to immortality." The warm leisure of their holiday has been transmuted by Seurat into the transcendent reality that eluded the narrators of Schwartz's earlier poems. Invoking John Keats—"O happy, happy throng,/ It is forever Sunday, summer, free"—whose urn depicted figures immortalized by the painter's art, Schwartz affirms the primacy of immediate sensory experience. The world evoked on Seurat's canvas is ultimate reality; but does reality consist of life's everyday actions, or the formal expression of those actions in works of enduring art?

"Seurat's Sunday Afternoon Along the Seine" may owe something to Wallace Stevens's idea, most poignantly expressed in the similarly titled "Sunday Morning," that the poet must rediscover the earth. He does so by creating a "supreme fiction" which endows life with the value once conferred by religion. Stevens, who ranked with William Butler Yeats and Eliot among Schwartz's heroes of modern poetry, treated reality as an extension of the artist's imagination and thereby bridged the gulf between the self and the world. In the penultimate stanza of his poem, Schwartz seems in like manner to have resolved the dualism that provided the imaginative framework for so much of his previous poetry. It only remains for the last stanza of "Seurat's Sunday Afternoon Along the Seine" to reestablish the unity of Schwartz's best work and, in the haunting tragedy of its conclusion, provide a fitting coda to his achievement.

The last stanza begins with a final affirmation of the immutability of art, which defies time and change. Although the nineteenth century has yielded to the twentieth and Seurat's painting has been transplanted to Chicago, his art endures: "All of his flowers shine in monumental stillness fulfilled." Abruptly, Gustave Flaubert's voice cries, "Ils sont dans le vrai," referring to people such as those in Seurat's painting, who have apparently discovered the truth—"The kingdom of heaven on earth on Sunday summer day"—and incidentally confirming the ultimate reality of the visible world. Franz Kafka repeats Flaubert's phrase, but in a voice "forever sad, in despair's sickness," fatally poisoning the poem's context. The everyday pleasures of forebears, marriages, and heirs, he suggests, are unavailable to the likes of Flaubert, Kafka, and, of course, Schwartz. As in "Prothalamion," when the invocation of Robinson Crusoe and Charlie Chaplin shattered the Spenserian moment, the voices of Flaubert and Kafka confirm Schwartz's eternal alienation. The closing lines of "Seurat's Sunday Afternoon Along the Seine" ironically redefine "summer knowledge" as a devastating epiphany of human defeat.

Other major works

short fiction: *The World Is a Wedding*, 1948; *Successful Love, and Other Stories*, 1961.

play: *Shenandoah*, pb. 1941.

nonfiction: *Selected Essays of Delmore Schwartz*, 1970; *Letters of Delmore Schwartz*, 1984; *Portrait of Delmore: Journals and Notes of Delmore Schwartz, 1939-1959*, 1986.

children's literature: *"I Am Cherry Alive," the Little Girl Sang*, 1958.

Bibliography

Atlas, James. *Delmore Schwartz: The Life of an American Poet*. San Diego, Calif.: Harcourt Brace Jovanovich, 2000. A full-length, comprehensive biography that attempts to cut through the poses and personae of Schwartz. Contains enriching details of Schwartz's life and extracts of his poems illustrating his development as a poet.

Carruth, Hayden. "Comment." *Poetry* 112 (September, 1968): 417-427. Reviews *Summer Knowledge* and notes that while Schwartz is capable of producing very good poetry, his work is uneven. Likens the good poetry to "wild roses in a bank of weeds."

McDougall, Richard. *Delmore Schwartz*. New York: Twayne, 1974. A straightforward account of Schwartz's work, commenting on his theme of alienation—that is, his self-concept as a Jew and the Jewish influence on his work. Attends to his later more successful poems. A useful introduction to Schwartz.

Phillips, Robert. *Letters of Delmore Schwartz*. Princeton, N.J.: Ontario Review Press, 1984. A collection of important letters by Schwartz that reflects not only his thinking but also the issues of the times. The introduction is sympathetic to Schwartz, noting that he is a man who "put his talent into his work and his genius into conversation." A must for Schwartz scholars.

Pollet, Elizabeth, ed. *Portrait of Delmore: Journals and Notes of Delmore Schwartz, 1939-1959*. New York: Farrar, Straus & Giroux, 1986. Edited by Delmore's second wife, this important collection of journals, notes, and poems will enlighten scholars and readers of Schwartz. In the introduction, Pollet offers some insights into her life with Schwartz and her perceptions of him.

Schwartz, Delmore. *Delmore Schwartz and James Laughlin: Selected Letters*. Edited by Robert Phillips. New York: W. W. Norton, 1993. A collection of correspondence offering insight into the lives and work of Schwartz and Laughlin. Includes bibliographical references and index.

Lawrence S. Friedman;
bibliography updated by the editors

Sir Walter Scott

Born: Edinburgh, Scotland; August 15, 1771
Died: Abbotsford, Scotland; September 21, 1832

Principal poetry

The Eve of Saint John: A Border Ballad, 1800
The Lay of the Last Minstrel, 1805
Ballads and Lyrical Pieces, 1806
Marmion: A Tale of Flodden Field, 1808
The Lady of the Lake, 1810
The Vision of Don Roderick, 1811
Rokeby, 1813
The Bridal of Triermain: Or, The Vale of St. John, in Three Cantos, 1813
The Lord of the Isles, 1815

The Field of Waterloo, 1815
The Ettrick Garland. Being Two Excellent New Songs, 1815 (with James Hogg)
Harold the Dauntless, 1817

Other literary forms

Sir Walter Scott's literary reputation rests firmly on his monumental collection of Waverley novels, the final revision of which was issued, in forty-eight volumes, between 1829 and 1833. The novelist produced those classics on a regular basis during the last eighteen years of his life—beginning with the three-volume *Waverley: Or, 'Tis Sixty Years Since* in 1814 and concluding, shortly before his death, with *Count Robert of Paris* and *Castle Dangerous* (under the collective title *Tales of My Landlord*, fourth series), both in 1831. In addition to the novels, Scott produced or adapted eight plays between 1799 and 1830: *Goetz of Berlichingen* (1799, translation), *The Iron Hand* (1799, translation), *Guy Mannering* (1816), *Halidon Hill* (1822), *Macduff's Cross* (1823), *The House of Aspen* (1829), *Auchindrane: Or, The Ayrshire Tragedy* (1830), and *The Doom of Devorgoil* (1830).

Scott's nonfiction prose includes *Provincial Antiquities of Scotland* (1826), *Religious Discourses by a Layman* (1828), *The History of Scotland* (1829-1830), and *Letters on Demonology and Witchcraft* (1830). He also produced three biographies of note: *The Life and Works of John Dryden*, first published in 1808 as part of his eighteen-volume edition of that poet's works; *The Memoirs of Jonathan Swift* (1826; originally included in the nineteen-volume *The Life of Jonathan Swift*, 1814); and *The Life of Napoleon Buonaparte: Emperor of the French, with a Preliminary View of the French Revolution* (1827, 9 volumes). In addition, as editor of *Ballantyne's Novelist's Library* 1821-1824 (10 volumes) Scott wrote biographical essays on each writer in the series (including Henry Fielding, Tobias Smollett, Samuel Richardson, Ann Radcliffe, Charlotte Smith, and Fanny Burney); he published those sketches separately in 1825 (2 volumes).

Finally, Scott expended considerable energy on a long list of editorial projects carried out between 1799 and 1831: In addition to the works of John Dryden and Jonathan Swift and the *Novelist's Library*, one may note *Minstrelsy of the Scottish Border* (1802-1803, 32 volumes), *A Collection of Scarce and Valuable Tracts* (1809-1815, 13 volumes), *Chronological Notes of Scottish Affairs from the Diary of Lord Fountainhall* (1822), and *Lays of the Lindsays* (1824). Various editions of *The Journal of Sir Walter Scott* have appeared, beginning in 1890.

Sir Walter Scott (Library of Congress)

Achievements

Sir Walter Scott's literary reputation still rests on thirty novels. Few twentieth century readers and scholars have been interested in his poetry or have taken the time to examine the distinct stages of his literary career. With the publication of *Waverley* in 1814, Scott's literary life as a novelist began and his period of intense poetic production terminated. At the outset, then, one is tempted to view the poetry only in the context of its effect on the fiction—or, from another perspective, the effect of Scott the poet on Scott the novelist.

Ample reason exists, however, for studying the poetry on its own merits, for the imaginative power to be found in Scott's metrical romances, lyrics, and ballads. Some contemporary scholars support the claims of their Victorian predecessors, who argued that Scott, among all of his "British" contemporaries, emerged as the first writer of the Romantic movement. Indeed, although literary historians correctly offer William Wordsworth's *Lyrical Ballads* (1798)—and its significant preface—as the key to understanding British Romanticism, Scott's *The Lay of the Last Minstrel*, published seven years later, reached a far wider audience (in both England and Scotland) than Wordsworth's collection and achieved a more noticeable impact among the poet's contemporaries than did the earlier work. In fact, no previous English poet had managed to produce a work that reaped such large financial rewards and achieved so much popular acclaim.

Interestingly enough, Scott's poetic achievements came in a form radically different from those qualities that marked the traditional "giants" of his age—Wordsworth, Samuel Taylor Coleridge, John Keats, Percy Bysshe Shelley, and Lord Byron. True, Scott considered, at a variety of levels, the prevalent Romantic themes: the rejection of scientific dogmatism, a return to the glamour of past ages, the discovery of happiness in primitivism rather than in modernity, the enjoyment of emotion, a basic belief in humanitarianism. He rejected, however, the radical sentiments of the Romantic movement. By nature and upbringing a conservative, Scott clung to Tory politics and to the established Church of England rather than rising up in actual or intellectual rebellion against such institutions. He had little or no interest in mysticism, overzealous passion, or the dark unconscious. Scott's poetry is distinguished by its considerable clarity and directness; it is the product of a gentlemanly and reasonably satisfied attitude toward promoting the values of his own social class. He did rush back into an imaginary past to seek out heroes and adventurers whom he found lacking in his own early nineteenth century cultural and artistic environment. Such escapes, however, never really detracted from his belief in the challenge of the present intellectual life and the present world, where, if everything else failed, courage would support the intellectually honest competitor.

Chronologically, Scott belongs with the early Romantics; culturally and intellectually, he occupies a middle ground between Scotland and England, and therein, perhaps, lies his ultimate contribution to poetry in English. He captured, first in the poems and later in his prose fiction, the essence of Scottish national pride; that pride he filtered through the physical image of Scotland, through its varied and conflicting scenery and its traditional romantic lore. The entire area—joined politically to Great Britain in 1707, but still culturally free and theologically independent during Scott's day (as it remains even to this day)—stimulated and intensified his creative genius and supplied the substance first for his poetry, then for his prose fiction. Nevertheless, Scott remained distinctly aware of England and receptive to the demands of the English public—his largest reading audience. For them he translated the picturesqueness of the Highlands and the Lowlands, the islands and the borders. While photographing (or "painting," as his contemporaries maintained), through his imagination, the language and the sentiment of Scotland, Scott gave to his English readers scenes and characters that could be observed as partly English. His poetry has a freshness, a frankness, a geniality, and a shrewdness peculiar to his own Scottish Lowlands. Still, as observers of that part of the world quickly appreciate, there is little difference between a southern Scotsman and a northern Englishman—which, in the end, may also be an apt commentary on Scott's poetry.

BIOGRAPHY

The fourth surviving son of Walter Scott and Anne Rutherford, Walter Scott was born on August 15, 1771, in a house in the College Wynd, Edinburgh. At the age of eighteen months, the infant contracted a fever while teething and, in the end, lost the use of his right leg. The circumstance became noteworthy not only for its effect on Scott's personality and his writing, but also as the first fully authenticated case of infantile paralysis in medical history. After the failure of various attempts to remedy the malady, Scott's father sent him to Sandy Knowe, near Kelso (Roxburgh), to live with his grandfather (Robert Scott) and his uncle (Thomas). Although the five years spent there contributed little or nothing toward curing the boy's lameness, they provided some experiences with lasting influence: subjection to republican and Jacobite prejudices; songs and legends taught to him by his grandmother (Barbara Haliburton); a trip to the spas at Bath, with a stopover at London on the way; sea-bathing at Prestonpans, near Edinburgh (and site of one of the key engagements of the Jacobite uprising of 1745), where he learned of the German wars from an old veteran of Invernahyle, one Captain Dalgetty.

In 1778, the boy returned to his father's house in George's Square, Edinburgh, and later that year entered the high school at Edinburgh. From his principal tutor, a strict Presbyterian named James Mitchell, Scott gained a knowledge of Scottish church history, while his mother encouraged him to read William Shakespeare. His health, however, continued to be a problem, so again the elder Scott sent his son off, this time to Kelso to live with an aunt, Jenny Scott. During his half-year's stay there, he met James Ballantyne and the blind poet Thomas Blacklock; there, also, he read James Macpherson's Ossianic poems, Edmund Spenser's *The Faerie Queene* (1590-1596), and Thomas Percy's *Reliques of Ancient English Poetry* (1765). Most important, however, he began to collect ballads, a form and a tradition that would remain with him and influence his own literary and cultural directions. By November, 1783, Scott had prepared himself sufficiently to begin studies at Edinburgh University; he pursued only those disciplines, however, that aroused his interest (law, history, romantic legends, and literature). Further illness reduced his stamina, and his education was interrupted once more when he apprenticed himself to his father, copying legal documents. Eventually he did manage to earn a degree in law (1792) and gain admission to the Scottish bar.

Although Scott did indeed practice law and, after a reasonable period as a novice, did manage to earn a fair income from his labors, his interest focused more sharply than ever on literature, ballads, and Scottish folklore. Thus, between 1792 and 1799—first merely as a companion to the sheriff-substitute of Roxburghshire, then as sheriff-deputy of Selkirkshire—he engaged in his "border raids," exploring the country, collecting ballads and tales, and generally enjoying the hospitality of many and various true and traditional Scottish characters. To that activity he added a deep interest in German literature; he learned the language (but not the formal grammar) well enough to read and to translate, publishing in 1799 an edition of Johann Wolfgang von Goethe's *Goetz von Berlichingen* (1774), one of that writer's earliest heroic creations in which an old knight bows to the forces of decay about him. Scott did not emerge as a public figure, however, until about six years later, when he published *The Lay of the Last Minstrel*. In rather quick succession he became a partner in and large contributor to James Ballantyne's publishing house, gained a permanent appointment (1806) as Clerk of Session at Edinburgh, and was a principal founder (along with John Murray the younger) of *The Quarterly Review*, the Tory rival to *The Edinburgh Review*. In 1813, he declined the honor of being named Poet Laureate of England in favor of Robert Southey. A year later his first novel, *Waverley*, was published.

As Sheriff of Selkirkshire, Scott went, in 1804, to live at Ashestiel, on the banks of the River Tweed (dividing England and Scotland); there he wrote, between 1805 and 1813, *The Lay of the Last Minstrel, Marmion, The Lady of the Lake, The Vision of Don Roderick, The Bridal of Triermain*, and *Rokeby*. In 1812 he had begun the construction of a baronial mansion at Abbotsford (near Melrose in Roxburghshire)—once known as the little farm of Cartleyhole belonging to the monks of Melrose. After taking up residence there he could, indeed, lay claim to the title of "Gentleman." He continued to reap financial benefits from his writing, and in 1820 he received a baronetcy. He would, however, be denied the luxury of lasting contentment. Economic depression swept the British Isles in 1825; a year later, the firm of John Ballantyne and Company collapsed, and Scott found himself being left responsible (morally and actually) for most of the publishing house's debts. Rather than declaring bankruptcy, the poet-novelist pressed forward on a number of literary projects in order to pay his creditors. To compound the emotional strain and the problems of failing health, Scott's wife, Charlotte Carpentier, died in the same year.

Thus, the last several years of Scott's life were marked by struggle and overwork; he was kept afloat, so to speak, on the strength of his pride and personal integrity. By 1831, his health had declined seriously; an Admiralty frigate carried him on a sea voyage through the Mediterranean; he had been sent off from Abbotsford with a fresh sonnet by Wordsworth. While on board, he suffered a stroke of apoplexy resulting in paralysis and was forced to return to Abbotsford. There he lingered, from mid-July, 1832, until September 21, when he died quietly in the presence of all of his children.

ANALYSIS

Sir Walter Scott's poetry, unlike that of his Romantic contemporaries, is vigorous, high-spirited, and unreflective. Scott delighted in war and pageantry, in the rich traditions of antiquity. As a Scottish poet born among a people who sought action, he was drawn to his heritage, to his connections with the border chieftains and the House of Buccleuch. Thus, his narrative poems and ballads reflect the character of a strong and proud man who, though he was lame, dreamed of the ultimate masculine activities: of chivalry, adventure, the qualities of feudalism, and the military picturesqueness of another age.

BALLADS

Any survey of Scott the poet must consider his interest in the popular ballad, an interest that came naturally because of the love for the old, harsh times. Scott saw in the popular Scottish ballad a contrast to the relative serenity of his own early nineteenth century. He relished the clannish loyalties, the bravery, the cruelty, the revenge, and the superstitions of the old ballads. Thus, he began with "The Chase" and "William and Helen" (1796)—two translations from the German lyric poet (and, coincidentally, lawyer) Gottfried August Burger (1747-1794); next came three strange, almost mystical ballads contributed to Matthew Gregory ("Monk") Lewis's *Tales of Wonder* in 1801: "Glenfinlas," "The Eve of St. John," and "The Gray Brother." His interest in the ballad reached its height—a scholarly as well as a poetic pinnacle—with *The Minstrelsy of the Scottish Border*, wherein Scott the editor and poet gathered and polished the best examples of what will always be considered the true literature of Scotland.

The ballad, however, was not to be the end-all for Scott the poet, but rather a springboard to other forms and variations of ballad themes. He turned his poetic attention to a series of complex and ornamental romances wherein, instead of the harshness and rusticity of the border, lords, ladies, and even clerics came forth to expound lofty themes in elevated language. Still, the stuff from which the popular ballads sprang is there. In *The Lay of the Last Minstrel*, for example, romantic love blends easily with magic, dwarfs, and goblins, while in *Marmion*, the early sixteenth century battle at Flodden Field in Northumberland, where the English, in 1513, defeated the Scots under James IV, allowed Scott to develop elaborate descriptions of conflict and chivalry, of the detailed instruments of warfare and the awesomeness of border castles. More important in terms of the ballad influence, *Marmion* draws considerable poetic life from its thoroughly romantic narrative—from intrigue, disguise, and unfaithfulness (both clerical and secular). *The Lady of the Lake* intensifies those actions, featuring Highland clans rushing to battle after being summoned by a fiery cross. Scott carried his readers on a tour of chieftain's lodge and king's court, setting the stage for James Fitz-James to reveal himself as King James and to restore the noble Ellen to her true love, Malcolm Graeme. Although the later poems—*The Vision of Don Roderick*, *Rokeby*, and *Harold the Dauntless*—reveal Scott as more than ready to abandon verse for prose fiction, the worlds of knighthood, sorcery, and the ancient bards and minstrels continued to fascinate him—no matter that the locales and circumstances seemed far removed from that wild terrain north of the River Tweed.

HISTORY AND NARRATIVE

One must not too quickly assume that Scott's poetry contains little beyond historical or romantic re-creations. Although he himself readily admitted that his work did not rise to the levels of Wordsworth or Coleridge, he nevertheless remained a legitimate poet, not simply a compiler and reviser of historical verse tales. Scott fully realized the depth and complexity of human emotions; he chose, however, to portray the manifestations of those emotions within the context of his own historical knowledge and his own historical imagination. Thus, he could set forth value judgments and insights into history rather than simply displaying the past as mere background scenery. Scott knew only too well that he was living in the present—in a world marked by political and social revolution to which the romantic past must, for the sake of reason and order, subordinate itself. Nevertheless, history could continue to instruct the present; it could also amuse and it could momentarily ease the confusion within the minds of the poet's readers. History could help a restless and degenerate age to imagine the heroics of an older time.

With only a few exceptions, the poetry of Scott conveys action and excitement, for the poet had learned at an early age to master the conventions of narrative. But narration alone could not carry the essence of the poem. In *The Lady of the Lake*, he demonstrated the quality of painting lovely scenery, giving it dimension, and fusing it skillfully with the poetry of clan life. Scott opened the gates to the Scottish Highlands for his cultivated readers to the south. For the height of action and excitement, however, those same readers had to turn to *Marmion*, to the strong horse striding over green terrain in the fresh air, its shrill neighing and the sun's rays reverberating and reflecting from the shield and the lance of its rider. In fact, the poet stacked his details one upon the other in almost breathless fashion: "Green, sanguine, purple, red, and blue,/ Broad, narrow, swallow-tailed, and square,/ Scroll, pennon, pensil, brandrol."

Characters

The major weakness of Scott as a poet is his inability to create believable characters. Margaret of Branksome Hall (in *The Lay of the Last Minstrel*) exudes considerable charm, but she does little beyond fulfilling her function as the typical "fair maid," even amid a fast-paced series of armed encounters and magical spells. Roderick Dhu, Malcolm Graeme, and Lord James Douglas (*The Lady of the Lake*) appear active enough, but they have little else to do aside from their obvious responsibilities as fierce Highland chieftains, outlawed lords, and young knights. Also acting according to form (and little else) are Roland de Vaux (*The Bridal of Triermain*), Philip of Montham (*Rokeby*), and Edith of Lorn and Lord Ronald (both from *The Lord of the Isles*)—although Edith's disguise as a mute page, as well as the dangers she encounters, allows her some room for depth and variety. There is little doubt that Scott's best poetic characters assume the forms not of romantic heroes but of heroic scoundrels, such as the stately forger Marmion and the pirate Bertram Risingham (*Rokeby*), whose evil nature contains some elements of good. Scott addressed this problem himself, stating that no matter how hard he had tried to do otherwise, his rogues emerged as heroes. More accurately, the rogues had more life and depth than did the heroes.

Nature

Scott's ballads and verse tales are not, however, anchored to the issues of characterization, to the conflicts between good and evil, or even to the differences between heroes and villains. Virtually obliterating the shallowness of those characters, the poet's almost passionate love for the beauties of nature infuses practically every poem. In that sense, and within the context of his abilities to communicate that love to a relatively large and varied reading audience, Scott may indeed be identified with the early Romantic poets. Traditionally, his sophisticated English readership perceived Scotland—especially the Highlands—as a physical and intellectual wilderness; at best, readers of that day recalled only the Gothic descriptions of James Macpherson's Ossianic poems or the Addisonian sketches of the essayist Henry Mackenzie. Then, with *The Lay of the Last Minstrel, Marmion*, and *The Lady of the Lake*, Scott revealed the culture of his native land, and "Cold diffidence, and age's frost,/ In the full tide of my song were lost." He carried his readers on his poetic back "Across the furzy hills of Braid," through "all the hill with yellow grain," and over "To eastern Lodon's fertile plain"; through Scott's lines, his readers far to the south undertook a vicarious trek into a land that had been virtually shut off from their imaginations.

In addition to satisfying the imaginative needs of his Romantic-age readers, Scott conscientiously guided them through an almost microscopic study of physical nature, as if he were conducting a tour: going over each scene, textbook in hand, noting the various species of plants and shrubs, stones and rocks, surveying "each naked precipice,/ Sable ravine, and dark abyss" to uncover "Some touch of Nature's genial glow." For example, in the description of Lake Coriskin (in *The Lord of the Isles*), the landscape portrait captures the warmth of nature and the poet's feeling for color: In addition to the genial glow of Nature, "green mosses grow" atop Benmore, while "health-bells bud in deep Glencoe"—all of which serves up a sharp contrast to the "Black waves, bare crags, and banks of stone" that constitute the "bleakest" side of the mountain. Again, in depicting Edinburgh and the camp in *Marmion*, the poet directs his audience to the "rose on breezes thin" that clash headlong with "Saint Giles's mingling din" as he strives to document the specifics of the distance (topographical and imaginative) "from the summit to the plain."

Critical assessments

Critical response to Scott's poetry has ranged from kindness to indifference. Perhaps the fairest assessment of his poetry is Scott's own. He never aspired to equal Wordsworth or Coleridge or Byron; he wanted only to enjoy life and literature (indeed, even in that order), disclaiming everything beyond the love of Scotland and its traditions. That love obviously led him to poetry, as it did to prose fiction, to biography, to history, and to scholarly editing and collecting. When he finished with one of those aspects of the good, intellectual life, he simply went on to something else. Literary history must be prepared to accept Sir Walter Scott on his own terms and on that middle ground.

Other major works

LONG FICTION: *Waverley: Or, 'Tis Sixty Years Since*, 1814; *Guy Mannering*, 1815; *The Antiquary*, 1816; *The Black Dwarf*, 1816; *Old Mortality*, 1816; *Rob Roy*, 1817; *The Heart of Midlothian*, 1818; *The Bride of Lammermoor*, 1819; *A Legend of Montrose*, 1819; *Ivanhoe*, 1819; *The Monastery*, 1820; *The Abbot*, 1820; *Kenilworth*, 1821; *The Pirate*, 1821; *The Fortunes of Nigel*, 1822; *Peveril of the Peak*, 1823; *Quentin Durward*, 1823; *St. Ronan's Well*, 1823; *Redgauntlet*, 1824; *The Betrothed*, 1825; *The Talisman*, 1825; *Woodstock*, 1826; *The Highland Widow*, 1827; *The Two Drovers*, 1827; *The Surgeon's Daughter*, 1827; *The Fair Maid of Perth*, 1828; *Anne of Geierstein*, 1829; *Count Robert of Paris*, 1831; *Castle Dangerous*, 1831; *The Siege of Malta*, 1976.

PLAYS: *Halidon Hill*, pb. 1822; *Macduff's Cross*, pb. 1823; *The House of Aspen*, pb. 1829; *The Doom of Devorgoil*, pb. 1830; *Auchindrane: Or, The Ayrshire Tragedy*, pr., pb. 1830.

NONFICTION: *The Life and Works of John Dryden*, 1808; *The Life of Jonathan Swift*, 1814; *Lives of the Novelists*, 1825; *Provincial Antiquities of Scotland*, 1826; *The Life of Napoleon Buonaparte: Emperor of the French, with a Preliminary View of the French Revolution*, 1827; *Religious Discourses by a Layman*, 1828; *The History of Scotland*, 1829-1830; *Letters on Demonology and Witchcraft*, 1830.

TRANSLATIONS: *The Chase, and William and Helen: Two Ballads from the German of Gottfried Augustus Bürger*, 1796; *Goetz of Berlichingen*, 1799 (of Johann Wolfgang von Goethe).

EDITED TEXTS: *Minstrelsy of the Scottish Border*, 1802-1803 (3 volumes); *A Collection of Scarce and Valuable Tracts*, 1809-1815 (13 volumes); *Chronological Notes of Scottish Affairs from the Diary of Lord Fountainhall*, 1822.

Bibliography

Bold, Alan, ed. *Sir Walter Scott: The Long-Forgotten Melody*. London: Vision Press, 1983. Nine essays cover such subjects as the image of Scotland, politics, and folk tradition, and draw upon Scott's poetry for illustration; the essay by Iain Crichton Smith, "Poetry in Scott's Narrative Verse," shows appreciation for the art of the poetry. Includes end notes and an index.

Chandler, Alice. "Origins of Medievalism: Scott." In *A Dream of Order: The Medieval Ideal in Nineteenth-Century English Literature*. Lincoln: University of Nebraska Press, 1970. This important essay examines the role of Scott's poems in preparing the way for popularity of medievalism in the writing of the era. His poetry derived from his scholarly research in medieval literature, and his novels would derive from his success as a poet. Supplemented by footnotes, a bibliography, and an index.

Goslee, Nancy Moore. *Scott the Rhymer*. Lexington: University Press of Kentucky, 1988. Aiming to restore Scott as a poet, this book analyzes in detail his major poems. A discussion of *The Lay of the Last Minstrel* is followed by examinations of the long poems from *Marmion* to *Harold the Dauntless*. These poems are affirmations of romance within self-reflexive frames of irony. Contains ample notes and an index.

Lauber, John. *Sir Walter Scott*. Rev. ed. Boston: Twayne, 1989. Following a survey of Scott's poetry and his turn to fiction, seven chapters analyze major narratives: *Waverly*, *Guy Mannering*, *The Antiquary*, *Old Mortality*, *Rob Roy*, *The Heart of Midlothian*, *The Bride of Lammermoor*, and *Ivanhoe*. The final chapter assesses the reputation of the Waverly novels.

Complemented by a chronology, notes, an annotated bibliography, and an index.

Mitchell, Jerome. *Scott, Chaucer, and Medieval Romance: A Study in Sir Walter Scott's Indebtedness to the Literature of the Middle Ages*. Lexington: University Press of Kentucky, 1987. Describes the influences of Geoffrey Chaucer and medieval romances at work in Scott's narrative poetry, early novels, middle novels written during his financial collapse, and novels of the darkly declining years. The style and structure of the novels are analyzed before a conclusion is drawn. Augmented by preface, notes, and an index.

Scott, Sir Walter. *The Journal of Sir Walter Scott*. Edited by W. E. K. Anderson. Edinburgh, Scotland: Canongate, 1998. Scott's journals offer invaluable biographical insights into his life and work. Includes bibliographical references and index.

Shaw, Harry E. *Narrating Reality: Austen, Scott, Eliot*. Ithaca, N.Y.: Cornell University Press, 1999. A provocative critique of nineteenth century British realist fiction. Shaw challenges the denigration of realism in critical writing of the 1980's and 1990's.

Sutherland, John. *The Life of Walter Scott*. Cambridge, Mass.: Blackwell Publishers, 1995. A narrative account that penetrates into the darker areas of Scott's life. The value of Scott's writing today as much as in his heyday is justified by Sutherland's account.

Todd, William B., and Ann Bowden. *Sir Walter Scott: A Bibliographical History, 1796-1832*. New Castle, Del.: Oak Knoll Press, 1998. Lists variant editions of the verse as well as the fiction, and casts light on his occupations as advocate, sheriff, antiquarian, biographer, editor, historian, and reviewer.

Tulloch, Graham. *The Language of Walter Scott: A Study of His Scottish and Period Language*. London: Andre Deutsch, 1980. In eight chapters and two appendices, Tulloch examines Scott's use of Scotch-English in his poetry and fiction. The special features of the language are analyzed in terms of vocabulary, grammar, and spelling. Scott's reading is also examined as a source of his language materials. Includes a bibliography and an index.

Samuel J. Rogal;
bibliography updated by the editors

Winfield Townley Scott

Born: Haverhill, Massachusetts; April 30, 1910
Died: Santa Fe, New Mexico; April 28, 1968

Principal poetry

Biography for Traman, 1937
Wind the Clock, 1941
The Sword on the Table: Thomas Dorr's Rebellion, 1942
To Marry Strangers, 1945
Mr. Whittier and Other Poems, 1948
The Dark Sister, 1958
Scrimshaw, 1959
Collected Poems, 1937-1962, 1962
Change of Weather, 1964
New and Selected Poems, 1967

Other literary forms

A Dirty Hand: The Literary Notebooks of Winfield Townley Scott (1969) is a collection of the notes Scott made about people (including other poets), places, and events. His *Exiles and Fabrications* (1961) is a collection of essays on Newport, Rhode Island, and Santa Fe, New Mexico, as well as commentary on E. A. Robinson, Amy Lowell, Booth Tarkington, Mark Twain, and Emily Dickinson. *Alpha and Omega* (1971) is Scott's account of his Newport boyhood, to which some late poems have been added. He also wrote several critical essays as well as countless book reviews for the Providence *Journal*, the New York *Herald-Tribune*, and *The New York Times*. He edited a collection of Emily Dickinson's poems, *Letter to the World* (1966), and Oliver La Farge's *The Man with the Calabash Pipe* (1966). Scott also compiled the *Poems of Robert Herrick* (1967).

Achievements

George Elliott, who edited the anthology *Fifteen Modern American Poets* (1956), maintained that Winfield Townley Scott was as good or better than any of the other poets in that collection. Although Scott never won the top prizes for poetry, his work did receive recognition. As a Brown University undergraduate, he was a cowinner of the Glascock Prize for poetry. In 1937 he won the Guarantors Prize, which is awarded annually for the best poem or poems published in *Poetry* the preceding year. Three years later he was one of two recipients of the annual Shelley Memorial Award for Poetry. His *Collected Poems, 1937-1962* was nominated for the National Book Award the year that Macmillan published it. Five years later *Poetry* awarded him the Harriet Monroe Memorial Award. Scott also received honorary doctorates from Rhode Island College and the University of New Mexico.

Biography

Winfield Townley Scott was born April 30, 1910, in Haverhill, Massachusetts, to Douglas and Bessie Scott. He spent the first ten years of his life in Newport, Rhode Island, where his father was a clerk in his family's hardware store, before moving back to Haverhill, where his father found employment in a shoe factory. In school and at home, Scott was shy, withdrawn, and eager to please. Scott Donaldson writes, "The boyhood habit of withdrawing from physical conflict, of avoiding the showdown, was encouraged and applauded by the women—his mother, Essie and Grammie Wilbar, and his schoolteachers—who dominated his existence." According to Scott, this feminine influence caused him to "call his maleness into question"; this concern is reflected in his poetry.

At fourteen, Scott had a school experience that shaped his life. His reading of Samuel Taylor Coleridge's "The Rime of the Ancient Mariner" left him transfixed, and he knew then that he would be a poet. From that time on, he regularly wrote poetry and sought out the company of established poets. As the editor of his high school paper, he shared his enthusiasm for the works of Robert Frost and Edgar Arlington Robinson, which remained the most significant influences on his poetry, with his classmates, who considered him a bit of an "odd stick," as one said. Scott attended Brown University from 1927 to 1931. There, he joined the Liberal Club, which reflected his political leanings; he was a lifelong Democrat. He also wrote regularly for the *Brown Literary Quarterly* and the *Brown Daily Herald*. The highlight of his college years was his meeting with his idol E. A. Robinson and their subsequent correspondence. Scott's outstanding academic performance gained him membership in Phi Beta Kappa. After graduation he married Savila Harvey, took a position with the Providence *Journal*, and supplemented his income by working as a newscaster. As a reviewer of movies and books, Scott made the acquaintance of several prominent poets, including Robert Hillyer and Horace Gregory. Gregory was instrumental in getting *Biography for Traman*, Scott's first book, published in 1937.

Wind the Clock, his second book, appeared in 1941, and Scott was publishing poems in leading poetry journals, giving readings, and receiving positive reviews of his work. In 1942 *The Sword on the Table* was published. That year Scott continued to write and became acquainted with Wallace Stegner, Louis Untermeyer, Bernard De Voto, and Robert Frost. In 1943 Scott met Eleanor Metcalf, a rebellious young woman from a wealthy family, while she was working on the *Journal* with him, and began an affair with her that led to his divorce from Savila in 1946. He married Eleanor the same year. *To Marry Strangers* is Scott's celebration of his love for Eleanor. *Mr. Whittier, and Other Poems* appeared in 1948, and he was one of fifteen poets selected for inclusion in *Mid-Century American Poets* (1950). However, he still lacked the recognition he sought and doubted that he would receive it if he remained at the *Journal*. Because of his wife's wealth, he could afford to quit his newspaper job and devote himself to full-time writing, even though he had some qualms about what he considered to be "selling out."

The years between 1948 and 1959, the year Macmillan published his *Scrimshaw*, were unproductive—he published no books during those ten years. In 1954 he and Eleanor moved from Hampton, Connecticut, to Santa Fe, New Mexico, and Scott had a surge of productivity, but his drinking and his fears about his mortality increased; he produced only one more volume of poetry, *Change of Weather*, though two collections of his poems were published, one posthumously in 1967. He died April 28, 1968, of a massive circulatory collapse due to an overdose of sleeping pills combined with a substantial amount of alcohol.

Analysis

Winfield Townley Scott never seemed able to live up to the expectations of others and of himself. Although he received recognition in 1956, when he was included in the anthology *Fifteen Modern American Poets*, he has virtually disappeared from the American literary canon. As a reviewer of poetry, he came to know all of his poetic contemporaries, but he was not in the mainstream. After he moved to New Mexico, he saw himself as a national, rather than regional, writer. Aside from a few poems, he continued to be squarely rooted in the New England literary tradition. He wrote two long narrative poems and sought funding to write other "epic" works. However, after he had enough money to devote himself to full-time writing, he failed to write any of the projected long poems. His lyric poetry, incredibly autobiographical and personal, is quite good, but his frequent poetic allusions to the seventeenth century become problems for many readers. His themes, mourning the past and coping with failure, are those of his hero and model E. A. Robinson, and his poetic persona is Robinsonian. Sexual and creative impotence, sometimes merged metaphorically, figure prominently in the poetry, which became increasingly preoccupied with death.

Biography of Traman

Biography of Traman, Scott's first volume of verse, contains poems about Traman, an anagram of Art Man, or Scott himself as artist. The poems, which cover Traman from childhood through university experiences and the world of work, were intended to form a kind of American parallel to James Joyce's *A Portrait of the Artist as a Young Man* (1916). Many of Scott's recurrent themes may be found in this early work. In "Traman Walks to Work," Traman's "twenty-ninth winter" finds him mired in grief and despair: "Traman faces/ More than loss of leaves and coming of snow." Tormented and "half mad yet from night insanity," Traman "cartwheels," or alternates, between "Triumph disaster triumph disaster," which critic Scott Donaldson reads as Scott's lifelong preoccupation with thwarted success. The first part of the poem concludes with Traman's concern about his future, which may be subject to a "larger failure than his own," or be beyond his control. The second part of the poem concerns his attempts to play a game in which he assumes the role of someone else. This reflects Scott's persistent efforts to please others and to avoid conflict. The attempt to walk in someone else's steps ends in failure because "His balance wasn't ever strong," a line that suggests Scott's own instability. The poem ends with lines that imply that Traman will be his own person: "With only his own legs to please/ He goes again—goes his own gait." Later poems indicate that Scott had trouble "going his own gait."

To Marry Strangers

This volume of verse has two subjects, his love for Eleanor Metcalf and his poetry. In one of the many sonnets in the book, Scott merges sex and art. "Sonnet XI (Lie There, My Art)" uses the sexual act as a metaphor for the writing of poetry. The "sheets" are both bed sheets and writing paper in "Must I Stay in Your Sheets Until I Starve?" The poem ends with references to castration and impotence, which apply to "writer's block," as they do to sex. In the sonnets, with their references to seventeenth century poets such as John Donne ("lovers who die together . . . and make one") and William Shakespeare ("My mistress' hair is something like the sun"), there is also the theme of unattained poetic achievement. "Sonnet II" concerns a man of promise at twenty who, at thirty, asks himself, "what have I done?" Youthful lyric poets such as Percy Bysshe Shelley and John Keats dishearten him in contrast; "Only Yeats and Hardy [who wrote in later life] comfort me."

Scrimshaw

Part 3 of *Scrimshaw* is titled "The Man at Mid-Century," which suggests that it is a kind of self-evaluation, and two poems in this section, one the title poem and the other "What I Assembled and Dissemble," take stock of Scott's progress. In the title poem, the "man" searches in vain for answers and solutions to his "inarticulate questioning." Hurrying home to "expectancy of dreams and drink," he desires others to give him his identity. He wants "someone" to tell him what to do, what to think, what to feel. Although the man is not supposed to be Scott, who maintains some distance from his protagonist, the references to "drink," the uncertainty about identity, and the hurried quest for answers all relate closely to Scott's own concerns. In "What I Assembled and Dissemble," the use of "dissemble" (to conceal, to hide) instead of "disassembled" implies that the poet's creations may not reveal the whole truth. "How useless is the lie of rhyme" suggests that poetry itself distorts the truth and those distortions are themselves limited in their power: "What I invent and what remember/ Will never save me from the sod." Scott again returns to his "intimations of mortality."

New and Selected Poems

The "new" poems in this volume reflect Scott's dampened enthusiasm, his discouragement with the political direction of the United States, and a sense of failure. His "Electric Silence" concerns President John F. Kennedy's assassination and ends with a line that implies the end of Camelot and liberal politics: "O with his Irish that night, we cried-down the rain." In several poems Scott writes about waning poetic and sexual potency. His "Middle-Aged Poet" is not middle-aged; he is an old man sitting on the sidelines in Florida. The last line of the poem reflects on Scott's own fears: "Knowing only how hard a man must stay to make love or poems." His inability to recapture the past is expressed in images of drought. In "Lyric Love" he returns to what had been a "blossoming orchard," but now it is "in a leafless season," and the woman who was there has vanished. "Year of Drought" concerns another "middle-aged" couple who want to rekindle their love, but they have lost their faith: "They bowed like two that had lost belief in rain/ Even under a sky swollen with thunder." In "The Uses of Poetry," Scott writes that poetry, written with a "craftsman's skill," serves only as an aphrodisiac for a boy intent on having sex with his girlfriend. Appropriately, the new poems include Scott's "Epitaph on Himself," which anticipates his death and reveals his final uncertainty about himself and his poetry: "He staggered into death/ Before death sought for him/ And still wondering 'Why?'"

Other major works

nonfiction: *Exiles and Fabrications*, 1961; *"A Dirty Hand": The Literary Notebooks of Winfield Townley Scott*, 1969; *Alpha Omega*, 1971.

edited texts: *Letter to the World*, 1966; *The Man with the Calabash Pipe*, 1966; *Poems of Robert Herrick*, 1967.

Bibliography

Donaldson, Scott. *Poet in America: Winfield Townley Scott.* Austin: University of Texas Press, 1972. A critical biography, essentially a biography "illuminated" with Scott's poetry but also a critique of the culture within which the American artist exists. Donaldson says Scott was cruelly criticized by people who did not appreciate his work and who disapproved of his willingness to be supported by his wife. Scott, who shared his critics' views even though he knew they should not matter, began to doubt himself and died the "emasculated victim" of his doubts and fears. The book contains a helpful bibliography of Scott's writings, including a section on the recordings Scott made of his own poetry. Essential reading for Scott research.

Frohock, W. M. "Win Scott on College." *Southwest Review* 58 (1973): 105-114. Frohock, who was a year behind Scott at Brown University, discusses Scott's "so-called failure" in terms of his experiences at Brown, where, except for Saunders Redding, an African American writer who isolated himself from his classmates, he was the only undergraduate "poet." Frohock believes that the English faculty "led him to expect more of himself than was good for him or than would have been good for anyone." As a result, when Scott began to feel that he was falling short of expectations, "there was really no place for him to hide."

Goldstein, Laurence. "The American Poet at the Movies." *Centennial Review* 24 (1980): 432-452. Goldstein juxtaposes Vachel Lindsay, who saw that film could "usurp the ancient prerogatives of the seer-bard," with Winfield Townley Scott, who ruefully acknowledged the "diminished public role he saw for the modern poet." In his analysis of Scott's "Dream Penny in the Slot at 6 a.m.," Goldstein contrasts the poet's cognitive way of knowing with film's "more elemental viewing-into that uncovers the crude instincts boarded up in man's inmost being."

Masters, Hilary. "Winfield Townley Scott: The Exile as Mentor." *Ohio Review*, no. 51 (1994): 10-24. Interesting and informative biographical account of the mentoring relationship between Scott and Masters. Discusses Scott's middle-class background and unease with the privileged class as influences affecting his writing and his life. Masters focuses on Scott's retirement from journalism and his self-exile from Providence, Rhode Island, and the workaday world, especially after Scott's second marriage and move to Santa Fe, New Mexico. Masters traces Scott's later career with its disappointments and political disillusionment as well as his alcoholism.

Thomas L. Erskine

SIR CHARLES SEDLEY

Born: Aylesford, Kent, England; March, 1639
Died: Hampstead, London, England; August 20, 1701

PRINCIPAL POETRY

"Song: Not *Celia*, that I juster am," 1672
"To Cloris: *Cloris*, I cannot say your Eyes," 1672
"Song: Love still has something of the Sea," 1672
"The Indifference: Thanks, fair *Vrania*, to your Scorn," 1672
Prologue to *Epsom Wells*, 1673 (Thomas Shadwell's play)
"Advice to the Old Beaux: Scrape no more your harmless Chins," 1693
Prologue to *The Wary Widow or Sir Noisy Parrat*, 1693 (Henry Higden's play)
"The Knotting Song: Hears not my *Phillis*, how the Birds," 1694
"Song: Smooth was the Water, calm the Air," 1702
"Song: *Phillis* is my only Joy," 1702
The Miscellaneous Works of the Honourable Sir Charles Sedley, Bart., 1702
The Happy Pair, 1702

OTHER LITERARY FORMS

Sir Charles Sedley was also known for his plays during his lifetime. His first theatrical venture was translating an act of Pierre Corneille's *La Mort de Pompée* (pr. 1643; *The Death of Pompey*, 1663) as a joint project with Edmund Waller, Robert Filmer, Baron Buckhurst, and Sidney Godolphin; it was performed in 1664 as *Pompey the Great*. Later plays include *The Mulberry Garden* (1668), *Antony and Cleopatra* (1677), and *Bellamira: Or, The Mistress* (1687). Sedley's plays were treated with respect during the Restoration and proved moderately successful at the box office, but they have not survived their era in performance. They are available in Vivian de Sola Pinto's 1928 edition of Sedley's works.

ACHIEVEMENTS

Sir Charles Sedley is remembered today as an important figure in a minor literary group: the Restoration court poets, sometimes known as the court wits or "the merry gang" of Charles II. The earl of Rochester is the most prominent poet in this group; Sedley ranks immediately after him. In his own time, Sedley was known as a man of taste and was as famous for his wit and conversation as for his writings. His judgment on a new play or poem could help to establish or destroy a literary reputation. Today, Sedley is best known for his lyric love poetry. The most immediately apparent elements in his songs are a clever use of persuasion and an underlying Epicurean philosophy. In his biography of Sedley (1927), Vivian de Sola Pinto has noted that as a group the Restoration court poets represent "the triumph of the intellectual and logical side of the Renaissance over the imaginative and emotional elements." This generalization surely applies to Sedley, who was a poet of direct statement and controlled feeling rather than of elaborate conceits and grand passion.

BIOGRAPHY

Sir Charles Sedley was born into a Cavalier family and grew up during Oliver Cromwell's Protectorate. In 1656 he inherited his title on the death of his brother, and in February, 1657, he married Katherine Savage. In December, 1657, they had a daughter, Katherine, who would become the mistress of James II. Sometime during the decade of the 1660's, Lady Sedley, suffering from the delusion that she was a queen, went permanently insane. In 1672 Sedley arranged for her to be removed to a convent in France, where she died in 1705, outliving her husband by four years. After her departure, Sedley formed a permanent relationship with Ann Ayscough, with whom he had a son, Charles, in 1672.

Sedley was among the group of young gentlemen who became the court favorites of Charles II upon his restoration to the throne in 1660. He quickly established himself in the vanguard of the king's "merry gang," a group known for its riotous living and dangerous atheistic views. His most scandalous behavior occurred at the Cock Tavern in 1663. Sedley had been drinking with several gentlemen when he appeared nude on the balcony of the tavern before a crowd and proceeded to deliver a mock sermon, which was offensive in both its content and mode of delivery. A trial followed, and for his indiscreet behavior Sedley was fined two thousand marks, half of which is believed to have been remitted by the king. Sedley's behavior during the 1660's was by all accounts fairly wild, but by the early 1670's he had reformed, quite possibly as a result of the good influence of Ann Ayscough.

Despite his reputation for debauchery in the first decade of the Restoration, Sedley was not given solely to the pursuit of pleasure. Early in his life, he involved himself in public affairs. He was elected to Parliament in 1668 and was apparently sent to France in 1670 on an important diplomatic mission with the earl of Buckingham, Buckhurst, and Sir George Savile. He retained his seat in Parliament for most of his life, performing his

Sir Charles Sedley (Hulton Archive)

most distinguished service during the reign of William III.

Sedley also pursued a second career in letters. He was not a prolific poet, but there is a consistent production of poems and plays from each decade of his life beginning with the 1660's. He may well have written more poems than have actually survived, for most of his verse was not written for publication. When his poems did appear in print, they were frequently anonymous. Since Sedley made no effort to collect his writings during his lifetime, undoubtedly much of his work was lost. The extant poems were intended to entertain a small group who belonged to the same class and knew one another personally. Poetry was a necessary accomplishment for a courtier, and poems were passed in manuscript within the court society.

Sedley's poems were remarkably consistent throughout his life, the poems dating from the 1690's appearing to be cut from the same cloth as those written in the 1660's. Even though Sedley's world changed radically during his lifetime and most of his contemporaries had either died or stopped writing by the 1690's, these changes are not reflected in the substance or style of Sedley's poetry. In like manner, the changes in Sedley's personal life are not reflected in his poetry. At first glance the poems appear to be graceful exercises on a variety of familiar literary themes, as noteworthy for the well-turned phrase as for any probing insights into the human experience, but they do reflect the spirit of an age. In *Restoration Carnival* (1954), Pinto notes that Sedley's poems "grew directly out of his life and are a natural product of the society in which he lived." Nowhere in his life or writings is there any indication that Sedley seriously challenged the values or customs of Restoration society. He lived his life in accordance with the rational skepticism of his class and era and is reported to have "died like a philosopher without fear or superstition." Thus, the consistency of his poetry may well be a reflection of the consistency of his life.

Analysis

Most of Sir Charles Sedley's songs deal with familiar love themes. There are a number of ladies who are alternately encouraging or discouraging, and whose beauty is so striking that it has turned the poet's fancy. The poet is concerned not so much to praise the lady's charms as to persuade her to yield to the pressing demands of time and nature. Sedley was known in his day for the love invitation. Rochester in "An Allusion to Horace: The 10th Satyr of the 1st Book" praises Sedley as a master of persuasion: "*Sidley*, has that prevailing, gentle Art,/ That can with a resistless Charm impart,/ The loosest wishes, to the chastest Heart." A number of Sedley's poems are obviously intended to encourage a lady to yield her virtue. Here, for example, is a short untitled piece on the way the poet passes lonely nights:

> Awake, my Eyes, at Night my Thought[s] pursue
> Your charming Shape; and find it ever new;
> If I my weary Eyes to Sleep resign,
> In gaudy Dreams your Love and Beauty shine;
> Dreams with such Extasies and Pleasures fill'd,
> As to those Joys they seem can only yield;
> Nor do they yield perhaps, wou'd you allow,
> Fair *Amidea*, that I once might know.

Rochester might have been thinking of this poem when he wrote his tribute to Sedley's art. The poem could be part of the sophisticated love games which were played in the comedies of the day, including Sedley's *The Mulberry Garden* and *Bellamira*. To create a feeling of longing within Amidea's heart, the poet employs an argument involving the lover's thwarted expectations of "Extasies," "Pleasures," and "joys," which are only realized in dreams. If one were to extend the argument beyond the poem, one would say that it goes against nature to thwart the fulfillment of such pleasures.

This argument is one more version of an important theme in most of Sedley's love lyrics: the pursuit and realization of pleasure. In a Sedley lyric there are no metaphysical flights which take the reader into another country; the poet is concerned with securing his ease and pleasure in this world. In "An Essay on Satyr," John Sheffield, earl of Mulgrave, later duke of Buckinghamshire, notes that "little *Sid*" "Pleasure has always sought, but seldom found:/ Tho' Wine and Women are his only Care,/ Of both he takes a lamentable Share." Most of Mulgrave's portrait, which dates from 1679, involves a nasty attack on the reforms in Sedley's personal life. Nevertheless, for all its venom, it contains a basic truth about Sedley the poet: He always sought pleasure. This statement applies to the late as well as the early works.

"Out of Lycophron" and "To Liber"

This strain of Epicureanism is more than only a ploy in the love game; it is a philosophical principle that was widely held in the Restoration. Sedley presents an Epicurean philosophy most explicitly in two translations from the ancients: "Out of Lycophron" and "To Liber." Sedley's translation of Lycophron, an Alexandrian dramatist who lived in the third century B.C.E., stresses the limits of human understanding. Man does not know

> Whither he goes to Heaven or Hell;
> Or after a few moments dear,
> He disappear,
> And at last,
> Perish entirely like a Beast.

He should therefore, not waste his time pondering what is unknowable; rather, he should give himself over to "Women, Wine and Mirth." The tone of this poem is complacent and urbane. There is none of the questioning and rage that one finds in Rochester when he confronts the possibilities of "Nothing." For Lycophron, life is reduced to "a few Moments dear." Even though man in death may be reduced to the status of a beast, Sedley's smooth verse takes the rough edges off this grim knowledge. He uses the possibility of nothing only as an argument to encourage man to secure his pleasure in this life. This Epicurean philosophy is even more emphatically stated in "To Liber," a translation of a Martial epigram. The speaker could be one Restoration gentleman giving another gentleman advice on how to spend his time most profitably. Thus, Liber should think "on charming Objects" and let "easie Beauty warm" his heart. The pursuit of pleasure and the easy satisfaction of appetite are sufficient as guiding principles.

Love: pleasure and flirtation

The love lyrics fall into two main categories: those in which the speaker self-consciously considers his own pleasure and ease and how well they are served, and those in which the speaker is an active participant in a flirtation, using his art and cleverness to secure the interest of a particular lady. Part of the charm of the poems in this second category is Sedley's obvious delight in the progress of a flirtation.

Two songs addressed to Phillis—"Phillis, let's shun the common Fate" and "*Phillis* is my only Joy"—fall into the first category. The speaker is as concerned with his own pleasure and ease as with the feelings or needs of Phillis. In the first song, the speaker states his theme in the opening lines: "*Phillis*, let's shun the common Fate,/ And let our Love ne'r turn to Hate." The speaker defines the limits of love, the point at which love ceases to be a pleasure and becomes a burden. The only way to avoid love turning to hate is to leave off loving at the first signs of boredom or disinterest. Thus, the speaker will "dote no longer" than he can, and the couple will part when they begin "to want Discourse,/ And Kindness seems to taste of Force." The speaker envisions love in terms of mild, if delectable, pleasures: "A Smile of thine shall make my Bliss,/ I will enjoy thee in a Kiss." If Phillis should stop loving first, the speaker will "the Blame on Nature lay" and accept his fate without rancor but rather with pride "in Parting well." Love, then, is a kind of bargain. If one does not invest too much of himself in a love relationship, he will experience a fine pleasure and avoid needless pain and suffering.

In "*Phillis* is my only Joy," Sedley celebrates the pleasures that are secured at the price of self-deception. In the second line, the speaker announces that Phillis is as "Faithless as the Winds or Seas," but the rest of the first stanza is about the pleasure he receives from Phillis: She "never fails to please," and she makes him "Happier than before." In the second stanza, the speaker deals with the problems of Phillis's faithlessness, but he reduces it to a game, perhaps best suggested by the telling couplet, "She deceiving,/ I believing." The sense of balance in these two lines and elsewhere suggests that the speaker's self-deception is simply the price he knowingly and willingly pays to secure his own pleasure. When he asks in the final line, "What need Lovers wish for more?" the obvious answer is "Nothing."

In the second main category of Sedley love lyrics, the speaker is an active participant in a flirtation. In such poems, he does not analyze how well his ease and pleasure are served. Rather, his pleasure is revealed by his obvious delight in the business at hand. A number of these verses appear to be designed for real occasions. The most obvious example is "To Amaranta Whom He Fell in Love with at a Play-House." Pinto suggests that the occasion for this poem may have been an encounter between Sedley and a masked lady at the King's House in Drury Lane, which was reported by Samuel Pepys in his diary. The conversation between the two was so sparkling and entertaining that it proved more interesting to Pepys than the performance of *The Maid's Tragedy* (1619). The situation in the poem is dramatic. The speaker encounters a beauty at a playhouse; he soon finds himself experiencing the emotions of the "feigned Love" on the stage: "The Hopes and Fears, in every Scene exprest,/ Grew soon th' uneasie Motions of my Breast." The poet first engages in some idle banter; "And if I ventur'd on some slight Discourse,/ It should be such as could no Passion nurse." Soon he finds himself ensnared ("At last I play'd too near the Precipice"), and then love breaks through like a force—a cultivated force—of nature:

> Your Words fell on my Passion, like those Showers,
> Which paint and multiply the rising Flowers;
> Like *Cupid's* self, a God, and yet a Child,
> Your Looks at once were awful, and yet mild.

Not all Sedley's poems deal with such casual flirtations. Many pay direct compliments to a lady of virtue; some even declare an undying fidelity. Yet even in these poems there is frequently an underlying Epicureanism marking them as the work of Sedley. In one of Sedley's most famous songs, "Not *Celia*, that I juster am," the speaker declares his devotion to Celia. He "would change each Hour" like the rest of humankind, but such are the charms of Celia that he has no choice but to stay where his heart is "at rest." When he concludes that "'Tis easie to be true," it is clear that ease is the condition which permits him to be true.

The presence in the Sedley canon of this poem and several others declaring the speaker's faithfulness creates a minor problem. It is possible to read most of the poems simply as graceful exercises on a variety of common literary themes with no biographical relevance. After all, Sedley wrote lyrics into the 1690's which celebrate the pleasures of flirtation and inconstancy. Nevertheless, there are some poems which invite a more personal interpretation. For example, in *Restoration Carnival*, Pinto calls "Not *Celia*, that I juster am" Sedley's "one great love song" in which he sings of his "real ideal . . . the tranquility of a happy marriage of true minds." Such an assertion is not warranted by the poem itself. Why should the speaker in the Celia poem be closer to Sedley's own feelings than the speaker in one of the Phillis poems?

There are at least two ways to explain this phenomenon. First, all Sedley's poems may have a degree of personal relevance, the seeming contradiction between the speaker of different poems being more apparent than real. The courtiers of the Restoration considered libertinism and marriage as two separate areas of their lives. Rochester, famous for his many sexual escapades, was by all accounts a devoted and affectionate husband and father. Heroes in Restoration comedies such as Dorimant in *The Man of Mode* (1676) also display the same balance between the life of the libertine and the life of a husband. At the end of George Etherege's play, Dorimant is not so much reforming as adding to his life by taking on a wife and engaging in a richer, fuller love relationship than he had experienced before. Second, the sentiments expressed in the Celia poem do appear to have a relevance to certain events in Sedley's life. He may have led the life of a libertine in the early years of his marriage, but when he found the right woman, he publicly declared his devotion to her and committed himself to her for life by going through a form of marriage in 1672 and treating her as his wife for the next thirty years. For Sedley, the concept of marriage was far more important than its legal definition.

LOVE AND MARRIAGE

Some of Sedley's poems, such as "Constancy," deal with a "marriage of true minds" in which physical attraction is simply the beginning of a long-lasting relationship. This understanding of marriage is at the heart of "To Cloris: *Cloris*, I justly am betray'd," which Pinto sees as being addressed to Ann Ayscough. The poet begins by frankly admitting that he had laid a trap for Cloris, thinking "at first with a small Sum/ Of Love, thy Heap to overcome." The reverse happens, and the poet makes a full declaration of his love, even though he is prevented from marrying Cloris:

My Hand, alas, is no more mine,
Else it had long ago been thine;
My Heart I give thee, and we call
No Man unjust that parts with all.

So ends the poem in the 1702 edition. In the original 1672 publication of the poem there was an additional couplet: "What a priest says moves not the mind,/ Souls are by love, not words, combin'd." In this couplet, Sedley presents his basic view of marriage, which remained consistent throughout his life: Love, rather than social custom, determines a marriage. In *The Happy Pair*, a late poem written in the ratiocinative style of John Dryden's *Religio Laici* (1682), the poet dwells on the horrors of the marriage bed when love is not present:

With feign'd Embrace they seem Love's Joys to crave,
But with their Bed, converted to a Grave:
And whilst their backward Hearts like Load-stones meet,
They wish their Linnen were the Windingsheet.

The imagery is surprisingly vivid. Sedley is rarely as explicit about the joys of love as he is about the miseries of a mercenary marriage in these lines. His poem ends with a paean to the joys of a lowly marriage where both partners are poor but truly in love. Such a union may belong to a pastoral ideal, but in *The Happy Pair*, it is set against the distorted emotions and values of upper class life, which destroy the chances for true love.

Sedley's views on marriage are consistent with his Epicureanism. If pleasure is the be-all and end-all of existence, love in marriage is the most satisfying pleasure. When love is missing, the marriage is a mockery. Presumably Sedley's unfortunate experience in marrying at a young age for the wrong reasons had taught him this lesson. In *The Restoration Court Poets* (1965), Pinto notes that the conclusion of *The Happy Pair* "with its praise of quiet domesticity shows that the wild gallant of the sixteen-sixties had by the end of the century developed into an Augustan 'man of feeling.'"

LEGACY

Sedley, however, is not remembered today as a forerunner of eighteenth century sentimentalism. He was a poet of his times. To a certain extent, he lived the life that is portrayed so vividly in the world of Restoration comedies, where style, wit, and pleasure are important ends in themselves. This world may not have been quite as amoral as is sometimes thought. The pursuit of pleasure does not rule out the cultivation of sentiment and deep, lifelong attachments, but in the Restoration, it did rule out pomposity and sentimentality. Sedley's poetry exemplifies the grace and wit of an age that too often is remembered only as a time of license and immorality.

OTHER MAJOR WORKS

PLAYS: *Pompey the Great*, pb. 1664 (translation of an act with Edmund Waller, Robert Filmer, Baron Buckhurst, and Sidney Godolphin); *The Mulberry Garden*, pr., pb. 1668; *Antony and Cleopatra*, pr., pb. 1677; *Bellamira: Or, The Mistress*, pr., pb. 1687.

BIBLIOGRAPHY

Pinto, Vivian de sola. *Restoration Carnivals, Five Courtier Poets: Rochester, Dorset, Sedley, Etherege, and Sheffield*. London: Folio Society, 1954. By the compiler of the 1928 edition of Sedley's plays, this is a thoroughly illuminating analysis that reveals much about the poets and their works. Offers a worthy overview of Sedley and his poetic achievements. Complemented by a bibliography.

_______. *The Restoration Court Poets: John Wilmot, Earl of Rochester; Charles Sackville, Earl of Dorset; Sir Charles Sedley; Sir George Etherege*. London: Longmans, Green, 1965. This volume compares and examines the critical and theoretical views of these four Restoration Court literary figures. The section on Sedley provides criticism helpful to an appreciation and understanding of Sedley's works.

_______. *Sir Charles Sedley, 1639-1701: A Study in the Life and Literature of the Restoration*. London: Longmans, Green, 1965. One of the few book-length works devoted to Sedley, by the well-known scholar of Restoration literature. Bibliography.

Vinson, James. ed. *Great Writers of the English Language: Poets*. Vol. 1. New York: St. Martin's Press, 1979. The entry by John H. Perry notes that Sedley, one of the chief poets of Charles II's reign, was primarily known for his love poems and songs. He claims that it was Sedley's satires, which betrayed the cynicism of the court, that made him less popular. Praises Sedley for his "perceptive eye and cutting pen."

Wilson, John Harold. *The Court Wits of the Restoration: An Introduction*. Princeton, N.J.: Princeton University Press, 1948. Wilson provides a worthy overview and analysis of early modern English literature from 1500 to 1700 and offers a history and criticism of English wit and humor. Supplemented by a bibliography.

Edward V. Geist;
bibliography updated by the editors

GEORGE SEFERIS

Giorgos Stylianou Seferiades

Born: Smyrna, Ottoman Empire (now İzmir, Turkey); February 29, 1900

Died: Athens, Greece; September 20, 1971

PRINCIPAL POETRY

Strophe, 1931 (*Turning Point*, 1967)
E sterna, 1932 (*The Cistern*, 1967)
Mythistorema, 1935 (English translation, 1960)
Gymnopaidia, 1936 (English translation, 1967)
Emerologio katastromatos I, 1940 (*Logbook I*, 1960)
Tetradio gymnasmaton, 1940 (*Book of Exercises*, 1967)
Emerologio katastromatos II, 1944 (*Logbook II*, 1960)
Kichle, 1947 (*Thrush*, 1967)
Emerologio katastromatos III, 1955 (*Logbook III*, 1960)
Poems, 1960 (includes *Mythistorema*, *Logbook I*, *Logbook II*, and *Logbook III*)
Tria krypha poiemata, 1966 (*Three Secret Poems*, 1969)
Collected Poems, 1967, 1981, 1995 (includes *Turning Point*, *The Cistern*, *Gymnopaidia*, *Book of Exercises*, *Thrush*, and others)

OTHER LITERARY FORMS

George Seferis earned distinction as a literary critic and translator in addition to his achievements as a poet. His collection of essays, *Dokimes* (1947), is regarded as one of the finest volumes of modern Greek literary criticism. His other principal prose works include *Treis meres sta monasteria tes Kappadokias* (1953; three days in the monasteries of Cappadocia), *Delphi* (1962; English translation, 1963), *Discours de Stockholm* (1964), and *'E glossa sten poiese mas* (1965). A selection of his essays was published in English as *On the Greek Style: Selected Essays in Poetry and Hellenism* (1966). Seferis translated T. S. Eliot's *The Waste Land* (1922; as *E Erema Chora kai alla poiemata*) and *Murder in the Cathedral* (1935; as *Dolophonia sten ekklesia*) into Greek, an achievement called "brilliant." Following Eliot's death in 1965, Seferis published a brief commemorative diary of their friendship. Seferis also "transcribed," as he put it, the biblical Song of Songs and the Revelation of Saint John the Divine into modern language. Finally, Seferis's *A Poet's Journal: Days of 1945-1951* was published in English in 1974.

ACHIEVEMENTS

George Seferis initiated a new spirit in Greek poetry with the publication, in 1931, of his first book, *Turning Point*. Influenced by the styles of French and English poets, Seferis freed his verse from the excessive ornamentation which then encumbered Greek poetry, creating a simple, direct style in the modern idiom and bringing Greek poetry into a closer relationship with the modernism of Western Europe. Insisting that poetry should be written in the language of everyday speech, he exploited the forms, themes, and diction of folk verse. Very much aware of his heritage, he integrated the mythology and history of Greece with the situation of his country and of humanity in general in the twentieth century. Like Eliot, Seferis weaves a complex tapestry of allusion in deceptively simple language; like Eliot, he universalizes his profound sense of alienation, so that his poetry, though distinctively Greek, speaks to readers of all nationalities. The Greek sense of tragedy that informs Seferis's work is not out of place in the twentieth century.

George Seferis, Nobel laureate in literature for 1963.
(© The Nobel Foundation)

BIOGRAPHY

George Seferis was born Giorgos Stylianou Seferiades in Smyrna (now İzmir), Turkey. The city was largely populated by Greeks then, and Seferis's memories of it served as an inspiration to him for the rest of his life. It was in Smyrna that he wrote his first poetry, at the age of fourteen. Shortly thereafter World War I began, and the Seferiades family left for Athens. There, Seferis continued his secondary schooling at the First Classical Gymnasium and was graduated in 1917. His father, who also wrote a few poems and made a few translations, was an expert on international law and became a professor at the University of Athens in 1919. Seferis set out to follow in his father's footsteps, studying law at the Sorbonne in Paris from 1918 to 1924. During this period, he became familiar with French poetry, especially the works of Paul Valery, Jules Laforgue, and other Symbolists, while continuing to write a few poems of his own.

After obtaining his degree at the Sorbonne, Seferis spent a year in London; anticipating a career in the Greek foreign service, he hoped to perfect his English. Thus, seven crucial years in Seferis's young manhood were spent away from Greece. In 1922, while Seferis was abroad, the city of Smyrna was burned and the Greek population there displaced. The "home" to which he had clung in his memories had ceased to exist, and he began to see himself in an Odyssean light, as a wanderer in search of home. After his return to Athens, he began a long career as a diplomat, working in the Ministry of Foreign Affairs. While serving as vice-consul in London in 1931, he first became acquainted with the works of T. S. Eliot and Ezra Pound, which would play an important role in the development of his art. In the same year, he also published his first book of poetry, *Turning Point*, a volume that heralded the beginning of a new generation of poetry in Greece. His second volume, *The Cistern*, appeared in 1932; then, between 1934 and 1936, while Seferis was living in Athens, two more volumes of his poetry were published, *Mythistorema* and *Gymnopaidia*.

From 1936 to 1938, Seferis served as consul in Koritsa, Albania, and then became a press attaché to the Ministry of Foreign Affairs. He married Maria Zannou in 1941. As the Nazis rolled over Greece, Seferis joined the government in exile, spending the war in Cairo, Johannesburg, Pretoria, and Italy. After Greece was liberated, he returned to Athens, receiving the Palamas Prize for Poetry in 1946. He worked there until 1948, when he became consul attached to the Greek embassy in Ankara. In 1951, he was appointed to the same position in London, where he became a personal friend of Eliot. In 1953, he was promoted to ambassador to Lebanon, Syria, Jordan, and Iraq and took up residence in Beirut. During his three years as ambassador, he visited Cyprus on several occasions, visits that would prove important not only in inspiring his later poetry but also in his diplomatic role as a member of the Greek delegation to the United Nations during the 1957 discussion concerning Cyprus.

Seferis was rewarded for his efforts with the ambassadorship to Great Britain. During his tenure there, he was awarded an honorary doctorate from Cambridge University, and in 1963, a year after he retired, he became the first Greek to receive the Nobel Prize. Many other awards soon followed, including honorary doctorates from Oxford, Thessaloniki, and Princeton. He was made an honorary foreign member of the American Academy of Arts and Letters and an honorary fellow of the Modern Language Association in 1966. Living in Athens at the end of his life, Seferis published very little, except for his *Three Secret Poems*. In March, 1969, he courageously attacked the Greek military dictatorship in a public statement; in the same year, he published one of his last poems, "The Cats of St. Nicholas," in an anthology of antigovernment poetry and prose, *Eighteen Texts*. He died in the fall of 1971 of complications following an operation for a duodenal ulcer. His funeral provoked a large public demonstration against the ruling junta, with thousands of people shouting "Immortal!" "Freedom!" and "Elections!"

Analysis

George Seferis revitalized Greek poetry and brought it into the mainstream of twentieth century Western poetry. In his work, the long tradition of Greek poetry is wedded to the European avant-garde, producing (in the words of the Nobel Prize committee) a "unique thought and style." As an "orphan" of Smyrna, Seferis experienced at first hand the sense of alienation that characterizes much of the poetry of the twentieth century. The Smyrna he had known was destroyed, and there was no "home" to which he could return; the world was therefore strange and unfamiliar to him, distorted in some fundamental way. Seferis's life as a diplomat perhaps intensified his sense of alienation; at the same time, his wide experience allowed him to transcend individual sorrow to speak to the larger problems of the human condition.

Seferis was keenly interested in the stylistic and tonal experiments of the French Symbolists, especially Paul Valéry and his "pure" poetry. In London, Seferis became acquainted with the poetry of Pound and Eliot, recognizing in their works the next step in the stylistic evolution that he had already begun. He abandoned strict meter and rhyme and avoided any sort of embellishment, keeping his imagery sparse.

Fundamentally, however, Seferis was Greek. His poetry springs from the traditions and heritage of his people, and though he altered substantially the shape of Greek poetry, he always worked from the raw materials provided by Greek folk songs, poetic forms, and mythology. In this approach, one immediately recognizes Seferis's kinship with Pound and Eliot, who also layered their texts with allusions, quotations, and mythological and historical parallels, though Seferis is more scrupulous in his treatment of his sources. He attempted to use the traditional decapentasyllable (a line of fifteen syllables with a caesura after the eighth and main accents on the sixth or eighth and on the fourteenth) in the expression of a contemporary sensibility, though it is the principal meter of folk poetry, dating back to the Byzantine period. In addition, he was influenced heavily by Cretan literature of the sixteenth and seventeenth centuries, especially the seventeenth century epic romance *Erotokritos*, by Vitzentzos Kornaros. In this work, Seferis saw the possibilities of demotic Greek as a language for poetry. In addition to writing a brilliant commentary on *Erotokritos*, he incorporated phrases from it in his poem "Erotikos Logos," establishing links between the language of modern Greece and the Greek past, much as Eliot incorporates in his verse phrases from Geoffrey Chaucer, William Shakespeare, and numerous other major English authors.

As Lawrence Durrell has written, "When Eliot speaks of 'getting every ounce of tradition behind each word,' one thinks of Seferis, so deeply steeped in the ancient Greek tragedies, and yet so modern in his approach." Fragments of the past litter the landscape, and in attempting to find what they mean, Seferis, like Eliot, finds himself face-to-face with the vacuum at the core of modern existence.

Seferis published little in the last fifteen years of his life. His credo as a poet, at once consciously Greek and consciously international, is concisely stated in *A Poet's Journal:* "The free man, the just man, the man who is the 'measure' of life; if there is one basic idea in Hellenism, it is this one." Seferis's vision is dark, full of suffering and haunted by a sense of estrangement, but it is redeemed by his humanistic faith that man is the "measure" of life.

Turning Point and The Cistern

Turning Point and *The Cistern*, Seferis's first two collections, marked a dramatic departure from the decadent poetry of the 1920's. Readers recognized in Seferis a different voice with something new to say. The poetry was stark, "Doric," but filled with original and surprising imagery. Seferis later commented that when he published *Turning Point*, he was aware of two things: He knew that he wanted to write simple poetry, and he knew that people would not like it. Seferis had not yet discovered the creative possibilities of free verse, and despite the demotic, conversational quality of the two collections, they show a careful attention to rhyme and meter. The characteristic starkness and sharpness of Seferis's work is already apparent in the first stanza of "Turning Point": "Moment, sent by a hand/ I had loved so much,/ you reached me just at sunset/ like a black pigeon." Consisting of only seventeen words (in the original Greek), the stanza is strongly evocative, emotionally powerful, yet finally enigmatic. As Peter Levi has observed, "There is a level at which the language of Seferis is simple, but with the apparent simplicity of ballads and chronicles, which is not simple at all."

This deceptive simplicity is further illustrated by the long poem "Erotikos logos," which is included in *Turning Point*. Composed of decapentasyllables in stanzas of four lines, the poem ends with the words, "The world is simple." Like Seferis's verse, which strives to appear simple yet is not, the world itself is simple yet opaque. In one sense, each line of the poem is clear, but if one tries to pin down the *meaning* of a given line or phrase, one finds oneself in a labyrinth of inferences, connotations, and allusions whose relationships to one another are as complex as the relationships among things in the world. Life is ultimately a mystery, out of human control, and pretensions to understand it (its "simplicity") finally only confirm humanity's terminal alienation. The imagery of "The Cistern" expresses this modern sensibility: "We are dying! Our gods are dying!/ The marble statues know it, looking down/ like white dawn upon the victim/ alien, full of eyelids, fragments,/ as the crowds of death pass by."

Mythistorema

Seferis's third collection, *Mythistorema*, was the first work of his maturity. In this volume, he abandoned strict meter and rhyme to work in his idiosyncratic free verse. Aware of the building political tensions and the rise of totalitarianism in Europe, Seferis conflated Greek myth and history in twenty-four concise poems with disturbingly violent imagery and an extraordinary number of allusions to classical myth and ancient literature. In Seferis's vision, the present is a desolate landscape of fragments. A coherent understanding of it is impossible, and one is left with the mere reverberations of voices from the past, echoes without meaning.

"The King of Asine"

One of the finest examples of Seferis's mature poetry is "The King of Asine," which ends *Logbook I*. The speaker of the poem relates that he has spent two years seeking the King of Asine, a Mycenaean ruler mentioned only once in the *Iliad* (c. 800 B.C.E., book 2, line 560), during the famous catalog of ships. The speaker has found a citadel covered with vines and a long beach, but even the wild doves have gone. He and his party have also found a gold burial mask that, when touched, makes an empty sound: "Hollow in the light/ like a dry jar in dug earth/ the same sound that our oars make in the sea." The King of Asine is a "void under the mask." His children are statues, his desires "the fluttering of birds." Though the mask replicates his face, a dark spot lies behind it—a dark spot symbolic of loss and the "void everywhere with us." Nothing is left but "nostalgia for the weight of a living existence/ there where we now remain unsubstantial. . . ." The poet, too, is a void. Nothing exists behind the words, just as the King of Asine exists only because of two words in Homer. Language itself thus becomes reality; behind it, there is nothing.

Book of Exercises and Logbook II

Before fleeing the German invasion, Seferis published *Book of Exercises*, a collection of various poems written between 1928 and 1937 that had not been included in his previous collections. A number of these poems involve a fictional character, Stratis Thalassinos (Stratis the Mariner), a persona used much as Eliot's J. Alfred Prufrock and Pound's Hugh Selwyn Mauberly are used. The collection also includes sixteen haiku, which, although not notably successful, are distinctively Seferis's work. In particular, number 4 expresses his vision of the mystical relationship between past and present: "Is it the voice/ of our dead friends or/ the gramophone?"

Logbook II was written in the various places of Seferis's exile with the Greek government; here, one finds the poet chronicling his wanderings, giving impressions of the many locales, some very exotic, to which his odyssey took him. Stratis Thalassinos appears again; in "Stratis Thalassinos on the Dead Sea," Seferis creates an image of Jerusalem during the war as a city of refugees with a Babel-like confusion of languages. People are shown as having little or no understanding of the city and its past and are led about like tourists with the refrain, "This is the place gentlemen!" One is reminded of T. S. Eliot's repetition of "Hurry up please its time" in *The Waste Land* and the imagery of "Unreal City," which Eliot derived from Charles Baudelaire.

"Last Stop"

"Last Stop," written at the last place where Seferis waited before returning to Greece at the war's end, has been called the most significant poem in the collection. His memories are painful, and it is not at all clear to him that the suffering of the war has been justified by the result. Nations lie in ruins, as they have in the past, some of them to be forgotten. Yet, despite this, the poem's closing lines recall a hero who left the hospital with his wounds still open; Seferis quotes this hero's emblematic words: "'We advance in the dark/we move forward in the dark. . . .'"

Other major works

nonfiction: *Dokimes*, 1947; *Treis meres sta monasteria tes Kappadokias*, 1953; *Delphi*, 1962 (English translation, 1963); *Discours de Stockholm*, 1964; *Ē glossa sten poiese mas*, 1965; *On the Greek Style: Selected Essays in Poetry and Hellenism*, 1966; *A Poet's Journal: Days of 1945-1951*, 1974.

translations: *Phoniko sten ekklesia*, 1935 (of T. S. Eliot's *Murder in the Cathedral*); *T. S. Eliot*, 1936; *Asma asmaton*, 1966 (of *The Song of Songs*); *E Apokalypse tou Ioanne*, 1966 (of *The Apocalypse of St. John*).

Bibliography

Beaton, Roderick. *George Seferis*. Bristol, England: Bristol Classical, 1991. A critical study of selected works by Seferis. Includes bibliographic references.

Hadas, Rachel. *Form, Cycle, Infinity: Landscape Imagery in the Poetry of Robert Frost and George Seferis*. Lewisburg, Pa.: Bucknell University Press, 1985. Compares the literary style and similarities of Frost and Seferis. Includes a bibliography and an index.

Kaiser, Walter. Introduction to *Days of 1945-1951: A Poet's Journal*. Translated by Athan Anagnostopoulos. Cambridge, Mass.: Harvard University Press, 1974. Kaiser provides some biographical and historical background to the life of George Seferis.

Kapre-Karka, K. *Love and the Symbolic Journey in the Poetry of Cavafy, Eliot, and Seferis: An Interpretation with Detailed Poem-by-Poem Analysis*. New York: Pella, 1982. A critical study of selected works by three poets. Includes an index and bibliography.

_______. *War in the Poetry of George Seferis: A Poem-by-Poem Analysis*. New York: Pella, 1985. A critical study of selected works by Seferis. Includes an index and bibliography.

Thaniel, George. *Seferis and Friends*. Toronto, Ont.: Mercury Press, 1994. Entertaining and informative correspondence from Seferis's wide circle of friends and acquaintances, including Henry Miller, T. S. Eliot, and Lawrence Durrell.

Tsatsou, Ioanna, and Jean Demos, trans. *My Brother George Seferis*. St. Paul, Minn.: North Central, 1982. An in-depth biography. Includes index.

J. Madison Davis;
bibliography updated by the editors

Jaroslav Seifert

Born: Prague, Czechoslovakia; September 23, 1901
Died: Prague, Czechoslovakia; January 10, 1986

Principal poetry

Město v slzách, 1921
Sama láska, 1923
Svatební cesta, 1925
Na vlnách TSF, 1925
Slavík zpívá špatně, 1926
Poštovní holub, 1929
Jablko z klína, 1933
Ruce Venušiny, 1936
Zpíváno do rotačky, 1936
Osm dní, 1937
Jaro sbohem, 1937, 1942
Zhasněte světla, 1938
Světlem oděná, 1940
Kamenný most, 1944
Přilba hlíny, 1945
Chlapec a hvezdy: Verse k obrazum a obrázkum Josefa Lady, 1956
Verse o Praze, 1962
Koncert na ostrově, 1965
Halleyova kometa, 1967
Odlévání zvonů, 1967 (*The Casting of Bells*, 1983)
Zpevy o Praze, 1968
Morový sloup, 1978 (*The Plague Column*, 1979)
Deštník z Piccadilly, 1979 (*An Umbrella from Piccadilly*, 1983)
Zápas's andelem, 1981
Býti Básníkem, 1983
The Selected Poetry of Jaroslav Seifert, 1986
The Early Poetry of Jaroslav Seifert, 1997
Ruce Venusiny, 1998
A sbohem, 1999
Treba vám nesu ruze, 1999

Other literary forms

For much of his life, Jaroslav Seifert worked as a journalist, and he wrote countless newspaper articles. During the decade after World War II, Seifert was under attack, vilified by the adherents of Socialist Realism, and withdrew from public life. His publications were limited to editing the works of various Czech authors, to translating—his translation of the biblical Song of Songs is outstanding—and to writing poetry for children.

Seifert's memoirs, titled *Všecky krásy světa* (all the beauties of the world), were first published in Czech in Toronto in 1981; a parallel edition under the same title, with minor deletions and alterations, was published shortly afterward in Prague. Seifert also produced children's literature in *Maminka: Yybor básni* (1954).

Achievements

The critic René Wellek once observed, "Lyrical poetry was always the center of Czech literature." One reason for this is that poets have probably expressed the concerns and aspirations of the Czech people better than writers in other genres.

Jaroslav Seifert was the author of nearly thirty volumes of poetry, and he won the Nobel Prize in Literature for 1984. He was a member of one of the most remarkable groups of poets in the history of Czech literature,

Jaroslav Seifert, Nobel laureate in literature for 1984.
(© The Nobel Foundation)

along with Vítězlav Nezval, Konstantin Biebl, František Halas, and Vladimír Holan. They were all born around the turn of the century, began to write when Czechoslovakia gained its independence after World War I, and took part in the numerous literary movements that flourished during the next two decades. They also lived through World War II, which their work records in depth, as well as the imposition of Communism on Czechoslovakia. Seifert survived the period of Stalinism, participating in the Prague Spring of 1968. He was honored by the government in 1966 and was named a National Artist; he served as acting chairman of the Union of Czechoslovak writers in 1968; and he was its chairman in 1969-1970. In addition, he received state prizes for his verse in 1936, 1955, and 1968. Holan, Halas, Biebl, and Nezval all died before Seifert; he was the last surviving member of this extremely talented group of poets, dying at the age of eighty-four.

Seifert was remarkably popular in Czechoslovakia, both as a poet and as a symbol of freedom of expression for writers under an oppressive regime. In 1968, he condemned the Soviet invasion of his country and was one of the original signers of the Charter 77 Civil Rights movement.

Biography

Jaroslav Seifert was born in 1901 in Prague, in a working-class neighborhood called Žižkov. Throughout his life, Seifert liked to recall his childhood in this part of Prague with its strong proletarian flavor, many tenements, railroad tracks, taverns, and its own dialect. Seifert's mother was Catholic, his father an atheist and Socialist. Although his parents were poor, Seifert was able to attend a *gymnasium* (academic secondary school), from which, however, he was not graduated; he left the *gymnasium* early and started working as a journalist.

Seifert wrote his first poems during World War I, when the future Czechoslovakia was still a province of Austria-Hungary. Czechoslovakia became independent in October, 1918; Seifert was associated with the left wing of the Social Democratic Party, and became one of the first members of the Communist Party when it was organized in 1921. Although "workers' poetry" was fashionable at the time, Seifert was one of the few practitioners who actually came from a working-class background.

The evolution of Seifert's poetry in the 1920's and 1930's is almost identical to the general evolution of Czech poetry during the period, proceeding from one major movement to the next. Seifert's friends, especially Karel Teige and Stanislav Neumann, weaned him from his earlier "proletarian poetry" and brought him closer to avant-garde artistic circles. Seifert joined them in founding a group called Devětsil; the name comes from a medicinal herb and flower that means, literally, "nine strengths." The group was inspired both by the Russian Revolution and by the heady atmosphere of freedom and national independence at the end of World War I. Its aim was nothing short of the rebuilding of the world.

Seifert also took part in the important movement of "Poetism" that left its imprint on almost all the arts in

Czechoslovakia after 1924. Poetism was influenced both by Franco-Swiss Dada and by Surrealism. It was an avant-garde movement oriented toward the future, considering all aspects of life as art forms—in the future, art would become life, and life would become art. For the Poetists, poetry became an imaginative game of chance associations of ideas, images, and words, often illogical and paradoxical. Sound effects were strongly emphasized in poetry, as well as fresh, startling rhymes; logical connections were loosened. The subject matter of poetry was broadened to include areas previously considered to be nonpoetic, such as science, technology, and exotic information. The poets drew on all the arts for their inspiration: film, music, the ballet, pantomime, the circus, and the music hall. The movement represented a sharp break with proletarian poetry. In morality, the poets tended to be skeptical; they were indulgent in sensual aspects of life and art, and often generalized their enthusiasms. They are sometimes accused of artistic insincerity, but they performed the great service of expanding the frontiers and technical devices of poetry.

In the early 1920's, Seifert wrote for a variety of newspapers and reviews. He was a reporter for a Communist newspaper in Prague, then in Brno, the Moravian capital; later, he worked for a Communist bookstore and publishing house in Prague, and edited a Communist illustrated magazine. During this time, Seifert also traveled; he went to northern Italy and France. He also went to the Soviet Union in 1925 and 1928.

By 1929, Seifert believed that the closely knit circle of Devětsil had outlived its purpose, and he became disenchanted with the new leadership of the Communist Party. With eight other Czech Communist writers, he signed a letter protesting the new party line and cultural program. He was expelled from Devětsil and the Party, which he never rejoined.

The 1930's saw a great shift of taste in Czech literature. The previous decade had sought liberation from tradition in theme, form, and style. The pendulum began to swing back, and there was a decline in free verse, a return to punctuation in poetry, and formerly avant-garde writers began to use classical forms such as the sonnet and rondel. Seifert, too, used regular, compact, stanzaic verse forms during the 1930's, with ingenious rhymes and frequent refrains. He showed an unsuspected gift for pure lyrical poetry, especially the poetry of love, with a new sense of spiritual or moral values. It was during this beleaguered decade that Seifert found and developed the two major themes that were to mark his poetic output and were to become the basis of his reputation: the theme of love for women and his stance as a national poet. He wrote his cycle of elegies on T. G. Masaryk, *Osm dní* (eight days), in 1937. Masaryk, the president-liberator, symbolized the independence of Czechoslovakia, and his somber funeral was an occasion for both nationalistic pomp and an outburst of lyric verse. Seifert's volume was reprinted six times before it satisfied popular demand. Seifert's next collections turned to children's poetry, and the writer Božena Němcová; during World War II, Seifert published three collections, and most of the poems are about Prague, which comes to symbolize the continuity of Czech history. *Přilba hlíny* (helmut of clay) celebrates the May, 1945, uprising in Prague and the subsequent liberation of the city.

After the liberation, Seifert again became active in journalism, but he was attacked by the new Communist regime; in an article titled "Not Our Voice," one minor critic accused him of being alien, bourgeois, and even un-Communist. Seifert was forced to withdraw from public life. It was only after 1954, following the death of Joseph Stalin, that he was able to publish selections from his past works and some new poetry. In 1956, he spoke from the platform at the Second Congress of the Union of Czechoslovak writers, advocating that writers express ethical conscience, civic consciousness, and public commitment—in his words, "May we be truly the conscience of our people."

After a decade of serious illness, Seifert emerged with a surprising new poetic manner. In *Koncert na ostrově* (concert on the island), he gave up much of his songlike intonation, rhyme, and metaphor for the sake of simpler, declarative free verse. It was during the Prague Spring, the time of maximum liberalization, when Alexander Dubček became leader of the Czech Communist Party, that Seifert was named a National Artist of Czechoslovakia. In August, 1968, after the invasion of the country by the Soviet Union, Seifert rose from his sickbed, called a taxi, and went to the building of the Union of Writers. Those present elected him acting chairman of the independent Union of Writers. A year later, the union was dissolved. Isolated and sick, Seifert continued to write; his poems were typed and distributed in copies by individual readers. He lived in a suburb of Prague, Břevnov, helping anyone who called on him and writing reminiscences of his long life as a poet. Between 1968 and 1975, only sections from his old works were published in Czechoslovakia, but some new poems were published in Czech in periodicals abroad. He became an original signer of Charter 77. Illness required him to be frequently hospitalized; in 1984, he received the Nobel Prize in his hospital bed, where television crews and reporters descended on him, asking for interviews. His son-in-law and secretary, Daribor Plichta, was to go to Stockholm to receive the Nobel Prize on behalf of the ailing Seifert, but the Czechoslovak government refused to give Plichta an exit permit. In 1985, Seifert was well enough to leave the hospital and return home, where he continued to write poetry. He died a year later.

Analysis

Jaroslav Seifert's life and poetry are closely interwoven, and it is a mistake to separate them. He took part in all the major poetic movements of his long life. During some of these phases, it is possible to say that he was surpassed by a friend and colleague. Perhaps Stanislav Neumann wrote superior poems of political commitment during the 1920's, and in the 1930's perhaps Josef Hora expressed the sense of attachment to the native land better than anyone else in his monumental poem "Zpěv rodné zemi" ("Song of the Native Land"). Indignation at the violent excesses of Communism was the most powerfully rendered in František Halas's superb "Potopa" ("The Deluge"). Vladimír Holan's output of meditative lyrics, published during the decade after World War II, was especially impressive. Yet it is futile to contrast Seifert to these poets as if they were competitors: They were often remarkably close and engaged in similar endeavors, and Seifert wrote poems addressed to most of these poets. Seifert's own poems are consistently interesting, remarkably high quality, and unique.

Seifert's main themes were the love of woman and the celebration of what is most positive in life. His finest collections were probably written after World War II, when these themes were increasingly associated with his defense of the individual conscience. Before the war, in the words of Arne Novák, Seifert was "a poet readily inspired by contemporary events and an unusually fluent improviser; he was a master of intimate, emotional, and highly musical verse." It should be added that he was able to express the feelings and aspirations of a remarkably broad audience. After the war, unable to publish regularly, he was to increase the depth and resonance of his poems until the end of his life.

Love as politics

In Western European countries and the United States, there has been some confusion about Seifert's emphasis on women, on the sensual love for them and their beauty, which he consistently expressed in his poems from 1930 onward. Sensuality, sexuality, love: These are often thought to be asocial, purely private concerns. In Eastern Europe, however, they assume a much greater importance. They are central to that domain where the individual man or woman still has freedom, where the state is unable to intrude, and where a human being is able to wrest a small, habitable space from a hostile environment. There he is able to express love, intimacy, and his most positive values. Love becomes a form of protest and of personal commitment, even of heroism. Seifert was able to express this theme in language that is not abstract but very concrete and specific, not moralistic or sanctimonious but frequently erotic. This is the unique synthesis of Seifert: The poems appear to be about specific experiences, but at the same time they are always more than this. He could define heaven and hell in these concrete terms, from "Jen jednou" ("Once Only"):

> Hell we all know, it's everywhere
> and walks upon two legs.
>   But paradise?
> It may be that paradise is only
> a smile
>   we have long waited for,
> and lips
>   whispering our name.
> And then that brief vertiginous moment
> when we're allowed to forget
> that hell exists.

"Merry-Go-Round with White Swan"

Although many of Seifert's poems about women may appear at first glance to be simply erotic, about his desire for an individual woman, he almost always manages to raise that desire to a higher degree of generality, simultaneously maintaining the utmost concreteness and specificity. He writes in his poem, titled "Vlastní životopis" ("Autobiography"), "But when I first saw/ the picture of a nude woman/ I began to believe in miracles." This notion of a "miracle" stayed with him as a measure of what was most positive, of the highest value. Toward the close of his life in "Merry-Go-Round with White Swan," he wrote:

> Goodbye. In all my life I never committed
> any betrayal.
> That I am aware of,
> and you may believe me.
>
> But the most beautiful of all gods
> is love.

The notion of a principle, and fidelity to it, might be easily missed. The strength of Seifert's notion of love is that it is both a positive moral concept and concretely erotic (entirely un-Calvinistic) at the same time.

A skeptical reader might ask, Is this love singular or plural? Does Seifert write of one woman, or several, or many? Or all women? Seifert moves from the singular to the plural with great ease, and the answer is that love is both singular and plural, one woman and many, concrete and universal. In addition, the concept is expanded in Seifert's many poems about Prague, which becomes "her," a distinctly feminine presence.

Opposites

The notion of love is often defined in terms of its opposite:

> Those who have left
> and hastily scattered to distant lands
> must realize it by now:
> The world is horrible!
>
> They don't love anyone and no one loves them.
> We at least love.
>
> So let her knees crush my head!

A passage such as this one might be misread by a Western reader, who lives in a democracy and assumes a sharp dividing line between private life and society; this dichotomy is upheld by democratic laws, rights, and institutions. In a totalitarian society, however, the division is abolished. The individual must create his freedom and positive values by his own efforts on a daily basis.

In another passage, love is again defined in terms of its opposite. Here it is opposed to war, presumably World War II; once again the love is not escapist, but raised to a higher level of generalization and affirmation:

> The many rondels and the songs I wrote!
> There was a war all over the world,
> and all over the world
> was grief.
> And yet I whispered into bejewelled ears
> verses of love.
> It makes me feel ashamed.
> But no, not really.

Although such a passage might seem, on a superficial level, to mock feats of armed resistance, it should be read carefully. The love here is raised to a principle, it is almost a weapon used against war. Seifert is modest and shies away from large claims or abstract words; usually he seems whimsical, his agile verse leaps from image to image, but the reader should not be fooled by the self-demeaning manner. The jeweled earrings do belong not only to a soft, attractive body (here unseen, carefully removed from the picture) but also to an object of intense devotion, menaced by the war but momentarily beyond its reach.

"A Requiem for Dvořák"

Love is also defined and contrasted to another opposite—death. Especially in his 1967 volume *The Casting of Bells*, Seifert looks forward to his own death, which serves as a foil for his theme of love. In his poem "Dvořákovo requiem" ("A Requiem for Dvořák"), he describes a place on the Vltava River where two lovers killed themselves by drowning. Most of the poem describes the efforts to drag for the couple with hooked poles, and the reactions of the men as they finally see the naked body of the girl. In the hands of another poet, this might easily degenerate into an exercise in necrophilia or voyeurism. Yet Seifert maintains—surely, deliberately—the contrast between death and the beauty of life throughout:

> The men in the boat called to the shore:
> "Drag it out, boys!"
> Well, you know, there were many of them.
> As if stuck to the ground in iced terror,
> not one of them moved.

The ending of the poem occurs not with the conclusion of this scene but the next day, "a peaceful, normal day" when "The grass-pillows smelled hot/ and invited lovers again/ to the old game." The entire volume of *The Casting of Bells* is a sustained meditation on imminent death and on life. The notion of the "casting" of a bell is a metaphor for the body which is "cast" or formed by sexual desire. Paradoxically, some poems in the volume are among Seifert's most positive.

"The Blow"

Seifert creates a similar structure of contrasts in his cycle of poems on the bombing of the town of Kralupy during World War II. He was forced to take cover in a cemetery, behind a low grave in "Uder" ("The Blow"). When the dead girl buried there "gave me her hand," Seifert "held" it and was able to resist the explosions coming from the town nearby. The gesture became an affirmation of life, and of Seifert's strong ties to what is most positive in life: Even the dead, through the feeling of love they once felt—human, sexual, and erotic—are able to participate in these ties.

The Plague Column

Seifert most explicitly contrasts love to totalitarian politics in his volume *The Plague Column*. As in Albert Camus's novel *La Peste* (1947; *The Plague*, 1948), Seifert's concept of a plague is allegorical and refers to contemporary history. The plague goes on and on:

> Don't let them dupe you
> that the plague has come to an end:
> I've seen too many coffins hauled past.
>
> The plague still rages and it seems the doctors
> are giving different names to the disease
> to avoid panic.

The "plague" is the Communism of the 1970's; it is also a grisly time of burning corpses and "cynical drinking songs." Like the young Seifert, the older poet again has an oppositional politics "in the name of love," though his politics is now anti-Communist rather than pro-Communist. Love is given its maximal meaning not only as a foil to death, and to war, but also to the rampant "plague" of political terror.

Late poems

This theme of love also has its special style. It closely resembles the alert and highly agile style that Seifert developed in his last three volumes. It is flexible and allusive, moves in unexpected directions, and is always surprising. Seifert is an extremely subtle poet. The translations of his work vary widely in quality; different translations of the same passage in Czech can give rise to totally different interpretations—what might seem whimsy to one reader may appear to be sharp irony to another, and the American or English reader relying on translations of Seifert should beware. The unique style of Seifert's last volumes is characterized above all by intimacy, also by freedom and sensuality. He harks back to his style during the period of Poetism, with its Surrealist and Dada overtones, but it has more depth and follows the contours of thought, the rhythms of intimate impulse and feeling, with far greater closeness and fidelity. As Seifert told a French interviewer near the end of his life:

> As one grows older, one discovers different values and different worlds. For me, this meant that I discovered sensuality. . . . All language can be thought of as an effort to achieve freedom, to feel the joy and the sensuality of freedom. What we seek in language is the freedom to be able to express one's most intimate thoughts. This is the basis of all freedom.

Style, too, can be a function of a principle of love, of those most positive values that Seifert opposes to political repression. Professor Eduard Goldstücker, chairman of the Czech Writers' Union in 1968 and subsequently exiled, emphasized Seifert's consistent role as a poet of resistance when he wrote in 1985: "Seifert's poems were always in the front line of resistance. In those dark years [of occupation by the Germans] he became the poet of his people, and he has remained so until this day."

OTHER MAJOR WORKS

NONFICTION: *Všecky krásy světa*, 1981 (autobiography).

CHILDREN'S LITERATURE: *Maminka: Yybor básni*, 1954.

ANTHOLOGY: *Dílo*, 1953-1970.

BIBLIOGRAPHY

Gibian, George. Introduction to *The Poetry of Jaroslav Seifert*. North Haven, Conn.: Catbird Press, 1998. A brief biography that focuses primarily on Seifert's literary activities and explores his literary ancestry and evolution as a poet. In a country in which poetry is highly regarded, Seifert achieved the status of a national poet who was widely respected and loved.

Harkins, William E. "The Czech Nobel Laureate Jaroslav Seifert." *World Literature Today* 59, no. 2 (Spring, 1985): 173-175. In response to questions evoked by Seifert's winning the Nobel Prize in Literature, Harkins affirms the merit of the award. Seifert's work spanned much of the twentieth century, uniting two great periods in Czech literature—"the interwar period of the twenties and thirties, and the 'thaw' period of the sixties." His "cult of optimism and love" reflected the mood of his countrymen.

Holub, Miroslav. "A Song Under All Circumstances." *Parnassus: Poetry in Review* 14, no. 1 (1987): 209-227. An exploration of the lyrical qualities of Seifert's poetry. Seifert's frequent use of the word "song" in the titles of his poems reflects its significance as a metaphor for all of his writing. His best poetry is "untranslatable and incomprehensible; he is hermetically national." He maintained a lyrical voice throughout his life and "represented the nation's positive spirit, consistently, steadfastly, and to the end."

Iggers, Wilma A. "The World of Jaroslav Seifert." *World Literature Today* 60, no. 1 (Winter, 1986): 8-12. An excellent overview of Seifert's literary career, including an examination of the relationship between his writing and his involvement in politics. The article also analyzes the differences between Seifert's poetry and prose, noting that his poetry generally "hovers *above* mundane reality" and "reflects his longing for beauty and goodness in the midst of evil."

Loewy, Dana. Introduction to *The Early Poetry of Jaroslav Seifert*. Translated by Dana Loewy. Evanston, Ill.: Northwestern University Press, 1997. Despite winning the Nobel Prize, Seifert remains relatively unknown in the English-speaking world and no extensive body of scholarly work exists in English. The lack of good translations dampened enthusiasm for his work outside his native country, but Loewy disavows claims by Seifert critics that his early work is untranslatable. Although some aspects of his poetry will be lost, his "musicality, playfulness, and lyricism can be imitated in English with the help of internal rhymes, half-rhymes, and assonance." Important influences on Seifert's early work included French poetry; movements in fine art such cubism, Futurism, and Dada; and the "poetism" movement in Czechoslovakia. By the end of the 1920's Seifert had become disillusioned with politics and turned inward with his poetry, but he consistently spoke out against political oppression.

Pešat, Zdenek. *Jaroslav Seifert*. Prague: Ceskoslovenský spisovatel, 1991. A full-length study of the life and work of Seifert. With a mother who was a practicing Catholic, a father who was a socialist and atheist, and a country which was in political turmoil, Seifert attempted in both his life and his poetry to avoid extremes and to embrace all of life. In Czech.

John Carpenter;
bibliography updated by Verbie Lovorn Prevost

LÉOPOLD SENGHOR

Born: Joal, Senegal; October 9, 1906
Died: Verson, France; December 20, 2001

PRINCIPAL POETRY

Chants d'ombre, 1945
Hosties noires, 1948
Chants pour Naëtt, 1949
Chants d'ombre—Hosties noires, 1956

Éthiopiques, 1956
Nocturnes, 1961 (English translation, 1969)
Poèmes, 1964
Selected Poems, 1964
Élégie des Alizés, 1969
Selected Poems of Léopold Sédar Senghor, 1977
Œuvre poétique, 1990 (*The Collected Poetry*, 1991)

OTHER LITERARY FORMS

Léopold Senghor was a poet and a politician, a combination of professions unusual in the Anglo-Saxon world but not uncommon in French literary history. As one of the leaders of the emerging nationalism of the former French African colonies and later, as President of Senegal, Senghor was called upon to make speeches, prepare reports, and write articles in newspapers, reviews, and periodicals. These many articles deal with a variety of topics: political, cultural, economic, judicial, and social, as well as literary. In 1948, Senghor edited *Anthologie de la nouvelle poésie nègre et malgache de langue française*, with a preface by Jean-Paul Sartre titled "Orphée noir." Among Senghor's prose works are *Congrès constitutif du P.F.A.: Rapport sur la doctrine et le programme du parti* (1959; constituent congress of the P.F.A.: report on the principles and programme of the Party) and *La Préhistoire et les groupes éthniques* (1960; prehistory and ethnic groups). Senghor's interest in socialism and its application in Africa was expressed in *Nation et voie africaine du socialisme* (1961; as volume 2 of *Liberté*, 1971; *Nationhood and the African Road to Socialism*, 1962; abridged as *On African Socialism*, 1964) and *Théorie et pratique du socialisme sénégalais* (1964). In the works of the Catholic thinker Pierre Teilhard de Chardin, Senghor found a synthesis of Catholicism and socialism which fit his personal beliefs, reflected in *Pierre Teilhard de Chardin et la politique africaine* (1962). *Liberté: Négritude et humanisme*, 1964 (*Freedom I: Negritude and Humanism*, 1974) collects a wide range of Senghor's articles and lectures.

ACHIEVEMENTS

As a result of his multitude of activities, Léopold Senghor presented a problem for critics assessing his poetic works. Does the fact that he was a black African

Léopold Senghor

make him a mouthpiece of black African peoples, or should he be judged only as a poet who happened to be black? Does the fact that Senghor wrote in French mean that he must be judged as a French poet or as an African—more specifically, a Senegalese poet—who happened to write in French? Must the fact that Senghor was a successful politician interfere with the way his poetry is judged?

There are no easy answers to these questions. Senghor himself was torn between the various worlds he inhabited, and—as is obvious in his poetry—he was not always successful in separating his different interests or in properly synthesizing them. As an educated, intelligent young Senegalese—he was the first African to receive the very competitive French *agrégation* (the equivalent of a doctorate for teachers) and thereby able to teach French in French *lycées*—Senghor became one of the leaders of the expatriate blacks in Paris during the 1930's. With Aimé Césaire and Léon Damas, he founded the magazine *L'Étudiant noir.* After the war, he published his first collection of poems, *Chants d'ombre*, and three years later, his second, *Hosties noires*. It was not, however, until he edited an anthology of black poetry that same year, *Anthologie de la nouvelle poésie nègre et malgache de langue française*, that he attracted the attention of French critics, and even then it was probably the preface by Jean-Paul Sartre, then at the height of his career, which earned the book notice.

In 1960, he was elected President of Senegal, a post he held until 1981. The demands of political office kept the poet too busy to be prolific. As president of Senegal, Senghor encouraged the study of African literature at the University of Dakar, which he was instrumental in founding, and made Dakar, the capital of Senegal, the intellectual capital of Africa. During his presidency, Senghor also initiated an ambitious campaign to eradicate illiteracy and promote books and reading in his country.

Senghor's honors and awards are almost too numerous to mention, flowing from institutions around the world and acknowledging his many accomplishments, both literary and political. In 1968, he received the Peace Prize of the German Book Trade Association; in 1970, the Knokke Biennial International Poetry Grand Prix; in 1971, the membership in Academy of Overseas Sciences; in 1971, the membership in Black Academy of Arts and Sciences; in 1972, the Grenoble Gold Medal; in 1973, the Haile Selassie African Research Prize; in 1973, the Cravat of Commander of Order of French Arts and Letters; in 1974, the Apollinaire Prize for Poetry; in 1977, the Prince Pierre of Monaco's Literature Prize; in 1978, the Prix Eurafrique; in 1979, the International Book Award sponsored by UNESCO's International Book Committee; in 1981, the Alfred de Vigny Prize; in 1981, the Aasan World Prize; in 1983, the election to the Academie Française, the first African to be so honored; in 1984, the Jawaharlal Nehru Award; and in 1985, the Athinai Prize. He also received the Grand Cross of the French Legion of Honor, was named Commander of Academic Palms, and received the Franco-Allied Medal of Recognition. He was the recipient of many honorary doctorates from academic institutions the world over.

BIOGRAPHY

Léopold Sédar Senghor was born on October 9, 1906, in Joal, a small coastal village south of Dakar, in Senegal. The Serer tribe to which Senghor's family belongs is a Catholic enclave in a predominantly Moslem region; the name Léopold was Senghor's Catholic name, while Sédar is his Serer name. Senghor's father, Basile Diogoye Senghor, and mother, Nyilane, were a well-to-do couple. Until the age of seven, Senghor was allowed to grow up wild and free in the lush nature which he recalls fondly as the kingdom of childhood in *Chants d'ombre*. At seven, Senghor was plucked from his kingdom and—to the chagrin of his mother, who thought he was much too young—sent to a Catholic mission school at N'gasobil, a few miles north of Joal. There, Senghor was still close to the nature he loved, but for the first time the future Socialist and politician became aware of the poverty of many black Africans. In 1922, Senghor was sent to the Catholic seminary in Dakar, where he hesitated between becoming a priest and becoming a professor. Told that he lacked the dedication to be a priest, he prepared for a career as a professor. Upon graduation in 1928, he left Senegal for the first time and traveled to Paris, where he entered the Lycée Louis-le-Grand. There, he met such future French luminaries as Paul Guth and Georges Pompidou, as well as fellow black expatriates from Africa and the West Indies, including Aimé Césaire and Léon Damas.

In Paris, a whole new world opened up for Senghor. For the black expatriates of the 1930's, France was both an adopted mother and an enemy. Blacks living in France did not face the legalized discrimination which existed at that time in the United States; instead, they were the victims of a polite, unofficial policy of segregation. In response, the expatriates banded together to analyze their situation; one product of such analysis was the concept of *négritude*, a word coined by Césaire and adopted by Senghor.

It was during these years in Paris that Senghor began developing his talents as a poet, writing the poems that were later to be published in *Chants d'ombre*. In 1932, Senghor received his *diplôme d'études supérieures* (the equivalent of the master's degree) with a dissertation on exoticism in the works of Charles Baudelaire, and in 1935 he took French citizenship to be able to receive his *agrégation*, which allowed him to teach French to French children. After his military service, Senghor began his career as a teacher at the Lycée Descartes in Tours, a city important to the Popular Front; the children he taught were workers' sons. In this atmosphere, Senghor's Socialist inclinations were reinforced. After Tours, Senghor taught at the Lycée Marcelin Berthelot at Saint-Maur des Fosses. Just before the war, he participated with Jacques Roumain and others in compiling a special edition for Editions Plon devoted to ethnic subjects. In 1939, Senghor was drafted; taken prisoner by the Germans in 1940, he was released in 1942 because of frequent illness. He returned to teaching and joined the Resistance. These unhappy times of war and suffering were the inspiration for his second volume of poetry, *Hosties noires*.

After the French liberation, Senghor's political activities intensified. Besides becoming professor of African language and civilization at the École Nationale de la France d'outre-mer in Paris, he was elected to the French National Assembly. In 1946, he married Ginette Eboué, daughter of the Governor of French Equatorial Africa. He was accused by some of marrying to enhance his career. In 1948, Senghor left the Socialist Party and created a new party, the Bloc Démocratique Sénégalais. In the 1950's, Senghor's political career continued to advance. He was part of the Edgar Fauré Cabinet and later a member of the Constitutional Assembly of Senegal. Finally, on September 5, 1960, he became the first president of the new, independent country of Senegal.

During the years between the war and his election, Senghor had traveled widely and had made many trips back to Serer country, where he participated in village feasts, the inspirations for several of his poems. When, in 1956, Senghor's first marriage failed, he married Colette Hubert, a white Frenchwoman who had been secretary to his first wife.

In 1981, Senghor voluntarily retired as president of Senegal, a rare act for an African head of state, to devote himself to writing and to promoting the Socialist International Organization, of which he has been vice president.

It is a testament to his preeminence as a politician, a poet, and a philosopher that, on October 18, 1996, UNESCO organized a three-day ceremony in Paris to honor Senghor on his ninetieth birthday. The celebration consisted of art exhibits and tributes by world dignitaries such as French president Jacques Chirac, King Hassan II of Morocco, Pope John Paul II, and winner of the 1986 Nobel Prize in Literature Wole Soyinka of Nigeria. Unable to attend in person, Senghor opened the festivities with a videotaped message pleading for solidarity among peoples and universal synthesis of cultures, a note that echoes his enduring dream of reconciling French-language culture and its humanism with *négritude*, the embodiment of the values of the black world.

As creator of the Organization of African Unity, Senghor was a champion of pan-Africanism, and as a pivotal architect in the creation of the International Francophone Community he bolstered his vision of a cultural community. Senghor died in late 2001, but many biographies of this man of uncommon destiny have appeared, and his poetry lives on in the many republications of his works which have been translated into some thirty languages. His poetry has strongly influenced the literary world and continues to do so as young readers discover a body of work which has stood for hope and unity.

Analysis

Léopold Senghor was at once a politician and a poet, a combination which he regarded as a logical marriage because, as he stated in an interview with Armand Guibert, culture—of which poetry is the highest expression—is the foundation and at the same time the ultimate goal of politics. When he was a student in the 1930's, Senghor, unlike his West Indies friends, believed that a cultural revolution should precede a political one. He wanted to be the *dyali* (Sengalese troubadour) of his country. In Senghor's experience, however, other dichotomies were not as easy to resolve. These dichotomies are expressed in his poems; indeed, they are the heart of many of them. During his years in France, Senghor was torn between his love for his native land (his "sister," as he sometimes calls it in his verses) and his love for his adopted country (his "foster sister"). He was caught between two very dissimilar civilizations, each with its own merits and faults. Repelled by French colonialism and by the racial prejudice that he encountered at first hand, he nevertheless admired French culture and the French language. When he was in Paris, he missed Senegal, and when he was back in Serer country, he missed "la douce France." He was a black man in a white world, and while many of his poems reflect his sensuous admiration of the black woman, who for him symbolizes Africa, several other poems express his love of a white woman (his first wife was black; his second, white). Finally, Senghor's poetry, especially his first volume, *Chants d'ombre*, is marked by nostalgia for the magic kingdom of his childhood, associated with a mythical, primeval Africa.

One of the major influences on Senghor's poetry was the Serer poet Maronne, whose songs introduced Senghor to the traditional literature of his native area. Even earlier, as a child, he had listened to the *gymnique* poets, whose songs accompany the wrestling matches so popular in Senegal and serve as work songs and lullabies as well. Senghor was also familiar with the poetry of the *griots*, professional and learned oral poets. Music was another major influence on Senghor's poetry. Under the titles of most of his poems, Senghor indicated the African musical instruments that should be used to provide accompaniment. In an interview with Armand Guibert, Senghor stated that there is a double reason for this: Musical accompaniment both enhances the effect of the poetry and revives the African oral tradition, in which poetry was song. Images of music abound in Senghor's poetry. He referred, for example, to the rhythm of the world, and a beloved is described as a flute. Senghor's French education was inevitably an influence also. From poets such as Charles Baudelaire and his successors Arthur Rimbaud, Paul Verlaine, and Stéphane Mallarmé, Senghor learned to use Symbolism "to express complex sensations," as Abiola Irele observes in her introduction to *Selected Poems of Léopold Sédar Senghor.* Paul Claudel's influence is evident in Senghor's religious poems extolling the mysteries of the Catholic faith. Irele believes that Senghor took up Paul Claudel's distinctive verse form, the *verset*, and infused it with elements of African oral tradition. There are also affinities between Senghor and St.-John Perse, but Senghor said that he first read Perse only after his own style was formed; thus, the similarities between them reflect a convergence rather than the influence of one on the other.

When Senghor started writing poetry, Surrealism was in full bloom. S. Okechukwu Mezu, in *Léopold Sédar Senghor et la défense et illustration de la civilisation noire* (1968), analyzes at great length the influence of Surrealism on Senghor's poetry—though here again, it may be more accurate to speak of a convergence than of an influence. The 1930's were marked by a renaissance of black awareness in Europe while the Surrealist revolt against Cartesian rationalism glorified the so-called primitive civilizations; thus, Senghor's proclamation of the purity of the black race—a purity that the white race had lost—was perfectly in accord with Surrealist dogma. What André Breton sought in the subconscious, Senghor sought by going back to his African roots. The European Surrealist had to delve deep into his subconscious to find his instincts and natural desires, but the black African had only to be himself. While Surrealist poets such as Paul Éluard tried to merge the real and the fantastic to avoid paranoia, Senghor saw no need for this synthesis. It already characterized the bushman, who knew neither insanity nor psychosis and in whom the body and the mind were one. Even in methods of composition, Senghor and the Surrealists followed the same path: The poetry of the Senegalese *griots* was spoken thought, a practice stemming from an oral tradition, a sort of psychic automatism. Describing the process he followed to write his poetry, Senghor said that he begins with an expression that is whispered in his ear like a leitmotif; when he began to write, he did not know what form the poem would take.

This new view of the black African corresponded to Senghor's definition of the term *négritude*, meaning the entire cultural heritage of the black civilizations of Africa. In Senghor's view, the black man, as a result of his heritage, enjoys a greater capacity for feeling and a closer relationship with the natural world than that bequeathed to the white man by European civilization. In general, Anglophone African writers have rejected the concept of *négritude*; the Nigerian poet, playwright, and novelist Wole Soyinka has observed that a tiger does not speak of its *tigritude*. Indeed, in recent decades, during which Africa has achieved independence from the colonial powers, the notion of *négritude* has lost much of its appeal in Francophone regions as well.

Chants d'ombre

More than any other African poet, Senghor was classical in his poetic style. The first poem of *Chants d'ombre* has a Latin title, and many of his poems contain classical allusions; for this he was criticized by other African writers. On the other hand, French critics have objected to African elements in his verse, ranging from his frequent use of repetition (a legacy of the oral tradition) to his sentence structure and his diction. Senghor liked to use words drawn from the two major languages of Senegal, Wolof and Serer. In an interview with Guibert, Senghor defended this practice, saying that he did not indulge in exoticism but had merely drawn on the vocabulary used by the French-speaking Senegalese and even by the French living in Senegal.

According to Senghor, rhythm is the key element of African art. He quoted American jazz great Duke Ellington to describe his own poetry: "popular Negro music." Senghor used several devices to achieve rhythm, including alternation of accented and atonal syllables instead of long and short, as well as more conventional devices, such as alliteration and assonance. Another quality of Senghor's poetry which marked him as an African poet is his imagery. He has been called "the Poet of the Night" because of his many references to night and darkness as symbols of good. Like many other black writers, especially the black American poets, Senghor reversed the solar hierarchy of white poets, who glorify the sun and the color white as good and depict night and black as evil.

Chants d'ombre, a collection of poems written during Senghor's early years in Paris, reflects the poet's nostalgia for his African home and his childhood, as well as his growing awareness of his own alienation in a country whose duplicity as a colonizer he could not ignore. The first poem in the collection, "In memoriam," is written in the form of a prayer. Despite the poet's religious fervor, however, his alienation is obvious. He feels set apart from the people with whom he goes to church in Paris; his prayer is to the dead, to his ancestors, as is the custom in his native land. He is further distinguished from the other churchgoers by his color. They, whom he calls his brothers, have blue eyes and "hard hands," a term that, in Africa, is a metaphor for hate, meanness, and inhospitality. "In memoriam" sets the tone of the entire collection. What follows is reminiscence. In "Tout le long du jour" (all day long), as the poet travels on the European train, he remembers his native land, the little uniform railroad stations, and the chatty, nubile young black girls. In these reminiscences, he seeks to forget Europe, and in so doing he idealizes his homeland. "Joal" reflects the same theme. Eight times, the words "I remember" are used, and what the poet remembers is an innocent Africa whose rhythm of life is simple and whose awareness of the divine presence in the universe is unique. The sacrifices to the gods, the pagan singing of the *Tantum ergo*, and the little parish church complement rather than oppose one another. The style of the poem is simple, as befits the subject matter; it ends, however, with a return to reality and the poet's awareness of his exile.

"For Koras and Balafong"

"For Koras and Balafong" is a long poem, a solemn chant in nine stanzas embracing all the themes of the collection. The poet examines the conflicts that tear at him, celebrating the African past and mourning its passing at the hands of the colonizers. The title immediately sets the African mood. The *kora* is a musical instrument similar to the harp, while the *balafong* is an African xylophone. The poem is dedicated to René Maran, a French West Indian writer whose novel *Batouala* (1921) dealt for the first time in literature with French colonial policy. "For Koras and Balafong" was written when Europe was on the brink of World War II. Stanza 1 is an idyllic description of Europe and of the poet's childhood. In stanzas 2, 3, and 4, the poet remembers his French schooling and the beginnings of his alienation, leading him to make comparisons between old France and young Africa. Stanzas 5, 6, and 7 celebrate Africa before the white man altered it; Senghor compares his continent to a black princess. In stanza 8, the Socialist Senghor views the future as a solemn procession of seven thousand peasants carrying the riches of his race, no longer slaves as in the days of colonialism. Stanza 9, a lyric paean to Africa, is dominated by the color black. Africa is a dark beauty, a black night. Night delivers the poet from the arguments and sophistries of salons, from the butchery rationalized by the colonizers. In "For Koras and Balafong," the language is French, but the poet is undeniably African.

"Paris in Snow"

The dominant color of "Paris in Snow" is white—here, the color of death: the white of the snow on the roofs of Paris, white sheets, and the white hands that whipped the slaves and cut down the forests of Africa. An indictment of Western civilization, "Paris in Snow" establishes a bitter contrast between the message of peace of the Christmas season and the rumbles of war presaged in the destruction of Spain and the persecution of the Jews. Ultimately, however, the theme of the poem is religious. In the first line, the speaker addresses Christ ("Lord, you visited Paris on the day of your birth"), and the entire poem is cast in the form of a prayer. The speaker's ambivalence and spiritual torment are revealed in contrasting images of white: Christ's "snow of peace" and the "white cold" of his demanding love versus the brutal "white hands" of the colonizers. The paradoxical images of Christ recall the poetry of John Donne and George Herbert: Senghor's Christ is dark (the Saras, a people from Chad, are "beautiful like the first men that were created by your brown hands"), yet the speaker of the poem, seeking to overcome his hatred of the white colonizers, concludes:

My heart, oh Lord, has melted like the snow on the
roofs of Paris

In the sun of your Goodness,

It is kind to my enemies, my brothers with the snowless
white hands. . . .

"Black Woman"

The most impressionistic and most sensuous poem of the volume is "Femme noire" ("Black Woman"). Senghor observed that in black Africa the woman holds a particularly high standing: She is both the giver of life and the repository of tradition, and she assures the clan's future. When a woman marries in Africa, she does not renounce her clan to become integrated into her husband's family; she continues to belong to her own clan. She also runs the household and has her own property. In 1950, in an article on Negro-American poetry, Senghor wrote that American blacks have a cult of the black woman, who symbolizes *négritude*. The woman more than the man is sensitive to the mysteries of life and the cosmos; she is also more sensitive to joy and pain. "Black Woman" is not about a particular woman but about a generic woman: a lover, a mother, and finally Africa herself. The poem is a succession of images; the black woman is a promised land, a savannah, a tom-tom, and a gazelle. Mezu compares Senghor's poem to André Breton's *L'Union libre* (1931; *Free Union*, 1982), in which Breton appropriates the manner of the litany. Senghor's "Black Woman" is also faithful to the tradition of the African praise poem.

Hosties noires and Éthiopiques

Hosties noires, Senghor's second volume of poems, was written as a result of Senghor's experiences as a prisoner of war. With this volume, Senghor moved from personal to collective poetry and from lyric and nostalgic to nationalistic poetry. Two recurring themes in *Hosties noires* are the sacrifices of black soldiers and the poet's ambivalent relation to France and the European tradition. The title, with its religious overtones—*hostie* refers to the Host in the Catholic Mass—unequivocally designates the most important theme of the volume, the black soldiers who died for France as sacrificial victims.

In *Éthiopiques*, Senghor adopted a more hermetic style displaying strong affinities with Surrealism. The four major long poems of the volume are "Chaka," "Letters to the Princess," "Congo," and "To New York." Chaka, an early nineteenth century Zulu chieftain, was an effective but ruthless soldier and leader who quickly rose to power and was driven insane by the nightmares of his crimes. He was finally assassinated by his brothers. Thomas Mofolo had written a novel on Chaka, and Senghor, in his poem, takes up where Mofolo left off—that is, at the end of Chaka's regime. In "Chaka," Senghor concentrates on the conflict between Chaka's political love and his personal love; the Zulu leader had to sacrifice his beloved Noliwe for his people. Senghor the African expresses his admiration for Chaka's nationalism and resistance to oppression, but Senghor the educated politician speaks as the "White Voice" in the poem and expresses his hatred of fanaticism and extremism. The White Voice calls Chaka the provider of hyenas and vultures. Nevertheless, what followed Chaka's regime was even more barbaric: colonialism.

"Letters to the Princess" deals with the conflict between love and politics; unlike Chaka, Senghor does not sacrifice his love to his political ambitions. The title figure of the poem is called "the Princess of Belborg," denoting a northern woman of noble blood, possibly an illicit love, since, as Mezu surmises, in chivalrous literature, the conventions of which this poem imitates, passion is usually illicit. Senghor wrote "Letters to the Princess" in the period during which he divorced his first wife, a black West Indian, and married a white Frenchwoman. Senghor, writing in Senegal, addresses letters to his distant love; he expresses nostalgia for Paris, for the neighborhoods where he once lived and which he associates with her. The bitterness he once felt toward Europe is assuaged; he feels the pain of the war-devastated continent. He hopes that his loved one will come to be with him in the land of his mother, "where the soil is black and the blood is dark and the oil is thick." The sensuality that prevails in "Black Woman" is repeated here when Senghor describes Lilanga, who symbolizes Africa:

> Lilanga, her feet are two reptiles, hands that gather the pestles that
>
> beat the males that till the earth
>
> And from the earth wells up the rhythm, sap and sweat, wave and smell
>
> of the damp earth
>
> That shudders the legs of the statue, the thighs that open to the secret
>
> Flows over the buttocks, hollows the loins stretched the belly gorges and
>
> hills
>
> Prows of drums. . . .

The same sensual and female images occur in "Congo." The Congo of the title is the river which Senghor calls "Queen over Africa." This queen has tamed "Phalli of mountains" and is the mother of all things. The Congo is another variation of the feminine archetype dear to the son of a matriarchal regime. In "To New York," perhaps the finest poem in the collection, Senghor distinguishes between two New Yorks: Manhattan, the white section—which is male, sterile, and livid, and where there is no child's laughter, no mother's breast—and Harlem, the black section—which is female, alive with sounds and color. New York's only hope is to allow the black blood to flow into the white. In this poem, as he did in "Paris in Snow," Senghor refers to the blackness of God: "God who with a burst of saxophone laughter created the heavens and the earth in six days./ And on the seventh day, he slept his great negro sleep." Similarly, in the second stanza of the poem, he proclaims that "there is more truth in the Night than in the day."

NOCTURNES

Nocturnes was published one year after Senghor became president of Senegal; the volume is made up of two parts: "Chants pour Signare" ("Songs for Signare") and "Élégies" ("Elegies"). The former is a group of love poems originally published in 1949 under the title *Chants pour Naëtt*. Written with Senghor's first wife in mind, they were revised for the later publication, and the name Naëtt was changed to Signare in deference to Senghor's second wife. (In Senegal, *signare*, from the Portuguese *senhora*, designates a woman of quality.) Among other revisions, Senghor substituted African words for French words, omitted some secondary words (such as articles), and changed the punctuation to give his poems a more African rhythm. The "Songs for Signare" are no longer concerned with the conflicts that tormented the poet in his earlier volumes. They are primarily love poems wherein the poet addresses an unnamed beloved and seeks her solace to soothe his weariness. The loved one is, as in previous poems, the archetypal woman, the nurturer and the giver of life; she is black and she is white, she is alive and she is abstract. The poet is now in his native land, but he longs for earlier, simpler days of childhood, and the woman symbolizes for him not only Africa, but also the Africa of his childhood. If the conflicts seem to be resolved, the contrasts remain. The key words for the entire collection are "night" and "light," beginning with the first line of the first poem: "A hand of light caressed my eyelids of darkness." The title of the collection, *Nocturnes*, indicates night for Senghor is peaceful, a time to be with his beloved; light is associated with the white man and political duties. In these poems, the contrasts of light and dark are set against a multitude of colors: the green smell of rice fields, the trees with golden leaves, the red African soil, and the blue city of the dead.

In "Elegies," the second part of the volume, the poet is more self-confident, more conscious of being a leader.

As John Reed and Clive Wake point out in their introduction to their translation of *Nocturnes*, even though the "Elegies" recall some of the early conflicts, they incorporate a more recent viewpoint which recognizes the importance of the creative act and of reconciliation. "Élégie de minuit" ("Elegy of Midnight") begins with the poet's discontent with what fame has brought him. The third stanza of the poem depicts in very erotic terms the despair that not even the music of love can calm. In the last stanza, the poet asks to be born again in the Kingdom of Childhood, to be shepherd to his shepherdess, to dance like the athlete, but then he calms down and accepts the fact that peace will come, that "I shall sleep the sleep of death by which the Poet is fed." "Élégie de l'eau" ("Elegy of Water"), as Reed and Wake observe, is Senghor's "supreme poem of reconciliation." Here, fire and water are symbols of purification; Chicago and Moscow are burning, and the poet calls for rain, on New York, on Pompidou, on Paris: ". . . China—four hundred thousand Chinese are drowned, twelve million Chinese are saved. . . ." Finally, he calls for rain "on straw heads and wool heads./ And life is born again color of whatever is."

Other major works

NONFICTION: *Congrès constitutif du P.F.A.: Rapport sur la doctrine et le programme du parti*, 1959; *La Préhistoire et les groupes éthniques*, 1960; *Nation et voie africaine du socialisme*, 1961 (as vol. 2 of *Liberté*, 1971; *Nationhood and the African Road to Socialism*, 1962; abridged as *On African Socialism*, 1964); *Pierre Teilhard de Chardin et la politique africaine*, 1962; *Liberté: Négritude et humanisme*, 1964 (*Freedom I: Negritude and Humanism*, 1974); *Théorie et pratique du socialisme sénégalais*, 1964; *Les Fondements de l'Africanité: Ou, Négritude et arabité*, 1967 (as *Négritude, arabisme, et francité: Réflexions sur le problème de la culture*, 1967; *The Foundations of "Africanité": Or, Négritude and "Arabité,"* 1971); *La Parole chez Paul Claudel et chez les négro-africains*, 1973; *Pour une relecture africaine de Marx et d'Engels*, 1976; *Liberté: Négritude et civilisation de l'universel*, 1977; *Liberté: Socialisme et planification*, 1983; *Liberté: Le Dialogue des cultures*, 1993.

EDITED TEXT: *Anthologie de la nouvelle poésie nègre et malgache de langue française*, 1948.

MISCELLANEOUS: *Prose and Poetry*, 1965.

Bibliography

Bâ, Sylvia W. *The Concept of Negritude in the Poetry of Léopold Sédar Senghor.* Princteon, N.J.: Princeton University Press, 1973. Examines issues of race identity in Senghor's works. Includes translations of selected poems. Bibliography.

Hymans, Jacques. *Leopold Sédar Senghor: An Intellectual Biography.* Edinburgh: Edinburgh University Press, 1971. This substantial biography of more than three hundred pages pays particular attention to Senghor's philosophical and literary development. Considers, among other things, the influence of Pierre Teilhard de Chardin, Paul Claudel, Marc Chagall, and Jacques Maritain. Bibliography.

Kluback, William. *Léopold Sédar Senghor: From Politics to Poetry.* New York: P. Lang, 1997. A book of imagined conversations based on Senghor's philosophy regarding humanity's moral evolution.

Markovitz, Irving Leonard. *Leopold Sédar Senghor and the Politics of Négritude.* New York: Atheneum, 1969. A three-hundred-page consideration of Senghor's philosophy of leadership and issues of race identity. Bibliography.

Mezu, Sebastian Okechukwu. *The Poetry of Leopold Sédar Senghor.* Rutherford, N.J.: Fairleigh Dickinson University Press, 1973. A rare monograph focusing on Senghor's poetry.

Rasmussen, R. Kent. *Modern African Political Leaders.* New York: Facts On File, 1998. Covers leaders, including Senghor, representative of the major regions of Africa during a period when many African nations moved from colonial rule to independence.

Spleth, Janice. *Léopold Sédar Senghor.* New York: Macmillan Library Reference, 1985. A detailed overview of Senghor's poetry, his development as poet and statesman, and the conflicts of those two roles. This discussion involves the author in extending her coverage beyond Senghor to examine the relationship between French and francophone African literature in general. Readable and balanced—an excellent starting point.

_______, ed. *Critical Perspectives on Léopold Sédar Senghor.* Washington, D.C.: Three Continents Press, 1993. A collection of critical essays on Sédar's works. Includes bibliographical references.

Vaillant, Janet G. *Black, French, and African: A Life of Leopold Sédar Senghor.* Cambridge, Mass.: Harvard University Press, 1990. A biography that adds to previous literature an extended examination of Senghor's childhood, including interviews with his extended Senegalese family. More material on his poetry than on his presidency of Senegal. The first major biography in English.

Monique F. Nagem,
updated by Nagem and the editors

ROBERT W. SERVICE

Born: Preston, Lancashire, England; January 16, 1874
Died: Lancieux, France; September 11, 1958

PRINCIPAL POETRY

Songs of a Sourdough, 1907
Ballads of a Cheechako, 1909
Rhymes of a Rolling Stone, 1912
The Rhymes of a Red Cross Man, 1916
The Shooting of Dan McGrew and Other Verses, 1920
Ballads of a Bohemian, 1921
Twenty Bath-Tub Ballads, 1939
Bar-Room Ballads, 1940
Songs of a Sun-Lover, 1949
Rhymes of a Roughneck, 1950
Lyrics of a Lowbrow, 1951
Rhymes of a Rebel, 1952
Songs for My Supper, 1953
Carols of an Old Codger, 1954
Rhymes for My Rags, 1956
Songs of the High North, 1958
The Complete Poems, 1933, enlarged 1938, enlarged 1942
Collected Poems, 1940
Later Collected Verse, 1965

OTHER LITERARY FORMS

Robert W. Service's novels never achieved any degree of literary significance or even popular acceptance; perhaps fiction simply allowed him some diversion from writing verse. The following titles, however, suggest the relationship between Service's poetry and his fiction: *The Trail of '98* (1910), *The Pretender* (1914), *The Poisoned Paradise* (1922), *The Roughneck* (1923), *The Master of the Microbe* (1926), and *The House of Fear*, 1927. Of greater value to the student are the three major autobiographical pieces, since each helps to cast some light upon both the poet and his work: *Why Not Grow Young? Or, Living for Longevity* (1928), *Ploughman of the Moon: An Adventure into Memory* (1945), and *Harper of Heaven: A Record of Radiant Living* (1948).

ACHIEVEMENTS

Perhaps the simplest way to come to grips with the poetry of Robert W. Service is to avoid the issue entirely and dismiss the man as little more than a terribly prolific balladeer, the writer of popular frontier verses that rhymed well enough to be memorized by schoolboys and sentimental adults, but which generally lacked poetic merit. A more reasonable approach would be to read the poetry in the light of Service's own intentions. Service saw himself as a grand combination of journalist and teller of tales (a twentieth century Scottish bard, if you will), whose medium was verse rather than the newspaper article or the short story. He preferred to roam certain parts of the world in search of characters whose stories had never really been told—or, at least, whose experiences had never reached a wide audience. In a sense, he listened to people who were themselves glad to come upon an eager listener; he transformed the details of those stories into rhythmic ballads for the benefit of still other listeners—his readers.

Apart from his poetry, he desired nothing more from life than to dream, to live as a recluse and a lover of liberty, to gaze in wonder at the beauty of the world, to observe the complexities and the varieties of the human condition. At the same time, he was a practical man who realized early in life that freedom had to be bought with hard cash; thus, he wrote and worked for that freedom, and in the end he achieved it. His verse remained the natural outlet for his dreams, visions, and observations,

Robert W. Service (Hulton Archive)

the means by which he could share, with ordinary people, the mysteries and joys of human life. As a poet, Service wanted to record, as quickly as possible, the actions and atmospheres of the moment; he did not waste time thinking—he simply saw and then he wrote. Thus, his readers were not required to approach his verse with any complex intellectual, cultural, or historical prerequisites; they needed only to read, to listen, and to imagine.

The achievement of Robert W. Service may well be the triumph of a paradox, of a writer who wanted, essentially, to be left alone with himself and with his thoughts. Nevertheless, he knew that somehow he had to communicate with those around him, to convey to people the essence of myriad experiences (real and imagined) that otherwise they would never see or imagine. He would serve as the surrogate romantic for thousands of people inclined toward romanticism and independence yet rooted to practicality and convention. Service wrote easily, quickly, rhythmically—almost too simply. The boys whooping it up at the Malamute saloon, Sam McGee from Tennessee, the water where the silver salmon play, the great white silence of the wild, the absinthe drinkers of the Café de la Paix, the three grim and gory British Tommies, the grimy men with picks and shovels—all came from the real world of his experience, but all belonged to the private world of his imagination as well.

Bret Harte and Eugene Field were Service's principal models. His poetry was strongly influenced by journalism; like the newspapermen who reported from Africa and the Far East, he sent poetic dispatches from the streets of Paris, the rough terrains of the Yukon, the Mackenzie basin, and the Arctic. Service's achievement was the triumph of *verse* as opposed to poetry; his poems appealed to the romantic young man in the tavern and to the equally romantic old spinster in the parlor. He thrust his heavily rhythmic songs into the hands of the schoolboy, who would recite them, and into the mind of the laborer, who would remember them. By his own admission, however, although he wrote for these people, he intended to please no one but himself.

Biography

The eldest in a family of seven boys and three girls, Robert William Service was born in Preston, Lancashire, England, on January 16, 1874. His father, also Robert Service, worked in a Scottish bank; his mother, Emily Parker, was the daughter of the English owner of a Lancashire cotton mill. From 1880 until 1895, young Service lived in Glasgow, where he received an education of some substance at the Hillhead High School; he also attended some classes at the University and engaged in a self-prescribed reading program at the public library and by way of Miss Bell's Circulating Library. The latter contributed significantly to his taste for literature and to his urge to travel abroad. Early realizing man's dependence upon money, Service worked at the Commercial Bank of Scotland. The drudgery of Glasgow, the bank, and schoolboy athletics, however, quickly gave way to romantic visions of Canada—of cowboys, gold prospectors, and beachcombers. The young man read pamphlets about Canada and set his sights on becoming a sturdy settler in a hard land—on raising grain, riding broncos, and roping steers. In 1895, he crossed the Atlantic aboard a tramp steamer, proceeded to British Columbia, and partook of the freedom of a backwoods ranch in the rough "wild west." From there he made his way up and down the West Coast of the United States, enjoying still more freedom and learning about life on the road.

Despite his love for the vagabond life, Service had a strong practical streak, and in 1903 he determined that a steady job would allow him to save some money, which in turn would provide the necessary independence for writing, travel, and general leisure. After securing a position with the Canadian Bank of Commerce, he moved through its various branches: Victoria and Kamloops in British Columbia, and Dawson in the Yukon. This job was to provide him with more than a solid bank account. Between 1904 and 1912, Service witnessed as a bank clerk and recorded as a writer the decline of the Klondike gold rush that had begun three years after his arrival in Canada. Ironically, his own fortunes ran directly against the tide of the times; such poems as "The Shooting of Dan McGrew" and "The Cremation of Sam McGee" signaled the beginning of his own literary and financial strike.

"The Shooting of Dan McGrew" and "The Cremation of Sam McGee" were published in 1907, in Toronto, as parts of a larger collection titled *Songs of a Sourdough* (or, in New York, *The Spell of the Yukon and Other Verses*). An insignificant novel followed in 1910, *The Trail of '98*, and then a successful collection, *Rhymes of a Rolling Stone*, two years later. No longer in need of a banking career, Service left Canada in 1912 to cover, for the Toronto *Star*, the brief scuffle involving Turkey, Montenegro, Bulgaria, and Serbia, known as the Balkan War. That experience introduced him to France and Paris; in 1913, he married Germaine Bourgoin, whose father owned a distillery outside Paris, and from that year he maintained residences in France without renouncing his British citizenship. When World War I erupted, Service served first with an American ambulance unit and then with Canadian army intelligence, experiences recorded in *The Rhymes of a Red Cross Man*. After the war, he returned to the highways of the world: The circle began and ended at Paris, with intermediate stops in Hollywood and Tahiti.

Although his Hollywood experience encouraged him to write, between 1922 and 1927, four additional pieces of pure melodrama, those efforts did little to win Service a reputation as a writer of serious fiction. Nevertheless, he continued to reap financial harvests from new verse collections and from complete editions of his poems. He determined to spend the remainder of his days in relative leisure, becoming a quiet and contented gentleman far different from the rough-and-tumble characters who roamed the lines of his ballads and autobiographical verse.

Between the wars, Service found time for two Russian journeys. Returning from the second one, he found himself cut off from his beloved France by World War II; he and his family spent the war years in Hollywood. In 1945, he returned once again to Brittany and Nice, purchased a villa at Monte Carlo, and published, between 1949 and 1956, seven separate volumes of verse and two volumes of his collected poetry. Service died of a heart attack on September 11, 1958—at the age of eighty-four—at his home (appropriately named "Dream Haven") in Lancieux, Brittany.

Analysis

The real difficulty in analyzing the poetic output of Robert W. Service is trying to separate the man from his work—if, indeed, such separation is possible or even necessary. No matter what the poem (for so many of them read as carbon copies of one another), there remains, at the end, the vision of the poet. The reader invariably sees the man of adventure and courage, the headstrong seeker of fame and fortune who, as a relatively young man, left Scotland and sailed for the American continent, there to see and to live with the last generation of pioneers, explorers, and true adventurers. Service detested any reference to himself as a "poet"; the word meant something higher than that to which he aspired or believed he could manage intellectually. To the last, he preferred to be known only as a verse writer, as one who had, since childhood, been talking and thinking in rhyme. In fact, he seemed more inclined toward the talking and the thinking than to expressing his observations and experiences on paper.

In many ways, Service's attitude and actions typified the wandering minstrel of another age, the vagabond strumming on the guitar, singing his own songs, talking about the old times, and telling of countless adventures (actual or imagined). Thus, from the pages of his collected works echo the vigor and the harshness, the tragedy and the ribaldry of the fascinating northern wilderness of Canada. Service virtually immortalized a hundred treks of men and animals through snow and blizzard, privation and suffering, injury and death; yet he also captured in rhyme the sheer glamour and romance of a time when his distant readers equated money with gold dust, love and beauty with a heavily bespangled saloon girl, and art with a whiskey-reeking prospector banging away at an old barroom piano in the corner of a smoke-filled, noisy room. For Service, these were real people in the midst of real experiences—"comrades," he called them, persons with whom he had "tramped God's land together." The triteness and the clichés would come later, from the minds and pens of those who had never seen that about which they were to write and speak.

Yet, the "land God forgot" proved merely a single stop on Service's personal poetic trek. France captured his heart and his rhythmic imagination, first during his bohemian days on the Left Bank, then while he served as a Red Cross ambulance driver during World War I. The songs written in the spring of 1914 reflect his bouts with poverty, when he had to write not for his living, but for his life. Nevertheless, the lines of those pieces are quick and happy attempts to shape the mood of one all too willing to spend his last sous not prudently on bread, but prodigally on beer. In "L'Escargot D'or," Service strolls down the Boul' Mich' in a lingering light that has all the exquisite tenderness of violet. The trees bow to him in their first translucent green; beneath, he sees lamps lit with the purest gold, while from the Little Luxembourg emanates a silver tingle of tiny voices. Boldly, he heads for the gay side of the street and enters the café, a place frequented at one time by Oscar Wilde and John Millington Synge, a place where one may "dream and drain,/ And drown despair." The strength of such poems lies in the reader's awareness that Service has no illusions about his mind or his art. Throughout the first part of *Ballads of a Bohemian* he admits to not being fool enough to think of himself as a poet in the classical sense. Instead, he comes forth as one with a knack for rhyme and an intense love for making verse—or, from another point of view, for "tootling, tin-whistle music." He asks only that his muse bring him bread and butter; if rhyme has been his ruin, he wants only to rhyme until the bitter end—to go down with what he wants to do, rather than be tied to what he has to do.

World War I

In August, 1914, however, the happy-go-lucky Bohemian from Glasgow saw the beginning of a world war. At forty, Service felt obliged to pack his happiness away in storage and apply his rhyme to a far different strain. Until that time, he later confessed, his verse had come from a land of his own making—a composite ground of hope, faith, and enthusiasm, of struggle, failure, and eventual triumph. With the coming of war, he believed he saw the end of what he termed "the exultant sunshine [of] our spirits" and the approach of "a deepening shadow of horror and calamity." While the poems of the Yukon carry a noisy, devil-may-care attitude ("there's 'hootch' in the bottle still"), the noise from France on the eve of World War I rings of frustration and fear and uneasiness, emanating from "nightmares of the past." In France, Service saw the shaping of minds in preparation for the battle; he comprehended the heredity and the discipline that sent village men out of their homes to seek barracks and battlefields and, eventually, death. His poems thus bemoan the docility with which farmers and tradesmen don baggy red trousers so as to let "some muddle-headed General" hurl them to destruction for some unknown cause or gain. To be shot in a saloon brawl in Dawson—"pitched on his head, and pumped full of lead"—is one thing; to be a father, a provider, and "fodder for cannon" is quite another matter.

Songs of a Sourdough

Rudyard Kipling's influence on Robert W. Service (who at times seems to have committed the former's 1892 *Barrack-Room Ballads* to memory) is quite apparent. Generally, Service favored vigorous description and narrative in long, swinging lines. In his first collection, *Songs of a Sourdough*, he illustrated fully the landscape of northern Canada, while at the same time capturing the fresh atmosphere of an almost unknown land. He wrote of lonely sunsets flaring forlornly down dreary and desolate valleys; of lordly mountains soaring scornfully, as still as death and as stern as fate; of the flames of lonely sunsets and giant valleys that consumed the night (except that his verb is "gulp"); of monster mountains scraping the sky; of an outcast, leper land that only the cry of the wolf can express, the lonely, "fell archspirit of the Wild." The poems of that place and of that period almost mirror one another ("Great White Silence," "The Call of the Wild," "The Spell of the Yukon," "The Law of the Yukon"), and the reader should notice particularly the violence of Service's adjectives, the crude satire in reference to men of a more normal and formal mode of existence, and the strong visual images of the naked grandeur of the land that the poet loved—even though God had forgotten it.

This land to which Service committed the early part of his adulthood made him a popular poet—and thus made him a wealthy man. However, he was able to extend his verse beyond the obvious level of "local color." Such poems as "The Shooting of Dan McGrew," "The Cremation of Sam McGee," and "The Ballad of the Black Fox Skin" became popular not only for the entertainment of their stories but also because the poet captured them in sound and rhythm. No doubt Service's yarns would have made first-rate short stories *à la* Bret Harte, Ambrose Bierce, or even Mark Twain. He chose, however, to condense and to versify those tales, giving them the force of brevity and rhyme, and wrapping them in neat packages of his own grim humor and quick command of alliterative phrasing.

Service is sometimes criticized for his failure to provide an accurate reflection of Canadian life. The error rests not with the poet, but with his audience. Service never sought to represent all aspects of Canadian existence. Instead, he chose to depict isolated conditions that prevailed at certain moments in the history of a remote section of the world; he captured with splendid specificity and rhyme the popular conception of the Canadian north.

Service the incurable romantic, the agent of free spirits everywhere, transported his fairly staid audience to the places where they could exercise their suppressed passions, their subconscious enthusiasm for the dangerous and the exciting. He carried to tens of thousands, in clear language and quick meter, the extreme Canadian north, the streets of Paris, the trenches of Flanders. Service possessed a limited but very practical poetic vision. Theories concerning poetry did not interest him. He sought only verse, and seemed quite content to follow the likes of Thomas Hood and Bret Harte, the real fashions of his day. He wanted, simply, to spend his days in the relative calm of his own privacy, testifying to "the rhapsody of existence," where youth and age might affirm, "the ecstasy of being."

OTHER MAJOR WORKS

LONG FICTION: *The Trail of '98*, 1910; *The Pretender: A Story of the Latin Quarter*, 1914; *The Poisoned Paradise*, 1922; *The Roughneck*, 1923; *The Master of the Microbe*, 1926; *The House of Fear*, 1927.

NONFICTION *Why Not Grow Young? Or, Living for Longevity*, 1928; *Ploughman of the Moon: An Adventure into Memory*, 1945; *Harper of Heaven: A Record of Radiant Living*, 1948.

BIBLIOGRAPHY

Athern, Stanley S. "The Klondike Muse." *Canadian Literature: A Quarterly of Criticism and Review* 47 (Winter, 1971): 67-72. Athern encourages critics to examine the Klondike works of Service as a pioneering attempt to mythologize the Canadian gold rush as early environmental history. While not speaking highly of Service's talents, Athern gives valuable insight into Service's initial publications.

Bucco, Martin. "Folk Poetry of Robert W. Service." *Alaska Review* 2 (Fall, 1965): 16-26. Bucco analyzes Service's Yukon poetry from the viewpoint that it used the search for gold as a metaphor for the quest for self. With this as his overriding theme, Bucco shows how Service created a vivid sense of tradition for the men who sought out the elusive riches buried in the forbidding North.

Burness, Edwina. "The Influence of Burns and Fergusson on the War Poetry of Robert Service." *Studies in Scottish Literature* 12 (1986): 135-146. Concentrates only on Service's war poetry and explores the influences that Robert Burns and Robert Fergusson had on Service. Burness draws interesting parallels between the men as she details the effects of realism, humor, and symbolism on the "universal" Scottish mind.

Hirsch, Edward. "A Structural Analysis of Robert Service's Yukon Ballads." *Southern Folklore Quarterly* 40 (March-June, 1976): 125-140. Hirsch suggests that Service's poetry should be judged by the aesthetics of oral traditions and not as literary artifacts.

He analyzes some of Service's Yukon ballads as monologue compositions.

Klinck, Carl F. *Robert Service: A Biography*. New York: Dodd, Mead, 1976. Klinck's biography is invaluable in studying the life of this amazing poet. Drawing heavily on Service's two-volume autobiography, Klinck follows the poet's career, commenting on the influences that led to such a variance in the subject matter of Service's works.

Lockhart, G. W. *On the Trail of Robert Service*. Edinburgh, Scotland: Luath Press, 1999. A short biography of Service and a narrative of his travels.

Mackay, James A. *Vagabond of Verse: Robert Service*. Edinburgh: Mainstream, 1995. An in-depth biography of Service. Includes bibliographical references and index.

Whatley, W. A. "Kipling's Influence in the Verse of Robert W. Service." *Texas Review* 6 (July, 1921): 299-308. Whatley, while recognizing and commenting on Kipling's influence on Service, expresses admiration for the native talents of Service. Through analyzing several ballads, Whatley presents Service's war poetry as nonpropaganda ballads written in the true "carry-on" spirit of Britain.

Samuel J. Rogal;
bibliography updated by the editors

Vikram Seth

Born: Calcutta, India; June 20, 1952

Principal poetry

Mappings, 1981
The Humble Administrator's Garden, 1985
The Golden Gate: A Novel in Verse, 1986
All You Who Sleep Tonight, 1990
Beastly Tales from Here and There, 1992
The Poems, 1981-1994, 1995

Other literary forms

Vikram Seth is best known for his novels. *A Suitable Boy* (1993), a family epic set in postcolonial India, is a monumental 1,349-page work which received mixed reviews but which became one of Seth's best-known works. *An Equal Music* (1999), set in contemporary London, is a love story about the members of a string quartet. Seth wrote a prizewinning travel book, *From Heaven Lake: Travels Through Sinkiang and Tibet*, published in 1983, and translated Chinese poetry in *Three Chinese Poets: Translations of Poems by Wang Wei, Li Bai, and Du Fu* (1992). *Arion and the Dolphin* (1995), written as the libretto for an opera, was also published as a children's book.

Achievements

Seth won the Thomas Cook Travel Book Award in 1983 for *From Heaven Lake*, the Commonwealth Poetry Prize in 1985 for *The Humble Administrator's Garden* (1985), the Quality Paperback Book Club New Voice Award and Commonwealth Poetry Prize, both in 1986, for *The Golden Gate*, the W. H. Smith Award in 1994 for *A Suitable Boy*, and the Commonwealth Writer's Prize in 1994. He received an Ingram Merrill Fellowship in 1985-1986, a Guggenheim Fellowship in 1986-1987, and the Order of the British Empire in 2001.

Biography

Vikram Seth was born in Calcutta, India, in 1952, the oldest of three children. His father, Prem Seth, was a shoe company executive and his mother, Laila Seth, served as a judge. Seth left India to study at Oxford University in England, earning degrees in philosophy, economics, and politics. He enrolled at Stanford University in California, intending to complete a Ph.D. in economics. While at Stanford, Seth was a Wallace Stegner Fellow in creative writing. He wrote the poems collected in *Mappings* during this time. From 1980 to 1982, Seth was in China for two years of travel and economic research. While there, he studied classical Chinese poetry and language at Nanjing University. He wrote an account of a hitchhiking journey to India during this time, published as *From Heaven Lake*.

Seth's works present a variety of subjects based on his experiences and travels. The poetry collections *The Humble Administrator's Garden* and *All You Who Sleep Tonight* (1990) merge Chinese, Indian, and Californian influences; *From Heaven Lake* details the hitchhiking

Vikram Seth in 1996. (Hulton Archive)

trip through Nepal and Tibet that Seth took while a student in China; and *The Golden Gate* is about young professionals in San Francisco, searching for love and identity.

Translation has played an important part in Seth's life, reflecting the multicultural sources of his material. His earliest book of poetry includes works translated from Chinese and Hindi. In 1992, *Three Chinese Poets: Translations of Poems by Wang Lei, Li Bai, and Du Fu*, was published, illustrating again the deep understanding of Chinese culture that critics appreciated in *From Heaven Lake*. In the introduction to *Three Chinese Poets*, Seth acknowledges his debt to works in translation, particularly Russian, French, and Greek, and presents the book as an offering of thanks to other translators.

After publishing *The Golden Gate* in 1986, Seth returned to India to live with his family and work on his major epic, *A Suitable Boy*. This novel, published in 1993, propelled him into the public spotlight. The book launched Seth into a series of interviews, talk shows, and book signings. However, critical reviews were mixed, and the public and his publishers were dismayed when the book was not considered for the Booker Prize in 1993.

After *A Suitable Boy*, Seth returned to London, where he was commissioned by the English National Opera to write a libretto based on the Greek legend of Arion and the dolphin. His 1999 novel, *An Equal Music*, was also set in London, and in 2001 Seth was awarded the Order of the British Empire for his achievements.

Analysis

Vikram Seth is a versatile writer who is at ease in a variety of genres. He is known for his clear, readable style, joyful use of language, irony, and technical mastery. He has made a place for himself as an Indian writing in the English language. Though his published works reflect his versatility, set in London, San Francisco, and China, as well as India, his best-known work is his epic of Indian culture, religion, family life, and postcolonial politics, *A Suitable Boy*.

Vikram Seth's work can be analyzed in terms of several distinctive factors. One is his multicultural identity. His books of poetry contain material influenced by his residence and familiarity with the literature of Eastern and Western countries and cultures: India, England, the United States, and China. He is further influenced by literature in translation from Russia and Greece. This cultural diversity is reflected in his variety of themes and material. Nevertheless, Seth remains ultimately an Indian writer.

A second distinctive factor in Seth's poetry is his technical mastery of traditional forms of rhyme and meter, unusual in a poet of the modern age. Seth has written that since his academic training was in economics rather than English, he followed his own inclinations and tastes in his own poetry. Verse "in form" is what he reads and recalls, and therefore writes.

Critics have noted the simplicity of style and unassuming tone of his poetry. The sheer joy of some of his use of language, his sense of humor, ease, and fun, his joy in small daily moments, and his strong sense of irony characterize the best of his work. While Seth's form is traditional, he is thematically a postmodernist. Coming through the irony and humor is a theme of the loneliness of late twentieth century life, the difficulty of forming relationships, the ultimate failure of love as a bond. His familiarity with contemporary idiom and culture further reflects his time and place. He has a postmodern self-consciousness as well, transparently revealing his writing technique and his presence as narrator throughout his work.

MAPPINGS

Seth's first published book of poetry reflects mixed feelings of nostalgia for India after studying for years in England and the United States. The book includes translations of poems from Hindi, German, and Chinese. His original work expresses youthful restlessness, the sadness of unfulfilled love, and ambivalent feeling toward family. These lines from "Panipat" show the poet's sense of being caught between two cultures:

Family, music, faces,
Food, land, everything
Drew me back, yet now
To hear the koyal sing

Brings notes of other birds,
The nightingale, the wren,
The blackbird; and my heart's
Barometer turns down.

THE HUMBLE ADMINISTRATOR'S GARDEN

This book is divided into three sections, "Wutong," "Neem," and "Live-Oak," which identify their influences, Chinese, Indian, and Californian. As in *Mappings*, Seth reports on surfaces and the trivia of life while using the traditional forms of the sonnet, quatrain, and epigrammatic couplet. Critics liked the book for Seth's unassuming tone and technical discipline. Themes of the poems include a refusal to look inward and a celebration of the simple pleasures of life. The California poems refer to loneliness and the dangers of a superficial life. Seth sometimes uses a deceptively simple form to mock emotion, as these lines from "Love and Work":

There is so much to do
There isn't any time for feeling blue.
There isn't any point in feeling sad.
Things could be worse. Right now they're only bad.

Although some of the poems appear so offhand as to be trivial, Seth's irony, humor, and ease with language express the ethic of an unromantic and eclectic contemporary mind.

THE GOLDEN GATE: A NOVEL IN VERSE

The Golden Gate, published in 1986, widely reviewed and critically well received, established Seth's reputation as a poet and popular writer. The novel is a 307-page series of nearly six hundred sonnets of iambic tetrameter. The long narrative poem is loosely modeled on Russian poet Alexander Pushkin's *Evgeny Onegin* (1825-1832, 1833; *Eugene Onegin*, 1881).

The novel is driven by the lives and entanglements of its characters, John, a self-controlled white Anglo-Saxon Protestant yuppie computer designer; Phil, a sensitive Jewish intellectual; Janet, a Japanese feminist rock musician; Liz, a career-driven Italian corporate lawyer; and her brother Ed, a troubled Roman Catholic homosexual. Each character is a part of a subculture of San Francisco life, and through them Seth demonstrates his thorough familiarity with the setting, the coffee houses, singles bars, and bookshops of 1980's San Francisco.

As in *The Humble Administrator's Garden*, central themes are loneliness, the failure of romantic love to resolve the need for others, and the significance of ordinary life. The narrative is witty and amusing and demonstrates Seth's skill and flexibility with language and mastery of verse form. While some critics found it unusual to depict 1980's yuppies through narrative verse, many found the form's unconventionality appropriate for a work that is both lightly comic and reflective. Despite the traditional model and form, *The Golden Gate* employs techniques of postmodernism in which the act of writing is self-consciously present, as the author comments upon himself and his technique and employs unexpected coincidences and interweaving of plots.

ALL YOU WHO SLEEP TONIGHT

The poems in this volume continue the Seth hallmarks of rhyme and traditional form. The book is divided into several distinct thematic sections, reflecting Seth's diversity of material. The section "Romantic Residues" reinforces some of the themes of *The Golden Gate:* the quality of love and the reluctance to make commitments and take risks. The second section, "In Other Voices," brings a new element of high seriousness into Seth's poetry, including poems about the Holocaust, the atomic destruction of Hiroshima, and AIDS. "In

Other Places" is a series of vignettes about varied places including China; "Quatrains" is a series of clever presentations of Seth's perspective on life; and the final section, "Meditations of the Heart," while also witty, presents a perspective that is saddened by death, loss, and solitude. The final section includes the title poem:

> Know that you aren't alone.
> The whole world shares your tears,
> Some for two nights or one,
> And some for all their years.

Beastly Tales from Here and There

This 1992 book is a collection of animal fables retold by Seth in lively tetrameter couplets. Once again Seth reveals his versatility and multicultural influences, including two tales each from India, China, Greece, and the Ukraine, along with two original tales. The tales are characterized by their fluent storytelling and combination of the comic and the tragic. On one level, these are children's tales, but they are more than simple retellings, as Seth gives the fables a moral twist all his own. The reader is left with a sense of ambiguity. What is the true moral?

The final story in the volume is Seth's original "The Elephant and the Tragopan." This fable has a thoroughly contemporary feel, as its theme is the protection of the environment, and the head of the council, Bigshot, is more concerned with money and votes than with saving Bingle Vale. The resolution is left open:

> And so I'll end the story here.
> What is to come is still unclear.
> Whether the fates will smile or frown,
> And Bingle Vale survive or drown,
> I do not know and cannot say;
> Indeed, perhaps, I never may.

Other major works

LONG FICTION: *A Suitable Boy*, 1993; *An Equal Music*, 1999.

NONFICTION: *From Heaven Lake: Travels Through Sinkiang and Tibet*, 1983.

TRANSLATION: *Three Chinese Poets: Translations of Poems by Wang Lei, Li Bai, and Du Fu*, 1992.

MISCELLANEOUS: *Arion and the Dolphin*, 1995.

Bibliography

Agarwalla, Shyam S. *Vikram Seth's "A Suitable Boy": Search for an Indian Identity*. New Delhi: Prestige Books, 1995. While not about Seth's poetry, this is the only book-length source on Seth and, employing the techniques of literary criticism, includes general cultural information and discussion of his role as an Indian writer. The chapter on linguistics and the Indo-English creative writing is particularly relevant to the study of Seth's poetry.

Corey, Stephen. Review of *All You Who Sleep Tonight*, by Vikram Seth. *The Ohio Review*, no. 47 (1991): 132-139. Critical review of the volume. Corey's conclusion is that the poetry is often trivial, singsongy, and oversimplified.

Davis, Dick. "Obliquities." Review of *The Humble Administrator's Garden*, by Vikram Seth. *The Listener* 114, no. 2938 (December 5, 1985): 33-34. Davis summarizes the collection's tone as "modest, ordered, well-mannered and well-planned, with a trace of deprecatory self-pity."

Perloff, Marjorie. "Homeward Ho!: Silicon Valley Pushkin." *The American Poetry Review* 15, no. 6 (November/December, 1986): 37-46. Critical review of *The Golden Gate*. Perloff asserts that Seth's concern with rhyme weakens the novel's characterization, plot, and satirical force. A scholarly article, with detailed analysis, and extensive references to poetic form and poets in history.

Perry, John Oliver. "World Literature in Review: India." Review of *All You Who Sleep Tonight*, by Vikram Seth. *World Literature Today* 65, no. 3 (Summer, 1991): 549-550. Perry discusses the content and form of several specific poems and concludes "It is a tribute to the poems . . . that often they can sound a bit like Frost or Hardy."

_______. "World Literature in Review: India." Review of *Beastly Tales from Here and There*, by Vikram Seth. *World Literature Today* 67, no. 2 (Spring, 1993): 447-448. Perry refers to issues for critical readers of Seth's previous volumes. *Beastly Tales* incorporates essential elements of Seth's art; the "pleasure, after the sheer joy of verbal play, consists of cultural twists of plot, character, and moral."

Seth, Vikram. Introduction and foreword to *The Poems, 1981-1994*. New York: Viking Penguin, 1995. A primary source, the poet's foreword reprinted in a volume of selected poems. Seth discusses his poetry and influences and reveals themes and insight into his priorities and thought process.

Susan Butterworth

ANNE SEXTON

Born: Newton, Massachusetts; November 9, 1928
Died: Weston, Massachusetts; October 4, 1974

PRINCIPAL POETRY

To Bedlam and Part Way Back, 1960
All My Pretty Ones, 1962
Selected Poems, 1964
Live or Die, 1966
Poems, 1968 (with Thomas Kinsella and Douglas Livingston)
Love Poems, 1969
Transformations, 1971
The Book of Folly, 1972
The Death Notebooks, 1974
The Awful Rowing Toward God, 1975
Forty-five Mercy Street, 1976
Words for Dr. Y: Uncollected Poems with Three Stories, 1978
The Complete Poems, 1981
Selected Poems of Anne Sexton, 1988

OTHER LITERARY FORMS

In addition to several articles on the craft and teaching of poetry, Anne Sexton wrote a play that ran successfully at the American Place Theatre of New York and several children's books produced in collaboration with Maxine Kumin. The play, *Forty-five Mercy Street* (1969), presents the struggle of a woman named Daisy to find meaning in a past and present dominated by religious and sexual conflicts objectified as demons and disembodied voices. Its success suggests that the poet also had talent as a playwright, and critics find the thematic material important biographically and artistically in an analysis of Sexton's career. An important collection of her prose is *Anne Sexton: A Self-Portrait in Letters* (1977); also, a recording of twenty-four poems read by the poet is available as *Anne Sexton Reads Her Poetry*, recorded June 1, 1974.

ACHIEVEMENTS

With little formal training in literature, Anne Sexton emerged as a major modern voice, transforming verse begun as therapy into poetic art of the first order. Important for refining the confessional mode, experimenting with new lyrical forms, and presenting themes from the female consciousness, Sexton's work has the controversial impact of any pioneering artist. Despite periodic hospitalization for depression ultimately culminating in her suicide at age forty-six, Sexton contributed richly to her craft, receiving much critical recognition and traveling widely.

Awarded fellowships to most of the major writing conferences, she worked closely with John Holmes, W. D. Snodgrass, Robert Lowell, Maxine Kumin, and others. She taught creative writing at Harvard, Radcliffe, and Boston University, and she served as editorial consultant to the *New York Poetry Quarterly* and as a member of the board of directors of *Audience* magazine. In 1963, her second collection of poetry, *All My Pretty Ones*, was nominated for a National Book Award; in 1966, she was awarded The Shelley Memorial Award: and in 1967, her fourth collection, *Live or Die*, received a Pulitzer Prize. Sexton also received a Guggenheim Fellowship in 1969 and many honorary degrees from major universities.

Although most critics believe the quality of her work deteriorated toward the end of her life, she had achieved by that time success with a new, highly personal voice in poetry and expanded the range of acceptable subjects to include the intimate concerns of women. In presenting the theme of female identity, Sexton began with a careful lyric formalism and then progressed throughout her career to experiment with open, dramatic forms, moving from the confessional to the surreal. She explored the limits of sanity and the nature of womanhood more fully than any poet of her generation.

Biography

The daughter of upper-middle-class parents, Anne Gray Harvey attended the public schools of Wellesley, Massachusetts, spent two years at Rogers Preparatory School, and one year at Garland Junior College, before marrying Alfred Muller Sexton, whose nickname "Kayo" provides the dedication for her first volume of poems. Although a strictly biographical approach to Anne Sexton's work is dangerously limiting, the significant events of her life serve as major subjects and impetus for her art.

After her marriage, she worked briefly as a model at the Hart Agency of Boston. Then, when she was twenty-five, her first daughter, Linda Gray Sexton, was born. The next year, Anne Sexton was hospitalized for emotional disturbance and several months later suffered the loss of her beloved great-aunt, Anna Ladd Dingley, nicknamed "Nana," in various poems and remembrances. The next year, Joyce Ladd Sexton was born, but within months her mother was again hospitalized for depression culminating in a suicide attempt on her twenty-eighth birthday.

Anne Sexton in 1967. (Library of Congress)

Following her first suicide attempt, Sexton began writing poetry on the advice of her psychiatrist, Dr. Martin, whose name appears in her first collection of poems. On the strength of her first work, she received a scholarship to the Antioch Writer's Conference where she worked with W. D. Snodgrass. Then she was accepted into Robert Lowell's graduate writing seminar at Boston University, soon developing friendships with Sylvia Plath, Maxine Kumin, and George Starbuck. The next year, both of Sexton's parents died in rapid succession. She continued her work, attending the Bread Loaf Writer's Conference and delivering the Morris Gray Poetry Lecture at Harvard, although she was hospitalized at intervals for pneumonia, an appendectomy, and an ovariectomy. In 1960, Sexton studied with Philip Rahv and Irving Howe at Brandeis University and developed a friendship with James Wright. She was appointed, with Maxine Kumin, to be the first scholars in poetry at the Radcliffe Institute for Independent Study. In 1962, she was again hospitalized for depression, but by the end of the year, she recovered and toured Europe on the first traveling fellowship of the American Academy of Arts and Letters. She also received a Ford Foundation grant for residence with the Charles Playhouse in Boston.

In 1966, Sexton began a novel that was never completed. She again attempted suicide in July, 1966. In August, she took an African safari with her husband, but in November, she was hospitalized again when she broke her hip on her thirty-eighth birthday. In May of that year, she received the Pulitzer Prize for *Live or Die* and the Shelley Memorial Award from the Poetry Society of America. She taught poetry as a visiting professor in many schools and received many honorary degrees before again attempting suicide in 1970. In 1973, she divorced her husband during another period of hospitalization for depression. Although she continued to write and teach despite frequent intervals of hospitalization, in 1974, she committed suicide by carbon monoxide poisoning in the garage of her home.

Analysis

Anne Sexton's poetry presents a search for self and meaning beyond the limits of conventional expression and form. Although viewing her work autobiographically limits critical understanding of it, readers discover in her work a chronicle of experience that is intensely personal and genuine. Her poems are confessional in that they present statements about impulses formerly unknown or forbidden. Begun for self-revelation in therapy and initially sustained for the possible benefit of other troubled patients, Sexton's poems speak with penetrating honesty about the experience of mental illness, the temptation of suicide, and the dynamics of womanhood. Although less strident in tone than the work of Sylvia Plath, Sexton's work occasionally alienates readers who, like James Dickey, find her work too personal for literary evaluation. At its best, however, Sexton's poetry develops the confessional lyric into an effective modern form.

To Bedlam and Part Way Back

In her first collection, *To Bedlam and Part Way Back*, scenes from an asylum are set against those of life before and after the speaker's hospitalization. The perspective of these early poems is a daring interior one, underscored by the book's epigraph taken from a letter of Arthur Schopenhauer to Johann Wolfgang von Goethe, including the phrase "But most of us carry in our heart the Jocasta who begs Oedipus for God's sake not to inquire further." Sexton's poems pursue the inquiry into the mental hospital and the mind of the patient as well. In the chantlike poem "Ringing the Bells," for example, Sexton projects the senseless rhythm of institutional life through the consciousness of a patient in the bell choir of a mental ward. The troubled women who "mind by instinct" assemble, smile, ring their bells when pointed to, and disperse, no better for their weekly music lesson. Another well-known portrayal of institutional life, "Lullaby," shows the figure of the night nurse arriving with the sleeping pills that, like splendid pearls, provide a momentary escape for the patients who receive them. Observing the moths which cling to window screen, the patient of "Lullaby" imagines that he will become like them after taking the sedative. "You, Doctor Martin" presents other figures in the mental hospital, including the large children who wait in lines to be counted at dinner before returning to the labor of making moccasins all day long. Although the portrayal of the mental hospital from an insider's perspective provides a fresh subject for experimental lyrics, Sexton's poems of the journey and return (suggested by the volumes title) are among her most complex and effective.

"The Double Image," for example, is a composite of experiences parallel to Sexton's own biography. In the poem, the speaker's hospitalization brings about a separation from her young daughter; the speaker's return to live in the home of her childhood coincides with the final illness of her own mother. Weaving together the present moment of her return home for a reunion with her daughter and events of the past, the speaker reflects on the guilt bounded by past and present sorrow. The three autumns explain her trouble better than any medical theories, and she finds that despair and guilt transform attempts at ordinary life into artifice. Portrait painting becomes a metaphor for control of time and emotions through the rest of the poem. Unable to adjust to the awkward period spent as a grown child in her parents' home, the speaker states repeatedly "I had my portrait done instead." The same response belongs to her mother, who cannot forgive the speaker's attempt at suicide and so chooses to have the daughter painted as a measure of control. A double image forms when the mother learns of her own incurable illness and has her portrait done "instead." The portraits, facing each other in the parental home, serve as a mirror reflection with the figure of the speaker's child moving between them. As the speaker had been "an awkward guest" returning to her mother's home, so the young daughter arrives "an awkward guest" for the reunion with her recovering mother. The child provides both a measure of final identity and guilt.

In "The Division of Parts," the bitterness of inheritance replaces grief as a response to the death of the speaker's mother. As in "The Double Image," the coincidence of the speaker's recovery with her mother's suffering suggests an apparent exchange of death for life. Equipped with the lost one's "garments" but not with grief, the speaker recalls the suffering of her mother, overshadowed now by the ceremonies of the Lenten season. Division of property replaces the concerns of the Christ who waits on the crucifix for the speaker. Her dreams recall only the division of ways: the separation of death and inevitable division of property.

Other poems in the first volume experiment with the voices of experience different from the poet's. "The

Farmer's Wife," for example, reveals the isolation and loneliness of a young wife on an Illinois farm. The poem presents the ambivalence of the woman toward her husband, whose work and bed are her lifelong habit. "Unknown Girl in the Maternity Ward" attempts to voice the feelings of an unmarried girl who has just given birth. The emotions and imagery are generalized and undefined in presenting the setting of an urban hospital and the typical unmarried girl in trouble. According to Sexton, the poem marks a pivotal moment in her career, for after reading it, Robert Lowell advised her to develop the more personal voice that gives her finest poetry its power. A poem reflecting conflicting advice is "For John, Who Begs Me Not to Enquire Further." John Holmes, Sexton's teacher for a Boston University poetry workshop, recommended that she avoid the self-revelation becoming characteristic of her work. The directly personal voice won out, not only in this poem of apology to Holmes but also throughout her career. Another early poem, "Kind Sir: These Woods," indicates an awareness that readers in general may disapprove her probing of the psyche, "this inward look that society scorns." The speaker finds in her inward search, however, nothing worse than herself, "caught between the grapes and the thorns," and the search for herself continued to the end of her life.

All My Pretty Ones

An epigraph for Sexton's second collection, *All My Pretty Ones*, suggests a reason for the poet's insistence on inner exploration. According to a letter of Franz Kafka, "a book should serve as the ax for the frozen sea within us." Sexton similarly asserted in a later interview that "poems of the inner life can reach the inner lives of readers in a way that anti-war poems can never stop a war." The inner life revealed in *All My Pretty Ones* is primarily the experience of grief, the response to loss of the most precious others expressed in the lines from *Macbeth* (1606) that form the title. "The Truth the Dead Know" and the title poem deal with the death of Sexton's parents during the same year. The first poem eliminates personal references except for a dedication to the parents and simply contrasts the intensity of life and grief with the emptiness and stoniness of the dead. "All My Pretty Ones" addresses the lost father with memories of his belongings, his habits, and his hopes. Disposition of scrapbook photographs provides a way to accept and forgive the disappointments of the past, including the secret alcoholism his daughter can never forget.

The strongest poems of the second volume arise from Sexton's own experience. In "The Operation," the speaker's confrontation with death parallels the illness of her mother, and the speaker considers the uncertainty of life as much as the reality of death. Knowing that cancer, the disease of her mother, the "historic thief" that plundered her mother's home is now invading her own domain, the speaker proceeds helplessly through the preparations for surgery, the experience of losing consciousness, and the recovery phase in doubt of her survival. Then, pronounced better, perhaps cured, by the doctors, she is sent home like a child, the stitches in her abdomen reminding her of the lacing on a football ready for the game. A similar sense of vulnerability appears in "The Fortress," wherein the speaker admits to her sleeping child that a mother has no ability to control life and that eventually it will overtake the child through the suffering of "bombs or glands" ending in death. Beyond the sense of relationships, especially those connected with motherhood, controlling many of Sexton's poems, there looms a sense of dark knowledge gained through poetry as a secret or forbidden art. In "The Black Art," for example, the speaker asserts that a woman who writes will not fit into society, for she "feels too much, these trances and portents." Home, family, social life are inadequate expressions for the one who wishes to know and control the mysterious forces of existence. The poem recalls an earlier statement of identity, "Her Kind," in which the speaker presents herself as a witch who is lonely, misunderstood, insane, and unashamed to die in the course of her journey. The comparison of Sexton's poetry with the black arts places her work on the level of myth, particularly in her pursuit of death itself.

Live or Die

Live or Die, Sexton's third collection, marks a high point in her career for handling intimate or despairing material with sure control and an element of self-irony. The epigraph for this book, taken from Saul Bellow's *Herzog* (1964), records the admonition to "Live or die, but don't poison everything." Certainly, the poems of this group reflect the impulse toward love and life as well as the impulse toward despair and death. The institutional setting appears in the volume but so does the home and family relationships of Sexton. "Flee on Your Donkey," one of her best-known poems, develops the tension between the worlds of private and institutional life. In the poem, a flood of scenes from the hospital culminates in a desire to escape back to the normal world that patients enter the hospital to avoid. Similarly, in "For the Year of the Insane," structured as a prayer to Mary, the speaker struggles to escape her mental as well as physical confinement. No longer at peace in the refuge of therapy, a mind that believes itself "locked in the wrong house" struggles in vain for expression and release. Poems of similar desperation, "The Addict" and "Wanting to Die," develop other means of escape. The speaker of the former poem yearns for the hallucinatory realm where drugs parcel out moments of deathlike experience. "Wanting to Die," another of Sexton's best-known poems, strives to explain for the uninitiated the hunger for death haunting the potential suicide. The obsession with methods of dying replaces the desire for experience of life. Love itself becomes "an infection" to those seeking the secret pleasure that final escape from the body will bring.

Poems of the third collection that deal with survival include those concerned with children and birth. In "Little Girl, My String Bean, My Lovely Woman," the speaker identifies with the approaching womanhood of her daughter Linda, beautiful even in the uncertain changes adolescence creates. The poem celebrates the body in its growth and capacity for becoming; the figure of mother and daughter share the mystery of reproduction that is spiritual, "a white stone," as well as physical, "laughter," and joy. In "Pain for a Daughter," the mother discovers in her injured child's suffering a universal misery that transcends their relationship. The child's foot torn by the hoof of a horse, she cries out to God, not her mother, and the isolation of the cry suggests not childhood misery but the future pangs of childbirth and death itself. The decision to survive, for the moment at least, appears in "Live," the final statement of the volume. The speaker recounts a shift from life as a dark pretense or game to a moment when the sun rose within her, illuminating the figures of her husband and daughters. The speaker determines herself no longer the murderer she thought, allowing the newborn Dalmatian puppies to live and deciding to survive herself.

Love Poems

Love Poems, Sexton's fourth collection, examines the cycle of roles women play in life and love. Poems of separation and return, for example, include "Touch" and "Eighteen Days Without You," lyrics in which love between a woman and her lover controls survival and existence beyond their union. Throughout the volume, individual body parts achieve significance beyond their function in the physical realm. "Touch" begins, "For months my hand had been sealed off/ in a tin box." Following the arrival of her lover, life rushes into the fingers, spreading across the continent in its intensity. Other celebrations of physical contact include "The Kiss," "The Breast," and "In Celebration of My Uterus." In this last poem, Sexton develops a great song which a whole catalog of women sing as they go about their daily work carrying the "sweet weight" of the womb. The negative side of experience returns in poems such as "The Break," which recounts the depression preceding a fall down the stairs which broke Sexton's hip and forced another lengthy hospitalization. Although the bones are sure to heal, the speaker's heart begins another building process to create a "death crèche," ready for the zeal of destruction when it returns.

Transformations

The theme of self-destruction is hidden in *Transformations*, Sexton's collection of rewritten fairy tales narrated by a "middle-aged witch," the poet's name for her persona in the tales. For some critics, this collection provides a more objective scheme for Sexton's mythic quest; for others, the subject matter is quaint and unoriginal. Certainly the retold tales are entertaining and effective in the dark, modern twists Sexton creates. "Snow White," for example, tortures the wicked queen without mercy before returning to gaze triumphantly in her mirror "as women do." "Rumpelstiltskin" develops the figure of the dark one within, the *Doppelgänger* trying to escape every man. Failing to gain the queen's child, he splits in two, "one part papa/ one part Doppelganger," completing the division of the psyche. "Briar Rose (Sleeping Beauty)" becomes a tortured insomniac after being awakened by her prince and never knows the sleep of death.

Last years

Sexton's last collections, *The Book of Folly*, *The Death Notebooks*, and *The Awful Rowing Toward God* contain many of her previous themes developed in experimental forms, including dramatic changes in style. Critics note a looser structure in the poems written late in Sexton's career; some believe it reflects a deterioration of her creative powers, while others find the experimentalism valuable for its innovation.

One of the well-known late poems, "Hurry Up Please It's Time," reflects the variety of thematic material, the variable stanza lengths, and the intrusion of dialogue, such as those between "Anne" and "The Interrogator." The poem reworks the approach of death and the obsessive derision of life on the part of the dying one. "Ms. Dog," one of Sexton's nicknames for herself, as well as "God" spelled backward, figures in the poem as the troubled one facing guilt and rejection, the mystery and futility of death. In "Frenzy," another of the last poems, the speaker describes herself "typing out the God/ my typewriter believes in."

Through the last years of Sexton's life, her writing sustained her even as her quest darkened. At the end of her life, she sought God when doctors, friends, and family were unable to help her; and her work reflected an outwardly religious search that had formerly been hidden. Although she never revealed that she found God within or without the lines of her poetry, she left behind a brilliant record of her heroic search.

Other major works

PLAY: *Forty-five Mercy Street*, pr. 1969.

NONFICTION: *Anne Sexton: A Self-Portrait in Letters*, 1977; *No Evil Star: Selected Essays, Interviews, and Prose*, 1985.

CHILDREN'S LITERATURE (with Maxine Kumin): *Eggs of Things*, 1963; *More Eggs of Things*, 1964; *Joey and the Birthday Present*, 1971; *The Wizard's Tears*, 1975.

Bibliography

Furst, Arthur. *Anne Sexton: The Last Summer.* New York: St. Martin's Press, 2000. A collection of Furst's photos of Sexton with letters and unpublished drafts of Sexton's poems written during the last months of her life, as well as previously unpublished letters to her daughters, giving unprecedented insight into the life of this legendary poet.

George, Diane Hume, ed. *Sexton*. Urbana: University of Illinois Press, 1988. According to M. Gillan, the reviewer for *Choice*, "a useful volume because the beautifully written essays provide contrasting viewpoints on the work, the influences on it, the relative merits of the religious poetry, the biographical aspects of the work, and the poet's craft."

Hall, Caroline King Barnard. *Anne Sexton*. Boston: Twayne, 1989. This useful introduction to Sexton examines her poetry and its chronological development. Describes the arc of her journey through the labyrinth of "madness, love, alienation, guilt and hope toward her answer." Worth noting is the chapter "*Transformations:* Fairy Tales Revisited."

McClatchy, J. D. *Anne Sexton: The Artist and Her Critics*. Bloomington: Indiana University Press, 1978. A collection of documentary and interpretative material—overviews, reviews, and reflections—on Sexton, including what are thought to be three of her best interviews. The volume sets out to establish a balanced critical perspective on this poet's work and includes reprints of journals.

Markey, Janice. *A New Tradition? The Poetry of Sylvia Plath, Anne Sexton, and Adrienne Rich*. Frankfurt am Main, Germany: Peter Lang, 1985. Discusses Sexton's label as a confessional poet and notes the criticism of repetition in her poems. In spite of this, cites Sexton's real wish to communicate something meaningful to her audience. This essay offers strong criticism, exploring Sexton's feminist roots and her perception of marriage as a failed institution.

Middlebrook, Diane Wood. *Anne Sexton: A Biography.* Boston: Houghton Mifflin, 1991. Middlebrook's biography of Sexton is based on tapes from Sexton's therapy sessions and the intimate revelations of Sexton's family. Middlebrook explores Sexton's creativity and the relationship between art and mental disorder.

Sexton, Linda Gray, and Lois Ames, eds. *Anne Sexton: A Self-Portrait in Letters*. Boston: Houghton Mifflin, 1977. A compilation of the best and most representative letters written by Sexton, who was an exceptional correspondent. Contains a wonderful collection of letters, arranged chronologically and interspersed with biographical details, and providing much insight about this poet's imagination.

Steele, Cassie Premo. *We Heal from Memory: Sexton, Lorde, Anzaldúa, and the Poetry of Witness*. New York: St. Martin's Press, 2000. Addresses the ways society carries a history of traumatic violence, from child sexual abuse, through slavery, to the transmission of violence through generations and the destruction of nonwhite cultures and their histories through colonization.

Wagner-Martin, Linda, ed. *Critical Essays on Anne Sexton*. Boston: G. K. Hall, 1989. An important volume of selected critical essays, gathering early reviews and modern scholarship, including essays on Sexton's poems and her life. All the essays offer significant secondary material on Sexton; the introduction by Wagner-Martin is particularly helpful, giving an overview of Sexton's poems. Includes a reminiscence by poet Maxine Kumin, a former teacher and friend.

Chapel Louise Petty;
bibliography updated by the editors

William Shakespeare

Born: Stratford-upon-Avon, England; April 23, 1564
Died: Stratford-upon-Avon, England, April 23, 1616

Principal poetry

Venus and Adonis, 1593
The Rape of Lucrece, 1594
The Passionate Pilgrim, 1599 (miscellany with poems by Shakespeare and others)
The Phoenix and the Turtle, 1601
A Lover's Complaint, 1609
Sonnets, 1609

Other literary forms

William Shakespeare is perhaps the world's greatest dramatist—certainly, at the very least, the greatest to write in English. Of his thirty-seven plays, written over a career in the theater that spanned, roughly, the years 1588 to 1613, the most important are *Romeo and Juliet* (c. 1595-1596); *Henry IV, Parts I* and *II* (c. 1597-1598); *Hamlet, Prince of Denmark* (c. 1600-1601); *Othello, The Moor of Venice* (1604); *Measure for Measure* (1604); *King Lear* (c. 1605-1606); *Macbeth* (1606); *Antony and Cleopatra* (c. 1606-1607); *The Winter's Tale* (c. 1610-1611); and *The Tempest* (1611).

Achievements

William Shakespeare also wrote some of the greatest love poems in English. His short erotic narratives, *Venus and Adonis* and *The Rape of Lucrece*, were typical examples of fashionable literary genres. Other minor poems include contributions to the miscellany *The Passionate Pilgrim* and *The Phoenix and the Turtle*, written for a collection of poems appended to *Love's Martyr* (1601), an allegorical treatment of love by Robert Chester. All of these pale alongside the sonnets, which, in an age of outstanding love poetry, attain a depth, suggestiveness, and power rarely duplicated in the history of humankind's passionate struggle to match desire with words.

Biography

William Shakespeare was born in the provincial town of Stratford-upon-Avon in 1564 and died there in 1616. He spent most of his adult life in the London theaters and quickly attained a reputation as a dramatist, actor, and poet. Shakespeare's company prospered under the reign of James I, and by the time of his retirement from playwrighting about 1612, Shakespeare had acquired a respectable fortune. His career as a poet, distinct from his more public career as a dramatist, was probably confined to perhaps a decade, between 1591 and 1601, although the sonnets were later collected and published (perhaps without his permission) in 1609. Because of the absurd controversies that grew, mainly in the nineteenth century, about whether Shakespeare actually existed, it is worthwhile pointing out that there are many official records (christening record, marriage license, legal documents, correspondence, and so on) which may be consulted by the skeptical.

ANALYSIS

One of William Shakespeare's great advantages as a writer was that, as a dramatist working in the public theater, he was afforded a degree of autonomy from the cultural dominance of the court, his age's most powerful institution. All over Europe, even if belatedly in England, the courts of the Renaissance nation-states conducted an intense campaign to use the arts to further their power. The theater, despite its partial dependency on court favor, achieved through its material products (the script and the performance) a relative autonomy in comparison with the central court arts of poetry, prose fiction, and the propagandistic masque. When Shakespeare briefly turned to Ovidian romance in the 1590's and, belatedly, probably also in the 1590's, to the fashion for sonnets, he moved closer to the cultural and literary dominance of the court's taste—to the fashionable modes of Ovid, Petrarch, and Neoplatonism—and to the need for patronage. Although the power of the sonnets goes far beyond their sociocultural roots, Shakespeare nevertheless adopts the culturally inferior role of the petitioner for favor, and there is an undercurrent of social and economic powerlessness in the sonnets, especially when a rival poet seems likely to supplant the poet. In short, Shakespeare's nondramatic poems grow out of and articulate the strains of the 1590's, when, like many ambitious writers and intellectuals on the fringe of the court, Shakespeare clearly needed to find a language in which to speak—and that was, necessarily, given to him by the court. What he achieved within this shared framework, however, goes far beyond any other collection of poems in the age. Shakespeare's occasional poems are unquestionably minor, interesting primarily because he wrote them; his sonnets, on the other hand, constitute perhaps the language's greatest collection of lyrics. They are love lyrics, and clearly grow from the social, erotic, and literary contexts of his age. Part of their greatness, however, lies in their power to be read again and again in later ages, and to raise compellingly, even unanswerably, more than merely literary questions.

VENUS AND ADONIS

In his first venture into public poetry, Shakespeare chose to work within the generic constraints of the fashionable Ovidian verse romance. *Venus and Adonis* appealed to the taste of young aristocrats such as the earl of Southampton to whom it was dedicated. It is a narrative poem in six-line stanzas, mixing classical mythology with surprisingly (and incongruously) detailed descriptions of country life, designed to illustrate the story of the seduction of the beautiful youth Adonis by the comically desperate aging goddess, Venus. It is relatively static, with too much argument to make it inherently pleasurable reading. Its treatment of love relies on Neoplatonic and Ovidian commonplaces, and it verges (unlike Christopher Marlowe's *Hero and Leander*, 1598, to which Shakespeare's poem is a fair but decidedly inferior fellow) on moralizing allegory, with Venus as flesh, Adonis as spiritual longing. The poem's articulation of the nature of the love that separates them is abstract and often unintentionally comic—although Shakespeare's characterization of Venus as a garrulous plump matron brings something of his theatrical power to enliven the poem. The poem was certainly popular at the time, going through ten editions in as many years, possibly because its early readers thought it fashionably sensual.

William Shakespeare (Library of Congress)

THE RAPE OF LUCRECE

The Rape of Lucrece is the "graver labor" which Shakespeare promised to Southampton in the preface to

Venus and Adonis. Again, he combines a current poetical fashion—the complaint—with a number of moral commonplaces, and writes a novelette in verse: a melodrama celebrating the prototype of matronly chastity, the Roman lady Lucrece, and her suicide after she was raped. The central moral issue—that of honor—at times almost becomes a serious treatment of the psychology of self-revulsion; but the decorative and moralistic conventions of the complaint certainly do not afford Shakespeare the scope of a stage play. There are some fine local atmospheric effects which, in their declamatory power, occasionally bring the directness and power of the stage into the verse.

The Phoenix and the Turtle

The Phoenix and the Turtle is an allegorical, highly technical celebration of an ideal love union: It consists of a funeral procession of mourners, a funeral anthem, and a final lament for the dead. It is strangely evocative, dignified, abstract, and solemn. Readers have fretted, without success, over the exact identifications of its characters. Its power lies in its mysterious, eerie evocation of the mystery of unity in love.

Sonnets

Probably more human ingenuity has been spent on Shakespeare's sonnets than on any other work of English literature. In his outstanding edition titled *Shakespeare's Sonnets* (1978), Stephen Booth briefly summarizes the few facts that have led to a plethora of speculation on such matters as text, authenticity, date, arrangement, and, especially, biographical implications. The sonnets were first published in 1609, although numbers 138 and 144 had appeared in *The Passionate Pilgrim* a decade before. Attempts to reorder the sonnets have been both varied and creative, but none represents the "correct" order. Such attempts simply fulfill an understandable anxiety on the part of some readers to see narrative continuity rather than variations and repetition in the sonnets. The "story behind" the sonnets has, as Booth puts it, "evoked some notoriously creative scholarship": speculation on the identity of the young man mentioned in many of the first 126 sonnets, of Mr. W. H., to whom the sequence is dedicated by the printer, of the "Dark Lady" of sonnets 127-152, and of the rival poet of some of the earlier sonnets—all of these matters have filled many library shelves.

Such speculations—which reached their peak in critics and readers wedded to the sentimental Romantic insistence on an intimate tie between literary and historical "events"—are in one sense a tribute to the power of the sonnets. They are arguably the greatest collection of love poems in the language, and they provide a crucial test for the adequacy of both the love of poetry and the sense of the fascinating confusion which makes up human love. In a sense, the sonnets are as "dramatic" as any of Shakespeare's plays inasmuch as their art is that of meditations on love, beauty, time, betrayal, insecurity, and joy. Each sonnet is like a little script, with (often powerful) directions for reading and enactment, with textual meanings that are not given but made anew in every performance, by different readers within their individual and social lives. What Sonnet 87 terms "misprision" may stand as the necessary process by which each sonnet is produced by each reader.

It is conventional to divide the sonnets into two groups—1-126, purportedly addressed or related to a young man, and 127-152, to the "Dark Lady." Such a division is arbitrary at best—within each group there are detachable subgroups, and without the weight of the conventional arrangement, many sonnets would not seem to have a natural place in either group. Sonnets 1-17 (and perhaps 18) are ostensibly concerned with a plea for a young man to marry; but even in this group, which many readers have seen to be the most conventional and unified, there are disruptive suggestions that go far beyond the commonplace context.

What may strike contemporary readers, and not merely after an initial acquaintance with the sonnets, is the apparently unjustified level of idealization voiced by many of the sonnets—an adulatory treatment of noble love which, to a post-Freudian world, might seem archaic, no matter how comforting. The continual self-effacement of the anguished lover, the worship of the "God in love, to whom I am confined" (110), the poet's claim to immortalizing "his beautie . . . in these blacke lines" (63), idealizations are all born out of a world of serene affirmation. Some of the most celebrated sonnets, such as "Shall I compare thee to a summer's day" (18) or "Let me not to the marriage of true minds" (116), may even seem cloyingly affirmative, their texts seemingly replete, rejecting any subtextual challenges to their idealism.

In the two hundred years since Petrarch, the sonnet had developed into an instrument of logic and rhetoric. The Shakespearian sonnet, on the other hand, with its three quatrains and a concluding couplet, allows especially for the concentration on a single mood; it is held together less by the apparent logic of many of the sonnets (for example, the "when . . . then" pattern) than by the invitation to enter into the dramatization of a brooding, sensitive mind. The focus is on emotional richness, on evoking the immediacy of felt experience. Shakespeare uses many deliberately generalized epithets, indeterminate signifiers and floating referents which provoke meaning from their readers rather than providing it. Each line contains contradictions, echoes, and suggestions which require an extraordinary degree of emotional activity on the part of the reader. The couplets frequently offer a reader indeterminate statements, inevitably breaking down any attempt at a limited formalist reading. The greatest of the sonnets—60, 64, 129, as well as many others—have such an extraordinary combination of general, even abstract, words and unspecified emotional power that the reader may take it as the major rhetorical characteristic of the collection.

In particular lines, too, these poems achieve amazing power by their lack of logical specificity and emotional open-endedness. As Booth points out, many lines show "a constructive vagueness" by which a word or phrase is made to do multiple duty—by placing it "in a context to which it pertains but which it does not quite fit idiomatically" or by using phrases which are simultaneously illogical and amazingly charged with meaning. He instances "separable spite" in Sonnet 36 as a phrase rich with suggestion; another example is the way in which the bewilderingly ordinary yet suggestive epithets sit uneasily in the opening lines of Sonnet 64. Often a reader is swept on through the poem by a syntactical movement which is modified or contradicted by associations set up by words and phrases. There is usually a syntactical or logical framework in the sonnet, but so powerful are the contradictory, random, and disruptive effects occurring incidentally as the syntax unfolds that to reduce the sonnet to its seemingly replete logical framework is to miss the most amazing effects of these extraordinary poems.

Shakespeare is writing at the end of a very long tradition of using lyric poems to examine the nature of human love, and there is a weight of insight as well as of rhetorical power behind his collection. Nowhere in the Petrarchan tradition are the extremes of erotic revelation offered in such rawness and complexity. Northrop Frye once characterized the sonnets as a kind of "creative yoga," an imaginative discipline meant to articulate the feelings that swirl around sexuality. Most of the conventional *topoi* of traditional poetry are the starting points for the sonnets—the unity of lovers (36-40), the power of poetry to immortalize the beloved (18, 19, 55), contests between eye and heart, beauty and virtue (46, 141), and shadow and substance (53, 98, 101). As with Petrarch's *Rime* (after 1327) or Sir Philip Sidney's *Astrophel and Stella* (1591), it would be possible to create a schematic account of commonplace Renaissance thinking about love from the sonnets. To do so, however, would be to nullify their extraordinary power of creation, the way they force ejaculations of recognition, horror, or joy from their readers.

After half a century of existentialism, readers in the late twentieth century understood that one of the most urgent subjects of the sonnets is not the commonplaces of Renaissance thinking about love, nor even the powerful concern with the power of art, but what Sonnet 16 calls our "war upon this bloody tyrant Time." It is no accident that the "discovery" of the sonnets' concern with time and mutability dates from the 1930's, when the impact of Søren Kierkegaard, Friedrich Nietzsche, and the existentialists, including Martin Heidegger, was starting to be widely felt in England and America. The sonnets' invitation to see man's temporality not merely as an abstract problem but as part of his inherent nature—what Heidegger terms man's "thrownness," his sense of being thrown into the world—seems central to a perception of the sonnets' power. Unpredictability and change are at the heart of the sonnets—but it is a continually shifting heart, and one that conceives of human love as definable only in terms of such change and finitude. The sonnets avoid the transcendentalism of Geoffrey Chaucer beseeching his young lovers to turn from the world, or of Edmund Spenser rejecting change for the reassurance of God's Eternity and his providential guidance of time to a foreknown, if mysterious, end. Shakespeare's sonnets rather overwhelm readers with questions and contradictions. In Sonnet 60, for example, time is not an impartial or abstract background. Even where it is glanced at as a pattern observable in nature or man, it is evoked as a disruptive, disturbing experience which cannot be dealt with as a philosophical problem. Some sonnets portray time as a sinister impersonal determinant; some thrust time at the reader as an equally unmanageable force of unforeseeable chances and changes, what Sonnet 115 calls man's "million'd accidents."

In Sonnet 15, it may be possible to enter into an understandable protest against time destroying its own creations (a commonplace enough Renaissance sentiment), and to accede to a sense of helplessness before a malignant force greater than the individual human being. When the sonnet tries, however, by virtue of its formally structured argument, to create a consciousness that seeks to understand and so to control this awareness, the reader encounters lines or individual words that may undermine even the temporary satisfaction of the aesthetic form. Such, for example is the force of the appalling awareness that "everything that grows/ Holds in perfection but a little moment." What is the application of "everything" or the emotional effect of the way the second line builds to a seemingly replete climax in "perfection" and then tumbles into oblivion in "but a little moment"? The sonnet does not and need not answer such questions. In a very real sense it cannot answer them, for readers can only acknowledge time's power in their own contingent lives. What is shocking is not merely the commonplace that "never-resting time leads summer on/ To hideous winter, and confounds him there" (5) but that each reading fights against and so disrupts the logical and aesthetic coherence of the reader's own sense of change and betrayal.

To attempt criticism of the sonnets is, to an unusual extent, to be challenged to make oneself vulnerable, to undergo a kind of creative therapy, as one goes back and forth from such textual gaps and indeterminacies to the shifting, vulnerable self, making the reader aware of the inadequacy and betrayal of words, as well as of their amazing seductiveness. Consider, for example, Sonnet 138. When one falls in love with a much younger person, does one inevitably feel the insecurity of a generation gap? What is more important in such a reading of the sonnets is the insistence that age or youthfulness are not important in themselves: It is the insistence itself that is important, not the mere fact of age—just as it is the anxiety with which a man or woman watches the wrinkles beneath the eyes that is important, not the wrinkles themselves. The note of insistence, in other words, is not attached merely to the speaker's age: It stands for an invitation to participate in some wider psychological revelation, to confess the vulnerability which people encounter in themselves in any relationship that is real and growing, and therefore necessarily unpredictable and risky.

Without vulnerability and contingency, without the sense of being thrown into the world, there can be no growth. Hence the poet invites the reader to accept ruefully what the fact of his age evokes—an openness to ridicule or rejection. The sonnet's insistence on being open to the insecurity represented by the narrator's age points not merely to a contrast between the speaker and his two lovers but rather to a radical self-division. This is especially so in the Dark Lady sonnets, where there is a savage laceration of self, particularly in the fearful exhaustion of Sonnet 129, in which vulnerability is evoked as paralysis. At once logically relentless and emotionally centrifugal, Sonnet 129 generates fears or vulnerability and self-disgust. Nothing is specified: The strategies of the poem work to make the reader reveal or recognize his own compulsions and revulsions. The poem's physical, psychological, and cultural basis forces the reader to become aware of his awful drive to repress words because they are potentially so destructive.

Even in the seemingly most serene sonnets there are inevitably dark shadows of insecurity and anxiety. In Sonnet 116, for example, the argument is that a love that alters with time and circumstance is not a true, but a self-regarding love.

The poem purports to define true love by negatives, but if those negatives are deliberately negated, the poem that emerges may be seen as the dark, repressed underside of the apparently unassailable affirmation of a mature, self-giving, other-directed love. If lovers admit impediments, and play with the idea that love is indeed love which "alters when it alteration finds," that it is an "ever-fixed mark" and, most especially, that love is indeed "time's fool," then the poem connects strikingly and powerfully with the strain of insecurity about the nature of change in human love that echoes throughout the whole collection. Such apparent affirmations may be acts of repression, an attempt to regiment the unrelenting unexpectedness and challenge of love. There are poems in the collection which, although less assertive, show a willingness to be vulnerable, to reevaluate constantly, to swear permanence within, not despite, transience—to be, in the words of St. Paul, deceivers yet true. Elsewhere, part of the torture of the Dark Lady sonnets is that such a consolation does not emerge through the pain.

In short, what Sonnet 116 represses is the acknowledgment that the only fulfillment worth having is one that is struggled for and which is independent of law or compulsion. The kind of creative fragility that it tries to marginalize is that evoked in the conclusion to Sonnet 49 when the poet admits his vulnerability: "To leave poor me thou hast the strength of laws,/ Since, why to love, I can allege no cause." This is an affirmation of a different order—or rather an acknowledgment that love must not be defined by repression and exclusion. Lovers can affirm the authenticity of the erotic only by admitting the possibility that it is not absolute. Love has no absolute legal, moral, or causal claims; nor, in the final analysis, can love acknowledge the bonds of law, family, or state—or if finally they are acknowledged, it is because they grow from love itself. Love moves by its own internal dynamic; it is not motivated by a series of external compulsions. Ultimately it asks from the lover the *nolo contendere* of commitment: Do with me what you will. A real, that is to say, an altering, bending, *never* fixed and unpredictable love is always surrounded by, and at times seems to live by, battles, plots, subterfuges, quarrels, and irony. At the root is the acknowledgment that any affirmation is made because of, not despite, time and human mortality. As Sonnet 12 puts it, having surveyed the fearful unpredictability of all life, lovers must realize that it is even "thy beauty" that must be questioned. At times this thought "is as a death" (64), a "fearful meditation" (65)—that even the most precious of all human creations, will age, wrinkle, fade, and die. Just how can one affirm in the face of that degree of reality?

Under the pressure of such questioning, the affirmation of Sonnet 116 can therefore be seen as a kind of bad faith, a false dread—false, because it freezes lovers in inactivity when they should, on the contrary, accept their finitude as possibility. Frozen in the fear of contingency, which Sonnet 116 so ruthlessly represses in its insistent negatives, readers may miss Shakespeare's essential insight that it is in fact the very fragility of beauty, love, poetry, fair youth, and dark lady alike, that enhances their desirability. Paradoxically, it is precisely because they are indeed among the wastes of time that they are beautiful; they are not desirable because they are immortal but because they are irrevocably time-bound. One of the most profound truths is expressed in Sonnet 64: "Ruin hath taught me thus to ruminate/ That Time will come and take my love away./ This thought is as a death, which cannot choose/ But weep to have that which it fears to lose." The power of such lines goes far beyond the serene platitudes of Sonnet 116. At his most courageous, man does not merely affirm, *despite* the forces of change and unpredictability which provide the ever-shifting centers of his life; on the contrary, he discovers his greatest strengths *because* of and within his own contingency. To accept rather than to deny time is to prove that man's deepest life ultimately does not recognize stasis but always craves growth, and that fulfillment is built not upon the need for finality, for being "ever fixed," but on the need to violate apparent limits, to push forward or die.

Against a sonnet such as 116, some sonnets depict love not as a serene continuation of life but rather as a radical reorientation. Readers are asked not to dismiss fears of limitation, but to affirm them. It is in the midst of contingency, when meditations are overwhelmed by the betrayals of the past, while "I sigh the lack of many a thing I sought,/ And with old woes new wail my dear Time's waste" (Sonnet 30), that love may open up the future as possibility, not as completion—so long as one accepts that it is time itself that offers such possibility, not any attempt to escape from it.

The typical Renaissance attitude to time and mutability was one of fear or resignation unless, as in Spenser, the traditional Christian context could be evoked as compensation; but for Shakespeare the enormous energies released by the Renaissance are wasted in trying to escape the burden of temporality. The drive to stasis, to repress experiences and meanings, is a desire to escape the burden of realizing that there are some transformations which love cannot effect. Ultimately, it is impossible to get inside a lover's soul no matter how much the flesh is seized and penetrated. The drive to possess and so to annihilate is a desire derived from the old Platonic ideal of original oneness, which only Shakespeare among the Renaissance poets seems to have seen as a clear and fearful perversion—it certainly haunts the lover of the Dark Lady sonnets and we are invited to stand and shudder at the speaker's Augustinian self-lacerations. In Sonnet 144 the two loves "of comfort and despair,/ Which like two spirits do suggest me still" are not just a "man right fair" and a "woman, colour'd ill": They are also aspects of each lover's self, the two loves that a dualistic mind cannot affirm and by which people may be paralyzed.

Throughout this discussion of the sonnets, what has been stressed is that their power rests on the seemingly fragile basis not of Shakespeare's but of their readers' shifting and unpredictable experiences. They are offered not in certainty, but in hope. They invite affirmation while insisting that pain is the dark visceral element in which man must live and struggle. Many of the Dark Lady sonnets are grim precisely because the lover can see no way to break through such pain. What they lack, fundamentally, is hope. By accepting that, for a time, "my grief lies onward and my joy behind" (Sonnet 50), the lover may be able, however temporarily, to make some commitment. Sonnet 124 is particularly suggestive, categorizing love as "dear," costly, not only because it is "fond," beloved, but also because it is affirmed in the knowledge of the world. Moreover, while it "fears not Policy" it is nevertheless "hugely politic." It is as if love must be adaptable, cunning, even deceptive, aware of the untrustworthiness of the world from which it can never be abstracted: "it nor grows with heat, nor drowns with showers." Finally, the poet affirms with a strong and yet strangely ironic twist: "To this I witness call the fools of Time,/ Which die for goodness, who have liv'd for crime."

As Stephen Booth notes, Sonnet 124 "is the most extreme example of Shakespeare's constructive vagueness," its key the word "it," which, "like all pronouns, is specific, hard, concrete, and yet imprecise and general—able to include anything or nothing." "It" occurs five times, each time becoming more indeterminate, surrounded by subjectives and negatives: In this sonnet "composed of precisely evocative words in apparently communicative syntaxes which come to nothing and give a sense of summing up everything, the word *it* stands sure, constant, forthright, simple and blank." The blankness to which Booth points has been filled very specifically by generations of readers to force the poem into a repressive argument like that of Sonnet 116. For example, the key phrase "the fools of time" is usually glossed as local, historical examples of political or religious timeservers—but the phrase contains mysterious reverberations back upon the lovers themselves. There is a sense in which men are *all* fools of time. When Sonnet 116 affirms that "Love's not Time's fool," it betrays a deliberate and fearful repression; an unwillingness to acknowledge that Love is not able to overcome Time; time is something that can be fulfilled only as it presents opportunity and possibility to us. People rightly become fools—jesters, dancers in attendance on Time, holy fools before the creative challenge of man's finitude—and men die, are fulfilled sexually, existentially, only if they submit themselves, "hugely politic," to the inevitable compromises, violence, and disruption which is life. Men "die for goodness" because in a sense they have all "lived for crime." People are deceivers yet true; the truest acts, like the truest poetry, are the most feigning.

The twelve-line Sonnet 126 is conventionally regarded as the culmination of the first part of the sequence. Its serenity is very unlike that of 116. It acknowledges that, even if the fair youth is indeed Nature's "minion," even he must eventually be "rendered." Such realism does not detract from the Youth's beauty or desirability; it in fact constitutes its power.

Whether one considers the Fair Youth or the Dark Lady sonnets, or whether one attempts to see a "hidden" order in the sonnets, or even if one wishes to see a story or some kind of biographical origin "within" them, perhaps their greatness rests on their refusal to offer even the possibility of "solutions" to the "problems" they raise. They disturb, provoke, and ask more than merely "aesthetic" questions; read singly or together, they make readers face (or hide from) and question the most fundamental elements of poetry, love, time, and death.

Other major works

plays: *Henry VI, Part I*, wr. 1589-1590, pr. 1592; *Edward III*, pr. c. 1589-1595, pb. 1596; *Henry VI, Part II*, pr. c. 1590-1591; *Henry VI, Part III*, pr. c. 1590-1591; *Richard III*, pr. c. 1592-1593, revised 1623; *The Comedy of Errors*, pr. c. 1592-1594; *The Taming of the Shrew*, pr. c. 1593-1594; *Titus Andronicus*, pr., pb. 1594; *The Two Gentlemen of Verona*, pr. c. 1594-1595; *Love's Labour's Lost*, pr. c. 1594-1595, revised 1597 for court performance; *Romeo and Juliet*, pr. c. 1595-1596; *Richard II*, pr. c. 1595-1596; *A Midsummer Night's Dream*, pr. c. 1595-1596; *King John*, pr. c. 1596-1597; *The Merchant of Venice*, pr. c. 1596-1597; *Henry IV, Part I*, pr. c. 1597-1598; *The Merry Wives of Windsor*, pr. 1597, revised c. 1600-1601; *Henry IV, Part II*, pr. 1598; *Much Ado About Nothing*, pr. c. 1598-1599; *Henry V*, pr. c. 1598-1599; *Julius Caesar*, pr. c. 1599-1600; *As You Like It*, pr. c. 1599-1600; *Hamlet, Prince of Denmark*, pr. c. 1600-1601; *Twelfth Night: Or, What You Will*, pr. c. 1600-1602; *Troilus and Cressida*, pr. c. 1601-1602; *All's Well That Ends Well*, pr. c. 1602-1603; *Othello, the Moor of Venice*, pr. 1604, revised 1623; *Measure for Measure*, pr. 1604; *King Lear*, pr. c. 1605-1606; *Macbeth*, pr. 1606; *Antony and Cleapatra*, pr. c. 1606-1607; *Coriolanus*, pr. c. 1607-1608; *Timon of Athens*, pr. c. 1607-1608; *Pericles, Prince of Tyre*, pr. c. 1607-1608; *Cymbeline*, pr. c. 1609-1610; *The Winter's Tale*, pr. c. 1610-1611; *The Tempest*, pr. 1611; *The Two Noble Kinsmen*, pr. c. 1612-1613 (with John Fletcher); *Henry VIII*, pr. 1613 (with Fletcher).

Bibliography

Bate, Jonathan. *The Genius of Shakespeare*. New York: Oxford University Press, 1998. Explores the extraordinary staying-power of Shakespeare's work. Bate opens by taking up questions of authorship, asking, for example, Who was Shakespeare, based on the little documentary evidence we have? Which works really are attributable to him? How extensive was the influence of Christopher Marlowe? Bate goes on to trace Shakespeare's canonization and near-deification, examining not only the uniqueness of his status among English-speaking readers but also his effect on literate cultures across the globe.

Burgess, Anthony. *Shakespeare*. London: Jonathan Cape, 1970. A prolific novelist, linguist, and literary analyst, Burgess here presents an attractive, copiously illustrated, and immensely readable volume. Although many of his insights are conjectural, he is tremendously persuasive. A highly recommended first reference, though the bibliography is limited.

Campbell, Oscar James, and Edward G. Quinn. *The Reader's Encyclopedia of Shakespeare*. New York: Thomas Y. Crowell, 1966. The most comprehensive single-volume reference, this illustrated work remains unsurpassed. Not only does it arrange an immense array of Shakespeare topics in alphabetic order, but it also includes excerpts of the full range of literary criticism and surveys of stage history. A widely used reference by both experts and amateurs.

Donno, Elizabeth Story. "The Epyllion." In *English Poetry and Prose, 1540-1674*, edited by Christopher Ricks. New York: Peter Bedrick Books, 1987. This brief introductory survey provides an excellent approach to Shakespeare's mythological poems, placing them securely in their contemporary literary context. Includes basic documentary notes and a complete bibliography of all relevant materials. Fully indexed.

Hulse, Clark. *Metamorphic Verse: The Elizabethan Minor Epic*. Princeton, N.J: Princeton University Press, 1981. Hulse surveys with great learning and enlightening insights the entire range of the Elizabethan mythological poem. Shakespeare's narrative poems are examined in detail and integrated with their literary and cultural backgrounds. Contains sound notes, a complete bibliography, and a thorough index.

Kasten, David Scott. *A Companion to Shakespeare*. Malden, Mass.: Blackwell, 1999. Offers an innovative and comprehensive picture of the theatrical, literary, intellectual and social worlds in which Shakespeare wrote and in which his plays were produced. Each individual essay stands as an authoritative account of the state of knowledge in its field, and in their totality the essays provide a compelling portrait of the historical conditions, both imaginative and institutional, that enabled Shakespeare's great art.

Reese, M. M. *Shakespeare: His World and His Work*. Rev. ed. London: Edward Arnold, 1980. Reese's essays on various aspects of Shakespeare, his life, his background, and his writings, constitute one of the best introductions to these topics available in one volume. Although they are best for intellectual and cultural backgrounds, they offer illuminating comments on the poetry. The directions for further reading are helpful.

Roche, Thomas P., Jr. *Petrarch and the English Sonnet Sequences*. New York: AMS Press, 1986. This is a comprehensive study of the phenomenon of the Elizabethan sonnet sequence, considered primarily from the point of view of its source in Petrarch. It covers the subject completely, and its consideration of Shakespeare's sonnets is unrivaled. The bibliographical apparatus is complete.

_______. "Shakespeare and the Sonnet Sequence." In *English Poetry and Prose, 1540-1674*, edited by Christopher Ricks. New York: Peter Bedrick Books, 1987. The title of this excellent introductory essay is misleading. In fact it is almost entirely about Shakespeare's sonnets, and the material is concisely presented and rewarding. The bibliographical material is excellent for beginners.

Wilson, John Dover, ed. *The Sonnets*. 2d ed. New York: Cambridge University Press, 1967. The introductory essay of twenty-four pages and the notes and commentary are simply the best ever done on this poetry. The bibliographical material is dated but sound.

Gary F. Waller;
bibliography updated by the editors

Alan Shapiro

Born: Boston, Massachusetts; February 18, 1952

Principal poetry

After the Digging, 1981
The Courtesy, 1983
Happy Hour, 1987
Covenant, 1991
Mixed Company, 1996
The Dead Alive and Busy, 2000

Other literary forms

Alan Shapiro has confined his work mostly to poetry and poetic prose, but his 1993 collection of essays *In Praise of the Impure: Poetry and the Ethical Imagination—Essays, 1980-1991* includes discussions of his poetic theory concerning the way imaginative literature can test the reader's moral certitudes and the narrative element in lyric poetry. The collection also includes some discussion of poets J. V. Cunningham, Robert Hass, James McMichael, Robert Pinsky, and John Berryman, as well as some discussion of the New Formalism, a poetic school which particularly affected Shapiro's early work.

The Last Happy Occasion (1996) is a collection of essays, partly biographical, mixed with literary criticism. In it Shapiro uses individual poems as starting points for discussing literary theory as well as for discussions of the poems' impact on his life. His memoir *Vigil* (1997) chronicles the death of his sister Beth from breast cancer. The death is agonizing for the whole family, and Shapiro examines the various ways individual members deal with it, ranging from her African American husband's self-imposed isolation to her brother's dark humor.

Achievements

Alan Shapiro's reputation has risen steadily as his body of poetry has increased. His earlier work was mostly formal; later work is less given to form. Shapiro received a fellowship from the National Endowment for the Arts in 1984. He was a Guggenheim Fellow in 1986. *Mixed Company* (1996) won the *Los Angeles Times* award for poetry. *The Last Happy Occasion* was a finalist for the National Book Critics Circle award. In 1999, Shapiro won the O. B. Hardison, Jr., Poetry Prize from the Folger Shakespeare Library. In 2001 he won the Kingsley Tufts Poetry Award for *The Dead Alive and Busy.*

Biography

Alan Shapiro was born in Boston, Massachusetts, on February 18, 1952, the son of Harold and Marilyn Shapiro. Many of his poems portray his extended Jewish American family, whose presence informed his early life with their rich tangle of rivalry, jealousy, love, and devotion. He has described himself as a baby-boom child of the middle class. His undergraduate work was done at Brandeis University, where he began to write poetry seriously while studying under the stringent gaze of J. V. Cunningham and Galway Kinnell.

Shapiro has followed an academic career, teaching creative writing at Northwestern University, Evanston; the University of North Carolina, Greensboro; and the University of North Carolina, Chapel Hill. In *In Praise of the Impure*, Shapiro records an experience from early in his teaching career when a talented student who seemed to read poetry with an unusually deep level of understanding succumbed to cancer. She seemed to use her understanding of poetry to interpret her mortality, a gift poetry can offer all its readers. The 1995 death of Shapiro's older sister, Beth, from cancer, and the death of his older brother, David, in 2000, have led him to similar insights, as his memoir *Vigil* attests.

Analysis

Alan Shapiro's poetry takes as its subject all the nuances of human relationships. It examines the interaction between husbands and wives and lovers and neighbors, and all the modulations of feeling fostered by our earliest relationships with our parents, siblings, aunts, uncles, and cousins. Shapiro watches love matches made and dissolved; he explores the threads of memory leading back to childhood but still binding adult emotions. He is always attentive to the layers of motive which inform human interactions; the people in his poems are simultaneously jealous and generous, loving and vengeful, bitter and compassionate.

The people of Shapiro's poems are sometimes autobiographical, as he notes in his readings; never sentimental about them, Shapiro treats them tenderly, even when he is recording the sad truths of their worst moments. Some of the appeal of this poetry rises from the reader's gratitude for Shapiro's compassion for these characters. Whatever their artistic origins, they seem to have come from everyone's family; the events of their lives are part of the fabric of all modern American life. Such intimate poetry is often termed confessional, but Shapiro's poems go beyond the exorcising of private curses to examine larger issues, an achievement that led one reviewer to call him "a shrewd and sympathetic moralist."

The Courtesy

The Courtesy introduces some qualities that are fundamental to Shapiro's work. His roots in formalism are apparent here, with poems in rhyming quatrains and blank verse. The vivid family portraits of the first section announce the sense of character as one of Shapiro's great strengths. In this volume, several poems focus on family tensions—the ancient rivalry between two sisters, a son's desire to please a demanding father. Several others deal with the stresses attendant on being a Jew in a Gentile world. In "Simon, the Barber," the speaker recalls his childhood history with the barber who disapproved of his secular ways. His rejection of the sidelock haircut of traditional Judaism foretells his leaving the law that Simon represented. When later he learns that Simon's son has been arrested in a drug raid (the hallmark crime of secular America), he recognizes Simon's pain at having been failed by his own seed, a pain that stands as "mere ashes in our prayer for the dead."

Happy Hour

The long poem "Neighbors" in *Happy Hour* furthers the presentation of Shapiro's interests. A narrative poem, it describes a woman whose emotional crisis is dipping into madness and how living upstairs from her affects an unnamed man and his unspecified lover, perhaps his young wife. They meet the woman as they move in; she stands at the window in her nightgown, singing along with a pounding stereo. He and his wife set to work cleaning and painting their rooms, all to the relentless accompaniment of the thumping music, evidently a rock love song: "'If you'll hold/ the ladder, baby, I'll climb to the top.'" They bang on her door, but she refuses to answer and sends them a note claiming that the music is an effort "to cure a paralyzed kid."

When the man breaks his wife's favorite coffee cup, the loss suggests the fissures growing in their relationship, amplified perhaps by the unremitting music which seems to have taken control of all they do. Once, in front of the apartment, the woman shouts out that her man is coming soon, just as the song has implied, and that they should all get together then. With this claim in the back of his mind, the man recalls his lovemaking with his wife and begins to fear that sex may be inadequate to sustain their relationship: "Capricious pleasure/ frail craft, how long, he wonders,/ how far will it carry them?"

When the woman orders a load of firewood in May and builds a roaring fire that goes on for days, smoking up the apartment's hallways, someone calls the police, and she is taken away, leaving the man to wonder at their desire to watch her crisis and to speculate on how the woman herself might have viewed the event: ". . . the song/ was playing, and her man, her one/ desire, was climbing up the blazing/ ladder no one else could see[.]"

Shapiro's finely tuned sense of emotional weather is present in many of these poems. In "Bedtime Story," a child longs for security in a world peopled by witches and wolves in the form of "that new man" who calls his mother away from reading to him. "Mortmain" depicts a mother's passive-aggressive anger at the son for whom she insists on suffering even while she refuses his offers of help. The son, the speaker in this poem, is angry and baffled in return. The bits of dialogue are a great strength here. The mother's aggrieved "Look/ at the trouble I've gone to/ to buy you this. Here take it" captures real speech rhythms in the poem's short lines.

Covenant

Shapiro's 1991 volume *Covenant* demonstrates his growing sureness in considering painful and intimate events thoughtfully but without self-indulgence. The long poem "The Lesson" is a particularly good example of this growth. The adult narrator records his experience as a ten-year-old dealing with a sexual predator, Rich, who picks up boys at the ball field and entices them into his golden Sting Ray with his friendly charm and tantalizingly sexy talk. The poem's short lines draw out the speaker's infatuation with this dashing fellow who, unlike their fathers, seems to have plenty of time for these boys, and they suggest the tense energy of the speaker's envy of the boys Rich seems to favor:

> How's it hanging, boys?
> he'd ask, and tap
> the wheel, jiggle the stick,
> the engine revving
> gently, not so gently,
> to remind us of all
> the other things
> he could be doing.

Each day, Rich selects a boy to ride in the golden car. "Each day it wasn't me." On their return, the privileged boys are curiously silent about the experience. When at last the speaker is summoned, the ride includes what the reader now expects. Unzipping the boy's trousers, Rich fondles him: "My boyhood ended/ there, that day." Eventually Rich is driven away from the ball field by a furious mother, but the event has marked the boy in an indefinable way. If he is not any longer a boy, neither is he a man, nor is he sure what being a man might mean in the light of what Rich has done to him.

In the book's last section, Shapiro turns to themes that will grow in importance in his subsequent work—the way memory of the past affects understanding of the present. In "Home Movie," a mother's running commentary on a movie picturing her, the father, and their baby daughter blends into the speaker's commentary, which reveals how the mother has fictionalized and romanticized the family's history. In the movie, as the mother waves the baby's hand to the future viewers, the speaker comments "Bitter, and long, and unforeseeable—what changes,/ what survives!"

Other poems in the section deal with death. "Two Elegies" shows miniature pictures of Irma and Dotty; "Purgatory" recalls Dante as it pictures the dead moving lost and anonymous, along a train platform. "Covenant" offers a masterful portrait of the angry older sister who now cares for the younger after a stroke. It includes conversations which capture the rhythms of Jewish American speech: "That one, she didn't care/ how sick she got, she always had her hair done."

Mixed Company

The titles of the poems in *Mixed Company* suggest its themes: two include the word "mother"; three include "wife"; two more include "ex-wife." "Widows," "Matriarchs," "Sisters," "Lover," "Girlfriend," "Woman Friend"—this is a volume of portraits, dramatic monologues, and conversations. Shapiro is always interested in personality but rarely rests with a mere picture. In "Girlfriend," for instance, he records an adolescent sexual experience, concentrating first on the speaker's eagerness to please his partner. In a typical Shapiro shift, the speaker then overhears the girl giggling on the phone to a friend. Her "girlish tune/ of scorn" has left the speaker with a lifelong expectation of disaster. In "Manufacturing," Shapiro again examines the sometimes humiliating requirements of manhood as he watches his father at the family business.

The Dead Alive and Busy

The Dead Alive and Busy is the volume for which Shapiro received the prestigious Kingsley Tufts Poetry Award; it continues the qualities that one reviewer has labeled "meditative and elegiac." The book's first section contains poems that picture his parents in old age. One of the most successful is "New Year's Eve in the Aloha Room," in which the aged parents' dancing somehow recalls their whole history together. "Vase of Flowers" looks to the book's last section by adapting the Persephone myth to represent a mother's view of a daughter's death.

The poems of the last section deal with the death of Shapiro's sister Beth and first appeared in his memoir *Vigil*. Like the memoir, they make a painfully detailed picture of a death from cancer. In "Hand," the speaker notes how each stage in the dying woman's decline becomes, in retrospect, "too brief a heaven// once it had passed." Now her whole ability to respond to human contact is reduced to the slight flexing of her fingers. "Rose" chronicles the speaker's temptation to use the rose-colored button on the morphine pump to give his sister the release she seems to desire. "I'd walk the halls/ to . . . quell the shame of what I wanted/ to do, the shame of being too afraid to do it." "Scarecrow," the last poem of the volume, uses the scarecrow and the crows of the written word to make a remarkable image of one whose excoriating experience has left him both empty and yet ready to look into the heart of the mysterious and painful world.

Other major works

nonfiction: *In Praise of the Impure: Poetry and the Ethical Imagination—Essays, 1980-1991*, 1993; *The Last Happy Occasion*, 1996; *Vigil*, 1997.

Bibliography

Gordon, Audrey K. *Perspectives in Biology and Medicine* 41, no. 4 (1998): 606. This thoughtful review of *Vigil* discusses the memoir from a medical perspective, concentrating particularly on the way the medical community is portrayed in the work. The writer is also interested in the poetic qualities of the book and praises Shapiro's sensitive responses to the various ways his family responds to the crisis.

Hadas, Rachel. "Three Lives." *Yale Review* 85, no. 3 (July 1997): 119-129. Hadas considers how a writer's life can shape the events in his or her work. Her discussion considers Shapiro along with Bernard Cooper and Nick Papandreau.

Keen, Suzanne. *Commonweal* 120, no. 4 (February 26, 1993): 26-29. In this article, Keen discusses *Covenant*. She says that Shapiro's poems range "from the uncomfortable to the ecstatic to the excruciating" and offers close reading of several of its poems—"The Sweepers," "The Visitation," and "The Lesson"—as evidence.

Ratner, Rochelle. Review of *The Dead Alive and Busy*, by Alan Shapiro. *Library Journal* 125 (February 1, 2000): 90. This short review considers the major strength of *The Dead Alive and Busy* the honesty of its first section, which pictures Shapiro's parents in their old age. The reviewer says that the poems of the middle section seem pallid by comparison and that the poems dealing with his sister's death are too unspecific to let the reader form a bond with their subject.

Williamson, Alan. Review of *Covenant*, by Alan Shapiro. *The American Poetry Review* 22, no. 2 (March/April, 1993): 33-36. This lengthy review praises Shapiro's cinematic use of narrative, a quality the author sees as characteristic of a new sort of American poetry. He also praises Shapiro's use of form, which employs its control without self-consciousness.

Ann D. Garbett

Karl Shapiro

Born: Baltimore, Maryland; November 10, 1913
Died: New York, New York; May 14, 2000

Principal poetry

Poems, 1935
Person, Place, and Thing, 1942
The Place of Love, 1942

V-Letter and Other Poems, 1944
Trial of a Poet and Other Poems, 1947
Poems, 1942-1953, 1953
Poems of a Jew, 1958
The Bourgeois Poet, 1964
The White-Haired Lover, 1968
Selected Poems, 1968
Adult Bookstore, 1976
Collected Poems, 1940-1978, 1978
Love and War, Art and God, 1984
Adam and Eve, 1986
New and Selected Poems, 1940-1986, 1987
The Old Horsefly, 1992
The Wild Card: Selected Poems, Early and Late, 1998 (Stanley Kunitz and David Ignatow, editors)

OTHER LITERARY FORMS

Karl Shapiro wrote one novel, *Edsel* (1971); four books of literary criticism, *Essay on Rime* (1945), *Beyond Criticism* (1953), *In Defense of Ignorance* (1960), and *To Abolish Children and Other Essays* (1968); and several works on prosody. He also coedited three books on the activity of writers, one with W. H. Auden, *Poets at Work* (1948); a second one with James E. Miller, Jr., and Bernice Slote, *Start with the Sun: Studies in Cosmic Poetry* (1960); and a third volume, *The Writer's Experience* (1964), with Ralph Ellison. *The Poetry Wreck: Selected Essays 1950-1970* (1975) is an anthology of his criticism. He published two volumes of a projected three-volume autobiography before his death in 2000: *The Younger Son* (1988), which covered his youth and experiences in World War II, and *Reports of My Death* (1990), which covers the years from 1945 to 1985.

ACHIEVEMENTS

Karl Shapiro's literary career was marked by both success and controversy. He has been labeled polemical, ambiguous, vulgar, inconsistent, uncommitted, and schizoid, yet most critics are agreed upon the vibrant, precise, no-nonsense deployment of language and style in his writings, securing for him a place of eminence in contemporary American letters. Shapiro became famous *in absentia* while serving in the United States Army during World War II, receiving the Pulitzer Prize in poetry in 1945 even before he was discharged. Before being inducted in March, 1941, Shapiro had published, besides the little-circulated *Poems*, only a handful of poems, including "Necropolis," "University," and "Death of Emma Goldman" in the *Partisan Review* and *Poetry*. By the end of 1941, he had several more poems accepted by those magazines, and the following year he won the Jeanette Sewell Davis Prize, awarded by *Poetry*. In 1942 he wrote, from "somewhere in the Pacific," *The Place of Love* and *Person, Place and Thing*, which brought him to the attention of the public. In 1943 he was included in the anthology *Five Young American Poets*, put out by New Directions, won the Contemporary American Poetry Prize, and was awarded the Levinson Prize by *Poetry*; his poems were circulated many times over in America's leading literary publications. In 1944, he published *V-letter and Other Poems* and obtained a grant from the American Academy of Arts and Letters. With the Pulitzer Prize in poetry in 1945, he became a Guggenheim Fellow and a Fellow in American Letters, Library of Congress.

Karl Shapiro with his wife Evelyn in 1946. (AP/Wide World Photos)

The same year, he published the highly controversial *Essay on Rime*, which the critic Dudley Fitts called his *ars poetica*. Shapiro distanced himself from the modernist poetics of William Butler Yeats, T. S. Eliot and Ezra Pound, and criticized both mainstream and university-backed poetry. Nevertheless, in 1945 he was honored with the Shelley Memorial Award, and became Consultant in Poetry at the Library of Congress from 1946 to 1947. Shapiro's reputation was on solid ground, and with the publication of *Trial of a Poet and Other Poems* in 1947, he was offered an associate professorship of English at The Johns Hopkins University, the school from which he had dropped out as a sophomore in 1939. He precipitated a controversy by voting against the awarding of the first Library of Congress Bollingen Prize to Ezra Pound in 1948 and defended his position in an article in the *Partisan Review*. His conviction that poetry is the "enemy" of literature and is not meant to be analyzed coldly for ulterior motives by academics and cultural critics was argued most convincingly during the Montgomery Lectures on Contemporary Civilization, published later under the title *Beyond Criticism*.

In 1950, Shapiro moved to Chicago to edit *Poetry* magazine, a position he held until 1956, when he moved to Nebraska and began a ten-year editorship of *Prairie Schooner*. He was awarded a second Guggenheim Fellowship in 1953, and taught at various universities, including the University of California, Berkeley, the University of Indiana, and the University of Nebraska. He also lectured overseas under the auspices of the State Department. In 1959, he delivered the Ellison Lectures at the University of Cincinnati. His collection of prizes was augmented by the Eunice Tietjens Memorial Prize in 1960 and the Oscar Blumenthal Prize in 1963; in 1969, Shapiro shared the Bollingen Prize for Poetry with John Berryman. He was Professor of English at the University of Illinois, Chicago Circle, from 1966 to 1968, when he took a position at the University of California, Davis, where he remained until his retirement in 1985. He received the Robert Kirsch Award from the *Los Angeles Times* in 1989 and the Charity Randall Citation in 1990.

Biography

Karl Jay Shapiro was born in Baltimore, Maryland, on November 10, 1913. His father, of Eastern European ancestry, was a customhouse broker and subsequently the owner of a moving and storage company. After his first two years of school, his family moved to Chicago for another two years, and then returned to the South, to Norfolk, Virginia, where Shapiro received most of his secondary education. In 1929, like many other small businessmen, Shapiro's father had to sell out, and the family moved back to Baltimore. Shapiro, a senior, enrolled at Forest Park High School and completed his credits for graduation at Baltimore City College. Apparently he was a poor student, and when he entered the University of Virginia he had to resign after one semester. His performance and attitude were inexplicable to his family, who counted on Shapiro to follow in the footsteps of his older brother, who was dedicated and successful and the winner of many literary awards. It was during this period that Shapiro became aware of such realities as social class, religious animosity, and ethnic differences: As a Russian Jew he was not allowed to mingle with German Jews, and as a middle-class student he was snubbed by the predominantly WASP faculty and classmates. He turned inward, began to write ever more assiduously, studied French for a while, and was privately tutored in Latin. He also studied piano for about two years but had to give it up for lack of money. He was employed in all sorts of odd jobs, in drug and hardware stores, in bars, and eventually as a filing clerk in his father's firm.

During this time, Shapiro saved enough money for a trip to Tahiti, and wrote the *Tahiti Poems*, now lost. Upon his return, he managed to obtain a scholarship to The Johns Hopkins University on the merit of *Poems*. There he went through a religious crisis, and approached Catholicism. At the same time, he gave some thought to changing his name to Karl Camden, in order to appear more Anglo-American and thus more acceptable.

In 1939, Shapiro was asked to leave the University for lack of academic achievement. Ironically, this was also the beginning of a literary success story. His poems were published in *The New Anvil* and *Poetry World*. One in particular, "Self History," appeared in five different newspapers on the East Coast, from Florida to Rhode Island. At a party in 1940, he met his future wife, Evelyn Katz, who became a staunch supporter of his work and acted as his agent while he was in the service. At this time he took up an intensive, salaried training course at the Enoch Pratt Library School in Baltimore, which helped him to secure his first postwar job and exposed him to all kinds of publications.

While in the service, the poet held a desk job, but he saw enough of the incongruities and cruelties of war to mark his sensibility forever. It was here that he developed the tone of the impotent, tragically detached observer, typical of one who "has seen too much." He returned from the war to find himself a literary celebrity, and soon was embroiled in the polemics which have marked his career.

Shapiro's life since 1945 can be viewed from two perspectives. The first would follow his activities on the college and university lecture circuit and as the editor of two important literary magazines. The second would take the unabashed exposés of *The Bourgeois Poet* and of *Edsel* as literal transcriptions of how he lived his life: nonchalantly denouncing the contradictions of the establishment, playing ambiguous games with poorly defined sociological stances, and almost sadomasochistically returning time and again to his own most private problems and encounters. When, in 1967, Shapiro left Evelyn for Teri Kovach, whom he married the same year, the "white-haired" poet appeared to have mellowed somewhat. It turned out, however, that in the 1960's and early 1970's Shapiro, more than a poet, was a true cultural critic "despite himself"; his views on the changing mores and the built-in nihilistic obsessions of American society were brutally expressed in the essay "To Abolish Children," whereas a less harsh but satirized vision of those turbulent years, 1967 to 1969, can be found in *Edsel*.

Analysis

"Everything I've ever known I've *felt*. Maybe my brain is in my fingertips," says the autobiographical protagonist in *Edsel*. Karl Shapiro's poetry can in fact be characterized as a poetry of feeling, of pure, spontaneous, unadulterated sensation. The poet is constantly preoccupied with saying exactly what he perceives at a given moment, and the nature and structure of the poetic text will be of primary importance. In poetry, says Shapiro, all statements concerning morality, politics, the greater social good, religion, and any other function which makes the poem *for* something or somebody are to be avoided as unimportant to the essence of the poem itself. From this perspective, all his books can be read as a series of impressionistic sketches and reveries, deeply grounded in his personal experiences, concerned only with saying what is being felt, concisely and with immediacy.

Early poems

The early poems, "Washington Cathedral," "Auto Wreck," "Hospital," and "University," are representative of this "gut" response to the world. The themes range from social injustice, decay, and the passing of life to man's alienation from his world. The stanzas of these poems are self-sustaining paragraphs proceeding from an external, almost naturalistic description of what has entered the poet's mind to a reflection on what seems to be happening, often spoken in the first-person plural, and concluding with a comment about the human condition. In other poems, he speaks in the first person, evidencing a tendency to set himself apart from the world, often taking a metaphysical view, as in the emblematic "The Dome of Sunday." Shapiro's concern with the right word, the only word that crystallizes his feelings and renders them real, is clear from his earliest exercises. Concerning the language suited to poetry, Shapiro explains that, since current speakers have inherited the English language quite by chance—downplaying history, as it were—there is no need to express oneself in "high" or "literary" English; rather, the poet should employ the current idiom of everyday life, a "low" and "common" American English that in the poem turns out to be more true and precise than any other mediated and contrived pattern.

"Lord, I've seen too much"

The documented yet inexplicable realities of everyday life confirm a recurrent conclusion in Shapiro: Everything is arbitrary. The notion slowly emerges that he is an alienated observer, a passerby whose life proceeds with a will all its own, and whose relationship to events and specific situations is casual, chancy, irrelevant, the ultimate causes being infinite and not given to man—to the poet—to fathom. This is apparent, for example, in a poem such as "Lord, I've seen too much," where Shapiro, referring to his own duty while in the service, spells out his feeling:

Lord, I have seen too much for one who sat
In quiet at his window's luminous eye
And puzzled over house and street and sky,
Safe only in the narrowest habitat.

The sincerity of the soldier becomes the purity of a child, who wonders in amazement about the mysteries of the cosmos, and finds that he only knows, and feels comfortable and safe in, his immediate surroundings. The poet has in fact "studied peace as if the world were flat," and "faltered at each brilliant entity/ Drawn like a prize from some magician's hat." The second and last stanza of the poem brings the poet's astonishment to universal levels, suggesting an analogy between the poet's experience and Adam's expulsion from Paradise.

Materializing the world

Shapiro generally attempts to render his moods and perceptions honestly and dispassionately in a language that becomes increasingly plain, approaching conversation, and richer in emotional intensity. There is no pity or pathos to be encountered, just the crystallization of a moment's feeling, a fleeting moment from life forever framed. Shapiro does not philosophize in his poetry, for poetry, as he frequently insists, is not a tool or servile guinea pig for academicians. Poetry, in his view, is the materialization of the world, the exact opposite of philosophy, which abstracts reality. He believes that poetry is an antilanguage, a counter-language, constituting the only mode in which he can be himself, independent and unique. When, in 1964, he published *The Bourgeois Poet*, the metamorphosis was complete. Shapiro was finally close to the art of children, the untrained, the hallucinated: He assembled the book by picking up at random all the autobiographical passages he had been writing.

Adult Bookstore

In *Adult Bookstore*, Shapiro registers events and impressions with a crystal-clear vision, very sardonic and emotionally detached from the sharp contours of reality; the titles themselves suggest a casual glance at what is going on in the world: "Girls Working in Banks," "Flying First Class," "The Humanities Building," and the "Adult Bookstore." The poems usually end with a casual remark, almost as if to seal the frame of the picture just given. Despite his drive to plunge into the intensity of language, Shapiro here conveys a sense of the playful and the gratuitous, the uncaring attitude of one who has long decided that the work of art is totally independent of both writer and society: He can say, with the protagonist of "The Piano Tuner's Wife," that "He plays his comprehensive keyboard song,/ The loud proud paradigm,/ The one work of art without content."

Later poetry

Shapiro himself felt that he gained too much fame too early in life, and in the 1970's and 1980's suffered from critical neglect. However, the publication of his autobiographies in 1988 and 1990 began to put him back in the public eye, and his final volume of poetry, *The Wild Card*, edited by Stanley Kunitz and David Ignatow in 1998, allowed readers to rediscover his work and trace the development of his craft from the early years until just before his death.

Other major works

LONG FICTION: *Edsel*, 1971.

PLAYS: *The Tenor*, pr. 1952 (libretto); *The Soldier's Tale*, pr. 1968 (libretto).

NONFICTION: *Essay on Rime*, 1945; *English Prosody and Modern Poetry*, 1947; *A Bibliography of Modern Prosody*, 1948; *Beyond Criticism*, 1953; *In Defense of Ignorance*, 1960; *Start with the Sun: Studies in Cosmic Poetry*, 1960 (with James E. Miller, Jr., and Bernice Slote); *Prose Keys to Modern Poetry*, 1962; *A Prosody Handbook*, 1965 (with Robert Beum); *To Abolish Children and Other Essays*, 1968; *The Poetry Wreck: Selected Essays, 1950-1970*, 1975; *The Younger Son*, 1988; *Reports of My Death*, 1990; *Poet: An Autobiography in Three Parts*, 1988-1990 (includes *The Younger Son* and *Reports of My Death*).

EDITED TEXTS: *Poets at Work*, 1948 (with W. H. Auden); *The Writer's Experience*, 1964 (with Ralph Ellison).

Bibliography

Bartlett, Lee. *Karl Shapiro: A Descriptive Bibliography, 1933-1977*. New York: Garden Publishing, 1979. A bibliographic record of all Shapiro's work up to 1977. Includes articles and poems in periodicals, translations of his works, contributions to anthologies, and so on. The annotations include quotations and excerpts from an interview with Shapiro on his publishing history. An appendix lists Shapiro's criticism and reviews. Includes a chronology.

Engels, Tim. "Shapiro's 'The Fly.'" *Explicator* 55, no. 1 (1991): 41-43. A close reading of one of Shapiro's better-known poems.

Hammer, Andrea Gale. "Poetry and Family: An Interview with Karl Shapiro." *Prairie Schooner* 55 (Fall, 1981): 3-31. This is a long, very personal and intriguing interview with the poet, interesting for the insight it sheds on the man and his thought. An excellent portrait of Karl Shapiro.

Mills, Ralph J., Jr. *Contemporary American Poetry.* New York: Random House, 1965. A chapter on Shapiro presents a broad, sympathetic view of his work with frequent quotations from the poems. This excellent introductory essay explores the interplay of influences and ideas on the poet. Includes an introduction, a reading list, and a good bibliography.

Reino, Joseph. *Karl Shapiro.* Boston: Twayne, 1981. The first full-length study of Karl Shapiro, this volume closely analyzes representative works showing the range of Shapiro's thought and craft. The text is replete with line-by-line explications. Contains an annotated bibliography which includes essays and reviews on Shapiro and his work.

Richman, Robert. "The Trials of a Poet." *The New Centurion* 6 (April, 1988): 74-81. This review of Shapiro's *New and Selected Poems 1940-1986* does more than simply report on the collection. Provides quick observations of a number of poems as well as a commentary on development and theme. The critic also pulls from Shapiro's nonpoetic writing for elaboration. A good, quick review.

Shapiro, Karl, and Ralph Ellison. *The Writer's Experience.* Washington, D.C.: Library of Congress, 1964. An essay by Shapiro, "American Poet?" is included in this pamphlet. It is autobiographical in part and personal in that it is a commentary on the process of writing poetry. Shapiro also shares a retrospective of his career and his personal struggles. He mentions influences and colleagues, and he comments on the state of poetry in America and in the modern world. An excellent and revealing essay.

Peter Carravetta,
updated by Leslie Ellen Jones

Percy Bysshe Shelley

Born: Field Place, Sussex, England; August 4, 1792
Died: Off Viareggio, Italy; July 8, 1822

Principal poetry

Original Poetry by Victor and Cazire, 1810 (with Elizabeth Shelley)
Posthumous Fragments of Margaret Nicholson, 1810
Queen Mab: A Philosophical Poem, 1813 (revised as *The Daemon of the World*, 1816)
Alastor: Or, The Spirit of Solitude and Other Poems, 1816
Mont Blanc, 1817
The Revolt of Islam, 1818
Rosalind and Helen: A Modern Eclogue, with Other Poems, 1819
The Cenci: A Tragedy in Five Acts, 1819
Letter to Maria Gisborne, 1820
Oedipus Tyrannus: Or, Swellfoot the Tyrant, a Tragedy in Two Acts, 1820
Prometheus Unbound: A Lyrical Drama in Four Acts, 1820
Epipsychidion, 1821
Adonais: An Elegy on the Death of John Keats, 1821
Hellas: A Lyrical Drama, 1822
Posthumous Poems of Percy Bysshe Shelley, 1824 (includes *Prince Athanase*, *Julian and Maddalo: A Conversation*, *The Witch of Atlas*, *The Triumph of Life*, *The Cyclops*, *Charles the First*)
The Mask of Anarchy, 1832
Peter Bell the Third, 1839
The Poetical Works of Percy Bysshe Shelley, 1839
The Wandering Jew, 1887
The Complete Poetical Works of Shelley, 1904 (Thomas Hutchinson, editor)
The Esdaile Notebook: A Volume of Early Poems, 1964 (K. N. Cameron, editor)

Other literary forms

Except for *A Defence of Poetry* (1840), Percy Bysshe Shelley's essays are not classics of English prose, but they have influenced writers as diverse as George Bernard Shaw, H. G. Wells, and Bertrand Russell, and they are very useful as glosses on the poetry. "On Love," for example, introduces Shelley's concept of the "antitype," the perfect mate, uniquely suited to one's intellect, imagination, and sensory needs, a "soul within our soul," but purged of all one finds unsatisfactory within oneself. Love is defined as the attraction to the antitype. Shelley movingly describes this longing for a mirror image of perfection:

> If we reason, we would be understood; if we imagine, we would that the airy children of our brain were born anew within another's; if we feel, we would that another's nerves should vibrate to our own, that the beams of their eyes should kindle at once and mix and melt into our own, that lips of motionless ice should not reply to lips quivering and burning with the heart's best blood. This is Love.

Love, as the attraction toward refined idealism, figures as well in Shelley's theory of the formative power of poetry.

In *A Defence of Poetry*, he argues that "the great secret of morals is Love." Through identification with the "beautiful which exists in thought, action, or person, not our own," one becomes moral through the process of empathizing. Love is thus an act of the sympathetic imagination. Because poetry, and literature in general, enhances and exercises the ability to empathize, it is an agent of tremendous potential for the moral regeneration of humankind. It goes without saying that the poet thus has a high office in the government of morality; he is Shelley's "unacknowledged legislator." By this phrase Shelley did not primarily mean that poets are unacknowledged for the good they do, but rather that they themselves were not and could not be aware of the power of their beauty. Shelley's poet is not in control of his power, for, in the language of his great metaphor of the creative process,

> the mind in creation is as a fading coal which some invisible influence, like an inconstant wind, awakens to transitory brightness: this power arises from within, like the colour of a flower which fades and changes as it is developed, and the conscious portions of our natures are unprophetic either of its approach or its departure.

Hence, poets do not control their inspiration—in fact, when writing begins, the most intense phase of inspiration has already passed; they express more than they understand; they feel less than they inspire; they are "the influence which is moved not, but moves. Poets are the unacknowledged legislators of the World."

Achievements

One of the six greatest English Romantic poets, Percy Bysshe Shelley is arguably the most versatile stylist among all English poets. His genius for versification enabled him to employ an astonishing variety of stanzaic patterns and poetic forms with equal facility. He has two basic styles, however—the sublime or rhapsodic, heard in such poems as *Alastor*, "Hymn to Intellectual Beauty," *Prometheus Unbound*, and *Adonais*; and the urbane or conversational style, found in poems such as *Julian and Maddalo: A Conversation, Letter to Maria*

Percy Bysshe Shelley (Library of Congress)

Gisborne, and *Epipsychidion*. In this latter mode, especially in the standard pentameter line with couplets, Shelley grew increasingly conservative prosodically, achieving a control almost neoclassical in balance and poise. Lyrical, unremitting intensity, however, is the defining quality of Shelley's verse.

Biography

In *Great Expectations* (1860-1861), Charles Dickens has the convict Magwitch put his life's story, as he says, into a mouthful of English—in and out of jail, in and out of jail, in and out of jail. Percy Bysshe Shelley's life falls into a similar pattern—in and out of love, in and out of love, in and out of love. Shelley admitted as much in a letter to John Gisborne, written the year he was to drown in a boating accident, and expressive of a truth he discovered too late: "I think one is always in love with something or other; the error, and I confess it is not easy for spirits cased in flesh and blood to avoid it, consists in seeking in a mortal image the likeness of what is perhaps eternal." At the age of twenty-nine, Shelley was still looking for his antitype; he believed he had found her, at last, in a nineteen-year-old Italian girl imprisoned in a nunnery, and had written one of his greatest poems, *Epipsychidion*, in celebration, typically disregarding the impact the poem would have on his wife Mary. Mary, however, had been party to a similar emotional event five years earlier when Shelley had abandoned his first wife, Harriet Westbrook Shelley, then pregnant with his second child, to elope with Mary. Both times Shelley speculated that the women could live with him, together, in harmony—the first combination, wife Harriet as sister, lover Mary as wife; the second combination, as stated metaphorically in *Epipsychidion*, wife Mary as Moon, Teresa Viviani as Sun to Shelley's earth, with a comet, Claire Claremont, Mary's half-sister, zooming into their "azure heaven" as she willed.

One of Shelley's great biographers, Kenneth Neill Cameron, says that Shelley was rather ahead of his time, at least ahead of today's liberal divorce laws, but most readers still find the facts of Shelley's love-life disturbing. His vision of love is wonderful; his idealism that sought to change the world through love and poetry is wonderful; the reality of that vision and idealism translated into life was a disaster. Shelley knew it and this awareness caused him to seek self-destruction.

His intense fits of love aside, Shelley could be the most thoughtful and loving of men. He was selfless, generous to a fault, a brilliant radical devoted to saving the world and just as passionately devoted to the pursuit of Metaphysical truth. Edward John Trelawny provides a description of Shelley in his study, German folio open, dictionary in hand (Shelley always read literature in the original—Greek, Latin, Spanish, Italian, German—so that he could be sensitive to the style and linguistic nuances of the art), at 10 A.M., and the identical picture at 6 P.M., Shelley having hardly moved, forgetting he had not eaten, looking tired and pale. "Well," Trelawny said, "have you found it?," referring to some Truth Shelley sought. "Shutting the book and going to the window," Shelley replied, "'No, I have lost it': with a deep sigh: 'I have lost a day.'"

Shelley was born into a family of landed gentry. His father Timothy was a member of Parliament and his grandfather Bysshe Shelley was a very wealthy landowner. Shelley studied at Eton, where he rebelled against the hazing system; fell madly in love with a cousin, Harriet Grove; attended Oxford, briefly, until his expulsion for printing a pamphlet defending atheism; and completed his teenage years by eloping with sixteen-year-old Harriet Westbrook, the daughter of a wealthy merchant. Harriet and Shelley had two children, Ianthe and Charles, the latter born after Shelley had left Harriet to elope with Mary Godwin, the sixteen-year-old child of Mary Wollstonecraft, author of *A Vindication of the Rights of Woman* (1792), and William Godwin, author of *The Inquiry Concerning Political Justice and Its Influence on General Virtue and Happiness* (1793). After Harriet committed suicide by drowning, probably because of her pregnancy with another man's child, Shelley married Mary. The couple lived in England for a while, but left for Italy to protect Shelley's health and to escape the group of friends, including William Godwin, who had come to depend on Shelley for financial support.

In Italy, they settled near Lord Byron, who had fled England for his own personal reasons—a divorce and a child allegedly by his half-sister. Mary and Shelley had two children, Clara and William. When Clara died from an illness exacerbated by the traveling that Shelley forced upon his family in Italy, the love-light seemed to wane in the Shelleys's marriage. The following year, 1819, Shelley's son died, and even greater despondency descended on them. Shelley was also disheartened by his ineffectiveness as a poet—no popularity, no audience, no hope of saving the world through his poetry. In *Adonais*, his eulogy for John Keats, Shelley tempts himself to put the things of this world aside, to die. On July 8, 1822, Shelley and Edward Williams set sail from Leghorn, too late in the afternoon considering their destination and with a storm pending. They drowned in the brief tempest. Several weeks later the two bodies were discovered on separate lonely beaches. In Shelley's pockets were a book of Sophocles and Keats's latest volume of poems, opened as if he had been reading. Byron, Trelawny, Leigh Hunt, and some Italian health officials cremated the bodies, Hellenic style, on the beach. Trelawny claims that Shelley's heart would not burn, or at least did not burn, and that he salvaged it from the ashes. Shelley, who likened the poet to fire and who prominently used the image of releasing one's fate to the stream, thus lived and died the myth of his poetry.

Analysis

Percy Bysshe Shelley mutedly noted in his preface to *Prometheus Unbound* that he had "what a Scotch philosopher terms, 'a passion for reforming the world.'" One might think that this would have endeared his work at least to the reading public left of center and to later readers who value the reforming spirit in humankind. Yet Shelley was almost able to name his readers, they were so few, and today, of the six major poets who dominate the canon of British Romanticism—William Blake, William Wordsworth, Samuel Taylor Coleridge, Byron, Keats, and Shelley—it is still Shelley who remains the least popular. For one reason or another, and though Shelley will always have a cadre of eloquent apologists, dedicated scholars, and brilliant explicators, he is usually out of favor with a significant group of readers. He has been criticized for bad thinking, for bad writing, and for bad living. Devaluations of his thought and poetry have largely been overcome, but this last—especially when made by sensitive feminist readers who find his narcissistic theory of love stupidly, if not heartlessly, destructive to the women in his life—is difficult to refute, if one grants its relevance to his art.

Shelley's theme of self-destructiveness leads to his poetry's most brilliant moments, but perhaps the weakness in Shelley's use of the antitype motif is that it fails to recognize even the possibility that the mate—the woman—exists in her own right, and that her likeness to the fiction of the poet's imagination might not be the best or safest evidence of her worth. In Lord Byron's *Manfred* (1817), the concept of the antitype is also used, but Byron is critical of the theme from the woman's point of view—Manfred has destroyed his lover, Astarte, with this dangerously egotistical love and madly strives to win her forgiveness. Shelley seems incapable of such a critique of his most important theme; therein may lie the weakness in his work. Except in this respect, Shelley was not in the least simpleminded concerning the problem of reforming the world according to his standards. Shelley desired more than the world could ever offer; he knew it, but he could not stop trying to close the gap between the ideal and the real, the vision and the fact. So powerful is his honesty that tension pervades his poetry, idealism playing against skepticism, irony hedging assertion. He ardently believed that man was perfectible, if man would only will it. At its most optimistic, his poetry seeks to arouse the reader's will to strive for perfection; at its most pessimistic, it is the poet's private struggle with the desire to escape through death.

Julian and Maddalo

One might take a poem of balanced opposites as a synecdochic introduction to Shelley's thought and art. *Julian and Maddalo: A Conversation* presents the issues, the imagery that typically embodies them, and the quest to dissolve division in nature, society, and personal life. The conversants in this urbane, sophisticated debate are Julian, a thin disguise for Shelley, and Maddalo, or Lord Byron. Julian, the Preface suggests, is the idealist, "passionately attached to those philosophical notions which assert the power of man over his own mind, and the immense improvements of which, by the extinction of certain moral superstitions, human society may be yet susceptible." Maddalo is the card-carrying cynic, and the tragedy from Julian's point of view is that Maddalo is one of the few who might be capable of changing the world, if he would only will it. It is Maddalo's weakness to be proud; he does not think the world worth the effort. A maniac also enters the poem as a character who was destroyed through unrequited love. Finally, Maddalo's little daughter is the ever-present, romantic image of humankind's potential.

The poem opens with a vision of harmony. Julian and Maddalo have been riding along the Lido of Venice, a waste of a beach, at sundown, and Julian responds to the correspondence he senses between the inner and outer worlds:

> . . . I love all waste
> And solitary places; where we taste
> The pleasure of believing what we see
> Is boundless, as we wish our souls to be:
> And such was this wide ocean, and this shore
> More barren than its billows.

Not much later, Maddalo will offer a constricted image of the soul, but for now, Shelley allows his better half to continue. Disagreeing with earlier Romantic work of Wordsworth and Coleridge, which argued for the sufficiency of man's relationship with nature, Julian/Shelley adds a companion to the landscape experience: "and yet more/ Than all, with a remembered friend I love/ To ride as then I rode." The friends are in perfect accord with each other as well as with nature. As they gallop along the beach, the wind brings the "living spray" into their faces, the blue heavens open, "stripped to their depths," and the waves send forth a "sound like delight . . ./ Harmonizing with solitude," carrying into their hearts "aereal merriment." The personal relationship is as perfect: "the swift thought,/ Winging itself with laughter, lingered not,/ But flew from brain to brain." As they turn homeward, however, division slowly enters the poem, beginning with a discussion on "God, freewill and destiny:/ Of all that earth has been or yet may be." Julian takes the brighter side, Maddalo, the darker. Shelley represents the argument metaphorically as two perceptions of landscape. Julian first offers a perception of the dissolution of the landscape's natural boundaries created by the light of the setting sun; Maddalo then counters with a brilliant image of the constricted soul and the madding passions, the bell of the insane asylum.

Julian first calls attention to the division between East and West, earth and sky. The Alps are a "heaven-sustaining bulwark reared/ Between the East and West"; only "half the sky/ Was roofed with clouds of rich emblazonry"; the sun pauses in a "rent" between the clouds; the hills are separate like a "clump of peaked isles." Then quite dramatically light begins to do its work of transformation:

> . . . as if the Earth and Sea had been
> Dissolved into one lake of fire were seen
> Those mountains towering as from waves of flame
> Around the vaporous sun, from where there came
> The inmost purple spirit of light, and made
> Their very peaks transparent.

This diffusion of water with fire, earth with air, air with fire, and water with earth, completed in the fleeting intensity of the sun's pause, becomes a vision of hope for human reconciliation through love. The sun's light is love and just as it can dissolve the perception of landscape boundaries so can the emotion dissolve boundaries in personal life and society. Nature teaches a lesson; even the city becomes a divine illusion, "Its temples and its palaces did seem/ Like fabrics of enchantment piled to Heaven."

Maddalo, however, is not taken by the vision. He insists on observing the sunset from a "better station." Between them and the sun is now imagined the madhouse, "A windowless, deformed and dreary pile," its bell tolling "In strong and black relief" for the maniacs to begin their evening prayers. Looking at his image of the bell and the asylum, Maddalo interprets:

> And such . . . is our mortality
> And this must be the emblem and the sign
> Of what should be eternal and divine—
> And like that black and dreary bell, the soul,
> Hung in a heaven-illumined tower, must toll
> Our thoughts and our desires to meet below
> Round the rent heart and pray—as madmen do
> For what? they know not,—till the night of death
> As sunset that strange vision, severeth
> Our memory from itself, and us from all
> We sought and yet were baffled!

If Byron literally spoke these lines, they are among the best lines of poetry he ever composed. The soul is no beach stretching to the horizon; it is finite, and dreary, and obfuscating. It provokes the heart with its spirituality to strive for the infinite in complete bewilderment, till death closes the quest. There is nothing eternal and divine; it is simply mortality at odds with itself. In the twilight, the "black bell became invisible" and the enchanted city "huddled in gloom," its ships, towers, palaces—emblems of commerce, church, and government—faded into the absurdity of night.

The following day, Julian argues that

> . . . it is our will
> That . . . enchains us to permitted ill—
> We might be otherwise—we might be all
> We dream of . . .
> Where is the love, beauty and truth we seek
> But in our mind? and if we were not weak
> Should we be less in deed than in desire?

Maddalo counters that such human weakness is incurable, that no matter how strong an argument Julian can make to prove the perfectibility of humankind, empirical evidence and experience will undermine it. Maddalo adduces as evidence the case of a maniac, who was like Julian an idealist but has been destroyed by unrequited love. Their visit to the maniac's cell in the asylum whose bell they had heard the preceding night reveals a man of rent heart, musing disjointedly and pathetically on his suffering. Still in love, he refuses to commit suicide because he does not want his former lover to feel responsible for his death. Julian feels that if he had the opportunity to befriend the man, he might save him, but the strength of Maddalo's argument has been felt. After many years, Julian returns to Maddalo's castle and learns from his grown daughter that the maniac's lover returned and he recovered; then, however, they separated once more. At Julian's entreaty, she reveals the whole story, but out of bitterness toward the world he refuses to disclose the resolution (as Shelley refuses to disclose it to his readers): "the cold world shall not know," concludes the poem. The debate has not resolved the issue. The maniac's recovery, although temporary, indicates that love is in the force that Julian has maintained, *if* one can sustain the will to love. Thus the poem returns to its starting point: Clearly one can will to love, or, at least, act as if one loved, but constancy is the problem, as the maniac's lover indicates.

ALASTOR

The same tensions that animate *Julian and Maddalo* inform Shelley's first major poem, *Alastor*. The poet-persona of *Alastor* begins as a happy youth. He seeks knowledge and truth from philosophy, nature, history, and travel, and experiences moments of high inspiration, as when, standing amidst the ruins of the cradle of civilization, "meaning on his vacant mind/ Flashed like strong inspiration, and he saw/ The thrilling secrets of the birth of time." On his quest he has been cared for by an Arab maiden, who brings food to him from her own plate and watches him dream innocently throughout the night, till to her father's tent she creeps "Wildered, and wan, and panting," but he does not recognize her love for him. Then, one night after leaving her locale, he has "a dream of hopes that never yet/ Had flushed his cheek." He dreams of his antitype, the perfect female of intellect, imagination, and sense to match his own. She speaks in low solemn tones of knowledge, truth, virtue, liberty; she next breathes the "permeating fire" of her pure mind in a song of passionate poetry; then, in the most erotic passage one will find in the Romantic canon, they join in sexual climax. She arises and the dreamer sees

> . . . by the warm light of their own life
> Her glowing limbs beneath the sinuous veil
> Of woven wind, her outspread arms now bare,
> Her dark locks floating in the breath of night,
> Her beamy bending eyes, her parted lips
> Outstretched, and pale, and quivering eagerly.

He receives her, "yielding to the irresistible joy,/ With frantic gesture and short breathless cry," folding his frame in "her dissolving arms." At the moment of climax, "blackness veiled his dizzy eyes, and night/ Involved and swallowed up the vision; sleep,/ Like a dark flood suspended in its course,/ Rolled back its impulse on his vacant brain."

One would wish to sleep forever to have such dreams, for how can such a dream be fulfilled? The world, which was once so beautiful to the poet, now appears vacant when he awakens. Cryptically, the narrator tells us that "The spirit of sweet human love has sent/ A vision to the sleep of him who spurned/ Her choicest gifts." Was the Arab maiden one of those gifts, or was she merely the catalyst of an awakening sexuality? Regardless, he now "eagerly pursues/ Beyond the realms of dream that fleeting shade," knowing that the realm beyond dream is most likely death. He moves madly through society and nature more to burn out than to seek a likeness of the veiled maid. When he tires or seeks infrequent nourishment, an image of the maid's eyes forces him on. In a passage that underscores the narcissism of his quest, the reflection of his own eyes in a fountain where he drinks provokes her shadowy presence.

He moves on, following a stream to its unknown source, for he has dimly perceived an analogue between "What oozy cavern or what wandering cloud" contain its waters and what mysterious source his own thoughts and visions may have. He finally stops in a virginal nook above the perilous mountain landscape and prepares to die. He is "at peace, and faintly smiling" as the crescent moon sets on his life: "His last sight/ Was the great moon," which as it declines finally shows only the tips of its crescent:

> . . . the alternate gasp
> Of his faint respiration scarce did stir
> The stagnate night:—till the minutest ray
> Was quenched, the pulse yet lingered in his heart.
> It paused—it fluttered.

The moon sets, and he dies. Why does his heart pause and flutter? Is he duped by the moon's tips appearing to be eyes, or does he smile faintly because he is aware of the irony? Or does he move from irony to the excitement of belief at the moment before final truth? The reader cannot know, but the poem's narrator finds little hope for the world when "some surpassing Spirit,/ Whose light adorned the world around it" dies an untimely death not with "sobs or groans,/ The passionate tumult of a clinging hope;/ But pale despair and cold tranquillity."

As he moved like a phantom through the landscape, the poet of *Alastor* recognized that nature provided a condition like love for its animate and inanimate beings—swans floating in pairs, "Ivy clasp[ing]/ The fissured stones with its entwining arms"—but that he belonged outside the circle. Shelley could not maintain the romantic myth that, as Coleridge wrote in "This Limetree Bower My Prison," "Nature ne'er deserts the wise and pure," or, as Wordsworth wrote in "Lines Composed a Few Miles Above Tintern Abbey," "In nature and the language of the sense,/ [is] the anchor of my purest thoughts, the nurse,/ The guide, the guardian of my heart, and soul/ Of all my moral being." Shelley did write in his essay "On Love" that one seeks correspondence with nature when one is denied human love; he paraphrased an unknown source to the effect that, if one were in a desert, "he would love some cypress." As is evident in *Julian and Maddalo* and *Alastor*, Shelley preferred human companionship, because there is a force impelling the physical world which is antithetical to love. Shelley called this force Necessity, or physical determinism. *Mont Blanc* provides its principal image.

Mont Blanc

In what becomes a showdown of sorts between mind and matter, imagination and necessity, Shelley beings *Mont Blanc* by recognizing that mind shares with matter a significant feature. The sense impressions that flow through the mind's stream of thought are impelled by a force as mysterious as that which drives the river from its home in the clouds down the mountain's ravine. Is it the same force? Critics have struggled with this problem, for Shelley did not make the matter very clear, or perhaps it is as clear as possible without being reductive of a difficult metaphysical question. On the one hand, Shelley imagines the Power as residing above the world of mutability, "Remote, serene, and inaccessible," but not without profound effect on the world below. The Power's image is the mountain's summit, which none can see but which all can feel in the form of the forces it releases that destroy and preserve, its glaciers and its rivers. Its position is amoral, perfectly nonanthropomorphic. The glaciers wreak their havoc, "The dwelling-place/ Of insects, beasts, and birds" their spoil. "The race of man," too, "flies far in dread; his work and dwelling/ Vanished, like smoke before the tempest's stream." On the other hand, majestic rivers, such as the Arve of Mont Blanc, derive from the same source and are "The breath and blood of distant lands." Can the mind of man be a manifestation of such a power? This is the question to which the poem leads, but just as Shelley offers the answer in the final stanza, he undermines it.

Addressing the mountain he says, "The secret strength of things/ Which governs thought, and to the infinite dome/ of heaven is as a law, inhabits thee!" While thought may be governed by a psychological determinism, Shelley seems to imply a distinction between causally determined thought and the products of imagination—poetry and value. He stresses that "Mont Blanc yet gleams on high," above the vicissitudes of our world, where "In the calm darkness of the moonless nights,/ In the lone glare of day, the snows descend/ Upon that Mountain, none beholds them there," and without fanfare he begins describing, valuing, and symbolizing what he has just indicated none behold:

> Winds contend
> Silently there, and heap the snow with breath
> Rapid and strong, but silently! Its home
> The voiceless lightning in these solitudes
> Keeps innocently, and like vapour broods
> Over the snow.

The winds pile the snow for the coming glacier with the quality of "breath," because, while the glacier will bring death, its next state of being as river will bring life—"The breath and blood of distant lands." Likewise emphasizing the absent force of mind that now interprets and values the cold causality of the mountain's secret summit is the acknowledgment that all of this is happening "Silently . . ./ . . . but silently!" No ears, no sound; no perceiver, no value. The poem concludes: "And what were thou, and earth, and stars, and sea,/ If to the human mind's imaginings/ Silence and solitude were vacancy?"

Something in the human mind renders value, recognizes or makes meaning for this universe, or decides there is no meaning. These are acts of ultimate power; the rest is a "dull round," as the human mind itself may enact when it refuses to transcend the path of association with its power to create, to vision, and to will. Shelley does not make this case as forcefully as it is presented here, however; he concludes with a question, not the strong declarative the reader might wish. The imagining undermines the assertion of "The secret strength of things"; the surmise of the conclusion undermines the imagining. This ambivalence does not derive from some precious sense of caution, but from Shelley's genuine uncertainty.

Prometheus Unbound

Shelley's belief in the power of love was unequivocal, however, and *Prometheus Unbound* reveals on a mythic scale the transformation that will occur when love rather than fear and hatred binds relationships among nations and humankind. *Prometheus Unbound* is a psychological drama that, along with other works of the Romantic period, asserts the power of mind in transforming the world. The French Revolution having failed to rid France of despotism, British writers sought to fulfill by individual transformation the apocalyptic hopes it had aroused. The logic was simple: If the mind and heart of the reader could be changed, the world would be changed. Thus Wordsworth, the major poet of the period, writes at the height of his optimism: "Paradise, and groves/ Elysian, . . ./ . . . why should they be/ A history only of departed things" (Prospectus to *The Recluse*). The hope of the Romantics was not naïve, but rather a variation of an eternal hope to improve the world.

Shelley's promise was that if humanity could just will to love, everything wonderful would follow. Thus, Prometheus, the mythic champion of humankind, chained to a rock in the Indian Caucasus for three thousand sleepless years, finds that he no longer hates the tyrant, Jupiter, and as a consequence the universe swells with the love, the growth, and the energy of springtime.

Ironically, Prometheus's transformation begins, not more than fifty-five lines into the first act, as he dwells on the satisfaction he will feel when Jupiter is dethroned and made to kiss "the blood/ From [Prometheus'] pale feet," which could then trample him, except that he would disdain Jupiter too much to do so. Then he says: "Disdain? Ah no! I pity thee," for the suffering Jupiter will endure at his demise, and his pity leads to grief: "I speak in grief,/ Not exultation, for I hate no more,/ As then, ere misery made me wise." There is a significant relationship between Jupiter's power and Prometheus's hatred, Jupiter's demise and Prometheus's love: Though he has been the hero of humankind, Prometheus has been responsible for the tyranny of the universe, because he empowered Jupiter with his hate—in fact, willed the inflictions of Jupiter upon humankind. When he transcends his hatred to love, Jupiter inevitably falls. It is the dialectic of the master and the slave; the slave's willed obeisance gives the master his power. Prometheus recalls his curse, which began the reign of Jupiter, and the reader begins to understand one half of the dialectic.

On a literal level, perhaps it appears foolish that the sufferer could hold power over the oppressor, as Prometheus claims, but, if one considers the action on the psychological level, where Shelley intended the battle to be fought and won, one can understand that a mind indulging in hatred blights the potential joy of life. At some level, Prometheus understands this, and retracts his curse, yet he must still undergo a test from the furies (perhaps representing his historical consciousness) which brings to his sight the truth of humankind's condition. The Reign of Terror of the French Revolution, the rejection and murder of Christ, the general wave of personal violence and horror, are all summoned to reveal this darkest truth: "those who endure/ Deep wrongs for man, and scorn and chains, but heap/ Thousand-fold torment on themselves and him." The plight of humankind is absurdly tragic: "The good want power, but to weep barren tears./ The powerful goodness want: worse need for them./ The wise want love, and those who love want wisdom;/ And all best things are thus confused to ill."

Prometheus's response to this futility is: "Thy words are like a cloud of winged snakes/ And yet, I pity those they torture not." "Thou pitiest them?" the fury cries: "I speak no more," and vanishes defeated. Prometheus's love has endured. From this moment on, the action of the play moves forward, as if on its own pattern of necessity, to overthrow Jupiter and rejuvenate humankind. As love trickles down through the universe and the society of humankind, there are "thrones . . . kingless," men walking together without fawning or trampling, all "Scepterless, free, uncircumscribed." Though still subject to chance, death, and mutability, ruling over them like slaves, man is free, liberated consciousness, "The King/ Over himself." The "mind-forg'd manacles," to quote William Blake's "London," are sundered. The mind of man is now "an Ocean/ Of clear emotion/ A heaven of serene and mighty motion."

Yet, as wildly joyous and supremely optimistic as *Prometheus Unbound* is, the reader is warned at the close that even this mythic bliss cannot remain unguarded. Should the world fall again into its tyranny, the morality that will reincarnate her beauty, freedom, and joy again must be this:

To suffer woes which Hope thinks infinite;
To forgive wrongs darker than Death or Night;
To defy Power which seems Omnipotent;
To love, and bear; to hope, till Hope creates
From its own wreck the thing it contemplates;
Neither to change nor falter nor repent:
This . . . is to be
Good, great and joyous, beautiful and free;
This is alone Life, Joy, Empire and Victory.

Prometheus Unbound is a difficult reading experience, a highly pitched lyric extended over four acts, without tonal relief, but it is essential reading for the student of Shelley and the Romantic period.

Part of Shelley's vision in *Prometheus Unbound* is that man would be passionate, "yet free from guilt or pain/ Which were, for his will made, or suffered them," and that women would be

. . . gentle, radiant forms
From custom's evil taint exempt and pure;
Speaking the wisdom once they could not think,
Looking emotions once they feared to feel
And changed to all which once they dared not be.

EPIPSYCHIDION

Many might find Shelley a prophet of modern morality, or immorality, depending on point of view, but it is certain that even the most liberal in the nineteenth century could not quite live this ideal, not even Shelley's handpicked women. In *Epipsychidion*, however, he allows himself a pure fantasy of relational perfection that celebrates his discovery, at last, of his antitype. The chief skepticism of the poem is not that he might be excessive in his rapture, but rather that language is not capable of adequately expressing his rapture, its object being perfection. The poem opens with a rhapsodic invocation without parallel in English literature, and struggles throughout with its diction to aggregate images and symbols that might invoke a rhetoric of infinity. Shelley has found the veiled maid of *Alastor:* "I never thought before my death to see/ Youth's vision thus made perfect. Emily,/ I love thee; . . . Ah me!/ I am not thine: I am a part of *thee*."

This perfect woman was Teresa Viviani, the teenage daughter of the governor of Pisa, who had confined her in a nunnery. The Shelleys became interested in her plight and this lovely victim of paternal tyranny inflamed Shelley's soul. He imagines how perfect it would be if Emily/Teresa could join him and Mary in a *ménage à trois*, for he has never been one of the "great sect,/ Whose doctrine is, that each one should select/ Out of the crowd a mistress or a friend,/ And all the rest, though fair and wise, commend/ To cold oblivion," though the moral code might demand such behavior. "True Love in this differs from gold and clay,/ That to divide is not to take away." Thus, if Mary would be the Moon—"The cold chaste Moon . . ./ Who makes all beautiful on which she smiles,/ . . ./ And warms not but illumines"—Emily would be the Sun and together they would form those spheres of influence "who rule this passive Earth,/ This world of live, this *me*." Finally, however, he and Emily both fly out of orbit, leaving the moon behind, to dwell in a paradisal isle.

Language cannot deal with the infinite limits of this vision: "The winged words on which my soul would pierce/ Into the height of love's rare Universe,/ Are chains of lead around its flight of fire.—/ I pant, I sink, I tremble, I expire!" Sympathetic readers of Shelley wince at these moments; his detractors triumph. Even Shelley was a bit embarrassed by the emotion of this poem, because the woman it celebrated finally married a boor. Shelley wrote to John Gisborne: "The 'Epipsychidion' I cannot look at." Mary Shelley also had a difficult time looking at it; *Epipsychidion* is the only poem in her excellent edition of Shelley's poems on which she does not comment.

"Hymn to Intellectual Beauty"

Shelley often wore his heart on his sleeve for daws to peck at, to paraphrase William Shakespeare's Iago, especially in the great series of poems representing himself as the *poète maudit*, the suffering poet vainly striving to save those who reject him. "Hymn to Intellectual Beauty," "Ode to the West Wind," and *Adonais* constitute the constellation and farthest reaches of this personal myth. Of course there is a great deal of vanity involved. One perceives that the world is not perfect; one attempts to save it and fails, thereby proving that the world really is bad, even worse than one thought. One then strives harder, becoming more assured that one is needed and that one's work is essential, rejection feeding vanity in a wicked, self-defeating cycle. Throughout, one retains one's heroic self-image.

In "Hymn to Intellectual Beauty," Shelley describes the dynamics of his dedication to poetry. While on a youthful search for truth, in much the manner of the poet of *Alastor*, he calls on the "poisonous names with which our youth is fed," God, ghosts and heaven, without success; he sees nothing, he hears nothing that responds to his Metaphysical anxieties in a direct way. He experiences something, however, that profoundly moves him. As he muses deeply "on the lot/ Of life" within the context of nature's springtime regeneration, "Sudden, thy shadow fell on me;/ I shrieked, and clasped my hands in ecstasy." The shadow is that of the spirit of beauty, an inexpressible something that transiently brings value to life—life's only value—by evoking in the receiver, its guest, a pulse of spiritual joy. If it could be a permanent experience, "Man were immortal, and omnipotent." The poet says that his life has been dedicated to creating a medium for evoking this spiritual condition. He vows that he will dedicate his "powers/ To thee and thine—have I not kept the vow?" he asks the spirit. His hope has been that if others could be given the experience of spiritual ecstasy, the world would be reborn. The time he has spent in reading, thinking, writing—those hours know, he says, that joy never

> . . . illumed my brow
> Unlinked with hope that thou wouldst free
> This world from its dark slavery,
> That thou—O awful Loveliness,
> Wouldst give whate'er these words cannot express.

In seeking to suggest this evanescent condition, Shelley creates several of the most alluring similes in English, such as, in the fourth stanza: "Thou—that to human thought art nourishment,/ Like darkness to a dying flame!" As the mind is a fading coal, so the darkness intensified makes thought appear brighter, thereby nourishing its waning condition so that it does not appear to be waning at all. The loveliness of verse makes the mind seem as full of beauty and intensity as the moment of inspiration had promised. The poem's opening lines, however, are the ultimate of Shelleyan perfection: "The awful shadow of some unseen Power/ Floats though unseen amongst us!" It is "Like clouds in starlight widely spread,—/ Like memory of music fled,—/ Like aught that for its grace may be/ Dear, and yet dearer for its mystery." These lines are Shelley in his power, for no other poet has so effectively failed to express the inexpressible and thereby succeeded in his attempt to evoke it. While Shelley was curiously winning the battle of expression, however, he was losing the war.

"Ode to the West Wind"

Unlike the modern age, which conceded, in the words of W. H. Auden, that "poetry makes nothing happen," the Romantic and Victorian periods permitted their artists to believe that they could and ought to be effectual. Several seemed to be: Wordsworth, Charles Dickens, Alfred, Lord Tennyson, and Robert Browning had enormous moral influence. Shelley did not; in fact, Matthew Arnold, the great social and literary critic of Victorian England, likened Shelley to an "ineffectual angel, beating in the void his luminous wings in vain." In 1819, at the age of twenty-seven, Shelley wrote his most perfect poem on his ineffectuality. "Ode to the West Wind" is a prayer for power to further the vision of *Prometheus Unbound* in nineteenth century England and Europe, by a poet who has been battered with failure.

In its five terza rima sonnet stanzas, which describe the autumn of earth, sky, sea, and poet—the elements of earth, air, water, and fire—Shelley's impassioned ode takes the literal cycle of the seasons through metaphorical transformations to approach an answer to the question: "If rebirth happens in nature, can it happen in society, with my verse, like the west wind, as the catalyst of the transition from near death to new life?" The first and last stanzas are illustrative of the metaphorical union the poet seeks with the regenerative wind. Stanza one presents the west wind in its dual function of destroying and preserving, driving dead leaves "like ghosts from an enchanter fleeing," and blowing seeds to "their dark wintry bed" where they will "lie cold and low,/ Each like a corpse within its grave, until/ [the wind of spring] shall blow/ Her clarion o'er the dreaming earth" to awaken the seeds to life. Of course, the dead leaves have the function of preserving the seed beds.

In the final stanza, the poet prays that his "dead thoughts" might be driven "over the universe/ Like withered leaves to quicken a new birth!" His seeds are his words, and because he is the equivalent of fire, his words are likened to ashes and sparks—some merely functional, some inspirational—that are now dormant in the waning hearth that is his life. Thus, if his verse could be sufficiently empowered by spirit, like a wind, he might produce a conflagration through the blowing about of ashes and sparks. As the spring of stanza one had her clarion, his verse will be "to unawakened Earth/ The trumpet of a prophecy." "O Wind," he closes, "If Winter comes, can Spring be far behind?" Clearly, if those leaves of stanza one—"Yellow, and black, and pale, and hectic red,/ Pestilence-stricken multitudes"—which have been accurately interpreted as the suffering races of humankind, and those leaves of stanza five—the poet's "dead thoughts"—can both be set afire by the spark of the poet's verse, both may rise from the ashes to new life. The final question, however, is threatening to the dream, for though it is certain that spring follows winter in nature, it is not at all certain that if total spiritual darkness covers humankind, a springtime of recovery will follow.

In stanza four of "Ode to the West Wind," Shelley represents himself as praying to the wind "in my sore need": "Oh! lift me as a wave, a leaf, a cloud!/ I fall upon the thorns of life! I bleed!/ A heavy weight of hours has chained and bowed/ One too like thee: tameless, and swift, and proud." He finally shed the weight of hours to join, not the wind, for that is to be bound still in the world of process, change, and dying hopes, but a poet of his generation who preceded him into the realm "where the eternal are." His elegy for John Keats, *Adonais*, signaled the final shift of his quest from social and personal visions of resurrected worlds and discovered antitypes to transcendence of human life and care.

Adonais

Shelley believed that Keats had been mortally wounded by a scurrilous review of his early work, *Endymion* (1818). "The savage criticism," he says in his Preface to *Adonais*, "produced the most violent effect on his susceptible mind; the agitation thus originated ended in the rupture of a blood-vessel in the lungs; a rapid consumption ensued, and the succeeding acknowledgments . . . of the true greatness of his powers, were ineffectual to heal the wound thus wantonly inflicted." This is not casebook medicine, but it does say something about the doctor who provides such an empathic diagnosis. Shelley self-consciously identified with Keats's early rejection and sought as well to identify with his early death.

Through the first thirty-seven stanzas of the poem, Shelley's narrator mourns Adonais's untimely death, culminating with the fancy of Shelley's image visiting the tomb in homage to a dead fellow-poet. The group of mourning poets stands aside to smile "through their tears" at this maudlin creature "Who in another's fate now wept his own." The muse, Urania, among the mourners for one of her most gifted, asks him his name; his response is to make "bare his branded and ensanguined brow,/ Which was like Cain's or Christ's." Then, in a moment of intense self-consciousness, Shelley disrupts this indulgent self-projection to criticize with truth—"Oh! that it should be so!" He is no important, mythical sufferer; though it has been his dream to be one, the comparison will not hold. Shortly, the poem moves to the second phase of its development, the realization that the living must not mourn for Adonais, who has "awakened from the dream of life," but for themselves: "*We* decay/ Like corpses in a charnel; fear and grief/ Convulse us and consume us day by day,/ And cold hopes swarm like worms within our living clay."

The second movement concludes with a pivotal question: "What Adonais is, why fear we to become?" The poem's third movement, stanzas 52-55, becomes darkly suicidal, but triumphant in its grasping of a new direction, a new vision. Life is imaged as a "dome of many-coloured glass" which "Stains the white radiance of Eternity,/ Until Death tramples it to fragments." Beyond Life is the Platonic "One," the blinding light of truth which humankind knows only from its shadows manifested in material form. "Die," the poet challenges, "If thou wouldst be with that which thou dost seek!" The beauties of natural, human, and aesthetic forms are "weak/ The glory they transfuse with fitting truth to speak." The challenge then becomes personalized as the poet addresses his heart, the image of his mortality and emotional life: "Why linger, why turn back, why shrink, my Heart?" Its hopes are gone, its love is gone, "what still is dear/ Attracts to crush, repels to make thee wither." The sky smiles, the wind whispers the invitation of Adonais: "oh, hasten thither,/ No more let Life divide what Death can join together." He feels the source of the fire he has represented as a poet, beaming, "Consuming the last clouds of cold mortality." Finally, the poem's concluding stanza aggregates the principal imagery of Shelley's major poetry to illustrate that throughout his work an undercurrent has been moving to this moment of poetic self-annihilation: The West Wind descends to blow; as in *Alastor*, the "spirit's bark is driven,/ . . . far from the trembling throng/ Whose sails were never to the tempest given"; the earth and skies, in contrast with the vision of *Julian and Maddalo*, are "riven" to accept the poet, rather than fused to involve him with a romantic vision of earth; he is now "borne darkly, fearfully, afar:/ Whilst burning through the inmost veil of Heaven,/ The soul of Adonais, like a star,/ Beacons from the abode where the Eternal are." The vision was shortly to descend to fact with Shelley's death by drowning.

Shelley admitted to a "passion for reforming the world." He sought an aesthetic medium that would inspire the will of man to close the gap between vision and reality. Shelley's art and thought are unique in the extremes that they bring to English literature; indeed, their fragile loveliness represents the hope and despondency possible only in an age that fervently believed in the infinite potential of man. He was a child of his age, and succeeding generations and imaginations will always need to be challenged by his visions.

Other major works

Long fiction: *Zastrozzi: A Romance*, 1810; *St. Irvyne: Or, The Rosicrucian*, 1810.

Nonfiction: *The Necessity of Atheism*, 1811 (with Thomas Jefferson Hogg); *An Address to the Irish People*, 1812; *Declaration of Rights*, 1812; *A Letter to Lord Ellenborough*, 1812; *Proposals for an Association of . . . Philanthropists*, 1812; *A Refutation of Deism, in a Dialogue*, 1814; *History of a Six Weeks' Tour Through a Part of France, Switzerland, Germany, and Holland*, 1817 (with Mary Shelley); *A Proposal for Putting Reform to the Vote Throughout the Kingdom*, 1817; *An Address to the People on the Death of the Princess Charlotte*, 1817?; *Essays, Letters from Abroad, Translations, and Fragments*, 1840; *A Defence of Poetry*, 1840; *Shelley Memorials*, 1859; *Shelley's Prose in the Bodleian Manuscripts*, 1910;

Note Books of Shelley, 1911; *A Philosophical View of Reform*, 1920; *The Letters of Percy Bysshe Shelley*, 1964 (2 volumes; Frederick L. Jones, editor).

TRANSLATIONS: *The Cyclops*, 1824 (of Euripides' play); *Ion*, 1840 (of Plato's dialogue); "The Banquet Translated from Plato," 1931 (of Plato's dialogue *Symposium*).

MISCELLANEOUS: *The Complete Works of Percy Bysshe Shelley*, 1926-1930 (10 volumes; Roger Ingpen and Walter E. Peck, editors); *Shelley's Poetry and Prose: Authoritative Texts and Criticism*, 1977 (Donald H. Reiman and Sharon B. Powers, editors).

BIBLIOGRAPHY

Bloom, Harold. ed. *Percy Bysshe Shelley.* New York: Chelsea House, 1985. An excellent selection of some of the most important works on Shelley published since 1950. Bloom's introduction, an overview of Shelley's poetry, is highly recommended. Of the ten other essays, the most useful for the student are probably "Scepticism and Platonism," by C. E. Pulos, the essays on *Prometheus Unbound*, by Frederick A. Pottle, and *Adonais*, by Jean Hall, "Orpheus and the West Wind" (on Shelley's esotericism), by James Rieger, and "Shelley's Last Lyrics," by William Keach. Essays by Leslie Brisman, Paul de Man, and Paul Fry are suitable only for advanced students.

Cameron, Kenneth Neill. *Shelley: The Golden Years*. Cambridge, Mass.: Harvard University Press, 1974. This major, lengthy work of biography and criticism covers the later period of Shelley's life, from 1814 to 1822, when all of his great poetry was written. Cameron examines Shelley's prose works and gives crystal-clear readings of all the major poems. He views Shelley's work in a historical context, and this acts as a necessary counterweight to Earl R. Wasserman's philosophical readings.

Everest, Kelvin, ed. *Percy Bysshe Shelley: Bicentenary Essays*. Cambridge, England: D. S. Brewer, 1992. A collection of biographical and critical essays on the life and works of Shelley. Includes bibliographical references.

Höhne, Horst. *In Pursuit of Love: The Short and Troublesome Life and Work of Percy Bysshe Shelley.* New York: Peter Lang, 2000. A biography of Shelley offering insights into his life and work. Includes bibliographical references and index.

Holmes, Richard. *Shelley: The Pursuit*. London: Weidenfeld & Nicolson, 1974. Reprint. London: Quartet Books, 1976. By far the liveliest and most readable of Shelley's biographies. Holmes's Shelley is not the ethereal, Ariel-like creature of Romantic tradition, but a more human, if not always so likable, figure. Some reviewers objected to what they felt was a too sensational treatment of some of the controversial episodes in Shelley's life, and there was general agreement that Holmes's discussions of the poetry lacked balanced critical judgment.

Pulos, C. E. *The Deep Truth: A Study of Shelley's Scepticism*. Lincoln: University of Nebraska Press, 1954. This brief volume can still be recommended as one of the best introductions to Shelley's philosophical thought. Pulos reads Shelley in the light of the skeptical tradition, and this acts as a corrective to studies which may have overemphasized Shelley's Platonism. Written when it was still necessary to rescue Shelley from charges of incoherence, Pulos shows that apparent inconsistencies in Shelley's thought can be attributed to his refusal to be dogmatic and to his attempt to balance idealism and empiricism.

Rogers, Neville. *Shelley at Work: A Critical Inquiry.* 1956. 2d ed. Oxford, England: Clarendon Press, 1967. Much of this volume is based on an examination of Shelley's notebooks. Rogers traces the evolution from drafts to finished poem, which is particularly useful for the "Ode to the West Wind" and "To a Skylark." Rogers views Shelley as a Platonic thinker, and this is probably the best exposition of this aspect of Shelley's work. This approach is no longer very fashionable (it is not represented in Harold Bloom's anthology), but it needs to be taken seriously.

Sperry, Stuart M. *Shelley's Major Verse: The Narrative and Dramatic Poetry.* Cambridge, Mass.: Harvard University Press, 1988. This excellent study of *Queen Mab*, *Alastor*, *The Revolt of Islam*, *Prometheus Unbound*, *The Cenci*, *The Witch of Atlas*, *Epipsychidion*, and *The Triumph of Life* attempts to synthesize philosophical, psychological, and biographical approaches to Shelley. Traces the source of Shelley's poetic impulses to his emotional experiences as a child—of the power of love, largely—but this psychoanalytic approach is never jargon-ridden and Sperry is too good a scholar not to vary his approach when the poem demands it.

Wasserman, Earl R. *Shelley: A Critical Reading*. Baltimore: The Johns Hopkins University Press, 1971. Wasserman's massive, detailed readings of virtually all Shelley's major poems ("To a Skylark," *The Witch of Atlas*, and *The Triumph of Life* are omitted) have been extremely influential. Wasserman emphasizes Shelley's metaphysical skepticism and discusses his conceptions of existence, selfhood, reality, causation, and their relation to transcendence. Some of the readings are very dense and may be intimidating for the beginning student, but no serious student of Shelley can ignore them.

Wheatley, Kim. *Shelley and His Readers: Beyond Paranoid Politics*. Columbia: University of Missouri Press, 1999. Examines Shelley's reception in major British periodicals and the poet's increasingly idealistic passion for reforming the world.

Richard E. Matlak;
bibliography updated by the editors

Enid Shomer

Born: Washington, D.C.; February 2, 1944

Principal poetry

The Startle Effect, 1983
Florida Postcards, 1987
Stalking the Florida Panther, 1987
This Close to the Earth, 1992
Black Drum, 1997
Stars at Noon: Poems from the Life of Jacqueline Cochran, 2001

Other literary forms

Enid Shomer has also published award-winning fiction, including the short story collection *Imaginary Men* (1993). She has also provided interviews and written nonfiction essays for a variety of journals. A dance interpretation of her poem series "Pope Joan," choreographed by Mark Taylor and with music by Anne LeBaron, was presented in Pittsburgh in 2000.

Achievements

Enid Shomer has received numerous prestigious grants, prizes, and awards in both her genres, poetry and fiction, beginning with the Eve of St. Agnes Prize awarded by Negative Capability in 1985 for "Women Bathing at Bergen-Belsen." Recognition for her poetry has been wide. She has been granted Artist Fellowships by the state of Florida in 1985, 1991, and 1996. She won the Washington Prize in Poetry in 1986, for "Stalking the Florida Panther"; the Cincinnati Poetry Review prize in 1986, for best poem series; the Jubilee Press Prize in 1986, for her collection *Florida Postcards*; the Word Works Washington Book Prize in 1987, for *Stalking the Florida Panther*; and the Apalachee Quarterly long poem prize in 1989, for "Datelines: Jacqueline Cochran at War's End." In 1989 and again in 1996, she received National Endowment for the Arts Poetry fellowships, and in 1990, the Celia B. Wagner Award, given by the Poetry Society of America. In 1992 she received the Randall Jarrell Poetry Prize for "My Friend Who Sings Before Breakfast." She is also a recipient of the Wildwood Poetry Prize and the Eunice Tietjens Memorial Prize in Poetry, and her work has been included in many anthologies, including *Best American Poetry, 1996*. She has also won major awards for her fiction. Shomer is one of the ablest practitioners of intellectually complex but emotionally accessible poetry.

Biography

Enid Shomer, whose surname is pronounced shoh-MER, was born on February 2, 1944, in Washington, D.C., the daughter of Philip and Minnie Steine; her father was a house painter and her mother, a homemaker. She frequently wrote poetry while growing up in Washington, and after showing great promise in high school she attended Wellesley College, from which she was graduated in 1965, Phi Beta Kappa. Her major in college was sociology/anthropology, as she did not find herself in sympathy with current practices of literary analysis. She followed this degree with a master of arts degree in American studies from the University of Miami. She married, had two children, and then after twenty-five years of marriage, divorced.

Shomer's career has been in both teaching and writing. She has taught in writing programs throughout the country; her teaching experience includes posts at Florida State University, the Antioch Writers' Workshop, and Ohio State University, among institutions. Scenes of Florida have particularly nourished her poetry from the outset; she used to rent a cottage at Cedar Keys where the beach, sea, and birds could invade her unconscious and resurface in the many sea images that form the basis of many of her poems. She spends part of her time in New York and part in Arkansas, where she teaches creative writing in the University of Arkansas master of fine arts program as Distinguished Visiting Writer each spring semester.

Analysis

Enid Shomer's poetry avoids the extremes of contemporary schools. Her work is layered and provocative, but it is accessible to all those who read literature, not just other poets trained in the same manner. Its many themes and subjects tend to coalesce around investigation of the mind-body problem from philosophical, physical, and feminist perspectives. The result is a physical metaphysics, a peace that comes from acceptance of the world matter, but matter shot through with spirit.

Her style is refreshingly various; she uses forms flexibly as well as blank verse that includes nonmetrical devices to center the poem and suggest form. Each carefully crafted poem is fully complete; her poems do not require others to explicate them. Their cumulative effect is, however, something beyond the sum of the individual poems, because her rhythms and characteristic metaphors engrave themselves deeper with repetition. She is particularly effective with long poems or sequences; her later books give these longer works increasing prominence. *This Close to the Earth* features "Pope Joan," *Black Drum* provides "From the Notebooks of Gustave Klimt," and *Stars at Noon* is devoted entirely to the life of Jacqueline Cochran, a pioneer woman aviator who has been virtually forgotten by the public. In each of Shomer's poems or sequences, a major personality is developed through the poem in such a way as to provide a vital reinterpretation of the subject's life and work. The trajectory of Shomer's work has taken her away from the vivid regional poems of *Florida Postcards* and *This Close to the Earth* to a wider exploration of womanhood and its capabilities and constraints.

This Close to the Earth

This Close to the Earth is a series of intensely physical poems with a spiritual dimension; the feminism of these poems is layered and subtle. The book has three parts, the first containing passionate poems of love, the second containing a long poem or sequence, and the third composed of poems with an elegiac tone. Perhaps the most exciting part of the book is the middle section, the sequence "Pope Joan," which is based on the legend of the ninth century woman who lived disguised as a man, became pope in the ninth century, and was stoned to death after giving birth in a papal procession. With the background of a fabled medieval figure, the body-mind issues are thrown into relief. The legendary rebel comes alive in the specifics of her preoccupations. The poems run the gamut of form, including a sonnet and a sestina as well as other formal and free-verse forms, and the poems catch the nature of a conflicted, passionate soul, comparing the life allowed her with the life she desires. "Sestina of Visions" compares her life with the nuns':

> O nuns,
> my sisters, do you love the fiery sky or must you blacken
> the lilies with faith and lay over everything a chaste
>
> gray pall? At midnight, a demon chased
> me with a copper comb to flay my flesh to ribbons.

The sequence celebrates the female courage expressed through the story of Pope Joan, evoking the extreme constraints that have been placed on women.

The shorter poems, also, often use particular instances to speak of female vulnerability and courage. An excellent example, which sparkles with humor despite its serious point, is "Learning CPR," a skilled sestina about a group of young people who are using "dummies, all named Annie" to learn the lifesaving moves of the CPR system. The group goes through the motions, during which the dummies become for them real people. "Annie! Annie! our small/ voices cry from all corners, tightening the springs/ in our thighs. We slap her, lightly, solely/ because it's required." As they work on the dummies, they recognize their own fragility; they are saving each other and themselves. In their vulnerability is their strength. The book's title comes from a line in another powerful poem, "Among the Cows," in which the woman speaker is told to "breathe with the Holsteins/ as a form of meditation" and finds this exercise therapeutic, a way of getting in touch with the natural verve of earth: "I want to believe I could live/ this close to the earth, could move with/ a languor so resolute it/ passes for will. . . ." The book provides satisfying explorations of the groundings of women's power.

Black Drum

The collection *Black Drum* explores the body-soul split in formal and free-verse poems, often with titles related to the ethereal and spiritual while the poems themselves are rooted to the earth. The poems accept the needs and desires of the body while longing for the spiritual satisfactions that would provide completion. The first of the collection's three sections consists mostly of family poems, on the death of a father with whom a difficult relationship is implied and the forgiveness of this father, and on the approach of death to a mother who seems never to have had the strength to resist life's obstructions. The second section contains mostly poems about art, poems that vividly re-create the works they describe at the same time that they both historicize and reinterpret them, reading them into the lives of both poet and reader. These poems often juxtapose the holy and the daily in such a way that the two blend into each other.

The sequence "Notes from the Sketchbook of Gustav Klimt," for example, brings the artist and his work to the reader with a vibrancy that is close to physical. "Country Garden with Crucifix" is one of the paintings described, highlighting the juxtaposition of the holy and the daily as the ethereal and spiritual are superimposed upon and blended with the natural world until the two are nearly indistinguishable. Christ on the Crucifix is described as a "pale/ stalk among the massed, brilliant vines and thick pigments," while the Virgin Mary, a face gazing out from her blue garments, "pooled beneath him like his shadow." Both holy figures are submerged in the natural scene, omnipresent yet grounded in the mundane:

> The pair hung there for decades,
> touched up, I'm told, with leftover
> housepaint, his stigmata one year
> barn-red, the next, scabbed over
> with chair-rail brown.

In Shomer's work part of the appeal comes from these ironies of her juxtapositions: human and holy, flesh and soul, casual and formal, vulnerability and power. Always that juxtoposition creates a paradox: power in vulnerability, soul in flesh, and often vice versa.

Stars at Noon: Poems from the Life of Jacqueline Cochran

Stars at Noon: Poems from the Life of Jacqueline Cochran is a poem series describing the life of an early aviator whose rise from obscurity to fame was ironically followed by her disappearance from the public eye; everyone remembers Amelia Earhart, but the name of Jacqueline Cochran, who did many of the same things as Earhart and more, has been forgotten. This collection introduces Cochran to a new readership, and the poems provide the satisfactions of several genres: poetry, autobiography, biography, and fiction. Although some of Shomer's characteristic forms are represented here, free verse is more common. The poems illuminate significant events in Cochran's life, including her abandonment as a baby, adoption, an impoverished childhood, her running away and taking care of herself independently while still a child, her success at being trained as an aviator, her breaking of all speed records, and her marriage, friendship with Amelia Earhart, retirement, and death.

The previously almost unchronicled life is made vital through poems that get under the skin of the aviator and give glimpses of those who played a major part in her life, as well as of the time period that made such achievements for a woman nearly impossible. Unlike many attempts to flesh out history, this collection has an immediacy that makes Cochran live: Poet Maxine Kumin commented:

> This book not only makes a major contribution to the annals of women and the turbulent era Cochran lived in, but because it is immensely readable, it may break the sound barrier between historical facts and passionate feelings.

David Wojahn called it "a work of visionary hagiography." Cochran, who flew in competitions until she was sixty, ran for Congress, and also was a cosmetician with her own company, is shown in this book as both a passionate and a sensible woman, with her quirks and feelings of inadequacy. In the "Ascent" portion of "The World Goes Black," a poem describing the flight in 1953 in which the pilot attained Mach 1 speed, she thanks God for her hands, which in feminine situations had not served her well. Shomer, focusing on the hands, reveals the female concerns of her subject as she contemplates how her hands have undermined her femininity at the same time that they symbolize her success in a world of men:

> Big fidgety anchors . . .
>
> . . . .
>
> I've tried dark gloves so women
>
> wouldn't notice. It made things
> worse when I took them off.
> In WASP dress white gloves,
> clown hands waved.
>
> They should see my feet.

"Afterword" is an acute discussion, in poems, of the relationship between the biographer and her subject, illuminating the process of researching a poem and showing the pull of the past on the present. Shomer describes listening to Cochran's voice "recorded/ fifty years ago/ on red wax cylinders" and how it was, listening to it:

> Stored like honey in a hive, now her voice
> flows again, deep
>
> amber and smoky. A sergeant's bark for the times
> when a voice soft as a skein
>
> of wool would be ignored.

It is the poet's own voice, then, concluding the collection, showing how the voice of the dead Cochran was able to speak to the poet, through her:

> Sometimes her voice carries me past all
> the wartime dying, as a mother
>
> carries a sleeping child, not so much
> to keep the child from waking
>
> as to be there when she wakes.

The book *Stars at Noon* has an unusually attractive and appropriate format, which includes photographs of Cochran throughout her life, including an especially winsome one of her sitting on a diving board at her home with Amelia Earhart. Other illustrations include a rosette of photographs of Cochran in her various roles and varied uniforms, surrounding a cameo of a sad child, photographs of planes in the outer rim. The photographs and plane icons give the layout an energy that is reinforced by the energy of the poems and of their subject.

Shomer's longer poems and sequences, especially *Stars at Noon*, weave history with the present and unite author, reader, and subject. They marry narrative and lyric to produce a lucent hymn to human persistence.

OTHER LITERARY FORMS

NONFICTION: *Imaginary Men*, 1993.

BILBLIOGRAPHY

Mason, David. "Subdividing Parnassus." *The Hudson Review* 51, no. 1 (Spring, 1998): 265-275. Discusses Shomer's work in connection with that of other contemporary poets to define trends and directions.

Yezzi, David. "Black Drum." *Poetry*, 171, no. 5 (1998): 291-293. This analytical review defines some of Shomer's themes.

Janet McCann

JANE SHORE

Born: Newark, New Jersey; March 10, 1947

PRINCIPAL POETRY

Lying Down in the Olive Press, 1969 (chapbook)
Eye-Level, 1977
The Minute Hand, 1987

Music Minus One: Poems, 1996
Happy Family: Poems, 1999

Other literary forms

As a coeditor for *Ploughshares* magazine, Jane Shore has written reviews and commentary in several issues, bringing her keen perception and careful analysis to the articles and poems in each volume. Her discussion of Elizabeth Bishop's use of metaphors in the Spring, 1979, issue is typical: "In a world full of mangoes, hurricanes, armchairs and muskrats, how does a poet choose just two things for an original and truthful comparison?" She examines several of Bishop's poems from the perspective of another poet, addressing mechanics and depth of insight.

Achievements

Jane Shore was noted and praised for her poetic ability upon the appearance of her first book of poetry in 1977: *Eye-Level* won the 1977 Juniper Prize. *The Minute Hand* was a Lamont Poetry Selection in 1986 (reviewed prior to publication), awarded by the Academy of American Poets, and *Music Minus One* was a 1996 National Book Critics Circle Award finalist. Shore was further honored with two National Endowment for the Arts (NEA) grants and a variety of university fellowships. She accepted a fellowship from the John Simon Guggenheim Foundation and was a fellow in poetry at the Mary Ingraham Bunting Institute (formerly the Radcliffe Institute for Independent Study), a Briggs-Copeland Lecturer at Harvard University, an Alfred Hodder Fellow at Princeton University, a Goodyear Fellow at the Foxcroft School in Middleburg, Virginia, a visiting distinguished poet at the University of Hawaii, and a Jenny McKean Moore Writer in Washington at George Washington University in Washington, D.C.

Biography

Jane Shore was born in New Jersey, the daughter of George and Essie Shore. She grew up above her parents' clothing store in 1950's New Jersey among the Jewish-owned shops along the Newark city streets. Shore's father, George, who had creative yearnings, played clarinet and saxophone with big bands of the 1930's and 1940's. Beginning in 1965, Shore attended Goddard College. It was during her university years that she discovered her intense interest in poetry and formed her lifelong friendship with fellow poets Barry and Lorrie Goldensohn. Although the 1960's was not an era to encourage precision of meaning or dedication to craft, and although Goddard College was noted by faculty members as a place of sexual and drug experimentation, Shore worked to create deeper meaning and careful structure as well as intensity of emotion in her poetry.

After graduating from Goddard with a bachelor's degree in 1969, Shore moved from Vermont to the Iowa Writers' Workshop. She received her master of fine arts degree in 1971 from the University of Iowa, finishing her education in the study and creation of poetry. Flourishing as a poet in the academic world, Shore earned a Briggs Copeland Lectureship at Harvard, where she would meet Elizabeth Bishop. The elder poet guided Shore, strengthening her originality of expression and encouraging her to continue exploring her personal history through the vehicle of her poetry. Like Bishop, Jane Shore made her later poems dramatic narratives which, memory-laden, dragged the lessons of the past into a meditative present. After Harvard, Shore went on to New York, Princeton, and Washington, D.C., through Guggenheim, Hodder, and NEA fellowships, and produced three books of poetry. During the 1980's she lived in Manhattan, teaching at such diverse places as Sarah Lawrence College, the 92d Street YMCA, and Tufts University.

Shore's literary career had roots in both publishing and education. Her poems were published in numerous magazines, including *Poetry* (for which she received the Bess Hokin Award), *The New Republic*, *Ploughshares*, and *The Yale Review*. She was a guest editor for *Ploughshares* in 1977, 1984, and 1997 and taught at a wide variety of universities. The recipient of two grants for literature from the National Endowment for the Arts, Shore was one of NEA's grants panelists for literature for the year 2001.

Analysis

In all of Jane Shore's poetry, two themes dominate: family and history. The first, family, is the most significant in that scenes of family members and family interactions serve as the subject for the vast majority of her poems. Her parents, cousins, aunts, and uncles play a pivotal role in all of her volumes in shaping the young Shore and guiding her toward universal truths. The second theme, that of history, is the vehicle by which Shore makes comparisons between her contemporary existence and her memories of the past, implying that her perception of the former necessitates and shapes her continuing hold on the latter. The two themes, when intertwined, form a view of life with which any reader can connect: that it is how one perceives the past, rather than the past in and of itself, that forms the largest part of one's self-awareness. Current perceptions shape memories, which define who we are as individuals.

Lying Down in the Olive Press

George Starbuck, introducing her in *Lying Down in the Olive Press*, the chapbook she published at twenty-one, said:

> Jane Shore knows us, gets us, talks of us or hears us talk of ourselves, with a faultless, unsettling, illuminating *interest*. And of herself . . . [I]t's a good voice and good judgment. Not only, not even mainly, in the comic vignettes, there's the *joy* of precise observation.

It seems obvious in retrospect that Shore's powers of observation are exactly what always drove her to create such vivid images of her personal history. The people inhabiting even her earliest poems are fascinating in their variety, from the soldier poet Archilochus, halted in an archaic olive grove, to Shore's vision of herself in the future, wheeling a shopping cart in some suburban community. Shore's characters bring an essential liveliness to verse which celebrates the diversity of human experience.

While *Lying Down in the Olive Press* is a small book of verse that represents only the embryonic form of Shore's vision, it nevertheless serves to demonstrate the compelling nature of her poetic gift. Even at the age of twenty-one, Shore felt that her family and her experiences somehow transcended the level of the individual and could be reshaped to give a reader, any reader, a sense of his or her own history's importance.

Eye-Level

Shore's second volume of poetry, *Eye-Level*, was published by the University of Massachusetts Press as the winner of the Juniper Prize in 1977. The book is concerned largely with miracles of human life: transformations, alterations, and adaptation. One poem describes the adaptation of the blind albino fish to the underground cavern that is its native habitat. Another poem creates a miracle of "resurrection," transforming a corpse into a living, breathing human being, as her father's movie camera stops and rewinds a trapeze artist's fatal fall. A third poem sends a chained and restrained Harry Houdini, the magician, underwater to escape his bonds. Each of these images allows the body to change and, sometimes miraculously, overcome its restrictions. Shore's work is deep and reflective but still more accessible than that of many poets who write in a more academic style.

Shore reflects on the truths of existence but manages to reach down to the level of common life. "An Astronaut's Journal" makes this point aptly:

> Because we landed on the moon, all Americans
> can walk a little taller.
>
> Planting our carpet roll of flags,
> one for each state in the Union!
> I feel so proud of my own Garden State
> with vegetables stitched onto the blue field
> of sky instead of stars.

Shore takes the quintessence of human achievement, the moonwalk, and relates it to a walk around her garden. The "Garden State," her own birthplace of New Jersey, becomes a "garden state" in which she grows her vegetables. She moves from the grandiose to the small in a pattern of simple images. Even the common vegetable is compared to the celestial star. It is a trait Shore continued to develop in later books of verse.

The Minute Hand

The Minute Hand, Shore's third collection of verse, displays a cover painting that epitomizes the blend of familiar and alien that won for this book it status as a Lamont Poetry Selection for 1986: an uneasy child in old-fashioned formal clothes whose haunted eyes and fearful mouth contrast with her domestic setting, the rocking chair so common to old-time photography. The poems within similarly demonstrate domestic settings inlaid with eerie symbols:

> . . . at last, the two littlest dolls,
> too unstable to stand upright,
> are cradled in her cavity, as if waiting to be born.
> Like two dried beans, they rattle inside her;
> twin faces painted in cruder detail,
> bearing the family resemblance
> and the same unmistakeable design.
>
> The line of succession stops here.
> You can pluck them from her belly
> like a surgeon . . .
> thus making the choice between fullness
> and emptiness . . .

The poem advances over and through the contours of a familiar object made ghoulish by close examination. The nesting dolls, an image of pregnancy and generational ties, become the poem's metaphor for femaleness and female connection.

MUSIC MINUS ONE

The title poem of Shore's fourth volume of poetry, *Music Minus One*, refers to a record album that provides orchestral accompaniment for a person who plays a solo instrument at home. Constructed like a novel comprising interwoven narratives, *Music Minus One* entwines Shore's memories of childhood tightly around her perceptions of adult life. In the title poem, "Music Minus One," Howard Norman, Shore's novelist husband, presses Shore to embrace the developing autobiography inherent in these poems. Said Shore of the evolving work,

> There was a template in my head for this book. I'd write an early childhood poem and there'd be another poem that would balance it, or fill in about a later part of my life. It was an arc, and there were points along this arc that needed to be told.

These poems incorporate the various personages of her deceased parents, George and Elsie, with her young daughter Emma and her husband. They combine the family home above the clothing store with an old farmhouse just a short distance from Goddard. Old memories blend seamlessly with new thoughts while Shore tries to formulate a world in which the two can coexist. Thus, in one of the early poems, the young Shore is moved by Anne Frank's famous diary to invent a game called "Washing the Streets of Holland," and readers are reminded of one of the poems in the book's end section. In it, Shore, as a grown woman, overcome by her visit to a Holocaust museum, "descend[s] floor by floor/ year by year, into history." Similarly, readers are treated to an image of Shore watching her father shave, only to observe later the adult Shore opening her father's safe after his death with the combination he has taught her. Finally, in "The Visible Woman," Shore makes the moving comparison of her mother's terminal illness and her daughter's slow, painstaking assembly of a plastic model of a woman's body. The thirty-one poems together formulate the "arc" of Shore's life in two parts: past and present.

HAPPY FAMILY

Shore's volume *Happy Family*, like her previous volumes, follows her life from childhood in a closely knit Jewish family in 1950's New Jersey to her marriage and parenthood. Her light verse links common experiences in the lives of women. Further, *Happy Family* continues the story of Jane Shore's life where previous volumes (*Eye-Level*, *The Minute Hand*, and *Music Minus One*) left off. "Not all Happy Families are alike," Shore says in the title poem, reminding the reader poignantly of the opening line of Leo Tolstoy's novel *Anna Karenina* (1875-1877; English translation, 1886). The resulting series of domestic scenes demonstrate a variety of "happy" incidents experienced by the citizens of Shore's 1950's New Jersey neighborhood: amusing, desperate, simple, or complicated. Shore shows the reader amazingly vivid scenes of her parents, aunts and uncles, cousins, and schoolteachers in a manner similar to that of a pair of friends flipping through an album of her family's old photographs. In poems—intimate, personal, and accessible—she combines the dual voices of past and present, the dual portraits of childhood and adulthood, and the dual realities of daughter and mother. Whether light in tone, elegiac in form, or despondent in theme, Shore's poems embrace memory through painstaking attention to all remembered details. Memory, she seems to suggest, is the only thing in life that lasts.

BIBLIOGRAPHY

Goldensohn, Lorrie. "About Jane Shore: A Profile." *Ploughshares* 23, no. 4 Issue (Winter, 1997): 209.

Goldensohn relates early biographical information about her friend and fellow poet Shore and paints a picture of the young woman while Shore was attending Goddard University. Goldensohn shared meals and poetry readings with Shore, helping her find her voice in her poetry and in her life. A portrait of the poet as a young artist.

Hadas, Rachel. "Four Voices Talking Out Loud." *The Kenyon Review* 20, nos. 3/4 (Summer/Fall, 1998): 157. Hadas finds that Shore ruminates, remembers, questions, explains, and describes, making splendid use of the range of the speaking voice. In order to do this, poets must first somehow create an attentive quiet in which their poems can be heard.

McFall, Gardner. "Toward a Visible Woman," *The New York Times Book Review*, February 23, 1997, p. 16. McFall describes Shore's *Music Minus One* as a strongly autobiographical work that uses material from her childhood in 1950's New Jersey to the birth of her daughter Emma and her parents' deaths. He details the volume as a series of thirty-one poems that shift perspective along the continuum of time and maturity, creating a history both personal and artistic.

Murphy, Bruce F. "Verse Versus Poetry." *Poetry* 127, no. 3 (January, 2001): 279. Murphy describes the works of several poets in this review, including Jane Shore's *Happy Family*. Although Shore's title refers to a common dish served in Chinese restaurants, he finds a secondary and ironic meaning as well. Murphy says that Shore's poems describe domestic scenes, meditating on childhood, aging, the disappointment of dreams, and how relationships further or blunt the energies of one's life. Murphy examines Shore's mechanics, placing her verse in the category of prose based on its rhythms and lack of rhyme.

Tabor, María García: "The Truth According to Your Characters: An Interview with Julia Alvarez." *Prairie Schooner* 74, no. 2 (Summer, 2000): 151. In this extensive interview with Julia Alvarez, Tabor makes several comparisons between the styles of Alvarez and Shore. Alvarez relates her poetic development as having been shaped by Shore's use of image and ethnicity.

Julia M. Meyers

Sir Philip Sidney

Born: Penshurst, England; November 30, 1554
Died: Arnhem, The Netherlands; October 7, 1586

Principal poetry

Astrophel and Stella, 1591 (pirated edition printed by Thomas Newman), 1598 (first authorized edition)
Certaine Sonnets, 1598
The Psalmes of David, Translated into Divers and Sundry Kindes of Verse, 1823 (with Mary Sidney Herbert, Countess of Pembroke)
The Complete Poems of Sir Philip Sidney, 1873 (2 volumes)
The Poems of Sir Philip Sidney, 1962 (William A. Ringler, Jr., editor)
The Psalms of Sir Philip Sidney and the Countess of Pembroke, 1963 (J. C. A. Rathmell, editor)

Other literary forms

Although Sir Philip Sidney's best-known work is *Astrophel and Stella*, his major work and the one to which he devoted most of his literary energy and much of his political frustration was *Arcadia* (originally titled *The Countess of Pembroke's Arcadia*). This long, much-revised epic prose romance was written and revised between 1578 and 1586; it was first published in an unfinished version in 1590, again in 1593 in a revised and imperfect version, and repeatedly in many editions for more than a century. The equivalent in prose of Edmund Spenser's *The Faerie Queene* (1590-1596), it is an encyclopedic romance of love, politics, and adventure, incorporating many stories and discussions of philosophical, theological, erotic, and psychological issues. Almost as important is Sidney's critical treatise, *Defence of Poesie* (1595; published in another edition as *An Apologie for Poetry*), written about 1580, and setting forth in a seductive, if never quite logically coherent argument, a celebration of the nature and power of poetry, along with some prescriptive (and perceptive) comments on the current malaise of English poetry, drama, and the literary scene generally. Other works Sidney wrote include *The Lady of May* (1578), a pastoral entertainment; the first forty-four poems in a translation of the Psalms, later revised and completed by his sister Mary; a number of other miscellaneous poems, prose treatises, and translations, mainly designed to further the cause of the Protestant faction in Elizabeth's court.

Achievements

"Our English *Petrarke Sir Philip Sidney* . . . often comforteth him selfe in his sonnets of Stella, though dispairing to attaine his desire. . . ." Thus Sir John Harington in 1591, and generations of readers have similarly sighed and sympathized with Astrophel's tragicomic enactment of "poore Petrarch's long deceased woes." In literary history, *Astrophel and Stella* marks a poetical revolution no less than William Wordsworth's *Lyrical Ballads* (1800) or T. S. Eliot's *The Waste Land* (1922); the poem is the product of a young, ambitious poet, acting upon his impatience with the poetry he criticized in his manifesto, *Defence of Poesie*. "Poetry almost have we none," he wrote, "but that lyrical kind of songs and sonets," which "if I were a mistresse would never persuade mee they were in love." Sir Philip Sidney has also had a special place in England's broader cultural history. Part of his fascination has been the ways succeeding ages have appropriated him: as a lost leader of the golden Elizabethan age, Victorian gentleman, anguished Edwardian, committed existentialist, apolitical quietist, even a member of the Moral Majority. Like all great writers, Sidney and his works have been continually reinterpreted by successive ages, his poems and his life alike inscribed into different literary, political, and cultural discourses. As contemporary scholars have become more attuned to both the linguistic and ideological complexity of Renaissance literature generally and to the new possibilities of contemporary critical methods, Sidney's writing has been seen, both in its seemingly replete presence and its symptomatic gaps and absences, as central to an understanding of Elizabethan poetry and culture.

None of Sidney's poetry was published in his lifetime, and yet along with his other writings it circulated among a small coterie of family and court acquaintances during the 1580's. Sidney's vocations were those of courtier, statesman, Protestant aristocrat, and patriot before that of a poet, and his poetry encourages the piecing together of a more problematic Sidney than that afforded by conventional hagiography. Sidney's writings often served, as A. C. Hamilton argues, "as a kind of outlet for political interests, compensating for the frustrations and failures" of his life: "problems that prove insurmountable in his career" were transposed and wrestled with in his fictions.

Sidney's major poetic work, *Astrophel and Stella*, in particular marks the triumphant maturity of Elizabethan court poetry, the belated but spectacular adaption of Petrarchanism to English aristocratic culture. It remains one of the most moving, delightful, and provocative collections of love poems in the language, all the more powerful in its impact because of the variety of needs that strain within it for expression—erotic, poetic, political, religious, cultural. One may read it, as Harington did, as the expression of thwarted, obsessive love, but it opens itself, like its author, to much richer readings, which reinforce Sidney's position as the central literary

Sir Philip Sidney (Library of Congress)

and cultural figure in the English Renaissance before William Shakespeare.

Biography

Sir Philip Sidney was born into one of England's leading aristocratic families. His father was one of Elizabeth I's most loyal civil servants, serving as Lord President of Wales and Lord Deputy of Ireland. On his mother's side, Sidney was related to the influential Leicester family, one of the major Protestant powers in the country. He was educated under the stern Calvinist Thomas Ashton at Shrewsbury School, along with his lifetime friend and biographer Fulke Greville; in 1568 he went to Oxford, but he left without a degree in 1571 and in 1572 went on a Grand Tour through Europe, where he was introduced to and widely admired by major European scholars and statesmen, especially by leading Huguenot and German Protestants. In 1575 he returned to England and joined Elizabeth's court. He contributed a masque, *The Lady of May*, to one of the royal entertainments in 1578 and was employed by the queen in a number of minor matters. Unfortunately, he alienated Elizabeth, partly because he was so forthright in his support of European and English Protestant ideals and partly because of his own personal charisma. In a stormy career at court, he alternated between periods of willing service and periods of retirement to his sister's house at Wilton, near Salisbury, where an increasing number of Elizabethan poets, intellectuals, and thinkers were gathering—almost as an alternative to the queen's court. In 1580 he quarreled with the earl of Oxford over whether the queen should consider marrying the French Catholic duke of Anjou. His advice on the matter was ignored, or played down, and he contemplated going illegally to the New World. Elizabeth's attitude to the man the English court so much admired (almost as much as many Europeans) was an ambivalent one: Sidney was probably too much a man of outspoken principle to be of use to her in her devious political dealings.

Sidney's literary career therefore developed in part out of the frustrations of his political career. Most of his works were written in his periods of chosen, or enforced, retirement to Wilton, and often grew out of discussions with friends such as Fulke Greville and Edward Dyer and his sister, Mary. He looked at the poetry being written in England, contrasted it most unfavorably with that of European courts, and so set out deliberately, by precept and example, to improve it. The result was an outburst of writing that marked a literary revolution: *Defence of Poesie*, probably started by 1578, was a sophisticated, chatty, and persuasive theoretical treatment. *Astrophel and Stella*, written in 1581-1582, is the first major Petrarchan sonnet collection written in English; the continually revised romance, *Arcadia*, dedicated to his sister, was started in 1578, and was still being revised shortly before his tragic death in the Battle of Zutphen in 1586. Sidney was given a hero's funeral in London. Monarchs, statesmen, soldiers, and poets from all over Europe sent condolences, wrote memorials, and for the next sixty years or so Sidney's person, prestige, and power hung over the English court and culture as a reminder of how the Renaissance ideal of the courtier could be combined with Protestant piety.

Analysis

Sir Philip Sidney was educated to embrace an unusual degree of political, religious, and cultural responsibility, yet it is clear from his comments in *Defence of Poesie* that he took his literary role as seriously. Both this critical treatise and *Astrophel and Stella* are manifestos—not only of poetic but also of broader cultural practice. Both look forward to a long-needed renaissance of poetry and culture generally. For Sidney, poetry and its broader social uses were inseparable. Indeed, it is only with distortion that one can separate a "literary" from a "social" text, even with a Petrarchan love sequence such as *Astrophel and Stella*. Like other Elizabethan court poets, Sidney wrote his poetry within a structure of power and tried to carve out a discursive space under ideological pressures that attempted to control and direct the languages by which the court operated.

The Elizabethan court

The court was more than a visible institution for Sidney and his contemporaries: It was a felt pressure which attempted to fix and determine all that came within its reach. Sidney's life and poetry are especially interesting examples of how the Elizabethan court's power operated upon poetry. The court poets—for example, Sir Walter Ralegh and the earl of Oxford—acted as spokesmen for the court's values, yet inevitably the strains and tensions of their roles show through in their poetry. Poetry was both an expression of the power of the court and a means of participating in that power. Where a poem like Ralegh's "Praised be Diana's Fair and Harmles Light" shows the court contemplating its own idealized image, Sidney's poetry has a more uneasy relation to the court's power. Although on the surface his writing appears to embody, in Terry Eagleton's words, a "moment of ideological buoyancy, an achieved synthesis" of courtly values, Sidney's own position in the court makes his poetry an especially revealing instance of the struggles and tensions beneath the seemingly replete surface of the court and court poetry alike.

More than any of his contemporaries before John Donne and Shakespeare, Sidney in his poetry evokes a felt world of bustling activity, psychosocial pressure, cultural demand—in short, the workings of power upon literary and historical discourse. The institutions that shape the poetry—the court, its household arrangements, its religious and political controversies—are evoked in the tournaments (41), the gossip of "curious wits" (23) and "courtly nymphs" (54), and make up an atmosphere of energetic worldliness. What distinguishes Sidney's poetry is the forceful way that something more than the glittering surface of the court energizes it. Despite his posthumous reputation as the perfect Renaissance courtier, Sidney's public career was one of political disappointment and humiliation; he seems to have been increasingly torn between public duty and private desire, much in the way the hero of his sonnet sequence is.

As Richard McCoy has shown, all Sidney's works are permeated with the problem of authority and submission. Like himself, all his heroes (including Astrophel) are young, noble, well-educated and well-intentioned, but as they become aware of the complexities and ambiguities of the world, they become diverted or confused, and Sidney finds himself caught between compassion and condemnation of their activities. In *Arcadia*, Sidney attempted to solve in fiction many of the tensions that beset his life, and *Astrophel and Stella* similarly served as an outlet for political and social frustration. In the prose romance, Sidney's narrative irresolution and (in an early version) premature and repressive closure reveal deep and unsettling doubts; similarly, the ambivalences and hesitations, the shifting distance between poet and character, the divided responses to intellectual and emotional demands in *Astrophel and Stella*, articulate Sidney's ambivalent roles within the court.

Protestantism

One of the fundamental influences giving Sidney's life and poetry their particular cast is Protestantism. Indeed, perhaps the most potent factor disrupting the repleteness of the court poetic was Sidney's piety and his struggle with creating a Protestant poetic. In A. C. Hamilton's phrase, Sidney was "a Protestant English Petrarch." Unlike his close friend Fulke Greville, for whom a radical Augustinian suspicion of metaphor and writing itself consistently undermined poetry's value, Sidney tried to hold together what in *Defence of Poesie* he terms man's "erected wit" and his "infected will." Indeed, what Sidney perhaps uniquely brought to the Petrarchan lyric was a self-conscious anxiety about the tension between courtly celebration and Protestant inwardness, between the persuasiveness and rhetoric and the self-doubt of sinful man, between the insecurity of man's word and the absolute claims of God's.

The tension in Sidney's writing between the courtly and the pious, John Calvin and Baldassare Castiglione, disrupts *Astrophel and Stella* most interestingly. Sidney's own theory sees poetry focusing on the reformation of will and behavior, and it is possible to read his own sequence as an exemplum of the perils of erotic love, or, in Alan Sinfield's words, "the errors of unregulated passion." Sidney displays Astrophel deliberately rejecting virtue, treating Stella as a deity in a "direct challenge to Christianity" and to right reason. His cleverness is displayed in trying to avoid or repel the claims of reason and virtue, and the outcome of the sequence is the inevitable end of self-deception. The inwardness of *Astrophel and Stella*—not necessarily, it should be noted, its supposed autobiographical dimension, but its concern with the persona's self-consciousness, even self-centeredness, as lover, poet, courtier—is thus a fascinating blend of Petrarchan convention and Protestant self-concentration, and one which points to a distinctive late sixteenth century strain within the inherited vocabulary and rhetoric of the poet in his role in the court.

The court poet

When Sidney returned from his Grand Tour, he looked back across the Channel to the sophisticated academies and court circles that were encouraging writers, scholars, and musicians, and that were united by a synthesis of Christian, usually Protestant, piety and high Neoplatonism. The French academies, in particular, displayed a self-consciousness that distinguished them very strongly from the medieval courts. Shortly after Sidney's return, his sister Mary became the countess of Pembroke and established at Wilton what one of her followers was to term a "little Court," dedicated, both before and after his death, to continuing the renaissance of English courtly culture. Sidney's whole literary career became a frustrated attempt to realize a new role for the court poet, one based upon the integrity and responsibility of values which he was unable to embody in his public life, and which more and more he poured into his writing. His remark to the earl of Leicester that he was kept "from the courte since my only service is speeche and that is stopped" has wider application than to its occasion, the French marriage crisis. It articulates a frustration toward the traditional subservience of a poet to the court, a stubborn insistence on forging a distinctive role for the poet.

Part of the fascination Sidney has traditionally evoked is what is often perceived as his ability to balance opposite ideological, rhetorical, or vocational demands upon him. Certainly in *Defence of Poesie* and *Astrophel and Stella* the elements of such a dialectic can be found. The promise of divinity that Astrophel perceives in Stella's eyes is, in Sidney's sympathetic comedy, wittily undermined by his self-consciousness, bashfulness, physical overeagerness, and human imperfection. In *Defence of Poesie*, Sidney describes poetry as a fervent reaching for the sublime, veiling truth in order to draw its reader toward it, and asserts that the power to move and so to bring about an enactment of poetry's transforming powers certainly lies within man's godlike nature. Yet for Sidney there was the seemingly inseparable problem of man's "infected will," and the reformed emphasis on man's depravity and the untrustworthiness of the mind seems to have posed crucial problems for him and for the possibility of creating a Protestant poetic. While elements of an opposition between rhetoric and truth, humanism and piety, Calvin and Castiglione, can be isolated, despite his most anxious intentions, Sidney does not manage to hold them together satisfactorily. In fact, his very fascination for later ages and his centrality for understanding sixteenth century poetry are grounded in such contradictions. "Unresolved and continuing conflict," in Stephen Greenblatt's phrase, is a distinctive mark of Renaissance culture, and Sidney's is a central place in that culture.

The Psalmes of David

The versification of the Psalms, started by Sidney about 1579 and revised and completed by his sister, the countess of Pembroke, after his death, comprises the first post-Reformation religious lyrics that combine the rich emotional and spiritual life of Protestantism with the new rhetorical riches of the secular lyric. There are distinctive Protestant notes—a strong stress on election in Psalm 43, echoing Théodore Bèze's and Calvin's glosses rather than the original text, for example—and other Psalms, where a strain of courtly Neoplatonism is highlighted, notably in Psalm 8, which (like Pico della Mirandola rather than Calvin) presents man as a privileged, glorious creation "attended" by God, an "owner" of regal and "crowning honour." Man emerges as a free and wondrous being, like his creator, "freely raunging within the Zodiack of his owne wit," as Sidney put it in *Defence of Poesie*. Here Sidney juxtaposes, without integrating them, the great contraries of his age.

It is now generally believed that the Psalms were originally drafted by Sidney early in his career, perhaps about 1579. Also written in this early period are a number of miscellaneous poems, including the so-called Certain Sonnets and many of the poems inserted into *Arcadia*. These are mainly of interest for showing Sidney's eager experimentation—with quantitative verse, pastoral dialogue, song, metrical and stanzaic patterns, and above all the appeal to the feelings of the reader, notably in "Leave me ô Love, which reachest but to dust" and the magnificent double sestina from *Arcadia*, "Yee Gote-heard Gods."

Astrophel and Stella

Sidney's most sustained and most celebrated work is his sonnet sequence *Astrophel and Stella*, probably written in 1582, which dramatizes a frustrated love affair between a courtier and an admired lady. As Germaine

Warkentin has shown, Sidney may have been tinkering with his "Certain Sonnets" during 1581-1582, abandoning them the next summer "to compose one of the three most distinguished sonnet sequences of the English Renaissance." Certainly *Astrophel and Stella* conveys an intensity that suggests a short burst of concentrated writing.

This sequence of 108 sonnets and eleven songs anatomizes the love of a young, restless, self-conscious courtier, Astrophel, for a lady, Stella, his star. His purpose is set out in the opening sonnet, in which he claims, "I sought fit words to paint the blackest face of woe/ Studying inventions fine, her wits to entertaine." The reader is taken into the familiar world of Petrarchan convention and cliché: Astrophel the doubting, self-conscious, aggressive lover; Stella, the golden-haired, black-eyed, chaste and (usually) distant and (finally) unobtainable lady. The figures are equally familiar—debates between Hope and Absence, denials of loving at first sight, the frustrated desire alleviated by writing, the beautiful woman with the icy heart who pitilessly resists siege, and the final misery of the lover who ends his plaints in anguish, swearing in the end by all he has left, her "absent presence." Like the best *Petrarchisti*, Sidney makes the traditional motifs intensely dramatic. For the first time in English poetry since Geoffrey Chaucer, C. S. Lewis suggests, "a situation is not merely written about: it is created, presented, so as to compel our imaginations." Earlier Petrarchan poets such as Thomas Wyatt had conveyed urgency and conversational informality, but, read as a whole, English poetry had not, since Chaucer, been distinguished by such continual, even restless, conflict and energy.

USES OF RHETORIC

Modern critics, reacting against earlier impressionistic, Romantic criticism, have shown how the energy and variety of Sidney's poetry rests on a thorough exploitation of the riches of Renaissance rhetoric—through his use of apostrophe, dialogue, irony, shifts in decorum, and modulations of voice. As Ringler points out, perhaps "the most valuable product of his studies and disputations in Oxford was the thorough training he received in logic and formal classical rhetoric"; to these he added intense study and practice in ways of loosening the rhythmic movement of English line and working within the formal demands of stanzaic and metrical form. By a thorough familiarity with the conventional techniques of Renaissance love verse—which he parodies in 6, 9, and 15, for example—Sidney works within the eloquent courtly poetic, mocking and adapting it where necessary. Sidney uses his poems as workshops, experimenting with a great variety of stanzaic patterns and with devices such as inversion and feminine rhyme. Above all, he tries continually to juxtapose the movement of formal verse with an immediacy of idiom and logical development to involve his reader in the often tortuous movements of his character's broodings, arguments, and self-deceptions. Especially notable is the lightness and wit with which even Astrophel's most tortured self-examination is presented. Parody, the exaggerated use of erotic or literary clichés and puns, are all obvious enough, but the whole sequence is characterized by a sophisticated playfulness—the outrageous puns on "touch" in 9 leading to the self-pity (Astrophel's, not Sidney's) of the last line, the tongue-in-cheek anguish of the sonnets on Cupid, and the uproariousness of some of the erotic sonnets. Above all, the humor of the poet, indulging in his own mastery of language and able to dramatize his character, invites his readers to share his enjoyment at the varied follies and complexities of human love.

PETRARCHANISM

If the Petrarchan tradition and the resources of Elizabethan rhetoric afforded Sidney a wonderfully flexible and rich poetic vehicle, there is nevertheless something limiting, even disturbing, about the literary mode in which he is working. Petrarchanism purports to be about love, and specifically about the obsession of a lover for a lady before whom he feels inferior, humble, and yet ennobled. Paradoxically, the sonnets become a weapon in an attempted mastery of the woman and their focus is exclusively upon the anguish and achievements of the male lover. The conventions of Petrarchanism are those of a male-dominated society and its rhetorical strategies serve to elevate the woman only to subjugate her.

As Ann Jones and Peter Stallybrass have argued, "to Stella, Astrophel may speak of love as service," but outside his devotion to friends, "he can suggest a sub-text of masculine domination." Within the struggle for mastery, rhetoric and erotic convention alike becomes means of domination. Stella herself is, like other Petrarchan mistresses, reduced to a disconnected set of characteristics, acknowledged only as they are manipulable or impinge on her lover's consciousness. She is entirely the product of her poet-lover's desires. *Astrophel and Stella* is a theater of desire in which the man has all the active roles, and in which she is silent or merely iconic, most present when she refuses him or is absent. Astrophel does not want—although it is arguable that Sidney might—to call into question the power of his anguish or the centrality of his struggles of conscience, yet it seems legitimate to ask what Stella might reply to Astrophel's earnest self-regarding pleas for favor. Even if her replies are not "in" most of the poems (and where they are, as in Song 8, they are reported through Astrophel), what might she say? Is her silence the repression of the character or of Sidney? Does her silence reflect a whole cultural blindness that fixes women as objects of gaze and analysis within a society they did not invent and could not control? When one considers in these ways how the dynamics of Sidney's text function, once again one finds "literary" and "cultural" texts interacting.

Biographical elements

An older criticism faced (or perhaps avoided) these issues by focusing on the biographical "origins" of the sequence. In part an outcome of the Romantic valorization of poetry as the overflow of sincerity or genuine experience, criticism sentimentalized the obvious connections between Sidney's life and the fiction of Astrophel and Stella into a poetic *roman à clef*. Undoubtedly, Sidney plays with his reader's curiosity about some kind of identification between himself and Astrophel and between Stella and Lady Penelope Rich (née Devereux) to whom as a youth Sidney's family nearly arranged a betrothal and in whom he may possibly (though there is no firm evidence either way) have had more than a literary interest. Sidney certainly builds into his sequence references to his career, to his father, to contemporary politics, to his friends, and—of most interest to the curious—to Lady Rich's name in two sonnets (24, 37) which were omitted from the first publication of the collection, perhaps for fear of embarrassing repercussions. Even so, the relationship between Sidney and his characters and between the events of his life and those seemingly within his poems should not be simplified. Just as Sidney manages simultaneously to have much in common with Astrophel, be sympathetic with him, and yet to criticize or laugh at him, so the gap between Stella and the historical Lady Rich is even wider—at best one can regard some of the references to Stella as sly or wistful fantasies. As to whether Sidney and Lady Rich were sexually involved, *Astrophel and Stella* gives no firm evidence.

Love and courtly behavior

A more rewarding approach is to try to trace the way the poems are traversed by a variety of overlapping and in many cases contradictory influences, including court politics, the psychology of love, poetry, rhetoric, and Christianity. Within its confusions, tensions, and contradictions, *Astrophel and Stella* highlights the diverse and often contradictory pressures and possibilities which constitute the situation of an Elizabethan poet and lover. One of the distinctive possibilities of Petrarchanism was to set the traditional medieval debate on the nature of love in terms of the lover's psychology and within the demands of the codes of courtly behavior. Part of the fascination Petrarch had for English poets in the late sixteenth century was their puzzlement about how the Petrarchist conventions might fit their experiences. The prestige and suggestiveness of Petrarchanism allowed poets to examine not only the relationship between love and poetry, but also the way its worldview, its rich schematization of human experience, and their own changing social and individual realities intersected.

Erotic love

One of the dominant concerns of the sequence is undoubtedly that of the problems and difficulties of erotic experience—although depicted entirely from the male viewpoint. *Astrophel and Stella* typically focuses on the "thrownness" of love—on the lover finding himself within a preexisting structuring of experience, a "race" that "hath neither stop nor start" (23), but which continually disrupts his sense of a preexistent self. Sexuality becomes an object to be examined, supervised, confessed, and transformed into poetry. It should be noted, however, that the "self" that is put into question in *Astrophel and Stella* is not, or not primarily, that of Sidney. The poet offers his poems to an audience of sympathetic listeners as a mirror less of his experiences than of theirs. The intellectual tensions observable in *Astrophel and Stella* are dramatized as paradigms, the effect of which is to highlight the readers' or hearers' awareness of their own experiences. Sidney's poems work upon their readers, suggesting and manipulating although never compelling into meaning. At times he refers to quite specific members of his audience—to other lover-poets in 6, in which Astrophel distinguishes his own "trembling voice" and the sincerity of his love from those of other lovers and so provokes them to respond by praising their own mistresses or talents. At times his suffering hero will ostensibly address a rather special audience—"I Stella's ears assayl, invade her ears," he says in Sonnet 61; or he (or Sidney) will address a friend (as in Sonnet 14), and even occasionally himself (as in 30). Yet the most important audience is unnamed: the readers who, through the poem's history, will read them, meditate upon and act out their drama.

Critical response

Surveying the history of Sidney criticism, especially that of the modern era, one discovers a curious anxiety to find a coherent, sequential organization not merely made possible by the poems, but as a required means of reading them. *Astrophel and Stella* is thus often read as if it were a poetic novel. C. S. Lewis cautions against treating the Petrarchan sequence as if it were "a way of telling a story"; *Astrophel and Stella* is, he says, "not a love story but an anatomy of love," while Max Putzel speaks of the poems' "careful disorder." On the other hand, A. C. Hamilton argues that "the sonnets are organized into a sequence with a unifying structure," and other critics have written of what they see as careful structure and sequence. In Hamilton's scheme, sonnets 1-12 form an introduction, 13-30 concentrate on Astrophel's isolation, with 41-68 concerned with his moral rebellion, 71-85 with his attempt at seduction, and the remainder with his failure. Such divisions differ radically among the proponents of a narrative structure; in short, if a reader wishes to find a narrative development and final irresolution rather than an exercise in love's variety, then *Astrophel and Stella* is open to such a reading. Perhaps the most satisfying sequential reading of the collection is that by Ann Rosalind Jones, who stresses that although it is possible (and peculiarly satisfying) to see Astrophel as undergoing a gradual disintegration and loss of control, Sidney's sequence does not use the linking devices of other poets, such as Dante or Maurice Scève, which might strongly encourage a reading of the sequence as a growth in self-knowledge. Even when one constructs a sequence, it is primarily characterized by an unstable, eddying movement, "dramatically *dis*ordered," as Jones argues. "Even at the end of his experience," Astrophel can "predict the course of his writing no better than the course of his love" and so each sonnet becomes a new starting place. In short, while *Astrophel and Stella* allows for a linear development, it does not force one upon a reader, encouraging one just as readily to view Astrophel's experience as unpredictable, random, and even as an exemplum of failure.

One recurring pattern is a tension between the demands of the public world of politics and responsibility and the private world of erotic desire. In many sonnets, Astrophel presents love in terms of a debate between traditional abstractions such as desire and reason, love and duty. Part of the reader's enjoyment lies in watching him, through Sidney's fond but penetrating perspective, indulging himself in false logic (52) or in seeing his dutifully constructed arguments against love undermined by the simple appearance of his beloved, as in 5, 10, or in the amusing self-contradictions of 47. Astrophel tries in vain to keep his two worlds and their demands separate. He claims that love gives him a private place, a sense of self from which the demands of courtly responsibility are shown to be trivial, but caught between conflicting worlds of self-indulgence and political responsibility, he ends by succeeding in neither. The reader watches him corrupting his avowedly pure love into sensuality by the deviousness of political rhetoric. In Sonnet 23 he appears to reject the world, but in Sonnet 69 he expresses Stella's conditional encouragement of his advances in terms of the court's own language. Since, he argues, she has "of her high heart giv'n" him "the monarchie," as a king, he too can take some advantage from that power.

At the root of Astrophel's self-deception is the structure of Petrarchanism itself, which, as John Stevens and others have pointed out, was at once a literary convention and a very serious courtly game, one "in which three powerful discourses meet and join hands: love, religion, and politics." *Astrophel and Stella* is based on a formula by which the man is subjected to his lady while, at the same time, the situation enables him to pour fourth his eloquence in an attempt to influence her. The relationship is parallel to the relationship between courtier and monarch—built on absolute loyalty and subjection, frustration and rejection—interlaced with devious manipulation for the favors of the capricious, distant beloved. Thus while Astrophel speaks of the "joy" inspired by Stella and of his own "noble fire," he is attempting to manipulate Stella's vulnerability, seeking power over her in the way the devious courtier seeks hidden but real power over the monarch. In terms of sexual politics of the Renaissance court, Astrophel's world is one shared primarily by other male courtiers, using language as a means of domination and treating women as subject to their desire, much in the way courtiers themselves were at the mercy of the monarch.

Thus the reader watches Astrophel indulging himself in small subtle ways—playing on grammar in 63, twisting Stella's words, speaking openly to her in a kind of "manic playfulness," and allowing (or being unable to prevent) the emergence of the underlying physicality of his desires in a series of fantasies of seduction (71, 72, 74, 79, 80, 81). The songs serve especially well to highlight the wish-fulfillment of Astrophel's frustrations—especially the dramatization in Song 5 of Astrophel's self-involvement, and the graceful fantasy of Song 8, viewed wistfully by the narrator from a distance and culminating in Sidney's clever and moving breaking down of the distance between narrator and character in the final line, where he confesses that "my" song is broken.

As the sequence draws to its inevitably inconclusive end, Astrophel's fantasies become less and less realizable. He indulges in self-pity and then more realistically accepts the end of the relationship, vacillating between joy and grief, optimism and despair, dedication and unfaithfulness. As Hamilton points out, the mutability of human love which haunts so many Elizabethan sonnet sequences, especially Shakespeare's, enters Sidney's only indirectly, but where he immerses himself in the intensity of the living moment, as the sequence ends, he realizes he is "forever subject to love's tyranny, a victim of *chronos* forever caught in time's endless linear succession."

Readings of *Astrophel and Stella* inevitably point to it as a quintessential ideological and literary struggle, where a variety of impulses struggle for mastery. Like the best love poems, it asks its readers to look at themselves. Stella herself, the guiding metaphor of the sequence, is distinguished by her nature, behavior, influence, and power, always requiring, like a text, interpretation. Astrophel, like the reader of his creator's sequence, is an exegete of love. "What blushing notes doest thou in margin see," he asks, and goes on, as all readers do with the whole sequence, to choose his own convenient misunderstanding of Stella. Astrophel may state that all his "deed" is to "copy" what in Stella "Nature writes" (3) or assert that "Stella" is, literally, the principle of love in the cosmos (28), and that the words he utters "do well set forth my mind" (44), but Sidney knows, as his readers do, that love and its significance and its expression in language are far more complex matters.

Astrophel and Stella is what Roland Barthes terms a "playful" text, one that depends strongly on its audience, inviting participation both to reproduce the process, intellectual and emotional, by which the poem's struggles came to be verbalized and to go beyond them, adding one's own preoccupations. *Astrophel and Stella* has a capacity to invade its readers, to direct and inform their responses, but as well, to open them to an awareness that it functions only through a process of deliberate reciprocity. It is this joyful welcome to its readers that makes it such a landmark in English poetry.

Other major works

LONG FICTION: *Arcadia*, 1590, 1593, 1598 (originally titled *The Countess of Pembroke's Arcadia*).

PLAY: *The Lady of May*, pr. 1578 (masque); "Fortress of Perfect Beauty," 1581 (with Fulke Greville, Lord Brooke; Phillip Howard, the earl of Arundel; and Baron Windsor of Stanwell).

NONFICTION: *Defence of Poesie*, 1595 (also published as *An Apologie for Poetry*).

MISCELLANEOUS: *Miscellaneous Prose of Sir Philip Sidney*, 1973.

Bibliography

Berry, Edward I. *The Making of Sir Philip Sidney*. Toronto: University of Toronto Press, 1998. Explores how Sidney created himself as a poet by making representations of himself in the roles of some of his most literary creations: *Astrophel and Stella*, and the intrusive persona of *Defence of Poesie*. Focusing on the significance of these and other self-representations throughout Sidney's career, Berry combines biography, social history, and literary criticism to achieve a carefully balanced portrayal of the poet's life and work.

Connell, Dorothy. *Sir Philip Sidney: The Maker's Mind.* Oxford, England: Clarendon Press, 1977. A thoughtful text that considers Sidney's life and art in a biographical and historical context. Connell discusses in detail important historical influences on Sidney. Supplemented by maps, a bibliography, and an excellent index.

Garrett, Martin, ed. *Sidney: The Critical Heritage.* New York: Routledge, 1996. A collection of essays that gather a large body of critical sources on Sidney. Includes bibliographical references and index.

Hamilton, A. C. *Sir Philip Sidney: A Study of His Life and Works*. New York: Cambridge University Press, 1977. A strong study of Sidney's life, poetics, and selected works and an excellent general survey that places his work in a biographical context. Includes an appendix, notes, a bibliography, and an index.

Kay, Dennis, ed. *Sir Philip Sidney: An Anthology of Modern Criticism.* Oxford, England: Clarendon Press, 1987. A frequently insightful collection of scholarly criticism: Kay's comprehensive introduction places Sidney in a cultural heritage and surveys the changes that have occurred in the critical approaches to Sidney's work. Complemented by a chronology, a bibliography, an index, and a list of early editions.

Kinney, Arthur F., ed. *Essential Articles for the Study of Sir Philip Sidney.* Hamden, Conn.: Archon Books, 1986. A collection of twenty-five insightful articles with a wide range of critical approaches. Topics include Sidney's biography, *The Lady of May*, *Defence of Poesie*, *Astrophel and Stella*, *Arcadia*, and *The Psalmes of David, Translated into Divers and Sundry Kindes of Verse*. Supplemented by a bibliography.

Myrick, Kenneth. *Sir Philip Sidney as a Literary Craftsman.* Lincoln: University of Nebraska Press, 1965. A very informative survey of Sidney's work as it reflects a critical project and approach to poetics. Specific attention is given to *Arcadia*, including a summary of plot and a character list. Contains notes and an index, as well as a valuable list of studies on Sidney from 1935 to 1964.

Sidney, Philip, Sir. *Sir Philip Sidney: Selected Prose and Poetry.* Edited by Robert Kimbrough. Madison: University of Wisconsin Press, 1983. In this lengthy and thorough work, Kimbrough gives detailed attention to *Defence of Poesie*, *Astrophel and Stella*, and *Arcadia*. Kimbrough also surveys the critical approaches to Sidney. Contains a chronology and a select bibliography.

Gary F. Waller;
bibliography updated by the editors

Sir Robert Sidney

Born: Penshurst Place, Kent, England; November 19, 1563

Died: Penshurst Place, Kent, England; July 13, 1626

Principal poetry

The Poems of Robert Sidney, 1984 (Katherine Duncan-Jones, editor)

Other literary forms

Unlike his more famous brother Philip and his sister Mary, Sidney was not a prolific writer. Indeed, his career as a poet was probably confined to a few years, possibly as few as two. There are many letters by him in the Sir Robert Sidney papers, but he published no literary work in his lifetime. Likewise, his poetry remained in manuscript, probably at Penshurst, until the early nineteenth century, when it found its way into the Warwick Castle Library. The manuscript was first positively identified by P. J. Croft in 1973 and purchased by the British Library in 1974. It was subsequently printed in a modern-spelling version by Katherine Duncan-Jones, published as *The Poems of Robert Sidney* in 1984 by Oxford University Press.

Achievements

The discovery of the manuscript of Sir Robert Sidney's poetry in the 1970's added a distinctive voice to the courtier poets of the late sixteenth century. In his manuscript's ninety pages of nervous, often corrected handwriting are the works of a new Elizabethan poet of outstanding interest. Sidney does not quite possess Philip's variety or intimate control of tone and mood within a poem (the emotions of his verse are expressed in broader sweeps) but his ear is highly sensitive, and his poems reverberate with the great commonplaces of Elizabethan life and literature—time, absence, grief, and deprivation. Like his contemporary Sir Walter Ralegh, Robert Sidney turned to poetry only occasionally, yet he found in it a commitment that went beyond emotional solace; and, like Ralegh's, Sidney's verse reveals the ideological power of the Elizabethan court over those who struggled for articulation within its frantic center or (in Robert's case) on its anxious margins.

Biography

During his life and after, Sir Robert Sidney was overshadowed by the brilliance of his elder brother Philip. He was a dutiful son of a family that was ambitious but relatively new to the power-struggles of the Elizabethan aristocracy. In his early life, Robert had none of the prestige or flamboyance of Philip. He dutifully went on his Grand Tour of Europe, pursued by letters of advice from his brother as to his reading, chivalric bearing, acquaintances, and finances. In 1585, he accompanied Philip, who had been appointed governor of Flushing, to the Low Countries, and was present at the Battle of Zutphen, where Philip was mortally wounded. Philip's death seemed to represent the death of an entire age. From the late 1580's, Elizabethans became increasingly bewildered and disillusioned, as the Armada victory turned sour, court infighting grew more and more frenetic, and the queen cultivated the trappings of high Neoplatonism to hold in check the corruption and confusion beneath the surface of the court.

In the shadow of his brother, Robert had undergone the usual initiation of the Elizabethan courtier. In 1584, he married Barbara Gamage, a young Welsh heiress—after some rather sordid negotiations. Their letters later show them to have grown into a most loving couple. He constantly addresses her as "sweet heart" or "dear heart," and the letters are full of sadness at his absence from her. In 1594, he wrote that "there is no desyre in me so dear as the love I bear you and our children . . . you are married, my dear Barbara, to a husband that is now drawn so into the world and the actions of yt as there is no way to retire myself without trying fortune further."

The intense strain of being an honest courtier during the 1590's is evident throughout his letters. Indeed, it might be said that Philip had the good fortune to die in 1586; Robert had to live on. In 1587, he was his brother's chief mourner, and, like his sister Mary, may have turned to poetry at this time partly in order to continue his brother's literary ideals. In 1588, he was appointed to Philip's old position of governor of Flushing, and, with only a few brief breaks, usually to carry out some unpalatable diplomatic task imposed by Elizabeth, he spent most of the next decade in the Low Countries, his chief interest being to return home. Constantly exhorted to live up to his brother's standard, he seems to have been regarded by the queen as a convenient workhorse.

After years of frustration, Robert Sidney's fortunes improved under James's reign. Life at Penshurst in the early seventeenth century was celebrated in that most harmonious of poems by Ben Jonson, "To Penshurst," in which he praised what appeared to its aristocratic proprietors to be the rich, cooperative life of an organic and humane community. Incidentally, Jonson does not here explicitly mention Sidney as a poet—although this would not have been entirely unusual, as outside his immediate circle even Philip's reputation as a poet had hardly been mentioned before his death. In 1605, Sidney was created Viscount de Lisle, and in 1618, earl of Leicester. He died in 1626, age sixty-two, having survived his elder brother by forty years and his elder sister by five.

Analysis

The retrieval of the manuscript poems written by Sir Robert Sidney was one of the most important Renaissance discoveries of the past one hundred years. The Sidney manuscript is the only extant substantial body of verse by an Elizabethan poet in his own handwriting and incorporating the poet's own revisions. In addition to their intrinsic interest, these poems dramatically change the present view of the literary activities of the Sidney circle—that unique, closely connected family group inspired by the genius and person of Sir Philip Sidney, Robert's brother.

Although references to the literary interests of all the Sidneys, including Robert, are found in many dedications, letters, and prefaces of the period, there are few references to him as a poet. George Chapman wrote of him in 1609 as "the most Learned and Noble Concluder of the Warres Art, and the Muses." There is a tradition that he wrote the lyrics for his godson Robert Dowland's *Musicall Banquet*, and he may have written verses in honor of his daughter's marriage. Certainly, like the rest of his family, Sidney was widely praised as a generous patron of literature. It is significant that the distinctive note of the other Sidneys's encouragement of poets was that they were poets themselves. "Gentle *Sir Philip Sidney*," wrote Thomas Nashe, "thou knewest what belonged to a schollar, thou knewest what paines, what toyle, what travel, conduct to perfection."

MARY SIDNEY

Like that of his sister Mary, Sidney's poetic career may have started seriously only after his brother's death. It is clear that she did not begin to write seriously until after 1586, when she took upon herself the vocation to continue his work in forwarding the Elizabethan poetic Renaissance. The bulk of her work, an impressive body of poetry and prose, grows directly out of Philip's inspiration: She edited his manuscripts, completed his versifying of the psalms, and wrote or translated a number of works directly influenced by his critical theories or dedicated to his memory. It may be that Robert also wrote his verse as a similar, although less public, attempt to continue his brother's poetic intentions. He may have decided that Mary, more permanently settled at Wilton in the 1580's with the increasing comings and goings of Fulke Greville, Edmund Spenser, Samuel Daniel, and other poets, was better placed to forward the literary revolution of the Sidneys. It was to her that he sent the one extant copy of his manuscript, possibly during one of his much-desired but infrequent visits to England.

SONNETS AND SONGS

The obvious comparisons are, then, between Sidney's poetry and that written by Philip and Mary. Like his brother's, Sidney's poems are in the form of a Petrarchan miscellany of sonnets and songs, although they show a greater variety of metrical and stanzaic patterns than the normal sonnet sequence of the 1580's and 1590's, a characteristic he may have derived from Mary, whose psalms are the most impressive formal experimentation in English verse before Gerard Manley Hopkins. In the countess's 165 psalms, there are 164 distinct stanzaic and metrical patterns, some of them being remarkably complex and subtle.

Robert's are technically less ambitious, although they certainly reflect a similar interest in working with complex patterns of verse—as evidenced by the three unusual thirteen-line stanzas of "Upon a wretch that wastes away/ Consumed with wants." Here the complex rhyme scheme (*aab cccb ddeeb*) and the varying line length (886886-33666 syllables) are reminiscent of the countess's experiments, as indeed are many of Sidney's pastorals and songs. None of the patterns exactly matches those of Mary and the diction is naturally closer to the typical love poetry of the era (such as in *England's Helicon*, 1600) than to her *Psalms*, but they arise from the same fascination with formal experimentation: Just as in Mary's Psalms only once is the stanzaic pattern repeated, so in Sidney's twenty-four songs he never repeats a pattern, and within particular poems, too, he displays a technical virtuosity comparable to that of his brother and sister.

Song 1, "O eyes, a lights devine," for example, skillfully mixes lines of varied length, with a predominantly iambic beat. Like both Philip and Mary, he uses feminine rhyme very skillfully in the songs (as in Song 10, "You whoe fauor doe enioy"), and his technical skill is seen in such sophisticated mixtures as blending of rhyming anapests with the regular iambics in Song 4 ("My soule is purest fine/ doth not aspyre"). Like Mary, Sidney shows an excellent control of movement and balance within single lines, as, for example, in the final lines of Sonnet 21: "Or if on mee from my fayre heauen are seen/ Some scattred beames: Know sutch heate giues theyre light/ as frosty mornings Sun: as Moonshyne night."

PHILIP'S INFLUENCE

If Sidney shares something of Mary's technical daring, the most important influence is nevertheless that of his brother. Sidney's sequence is clearly modeled on *Astrophel and Stella* (1591): It mingles sonnets with longer, more emotionally diffuse songs, and like Philip's, Sidney's sequence contains an interesting transformation of biographical reference into a devious fiction. The whole sequence is characterized by an opaque melancholy, a mood of disturbance and brooding which, while endemic to Petrarchan sonnets in general, nevertheless takes as its subject Sidney's reading of his own political and personal career. While the collection is a typical Petrarchan miscellany, it is united even less than *Astrophel and Stella* by narrative or personae and is held together, more explicitly than in any other collection of late Elizabethan lyrics, by that most powerful of institutions and ideological forces, the Elizabethan court.

Writing from the Low Countries

Robert's poetry was probably written during his long, frustrating tour of duty in the Low Countries, perhaps begun (like Mary's) in the late 1580's but (at least in the one extant copy) copied probably at some time between 1596 and 1598. Perhaps Sidney's poetry was a reaction not only to his depressing exile from England but also to the melancholy duty of occupying his brother's old post. Much of Sidney's verse could be read as a moving expression of a frustrated politician's world of escape, yearning for his wife and children and home at Penshurst.

Sonnet 7, "The hardy Captein vnusde to retyre," speaks directly of his turning from the Low Countries "to the West" where "loue fast holds his hart" (Song 6). The sixth Song of the collection is an especially revealing piece—as well as being the most impressive poetically. Like Ralegh's famous and haunting "As you Came to the Holy Land," it is based on the traditional lost ballad of a pilgrim traveling to Walsingham. Sidney's version is a 136-line poem, hauntingly evocative in its use of the ballad with its traditional dialogue, here occurring between a Pilgrim and a Lady who presumably represents Sidney's wife. Certainly, "the knight that loves me best," who "greefs liuerie weares," who "to the west . . . turns his eyes," to whom she refers is Sidney's wistful projection of his own exiled self held by duty to the Low Countries away from what later in the poem he terms: "the lady that doth rest near Medwayes sandy bed." Penshurst Place, the Sidney home, stands on the Medway River just outside Tonbridge and almost due west of Flushing. Interestingly enough, Sidney revised this particular line to read "near ritch Tons sandy bed," which of course refers to Tonbridge.

Petrarchanism

Song 6 is the most clearly autobiographical poem in the sequence, projecting a partly calculated, partly wistful view of Sidney's frustrated personal and political career. The bulk of the collection, in traditional Petrarchan fashion, is ostensibly concerned with love and is similar to a host of sequences written in the 1590's, such as Daniel's *Delia* or Michael Drayton's *Idea*, although no poem mentions any identifiable or even coherently fictional mistress. The diction is typical of the English *petrarchisti*. The lovers "sowle" exists "in purest fyre" (Song 4); he accepts both the joys and griefs of love, in his "bands of service without end" (Sonnet 13). Readers encounter the familiar world of Petrarchan paradox: On the one hand, there is the high idealism of the lover who affirms the beauty of "those fayre eyes" which "shyne in theyr former light" (Song 12); on the other hand, there are the "paines which I vncessantly susteine" (Sonnet 2). The lady's beauties are "born of the heauens, my sowles delight" (Sonnet 3), while the lover's passions are "purest flames kindled by beauties rare" (Sonnet 4), as he contemplates in pleasurable agony how she takes "pleasure" in his "cruelty" (Sonnet 25), asking her why she "nowrishes" poisonous weeds of cold despair in love's garden instead of the plants and trees of love's true faith and zeal (Song 22).

This basic Petrarchan situation of frustration, contradiction, and paradox is decked out in familiar Neoplatonic garb. The world is a dark cave where love's lights never shine except through the beloved's eyes, the "purest stars, whose neuer diying fyres" (Sonnet 1) constantly burn a path between the heavens and the lover's soul. Sexual desire is rarely explicitly mentioned: the dominant mood is that of melancholy, the recurring emphasis on the lover's self-torturing helplessness, and to an unusual degree, on torture, disease, and violence. The lover is a continually lashed slave, flung from rocks, a leper, racked by gangrene, or in violent wars.

Even with the marked emphasis on violence, this is a world familiar to readers of Renaissance lyrics. Sidney's work is less versatile, metrically and metaphorically, than

Philip's, with no double sestinas or quantitative verse and little of Philip's sly humor. What distinguishes Sidney's poems from the mass by second-rate poets such as Thomas Watson and Henry Constable and from the anonymous verse of a miscellany like *England's Helicon* is his remarkable control of form and tone, and his frequent use of a cryptic and direct address, not unlike the aphoristic tone of some of Greville's poems. Typical is the brief, pessimistic Song 17, which seems to reflect upon deeply tragic events in the poet's experience.

Well-crafted lines

Robert's poetry, like the work of Philip and Mary, shows a deep commitment to the craft of poetry as well as to its inspiring or calculated consolations of erotic or political favor. It is more than conventional Petrarchan regret when he asserts that even "the most perfect stile cannot attaine" the expression of the mistress's beauties or the pangs of love. The poems are the work of a poet with a highly sensitive ear, and a range of tone that, while not broad, is deeply resonant, especially receptive to the way emotions may be attached to metaphors of absence and loss. In his *Caelica*, Greville often takes up the conventional assertion that, when apart, true lovers are paradoxically closer because of the spiritual nature of their love; but he places the motif in a grimly realistic context, affirming instead that "absence is pain." Similarly, Sidney's brooding over absence, delay, and loneliness have more than a conventional "feel" to them. Over and over again, the poet suffers from "greefs sent from her whom in my sowle I bless" (Song 23); constantly he feels that "delaies are death" (Song 18), as he waits "on unknown shore, with weather hard destrest" (Song 22). Such common Petrarchan motifs are made peculiarly effective especially through the grave, deliberate melancholic movement of the lines, which convey the passion, the hopelessness, and yet the continuing devotion of the lover.

Neoplatonism and Calvinism

Intellectually, Sidney's verse is as rich a revelation of the peculiar strains and repressions of the Elizabethan aristocracy as that of Philip or Mary. His poetry, however, seems more detached from their particular religious interests. One of the most revealing notes of the literature of the Sidney circle is its continual attempt to balance the idealism of high Neoplatonism, and its emphasis on the autonomy of the human will and man's desire for perfection, with the psychological and political demands of a strong Calvinistic piety, emphasizing God's transcendence of humanity and the corruption and worthlessness of human aspirations. It is interesting that Sidney seems relatively indifferent to this great intellectual debate; nor is there any sense that he was especially interested in the more extreme varieties of Neoplatonic or magical philosophy associated with John Dee or Giordano Bruno, which were current in the 1580's. Perhaps living isolated from the mainstream of English philosophical developments in the 1580's and 1590's, he was untouched by such speculation; altogether, Sidney's character and interests were more pragmatic and less speculative. His poetry had more immediate ends in view. A typically aspiring courtier, directing his poems at particular (never, of course, stated) ends, the intellectual tensions of his verse remain the stock-in-trade of the Petrarchan poet; his sequence is poetically but not intellectually sophisticated.

The Elizabethan court

The particular feature of Sidney's poetry which makes his work important to readers of the ideologically opaque power struggles of the Elizabethan aristocracy is the intense way it articulates the silent power of the dominant institution of the age, the court. The basis of the Petrarchan sonnet collections of the late sixteenth century is not primarily erotic, despite their Petrarchan apparatus. Sexual desire is used—by Sidney's brother, as well as by Spenser, Daniel, Ralegh, and others—as a metaphor for political desire and frustration. Most of Sidney's poems do not evoke the frustrated sexual passion of a lover; they use that basic Petrarchan situation as a metaphor for political powerlessness and aspiration. The "lights divine" from which the lover is "exiled," "the only cause for which I care to see," and "these purest flames kindled by beauties rare," may be read as conventional Neoplatonic complements of a beloved only if the realities of Elizabethan politics and the court's control of the discursive structures of both politics and poetry are ignored.

No less than Ralegh's "Cynthia" or "Praised be Diana's Fair and Harmless Light," Sidney's sonnets articulate the ideological dominance of the Elizabethan court; unlike Ralegh's—except in their intense anxiousness and their overly insistent protest of absolute devotion—they do not articulate any opposition to that hegemonic discourse. As his brother Philip's *Astrophel and Stella* so triumphantly shows, one of the distinctive features of the Petrarchan sequence is its encouragement to readers to decode it in a variety of ways—as erotic self-evaluation, philosophical meditation, or moral debate. Sidney's poems can be read as intense, extreme Neoplatonic poems of compliment and frustration, but they acquire an urgency and become rooted in the material life of late Elizabethan society when they are read as compensations for political powerlessness.

Not all of Robert Sidney's poems can be read so directly in this way—there are a variety of translations, songs, and other miscellaneous pieces which may be seen as typical "workshop" exercises designed to show or practice his skills—but through the whole collection, one senses the enormous power of the Elizabethan court, creating and controlling its subjects by exerting power over their language, over their metaphors of political as well as poetical expression. The political world in which Sidney had, between 1586 and 1598, a marginal part, can be read from his poetical text: Finally the poetical text (the poems extant in his slim notebook) and the social text (the events which constitute the milieu in which he wrote) are indistinguishable, each flowing into the other to articulate the material and metaphorical dominance of the Elizabethan court.

A true Sidney

It is fascinating to see the emergence into literary and critical consciousness of such an interesting poet almost four hundred years after he wrote. When it was written, Sidney's poetry aimed to demonstrate his fitness to take part in the power of the court, but it demonstrated as well that he was a Sidney in another way—in his devotion to the craft and the importance of poetry. A decade or more after he wrote these poems, Sidney was praised by Ben Jonson as a man of generosity, responsibility, and piety. Jonson speaks of how his children might "Reade, in their vertuous parents noble parts,/ The mysteries of manners, armes, and arts." Sidney's distinction in "armes and manners" was no mystery; he was a Sidney, a name which, as Jonson put it, was in "the impresse of the great." Until the rediscovery of his manuscript, however, Sidney's "arts" were indeed unknown. Perhaps by the time Jonson wrote "To Penshurst," Sidney himself had all but forgotten his youthful poetry. He had, after all, achieved his comfortable if minor place in the Jacobean aristocracy. One can only be glad that the longer span of history sometimes uncovers what the short time of individual men happens to bury.

Bibliography

Croft, Peter J. *The Poems of Robert Sidney: Edited from the Poet's Autograph Notebook*. Oxford, England: Oxford University Press, 1984. This important book-length edition includes an extended introduction which concerns the life and work of Sidney. For this alone, the text is invaluable. This work also, however, contains a chronological table of the life and times of Sidney and his complete works. The poems are supplemented by extended notes and commentaries which aid greatly in their explication. This is a valuable source for the study of Sidney.

Hay, Millicent V. *The Life of Robert Sidney, Earl of Leicester, 1563-1626*. Washington, D.C.: Folger Shakespeare Library, 1984. This rather pedestrian book-length account of Sidney is of value because of its extensive bibliography. Each of its chapters contains notes, and there is a good account given of his poetry. The work also contains a genealogical table and a thorough index.

Sidney, Sir Robert. "The Poems of Robert Sidney." *English* 136 (1981): 3-72. This unique article, edited by Katherine Duncan-Jones, presents a thorough collation of the poems of Robert Sidney. It is important because it modernizes the spelling in the poems. While it is rather complete and the changes appear accurate, the modernization of the verse is somewhat disappointing.

Waller, Gary F. "Sir Robert Sidney." In *Early Poetry of the Sixteenth Century*. London: Longman, 1986. Waller puts the short literary life of Sidney into perspective in this fine essay. Short, yet thorough, this work centers on the strain of Sidney's life as a courtier, his comparison with his more widely known, flamboyant brother Philip and his sister Mary. The work contains a concise chronology, general bibliography, and notes.

Gary F. Waller

Jon Silkin

Born: London, England; December 2, 1930
Died: Newcastle upon Tyne, England; November 25, 1997

Principal poetry

The Peaceable Kingdom, 1954
The Two Freedoms, 1958
The Re-ordering of the Stones, 1961
Nature with Man, 1965
Poems, New and Selected, 1966
Amana Grass, 1971
The Principle of Water, 1974
The Little Time-Keeper, 1976
The Psalms with Their Spoils, 1980
Selected Poems, 1980, 2d revised edition 1988, new edition 1993
The Ship's Pasture: Poems, 1986
The Lens-Breakers, 1992
Watersmeet, 1994

Other literary forms

Not only was he a noted poet, Jon Silkin was also an important literary critic, authoring a study of English poetry from World War I, *Out of Battle: The Poetry of the Great War* (1972, revised 1987), and a study of modern twentieth century poetry, *The Life of Metrical and Free Verse in Twentieth-Century Poetry* (1997). Related to his criticism was his editing of the significant collections *The Penguin Book of First World War Poetry* (1979, revised 1981), *Wilfred Owen: The Poems* (1985), *The Penguin Book of First World War Prose* (coeditor with Jon Glover; 1989), and *The War Poems of Wilfred Owen* (1994). Silkin also wrote one play, *Gurney*, published in 1985 and produced in London, as *Black Notes*, in 1986.

Achievements

As important as his awards (Faber Memorial Prize, 1965; C. Day Lewis Fellowship, 1976-1977; Fellow of the Royal Society of Literature, 1986) is Silkin's inclusion in such prestigious anthologies as *New Poets of England and America* (editions of 1957 and 1962), *The New Poetry* (second edition, 1966), *Poems of Our Moment* (1968), *British Poetry Since 1945* (1970), *The Norton Anthology of Modern Poetry* (1973), *The Oxford Book of Twentieth-Century English Verse* (1973), *The Hutchinson Book of Post-War British Poets* (1989), and *Anthology of Twentieth-Century British and Irish Poetry* (2001). Finally, his role as founder and continuing editor of the magazine *Stand*—devoted first to publishing modern poetry and its criticism, and later including modern fiction—also ensures Silkin a lasting place in the history of modern British literature.

Biography

Silkin was the son of Jewish parents, Joseph, a lawyer, and Dora Rubenstein Silkin. War made a deep impression on Silkin as a child; as a youngster, one of Silkin's most vivid memories, referred to in his poetry, was of being evacuated from London to the countryside during the German bombing of World War II. After National Service in the Education Corps (1948-1950), during which he reached the rank of sergeant, Silkin spent the years between 1950 and 1956 as a manual laborer in London, an experience partly reflected in his first-person poems about cemetery groundskeeping and about workingmen. During this period, he founded the literary periodical *Stand* in 1952 and published his first major poetry collection in 1954.

After working as an English teacher to foreign students in 1956-1958, Silkin was appointed Gregory Fellow in Poetry at the University of Leeds, a position he held from 1958 to 1960. He came relatively late to a formal college education, earning his B.A. from the University of Leeds as a mature student. The degree, awarded in 1962, took him only two years to complete. In 1964, he became founding coeditor of Northern House Publishers in Newcastle upon Tyne and subsequently, as reflected in the locales of his poetry, held a variety of teaching, visiting instructor, and visiting writer in residence posts at universities and colleges in England, the United States (in Ohio, Iowa, Idaho, Kentucky, and Washington, D.C.), Australia, Israel, Japan, and Korea.

Married to the writer Lorna Tracy in 1974, Silkin had four children; the death of the first, Adam, and birth of the second, David, had profound impacts on Silkin, manifested in his poetry, which likewise indicates how

Jon Silkin

important love, marriage, children, and parenting remained throughout his life.

Analysis

Humanity versus nature

A third or more of Silkin's approximately 350 poems deal with or touch on the subject of the natural world and humanity's relation with it, through concord, discord, or symbolic parallels. Animals, such as the persecuted fox of Silkin's anti-hunting poems, or various caged or free birds; insects, such as the bees, butterflies, moths, ants, and flies, with their interesting symbolism applicable to nature and humanity; plants, such as the various flowers of Silkin's distinctive "flower poems"; and inanimate nature, especially stones, river, sea, sky, and stars—all pervade Silkin's poetry both as subjects and repositories of imagery and symbolism. The poems most often anthologized have been selections from the fifteen "flower poems" (so named by Silkin himself) in *Nature with Man:* "A Bluebell," "Crowfoot (in Water)," "A Daisy," "Dandelion," "Goat's Beard and Daisy," "Harebell," "Iris," "Lilies of the Valley," "Milkmaids (Lady's Smock)," "Moss," "Peonies," "Small Celandine," "The Strawberry Plant," "The Violet," and "White Geranium." As Silkin himself explains in "Note on 'Flower' Poems" in *Nature with Man*, the flowers are either wild or cultivated, suggesting certain relationships with humanity, and the garden is "a kind of human bestiary, containing in the several plants earlier developed and anticipatory examples of human types and situations." Silkin goes on in his note to discuss almost every flower poem, explaining for example that "'Dandelion' . . . sees its subject as a seizer of space, and asks for political parallels to be made," including the idea of "nature being a 'preying upon.'" While Silkin's analyses of his own flower poems are perceptive (not always true of writers about their own work), they are not exhaustive: for example, lurking in the background of "Dandelion" is the etymology of the flower's name, from "lion's tooth." As meritorious as these flower poems but not as well known are the ones from Silkin's later books: "Snow Drop" from *Poems, New and Selected*, which suggests the paradoxes of a flower having insectlike qualities and appearing in sunshine, despite its name; "Ajuga" from *The Ship's Pasture*, which explores the flower's intercontinental intermixture, the paradox of a mineral appearance of a plant, and the powerful psychological effects on the viewer; and "Inside the Gentian" in *The Lens-Breakers*, suggesting the flower's combination of visual art, mystery, magic, violence, and communicativeness.

Humanity versus humanity: love, marriage, children, society, war

A third or more of Silkin's poems deal with romantic love, including marriage and the parent-child relationship, and an even higher proportion of his poems deals with all the varied relationships between human beings individually and in groups, societies, or nations. Romantic love, frequently with marriage implied, is celebrated in physical terms, sometimes quite sexually explicit, in poems such as "Community" (1965), "Processes" (1965), "Opened" (1971), "Our Selves" (1971), "Untitled Poem: 'The Perfume on Your Body'" (1977), "Acids" (1980), "Going On" (1980), "Water" (1980), "Given a Flower"

(1986), "The Lamps of Home" (1986), "Beings" (1992), "The Hand's Black Hymns" (1992), "Juniper and Forgiveness" (1992), and "Psalmists" (1992). Such love may sometimes emphasize a triumph of life over death, or reach to the spiritual beyond the physical, an issue that is recurrent in Silkin's poetry, as are the words "flesh," "mind," and "spirit." Such physical love gone wrong is shown in one of Silkin's poetic sequences, "Poems Concerning Salome and Herod" (1986). Another difficult issue in romantic love includes separation, as in "Absence and Light" (1986), "A Hand" (1986), and "A Psalm Concerning Absence" (1992). Other recurrent words in Silkin's poetry are "absence" and "space," which refer to lovers' separation as well as death. Also problematic in love may be constancy or fidelity, as in "Fidelities" (1992).

For many couples, with love and marriage come children, and Silkin's responses to them range from elegy on their tragically premature death, as in "Death of a Son: Who Died in a Mental Hospital Aged One" (1954), to wonder and celebration at their birth, as in "For David Emanuel" (1954)—both autobiographical poems. A link between children and social criticism is shown in the poetic sequence "The People" (1974), in which a couple have difficulties with obtuse governmental authorities about the institutionalization and treatment of their disabled child in a case resembling that in "Death of a Son" and "For a Child: On His Being Pronounced Mentally Defective by a Committee of the LLC" (1961). Lastly, the other side of the relationship—child to parent, rather than parent to child—is explored in "Fathers" (1992), in which the speaker deals with his father's death and cremation.

Unlike the passionless poet-critics he censures in "Three Critics" (1961), Silkin is emotionally and socially engaged, writing poetry with social criticism of a government's or a society's mistreatment of parents and children, as in "For a Child: On His Being Pronounced Mentally Defective by a Committee of the LLC" (1961); of the working poor, as in "And I Turned from the Inner Heart" (1958), "Bowl" (1958), "Furnished Lives" (1958), "Savings" (1961), and "Killhope Wheel, 1860, County Durham" (1971); of whole groups of people, as in "Cherokee" (1992); or of pollution of the environment, as in "Crossing a River" (1986) or "The Levels" (1992). Worst of all, perhaps, is the failure of societies and nations to stop wars, spanning history from ancient times to the future nuclear war complacently lectured about by a government bureaucrat in "Defence" (1965). The epigraph to *The Peaceable Kingdom*, drawn from the Biblical book of Isaiah about the wolf dwelling with the lamb, and the poem "Isaiah's Thread" (1974) show Silkin's continual awareness and criticism of the injuries inflicted in war throughout history: the Romans' war against the Jews in "Footsteps on the Downcast Path" (1986); the wars of the English against the Irish or Scots, in "Famine" (1992), "What Can We Mean?" (1972), or "Poem: 'At Laggan'" (1971); the American Civil War, in "Paying for Forgiveness" (1992) and "Civil War Grave, Richmond" (1992); World War I, in "Mr. Lloyd's Life" (1992); and World War II, in "We Stock the Deer-Park" (1986) and numerous poems about the Holocaust.

Jewish heritage and history

Related to Silkin's Jewish heritage are nearly fifty poems referring to the history and culture of the Jewish people from ancient to modern times, scattered throughout all of Silkin's works. In "First It Was Singing" (1954), Silkin equates the outcries of hunted animals and persecuted Jews, which motivate the "singing" of the animals and the Jewish poet. The suffering of Jews and the guilt of Christian societies involved in their massacre and oppression in medieval England is the subject of "Astringencies No. 1: The Coldness" (1961), "The Malabestia" (1974), and "Resting Place" (1980), while the Holocaust of World War II is a focus of "Culpabilities" (1961), "Jaffa, and Other Places" (1971), "The People" (1974), "The Plum-Tree" (1977), "Footsteps on the Downcast Path" (1986), "Fidelities" (1992), and "Trying to Hide Treblinka" (1992). An eight-poem section of *Amana Grass* ("A Word about Freedom and Identity in Tel-Aviv," "Reclaimed Area," "Jaffa, and Other Places," "What are the lights, in dark," "Conditions," "Ayalon," "Bull-God," "Divisions") is devoted to Israel, and in these poems, as well as "Communal" (1986), "Climbing to Jerusalem" (1986), and "Jews without Arabs" (1992), Silkin considers how, from ancient through modern times, Jews have confronted the issues of struggling with the natural world to make the land more habitable or living in harmony with non-Jewish fellow inhabitants.

Metapoetics, language, and communication

More than fifty of Silkin's poems deal with the topics of metapoetics (poetry about the nature, effects, or creation of literature or art), language, and communication. In *The Peaceable Kingdom*, Silkin suggests not only that the suffering and persecution of animals and Jews create their "singing," but also, in "Prologue" and "Epilogue," the poems that open and close the book, that his poetry may function as a kind of Noah's ark to save the animals from injury by human beings as well as, perhaps, to unite all in enlightened, considered, and considerate harmony. In "From . . . the Animal Dark" (1958), each of whose two sections is a partly disguised sonnet, appropriate to love poetry, the poet-speaker suggests that language charged by the poem may help create light, enlightenment, and the reunion of lovers. Likewise, in "Amber" (1992), the poem is equated to an amber pendant, a combination of art, nature, and preserver, whose beauty, warmth, electrical charge, and electrical attraction may touch the beloved both literally and metaphorically.

In contrast with the power of literature and language to enrich or unite, or to communicate with the divine, are the thwarting of this potential in sterility and divisiveness. "Three Critics" (1961), with implied ironic tautology, criticizes poet-critics who, following theory and social class, separate intellect from feeling and thus drain their verse of emotion, warmth, and conviction. "The Uses of Man and the Uses of Poetry" (1980), with similar social criticism, laments the prison inmate who learns lyric and then satiric poetry but is rewarded with beating by the "warders" (guards). In "Crowfoot (in Water)" (1965), one of Silkin's celebrated "flower poems," details suggest that the flower is "articulate," has a capacity for communication, but this communication is "smutched" in the mouths and throats of hungry cattle that devour it. Also, in "Douglas of Sorbie and the Adder" (1992), based on a folktale, a mother is horrified by the realization that her young son and an adder are not only sharing food but communicating. She orders the farm's day laborers to kill the snake, hoping for the child's success in Georgian London, but, in an example of Silkin's ironic social criticism, causes the death of her son through grief as well as that of the snake.

Other major works

play: *Gurney*, pb. 1985, pr. 1986 (as *Black Notes*).

nonfiction: *Out of Battle: The Poetry of the Great War*, 1972, revised edition 1987; *The Life of Metrical and Free Verse in Twentieth-Century Poetry*, 1997.

translation: *Against Parting*, 1968 (by Nathan Zach).

edited texts: *Poetry of the Committed Individual: A "Stand" Anthology of Poetry*, 1973; *The Penguin Book of First World War Poetry*, 1979, revised edition 1981; *Wilfred Owen: The Poems*, 1985; *The Penguin Book of First World War Prose*, 1989 (with Jon Glover); *The War Poems of Wilfred Owen*, 1994.

Bibliography

Bell, Arthur, Donald Heiney, and Lenthiel Downs. *English Literature: 1900 to the Present*. 2d ed. New York: Barron's Educational Series, 1994. A separate section in Chapter 12, "Varieties of Experimental Verse," gives a brief overview of Silkin's career through 1986, with comments on "Death of a Son" and the flower poems.

Brown, Merle. *Double Lyric: Divisiveness and Communal Creativity in Recent English Poetry*. New York: Columbia University Press, 1980. Chapter 6, "Stress in Silkin's Poetry and the Healing Emptiness of America," is a thirty-three-page survey of Silkin's work up to 1979 from the perspective of the "stress between imaginative realization and ideological commitment" by Silkin's most appreciative critic. Brown's brief "Afterword" is included in the 1975 edition of *The Peaceable Kingdom*, indicating themes of that book. Silkin composed an elegiac poem about Brown, "Wildness Makes a Form: In Memoriam the Critic Merle Brown" (1980).

Cluysenaar, Anne. "Alone in a Mine of Reality: A Matrix in the Poetry of Jon Silkin." In *British Poetry Since 1960*, edited by Michael Schmidt and Grevel Lindop. Oxford, England: Carcanet, 1972. A seven-page survey of Silkin's poetry books from 1954 to 1971 stresses Silkin's awareness in his poetry of the interconnectedness of things.

Huk, Romana. "Poetry of the Committed Individual: Jon Silkin, Tony Harrison, Geoffrey Hill, and the Poets of Postwar Leeds." In *Contemporary British*

Poetry: Essays in Theory and Criticism, edited by James Acheson and Romana Huk. Albany: State University of New York Press, 1996. Taking her title from the title of Silkin's anthology from *Stand* magazine, Huk analyzes the poetry from the perspective of political engagement.

Schmidt, Michael. *An Introduction to Fifty Modern Poets*. New York: Barnes and Noble, 1979. A five-page survey of Silkin's poetry books from 1954 to 1974 stresses the progression from book to book, as well as the worth of the poetry because of what it attempts despite the "unfinished" quality of individual poems.

Norman Prinsky

Leslie Marmon Silko

Born: Albuquerque, New Mexico; March 5, 1948

Principal poetry

Laguna Woman: Poems, 1974
Storyteller, 1981 (includes poetry and prose)

Other literary forms

Leslie Marmon Silko published her first and most critically acclaimed novel, *Ceremony*, in 1977. Later novels include *Almanac of the Dead* (1991) and *Gardens in the Dunes* (1999). She has also published many short stories, most notably "The Man to Send Rain Clouds" (1969), "Yellow Woman" (1974), and "Lullaby" (1974).

Nonfiction works include *Sacred Water: Narratives and Pictures* (1993) and a collection of her essays, *Yellow Woman and a Beauty of the Spirit: Essays on Native American Life Today* (1996). The letters between Silko and the poet James Wright were published in 1986 as *The Delicacy and Strength of Lace: Letters Between Leslie Marmon Silko and James Wright*.

Achievements

Leslie Marmon Silko is generally considered the first important Native American woman writer. She is best known for her fiction, especially her first novel, *Ceremony*. However, her first collection of poetry, *Laguna Woman*, was also very well received, and in 1977 she won a Pushcart Prize for Poetry. Her short story "Lullaby" was selected as one of the best short stories of 1975. She earned a MacArthur Prize Fellowship in 1981, and in 1988 New Mexico named her a "Living Cultural Treasure." In 1994 she won the Native Writers Circle of the Americas lifetime achievement award, an honor previously bestowed upon such Native American literary luminaries as N. Scott Momaday and Simon J. Ortiz.

Biography

Of Native American, Mexican, and Caucasian descent, Leslie Marmon Silko was born in 1948 to Leland Howard Marmon and Mary Virginia Leslie. She spent most of her childhood among her extended family on the Laguna Pueblo reservation, which later provided the setting for much of her poetry and fiction. Silko first was educated at an Indian boarding school and later graduated from a Catholic high school in Albuquerque. In 1964 she enrolled at the University of New Mexico. While still an undergraduate, she married, had her first child, and published her first short story, "The Man to Send Rain Clouds" (1969). After graduating in 1969, she briefly attended law school in hopes of becoming a legal advocate for the people of the Laguna reservation but dropped out after becoming disillusioned with the criminal justice system.

After returning to the University of New Mexico for several graduate courses in English, she taught for several years at Navajo Community College in Arizona while continuing to write and publish poems and short stories. Having divorced her first husband, she married John Silko and in 1972 and had her second child. In 1974 her first book of poems, *Laguna Woman*, was published. Having moved with her husband to Alaska, she began work on her first novel, *Ceremony*, in part, she said, as a way of managing the homesickness she felt for her native New Mexico.

In 1978 Silko returned to the American Southwest, residing at Tucson and teaching at the University of Arizona. While going through a painful divorce and custody battle, she put together her next book, *Storyteller*, which consists of previously published short stories interwoven with old and new poems, passages of prose autobiography, and photographs. In the early 1980's she became interested in film and produced an adaptation of a Laguna myth, *Estoyehmuut and the Gunnadeyah* (1980). Throughout the rest of the 1980's Silko became somewhat more reclusive. With the support of a MacArthur Foundation grant, she spent most of her time alone writing her second novel, *Almanac of the Dead.* A darker novel than *Ceremony*, it reflects her growing frustration over the continued injustices suffered by Native Americans.

Throughout the 1990's, Silko continued living alone on her ranch outside Tucson. In 1993 she produced a self-published book, *Sacred Water: Narratives and Pictures*, which consists of an essay printed alongside her own photographs. Three years later she collected her previously published nonfiction in *Yellow Woman and a Beauty of the Spirit.* In 1999 she published her third novel, *Gardens in the Dunes*.

Analysis

In her poetry's form and themes, Leslie Marmon Silko consciously reflects her mixed cultural heritage. Part Caucasian, part Mexican, part Laguna Pueblo, Silko attempts to break down boundaries of all kinds in her poetry—poetic, generic, racial, national, gender—in order to emphasize the universal interconnectedness and interdependence of all things.

Often in her poetry she depicts herself as a new breed of storyteller. As a poet and fiction writer who has dedicated her life to the written word, Silko acknowledges the influence of her Western, Europeanized education. She also, however, sees herself as another in a long line of Laguna Pueblo storytellers. In an oral culture such as that of the Laguna Pueblo, the storyteller is the repository of the communal history and the preserver of the communal identity. Thus, many of Silko's poems represent her attempt to put the central Laguna Pueblo myths into verse, and into a verse form that in its stanza formations, indentations, and parenthetical asides retains as many of the characteristics of oral storytelling as possible. Even those of her poems that are not verse retellings of traditional stories often depend upon figures and images drawn from these myths. The act of storytelling in Laguna culture is, however, communal and highly democratic; no one storyteller can know all the stories, or all the versions of each story. In order to re-create this sense of community Silko often prefaces her poems by informing the reader about who first told her the story in the poem or by noting that other versions of the story exist within the oral tradition.

Another characteristic of Silko's poetry is its emphasis on sense of place. The setting for almost all her poems is the Laguna reservation and its environs. Like Laguna mythology, her poems often incorporate very specific Laguna landmarks as a way of emphasizing the connection of the people to the land on which they live. Additionally, Silko's poems reflect the Laguna people's profound reverence for the natural environment as that on which they depend for their very survival. Not surprisingly, her poetry often carries an implicit environmental agenda and a criticism of what she sees as the destructive and proprietary attitude of white people toward the land.

Laguna Woman

Although well received on its initial publication, Silko's first book of poetry garnered relatively little critical attention, in part because many of the strongest poems in the collection were later republished in *Storyteller.* A slim volume containing only eighteen poems, *Laguna Woman* introduces many of the themes and motifs that lie at the heart of all Silko's works. The poems focus particularly on the interwoven themes of nature, time, and love. In "The Time We Climbed Snake Mountain," for instance, the speaker warns her fellow climbers to "watch out" for "the spotted yellow snake," not because the snake presents a threat but because "he lives here./ The mountain is his." In Silko's poems the indifference of people toward nature poses the real threat, not poisonous snakes.

Like other Native American poets, Silko also emphasizes the cyclical nature of time. "Preparations" describes in graphic detail crows feeding on the carcass of a sheep. They "Pull wool from skin/ Pick meat from bone/ tendon from muscle." The poem, however, is not a lament but the description of an endlessly repeated and cleansing ritual. The speaker informs us that "The body is carefully attended" by the crows who "gather/ to make preparations." Only "Let wind polish the bones" and "It is done." The destruction of the sheep does not make an end but becomes the life of the "fat" crows with their "long black wings" and "shining eyes."

"Indian Song: Survival" is typical of the way Silko's poems explore the paradoxical nature of sexual love with its elements of conquest and domination being inseparable from the pleasure and transformation it can bring. The "mountain lion man" stalks the speaker, who has "slept with the river" and who knows that "he is warmer than any man." Nevertheless, once the mountain lion man conquers the speaker she finds contentment, feels "sunlight warmth," and is transformed into "the lean gray deer/ running on the edge of the rainbow."

Storyteller

As a part of her attempt to tear down traditional literary boundaries, Silko mixes many genres in her 1981 collection *Storyteller.* The poems contained in this collection vary widely. Some seem to be straightforward records of Silko's memoirs, while others relate family stories she heard as a child. Still others are versifications of powerful Laguna Pueblo myths drawn from the oral tradition.

The various pieces are interwoven in no immediately apparent order and without any of the organizational divisions (such as chapters or section headings) that one finds in more conventional collections. Most of the new poems even lack titles. Silko herself has often compared Pueblo storytelling (and likewise the effect she hopes to achieve in her poetry) to a spiderweb, whereby each storyteller makes a contribution and meaning can be found only in the larger, interconnected design. Silko thus leaves it to her reader to trace the individual threads of her collection and to make out the larger design or designs. The effect of the entire collection is dialogic, with each of the poems and stories responding to one another to form a complex, multilayered fabric.

"I always called her Aunt Susie"

The untitled poem focusing on Silko's Aunt Susie found at the beginning of *Storyteller* is typical of the poems found throughout that directly relate Siko's personal and family history. An appropriate beginning, this poem describes one of Silko's early role models. Like Silko, Aunt Susie had gone away to college and "had come to believe very much in books/ and in schooling." Although dedicated to the written word, Aunt Susie was also "the last generation here at Laguna,/ that passed down an entire culture/ by word of mouth." Silko learned from Aunt Susie that the Laguna require a new kind of storyteller, since, as she understood, "the atmosphere and conditions/ which had maintained this oral tradition in Laguna culture/ had been irrevocably altered by the European intrusion." Silko then explains that in Laguna culture each storyteller remembers a portion of the oral tradition. She thus ends her poem—and begins her collection—by writing, "this is what I remember."

"A Ck'o'yo medicine man"

Another untitled poem, this one is found at the heart of the collection and recounts the Laguna myth of the "Ck'o'yo medicine man," who uses flashy magic to distract the people from their ritual maintenance of "the Mother Corn altar." This causes the Mother who gives life to the natural world to retreat to "the fourth world below." "She took the/ rain clouds with her," and soon "The people were starving." In order to restore life on the surface world, or "fifth world," the people rely on Hummingbird as a messenger to beg their forgiveness. He in turn relies on the help of Fly, and together they must get help from Buzzard and Caterpillar before Mother is appeased. On its surface the poem explains in mythological terms the cycle of drought and rain typical of the Laguna region, but it also emphasizes the interdependence of all earthly life and the reverence and attention human beings owe to nature.

"COTTONWOOD Part Two: Buffalo Story"

The two "COTTONWOOD" poems found in *Storyteller* relate the adventures of Kockininako or Yellow Woman, a crucial character in Laguna mythology and a frequent figure in Silko's poetry and fiction. Yellow Woman is a figure of transgression but also of renewal. In "Part Two: Buffalo Story," Yellow Woman is seduced and kidnapped by the Buffalo Man at a time when her people are starving for lack of meat. Her husband, Arrow Boy, recaptures her and in the process kills all the buffalo and even Yellow Woman herself when he realizes that she loves the Buffalo People and wants to remain with them even in death. Thus begins the tradition of the buffalo hunt, which saves the people from starvation. Although Yellow Woman abandons her pueblo out of sexual longings, she also brings the people new sustenance and continued life. Like the Yellow Woman, Silko has gone outside the traditions of the Pueblo through her embrace of literature and poetry but only in an attempt to renew it and to ensure its survival through the recording of its traditions.

Other major works

long fiction: *Ceremony*, 1977; *Almanac of the Dead*, 1991; *Gardens in the Dunes*, 1999.

short fiction: *Yellow Woman*, 1993.

nonfiction: *Sacred Water: Narratives and Pictures*, 1993; *Yellow Woman and a Beauty of the Spirit: Essays on Native American Life Today*, 1996; *The Delicacy and Strength of Lace: Letters Between Leslie Marmon Silko and James Wright*, 1986; *Conversations with Leslie Marmon Silko*, 2000 (Ellen L. Arnold, editor).

Bibliography

Barnett, Louise K., and James L. Thorson, eds. *Leslie Marmon Silko*. Albuquerque: University of New Mexico Press, 1999. A collection of critical essays, this text offers biographical information on Silko as well as an extensive bibliography of primary and secondary sources complete with a helpful bibliographical essay. The collection also includes Linda Krumholz's essay "Native Designs: Silko's *Storyteller* and the Reader's Initiation," in which the author argues that Silko's text "resists appropriation by initiating the reader into a Native American reading practice that defies and subverts the Master Narratives."

Graulich, Melody, ed. *"Yellow Woman": Leslie Marmon Silko*. New Brunswick, N.J.: Rutgers University Press, 1993. An important addition to Silko scholarship, this collection of critical essays contains a great deal of useful background information on the Yellow Woman myth so central to Silko's *Storyteller* collection. In addition, it gathers some of the most influential Silko scholarship, including Bernard A. Hirsch's "'The Telling Which Continues': Oral Tradition and the Written Word in Leslie Marmon Silko's *Storyteller*." Hirsch meticulously analyzes Silko's strategies for bringing alive Laguna oral mythology in writing when written language by its nature "does not allow the living story to change and grow, as does the oral tradition."

Jaskoski, Helen. *Leslie Marmon Silko: A Study of the Short Fiction*. New York: Twayne, 1998. Although Jaskoski devotes her analysis only to the short fiction, this text remains useful to those interested in her poetry because of the inclusion of four interviews. For a poet, Silko is unusually forthcoming in interviews about the themes found in her work and the sources of her creativity. Thus her published interviews offer some of the best introductions to her poetic works.

Salyer, Gregory. *Leslie Marmon Silko*. New York: Twayne, 1997. Because Silko is best known for her fiction, there is little criticism that focuses on her poetry alone. One of the few single-author books on Silko, Salyer's is the only one to discuss Silko's first collection of poems, *Laguna Woman*, at length. He devotes an entire chapter to it, offering useful insights on both the individual poems and the collection as a whole. Salyer's book is the most complete introduction to Silko's work available, containing a chapter of biography, a selected bibliography, and a thorough analysis of *Storyteller*.

Silko, Leslie Marmon. "Landscape, History, and the Pueblo Imagination." In *The Ecocriticism Reader*, edited by Cheryll Glotfelty and Harold Fromm. Athens: Georgia University Press, 1996. Clear and remarkably concise, Silko's own essay offers one of the best, and quickest, introductions to the Pueblo attitudes that thoroughly inform her poetry. Silko explains the crucial importance of place within the communal Pueblo oral tradition and explains how the Pueblo came to envision themselves as dependent on nature rather than as owners of it.

Christopher J. Stuart

Charles Simic

Born: Belgrade, Yugoslavia; May 9, 1938

Principal poetry

What the Grass Says, 1967

Somewhere Among Us a Stone Is Taking Notes, 1969

Dismantling the Silence, 1971
White, 1972, revised edition 1980
Return to a Place Lit by a Glass of Milk, 1974
Biography and a Lament: Poems, 1961-1967, 1976
Charon's Cosmology, 1977
Brooms: Selected Poems, 1978
Classic Ballroom Dances, 1980
Austerities, 1982
Shaving at Night, 1982
The Chicken Without a Head, 1983
Weather Forecast for Utopia and Vicinity: Poems, 1967-1982, 1983
Selected Poems, 1963-1983, 1985, revised 1990
Unending Blues, 1986
The World Doesn't End: Prose Poems, 1989
The Book of Gods and Devils, 1990
In the Room We Share, 1990
Hotel Insomnia, 1992
Night Mail: Selected Poems, 1992
A Wedding in Hell, 1994
Frightening Toys, 1995
Walking the Black Cat, 1996
Looking for Trouble, 1997
Selected Early Poems, 1999
Jackstraws, 1999
Night Picnic, 2001

OTHER LITERARY FORMS

Charles Simic edited, with Mark Strand, *Another Republic* (1976), an influential anthology that provided many American readers with an introduction to contemporary poetry in Europe and Latin America. Simic also edited *The Essential Campion* (1988), a selection of the lyrics of Thomas Campion. His essay collections include *The Uncertain Certainty: Interviews, Essays, and Notes on Poetry* (1985); *Wonderful Words, Silent Truth: Essays on Poetry and a Memoir* (1990), *The Unemployed Fortune-Teller: Essays and Memoirs* (1994), and *Orphan Factory: Essays and Memoirs* (1998). *A Fly in the Soup: Memoirs* (2000) focuses on Simic's childhood. Simic is also a prolific translator of poetry from eastern Europe.

ACHIEVEMENTS

Among Charles Simic's many awards are a Guggenheim Fellowship (1972-1973), grants from the National Endowment for the Arts (1974-1975 and 1979-1980), the Edgar Allan Poe Award (1975), a National Institute of Arts and Letters and American Academy of Arts and Letters Award (1976), and an International Association of Poets, Playwrights, Essayists, and Novelists (PEN) International Award for Translation (in 1970 and 1980). In 1984 he was awarded a MacArthur Foundation Fellowship, and his book of prose poems *The World Doesn't End* received the Pulitzer Prize in poetry in 1990. *Walking the Black Cat* was a finalist for the National Book Award. In 1998, he was granted an Academy of American Poets Fellowship. Jackstraws was named a Notable Book of the Year by the New York Times.

Charles Simic

BIOGRAPHY

Charles Simic was born in Belgrade, Yugoslavia, in 1938, and emigrated to the United States in 1954. "My travel agents were Hitler and Stalin," he has said. When Simic was three years old, a house across the street from his family's home was destroyed by a bomb. For young Simic and his friends, the war (so serious and terrible for adults) was often a source of fun. There were guns and air-raid sirens to imitate—and, toward the end, a thriving salvage business in gunpowder. The chaos and menace of that time survive in Simic's poems, along with its variety, wonder, comedy, and sadness. For Simic, the city survives as well. "My mother is calling my name out of a tenement window," he has said. "She keeps calling and calling. My entire psychic life is there."

Simic settled in Chicago, where he attended Oak Park High School and the University of Chicago. After finishing a stint in the army, he lived in New York, working at a variety of jobs (shirt salesman, house painter, payroll clerk) and attending New York University, where he earned his B.A. Another part of his education took place in the New York Library, where he read all the folklore and anthropology he could find, as a way of introducing mythic consciousness into his poetry. He ended up making his own myths of things common and close to home: brooms, ballroom dances, the fingers of a hand. Simic published his first two books, *What the Grass Says* and *Somewhere Among Us a Stone Is Taking Notes*, with Kayak Press; *Dismantling the Silence* (composed of some poems from the first two books, plus new ones) was issued by the publisher George Braziller in 1971.

To his surprise, Simic's increasing reputation brought him invitations to teach. He has taught at the California State University at Hayward and became a professor of English. In 1973, he began his long tenure at the University of New Hampshire teaching English. He served as guest editor of *The Best American Poetry 1992* and in 2000, he was elected a Chancellor of The Academy of American Poets.

Analysis

In his autobiographical essay "In the Beginning . . . ," Charles Simic describes one of the first great influences on him, the family radio:

> The nights of my childhood were spent in the company of that radio. . . . Once I heard beeps in Morse code. Spies, I thought. Often I'd catch a distant station so faint I'd have to turn the sound all the way up and press my ear against the rough burlap that covered the speaker. Somewhere dance music was playing or the language was so attractive I'd listen to it for a long time, as if on the verge of understanding.

This solitary attentiveness, this fascination with the barely intelligible, with speech so far away that it seems transmitted from silence, has characterized Simic's poetry from the beginning. In attentive silence, he says, he can come closer to "the way things are."

Simic's poetic sensibility combines a surrealistic fascination with recurring archetypes and an imagist concern for precise observation of things. His first influences were poets with a gift for the primitive and a knack for using language to evoke origins: Vachel Lindsay, Hart Crane, Carl Sandburg, Theodore Roethke (in particular his poem "The Lost Son"), and the Yugoslav Vasko Popa (whose work Simic has translated). He has also been influenced by the blues, with its verbal inventiveness, eroticism, and tragic sense of life.

"Butcher Shop," like many of Simic's poems, ushers the reader into a mysterious world: late night, after hours. Here the implements of butchery take on their own dark lives. The blood on the butcher's apron becomes a map "of the great continents of blood," while glittering knives are reminiscent of altars in some ominously dark church where "the cripple and the imbecile" are brought "to be healed."

Simic's love for ordinary objects enables him again and again to rebuild the universe with them at the center. When he describes a butcher's bloody apron, nothing but it exists. It emerges anew from its mysterious origins, part of a myth of nourishment—a river where the reader, with Simic, can be fed.

Simic's "object poems" are justly among his most celebrated works. In "Bestiary for the Fingers of My Right Hand," the thumb becomes a "fat worm/ They have attached to my flesh"; the middle finger is stiff, a querulous, questing old man; the fourth, with its occasional inexplicable twitches, "is mystery." The hand's transformation is nothing so simple as mere personification. Rather than being made human simulacra, the fingers are animated—that is, they assume their own vibrant lives, the equal of any animal or human.

"Brooms"

The imagination animates all Simic sees. Why should people, Simic's poems assert, have a monopoly on lives? His poems turn the pecking order upside down, reserving special reverence for the ugly, the ignominious. "Brooms," from *Return to a Place Lit by a Glass of*

Milk, is a lavish celebration of brooms, a compendium beginning with their knowledge (including self-knowledge): they know of the Devil's existence, and they are aware of their own mysterious life, which Simic suggests in images of trees in an orchard. Section 2 moves to broom lore, explaining that in dream analysis they are interpreted as "omens of approaching death." In public they resemble "flat-chested old maids"—a comparison both wildly imaginative and devilishly accurate.

One secret of this poem's liveliness is that while the subject remains constant, the context veers wildly, from dream books to jails to tenements. In section 3, the lives of saints and astronomers are shown to contain the origins of brooms. To make "the first ancestral broom," arrows were harvested from Saint Sebastian's back and bound together with the rope that Judas Iscariot used to hang himself. The broom's handle was one of the stilts on which Nicolaus Copernicus mounted to touch the morning star.

Section 4 presents the teachings of brooms, ending with advice on levitation: "I suggest remembering:/ There is only one God/ And his prophet is Mohammed." This reference seems at first a hilarious red herring—but then the reader remembers that Muhammad is said to have levitated. Simic is interested, first and last, in the sense of nonsense, the wedding of the ordinary with the sweepingly important. Here, as so often in his poems, the holy and the silly are intertwined.

Simic loves to create worlds, then dismantle them to silence and invisibility. In the end, the Brooms disappear into their origins in mythic time: "Once, long ago."

Simic's fascination with combining the intricate and the simple has a connection with philosophy. He reads philosophy—particularly Martin Heidegger, for he admires that thinker's determination to reexamine what is simple and taken for granted. Simic sees the poet's task as similar.

Charon's Cosmology

In *Charon's Cosmology*, Simic keeps his mythic tone but reveals a growing sense of history. The menace and destruction he witnessed as a boy make their way into his work. "Eyes Fastened with Pins" has Death as its main character—personified, with unsettling humor, as an ordinary working stiff, having to prowl unfamiliar parts of town in the rain while his neighbors relax on the backyard steps drinking beer. In "Charon's Cosmology," Death's boatman gets confused about which side of the river is which—each side has an identical pile of corpses.

Classic Ballroom Dances

Classic Ballroom Dances contains even more history. A poem called "Baby Pictures of Famous Dictators" marvels quietly at history's constant odd juxtapositions, its strange plots and casting: carnival freaks, Thomas Alva Edison inventing the light bulb, a famine that rages in India. The infant dictators pose in their sailor suits, lovable and innocent as any other babies. Yet the photographer's black hood, trembling in the breeze, is silently ominous.

For Simic, history is made of small moments, inconsequential but resonant. "Classic Ballroom Dances" shows grandmothers wringing chickens' necks and nun schoolteachers pulling boys' ears. The poem is, in fact, a dance, a box step of four-line stanzas that lead the reader through a list of ordinary rituals, ancient patterns of habit, from pickpockets' crafty steps as they work a crowd that has gathered at the scene of an accident to "the ancient lovers, cheek to cheek,/ On the dancefloor of the Union Hall." To see all these gestures in the same light changes them, makes the reader reconsider their identities.

Simic calls the list poem "the poetic equivalent of quilt-making. One cuts the patches into signs and symbols of one's own cosmology, then one covers oneself with it on a cold winter night." He remembers his elders as they reverently learned dances from foot patterns traced on the floor with chalk, so they could repeat time-hallowed movements. "The world," Simic says, "is a ballroom full of mirrors and we are the inspired or awkward dancers."

White

Also in 1980, Simic published the revised version of his long poem *White*, which explores and dramatizes the source of his poetic impulse, personified as White—"his muse," Peter Schmidt has written, "of strangeness and new selfhood." The poem's task is set in its first lines: "Out of Poverty/ To begin again"—the implicit task of every poem. In the first two parts of *White* the poet speaks; the third and last belong to White herself. She is identified with what Simic has called "a state that precedes verbalization," which embraces all possibilities. White will always remain beyond him: "I thought of you long before you thought of me," she reminds the poet. Yet her elusiveness is not to be mourned: "the most beautiful riddle has no answer."

Austerities

Austerities intensifies an impulse central to Simic's work: the desire to use the fewest possible words to produce the largest possible effect. He exercises once again his gift for combining the archetypal with the everyday, as in "Drawn to Perspective," a painterly poem that renders one hushed moment on a summer evening with pared-down images of a parent calling a child, a boy on skates, and a couple poised to embrace.

Unending Blues

In *Unending Blues*, Simic adopts a more personal, relaxed voice than ever before. In "To Helen," he announces in blues style,

> Tomorrow early I'm going to the doctor
> In the blue suit and shirt you ironed.
> Tomorrow I'm having my bones photographed
> With my heart in its spiked branches.

He fashions a setting for the heart—it will resemble an old nest in a bare crabapple tree in autumn—that spins out further and further until a new world is complete. A poetic phenomenologist, Simic writes poems that demonstrate the notion (derived from Edmund Husserl and Martin Heidegger) that the world is made of objects people intend through their attention. That is, the human act of attention reveals and creates their significance. This attention operates in the book's other poem addressed to Helen, this time in praise of a sea cucumber. He has never seen one but likes the "cold and salty" sound of its name, so he proposes diving into a dark, treacherous ocean to harvest some of these "lovely green vegetables" for a salad. Like many Simic poems, this one exhibits a childlike spirit that takes delight in creating a vivid world and then imagining an adventure in it.

The World Doesn't End

The World Doesn't End, a volume of prose poems, received the Pulitzer Prize for Poetry in 1990. Simic found this hybrid form congenial because of its versatility. Whereas the lyric poem is essentially static, focusing on only one moment, the prose poem is mobile. "You write in sentences, and tell a story, but the piece is like a poem because it circles back on itself."

In contrast to the finite, boxlike forms of Simic's lyrics, these poems seem to speak out of an unseen, infinite story, the spaces between them no more than pauses for breath. Titles appear at the tops of pages only for the four tiny lyrics the book includes, which function as resting places amid the striding prose. The table of contents features the first phrase of each poem, followed by an ellipsis, the notation for silence. Indeed, these prose poems create their context directly from silence. "Where ignorance is bliss . . ." creates a world from a proverb:

> Where ignorance is bliss, where one lies at night on the bed of stupidity, where one prays on one's knees to a foolish angel . . . Where one follows a numbskull to war in an army of beatific dunces . . . Where the roosters crow all day. . . .

The Book of Gods and Devils

In *The Book of Gods and Devils*, Simic returns to the lyric, writing poems that hark back to his years as a young man in New York, reading and wandering Fourteenth Street, Hell's Kitchen, the old Fourth Avenue booksellers' row. As he wrote the book, he has said, he was aware of an impulse to follow the custom of pagans: to create gods or demons for places where he had had particularly intense experiences. He marvels at the many "gods" that populate a large city such as New York: objects of worship, objects of fear.

In "Shelley" he remembers reading the poet first on a rainy New York evening, having bought a tattered volume at a secondhand bookstore. Though he still speaks English with an "atrocious Slavic accent," he is captivated by the Romantic poet's flowing language. Flush with Percy Bysshe Shelley's sense of the phantasmagorical, he begins to see the people around him as portentous and archetypal. In a rundown coffee shop, the owner, a retired sailor, gladly refills Simic's cup "with a liquid dark as river Styx"; he has dinner in his accustomed Chinese restaurant, with its silent "three-fingered waiter." The poem captures the deep sense of the world's strangeness experienced by the intense youth who reads Shelley's "Splendors and Glooms" by the light of city storefronts. Even Simic's rented room, to which he contemplates returning, has become strange and fearful, "cold as a tomb of an infant emperor."

With this volume Simic discovers how to use this archetypal method to illuminate lived experience. These poems are anecdotal, but not slack. Their luminous details enrich the world. As always, Simic dwells on the inconsequential detail that means the world: a "pale little girl with glasses" who appears in the door of a Chinese restaurant, a "little white dog" that "ran into the street/ And got entangled with the soldiers' feet," a woman who runs by shrieking, "hugging a blood-stained shirt."

The early impulses are all here, but amplified and extended—made more accessible. Speaking of this volume, Simic has described himself as both a realist and a surrealist, pulled between two ways of seeing. Never before in Simic's work have the real and surreal had such equal voices. The world is here, attended by its mysteries—a strange union of time and timelessness. Increasingly, the poet's attitude is one of astonishment and awe before the world. As in all Simic's work, there is between and behind the lines the pressure of the unspeakable, that which belongs to silence. Simic's poems do not lift silence, but tantalizingly part its ineffable curtains. "We are always at the beginning," he says, "eternal apprentices, thrown back again and again into that condition."

Walking the Black Cat

Through the 1990's Simic continued to write almost nonstop, publishing a new collection every two or three years. *Walking the Black Cat* consists of highly visual, brief narratives. It is almost as if Simic is writing scenarios for tiny films in the manner of Jean Cocteau. The poems here are mostly quick flashes, mysterious, oddly humorous scenes in which perceptions are adjusted by verbal feints and dodges. There are almost as many poems as pages.

Many of them conjure up nightmarish situations. In "Cameo Appearance," the speaker finds himself having a "nonspeaking part/ in a bloody epic" of military carnage. He replays the footage hundreds of times, trying to convince viewers that he's really there (though who would want to be?), pointing out just where he is—or is supposed to be. The speaker's need to prove his existence in the film, which would make him a victim among victims, transforms into a desperate and frustrated insistence on his participation in life itself. Has he, have we all, been playing our parts when the camera has been turned off or pointing elsewhere?

Throughout the collection, Simic's understated delivery forces acceptance of the absurd, the outlandish, and the undesirable circumstances that we would prefer to shun. His strange mixture of the mundane and the surreal captures our harshest anxieties about our unpreparedness for what our lives might, at any moment, become.

Jackstraws

The randomness of the childhood game jackstraws points to Simic's preoccupation in this volume: the arbitrariness and precariousness of everyday life. Here he mystifies the quotidian (as in "Vacant Rooms": "Emptied and swept clean,/ Their windows like eyeglasses/ Raised to the light/ With no one squinting behind them"), becomes darkly involved in the bug world (as in "Bug Doctor" in which he considers humans in the role of torturers: "Night visitor, do you know about fear?/ Are you astounded to be in pain/ When they crucify you with pins,/ Or when I squeeze you tight/ Between a thumb and a forefinger?"), and sharply unites haunting memories of and fresh concern about the horrors of Eastern Europe with affectionately sardonic impressions of his second home, America. In *Jackstraws*, he offers consolation to those disconsoled, a solace which doesn't erase the discomfort but uses humor to assist in finding the promise of its own redemption.

Night Picnic

Simic draws his attention to the mundane in *Night Picnic*: objects on a dresser, unmade beds, a gas station. His dark outlook and affinity for foreboding themes abates slightly here, ushering in a new strain of sardonic humor and a keen sense of the entanglement of the erotic and the doomed. Unexpected juxtapositions focus on mixed messages: a thread of opera set against "the city boiling in its bloody stew," a couple French-kissing while the homeless lie in "dark doorways," unlikely Christ figures, including a "Jesus lookalike/ who won a pie-eating contest in Texas." The final section of the book's three parts departs from Simic's usual pattern, offering saddened epigrams followed by powerful meditations on death and old age, considered as a raindrop, as a kitchen or as a restaurant ("The check is being added in the back/ As we speak").

Other major works

nonfiction: *The Uncertain Certainty: Interviews, Essays, and Notes on Poetry*, 1985; *Wonderful Words, Silent Truth: Essays on Poetry and a Memoir*, 1990; *Dime-Store Alchemy: The Art of Joseph Cornell*, 1992; *The Unemployed Fortune-Teller: Essays and Memoirs, 1994; Orphan Factory: Essays and Memoirs*, 1997; *A Fly in the Soup: Memoirs*, 2000.

translations: *Four Yugoslav Poets: Ivan C. Lalic, Brank Miljkovic, Milorad Pavic, Ljubomir Simovic*, 1970; *The Little Box: Poems*, 1970 (of Vasko Popa); *Homage to the Lame Wolf: Selected Poems, 1956-1975*, 1979, enlarged edition 1987 (of Popa); *Roll Call of Mirrors: Selected Poems*, 1988 (of Ivan V. Lalic); *Some Other Wine and Light*, 1989 (of Aleksandar Ristovic); *The Bandit Wind*, 1991 (Slavko Janevski); *The Horse Has Six Legs: An Anthology of Serbian Poetry*, 1992 (anthology of Serbian poetry); *Devil's Lunch: Selected Poems*, 2000 (of Ristovic).

edited texts: *Another Republic*, 1976 (with Mark Strand); *The Essential Campion*, 1988.

Bibliography

Contoski, Victor. "Charles Simic: Language at the Stone's Heart." *Chicago Review* 48 (Spring, 1977): 145-157. This excellent article outlines Simic's efforts "to interpret the relationship between the animate and inanimate" in his poems. Contoski analyzes Simic's use of language from *What the Grass Says*, his first book, up to *Return to a Place Lit by a Glass of Milk*.

Hart, Kevin. "Writing Things: Literary Property in Heidegger and Simic." *New Literary History: A Journal of Theory and Interpretation* 21 (Autumn, 1989): 199-214. Especially useful for readers wishing to explore the relationship between Simic's poetry and the philosophy of Martin Heidegger. Citing examples from Simic's poems, Hart extensively explores Simic's affinity with Heidegger's phenomenological philosophy.

Jackson, Richard. "Charles Simic and Mark Strand: The Presence of Absence." *Contemporary Literature* 21 (Winter, 1980): 136-145. This article persuasively links the "surrealist moods" of Charles Simic and Mark Strand, exploring (with frequent references to Martin Heidegger and Jacques Lacan) the "absolute priority these two poets give to the ontological function of language."

Nash, Susan Smith. Review of *Walking the Black Cat*. *World Literature Today* 71, no. 4 (Autumn, 1997): 793-794. This is an enthusiastic appraisal that views this collection as a cohesive and focused expression of Simic's major themes.

Orlich, Ileana. "The Poet on a Roll: Charles Simic's 'The Tomb of Stéphane Mallarmé.'" *Centennial Review* 36, no. 2 (Spring, 1992): 413-428. Orlich examines Simic's relationship to the Surrealists, and in particular the role of chance, through a close reading of a key poem. Orlich considers the poem to be an aesthetic manifesto.

Schmidt, Peter. "*White*: Charles Simic's Thumbnail Epic." *Contemporary Literature* 23 (Fall, 1982): 528-549. Schmidt analyzes the revised version of Simic's long poem *White*, illuminating its importance to Simic's work as a whole. While centering on *White*, Schmidt's discussion provides a thorough orientation for readers of Simic's poetry. Walt Whitman and Ralph Waldo Emerson, "those ambiguous foster-parents," are shown to have played a central role in the poet's development.

Simic, Charles. Interview by Molly McQuade. *Publishers Weekly* 234 (November 2, 1990): 56-57. This lively interview focuses on Simic's origins as a poet and on the autobiographical basis of *The Book of Gods and Devils*.

________. *The Uncertain Certainty: Interviews, Essays, and Notes on Poetry*. Ann Arbor: University of Michigan Press, 1985. This volume collects much of what Simic has said about poetic theory and practice. Of these interviews and essays, particularly noteworthy are the interview with Sherod Santos, in which Simic discusses the genesis and development of his work, and Simic's essay "Negative Capability and Its Children," in which he explores John Keats's notion of the poet as "capable of being in uncertainties." *The Uncertain Certainty* is an invaluable aid to understanding not only Simic's work but also the nature of poetry itself.

Stitt, Peter. "Charles Simic: Poetry in a Time of Madness." In his *Uncertainty and Plenitude: Five Con-*

temporary Poets. Iowa City: University of Iowa Press, 1997. Though Simic's imagery suggests a surrealist orientation, he is essentially a realist who reflects his Eastern European heritage. A close reading of several poems establishes the archetypal nature of Simic's speakers and the displacement of the poet's own ego.

Vendler, Helen. "A World of Foreboding: Charles Simic." In *Soul Says: On Recent Poetry.* Cambridge, Mass.: Harvard University Press, 1995. Focusing on *Hotel Insomnia*, Vendler provides a comprehensive overview of Simic's themes and methods. She charts a "master list" of key words that run through this collection. Astute analysis by a major critic.

Weigl, Bruce. *Charles Simic*. Ann Arbor: University of Michigan Press, 1996. Traces the critical reception of Simic's poetry across a quarter century, in an effort to delineate Simic's aesthetic. Bibliography.

Angela Ball,
updated by Philip K. Jason and Sarah Hilbert

Louis Simpson

Born: Kingston, Jamaica, British West Indies; March 27, 1923

Principal poetry

The Arrivistes: Poems, 1940-1949, 1949
Good News of Death and Other Poems, 1955
A Dream of Governors, 1959
At the End of the Open Road, 1963
Selected Poems, 1965
Adventures of the Letter I, 1971
Searching for the Ox, 1976
Caviare at the Funeral, 1980
The Best Hour of the Night, 1983
People Live Here: Selected Poems, 1949-1983, 1983
Collected Poems, 1988
In the Room We Share, 1990
Jamaica Poems, 1993
There You Are, 1995

Other literary forms

Louis Simpson's contributions to criticism and literary analysis include *The New Poets of England and America* (1957) and *James Hogg: A Critical Study* (1962). These two studies pointed the direction poetry was to take in subsequent years, especially Simpson's own. Simpson wrote several other works of literary criticism in following years, including *Three on the Tower: The Lives and Works of Ezra Pound, T. S. Eliot, and William Carlos Williams* in 1975. Another volume of criticism, *A Revolution in Taste: Studies of Dylan Thomas, Allen Ginsberg, Sylvia Plath, and Robert Lowell*, appeared in 1978. This work was followed by two other volumes, *A Company of Poets* (1981) and *The Character of the Poet* (1986), which expanded and defined Simpson's literary tastes, principles, and objectives. Prolific into the 1990's, Simpson published more literary studies in *Ships Going into the Blue: Essays and Notes on Poetry* in 1994.

Simpson's only novel, *Riverside Drive* (1962), won critical respect but convinced him that his talent was better suited to poetry, although his reputation as a literary critic brought him much respect in later years. *North of Jamaica* (1972) is a prose account of his childhood in Jamaica, his wartime experiences, and his teaching career at Columbia University and the University of California at Berkeley. This autobiography introduces the reader to Simpson's ideas on poetry as he saw it being practiced and as he thought it should be written. The book shows how much of Simpson's poetry derives from his own life and how seamlessly the two are joined.

Achievements

Louis Simpson's literary career has generated enough commentary to rank him among the major poets of the second half of the twentieth century. His war poems have been called the best to come out of World War II, and his literary criticism has gained him additional respect. His poetic reputation was barely established when he was awarded the Prix de Rome in 1957, and this award was followed in 1964 by a Pulitzer Prize for his collection of poems *At the End of the Open Road.* His work continues to win critical praise, which extends to his translations. His *Modern Poets of France: A Bilin-*

gual Anthology garnered the Harold Morton Landon Translation Award in 1998. Perhaps much of the respect he has earned as a critic stems from his not aligning himself with any literary school or movement.

Biography

Louis Simpson's life is especially important because of its relation to his poetic development. He was born Louis Aston Marantz Simpson in Kingston, Jamaica, on March 27, 1923. His father was a lawyer of Scottish descent, his mother a Jewish immigrant from southern Russia. His parents had met when Rosalind de Marantz went to Kingston from New York City to appear in a film. A brother had been born first, then Louis. Following the breakup of the marriage in 1930, Rosalind went to Toronto. Louis was sent with his brother to Munro College, a private school a hundred miles from Jamaica. Louis was to remain at Munro College until he was seventeen years old. His father remarried, and another child was born. When Louis was near graduation, his father died, leaving most of his estate to his new family. Louis and his brother were made to leave their parental home immediately. On his own, Louis returned to school, where he excelled in literary studies and developed two goals: to be a writer and to leave Jamaica. At sixteen, he was already writing and publishing poetry and prose. This principle would guide him in writing about all the "real wars" he was to wage back in the United States.

Louis Simpson (© Marianne Zittau)

In New York, Simpson entered Columbia University, where he studied under Mark Van Doren. In 1943, he joined the army and was sent to Texas. Military life turned him into a dog soldier with little respect for officers. The army also enabled him to see Texas, Louisiana, and Missouri. He took part in the Normandy invasion, fought at Bastogne, and visited London and Paris. By war's end he had gained United States citizenship, won the Bronze Star with cluster, twice earned the Purple Heart, and grown cynical. After winning the Pulitzer Prize while teaching at the University of California in Berkeley, he took a teaching position in 1967 at the State University of New York at Stony Brook. Making his permanent residence in Setauket, New York, he has traveled extensively, going to Australia and several times to Europe, visiting his ailing mother, who lived near Pisa, Italy.

Simpson retired from teaching in the early 1990's but continued to write literary essays and poetry and to translate French poetry. He remains outspoken as always, bemoaning the neglect of poetry in the United States and the scarcity of good translations of French poetry, a scarcity that he has set himself to remedy in his own translations.

Analysis

Simpson's development as a poet encompasses virtually the entire second half of the twentieth century. At a time when the Academic poets warred with the Beat poets, Louis Simpson marched to his own poetic rhythms. He passed through the waters of the Deep Image without being caught in its currents. Wordsworthian influences have been noted in his poetry, and Simpson gives important attention to Walt Whitman in both his poetry and prose, but Whitman's influence is perhaps more psychological and theoretical than overt. Using forms and devices that were necessary to express his poetic vision and to speak in a voice that was his own, Simpson has stood apart from literary traditions and popular trends, finding a unique voice and vantage point to illuminate a common humanity.

THE ARRIVISTES

Simpson's first volume, *The Arrivistes*, includes poems of mixed forms and subjects. A sestina, a ballad, and a versified dialogue are found among lyrics on war, love, and death. In the book's mixture of classical and modern materials, one finds Simpson's major interests—the city, love, war, and art—all explored with irony and wit. His images have sharpness and emotive force: for example, "the sun was drawn bleeding across the hills" ("Jamaica"). Simpson's interest in the wanderer is evident in "The Warrior's Return" (the warrior being Odysseus) and in "Lazarus Convalescent," in which the biblical Lazarus faintly suggests the poet coming from the "hell" of war to speak to the living. Succinct to the point of aphoristic, many lines cut through literary self-consciousness. "Room and Board" creates a somber city scene; set in France, it expresses genuine feelings through vivid imagery.

GOOD NEWS OF DEATH AND OTHER POEMS

In *Good News of Death and Other Poems*, Simpson continues to show interest in romantic love, war, death, the loss of hope, and the ironic contrast between classical and modern values. Here the rhythms are less regular, and the rhymes have loosened. Simpson's characteristic irony and wit are well represented, along with a sensitivity to the seasons, a softening of war's disillusionment, and a corresponding emphasis on lyrical love tinged by a sense of loss or mild sorrow. "The Man Who Married Magdalene" demonstrates the confident handling of voice, tone, and manner that is found increasingly in the poems: "But when he woke and woke alone/ He wept and would deny/ The loose behavior of the bone/ And the immodest thigh." In "Memories of a Lost War," Simpson has discovered a way to shape experience into a form that releases sharp meaning: "The scene jags like a strip of celluloid,/ A mortar fires,/ Cinzano falls, Michelin is destroyed,/ The man of tires." Simpson's gift for juxtaposition has given him a way to mix disparate bits of information into a vivid, moving collage.

Literary portraiture, another of Simpson's strengths, often combines with his interest in objective reality. In "American Preludes," America's past comes under scrutiny, and "West," in open stanza and irregular line, shows a growing interest in modern America. The social commentary in many of the poems hints at a growing interest in the direction American society is taking and an interest in the lives of those who inhabit the land. He finds that boredom is widespread and that many people have founded their lives on values that are false or fragile. "Good News of Death," a pastoral, returns to the bucolic past in rhyme and regular lines to express the idea that the classical past is reborn in the birth of Christ. The "good news" is that Christ offers salvation to humankind.

A DREAM OF GOVERNORS

A Dream of Governors is the first collection to be divided into sections, each titled, reflecting the poet's concern with the arrangement of the poems. In the first group, poems are cast mainly in regular lines and rhymed stanzas, and there is a mixture of classical and modern. The classical lovers in "The Green Shepherd" remain unaffected by the great westward thrust of empire, while the "dragon rises crackling in the air" over the Western Hemisphere. The dragon as symbol of ensuring devastation of the land appears again in the title poem, "A Dream of Governors," the dream being "The City," which the Knight rescues from the dragon, only to become king and grow "old/ and ludicrous and fat." The poem ends as the dragon rises again. Demonic characters and gloomy overtones are to be found in other poems in this collection as well. "To the Western World" concludes grimly: "And grave by grave we civilize the ground." "The country that Columbus thought he found . . . looks unreal," the poet muses in "Landscape with Barns." "Only death looks real." Even America's vaunted freedom "is the basilisk," and the poet's reaction to the Land of Opportunity is to realize that "the melancholy of the possible/ Unmeasures me" ("Orpheus in America").

The idyllic past, only a fantasy, sends the poet to the Old World, where he finds a graveyard. The poetry is becoming more autobiographical as the lines and stanzas continue to open. The poet's voice sounds more like natural speech: "But I am American, and bargain . . . where the junk of culture/ Lies in the dust" ("An American in the Thieves' Market"). In "The Runner," which occupies roughly a third of the entire volume, war is seen through the eyes of a soldier whose journey takes the reader through war as Simpson saw it himself. Following it, "The Bird" injects a fairy-tale quality into the grim aspect of war. Simpson's interest in the surreal may have suggested the vision of a young German soldier who is sent to work in a concentration camp, all the while singing the refrain, "I wish I were a bird." The rhymed quatrains with their three-stress lines create an otherworldly atmosphere. There are Russian tanks, and there is "a little bird . . . flitting"—the transformed soldier. The same stanzaic pattern is used in one of Simpson's most celebrated war poems, "Carentan O Carentan," which reads somewhat like a ballad and focuses on the poignancy of death in war with ironic overtones.

The love poems in the final section continue the mixture of pastoral and classical with modern characters and scenes rendered in regular rhymed stanzas. The volume ends with "Tom Pringle," a poem spoken in the voice of a young man who "will watch the comets' flight . . . And wonder what they mean." Tom Pringle could watch the comets' flight, but Simpson had to return to America.

At the End of the Open Road

At the End of the Open Road looks squarely at modern America and its recent past. The voice is often conversational, classical allusions have been dropped, and the lines and stanzas are unrhymed and irregular. Simpson's penchant for focusing on the objects of his world and its people is clearly evident. The mood is serious, and the irony is restrained. "In California" begins with the poet speaking in his own voice—"Here I am"—but by the end, the "I" has become "we." He has joined those who travel the open road and come to the western gate, where they must "turn round the wagons." He discovers that "there's no way out" ("In the Suburbs"). The suburbs trap the body and spirit, and the seeking continues: "I tread the burning pavement. . . . I seek the word. The word is not forthcoming" ("There Is").

Turning to his own past, the poet remembers his grandmother's house, where "there was always chicken soup/ And talk of the old country" ("A Story About Chicken Soup"). He has learned "not to walk in the painted sunshine/ . . . But to live in the tragic world forever." Simpson employs again the narrative form to reveal his vision of the world, blending the open form with a voice closer to his own, as in "Moving the Walls," in which a modern voyager, collecting gewgaws, misses the deeper mystery of the world. The men who sought the golden fleece sought the grand and beautiful mysteries. Looking around, the poet doubts that he sees "any at sea."

Many of the poems reflect the poet's journey from Europe to Japan as if in search of fulfillment, a deeper perception. Searching is thematic and culminates thus: "I am going into the night to find a world of my own" ("Love, My Machine"). Simpson has found that Whitman's open road "goes to the used-car lot"; in "Walt Whitman at Bear Mountain," the angel from "In California" appears again, dancing "like Italy, imagining red," still ambiguous. The search is for a way out of a spiritual cul-de-sac. In the final poem, "Lines Written near San Francisco," the American dream turns out to be "cheap housing in the valleys// Where lives are mean and wretched."

Selected Poems

A dozen new pieces in *Selected Poems* revive thoughts of impending disaster, rendered in striking imagery. In "The Union Barge on Staten Island," the poet sees a threat in nature itself: "Under your feet, the wood seems deeply alive./ It's the running sea you feel." The animals "felt the same currents," and ominous clouds drift "over the Wilderness, over the still farms." The poet discovers in "Things" that "machines are the animals of the Americans." Yet he finally feels a kinship with those whom he has been observing from a distance: "Who lives in these dark houses?/ I am suddenly aware/ I might live here myself" ("After Midnight").

Adventures in the Letter I

The eye turned inward becomes the basis of *Adventures in the Letter I*, in which Simpson looks beyond contemporary America and finds the Russia his mother used to describe. The poems are often autobiographical, freed of rhymed stanzas and regular lines. The lines do not invariably begin with capital letters. Simpson wants his poetic language to look more like the speech it is becoming. "Adam Yankev" creates a portrait of the artist looking at himself, realizing that, though his head is "full of ancient life," he sees "houses,/ streets, bridges, traffic, crowds," people whose "faces are strangely familiar." No longer alienated by what he sees, the poet finds that "things want to be understood."

Though still somewhat disengaged from the world, the poet feels a kinship. In "The Photographer," a still life gives ideas "a connection." Simply to look is to find meaning, a kinship. In a longer poem telling of a man having an affair that ends in the grim reality of paying alimony and child support, the poet's sympathy is evident in the final vision of the man's life: "Maybe/ he talks to his pillow, and it whispers,/ moving red hair" ("Vandergast and the Girl"). Kinship is also evident in the poet's speaking as the ghost of a dead man: "And I, who used to lie with the moon,/ am here in a peat-bog" ("On a Disappearance of the Moon"). In "An American Peasant," the poet shares the peasant's trust in "silence" and distrust of "ideas."

Some of the poems read like letters to the reader: "My whole life coming to this place,/ and understanding it better" ("Port Jefferson"). In the poet's ancestral past lies the meaning he has been seeking. In "A Friend of the Family," the technology that deadens the spirit of America spreads to Asia while the speaker envisions nights in Russia, where a "space-rocket rises" and is called "Progress." The poet realizes that Anton Chekhov "was just a man," that the world is peopled by Vanya and Ivanov, that "people live here . . . you'd be amazed." As Simpson says in "Sacred Objects," people find their "sacred objects" by living in the moment and for the moment.

Searching for the Ox

Searching for the Ox opens with Simpson reminiscing about his boyhood on the shore of Kingston harbor and tracing his life to the present. The wanderer's life has been poetically circular. To advance is to come back to the starting place, though one continues to change, to discover. In many of the poems, the poet's life unfolds without a sense of kinship or connection with the objects and people that earlier had taught him where the mystery lies and perhaps how to engage with it. "Words are realities," he reminds the reader. "They have the power/ to make us feel and see" ("The Springs of Gadara"), as do people, places, things. Mechanical lives and repetitious rounds continue as though waiting for some meaning to break the cycle; when they are transformed into a poetic vision, their meaning becomes felt, implicit.

The poet's sense of pointless repetition and continued disengagement threads through places, times, and the lives of the people remembered or envisioned. "Cliff Road" ends at "a fence on a cliff,/ looking at the lights on the opposite shore." The way through and beyond this impasse lies in the word. Baruch always wanted to study the Torah ("Baruch"). Like the old man, the poet says, "We have been devoted to words." With this faith in the word and its redemptive power goes a continuing attachment to the real world just beyond the senses. Abstractions lead away from the objects that give meaning. In "Searching for the Ox," the speaker says, "I find my awareness/ of the world . . . has increased." The search ends in the discovery: "There is only earth."

The final section includes more snapshots of the world the poet is journeying through, recording, a journey that shifts to his ancestral past and forward to the present. At the same time, the poet looks outward and inward. Changed by what he sees, he changes it, the part humankind imposes on the world, the "Machine." By recognizing the monotonous, mechanical nature of a shelling machine, for example, he has changed it. Recognition by "a total stranger" of the thing that makes human life mechanical gives character, even life, to both.

Caviare at the Funeral

In this collection, Simpson continues seeing kinship between the inner and outer worlds, and he finds a connection between the past and present. The opening poem, "Working Late," weaves memories of the poet's father with images from nature that suggest the poet's mother. The moon "has come all the way from Russia," as the mother had done, a sojourner like her son. Still, the son feels a kinship with his father, whose light shines in the study—it "now shines as late in mine." Shards from the everyday world resonate in his memory as the portraits of individuals unfold around and through them. As the artist's sensibility gives them meaningful shape, a world of meaning is created. Poetry gives the poet what he seeks: meaning from the inert objects that claim his attention.

The poet remains the outsider, observing events and individuals and occasionally commenting on them, though he often lets a description of a scene make the comment. In "Little Colored Flags," the poet envisions the bland typicalness of small-town life; the sea is tucked away "behind the last house at the end of the street," all but unnoticed, suggesting that those who do not see the world around them become prisoners of their own limited vision. The poet paints scenes in which people sense the futility of life, having surrendered to the mechanical motions of a technological world. "Unfinished Life" provides a telling symbol: "A hubcap went rolling in circles, ringing as it settled." The sound is not the music of the spheres, nor the Sirens's call. It is the shrill voice of trapped spirits.

Simpson reiterates his faith in the redemptive power of words in "Profession of Faith" and again in "Why Do You Write About Russia?" The soul of poetry is the "voice." That voice deserves to be heard, for it expresses the poet's "love," his "infinite wonder." Only it, the poet suggests, offers a way out of the "dream" everyone lives. The quest is for "a life in which there are depths/ beyond happiness." A kinship with the past, geographical and ancestral, is nurtured by sound, "such as you hear/ in a sea breaking along a shore." The sounds of nature, of the past, and of people form a universal bond.

In the final section of the volume, Simpson's trip to Australia is presented in poetic snapshots and a prose piece. The theme of the outsider persists in "Out of Season": "when I am away from home/ . . . it is as though there were another self/ . . . waiting to find me alone." Persisting too is the faith that there may be a reason for being "in one place rather than another."

The Best Hour of the Night

This series of poems reflects an ongoing interest in the scenes and characters that Simpson encountered in Russia and the United States. The forms remain free, and the dramatic narrative continues to weave commentary and image out of ordinary things and people. "Quiet Desperation" portrays another individual trapped in the monotony of modern life. All his searching can accomplish is a "feeling of pressure" that leads to a vague idea of the depths, the wonder and mystery, beyond the surface world, but they evade him. "The Previous Tenant" offers a similar portrait, that of a man in yet another suburb whose illicit affair has destroyed his marriage. The speaker approves of the affair, for in "such ordinary things" the vigor, if not the beauty, of life can be seen. Modern life still exacts a heavy price: One's spirit is buried "under the linoleum," ingested by the things the culture has disgorged, "brown material/ grained like wood, with imitation knotholes" ("In Otto's Basement").

People Live Here

The poems in *People Live Here* are grouped without attention to chronology, Simpson points out. He ends with a prose reflection on his early life, up to World War II, and his artistic credo: "I don't write for myself. . . . I write poems in order to express feelings I have had since I was a child . . . to express the drama, the terror and beauty of life." The close affinity between Simpson's poetry and prose reflections is evident in the final section of *People Live Here* and *In the Room We Share*. Fully a third of this latter volume is given over to journal entries describing a trip to visit his mother in Italy. In both his poetry and his prose, Simpson continues to record the world. The poetry, because it is more compressed and focused than the prose, becomes a window through which the reader sees what the poet sees. The elements synthesize; poetry is achieved.

In the Room We Share

Simpson has always been keenly aware of nature's presence—the trees, the sea, the wind. These elements surround many of his experiences, like ministering spirits. The poems in *In the Room We Share* show him returning again and again to his past, to his search beyond happiness, to the drama of life and the scenes and characters that generate it. In "Words," the poet is reading his poems to a group of students, talking to them as through a glass, seen but not heard. Memories of his own youth return to the room he is sharing with the young people, who wonder what he might have to say that might have meaning to them. He tells them how he began to write: When his senses were stirred by an image of "gray eyes, long golden hair," he found the genesis of poetry, "a vision of beauty." Are the youths listening to him? Likely not.

Simpson recapitulates familiar subjects: his war experiences, life in New York City and the suburbs, experiences in Germany, France, Italy, Jamaica, Russia, scenes from the American landscape. The poet is the transcontinental observer, giving life to what he sees, voice to nature and people, meaning to everything, though he is always the outsider, the other person in the room "we" share. Considering the lives of his neighbors (in "Neighbors"), the poet remains attuned to sights and sounds, "as though a world were building/ its likeness through the ear."

Simpson's circular journey has taken him from gloomy predictions of disaster and a sense of alienation to an enfolding vision. In sound, the sea, the word, Simpson sees kinship. The walls of his world form concentric circles from the poet outward, enclosing himself, his neighborhood, city, country, the whole world, but these walls dissolve in the poem. Form both encloses and releases. The poem is a glass that alternates as a mirror and a transparent pane. Simpson's poetic has constructed a room shared by all those who read him, but a room without walls. The past and present are interwoven, and a kinship is achieved in the shared vision. By speaking in his own voice, speaking in the language of the "common man," Simpson has made his poetry an experience that synthesizes thinking and feeling into a common humanity. In the end, he comes back to himself, the end of the open road, and finds a world of things and individuals in a room constructed out of his memory—seeing through the used car lot, beyond the empty dreams, like an angel in the gate.

Essays and translations

Simpson's interest in both literary theory and French poetry is manifest in his later essays and translations. His essay, "'The Man Freed from the Order of Time'" (1990), for example, is a study of the poetic theory of the British poet William Wordsworth and the French novelist Marcel Proust. Simpson sees in the work of these two writers the expression of a power of mind that transcends time and place, making their theories of literary creation as relevant today as when they wrote. Simpson has also continued to be interested in the work of Walt Whitman, addressing the nature of Whitman's sexuality in *Leaves of Grass* (1855) in an essay published in 1994. In an interview given after his retirement from teaching, he reveals a familiarity with literary history and contemporary poetry that gives his views both substance and authority.

Despite this prolific output, all the while keeping up with his own poetry, Simpson devoted much of his literary effort in the 1990's to translating French poets. These translations represent considerable effort and scholarship on Simpson's part as well as a desire to bring French poetry to the English reader. He translated some poems by Stéphane Mallarmé when he found the available translations beneath the quality that he thought he himself could achieve. In his introduction to those poems, he also explained Mallarmé's influence on major poets writing in English. He followed this publication with a translation of seven poems by Robert Desnos, giving a brief biography of the poet in the introduction. When Simpson published his translations of two poems by Jules Laforgue in 1996, he again explained in an introduction the poet's importance to English literature and the freshness of Laforgue's subjects—the experience of adolescence, for example. This time, Simpson included the original poems alongside his translation. He repeated this practice in his next translations, two poems by Charles Baudelaire, two by Léon-Paul Fargue, and four by Marceline Desbordes-Valmore. In all of these translations, Simpson's aim seems to be to keep French poetry fresh in the American mind and, one may imagine, indulge his own literary tastes at the same time.

Simpson's crowning achievement in this kind of writing, however, was his translation of François Villon's *The Legacy* and *The Testament* in a dual-language edition with a brief introduction and notes. His versions of these two famous poems are marked by simplicity of language and stylistic informality. Simpson sought to make the poems as close to the original as English allowed without sacrificing the music of poetry and losing the special quality of Villon's language and imagery. Since his own poetry excels in these qualities, and since his other translations had given him much experience in translating French poetry, one can only assume that he succeeded with Villon.

Other major works

long fiction: *Riverside Drive*, 1962.

nonfiction: *James Hogg: A Critical Study*, 1962; *North of Jamaica*, 1972; *Three on the Tower: The Lives and Works of Ezra Pound, T. S. Eliot, and William Carlos Williams*, 1975; *A Revolution in Taste: Studies of Dylan Thomas, Allen Ginsberg, Sylvia Plath, and Robert Lowell*, 1978; *A Company of Poets*, 1981; *The Character of the Poet*, 1986; *Ships Going into the Blue: Essays and Notes on Poetry*, 1994; *The King My Father's Wreck*, 1995 (autobiography).

translations: *Modern Poets of France: A Bilingual Anthology*, 1997; "The Legacy" and "The Testament," 2000 (of François Villon).

EDITED TEXT: *The New Poets of England and America*, 1957 (with Donald Hall and Robert Pack); *An Introduction to Poetry*, 1967.

MISCELLANEOUS: *Selected Prose*, 1989.

BIBLIOGRAPHY

Lazer, Hank. "Louis Simpson and Walt Whitman: Destroying the Teacher." *Walt Whitman Quarterly Review* 1 (December, 1983): 1-21. Lazer believes that Simpson's poetic development since 1963 has been shaped by Simpson's "dialogue" with Whitman.

_______, ed. *On Louis Simpson: Depths Beyond Happiness*. Ann Arbor: University of Michigan Press, 1988. Simpson himself says that one "should definitely have" this book, which runs to almost four hundred pages. Lazer's introduction surveys the criticism of Simpson's work from the beginning. The book itself offers shorter reviews and longer essays that would otherwise remain beyond the reach of most readers, enabling the reader to see how all Simpson's writing and thinking bear on the poetry.

Mason, David. "Louis Simpson's Singular Charm." *The Hudson Review* 48, no. 3 (Autumn, 1995): 499-507. Mason examines Simpson's literary theories and ideas as they are revealed in his poetry, criticism, and memoirs, particularly his latest publications.

Moran, Ronald. *Louis Simpson*. New York: Twayne, 1972. Chiefly important as the only book-length study of Simpson's literary career, this work opens with a brief biography and then examines the first five collections of poems and Simpson's one novel, *Riverside Drive*. Moran discusses critical response to each of the publications and places many of the poems in the larger context of Simpson's thought, emphasizing the development of the "emotive imagination" in his poetry. A brief annotated bibliography concludes the nearly 200 pages.

_______. "Louis Simpson: An Interview." *Five Points* 1, no. 1 (Fall, 1996): 45-63. Moran's questions lead Simpson through a wide range of subjects, including his views on other poets, such as Sylvia Plath, themes in his own poetry, some favorites of his own poems, and contemporary poetry.

Roberson, William H. *Louis Simpson: A Reference Guide*. Boston: G. K. Hall, 1980. This book attests the importance of Simpson's contribution to contemporary poetry. Lazer describes this reference work as "an invaluable book for anyone interested in Louis Simpson's writing and in critical reactions to that body of writing." The 172-page volume begins with a survey of Simpson's poetic career and critical reputation. Part 1 lists the writings by Simpson, and part 2 lists writings about him. Two indexes help the reader through the myriad titles and references.

Stitt, Peter. "Louis Simpson: In Search of the American Self." In *The World's Hieroglyphic Beauty: Five American Poets*. Athens: University of Georgia Press, 1985. Stitt follows Simpson's development through "three distinct phases" and traces the unifying sensibility in the poetry, looking closely at a number of the poems along the way. One of the longer essays on Simpson, this is one of the most illuminating as well.

Bernard E. Morris

L. E. SISSMAN

Born: Detroit, Michigan; January 1, 1928
Died: Boston, Massachusetts; March 10, 1976

PRINCIPAL POETRY

Dying: An Introduction, 1968
Scattered Returns, 1969
Pursuit of Honor, 1971
Hello, Darkness: The Collected Poems of L. E. Sissman, 1978 (Peter Davison, editor)

OTHER LITERARY FORMS

The publishing firm Little, Brown published *Innocent Bystander: The Scene from the '70's* in 1975, a collection of L. E. Sissman's "Innocent Bystander" columns from *The Atlantic Monthly*.

ACHIEVEMENTS

L. E. Sissman garnered significant recognition in his tragically short career: a Guggenheim Fellowship in

1968, followed in 1969 by an award from the National Institute of Arts and Letters. In 1971 he was asked to be Phi Beta Kappa Poet for Harvard University.

Biography

Louis Edward Sissman was born in Detroit, Michigan, on January 1, 1928, the only child of Edward James and Marie (née Anderson) Sissman, though his father apparently had children during a former marriage. Edward Sissman was in advertising, and his wife, according to "Parents in Winter," had run away from Ontario at the age of seventeen to go on the stage, eventually playing the Palace Theater in New York, taking up the piano and winning the Bach prize before settling down to marriage. In his introduction to *Hello, Darkness*, Peter Davison summarizes Sissman's parents as "peripatetic, homiletic, and remote," the father renting rather than buying the large dilapidated building in downtown Detroit that served as their home and his commercial art studio because of his fear of being restricted by ownership.

Money was not a problem, however, and Sissman attended the Detroit Country Day School between 1937 and 1944. He was one of the Quiz Kids on national radio and won the National Spelling Bee Prize in 1941, but he resented his parents and teachers for pushing him into such exhibitions, as an essay titled "Confessions of an Ex-Quiz Kid" makes clear. Ambivalent feelings about his father, which contained a fair degree of Oedipal resentment, lasted until his father's death in 1974, a year after his mother had died.

In 1944, not yet seventeen, Sissman entered Harvard, but two years later he was expelled, the causes given in "Guided Missiles" as "laziness and insubordination." He remained in the area, however, working as a stack boy at the Boston Public Library, and was readmitted the next year. He also began writing poetry, mostly imitations of English Renaissance poets, and studied under John Ciardi, Andrew Wanning, and Theodore Morrison. When he graduated cum laude in 1949, he did so as Class Poet and winner of the Garrison Poetry Prize. A year earlier, he had also been married, but the union was brief and childless.

After leaving Harvard, Sissman worked for a year as a copy editor at Prentice-Hall, then took a job as production manager with the A. S. Wyn publishing house in New York. He returned to Boston in late 1952 to serve as a campaign aide with the John F. Kennedy staff and, in 1953, became a senior writer with Boston's John C. Dowd advertising firm, where he would remain until 1956. That year he was appointed vice president and creative director for the Kenyon and Eckhardt advertising company, also in Boston. On November 27, 1958, he married Anne Bierman, and they moved to the rural town of Still River, an hour's drive west of the city. Their marriage lasted until his death.

In the 1960's, while still a successful advertising executive, Sissman's poems started appearing with increasing regularity in *The New Yorker* and elsewhere, but it was the frightening diagnosis of Hodgkin's disease in 1965 and subsequent radiation treatments that drove him into verse-writing with renewed vigor, almost desperation. In 1966 he wrote the title poem for *Dying: An Introduction*, his first effort to join autobiographical candor with traditional formulas. The collection itself was published in 1968; the same year he was given a Guggenheim Fellowship, which was followed in 1969 by an award from the National Institute of Arts and Letters. His most treasured honor came in 1971 when he was asked to be Harvard's Phi Beta Kappa Poet.

The period between 1970 and his death was a period of extraordinary achievement: He served as contributing editor at *The Atlantic Monthly*, where his "Innocent Bystander" column was a regular feature for five years; he contributed poems and reviews to *The New Yorker*; and he wrote the potent verses of the "Hello, Darkness" sequence under the gun of progressive physical deterioration. Davison has pointed out that Sissman could no longer write poetry after the end of 1974, although his prose was unaffected. As predicted by "Dying: An Introduction," his death came in a Boston hospital a few months after his forty-eighth birthday.

Analysis

In a tragically shortened career, L. E. Sissman managed to create a substantial, if not major, body of work that illustrates the way in which very traditional forms can be harnessed to intensely autobiographical, often mundane material to produce poetry of a high order. Confronted in his late thirties by death as an immediate, oppressive reality—"Very few people know where they will die,/ but I do: in a brick-faced hospital"—his verses dwell, too excessively at times, upon the clinical details of standard medical procedures, hospital dramas, burnishing them with wit, irony, and a sheen of erudite lyricism: "My awesome, glossy x-rays lay me bare/ In whited spaces: my skull glows like a moon/ Hewn, like a button, out of vivid bone" ("Hello, Darkness").

Sissman was both modest and precise about his aesthetic stance: "I write traditional, scanning, stanzaic verse, with special emphasis on iambic pentameter and the couplet." Yet, this adamantly conservative commitment to conventional techniques, which included a playful tendency to paraphrase admired contemporaries and past masters in his work, was fused with a refreshing willingness to take advantage of the new thematic freedom featured in the confessional lyrics of Robert Lowell, Anne Sexton, and Sylvia Plath, fellow New Englanders who also favored, in the main, a formalist style. Consequently, despite an early, lifelong allegiance to W. H. Auden and Auden's deft merger of private experience and public commentary, Sissman's best poetry, at its peak when contemplating family history or imminent personal dissolution, depends heavily upon a sense of autobiographical exactitude and diary-like fidelity to realistic detail, however fictional or transfigured.

In line with John Donne's and Andrew Marvell's ventures in the same area, seduction was another subject that seemed to elicit Sissman's strongest efforts, as in "In and Out: A Home Away from Home, 1947" and the punning "Pursuit of Honor," but the poems most likely to endure are those keyed to the pressure of a terminal illness, poems such as "Dying: An Introduction," "A Deathplace," and the harrowing "Hello, Darkness" sequence, where all the impressive resources of the poet are thrown into battle against the hovering specter of oblivion. Other poems have their charms and moments of undeniable power, among them "The Big Rock Candy Mountain," an elegy for a half-brother, but these too frequently dissipate their emotive energies at crucial moments, as well as their author's gift for clever metaphors, by retreating into self-indulgent pyrotechnics, piled-up images, literary distractions, and the kind of preciousness that can result when laboring with received modes without firm control.

Neither pioneer nor genius, Sissman's main contribution lay in the production of a series of skillful narrative and lyric poems that chronicle, with wit and grace, a single life's unfolding dimensions, a body of verse which should, as X. J. Kennedy has suggested in his perceptive and touching retrospective for *Parnassus* (Fall/ Winter 1979), be read as "one enormous poem: an effort to recapture his past, interpret it, fix it, set it in order." This represents a significant achievement, if only as a reminder that poetry's essential humanity still wells from just such a constant reification of ordinary existence for communal benefit.

Dying: An Introduction

Aside from the title poem, which has the fear of death behind its fierce drive, the poetry in L. E. Sissman's first collection rarely manages to attain the kind of intensity that generates first-class art. Confessedly obsessed with the challenge of using difficult forms, such as villanelles and canzonis, in a language where there is a relative paucity of rhymes, the poet's devices, many of them clever, draw too much attention to themselves, as in the playful "Just a Whack at Empson," where at least the subject matter suits its light verse jacket: "Each greening apple has its browning spot:/ 'The rank of every poet is well-known." The pun on Browning and its shrewd denial of Empson's offensive sentence in the second line demonstrate the delightful talent for apt connections and sly technical tricks that are evident throughout *Dying: An Introduction*.

"Two Encounters"

When dealing with more serious matters, however, the habitual resort to puns and obtrusive rhymes, to endless tag lines from other poets and ceaseless amplification of tropes, can create a humorous detachment that destroys the poem's quest for transcendence, even as it wins the reader's admiration. In "Two Encounters," for example, which is divided into halves, "At the Inn, 1947" and "At the Fair, 1967," stressing Sissman's concentration upon a scrapbook past and his love of William Wordsworth, the opening lines exemplify the strengths and limitations of such a modus operandi:

> Your mink scarf smells as if it smoked cigars,
> And soot clings in the corners of your eyes,
> And cold has cancelled your pale cheeks in red,
> And you stand faintly in a veil of Joy.

The list continues, affirming Sissman's habit of never knowing when enough is enough, and the tenor of the lines, arch images of a cigar-smoking dead mink and cheeks stamped by red ink, establishes a mood of youthful insouciance appropriate to the time and place, the speaker's undergraduate days—aided by the borrowing from Randall Jarrell—but in the "altered circumstances" of meeting his "Dark lady of a dozen sonnets" twenty years later, the tone is capable of evoking rue, nothing deeper, even though the ending is salvaged by a beautiful closing on a Ferris wheel: "To hold your airborne arm/ Twenty years later is to ride the calm/ World's rim against the gravity of time."

"Two Encounters" is a good poem, generally successful in what it attempts and accomplishes, yet the very nature of its professional performance, its studied self-consciousness, appears to preclude leaps into the sublime. It favors, instead, literature over life, in the sense that risks—of self, of comprehension—are usually avoided, and felt responses are tuned to a distancing knowledge of other poets, other poems, so that poems titled "Peg Finnan's Wake in Inman Square" and "Sweeney to Mrs. Porter in the Spring" are inescapable presences, inviting possibly fatal separations between experience and artifice. Even in "Parents in Winter," where the portraits of his mother and father might be expected to tap richer feeling, Sissman cannot resist ending "Mother at the Palace, 1914" with coy echoes: "And winning the Bach prize, and having sowed/ Such seeds and oats, at last to marriage./ And so to me? But that's another story."

"Dying: An Introduction"

Only in the title poem to his collection do Sissman's narrative gift and comic reflexes find an appropriate vehicle, the wry perspective of the persona accentuating the tension supplied by the bleak situation, which involves three visits to the doctor, once for an examination, the second time to have a slice of a dangerous lump removed for a biopsy, and the third visit to hear the dreaded results: cancer of the lymph nodes or Hodgkin's disease. Divided into five sections, the poem moves from "Summer still plays across the street" to the last section's November setting, which, ironically, has "a thick smell of spring," heightened by laughing "college girls" parading in "ones and twos" and "twos and threes" down the street. The previous section's humorous details—"One *Punch* and two/ *Times* later comes the call" in the waiting room, culminating in "one *Life* further on"—resolves into a series of lean lines that melds unaccustomed spring awareness with memory (of a young sexual episode) and meditative slowness, the autumn world viewed through a new veil of "finity" as

> . . . oddly, not as sombre
> As December,
> But as green
> As anything:
> As spring.

Death's grip, "mixing memory and desire," to quote from T. S. Eliot, a Sissman favorite, has instilled new life.

Scattered Returns

In many ways, *Scattered Returns* is a duplicate of *Dying: An Introduction*: the same olio of charming, witty, often facile versifications of vagrant experience and recovered "spots of time," perceived, as usual, through a net of literary associations—the third poem in the title sequence is "Three Derivative Poems," inspired by Eliot.

To match the starkness of "Dying: An Introduction," there is "A Deathplace," which foretells: "A booted man in black with a peaked cap/ Will call for me and troll me down the hall/ And slot me into his black car. That's all." Assisted by monosyllabic deliberateness, the simple diction and matter-of-fact attitude underlines the fearful banality of death's impact, its routine quality to others, while the terse last sentence simulates its abrupt finality. Unfortunately, the sequence itself climaxes with "Sonatina: Hospital," which represents Sissman at his precious worst, straining after a sardonic conceit that eludes sought-for reverberations.

The sole thematic difference between *Scattered Returns* and *Dying: An Introduction* might be seen in the ambitious sequence, "A War Requiem," that concludes the former. Composed in 1969, a year after the assassinations of Martin Luther King and Robert Kennedy when antiwar feelings were reaching fever pitch, the sequence contains thirty-two sections or individual poems and ranges from "New York, 1929" through four decades to "Twelfth Night, 1969." Not too surprisingly, the whole is less than its parts, since it is a case of a minor talent struggling to encompass an awesome theme: the manner in which American history had conspired to produce the disasters of the late 1960's. When read as narrative, a string of dramatic and lyric moments from the author's past as that past intersected with and humanized crucial national events, "A War Requiem" unwinds like a slowly flipping comic strip, broad and fine strokes blurred at times into caricature.

Most often, the sequence functions efficiently where Sissman is content to isolate his governing metaphor without forcing extra literary or political implications upon it, as in section 28, "New York, 1967," when reflections in Manhattan's ubiquitous plate glass windows and a lowered glance captures the city's dehumanizing patterns, "an absurd/ Theatre without end and without word." Another successful section, 14, "The '46s, 1945," briefly encapsulates the hungry delight with which crowds, weary of war's deprivations, greet the new car models in Detroit and "sniff the fruit of peace." A portrait of the Kennedys, disguised as the "O'Kanes" in section 17, "The Candidate, 1952," is also generally on target, especially the final picture of John F. Kennedy, "moody, willful, and mercuric man," as prisoner to ambition, "easy in his bonds, under the dour/ And time-releasing sedative of power."

Other sections are much less felicitous in their convergence of private recollections and historic dramas, once again exposing Sissman's weakness for misplaced witticisms and easy literary allusions—Eliot is echoed several times. In section 25, "Talking Union, 1964," for example, in trying to convey the new television image pursued by contemporary labor leaders, which entails smoothness and lies or non sequiturs, he cannot help subsiding into: "So gentlemen/ Are made, not born, with infinite labor pains." Section 30, "New York, 1968," a short, impressionistic sketch of Manhattan's clamor, glibly appeals to "The Love Song of J. Alfred Prufrock" for its climax, small voices connecting, "and we come true/ To one another, till the rising town's/ Unhuman voices wake us, and we drown." Probably the surest indicator of "A War Requiem's" larger failure, which does not detract from the brilliance of many of the sections, can be found in the image chosen to complete the entire poem, that of a snowy owl glimpsed planning "down its glide path to surprise a vole." This is not only familiar, owing a debt to Sylvia Plath and, no doubt, others; it is also trite and inadequate to its complex subject, however well executed.

With the exceptions already noted, the same can be said of the collection as a whole and emphasizes that Sissman, for good or ill, epitomizes *The New Yorker*-type poet in full flight, as roughly defined by the deft verses published in that journal during Howard Moss's long tenure as its poetry editor. (*Scattered Returns* is dedicated to Moss, whom Sissman had met at Harvard.) The specimen virtues are real and worthy of praise, among them accessibility, formalist intelligence, and an educated predilection for irony, but they do encourage elitist conformity, a poetry of exquisite sensibility (the adjective is instructive) that mandates a voice of muted nuance and wry detachment so persistent as to ensure monotony and, worse, a narrow vision of life's (and poetry's) vigorous variety. For Sissman, being a *New Yorker* poet meant repeated reinforcement of serious defects in style and substance which undermined the bulk of the poetry appearing in the three volumes published during his lifetime.

Hello, Darkness

When putting together *Hello, Darkness: The Collected Poems of L. E. Sissman* a few years after its author's death, Peter Davison, literary executor, decided to group all of the poems written after 1971, except for some occasional verse, at the end of the volume. These appear as "A Posthumous Collection" and are broken down into four divisions: "Descriptive and Satirical," "Nostalgic and Narrative," "Light and Dreamy," and "Hello, Darkness," the latter being probably among the latest. The first group occupies the middle range of Sissman's achievement, although several of the poems are marked by an appealing retreat from mere virtuosity, as in the pleasantly chilling fable of "The Clearing in the Woods" and "Spring Song," a more ragged quest to configure death's approach that overcomes self-indulgence to soar into bitter hatred for the notion of perishing like "a leafless log of body" thrown on a December fire. "The Persistence of Innocence" also strikes a responsive emotional chord, despite lapses into preachy rhetoric.

The verses in the "Nostalgic and Narrative" section

are further stories from the past reworked into typical pastiches of astute observation, extended tropes, and time-softened sentiment. "At the Bar, 1948" can serve for the rest, replete with wit and genuine skill and charm, but it reminds the reader that autobiography requires more from poetry, that the specifics of someone else's life can be as dull as home movies, unless transmuted into universal terms. The best of this lot is actually "A Late Good Night," which shuns confession to record a frustrated man's passage into suicidal ends.

The small handful of fragments and whole poems in "Light and Dreamy," true to their Hollywood name, are dominated by characteristic playfulness, urbane resistance to the banal impositions and surreal possibilities inherent in ordinary existence. "To Your Uterus: An Uncompleted Call" is one worth a quick look, and "Dear John," an amusing versified letter, is another. The last two, "Cockaigne: A Dream" and "Three American Dreams: A Suite in Phillips House," are weightier endeavors. The former flows along with customary smoothness; a series of dream perspectives upon city scenes from the dreamer's past manages to vivify the anticipated waking up to middle-of-the-night reality and feelings of loss, the dream's "only evidence being my tears/ Of joy or of the other, I can't tell." More hungry for significance, "Three American Dreams" sees America through biography, the nightmare of success, failure, and death's ever-threatening erasure of both. It is of a piece in the Sissman mode, excessive in its language and metaphors at times, but far from inert.

The central texts of "A Posthumous Collection" surface, however, in the "Hello, Darkness" portion of the book, starting with the first poem, "Negatives," which makes a virtue of Sissman's worst flaw, his sways into dense language and image, as if afraid to prune away potential meaning. The tone is bravely jocular—"Hello, black skull. How privily you shine/ In all my negatives"—and exaggeration is a logical evolution of such a voice as it searches for the right figures of speech to convey the negatives' inner design and purpose:

> The tubular members of my rib cage gleam
> Like tortile billets of aluminum;
> My hand shines, frozen, like a white batwing
> Caught in a strobe.

When the climax comes, it brings the necessary release of irony and insight, diminishing death's menace; future "coroners" are imagined as accepting his mere hunk of dead meat as his "true bills," instead of the fluorographs and X rays which reveal the beauty and plan beneath flesh's frail husk. "December 27, 1966" is less sharp, less impressive, because it is hampered by so many tired comparisons, speaking of the moon as a half-dollar, of death's temptation in terms of high stakes and "the veiled dealer" vending "bad cards." Even so, the slowly building drift into a closing image of the same moon floating past in dead serenity, "tailed by her consort of stars," has the merit of a sudden, fertile disjunction in its clash with the shivering night watchman (himself) "pressed against the falling glass."

"Homage to Clotho: A Hospital Suite"

The third poem, "Homage to Clotho: A Hospital Suite," a set of seven stanzas or sections that follow the speaker from a hospital stay and operation to an uncertain future at home, demonstrates Sissman's easeful mastery of form and language when pressed by consciousness of death into more telling brevity, a use of abundant poetic resources for needed structural variations, not mere display or compulsion. The initial section reifies the threat, airless and tense, enveloping the entire sequence, "a vacuum waiting for a rupture in/ The tegument," while he resides, in life, in the hospital, upon the sufferance of authorities until "my vistas wither, and I die."

Governed by contraries, the poem is effective, and the second section introduces a change in tone and tenor, a wish for a woman poet, who sounds like a parody of Marianne Moore, to be singing his song at this brief and fleeting hour. Section 3 resumes a direct address, thinking how easy it is to be watching a film, how easy to accept its end, which acts as preamble to the persona suffering a long needle injected into his pelvic arch in pursuit of bone-marrow in front of "starched and giggling girls." Roles are reversed, and he is the movie star.

Though still intent upon the idea of passive anguish and spectacle, of helplessness under the care of others, section 4 returns to the eight-line formula of section 2 to observe, from a calm distance, a male nurse shaving him for the operation. The nurse's casual reassurances are obviously resented for masking indifference, but the overt response is the language (prose) and common sense of the street: "It is that he must make his living, too." The lack of stress on "living" gives it added sarcasm in a hospital context.

Another variation in the "suite" of verses comes with the startling switch into full-blooded protest in the fifth section, which begins: "If Hell abides on earth this must be it." The "it" refers to the recovery room, where he lingers in pain and uncertainty between life and death, a metaphor for the whole experience, where he can finally resort to the gift for analogy he delights in exhibiting without violating formal restraints, as in describing the dryness overwhelming him, "his own/ Throat-filling Gobi, mucous membrane gone/ Dry as Arabia." The images pile up and are explained in a well-deserved climax: "such wet dreams/ Afflict the dessicate on their interminable way/ Up through the layers of half-light to day"—contraries persist, unifying the sequence, but tonal alterations avoid monotony.

A conversational style prevails in section 6, which is constructed around a basic comparison between walking to the bathroom with his "wheeled I. V. pole" and the riddle of Sphinx, which Oedipus solved, that saw man in the last state of his life as a three-legged creature attached to a cane. Unable to urinate, the persona must accept defeat and return to his bed to await the aid of a young man with "his snake-handler's fist of catheters." The ultimate image welds together further contrasts with harrowing precision, his body kept alive by being "tethered" to various "bottles, bags, and tubes," to the point where its importunities dun the mind "in this refined,/ White-sheeted torture, practiced by a kind,/ Withdrawn white face trained in the arts of love." Besides once more using irony to amplify polar reversals and displacements, the arts of love as kindness, survival rituals, not sexual manipulations, the poem has established a schema that incorporates ancient Greece, the antithesis of the arctic modern hospital where the body and rote rule, which patently prepares the reader for the last section.

Clotho, one of the three Fates in Greek mythology charged with determining each person's life span by the length of the thread they sever, is finally granted her homage, after the persona has been released and is met at home by autumn leaves, "fat, sportive maple leaves" that are blown on his shoes, as if including him "in their great fall." A subtle undercurrent might be adduced here in conjunction with the earlier Sphinx reference, since his fall from health is hardly of the stature of Greek tragedy. Unrepentant punster, he must clamber up "enneads of stairs" to the bedroom where he will recompose himself to enduring existence, a "world of voices and surprises," for as long "as Clotho draws my filament," until "her sister widows" cut it off and "send me to befriend the winter leaves." This quiet, seasonally cyclical climax to the poem and to the sequence articulates a thoughtful decline into civilized acceptance of death and its modern lack of drama as the sole sane reaction contemporary art can muster.

In the first five sections treated as film scenes, "Cancer: A Dream," Sissman shapes a more surreal drama. The setting is a movie studio, with the persona envisioned as an actor repairing to his dressing room after a wearying piece of acting, Shakespearean rage "torn to dated tatters" for an audience of "cavefish." All he can do, like a patient after surgery, facing death and constant, humiliating observation, is to "undress shakily and lie me down/ In dust on the vast desert of the bed." What ensues in the next four scenes, skillfully handled to join literal and fantasy elements with a minimum of shock, entails a shift of scene and directions from a script girl, plus an embarrassing inability to respond to the sexual advances of an aged female poet, all of which can be associated with the conditions of a man in the death-throes of a debilitating disease. The climax, a brilliant bit of grotesque maneuvering, has him center stage, performing the dance of death with cancer's crab—perhaps it is another self as well, certifying Sigmund Freud's death instinct and affirming the poem's deeper dimensions.

"Tras Os Montes," the final poem in "A Posthumous Collection," equally well sustained, may be the strongest Sissman ever wrote. After two memorial sections devoted to dead parents, illuminating their dying more than their lives to echo his own disintegration, the mountain allusion is realized in an allegorical assault upon mountains "In Company" with eleven friends, actual people whom the author expected to attend his funeral. This section, first of three in the poem titled for the sequence, concludes with death as a form of military disgrace, a body thrown from a parapet,

. . . gaining weightlessness
As its flesh deliquesces, as its bones
Shiver to ashes—into an air that crawls
With all the arts of darkness far below.

"A Deux" is the heading for the second section, a farewell to a beloved mate, a "new scenario" in which his death is falling upward, into a "stormcloud from the springing field," where he can spy on her "and rain farewells/ And late apologies on your grey head" before, with a bold, haunting metaphor, the sun lights up his remains as "a tentative rainbow,/ An inverse, weak, and spectral kind of smile."

Dying is a solo act, however, as Sissman knew, and the third section, "Alone," reverts to the dependence upon paradoxes, a series of ironic oppositions, that motored the other death poems. The persona's climb to death is now in the guise of an isolated infiltrator, casting off his human ties in "the same selfish spirit" that had inspired Sissman's "lifelong journey" in the first place.

Thus, death is birth, the primal paradox, the egoistic art that reared "imperial Rome" returning to earth, "its inveterate love/ For the inanimate and its return." If too dense, on occasion, to match the achievement of its predecessors, "Alone" does not disgrace them, and the sequence, like the collection, manifests sufficient emotional and artistic energy to guarantee Sissman's poetic survival.

Other major work

nonfiction: *Innocent Bystander: The Scene from the '70's*, 1975.

Bibliography

Gunton, Sharon R., ed. *Contemporary Literary Criticism*. Vol. 18. Detroit: Gale Research, 1981. The entry on Sissman notes that in an era of experimentation, he "clung to stanzaic verse, the iambic foot, couplets, and sonnets."

Kennedy, X. J. "Innocence in Armor." *Parnassus: Poetry in Review* 8 (Fall/Winter, 1979): 48-63. Reviews *Hello, Darkness: The Collected Poems of L. E. Sissman* and *Innocent Bystander: The Scene from the '70's*. Also discusses Sissman's "other" life as an advertising executive and how this counted against him as a poet. By and large a sympathetic review that sees Sissman's strength in the narrative poem. Calls his poem "Cancer: A Dream" harrowing in its description of hospitals and praises it for its "sustained length, in such cold intensity."

Leithauser, Brad. "The Fixed Moment: The Poetry of L. E. Sissman." *The New Criterion* 2, no. 2 (October, 1983): 36-42. A critical assessment of Sissman's poetic works.

Pritchard, William H. "Innocence Possessed." *The Times Literary Supplement*, no. 3982 (July 28, 1978): 847. Discusses Sissman's poem "Dying: An Introduction" and the impact it has coming from Sissman's own experience of being "introduced" to his death. Says that in many ways Sissman was "possessed by his past." Cites his last poems as his best, especially "Tras Os Montes."

Updike, John. "Witness to His Dying." *The New York Times Book Review*, May 14, 1978, p. 10. In reviewing *Hello, Darkness: The Collected Poems of L. E. Sissman*, Updike defines the "Sissmanesque" mode as being one with "fascinating specificity" and describes it as "dense but dancing blank verse varied by spurts of rhyme." He says Sissman's poetry is less American than British in form and style. The three volumes of Sissman's poetry sum up a world in themselves, a rarity in modern poetry.

Williamson, Alan. "Comment: *Hello, Darkness: The Collected Poems of L. E. Sissman*." *Poetry* 132, no. 1 (November 1, 1978): 100-102. Notes Sissman's "indiscriminate curiosity about how life is lived on the surface," an unusual approach for a poet. Reveals that this poet's strength is his power to suggest the "symbolism of incidentals." On the other hand, notes his struggle to bring his verse to the level of "truly private feeling."

Edward Butscher

Edith Sitwell

Born: Scarborough, England; September 7, 1887
Died: London, England; December 9, 1964

Principal poetry

The Mother and Other Poems, 1915
Twentieth Century Harlequinade and Other Poems, 1916 (with Osbert Sitwell)
Clown's Houses, 1918
The Wooden Pegasus, 1920
Façade, 1922
Bucolic Comedies, 1923
The Sleeping Beauty, 1924
Troy Park, 1925
Poor Young People, 1925 (with Osbert Sitwell and Sacheverell Sitwell)
Elegy on Dead Fashion, 1926
Rustic Elegies, 1927
Popular Song, 1928
Five Poems, 1928
Gold Coast Customs, 1929
Collected Poems, 1930
In Spring, 1931
Epithalamium, 1931
Five Variations on a Theme, 1933
Selected Poems, 1936
Poems New and Old, 1940
Street Songs, 1942
Green Song and Other Poems, 1944
The Weeping Babe, 1945
The Song of the Cold, 1945
The Shadow of Cain, 1947
The Canticle of the Rose, 1949
Façade and Other Poems, 1950
Gardeners and Astronomers, 1953
Collected Poems, 1954
The Outcasts, 1962
Music and Ceremonies, 1963
Selected Poems, 1965

Other literary forms

In addition to her many collections of poetry, Edith Sitwell wrote several volumes of critical essays, biography, autobiography, social history, and fiction. Foremost among her critical studies are *Poetry and Criticism* (1925), *Aspects of Modern Poetry* (1934), and *A Poet's Notebook* (1943). Her critical biography *Alexander Pope* (1930) was meant to serve as a vindication of the man and poet. Having as much of an affinity for Queen Elizabeth as for Pope, she wrote of England's controversial monarch in *Fanfare for Elizabeth* (1946) and *The Queens and the Hive* (1962). *Bath* (1932) is a work of social history. *I Live Under a Black Sun* (1937) is a fictionalized biography of Jonathan Swift. She also edited several anthologies, of which *The Pleasures of Poetry* (1930-1932, 1934), *The American Genius* (1951), and *The Atlantic Book of British and American Poetry* (1958) are the best known. Her rather acerbic autobiography, which was posthumously published, is titled *Taken Care Of* (1965).

Achievements

In 1933, Edith Sitwell was awarded a medal by the Royal Society of Literature. Honorary degrees from Oxford, Leeds, Durham, and Sheffield universities followed, and she was made an associate of the American National Institute of Arts and Letters.

The best compliment ever paid to Sitwell was Evelyn Waugh's statement that she took the dullness out of poetry. Never boring or tiresome, the worst her adverse critics could say about her was that she was eccentric and exhibitionistic, her poetry too experimental. A few

Edith Sitwell (Hulton Archive)

of her literary enemies—and at one time they were almost as numerous as her friends—did go a step further, however, and labeled her early poetry pretentious, rambling, vacuous. Geoffrey Grigson, Julian Symons, and F. R. Leavis are only a few of the critics who thought her a dreadful poet; but William Butler Yeats, Cyril Connolly, Stephen Spender, Dylan Thomas, and T. S. Eliot believed she was one of the most creative artists of the twentieth century. Allen Tate summarized Edith Sitwell best when, shortly after her death, he commented that she was "one of the great poets of the twentieth century . . . a remarkable and independent personality."

Biography

Edith Sitwell, daughter of Sir George and Lady Ida Sitwell and sister of the two writers Osbert and Sacheverell, was born at Scarborough, Yorkshire, in 1887. Though reared in an atmosphere of wealth and culture, her early years, as her brother Osbert wrote in his *Left Hand, Right Hand* (1944), were emotionally trying. An unwanted child, she suffered considerable physical and nervous anguish in being reared by a tyrannical father, who, among other things, made his only daughter wear a painful device to improve the shape of her aquiline nose. At an early age she announced her intention of becoming a genius, and soon after she learned to write, she tried her hand at poetry. Physically, she grew to be a tall, pale, distinguished-looking young woman with heavy-lidded eyes and a Plantagenet presence.

Early in the 1920's, Edith, Osbert, and Sacheverell emerged as a literary cult of three. Their circle was graced by such figures as Yeats, Virginia Woolf, Aldous Huxley, and Eliot. The most prolific of the three Sitwells, Edith produced volume after volume of poetry, and she took to reading her work to literary groups. *Wheels*, an iconoclastic annual publication which she founded and edited, outraged many. Critics and philistines not appreciative of her efforts often felt the sting of her tongue.

Between 1914 and 1929, in what might be called her initial period, she reacted strongly against the "banal bucolics" of the Georgian poets and wrote a great deal of nonrepresentational verse, which to some extent parallels the paintings of Pablo Picasso and the cubists. During her middle period, which extended from 1930 to 1940, she abandoned her dream world of sensuous mood and tonal patterns, her "pure poetry," to write poems that, like Eliot's *The Waste Land* (1922) denounced the barbarism, the hypocrisy, the misdirection of modern society. At the time, she regarded poetry as akin to moral wisdom, and she delighted to play the role of a Sibyl or Cassandra. To accentuate her six-foot frame, she dressed in long flowing gowns, sometimes of startling Chinese red, sometimes of intricate brocade, and she swathed her head with tall turbans. To make herself even more notoriously recognizable, she wore heavy jewelry and gold amulets. She painted her long nails with bright silver polish and adorned her thin fingers with marble-sized rings. All this was done, she said, as a gesture of defiance of her upbringing and as an act of faith in herself. For the sake of variety, however, she would often dress simply and entirely in black. One day, when asked for whom she was mourning, she responded: "For the entire world."

An eccentric but fascinating woman, Sitwell attracted the attention of many major celebrities and moved among them. Her famous friends and foes were legion. She was especially fond of such diverse personalities as Pavel Tchelitchew, Cecil Beaton, Gertrude Stein, Jacob Epstein, Alec Guinness, and Marilyn Monroe. She had little use for D. H. Lawrence, Lytton Strachey, H. G. Wells, George Moore, and John Galsworthy. It took her almost forty years to forgive Noël Coward for a devastating spoof, *London Calling* (1923), of her and her brothers. Friendships, rivalries, and public spats made her life interesting, but the central theme of her life remained poetry.

In 1941, she entered her final period and turned, like Eliot, to traditional values, spiritual matters, and orthodox Christianity. Thirteen years later she was made a Dame Commander of the Order of the British Empire. The following year, Dame Edith Sitwell was received into the Roman Catholic church. Evelyn Waugh, who served as her godfather, cautioned her at the time that all too many Catholics were bores and prigs, crooks and cads, and that he himself was really pretty awful; but he added, mainly for Dame Edith's edification, how much worse he should be without the Faith. She took Waugh's words to heart, and shortly after her reception, when questioned what meant most to her, with the zeal of a convert she replied: "The love of God, the love of mankind, and the future of humanity."

With such ideals uppermost in mind, she spent her final years in London, devoting herself even more zealously to literature. She continued to create and to encourage fledgling writers to do likewise, often writing warm introductions to their books. She died on December 9, 1964, after several months of illness.

Analysis

Edith Sitwell's early poems produced a series of shocks. To some, her verse was artificial; others could see that she purposefully created an artificial world. Her teeming imagination fashioned a luscious, semimechanical microcosm, one having "furry light" from "a reynard-coloured sun," trees that "hissed like green geese" with leaves as "hoarse as a dog's bark," a domain populated by "poor flaxen foundlings . . . upon a darkened stair." The world she wrote about in her poetry was, as she put it, "like a bare egg laid by the feathered air."

Of her seriousness as an artist, there is no doubt. A childless woman, she actually lay in her bed and labored for as long as six hours a day for more than forty years to bring forth reams of poetry. A few of her creations may be idiot brainchildren afflicted with echolalia; more are precocious offspring of her metaphysical imagination; most are somewhere between these extremes. In short, though she was wildly eccentric in all she did and wrote, she was still a poet of emotional depth and sincere human concerns. What she wrote was hardly for the common man, but she often maintained that the public enjoys poetry, "unless it is lethally boring or they are frightened out of doing so by bad critics." The matter, the form, the method employed by so many of her contemporaries aroused her ire. Like an electric eel in a pond full of catfish, she attacked such poets for their lack of tactile and visual sensibility and their inability to please those sensibilities by means of the written word.

Most admirers of her work rank the poems of her last years higher than the verbal legerdemain of her experimental period. Louise Bogan is one of the few who prefers Sitwell's earlier efforts to her later brooding reflections on the world's evils. In many of her early poems, Sitwell was more concerned with evoking beauty, with producing sonorous effects, than with communicating ideas; but in her later work she manifested a somberness and intensity, an almost grieving understanding of, and compassion for, the sufferings of humanity.

The Mother and Other Poems

The pattern for much of Sitwell's early verse can be found in her first published work, *The Mother and Other Poems*, wherein she deals with a prissy, dollhouse world full of such exotic objects as tambourines, mandolins, parakeets, nutmeg trees, and chinoiserie. Technically, the third poem in the collection, "Serenade," is one of the best. In its music of evening, the primacy of darkness is established in the opening lines: "The tremulous gold of stars within your hair/ Are yellow bees flown from the hive of night." In attributing the sun's color to the stars, she suggests a causal relationship between darkness and light, night and day. The yellow bees, born from the mothering hive of night to experience the darkness of the evening world, find the blossoms of the eyes of the beloved more fair "Than all the pale flowers folded from the light." Finally, "Serenade" pleads that the loved one open dreaming eyes "Ere those bright bees have flown and darkness dies."

Bucolic Comedies

Most of the poems in *Clown's Houses* and *The Wooden Pegasus* are similar to those in *The Mother and Other Poems*, but the poems making up *Bucolic Comedies* deal less with rhythm and exotica and more with what Sitwell labeled "sense transfusions." Though at first glance most of these poems may seem comedic nonsense, a careful reading indicates that even their oddest images have a purpose.

In "Aubade," for example, Sitwell depicts the sad stupidity of a servant girl on a country farm coming down to light a morning fire: "Jane, Jane,/ Tall as a crane,/ The morning-light creaks down again." The dawn "creaks" about Jane because early light does not run smoothly. It is raining and Jane imagines each drop of moisture hardening into a "dull blunt wooden stalactite." Facing daily chores of weeding "eternities of kitchen garden," she senses flowers that cluck and mock her. (The flowers "cluck" for they are cockscombs.) The flames of the fire remind her of the carrots and turnips she has continually to clean and cook. Her spirits hang limp as "the milk's weak mind." Like so many of Sitwell's early poems, "Aubade" contains recollections of her own childhood. Thinking of the servant, Jane, brings to the poet's mind "The shivering movement of a certain cold dawn light upon the floor suggestive of high animal whining or whimpering, a half-frightened and subservient urge to something outside our consciousness."

Façade

Sitwell's early volumes caught the attention of only a limited number of readers, but on June 12, 1923, after reciting her *Façade* at London's Aeolian Hall, she achieved instant notoriety. Everything about her performance provoked controversy. She sat with her back to the audience, barely visible behind a transparent curtain adorned with a crudely painted moon face. The ostensible purpose of the curtain was to allow the audience to concentrate chiefly on the auditory qualities of the poems. The moon face was in keeping with the dreamlike world of apes, ducks, grotesque lords and ladies, clowns, peasants, and servant girls she had written about. Rumors of the nature of *Façade* had reached the literary world after one or two private recitations, and on opening night a large and curious audience was present.

Sitwell chanted her poems through an instrument called a "Sengerphone" (named after its inventor, George Senger). Out of the Sengerphone, which was made of compressed grasses meant to retain the purity of magnified tonal quality, came such baffling words as "The sound of the onycha/ When the phoca has the pica/ In the palace of the Queen Chinee!" Music may have the power to soothe the savage breast—and there was little adverse reaction to William Walton's orchestration—but the response to Sitwell's poetry bordered on the primitive. After the performance the audience became so threatening that the poet had to remain on stage behind the curtain. Someone whispered to Sitwell that an old lady was waiting to hit her with an umbrella. Disgruntled spectators complained loudly that they were victims of an enormous hoax. They had come to *Façade* expecting to enjoy Walton's music and hear some edifying verse. What they heard sounded like gibberish. Had they listened more attentively they might have found subtle criticisms of modern life, innuendoes of decay, death, nothingness.

Never had more brickbats been hurled at a poet. In her defense, when Sitwell wrote *Façade* she believed a change in the direction, imagery, and rhythms of poetry had become necessary, owing, as she expressed it, "to the rhythmical flaccidity, the verbal deadness, the dull and expected patterns" of modern poetry. The poems in *Façade*, consequently, are in most cases virtuoso exercises in verbalizing, studies in rhythmical techniques. "Fox Trot," "Assface," "Sir Beelzebub," "Waltz," and "Hornpipe" are excellent examples of her rhythmical techniques; these poems, in particular, consist of experiments concerning the effect that sound has on meaning.

One trisyllabic word, Sitwell discovered, had greater rapidity than three monosyllabic words. Two rhymes placed immediately together at the end of each of two lines, furthermore, would be like "leaps in the air." In "Fox Trot," for example, she wrote: "'Sally, Mary, Mattie, what's the matter, why cry?'"/ The huntsman and the reynard-coloured sun and I sigh." Other experiments were made to discover the influence of rhythm on the thickening and thinning, sharpening and softening, of consonants, as in certain lines of "Waltz": "The stars in their apiaries,/ Sylphs in their aviaries. . . ." These lines in turn are followed by others which end at times with a dissonance, at other times with a rhyme. To produce a waltz rhythm she used disyllabic rhymes to begin as well as to end lines, "Daisy and Lily,/ Lazy and silly," followed by two long lines with assonance: "Walk by the shore of the wan grassy sea—/ Talking once more 'neath a swan-bosomed tree."

When Sitwell published *Façade* she attempted in a long and complicated preface to rebut the protests and complaints of her critics. Those willing to accept her prosodic theories were still troubled by her startling imagery. Such conceits as "wan grassy sea," "swan-bosomed tree," "foam-bell of ermine," and "asses' milk of the stars," she maintained, were partly the result of condensations where the language of one sense was insufficient to cover meaning or sensation. The use of such imagery, she hoped, would "pierce down to the essence of the thing seen," revealing attributes which at first might appear alien to a tired eye or unresponsive ear. Perhaps the chief reason why *Façade* was so widely misunderstood was that Sitwell experimented with abstract patterns. Then, too, the apparent vacuity of some of the poems caused them to be suspect.

They were useless; they were butterflies; but butterflies, she protested, can adorn the world and delight the beholder.

No two poems in *Façade* are alike; indeed, they differ radically from one another. "Hornpipe" is a jaunty piece set to nautical music. "Trio for Two Cats" has more than an amusing title; its fast rhythm creates an eerie mood accentuated with castanets. "I Like to Do Beside the Seaside" is set to a tango rhythm. "Scotch Rhapsody" begins with "Do not take a bath in Jordan, Gordan," and a heavy drumbeat sounds throughout. "By the Lake" has a slow pace and its cold imagery depicts a lonely winter night with two estranged lovers recalling a happy past. "Polka" has such clever running rhymes as "Robinson Crusoe rues so" and the "poxy, doxy dear." "Popular Song" is a joyful and carefree lyric about "Lily O'Grady,/ Silly and Shady,/ Longing to be/ A lazy lady." "Sir Beelzebub," who calls for "his syllabub in the hotel in Hell/ Where Prosperine first fell," is meant to mock the Victorians and their poet laureate, "Alfred Lord Tennyson crossing the bar."

In "The Drum" the verse conveys a sense of menace, of deepening darkness, through the use of subtle dissonances. It opens: "In his tall senatorial,/ Black and manorial/ House where decoy-duck/ Dust doth clack—/ Clatter and quack/ To a shadow black." The words "black," "duck," "clatter," and "quack" with their hard consonants and dead vowels, Sitwell explained, are "dry as dust, and the deadness of dust is conveyed thus, and, as well, by the dulled dissonance of the 'a's,' of the 'u' in 'duck' followed by the crumbling assonance of 'dust.'" A duck's quacking, she obligingly added, was for her one of the driest of sounds: "It has a peculiar deadness." In such Sitwellian fashion she explained other aural qualities of "The Drum." As for its essential meaning, she noted that it sprung from a story about witches and witchcraft told by the seventeenth century Neoplatonist Joseph Glanvill:

> Black as Hecate howls a star
> Wolfishly, and whine
> The wind from very far . . .
> Out go the candles one by one,
> Hearing the rolling of a drum . . .
> Where the drum rolls up the stair, nor tarries.

Sitwell's verse was so radical that she often had to supply instructive analyses of individual poems. "Said King Pompey," she was kind enough to explain, is built upon "a scheme of *R*'s . . . to produce a faint fluttering sound, like dust fluttering from the ground, or the beat of a dying heart." There are obvious *r* sounds in the opening lines of the poem, but to what extent, it is reasonable to ask, do the *r*'s suggest "dust fluttering from the ground"? Sitwell would respond by expatiating upon affective language and synaesthetic exchange. A reader willing to consider the poem with an open mind is likely to fathom her technical experimentation with synaesthesia, but whether the reader will affirm her theories about echo and meaning is another matter.

As soon as a reader is willing to accept her theory of *r* sounds, he is then asked to consider other aural impressions. Certain words ending in *ck*, she goes on, "cast little imperceptible shadows." In "The Bat" she plays upon such words as "black," "quack," "duck," and "clack," in order, she says, to contrast shadows "so small yet so menacing, with . . . flat and shadeless words that end with 't' and with 'd.'" Some of the *a*'s, she contends, have neither depth nor body, are flat and death-rotten, though at times the words in which they occur cast a small menacing shadow because of the *ck* ending, and frequently these shadows are followed almost immediately by flatter, deader, more shadeless words.

Metamorphosis

A few years after *Façade*, Sitwell turned from phonological hypothesizing to conceptualizations of time. Between 1924 and 1928, she devoted three long poems to finite time–*The Sleeping Beauty, Elegy on Dead Fashion*, and *Metamorphosis*. Each of these works has a richness that deserves critical attention; but, more important, she slowly overcame an agonized preoccupation with the destructiveness of time. Of the three poems, *Metamorphosis* is the most important. Time initiates the metamorphosis of the poem's title, and in her verse Sitwell searches for a solution to the infernal behavior of contemporary man. Her hope at the end of the poem lies in the generative power of the sun, and she writes: "To rouse my carrion to life and move/ The polar night, the boulder that rolled this,/ My heart, my Sisyphus, in the abyss." The writing of *Metamorphosis*, however, left Sitwell in an even deeper spiritual abyss.

Gold Coast Customs

Sitwell followed *Metamorphosis* with one of the strongest poems of her early period, *Gold Coast Customs*. Admirers of her poetry thought it a sensation. William York Tindall labeled it "her *Waste Land*, footnotes and all." Yeats wrote that it was ennobled by the "intensity . . . endurance . . . wisdom" missing from much of contemporary poetry, the "something absent from . . . literature being back again. . . ." What Yeats especially liked about *Gold Coast Customs* was its concentration on the sterility of modern life. Relying on G. F. W. Hegel's *The Philosophy of History* (1932) and anthropological findings as sources, Sitwell began *Gold Coast Customs* by drawing parallels between an African tribe of cannibals and a Lady Bamburgher, a metaphorical goddess of materialism overly concerned with social rites. Convulsive rhythms suggest a *danse macabre*.

At the close of the poem, there is an intimation of the sacred, a quest for belief, some resolution of the futility of contemporary life. Sitwell's direction, broadly hinted at in the conclusion, was toward Christianity. Her lines allow the inference that she had become fully cognizant of the evil continuously erupting in the hearts of men. Convinced that there must be a greater design for life, that all moves toward a Day of Resurrection, she ends *Gold Coast Customs* with the words:

Yet the time will come
To the heart's dark slum
When the Rich man's gold and the rich man's wheat
Will grow in the street, that the starved may eat—
And the sea of the rich will give up its dead—
And the last blood and fire from my side will be shed.
For the fires of God go marching on.

Religious imagery

During the time that Sitwell wrote *Gold Coast Customs*, she began to reflect upon the sufferings of Christ, "the Starved Man hung upon the Cross, the God . . . who bears in his heart all wounds." Suffering became a dominant theme in several of her poems. In "Still Falls the Rain" she wrote of the bombing of London during World War II. A red flare dripping from the sky to the earth symbolizes blood—blood that stains the sky. On earth, where the bombs find their mark, actual bloodshed takes place, a slaughter comparable to the crucifixion of Christ. The rain of Nazi bombs falls upon guilty and innocent alike, upon Dives and Lazarus. Despite man's horrendous deeds, his shedding of blood, Christ stands willing to forgive: "'Still do I love, still shed my innocent light, my Blood for thee.'"

"The Shadow of Cain," as its title indicates, is about modern fratricide. Its narrative concerns the second Fall of Man, symbolized by the dropping of the first atomic bomb on Hiroshima. The poem had its origin on September 10, 1945, when Edith and her brother Osbert were on a train going to Brighton, where they were to give a reading. Osbert pointed out a paragraph in the London *Times*, a description by an eyewitness of the actual dropping of the bomb. What most impressed the witness was "a totem pole of dust that arose to the sun as testimony to the murder of mankind. . . . A totem pole, the symbol of creation, the symbol of generation." Although most of the poem came into Edith's head as Osbert read the *Times* report, she did not write it down for several months. She continually revised it in her mind, and the poem passed through several stages. When she finally put pen to paper, she wrote how, after "that epoch of the Cold," the victims of the immolation reached an open door. All that was left to them were primal realities:

The Fate said, "My feet ache."
The wanderers said, "Our hearts ache."
There was great lightening
In flashes coming to us over the floor:
The Whiteness of Bread
The Whiteness of the Dead
The Whiteness of the Claw—
All this coming to us in flashes through the open door.

The foregoing lines, Sitwell claims, came to her in a dream. The three flashes of lightning she explains as three primal realities of preservation, death, and struggle. Beyond the open door she saw spring returning; for there was still the grandeur of the sun and Christ returning with the life-giving wheat of harvest. Then came the horror, the symbol of which was seen by the eyewitness at Hiroshima. A gulf was torn across the world, stretching its jaws from one end of the earth to the other. Loud were the cries in the hollow from those who once were men, and yet "those ashes that were men/ Will rise again."

The horror of Hiroshima affected Sitwell deeply. Did God in some mysterious way declare himself through such suffering? She began to incorporate into her work the re-creating energy of divine love. Her interest in prosodic experimentation was over. No longer would she tinker with sound effects, with the mechanics of rhyme. She encapsulated all of her principles of versification into one central dictum: "Poetry should always be running on pleasant feet, sometimes swift, sometimes slow."

As a poet she now wanted to vent the depths of her heart in sonorous, free-flowing lines that would touch the hearts of others. To express truths about human beings and the universe, to point them in the direction of salvation, became her purpose. In her final period, her poems were hymns to the glory of life.

Other major works

LONG FICTION: *I Live Under a Black Sun*, 1937.

NONFICTION: *Poetry and Criticism*, 1925; *Alexander Pope*, 1930; *Bath*, 1932; *The English Eccentrics*, 1933; *Aspects of Modern Poetry*, 1934; *Victoria of England*, 1936; *Trio*, 1938 (with Osbert Sitwell and Sacheverell Sitwell); *A Poet's Notebook*, 1943; *Fanfare for Elizabeth*, 1946; *A Notebook on William Shakespeare*, 1948; *The Queens and the Hive*, 1962; *Taken Care Of*, 1965; *Selected Letters of Edith Sitwell*, 1998 (Richard Greene, editor).

EDITED TEXTS: *Wheels*, 1916-1921; *The Pleasures of Poetry*, 1930-1932, 1934; *Planet and Glow Worm*, 1944; *A Book of Winter*, 1950; *The American Genius*, 1951; *A Book of Flowers*, 1952; *The Atlantic Book of British and American Poetry*, 1958.

Bibliography

Brophy, James D. *Edith Sitwell: The Symbolist Order.* Carbondale: Southern Illinois University Press, 1968. Brophy examines the themes and techniques of Sitwell's admittedly difficult poetry. He finds in her work a coherent use of modernist symbolism. The imagery of darkness and shadow connects her with English seventeenth century Metaphysical poets. A valuable study for close analysis of her poems and critical views. Supplemented by a select bibliography and an index.

Cevasco, G. A. *The Sitwells: Edith, Osbert, and Sacheverell.* Boston: Twayne, 1987. Edith and her younger brothers, all writers and famous personalities, are brought together in an excellent, compact survey of their writings and family life. Their texts are shown to respond to the major events that shaped the twentieth century: two world wars, a depression, and the opening of the atomic age. Contains a chronology, notes, a select bibliography, and an index.

Elborn, Geoffrey. *Edith Sitwell: A Biography.* London: Sheldon Press, 1981. An intimate portrait of the woman, poet, and publicity seeker, this useful book traces Sitwell's life from her birth as an unwanted female to her solitary death (by her own command). Early travels exposed her to the world and many friendships with famous people brought her into literary and artistic circles in England and the United States. Includes memorable photographs that illustrate her life, twelve half-plates, two plates, notes, a bibliography, and an index.

Glendinning, Victoria. *Edith Sitwell: A Unicorn Among Lions.* London: Phoenix, 1993. The major work on Sitwell's life and times, this revisionary appraisal separates the myths from the newer status of her work. Glendinning discusses her poetry, her criticism, and her seriousness and sensational literary relationships. Two groups of photographs, one a series of portraits in color, illustrate the beauty and eccentricity that were hers. Complemented by six plates, seventeen half-plates, notes, and an index.

Pearson, John. *Façades: Edith, Osbert, and Sacheverell Sitwell.* London: Macmillan, 1978. A detailed, year-by-year account of the literary activities, travels, and relationships of the famous sister and her brothers, which places Sitwell in her literary environment. Her conversion to Roman Catholicism and its effects on her proud soul fills a poignant chapter. Photographs are placed throughout the text. Contains seventeen plates, notes, and an index.

Salter, Elizabeth. *The Last Years of a Rebel: A Memoir of Edith Sitwell.* London: Bodley Head, 1967. Salter was secretary to the poet from the time Sitwell was sixty-nine until her death. The author brings out Sitwell's humor, her loyalty, and her creative power. Salter has also published a companion book of extraordinary photographs and drawings. Presents an inside view from a devoted friend. Includes five plates, and six half-plates.

Sitwell, Edith. *Selected Letters of Edith Sitwell.* Edited by Richard Greene. Rev. ed. London: Virago, 1998. A collection including previously unpublished letters to a remarkable array of notables, including Bertrand Russell, Gertrude Stein, Cecil Beaton, Kingsley Amis, T. S. Eliot, and Virginia Woolf. The cutting wit and stunning clarity of Sitwell's prose renders *Selected Letters* an important contribution to the canon of her literary works.

G. A. Cevasco;
bibliography updated by the editors

John Skelton

Born: Northern England, possibly Yorkshire; c. 1460
Died: London, England; June 21, 1529

Principal poetry

The Bowge of Court, 1499
Phyllyp Sparowe, c. 1508
Ware the Hawk, c. 1508
The Tunnyng of Elynour Rummyng, 1508
Speke, Parrot, 1521
Collyn Clout, 1522
Why Come Ye Nat to Courte, 1522
The Garlande of Laurell, 1523
Pithy, Pleasaunt and Profitable Workes of Maister Skelton, Poete Laureate, 1568
The Complete Poems of John Skelton, Laureate, 1931 (Philip Henderson, editor)

Other literary forms

In addition to the poems listed above, John Skelton wrote a play, or, more properly, an interlude (a short allegorical morality play), called *Magnyfycence* (1516), which counsels monarchs against excessive liberality. Skelton also participated in a popular form of court entertainment called "flyting," in which two courtiers trade insults before an audience of their peers. In particular, Skelton flyted one Christopher Garnish, and some of his "insults" persist in the *Poems Against Garnish* (1513-1514).

Finally, Skelton translated a significant number of works and had a reputation as an excellent Latinist. His translations apparently included the works of Diodorus Siculus, Cicero's *Familiar Letters* and Guillaume Deguilleville's *La Pélerinage de la vie humaine*. The latter two works, mentioned in *The Garlande of Laurell*, do not survive. Skelton also composed a moral guidebook: *Speculum Principis* (1501, also known as *A Mirror for Princes*).

Achievements

Modern readers find John Skelton's work hard to understand and appreciate. He lived and wrote just as the literary Renaissance and political Reformation began to reshape England. Skelton reveals in *The Garlande of Laurell* that he perceived himself to be the heir of the medieval poets Geoffrey Chaucer, John Gower, and John Lydgate. His language resembles the Middle English of these three forebears but, like the English of his contemporary Sir Thomas Malory, borders on what is now termed "Modern" English (the conventional boundary date between Middle and Modern English is 1500). The difficulty in reading Skelton, then, comes not from the archaic quality of his language but from its deliberate, often playful, polyglot tendencies and its unusual metrical properties. Skelton intermingles French and Latin words and phrases in many of his poems, often producing the kind of interlingual mix known as "macaronic" verse. He also loads his poems with allusions to the Bible and to contemporary political events. Metrically, Skelton's poetry surprises readers used to the iambic pentameter line that became the norm for English poetry after William Shakespeare. In many poems Skelton uses trimeter (six-syllable) couplets with irregular rhythm. This meter is so characteristic of his poetry that it has become known as Skeltonic.

In his lifetime, Skelton was well rewarded and admired, although perhaps not as completely, or as consistently, as he might have liked. He is thought of today as the first poet laureate of England: That honor, however, was conferred upon him not by the king but by the Uni-

John Skelton (Hulton Archive)

versity of Oxford (1488) and later by the University of Louvain (1493) and the University of Cambridge (1493). The laureateship, which today implies particular patronage of the king or queen and entails the responsibility of writing public occasional verse, titled Skelton to be recognized as a graduate with a degree in rhetoric. Although the implications of laureateship were not the same for Skelton as for a poet such as Alfred, Lord Tennyson (laureate to Queen Victoria), the honor was nevertheless great, and Skelton doted on the accomplishment for the rest of his life. Indeed, he named his last major work, which sums up his poetic career, *The Garlande of Laurell*. Skelton did enjoy the special attention of Henry VII, by whose grace he wore a robe of green and white, the Tudor colors, embroidered "Calliope," for the muse of epic poetry.

The first collected poems of Skelton appeared in 1568, were edited by Thomas Marshe, and were reissued in 1736. A two-volume edition, produced by the Reverend Alexander Dyce (1843), bridged the gap between the Renaissance and the current editions, notably *The Complete Poems of John Skelton, Laureate* (1931), edited by Philip Henderson.

BIOGRAPHY

John Skelton's life and poetry are closely bound up with the world of the Tudor court under Henry VII and Henry VIII. The first sure facts about his life have to do with the laureate degrees discussed above. Two years after the award from Oxford, Skelton received glowing praise in William Caxton's preface to *The Boke of Eneydos* (1490). Caxton made clear his admiration for Skelton's immense knowledge of Latin, his translations, and his ability to write in English. Thus, by about the age of thirty, Skelton was known as a scholar and poet. At about this time he became officially connected with the court of Henry VII, writing occasional state poems and eventually becoming official tutor to Prince Henry, who was intended to become a priest. Skelton himself took holy orders in 1498.

In 1502 Henry's older brother Arthur, the heir to the throne, died. Young Henry, now the next in line for the throne, no longer needed quite the same kind of instruction, and Skelton was sent from the court to be the rector of Diss, an area on the borders of Suffolk and Norfolk, ninety miles from London. It is uncertain how Skelton took this "exile." On the one hand, he clearly enjoyed the prestige of his royal connection. On the other, his first major poem, *The Bowge of Court*, written before his removal to Diss, established his recognition of the traditional problems of a courtier's life, including battles with hypocrisy, deceit, flattery, and despair.

At Diss, Skelton continued to write satirical poems as well as perform his clerical duties with apparent gusto. Skelton's life at Diss has been immortalized in a collection of stories by an anonymous author or authors, *The Merie Tales of Skelton* (1567). It is difficult to say how much truth is contained in this group of stories, which show Skelton teasing his puritanical bishop and flaunting his wife and child before his parish. In general, Skelton emerges in these tales as lusty, witty, and mischievous. If the tales are not true in fact, many biographers have assumed that they are true in spirit.

In 1509, Henry VIII became king, and Skelton initiated a campaign of compliments and requests designed to bring him back to court. In 1512, he returned to London officially titled *Orator Regius*—orator to the king. From that time on, Skelton lived in London and flourished as a satirist, attacking the evils of court life, particularly the abuse of power by figures such as Thomas Wolsey, whose rise to power apparently made Skelton jealous and certainly angered him. In 1521 and 1522, he wrote three satires directed at Wolsey: *Speke, Parrot*, *Collyn Clout*, and *Why Come Ye Nat to Courte*. Despite the bitterness of these poems, Skelton's wrath toward Wolsey seems later to have abated—or, at least, he lost his willingness to embarrass publicly the powerful man. His last known work, a part-prose, part-Skeltonic critique of Lutheranism, includes a dedication praising Wolsey.

Skelton died on June 21, 1529, and was buried at St. Margaret's Church in Westminster.

ANALYSIS

In 1490, William Caxton described John Skelton in glowing terms. He apparently viewed Skelton as a perfect example of a rising court scholar and poet, one worth praising in print. Desiderius Erasmus, who epitomizes the early Renaissance humanist, met Skelton in 1499 and admired him. Yet the poet fell rapidly into obscurity after his death, surfacing in literary surveys only to be described as "beastly" or "scurrilous." These contradictions are easier to explain than might be supposed. First, Skelton's literary career underwent a marked shift beginning with the publication of *The Bowge of Court* in 1499. Until that time, Skelton's work had been what Caxton's remarks suggest: scholarly, patriotic, sagacious. As he began to criticize political and religious changes in England, a new persona emerged. Subtly in *The Bowge of Court*, more fully in *Ware the Hawk*, and full blast in *Speke, Parrot*, Skelton reveals a sensibility by turns bitter, vitriolic, ribald, self-righteous, and intolerant.

Second, Skelton's reputation changed because his fundamental values were misperceived by later generations. Since he wrote in an unusually diffuse, free-spoken, irreverent manner, readers, especially in the nineteenth century, lost sight of the essentially conservative values that underlie his work. Skelton became accustomed, while relatively young, to certain habits of life. He associated himself with the Tudor court, he was devoutly religious, and he was committed to a certain kind of learning and literature which emphasized knowledge of Latin. When his stability was challenged by changes in government, church, and education, his poetry changed drastically. All of his major work treats the theme of personal instability in a shifting world.

THE BOWGE OF COURT

Thus, in *The Bowge of Court* the condition of a courtier is revealed as "Dread"; in *Phyllyp Sparowe* language and convention are twisted to reveal new, ironic possibilities of expression; in *Ware the Hawk* the sanctity of the church is defended with a kind of comic hysteria. *Speke, Parrot* is the culmination of his stylistic experimentation; for many students today, this poem is unreadable, an impenetrable jungle of Latin, French, random allusion and odd statement. Skelton's poems after *Speke, Parrot* retain some of these macaronic devices but are not quite as difficult, and in *The Garlande of Laurell* he returns to the relatively straightforward form of the dream vision.

The Bowge of Court, Skelton's first long poem, is an allegorical dream vision in the tradition of Chaucer's *Hous of Fame* (1372-1380). The title might be translated as "Patronage of Court" since "bouge" means free rations or board, as in the kind of stipend given to courtiers. The pattern of the poem resembles the Chaucerian dream vision as it was imitated in fifteenth century works such as *The King's Quair* and *The Court of Love*.

The poem's prologue introduces the speaker as a poet who is having trouble writing. When he falls asleep, he dreams of a stately ship, the *Bowge of Court*, carrying a cargo of Favor. The dreamer meets a lady-in-waiting to the owner of the ship; he tells her his name is Dread. The allegorical situation becomes apparent. The main character, Dread, represents anxiety: Like the poet-narrator, he cannot gain a firm foothold in life, and he seeks aid or reassurance from outside himself. Dread, unfortunately, has come to a very bad place for stability. Not only is the *Bowge of Court* a ship, but its favors are also dispensed only for money and only at the command of the ship's pilot, Fortune.

Dread's very nature—his fearfulness—makes him the target of attack by his fellow passengers on the ship. Almost immediately he is caught up in a network of intrigue involving Favell (Flattery) and Suspect. Similarly, five other characters (ranging from the pickpocket Harvy Hafter to Deceit) increase Dread's anxiety, until he jumps overboard to escape them. At this point the dreamer awakens, and the poem ends.

The Bowge of Court differs significantly from dream visions by earlier writers, which usually provide a "psychopaunt," or dream guide, for the narrator. Dread is alone, and no one helps him draw a moral from his experience. *The Bowge of Court* criticizes court folly in the typical fashion of satire, but it also, perhaps more significantly, provides an analysis of Dread as a state of mind, and throws an emphasis on the speaker's insecurities.

Phyllyp Sparowe

While Skelton was rector of Diss he composed ironic elegies for two of his parishioners. Witty as these are, they are surpassed in whimsicality by the long, unusual poem *Phyllyp Sparowe*, in which Skelton eulogizes the pet bird of Jane Scrope, a young neighbor. The poem, written in Skeltonic trimeter, has been said to imitate the quick jerky movement of a sparrow.

The poem begins with a version of the Catholic burial mass, lamenting the death of the pet bird. Much of the poem is filtered through the mind of Jane, who both laments Philip lavishly and remembers with pleasure his charming habits in life. She imagines all the birds holding a mass in his honor, and she searches her memory for books that might provide him with an epitaph. In this section of the poem Skelton relies on the reader's knowledge that parodies of the mass are traditional; he also assimilates Philip into the tradition in which Ovid and Catullus exploit the sexual implications of a sparrow who hops around in his mistress's lap and tries to get under the covers of her bed.

Furthermore, the poem contains a section headed "Commendations"; here Skelton, abandoning Philip, praises Jane herself. In all sections of the poem Skelton freely adds snippets of Latin or French. *Phyllyp Sparowe* ends with an epilogue, clearly written after the rest of the poem had circulated, defending what had apparently struck many critics as blasphemous or inappropriate. Although Skelton does not offer a detailed defense of his own work, he might well have argued for its essential conservatism in religious matters. Skelton does not burlesque the burial mass or use it for vulgar purposes; he simply includes it among the devices by which he pokes fun at Jane's excessive mourning. Ultimately, the poem encourages a turning away from bathetic grief either to a happy contemplation of the past or to the celebration of Jane herself, who is young, alive, and human. Thus the poem's values and moral lesson are quite conservative; only the poem's exterior form is new and "shocking."

Ware the Hawk

Ware the Hawk shows Skelton, in his role as rector of Diss, calling down God's wrath upon another parson who brought his hawk into Skelton's church and allowed it to defecate on the altar. The poem is simultaneously scathing and funny, although the humor is of a distinctly learned kind; for example, Skelton puns on "hawk" and the Latin word *hoc*. He invokes a catalog of the great tyrants of history in order to convey the enormity of his scorn for the offending parson and his hawk. The incident, whether real or fictional, gave Skelton an excuse to list what he considered various licenses taken by the parish priests. His wrath grows out of all proportion to the comic absurdity of the particular offense. Skelton seems to criticize both the speaker, who rants so futilely, and the man who allows his falcon to defile the sacred altar of God. Skelton puts his understandable sentiments into the mouth of a near-lunatic, again demonstrating the typical split in his work between conservative subject and unorthodox method.

Speke, Parrot

Fourteen years after writing *Ware the Hawk* and *Phyllyp Sparowe*, Skelton produced his series of political poems attacking Cardinal Thomas Wolsey, who symbolized for Skelton the corruption of power in both church and state. In Wolsey, Skelton saw the decline of the old political and religious order he respected. Moreover, Skelton disliked the changing attitude toward education in the 1520's (in particular he lamented the decline of Latin studies in favor of Greek, and Wolsey himself established in 1520 a professorship of Greek at Oxford). Skelton thus had moral, political, and literary grudges against Wolsey, and they all came spilling out in *Speke, Parrot*, a macaronic mélange of history, biblical allusion, and moral reflection.

The speaker is Parrot, a natural mimic, who stands for the poet himself. The parrot is traditionally both poet and pet, and these dual identities suggest the duplicity of living at court while satirizing the court. The flexible pose allows Skelton to shift between scathing critical statements and sycophantic requests for food and treats. Description cannot do justice to the baffling effect of reading this poem, created by the mix of riddle, proverb, lyric, oath, and allusion. Throughout the poem, Parrot praises himself and indirectly criticizes Wolsey without naming him. He veils his criticism by using biblical names to stand for Henry and Wolsey.

Speke, Parrot attacks more than Wolsey alone. It attacks the world at present, the instability of fortune, the vanity of human wishes, and the inadequacy of eloquence. Parrot touches bitterly on all of these pitfalls of the human condition. Insofar as Parrot offers Skelton's views, the poem again shows him using a radically new—nearly opaque—poetic technique to defend the ideas and systems to which he has become accustomed.

COLLYN CLOUT

After the exuberant chaos of *Speke, Parrot*, *Collyn Clout* appears as a plain-spoken, modest attempt to assert much the same values. Like Dread and Parrot, the heroes of Skelton's earlier poems, Colin Clout knows that the world is in trouble; unlike them, he knows that he is part of the world. Since Colin is himself a minor cleric he is implicated in the current problems he perceives in the Church. He seems to hold two positions at once (much like Parrot as poet and pet), both reporting overheard evil tidings about clerical abuses, and pointing out that these rumors may be false. Although his manner of doing so is new, he resembles Parrot in his tendency to back away from criticism to the safe pose of naïveté.

The poem depicts a world gone awry. The higher-placed clergy are corrupt, and the lower ones (such as Colin), who may themselves be good, are afraid to speak out. The aristocrats, unwilling to assert their power, give themselves over to leisure. The poem focuses criticism on the bishops and on one bishop in particular, who, Colin prophesies, is headed for a fall despite his present power. It becomes certain that this man is Wolsey when Colin describes both his typically elaborate clothing and the tapestries that adorn the walls of his home, Hampton Court.

The specific abuses which Colin laments are predictable: He claims that the clergy are greedy, ignorant, lascivious. The bishops live in luxury while the common people suffer. On the other hand, it is clear that Colin respects the sincere clergy, and he particularly laments that the nuns and monks have been turned out of their cloisters under Wolsey's regime.

After Colin has gone on for more than a thousand lines, the opposition is given a chance to speak for itself. Rather than offering a defense, however, Colin's respondent simply acknowledges the criticism and threatens to punish and condemn the critics. Colin's only possible escape at this point is to commit himself to Christ, stop writing, and disappear from view. As did Dread, he finally gives up and escapes, leaving behind his poem as a record of experience. Not resigned to the world's decay, he is nevertheless powerless to stop it.

WHY COME YE NAT TO COURTE

The third of Skelton's attacks on Wolsey concentrates on the cardinal's political abuses. *Why Come Ye Nat to Courte* has neither the plain-speaking voice of Colin Clout nor the wise folly of Parrot. Instead, the poem seems to be a pastiche of satirical ballads unified only in their criticism of Wolsey. Among other things, Skelton blames Wolsey for misusing the Star Chamber (Henry's advisory council) and for inciting the war with France that began in 1522 and resulted in unpopular new taxes.

Whereas *Collyn Clout* and *Speke, Parrot* juxtapose the attitudes of a self-righteous speaker against the ill-doings of Wolsey as a symbolic monster, *Why Come Ye Nat to Courte* resembles a flyting, or insult match, in which both parties swing wildly at each other and everything; even Wolsey's physical deformity is fair game for attack. To the reader familiar with the other anti-Wolsey poems, little in this one seems new, and the very length of the poem (some twelve hundred lines) underscores its lack of structure. This lack is, arguably, in itself a key to the poem's meaning: Enraged and baffled by Wolsey's complete moral corruption, which seems responsible even for the cardinal's diseased eye, the speaker has lost the capacity both for objective judgment and calm reportage. Like the cardinal, the poet has developed limited vision, and only by a deliberate widening of perspective is he able to go on to write *The Garlande of Laurell*.

The Garlande of Laurell

As the title suggests, Skelton here forcefully reminds the reader of his own claim to wear the garland of laurel, symbol of the poetic vocation as handed down by Apollo. Unlike Chaucer and other medieval poets who dismiss their own claims to greatness and affect a modesty about their work, Skelton heralds himself as the new Homer of England. Like Dante in the fourth canto of the *Inferno* (c. 1320) joining the band of great classical poets, Skelton depicts himself as being welcomed into the Court of Fame by his great English predecessors Chaucer, Gower, and Lydgate, none of whom, he carefully points out, officially earned the right to wear the laurel.

Despite Skelton's ultimate inclusion in the Court of Fame, he acknowledges that some might carp at his being so honored. The poem takes the form of a dream vision in which Skelton's candidacy for Fame is assessed at the recommendation of Pallas. The Queen of Fame, however, disapproves of him because of his stylistic experimentation: He has not written in the ornate aureate style of which she approves. He partially assuages her by actually introducing, in this poem, a series of lyrics in honor of the countess of Surrey and other noble ladies.

Later, Skelton's accomplishments as a poet are reviewed, after which he is so cheered by the crowd (whose fickle favor he scorns) that he ascends to Fame without a formal judgment. *The Garlande of Laurell* also presents a loftier vision of poetry than that which pleases the fickle Queen of Fame and the rabble who crowd about her gates. For part of the poem Skelton walks with Occupation (who represents his calling as a poet) through a paradisiacal landscape where he sees Apollo himself playing the harp. Compared with this serenity, the ironically intoned list of Skelton's works, in which *Speke, Parrot*, for example, is described as a commendation of ladies (which it is not), seems beside the point. In fact, it is surprising that Skelton, whose later poetry was so caught up in the incidental events of his day, saw his vocation as originating in a divinely ruled pastoral grove. Even more surprising, the poem offers itself, at the end, to the correction of Cardinal Wolsey, as if Skelton were pulling back somewhat from his recent harsh criticism.

Skelton's identification with Apollo and the great poetic tradition of England confirms that he is a literary, as well as a political and religious, conservative. In stressing the importance of the poet as visionary seer, he gives even more power to the predictions and complaints made in his earlier works. Unlike Dread in *The Bowge of Court*, Skelton is a dreamer with a guide and mentor—not only Occupation but also Pallas, goddess of wisdom.

Other major works

play: *Magnyfycence*, pb. 1516.

nonfiction: *Speculum Principis*, 1501 (also known as *A Mirror for Princes*).

Bibliography

Carpenter, Nan Cooke. *John Skelton*. Twayne's English Authors Series 61. New York: Twayne, 1968. This introduction contains a preface, a chronology, and an outline of Skelton's life. Carpenter discusses all of his important poetic works and highlights in a very useful way the poet's intimate technical knowledge of music, dance songs, and popular song tags. Skelton's reputation and influence is also discussed. Includes notes and references.

Fish, Stanley Eugene. *John Skelton's Poetry*. New Haven, Conn.: Yale University Press, 1965. This volume in the Yale Studies in English series is an overview of the work which presents Skelton as a poet interested in invoking reader-response by personally engaging his subjects. Medium-length (268 pages), with an introduction by the author.

Heiserman, Arthur R. *Skelton and Satire*. Chicago: University of Chicago Press, 1961. The first chapter gives some background on Skelton's scholarship and outlines the theory of this book: that satire focuses on an object of attack, using a mixture of devices, personae, and careful diction to control the audience's response. Heiserman applies this definition to the poetry, declaring that *The Bowge of Court* is his most successful poem, *Speke, Parrot* his most interesting failure, and *Collyn Clout* the least challenging artistically.

Kinney, Arthur F. *John Skelton, Priest as Poet: Seasons of Discovery*. Chapel Hill: University of North Carolina Press, 1987. Maintaining that Skelton's primary vocation—the priesthood—was fundamental to his literary work, Kinney attempts to give a comprehensive evaluation of his poetry. The five chapters follow the development of Skelton's poetics chronologically. Kinney reads the poems with enjoyment, simplicity, and elegance. Supplemented by notes and a thorough index.

Lloyd, Leslie John. *John Skelton: A Sketch of His Life and Writings*. 1938. Reprint. New York: Russel & Russel, 1969. This volume is a reprint of a 1938 edition, with a new preface by the author. Lloyd discusses Skelton's early years and the early poems, as well as *Phyllyp Sparowe*, *Magnyfycence*, and the satires. The last chapter, "A Poet's Faith," covers *The Garlande of Laurell* and "A Replycacion." Includes appendices of Skelton's translation and his "Lost Works," as well as a glossary and an index.

Pollet, Maurice. *John Skelton (c. 1460-1529): Contribution à l'Histoire de la Pre'renaissance Anglaise*. Paris: Didier, 1962. Translated as *John Skelton: Poet of Tudor England* by John Warrington. Lewisburg, Pa.: Bucknell University Press, 1971. An introduction to Skelton, his poetry, and his age, which follows his career from cleric-poet in the court of King Henry VII through the satires written against Thomas Wolsey to his last years and his struggle against the Lutherans. Complemented by appendices, a bibliography, and an index.

Scattergood, V. J. *Reading the Past: Essays on Medieval and Renaissance Literature*. Portland, Oreg.: Four Courts Press, 1996. Includes a crittical essay on the works of Skelton, bibliographical references, and an index.

Spinrad, Phoebe S. "Too Much Liberty: *Measure for Measure* and Skelton's *Magnyfycence*." *Modern Language Quarterly* 60, no. 4 (December, 1999): 431-449. Spinrad explores the themes of liberty and restraint in William Shakespeare's "Measure for Measure" and John Skelton's early sixteenth century "Magnyfycence," a "governance" play. Skelton's drama remained in print well into Shakespeare's life and may have influenced "Measure for Measure" and other plays.

Walker, Greg. *John Skelton and the Politics of the 1520's*. New York: Cambridge University Press, 1988. Part of the Cambridge Studies in Early Modern British History series. Discusses the political and social views of Skelton and gives a history of English political satire, as well as a view of the politics and government in England during the first half of the sixteenth century.

Diane M. Ross;
bibliography updated by the editors

David Slavitt

Born: White Plains, New York; March 23, 1935

Principal poetry

Suits for the Dead, 1961
The Carnivore, 1965
Day Sailing, 1968
Child's Play, 1972
Vital Signs: New and Selected Poems, 1975
Rounding the Horn, 1978
Dozens, 1981
Big Nose, 1983
The Walls of Thebes, 1986
Equinox and Other Poems, 1989
Eight Longer Poems, 1990
Crossroads, 1994
A Gift: The Life of da Ponte, a Poem, 1996
PS3569.L3: Poems, 1998
Falling from Silence, 2001

Other literary forms

David Slavitt has produced translations of Vergil, Ovid, Seneca, Prudentius, and other classical writers as well as works by Jewish writers from the Spanish Golden Age. He has written numerous books of fiction under his own name. These include *The Hussar* (1987), *Turkish Delights* (1993), *The Cliff* (1994), and *Short Stories Are Not Real Life* (1991). Other works are fiction have been published under the pseudonyms Henry Sutton, David Benjamin, Henry Lazarus, and Lynn Meyer. He has also written several books of nonfiction. Slavitt served as a writer at *Newsweek* from 1958 to 1965.

Achievements

One of David Slavitt's unique accomplishments has been to bring the recaptured wisdom, vistas, and decorum of his classical learning into contemporary discourse through a refined poetic instrument capable at once of formal dexterity and authentic—often playful—contemporary idiom. Slavitt has won several awards, including the Pennsylvania Council on the Arts Individual Artist Fellowship in fiction (1985) and poetry (1987), a National Endowment for the Arts Fellowship in Translation (1988), the National Academy and Institute of Arts and Letters Award (1989), and the Rockefeller Foundation Artist's Residence at Bellagio (1989).

Biography

The son of Samuel Saul and Adele Beatrice Rytman Slavitt, David was born in White Plains, New York. Slavitt attended Phillips Academy in Andover, Massachusetts, during which time he published his first poem, a parody of John Greenleaf Whittier's "Snowbound," in *Providence Journal*. In 1952 he entered Yale University, where he studied with Cleanth Brooks, Robert Penn Warren, Richard Sewall, and Paul Weiss. Slavitt was Scholar of the House at Yale and followed William F. Buckley, Jr., as anchor of the Yale debate team. Slavitt was graduated magna cum laude in 1956. That year he married Lynn Nita Meyer, with whom he has had three children, Evan, Sarah, and Joshua. After divorcing his first wife in 1977, Slavitt was married to Janet Lee Abraham, a physician, in 1978.

In 1957 Slavitt received an M.A. at Columbia University, writing his master's thesis on the poetry of Dudley Fitts, who had taught Slavitt at Phillips Academy. Slavitt taught in the English department of Georgia Technological University in 1957-1958 prior to taking a job at *Newsweek*. Since then, Slavitt has taught, lectured, given poetry readings, and led writing workshops at such institutions as Yale, Harvard University, Bennington College, Hollins College, the University of Texas, the American University, the Folger Shakespeare Library, and the Library of Congress. In 1977, he was a visiting lecturer at the University of Maryland; from 1978 to 1980, he was a visiting associate professor at Temple University. In the years since he has taught at Columbia University, Rutgers University, and, in 1991, began his tenure teaching English and classics at the University of Pennsylvania.

Analysis

David Slavitt has written in a range of poetic styles, from tightly crafted poems treating mythical or historical subjects to poems in looser forms better suited to more contemporary concerns such as his family, the nightly news, and visits to F. A. O. Schwarz. Slavitt's wide vision of humankind is enhanced by his formal study in history and classical literature, his translations of Vergil, his work as "*Newsweek*'s witty, offbeat, irreverent movie critic," and his writing of popular novels under the pseudonyms Henry Sutton, David Benjamin, Lynn Meyer, and Henry Lazarus. He has been praised for his ability to find poetry not only in the domestic occasion but also simultaneously in his understanding of current affairs and historical events. As a result, there is a dark side to Slavitt's poetry, a side that seems almost fearful of death, no doubt concerned about the

David Slavitt (© Bernard Gotfryd)

world as it must appear when viewed and analyzed by the historian-classicist. For a poet such as David Slavitt with an impressive intellectual range that renders him uniquely aware of the continuous reenactment of grave mistakes because human beings rarely learn from history, the only certitude ultimately is form, and the only objective validation for behavior is not one's performance itself, but how one's behavior is reported later, most often by others.

Suits for the Dead

Examining Slavitt's first collection of poetry, *Suits for the Dead*, John Hall Wheelock, editor of the Scribner Poets of Today series, notes among other qualities the poet's command of form and point of view, two characteristics that continued to distinguish Slavitt's poems. Wheelock stresses "the brilliance and clarity of [Slavitt's] work, its brisk pace and taut resonance of line, its sardonic counterpoint, and, above all, its dramatic tensions." *Suits for the Dead* is remarkable, as are the first books of many first-rate poets, for the territory it marks off as Slavitt's own, the juxtaposition of the historical and mythological to images of the contemporary world. Such juxtapositions are subtle reminders of the cyclical nature of history, the arbitrariness of what is regarded as significant about events from the past, the contrariness concerning which of these events to celebrate and which to ignore, and, finally, the necessity of questioning authorities to determine why certain events and not others have been judged historically significant and whether they have been accurately portrayed.

The Carnivore

While these concerns are brought to light in *Suits for the Dead*, they receive a greater depth of treatment and clarity of articulation in Slavitt's second volume, *The Carnivore*. Here again Slavitt deftly juxtaposes scenes from contemporary life to images of lasting historical import. "Item from Norwich" expresses the predicament a poet who has been strongly influenced by his classical background must confront. The poem depends for its success upon a series of images. For example, "the bit before the baseball scores: the man/ seventy-two, found in a tarpaper shack" sets up in Slavitt's mind a comparison with Athe Syrian, Simeon Stylites, [who] raised near "ntioch/ a column three feet around and sixty high," upon which he perched for thirty years, until his death. Slavitt then moves in this same poem to "the regimen of the Egyptian monasteries" and then back to "the man by the dump" in Norwich. The images Slavitt rolls before the reader suggest an ongoing motion picture of history and significant events, and he questions whether they are, in fact, the same. The poem concludes by noting how natural, how futilely human it is to record such senses: "The impulse [to make such records] is always with us." What is history? Slavitt seems to ask. What is news? Which events merit reenactment, even celebration? Do the historical events that are remembered rise above the "traditional mortifications" of events found newsworthy today?

Yet there are more than these epistemological concerns in *The Carnivore*, since history is full of reminders of aging and death and the inevitable hardship of endings. Slavitt writes in this volume about aging film heroes in old Westerns, Leonardo da Vinci's last years, wreckers smashing gables, the practice of fishing with grenades, and Eskimos floating away on ice floes. An excellent example of his concerns comes in "The Lemmings," where Slavitt writes that "they begin to swim/ westward in the nobility of despair." Then, however, he adds an overlooked complication: "who can say the conclusion/ is the obvious drowning . . . ?" Slavitt reinforces here and elsewhere in the volume the notion that the writer-recorder and not the actor is the maker of history. In "On Realpolitik and the Death of Galba," he writes, "There are some that say/ the death of Galba was noble, some say not." After all, in reviewing historical occurrences, historians must either record accurately and without the filter of subjectivity, so that later generations can interpret and evaluate such events themselves (which means that they must record all events), or sit among poets in a Platonic celebration of the event, recreating it with the republic and its hero in mind, with the lone goal of making the event memorable. No doubt history, like the news it immortalizes, depends on who tells the story.

The question of authority permeates *The Carnivore* since it spells some kind of death, not only of the historical figure but also potentially of self-determinacy in interpreting events. In "Planting Crocus," the speaker's son "is certain the flowers will come, because I have said/ they would." Readers are required as they read such poems to ask not only who has authored their past and the history of their species but also who has authored their future, their expectations. For many children, Benjamin Franklin is portrayed in school as a historical figure who provided a model for earnest endeavor; the truth of his past is only whispered behind their backs. Slavitt writes with typical wit in "Financial Statement": "Benjamin Franklin, egomaniac, lecher,/ a penny saved is a penury earned."

Day Sailing

Day Sailing is equally concerned with the theme of authority and self-determinacy. Though Slavitt rises to a more hopeful note in many of these poems, he is somewhat concerned that his craft may be, ultimately, no better than other kinds of crafts, including in the title poem, "a skill, a trade, a duplicity,/ a small boat." He admits in this poem, "I am no sailor, but there is no virtue/ wholly irrelevant," as if to suggest a continued search for the causes of this captivity he is beginning now to understand. He describes this captivity in "Another Letter to Lord Byron" as a lack of "something to do." He writes, "It must be dull to be dead. You can't write,/ or, if you do, you can't send it off to the printer/ the way you used to." Slavitt is concerned still with the issue of authority as he perceives it, and the poems in this collection are often concerned with the act of creativity as a kind of breaking free of captivity, the deathlike state that prevents one from finding "something to do." In "Cape Cod House," he writes about "the builder of this room who had a sense/ of grace and gave more than a thought to grandeur." In "Three Ideas of Disorder," he models his behavior after that of his son, "who has learned the tough/ tyranny of blocks" by stooping himself "to make an architectural monster of some kind." For Slavitt these are expressions that break free from the prison-house of self-consciousness and silence. As he says to George Garrett in "Upon Receiving a Book of Poems," comparing Garrett's gift of his book to another friend's gift of a crystal bowl, "I have read your book, and flicked my nail/ against its rim, and having done so, thank you,/ for the air rings, sings with a clear tone." Sometimes one can break free of captivity in that way. Sometimes one cannot.

The problem is a matter of articulation, as it is described for historians in *The Carnivore* and the tales they tell. In "Plymouth Rock," the true story of what happened "is suppressed/ because we prefer to derive from the rock its gray/ certainties than to romp on the sand. Half-dressed/ little sailors and whores in the school's Thanksgiving play/ wouldn't be right." Slavitt, though in a lighter tone, has not progressed substantially from his earlier position in *The Carnivore:* history is the record someone chooses to keep. Without truth, one is a victim, a captive of another's fiction. There seems to be little protection in *Day Sailing*. When some sort of protection is built, the result is ironic, as in "Precautions," where the poet recounts efforts to protect his boat against a promised hurricane. When the hurricane does not appear, he bemoans the fact that the unsecured boats of the "careless weekenders" have survived: "Battered to bits/ they should have been, all wrecked, and only mine/ secure in a just world." In this unjust world, the poet likens the person who takes precautions to a Noah who might have awakened to find that the promised rain never developed, or a Lot who might have left a city "to which nothing at all happens." Fortunately, Slavitt's sense of irony permits him an acceptance of his place among other captives. All humans are somewhat like the seals, in a poem of that title, that, trapped inside a zoo, lose their "natural seal sense,/ and being captive,/ acquire dependence." There is ample recompense for Slavitt, however, in "Pruning," where the reader is reminded that he or she can "read/ with prickered fingers some of the rose's poems." Again, there is a hopeful moment in Slavitt's "The Covenant," which begins, "Let the world be wary of my son,/ be gentle with him, be reverent."

Child's Play and Vital Signs

The logical extension of such thinking, however, leads one back to form, to appearance, to the way the intensity of color changes depending on what is held beside it. These concerns seem to have occurred to Slavitt in his next two volumes of poetry, *Child's Play* and *Vital Signs: New and Selected Poems*. Between the publication of *Day Sailing* and *Child's Play*, Slavitt published two books of translations, Vergil's *Eclogues* (1971) and *Georgics* (1972), the product of seven years' hard work. Slavitt approached these translations wholly as a matter of challenge, not simply of technique but of understanding as well. The poet's understanding of the *Eclogues* was to influence his sense of his own time and the place of the writer among daily events as being inescapably exhilarating, almost unbelievable; his notion of the importance of form and juxtaposition was also influenced by Vergil. The central concern of the *Eclogues*, what Slavitt describes as "the lit biz," enabled Slavitt to recognize Vergil's anguish over his own reading public. Slavitt's translations—which involve summary, critical interpretation, and commentary, often through direct address of the present-day audience—made him aware of form as a kind of salvation, a method for overcoming the subjectivities that surround him, as apparent in the heavy reliance on forms in *Child's Play*.

Child's Play articulates an unmistakably darker vision for Slavitt. The poet attempts to fall back upon old and trusted remedies for his increasingly cynical view of the modern world, children and form, but those methods fail. For example, his three "children's stories" and the title poem all look to the innocent and childlike vision as redemptive, but come up instead with the coarse understatement that "kings are always whimsical" and apt to suffer the rebellion of their minions: "It always happens. The leader knows it will,/ next time be worse." Not even Peter Pan, in "Child's Play," is spared. Most viewers respond to the appearance, the form, the certainty their experiences tell them to trust: "They ooh and ah delight, surprise,/ who do not see the piano wire/ or the rigging in the flies." Slavitt seems to suggest that history is a tale of loss, rejection, deception, and uncertainty. The question is, "What/ do you tell your children?"

The answer in *Vital Signs* is that one tells them one's personal history and arranges history to reflect in its very form, in its continuous efforts to clarify, who, exactly, one is. The section of "selected poems" includes all the poems from his previously published books, as is often the case in such collections. Yet though Slavitt said in an interview with John Graham in *The Writer's Voice* that arranging poems in a volume is "about the same sort of thing as determining what order the acts ought to go on, say, an Ed Sullivan show," here he carefully arranges his poems by subject and theme. By viewing his life's production in this way, Slavitt is able to tell his children—and his readers—"This is the way I thought about the cello," for example, "as a young man, but this is the way I think about it now." *Vital Signs* reads like home films, carefully edited not to show the random events of passing years, but to reveal the changing perception, the certainty turned uncertainty in the growth of the poet's mind. Even the new poems are so grouped, in a careful effort to re-create the formal rendering of the changing mind, perhaps offering a truer picture of history than the events others have recorded for posterity and study. As Slavitt writes in "Wishes," "who can be so knowing/ and still believe there is luck in a meteorite?" The arrangement of poems in *Vital Signs* might be seen as exactly this statement aesthetically applied, a commitment to the form as one way of knowing and to the content of knowledge or theme as something more changeable, less dependable.

ROUNDING THE HORN

Rounding the Horn reinforces Slavitt's continuing concern with form. In this collection of fifty-five poems, all of them written in different forms, Slavitt is committed in some epistemological way to rhyme while dealing with some of the old subjects and themes, built around the metaphors of voyaging, escape, and adventure. Many of these poems seem simpler, though darker in their simplicity: "The clown is supposed to be sad," writes an earnest Slavitt, "but what about the xylophone player/ who has more reason . . . ?" Slavitt calls attention to his learning less in this collection, perhaps, than in his earlier books. Still, he is a disciplined craftsman, writing with humor and wit about life and its complexity. He deals with people, including a vandal, an old woman with a cane, the painter Claude Monet, a pitcher. He deals with events, such as college reunions, Youth, Age, and Life. He takes his reader abroad, to Poland and Italy, to Greece and Charles Dickens's inkwell. There is still an urge to find something permanent, but in the world of this collection, one sees the product and wonders whether one will become a part of it. "Garbage" notes "the tendency of/ things to turn sooner or later into junk,/ scrap, detritus" and clarifies that this tendency exists not only among "objects and ornaments" but also "ideas and people."

DOZENS

Dozens seems to be an effort to eschew as garbage all ideas and people and hold instead to the certainty of form. The collection is exactly what the title suggests, a book-length poem of 144 twelve-line stanzas. What is clearly of greatest importance about *Dozens* is not the subject, which has failed to impress some of Slavitt's critics, but the power of form when put to the use Slavitt intends in this collection. There is a narrative plan here, and the narrative is spoken in a voice not always reminiscent of the earlier Slavitt, the poet who has served as a resigned observer of the human condition against a background of history and classical literature. Slavitt's invective in this long poem would be incorrectly approached, however, if one were to try to separate it altogether from his earlier work. In "Touring," the opening poem in *Child's Play*, Slavitt wrote, "Architecture, painting, tapisserie . . . / but gore is what we tour. The seriousness/ of a nation comes from the seriousness of its crimes." In stanza 18 of *Dozens*, he describes "a dreadful city, as Whitman's/ Camden is a dreadful city. The worse/ it is, the better it is."

Perhaps the persistence of this view sets critics on edge. The poem seems to take place in Central America (though it might be any number of other places). A revolution is taking place outside a hotel. The point of it all is "not the end of the world but, say, the fun/ of the end of the world." No doubt one can hear irony in this statement, but the argument is unrelenting, forcing the reader to recall "Garbage" from *Rounding the Horn* in an effort to understand this particular assault on the human condition. At the end of "Garbage," the speaker claims that he tries to believe in God, and pictures God as a garbage-picker with gloved hands, who comes across the speaker as he sifts through debris. Perhaps God will pause and remember, says the speaker, "that I/ was once supposed to fit somewhere, that I was/ not always garbage." *Dozens* captures a world-turned-rubble: "Let the grubby truth/ be carted away with New Haven, a grubby place." If one does not look too long at dismal reality, the poem says cynically, one may be able to imagine that "the broken down world" can "heal/ as the poets have taught us to think it may. It may/ if we say so often enough and loud enough."

Big Nose

Big Nose, Slavitt's next collection of poems, does not "say so often enough and loud enough." In fact, the introductory "To His Reader" is hardly charming. The voice, once again, rings with invective that jolts the relaxed reader into defensiveness. Slavitt concludes, "You and I depend thus on one another, and serve, but you are not my friend. Nor am I yours." Slavitt does not seem to be in the "lit biz" to make friends, but he is clearly able to stimulate readers and tell stories. "Big Nose" is an excellent narrative of a Western criminal, Big Nose George Parrott, who is hanged and then made into a pair of boots to be worn by the sheriff. Soon the sheriff, who wears the boots proudly at first, becomes the object of horror and leaves town still trapped, however, by his past. This narrative represents something new for Slavitt, though it was foreshadowed by the long narration of *Dozens*. One must wonder why the introductory material was so long in coming, considering Slavitt's long affection for Vergil.

The Walls of Thebes

The Walls of Thebes brings Slavitt at perhaps his best. This collection walks a higher ground, passing through personal graveyards, forcing the poet to confront episodes of his past, which he does with clarity and surprising objectivity. As he says in "Reading," in looking through his poems before reading them to an audience, "They're an album of my life." This is a sobering collection of poems, often offering accounts of personal nightmare, but unsentimentalized and earned: "Each of us has suffered losses, each/ has felt the terrible wrench of the earth/ shrinking beneath his feet." In some ways, the old themes return, a search for the appropriate form as well as a search for answers to questions Slavitt has been asking all along: What is of permanent value? What authors one's understanding of history? When does the simple event become historically significant? Perhaps the most affectively moving of Slavitt's poems in this collection is "Bloody Murder," in which he speaks with unquestionable discipline of events that came "after the burglar bludgeoned my mother/ to death with a bathroom scale and a large/ bottle of Listerine." At the recommendation of the police, he hired "Ronny Reliable's/ Cleaning Service" to clean up afterward. "I still wonder/ who would choose that kind of employment," Slavitt says and, more than that, who of that occupation could leave behind a bloodstain. More than any other of Slavitt's collections, this poem reveals a turning inward, relying on snapshots, vignettes, and a variety of reminiscences that force the poet to reevaluate his personal history, much as he did in a more objective manner in *Vital Signs*.

EIGHT LONGER POEMS

The later collections seem to flow from a kind of meditation hinted at in *The Walls of Thebes. Equinox* and *Eight Longer Poems* tend to focus somewhat more than Slavitt's earlier works on domestic events as well as on the time-tested subject of historical and classical study. "Monster Dance," in *Eight Longer Poems*, concerns the dance Slavitt's grown son performs each night at bedtime to reassure the poet's younger son that there is nothing to fear. Slavitt takes on subjects such as his own partial deafness as a means of exploring larger questions. Naturally, Slavitt looks back in these collections as well, considering "a whole decade/ of what I thought of as civilization."

A GIFT

Amazingly, Slavitt's productivity accelerated in the 1990's. He turned out important translations of both familiar and unfamiliar work nonstop; he continued to produce a substantial body of fiction, and his own poetry—often informed by his scholarly pursuits—continued to flourish. While *Crossroads* and *Falling from Silence* are strong collections focusing on important themes of identity, suffering, and forbearance, *A Gift: The Life of da Ponte a Poem* is perhaps Slavitt's most remarkable and most original creation of the decade. This long poem treats the life of an obscure writer, Lorenzo da Ponte, a man of grand and frustrated ambition. A contemporary of Mozart's, for whose works he wrote several librettos, da Ponte touched greatness but never achieved it. Slavitt's episodic biography has an intriguing cast of characters among whom da Ponte finds his footnote fate. There is more than a touch of identification, one must feel, in Slavitt's sympathetic treatment of the unrecognized artist.

PS3569.L3: POEMS

Slavitt's later work becomes slightly more introspective than earlier in his life, as though now that he has a life to reflect upon, and not merely an intellect to play with, the time has come to reevaluate his relationships with those closest to him, including himself.

Taking its title from the author's Library of Congress number, *PS3569.L3* offers a satiric and witty exploration of several themes, the predominant being the role of God in a profane contemporary landscape. He also examines history—legendary figures like Helen of Troy, the Comte de Nesselrode, and James V. Forrestal make appearances—and the blending of past and present, evident in "Reading Pindar," a whimsical piece based on a thorough reading of Pindar's texts. A range of sensibility and response to the various occasions of chaotic existence in our time is clearly present here, and Slavitt offers us his reactions to those stresses and cultural shocks that have snared his attention.

FALLING FROM SILENCE

A lamentation of Slavitt's limitations as he ages and experiences loss is the dominant theme in the collection titled *Falling from Silence.* The poems here examine death and aging and explore what is, for Slavitt, the reassuring connection between the generations. With his characteristic wry wit, he turns to religion, reads the classics, and engages in a cheerful wordplay to assuage his physical failings, but none of these pastimes bring a stop to the passage of time. His passion is the act of argument and here he questions beauty and its satisfactions, whether the beauty produced by honed talent in "Performance: An Eclogue" or the beauty discovered by honed perceptions in "Against Landscape." He speculates that Moses was barred from the promised land because by bringing down the Torah, he "did not/ diminish heaven so much as elevate earth." A spectrum of sentiment also finds a place here, including angry humor ("Spite"), bittersweet resignation ("Culls"), and a grandfather's love.

OTHER MAJOR WORKS

LONG FICTION: *Rochelle: Or, Virtue Rewarded*, 1966; *The Exhibitionist*, 1967 (as Henry Sutton); *Feel Free*, 1968; *The Voyeur*, 1969 (as Henry Sutton); *Anagrams*, 1970; *Vector*, 1970 (as Henry Sutton); *A B C D*, 1972; *The Liberated*, 1973 (as Henry Sutton); *The Outer Mongolian*, 1973; *The Killing of the King*, 1974; *King of Hearts*, 1976; *That Golden Woman*, 1976 (as Henry Lazarus); *Jo Stern*, 1978; *The Sacrifice*, 1978 (as Henry Sutton); *The Idol*, 1979 (as David Benjamin); *The Proposal*, 1980 (as Henry Sutton); *Cold Comfort*, 1980; *Ringer*, 1982; *Alice at 80*, 1984; *Secrets*, 1985 (with Bill Adler); *The Agent*, 1986; *The Hussar*, 1987; *Salazar Blinks*, 1988; *Lives of the Saints*, 1989; *Turkish Delights*, 1993; *The Cliff*, 1994; *Bank Holiday Monday*, 1996 (as Henry Sutton).

short fiction: *Short Stories Are Not Real Life*, 1991.

nonfiction: *Understanding Social Life*, 1976 (with Paul F. Secord and Carl W. Backman); *Physicians Observed*, 1987; *Virgil*, 1991.

translations: *The Eclogues of Virgil*, 1971; *The Eclogues and the Georgics of Virgil*, 1972; *The Tristia of Ovid*, 1986; *Ovid's Poetry of Exile*, 1990; *Five Plays of Seneca*, 1991; *The Metamorphoses of Ovid*, 1994; *Sixty-one Psalms of David*, 1996; *Hymns of Prudentius*, 1996; *Epic and Epigram: Two Elizabethan Entertainments*, 1997 (of John Owen's *Epigrammata*); *A Crown for the King*, 1998 (of Ibn Gabirol); *The Oresteia*, 1998 (of Aeschylus); *The Poem of Queen Esther*, 1999 (of João Pinto Delgado); *The Voyage of the Argo: The Argonautica of Gaius Valerius Flaccus*, 1999; *The Book of the Twelve Prophets*, 2000; *The Latin Odes of Jean Dorat*, 2000; *Sonnets of Love and Death*, 2001 (of Jean de Sponde).

edited texts: *Land of Superior Mirages: New and Selected Poems*, 1986 (by Adrien Stoutenburg); *Aristophanes*, 1998-1999 (with Palmer Bovie); *Euripides*, 1998-1999 (with Bovie); *Menander*, 1998 (with Bovie); *Sophocles*, 1998-1999 (with Bovie); *Aeschylus*, 1998-1999; *Plautus: The Comedies*, 1995 (with Bovie).

Bibliography

Booklist. Review of *The Walls of Thebes*, by David Slavitt. *Booklist*, October, 1986. Discusses life and art ("the cruel injustices of the former and the inadequate consolations of the latter") as the themes of Slavitt's book. Praises the volume as touching while noting that it is also "often troubling."

Garrett, George. "An Amoebaean Contest Where Nobody Loses: The Eclogues of Virgil Translated by David R. Slavitt." *Hollins Critic* 8 (1971): 2-14. This review-article deals with Slavitt's translations of Vergil's *Eclogues*. In it Garrett comments extensively about Slavitt's approach to the translations.

Kaganoff, Penny. Review of *Eight Longer Poems*, by David Slavitt. *Publishers Weekly* 237 (March 30, 1990): 56. Praises Slavitt's "inventiveness and proficient manipulation of language" while alleging his "excessive" references to "blood" and "wounds." Also discusses Slavitt's effort to transform "personal suffering into universal circumstance."

Slavitt, David. Interview by George Garrett and John Graham. In *The Writer's Voice: Conversations with Contemporary Writers*, edited by George Garrett. New York: Morrow, 1973. This interview is often cited for its reliable insights into Slavitt's broad range of interests as a writer of fiction, poetry, and essays. It highlights many of his adjustments that follow his translations of Vergil.

Taylor, Henry. "The Fun of the End of the World: David R. Slavitt's Poems." *Virginia Quarterly Review* 66, no. 2 (Spring, 1990): 210-248. Taylor's comprehensive overview explores Slavitt's wit, erudition, and "neoclassical attention to form." Slavitt's tonal variety and his ability to take successful risks in tonal shifts are hallmarks of his technical mastery. His narratives transform their historical materials, revealing the repeated bad news of history, included failed relationships and diminished love, in delightfully inspiring art.

Wheelock, John Hall. "Introductory Essay: Man's Struggle to Understand." In *Poets of Today VII*, edited by John Hall Wheelock. New York: Scribner, 1960. This is the introduction to Slavitt's first full collection of poems, published in the Scribner's Poets of Today series. Wheelock identifies themes and techniques used by the young Slavitt—an identification remarkable for its continuing applicability.

Patrick Bizzaro,
updated by Philip K. Jason and Sarah Hilbert

Antoni Słonimski

Born: Warsaw, Poland; November 15, 1895
Died: Warsaw, Poland; July 4, 1976

Principal poetry

Sonety, 1918
Czarna wiosna, 1919
Harmonia, 1919

Parada, 1920
Godzina poezji, 1923
Droga na Wschód, 1924
Z dalekiej podróży, 1926
Oko w oko, 1928
Wiersze zebrane, 1929
Okno bez krat, 1935
Alarm, 1940
Popiól i wiatr, 1942
Wybór poezji, 1944
Wiek klęski, 1945
Poezje, 1951
Liryki, 1958
Nowe wiersze, 1959
Rozmowa z gwiazda, 1961
Wiersze 1958-1963, 1963
Poezje zebrane, 1964
Mlodość górna: Wiek klęski, Wiek meski, 1965
138 wierszy, 1973
Wiersze, 1974

Other literary forms

The poetic output of Antoni Słonimski forms a relatively small part of his voluminous work. He was especially prolific as an author of nonfiction. During the 1930's, and again during the 1960's and 1970's, Słonimski's name was associated with the feuilleton even more than with poetry. He undoubtedly was one of the most accomplished masters of the *felieton*, a specifically Polish hybrid consisting of elements of literary essay, political column, and satirical lampoon. Before World War II, his popularity was also the result of his vitriolic criticism (particularly theatrical reviews), comedies in the manner of George Bernard Shaw, and science-fiction novels with some of the flavor of H. G. Wells. In 1966, he published *Jawa i mrzonka*, two short stories consisting of first-person monologues. Toward the close of his life, he published his memoirs, *Alfabet wspomnień* (1975).

Achievements

Throughout the sixty years of his literary career, Antoni Słonimski successfully reached a large readership and exerted a powerful moral influence on opinions and attitudes in Polish society. His political position was that of an independent intellectual with pronounced liberal and democratic views. Especially in the 1930's, as both right-wing and left-wing groups in Poland grew dangerously radical, Słonimski stood out as the most prominent defender of common sense, human rights, and civil liberties, always the first to ridicule totalitarian or chauvinist follies in his immensely popular feuilletons. He maintained the same position during the war, which he spent in exile; in postwar Poland, his intransigent stance exposed him more than once to the ill will of the Communist regime. In the last decades of his life, Słonimski, while he was still actively participating in Poland's literary life, was generally considered to be a living symbol of the best traditions of the Polish liberal intelligentsia. His funeral in Laski, near Warsaw, underlined his influence as it became a silent demonstration by independent-minded intellectuals.

Unlike Słonimski's unquestionable moral authority, his reputation as a poet has been subject to many critical revaluations. He entered the literary scene in approximately 1918, as cofounder of an iconoclastic poetic group, Skamander, whose innovation consisted primarily of denying the validity of the post-Romantic tradition under the new circumstances of regained national independence. Very soon, however, the young rebels from Skamander, acclaimed as the Polish Pléiade, achieved prominent positions in the literary establishment while becoming artistically more and more conservative, especially if compared with various avant-garde movements of that time. Słonimski, in particular, could have been viewed as the most rationalistic, traditional, direct, and "public" among the Skamander poets.

By no means an artistic innovator, he was still highly esteemed for his integrity and immediacy of appeal; his "Alarm," for example, written in 1939 in Paris and repeatedly broadcast to Poland, has certainly become the most remembered Polish poem of the entire war period. In the postwar years, Słonimski's willful defense of traditional artistic devices did not obstruct his own interesting development as a poet, and his final rapprochement with the Christian philosophical tradition (although he remained an agnostic) enriched his late poetry with a new, metaphysical dimension. Against the background of twentieth century Polish poetry, his appears, even in the eyes of his opponents, as an unmatched example of clarity, precision, and moral sensitivity, happily married to a sense of humor.

Biography

The son of a Warsaw physician, Antoni Słonimski was born and reared in a family proud of its Jewish ancestors, including an eighteenth century inventor and mathematician. The poet's father was a member of the Polish Socialist Party and professed the progressivist and rationalistic ideology of Polish Positivism. Initially, Słonimski chose the career of an artist rather than that of a writer. He studied painting in Warsaw and Munich, and although his first poem was published as early as 1913, he was not yet giving his writing any serious thought. Instead, he was making his living by drawing cartoons for satirical weeklies. Only in 1918 did he publish his first sonnets, which he later considered his actual debut.

In the last years of World War I, Słonimski entered into friendly relations with several other young poets, especially Julian Tuwim and Jan Lechoń. Together they created in 1918 a poetic cabaret, "Picador," which two years later evolved into a poetic group called Skamander (joined also by Jaroslaw Iwaszkiewicz and Kazimierz Wierzyński). In a few years, the five Skamander poets gained an astonishingly large following; for the next two decades, if not more, the mainstream of Polish literary life was dominated by them and their informal school. Their influence found a particularly efficient outlet in *Wiadomości Literackie*, a literary weekly of liberal orientation, to which Słonimski was perhaps the most prolific contributor. Not only were most of his poems and articles published there, but also his caustic theatrical reviews and, above all, his "Kroniki tygodniowe," the enormously popular weekly "chronicles" or feuilletons. The success of these chronicles reduced for a while Słonimski's lyrical productivity. While between 1918 and 1928 he had published many books of poems, during the next decade only one new collection appeared. Instead of poetry, in the 1930's he wrote mostly nonfiction of various sorts, ranging from purely nonsensical parodies to serious publications, including a report on his trip to the Soviet Union, *Moja podróż do Rosji* (1932), interesting as a document of his fascination with "progress" and, at the same time, his unequivocal repugnance for the horrors of totalitarianism. At that time, his uncompromising liberal stance earned for him many violent attacks from both Left and Right.

As a Jew and an outspoken liberal, Słonimski had every reason to fear both Nazis and Communists; Słonimski left Warsaw in September, 1939, and found his way to Paris via Romania and Italy. After the fall of France, he escaped to London. He stayed there with his wife until 1946, editing the émigré monthly *Nowa Polska*; his wartime poetry collection, *Alarm*, was reedited several times during the early 1940's. While in London, he also began to work for UNESCO (United Nations Educational, Scientific, and Cultural Organization). Even though he was officially repatriated in 1946, he soon returned to the West, to serve, until 1951, first as chairman of the literary section of UNESCO, then as director of the Polish Cultural Institute in London.

In 1951, Słonimski again returned to Poland with his wife, this time for good. Initially a cautious supporter of the new political order, he soon began to find himself more and more at odds with the Communist regime. His spectacular comeback to public life occurred in 1956, when, in the celebrated "thaw," he was elected president of the Polish Writers' Union, a position he held until 1959. In the 1960's he returned to his favorite genre, writing a new series of feuilletons for a satirical weekly, *Szpilki*.

The year 1968 brought about the culmination of Słonimski's fame as the grand old man of Poland's intellectual opposition. After having courageously contributed to the protest of Polish writers against the regime's anti-Semitic and anti-intellectual campaign, the poet became a target for personal attacks from the Communist Party leader, Wladyslaw Gomulka. Słonimski was all but blacklisted, at least until the early 1970's, when he found a shelter in a Catholic weekly, *Tygodnik Powszechny*. There, in 1972, he began publishing his last series of feuilletons, later collected in *Obecność* (1973) and *Ciekawość* (1981). The publication of *138 wierszy* in 1973 initiated the public reappearance of his poetry as well. His continuing participation in the protests of intellectuals, however, made him a target of state censorship until the end of his life. He died as a result of injuries suffered in a car accident.

Analysis

Antoni Słonimski occupies a unique place in twentieth century Polish poetry as a result of a fundamental paradox in his work: his self-contradictory attitude toward tradition. As a man of ideas, he had always been in favor of progress, common sense, and tolerance; he unflaggingly fought all forms of obscurantism. The course of contemporary history, however, turned such efforts into their opposite: What initially was a progressive and modern stance soon began to appear as a defense of traditional, old-fashioned, outdated values. Słonimski's poetry seems therefore to be a peculiar combination of modern problematics and conservative artistic means; the poet himself appears as a champion of the public weal who is paradoxically aware of his quixotic loneliness.

The Skamander poets

This apparent rift can be traced back to the very beginnings of Słonimski's literary career. As a member of a group of young poets, later called Skamander, he provided the chief battle cry in a couplet from one of his early poems: "My country is free, is free. . . . So I can throw Konrad's cloak off my shoulders." Konrad, the name of poet Adam Mickiewicz's Romantic hero, symbolizes here the whole tradition of national martyrdom as embodied in Messianic poetry of the great Polish Romantics. Under the circumstances of Poland's newly regained independence, such a tradition seemed nothing but a needless burden, and Słonimski, like the other Skamandrites, at first rejected the Romantic heritage ostentatiously and totally.

Parnassism

His individual way of doing this, however, was rather atypical. Apart from a long poem *Czarna wiosna* (confiscated by government censors in 1919), in which, by way of an exception, he gave vent to anarchic slogans in an Expressionistic style, he appeared in his early poems (most of them sonnets) as an utterly classical and harmonious Parnassist, very much in the spirit of José Maria de Hérédia. The only difference from the original Parnassism was that Słonimski was using the classical forms not for the art's sake, but rather in order to pose questions of an overtly ethical nature and to propound an active attitude toward contemporary reality. This peculiar manner, in which classical devices are used for anticlassical purposes and moral earnestness is disguised as aestheticism, remained a trademark of his poetry in later years.

This does not mean, however, that Słonimski's later work did not evolve. In fact, in his poems written in the mid-1920's, there is no trace of his youthful rejection of the Polish Romantic tradition. On the contrary, collections such as *Godzina poezji, Droga na Wschód*, and *Z dalekiej podróży* enter into an explicit dialogue with the shadows of the greatest poets of the Polish nineteenth century, even going so far as to imitate Romantic verse forms. What attracted Słonimski to Romanticism, however, was not its Messianic obsession. Rather, his rationalistic and liberal mind discovered in the native Romantic tradition a powerful current of humanism and universalism, according to which the brotherhood of humankind should always weigh more than nationalistic prejudices. This is explicit in one of Słonimski's most overt lyrical manifestos, "He Is My Brother."

Pessimism of the 1930's

In the 1920's, Słonimski could have been accused, not without justification, of being a naïve optimist who professed Wellesian confidence in progress and the ultimate triumph of reason. His beliefs, however, underwent an important modification in the course of the next decade. The ominous course adopted by the European powers in the 1930's forced the poet to give up, at least partly, his outdated positivist illusions. It was becoming more and more apparent that the development of science and technological progress did not necessarily go hand in hand with the ethical improvement of humankind. Therefore, the rapid growth of pessimistic and even catastrophic tendencies which marked Polish literature in the 1930's found its reflection also in Słonimski's work.

Nevertheless, his volume *Okno bez krat* is pessimistic only as far as its picture of the contemporary world is concerned; evil, though, is still seen as humankind's irrational and passing folly, capable of being overcome. Accordingly, Słonimski's poetry in this period became even more "public" and utilitarian; in *Okno bez krat*, he does not hesitate to resort to what could be termed poetic publicism, characterized by a didactic or satirical tone; an increased use of rhetorical devices; regular verse; and simple, transparent, sometimes quite prosaic language.

If such stylistic features seem to prove that, in the 1930's, Słonimski still believed in the didactic effectiveness of poetry, one must be aware that, on the other hand, some growing doubts were also often expressed in his poems of that period. His personal experiences (he constantly was being vilified, especially by the nationalistic Right, for his pacifism and supposed lack of patriotic feelings) certainly had much to do with his perplexity. At any rate, the theme of the poet's loneliness among a hostile crowd recurs in his poems written at that time. Since they alluded clearly to the archetypal image of the ostracized prophet, Słonimski's poems of the 1930's would have taken on a thoroughly Romantic aspect were it not for his infallible rationalism and ironic sense of humor.

Popiół i wiatr

If Słonimski ever relinquished his self-irony and detachment, it was perhaps in his wartime poetry, in which the fate of the exiled poet quite naturally found its precedents in the biographies of Polish Romantics. Especially in the long poem *Popiół i wiatr*, Słonimski attempted to revive the century-old genre initiated by Mickiewicz's *Pan Tadeusz* (1834; English translation, 1917): Like the latter, it is a nostalgic tale in which the exiled poet recalls the images of places and years that now seem to be irretrievably lost. What is striking is that Słonimski's rationalistic humanism remains intact, even in those poems in which he speaks with pain and indignation about the horrors of the war. Even at this darkest moment, he hopes against hope that, once the war is over, humankind will recover from its moral degradation and reconstruct the system of its fundamental ethical values.

The 1960's and 1970's

This belief seemed to be corroborated by the quite literal reconstruction of Poland in the immediate postwar years, which Słonimski greeted with enthusiasm and renewed hope. Very soon, however, his liberal principles—consisting, above all, in caring about the fate of the individual rather than some mythical "historical necessities"—prompted him to an ever-growing skepticism about the possibilities of the new political system and the truth of its slogans. It is worth noting that this time, his adoption of an independent stance as a defender of traditional values had something more to it than superficial common sense. In the 1960's and 1970's, Słonimski's poetry acquired a wider philosophical perspective. While remaining classical and rationalistic in its style and rhetoric, it became essentially tragic in its vision of existence. The symbolic figures of Hamlet and especially Don Quixote organize key images in these later poems, serving as metaphors for the unresolvable contradictions of human fate. Słonimski realized painfully that the human being is reduced to nothingness if placed against an indifferent universe and hostile history; he nevertheless refused to accept this situation, remaining, as he himself put it, "unreconciled with the absurdity of existence." The human spirit, doomed to fail in most cases, nevertheless must cope with adversity, not because there is any guarantee of victory, but because "only the human thought, free and fearless, can justify the subsistence of that feeding ground called 'the world.'" Within this existential context, the role of the poet is compared, with a certain amount of self-disparaging irony, to that of Don Quixote: His defense of illusory values may seem objectively useless and ridiculous, but it is precisely this hopeless struggle that makes him worth remembering.

In the last years of Antoni Słonimski's life, the supposedly outmoded poet was rapidly gaining in topicality and importance. His individual development coincided with society's tendency to seek genuine spiritual values in a world degraded by fear and deceit. Słonimski, old enough to ignore the postwar avant-garde yet young enough to grasp the spirit of the modern age, was able to contribute significantly to that spiritual revival.

Other major works

long fiction: *Teatr w więzienia*, 1922; *Torpeda czasu*, 1924; *Dwa końce świata*, 1937.

short fiction: *Jawa i mrzonka*, 1966.

plays: *Wieża Babel*, pb. 1927; *Murzyn warszawski*, pr. 1928; *Lekarz bezdomny*, pb. 1930; *Rodzina*, pb. 1933.

nonfiction: *O dzieciach, wariatach i grafomanach*, 1927; *Mętne łby*, 1928; *Moja podróż do Rosji*, 1932; *Moje walki nad Bzdurą*, 1932; *Heretyk na ambonie*, 1934; *W beczce przez Niagare*, 1936; *Kroniki tygodniowe 1927-1939*, 1956; *Wspomnienia warszawskie*, 1957; *W oparach absurdu*, 1958, 1975 (with

Julian Tuwim); *Artykuły pierwszej potrzeby*, 1959; *Gwalt na Melpomenie*, 1959; *Załatwione odmownie*, 1962, 1964; *Jedna strona medalu*, 1971; *Obecność*, 1973; *Alfabet wspomnień*, 1975; *Ciekawość*, 1981.

Bibliography

Gillon, Adam, and Ludwik Krzyzanowski, eds. *Introduction to Modern Polish Literature*. New enlarged ed. New York: Hippocrene Books, 1982. Provides translations of selected works and brief biographical background of Słonimski.

Miłosz, Czesław. *The History of Polish Literature*. 2d ed. Berkeley: University of California Press, 1983. Offers a historical background for the works of Słonimski. Includes bibliographic references and an index.

Stanisław Barańczak

Juliusz Słowacki

Born: Krzemieniec, Poland; September 4, 1809
Died: Paris, France; April 3, 1849

Principal poetry

Poezye, 1832 (2 volumes), 1833 (3 volumes; includes *Żmija*, *Arab*, *Lambro, powstańca grecki*, and *Godzinna myśli*
Anhelli, 1838 (English translation, 1930)
Trzy poemata, 1839 (includes *Wacław*, *W Szwajcarii* [*In Switzerland*, 1953] and *Ojciec zadżumionych* [*The Father of the Plague-Stricken*, 1915])
Poema Piasta Dantyszka herbu Leliwa o piekle, 1839
Grób Agamemnona, 1840 (*Agamemnon's Grave*, 1944)
Beniowski, 1841
Genezis z ducha, 1844
Król-Duch, 1847

Other literary forms

The dramatic works of Juliusz Słowacki are among the most highly esteemed offerings in the repertory of the modern Polish theater. Despite his early death, Słowacki managed to complete close to twenty full-length plays of great variety. Six of these works are especially popular with Polish audiences: *Maria Stuart* (pr. 1832, pb. 1862; *Mary Stuart*, 1937), *Kordian* (pb. 1834, pr. 1899), *Balladyna* (pb. 1834, pr. 1863 ; English translation, 1960), *Lilla Weneda* (pb. 1840, pr. 1863), *Mazepa* (pb. 1840, pr. 1847; *Mazeppa*, 1930), and *Fantazy* (wr. 1841, pb. 1866, pr. 1867; English translation, 1977). The subject matter of these plays stemmed more from his literary and historical studies than from his personal experiences. Among the literary influences which shaped these works, those of Greek drama, William Shakespeare, and the French Romantic theater are especially prominent. Elements derived from Polish balladry and Slavic folklore also contribute to the stylistic diversity manifested in these plays. Later in life, Słowacki came increasingly under the influence of the seventeenth century Spanish playwright Pedro Calderón de la Barca, an influence evident in works such as *Ksiądz Marek* (pb. 1843, pr. 1901; Father Mark) and *Sen srebrny Salomei* (pb. 1844, pr. 1900; the silver dream of Salomea). Although both of these works are set in the Polish Ukraine, they combine elements of Spanish mysticism and Christian self-sacrifice in a manner which is reminiscent of Calderón's sacramental dramas. Also noteworthy is Słowacki's free-verse adaptation of Calderón's *El príncipe constante* (1629; *The Constant Prince*, 1893), which has become one of the featured plays in the repertory of the Laboratory Theater in Wrocław in the production directed by its founder, Jerzy Grotowski. It is important to remember that none of these dramatic works was ever performed onstage during Słowacki's lifetime; his writings were prohibited from being published in his homeland as a result of his political activities as an émigré. One of the positive literary by-products of this political exile can be found in the letters which Słowacki wrote to his mother during a period of nearly two decades. Now regarded as masterworks of Polish Romantic prose, they also contain instructive comments pertaining to the poet's works in progress.

Achievements

Juliusz Słowacki, like Adam Mickiewicz, is honored in his homeland not only for his literary genius but also for his lifelong dedication to the cause of freedom. In 1927, the newly independent Polish state arranged for his remains to be transported from a cemetery in Paris back to Poland for reinterment in the royal crypt of the Wawel Castle in Cracow, amid the tombs of Poland's kings and national heroes. Słowacki's sarcophagus is to be found alongside that of Mickiewicz, the man whom he had always regarded as his arch rival for the title of national *wieszcz* (bard). Although Mickiewicz is universally regarded as Poland's greatest poet, Słowacki, especially in his later works, transcended the limits of Romanticism and developed poetic techniques which anticipated those used by the French Symbolists and the English Pre-Raphaelites. Because he was a herald of future artistic trends, Słowacki became the guiding star for those Polish poets who were adherents of a neo-Romantic literary movement known as Młoda Polska (Young Poland), a group of writers who came of age around 1890. For them, his work was a source of inspiration for both theme and technique.

Oddly enough, very few of Słowacki's lyric poems were published in his lifetime. It was only from 1866 onward, when Antoni Malecki began to bring out an edition of the poet's collected works which incorporated many unpublished manuscripts, that the reading public in Poland became aware of Słowacki's lyric as well as epic and dramatic genius. By virtue of his accomplishments in all three genres, he is now ranked second only to Mickiewicz in the pantheon of Polish poets. If Mickiewicz may be said to be the Byron of Polish literature, then Słowacki must surely be its Shelley.

Biography

Juliusz Słowacki left his homeland in 1831 when he was only twenty-two years of age and was destined to spend the rest of his life in exile. Up to that year he had lived in three Polish cities. He was born in the town of Krzemieniec on September 4, 1809 (August 23rd, Old Style). Located in the province of Volhynia, Krzemieniec was an important cultural center in eastern Poland at the time of Słowacki's birth, because, in 1805, a prestigious lyceum had been established there. The poet's father, Euzebiusz Słowacki, taught literature and rhetoric at the lyceum, and his mother, Salomea né Januszewska, was a highly cultivated woman of sentimental temperament. Both parents were passionately devoted to their only child. When Słowacki was a few years old, the family moved to the city of Wilno so that his father could assume a professorship at the university there. The elder Słowacki died suddenly in 1814, and three years later the boy's mother married Dr. August Bécu, a medical professor at the University of Wilno, who was himself a widower and the father of two young daughters. Słowacki, somewhat frail in health and the only male child in the new household, led a pampered life and was strongly encouraged to pursue his musical and literary interests. In 1824, however, this sheltered life came to an abrupt end when Dr. Bécu was struck by lightning and killed. Słowacki's mother decided to return to Krzemieniec, leaving her son in Wilno, where he could train for a career in law at the university. Słowacki completed the prescribed course of studies in three short years and, at the young age of nineteen, became an employee of the ministry of finance in Warsaw, capital of the Russian-dominated kingdom of Poland.

Słowacki frequently attended the theater in Warsaw and soon completed two plays which he planned to publish in an edition of his works to date. Before arrangements for the printing of this two-volume set could be completed, an armed insurrection against the country's Russian overlords broke out in November, 1830. Although Słowacki had been largely apolitical up to that time, he immediately embraced the insurrection's cause as his own and composed an ode to freedom in its honor. Because of his delicate physical constitution, he was unfit for military service; he did, however, place himself at the disposal of the Polish revolutionary government and was eventually sent on a diplomatic mission to London during the summer of 1831. While in London, he mixed business with pleasure and managed to see Edmund Kean in a performance of Shakespeare's *Richard III*. After several weeks in London, Słowacki moved to Paris. By this time, it was clear that the November Insurrection was doomed to defeat, and he made no attempt to return to Warsaw. After the Poles capitulated to the Russians in September, 1831, Słowacki decided to settle in Paris, where he was soon joined by many of his compatriots; in a move that has come to be called the Great Migration, some ten thousand Poles left their homeland for sanctuary in the West and gathered in cities such as

Paris, London, Geneva, and Rome. Unlike most of the other émigrés who left Poland to escape Russian retribution, Słowacki always had sufficient funds to meet his living expenses, for his father had established an annuity for him. Moreover, he invested these modest sums wisely in stocks, and thus he acquired the wherewithal to pursue his literary ambitions free from any financial restrictions.

Słowacki made his belated literary début in Paris by publishing at his own expense the two-volume set of his works to date which he had planned to publish in Warsaw before the insurrection. He then anxiously awaited his compatriots' reaction. One of the few people interested enough to read his works was Adam Mickiewicz, slightly more than ten years Słowacki's senior and already regarded as the foremost Polish poet of his generation. Since Słowacki's verse was at this time almost wholly devoid of any political or religious ideology, Mickiewicz dismissed these volumes as being "a church without a God inside." In view of the indifference shown toward his work, Słowacki decided to leave for Switzerland toward the end of 1832 and spent the next three years there writing zealously. During the winter of 1836, Słowacki left Switzerland in order to join relatives from Poland on a grand tour of Italy. While in Rome, he met a Polish poet a few years his junior, Zygmunt Krasiński; it was Krasiński who first recognized Słowacki's literary genius. Much encouraged, Słowacki then decided to accompany two compatriots on a trip to Greece and the Near East. After his return to Europe ten months later, he remained in Florence for a year and a half before rejoining the émigré community in Paris in December, 1838.

Once back in Paris, Słowacki gradually gained recognition for his literary endeavors and also became a key figure in the political debates concerning the future of Poland. In 1846, amid all this activity, Słowacki discovered that he had contracted tuberculosis. Despite this affliction, he rushed off to the aid of his countrymen when an insurrection broke out in Prussian Poland in 1848. This revolt proved to be short-lived, but he did manage to arrange a meeting with his mother in the Silesian city of Breslau. The encounter was a sad one, for both realized that his days were numbered. Returning to Paris, he worked feverishly in an unsuccessful attempt to complete the epic poem *Król-Duch* (king-spirit). Death overtook him on April 3, 1849. Oddly enough, his compatriot Frédéric Chopin was to die in Paris a few months later from the identical malady and at exactly the same age.

Analysis

Juliusz Słowacki's life was destined to unfold amid the political turmoil which arose as a result of the partitioning of Poland by Russia, Prussia, and Austria during the closing decades of the eighteenth century. The annexation of Polish territory by its more powerful neighbors occurred in three stages. The first partition took place in 1772; the second, in 1793; and the third, in 1795. Each of the three cities in which Słowacki spent his youth—Krzemieniec, Wilno, and Warsaw—came under Russian occupation in 1795. Thus, the restoration of Poland's independence was the central concern of Słowacki's life and work. His fellow poets Adam Mickiewicz and Zygmunt Krasiński were similarly preoccupied with their country's fate, but Słowacki differed from them on a great many social and political issues. One crucial difference pertains to the status of the Polish nobility (*szlachta*) and its role in Poland's future national life. Up to the time of the partitions of Poland in the eighteenth century, all political power was vested in the nobility, and the masses were completely disenfranchised. The Polish nobility, otherwise known as the gentry, was a relatively large class constituing approximately ten percent of the population. They regarded themselves as the "nation" (*naród*) and felt that they had a moral right to exploit the "people" (*lud*). Although Słowacki himself was technically a member of the gentry, he held a highly critical attitude toward this social class. While both Mickiewicz and Krasiński wanted the gentry to dominate the political and cultural life of a reconstituted Polish state, Słowacki advocated a social revolution which whould give the people a greater stake in the cause of national liberation. It was thus in the people that he sought to find Poland's "angelic soul."

Słowacki's distrust of the political ambitions of the gentry, moreover, led him to take an extremely pessimistic view of the prospects for restoring Poland's independence in the immediate future. Mickiewicz believed that the task would be accomplished by his generation of

Polish émigrés. Indeed, in Mickiewicz's messianic vision, the émigrés were depicted as destined to be the saviors not only of Poland itself but also of the entire world. In response to such notions, Słowacki composed *Anhelli*, an epic which deals with a group of Polish exiles who are annihilated in the frozen wastelands of Siberia. It is clear that Słowacki, at least on a symbolic level, meant to equate the fate of these exiles with that of their counterparts in Western Europe. Since Poland did not regain its nationhood until after World War I, Słowacki's position has been vindicated by the judgment of history.

By the fall of 1831, following the failure of the November Insurrection of 1830, Słowacki had already settled down in Paris with numerous other Polish refugees, including Mickiewicz and Frédéric Chopin. In 1832, at his own cost, Słowacki published a two-volume set of his works to date, issued under the title *Poezye* (poems), the second volume of which consisted of the two plays that he had written in Warsaw, *Mindowe Król Litewski* (1829) and *Mary Stuart*. Among the narrative poems in the first volume were several juvenile verse tales of an exotic character enveloped in an atmosphere of Romantic pessimism reminiscent of Lord Byron. These works also reveal the strong influence of Mickiewicz's *Ballady i romanse* (1822; ballads and romances), the publication of which assured the triumph of the Romantic movement in Poland.

Żmija

Among these verse tales in which Słowacki's pessimistic frame of mind manifested itself are *Żmija* (the viper) and *Arab*. The plot of *Żmija* combines Turkish and Cossack milieus. The protagonist is a young Turk who is the son of a powerful pasha. The pasha is overthrown and imprisoned by an ambitious rival, and at the same time, the son's bride is abducted and placed in the culprit's own harem. The young Turk, obsessed by a desire for revenge, runs off and seeks refuge with the Cossacks. He adopts the name "Żmija" and eventually becomes a hetman. Returning to his homeland at the head of a Cossack army, he succeeds in subduing the opposing forces but dies during individual combat with his archenemy. The work is meant to dramatize the plight of an individual who is compelled by cruel circumstance to abandon his whole way of life, to fight unequal battles with utmost courage, and still to lose in the end despite all his great sacrifices.

Arab

Similarly bleak in outlook is *Arab*, a tale with an Islamic setting in which the central character is unable to tolerate the existence of human happiness. He therefore feels obliged to inflict injury on happy people whenever he encounters such individuals. On one occasion, for example, the Arab meets a man who is the only survivor of a caravan that was attacked by a band of robbers. Among the victims of the attack were the sons of the survivor, and he is so filled with remorse over his loss that he wishes to join his offspring in death. The Arab, true to his nature, prevents the bereaved father from embracing death and thereby forces him to continue living a life of unremitting sorrow. Słowacki never truly clarifies the motivation of this self-appointed tormentor, but the poem may be a reflection of the author's conviction that the reasons for man's terrestrial misfortunes are fundamentally inexplicable.

Lambro, powstańca grecki

Before leaving Paris for Switzerland at the end of 1832, Słowacki made arrangements for the printing of another volume of poetry; this third volume duly appeared in the following year, when Słowacki was residing in the outskirts of Geneva. One of the two major poems included in this volume, *Lambro, powstańca grecki* (Lambro, Greek insurgent), is a verse tale which describes a Greek hero's fight against the Turks for the sake of his homeland's independence. Lambro, after leading his countrymen in many a valiant battle, becomes disillusioned with the shortcomings of his Greek contemporaries and decides to retreat to the mountains in order to purge himself from petty thoughts through contact with the grandeur of nature. Instead of experiencing spiritual rejuvenation, however, Lambro finds that life in isolation merely increases his own moral vulnerability, and he soon dies under the euphoric effects of hashish. Thus, in the end, both the leader and the rank and file are found to be wanting in moral strength. It is quite apparent that Słowacki was criticizing his fellow Poles, rather than the Greeks. Here, the diffuse psychological pessimism of his earlier works acquired a concrete political focus: a somber assessment of the prospects for achieving the restoration of Polish liberty in the near future.

Godzinna myśli

Godzinna myśli (hour of thought), the other major poem in Słowacki's third volume, may be characterized as an elegiac autobiographical sketch in verse form. Set in Wilno and its environs, the poem depicts the trials and tribulations of an adolescent poet who is coming of age. The poem's sketchy plot reflects Słowacki's relationship with two people: Ludwik Szpicnagel, his first close friend, and Ludwika Śniadecka, his first (unrequited) love. Both were a few years his senior and had fathers who were professors at the university. Szpicnagel, despite the promise of a brilliant academic future, committed suicide for unknown reasons, while Śniadecka, already in love with a Russian officer, proved unresponsive to Słowacki's courtship. The poet's despair and melancholy are, for the most part, poured into a classical mould, but from time to time Słowacki's style reverts to the sensuous diction characteristic of the Baroque era. With this work, Słowacki may be said to have hit his stride as a poet of genius.

In Switzerland

Słowacki lived in Switzerland for three years—at first in a suburb of Geneva, later near Lausanne. During this period, he wrote five full-length dramas, including the masterworks *Kordian* and *Balladyna*. He did, however, interrupt his literary activity occasionally to visit the salon of Mrs. Wodzińska in Geneva in order to pay court to the Polish aristocrat's eldest daughter. This enchantress, named Maria, enjoyed a degree of celebrity herself, since it was common knowledge that Frédéric Chopin was madly in love with her. On one occasion, Słowacki went on a long excursion into the Alps with Maria and other members of her family, and this experience inspired him to write the love idyll titled *In Switzerland*, a work begun during his Swiss sojourn and later completed in Italy.

Set amid the scenic splendor of the Alpine countryside, the idyll consists of a number of episodes in the life of a pair of lovers. The reader is told of their meeting, their marriage, the premature death of the bride, and the young man's subsequent departure from Switzerland. Except for a hermit who marries them, there are no other characters in the poem but the young lovers themselves, and even they are never identified by name. The young woman is generally said to be modeled after Maria Wodzińska, but it is difficult to regard the lovers as full-blooded people, for neither their speech nor their movements are precisely defined. The same lack of definition pertains to the Alpine countryside itself, which appears as though recollected in a dream. In short, the idyll is a poem of great delicacy in which shifting moods are mirrored in a landscape of the mind. Słowacki's *In Switzerland* has often been likened to Percy Bysshe Shelley's *Epipsychidion* (1821) in terms of musical texture, and it is difficult to imagine how either work could be successfully translated into another tongue.

Wacław and The Father of the Plague-Stricken

The publication of *In Switzerland* was deferred until 1839, at which time it appeared in the volume titled *Trzy poemata* (three poems) along with the narrative verse tales *Wacław* and *The Father of the Plague-Stricken*. Conceived as a sequel to Antoni Malczewski's highly acclaimed epic poem *Maria*, *Wacław* is set in the Ukraine and delineates the treasonous activities and dreadful death of a powerful landowning magnate. It is generally considered to be the weakest of Słowacki's mature works. *The Father of the Plague-Stricken*, on the other hand, is one of his most popular narrative poems. During his visit to Egypt, Słowacki was quarantined for two weeks in a desert oasis, where a doctor told him a story about an Arab who, while in quarantine for a three-month period, lost his wife and all seven of their children. In his poem, Słowacki casts the father in the role of narrator and has him relate the circumstances accompanying each individual death. After his release from quarantine, the emotionally devastated father can find no further joy in life and simply wanders aimlessly. As time passes, however, the father gradually becomes reconciled to his fate, and he tells his tale with a certain degree of philosophical detachment. Many critics see the influence of Dante at work in this poem, directing attention to the parallels between Słowacki's theme and the situation described in the thirty-third canto of Date's *Inferno* (from *La divina commedia*, c. 1320; *The Divine Comedy*), in which Count Ugolino relates how he was compelled to watch his four sons die slowly from starvation. *Poema Piasta Dantyszka herbu Leliwa o piekle* (Piast Dantyszek's poem on Hell), Słowacki's subsequent attempt to imitate Dante more overtly, is far less successful, little more than a coarse political satire directed at contemporary Russian and Polish political figures, including Czar Nicholas himself.

Podróż na wschód and Anhelli

The pair of works titled *Podróż na wschód* (journey to the East) and *Anhelli* were the chief literary byproducts of Słowacki's ten-month trip to Greece and the Near East during the years 1836 and 1837. Composed in sestinas, *Podróż na wschód* is a loosely structured travel diary that records Słowacki's voyage from Naples to Greece as well as his subsequent wanderings in that country. The narrative is, however, interrupted frequently by digressions in which the poet expatiates on various topics of personal concern. Some of *Podróż na wschód* was written while traveling, and other parts were composed later, in Italy and France. Published posthumously, it is an unfinished work. In 1840, however, Słowacki published the eighth canto independently, under the title *Agamemnon's Grave*. Here the poet meditates at a grotto which was then believed to be the burial chamber of Agamemnon. Słowacki recalls the legendary heroism of the ancient Greeks and bemoans the defects in both his own character and that of his countrymen. With a fury reminiscent of the invective which Dante directs at Florence in his *Inferno*, Słowacki angrily denounces the Polish gentry and attributes Poland's extinction as a nation to its self-indulgent behavior. He then predicts that Poland will not be restored to independence until there is a transformation in the national psyche, and he appeals for the liberation of its angelic soul, still imprisoned within a hardened skull.

Departing from Greece, Słowacki continued to Egypt and then to Palestine. While in Jerusalem, he prayed all night in the church containing Christ's tomb and ordered a Mass to be said for Poland. Słowacki next visited Lebanon, where he decided to spend a few weeks in contemplation at a local monastery in order to work on the first draft of *Anhelli*. Written in poetic prose with biblical affinities, it describes the plight of Polish deportees in the frozen wastelands of Siberia during the years following the failure of the November Insurrection. Like the Polish émigrés who settled in Western Europe, the exiles depicted in *Anhelli* begin to quarrel among themselves and soon divide into three main political factions—those of the gentry, the democrats, and the religionists. On one occasion, in order to determine which of these parties has the blessing of God, the exiles decide to crucify a representative from each of the three competing ideologies in the belief that the individual who survives the longest will thereby demonstrate the rightness of the cause that he champions. This trial-by-ordeal miscarries, however, and the bickering continues. The one pure soul among the exiles is a youth known as Anhelli (a name which, incidentally, sounds very much like the Polish word for angel). This angelic soul is singled out by a Siberian shaman who initiates him into the mysteries of the occult. Late in the story, Anhelli is visited by two angels, who inform him that all his fellow exiles have perished and that the darkness of winter is about to descend upon his homeland for eternity. He immediately offers his own life as a sacrifice, in the hope that Poland will be resurrected at some future date. The Lord deigns to accept his sacrifice but makes no commitment concerning Poland's final fate. Before Anhelli's corpse is cold, however, a mysterious knight on a fiery steed appears and sounds a call to arms. Thus, the reader concludes that Anhelli's sacrifice of the heart has not been in vain, and that the resurrection of Poland will someday come to pass.

Beniowski

Up to the time of the publication of the first five cantos of *Beniowski*, a mock-heroic epic composed in ottava rima, the Polish émigré community paid scant attention to any of Słowacki's writings. With the appearance of *Beniowski* in 1841, however, Słowacki achieved not only personal fame but also a degree of notoriety. Popular response to *Beniowski* centered on the satirical attacks against well-known persons, periodicals, and political factions that were made within its pages. In order to create a vehicle that would accommodate such freewheeling criticism of his countrymen and their follies, Słowacki decided to pattern his poem after Byron's *Don Juan* (1819-1824, 1826). Thus, he was able to insert materials unrelated to the formal narrative. Because of the frequently scandalous character of these digressions, the reader soon becomes more interested in Słowacki's personal views on sundry topics than in the actual adventures of the epic's eponymous hero. At the conclusion of the fifth canto, for example, Słowacki stages an inspired "gigantomachy" in which Adam Mickiewicz is cast as Hector, a symbol of Poland's past, and he himself is depicted as Achilles, a herald of his country's future. Even though he defeats Mickiewicz in this poetic duel, he is magnanimous in victory, according his beaten rival an honored place on the heavenly scroll where the names of great poets are inscribed.

The main character in this epic is a historical personage, Maurycy Beniowski, a man of mixed Polish and Hungarian ancestry and a former officer in the Austrian army. In the 1760's, Beniowski decided to go to the Polish Ukraine to join members of the gentry class in an armed insurrection against the Russian-dominated Polish government. The Russians intervened, and Beniowski was arrested and exiled to the island of Kamchatka. He escaped to Japan and, after a brief stay in France, went to Madagascar, declaring himself to be the island's king. He died while leading the natives in a revolt against the French. Słowacki, however, departs from the historical facts and transforms Beniowski into a young Polish nobleman who, after losing his estate, joins the anti-Russian conspiracy. He is then sent to the Crimean peninsula on a diplomatic mission for the conspirators. Despite many perilous adventures, Beniowski manages to return to Poland at the head of a regiment of Tartar cavalry. A romantic interlude in which Beniowski falls in love with the daughter of a comrade-in-arms completes the plot of Słowacki's epic. Słowacki probably intended to add further cantos, but he apparently lost interest in continuing the epic once he had been converted to Andrzej Towiański's mystical theological doctrines.

Genezis z ducha

On July 12, 1842, Andrzej Towiannński, a religious mystic from Wilno, had a long talk with Słowacki and succeeded in converting him to his doctrine. Towiański had been in Paris since September, 1841, and had already converted Mickiewicz to his inner circle. His teachings emphasized the central importance of the Hebrew, French, and Polish peoples in God's scheme for establishing the Kingdom of Heaven on Earth as well as the crucial role to be played by great individuals in furthering the historical manifestation of the Divine Will. Even though Słowacki broke with his spiritual mentor over a political question in November, 1843, he never abandoned the basic tenets of Towiański's religious credo. Using these precepts as a point of departure, Słowacki went on to develop a highly original philosophy of his own, set forth in *Genezis z ducha* (genesis from the spirit) and *Król-Duch*. Both of these works are based on Słowacki's belief in the supremacy of spirit over matter.

In the prose poem *Genezis z ducha* Słowacki presents his readers with a vision of cosmic evolution that has strong affinities with the theories propounded in the twentieth century by the French Jesuit Pierre Teilhard de Chardin. Written at Pornic on the Atlantic coast, it opens with a meditation on the ocean, the cradle of life. Inspired by its protean form and erratic sound, the poet proceeds to explore the mysteries of evolution from inorganic matter to man himself. All existing forms, he argues, are progressive manifestations of spiritual forces that pervade the universe. This evolutionary process, moreover, will not be complete until humankind assimilates the spiritual force of Christ's nature. To reach this goal, humankind needs leaders, for whom Słowacki invents the term "king-spirits." At times, whole nations may perform the function that he attributes to the "king-spirits," and Słowacki asserts that Poland, purified by her sufferings, has assumed this role.

Król-Duch

The manifestation of the spirit on the historical level is examined in *Król-Duch*, an epic poem written in ottava rima and divided into segments called "rhapsodies." Here, Słowacki employs the concept of metempsychosis that is derived from the tenth book of Plato's *Republic* (c. fourth century B.C.E.), in which the Orphic doctrine of reincarnation is propounded in the section titled "The Myth of Er." In Słowacki's vision, a Greek warrior named Er embraces the idea of Poland while awaiting his next reincarnation, and upon rebirth he assumes the identity of Popiel, the legendary Polish king of prehistory. This semimythical figure is reputed to have been a cruel tyrant, but Słowacki assigns him the task of hardening the minds and bodies of his placid Slavic subjects in order to prepare them to do battle with the German marauders, who threaten the Polish nation with extinction. The series of reincarnations continues, the king-spirit passing on from Popiel to Mieszko, the king who brought Poland into the comity of Christian nations in 966. Other reincarnations follow, carrying on the historical mission of Poland. The figures that Słowacki selects to embody the king-spirit were well-known to Polish readers, and this work may be read as a historical romance if one chooses to do so—just as one may appreciate Dante's *The Divine Comedy* without subscribing to his theological presuppositions. *Król-Duch* is, in fact, the closest counterpart to *The Divine Comedy* in Polish literature, and many regard it as Słowacki's finest work, despite the fact that he was only able to give final form to the first of the five rhapsodies which constitute its text.

Lyric poems

Słowacki's lyric poetry makes up a relatively small part of his total work. He wrote approximately 130 lyric poems, of which only thirteen appeared in print during his lifetime. A large number of the unpublished poems remain unfinished, but some are highly polished, and it is difficult to understand why he made no attempt to publish them. Słowacki's language is highly creative, owing its unconventional character to his preference for unusual words, neologisms, uncommon rhymes, and metrical virtuosity. His work in this genre, moreover, covers a wide range of themes, Perhaps the weakest are those that treat love, for it is always thwarted love, not its triumph, that interests the poet. More varied are those poems dealing with friendship, such as the ones written for Ludwik Szpicnagel and Zygmunt Krasiński, as well as those pertaining to historical figures and contemporaries in the émigré community. There are, strangely enough, two poems addressed to Słowacki's mother. Patriotic revolutionary themes first make their appearance in connection with the November Insurrection and become an inexhaustible source of poetic inspiration from then on. After the summer of 1842, when Słowacki became a convert to Andrzej Towiański's messianic doctrines, his lyric poems undergo a marked change in tone. The pessimism recedes and is replaced by a mood of mystical exaltation. With a newly found faith in his mission and in himself, Słowacki enters into a close communion with God—viewing God as his ally in the cause of Poland and expressing gratitude for his own transformation into "a vessel of grace."

There are, it is interesting to note, four poems in which Słowacki expresses resentment toward the Papacy for its failure to support Poland's struggle for freedom. In a poem on this theme composed in 1848, Słowacki actually makes a prophecy to the effect that a Slavic pope will someday occupy the chair of Saint Peter.

> In the midst of dissension the Lord God suddenly
>   rings an enormous bell.
> Behold! He throws open his earthly throne to a pope
>   from Slavic realms.
> . . . .
> We need strength so as to rejuvenate this lordly world
>   of ours:
> A Slavic pope, a brother to humankind, comes to aid
>   us in this task.
> Look and see how he anoints our bodies with the
>   balms of the world,
> While a celestial choir of angels bedecks his throne
>   with resplendent flowers.

This untitled poem is among the last that Słowacki wrote, and nowhere does he demonstrate the vatic powers of a national bard more fully. When the announcement "Habemus Papam!" was made on October 16, 1978, the world learned to its astonishment that the papal designate was a cardinal from Cracow named Karol Wojtyła.

A fruitful insight into the nature of Słowacki's approach to poetry is contained in an article titled "A Few Words About Juliusz Słowacki," written by his friend Zygmunt Krasiński. Here, Krasiński compares Słowacki with Mickiewiez and contends that the former's poetic style is "centrifugal" while the latter's is "centripetal." In place of the concreteness and tangibility that characterizes Mickiewicz's work, Słowacki's poetry manifests a dispersing tendency that is cosmic in its range. In Mickiewicz, moreover, one senses a poet who is exercising strict control over his language, while Słowacki appears at times to be engaged in a form of automatic writing. His imagery, as a consequence, is frequently diffuse and indistinct in a way that is reminiscent of the aesthetic qualities embodied in the paintings of the nineteenth century English artist J. M. W. Turner. Like Turner, Słowacki has a profound interest in color, and his poetry therefore shares many of the coloristic attributes of that written in Poland during the Baroque period. Musicality is, by the same token, another feature of Słowacki's verse that sets it apart from the more natural speech intonations to be found in that of Mickiewicz. Because of such significant stylistic differences, the poetical works of Słowacki and Mickiewicz are best viewed as complementary. It is, therefore, highly appropriate that the mortal remains of Słowacki and Mickiewicz now rest side by side in the royal crypt of the Wawel Castle in Cracow. They are, it should be noted, the only poets who have been accorded the signal honor of interment at the site of this Polish equivalent to Westminster Abbey.

Other major works

plays: *Mindowe Król Litewski*, wr. 1829, pb. 1832, pr. 1869; *Maria Stuart*, pb. 1832, pr. 1862 (*Mary Stuart*, 1937); *Kordian*, pb. 1834, pr. 1899; *Balladyna*, wr. 1834, pb. 1839, pr. 1862 (English translation, 1960); *Horsztyński*, wr. 1835, pb. 1866, pr. 1879; *Beatrix Cenci*, wr. 1839, pb. 1866; *Lilla Weneda*, pb. 1840, pr. 1863; *Mazepa*, pb. 1840, pr. 1847 (*Mazeppa*, 1930); *Fantazy*, wr. 1841, pb. 1866, pr. 1867 (English translation, 1977); *Złota czaszka*, wr. 1842, pb. 1866, pr. 1899; *Ksiądz Marek*, pb. 1843, pr. 1901; *Książę niezłomny*, pb. 1844, pr. 1874; *Sen srebrny Salomei*, pb. 1844, pr. 1900; *Agezylausz*, wr. 1844, pb. 1844, pr. 1927; *Zawisza Czarny*, wr. 1844, pb. 1889, pr. 1910; *Samuel Zborowski*, wr. 1845, pr. 1911, pb. 1928.

Bibliography

Dernalowicz, Maria. *Juliusz Słowacki*. Warsaw, Poland: Interpress, 1987. A short biographical study of the poet's life and work. Includes an index.

Kridl, Manfred. *The Lyric Poems of Julius Słowacki*. The Hague, the Netherlands: Mouton, 1958. A critical assessment of the poetic works of Słowacki. Includes bibliographic references.

_______. *A Survey of Polish Literature and Culture*. New York: Columbia University Press, 1956. Provides some historical and cultural backgroung to Słowacki's poetry. Includes bibliographic references.

Treugutt, Stefan. *Juliusz Słowacki: Romantic Poet*. Warsaw, Poland: Polonia, 1959. A critical analysis of Słowacki's poetic works.

Victor Anthony Rudowski

Christopher Smart

Born: Shipbourne, near Tunbridge, England; April 11, 1722

Died: King's Bench Prison, London, England; May 2, 1771

Principal poetry

On the Eternity of the Supreme Being, 1750
On the Immensity of the Supreme Being, 1751
On the Omniscience of the Supreme Being, 1752
Poems on Several Occasions, 1752
The Hilliad, 1753
On the Power of the Supreme Being, 1754
On the Goodness of the Supreme Being, 1755
Hymn to the Supreme Being, on Recovery from a Dangerous Fit of Illness, 1756
A Song to David, 1763
Poems, 1763
Ode to the Earl of Northumberland, 1764
Hymns for the Amusement of Children, 1772
Jubilate Agno, 1939 (as *Rejoice in the Lamb*, 1954)
Collected Poems, 1950 (2 volumes; Norman Callan, editor)

Other literary forms

In London Christopher Smart did hackwork for booksellers, wrote songs for Vauxhall Gardens entertainment, and edited the magazine *Midwife: Or, Old Woman's Magazine* from 1749 to about 1750. *The Works of Horace, Translated Literally into English* (1756) is a prose translation of the poems from the Latin; *A Translation of the Psalms of David Attempted in the Spirit of Christianity, and Adapted to the Divine Service, with Hymns and Spiritual Songs for the Fasts and Festivals of the Church of England* (1765) was rendered from the Hebrew in poetic form; another translation, *The Works of Horace Translated into Verse*, came out in 1767.

Achievements

Christopher Smart became a fellow of Pembroke Hall, the University of Cambridge, in 1745, and attained college office after receiving his master's degree in

1747. He won the Seaton Prize for poetry every year from 1750 to 1755, with the exception of 1754, when he did not enter.

Biography

Christopher Smart was born in Kent, where his father served as steward to William, Viscount Vane. His earliest love was Lord Vane's daughter Anne, but the two were forced apart. A precocious student, he was sponsored by the duchess of Cleveland for enrollment at Pembroke Hall, Cambridge. Her forty-pound annuity allowed him to concentrate upon both scholarship and social life in college, where he gained a reputation as a hard drinker and incurred heavy debts. He received his bachelor's degree in 1742, followed by a master's in 1747, with election to college office the same year. He also married Anna Marie Carnan; the marriage was kept secret until its discovery forced him to give up his position. Yet Smart was allowed to keep his connection in order to compete for the Seaton Poetry Prize each year. He won the prize in 1750, 1751, and 1753; after skipping a year of the competition in 1754, he came back to win again in 1755. The Seatonian odes are not considered successful, but they show the religious attitudes for which Smart was noted as well as his practice of the cataloging technique as a strategy.

Smart had left Cambridge for London in 1749 to make a living as a writer, taking various hack assignments in a variety of forms. On jobs for booksellers, mostly for his wife's stepfather John Newbery, he wrote humor, fables, lyric verses, and epitaphs. As a periodical writer he remained poor and undistinguished, even as editor of *Midwife: Or, Old Woman's Magazine*.

He was befriended by such noted figures as Samuel Johnson, Oliver Goldsmith, Thomas Gray, and David Garrick, who helped him during his periods of alcoholism and madness. Johnson supposedly did some of Smart's periodical writing, and Garrick performed in 1759 to raise money for him. Even with help from friends, however, Smart's family fell apart; his wife and two daughters moved to Ireland and remained there with his sister.

The study of Smart's life and his works has customarily revolved around his madness, which seems to have begun around 1756. He was confined several times for madness and for debts. Though there is no agreement on the causes or the exact label for his madness, it is generally considered to have been a religious form of monomania. His poem titled *Hymn to the Supreme Being, on Recovery from a Dangerous Fit of Illness* (1756) is considered evidence of the techniques that would make his later works worthy of note. This poem receives notice as pivotal in his literary development from religious and technical perspectives.

Christopher Smart (Hulton Archive)

His compulsiveness and his fixation seem to have a shared religious root, resulting in what was considered his most bizarre public behavior: praying aloud whenever and wherever the inclination struck him. He said once, "I blessed God in St. James's Park until I routed all the company." Such behavior was categorized as enthusiasm in the eighteenth century, and the adjective "enthusiastic" was applied to many Dissenters seized by religious fervor.

Although his friends did not agree on the necessity for Smart's confinement, he was kept in St. Luke's Hospital from 1757 through part of 1758. When released that year, he seemed to grow worse, and mental problems caused him to be placed in asylum from 1759 to 1763. Under these circumstances he seemed to behave quietly and occupy himself with religious activities, his writing, and domestic chores. Among his friends who visited, Johnson said, "I did not think he ought to be shut up. . . . His infirmities were not noxious to society. He insisted on people praying with him; and I'd as lief pray with Kit Smart as anyone else." During this second confinement he wrote his major works, *Jubilate Agno* (begun in 1759), which remained unfinished and unpublished during his lifetime, and *A Song to David* (1763), his most important work.

Upon returning to society, having lost all contact with his family, Smart became involved in a series of bitter conflicts with other journalists, in which he revealed an indignation or self-righteousness that has been frowned upon since that time.

Smart continued to deteriorate physically and behaviorally after he returned to London life, but he concentrated more and more on the writing of poetry and focused to an even greater extent on religious subjects. He published *A Translation of the Psalms of David* in 1765 and his verse translation of Horace in 1767, several years before his final incarceration, which began in 1769. A number of biographical questions exist relating to the actual composition of his religious poems, with some critics interested in whether several were written simultaneously. Smart seems to have hoped that some of his works would be adopted by the Church of England for its liturgy, since his psalms and their arrangement not only imitate the Hebrew and the Anglican prayer book of his day but also follow the sequence of the Christian year.

Because Smart was not only a literary scholar and linguist but also a student of natural phenomena, he drew these interests into his poetry. Much of what he knew about science came from books and reading, but he insisted upon studying God's works in nature so that he could celebrate all of creation.

The year 1769 brought further debt and lack of control, resulting in a final incarceration in King's Bench prison for debtors. During this year Smart wrote *Hymns for the Amusement of Children*, a book of verses sharing his knowledge of nature and his love of God. It was in this prison that he died, remaining outwardly optimistic and happy regardless of his problems. He seems to have been absolutely sure of his salvation; at least he asserted his certainty flamboyantly and repeatedly, often to the discomfort and irritation of others. His masterpiece, *A Song to David*, was the primary reason for his reputation as a writer and the work on which his reputation as a poet rests to this day.

ANALYSIS

A Song to David was first published in 1763, the year Christopher Smart was released from his second period of confinement. Such timing must have had more than a little to do with the speculation about the connection between madness and poetry which has remained a constant in criticism of Smart's literary productions. James Boswell, Samuel Johnson's famous biographer, seems to have begun the discussion that occupied Smart's contemporaries even when they were admiring of the work, as Boswell was. The Romantic poets William Wordsworth and Leigh Hunt were among the first to consider *A Song to David* a great lyric. Generally the Romantics were appreciative of Smart, but the Victorian Robert Browning is credited with reviving interest in his works. There is widespread agreement about the high quality of *A Song to David*, even though critical appreciation of Smart's other work waxes and wanes as tastes change.

A SONG TO DAVID

Writing a song of praise to the great Hebrew psalmist appears to have been a deliberate act of emulation on the neoclassical poet's part. Although he suggested that good poetry was inspired by God rather than the muse, it is known from his translations of Horace into both poetry and prose that Smart learned how to apply the theory and advice gained from his reading of the Roman poet. Typical of his era, however, he did not hesitate to combine classicism with Old Testament techniques and New Testament concepts. The trend toward imitation of Hebrew poetry seems to have been initiated by Bishop Robert Lowth's *Praelectiones de Sacra Poesi Hebraerorum* (1753, lectures on the sacred poetry of the Hebrews), published ten years earlier than *A Song to David*. This work attracted attention in scholarly and literary circles and even stimulated popular interest with its analysis of Hebrew poetics and the technical devices of Old Testament poetry.

A Song to David does more, however, than follow a trend. It is in some ways unique, and it expresses a personal exhilaration that illustrates the neoclassical concept of the sublime. This sublime, or grand and exalted effect, is never grandiose or bombastic. A look at the formal properties of the poem reveals that Smart was certainly in control, rather than insane, when he wrote this tribute to his hero and model, King David.

The poem is made up of eighty-six stanzas, each of which follows the same basic pattern: two lines of iambic tetrameter followed by an iambic trimeter line and then a repetition of this sequence, making a six-line unit. The rhyme scheme is *aabccb*, with all the end rhymes masculine. An outline of the poem's structure, made by Smart himself and labeled "Contents," is placed between the quotation from 2 Samuel 23:1-2 and the opening stanza.

The quotation introduces David as the subject capsules his life, from his ancestry to his anointing by Samuel and his sacred gift of poetry and song. Traditional interpreters of Hebrew Scripture will find in this passage allusions to the various subtopics addressed within the poem proper: David's ancestry, his monarchy, his sacred gift of poetry and song. David's lineage from the family of Jesse is essential to Smart's establishment of the connection between his Old Testament subject and Jesus Christ. Christian theology teaches that God became man in the form of Jesus of Nazareth, a descendant of the house of David, son of Jesse.

David was anointed King of Israel by Samuel, the same prophet who had anointed the first king, Saul. David, who was close friends with Jonathan, Saul's son, was not only the warrior who slew the Philistine giant Goliath but also served Saul's court as harpist, singer, and poet. The Book of Psalms in the Old Testament is traditionally considered the work of David. David was also the mastermind behind the design of the temple, which was built by his son Solomon (1 Chronicles 28). In the poem proper, Smart goes into more detail, establishing traditional biblical grounds for his treatment of David.

Identifying Smart's concept of David as well as the biblical allusions permeating the stanzas is essential in reading the poem. The David of this poem is not simply the David of the Old Testament and of Jewish history. The David addressed at the beginning of the poem combines the king, the harpist, and the Old Testament type (symbol) of Christ. Evidence from this poem and others, including translations of the Psalms, reveals that Smart incorporates into his David figure the Orpheus of classical mythology, the symbol of the poet as maker, who duplicates on the earthly plane God's act of creation. This creative power provides the thematic basis for the catalog of natural creation that dominates certain prominent sections of the poem. The singer-king is developed thus as the model for the way to praise God and the leader of Christendom in the various acts of praise, just as the psalmist or song leader might direct the congregation in communal praise. As a preliminary way of getting into a celebratory posture, Smart also praises David himself.

Stanza 5 begins the section on David's life, with each stanza from 5 through 16 developing details to support an adjective applied to David in the fourth stanza: "Great, valiant, pious, good, and clean,/ Sublime, contemplative, serene,/ Strong, constant, pleasant, wise!" The history and folklore traditionally associated with the hero are deftly introduced in this passage, with references to well-known characters and minor ones who were a part of David's rise to glory. The close friendship with Jonathan and the feats of the young hero are given more attention than the illicit love affair with Bathsheba, which Smart touches upon very briefly. The colorful story of sex, murder, and repentance from 2 Samuel 11 and 12 is mentioned only as "his fall" and is presented as an example of how David "rose [to] his eminence o'er all" by learning from his sin. David's first wife, Michal, and the young girl Abishag, who was supposed to be a comfort to his old age, are mentioned in stanza 17 as means to show the superior importance of his muse, whose influence was greater than that of any of David's women.

The subjects inspired by his muse are then treated generally in a succession of three stanzas: God, angels, man, and the world. Then he begins a catalog of creation, which he turns into his own hymn of praise, making vivid word pictures, especially in the lines describing precious stones. The power of this inspired musicianship to overcome not only human foes but also spiritual and demonic ones is the subject of the next three stanzas.

The next section of the poem, introduced by the thirtieth stanza's focus on seven "pillars of the Lord," refers to another creation of David, an architectural act of praise known as Solomon's temple. Allusions are made to the seven pillars of wisdom from the ninth chapter of Proverbs, the seven days of creation as recounted in the first chapter of Genesis, and the decorative pillars of the temple as described in 1 Kings 5-8. The majority of critics, however, see this passage as built upon the rites and symbolic system of Freemasonry, which is traditionally associated with the builders of the temple. Each stanza begins with the name of a letter of the Greek alphabet, with vowels and consonants alternating.

Two stanzas complimenting David's knowledge introduce what Smart calls "an exercise upon the decalogue," referring to the Ten Commandments received by Moses. Ever intent upon bringing the Hebrew vision of God and the Christian together, Smart reminds his reader to follow the advice of Saint Paul and "turn from old Adam [from the Book of Genesis] to the New [Jesus Christ]." A profusion of images forms the next catalog, which makes a glorious presentation of God's creatures participating in the grand impulse of nature to praise the Creator. This call to celebration and participation is developed under the heading of adoration, with David the singer as its leader. The word "ADORATION" is artfully placed in a different line within each stanza, so that it is given strategic emphasis. Certain of these stanzas reveal Smart's paraphrasing of psalms, including myriad details in the passages he had earlier labeled exercises upon "right use" of the seasons and "how to subdue" the senses. The abundance of creation, with its systematic and plenary chain of being, is suggested, creating a joyous and effervescent tone of love and unity.

Stanza 72 begins the crescendo that develops to the finale, which was described earlier in Smart's outline as "an amplification in five degrees," once again suggesting the Masonic Order. Repetition of a series of adjectives, much like the repetition of "ADORATION," precedes the nature imagery used to define and illustrate the individual words: "sweet," "strong," "beauteous," "precious," and "glorious." Each adjective is taken through its own degrees of comparison, with sentences built around its meaning.

The last stanza of the poem is also the final one in the adjectival series, with its focus upon the meanings of "glorious" as summed up in the person of Christ the King, who took upon himself human form. Having brought together the creation, the incarnation, and the resurrection, which are the foundation of traditional Judeo-Christian belief, Smart ends on a note of triumph that seems as much a personal declaration as a thematic one: "DETERMINED, DARED, and DONE."

Other major works

LIBRETTOS: *Hannah: An Oratorio*, 1764; *Abimelech: An Oratorio*, 1768; *Providence: An Oratorio*, 1777.

NONFICTION: *Mother Midnight's Miscellany*, 1751 (as Mary Midnight); *The Nonpareil: Or, The Quintessence of Wit and Humor*, 1757 (as Midnight).

TRANSLATIONS: *The Works of Horace, Translated Literally into English*, 1756; *A Poetical Translation of the Fables of Phaedrus*, 1765; *A Translation of the Psalms of David Attempted in the Spirit of Christianity, and Adapted to the Divine Service, with Hymns and Spiritual Songs for the Fasts and Festivals of the Church of England*, 1765; *The Works of Horace Translated into Verse*, 1767.

Bibliography

Bond, William H. "Christopher Smart's *Jubilate Agno.*" *Harvard Library Bulletin* 4 (1950): 39-52. This article is a comprehensive attempt to put the poem's fragments together. Examining the holograph manuscript leads Bond to believe that Smart took about four years to write these verses and originally set up an antiphonal structure but eventually lost control over it.

Devlin, Christopher. *Poor Kit Smart*. Carbondale: University of Illinois Press, 1961. This biography includes critical commentary on individual poems as well as an attempt to evaluate Smart's works as a whole. Devlin's emphasis follows his subject's paramount concern: religion.

Dillingham, Thomas F. "'Blest Light': Christopher Smart's Myth of David." In *The David Myth in Western Literature*, edited by Raymond-Jean Frontain and Jan Wojick. West Lafayette, Ind.: Purdue University Press, 1980. The biblical David is central to Smart's highest poetic achievements, says Dillingham, whether used as subject, as in *A Song to David*, or as a model for imitation, as in the translations and biblical paraphrases. Smart combines the Old Testament figure with the Greek Orpheus and Christian theology in seeking a unified vision for his faith.

Havens, Raymond D. "The Structure of Smart's *Song to David*." *Review of English Studies* 14 (1938): 178-182. This work is old but not outdated, and it is a highly regarded source with which to begin a study of Smart's major work. The poem's structure is analyzed from a mathematical and a mystical point of view. Attention is devoted, for example, to Smart's dependence upon the numbers three and seven and their multiples.

Hawes, Clement, ed. *Christopher Smart and the Enlightenment*. New York: St. Martin's Press, 1999. A reappraisal of Smart's legacy and his remarkable impact on twentieth century poetry and an analysis of the generative impact of Smart on modern poetry and music, demonstrating the reach of Smart's contemporary resonance.

Mounsey, Chris. *Christopher Smart: Clown of God*. Cranbury, N.J.: Associated University Presses, 2001. A biography of the poet detailing his confinement for mental illness. Includes bibliographical references and index.

Sherbo, Arthur. *Christopher Smart: Scholar of the University*. East Lansing: Michigan State University Press, 1967. This book-length work concentrates on biographical material interpreted through a detailed look at eighteenth century history. The poems are discussed in their contemporary setting without extensive analysis.

Emma Coburn Norris;
bibliography updated by the editors

Dave Smith

Born: Portportsmouth, Virginia; December 19, 1942

Principal poetry

Bull Island, 1970
Mean Rufus Throw Down, 1973
The Fisherman's Whore, 1974
Drunks, 1975
Cumberland Station, 1976
In Dark, Sudden with Light, 1977
Goshawk, Antelope, 1979
Blue Spruce, 1981
Dream Flights, 1981
Homage to Edgar Allan Poe, 1981
In the House of the Judge, 1983
Gray Soldiers, 1983
The Roundhouse Voices: Selected and New Poems, 1985
Cuba Night, 1990
Night Pleasures: New and Selected Poems, 1991
Fate's Kite: Poems, 1991-1995, 1995
Floating on Solitude: Three Volumes of Poetry, 1996
The Wick of Memory: New and Selected Poems, 1974-2000, 2000

Other literary forms

Dave Smith's productivity as a poet does not exhaust his pen. He has produced scores of reviews and essays on poetry and poetics, many of them as a columnist for *The American Poetry Review*. *Local Assays: On Contemporary American Poetry* (1985) collects many of these pieces. Smith's map of the contemporary scene is revealed in *The Morrow Anthology of Younger American Poets* (1985), which he edited. Smith also edited and wrote the introduction for *The Pure Clear Word: Essays on the Poetry of James Wright* (1982). In these activities, Smith has helped to define the critical context for his own work, for the poets of his generation, and for the canon of major influences on that generation. An enthusiastic reviewer, Smith has been faulted by some for excessive generosity. Nevertheless, his stature as a critic is rising to match his standing as a major poet of his era. He has also edited *The Essential Poe* (1991).

Smith's first novel, *Onliness* (1981), won critical acclaim. As Alan Bold wrote for the *Times Literary Supplement* (November 27, 1981), "*Onliness* is no tentative beginning, but an ambitious attempt to write the Great American Novel by bringing myth, archetype, allegory and abstraction to a fluent narrative." The usually sober-minded poet became an adept prose stylist who unveiled

Dave Smith (© Maurice Duke)

a comic wit not often realized in his poetry. At once erudite, folksy, and bizarre, *Onliness* fashions a version of the American South that owes more to Flannery O'Connor than to William Faulkner, yet Smith has made it a region of his own. *Southern Delights* (1984), a collection mixing stories and poems, is a less satisfying display of Smith's narrative skill.

Achievements

Dave Smith is a poet of inclusion. Working during a period characterized by emotional coolness and reductionism, Smith has been one of very few swimming in the opposite direction. His poetry is unashamedly passionate—exuberantly so. He almost never merely outlines a theme; he elaborates it with lavish care. Given these tendencies, it is not surprising that the characteristic Smith poem does not sit neatly on a single page. He has helped to bring back the long poem, both meditative and narrative. Smith is a brooder, a storyteller, and a moralist.

For these poems, Smith has created a rhetoric based on long lines and longer sentences—a rolling terrain of accumulating phrases and clauses. He is not, usually, a metrical poet, but rather a poet of sweeping cadences and accentual rhythms. His style is particularly Southern: affinities with Faulkner, Robert Penn Warren, and James Dickey are evident. Like them, Smith tends toward the baroque. He has built an ornamented and oratorical style that stands somewhere between colloquial idiom and grandiloquent rapture.

Much of Smith's work is a poetry of memory and yearning. The memories are personal, familial, and communal. In the best poems, they are also universal. Some of his work tries to give retrospective testimony to his (and everyone's) inarticulate youth. He is often sneaking up on the young boy, forcing him to explain himself, and encountering some kind of evocative silence or near-silence. To recapture the past is part of that severe yearning in Smith's poems. Passionate desire, however, can carry the poet in other directions: to see something clearly enough; to trust one's perceptions and one's heart; to answer nature's alternately strange and familiar glance. Smith, like the poets of ages past, is simply after the meaning of life. The intellectual life alone, without the felt underpinning of the physical life, is something that Smith distrusts, just as he has little patience for the questions of poetic form until there is the pulse of significant content.

A frequent device in Smith's work is the generative image or symbol. From the early "Medieval Tapestry" through such poems as "The Spinning Wheel in the Attic," "Under the Scrub Oak, a Red Shoe," "Blue Spruce," and "Crab," Smith uses his central image not merely for verbal accuracy or to invoke a single correspondence, but as a center for the intersection of many planes of thought and feeling. In such poems, as in the story poems with their enigmatic, fabulous glow, there is the hope—if not the proof—that all experience is connected in a way that one may ultimately grasp. Smith's vision is clearly in the romantic tradition.

Smith is a poet of full commitment to all that poetry can be. His long reach risks many things, including excess, but he does not choose to hold back. His special gifts and his special ambition are profoundly mated. His craft is in knowing when, and how, to go on. Norman Dubie's claim that Smith is the greatest poet of the American South is hard to dispute. Indeed, Smith may take his place among the foremost writers of any kind that the South has produced.

Recognitions of Smith's achievement have included fellowships from the Lyndhurst Foundation (three years), the John Simon Guggenheim Foundation, the National Endowment for the Arts (twice), and the Bellagio (Italy)/Rockefeller Foundation for Artistic Studies. He also received an Award for Excellence from the American Academy and Institute for Arts and Letters. He has been twice a runner-up for the Pulitzer Prize (1979 and 1981) as well as a finalist for the National Book Critic's Award (1979) and the Lenore Marshall Prize (1981).

Biography

David Jeddie Smith spent nearly all of his first thirty years in or near the tidewater region of Virginia. The collection of towns and villages clustered around the fishing and shipbuilding economy of the lower Chesapeake Bay formed the scenes of his childhood. Born in Portsmouth, he began rearing his own family in nearby Poquoson. It was there, after graduating from the University of Virginia in 1965, that Smith began his teaching career at Poquoson High School. Soon after his marriage in 1966 to Deloras Mae Weaver, Smith traveled to Edwardsville, Illinois, to work toward a master's degree at Southern Illinois University (1967-1969). Returning to Poquoson, Smith spent the next three years (January 1969-January 1972) on active duty in the Air Force, continuing to teach with night classes at local colleges.

Smith began writing in the late 1960's and ran his own small press, Back Door, for a number of years. The press's colophon, a dilapidated shack, was an emblem not only for a typical shoestring small press operation, but also for the shoestring lives of the characters that Smith would write about so often. The marginal but deeply felt and patterned lives of the Atlantic watermen provide the subject of Smith's first small collection, *Bull Island*, and of individual poems in later volumes. People living on the brink always appeal to Smith.

The geography of Smith's imagination embraces his own immediate region, his ancestors' mid-Atlantic wanderings, and the caldron of United States history: the Chesapeake from Norfolk to Baltimore, and the slow ascent westward to the mountains of Maryland, Virginia, and West Virginia. In much of Smith's work, the song of his time in this place becomes mixed with the lingering, ghostlike voices of landmarks and battlefields.

The traditions of this part of the South and his admiration for the common man and the physical life are aspects of the sensibility that Smith brings to his work. There is also Smith the man of letters: no noble savage at all, but rather the winner of graduate degrees in literature and the university teacher. The boy who had gone hunting year after year with his grandfather would find himself stalking the long commons of the contemporary American poet—academe. In his work, Smith has managed to subdue this bifurcation and, sometimes—as in "The Roundhouse Voices," in which words and deeds are explicitly measured against one another—to exploit it.

In 1972, Smith began a program of study at Ohio University that allowed him to earn a Ph.D. in 1976 with a creative dissertation. He was in residence for only the first and last years, spending 1973 to 1974 teaching at Western Michigan University and 1974 to 1975 at Cottey College in Nevada, Missouri. By the time the degree was completed, Smith had published his first two full-length collections and earned several important fellowships. While *Cumberland Station* was being readied for publication, Smith was offered the directorship of the creative writing program at the University of Utah. He held that position for four years. Life in the American West provided the landscape and inspiration for Smith's next book, *Goshawk, Antelope*. During 1980 and 1981, Smith brought to publication four books—three poetry collections and one novel—while working as a visiting professor at the Binghamton campus of the State University of New York. These collections, *Dream Flights* and *Homage to Edgar Allan Poe*, marked Smith's imaginative return to his tidewater roots, although with modifications of style and sensibility.

The imaginative return anticipated the actual one. After spending the academic year 1981-1982 as Director of Creative Writing at the University of Florida in Gainesville, Smith moved with his wife and three children to Richmond. There, as Professor of Creative Writing at Virginia Commonwealth University, Smith continued to write and to build upon the reputation that had risen meteorically in little more than a decade. *In the House of the Judge* contains some of Smith's most demanding work in longer forms. *The Roundhouse Voices*, an interim summary of his career as a poet, assured his permanence in the history of American letters. After what (for a writer as prolific as Smith) seemed like an unusual interval, *Cuba Night* appeared, a collection signaling the continued growth in craft, vision, and stature of the poet at middle age. In 1990, Smith and his family relocated to Louisiana State University where he continues to teach and is co-editor of *The Southern Review*.

Analysis

Generalizations about the memory-laden nature of much of Dave Smith's work have obscured the variety of ways in which his themes are developed, just as generalizations about his style do not reflect the wide range of experimentation in his work. The thorough reader will find many Smith poems that are short, lyric outbursts—and even poems in highly patterned stanzaics. *Mean Rufus Throw Down* contains pieces using full or subdued rhymes in couplets, tercets, and quatrains. In this volume, the variety of techniques may be accounted for as the searching experimentation of the young poet. Each volume, however, has its traditionally patterned efforts. "The Collector of the Sun," in *Goshawk, Antelope*, shows Smith at home with the difficult couplet quatrain. In *Homage to Edgar Allan Poe*, there is a studied return to the manipulation of older conventions (one aspect of the "homage"). For Smith, this kind of discipline is not always rewarding; it often seems that such strictures are at war with his truest poetic impulses. Still, one would not want to do without "The Abused (Hansel and Gretel)," a sonnet, or "Under a White Shawl of Pine," with its delicately flowing alternating rhyme quatrains.

Because Smith is usually expansive, the terse, compact sketches of film stars (such as "Doubling Back with Bogart") in *The Fisherman's Whore* are welcome surprises. Because he is often unrelievedly solemn, the grim whimsy of "The Suicide Eaters" (in *Goshawk, Antelope*) reminds readers that there is range to the emotive notes that Smith can strike. Smith's work is fully of his time (and place, one must add), yet fully transcendent. His is a voice that sometimes breaks stride with the patterns of standard written syntax as Smith grasps for the inclusive statement. He frequently sends parts of speech rolling into one another to form a redeemed mother tongue with some of the comfortable scaffolding torn away. Over and over again, however, Smith's magnetic cadences draw the reader in, focus our attention, lead the reader to resolve what he or she has rubbed up against, and then the voice is clear and penetrating. It is a voice that has a proper place in the timeless chorus.

"The Dark Eyes of Daughters"

The ongoing drama of being a husband and father often leads Smith to the backward-looking stance (as his own childhood and his own parents are recalled), but often enough such subjects leave him firmly planted in the present and looking to the future. In "The Dark Eyes of Daughters," one of Smith's poems of domestic concern (from *Goshawk, Antelope*), focus is achieved by a careful orchestration of images and figures of speech.

The poem recounts a moving instance of "love's division." The speaker, angered at his daughter's cat for attacking a tame quail, finds himself outside kicking the cat, and then, in almost the same instant, realizes that his young daughter is looking on, a witness to his brutality. In this moment of unplanned but decisive action, the father has become implicated in complex losses. Simply enough, the world will never be the same. He knows it and wishes against the change in his daughter's knowledge and heart; but the wish is futile.

The poem provides an experience focused by a series of similes and metaphors and by a careful metamorphosis of images. The heated action and the distance it has created are figured in the noise of "the back door/ still banging like a ripped/ shred of memory." The impulse to wish the truth away is like that of "a man in a car/ that's dropped something/ to howl down a quiet street." The oppressiveness of the truth is a "light/ banging hard overhead" and "this slow gouging/ of sparks that is the world." The "intense unloosening stare" of the cat's eyes gives way to consciousness of "the fixed and heart-dark/ pupils of the child startled/ to see what cruelty is." The revealing, vengeful sun, the cat, the daughter, and the painful truth she is learning are all brought together—in spite of the speaker's contrary wish: the "sun the color of a cat" falls "on her struck face that is/ learning to mouth these words/ without end." Finally, the sun, "like flint, strikes."

This same sun, at the beginning of the poem, was weakly invoked by the phrase "the dew dulls out." The sun as flint reaches back to the "gouging . . . sparks." The "spatter of quail feathers" at the poem's opening looks forward to the penultimate movement, the daughter's words "a beginning already long lost/ like pawprint or feather." The absorption of this tight structure of reverberating images into the illusion of artless, passionate utterance is characteristic of Smith's best work and especially of the more modulated passions of *Goshawk, Antelope*.

"Night Fishing for Blues"

More ambitious, and perhaps more central to Smith's developing manner, is "Night Fishing for Blues," in *Cumberland Station*. This poem exemplifies Smith's interest in the physical life, especially the actions of work and sport in the region he knows best. To that level of concern is added another dimension as the region's historical ghosts drift through the poem, helping to universalize its experience and revealing an unexpected theme. The urge to test one's self, to do some single thing well, excites Smith in a way that is reminiscent of Ernest Hemingway, although Smith's language is more emotionally charged. The black woman in "Night Fishing for Blues" is a version of Smith's heroic figure; heroic not in worldly stature, but in the full giving of herself to the task at hand. What she *does* defines her; no explanations are necessary. Yet, in this poem, the woman is something more. She is part of a loose allegory, for the poem is a complex fable.

The scene is Fortress Monroe, Virginia, where the "big-jawed Bluefish" slam "into banked histories of rock/ pile." This place is near "where Jefferson Davis/ hunched in a harrowing cell." Already, before the central event is under way, Smith has built a context that links the present experience with the long shadow of the Civil War. Military metaphors identify the masses of fish as "convoys, a black army, blue/ stained sequins rank after rank." To this place the speaker has "come back"—but how far back?

The fishing begins in the unexpected company of three African Americans: two men in "Superfly shirts" and "a grandmotherly obelisk." The speaker becomes involved in a pitched battle with the fish, and the intensity builds with the proliferation of the enemy and the fisherman's success: "I haul two, three at a time, torpedoes, moon-shiners. . . ." The woman watches, transfixed, "canting/ to Africa, a cluck in her throat, a chain/ song from the fisherman's house." The speaker cannot, or will not, take the time to understand this song or its meaning. He has reached a pinnacle of perfect action: "I know I have waited/ a whole life for this minute." The woman is fishing well, too, but the speaker pays no heed to her call for recognition: "*I ain't doing so bad/ for an old queen*."

In a wild crescendo of hauling and slinging lines, the speaker feels for a moment that he has "caught the goddamndest/ Blue in the Atlantic. She screams: *Oh my God!*" He has hooked the woman's face. In an instant the ignored fellow-fisher has become—or has been mistaken for—prey and enemy. Readers have seen a tragic accident of innocence, ignorance, and selfishness, as well as an act of fate.

When the hook is removed, the woman and the speaker set to fishing once again. Now, their lines tangle; they have "caught each other but we go on for the blue blood of/ ghosts that thrash in the brain's empty room"—a contest of old habit with no real aim. Then the two admit that nothing else has been caught; the fish have ceased to bite; they can untangle themselves at last. Says the woman, "*Sons they done/ let us go*." In her final action, the woman shows the others how to pack the caught fish. At dawn, as the speaker returns home,

> thousands of Blues fall from my head,
> falling with the gray Atlantic, and a pale veining light
> fills the road with sea-shadows that drift in figure
> eights, knot and snarl and draw me forward.

This vague epiphany is a movement forward in the speaker's moral life. "Night Fishing for Blues" is a compelling poem, a visually rich, taut narrative that suggests the reenactment of old passions and the redeeming power of passions of another order. The images of blue and gray, of weaponry, and of lines tangled and freed work their way through the poem with the hard tug of the inevitable.

Urgency is in every movement and in the hard rivets of sound and rhythm: "to pitch through tideturn and mudslur/ for fish with teeth like snapped sabers." This is torrential Smith in high gear, at the verge of excess, collapse, and presumption, but making a grandly successful world of words that is beyond the reach of craft alone.

"THE TIRE HANGS IN THE WOODS"

A representative poem of return, "The Tire Hangs in the Woods" (*Dream Flights*), may be one of Smith's best. In it the speaker journeys back to a place where he first "went to dream" and where, later, he and his friends "stared, with our girls, into the sky." While in many of his poems Smith's persona returns only in memory, in this piece memory is spurred by the actual return to that "secret place" whose totem is the hanging tire. The stream of memories is clustered around this central image, first introduced in juxtaposition to "somebody's rubber" which is "hung on a berry vine."

Once in focus, the hanging tire becomes the "black holes" of lifted mouths in the Churchland Baptist Church, and thus an evocation of religious mystery and yearning. The generative image is then likened, in turn, to genitals, "Poe's pendulum," "an arc of blackness/ gathering the hung world in its gullet," and the "sexual O" of a girl's mouth. In its cumulative power, the hanging tire is the "Ghost-heart of this place" where the speaker's present and past have intersected and where imagination has given memory a reality of the highest order. This poem is, at bottom, a romantic poem. The unpromising woods behind a friend's house take the place of a Tintern Abbey or a limetree bower.

Under the spell of the occasion, the mute but mysteriously charged adolescent is fused with the articulate, worldly-wise adult who returns. It is as if they have each longed for this meeting, each shoved his feet in the circular space and swung out to a point in the woods' darkness where time vanishes. The poem conjures up the touching of a truth—a miraculous truth—as present and past meet. The truth is not reducible, however, to direct utterance: It is pure, vital feeling willed and caught by the transcendent imagination.

These woods are, simultaneously, a place of death and of hope. They hold "thickets of darkness" and are marked by a "dead-end" and by "stillness . . . ticking like throat rattle." Paradoxically, they are also the setting for the trials and triumphs of *rites de passage:* the fistfight over a girl and love's early, earnest promises. In the present, the speaker gives the tire a shove "and sure enough I hear the tick and all that was/ is, and a girl straightening her skirt walks/ smack against you and screams." Transitions like these (note the pronoun shift) keep the poem suspended between now and then, life and death, time and timelessness. The hanging tire—still, spinning, or swinging—mediates the poem's potentially erratic flights. In its haunting shape and motions the movement toward revelation takes place: "me in the tire spinning my childish words" to "swinging like a secret in the dark/ woods" to "I . . . swing in absolute black./ The whine of the rope is like a distant scream./ I think, so this is it. Really it." In Smith's conclusion, colloquial idiom stands in place of the traditional romantic's ecstatic shriek, shrunk down to the simile of the rope's whine.

"The Tire Hangs in the Woods" carries forward and refines many of Smith's stylistic habits. In it, he makes use of the long, complex sentence that sprawls over many lines and gains power by accumulation. The first fourteen lines of the poem comprise only two sentences, and many other sentences roll on for five or six lines. As the poem moves toward its conclusion, however, the sentences become more and more compact until the final movement, in which there are four sentences in three lines. This increased frequency of full stops is an effective device for moving the poem toward closure, toward the silence that is left to speak after the words have done all they can. Syntactical complexity in this poem does not fall into the knotty opacity of some of Smith's earlier work, nor are his rhythms here as clotted with spondaic bursts. Still, Smith is lavish in his use of sound patterns to release and spring strong rhythms. A line such as "gone dull as soap-scum, the husband grunting" is reminiscent of Gerard Manley Hopkins and of the strong-stress lines of Anglo-Saxon poetry.

The yard in which the tire hangs is, until Smith's poetry touches it, a very ordinary place: a place, in fact, to be overlooked, if not avoided. It is to traditional poetic settings just what many of Smith's central characters are to heroes: solitary, obscured, abused, just barely surviving. It is a dying place whose dignity Smith senses and celebrates. Smith's treatment of place, image, and self in this poem links "The Tire Hangs in the Woods" to the great American tradition. Here, the singing and soaring of Walt Whitman blend with the down-to-earth speaking of the birch-swinger, Robert Frost. Yet it is entirely his own, the kind of masterpiece that only Smith could write.

"Southern Crescent"

Like many of the poems in *Cuba Night*, "Southern Crescent" can lay claim to being a new American masterpiece. It is a rich meditation etched out of narrative detail, dialogue, feeling-drenched thoughtfulness, and precise imagery. Riding the return train trip with his wife from her father's funeral, the poet records the desolate America through which only old track beds pass. The scene aggravates the sadness he feels for his wife's loss as its debris mixes with his guilt at never having liked his father-in-law. Still, searching for the right words, hovering near them, he manages to be of some use to his wife. They pass a poor shack where a man gives them the finger, his hovel lit up for Christmas, the lights flickering. Only the speaker sees this, and he is forced to laugh. In explaining what happened to his wife, in their interchange of question and answer, they reach a new intimacy beyond the formalities of the grievous occasion. An unexpected perspective is gained, and an unexpected peace. Like Smith's best work, this is a small story perfectly told—or shown. The reader is left to feel the connection between the woman's father, the man along the tracks, and the ways in which our actions may unexpectedly fulfill another's needs.

Fate's Kite

Smith's collections after *Cuba Night* show him to be working at a slower pace, but the poems themselves make it clear that there is no slackening of intensity. While both *Night Pleasures* and *The Wick of Memory* present new poems in the context of selections from earlier volumes (*The Wick of Memory* being a most comprehensive representation of Smith's career), *Fate's Kite* stands alone during this period as an orchestration of new work that seems conceived as an independent book-length project. Each poem is thirteen lines, and the lines keep to a fairly uniform length throughout. This extended use of a predetermined pattern is unique to Smith's work, lending a sense of compression and closure that, until this experiment, had not been characteristic. Like much of Smith's work, these poems trace a frustrated yearning for the sacred. Though they encompass a wide range of images, tones, and settings, Smith's restless, hungering spirit and the daring formal decision combine to forge a special unity.

Other major works

long fiction: *Onliness*, 1981.

nonfiction: *Local Assays: On Contemporary American Poetry*, 1985.

edited texts: *The Pure Clear Word: Essays on the Poetry of James Wright*, 1982; *The Morrow Anthology of Younger American Poets*, 1985 (with David Bottoms); *The Essential Poe*, 1991.

miscellaneous: *Southern Delights*, 1984.

Bibliography

Balakian, Peter. "Heroes of the Spirit: An Interview with Dave Smith." *Graham House Review* 6 (Spring, 1982): 48-72. Smith responds to questions about the large number of downtrodden characters in his work, his affinity with romantic tradition, his narrative impulse, and the complex issue of Smith's identity as a regional writer. Particularly useful are observations on the strong-stress rhythms of Anglo-Saxon poets and of Gerard Manley Hopkins as they influence Smith's own work.

Christensen, Paul. "Malignant Innocence." *Parnassus: Poetry in Review* 12 (Fall/Winter, 1984): 154-182. Christensen's article is one of the most comprehensive examinations of Smith's work, discovering in the poet's voice a version of an American and Southern archetype mediating between youth and age, initiate and elder. Christensen provides a rich understanding of the mythic taproots of Smith's career and of his major themes.

DeMott, Robert J. *Dave Smith: A Literary Archive*. Athens: Ohio University Libraries, 2000. Important for biographical and bibliographical research, this description of DeMott's personal collection of Dave Smith materials includes references to manuscripts, correspondence, Smith's contributions to periodicals, print editions both major and rare, and intriguing association items. The introduction, which traces DeMott's relationship to Smith, sheds a highly personal light on Smith's life and art. DeMott also describes the Ohio University Alden Library's Foundational Dave Smith Collection.

Millichap, Joseph K. "Dave Smith." *Contemporary Southern Writers*. Detroit: St. James Press, 1999. This brief overview of Smith's career stresses the "trend toward variety and diversity" in style and subject. Comments on each major volume through *Fate's Kite*.

Suarez, Ernest. "An Interview with Dave Smith." *Contemporary Literature* 37, no. 3 (Fall, 1996): 348-69. This excellent interview begins with an intelligent overview of Smith's art and an examination of a representative poem. Suarez's questions bring forth comments on influences, writing habits, the creative process, Smith's sense of the poet's role, and his own particular ambitions as a writer. Intriguing comments as well on form and on the term "confessional" poetry.

Swiss, Thomas. "'Unfold the Fullness': Dave Smith's Poetry and Fiction." *The Sewanee Review* 91 (Summer, 1983): 483-490. Swiss examines the architecture of *Dream Flights*, *Homage to Edgar Allan Poe*, and *In the House of the Judge*, collections that mark Smith's imaginative homecoming. In these and in his novel (*Onliness*), "Smith's strong attraction to violence, to stories of southern life marked by tragedy, is tempered by a vision which is fundamentally romantic."

Vendler, Helen. "Dave Smith." *The Music of What Happens: Poems, Poets, Critics*. Cambridge, Mass.: Harvard University Press, 1988. Vendler here modifies her original view that Smith is a regional Southern writer. She now argues, on the basis of *Goshawk, Antelope*, that he is "a distinguished allegorist of human experience." Vendler still admires the "torrential, impatient, exasperated" Smith whose "language is theatrical, even melodramatic." She notes Smith's clouded optimism, how he often "undoes his hopes as he utters them."

_______. "'Oh I Admire and Sorrow.'" In *Part of Nature, Part of Us: Modern American Poets*. Cambridge, Mass.: Harvard University Press, 1980. Originally published in *Parnassus* (Spring/Summer, 1977), this is the first extended statement by a major critic on Smith's work. Vendler enjoys the momentous energy in Smith's style, the range of his subjects, and his ambition. She praises especially his poems about the Civil War and about fishing. The essay examines several representative poems from Smith's earlier books.

Weigl, Bruce. "Forms of History and Self in Dave Smith's *Cuba Night*." *Poet Lore* 85 (Winter, 1990/1991): 37-48. In examining the long poem "To Isle of Wight," Weigl stresses Smith's mythmaking ability and his ongoing struggle with his Southern heritage. Smith's romantic attachment to the Old South is complicated by his "struggling against those racist tendencies so subtly woven into the fabric of a culture he is at once part of and at odds with." Weigl explores the range of Smith's prosodic virtuosity. He notes Smith's active recognition of the need to "embrace the whole of who and what we are personally and historically."

_______, ed. *The Giver of Morning: On the Poetry of Dave Smith*. Birmingham, Ala.: Thunder City Press, 1982. This first slender collection of comment on Smith's work fittingly assesses the amazing first dozen years of his career. The lead essay by Robert DeMott develops Smith's notion that the poem is a moral act, examining his ambition and success. Other essays are by Weigl, Helen Vendler, and Terry Hummer. Included also is an interview conducted by H. A. Maxson.

Philip K. Jason, updated by Jason

Stevie Smith

Born: Hull, Yorkshire, England; September 20, 1902
Died: Ashburton, England; March 7, 1971

Principal poetry

A Good Time Was Had by All, 1937
Tender Only to One, 1938
Mother, What Is Man?, 1942
Harold's Leap, 1950
Not Waving but Drowning, 1957
Selected Poems, 1962
The Frog Prince and Other Poems, 1966
The Best Beast, 1969
Two in One: Selected Poems and The Frog Prince and Other Poems, 1971

Scorpion and Other Poems, 1972
The Collected Poems of Stevie Smith, 1975
Selected Poems, 1978
Cats, Friends, and Lovers: For Women's Chorus, 1987 (music by Stephen Paulus)
New Selected Poems of Stevie Smith, 1988
Stevie's Tunes: An Anthology of Nine Songs for Mezzo-soprano and Piano, 1988 (music by Peter Dickinson)
Two Stevie Smith Songs: For Voice and Piano, 1990 (music by Geoffrey Bush)

Other literary forms

Stevie Smith published three autobiographical novels, the best-received of which was her first, *Novel on Yellow Paper: Or, Work It Out for Yourself* (1936). A book of her drawings (with captions) called *Some Are More Human than Others: Sketchbook by Stevie Smith* appeared in 1958. She also wrote short stories, essays, book reviews, and a one-act radio play.

Achievements

Stevie Smith's first novel received warm reviews in 1936, and she enjoyed a popularity that was sudden but relatively stable until the 1950's, when she fell out of fashion for a number of years. By the early 1960's, however, she was back in the public eye, and she remained popular, giving readings in which she sometimes sang her poems in an odd, singsong voice, until her death in 1971. She won the Cholmondeley Award for Poetry in 1966 and was awarded the Gold Medal for Poetry by Queen Elizabeth II in 1969.

Biography

Born Florence Margaret Smith, Stevie Smith belonged to a family made up of women from the time she was four, when her father disappeared to make a career for himself as a sailor. That year, 1906, she moved with her mother, sister, and aunt to a house on Avondale Road in the London suburb of Palmers Green. Smith lived there for the rest of her life. By 1924 her mother had died and her sister had moved to Suffolk. From then on, she shared the house with her adored Aunt Margaret, whom Smith affectionately called "the Lion Aunt."

Smith was not university educated and was never married. The nickname "Stevie," acquired when she was eighteen, is a reference to Steve Donaghue, a famous jockey. After her graduation from secretarial training college, she got a job as a private secretary at a publishing firm in 1923. She kept this job for thirty years, until she finally devoted herself to writing full time. She died of an inoperable brain tumor in 1971.

Analysis

Stevie Smith populated the margins of her poems with idiosyncratic drawings of swimmers and potted plants, ghosts and dogs, howling children and flirting couples. She doodled this art herself, when, as she explained, she was "not thinking too much. If I suddenly get caught by the doodle, I put more effort into it and end up calling it a drawing. I've got a whole collection in boxes. Some are on tiny bits of paper and drawn on telephone and memo pads." Smith insisted that the drawings be published with her poems, even though they do not technically "illustrate" the words on the page. Instead, she chose drawings which seemed to her to illustrate "the spirit or the idea in the poem."

In some ways, reading Smith's poetry is like fishing in one of her boxes filled with drawings on loose sheets and tiny bits of paper. As one moves from one drawing to another, one poem to another, the habits of her imagination become familiar. One can identify concerns (death, spinsterhood, sexuality) that appeared early and persisted late, name maneuvers (analysis of myth, parody of family roles) that recur again and again. One learns to recognize the spatialization of her impatience with categories through images of claustrophobia ("Souvenir de Monsieur Poop"), to expect her assumption of the proximity between love and hate ("I HATE THIS GIRL"), to look for the ways in which grief feeds the heart ("So to fatness come"). She moves back and forth among forms—from rapid stanzas with fixed rhyme schemes ("Nourish Me on an Egg," "Do Take Muriel Out") to long poems constructed of rhyming couplets ("The Passing Cloud," "The Hostage"), to looser, more narrative lines ("Dear Karl," "The Abominable Lake"). Yet the procedure from one poem to another—or one collection to another—does not present itself as neat linear development.

Inherited stories

It is possible, however, to sketch out a set of preoccupations that Smith found compelling enough to return to throughout her career. One of the most conspicuous of these concerns is her investigation of inherited stories: fairy tales, narratives from the Bible, legends, and myths. Smith takes as her premise that material culture and literary culture constitute overlapping territories and is at pains in many of her poems to demonstrate the ways in which Western culture has organized itself in response to certain famous stories.

In a late poem called "How Cruel Is the Story of Eve," for example, she argues the disturbing repercussions that Genesis, with its snake and its apple and its falling woman, set in motion: "What responsibility it has/ In history/ For cruelty." She goes on to address the collective resistance of skeptical readers, who might call her estimation of the effects of Eve's story exaggerated: What is the meaning of this legend, she asks, "if not/ To give blame to women most/ And most punishment?"

Smith is interested in stories and images that have saturated the cultural imagination of her society—stories that have defined and continue to influence the position of women, to shape attitudes about animals and wildness, to teach lessons about romance and relationships. Her poems refer back in literary history to William Blake (in her "Little Boy Sick") and across boundaries of genre when she appropriates fairy stories (in "The Frog Prince") or Arthurian legends (in "The Blue from Heaven"). As Smith points out, these stories color all human thought and are therefore important to anyone interested in disrupting some of those thoughts.

Inherited roles

If Smith's exploration of inherited stories uncovers some of the ways in which culture grids according to gender or species, her survey of the roles inherited and negotiated within families reduces the scale of the inquiry while maintaining precise attention to instances of ill fit between individuals and the roles in which they find themselves. Adults are irked at having to give up the colors and excesses of childhood ("To Carry the Child"); children with absent fathers are cynical from babyhood ("Infant"). Women with husbands and children weep over frying pans ("Wretched Woman") or lash out—"You beastly child, I wish you had miscarried,/ You beastly husband, I wish I had never married" ("Lightly Bound")—while women who refuse to compromise themselves by investing in less-than-adequate relationships doubt their own decisions and worry about isolation: "All, all is isolation/ And every lovely limb's a desolation" ("Every Lovely Limb's a Desolation"). Because Smith delights in circling round a situation, sizing it up from all angles, there also are poems that defend solitude—speakers who argue, for example, that the best personal prescription is to "shun compromise/ Forget him and forget her" ("To the Tune of the Coventry Carol"), despite the risks of isolation. The typical attitude of a wife toward her wifehood, a mother toward her motherhood, or a child toward her childhood is discomfort and cynicism. Figures in Smith's poems are perpetually chafed by the discrepancy between their needs and the roles into which they believe they have been, one way or another, stuck.

For all her self-consciousness about cultural slots, Smith feels no obligation to limit her renditions of them to tragic monotones. Her preference for reading Agatha Christie novels in translation, for example, clearly indicates that she relished the humor of a poor fit. "If you read her in French," she once remarked, "you get a most exotic flavor, because there never was anything more English than the stuff she's writing. It's great fun that the translations are rather poor." Smith administered her critical, antic judgment to anything in sight, including her own loyalties—to Anglicanism, for example. While she remained personally loyal to the church her whole life, she cheerfully poked poetic fun at the awkward positions into which God forces his underlings.

"Nature and Free Animals"

She argues in one early poem, for example, that the human impulse to make dogs into pets has always been prompted by the unbearably cramped space of the will to which people find themselves restricted when they see, on the one hand, "Nature and Free Animals" and on the other hand God himself. The poem begins with God's irate pronouncement that humans have committed the one moral error he cannot abide: "they have taught [dogs] to be servile . . . To be dependent touching and entertaining." Given human pride in legal systems that articulate and protect human rights, to complain that having "rights to be wronged/ And wrongs to be righted" insults a God-given wild dogginess might strike one as ludicrous. Yet Smith celebrates the possibility of uninhibited if violent life that animals represent while poking merciless fun at the ways in which human laws and orders actually trivialize death. The person God reprimands in this poem shoots back a feisty self-defense: "Nature and Free Animals/ Are all very fine," the speaker grants, but with them "on the one side/ And you on the other,/ I hardly know I'm alive." Squeezed from both directions, humans have no room to exercise either instinct or will, and it is precisely this unpleasant sensation that compels them to make dogs into pets. Having made her irreverent point, Smith undoubtedly chuckled at the anagrammatic joke of resisting God by putting a leash on his name spelled backwards.

"The Zoo"

Not being one to shy away from the unorthodox destinations toward which her unorthodox theories point her, Smith accepts the fact that her celebration of animals must accommodate violence. Thus, in a poem called "The Zoo," a lion "sits within his cage,/ Weeping tears of ruby rage" because he has been deprived of his natural capacity for violence. "His claws are blunt, his teeth fall out,/ No victim's flesh consoles his snout," the speaker reports sympathetically, concluding that it is no wonder that "his eyes are red/ Considering his talents are misused." Smith gives God due credit for having bestowed upon the lion "lovely teeth and claws/ So that he might eat little boys."

Oddly as such a compliment rings, other of Smith's treatments of animals suggest that it is not an entirely backhanded one. The reader may wince at being made politely to admire the lion's gift for making snacks of little boys, but when one is presented with the alternative of allying oneself with pet owners as depicted in poems such as "Jumbo," the crunching of bones begins to have a certain raw dignity:

> Jumbo, Jumbo, Jumbo darling, Jumbo come to Mother.
> But Jumbo wouldn't, he was a dog who simply wouldn't bother
> An ugly beast he was with drooping guts and filthy skin,
> It was quite wonderful how "mother" loved the ugly thing.

What Smith ridicules here is not the ugliness of Jumbo but rather the human compulsion to assert its will even over such a mangy beast. Jumbo's unwillingness to be bothered with his yodeling "mother" is a caustic enough comment on humans' clumsy interference with naturally occurring systems in which dogs, with wonderful indifference, eat dogs. Smith takes clear delight, however, in pushing the caricature one step further. In linking humans' desire to lord it over the likes of Jumbo with the sacred job of mothering, she insinuates that perhaps people are not as far removed from the harshness of nature as they wish to believe.

"A Mother's Hearse" and "The Wanderer"

Crass as one may find such an intimation, Smith doggedly pursues the possibility that "the love of a mother for her child/ Is not necessarily a beautiful thing" ("A Mother's Hearse"). "Mother, if mother-love enclosure be," one child protests, "It were enough, my dear, not quite to hate me." While another Brontë-like waif trails about tapping at windowpanes and crying that "you have weaned me too soon, you must nurse me again," the speaker corrects the misapprehension of the unhappy ghost. Would she indeed "be happier if she were within?" Smith guesses not: "She is happier far where the night winds fall,/ And there are no doors and no windows at all" ("The Wanderer").

Just as God and beasts are understood to restrict the possibility for human action by having prior claim on both divine instruction and animal instinct, claustrophobia of the will looms over the enterprise of motherhood. What Smith seems, in fact, to be suggesting is the unattractive possibility that domination is one of the primary (and primal) motivations of humankind. The desire to dominate warps even the best-intentioned of projects—warps even love.

"Papa Love Baby"

If mothers threaten to smother their little darlings, the conspicuous absence of paternal will allows children to rule in worlds of lopsided power. The gigantic quantity of control one presumes that parents wield over their toddlers, for example, dwindles rather rapidly in "Papa Love Baby" when the child administers judgment:

I sat upright in my baby carriage
And wished mama hadn't made such a foolish
marriage.
I tried to hide it, but it showed in my eyes
unfortunately
And a fortnight later papa ran away to sea.

Such radical shrinkage of adult presumption would be comic except for the child's disturbing admission that its keen and unforgiving wit carries with it the burden of responsibility: "I could not grieve/ But I think I was somewhat to blame."

Even more disturbing than this image of a preschooler having to shoulder the blame for her own abandonment, the articulate baby of "Papa Love Baby" tells her brief tale in a way that hints darkly at incest:

What folly it is that daughters are always supposed
to be
In love with papa. It wasn't the case with me
I couldn't take to him at all
But he took to me
What a sad fate to befall
A child of three.

The shrinking line lengths of this stanza, which ends with an admission of her tender age, remind us of the inevitable physical advantage that even a stupid papa enjoys over his little girl. The sexual suggestiveness of the poem stays, by all means, at the level of nebulous suggestion: The father "took to" the child who did not "take to him." Yet the reader can hardly help wondering why such a turn of events would constitute a "sad fate" and why, despite the fact that the poem concerns itself primarily with the child's disdain for her "unrespected" father, its title should highlight the fact that in spite of that childish contempt, "Papa Love Baby."

A Good Time Was Had by All

The place children occupy in the various structures they find themselves to have inherited from adults constitutes one of Smith's most persistent preoccupations. *A Good Time Was Had by All*, her first published volume of poetry, begins and ends with poems that treat this issue. "The Hound of Ulster" and "Louise" frame the collection, typifying her vision of how the tension between adulthood and childhood shapes most human relationships. Despite what is normally thought of as the distance separating grownups from youngsters, she was at perpetual pains to point out their complicated proximity. "We are," as she once remarked, "as much the child's old age as he is our youth."

"The Hound of Ulster"

In "The Hound of Ulster," a "courteous stranger" urges a little boy to "take a look/ In the puppy shop," with its tantalizing array of dogs: "Could anything be merrier?" This adult script, rendered instantly suspect by the ease with which it fits the pattern parents proverbially warn their children against (never accept rides, candy, or invitations from strangers), does not, however, turn genuinely sinister until the last lines of the poem. Upon the child's polite inquiry regarding what it might be that "lurks in the gray/ Cold shadows at the back of the shop," the stranger warns that Cuchulain, the legendary Irish warrior also known as the Hound of Ulster, "lies tethered there . . . tethered by his golden hair."

As a child, the legend goes, Cuchulain killed a fierce dog that attacked him. The dog belonged to Chulain, who grieved over the death of his pet. Upon seeing the owner's grief, the child took it upon himself to be watchdog for Chulain until a new dog could be found. Thus he earned the name of Cuchulain, which translates to "the hound of Chulain." Cuchulain is also known as "the Hound of Ulster" in reference to the Ulster cycle of Gaelic literature.

If, as "Nature and Free Animals" suggests, humans make pets of dogs as a way of securing for themselves a modicum of space within which their wills—bounded by animals from below and God from above—can operate, the childhood feat of Cuchulain represents a double seizure of power. Having been mortally threatened by the dog, the child first dispenses with the beast that dares to trespass beyond his already-liberal bounds, then appropriates the bestial vigor of the dog—but only temporarily. In Smith's structure of competing territories between people and animals, then, Cuchulain's ability to negotiate his way between those territories ensures a much more spacious scope for the exercise of his strength.

In the poem, however, the hound stands as an image of paralyzed will, "tethered by his golden hair/ His eyes are closed and his lips are pale/ Hurry little boy he is not for sale." Having asked too much, the curious child is sent on his way. Only the poem's speaker, familiar with the puppy inventory and protective of the shop's tethered secret, seems to exercise any genuine control in this poem, and it is a control of exhibition. The reader's or the boy's access to dogs of the will is strictly limited to spectatorship, while the speaker extends the invitation and controls the display, blending the roles of poet and zookeeper.

"LOUISE"

"Louise," the final poem in *A Good Time Was Had by All*, repeats the eerie childhood experience described in "Papa Love Baby": articulate intellectual power darkened by traces of sexual powerlessness. Louise sits on a suitcase in the "suburban sitting room" of Mr. and Mrs. Tease, having traveled all over Europe with her mother but having "never been long enough in any nation/ Completely to unpack." The only words she speaks in the poem are wistful ones—"Oh if only I could stay/ Just for two weeks in one place." Her thoughts are quickly followed by her mother's advice, "Cheer up girlie," because they will indeed be stopping here for at least two weeks, as it will take Louise's father that long to come up with the money they need to move on. The poem (and the collection) thus ends on a note of bewilderment colored by the reader's response to the idea of hosts called "Mr and Mrs Tease": "The poor child sits in a mazy fit:/ Such a quick answer to a prayer/ Shakes one a bit." That the near-instantaneous answer to her wish should send Louise down the emotional path of something as complicated as a "mazy fit" demonstrates part of what makes Smith's abnormally astute, hyper-intuitive children such disturbing combinations of sophistication and vulnerability. While their wishes conform to a formula of Cinderella simplicity, their intuitive gifts expose the problems inherent in reductive answers. A homesick child gets to stay in one house for two weeks, but how reassuring is it when that house is presided over by hosts by the name of "Mr. and Mrs. Tease"? The predicament of Louise, caught between her apparent powers of shaping the adult world and her childish susceptibility to the adults who nevertheless continue to rule it, haunts the body of Smith's work right up to her death.

"DUTY WAS HIS LODESTAR"

Sometimes children manage to elude adult authority—exhibiting, as a poem such as "'Duty Was His Lodestar'" gleefully demonstrates, particular skill in ducking out of verbal structures. As Smith herself has explained, the premise of this poem is a child's having "been told that duty is one's lodestar. But she is rebellious, this child, she will have none of it, so she says lobster instead of lodestar, and so makes a mock of it, and makes a monkey of the kind teacher." What we're presented with is "A song" (the poem's subtitle) in which speaker and lobster damage their relationship but then mend it and celebrate their reunification:

> Duty was my Lobster, my Lobster was she,
> And when I walked with my Lobster
> I was happy.
> But one day my Lobster and I fell out,
> And we did nothing but
> Rave and shout
>
> Rejoice, rejoice, Hallelujah, drink the flowing champagne,
> For my darling Lobster and I
> Are friends again.

The seriousness of duty as presented by adult to child is replaced by the celebration of relationship. Duty, meant to fix the child's respectful attention and serve as a sober guide, gives way to friendship, charged with gospel-choir enthusiasm.

"OUR BOG IS DOOD"

In "Our Bog Is Dood," Smith parodies the limits of the religious imagination in a humorous anecdote about the difficulties of achieving interpretive consensus. In this poem, the children chanting "Our Bog is dood" reveal to the speaker that they know their Bog is dood "because we wish it so/ That is enough." Here, Smith lays out for the reader's amusement (or admiration; the two are neighboring concepts as far as she is concerned) the acts of sheer and reckless will by which both children and children of God collapse the distance between wish and belief, constructing verbal worlds that they inhabit with collective placidity until prodded to articulate the specifics of those worlds. "Then tell me, darling little ones," the speaker inquires, feigning innocence, "What's dood, suppose Bog is?" This flummoxes them, for though they give the irritating speaker an answer quick enough ("Just what we think it is"), they soon began arguing with one another, "for what was dood, and what their Bog/ They never could agree." The speaker proves to be exempt from this hostility not by virtue of having answers to the issues of Bog or dood but rather by a willingness to let the questions lie unanswered, to walk beside rather than into "the encroaching sea,/ The sea that soon should drown them all,/ That never yet drowned me."

"To Carry the Child"

Yet it is irrepressibility that Smith celebrates in the children of "To Carry the Child," which suggests that the labor of carrying a child does not end at birth or even when the baby learns to walk but rather at the nebulous juncture separating childhood from adulthood. In this poem she describes the moment of being allowed to stand on one's own two feet not as a moment of independence but of diminishment. Grownups are "frozen," while children are "easy in feeling, easily excessive/ And in excess powerful." Growing in this poem is an act not of growing up but of growing into, a process of entrapment: What can the poor child, then, do, "trapped in a grown-up carapace,/ But peer outside of his prison room/ With the eye of an anarchist?" That Smith visualizes adults as a population of "handicapped" children speaks to the vigor with which she gripped onto the idea of children as a models for the independent imagination, gradually able to hold onto their mobility of vision only from within a claustrophobic space.

"Numbers"

If the encroaching rigidity of a carapace threatens to reduce the imaginative scope of a child to the rolling of eyeballs, then the architecture of domesticity constructs somewhat less restrictive but still idiosyncratic frames of reference. In "Numbers," that such frames of reference limit the bounds of the imagination becomes a matter of literal concern as well, since the information that fails to make its way into the boundaries of the poem's window frames is the small fact that the speaker's house sits on a four-hundred-foot cliff. The poem lists numbers of objects that romp about or spread outside one house:

> A thousand and fifty-one waves
> Two hundred and thirty-one seagulls
> A cliff of four hundred feet
> Three miles of ploughed fields.

Four windows provide views of the waves and the fields, while one skylight provides visual access to a square of sky. Thus the occupant of the house is able to perceive a little bit of most of what lies beyond the walls of the house: four windows' worth of the thousand and fifty-one waves; four windows' worth of the three miles of fields; one of the two hundred and thirty-one seagulls. Only the four-hundred-foot cliff upon which the house sits is invisible, suggesting that while frames of domestic reference may indeed offer access to snippets of the world at large, they ground themselves, obliviously, on the precarious edges of things. What is disturbing about this poem is not so much the cliff as the apparent unconsciousness with which the inhabitants of the house are perched upon it.

Attitude toward death

Harold's courage in not only confronting but in leaping such cliffs is what stirs the admiring eulogy of acrophobic Harold in the title poem of Smith's 1950 collection, *Harold's Leap*. "Harold was always afraid to climb high,/ But something urged him on." Smith lavishes the energy of this poem not on Harold's failure to accomplish anything beyond his own death-by-leap but on the dizzying height of the rocks, the sheer will Harold mustered. That she applauds his leap in spite of its futility suggests that since death is the project looming over all other projects anyway, to take one's death into one's own legs constitutes the only possible act of frank courage.

This unblinking attitude toward death constitutes, in fact, one of the most conspicuous stripes by which Smith's work may be recognized. Her stance toward it veers from the dismissive to the devoted but always takes careful account of its reliability as a solution. In "Death Bereaves Our Common Mother, Nature Grieves for My Dead Brother," an early poem from *A Good Time Was Had by All*, death is noted as a shift in verb tense: "He was, I am." The subject is a dead lamb, a drawing of which (lying on its back with its four legs straight up like a dead bug) decorates the poem. This ditty on death is casual to the point of flippancy, despite its professed compassion—"Can I see lamb dead as mutton/ And not care a solitary button?" Lest one suspect that she reserves this easy tone for animals, Smith describes the death of one Major Spruce in another poem in the same volume in nearly identical terms. "It is a Major Spruce/ And he's grown such a bore, such a bore. . . . It was the Major Spruce./ He died. Didn't I tell you?" ("Progression").

In the title poem of *Tender Only to One*, Smith borrows a familiar convention of gooey sentimentality to demonstrate her feelings for death. Here, the petalplucking speaker performs that hoary ritual of virginhood—loves me, loves me not—in order to discover the name of him to whom she is tender. In the end, the bald flower manages to convey the message: "Tender only to one,/ . . . His name, his name is Death." While it is difficult to tell precisely whether the speaker with such a quantity of tenderness to bestow is surprised by the outcome of her experiment, the ease with which the stanza contains the name of the beloved suggests that the news does not perturb her. The entire display, apparently, is presented for the reader's benefit.

Another poem in the same collection fancies death as stage two of a doctor's prescription. When the solicitous physician observes that "You are not looking at all well, my dear,/ In fact you are looking most awfully queer," my dear replies that yes, indeed, the pain is "more than I can bear, so give me some bromide." She will go away to the seashore, where the tides, naturally, will take care of the situation, carrying the speaker "beyond recovery" ("The Doctor"). "Come Death (I)," meanwhile, reprimands Christianity for teaching people to be brave in facing death, for courage is not even necessary. "Foolish illusion, what has Life to give?" the speaker inquires scornfully. "Why should man more fear Death than fear to live?" "From the Coptic" shapes the relationship between life and death into a narrative, as it describes three angels trying to coax clay into manhood. The first two angels promise the clay happiness, to little effect: "the red clay lay flat in the falling rain,/ Crying, I will stay clay and take no blame." Upon identifying himself as Death, however, the third angel produces immediate results: "I am Death, said the angel, and death is the end,/ I am Man, cries clay rising, and you are my friend."

"Not Waving but Drowning"

Given the array of instances in which Smith warmly clasps the hand of death, that her most famous poem draws on the human dread of dying may say more about the kind of poems people wish to anthologize than it does about any alteration of her sensibility. "Not Waving but Drowning" is, however, the title poem of the 1957 collection, suggesting at the very least that she wished her readers to take a look at this fable of how gestures of despair and even catastrophe get mistaken for something else:

> Nobody heard him, the dead man,
> But still he lay moaning:
> I was much further out than you thought
> And not waving but drowning.

This poem, with its disturbing pun on panicky signal and casual acknowledgment, suggests that civilized systems of communication fail to accommodate emergencies. Schooled in polite noninterference and having no mechanism for detecting anything outside the bounds of that inarticulate propriety, one simply assumes that any waves at all are bound to be waves of greeting. This sorry state of communicative affairs is further complicated by the fact that the swimmer's ability to articulate difference is overwhelmed by the very medium through which he swims: How can he be expected to clarify for others the distinction between waves of greeting and waves of alarm when all of his waves are immersed in even more and perpetual waves of water? The enterprise seems doomed from the beginning.

Smith's refusal to desert these individual victims of isolation, her cocking of the ear to the persistent voice of a dead man, offers a fragile consolation. Prodded and coached by this plucky mistress of lost voices, her readers learn at least to recognize the coarseness of their own powers of interpretation. If one fails to make out the words of the drowned swimmer, one can at least be assured that it is not for the lack of his having gurgled out a message.

Other major works

long fiction: *Novel on Yellow Paper: Or, Work It Out for Yourself*, 1936; *Over the Frontier*, 1938; *The Holiday*, 1949.

nonfiction: *Some Are More Human than Others: Sketchbook by Stevie Smith*, 1958, 1990.

miscellaneous: *Me Again: Uncollected Writings of Stevie Smith*, 1981; *Stevie Smith: A Selection*, 1985; *A Very Pleasant Evening with Stevie Smith: Selected Short Prose*, 1995.

Bibliography

Barbera, Jack, and William McBrien. *Stevie: A Biography of Stevie Smith*. London: Heinemann, 1985. Barbera and McBrien's literary biography is well researched and very readable.

Bedient, Calvin. "Stevie Smith." In *Eight Contemporary Poets*. London: Oxford University Press, 1974. Bedient's study is useful for its discussion of individual poems.

Pumphrey, Martin. "Play, Fantasy, and Strange Laughter: Stevie Smith's Uncomfortable Poetry." *Critical Quarterly* 28 (Autumn, 1986): 85-96. Pumphrey uses some of the basic assumptions of play theory to approach Smith's poems. He discusses her use of fairy-tale elements and describes her as an "anti-confessional" poet.

Severin, Laura. *Stevie Smith's Resistant Antics*. Madison: University of Wisconsin Press, 1997. Severin's extensive study challenges the notions of Smith as an apolitical and eccentric poet, instead portraying her as a well-connected literary insider who used many genres to resist domestic ideology in Britain. Severin explores the connections between Smith's work and mass media production; twentieth century historical events; her Romantic and Victorian predecessors; and such contemporaries as Virginia Woolf, Dorothy Parker, Aldous Huxley, and Evelyn Waugh.

Sternlicht, Sanford. *Stevie Smith*. Boston: Twayne, 1990. Sternlicht's book is a good introduction to Smith's work. It includes chapters on her novels and nonfiction as well as chronological descriptions of Smith's development. The book contains a chronology of Smith's life and a selected bibliography.

_______, ed. *In Search of Stevie Smith*. Syracuse, N.Y.: Syracuse University Press, 1991. A collection of biographical and critical essays on the life and works of Smith. Includes bibliographical references and index.

Storey, Mark. "Why Stevie Smith Matters." *Critical Quarterly* 21 (Summer, 1979): 41-55. Storey analyzes the ways in which Smith makes critics uncomfortable: her apparent lack of development, the drawings, the singing voice, the simplicity.

Williams, Jonathan. "Much Further Out than You Thought." *Parnassus: Poetry in Review* 2 (Spring/Summer, 1974): 105-127. This article is a meditation by a personal friend of Smith, most interesting for its quotations from a 1963 interview.

Allyson Booth;
bibliography updated by the editors

William Jay Smith

Born: Winnfield, Louisiana; April 22, 1918

Principal poetry

Poems, 1947
Celebration at Dark, 1950
Laughing Time, 1956
Poems, 1947-1957, 1957
Boy Blue's Book of Beasts, 1957 (juvenile)
Puptents and Pebbles, 1959 (juvenile)
Typewriter Town, 1960 (juvenile)
What Did I See? 1962
The Tin Can and Other Poems, 1966
Mr. Smith and Other Nonsense, 1968
New and Selected Poems, 1970
The Traveler's Tree: New and Selected Poems, 1980
Plain Talk, 1988
The World Below the Window: Poems, 1937-1997, 1998
Here Is My Heart: Love Poems, 1999
The Cherokee Lottery, 2000

Other literary forms

Although William Jay Smith published mainly original poetry for adults and children, he also compiled a number of volumes of poetry, including *The Golden Journey: Poems for Young People* (1965) with Louise Bogan and *Poems From France* (1967). He edited numerous books of poetry and adapted the Swedish poetry of Elsa Beskow, *Children of the Forest*, published in 1970. His publication of Valéry Larbaud's *Poems of a Multimillionaire* (1955) and *The Selected Writings of Jules Laforgue* (1956) established him as an important translator. He translated *Two Plays by Charles Bertin* in 1970.

In addition to poetry, Smith wrote essays and a study of well-known literary hoaxes and lampoons, *The Spectra Hoax* (1961). *The Streaks of the Tulip*, a collection of literary criticism, appeared in 1972. He published *Children and Poetry: A Selective Annotated Bibliography* in 1969. He has contributed to a vast number of poetry anthologies and has presented television programs on poetry for children.

Achievements

Probably the most impressive accomplishment of William Jay Smith is his poetry's great diversity in form and content. Although he demonstrates a conviction that poetic feeling can best be developed through submission to discipline and form, he expresses more expansive feelings in his free verse experiments later in his career. Despite the judgment of some critics that he sacrifices rhyme for wordiness, he apparently reached a point in his career that evoked a deepening range. His later complexity is evident in *New and Selected Poems*, a somewhat slender volume that indicates evolving sensibilities and a shift in his philosophy of composition.

William Jay Smith (© Lawrence B. Fink)

As diversified as his experience, his poetry has many voices. Sometimes delicate and aesthetic, and at others intense and compelling, his range of subject and tone can extend from rich, courtly, precise phrases to witty, nonsense verses for children. Smith has the power to rejuvenate his readers. Serious statements are frequently disguised as children's whimsy to gain distance from reality and thereby create a more complex imaginative realm.

In his long, distinguished career, he has produced more than fifty books of poetry in a carefully crafted array of verse forms and patterns. For his versatile talents, Smith has received numerous awards, including *Poetry* magazine's Young Poet's Prize (1945), a Ford Foundation Grant in drama in 1964, the Union League Prize in Poetry from *Poetry* magazine in 1964, three National Endowment for the Arts Grants (1972, 1975, 1989), an Ingram Merrill Foundation Grant in 1982, a California Children's Book and Video Awards recognition for excellence in 1990, and the French Academy's medal for Service to French Language in 1991. He served as the Poet Laureate Consultant to poetry from 1968 to 1970.

Biography

William Jay Smith was born in Winnfield, Louisiana, in 1918, the older of two sons, to Jay and Georgia Ella (Campster) Smith. His memoir *Army Brat* (1980), describes his early life at Jefferson Barracks, an Army post near St. Louis, Missouri, where his father was an enlisted clarinetist in the Sixth Infantry Band. Smith recounts his generally happy life on the base with his family, enlivened by his father's experiment with making and selling an illegal, alcoholic beverage, "home brew." It was there that Smith learned his mother was part Choctaw Indian, a revelation that answered some questions about his and his mother's striking physical characteristics and generated a lifelong interest in his heritage.

Because his father continued to reenlist in the Army, Smith lived at Jefferson Barracks until he graduated from Cleveland High School. He attended Washington University in St. Louis on a scholarship, where he developed a friendship with a shy, quiet student named Thomas Lanier Williams, who later became better known as the playwright Tennessee Williams. Together, they reveled in the works of T. S. Eliot, William Butler

Yeats, and other younger English poets, as well as those of Robert Frost and Wallace Stevens.

Smith earned his B.A. in 1939, and on the same day in 1941 on which he was awarded his master's degree in French, he received his draft notice. He was reassigned from naval reserve to regular duty in the Navy and was soon ordered to report to Pearl Harbor. While completing his training, he sent two recently written poems to *Poetry*, the Chicago magazine of verse and learned shortly before he left that one of them had been accepted for publication.

After the war, Smith pursued graduate study at Columbia University from 1946 to 1947, attended Oxford University as a Rhodes scholar from 1947 to 1948, and was at the University of Florence from 1948 to 1950. He became a lecturer in English at Williams College, Williamstown, Massachusetts, in 1951. He accepted the post of writer in residence at Arena Stage, Washington, D.C., and at Hollins College in Virginia.

Smith's impressive literary career spans various positions, including Library of Congress consultant in poetry (1968-1970), editorial consultant for Grove Press (1952-1953), poetry reviewer of *Harper's* (1961-1964), and Boy Scouts of America Committeeman (1962-1963). He was a freelance writer in Pownal, Vermont, and served a term in the Vermont House of Representatives from 1960 to 1962. In addition to numerous lectures at colleges, clubs, and book fairs, Smith presented the award-winning television program for children on National Educational Television, "Mr. Smith and Other Nonsense," in 1970.

Smith married Barbara Howes, a poet, on October 1, 1947, the two becoming parents of two boys, David Emerson and Gregory Jay. Following their divorce in June, 1964, Smith married Sonja Haussman. He has visited or resided in England, Italy, Haiti, and France, and has traveled on cultural exchange visits for the Department of State to Japan and East Asia in 1969, and to the Soviet Union, Eastern Europe, and the Middle East in 1970. An avid traveler and painter, he eventually settled in Cummington, Massachusetts.

ANALYSIS

As a lyric poet, William Jay Smith celebrates the things of this world with a sensuous delight. Yet, underlying his poems is a sadness and a helplessness in the face of ruin, decay, and death. Loving harmony and measure and hating sloppiness in any form, Smith restrains his emotional response to loss in somewhat muted and reflective statements. Distrusting emotional extravagance, he turns his attention to seasons, places, times of day, and creatures of the natural world with detailed precision. He seems obsessed with time, change, and ultimate deprivation, approaching these themes in his early poetry in conventional forms with polished, disciplined language.

Later in his career, his creative vision shifted from Romantic to the prophetic, from a concern (similar to John Keats's) with truth and beauty to a more prophetic tone suggestive of T. S. Eliot. His free-verse mode acquired black subject matter, darker imagery, and a more pessimistic view of individuals and society facing imminent death and destruction. Surrealistic images depict Smith's preoccupation with the darker side of experience that experimentation with open forms allows him to express.

POEMS, 1947-1957

This early collection of Smith's poetry contains a sampling of everything he had attempted to that time and demonstrates his range. Many poems echo the vivid imagery employed by Wallace Stevens, whom Smith admired, combined with Smith's own austere verses.

"American Primitive," one of his best-known poems, describes a man who commits suicide for some reason concerning money. Reminiscent of Edwin Arlington Robinson's poem "Richard Cory," the poem comments on the inability of money to supply happiness: "There he is in a shower of gold;/ His pockets are stuffed with folding money,/ His lips are blue, and his hands feel cold." The poem's events are recounted in a singsong voice of a child who observes the chilling sight of the man hanging in the hall:

> Look at him there in his stovepipe hat,
> His high-top shoes, and his handsome collar;
> Only my Daddy could look like that,
> And I love my Daddy like he loves his Dollar.

The same flat declaration is seen in "Plain Talk," a twelve-line poem that concerns the poet's recollection of his father's assessment of people "so dumb" that "they don't know beans from an old bedstead."

Laughing Time

At a time when few collections of poetry were being published, Smith wrote this 1956 volume with his son David in mind. Anxious to capture the way a four-year-old sees the world, Smith observed his son carefully, hoping to see things the way David saw them. Smith insists that children think in images and generally in rapid shifts and accordingly writes in a lively, playful manner. He maintains that, most important, children's poetry requires the skill, virtuosity, and technical expertise of poetry for adults; it should not just adapt writing and ideas to the needs of the young but should do more toward bringing children within reach of adult perception and thought.

Smith carries children's poems forward with nouns and verbs, not adjectives, and attempts leaps and connections similar to those characteristic of young children. Included are limericks, alphabets, and recipes, with fantastic description. A toaster is a "silver-scaled Dragon with jaws flaming red"; "Old Mrs. Caribou lives by a lake/ In the heart of darkest Make-Believe." Directions for reaching "The Land of Ho-Ho-Hum" are, "When you want to go where you please,/ Just sit down in an old valise,/ And fly off over the apple trees."

For children

Smith finds children's poetry, with its wide use of strange forms and the range of its nonsense, a liberating device. Dedicated to his two sons, *Boy Blue's Book of Beasts*, illustrated by Juliet Kepes, describes animals humorously and imaginatively and plays games, as in "Tapir."

> How odd it would be if ever a Tapir,
> Wrapped in gold and silver paper
> And tied with a bow in the shape of a T,
> Sat there in the corner beside the tree
> When I tiptoed down at six in the morning—
> A Christmas present from you to me!

Puptents and Pebbles, for Smith's son Gregory, and also illustrated by Juliet Kepes, contains delightful excursions into nonsense rhymes for letters of the alphabet: "M is for mask/ It changes a lot/ To add a new face/ To the face you have got;/ Then the person you are/ Is the person you're not."

One section of *Typewriter Town*, dedicated to Smith's two sons and for "all other aficionados of the typewriter," contains limericks about "Typewriter People," accompanied by humorous sketches of them done by typewriter keys:

> There was an Old Lady named Crockett
> Who went to put a plug in a socket;
> But her hands were so wet
> She flew up like a jet
> And came roaring back down like a rocket!

The Tin Can and Other Poems

Smith maintains that the poet should always venture into new things. In this 1966 volume of verse, his open form of poetry achieves depths unknown in his earlier work. The long, rambling lines of "The Tin Can" echo Walt Whitman's "Song of Myself": "O bodies my body has known! Bodies my body has touched and/ remembered—in beds, in baths, in streams, on fields and/ streets—will you remember?" The more personal subject matter of this poem perhaps lends itself better to free verse. The title refers to the Japanese custom of personal seclusion for meditation, called going into the "tin can." Through a series of surrealistic images, the poet takes the reader from a New England winter landscape to a descent into his subconscious in his effort "to confront the horrible, black underside of the world." Beginning with quiet, muted feelings, the poem builds to whirls of extravagant and convoluted self-recognitions and searches out his creative anxieties as he faces an "unseen immensity that will never be contained."

New and Selected Poems

Four poems in this 1970 volume are new and reflect Smith's more extensive use of free verse. "Fishing for Albacore" describes a fishing trip the poet took with his ten-year-old son, which serves as an initiation into manhood, as he began to understand the "beauty and terror of nature."

The darker themes of Smith's later poetry continue in "What Train Will Come?" The poem's title is taken from an inscription on a subway wall—"What train will come to bear me back across so wide a town?"—and is used as a refrain throughout the poem to suggests that the tracks foretell an individual and societal path to destruction. Intensification is achieved through the association of the underground train with death and dissolution.

The Cherokee Lottery

Smith relates the sad and disturbing story of the forced removal of Cherokee, Choctaw, Chickasaw, Creek, and Seminole Indians to the Oklahoma Territory. More than four thousand of the eighteen thousand died in the harrowing ordeal remembered as the Trail of Tears. Smith fashions imaginative and historical episodes. The title poem describes the lottery that determined the disposition of Native American lands. Other poems describe the first day of the move as the Indians mournfully begin their tragic journey. Other poems detail Sequoyah's creation of the Cherokee alphabet, the death of Seminole chief Osceola, and unforgettable images of starving Native Americans devouring pumpkins in a field. Vividly, Smith depicts a buffalo hunt, a Choctaw stick-ball game, and the theft of unattended baggage of a traveling Shakespeare troupe by Coachooche, who reappeared wearing Prince Hamlet's attire.

Other major works

plays: *The Straw Market*, pr. 1965; *Army Brat*, pr. 1980.

nonfiction: *The Spectra Hoax*, 1961; *Children and Poetry: A Selective Annotated Bibliography*, 1969; *The Streaks of the Tulip*, 1972; *Army Brat, a Memoir*, 1980; *Green*, 1980.

translations: *Poems of a Multimillionaire*, 1955 (of Valéry Larbaud); *The Selected Writings of Jules Laforgue*, 1956; *Children of the Forest*, 1970 (of Elsa Beskow); *Two Plays by Charles Bertin*, 1970; *The Pirate Book*, 1972 (of Lennart Hellsing); *The Telephone*, 1977 (of Kornei Chukovsky); *Agadir*, 1979 (of Artur Lundkvist); *The Pact: My Friendship with Isak Dinesen*, 1983 (of Thorkild Bjoernvig); *Moral Tales*, 1985 (of Jules Laforgue); *Wild Bouquet*, 1985 (of Henry Martinson); *Collected Translations: Italian, French, Spanish, Portuguese*, 1985; *Eternal Moment*, 1988 (of Sandor Weoeres); *The Madman and the Medusa*, 1989 (with Sonja Haussmann Smith).

children's literature: *My Little Book of Big and Little*, 1963 (3 volumes; illustrated by Don Bolognese); *Ho for a Hat!*, 1964 (illustrated by Ivan Chermayeff); *If I Had a Boat*, 1966 (illustrated by Bolognese); *Around My Room and Other Poems*, 1969 (illustrated by Don Madden); *Grandmother Ostrich and Other Poems*, 1969 (illustrated by Madden); *The Key*, 1982; *Birds and Beasts*, 1990 (illustrated by Jacques Hnizdovsky).

edited texts: *Herrick*, 1962; *The Golden Journey: Poems for Young People*, 1965 (with Louise Bogan); *Poems from France*, 1967; *Poems from Italy*, 1973; *Light Verse and Satires of Witter Bynner*, 1976; *Brazilian Poetry*, 1984 (with Emanuel Brasil); *Behind the King's Kitchen*, 1992 (with Carol Ra); *The Sun Is Up*, 1996 (with Ra).

Bibliography

Dickey, James. *Babel to Byzantium: Poets and Poetry Now*. New York: Farrar, Straus and Giroux, 1968. Dickey, an established poet himself, offers a brief but enthusiastic evaluation of Smith's place in American poetry.

Smith, William Jay. *Army Brat, a Memoir*. New York: Persea Books, 1980. Smith details his early life as a military child. This coming-of-age book contains insight into Smith's discoveries of language and his poetic talent.

_______. "A Frame for Poetry." In *Poets on Poetry*, edited by Howard Nemerov. New York: Basic Books, 1966. Smith explores several of his own poems, commenting extensively on their genesis, his writing process, and creativity.

"William Jay Smith." In *Contemporary Authors, New Revision Series*. Vol. 44. Detroit, Michigan: Gale Research Group, 1994. This article provides an excellent overview of Smith's life and career, focusing on critical attention to his later work, specifically *Army Brat*.

Mary Hurd

W. D. Snodgrass

Born: Wilkinsburg, Pennsylvania; January 5, 1926

Principal poetry

Heart's Needle, 1959

After Experience: Poems and Translations, 1968

Remains: Poems, 1970 (as S. S. Gardons)
The Führer Bunker, 1977
If Birds Build with Your Hair, 1979
The Boy Made of Meat, 1983
Magda Goebbels, 1983
D. D. Byrde Callyng Jennie Wrenn, 1984
A Locked House, 1986
Kinder Capers, 1986
Selected Poems, 1957-1987, 1987
W. D.'s Midnight Carnival, 1988 (with paintings by DeLoss McGraw)
The Death of Cock Robin, 1989 (with paintings by McGraw)
Each in His Season, 1993
The Fuehrer Bunker: The Complete Cycle, 1995

Other literary forms

Although W. D. Snodgrass is known primarily as a poet, he has also published criticism and translations. *In Radical Pursuit: Critical Essays and Lectures* (1975) offers original perspectives on the works of Homer, Dante, William Shakespeare, Fyodor Dostoevski, and others, but its greatest interest lies in several essays in which Snodgrass follows Edgar Allan Poe in giving his own "philosophy of composition." His translations are diverse and interesting. *Gallows Songs* (1967) and the translations included in *After Experience* (1968), *Miorita* (1975), and *Six Troubadour Songs* (1977), offer a diverse selection of poetry which includes the Rumanian folk poem "Miorita" and works by Christian Morgenstern, Gérald de Nerval, Arthur Rimbaud, Rainer Maria Rilke, and Victor Hugo. They are effective English poems that remain faithful to the originals. Snodgrass also became interested in autobiographical sketches, six of which have appeared in magazines.

Achievements

W. D. Snodgrass's first book, *Heart's Needle*, won the Pulitzer Prize in 1960. He was the recipient of numerous fellowships and grants, from *Hudson Review* (1958), the National Institute of Arts and Letters (1960), the Ford Foundation (1963), the National Endowment for the Arts (1966), the Guggenheim Foundation (1972), and the Academy of American Poets (1973). His output, though not as prolific as that of others, has nevertheless won numerous accolades and honors in addition to the prestigious Pulitzer: the Ingram Merrill Foundation Award in 1958; the Longview Foundation Literary Award in 1959; the Poetry Society of America citation in 1960; the British Guinness Award in 1961, for *Heart's Needle*; the Yaddo Resident Award in 1960, 1961, 1965, 1976, 1977; the Miles Poetry Award in 1966; the Bicentennial medal from College of William and Mary in 1976; the Centennial Medal from the government of Romania in 1977; and the first prize for translations of Romanian letters from the Colloquium of Translators and Editors, Siaia, Romania in 1995.

W. D. Snodgrass

Biography

William DeWitt Snodgrass was born in Wilkinsburg, Pennsylvania, on January 5, 1926. After a normal boyhood he enrolled at nearby Geneva College in 1944. Two years later, he was drafted into the Navy and sent to the Pacific. For the first time, he was truly on his own, away from home and familiar surroundings. World War II and its aftermath carved itself into his memory, and he would draw material from this experience for his poetry.

Following his discharge, two events occurred that were very important in his development as a poet: his marriage and his transfer to the University of Iowa to join the writers' workshop. At Iowa he found a group of talented students and skilled teachers who encouraged him to perfect his technique. Although he eventually broke with his teachers, who preferred highly intellectual poems following the traditions of the French Symbolists and the English Metaphysical poets, he would later tell an interviewer that he would never have written poetry if he had not gone there. He remained at Iowa for seven years, completing work for an undergraduate degree, an M.A., and an M.F.A. While his years there might have made him into a poet, they had a disastrous effect on his marriage, which ended in a divorce and separation from his young daughter in 1953. Snodgrass tried to adjust to this experience through his writing and through psychoanalysis; the result was the long poem "Heart's Needle," a two-and-a-half-year chronicle written while the events were taking place. The immediacy of the experience and the intensity of his feeling of loss help to give the poem its power.

After leaving the University of Iowa, Snodgrass was a college professor and writer in residence at several universities, including Cornell, Wayne State, and Syracuse, as well as a frequent participant in writing conferences. In 1979, he became Distinguished Visiting Professor of English at the University of Delaware in Newark, and he remained at that institution, retiring as Distinguished Professor Emeritus in 1994. He has since taught and lectured at writers' workshops and conferences across the United States.

Analysis

He once remarked that few American poets ever have a true "mature" period, and, perhaps to ensure such maturity, he has not rushed into print until he is thoroughly satisfied with what he has written. The result is that he has written comparatively little, although his work shows continued growth and variety. After the purely "confessional" poems of *Heart's Needle*, he developed distance and objectivity in *After Experience*, but without losing the human voice of the earlier volume. In *The Führer Bunker* he made a radical departure in an ambitious effort to draw believable portraits of Adolf Hitler and his principal associates during their final days. In *Selected Poems, 1957-1987* he collected the best poems from the three earlier volumes and added a number of new poems, which had mostly appeared in hard-to-find, limited editions. For his achievements he has received a number of poetry awards, and his poems are frequently included in anthologies.

Snodgrass's style has been equally innovative. Breaking from his teachers and from the prevailing trends of contemporary poetry, he chose a simple, lyrical style rather than the obscure, intellectual style his models provided. His language is plain, colloquial, and candid, and his images and symbols are drawn from nature or ordinary life and experience. In prosody he is a traditionalist, employing complex stanza forms and intricate rhyme schemes. In most of his poems the form is wedded to the content so that they work together to reveal the meaning. In addition, the poems are dramatic. They are concerned with real problems of this world—problems of identity, marriage, academia, art, war—and the persona is faced with a choice. What he decides is usually either the effect or the cause of the action. Snodgrass's reputation is secure because he speaks so directly about these universal problems.

Henry David Thoreau's words in *Walden* (1854), "I should not talk so much about myself if there were anybody else whom I knew as well," could easily be applied to most of W. D. Snodgrass's early poetry. It has been called "confessional poetry" because of the intense focus on the poet's private life and concerns. Snodgrass, often labeled one of the founders of the confessional movement during the 1950's, used himself as the subject of his first volume of poetry; but while his poems are an examination of his own experience, he does not fall into the role of the moralist, making generalizations about what he has learned and suggesting how others can find happiness through his example. One might think that such poetry would be of little interest to anyone other than the poet. Why should the reader be interested in his problems of adjustment, which are not really extraordinary experiences? Other confessional poets have written about insanity, homosexuality, and suicide, but Snodgrass is concerned with mundane affairs, many having to do with the family—leaving home for the first time, the loss of innocence, illusions, and love. It is this quality of familiarity, however, which accounts for the appeal of Snodgrass's first volume.

The persona developed in the poems is honest, candid, and sincere. Snodgrass says in his essay "Finding a Poem":

> I am left with a very old-fashioned measure of a poem's worth—the depth of its sincerity. . . . Our only hope as artists is to continually ask ourselves, "Am I writing what I *really* think? Not what is acceptable; not what my favorite intellectual would think in this situation; not what I wish I felt. Only what I cannot help thinking."

Most important, the persona is human with a voice that one might expect to hear in the world. At times he is pompous, absurd, and silly, but the poetry reveals that he is aware of this weakness. He speaks in this world, about this world, and the reader is better able to understand his own problems of adjustment by living through them with the poet.

HEART'S NEEDLE

Several of the poems in *Heart's Needle* are concerned with identity, with discovering one's own name. Far from being a mere label or external description, a name expresses the profound reality of the being who carries it. In the Old Testament, creation is not completed until all things brought into existence have a name. Further, a name carries with it the possibility of knowledge. By reason of its nature a name imparts knowledge, and by one's name one can reveal to others who he is.

In "MHTIS . . . OU TIS," which is dedicated to R. M. Powell, Snodgrass's psychotherapist, he uses the story of Odysseus escaping from the Cyclops by a trick, identifying himself as no man (*ou tis*): "I had escaped, by trickery, as no man." This surrender of his identity, he realizes, is a much worse fate, and he implores his psychotherapist to restore him. He calls him his "dead blind guide" because Powell's strategy with him was to remain out of sight at all times, forcing Snodgrass to speak and clarify his problems in his own way and in his own words. The poem closes with these lines: "My dear blind guide, you lead me here to claim/ Still waters that will never wash my hand,/ To kneel by my old face and know my name."

The problem of a name occurs again in "A Cardinal." It is about a poet who goes into the woods for inspiration but finds that he cannot complete his verses because he cannot escape the crass, materialistic world even there. In the underbrush are "beer cans and lover's trash." He hears the squeal of the mill whistles, the whine of the freight cars, the trucks on the super-turnpike, and the chant of the air cadets marching. When he sees a cardinal above him with a green insect in his beak, he recognizes it as a confirmation of the evil that is in all things. Nature is "red in tooth and claw," or, as Snodgrass says it, "celebrate(s) this ordinal/ of the red beak and claw." In the bird-eat-insect, man-eat-man world in which he lives, he is foolish to think that he can write poetry, but then comes the turning point in the poem. He realizes his absurdity in blaming his lack of energy and creativity on something outside himself. When he hears the cardinal sing, he hears it as a song of natural self-assertion: "The world's not done to me;/ it is what I do." In asserting himself, the bird sings his name, confident in his identity, announcing it to the world: "I music out my name/ and what I tell is who/ in all the world I am."

Snodgrass announces his own name in "These Trees Stand. . . ." The line "Snodgrass is walking through the universe" is the natural final step in the process of a very personal poet naming his own name. It is his announcement that he has found his identity and will proclaim it to the whole universe. Snodgrass admits that it is "one of the most absurd and pompous things" he has ever heard, but pomposity has its place in poetry too, as long as one is aware that he is being pompous. He may not be able to reconcile estranged lovers or alter civilization's downward course, but he can wipe his glasses on his shirt to see himself and the world around him more clearly.

Being able to name one's own name is an important concern of a confessional poet such as Snodgrass; acceptance of loss is another. A number of his early poems are about loss. "Ten Days Leave" has a young soldier return to his home to find that his childhood is gone forever. In "Orpheus," he assumes a literary mask in a futile but necessary attempt at rescuing Eurydice, whose only crime was to love, which is impossible in a world ruled "by graft and debt." His most sustained and profound treatment of loss, however, is in the ten-poem sequence, "Heart's Needle."

The title of the poem comes from an old Irish story of a man who, when told of his daughter's death, says, "And an only daughter is the needle of the heart." For Snodgrass, the "Heart's Needle" is the loss of his daughter Cynthia through divorce. The poem in ten parts chronicles a two-and-a-half year period that he spent trying to adjust to this loss. The poem records the two battles that the poet has to wage. The first is external, the fight with his former wife which led to the divorce and which continued afterward: "Our states have stood so long at war." The other is the internal one of love and guilt. He loves his child and does not want to give her up, but in the succeeding years he marries again and has another child. His attempts to maintain a close relationship with Cynthia are only causing her further emotional harm. He is left with the dilemma: "I cannot fight/ or let her go."

Images of war, trapped animals, blasted lives, newly planted seeds, and withered flowers are interspersed with the passing of the seasons, which show the breakup of the marriage and the growing distance between him and his daughter. It is the imagery rather than any overt statement that shows the reader that the poet was able to maintain his identity and establish a workable relationship with his daughter. The poem begins in the winter but ends in the spring. The first poem is set within the context of the "cold war," with soldiers falling and freezing in the snows of Korea, but the final poem is set in the park, where Snodgrass and his daughter roast hot dogs and feed the swans. Earlier, there is an image of a fox with his paw in a trap, but in the final poem the red fox is trotting around bachelor pens. Together, Snodgrass and his daughter look at the bears imprisoned behind bars, but he has found a way to liberate himself through the knowledge that even though they are separated, "You are still my daughter."

Each part of the poem is carefully crafted; the third section is a good example. It is still early in the separation, but the unrest and pain are apparent. The poem begins with the image of two parents holding the hands of a child and together swinging the child over a puddle; but as soon as the hurdle is successfully cleared, they "stiffen and pull apart." He recalls that they were reading in the newspapers about the Korean War, about the cold and pain, about the land that was won and lost, and about the prisoners that were taken. The outcome of the battles, paralleling those of his own marriage, was satisfactory to no one. Then he returns to the child's hands and remembers that once in a playful game he tugged too hard, dislocating her wrist. The resolution of the poem recalls the decision that Solomon once had to make in a dispute over a child between two women, each claiming to be its true mother. Like the real mother in that story, Snodgrass offers to give his daughter up for her own good. The three episodes and the conclusion are closely tied together and reflect the inner struggle of the poet. Even the rhyme scheme (*aabccb*) reflects it. Each stanza begins with a couplet, but the second rhyme is delayed in each to emphasize the separation and loss recorded in the last line of each stanza. To reinforce this, the sixth line of each stanza is shortened from four feet to three.

The seasons mark the passing of time and the changing relationships of a man and his daughter. It is not a sentimental recital of events but rather an honest treatment of hurt, shared blame, and a growing awareness of their separateness. Snodgrass has said that a poet must write what he really thinks and feels, and in "Heart's Needle" he has apparently been successful.

Much of Snodgrass's life has been in the world of academe, and he has written about it in a number of his poems. "The Campus on the Hill" is based on his life while teaching at Cornell, but it could represent many colleges during the 1950's, marked by the complacency of the students in a world that seemed to be falling apart. "The Men's Room in the College Chapel" suggests an inversion of the traditional view of man's spiritual nature triumphing over his animal nature. Whereas earlier cultures retired to caves to carve totemic drawings to their "dark gods" or to the catacombs to write "pious mottos of resistance," the subversive humans of today go into the four gray walls to "scribble of sex and excrement,/ draw bestial pictures and sign their name."

In "April Inventory" the poet turns to himself as a teacher to list his own weaknesses and strengths. Spring is an appropriate season to watch the catalpa tree and the cherry blossom; but then, so quickly, the blossoms fall. The poet realizes that his own period of productivity will be similarly brief, and so far he has not accomplished much that can be measured. The recognition goes to "the solid scholars" who "get the degrees, the jobs, the dollars," but they also get ulcers. He cannot bring himself to read secondary sources, plot summaries, or memorize dates. He prefers to teach "Whitehead's notions," or a song of Gustav Mahler, or to show a child the colors of a luna moth. He prefers to learn "to name my own name," to give enjoyment to the woman he loves, and to ease an old man's dying. At the end of the poem he seems content that gentleness and loveliness are also important, and that these will survive where other accomplishments will fail.

Snodgrass does not often write satire, but he does in "The Examination." At first reading, the poem appears to be a sinister fantasy of black-robed figures with single eyes and ragged nails performing a lobotomy on a bird man named Garuda. It seems to have happened long ago and far away because they mark on the brain "with a crow's quill dipped into India ink" and use silver saws to cut away the dangerous areas, but they have an anesthetic, which enables them to remove the brain from the skull and stitch up the incision so that there is no seam. It is only in the last few stanzas that one realizes just who these black-robed figures are, who Garuda is, and what are some of the greatest failings in educational institutions. Snodgrass's professors are those who fear any challenge to their own established systems and thus clip Garuda's wings so that he can "fly no higher than his superiors fly." The irony is that even after being stripped of his powers of creative thought, of his reproductive powers, and his sensitivity, their "candidate" will return to thank them and become a black-robed professor himself. Snodgrass's experience has taught him that too often it is the academic conformist who receives the high grades and is encouraged to go on to graduate school, where he is again dutifully rewarded for recalling his professor's opinions and returning them to him in an examination.

Art interpretation

A number of poems on specific paintings are also related to Snodgrass's teaching, since the idea for them grew out of his substituting, for one night, in an adult education course on art. He acknowledged that he knew very little about art, but that did not stop him from teaching that night or from writing poems about the paintings that interested him most. Snodgrass's poems on paintings raise questions that the viewer might have when first looking at a painting, and he offers a guide to understanding what the artist intended to say, a short course in art appreciation through the eyes of a novice art critic. Yet, he is writing poetry, not interpretive notes for a catalog of an art exhibition.

The five paintings he selects are carefully chosen and share a common theme. In the essay "Poems About Paintings," Snodgrass says that this theme was "the transformation of matter into energy." In "Matisse: 'The Red Studio,'" the paintings on the walls draw all the energy of the artist so that he disappears completely, leaving only a blank space at the center of the canvas: "His own room drank him." As his art objects become real, he becomes unreal and is transformed or absorbed into them. In "Vuillard: 'The Mother and Sister of the Artist,'" Snodgrass sees a devouring relationship between the mother and her daughter. All things in the room belong to her and even the child is being transformed into one of her mother's objects. The color of the daughter's dress is the same as the wallpaper behind her, and she appears to be vanishing into the wall. "Monet: 'Les Nympheas'" seems to absorb the viewer in the same way that it does the clouds, which appear to be beneath the lilies in the water.

The last two poems in the series are longer and add a wider significance to the theme. In "Manet: 'The Execution of the Emperor Maximilian,'" Snodgrass is concerned with the public's reaction to the work. Based on a historical event that deeply disturbed all of Europe, Édouard Manet's painting treated the execution with cold detachment. It is even comic in comparison to Francisco Goya's "The Executions of May 3, 1808," upon which it is based, and the public almost rioted when Manet's painting was first shown. Snodgrass's poem is a variation of the theme of "transformation of matter into energy" because its focus is on the energy aroused in the viewer.

In order to include the reaction to the painting in his poem, Snodgrass uses two voices. One, interspersed throughout the poem, gives a poetical prose account of the historical events of Maximilian's life and death. The major part of the poem is the voice of a viewer asking questions and making observations concerning the meaning of the painting in a colloquial, prosy sort of verse. He notes the strangeness of the three portrait groups. The dapper Mexican soldiers in the firing squad, "like ballet girls," are dressed in "natty" European uniforms. One of the soldiers, given a prominent place in the painting, looks "less like a penguin" than the others, but he seems totally unconcerned with what is happening as he inspects his gun. The second group, the peasants watching from the wall, are totally unconcerned with what is happening before their eyes. The viewer says, "Surely someone must come/ Declare significance, solve how these things relate/ To freedom, to their life's course, to eternity." The third group, Maximilian and the two men being shot with him, is the most perplexing because of their total insignificance in the painting. One cannot even be sure which one is the emperor: "Which IS the man? No doubt he should stand at the center,/ Yet who gets shot in a frock coat and sombrero?"

Snodgrass's interpretation of the painting emphasizes the complete breakdown of the order in the state as the Mexican soldiers are given European uniforms and the "Emperor of all the Firmament" is clad in a Mexican sombrero. The indifference of all the principals signals the rise of individualism and relativism where technology (the soldier inspecting his gun) is more important than a human life. By implication, Manet shows in his depiction of Maximilian's death the complete insignificance of any individual life. This bleak view of the world, perhaps more than anything else, caused the furor which first greeted the painting, and Snodgrass has captured it in his poem.

The last painting in the group, "Van Gogh: 'The Starry Night,'" is the clearest representation of pure energy engulfing matter, and Snodgrass emphasizes this in his poem with his contrast between the solidly built town and the swirling, rushing, violet sky overhead. The ordered rows of houses enclose the ordered lives within, while the sky is "a spume of ancient/ vacuum shuddering to reclaim/ its child." To capture the energy of the painting and to show its contrast between order and disorder, Snodgrass uses a form with two alternating styles: Simple, orderly blocks of words describe the town, and wild, disorganized arrangements of words depict the sky. In addition, he has interspersed throughout the poem quotations from Vincent Van Gogh's letters, as if to remind the reader that behind the colors and shapes there was an energetic mind fervently at work. In this last poem on paintings, Snodgrass effectively combines form and content to create a remarkable poetic equivalent for the charged energy of the painting.

Commentary on inhumanity

One theme that is pervasive in Snodgrass's poetry is man's inhumanity to man, especially as it is revealed in war. What is human nature when it is sorely tested? "After Experience Taught Me . . ." asks whether the most basic law is that of self-preservation. It is a poem using alternating voices, that of the philosopher Spinoza and that of a military drill officer. Contrasted as they are in language and approach, they nevertheless agree that man's ultimate wish is "to be, to act, to live." In the last stanza the poet's voice speaks for the first time to challenge them both: "What evil, what unspeakable crime/ Have you made your life worth?"

Snodgrass raises a similar question in "A Visitation," in which he allows the ghost of Adolf Eichmann to return and confront the speaker with the charge that had he been living in Eichmann's time and in his place he would have done the same things, for "You've chained men to a steel beam on command." Snodgrass is attempting to say that Eichmann was a human being who went terribly wrong, but he was a human being. One must remember that humans do have this possibility for evil, even great evil. To deny this possibility is to ignore a vital part of human nature, and so Eichmann's ghost returns to issue a warning.

The Führer Bunker

Snodgrass's fullest treatment of the evil brought out by war is in *The Führer Bunker* (originally published in 1977 and reissued in 1995 as *The Fuehrer Bunker: The Complete Cycle*). The book is an ambitious attempt to portray the last month of Adolf Hitler's life as he and his faithful followers huddle in the bunker preparing for their deaths. In twenty poems, Snodgrass allows them, through soliloquies and dramatic monologues, to reveal their true selves, which they have hidden from others and even from themselves. Moreover, for each speaker the poet selects a different verse form.

Contradictions, character flaws, and irrational acts are vividly portrayed. Magda Goebbels reveals her plan to kill herself and her six children "to preserve them from disloyalty." The contradiction inherent in killing someone to preserve him escapes her, and this is underscored by the modified villanelle form she uses. The complex but artificial verse form suits her character. Four of the poems are spoken by Albert Speer. He appears to be always in control; even his stanzas show the mind of the architect as each line becomes progressively longer to form a one-sided pyramid. Yet he is like his friend the cancer specialist who is unknowingly dying of cancer: "He neglects his knowing." Hermann Fegelein, Eva Braun's brother-in-law, deserves death for many reasons, but he is sentenced to die for the wrong reason, being accused of complicity in Himmler's treason. He says, "I wish/ to sweet shit Id of known." Eva considers her death as the reason for her living.

Adolf Hitler, quite predictably, is the most complex of the nine characters who are allowed to speak. He reveals his childhood fantasies, his sexual perversions, and his misplaced affections. He shows his concern for his dog Blondi, but he is oblivious to the torture and death of his own supporters, cursing them as being "Too gutless/ Even to get killed." On his last day, he is reckoning his place in history by the millions whose death he has caused. Hitler reveals himself as almost pure evil. He reveals almost nothing about himself that would explain the devotion his last followers give to him, unless it is the purity of his evil and his power to accomplish it.

The Führer Bunker is a remarkable work. It was published as "A Cycle of Poems in Progress," and Snodgrass has added fifty new poems to the twenty original ones. One of the later poems is "Magda Goebbels 30 April 1945," in which he creates a different, but nevertheless appropriate, verse form to fit her character. Based on the nursery rhyme, the mother speaks to her six children to the tune of "Here we go round the mulberry bush," preparing them for the spoonful of cyanide that she is offering them: "This is the spoon we use to feed/ Men trapped in trouble or in need,/ When weakness or bad luck might lead/ Them to the hands of strangers."

Heinrich Himmler, head of the SS, is a new character added to the cast. Since he based his extermination policies on pseudoscientific experiments and theories, his three poems are written on graph paper in twenty-five-line acrostics. The first line begins with the letter A, and each subsequent line begins with the next letter of the alphabet, omitting only the X. The form shows a methodical but simplistic mind, one interested in logic and order but which fails to see the paradox of slaughtering millions to "benefit humanity." His poems are a defense of "the fully rational mind." Most of the poems, in fact, could be called rational defenses of each character's participation in this inhuman drama.

If Birds Build with Your Hair

If Birds Build with Your Hair contains a series of realistic poems on nature in which Snodgrass celebrates elm trees, cheery saplings, owls, barns, and other things. "Old Apple Trees" is about the life and individuality shown in these old trees, which have deep roots and twisted but distinct characters. They are different from the pruned, identical nursery trees of his neighbor. The trees are like the battered lives of workmen "bent too long over desks, engines, benches," but they are still full of life. This life is shown by the poet's visit to the Greek bar with the belly dancers and the blessing by the trees when he returns. The trees stand as white-haired elders of Thebes swaying in a dance ritual to remind readers of the poem that they must cherish life and their own uniqueness.

A Locked House

A Locked House returns to the confessional poetry of *Heart's Needle*, with several poems describing the breakup of a marriage. "Mutability" is a villanelle that demonstrates that in human relationships the only certainty is that of change: "It was all different; that, at least, seemed sure." "One Last Time" reveals one last act of gentleness, when the one he had loved caressed him publicly, but that was three years earlier, and it was not repeated. One of the most beautiful and poignant poems in the series is "Old Jewelry." Bracelets, rings, and pins were bought as "emblems of what lasts." They were precious things with long histories, but now they are "Laid out for buyers in a glass showcase," another symbol of love that dies. The title poem, "A Locked House," shows that one can lock a house to keep it safe, but there is no such security for those who live within it. People care for and protect their possessions, but the love of man and wife is lost or stolen before either realizes it. Now, when he returns, the house still stands locked and untouched, because those who wished to protect it have abandoned it.

COCK ROBIN POEMS

Snodgrass's poems on Cock Robin, in collaboration with painter DeLoss McGraw, seem to be a radical departure from his earlier work. The partnership began in 1982, when McGraw wrote to ask permission to use W. D. Snodgrass as a character in some color lithographs he was painting. These then led to a series of poems on Cock Robin in which "W.D." plays a key role. Normally, McGraw would first do the painting and Snodgrass would write a poem to accompany it. Since the project involved two of the poet's primary interests, poems on paintings and children's verse, the result was more a continuation rather than a break from his earlier poems. In college he had written many children's poems, and in 1962, he wrote "The Boy Made of Meat," which answers the question, "Why do they make boys always eat meat?" by listing a number of other foods that are more tasty and just as nutritious.

The Cock Robin poems are difficult to analyze because some are written in nonsense verse, as in "W. D., Don't Fear That Animal": "My hat leaps up when I behold/ A rhino in the sky;/ When crocodiles upon the wing/ Perch on my windowsill to sing." Such verse sounds like William Wordsworth recorded by Lewis Carroll. The more serious problem, however, is access to the paintings that prompted the poems, since they appeared in limited, hard-to-find editions. The book jacket of *Selected Poems, 1957-1987* has a color photograph, *W. D. Creates a Device for Escaping*, which helps to explain the references in the poem to the green foot and the red foot, the blood-red hands, and the arm and leg through the spokes of a wheel. W. D.'s burden in carrying the dead Cock Robin is reinforced by the references to Ixion's wheel and "Sisyface" (in reference to the mythical figure Sisyphus) rolling a stone. The paintings do not present a unified narrative, according to McGraw, but Snodgrass has attempted to give it some coherent structure. He calls Cock Robin a comic version of Orpheus, the god of song, and he is, at times, the alter ego of W. D. Based on the nursery rhyme, Snodgrass universalizes the symbol to represent the poet's life, death, and resurrection.

One poem, "The Charges Against Cock Robin," lists his crimes: the content and range of his songs, his dress, and his nonconformity. In other poems, his friends either desert him or practice character assassination. W. D. warns him of his enemies: "The Brutish are coming; the Brutish;/ The Rude-Coats with snares and bum-drumming!" When Cock Robin is killed, unlike the original poem, no one will accept the blame, not even the sparrow. W. D. does escape, however, disguised as Cock Robin, and near the end of the sequence, phoenixlike, he rises from the ashes.

Despite the fact that the series of poems deals with serious issues, Snodgrass never loses the light touch of nursery rhyme. One of the poems in *Kinder Capers*, "A Darkling Alphabet," appears to be a children's alphabet rhyme, but it helps the reader to understand Snodgrass's poetic credo. For the letter *Y* he writes: "*Y* is for Yes and that's/ the poet's word. He must affirm/ What makes ideacrats/ and joiners itchy. He can't squirm." The common thread in all of Snodgrass's poetry is an affirmation: the celebration of life, wholeness, and humanity. His achievements entitle him to a secure place in the literature of the twentieth century.

DE/COMPOSITIONS: 101 GOOD POEMS GONE WRONG

In a move that redefines poetry criticism, Snodgrass illustrates how celebrated poems by famed poets could have been written differently—or worse, badly—in *De/Compositions: 101 Good Poems Gone Wrong*. Snodgrass actually rewrites poems by authors ranging from Elizabeth Bishop to William Shakespeare, and displays the reworked version side-by-side with the original, so readers can appreciate the subtle shifts that occur—word by word, line by line, stanza by stanza—and gain a better understanding of the astonishing merits of the original work. The "de/compositions" are divided into five categories: "Abstract and General vs. Concrete and Specific," "Undercurrents," "The Singular Voice;" "Metrics and Music," and "Structure and Climax."

He changes the specific words and syntax but retains the sense, meter, and length of various poems and asks students to compare the two versions. For example, Shakespeare's Sonnet 129 begins:

> The expense of spirit in a waste of shame
> Is lust in action; and til action, lust
> Is perjured, murderous, bloody, full of blame

while in Snodgrass's version, it reads:

> Vigor and spunk drain out to barren guilt
> In casual sex. To bring it off, we lie,
> Accuse, cheat, kill; first tears are split,
> Then blood; we slash, stab, gouge out groin or eye.

E. E. Cummings's "anyone lived in a pretty how town" (here "A certain man lived in a very nice town"), Robert Lowell's "Skunk Hour" ("Raccoon Time"), and Emily Dickinson's "I Never Lost As Much but Twice" (simply "I've Lost So Much")—each possesses a "particular excellence" that Snodgrass attempts to "dissolve or drive out," thereby laying bare the elements that make a poem great. The poems are humorous and instructive and serve well as a teaching tool for students of poetry.

Other major works

PLAY: *The Führer Bunker*, pr. 1980, pb. 1981.

NONFICTION: *In Radical Pursuit: Critical Essays and Lectures*, 1975; *The Four Seasons*, 1984 (translation); *W. D. Snodgrass in Conversation with Philip Hoy*, 1998; *After-Images: Autobiographical Sketches*, 1999; *De/Compositions: 101 Good Poems Gone Wrong*, 2001.

TRANSLATIONS: *Gallows Songs*, 1967 (with Lore Segal; of Christian Morgenstern); *Miorita*, 1975 (of Romanian ballads); *Six Troubadour Songs*, 1977; *Traditional Hungarian Songs*, 1978; *Six Minnesinger Songs*, 1983 (of high middle German poems); *The Four Seasons*, 1984 (of sonnets including Antonio Vivaldi's music score).

Bibliography

Gatson, Paul L. *W. D. Snodgrass*. Boston: Twayne, 1978. The first book-length study of Snodgrass, this volume is the fullest available introduction to his life and works. It offers insightful studies of the major poems in Snodgrass's first three volumes. The text is supplemented by a chronology, notes, a select bibliography, and an index.

Goldstein, Laurence. "*The Führer Bunker* and the New Discourse About Nazism." *The Southern Review* 24 (Winter, 1988): 100-114. This article raises a concern that poems about Hitler might elevate him to the stature of a charismatic figure because of the absoluteness of his power. A review of the form and content of the most important poems, however, shows how completely Snodgrass has revealed the twisted nature of Hitler and his supporters.

Haven, Stephen, ed. *The Poetry of W. D. Snodgrass: Everything Human*. Ann Arbor: University of Michigan Press, 1993. Gathers reviews and criticism on Snodgrass and his major collections, by poets and critics such as John Hollander, Hayden Carruth, J. D. McClatchy, Harold Bloom, Hugh Kenner, and Dana Gioia. Haven includes a chronology of the poet's life and work, as well as a bibliography. The first major book-length work on Snodgrass.

McClatchy, J. D. *White Paper on Contemporary American Poetry*. New York: Columbia University Press, 1989. A fellow poet writes a long chapter about the lyricism in Snodgrass's poetry. He sees the confessional mode as dominant in his early poems and then modified in the later works, but never abandoned.

Mazzaro, Jerome. "The Public Intimacy of W. D. Snodgrass." *Salmagundi* 19 (Spring, 1972): 96-111. Mazzaro shows that much of Snodgrass's early poetry has an existential philosophy, and he selects a number of poems to illustrate the themes of being, choice, self-deception, and despair. This existentialism is linked to his confessional mode to show how his poetry takes on a universality by its use of detail.

Phillips, Robert. *The Confessional Poets*. Carbondale: Southern Illinois University Press, 1973. Phillips defines the confessional mode in modern American poetry and discusses the six major poets in the movement. Snodgrass's central role is shown through a close study of the poems in *Heart's Needle* and *Remains*. His success results from his sincerity and his ability to communicate personal loss while avoiding sentimentality.

Raisor, Philip, ed. *Tuned and Under Tension: The Recent Poetry of W. D. Snodgrass*. Newark: University of Delaware Press, 1998. Essays examine Snodgrass's "poetic musics," his use of history, and his standing along with Walt Whitman as a constructor of the American consciousness. Index.

Snodgrass, W. D. "W. D. Snodgrass: An Interview." Interview by Elizabeth Spires. *The American Poetry Review* 19 (July/August, 1990): 38-46. The interview covers a wide range of topics, from the origin of Snodgrass's confessional poetry to his intentions in writing *The Death of Cock Robin*. Snodgrass mentions a number of other poets who have influenced him in his development.

_______. *W. D. Snodgrass: In Conversation*. London: Between the Lines, 1998. In one volume of the publisher's useful series of interviews with major poets and writers, Philip Hoy discusses with Snodgrass his life, works, and poetics.

Edwin W. Williams,
updated by Sarah Hilbert

GARY SNYDER

Born: San Francisco, California; May 8, 1930

PRINCIPAL POETRY

Riprap, 1959
Myths and Texts, 1960
Nanao Knows, 1964
Riprap, and Cold Mountain Poems, 1965
Six Sections from Mountains and Rivers Without End, 1965
A Range of Poems, 1966
Three Worlds, Three Realms, Six Roads, 1966
The Back Country, 1967
The Blue Sky, 1969
Regarding Wave, 1969, enlarged 1970
Manzanita, 1972
The Fudo Trilogy: Spel Against Demons, Smokey the Bear Sutra, The California Water Plan, 1973
Turtle Island, 1974
All in the Family, 1975
Axe Handles: Poems, 1983
Left Out in the Rain: New Poems, 1947-1986, 1986
No Nature: New and Selected Poems, 1992
Mountains and Rivers Without End, 1996

OTHER LITERARY FORMS

Gary Snyder's pioneering journal of personal environmental discovery, *Earth House Hold* (1969), was subtitled "Technical Notes and Queries To Fellow Dharma Revolutionaries," a descriptive invitation to examine the treasure of the planet and to consider how it might be employed for the benefit of all living species. It represents the culmination of the work Snyder began nearly two decades before when he conceived of a major in literature and anthropology at Reed College, and its somewhat tentative, propositional format expresses the spirit of a movement that recognized the destructive aspects of modern industrial society and sought alternative approaches to the questions of planetary survival. Although Snyder was sometimes referred to disparagingly as "a kind of patron saint of ecology" by critics trapped in more conventional social arrangements, his interest in the environment has proved to be as perceptive and enduring as his best poetry, and the publication of *The Practice of the Wild* (1990) has deepened the context of his interests, offering the wisdom and experience of a lifetime spent living in and thinking about the natural world. The book is a linked series of reflective essays, and its amiable, reasonable tone—similar to Snyder's conversational voice in his interviews, most notably those collected in *The Real Work: Interviews and Talks, 1964-1979* (1980)—permits the power of his intellectual insights, his scholarly investigations, and his political theories to reach an audience beyond the experts he hopes to equal in his argument. Combining energetic conviction and poetic eloquence, Snyder's essays are intended to be a "genuine teaching text" and "a mediation on what it means to be human." They demonstrate his philosophy of composition as it reveals a poetics of existence and have been written to stimulate "a broad range of people and provide them with historical, ecological and personal vision." *A Place in Space: Ethics, Aesthetics, and Watersheds* (1995) continues his exploration of these concerns.

ACHIEVEMENTS

Before "ecology" had become a password of political correctness, Gary Snyder was devising a program of study designed to create a language of environmental

Gary Snyder (Courtesy of Gary Snyder)

advocacy; after many trendy Westerners had long since recoiled from the rigors of Eastern thought, Snyder completed a curriculum of apprenticeship in Japan and went on to develop an American version of Zen applicable to his locality; as Native American life and lore gradually seeped into the area of academic interest, Snyder continued his examinations of the primal tribal communities that lived in harmony with the North American land mass for pre-Columbian millennia and worked to apply their successes to contemporary life; while hippies and dropouts returned to the button-down corporate culture after a brief dalliance with a counterculture, Snyder built his own home at the center of a small community that endures as an example of a philosophical position in action; and most of all, while some of the other voices that arose during the post-"Howl" renaissance of the New American Poetry have become stale or quaint, Snyder's use of a clear, direct, colloquial but literature-responsive language made it possible for his concerns to reach, touch, and move a substantial audience through his poetry.

Snyder's varied interests have given him extensive material for his poems, but the appeal of his work is not dependent on a program calculated to educate or persuade. Much more than argument, the poetry is an outgrowth of the processes of Snyder's life—his work, his family, his intellectual and athletic interests, his cultural convictions, and his rapport with the landscape. He has been able to illustrate effectively how art and life can be intertwined in a reciprocal interchange that does not depend on academic procedures or traditional schools (while not denying their usefulness as well), an interchange that enriches and expands both realms, and in this he joins Herman Melville (the sailor), Henry David Thoreau (the naturalist), Ralph Waldo Emerson (the philosopher and teacher), and Walt Whitman (the celebrator) in a line of American artists whose work was, in a profound sense, the spiritual and aesthetic expression of their life's focus. *Turtle Island* won the Pulitzer Prize in 1975.

Biography

Gary Snyder was born in San Francisco in 1930, the son of Harold Alton and Lois Wilkie Snyder. His parents moved back to their native Pacific Northwest in 1932, where they settled on a dairy farm near Puget Sound in Washington. Snyder's mother moved to Portland, Oregon, to work as a newspaper-woman when Snyder was twelve, and reared Snyder and his younger sister Anthea as a single parent, insisting that Snyder commute downtown to attend Lincoln High, the most intellectually demanding school in the Portland system. In 1947, he received a scholarship to Reed College, where he devised a unique major in anthropology and literature. Early in his college years, he joined the outdoor groups the Mazamas and the Wilderness Society and took up backcountry hiking and skiing and snow-peak mountaineering. His first poems were published in the Reed College literary magazine. He lived in an old house shared by a dozen other students similarly interested in art and politics, including the poets Philip Whalen and Lew Welch, who became his close friends. Snyder wrote for *The Oregonian* newspaper at night and spent the summer of 1950 on an archaeological dig at old Fort Vancouver in Washington. At about that time, he was briefly married to Allison Gass, a fellow student.

Upon graduation from Reed, Snyder completed one semester of graduate studies in linguistics at Indiana University before transferring to the University of California at Berkeley to study Oriental languages. During the summers of the years he pursued graduate work, he took a job first as a fire-watcher in the Cascade mountains and later, after he was fired in the McCarthy-era hysteria of 1954, as a choker-setter for the Warm Springs Lumber Company. Utilizing skills in woodcutting he had learned from his family and neighbors, Snyder "was often supporting himself" in his student years, and his first accomplished poems were related to these experiences as well as to his work on a trail crew in Yosemite in 1955.

That fall, Snyder met Allen Ginsberg and Jack Kerouac and became involved in the exploding art scene in San Francisco, where he took part in the historic Six Gallery reading where Ginsberg read "Howl" in public for the first time. Snyder followed this extraordinary performance with his own poetry in a very different vein and was also successful in capturing the attention of the audience. He and Kerouac shared a cabin in Mill Valley, California, through that winter and spring, and then Snyder traveled to Kyoto, Japan, to take up residence in a Zen temple, beginning a twelve-year sojourn in Japan that was broken by a nine-month hitch as a crewman on the tanker *Sappa Creek* and a brief return to San Francisco in 1958. His translations from the Chinese poet Han-shan, who lived in the seventh century, were published in the *Evergreen Review* in 1958 as "Cold Mountain Poems," and his first collection, *Riprap*, was published by Cid Corman's Origin Press in Japan in 1959.

Working as a part-time translator and researcher of Buddhist texts, Snyder eventually became a student of Rinzai Zen under Oda Sesso, Roshi (master), and established contacts with activist groups concerned with ecology, women's issues, and world peace. His next collection, *Myths and Texts*, was published in 1960, the same year he married the poet Joanne Kyger. In 1962, he traveled to India with Ginsberg, Peter Orlovsky, and Kyger, and his association with the poet Nanao Sakaki drew him into artistic circles in Tokyo in 1964. He returned to the United States to teach at Berkeley in 1965, won a Bollingen grant, and returned to Japan. His marriage with Kyger was over when he met Masa Uehara, a graduate student in English, and they were married in 1967.

With his wife and his son, Kai, who was born in Kyoto, Snyder returned to the Western Hemisphere, settling in the northern Sierra Nevada mountains, where he built a home (called "Kitkitdizze," meaning "mountain misery") in 1970 with a crew of friends. His first book of poems reflecting his commitment to his native country, *Turtle Island* (from an old Native American name for the continent), was published in 1974 and won the Pulitzer Prize. During this time, Snyder was traveling to universities three or four months a year to read poetry, working on the needs of his immediate mountain community, and serving the state of California as the chairman of its Arts Council. At the end of the decade, he published a collection called *The Real Work: Interviews and Talks, 1964-1979* (1980), and in 1983, he published *Axe Handles*, poems written during the previous ten years. In 1985, he joined the English department at the University of California at Davis, where he taught literature and ecological matters, and he began to travel widely, visiting Hawaii, Alaska, China, and parts of Europe to speak "on the specifics of Buddhist meditation, ecological practice, language and poetics, and bioregional politics." The poems he had written but left uncollected were published in *Left Out in the Rain: New Poems, 1947-1985*. In 1988, he was divorced from Masa Uehara and married Carole Koda, and in 1990, he completed a book that presented a program for personal renewal and planetary conservation called *The Practice of the Wild*. That same year, a compilation of comments, reminiscences, poems, and assorted other statements was published by the Sierra Club under the title *Gary Snyder: Dimensions of a Life* in celebration of the poet's sixtieth birthday. Snyder completed his epic "poem of process" *Mountains and Rivers Without End* in 1996 and continued to train students at Davis to deal with environmental crises. The hero-figure Kerouac patterned after Snyder in *The Dharma Bums* (1958), "Japhy Ryder," has become the source of wisdom, the poet Gary Snyder, now grown into an elder of the tribe.

Analysis

Among many evocative statements about his life and work, a particularly crucial one is Gary Snyder's claim that

> As a poet, I hold the most archaic values on earth. They go back to the late Paleolithic; the fertility of the soil, the magic of animals; the power-vision in solitude, the terrifying initiation and rebirth; the love and ecstasy of the dance, the common work of the tribe.

The social and philosophical principles he has expressed are the fundamental credo of his convictions as a man and an artist. He uses the word "archaic" to suggest "primal" or "original"—the archetype or first pattern from which others may evolve. His citation of the late Paleolithic era as source-ground stems from his belief that essential lessons concerning human consciousness have been learned and then lost. Thus Snyder devotes much time to the study of ancient (and primitive) cultures. The values he holds stand behind and direct his poetry, as it is drawn from his studies and experiences. His values include a respect for land as the source of life and the means of sustaining it; a respect for all sentient creatures and for the animalistic instincts of humans; a recognition of the necessity for the artist to resist social pressure in order to discover and develop power from within; an acknowledgment of the necessity for participation in both communal ritual and individual exploration of the depths of the subconscious to transcend the mundane and risk the extraordinary; an acceptance of the body and the senses—the physical capabilities, pleasures, and demands of the skin; and a feeling for the shared labor of the community, another version of "the real work" that unites the individual with a larger sense and source of meaning. Neither the poet as solitary singer nor as enlightened visionary is sufficient without the complex of relationships that joins the local, the bioregional, and ultimately the planetary in an interdependent chain of reliance, support, and enlightened use of resources. It is with these values in mind that Snyder defines an ethical life as one that "is mindful, mannerly and has style," an attitude that is crucial to the accomplishment of "the real work."

Each of these precepts has an important analogue in the technical execution of the poems themselves. As Jerome Rothenberg has observed, "where I continue to see him best is as he emerges from his poems." Poetically, then, "the fertility of the soil" is worthless without the labor that brings it to fruition, and as Snyder has commented, "the rhythms of my poems follow the rhythms of the physical work I'm doing and life I'm leading at any given time—which makes the music in my head which creates the line." The linkage between the rhythmic movement of the body, the larger rhythmic cycles of the natural world, and the structure of words in a particular poem follows the precepts that Charles Olson prescribed in the landmark "Projective Verse" essay (1950), and Snyder, like Ginsberg, Robert Creeley, and others, has always favored the creation of a particular shape or form to suit the purpose of the poem under attentive development. The rhythms of a particular poem are derived from an "energy-mind-field-dance" that, in turn, often results from labor designed to capitalize on the life of the earth.

Similarly, when Snyder speaks of "the magic of animals," he is identifying one of his central subjects, and the images of many of his poems are based on his observations of animals in the wild. The importance of wilderness and the manner in which animals seem to interact instinctively with their natural surroundings are, for Snyder, keys to his conception of freedom. The magic of their existence is part of a mystery that humans need to penetrate. Thus, as image and subject, animals and their ways are an important part of the "etiquette of freedom" Snyder's work serves.

The concept of the "power vision in solitude" is derived from both the shamanistic practices that Snyder has studied in primitive societies and the varieties of meditation he has explored in his research into and expressions of Buddhist thought. Its immediate consequence in poetry is the necessity for developing a singular, distinct voice, a language with which one is comfortable, and a style that is true to the artist's entire life. For Snyder, this has meant learning to control the mood of a poem through tonal modulation, matching mood to subject and arranging sequences of poems that can sustain visionary power as well as intimate personal reflection. "The terrifying initiation and rebirth" is a corollary of the power vision. It implies that once a singular voice has been established, it must be followed according to the patterns of its impulsive organization—in other words, to its points of origin in the subconscious. Snyder speaks of the unconscious as "our inner wilderness areas," and sees in the "depths of the mind" the ultimate source of the imagination. The exploration of the wilderness within is vital to the image-making function of poetry.

The "love and ecstasy" Snyder speaks of stems from the revolt that Snyder and his colleagues led against the stiff, formal, distant academic poetry favored by critics in the 1950's, and its application has been to influence the colloquial nature of his language, to encourage the use of primitive techniques such as chant to alter perceptive states, to permit the inclusion of casual data from ordinary existence to inform the poem, and, most of all, to confront the most personal of subjects with honesty and self-awareness. There is a discernible narrative consciousness present in Snyder's poetry even when he avoids—as he generally does—personal pronouns and definite articles. Yet his resistance to cultural authority is balanced by his praise for the "common work of the tribe," the artistic accomplishment that he treasures. As he has said, "I feel very strongly that poetry also exists as part of a tradition, and is not simply a matter of only private and personal vision." Explaining his interests in Ezra Pound, William Carlos Williams, Wallace Stevens, John Milton, and others, Snyder says he wants "to know *what* has been done, and to see *how* it has been done. That in a sense is true craft." Almost paradoxically, considering his emphasis on originality, he advocates (and practices) extensive examination of multidisciplinary learning, explaining that knowledge of the past saves one "the trouble of having to repeat things that others have done that need not be done again. And then also he knows when he writes a poem that has never been written before."

RIPRAP

Snyder's first two collections, *Riprap* and *Cold Mountain Poems*—which were published together initially in 1965 and reached a "fourth incarnation" in 1990—are evidence of the writing and thinking that Snyder had been doing through the mid-1950's. *Riprap* took shape while Snyder was working on a backcountry trail crew in 1955, and its title is at first a description of "stone laid on steep, slick rock to make a trail for horses in the mountains," then a symbol of the interlinkage of objects in a region and a figure for the placement of words in a poetic structure. It serves to connect language and action, reflective thought and the work that generates it. The poems in the collection are dedicated to the men Snyder worked with, the "community" of cohesion and effort he joined, men who knew the requirements of the land and who transmitted their skills through demonstration. *Riprap* includes elements of the oral tradition Snyder intersected, and the title "celebrates the work of the hands" while some of the poems "run the risk of invisibility" since they tried "for surface simplicity set with unsettling depths." Poems like "Above Pate Valley" and "Piute Creek" begin with direct description of landscape and move toward an almost cosmic perspective concerning the passage of time across the land over geological epochs. The specific and the eternal coalesce:

> Hill beyond hill, folded and twisted
> Tough trees crammed
> In thin stone fractures
> A huge moon on it all, is too much.
> The mind wanders. A million
> Summers, night air still and the rocks
> Warm. Sky over endless mountains.
> All the junk that goes with being human
> Drops away, hard rock wavers.

Poetry, as Snyder put it in "Burning: No. 13" from *Myths and Texts*, is "a riprap on the slick road of metaphysics," helping one find meaning and explaining why one reads "Milton by Firelight" (the title of another poem) and finds new versions of hell and "the wheeling sky" in the Sierras.

COLD MOUNTAIN POEMS

The *Cold Mountain Poems* are "translations" (in the Poundian sense) from Han-shan, a hermit and poet of the T'ang dynasty, and they represent Snyder's identification with a kind of nature prophet at home in the wild as well as his inclination to isolate himself from those aspects of American (or Western) society he found abhorrent until he could fashion a program to combat the social ills he identified. As in most effective translations, there is a correspondence in sensibility between the two artists, and Snyder's comfort with the backcountry, as well as his growing sense of a cross-cultural and transepochal perspective, may be seen in lines like

> Thin grass does for a mattress,
> The blue sky makes a good quilt.
> Happy with a stone underhead
> Let heaven and earth go about their changes.

Calling Han-shan a "mountain madman" or "ragged hermit," Snyder expresses through the translations his admiration for a kind of independence, self-possession, and mindful alertness that he saw as a necessity for psychic survival in the Cold War era, a husbanding of strength to prepare for a return to the social struggle. "Mind solid and sharp," he says, he is gaining the vision to "honor this priceless natural treasure"—the world around him ("the whole clear cloudless sky")—and the insight ("sunk deep in the flesh") to understand the complementary wonder within.

Myths and Texts

Written at about the same time as *Riprap*, *Myths and Texts* is Snyder's first attempt to organize his ideas into an evolving, complex structural framework. In it, Snyder's wilderness experience is amplified by the use of Pacific Coast Indian texts, which are set as a kind of corrective for the exploitation and destruction of the environment that Snyder sees as the result of misguided American-European approaches to nature. The crux of the matter is the failure of Judeo-Christian culture to recognize the inherent sacredness of the land, and Snyder uses what he feels is a kind of Buddhist compassion and a Native American empathy as a corrective thrust. The three books of the collection are called "Logging"—which uses the lumber industry as an example of "technological drivenness" that destroys resources and shows no respect for the symbolic or ritualistic aspect of the living wilderness; "Hunting"—which explores the intricate relationship between the hunter and the quarry (and between mind and body) in primitive societies; and "Burning"—which is somewhat less accessible in its intriguing attempt to find or chart a symbolic synthesis that integrates the mythic material Snyder has been presenting into a universal vision of timeless cycles of destruction and rebirth.

As Snyder defines the terms, in a preliminary fashion, the myths and texts are the "two sources of human knowledge—symbols and sense-impressions." The larger context at which he aims—the "one whole thing"—is built on the power of individual poems, and among the best are ones like "Logging: No. 8," in which the logged ground is likened to a battlefield after a massacre; "Logging: No. 3," in which the lodgepole pine is treated as an emblem of nature's enduring vitality; "Logging: No. 13," in which a fire-watcher reports a fire ("T36N R16E S25/ Is burning. Far to the west") and seems more interested in the abstract beauty of the landscape than in any specific situation; and among several hunting songs, the exceptional "No. 6," which carries the dedication, "*this poem is for bear.*"

Snyder read the original version of "The Woman who Married a Bear" in an anthropology text in Reed College and was fascinated by the interaction of the human and animal cultures. He devotes a chapter to the story in *The Practice of the Wild* (1990), lamenting that "the bears are being killed, the humans are everywhere, and the green world is being unraveled and shredded and burned by the spreading of a gray world that seems to have no end." His poem is placed at the convergence of several cultures and is structured by the different speaking "voices"—not specifically identified but clear from tone and context. First, in a quote from the anthropological text, the bear speaks: "As for me I am a child of the god of the mountains." Then, a field scientist, observing the data:

> You can see
> Huckleberries in bearshit if you
> Look, this time of year
> If I sneak up on the bear
> It will grunt and run.

This relatively matter-of-fact, outside position is replaced by a tale of the girl who married a bear: "In a house under the mountain/ She gave birth to slick dark children/ With sharp teeth, and lived in the hollow/ Mountain many years." A shift has been made to the Native American culture, and what follows is the burden of the legend, as the girl's tribe goes to reclaim her. The next voice is the hunter addressing the bear:

> honey-eater
> forest apple
> light-foot

> Old man in the fur coat, Bear! come out!
> Die of your own choice!

Now the poet enters, turning the tale (text) into poetry (myth): "Twelve species north of Mexico/ Sucking their paws in the long winter/ Tearing the high-strung caches down/ Whining, crying, jacking off." Then the tale continues, as the girl's brothers "cornered him in the rocks," and finally the "voice" of the bear-spirit speaks, as through a shaman perhaps, in the "Song of the snared bear":

> "Give me my belt.
> "I am near death.
> "I came from the mountain caves
> "At the headwaters,
> "The small streams there
> "Are all dried up.

In a deft conclusion, Snyder reduces the dramatic tension by the interposition of the disarmingly personal. As if inspired by the story, he begins to imagine himself a part of the Paleolithic hunter culture: "I think I'll go hunt bears." Yet he is too solidly grounded in reality to go beyond a reading of the text: "Why s— Snyder,/ You couldn't hit a bear in the ass/ with a handful of rice." Although, of course, in the poem, he has hit the target squarely by assimilating the different voices (as different strands of culture) into his own modern version of the myth.

REGARDING WAVE

With *Regarding Wave*, Snyder's work turned from the mythic and philosophical toward the intimate and immediately personal. He had begun a family (his son Kai was born in 1968) and returned to the United States, and the poems recall his last days in the Far East and his sense of how he had to proceed after returning to his native land at a time of strife and turmoil. The family poems are celebratory, written in wonder, open and exuberant in the first flush of parenthood, expressing his delight with his wife Masa and their infant son. There are poems that are like meditations on the sensual: "Song of the View," "Song of the Tangle," or "Song of the Taste," and poems that are drawn from the experience of rearing a child, like "The Bed in the Sky" or "Kai, Today," which is an awestruck reflection on the act of birth, or the supra-mundane "Not Leaving the House," in which Snyder admits "When Kai is born/ I quit going out," and justifies his inward angle of view by concluding "From dawn til late at night/ making a new world of ourselves/ around this life."

Yet since Snyder found in his return to the New World beyond "ourselves" that the political situation in America in 1969 was troubling ("Off the coast of Oregon/ The radio is full of hate and anger"), and even before landing was warned that "beards don't make money," he began to plan the outlines of a life as a poet and activist in the United States. The effects of his action become more clear in his next collection, but the cast of his mind is apparent in the transitional "What You Should Know to Be a Poet," which calls together what he had learned from his life to that point:

> all you can about animals as persons
> the names of trees and flowers and weeds
> names of stars, and the movements of the planets
> and the moon.
>
> your own six senses, with a watchful and elegant mind

and then blends it with a kind of resolution to confront the bestial nature of humans in order to prepare to engage the evil at large in the world, as expressed in the crucial central stanza beginning, "kiss the ass of the devil." From that point, the poem alternates positive aspects of existence ("& then love the human: wives husbands and friends") with an acceptance of the trials and burdens of life ("long dry hours of dull work swallowed and accepted/ and livd with and finally lovd") until it concludes with an unsettling sense of the future, "real danger. gambles. and the edge of death."

Snyder's ambivalent feelings about living in America are again expressed in the hilarious "Smokey the Bear Sutra," in which the familiar symbol of the forest service is depicted as a kind of Asiatic avenging demon protecting the environment and resisting polluters. Published in 1973 as a part of *The Fudo Trilogy*—a pamphlet that included "The California Water Plan" (a section of *Mountains and Rivers*) and "Spel Against Demons"—it combines Snyder's serious concerns about the environment and his continuing pursuit of Asiatic culture with his characteristically engaging high good humor. The chant, "Drown their butts; soak their butts" is presented in mock seriousness as a mantra of righteousness, while Smokey is depicted more as a lovable child's pet than the fierce scourge of evil that the archetype suggests. The comic conception works to keep Snyder's considerable anger under control, so that he does not turn his poetry into polemic. By then fully involved in the bioregional movement and committed to the local community of San Juan Ridge, where he had built a home, Snyder in the early 1970's followed a dual course in his poetry. The overarching theme of his work was to protect and preserve "Turtle Island—the old/new name for the continent, based on many creation myths," and it was expressed in poems that "speak of place, and the energy-pathways that sustain life" and in poems that decry the forces of destruction unleashed by the stupidity of "demonic killers" who perpetrate "aimless executions and slaughterings."

Turtle Island

These poems were published under the title *Turtle Island* (1974), sold more than 100,000 copies, and won the Pulitzer Prize. Among the most memorable poems Snyder has written, the ones that explore the "energy pathways" sustaining life include the unique "The Bath"—a Whitmanesque rapture in appreciation of the body that challenges the latent Puritanism and fear of the skin in American society by describing in loving detail the physical wonder of his son, his wife, and himself in a bath. The sheer glory of the body glowing with health and the radiant reflection of the natural world around them build toward a feeling of immense physical satisfaction and then toward a complementary feeling of metaphysical well-being. The frankness of the language may be difficult for some readers, but Snyder's tasteful, delicate, and comfortable handling of it makes his declaration "this is our body," an echoing chorus, an assertion of religious appreciation. In an even more directly thankful mode, the translation of a Mohawk "Prayer for the Great Family" unites the basic elements of the cosmos in a linked series of gemlike depictions, concluding with one of Snyder's essential ideas: that there is an infinite space "beyond all powers and thoughts/ and yet is within us-/ Grandfather Space/ The Mind is his Wife." Other expressions of "eternal delight" include "By Frazier Creek Falls," "Source," and "The Dazzle," as well as many poems in the book's last section, a kind of basic history primer called "For the Children," that convey considerable emotion without lapsing into obvious emotional tugging.

The more overtly political poems and sketches tend to be somber, frequently employing a litany of statistics to convey grim information that needs little additional comment, but in "The Call of the Wild," Snyder's anger is projected in language purposefully charged with judgmental fervor. Avoiding easy partisanship, Snyder condemns, first, "ex acid-heads" who have opted for "forever blissful sexless highs" and hidden in fear from what is interesting about life. His image of people missing the point of everything by living in trendy "Geodesic domes, that/ Were stuck like warts/ In the woods" is as devastating as his cartoon conception of advanced technology declaring "a war against earth" waged by pilots with "their women beside them/ in bouffant hairdos/ putting nail-polish on the/ gunship cannon-buttons." Snyder did not publish another book of poems until 1983, when *Axe Handles* was issued by North Point Press.

Axe Handles

The poems in *Axe Handles* have a reflective tone, moving inward toward the life Snyder has been leading in his local community, to which he dedicated the collection. His concerns do not change, but in a return to the more spare, lyrical poems of *Riprap*, Snyder condenses and focuses his ideas into "firm, clean lines of verse reminiscent of Ezra Pound's *Rock-Drill* cantos," according to critic Andrew Angyal. The title has a typically dual meaning, referring to language as an instrument for shaping meaning and to the entire meaning of tools in human life. The theme of "cultural continuity" is presented in terms of Snyder's passing his knowledge on to his family, friends, and readers and is explicitly explained in the parable of the title poem. The book evokes an ethos of harmony in cycles of renewal and restoration, rebirth and reconsideration. Snyder moves beyond his specific criticism of human social organizations in the late twentieth century and toward, in Angyal's words, his "own alternative set of values in communal cooperation, conservation, and a nonexploitative way of life that shows respect for the land." The compression and density of Snyder's thinking are evident in the poem "Removing the Plate of the Pump on the Hydraulic System of the Backhoe," which reads in entirety

Through mud, fouled nuts, black grime
it opens, a gleam of spotless steel
machined-fit perfect
swirl of intake and output
relentless clarity
at the heart
of work.

The pursuit of "relentless clarity" in everything characterizes Snyder's life and art, but the pressures of the search are alleviated by his congenial nature and sense of humor. While emphasizing the importance of Zen "mindfulness," Snyder has also stressed that "a big part of life is just being playful." In accordance with this approach, Snyder has kept dogmatic or simplistic solutions out of his work and has cherished the wild and free nature of humankind. In a recent poem, "Off the Trail," which he wrote for his wife Carole Koda, he envisions a life in which "all paths are possible" and maintains that "the trial's not the way" to find wisdom or happiness. "We're off the trail,/ You and I," he declares, "and we chose it!" That choice—the decision to go against the grain "to be in line with the big flow"—has led to a poetry of "deeply human richness," as Charles Molesworth puts it in his perceptive study of Snyder's work, in which "a vision of plenitude" leads to a "liminal utopia, poised between fullness and yet more growth."

Mountains and Rivers Without End

On April 8, 1956, Snyder began to work on a "poem of process" somewhat akin to Pound's *Cantos* (1970) or Williams's *Paterson* (5 volumes, 1946-1956) that he called *Mountains and Rivers Without End*. Initially inspired by East Asian brush painting (*sumi*) on a series of screens and by his own experiences with what he viewed as "a chaotic universe where everything is in place," Snyder brought in elements of Native American styles of narration, his continuing study of Zen Buddhism, Asian art and drama, and the varied landscapes that he traversed on several continents during the next four decades as the primary features of the poem. "It all got more complicated than I predicted and the poems were evasive," Snyder remarked in retrospect about the project. A particular problem involved the central narrative consciousness, since the traditional idea of an epic hero as a focal perspective seemed outmoded. As an alternate center of coherence, Snyder devised an elaborate structural arrangement built on ways in which "walking the landscape can be both ritual and meditation" so that the evolving perceptual matrix of the artist provided a fundamental frame for the materials of the poem.

Drawing on the "yogic implications" of mountains as representations of "a tough spirit of willed self-discipline" and rivers as a projection of "generous and loving spirit of concern for all beings" (as Snyder explained in "The Making of *Mountains and Rivers Without End*," an afterword to the poem), the epic is energized by the interplay between these elemental forces. The essential things of the poet's life—his practice of Zen meditation and action, his abiding concern for the "ark of biodiversity," his love and care for friends and family, his investigative interest in the previous inhabitants of the North American continent, and his sense of himself as an artist whose poetry is an extension of the patterns of his working world—provide the distinct subjects and incidents for the separately composed poems that constitute individual sections, written (as he notes in his signatory final line) from "Marin-an 1956" to "Kitkitdizze 1996."

Like Pound, whom Snyder calls "my direct teacher in these matters," Snyder wanted to include what he considered the most important intellectual, mythological, and cultural aspects of his times, but he noted that "big sections of the *Cantos* aren't interesting." To avoid the kind of obscurity that requires endless emendations, Snyder provided several pages of explanation in endnotes and included a record of publication of the individual parts, which functions as an accompanying chronology. Nevertheless, the technical strategies Snyder employs to "sustain the reader through it" are fairly intricate and designed to maintain a discernible structure that contributes to the cohesion of the poem. The guiding principle behind the entire enterprise depends on Snyder's conviction that, as he stated in a 1990 afterword to *Riprap*, the whole universe can be seen as "interconnected, interpenetrating, mutually reflecting and mutually embracing." Therefore, while some individual parts may contain names, ideas, and references that appear esoteric or strictly personal, "there will be enough reverberations and echoes from various sections so that it will be self-informing." Since the poem's progress is not chronological, arranged according to place rather than period, there is no ultimate sense of completion. For Snyder, the poem is not "closed up" but ideally should continue to maintain a "sense of usefulness and relevance" as it offers "stimulation and excitement and imagination" for the reader.

In addition to the widest patterns of intersection, Snyder uses several prominent technical devices to tie things together. Initially, he expected to have twenty-five sections, each centering on a key phrase. While this plan was not maintained for every part of the poem, there are some especially important key phrases, as in the seventh poem ("Bubbs Creek Haircut"), in which the third line from the last, "double mirror waver," is described by Snyder as a "structure point" conveying infinite reflection. Similarly, in "Night Highway 99," the third poem, the image of a "network womb" is described by Snyder as a reference to the Buddhist concept of "the great womb of time and space which intersects itself." The poem "The Blue Sky," which concludes part 1, contains what Snyder describes as a "healing" word, "sky/tent/curve," an image of an arc that connects the disparate horizons of isolated nations. This sense of joining is a crucial philosophical precept in the poem, since the original idea of landscape paintings on screens or scrolls is exemplified by Snyder's remark that he "would like to have the poem close in on itself but on some other level keep going."

The final form of the poem is clarified by the publication record, which indicates an unleashing of energy in the 1960's followed by an ingathering of strength during the mid-1970's to mid-1980's, when Snyder's travels took him to "most of the major collections of Chinese paintings in the United States." His sense of the poem was also "enlarged by walking/working visits to major urban centers," which became important social complements to the portrayals of the natural world. In the 1990's, Snyder says, "the entire cycle clicked for me" and he wrote sixteen of the poem's sections while revising the typography of some earlier parts and reorganizing the placement of the poems in the final version. While each individual poem can function as an independent entity, the completed poem has, as poet Robert Hass has commented, "the force and concentration of a very shaped work of art."

An overview of the poem reveals Snyder's shaping strategies. The first of the four parts deals with the origins of a voyage, the inner and outer landscapes to be traveled, and the ways in which the features of the terrain can be gathered into a personal vision. "Night Highway 99," for instance, is Snyder's *On the Road*, embracing the Pacific Coast route where Snyder hitchhiked south from his home ground and met people like Ginsberg ("A. G."), a road brother. The second part extends the journey to the concrete bleakness and compulsive energy of giant urban complexes. "Walking the New York Bedrock" revels in the sheer magnitude of a great city, which still recalls the "many-footed Manhatta" of Whitman's paean. The parallels Snyder draws here between geologic strata, canyons, and skyscrapers imply a commonality in disparate forms. The third part moves toward a reconciliation of forces and forms, while the fourth, containing poems written more recently, conveys the now mature poet's reflective estimate of enduring values. The poem for Snyder's wife Carole, "Cross-Legg'd," is a kind of prayer of appreciation for the rewards of the journey, an expression of serenity and alertness. As a demonstration of the qualities he esteems, its conclusion, "we two be here what comes," celebrates the condition of mindful awareness Snyder sought when he began his study of Buddhist ways.

Toward the poem's conclusion, "The Mountain Spirit" reframes the conception of mountains and rivers that launched the journey. Its declaration, "Streams and mountains never stay the same," is like a motto for the poet's way of being, while its statement "All art is song/ is sacred to the real" reemphasizes his fundamental credo. His quote "nothingness is shapeliness" is at the core of Zen practice, also echoing Ginsberg's claim, "Mind is shapely/ Art is Shapely." The final poem, "Finding the Space in the Heart," explores the infinity of space, which Snyder sees as a symbol of freedom, ending the poem in an ethos of gratitude epitomized by the "quiet heart and distant eye," which he acknowledges as the supreme gift of "the mountain spirit." Even with all of the evocative, vividly descriptive passages illuminating the natural world, Snyder's poetry remains firmly grounded on the human values he sees as the fundamentals of existence. As he has said, "In a visionary way, what we would want poetry to do is guide lovers toward ecstasy, give witness to the dignity of old people, intensify human bonds, elevate the community and improve the public spirit."

Other major works

nonfiction: *Earth House Hold: Technical Notes and Queries to Fellow Dharma Revolutionaries*, 1969; *The Old Ways*, 1977; *He Who Hunted Birds in His Father's Village: The Dimensions of a Haida Myth*, 1979; *The Real Work: Interviews and Talks, 1964-1979*, 1980; *Passage Through India*, 1983; *The Practice of the Wild*, 1990; *Gary Synder Papers*, 1995; *A Place in Space: Ethics, Aesthetics, and Watersheds*, 1995.

miscellaneous: *The Gary Snyder Reader: Prose, Poetry, and Translations, 1952-1998*, 1999.

Bibliography

Almon, Bert. *Gary Snyder.* Boise, Idaho: Boise State University Press, 1979. An analytical examination of Snyder's work in terms of his Buddhist background and interests. Sharply focused, somewhat esoteric, and occasionally narrow in approach. Knowledgeable and reliable on the poet's use of material from Asiatic culture.

Dean, Tim. *Gary Snyder and the American Unconscious.* New York: St. Martin's Press, 1991. An intelligent and careful reading of Snyder's work, somewhat limited by an academic style and perspective.

Faas, Ekbert, ed. *Towards a New American Poetics.* Santa Barbara, Calif.: Black Sparrow Press, 1978. Contains an informative critical essay and an interview that covers areas not usually touched.

Halper, Jon, ed. *Gary Snyder: Dimensions of a Life.* San Francisco: Sierra Club Books, 1991. A semibiographical tribute in which sixty-five friends, fellow-workers, and members of Snyder's family write about the poet and his work. Varying tremendously in quality and interest, there are many informative and revealing contributions by well-known (Allen Ginsberg, Ursula Le Guin) and unfamiliar individuals.

Molesworth, Charles. *Gary Snyder's Vision: Poetry and the Real Work.* Columbia: University of Missouri Press, 1983. An intellectually adept, stylishly written, and perceptive study of Snyder's writing through the early 1980's.

Murphy, Patrick, ed. *Critical Essays on Gary Snyder.* Boston: G. K. Hall, 1990. A comprehensive, well-chosen collection of critical essays by one of Snyder's most intelligent critics. Ranging from the earliest responses to the poet's work through three decades of criticism, this book is evidence of the variety of perspectives Snyder's work has brought forth.

Sciagaj, Leonard M. *Sustainable Poetry: Four American Ecopoets.* Lexington: University Press of Kentucky, 1999. Along with Snyder, discusses and compares A. R. Ammons, Wendell Berry, and W. S. Merwin and their treatment of nature and environmental concerns in their works. Bibliographical references, index.

Snyder, Gary. *The Real Work: Interviews and Talks 1964-1979.* Edited by William Scott McLean. New York: New Directions, 1980. A crucial collection of interviews and talks that indicate, in detailed and lucid prose, the direction of Snyder's thought and the principles of his poetics.

Steuding, Bob. *Gary Snyder.* Boston: Twayne, 1976. Steuding follows the format of the Twayne critical series, mixing biographical information with a critical examination of each book Snyder wrote through *Turtle Island.* In conversation with Snyder, he worked out his basic thesis, and his remarks are essentially accurate if a bit pedestrian. Biographical sketch of the poet's life through the mid-1970's and an annotated bibliography. For a more current bibliography, see Katherine McNeil's *Gary Snyder: A Bibliography* (New York: Phoenix Books), 1983.

Leon Lewis, updated by Lewis

Edith Södergran

Born: St. Petersburg, Russia; April 4, 1892
Died: Raivola, Finland; June 24, 1923

Principal poetry

Dikter, 1916 (*Poems*, 1980)
Septemberlyran, 1918 (*The September Lyre*, 1980)

Rosenaltaret, 1919 (*The Rose Altar*, 1980)
Brokiga iakttagelser, 1919 (*Motley Observations*, 1980)
Framtidens skugga, 1920 (*The Shadow of the Future*, 1980)
Landet som icke är, 1925
Min lyra, 1929
Edith Södergrans dikter, 1940 (*The Collected Poems of Edith Södergran*, 1980)
We Women: Selected Poems of Edith Södergran, 1977
Love and Solitude: Selected Poems, 1916-1923, 1980, 1985
Poems, 1983
Complete Poems, 1984

Other literary forms

Edith Södergran died of tuberculosis at the age of thirty-one, and fully half the titles listed above were published posthumously. She left behind her a remarkable collection of letters to Hagar Olsson, a critic and novelist whose favorable review of Södergran's *The September Lyre* led to a close friendship between the two young women. Södergran's correspondence with Olsson was published under the title *Ediths brev: Brev från Edith Södergran till Hagar Olsson* (Edith's letters: letters from Edith Södergran to Hagar Olsson) in 1955.

Achievements

Edith Södergran's poetry met with a baffled and even hostile reception in her own day, with a few notable exceptions, and even caused a journalistic debate as to her sanity. Writing in a period when Nordic verse still supported traditional values of regular meter and rhyme, Södergran espoused free verse and arrived—apparently on her own initiative—at something like the "doctrine of the image" laid out by Ezra Pound in 1912, derived by him in part from his study of the first poems of H. D. Therefore, shortly before her death, Södergran was hailed in the Finno-Swedish journal *Ultra* as the pioneer of Finnish modernism.

By the 1930's, Södergran's home in Raivola had become an unofficial shrine for younger poets, and Södergran's work was revered by a number of successors, among these Gunnar Ekelöf, the Swedish poet, and Uuno Kailas, the Finnish writer. Her courageous rejection of verse conventions inspired later poets to do the same. Her canon makes clear the expressionistic elements in the modernist temper, and in granting to irrational forces pride of place, Södergran (wittingly or not) aligned herself with such contemporaries as D. H. Lawrence, James Joyce, and André Breton. In the words of George Schoolfield, "Her simple directness, enlivened by her genius for the unexpected in language, is seen to best advantage when [she] is overwhelmed by forces outside herself." This primordial and homespun receptivity has proved to be a highly prospective stance, and accounts for Södergran's continuing popularity, enhanced by the feminist movement's reexamination of women's writing, spreading far beyond the boundaries of Norden, and gaining momentum more than sixty years after her death.

Biography

Edith Södergran was born on April 4, 1892, in the cosmopolitan city of St. Petersburg (called Leningrad during the years of the Soviet Union), the principal Baltic seaport and then capital of Russia. Her father, Mattias Södergran, came from a family of farmers who, while they lived in northwestern Finland, were of Swedish stock. Her mother, Helena Holmroos, Mattias's second wife, was the daughter of a prosperous industrialist, also of Finno-Swedish descent. When she was three months old, Södergran's family moved to Raivola (later Rodzino), a village in the Finnish province of Karelia, close to the Russian border. Thenceforth, the family divided their time between St. Petersburg, where they wintered, and Raivola. Södergran received a sound education at a German church school, studying the literature of France, Russia, and Germany. Her apprentice verse was written in German, which she learned not only in school but also at the sanatorium in Davos, Switzerland; she was a patient there from 1912 to 1913 and again from 1913 to 1914. Heinrich Heine provided the model for much of Södergran's early writing.

Södergran's father died of tuberculosis in 1907, after which his family ceased to reside in St. Petersburg. In 1908, Södergran was discovered to be tubercular, and between 1909 and 1911, she was on several occasions confined to a sanatorium at Nummela, in Finland.

Nummela was the only place she lived where Swedish was the primary language; otherwise, Södergran spoke Swedish mainly with her mother.

It is believed that the philologist Hugo Bergroth was instrumental in persuading Södergran to write in Swedish. Nevertheless, she had very little knowledge of the literature of that language, beyond the work of two nineteenth century authors, C. J. L. Almqvist, whose novel *Drottningens juvel-smycke* (1833; the queen's jewelry) she found fascinating, and Johan Ludvig Runeberg, with his aphoristic lyrical poems. Her interest, rather, lay elsewhere—in such German expressionists as Else Lasker-Schüler and Alfred Mombert, in Victor Hugo (whose *Les Misérables*, 1862, captured her attention), in Rudyard Kipling (particularly his *Jungle Book*, 1894), in Maurice Maeterlinck, in Walt Whitman, and in the Russians Konstantin Dmitrievich Balmont and Igor Severyanin.

A turning point in her life was her love affair, during her early twenties, with a married man, an affair of the kind customarily known as "unhappy." Presumably it was not consistently so. For a poet so able to live with paradox, the relationship may have been, after all, deeply inspirational. Certainly, the affair virtually coincided with an intense period of production, during which she wrote the first of her mature works. Södergran's sense of her own poetic powers had been waxing throughout these two years, 1915 and 1916, and had given her the impetus to visit Helsinki to show her manuscripts to Arvid Mörne, the poet, and Gunnar Castrén, the critic. Yet the literary world of Helsinki was unreceptive to her work; her first book, *Poems*, prompted one reviewer to wonder whether her publisher had wanted to give Swedish Finland a good laugh, and in general, reactions ranged from amused bewilderment to open ridicule. Södergran appears to have been taken completely aback by such uncomprehending hostility; her naïveté, one of the strengths of her poetry, was in this respect a major weakness of her person, and it caused her many painful passages.

Yet resilience was hers in equal measure, and before long, she regained equilibrium, coming to think of herself (indeed, quite properly) as a literary pioneer. Her sense of mission grew with her reading of Friedrich Wilhelm Nietzsche, whose influence may be traced throughout her subsequent work. Will in the sense of libido becomes a fundamental drive which her poetry not only acknowledges but also would advance. In a poem composed in 1919, Södergran writes:

> I am nothing but a boundless will,
> a boundless will, but for what, for what?
> Everything is darkness around me.
> I cannot lift a straw.
> My will wants but one thing, but this thing I don't
> know.
> When my will breaks from me, then shall I die:
> All hail my life, my death and my fate!

She praises the moment when these three abstract, powerful forces unite into the one action, the moment of discovery ("Ah, this is what I want, was wanting!"), when the alienation of categories is banished by the wholeness, the good health, of choice, when the will to choose and the will to be chosen fuse, banishing both subjective and objective, to disclose the truth: that life, death, and one's fate are all of a piece, compose one single motion. The "I" one was until that moment "dies" and is replaced by the "I" who has chosen, having discovered that "thing" which until then one had not known.

Resilient though she was, however, Södergran was increasingly ill, and it might have been literally the case that, on certain days, she could not "lift a straw." More than her personal world was in turmoil. World War I, in which Russia was then engaged, led to the Russian Revolution of 1917. Raivola, astride a trunk line of the railroad from St. Petersburg, witnessed both troop transports and refugee trains passing through, and, with the revolution, Södergran and her mother found themselves destitute, for St. Petersburg had been their source of funds. In this same year, 1917, Finland declared its independence from Russia, and the ensuing civil war resulted in near starvation for the poet and her family. Yet at the same time, to behold so many other substantially afflicted persons helped Södergran place her own hardships in perspective. She learned quickly from her experiences. Huge, irrational forces had been unleashed, yet Södergran had the grace to recognize her world. In her introduction to her next book, *The September Lyre*, she observes:

> My poems are to be taken as careless sketches. As to the contents, I let my instincts build while my intellect watches. My self-confidence comes from the fact that I have discovered my dimensions. It does not behoove me to make myself smaller than I am.

To some extent, this was surely a whistling in the dark. Two further books of poetry were met with tremendous hostility. There was one favorable review, however, by Hagar Olsson, and to this Södergran responded with incredulous joy. The two became fast friends, albeit mainly through correspondence. (Invited to visit Olsson in Helsinki, Södergran declined: "Insomnia, tuberculosis, no money. We live by selling our furniture.") They met only a few times, but their correspondence flourished.

Now Södergran became a convert to anthroposophy, the belief of Rudolf Steiner, and thence to a primitive Christianity, which replaced for her the writing of poetry. She returned to poetry however, shortly before her death, on June 24, 1923, at Raivola. The posthumous publication of her previously uncollected poems from 1915, under the title *Landet som icke är* (the land which is not), established her as a major poet. Subsequent collections and volumes of selected poems continue to appear, enhancing Södergran's reputation and securing for her an ever-widening audience.

Analysis

The power of Edith Södergran's poetry stems from the complex mixture of its elements. She gives the impression of being very straight-spoken, yet for all that, most of her poems are deeply enigmatic. Her choice of subjects is usually appropriate to this technique. One is reminded of a child just at that stage where puberty startles it out of one kind of consciousness into another. This is the age when the "big" questions come up: What is outside the universe? What was before time began? What is death? What shall be my destiny? And love—what is love?

Somehow, Södergran survived the subsequent stages of her life to produce virtually intact poems of a childlike naïveté wedded to a maturity that feels precocious—the precocious intelligence of the thirteen-year-old who has recently realized that she is more far-seeing than her elders and that she sees more clearly into the heart of adult life because she is so new to it. This image, subliminal in so many of her poems, of a gravely joyous child gazing directly into adulthood and finding it at once wanting and yet (wisely) sufficient, wreathes her poetry in an aura of heartbreak. All the mysterious grand abstractions—death, life, love, pain, happiness, grief, instinct, hell—framed by the pubescent as essential questions to be answered are answered in Södergran's poetry, as in life, with an image that may at first appear as basically haphazard but which one then comes to apprehend as intuitively adequate. Life proves to be not the wondrous thing one had at thirteen thought it to be; it turns out, however, in its difference from the ideal, to be *something* (a state of affairs that is recognized, by a sudden twist of maturity, to be in itself wondrous).

"The Day Cools . . ."

Södergran does not incorporate undigested personal experience into her work. Her experience is nearly always universalized, through either a symbol or (more interestingly) some less predicated distancing technique—or a combination of both, as at the end of part 2 of "The Day Cools . . .":

> You cast your love's red rose
> into my white womb—
> I hold it tight in my hot hands,
> your love's red rose that will shortly wilt . . .
> O thou master, with the icy eyes,
> I accept the crown you give me,
> that bends my head towards my heart.

This passage demonstrates Södergran's ability to qualify the symbol with realism and realism with its own stylization: "head" being a symbol for thought, rationality, as distinct from feeling, impulse, symbolized by heart, yet at the same time as she is using this symbolic language to imply that, in love, the head is brought nearer to the heart, she is also stating the fact that, in the act of love, the neck can bend the head forward, bringing it literally closer to the heart, but perhaps *only* literally. The physical undoes the symbolic, even as the latter transcends the physical. The same double movement is present throughout this poem: The presence of the physical both renders the symbolism ironic ("red rose" is so obviously a penis) and accounts for it, explains away its symbolism, even while the symbolic is raising the sad physical facts to a transcendent plane, as though from lust to love.

"DISCOVERY"

In this technique, the essential ambiguity of such a situation is preserved intact, preserved from the poet's intentions upon it and from the reader's everlasting demand for assurance. Is the "master" subject only to "higher" motives? That one may doubt this is suggested in a subsequent poem, "Discovery":

> Your love darkens my star—
> the moon rises in my life.
> My hand is not at home in yours.
> Your hand is lust—
> my hand is longing.

Here, Södergran lays out neatly the two halves of the picture, the "fifty-fifty" of the heterosexual fix. His love, although desired (in fact, "longed for"), threatens to overwhelm the woman, who senses that her own "star" (her own sense of self and particular destiny) is being obscured by the male presence, no doubt filled with assumptions and demands, obscured in the way that the light of a star is blocked when the full moon rises. Panicked, she retreats: "My hand is not at home in yours." Presumably she had felt otherwise about this man. Thus she leads herself to her "discovery": He lusts, while she longs. He also longs, as no doubt she also lusts; it is a question of which emotion is primary. Enlightened, however sadly, the poet, through observing this dynamic, gives herself back to herself and finds her star. Able to describe the process, she finds a power within herself to withstand it. It is noteworthy that Södergran is not deterred from her use of natural imagery by preexisting symbolic meaning: that the moon, for example, is customarily a symbol of the female.

"FOREST LAKE"

Such nature imagery permeates Södergran's work from start to finish. Whole poems are built from observations of the landscape and weather of Raivola. "Forest Lake" is a striking example of this:

> I was alone on the sunny strand
> by the forest's pale blue lake,
> in the heavens floated a single cloud
> and on the water a single isle.
> The ripening summer's sweetness dripped
> in beads from every tree
> and into my opened heart ran
> down one little drop.

Nature burgeons on all sides in supernumerous abundance, while in the felt middle of it all, the human singularity (which remarks not only the various signs of its own condition—cloud, island, lake, each one a singular—but also, the signs of its opposite state—the "beads" that drip from "every tree") inevitably, inescapably one feels, selects for itself that which most speaks to it of itself from out of the swarming possibilities. One senses at once the rightness of this as well as the sadness. In the phrase "one little drop" a pathos inheres: Why so little, when one is offered so much? Yet the poem offers also a sense of this as sufficient; it is characteristic of Södergran's poetry to play between senses of pathetic inadequacy and grateful, if humble, plenitude.

"THE DAY COOLS . . ." PART 4

Sometimes the speaker senses herself as the source of the inadequacy, as in part 4 of "The Day Cools . . . ":

> You sought a flower
> and found a fruit.
> You sought a well
> and found a sea.
> You sought a woman
> and found a soul—
> you are disappointed.

The irony of the situation, which she sees and names so clearly, does not completely expunge the guilt of the speaker. Somehow, one feels, she holds herself to blame for being so much more than the seeker expected to find. She is caught in the patriarchal trap, even as she would, with her vision and fluency, transcend it. Indeed, for her to testify otherwise would be an impossible distortion of reality, one which would demean her import and that of her fellow sufferers.

The simple symmetry of this poem reminds one of Södergran's courage in discarding so many of the conventional signs of verse. Perhaps it was as much a blind plunge forward as a reasoned decision; no matter, the result is the same. Whether the reader indeed interprets her poems, as she advised, as "careless sketches," or, disregarding that phrase as one born of a strictly temporary bravado, one views them as finished pieces is irrelevant. Certainly, she did not abjure regular meter and rhyme out of inability; while still a schoolgirl, she composed hundreds of verses in the manner typical of Heinrich Heine.

While at Davos, Södergran learned something of the current furor and ferment at work in European art and letters, and possibly of free verse. Above all, however, her writing is instinct with craft; Södergran has no need to make a display of her talent in more conventional terms because so many of her poems bear this out at the microscopic level.

"Nothing"

If there are infelicities in Södergran's poetry, they are those inherent in writing poetry whose rhythms are at times those of prose. One notes the occasional deafness to the echoes of what is being said. "Have you looked your dreams in the eye?" she inquires, her own eye on the object of her poem, distracting her from the faintly ridiculous literal picture presented. Because both "dreams" and "look in the eye" are clichés, it is not easy to remember that they allude to specifics. Her practice of personifying abstractions gets her into trouble sometimes: "My soul can only cry and laugh and wring its hands," for example, or "Will fate throw snowballs at me?" Yet there is a charm of sorts in these minor ineptitudes, some echo of the child just learning to put words together; surely this is one with her ingenuousness and directness. The person who senses her soul as real, as real as her body, is blind to the unintended image offered of a pair of bodiless hands "wringing" each other; this is the same person who can write (of the abstraction "Nothing" in the poem of that name)

> We should love life's long hours of illness
> and narrow years of longing
> as we do the brief instants when the desert flowers.

In this poem, Södergran is reminiscent of John Keats in "To Autumn"—the spiritual definition of "iron" circumstance which allows one room to live. It is a wonderful benignity, won at what cost from malign condition, and not at all ironic. There are certainly poems of less mitigated bitterness, but even with these, one feels that in the act of naming the enemy, Södergran has won the only release truly possible from the shadow of death and death-in-life. Through the storms within her own organism, as through the storms without (war, revolution, poverty, and hunger) she looked steadily into the heart of things. In a very late and striking poem, she wrote

> I long for the land that is not,
> because everything that is, I'm too weary to want.
> The moon tells me in silvery runes
> of the land that is not.
> The land where all our wishes shall be wondrously
> fulfilled,
> the land where our shackles drop off,
> the land where we cool our bleeding forehead
> in moon-dew.
> My life was a feverish illusion.
> But one thing I have found and one I have really won—
> the way to the land that is not.

The poem has a further stanza but should have ended here. Södergran's gift for discerning the positive in the negative has seldom been more strongly realized. Through her genius, the reader comes to understand how the negative is so qualified, somewhat as "faery lands forlorn" in Keats's "Ode to a Nightingale," and that a simple act of the imagination may transform nothingness into a vision more sustaining than anything which blank materialism affords.

Other major work

nonfiction: *Ediths brev: Brev från Edith Södergran till Hagar Olsson*, 1955.

Bibliography

Hird, Gladys. "Edith Södergran: A Pioneer of Finland-Swedish Modernism." *Books from Finland* 11 (1978): 5-7. A short historical and critical assessment of Södergran's life and works.

Jones, W. Glyn, and M. A. Branch, eds. *Edith Södergran*. London: University of London Press, 1992. A collection of nine biographical essays dealing with Södergran's life and works. Includes bibliographical references and indexes.

Katchadourian, Stina. Introduction to *Love and Solitude*, by Edith Södergran. 3d ed. Seattle, Wash.: Fjord Press, 1992. Katchadourian's introduction offers some biographical and historical background for Södergran's life and works.

Mossberg, Christer Lennart. "I'll Bake Cathedrals: An Introduction to the Poetry of Edith Södergran." *Folio: Papers on Foreign Language and Literature* 11 (1978): 116-126. A critical introduction to Södergran's poetic works.

Schoolfield, George C. *Edith Södergran: Modernist Poet in Finland*. Westport, Conn.: Greenwood Press, 1984. A biography of Södergran detailing the historical background of her life and works. Includes bibliographic references and an index.

David Bromige;
bibliography updated by the editors

Dionysios Solomos

Born: Zakynthos, Greece; April 8, 1798
Died: Corfu, Greece; November 21, 1857

Principal poetry

Rime improvisate, 1822
Imnos is tin eleftheria, 1823 (*The Hymn to Liberty*, 1825)
Is ton thanato tou Lord Byron, 1824
Lambros, 1834 (partial), 1859
Ta euriskomena, 1859 (collection of works including the foregoing as well as *Eleftheroi poliorkimenoi*, *To Kritikos*, and *Porphyras*)
Hapanta, 1880, 1948-1960 (collected works)
Faith and Motherland: Collected Poems, 1998
The Free Besieged and Other Poems, 2000

Other literary forms

Although verse was Dionysios Solomos's major form of expression, he published two works of prose. *Dialogos* (1824) is Solomos's defense of the demotic language of Greece, a kind of rebuttal to Adamantios Koras and other proponents of the *katharevousa*, the purist tongue. Solomos asserted that the language of the people belongs only to them, and no external forces can change it. It was also part of his credo that the poet, as a custodian of the language, must enrich and ennoble it from within. The twenty-five or thirty pages of *Dialogos* (one part of the work has been lost), written in the form of a conversation between a poet, a friend, and a philosopher, have served as the prototype of modern Greek prose. Solomos's other prose work is *I yineka tis Zakynthos* (1927, 1944; *The Woman of Zakynthos*, 1982), an enigmatic, fragmentary work set at the time of the fall of Missolonghi.

Achievements

Dionysios Solomos is the national poet of modern Greece. The first four stanzas of his *The Hymn to Liberty* were proclaimed by King Otto in 1865 as the Greek national anthem, and Greek schoolchildren have been learning and memorizing Solomos's verses for more than 150 years. His use of demotic Greek—the spoken language of everyday life—prepared the way for the extraordinary flowering of Greek poetry in the twentieth century.

Solomos has been the subject of studies in Italian, Dutch, French, German, Romanian, and Turkish, as well as English. The critic M. Byron Raizis has estimated that scholarly works on Solomos "approach the one-thousand mark." Because, in the early years of his apprenticeship, Solomos wrote in Italian, he has been especially interesting to Italian poets and critics.

Solomos's contemporaries acknowledged him as the founder of modern Greek poetry: He took it upon himself to become a Greek Dante, a poet who would use the vernacular, the language of the people, in order to praise his countrymen's struggle for liberation, in order to sing of the pains, the values, and the joys of the land of his birth. What Alexander Pushkin, who was born a year later, came to mean to the Russians, Solomos came to mean to the Greeks. Like Alexander Pushkin's lyrics, Solomos's Romantic verse lauded freedom and castigated tyranny. Solomos is regarded as the quintessence of the national genius; it is no wonder that upon his death, the Greek poet was given a state funeral which was followed by public mourning throughout Greece.

It is not only for his poetry, then, that Solomos is important. He was the bard of the Greek War of Independence; he introduced Romanticism to Greece; and, perhaps most important, he gave dignity to demotic Greek, the language of the people, at a time when pretentious literati in Greece were working hard to impose the purist tongue on the recently freed, tormented country.

In contemporary Greece, Solomos's appeal transcends ideological boundaries: He is loved by conservatives, for he represents that old spirit of the disciplined artist, the pioneer of Hellenic values; the leftists honor him for praising the virtues of struggle and for dramatizing the plight of the oppressed; the Greek Orthodox Church has embraced him for praising the religious values of his land and for his acceptance of the Church's role in the war of liberation from the Turks; finally, he is admired by Greek youth, who respond to the youthful energy and simplicity of his patriotic and romantic verse. Solomos's achievement as a Greek poet is unquestioned and unshakable.

Biography

After the fall of Constantinople in May, 1453, Greece, under oppressive Ottoman rule, remained for nearly four hundred years a cultural wasteland. When Crete fell to the Turks in 1669, the Solomos family migrated to the Heptanesian island of Zakynthos, having first been honored by the Venetian administrators in Crete with titles of nobility. After one generation, Count Nicholas Solomos, the poet's father (acknowledged as Count by the Venetian authorities of Zakynthos), succeeded in acquiring the tobacco monopoly of the island, and in a few years, the shrewd businessman amassed a large fortune. Dionysios Solomos was born to Count Nicholas in 1798; at his birth, his father was sixty-one and his mother, the count's maid, only seventeen years old. When Solomos was seven years old, he came under the tutelage of an Italian priest, Santo Rossi, then living in exile on Zakynthos because of his liberal views. Father Rossi taught the precocious boy not only the Italian language but also the culture and the literature of Italy.

After the death of his father, Solomos (accompanied by Rossi) was sent to Italy for a more sophisticated, more systematic education. In 1807 and 1808, in Venice and Cremona, the youth studied Latin and Italian philology. He was introduced to liberal ideas, to Romantic aestheticism, and to the works of Vergil, Dante, and Petrarch, who were to influence his poetry. In the period from 1812 to 1814, he wrote his first Italian verse. The fall of 1815 found the seventeen-year-old Solomos studying law at the University of Pavia. Although he received his first certificate of law, literature was his consuming interest. In Milan in 1817, Solomos met the famous poet and translator of Homer, Vincenzo Monti. Legend has it that the young Greek got into an argument with Monti over a certain passage in Dante's *Inferno* (c. 1320). "Nobody should rationalize so much," Monti chastised the youth. "One should feel, feel." Solomos's reply has been repeated with pride by his biographers: "First the mind must understand vigorously, and then the heart must feel warmly what the mind has comprehended."

Solomos's return to Zakynthos in August, 1818, presented him with a challenge: How could he thrive intellectually in a place that did not have the cultural fervor of the Italy of his adolescence? There were some intellectuals on the island, but not of the caliber of Ignazio Baretta, Mateo Butturini, or Vincenzo Monti. Nevertheless, Zakynthos was not intellectually barren: Andreas Kalvos, a contemporary of Solomos and a great poet himself, was born in Zakynthos, though there is no indication that he ever met Solomos. The island, too, was the birthplace of Ugo Foscolo (a half-Greek poet who wrote in Italian, a giant of the Romantic movement), whom Solomos did befriend, as in due course he befriended several other Zakynthos intellectuals.

Italian gave way to the Greek language in Solomos's verse soon after his return to Zakynthos. His sonnets and religious poetry still manifested his Romantic tendencies, along with the techniques of prosody that he had learned in Cremona and Venice. He had not yet achieved the mastery of the demotic which would distinguish his later verse.

Solomos's serious Greek verse began, in fact, when Spyridon Trikoupis visited Zakynthos. Trikoupis was a politician and the foremost historian of the Greek War of Independence. A relative of the Greek leader Alexandros Mavrokordatos, Trikoupis had come to Zakynthos to meet Lord Byron. When Trikoupis met Solomos, at the end of 1822, the latter read him his Italian "Ode per prima messa." Trikoupis fell silent for a moment and then told Solomos that what their country needed was a Greek poetry. "Greece is waiting for her Dante," exclaimed Trikoupis. Solomos must have been both flattered and challenged. He had not actively joined the fight against the Turks, partly because of his reclusive personality and partly because the Greek revolutionaries, though heroic, were cantankerous and uneducated villagers. There is no indication, in fact, that the poet ever visited the Greek mainland. The meeting with Trikoupis, however, sparked in the young poet a patriotic sense of literary duty. Though he never forsook his Italianate learning, he turned to Greek themes and the Greek language.

Some six months after meeting Trikoupis, Solomos completed the 158 quatrains which constitute *The Hymn to Liberty*. The long poem (whose first stanzas became the Greek national anthem) reenacts scenes from the Greek War of Independence and exalts the glory of Greece and of Greek freedom. Solomos's diligent effort to improve his Greek and to become the Greek poet par excellence must have also been inspired by the publication of Claude Fauriel's *Chansons populaires de Grece* (1824), in which the Frenchman praised the Greek language as "the most beautiful of the European languages and the one . . . suited to perfection." Fauriel further prophesied that "modern Greek will soon be a language which, without resembling ancient Greek more than it now resembles it, will have no reason to envy it." Years later, Solomos would collaborate with Fauriel.

In 1928, when most of Greece had been liberated, Solomos moved from Zakynthos to the island of Kerkyra (Corfu). By then, Solomos had become famous throughout Greece, and on Corfu, he found the solitude that he sought. There, he pursued more vigorously his studies in the German Romantic movement, in particular the works of Friedrich Schiller. Though a more prolific decade was behind him, the decade that followed was to be more impressive in terms of the quality of his work. On Corfu, Solomos honed and refined his poetry, working on his fragmentary *The Woman of Zakynthos*, on *Eleftheroi poliorkimenoi* (the free besieged), and on *To Kritikos*, revising his *Lambros*, and writing his serene "Funeral Ode" and "To an English Lady."

Temperamental, especially during his years on Corfu, Solomos manifested a disquieting propensity to leave his works incomplete. An extreme perfectionist, he destroyed almost as many manuscripts as he was able to complete. Kostis Palamas, Solomos's successor as the poet of the Greek people, discerned a duality in Solomos's nature: the dedicated, patient, profound creator opposed to the impetuous, bored, immature man who could not complete his work when he felt disheartened and unsatisfied. Other critics, in examining his character, have pointed to the distractions of a prolonged legal battle: John Leontarakis, Solomos's half brother, sued in order to prove, both for inheritance purposes and out of vindictiveness, that he, John, was the only legitimate son of Count Nicholas. The trial that ensued lasted from 1833 to 1838 and embittered Solomos greatly, since he had helped his half brother both socially and financially. This humiliating episode, and the poet's own restless nature, explain—as well as anything can explain—his inability to finish many of his poems.

The litigation with his half brother—finally won by Solomos—caused the poet to retreat even more into his solitude. "There is no doubt," he wrote to his friend George Markoras, "that one can live well only alone." It was probably at this time that Solomos began drinking, which may well have affected both the quality as well as the quantity of his subsequent work. Solomos's struggle for perfection, however, overcame all the crises that held him back. Indeed, he wrote his best poetry during the last twenty years of his life: *To Kritikos*, *Eleftheroi poliorkimenoi*, and *Porphyras* were written during this period. The obstacles in his life were counterbalanced by the recognition he received not only in Greece but also throughout Western Europe. In 1849, King Otto of Greece bestowed on Solomos the Golden Cross of the Royal Order of the Savior. By then, Solomos was respected even among the envious mainland writers.

Despite his preference for solitude, Solomos had a select group of friends while living on Corfu. James Polylas, who selflessly collected and edited the Solomos's works posthumously (in *Ta euriskomena*), was one of the most loyal; Nicholas Mantzaros, the composer who set the lyrics of *The Hymn to Liberty* to music, was another. Solomos never married, and no evidence of a love affair exists.

From 1847 to 1851, Solomos returned to writing verse in Italian, which some critics see as evidence of his disappointment with his output in Greek. Yet, even when he wrote in Italian, most of his themes remained Greek ("To Orpheus," "The Greek Mother," "The Greek Vessel"). It was also during this period, between 1847 and 1849, that he wrote one of his greatest works in Greek, *Porphyras*.

During the last decade of his life, Solomos's health deteriorated. He suffered a cerebral stroke in 1851, and his niece's suicide caused him further depression that year; fits of melancholy continued until his death. On November 21, 1857, he died of a stroke. It is alleged that on his deathbed, the poet remembered the beloved mentor of his youth, Santo Rossi, and that in gratitude to him, he recited stanza 95 of *The Hymn to Liberty*, where Liberty is seen allegorically in imagery of light:

Fiery gleams of flashing cluster
Hang from lip, eye, forehead bright,
Hand and foot are clothed in luster,
And around you all is light.

Analysis

It is unfortunate that Dionysios Solomos's poetry is almost totally resistant to translation. Just as Robert Burns's musical lines suffer greatly in translation into other languages, and just as Pushkin's lyric Russian is frustrating to translators, so Solomos and his lyric rhyming lines lose a great deal in translation. It is difficult to convey the exquisite music of his stanzas, his struggle to achieve perfection with each poem, his admirable development in diction and form. A good translation will communicate only in part the energy of his language, but even in translation, one can still appreciate Solomos's love of freedom and his loathing of oppression, his compassion for the humble and his bewilderment with the injustices of destiny.

Solomos started to write seriously upon his return from Italy in 1818. His early poems, written in Italian, are more mature and precise than the naïve and imperfect poems that he wrote when he first experimented with the Greek language. His earliest poems were written in short, flexible trochaic and iambic lines; when he attempted decapentasyllabic couplets, in imitation of the Greek folk song, the prosody appeared contrived and superficial.

Among these early poems, there are many which are pastoral in nature, such as "The Death of the Shepherd," "Eurykome," and "The Death of the Orphan Girl." Most typical of Solomos's work at this stage is "The Mad Mother," a moving poem about the tragic death of a child; the Romantic elements are obvious. Here, Solomos employs a favorite theme: the suffering of a gentle woman at the hands of fate. "The Unknown Woman" and "Xanthoula" are two more sophisticated poems with this theme. In the best of these early poems, Solomos avoids emotional description, though emotional connotations are cleverly insinuated.

The Hymn to Liberty

Solomos was profoundly inspired by the revolution of 1821. In his *Dialogos*, he exclaimed: "Have I anything else in my mind but liberty and the language?" In 1823, he completed *The Hymn to Liberty*, a vigorous paean to Greek freedom that bought instant fame to the twenty-five-year-old poet. Here, the poet, surveying the ordeals and ideals of the enslaved Greeks, intertwines the essence of freedom with the whole destiny of the Greek nation, as he recounts, one by one, both the sacrifices and the achievements of the Greek fighters.

The Hymn to Liberty begins as the poet, addressing Liberty, visualizes her rising from the bones of slain Greek heroes. He recognizes her from her gaze and from the sharpness of her sword; as she paces across the blood-soaked hills and valleys, he greets her with joy and pride: "Hail, oh Hail, Liberty!" The poem goes on to relate the Greeks' struggles for freedom, and the blood shed on Liberty's behalf—the battle of Tripolis, the destruction of Corinth, the naval victories. The tempo is rapid, robust, and rolling; the trochaic stanzas move from image to image without sacrificing smooth transitions or unity. For 140 or so of the poem's 158 stanzas, Liberty is both the inspiration and the unifying force.

In the last section, however, the poem loses direction as Solomos summons the great powers of Europe to help "the defenders of the Cross." The references to Liberty, her actions, words, and inspiring presence are abandoned as the poet chastises the larger powers of Europe for having turned their backs on Greece for centuries.

Is ton thanato tou Lord Byron and "To Psara"

Solomos's next patriotic work, *Is ton thanato tou Lord Byron* (on the death of Lord Byron), is inferior to *The Hymn to Liberty*, which it resembles in both meter and subject matter. Though artistically a failure, this long poem served its purpose in expressing the gratitude of the Greek nation to the famous philhellene. That

Solomos's craft was not deteriorating at this stage of his career is manifested by the short poems written during this period, from 1824 to 1827. "To Psara" is a short lyric that all Greek children learn by heart (the town of Psara had just been burned to the ground by the Turks when the poem was written):

> On Psara's dark and desolate stone
> Glory softly walks all alone
> Musing over her son's noble deeds
> As her hair is adorned by a wreath
> Made of some yet unrazed weeds
> That remained on the wasted heath.

Lambros

Lambros is a melodramatic tale about a young man (Lambros) who fathers three sons and a daughter out of wedlock with a teenage beauty named Maria. Lambros, while fighting the Turks, meets a young man who turns out to be a girl in disguise. He falls in love with her and seduces her, only to discover that she is the daughter he had long ago left behind. The daughter drowns herself in a lake, and Lambros returns to tell Maria what has happened. Grief is followed by their agreement to marry each other. As their three sons accompany them to the church, however, Lambros, overwhelmed by pain and shame, drowns himself, and Maria, after going insane, also drowns herself in the same lake. Though *Lambros* is maudlin by modern standards and though it lacks unity, there is robust emotion in it and much pathos. The Byronic influence is evident in the fifteen-syllable lines of its octaves.

To Kritikos

Like *Lambros*, *To Kritikos* (the Cretan) is a tragic narrative of romantic love. Its prosody and its theme were inspired by the Cretan epic *Erotokritos* (seventeenth century), and its musicality, simplicity, and skillful syntax have been highly praised by critics. An incomplete work, *To Kritikos* is oneiric in content and decapentasyllabic in meter. The passionate, musical, and well-controlled work is about a Cretan youth found at sea at night, trying to rescue his beloved. The girl is his only contact with life. Everyone in his family has been disgraced and destroyed by the Turks. His struggle with the irrational, unpredictable sea is juxtaposed to his struggle against the Turks in Crete.

Early in the poem, there appears to the youth a "moonlight-dressed" maid. When she stares at the stars, they stop twinkling, and she makes the light seem brighter. The youth feels that he has seen her before; indeed, the girl is a "Platonic memory." The Hungarian critic Andrei Horvat has said that she is an angel of beauty and goodness descended from the Platonic heaven. The young Cretan's epiphany is accompanied by a heavenly sound, as if to complete the harmony of the senses. In keeping with classical Greek notions of form and concept, Solomos here weds the ideal and the real—an endeavor which would be successful in many of his poems. What Solomos intended to symbolize with the moonlight-dressed girl may be suggested by his later poem, *Eleftheroi poliorkimenoi*, in which a "light-vested" maid symbolizes life and nature, which, along with freedom, are most dear and most inspiring to the Cretan lad.

After four thunderbolts strike the sea, a calmness reigns everywhere, and in his beloved's embrace the youth breathes a fragrance that he compares to a flower garden amid the silence. From that moment, the narrator-youth says, his hand can no longer grasp the knife: The warrior has turned poet and lover. In marvelous synesthesia, the youth hears his beloved's eyes within him and is touched by her smile. Both tears and smile are inspirational, and the Cretan becomes more eloquent, so that the lines that follow are among Solomos's most beautiful. Although the youth turns to his beloved only to find her dead, Solomos suggests that the Cretan has triumphed: He has experienced true wonder and beauty; he has become a poet. In both *To Kritikos* and *Lambros*, Solomos tried to prove that demotic Greek was capable of expressing the loftiest emotions and not merely mundane realities.

Eleftheroi poliorkimenoi

Eleftheroi poliorkimenoi is a long poem which many regard as Solomos's finest work. Solomos's intent was to show how moral strength triumphs over physical violence. The heroes of the poem are the masses, the people; the poet dramatizes the plight of the besieged at Missolonghi, who, for more than a year and against unbelievable odds, withstood the Turkish attacks. The lyricism of this work reaches heights unequaled in all Greek poetry. Though incomplete, *Eleftheroi poliorkimenoi* has the peculiar fascination of the fragmentary, a quality it shares with the Hermes of Praxiteles and the Venus de Milo. Solomos began the poem in 1826—the year when Missolonghi, after its inhabitants' heroic stand, fell to the Turks—and worked on it until his death.

The poem changes metric form as it moves along, and parts of it, in fact, are in prose. Spring in all its glory and the beauty of nature ("April of the golden hair is dancing with Eros") aim to weaken the resolve of the Missolonghians to die fighting for their freedom ("on such a day dying is death a thousand times"). It is a time of the year when human beings would love to live forever. The besieged are confronted with the temptation to embrace the loveliness and pleasure surrounding them. The patriotic sense of duty which sustains them in the face of such temptation is best exemplified in the scene with a young orphan girl. An angel descends and offers the doomed girl, whose lover has already been killed in battle, a pair of wings with which to escape. She proposes to accept the wings, not in order to fly away, but to wrap them round her and wait for death in solidarity with the other heroic women.

It was with such a sense of duty in mind that Solomos originally named his incomplete masterpiece "The Obligation." The defenders of Missolonghi, like their ancestors in ancient tragedy, place glory above hope and duty above expedience. The overriding moral imperative is to live free or die. The poem's theme is the struggle between ethical duty and merciless necessity. That the Greeks of Missolonghi will be defeated is not the issue; rather, the question is *how* they will be defeated.

Porphyras

During the last decade of his life, Solomos composed *Porphyras*, which some critics regard as his masterpiece. Though the poem is incomplete, its greatness is evident: Its rhythms, its diction, its humane theme, and its poetic treatment of ideas are superb. The poem was inspired by the news that an English soldier had been devoured by a shark (called *porphyras* by the islanders of Corfu) in the port of Corfu. Solomos makes the soldier, as he struggles between sea and sky, a symbol of spiritual strength fighting against the aggressiveness and obstinacy of matter—purity against barbarity. When the young Englishman is confronted with "reasonless and monstrous strength," he finds in a moment of self-awareness the strength to resist and to acknowledge his being: "Before the noble breath was spent, his soul was filled with joy./ Suddenly in a lightning flash the young man knew himself."

Solomos must be seen not only as a poet but also as a patriot and a humanist, a man who preached a higher sense of morality. He must also be recognized as one of the major pioneers of modern Greek poetry.

Other major works

nonfiction: *Dialogos*, 1824; *I yineka tis Zakynthos*, 1927, 1944 (*The Woman of Zakynthos*, 1982).

Bibliography

Coutelle, Louis, Theofanis G. Stavrou, and David R. Weinberg. *A Greek Diptych: Dionysios Solomos and Alexandros Papadiamantis*. Minneapolis, Minn.: Nostos Books, 1986. A historical and biographical study of two nineteenth century Greek authors. Includes bibliographical references.

Mackridge, Peter. *Dionysios Solomos*. New Rochelle, N.Y.: Aristide, 1989. A critical analysis of Solomos's works. Includes bibliographical references.

Polites, Linos. *A History of Modern Greek Literature*. Oxford, England: Clarendon Press, 1973. A historical and critical study of Greek poetry of the nineteenth and twentieth centuries. Includes bibliographic references.

Raizis, M. Byron. *Dionysios Solomos*. New York: Twayne, 1972. An introductory biography and critical study of selected works by Solomos. Includes bibliographic references.

Minas Savvas

Cathy Song

Born: Honolulu, Hawaii; August 20, 1955

Principal poetry

Picture Bride, 1983
Frameless Windows, Squares of Light, 1988

School Figures, 1994
The Land of Bliss, 2001

OTHER LITERARY FORMS

Cathy Song is primarily a poet. She first wrote short stories and published one, "Beginnings (For Bok Pil)," in the Spring, 1976, issue of *Hawaii Review*.

ACHIEVEMENTS

Cathy Song is the first native Hawaiian writer to receive national recognition for her work. She has also made significant contributions to Asian American literature. Her work is applauded by mainstream critics and scholars, and she has been included in a variety of important anthologies, including the *Norton Anthology of American Literature* and the *Heath Anthology of American Literature*. Individual poems have been published in numerous important journals, including *Michigan Quarterly Review*, *Poetry*, and *The Kenyon Review*.

Song's first book of poetry, *Picture Bride*, won her the 1982 Yale Series of Younger Poets Award and a nomination for a National Book Critics Circle Award. She also received the Shelley Memorial Award from the Poetry Society of America and the Hawaii Award for Literature, both in 1994.

BIOGRAPHY

Cathy Song was born in Honolulu, Hawaii, in 1955; her mother was Chinese American, her father Korean American. She grew up in Wahiawa, a small plantation town in a rural section of Oahu, then moved to Honolulu with her family when she was seven years old. She began writing as a high school student and spent two years at the University of Hawaii at Manoa, mentored by John Unterecker, a poet and critic. She then moved to New England, completing a bachelor's degree in English literature at Wellesley College in 1977 and a master's degree in creative writing at Boston University in 1981. She and her family lived on the mainland, in Boston and Colorado, for several years.

Song returned to Hawaii in 1987 with her husband, Dr. Douglas Davenport; they had two children. She has taught creative writing at various universities, including the University of Hawaii, and for the Poets in the Schools program, which she enthusiastically supports.

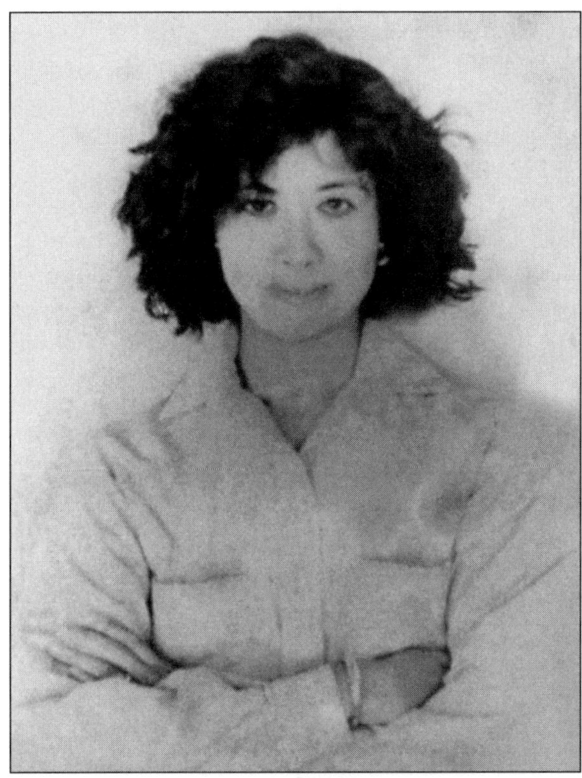

Cathy Song (Courtesy of Korea Times)

Song became a member of the Bamboo Ridge study group, a group of local Hawaiian poets and fiction writers. She has also worked for the Bamboo Ridge Press; in 1991, Song and Juliet S. Kono edited *Sister Stew*, a collection of poetry and fiction by a variety of Hawaiian women writers that was published by the press.

ANALYSIS

In their introduction to *Sister Stew*, Cathy Song and Juliet S. Kono make this observation about the works of other female Hawaiian writers:

> These writings are our voices. . . . the voices we grew up with. They are the moments of our mothers, our daughters, the intimate voices with which we speak when we speak to a loved one. . . . tell[ing] of the moments when we listened, watched, and understood, as if life, like a piece of music, could be apprehended in all its strangeness.

They could be talking about the poetry of Song, which features a woman's voice, often speaking for other women—her "picture bride" grandmother, the women in Japanese printmaker Utamaro's pictures, Georgia O'Keeffe—as well as for her children, siblings, father, grandfather, and ancestors both Chinese and Korean.

Picture Bride

Song's first book explores the relationships in her family, beginning with the title poem, which sees in imagination the arrival of her grandmother, a Korean picture bride, thirteen years younger than the "stranger/ who was her husband." Song makes her emotional connection to her grandmother clear in the first lines of the poem:

> She was a year younger
> than I,
> twenty-three when she left Korea.

Allusions to plantation control of her new environment and of the man who "waited/ turning her photograph/ to the light when the lanterns/ in the camp outside/ Waialua Sugar Mill were lit" cast doubt on the fate of the bride, whose dress, Song imagines, fills with dry wind from the fields where men like her grandfather were burning sugar cane.

"Easter: Wahiawa, 1959" revisits the grandparents and their Americanized family in the year that Hawaii gains statehood. The ambivalence that Song feels about the lives of her grandparents is clear in her paralleling of the grandfather's "long walks" in Korea with those through the sugarcane fields of Hawaii. His eighteen years cutting sugar have left their mark:

> His right arm
> grew disproportionately large
> to the rest of his body.
> He could hold three
> grandchildren in that arm.
> I want to think
> that each stalk that fell
> brought him closer
> to a clearing.

In addition to the numerous poems that relate to her family and their immigrant experience, Song devotes significant time to two visual artists to whom she feels a special connection: the nineteenth century Japanese printmaker Kitagawa Utamaro and the modern American painter Georgia O'Keeffe. The five sections of this book are named for flowers that are also paintings by O'Keeffe, and two poems address the connection Song feels to O'Keeffe: "Blue and White Lines After O'Keeffe," a poem in five sections, related from O'Keeffe's point of view, and "From the White Place," focused on O'Keeffe's reaction to her lover, photographer Alfred Stieglitz, whose "lens felt like a warm skull," and to the American Southwest.

The "Orchids" section contains three poems referring to Utamaro prints. In "Beauty and Sadness," Song describes some of the "hundreds of women/ in studies unfolding/ like flowers from a fan," women of "pleasure," including actresses, geishas, and courtesans:

> They resembled beautiful iridescent insects,
> creatures from a floating world.
> Utamaro absorbed these women of Edo
> in their moments of melancholy
> as well as of beauty.

Song relates to Utamaro and his "inconsolable eye"; his view of the "melancholy and beauty" in the lives of these women is reminiscent of her own sadness as she examines the lives of her grandmother and other women.

Frameless Windows, Squares of Light

Song's second book expands on her examination of her own experience and family. Critics have noted that it is more generalized and abstract than *Picture Bride*. In writing about this book, Song notes that these poems are about the "timeline that spans the length of your room. The window you occupy day after day. What frames the view is the mind in the diamond pinpoint of light of concentration, tunneling into memory, released by imagination."

The collection begins with "The Day You Are Born," which chronicles the sense of loss in the birth of a last child:

> There was an emptiness
>   waiting for you. The night
>   your mother knew you existed,
> she felt a flicker of sadness
>   for the life, no bigger than her thumbnail,
>   burrowing itself within her body.
> She knew you would be

her last child, the last flowering
before the pod, like a crippled hand,
withered shut; . . .

"Humble Jar," a poem that has attracted wide critical attention, focuses on a mayonnaise jar filled with buttons kept by Song's mother. Some of the buttons are useful, ready for "every emergency," but

Others were less practical,
the buttons that had been lost
and then retrieved,
only to reenter the orphanage,
the original setting (a cashmere coat,
a bottle-green evening gown) long gone,
shipped off to Goodwill
with the other ousted heirlooms:
the denture-pink Melmac plates and cups.

Although Song's mother displays other collections, her buttons were "oddly private"—the jar a place where Song's mother "retrieved a moment/out of a cluttered life—/ before I was born,/ before any of us had made our claims." Another frame from her mother's life is captured both in this poem and in a photograph from the "summer she wore that scalloped dress" and smiled "for life that was certain to be glorious."

School Figures

As the title poem of Song's third book makes clear, the reference is to the figures that ice skaters must practice repeatedly, a measure of discipline and "obedience traced into the crystalline structured,/ unadorned and essential as numbers." In her continued examination of complex family relationships, Song explores the world of her own past and the experience of her mother and other family members.

"The Grammar of Silk" recalls the Saturdays when her mother sent her to Mrs. Umemoto's sewing school and the trip to Kaimuki Dry Goods, where her mother bought her sewing supplies and where "Seamstresses waited at counters/ like librarians to be consulted." Song sees this as a "sanctuary" where mothers and daughters "consulted the oracle,/ the stone tablets of the latest pattern books." She realizes why her mother has sent her:

She was determined that I should sew
as if she knew what she herself was missing,
a moment when she could have come up for air—
the children asleep,
the dishes drying on the rack—
and turned on the lamp
and pulled back the curtain of sleep.

Themes and imagery

Song's poetry is rooted in her own experience and that of her family. She explores especially the role of women, often focusing on her mother and grandmother as well as on her own relationships with her children. Many of her poems focus on the female body—warm poems about pregnancy and sensuality such as "The White Porch"; troubled poems about aging such as "The Youngest Daughter"; poems about eating and eating disorders such as "Sunworshippers" and "Eat." Her love of music and the visual arts is clear in her images and striking use of color. She examines her relationships and her emotions honestly and clearly.

In his introduction to *Picture Bride*, Richard Hugo notes the last line of this book: "Someone very quiet once lived here." Hugo links this to the poet: "In Cathy Song's quietude lies her strength. . . . In her receptivity, passive as it seems, lies passion that is expressed in deceptive quiet and an even tone." There is also strength in the "quietude" and plain language, the images of household objects and lush nature. It is the strength of a careful observer, unafraid to examine who she is, where she comes from, and how the present moment of her life and her poetry connect to her past and her roots.

Other major works

EDITED TEXT: *Sister Stew: Fiction and Poetry by Women*, 1991 (with Juliet S. Kono).

Bibliography

Fujita-Sato, Gayle K. "'Third World' as Place and Paradigm in Cathy Song's *Picture Bride*." *MELUS* 15, no. 1 (Spring, 1988): 49-72. Fujita-Sato analyzes *Picture Bride* in terms of its examination of "relationships among ethnicity, culture, and writing." She defines "third world" in two ways: as place and as paradigm. She sees these two senses of the third world as interconnected and asserts that both are illustrated in *Picture Bride*. Her analysis of the text leads her to conclude that the Wahiawa porch represents third world as place, the white porch third world as paradigm.

Kyhan, Lee. "Korean-American Literature: The Next Generation." *Korean Journal* 34, no. 1 (Spring, 1994): 20-35. Kyhan reviews the history of Korean American literature and devotes the third section of his article to Song, the most widely known of those he considers the "next" or third generation of Korean American writers. Song typifies these writers with her focus on identity and the self in relation to her ethnic identity, her interest in the stories of her parents and grandparents, and her status as a woman examining the identity of ethnic women.

Song, Cathy. "Cathy Song: Secret Spaces of Childhood Part 2: A Symposium on Secret Spaces." *Michigan Quarterly Review* 39, no. 3 (Summer, 2000): 506-508. In response to an invitation from editors of this *MQR* special issue to "[d]escribe a private realm of your own early life that has left vivid images in your memory," Song reflects on her fascination with singing. In saying, "In singing I found my true voice," she makes the implicit connection between this lifelong love of singing and her dedication to her voice, her poetry.

Sumida, Stephen H. "Hawaii's Local Literary Tradition." In *And the View from the Shore: Literary Traditions of Hawai'i*. Seattle: University of Washington Press, 1991. In the final chapter of his book, Sumida focuses on two poems by Song to support his contention that her work has broken the "critical stranglehold" on local Hawaiian literature that considered it "insular, provincial, not universal." He views "Lost Sister" and "From a Georgia O'Keeffe Portfolio: Flower Series, No. 3, An Orchid (Makena Beach, Maui)" as demonstrating Song's "catholicity and range" and, by extension, the universality of Hawaiian writers.

Wallace, Patricia. "Divided Loyalties: Literal and Literary in the Poetry of Lorna Dee Cervantes, Cathy Song, and Rita Dove." *MELUS* 18, no. 3 (Fall, 1993): 3-20. Wallace examines the work of three contemporary American women poets and women of color from the perspective of their struggle to reconcile the presentation of a literal, historical, and often personal world with the wish to incorporate the literary elements necessary to poetry. The middle section of the article focuses on Song, analyzing two of her poems, "Humble Jar" and "Picture Bride," from this perspective. Wallace sees Song as able to "transform what seems simple or ordinary—including words themselves—by lifting things out of their ordinary settings." She offers "Humble Jar" as emblematic of this, the buttons an image both "wonderfully figurative and stubbornly literal." She concludes that in reading the work of Song, Cervantes, and Dove, "we find the most literary aspects of the poet's language bear the pressure of the actual."

Elsie Galbreath Haley

Gilbert Sorrentino

Born: Brooklyn, New York; April 27, 1929

Principal poetry

The Darkness Surrounds Us, 1960
Black and White, 1964
The Perfect Fiction, 1968
Corrosive Sublimate, 1971
A Dozen Oranges, 1976
White Sail, 1977
The Orangery, 1978
Selected Poems, 1958-1980, 1981
A Beehive Arranged on Humane Principles, 1986

Other literary forms

Although Gilbert Sorrentino started out writing poetry, his first novel, *The Sky Changes*, was published in 1966. *The Sky Changes* ignores time sequences and scrambles the past, present, and future. This was followed by a remarkable output of fiction: *Steelwork* in 1970, *Imaginative Qualities of Actual Things* the following year, and *Red the Fiend* in 1995, among others.

His fiction was experimental and won praise from critics, but it was only with the 1979 publication of *Mulligan Stew* that Sorrentino earned popular success. The novel is considered Sorrentino's masterpiece and won rave reviews in almost every influential newspaper. *Mulligan Stew* attacked the conventions of traditional novels with their linear plot lines, "real" characters, and language subordinated to story.

Sorrentino also published a play, *Flawless Play Restored: The Mask of Fungo* (pb. 1974), and a work of nonfiction, *Something Said*, in 1984.

ACHIEVEMENTS

The controversial Vietnam War and the social upheaval of the Civil Rights movement spurred an experimental writing movement that began in the 1950's and 1960's. Gilbert Sorrentino was among the literary avant-garde of the period, along with Thomas Pynchon, Robert Coover, John Barth, William Gass, and Everett LeRoi Jones (Amiri Baraka). In 1956, while at Brooklyn College, he founded the magazine *Neon* with college friends. The issues that Sorrentino edited contained contributions from prominent writers, including William Carlos Williams, Jones, Hubert Selby, Jr., and Joel Oppenheimer. From 1961 to 1963, Sorrentino wrote for and edited *Kulchur*, a literary magazine publishing writers from the Black Mountain school, the Beats, and the New School.

In addition to many grants, including Guggenheim Fellowships in 1973 and 1987, Sorrentino won the John Dos Passos Prize for Literature in 1981, an award for literature from the American Academy of Arts and Letters in 1985, and the Lannan Literary Award for fiction in 1992.

BIOGRAPHY

Gilbert Sorrentino was born in Brooklyn in 1929 to a Sicilian-born father and a third-generation Irish mother. He was raised in Roman Catholic milieus and blue-collar neighborhoods that form the setting for two of his novels. When he was eighteen he moved across the river to investigate the cultural centers of Manhattan and enrolled in Brooklyn College, but a stint in the U.S. Army Medical Corps in 1951 interrupted his education. He decided to become a writer after two years in the Army and started a novel that was eventually aborted. He returned to Brooklyn College in 1955 and founded the magazine *Neon* with, among others, Hubert Selby, Jr., with whom he formed a lifelong friendship based partly on their common background.

The Darkness Surrounds Us, his first book of poetry, appeared in 1960 and was followed by another collection, *Black and White*, in 1964. The following year, Sorrentino started what was to become a long and distinguished teaching career with a course at Columbia University and released his first novel, *The Sky Changes*, in 1966. He worked at Grove Press until 1970 as an assistant, then an editor, where his first editing assignment was Alex Haley's *The Autobiography of Malcolm X* (1965). This was followed by teaching stints at the Aspen Writer's Workshop, Sarah Lawrence College, and New School for Social Research. In 1979 he was appointed Edwin S. Quain Professor of Literature at the University of Scranton in Pennsylvania, and in 1982 he joined the faculty of Stanford University, where he taught creative writing until his retirement in 1999.

ANALYSIS

Although Gilbert Sorrentino is not usually identified with the Beat poets, he was contemporaneous with

Gilbert Sorrentino (© Thomas Victor)

them and published many as the editor of *Kulchur* magazine from 1961 to 1963. Significantly, Sorrentino's first published book of poetry appeared in 1960. The term "Beat poets" is applied to a loosely knit group of American lyric poets identified more by their shared social attitudes such as apolitical and anti-intellectual orientations, and romantic nihilism, than by stylistic, thematic, or formal unity of expression. They were centered in San Francisco and New York. The term "Beat" expressed both exhaustion and beautification. The writers were tired and disgusted with what they saw as a corrupt, crass, commercial world ruled by materialism and believed that by disassociating with that world they would provide a sort of blissful illumination for it, aided by drugs and alcohol. In the best of the Beats, such as Allen Ginsberg, Gregory Corso, and Jack Kerouac, there is a personal statement and power that goes beyond the jargon and "hip" vocabulary many of them used.

Sorrentino's poetry owes much to the Beat movement, although as his poetry continued to develop it became difficult to classify. Sorrentino has faith in the power of the word and its multiple technical possibilities, which may be the subject of all his works. The only rules that he adhered to were a rigorous parsimony for his poetic diction and a luxurious inventivenesss for his fictional language.

"Midnight Special" and "Nightpiece"

These two poems from Sorrentino's first book of poems, *The Darkness Surrounds Us*, use techniques that would be found again in his work. The title "Midnight Special" is taken from a song of that name and refers to a midnight special train ride, but in the poem it refers to a nightmare the poet has of his son in a snowy garden. In another ironic twist, the last line of the poem, "shine your everloving light on me" uses the last line of the song's chorus to address the child directly. The world of music will play an important part in Sorrentino's later poetry.

"Nightpiece" is a city poem ostensibly about rats who first are seen along a wall. One enters a house where it eventually finds itself trapped in a room and beset by fear and disorientation. The poem ends with the shocking comparison to men, who "have shot themselves// in the head/ for less reason. The poem uses images of bleak despair that are omnipresent in some of his later collections.

The Perfect Fiction

In an interview in 1994, Alexander Laurence asked Sorrentino about his interest in formalism. Sorrentino replied that he had always been interested in the formal, which in his sense is that "of a structure or series of structures that can, if one is lucky enough, generate 'content,' or, if you please, the wholeness of the work itself. Almost all of my books are written under the influence of some sort of preconceived constraint or set of rules."

In an early collection, *The Perfect Fiction* (1968), dedicated to his mother, who died in 1960, Sorrentino presents his vision of the city through a series of untitled poems written in three-line verse units called triplets and populated with shadowy, anonymous, vaguely threatening figures. The tone is uniformly dismal, creating a metropolis inhabited by lonely, lost souls, such as this image: "an old woman maybe// was kind to her cats is dying/ of loneliness. Hers is that face/ in the window, how impossibly// remote." Other characters that populate this city are "a huge black man/ riding on a motorcycle," "The stupid painter," and "stinking" people who "know that they/ are garbage and this fact/ somehow consoles them."

The triplet form of the work occasionally admits slight variations, such as "*(pentagram)*," a poem constructed of ten triplets arranged with five down each side of the page. Each stanza is very brief, the lines consisting of only one or two syllables, or only punctuation, until the last stanza, which begins with the word "nostalgia." Another variation is found in the untitled poem that begins with "Such a long walk to get out/ of any pocket, any abstract/ one," in which the third line of each triplet consists of only one word, spaced to the right of the first two lines.

Although the triplet form has never been used as widely as the couplet or the quatrain, it was used in the collection *The Desert Music and Other Poems* (1954) by William Carlos Williams, a poet whose work Sorrentino published in his literary magazine *Neon* during his college years and always admired.

A Dozen Oranges

A slim paper volume published in 1976, *A Dozen Oranges* contains twelve poems using the word "orange." It typifies the use of color in Sorrentino's poetry, which became increasingly important as he continued to write. All the poems published in *A Dozen Oranges* were reprinted in *The Orangery* (1978), to which Sorrentino added another sixty poems.

White Sail

White Sail, a collection saturated with color, was published in 1977. Although many of the poems feature other colors, such as "Drifting Blue Canoe" and "Navy Blue Room," there are also ten "Orange Sonnets" included here, each a fourteen-line poem using the color orange. One "Orange Sonnet" begins with the line "She was all in black" and expands the shade of black as symbol for the darkness of evil: "We know black here in America./ Why, it's a scream." By the third stanza the black becomes both color and metaphor: "Stick a point of orange in it/ just for fun. Just to see what comes of it." Another "Orange Sonnet" describes a town the poet sees or imagines "across the water," a town drenched in "lime-green haze" and filled with "Mothers and children in blue," where "the sky is blue." Yet the poem ends with a playful reference to orange in a direct address to the reader: "I forgot orange. There."

In a third "Orange Sonnet," subtitled "1939 World's Fair," the poet describes the fair with its "fake orange trees" and includes this image: "My mother was beautiful/ in the blue gloom." Yet by the end of the poem "She died ice-grey in Jersey City" after "Depression and loneliness/ dulled her soft bloom." Color is used here to signify emotional states, and the gentle rhyme of "gloom" with "bloom," echoed by "word" in the last line gives the poem a certain poignancy.

The Orangery

First published in 1978 and reprinted in the 1990's, *The Orangery* is one of Gilbert Sorrentino's most memorable collections of poetry. Each poem includes the word "orange," the "preconceived constraint" upon which the poet planned this book. Orange appears and reappears as a color, a fruit, a memory, an intrusion, a word seeking a rhyme, or an unexpected presence. On first publication William Bronk wrote, "In *The Orangery* Sorrentino makes things which are hard, gaudy, and sometimes scary. They are stark artifacts of our world. . . . They are made to last."

The poem titled "King Cole" takes two lines from the song which Nat King Cole made popular: "Wham! Bam! Alla Kazam!/ out of an orange colored sky," and focuses on the nonsense words. In two spare free-verse stanzas the poet brings the reader's attention to the way the words "Wham! Bam! Alla Kazam!" somehow achieve a meaning of their own within the "foolish song," a meaning wedded to the sound of the words even more powerfully than the image of "a sky colored orange." The poem is modern in its self-referential quality; it is basically about itself and the images contained within it. Yet the last word of the poem, "Fruitless," is ambiguous; the reader does not know if it refers to the "foolish song," to the analytic method of the poem itself, or to both. Sorrentino seems to be experimenting in this poem, trying out tricks to see how they work, such as the use of a parenthesis that is not closed.

Many of the poems in *The Orangery* experiment with form as well as meaning. There are sonnet variations, including the poems "Cento," "Fragments of an Old Song," and "One Negative Vote, " which keep the fourteen-line sonnet form but ignore the traditional iambic pentameter and rhyme scheme. One of the most charming poems in this collection is "Villanette," a word that doesn't exist yet and was presumably created by the poet to title this variation on the venerable villanelle, an old French form derived from Italian folk song. The villanelle is composed of five tercets (rhyming triplets) in the rhyme scheme *aba*, followed by a closing quatrain in the scheme *abaa*.

Sorrentino's "Villanette" contains only four tercets, which maintain the rhyme scheme, and closes with a rhymed couplet. The subject of the poem is certain words denoting a northern winter, compared to the pleasures of winter in Florida. The form lends a certain dignity to the topic, adds importance, and renders it more memorable.

Other major works

long fiction: *The Sky Changes*, 1966; *Steelwork*, 1970; *Imaginative Qualities of Actual Things*, 1971; *Splendide-Hotel*, 1973; *Mulligan Stew*, 1979; *Aberration of Starlight*, 1980; *Crystal Vision*, 1981; *Blue Pastoral*, 1983; *Odd Number*, 1985; *Rose Thunder*, 1987; *Misterioso*, 1989; *Under the Shadow*,

1991; *Pack of Lies*, 1997; *Red the Fiend*, 1995; *Gold Fools*, 1999.

PLAY: *Flawless Play Restored: The Masque of Fungo*, pb. 1974.

NONFICTION: *Something Said*, 1984.

TRANSLATION: *Suspiciae Elegidia/Elegiacs of Sulpicia*, 1977.

Bibliography

Mackey, Louis. *Fact, Fiction, and Representation: Four Novels by Gilbert Sorrentino*. Columbia, S.C.: Camden Housei, 1997. This critical work examines Sorrentino's long fiction but is informative for its exploration of his general themes. Includes bibliography.

McPherson, William. *A Descriptive Bibliography.* Elmwood Park, Ill.: Dalkey Archive, 1991. This catalogue is lavishly illustrated and, for each major entry, contextualized by extensive background notes. Many of these annotations amount to small essays, pulling together diverse information supplied by Sorrentino himself, as well as by colleagues, editors, publishers, and friends. The catalog of secondary writing on Sorrentino is thorough and full of surprises.

Mottram, Eric. "The Black Polar Night: The Poetry of Gilbert Sorrentino." *Vort*, 1974, 43-59. This is an exhaustive discussion of Sorrentino's poetry, focusing on his color imagery, his humor, and his poetic techniques. Especially strong in documenting the poet's bleak vision.

O'Brien, John, ed. *Gilbert Sorrentino Number.* Elmwood Park, Ill.: Dalkey Archive, 1981. Contains critical writings on Sorrentino's work.

Sheila Golburgh Johnson

Gary Soto

Born: Fresno, California; April 12, 1952

Principal poetry

The Elements of San Joaquin, 1977
The Tale of Sunlight, 1978
Where Sparrows Work Hard, 1981
Black Hair, 1985
Who Will Know Us, 1990
Home Course in Religion, 1991
New and Selected Poems, 1995
A Natural Man, 1999

Other literary forms

Living up the Street: Narrative Recollections (1985), *Small Faces* (1986), *Lesser Evils: Ten Quartets* (1988), *A Summer Life* (1991), and *The Effects of Knut Hamsen on a Fresno Boy* (2000) are collections of autobiographical essays that deal mainly with Gary Soto's memories of growing up in a Chicano community; he addresses issues such as race, class, and religion by relating personal vignettes. His adult fiction includes *Nickel and Dime* (2000) and *Poetry Lover* (2001). Soto has also become a prolific and influential writer of stories and novels for children and young adults.

Achievements

Gary Soto has received public and critical praise for his poetry and prose memoirs, which explore the pleasures and difficulties of life for working class Chicanos. Many readers respond to the direct emotional appeal of his writing and his ability to write clearly and imaginatively about his ethnic background. He received an award from *The Nation* magazine for his poem "The Discovery" in 1975 and the United States Award from the International Poetry Forum in 1976 for his first book, *The Elements of San Joaquin*. His second collection of poems, *The Tale of Sunlight*, was nominated for a Pulitzer Prize. His nonfiction writing has also garnered awards, including the American Book Award in 1985 for *Living up the Street*. Individual poems have won the Bess Hokin Prize and the Levinson Award from *Poetry.* Soto's *New and Selected Poems* was a National Book Award finalist.

Biography

Gary Soto was born into a Chicano family in 1952 in Fresno, where, according to his essay "Being Mean," his father and grandfather worked in blue-collar jobs at Sun-Maid Raisin and his mother peeled potatoes at Reddi-Spud. Because of the family's poverty, exacerbated by

Gary Soto (M. L. Martinelle)

the father's early death in a work-related accident, Soto was forced to earn money as an agricultural laborer in the San Joaquin Valley and at a tire-retread factory in Fresno. Soto's work, especially his early poems, focuses primarily on this personal history. Although he never mentions it in his poems, Soto does have an impressive academic background: He was graduated magna cum laude from California State University at Fresno (1974), received a master of fine arts degree in creative writing from the University of California at Irvine (1976), and has taught at the University of California at Berkeley in the Department of English and Chicano Studies. He has also been Distinguished Professor of Creative Writing at the University of California, Riverside. Soto married Carolyn Oda, a Japanese American, in 1975, and they have one daughter, Mariko. Since 1990, most of his writing has been fiction for young adults.

Analysis

Although Gary Soto was born into a Catholic family and attended parochial schools in Fresno, California, religious issues are discussed only in his late work; primarily, he is attracted to and obsessed by the issues of race and poverty that dominated his early life and the importance of memory for a poet.

The Elements of San Joaquin

The Elements of San Joaquin, Soto's first book, is divided into three sections that neatly compartmentalize his early experiences: He moves from urban portraits of Fresno to the agricultural landscape of the San Joaquin Valley and closes with memories of his childhood and adolescence.

The opening poem, "San Fernando Road," describes and is dedicated to Leonard Cruz, a Chicano working in a factory, and it sets the mood for the first section and the book as a whole. An allusion to the four natural elements of the title—earth, air, fire, and water—is made in the poem, but there is nothing invigorating or revitalizing here. The air Leonard breathes contains "the dust/ Of rubber" from the factory, the water sits in the "toilets/ No one flushed," the men's "arms/ Were bracelets/ Of burns," and the earth on which he sleeps (he is homeless) only makes him shiver "Like the machinery/ That went on and on." It is no wonder that Leonard's body is weakening as he works; he has lost contact with the earth that gives life. The only hint of life or vibrancy comes in the hideous image of a woman "Opening/ In her first rape." Soto evokes the hopelessness of the environment by suggesting that this is not the last time the woman will be violated.

"Mission Tire Factory, 1969" is another version of the opening poem of this collection in "San Fernando Road," Leonard "swept the dust/ Of rubber . . . into his nostrils" and "Went into ovens/ Squint-eyed," and in the later poem Soto recalls "the wash of rubber in our lungs" and "the oven we would enter, squinting." Clearly there are problems with returning to familiar sights too often: The language becomes predictable and stale. Soto manages to save the poem, however, by focusing the reader's attention on the particularized humanity of the workers without sentimentalizing them. Manny, injured on the job, is carried to the work shed by his fellow workers (including Peter, who pinches "at his crotch"), and all the bleeding man can say is, "Buy some sandwiches. You guys saved my life." Soto comments with candor and compassion that his ignorance was "outdone only by pain."

Section 2 looks at the lives of farm workers in the San Joaquin Valley, where "nothing will heal/ Under the rain's broken fingers." A typical poem, "Harvest," once again carefully details the importance of the four elements, but in this case they do affect the growth cycle. The fire of the sun works on "the vineyard that never failed," the wind moves the dust of the earth and Soto's own voice across the crops, and the "ropes of rain" fall on the "thick harvest." Unfortunately, the worker in the field, Soto himself, does not share in the natural production of wealth: "ropes of rain dropped to pull me/ From the thick harvest that was not mine."

Memories of friends in the neighborhood and family members are the focus of section 3. The oppressive mood of the poems about factory workers and agricultural laborers does not lift here. In fact, the deprivations become engraved in the poet, like the bracelets of burns on the factory workers' arms. In "Moving Away," addressed to Soto's brother, he remembers moments when "the one we hated/ Watched us from under a tree." That gaze is still on him; it belongs to the "white stepfather" who replaced Soto's own father. Although what troubled the stepfather "has been forgotten," Soto, speaking for his brother as well, concludes that "what troubled us has settled/ Like dirt/ In the nests of our knuckles/ And cannot be washed away." There are no purifying waters in this very powerful and depressing first book.

The second section contains another tire-factory poem which is both comic and disturbing. In "Mexicans Begin Jogging" (the title itself is flippantly comic), Soto is apparently working with undocumented immigrants; when the border patrol arrives at the factory, he runs from the shop at his boss's orders. Soto, who shouts that he is an American, does not object to the discrimination, because the boss presses "a dollar in my palm." "Since I was on his time, I ran/ And became the wag of a short tail of Mexicans." Soon he breaks into a yuppie jog and "a great silly, grin" because he has outwitted the prejudiced employer; an exploited worker enjoys few things more than getting paid an hourly wage plus a dollar bonus for doing no work at all. Soto later returns to the subject matter of Mexican immigrants in a prose piece, "Black Hair" from his book *Living up the Street*. Except for the metaphor of the wagging tail, the story is very similar to the poem except in one important detail: in "Black Hair" he is able to address the distance he feels from some of his fellow workers, a distance that is lessened somewhat when he runs with the undocumented workers. "Among the Mexicans I had few friends because I was different, a *pocho* who spoke bad Spanish. At lunch they sat in tires and laughed over burritos, looking up at me to laugh even harder." In the poems this honest recognition of the separation among the workers is absent.

The third section of *Elements of San Joaquin* contains a poem that suggests the new directions Soto's work will take in subsequent volumes. "Angel" leaves the world of the economically disfranchised and their tales of work woes and arrives in a gentler, more personal area. Here Soto watches his wife as she sleeps, "heavy/ And tilting with child," and he reflects not on his own grim past, but on the child's future. He pictures the tiny fingers, which "bloom like candles," even though it is still weeks before the baby "slides from water/ And blood, his blue hands/ Tightening on air." He does not despair about the child's future, perhaps because Soto has by this time escaped his old working-class life and joined the privileged world of academics; instead, he can only expectantly wait for "that good day/ When this child will kick/ His joints into place." After the arrival of that child, kicking *her* joints into place, Soto wrote a number of buoyantly hopeful poems about Mariko, his daughter.

The Tale of Sunlight and Where Sparrows Work Hard

His second book, *The Tale of Sunlight*, is distinctive in that the poet creates two characters, Molina and Manuel Zaragoza, who take the focus off Soto's own life experiences. Molina, a Chicano alter ego of Soto, and Manuel, a cantina owner in Taxco, Mexico, allow him to escape the solipsistic world of poems narrated in the first person. This is the only time in Soto's career when characters other than the poet become the principal focus of the work.

In *Where Sparrows Work Hard*, Soto returns to familiar sights: the neighborhood, the tire factory, the fields, and family. As this book progresses, however, there are some happy, sometimes comic moments that relieve the despair.

Black Hair

Black Hair examines familiar themes. There is the sense of resignation and bitterness that Soto feels when he recalls his early farm-worker experiences: "Work in dust, get up in dust. Beer makes it go." There are recollections of childish mischief directed against the "enemy": with a friend he "started/ Kicking a Republican's fence,/ The pickets working loose." In the title poem, "Black Hair," there is pride in having brown skin and being a Chicano: Soto, at age eight, worships a baseball player and fellow Chicano, Hector Moreno, and assumes "his crouch . . . before an altar/ Of worn baseball cards" in his room. There are wonderfully surprising metaphors throughout the poems: garbage is a "raffle of eggshells and orange peels"; a column of ants on the ground is a "loose thread to an old coat"; crying is like "rope/ Going taut."

The changes that do appear in this book derive from Soto's relationship with his daughter. The childlike quality of many of his earlier poems is redoubled here because of the young girl's presence. At times this childlike quality becomes too dull and almost puts the poems to sleep. In France they walk hand in hand, "smiling/ For no reason other than/ Everything is new"; when his daughter asks "What's that? . . . there's no greater/ Pleasure than saying,/ Beats me. Let's go see." This conversational, matter-of-fact diction can disappoint the reader who seeks sparkling or inventive language. Yet the presence of the daughter in these poems allows a new side of Soto's character to shine through. Instead of seeing himself as a victim and the enemy as Republicans, he includes himself in a catalog of human transgressions: While watching and admiring ants with his daughter he waxes philosophical for a moment and admits that "many people, whole countries,/ May go under because we desire TV/ And chilled drinks, clothes/ That hang well on our bodies." Ants are better than humans, and Soto is human. The daughter, however, also permits Soto to write fairly innocent, anger-free poems about simple joys. Instead of concentrating on the exploitation inherent in the economic system, Soto explains to his daughter that "if we buy a goldfish, someone tries on a hat." The exchange of wealth between buyer and seller seems almost like play; gone are the dust from rubber, the hot ovens the factory workers have to enter, and the injustice of substandard wages. Now "If we buy crayons, someone walks home with a broom"; with "a small purchase here and there,/ And things just keep going."

Soto avoids sentimentality in these generally happy poems by admitting the quirks of childhood. When he wants to walk in nature to a special spot with his daughter, she responds in a typically modern, spoiled way, "Daddy please, why/ Don't we get in the car/ And be over there." His amused annoyance is entertaining. The poems generally are admirable for the new range of emotions that Soto permits himself. With this collection, he is no longer solely the angry young man; now he is the proud father as well.

"Who Will Know Us?"—the title poem of Soto's fifth volume—asks the difficult question, "Who will know us when we breathe through the grass?" Despite the gravity of the question, thought up while he is "on a train, rocking toward the cemetery/ To visit the dead," the collection as a whole does not dwell on difficult or macabre questions; instead, it celebrates life in typical Soto fashion—by praising the quotidian and remembering the past.

Lesser Evils

In "Eve," the poet repeats a story that is similar to one in the prose collection *Lesser Evils: Ten Quartets*. In "Starting Young," the adolescent Soto meets a precocious thirteen-year-old, Sue, in a shed belonging to a neighbor, and they pull down their pants and touch each other. He worries needlessly about impregnating her, and the story of early investigative romance ends sweetly. In the poem "Eve" Soto goes all the way with a girl on her father's workbench in the barn; when she unfastens her skirt, her "kinked hair" is "thick as a child's black scribbling." Again he worries, needlessly, that he has impregnated her; the poem ends with no shotgun solutions to problems, but a melancholy dictum: people said that "it should hurt the first time,/ Then stop . . . how they lied." Pain goes hand in hand with love and sex—first time, every time. The comparison between the versions in prose and poetry reveals little more than the obsessive quality of Soto's work: He returns again and again to subjects that he finds worthy of his attention, not concerned that this is country he has already discovered. He wants to mine the mountain until the ore is gone.

One of the concluding poems in the book, "Evening Walk," is pleasantly self-effacing. Soto, while walking with his daughter, tries to tell her "poor stories" about the old days when he "picked/ Grapes like nobody's business" and "lugged oranges and shared plums with Okies." Mariko will have none of it. Soto concludes that he is "a bore to the end," while Mariko runs and skips ahead, dragging a branch that flutters "like a green fire." Her only eagerness is for an evening without him; the parent-poet-storyteller senses the inevitable hostility of the younger generation. In typical fashion, Soto accepts stoically and with humor the march and skip of time.

Home Course in Religion

Yet when it comes to religion, a subject that Soto largely ignored in his early poems, he nostalgically yearns for old-fashioned sanctity. In *Home Course in Religion*, published in 1991, Soto catalogs the items he misses in post-Vatican II Catholicism: pagan babies, holy water in the cupboard, Mass said in Latin, and meatless Fridays. The modernization of the church has even invaded the most primitive forms of worship: "At the altar of Mary, we have electric bulbs,/ Not candles, sitting in votive cups." The altar "lights up like a pinball machine" when one drops a quarter in the slot for each sin. The early radical Soto has become movingly conservative; he wonders, "How do we kneel and pray at such a place?" Many of these poems also recall his adolescent initiation into the sometimes mysterious, sometimes comic rites of the faith.

This collection also focuses considerable attention on Soto's relationship with his stepfather, Jim, but in this case the poet does not reminisce with pleasure. In contrast to the imaginative re-creations of his father, who died before Soto really knew him, the evocations of his stepfather are hauntingly realistic, almost naturalistic. The father is associated with his La-Z-Boy recliner, his Jack Daniels, his racism, and the "pounding of fists that pounded boxes all day." After Soto records on a cheap tape recorder an argument between his mother and Jim, he replays the vicious piece "until the voices slurred to a crawl/ And the tape recorder died." As the batteries fade, Soto notices that the plastic statue of Jesus, "marble white and hollow," captures the afternoon glow from the window, but it offers no consolation for the fear and anger the young boy is feeling. Soto appreciates the ritual of Catholicism, but he seems to suggest that the value of the faith for relieving anguish is minimal.

In the last few poems of the book, Soto escapes from memories of youth and evaluates his adult life, which seems to be packed with distracting facts and activities. He watches television, reads student papers, studies karate, and examines Japanese and Impressionist Art. A moving line positioned amid all this clutter is "I want very badly to know how to talk about Christ." Yet the faith is absent; instead, Soto finds whatever redemption there is in his daily existence—his daughter's games, his humor, his marriage.

A Natural Man

Soto's collections through the 1990's, some of which are aimed at children, find him walking the same path he set out on as a young poet. Though he has not stopped looking around him, and though he continues to examine the father-daughter relationship as the daughter matures, much of his work still conjures up memories of his boyhood. His short, staccato lines and gritty colloquialism create an ever-refined vehicle for his accurate eye, and he builds intriguing tensions through voices poised between innocence and experience, even the middle-aged voices of *A Natural Man*.

The subjects that Soto addresses in his poems are very similar; in many ways, however, the Soto of today is not the same poet who began writing in the 1970's. He has matured; he has established a very successful career by looking into his past, but his work published in the 1990's suggests that his main concern is trying to find spiritual sustenance in a middle-class, comfortable life. He says, "We invent misery for our bodies,/ Then our minds, and then, having nothing else to do/ Look for ways to make it stop." Soto's poems are trying to stop the pain through humor, through nostalgia, and through intense living in the present.

Other major works

long fiction: *Nickel and Dime*, 2000; *Poetry Lover*, 2001.

nonfiction: *Living up the Street: Narrative Recollections*, 1985; *Small Faces*, 1986; *Lesser Evils: Ten Quartets*, 1988; *A Summer Life*, 1991; *The Effects of Knut Hamsun on a Fresno Boy*, 2000.

CHILDREN'S LITERATURE: *Baseball in April and Other Stories*, 1990; *Taking Sides*, 1991; *Neighborhood Odes*, 1992 (poetry); *Pacific Crossing*, 1992; *The Skirt*, 1992; *Too Many Tamales*, 1993; *Local News*, 1993; *Crazy Weekend*, 1994; *Jesse*, 1994; *Boys at Work*, 1995; *Canto Familiar*, 1995 (poetry); *The Cat's Meow*, 1995; *Chato's Kitchen*, 1995; *Off and Running*, 1996.

EDITED TEXT: *California Childhood: Recollections and Stories of the Golden State*, 1988; *Pieces of the Heart: New Chicano Fiction*, 1993.

BIBLIOGRAPHY

Armour-Hileman, Vicki. Review of *Where Sparrows Work Hard*. *Denver Quarterly* 17 (Summer, 1982): 154-155. Armour-Hileman notes what many critics call attention to: the similarity between Soto and his teacher Philip Levine in subject matter, "a surrealistic bent," and short, enjambed lines. She finds fault with the "inaccuracy of the images" in many of Soto's poems and "their elliptical movement." She does admire the poems in which Soto "becomes not an ethnic poet, but a poet who writes about human suffering." His writing in the last third of this collection she considers a "great success."

Cooley, Peter. "Two Young Poets." *Parnassus* 7 (Fall/Winter, 1979): 299-311. In this extremely laudatory examination of Soto's two earliest collections, Cooley calls Soto "the most important voice among the young Chicano poets." He praises Soto's ability to re-create his lost world of San Joaquin with "an imaginative expansiveness." This is a crucial essay for understanding the initial praise given to Soto and how his work seemed to speak for a generation of Chicanos.

Mason, Michael Tomasek. "Poetry and Masculinity on the Anglo/Christian Border: Gary Soto, Robert Frost, and Robert Hass." In *The Calvinist Roots of the Modern Era*, edited by Aliki Barnstone, Michael Tomasek Manson, and Carol J. Singley. Hanover: University Press of New England, 1997. Manson carefully traces the evolution of notions of masculinity, "machismo," in Soto's work.

Paredes, Raymund A. "The Childhood Worries, or Why I Became a Writer." *Iowa Review* 25, no. 2 (Spring/Summer, 1995): 105-115. Soto recalls the formative influences later treated in his poetry and the initial motivations for expressing his experiences.

_______. "Recent Chicano Writing." *Rocky Mountain Review* 41, nos. 1/2 (1987): 124-129. Paredes admires Soto's writing because "ethnic and class consciousness constitutes an essential part of his literary sensibility." He faults Soto, however, for his portrayal of women: "As he depicts them, their roles are wholly conventional." He does not find the portrayals of women to be totally offensive, but he chides the poet for "performing unremarkably" on this issue.

Wojahn, David. Review of *Black Hair*, by Gary Soto. *Poetry* 146 (June, 1985): 171-173. In this review of Soto's fourth collection, Wojahn accuses him of displaying the "brooding confusions of the pubescent mind" and thereby creating a book that is a "distinctly minor achievement." Wojahn believes Soto's abandonment of the surrealistic poetics and mythmaking of his earlier books for "anecdotes of adolescence" was a mistake.

Kevin Boyle,
updated by Philip K. Jason

ROBERT SOUTHEY

Born: Bristol, England; August 12, 1774
Died: Greta Hall, Keswick, England; March 21, 1843

PRINCIPAL POETRY

Poems, 1795 (with Robert Lovell)
Joan of Arc: An Epic Poem, 1796, 1798, 1806, 1812
Poems, 1797-1799
Thalaba the Destroyer, 1801
Madoc, 1805
Metrical Tales and Other Poems, 1805
The Curse of Kehama, 1810
Roderick, the Last of the Goths, 1814
Odes to His Royal Highness the Prince Regent, His Imperial Majesty the Emperor of Russia, and His Majesty the King of Prussia, 1814

Minor Poems, 1815
The Poet's Pilgrimage to Waterloo, 1816
The Lay of the Laureate: Carmen Nuptiale, 1816
Wat Tyler: A Dramatic Poem, 1817
A Vision of Judgement, 1821
A Tale of Paraguay, 1825
All for Love, and the Pilgrim to Compostella, 1829
Poetical Works, 1829
The Devil's Walk, 1830 (with Samuel Taylor Coleridge)
Selections from the Poems, 1831, 1833
Poetical Works, 1839
Oliver Newman: A New-England Tale (Unfinished): With Other Poetical Remains, 1845
Robin Hood: A Fragment, 1847 (with Caroline Southey)

Other literary forms

Robert Southey's collected prose works comprise almost forty volumes, ranging from literary criticism to biography, from fiction to translations. *Letters from England by Don Manuel Espriella* (1807) is a satiric commentary on everyday life in contemporary England, while *Sir Thomas More* (1829) reveals Southey again examining society, this time by way of conversations between the spirit of the departed More and Montesimos (Southey himself). His so-called novel, the seven-volume *The Doctor* (1834-1847), concerns Dr. Daniel Dove of Doncaster and his horse Nobs; as a fantasy and a commentary on life, the excruciatingly lengthy piece reminds one of Laurence Sterne's *Tristram Shandy* (1759-1767)—without the artistic qualities of that remarkable work of fiction. Hidden within Chapter 129 of Southey's effort lies the first-known telling of the nursery classic "The Three Bears."

Life of Nelson (1813) and *Life of Wesley and the Rise and Progress of Methodism* (1820) head the list of Southey's biographical studies. Others of note include *A Summary of the Life of Arthur, Duke of Wellington* (1816); the *Life of John, Duke of Marlborough* (1822); *Lives of the British Admirals* (1833-1840); and *The Life of the Rev. Andrew Bell* (1844, one volume only), the Scottish-born educationist who founded the National Society for the Education of the Poor. Southey's historical writings include the *History of Brazil* (1810-1819), *The History of Europe* (1810-1813), and the *History of the Peninsular War* (1823-1832). In 1812, Southey published *The Origin, Nature, and Object of the New System of Education*. This was followed by *The Book of the Church* (1824), *Vindiciae Ecclesiae Anglicanae* (1826), and *Essays Moral and Political* (1832).

Southey was also an editor and translator. Among his edited works are *The Annual Anthology* (1799-1800), *The Works of Chatterton* (1803, with Joseph Cottle), *Palmerin of England* (1807), Isaac Watts's *Horae Lyricae* (1834), and *The Works of William Cowper* (1835-1837). Southey's notable translations include Jacques Necker's *On the French Revolution* (1797), Vasco Lobeira's *Amadis de Gaul* (1805), the *Chronicle of the Cid* (1808), Abbe Don Ignatius Molina's *The Geographical, Natural, and Civil History of Chili* (1808), and *Memoria Sobre a Litteratura Portugueza* (1809).

Achievements

During his lifetime, Robert Southey enjoyed moments of popularity and success; there were even those

Robert Southey (Hulton Archive)

among his contemporaries who believed that he ranked with the best of his nation's poets. He outlived Samuel Taylor Coleridge, Sir Walter Scott, Charles Lamb, William Hazlitt, Lord Byron, Percy Bysshe Shelley, and John Keats, yet rarely does one find mention of his name in a discussion of the significant figures and forces that shaped British Romanticism in the first part of the nineteenth century. Although Southey is deep in the shadows of William Wordsworth and Coleridge, appearing in literary histories only as their mediocre associate, his poetry deserves a careful reading, especially that written before 1801. This early work reveals an extremely high degree of versatility, not always appreciated by those who study only the first rank of nineteenth century British Romantics. The simplicity and directness of language found in Southey's early ballads and short narratives echo Wordsworth's *Lyrical Ballads* (1798), but the pieces succeed because the poet could rise above pure imitation. He could also write irregular odes and heroic epistles that demonstrated his knowledge of the Augustan Age; he knew how to create sublime imagery with the aid of biblical themes, and he could plunge downward to concoct playful exercises with pigs and gooseberry pies. He was adept in a variety of poetic forms: the elegy, the sonnet, the sapphic, the ballad, the metrical tale.

The content of Southey's poems is as varied as the form. While at Balliol College, Oxford, during the period of his enthusiasm for republicanism, he wrote a dramatic poem on Wat Tyler, the leader of the peasant revolt of 1381, while four years later his piece on the first Duke of Marlborough's victory at Blenheim (August, 1704) during the War of the Spanish Succession graphically underscored the poet's sentiments on the futility of war—"But what good came of it at last?" In what seemed a radical shift of poetical gears, Southey rode hard and fast upon the waves of the Gothic horror narrative in "God's Judgment on a Wicked Bishop" (1799), in which he adapted the legendary story of a tenth century German Bishop who was attacked and then devoured by a pack of rats. At the outset of the nineteenth century, he turned to a series of epic poems—*Thalaba the Destroyer* and *The Curse of Kehama* being two examples—that placed him alongside his contemporaries in the Romantic quest for glamour and the grandeur of distant places and even more distant times.

Southey's greatest weakness may have been his inability to recognize his own limitations as a poet. He remained unaware of what he could do best. He took his role as poet laureate of England far too seriously—especially in view of the fact that the honor came only because Sir Walter Scott refused to accept it. Not only did he exercise poor political and critical judgment by attacking Byron, but he also wrote, in 1821, the unnecessarily lengthy *A Vision of Judgement*, in which he attempted to transport the recently departed King George III into heaven. Byron, of course, replied in the preface to his similarly titled poem (*The Vision of Judgment*, 1822), "If Mr. Southey had not rushed in where he had no business, and where he never was before," paraphrasing Alexander Pope's *An Essay on Criticism* (1711), "the following poem would not have been written." Southey never appreciated his skill as a writer of shorter and less ambitious poems wherein, for example, he could calmly reflect upon his personal love of good books in his own large library, as in "My Days Among the Dead Are Past." Perhaps, also, he never realized the extent to which he could display his talent with language, as in the onomatopoetic and highly animated "The Cataract of Ladore." Interestingly enough, when Southey could isolate himself from the perils and problems of a large, ugly world, he achieved considerable maturity as a poet. Unfortunately, the periods of imaginative seclusion were both irregular and inconsistent.

BIOGRAPHY

Although born at Bristol, the son of Robert Southey and Margaret Hill Southey, Robert Southey spent most of his first fourteen years at Bath, in the company of his mother's half-sister, Miss Elizabeth Tyler. Biographers describe Tyler as a lady endowed with strong personal attractions, ambitious ideas, an imperious temper, and a significantly large library. The last-mentioned asset allowed young Southey early introductions to dramatic literature, classical poetry, and the epics of Edmund Spenser. Thus, his entrance into Westminster School in April, 1788—after shorter terms at small schools in Corston and Bristol—found him well prepared to pursue learning. Nevertheless, he demonstrated little interest in subjects outside the narrow limits of his own idiosyncratic reading tastes: ceremony, ritual, and world mythology and religion. Four years later, the school authorities expelled him for his published essays against Westminster's system of corporal punishment, specifically the flogging of students by their masters for trivial offenses. Through the efforts of his maternal uncle, the Reverend Herbert Hill, Southey gained entrance to Balliol College, Oxford (after first having been refused admission by Christ Church because of the Westminster School incident). The significant events during his undergraduate term proved to be friendships formed with Samuel Taylor Coleridge and Robert Lovell. The three determined to emigrate to the banks of the Susquehanna River in the United States, there to embark upon a scheme of an ideal life of unitarianism and pantisocracy (a Utopian community in which all members would rule equally). Interestingly enough, the relationship acquired even stronger ties (which would eventually cost Southey considerable money and labor) when the friends married the three daughters of the widow of Stephen Fricker, an unsuccessful sugar-pan merchant at Westbury. Southey's marriage to Edith Fricker occurred in November, 1795.

When Elizabeth Tyler heard of her nephew's proposal to leave England, she evicted him from her house. By that time, Southey had embarked upon several literary projects, and, fortunately, a young publisher, Joseph Cottle, came to his aid and purchased the first of his epic poems, *Joan of Arc*. Moreover, his uncle, Herbert Hill, invited him to visit Lisbon, resulting in *Letters in Spain and Portugal* (1808) and *Madoc*. Returning to London, he began to study the law, but soon abandoned that exercise (as he had turned from divinity and medicine at Oxford) and once more focused his attention on poetry. Seeking seclusion, Southey moved first to Westbury, then to Burton (in Hampshire), producing additional ballads and eclogues and working hard on his *History of Brazil*. In April, 1800, serious illness forced him to seek the temperate climate of Portugal, where he remained for a year, completing *Thalaba the Destroyer* and continuing to plod along with the Portuguese history. Back in England, he settled first at Keswick, then moved to Dublin as secretary to the chancellor of the Irish exchequer, Isaac Corry. He then moved to Bristol, but the death of his mother and infant daughter drove him away from his birthplace; in 1803, partly to satisfy his wife, Southey and his family took up residence at Greta Hall, Keswick; there, practically under the same roof as his brother-in-law Coleridge, he made his home for the remainder of his life.

Work and activity at Keswick brought Southey into close association with Wordsworth and, more important, provided the motivation to produce his most ambitious poetic works. Financial pressures (particularly the support of Coleridge's family in addition to his own), however, forced him to forsake poetry temporarily for more lucrative prose projects, which he churned out in significant quantity between 1803 and 1832. At Greta Hall, he amassed a library in excess of fourteen thousand volumes, including works that he eventually edited and translated. Between 1808 and 1839, he edited and contributed to the *Quarterly Review*, the result of his association with Sir Walter Scott. That relationship proved to be most advantageous to Southey's literary career, for although Scott could not arrange to secure for his friend the post of historiographer royal, he did, in 1813, transfer the offer to be poet laureate from himself to Southey. To his credit, the latter accepted the honor only on condition that he would not be forced to write birthday odes to the sovereign or to members of the royal family. Unfortunately, however, he did manage to get into trouble with Byron and others of the liberally inclined Romantic poets when he wrote *A Vision of Judgement* and seemingly challenged liberal opinion. Despite squabbles with his contemporaries, his reputation remained high, as witnessed by offers to edit the *Times* of London and to serve as librarian of the Advocates' Library, Edinburgh—both of which he declined.

In November, 1837, Edith Southey passed away—for years she had been failing mentally. The poet-essayist himself, according to contemporary accounts, had by this time become afflicted with softening of the brain, manifested by an obvious indifference to everyone and everything except his beloved books. Suddenly, near the end of his sixty-fourth year, Southey remarried (on June 4, 1839)—one Caroline Ann Bowles, a poet and hymnodist with whom he had maintained a close correspondence for more than twenty years. When the couple returned from their wedding tour, Southey's condition worsened; he passed gradually from insensibility to external matters into a complete trance and died on March 21, 1843. The poet laureate was buried in Crosthwaite churchyard, and friends placed memorials in Westminster Abbey and Bristol Cathedral.

Analysis

Robert Southey's poetical career proved, indeed, to have been a struggle: His desire to create from impulse and inspiration came into conflict with his duty to earn money from his pen. During his early period, he wrote a large number of ballads and metrical tales for the *Morning Post* at the then-going rate of one guinea a week. When he republished those in book form, money again became the principal motive, as it did once more in 1807 when he had to support Coleridge's family as well as his own. At that time he announced that, if necessary, he would take on more reviews and articles for the magazines and would write additional verses for the newspapers. Thus, judgment and analysis of his poetry must balance what Southey wanted to do with what he had to do. Throughout his professional life, he tried desperately to preserve the time for literary labors worthy of his talent; as long as that division existed, he could perform his hack work without fear of humiliation or sacrifice. Unfortunately, time and energy eventually failed him, and his poems—both serious and popular—became less salable; after 1820, he saw himself as more historian than poet.

In 1837, two years prior to the illness that would eventually incapacitate him, Southey prepared the last collected edition of his poems to be published during his lifetime. That task provided an opportunity for the poet to survey his own work, to rank as well as to analyze. Thus, concerning the narrative poems, he thought *Joan of Arc*, written when he was nineteen, to have the least merit, although the piece did constitute the first stage of his poetic development. *Thalaba the Destroyer*, published five years afterward, allowed Southey to achieve poetic maturity, to set aside the law of nature and permit his poetic fancy to wander freely. For that reason, he chose not to control the rhythmic structure of his blank verse; rather, the lines of that poem follow a spontaneous melody, dividing themselves into varying lengths. In addition, the poet tended to interrupt the ordinary iambic cadence with a sudden trochaic or dactylic movement: for example, "Lo! underneath the broadleaved sycamore/ With lids half closed he lies,/ Dreaming of days to come."

Religious epics

While a schoolboy at Westminster, Southey had formed the idea of a long poem, epic in form and content, based upon each of the important religions (he considered them to be mythologies) of the world. For Islam (then called Mohammedanism), he eventually wrote *Thalaba the Destroyer*; *The Curse of Kehama*, published in 1810, focused on Hinduism. In the later poem, he again allowed his fancy and his imagery to range freely, seemingly unconcerned with the orthodox notions and sympathies of the vast majority of his readers. For whatever the reasons, however, in *The Curse of Kehama* Southey returned to rhyme; more accurately, he attempted to compromise between the rambling blank verse of *Thalaba the Destroyer* and the symmetry of the traditional English epic form. *Madoc* had been begun before he set to work on *The Curse of Kehama*, but Southey, believing the former to have been his most significant poem, set it aside until he could devote his full attention to it. Finally published in 1805, *Madoc* evidences a pleasing melody and an easy, fluent, and graceful narrative diction. Unfortunately, it met with the least favorable reception of all his long poems.

Roderick, the Last of the Goths

The failure of *Madoc* did not deter Southey from his grand epic design. In *Roderick, the Last of the Goths*, he produced a long narrative poem that succeeded because the versification and theme managed to complement each other. Relying on the issue of subjugation and underlining it with moral grandeur and tragedy, the poet easily held the interest of his contemporary readers. He began with a single and momentary sin of the passions by an otherwise consistently virtuous monarch and proceeded to unravel the consequences: the slaughter of Christians by Moors in a battle lasting eight days; the king's escape after the battle and his deep remorse and self-inflicted penance of a long and solitary hermitage while others thought that he had been slain; the king's dream, in which his mother appears with instructions to deliver his country from the Moors; and the departure and eventual encounter with the sole survivor of a massacre, who tells the king of the tragedy and inspires him to both personal and patriotic revenge. Southey demonstrated, in *Roderick, the Last of the Goths*, his ability to sustain a narrative while at the same time developing a character, a hero, through a series of meaningful and related adventures: Roderick, in the guise of a priest, passes through the country, meets old friends, and is recognized only by his dog. Finally, the king leads his forces in triumph over the Moors, after which he disappears.

Southey achieved effective rhythm to complement the narrative of Roderick's adventures by taking full advantage of proper names derived from Spanish and from various Moorish and Gothic dialects. He sought diversity of both rhythm and language, knowing well how John Milton, for example, had underscored the substance of his theme in the opening book of *Paradise Lost* (1667) with his roll call of Satan's evil host. Thus, in a single passage of twenty-six lines from Book IV, the poet relies on the effect of a dozen or so proper names to vary his rhythm, as

> Skirting the heights of *Aguiar*, he reached
> That consecrated pile amid the wild
> Which sainted *Fructuoso* in his zeal
> Reared to *St. Felix*. on *Visionia's* banks.

Further, Southey reinforced his narrative with heavy descriptions of natural scenery, furnishing rhetorical respites from the action and the passion of events. He viewed such pauses as essential to the long narrative poem, particularly when they followed long episodes of emotional strain or exaltation. From a positive point of view, the descriptive respites filled the imagination with the sights and the sounds of the beauties of nature, allowing the long narrative poem to serve as a true work of creative art. Southey made such attempts in all of his long poems, but he reached the highest levels of perfection in *Roderick, the Last of the Goths*.

"Ode, Written during the Negotiations with Buonaparte, in January 1814"

Although Southey's occasional poetry includes his weakest efforts, there are rare moments of eloquence when the poet is able to give free rein to his emotions. Consider, for example, his "Ode, Written during the Negotiations with Buonaparte, in January 1814." Southey truly detested the diminutive emperor of the French, and he attacked his subject on moral grounds, as well as on the obvious political and patriotic levels. His passions were further aroused by the sight of those individuals who worshiped what they believed to have been the wonders of Napoleon's political and military successes. The poet saw the emperor only as a mean tyrant: "And ne'er was earth with verier tyrant curst,/ Bold man and bad,/ Remorseless, godless, full of fraud and lies"; for those personal and political crimes, demanded Southey, Napoleon must pay with his life.

"Funeral Ode on the Death of the Princess Charlotte"

Another of Southey's occasional poems should be mentioned—the "Funeral Ode on the Death of the Princess Charlotte"—for its lines are as sensitive and serene as those on Napoleon are harsh and bitter. The poet gazes about the burial grounds at Windsor, where, "in thy sacred shade/ Is the Flower of Brunswick laid!" Then, further surveying the scene, he comments on others lying there—Henry, Edward, Elizabeth, Ann Seymour, Mary Stuart. Nevertheless, the piece serves as more than a roll call of history, for Southey loses sight of neither his subject nor the tragedy of Charlotte's passing: "Never more lamented guest/ Was in Windsor laid to rest."

Legacy

In the final analysis, Southey must be seen as a nineteenth century child of the Augustan Age who contributed little to the poetry of Romanticism. Confusion arises when literary historians too quickly connect him with Wordsworth and Coleridge, forgetting, perhaps, that the relationship existed on a personal rather than an artistic level. Artistically and intellectually, Southey had almost nothing in common with the major figures among the first generation of British Romantic poets. He waited until practically the end of his literary life—in the preface to the 1837-1838 edition of his *Poetical Works*—before setting forth what amounted to his poetical and intellectual declaration of independence from the new literature of pre-Victorian England. Southey chose to spend a lifetime with his books, rather than in the company of men; he would retire to a life of literary pursuit, "communing with my own heart, and taking that course which upon mature consideration seemed best to myself."

Southey further maintained that he had no need for the new schools of poetry, for he had learned poetry from the masters, confirmed it in his youth, and exemplified it in his own writing. Indeed, few would deny Professor Renwick's assertion that "No poet since Dryden wrote such pure clean English so consistently." Unfortunately, unlike his contemporaries who set and then followed new trends, Southey seemed more inclined to practice and develop the *craft* of poetry rather than its art. He never really learned (either in or out of school) that poetry had to come from sources other than labor and learning. Nevertheless, he possessed an ardent and genial piety, a moral strength, a poetic power of depth and variety, and an ability to develop a range of literary forms and interests. In those respects, he deserved the name and the honor of poet laureate.

Other major works

LONG FICTION: *The Doctor*, 1834-1847 (7 volumes).

PLAY: *The Fall of Robespierre*, pb. 1794 (with Samuel Taylor Coleridge).

NONFICTION: *Letters from England by Don Manuel Espriella*, 1807; *Letters in Spain and Portugal*, 1808; *The History of Europe*, 1810-1813; *History of Brazil*, 1810-1819; *The Origin, Nature, and Object of the New System of Education*, 1812; *Life of Nelson*, 1813; *A Summary of the Life of Arthur, Duke of Wellington*, 1816; *Life of Wesley and the Rise and Progress of Methodism*, 1820; *History of the Expedition of Orsua and Crimes of Aguirre*, 1821; *Life of John, Duke of Marlborough*, 1822; *History of the Peninsular War*, 1823-1832; *The Book of the Church*, 1824; *Vindiciae Ecclesiae Anglicanae*, 1826; *Sir Thomas More*, 1829; *Essays Moral and Political*, 1832; *Lives of the British Admirals*, 1833-1840; *The Life of the Rev. Andrew Bell*, 1844.

TRANSLATIONS: *On the French Revolution*, 1797 (of Jacques Necker); *Amadis de Gaul*, 1805 (of Vasco Lobeira); *Chronicle of the Cid*, 1808 (of *Crónica del famoso cavallero Cid Ruy Diaz Campeador, La crónica de España*, and *Poema del Cid*); *The Geographical, Natural, and Civil History of Chili*, 1808 (of Abbe Don Ignatius Molina).

EDITED TEXTS: *The Annual Anthology*, 1799-1800; *The Works of Chatterton*, 1803 (with Joseph Cottle); *Palmerin of England*, 1807; *Horae Lyricae*, 1834 (by Isaac Watts); *The Works of William Cowper*, 1835-1837.

Bibliography

Bernhardt-Kabisch, Ernest. *Robert Southey*. Boston: Twayne, 1977. A study of *Joan of Arc* follows a sketch of Southey's early life. Chapter 3 assesses his personality and lyrical poetry. The central chapters analyze his epics and the verse of his laureate years. The last chapter is a survey of Southey's prose. Contains a chronology, notes, a select bibliography, and an index.

Carnall, Geoffrey. *Robert Southey and His Age: The Development of a Conservative Mind*. Oxford, England: Clarendon Press, 1960. Part 1 focuses on Southey as Jacobin, devoted to radical reform and democracy. Part 2 analyzes Southey as Tory, advocating strong government and conservativism. Finally, the question of whether Southey should be called an apostate is examined. Supplemented by illustrations, two appendices, and an index.

Chandler, Alice. "Broadening the Vision: The Lake Poets and Some Contemporaries." In *A Dream of Order: The Medieval Ideal in Nineteenth-Century English Literature*. Lincoln: University of Nebraska Press, 1970. This essay sets Southey in the context of his contemporaries. They share a common vision of medievalism as a corrective to threats of chaos from events of the French Revolution. Southey is interesting for having used medievalism for both his radical and his conservative writing. Includes footnotes, a bibliography, and an index.

Curry, Kenneth. *Southey*. London: Routledge & Kegan Paul, 1975. Part 1 reviews Southey's life: the formative years and the productive years. Part 2 surveys the prose: social and political criticism, biographies, autobiographies, histories, and journalism. Part 3 examines the poetry: early poems, long poems, laureate poems, and an estimate of Southey as a poet. Complemented by a bibliography and an index.

Simmons, Jack. *Southey.* London: Collins, 1945. A substantial biography of modest length, this book details Southey's education, his friendship with Samuel Taylor Coleridge, and his sojourn in Portugal. His fame leads to political controversies, and his declining years begin with the death of his daughter Isabel. Contains illustrations, a note on the Southey family, a list of Southey's works, notes, and an index.

Smith, Christopher J. P. *A Quest for Home: Reading Robert Southey.* Liverpool, England: Liverpool University Press, 1997. A historical and critical study of the works of Southey. Includes bibliographical references and index.

Storey, Mark. *Robert Southey: A Life.* New York: Oxford University Press, 1997. Storey tells the fascinating story of a complex and contradictory man, the mirror of his age, and sets him centre-stage to provide a new perspective on familiar events and figures of the Romantic period.

Samuel J. Rogal;
bibliography updated by the editors

Robert Southwell

Born: Horsham St. Faith, Norfolk, England; 1561
Died: London, England; March 4, 1595

Principal poetry

St. Peter's Complaint, with Other Poems, 1595
Moeoniae, 1595
The Complete Poems of Robert Southwell, 1872 (Alexander B. Grosart, editor)
The Poems of Robert Southwell, 1967 (James H. McDonald and Nancy Pollard Brown, editors)

Other literary forms

Besides writing poetry Robert Southwell wrote many religious tracts, including *Mary Magdalens Funerall Teares* (1591).

Achievements

Robert Southwell's reputation as a poet in his own time is difficult to determine, since he was a priest in hiding and a martyr for his Roman Catholic faith. It is natural that the five manuscript compilations of his verses do not name the author, and that the two printed volumes, both published in the year of his execution, likewise do not name the author; one of them, however, gives his initials. The publishers may have thought that readers would associate the poems with Southwell, who was of much interest at the time, although the government tried to keep his trial secret. Early references to his verse, however, with a single exception, do not indicate knowledge of authorship. Southwell's name did not appear in an edition until 1620.

The musical quality of his verse is remarkable, considering that he almost forgot his native English during his long education abroad and had to relearn it when he returned to England as a priest in hiding. He has been described by Pierre Janelle as the "leading Catholic writer of the Elizabethan age," and one who might have developed into one of the greatest English writers if it were not for his death at thirty-four. His best-known poem is "The Burning Babe," and Ben Jonson is reputed to have said that if he had written that poem, he would have been content to destroy many of his.

Biography

Robert Southwell was born toward the end of 1561, according to evidence gathered from his admittance to the Society of Jesus and from his trial. His family was prosperous, and he spent his boyhood at Horsham St. Faith, Norfolk.

In 1576, when he was about fifteen, he entered the English College of the Jesuit school at Douai; like many young Catholics of that period, he was sent to the Continent for his later education. He studied at the Jesuit College of Clermont in Paris for a short time for his greater safety, returning to Douai in 1577, the year in which he applied to enter the Jesuit novitiate at Tournai. He was at first rejected, but was accepted into the novitiate in Rome in 1578, where he was a student at the Roman College and tutor and precept of studies at the English College. Forbidden to speak English, he spoke Latin and Italian, becoming very fluent in the latter and reading a great deal of Italian literature. He wrote Latin poetry, including religious epics, elegies, and epigrams.

His poetry in English was written during his English mission, from his return to England in July, 1586, to his arrest in June, 1592. He was stationed in London, working under a superior, Reverend Henry Garnet. Southwell occupied a house in London and provided lodgings for priests, meeting those coming into the country. He corresponded with the Reverend Claudius Aquaviva, General of the Society of Jesus, giving him reports of the persecution. He received much help from the Countess of Arundel, and his prose works were printed secretly. He met at intervals with his superior and other priests; one such meeting was raided, but they managed to escape.

He was betrayed by a fellow Jesuit who had been arrested after arriving in England and who described the appearance of Southwell, and by the sister of a Catholic friend with whom he was staying in Uxenden, north of London. This Anne Bellamy, of a loyal Catholic family, had been imprisoned and become pregnant while in prison, probably having been assaulted by the priest-hunter Topcliffe; she married Topcliffe's assistant and betrayed Southwell on the condition that her family would not be molested, a promise which was not kept. Southwell was arrested on June 25, 1592. Topcliffe wrote an exultant letter to the queen about the importance of his prisoner and his intentions. Southwell was brought to Topcliffe's house and tortured many times. One of the tortures was being hung by the hands against a wall. He refused to identify himself or admit that he was a priest; in the absence of such identification, the family that had sheltered him could not be implicated. On Queen Elizabeth's instructions, he was moved to the Gatehouse Prison, where he was tortured and questioned by the Privy Council; but he always kept his silence. After he heard that there was other evidence against the Bellamys (they had been imprisoned on Anne's evidence), he wrote to Sir Robert Cecil, a member of the Council, that he was a priest and a Jesuit. He did not want his silence to be misinterpreted as fear or shame of his profession. Imprisoned in the Tower of London, he was arraigned under the Act of 1585 for the treason of returning to England as an ordained Catholic priest and of administering sacraments. Weak as he was, he had to conduct his own defense, but he was constantly interrupted. He was convicted, dragged through the streets, and hanged, drawn, and quartered at Tyburn Tree on March 4, 1595, after praying for his queen, his country, and himself. He was beatified by his Church in 1929 and canonized as a saint in 1970.

Robert Southwell (Hulton Archive)

ANALYSIS

Robert Southwell wrote his religious poetry with a didactic purpose. In the prose Preface to a manuscript, addressed to his cousin, he says that poets who write of the "follies and fayninges" of love have discredited poetry to the point that "a Poet, a Lover, and a Liar, are by many reckoned but three words of one signification." Poetry, however, was used for parts of Scripture, and may be used for hymns and spiritual sonnets. He has written his poetry to give others an example of subject matter, he says, and he hopes that other more skillful poets will follow his example. He flies from "prophane conceits and fayning fits" and applies verse to virtue, as David did. Perhaps his distaste for the stylized love poetry of his time explains the absence of sonnets in his writing. While Southwell's purpose in writing was didactic, he was often more emotional than purely intellectual. His poems are seldom tranquil. They tend to startle through his use of the unexpected, the fantastic, and the grotesque, and may thus be described as baroque. Southwell is also linked to the baroque movement in his use of Italian models and such themes as weeping, anticipating the seventeenth century Roman Catholic poet Richard Crashaw.

As might be expected, death is a recurring theme in his poetry, yet he makes the theme universal rather than personal, for his purpose was instructive and oral rather than merely self-expressive. In "Upon the Image of Death," for example, he speaks of what is apparently a *memento mori* kind of picture that he often looks at, but he still does not really believe that he must die; historical personages and people he has known have all died, and yet it is difficult to think that he will die. There are personal touches, such as references to his gown, his knife, and his chair, but all are reminders to him and to all of inevitable death, "And yet my life amend not I." The poem's simplicity and universality give it a proverbial quality.

His most inspired poems were about birth rather than death, the birth of the Christ-child. In Part VI of "The Sequence on the Virgin Mary and Christ," "The Nativitie of Christ," he uses the image of the bird that built the nest being hatched in it, and ends with the image of the Christ-child as hay, the food for the beasts that human beings have become through sin. His image of Christ is often that of a child, as in "A Child My Choice," where he stresses the superior subject he praises in the poem, compared with the foolish praise of what "fancie" loves. While he loves the Child, he lives in him, and cannot live wrongly. In the middle two stanzas of this four-stanza poem, he uses a great deal of alliteration, parallelism, and antithesis to convey the astonishing nature of this Child, who is young, yet wise; small, yet strong; and man, yet God. At the end of the poem, he sees Christ weeping, sighing, and panting while his angels sing. Out of his tears, sighs, and throbs buds a joyful spring. At the end of the poem, he prays that this Child will help him in correcting his faults and will direct his death. The prayer was of course meant to be didactic, but it assumes a very personal meaning because of Southwell's manner of death. The themes of the Nativity and of death are thus artistically linked.

"A vale of teares"

As Vincent Barry Leitch has stated, the Incarnation serves as a paradigm of God's love for human beings and signifies God's sanctification of human life. There is thus a strong sense of the divine in human life in most of Southwell's poems, yet some of the poems are referred to as "desolation poems" because this sense of God in human life is absent. Sin is prevalent, and the sinner feels remorse. In "A vale of teares," for example, God seems to be absent, leaving people alone to work things out for themselves. The poem is heavily descriptive, describing a valley of the Alps and painting a picture of a dreary scene that is in keeping with a sense of loneliness and desolation. It is wild, mountainous, windy, and thunderous, and although the green of the pines and moss suggests hope, hope quails when one looks at the cliffs. The poem ends with an apostrophe to Deep Remorse to possess his breast, and bidding Delights adieu. The poem has been linked to the conventional love lyric in which the lover, in despair, isolates himself from the world, but it has also been linked to the Ignatian Exercises of the Jesuits.

St. Peter's Complaint

Another poem on the theme of isolation and remorse is the long dramatic poem *St. Peter's Complaint*, comprising 132 stanzas of six lines each, based on an Italian work by Luigi Tansillo (1510-1568), *Le Lagrime di San Pietro* (The Tears of Saint Peter). Southwell wrote a translation of part of Tansillo's poem, titling it, "Peeter Playnt," and two other poems, "S. Peters complaint," a poem of eleven stanzas, and "Saint Peters Complaynte," a poem of twelve stanzas. These three apparently represent stages in the composition of the long poem. In the translation, there is an objective rather than a first-person point of view, and Peter's denying Christ was an action in the immediate past in the courtyard, while reference is made to the suffering Peter will experience in the future. In each of the three original versions, Peter is the speaker and the time and place are indefinite. Much of the material in "Saint Peters Complaynte" is incorporated in the long poem. The uneven quality of the long poem has caused Janelle to assign it to an early period of experimentation, but McDonald and Brown see it as an unpolished work left unfinished when Southwell was arrested.

In the long poem, St. Peter indulges in an extended nautical conceit, appropriate for this speaker, of sailing with torn sails, using sighs for wind, remorse as the pilot, torment as the haven, and shipwreck as the best reward. He hopes his complaints will be heard so that others will know that there is a more sorrowful one than they, and he lists all the unfortunate things he is, one to a line for a whole stanza, including "An excrement of earth. . . ." He says that others may fill volumes in praise of "your forged Goddesse," a reference to the literary fashion of praising some supposed love, who might not be real at all. St. Peter's griefs will be his text and his theme. Several times in his works, Southwell makes this distinction between the falseness of stylized love poetry and the reality of religious themes. St. Peter says that he must weep, and here Southwell employs hyperbole, for a sea will hardly rinse Peter's sin; he speaks of high tides, and says that all those who weep should give him their tears. The poem is heavily rhetorical, with many exclamations, parallelisms, repetitions, questions, and comparisons. St. Peter had not thought that he would ever deny Christ. In lines 673-677, Southwell characteristically begins a line with a word which had already appeared toward the end of the preceding line, thus patterning Peter's "circkling griefes." Peter compares himself to a leper with sores, and asks Christ's forgiveness. The taunts that Peter levels at the woman in the courtyard in the poem have been taken to suggest a parallel between her actions and those of Queen Elizabeth. Alice Mary Lubin, in a study of Southwell's religious complaint lyrics, says that this poem differs from the traditional complaint poem in that the complaining figure is separated from Christ rather than from a figure such as a lover, and that it differs from medieval religious complaint poems because it constitutes a statement of remorse rather than being simply a lament. A description of Peter's isolation occupies much of the poem. Lubin does not see the work as an ordered meditative poem; rather, it resembles an Italian "weeper" poem in subject, though not in treatment. She suggests analogues in *A Myrrour for Magistrates* (1559) and in the Old Testament Lamentations.

"The Burning Babe"

Southwell's most famous work, "The Burning Babe," combines several of his favorite themes, including the Nativity, isolation, guilt, and purification, into a vision poem that becomes a lament. He presents the material as a mystical vision. The occasion is presented dramatically, for it was a "hoary winter's night" and he was shivering in the snow when he felt the sudden heat that made him look up to see the fire. The dramatic contrasts continue, as he speaks of seeing a pretty baby; but it is in the air, not where a baby would be, and it is "burning bright," like a fire; the image is deliberately odd, ambiguous, and out of place. The next image, that the baby is "scorched" with great heat, turns the odd image into a horrible one, conveying the idea that the baby's body is no longer white but discolored from a fire that is not a mere metaphor. The fire is not from the air, but from inside the body, which means that there is no escape for the baby. The next image is ironic, for the baby cries copiously, as though the "floods" of tears could quench the flames, which they cannot do.

When the baby speaks, it is to lament that he fries in this heat although he has just been born, and yet no one seeks to warm the heart at this fire, and no one but the baby feels this fire. Here the Christ-child is very much alone. It is not until the next line, however, that the baby is clearly identified as Christ, when he says that the furnace (the place where the fire is) is his breast, and the fuel is "wounding thorns." The ironic crown of thorns of the Crucifixion becomes fuel for the fire. His breast is kept burning because people wound him with thorns and hurt him through their mocking actions. The Crucifixion was a specific event, but the fire is a continuing torment, so the "wounding thorns" must be not only the crown of thorns but also the sins that people are continuing to commit.

Vision poems have often had a guide figure, someone who leads the viewer and explains the allegorical significance of the vision. Here the baby is both the vision and the guide, resulting in a kind of ironic horror. The image throughout this section of the poem is that of a furnace, a piece of technology used for creating and working things. The baby explains that the fire is love, a rather complicated idea, for it is the "wounding thorns" that keep the fire (the love) alive. Christ's love feeds on the wrongs of human beings. He loves human beings despite their sins, and indeed because of their sins. The smoke is sighs, his emotional dissatisfaction with what is happening, how people are acting. The ashes are the residue, the residual shame and scorn. The shame is Christ's embarrassment at being crucified and the equal embarrassment of the constant crucifixion He suffers because of continuing sin. The scorn is the rejection of his reality and the mission that he came into the world as a baby to accomplish, the taking of sins onto himself. Thus the residue of the fire is the shame and scorn, not entirely consumed in the fire but left over and ever-present. Two personifications now enter the allegory. Justice puts the fuel on the fire, for it is not only that the sins and injustices of human beings be burnt, consumed, transformed in this way; it is also Mercy that "blows the coals," that keeps the fire of love going strong by blowing air onto it. The imagery has changed from the "wounding thorns" causing the baby to be on fire, to the necessity and justice of burning up and burning away the wrongs of humans in the heat of God's love, which is kept going by his mercy.

The metals that are worked in this furnace are the souls of human beings, which have been defiled, but which are to be changed in the fire, thus representing another change in the imagery. Christ is now on fire to change them into something better, and he says that he will "melt into a bath to wash them in my blood." A bath is a cleansing, a purification, and after feeling the love of God, they will be purified by a cooling liquid, ironically not water, but Christ's blood, another touch of horror but also of love and glory. Saying that he would melt, a term meaning depart or disappear, but having special imagistic significance here because of the burning, the Christ-child vanishes. The reader is conscious that the baby will become the crucified Christ, and the poet realizes that it is Christmas. Southwell here makes the Christ-child the isolated one, most ironically, and develops the symbolism to make the reader feel remorse for his sins. The poem's startlingly grotesque subject clearly links it to the baroque movement.

Joy and alienation

Southwell's main themes were the opposing ones of the joyous Incarnation, with its joining of God and human beings, and the tragic desolation of feeling the alienation of self from God through sin. Striking images with strong emotion achieve a religious purpose of affecting the reader. In his short life, Southwell wrote many fine poems in a language he had once forgotten. He referred very little in his poetry to the persecution that overshadowed his life, choosing to write instead of religious experiences that transcended time and place.

Other major works

nonfiction: *Epistle of Robert Southwell to His Father, Exhorting Him to the Perfect Forsaking of the World*, 1589; *Mary Magdalens Funerall Teares*, 1591; *His Letter to Sir Robert Cecil*, 1593; *A Humble Supplication to Her Majestie*, 1595 (written in 1591); *The Triumphs over Death*, 1596 (written in 1591); *A Short Rule of Good Life*, 1598; *An Epistle of Comfort*, 1605 (written in 1591); *A Hundred Meditations on the Love of God*, 1873 (written c. 1585; translation).

Bibliography

Brownlow, F. W. *Robert Southwell*. New York: Twayne, 1996. An introductory biography and critical study of selected works by Southwell. Includes bibliographic references and an index.

Janelle, Pierre. *Robert Southwell the Writer: A Study in Religious Inspiration*. 1935. Reprint. Mamaroneck, N.Y.: Paul J. Appel, 1971. Though a relatively "old" book, Janelle's biography—the first three chapters of the book—remains the standard account of the life of Southwell. The other chapters concerning Jesuit influence, Petrarchan origins, and Southwell's place among his contemporaries have stood the test of time. This scholarly volume contains an extensive bibliography, especially of primary sources.

Lewis, C. S. *English Literature in the Sixteenth Century, Excluding Drama*. Oxford: Clarendon Press, 1954. In a relatively brief overview of Southwell's poetic achievements, Lewis states that Southwell is of most historical interest as an early Metaphysical poet (his verse particularly resembles George Herbert's). Lewis also addresses the religious content of Southwell's poetry.

Martz, Louis L. *The Poetry of Meditation: A Study in English Religious Literature of the Seventeenth Cen-*

tury. New Haven, Conn.: Yale University Press, 1954. 2d ed. New Haven, Conn. Yale University Press, 1962. Martz examines Southwell's meditative poetry which looks ahead to the religious poetry of the seventeenth century in its adapting "profane" poetic devices to religious poetry, in its poetic meditations on the lives of Christ and Mary, and in its Ignatian self-analysis. He also demonstrates close ties between Southwell and George Herbert.

Moseley, D. H. *Blessed Robert Southwell*. New York: Sheed & Ward, 1957. A sympathetic biography drawn from late sixteenth century writings and records, which provides an understanding of the cultural, religious, and political climate in which Southwell lived and wrote. Supplemented by a chronological select bibliography of Southwell criticism.

Scallon, Joseph D. *The Poetry of Robert Southwell, S.J.* Salzburg, Austria: Institut für Englische Sprache und Literatur, 1975. Scallon's monograph provides chapters on Southwell's biography, his short poems (particularly those concerning Christ and the Virgin Mary), and the poems on repentance. *St. Peter's Complaint*, Southwell's best poem, receives extensive analysis. Contains a substantial bibliography.

Rosemary Ascherl;
bibliography updated by the editors

Stephen Spender

Born: London, England; February 28, 1909
Died: London, England; July 16, 1995

Principal poetry

Nine Experiments, by S. H. S.: Being Poems Written at the Age of Eighteen, 1928
Twenty Poems, 1930
Poems, 1933, 1934
Vienna, 1935
The Still Centre, 1939
Selected Poems, 1940
Ruins and Visions, 1942
Spiritual Exercises (To Cecil Day Lewis), 1943
Poems of Dedication, 1947
Returning to Vienna 1947: Nine Sketches, 1947
The Edge of Being, 1949
Collected Poems, 1928-1953, 1955
Inscriptions, 1958
Selected Poems, 1964
The Generous Days, 1971
Recent Poems, 1978
Collected Poems, 1928-1985, 1985
Dolphins, 1994

Other literary forms

Although best known for his poetry, Stephen Spender wrote a considerable body of drama, fiction, criticism, and journalism. The first of his six plays, *Trial of a Judge* (1938), was his contribution to the Group Theatre effort, in which his friend W. H. Auden was so heavily involved, and reflected the young Spender's socialist outlook. Most of the others—notably *Danton's Death* (1939), which he wrote with Goronwy Rees; *Mary Stuart* (1957), taken from the J. C. F. Schiller play; and *Rasputin's End* (1963), a libretto to music by Nicholas Nabokov—likewise dealt with broadly political situations and problems. Spender's published fiction consists of a collection of stories, *The Burning Cactus* (1936); a novel, *The Backward Son* (1940); and two novellas, *Engaged in Writing* and *The Fool and the Princess* (published together in 1958).

Spender's nonfiction prose comprises more than a dozen books, as well as hundreds of essays contributed to periodicals. The critical works have dealt mostly with the issues and problems of modern literature, beginning with essays written for *The Criterion* in the 1930's and *The Destructive Element: A Study of Modern Writers and Beliefs* (1935), and continuing through his study of T. S. Eliot (1975) and the selection of essays from various periods of Spender's career titled *The Thirties and After* (1978). Especially notable among his other critical books are *The Struggle of the Modern* (1963), a study of modernism's complicated relationship to twentieth century literature in general, and *Love-Hate Relations: A Study of Anglo-American Sensibilities* (1974), which examines the connections between American and English literary sensibilities. Spender's journalistic writings include *Citizens in War and After* (1945) and *European*

Witness (1946). He also published an autobiography, *World Within World: The Autobiography of Stephen Spender* (1951).

ACHIEVEMENTS

Several of Stephen Spender's poems stand among the most poignant of the twentieth century. Those anthology pieces with which his name is most often associated—"Not Palaces, an Era's Crown," "Beethoven's Death Mask," "I think continually of those who were truly great," "The Express," "The Landscape near an Aerodome," and "Ultima Ratio Regum"—have helped achieve for Spender greater recognition than for any of the other British poets who came into prominence in the late 1920's and early 1930's, with the notable exception of W. H. Auden. Spender's stature rests also on his peculiar position among poets writing through the Great Depression and after World War II. More than the others, he emerged as an authentic voice bridging the modernist and postwar periods. Even during the 1930's—when Auden was the leader of the loose confederation of young writers to which he and Spender belonged—it was Spender who in poem after poem voiced most honestly and movingly the tensions informing the writing of poetry in that troubled time. When Auden and Christopher Isherwood departed for America in 1939, Spender remained as the foremost representative of the liberal values and lyric intensity which had marked the best poetry of the prewar years. Later—especially with the death of the other figures making up the so-called Auden Group—Spender's verse, as well as his prose, took on special interest, as a last link between contemporary British literature and an earlier period crucial to its development.

In many respects Spender's outlook and poetry scarcely changed after the 1930's. While many critics regarded such want of development as a mark of failure, in a sense it represents a strength. Presumably, Spender saw little reason to change his poetic method or to go beyond those indisputably successful poems of his early adulthood because for him the fundamental problems—poetic, political, and personal—hardly changed since that time. Interestingly, an audience that grew up scarcely aware of Spender's poetic achievement became fascinated by Spender the essayist and lecturer. Because his most characteristic pronouncements to this more recently acquired audience were closely related to the viewpoint revealed in the early poems, they suggest the continuing value of those poems, not merely as artifacts from an increasingly distant past but as permanent sources of interest and pleasure.

BIOGRAPHY

Stephen Harold Spender was born in London on February 28, 1909. His father was Harold Spender, a noted journalist and lecturer, and his mother was Violet Hilda Schuster Spender, a painter and poet. The death of Spender's mother when he was fifteen and of his father two years later, in 1926, brought the four children, of whom he was the second-oldest, under the care of his maternal grandmother, a pair of spinster great-aunts, and an uncle.

After attending University College School in London, Spender went to University College, Oxford, in 1928, leaving in 1930 without a degree. Having begun to write poetry in childhood and having determined to be a poet, he sought out the somewhat older W. H. Auden even before beginning at Oxford. Their friendship, marked by a mutual awareness of their differences in temperament and outlook, apparently developed rapidly; Spender himself published Auden's first book of poems in 1928 on the same handpress he used to bring out his own first book. He spent the summer vacation of 1929 in Germany, meeting many young Germans and observing social and political developments that would set the stage for the next decade.

The 1930's were a time of tremendous literary activity for the young Spender, periodically punctuated by travels throughout Europe. He achieved prominence as a leading member of the group of rising young writers clustered around Auden. Although Spender has claimed a singular position among the Auden group, during that time he behaved in a fashion broadly similar to that adopted by the others, briefly joining the Communist Party in 1936, traveling to Spain in 1937 to observe the Civil War from the Republican side, and publishing poems and essays supporting a radical viewpoint and warning of the growing Nazi menace. By late 1939 he had joined Cyril Connolly as coeditor of *Horizon*, a post he held until 1941. The war years also saw

Spender in the National Fire Service and later in the Foreign Service. In 1941, he married Natasha Litwin, his 1936 marriage to Agnes Marie Pearn having ended in divorce.

After World War II, Spender focused on numerous writing, editing, and translating projects, on extensive travel and university lecturing—particularly in the United States—and on his family life. From 1953 to 1966, he served as coeditor of *Encounter*, resigning when he learned of the Central Intelligence Agency's financing of that magazine. Spender's many public and literary honors include being named a Companion in the Order of the British Empire (C.B.E.) in 1962, receiving the Queen's Gold Medal for Poetry in 1971, and being given an Honorary Fellowship to University College, Oxford, in 1973. In 1970, he was appointed to the chair of English literature in University College, London. He died in London on July 16, 1995.

ANALYSIS

Stephen Spender seems always to have struck his readers as halting. Even in the relatively confident writing of his youth, he was the most likely of the Auden Group to avoid the extreme pronouncements to which his seemingly more self-assured contemporaries—especially Auden himself—were prone. Taken as a whole, his poetry appears to reflect a perpetual debate, an unresolved tension over what can be known, over what is worth knowing, and over how he ought to respond as a poet and as a citizen of a modern society. Taken separately, his poems—particularly the best and most representative ones—exhibit an attraction or a movement sometimes toward one side of an issue, and sometimes toward the other. Almost always, however, such commitment at least implies its opposite.

This tension itself may account for the continuing appeal of so many Spender lyrics, decades after they were written and after their historical context has passed. Obviously they conform to the demand for irony and ambiguity begun in the late 1920's by I. A. Richards and William Empson and prolonged until recently by their American counterparts, the New Critics. In this respect, if not in others, Spender established a link with the seventeenth century Metaphysical wits so admired by T. S. Eliot. The qualifying tendency of Spender's poetry connects him also with the postwar movement among a younger generation of British poets—notably Philip Larkin, Donald Davie, and Kingsley Amis—who have taken issue with Eliot's modernist ambitions and with Dylan Thomas's romantic gesturing.

The tentativeness of Spender's writing connects with so many diverse and often opposing tendencies in modern literature because it has its roots in the Romanticism underlying all modern literature. Like Romanticism, Spender's verse embraces a variety of conflicting impulses. Whether to write about private subjects or to take on more public concerns, and whether to adopt a personal or an impersonal stance toward the selected subjects, become central problems for Spender. He finds himself at some times, and in some poems, drawn to life's simple, civilian joys; at other times he is moved toward the grand actions of politics. Stylistically, he can be seen vacillating between directness and obliqueness, literalness and figurativeness, and realism and imagism. The conflicting pulls of pragmatism and idealism so evident throughout his career suggest a sympathy with virtually all strains of Western philosophy, especially since René Descartes. Underlying this inability, or unwillingness, to project a set posture is the drive toward inwardness seen in nineteenth century literature, a drive at once hastened and opposed by the great Romantics. The legacy of this drive and its attendant struggle constitute much of the drama played out in Spender's poems.

His writing in the 1930's suggests the same sort of shift evident in the other Auden poets and in many prose writers, such as George Orwell. It suggests, too, a process more of accretion than of drastic change, since the seeds of Spender's discontent with the posture of his earlier political poems lay in the poems themselves. Auden's poetry probably encouraged the young Spender to move from the unfocused idealism of his teens and to write more about the real world. Spender's poetry thus became noticeably contemporary in reference, with urban scenes and crowds, to the point that he could devote entire poems to a speedy train ("The Express") or an airship ("The Landscape near an Aerodrome").

Just as Auden found Spender too romantic, Spender found Auden too cool and detached from the often grim world which Auden had induced him to consider in his poems. Even at his most topical, even when most under Auden's influence, Spender refused to indulge in Audenesque wit or satiric bite. The characteristic feeling of the *Poems* of 1933 is one of commitment and seriousness. Where Auden might concentrate on the ridiculousness of society, Spender concentrates on society's victims and their suffering.

"Moving Through the Silent Crowd"

"Moving Through the Silent Crowd" illustrates well the understated poignancy of which Spender was capable at this time in his career. Nearly empty of metaphor, it gains its effect through Spender's emphasis on emblematic detail and through the development of saddening irony. He frames the poem with his own vantage point, from which he observes the idle poor. The first stanza turns on his intimation of "falling light," which represents for him the composite disillusionment and wasted potential of the men silent in the road. In the second, he notices the cynicism implicit in such gestures as shrugging shoulders and emptying pockets. Such a scene leads him, in the final two stanzas, to develop the irony of the situation and to hint at a radical political stance. He notes how the unemployed resemble the wealthy in doing no work and sleeping late. Confessing jealousy of their leisure, he nevertheless feels "haunted" by the meaninglessness of their lives.

An equally strong element of social conscience colors many other Spender poems written before 1933. Generally they exhibit more eloquence and metaphorical sweep than the rather terse "Moving Through the Silent Crowd." For example, in "Not palaces, an era's crown" he catalogs those purely intellectual or aesthetic considerations which he must dismiss in favor of social action. Such action he significantly compares to an energized battery and illustrates in a bold program of opposition to social and political tyranny. The short, forceful sentences of the poem's second section, where this program is described, contrast with the longer, more ornate syntax of the beginning. The hunger that Spender hopes to eradicate is of a more pressing order than that addressed by aesthetics or vague idealism, which he characterizes as sheer indolence. Only in the poem's final line, once his moral and political ambitions have been fully expressed, can he permit himself a Platonic image, as light is said to be brought to life.

Such insistence upon social reform, shading into radical political action, probably peaked in the period of 1935 to 1938, when *Vienna* and *Trial of a Judge* were appearing. Perhaps more notable than Spender's eventual repudiation of the unsuccessful *Vienna* is the fact that in so many of the shorter poems written during these years, especially those concerned with Spain, he turned increasingly from the public subjects, the outwardly directed statements, and the didactic organization marking the earlier poems. Where his critique of life in England might be construed as supportive of Communism, the picture he draws of Spain during the Civil War largely ignores the political dimension of the struggle and focuses instead on the suffering experienced by civilians in all regions and of all political persuasions. While a strain of political idealism continues, the enemy is no longer simply capitalism or even Adolf Hitler; rather, for Spender it has become war and those persons responsible for inflicting a state of war on the helpless and innocent.

"Ultima Ratio Regum"

One of his most effective poems from Spain, "Ultima Ratio Regum," exhibits a didactic form, even ending with a rhetorical question; but it carefully avoids condemnation or praise of either side. Read without consideration for Spender's original reasons for going to Spain, his angry and moving account of a young Spaniard's senseless death by machine-gun fire condemns the Republicans no less than the Insurgents and ultimately centers on the impersonality of modern war, which reduces to statistical insignificance a formerly alive and sensitive young man. Similarly, "Thoughts During an Air Raid" deals with Spender's own feelings while taking cover and with the temptation to regard oneself as somehow special and therefore immune from the fate threatening all other people in time of war. If Spender here argues for a more collective consciousness, it is but a vague and largely psychological brotherhood. As in "Ultima Ratio Regum," the viewpoint here is wholly civilian and pacifist. Even "Fall of a City," which clearly and sadly alludes to a Republican defeat, suggests more the spirit of freedom which Spender sees surviving the fall than any political particulars or doctrine attending that spirit. There Spender derives his residual hope not from a party or concerted action, but from the simple handing down of memories and values from an old man to a child. If anything, this poem reflects a distrust of large-scale political ideologies and action and of the dishonesty, impersonality, and brutality that they necessarily breed.

In his autobiography Spender writes of having been puzzled by civilian enthusiasm for both sides in the Spanish struggle. Like Orwell, he was also disturbed by Republican atrocities against civilians. Such disillusioning discoveries no doubt contributed to the reluctance with which he viewed England's struggle against the Nazis even after the war had begun. Conceding the need to counter the German threat, Spender in his war poems nevertheless stressed the pain, rather than the glory, of that necessity. Such was his perception of that pain that he found it necessary in "The War God" to ask and answer questions which, after Munich or the invasion of Poland, even the most war-wary Englishman probably would no longer have considered. One almost gets the impression that Spender is concerned with convincing, or reminding, himself more than anyone else of the reasons behind the war, so obvious is the logic of the poem. Even "Memento," his more effective response to the death camps, betrays the same lingering pacifism as its surreal images describe the victims' horror and helplessness.

"June 1940"

Perhaps Spender's most remarkable—and his most reluctant—war poem is his response to the fall of France, "June 1940." Even as Britain is most threatened, he finds it necessary and appropriate to invoke the ghost of World War I to express his skepticism about the impending defense against Hitler. The first section of the poem combines a lyrical description of the delights of the English summer with suggestions of the war's distance from that pastoral scene. Spender has the "grey" survivors of the earlier war note the difference between the trench fighting of their youth and the newer, more mechanized European war of which they have heard only very little. He shows boys bicycling around village war memorials and the Channel "snipping" England from France. The scene and mood change drastically in the next section, with the slightly surreal account of the "caterpillar-wheeled blond" charging over birds' nests in France that very day, and with the lengthy series of voices arguing the need to counter the Nazi horde with armed resistance. Such arguments persuade the old soldiers, sitting in their deck chairs since the poem's beginning, that the struggle against Germany is just and that the alternative is an imprisoned England.

Even so, Spender characterizes the old veterans' response as "disillusioned" to prepare the reader for the poem's audacious ending. In six short lines he overturns the style, the premises, and the conclusion of the earlier dialogue. A dead soldier from the Great War suddenly testifies to the purgatory of guilt to which participation in that earlier struggle against Germany has doomed him, to imply that the arguments justifying the current war represent only a seductive parallel to earlier warmongering, and that even defeating Hitler will not wholly justify the impending struggle or absolve the English of war guilt. While the conclusion implied by the logic of the poem may not be that England ought to surrender, it certainly cuts very thin any moral advantage the English might claim in resisting. Again Spender ultimately focuses his attention on the burden—in this case a moral one—placed on the individual by collective action.

"June 1940" represents only the most blatant evidence of Spender's departure from the spirited socialism and anti-Nazism of his earlier poems. The general drift of his writing after 1934 had been clearly in that direction. His poems had dealt increasingly with personal problems and situations. In *Forward from Liberalism* (1937), he had articulated his dissatisfaction with the socialist creed, a dissatisfaction based principally upon what he saw as the necessary antipathy to the individual person which politics, and especially leftist politics, inevitably aroused. Before too long he was able, in *The Creative Element: A Study of Vision, Despair, and Orthodoxy Among Some Modern Writers* (1953), to attribute his earlier political orthodoxy to liberal guilt induced by the misery of the poor during the Great Depression.

"An Elementary School Classroom in a Slum"

The ease with which such renunciation and self-analysis seem to have come after the late 1930's suggests the limited nature of Spender's commitment to politics even when he seemed most political. The tension between individual and collective viewpoints which becomes central to the Spanish Civil War poems and to "June 1940" is at least implicit in most of his earlier writing, as well.

It is true that in his criticism Spender repeatedly questions the wisdom of the modernists' avoidance of politics, particularly that of T. S. Eliot and William Butler Yeats, whom he so admired as a young man. In this regard, "An Elementary School Classroom in a Slum" constitutes Spender's gloss on Yeats's "Among School Children," first in the type of school the younger poet chooses to visit, and second in his refusal to turn the visit into an occasion for personal theorizing, as Yeats did. Spender's allusion to "Sailing to Byzantium"—where he asserts that he will not transform the street beggars into "birds" on his "singing-tree"—attacks Yeats even more directly.

The grammar of this assertion, however—indeed, of many ostensibly political statements by the young Spender—guarantees, perhaps intentionally, some confusion of purpose and does it so often that it seems reflective of a confusion in Spender himself.

First-person perspective

"In railway halls, on pavement near the traffic" is the very poem in which he seems to mock Yeats for the Irishman's indifference to public affairs. The poem is governed by an "I" whose statement of poetic intent ultimately reflects more on himself than on the plight of the poor. Not only does the subject of the poem thus become poetry—something that Spender could deplore in Yeats—but also in a sense the poet becomes the hero. This is not to criticize Spender, but merely to point out, ironically, how much his focus approaches Yeats's after all. The first-person perspective of so many other early Spender poems ties the public to the private and prevents any purely political orientation from taking over.

"Moving Through the Silent Crowd" illustrates even more strikingly this same tension. While the observed poor are rendered sympathetically, the reader can never forget the observer. The marked return, in the final stanza, to his viewpoint and his troubles—where three of four lines begin with "I'm," and where each of the parallel clauses develops the poet's dilemma—clearly raises a question as to the ultimate object of sympathy here. This does not mean that the poem reflects merely self-pity or that Spender might not want to get outside himself; however, the poem finally becomes an exposure not only of poverty, but also of the poet's inability to close the perceived gap between himself and the poor. He concludes with a sense of his distance from them; all he can do is sympathize and be "haunted" by them. Because he appears as helpless as they, though in a somewhat different sense, his helplessness becomes at least as important as theirs as the subject of the poem. Without the personal perspective, the poem seems to ask, Of what validity is political or social criticism? At the same time, the poem's fixation with the observer's perspective places in serious doubt the efficacy of whatever criticism he may construct.

"The Express"

Another dimension of Spender's uncertainty comes in his treatment of contemporary civilization, particularly in those celebrated early poems dealing with technology. Although Auden probably influenced Spender in this direction, Spender seems never to have been so comfortable as Auden with the up-to-date world, particularly as an element of his poetry. Such discomfort largely escaped his first readers, who found his apparent acceptance of material progress a welcome departure from old-fashioned nature poetry. A. Kingsley Weatherhead rightly suggests, in *Stephen Spender and the Thirties* (1975), that many writers of that decade wrote a covert kind of nature poetry even as they purported to repudiate the values of the Georgian poets. They did so, Weatherhead says, by taking a critical look at contemporary civilization and thereby implying retreat as the only viable alternative.

While this no doubt is true of Spender, his retreat often takes very subtle forms. Sometimes it resides largely in the terms with which he commends an aspect of twentieth century technology. "The Express," for example, appears to celebrate the beauty and speed of a fast-moving train and, thus, to confirm the benefits of modern applied science. An examination of the poem's progression, however, reveals considerable dissatisfaction with the external world for which the train has been manufactured. Perhaps the whole idea of a lyric poem's appropriating something so utilitarian as an express train might seem an implied criticism of utility; certainly Walt Whitman's "To a Locomotive in Winter" and Emily Dickinson's "I like to see it lap the miles" can be seen as backhanded compliments. Even so, Spender's train poem seems of a different order in that it places the train much more realistically—with references to stations, to gasworks, and to Edinburgh. A good deal of the poem's language is very literal. Even Spender's initial nonliteral description ascribes utility to the train's beginning: It is cast as a queen issuing a "plain manifesto" to her subjects.

The image of such public action yields to more private behavior in the poem's second sentence, where "she" is said to "sing" with increasing abandon as she gathers speed. In the third and final sentence, she sings enraptured, exceeding the bounds of nature by flying in her music. The shape of the poem is thus the progression of its metaphors. Because that progression is vertical—away from the earth, into a state of Platonic grace suggested by music, again reminiscent of Yeats—the poem becomes a celebration of imaginative and self-absorbed retreat from the mundane and empirical reality in which the express actually resides. Even as Spender praises the train, he gives equal praise to a place where the express could not possibly exist. The two objects of praise coexist, as do the two kinds of language by which they are represented. There is no evidence that the speaker of the poem—significantly *not* represented as "I"—does not believe he is praising the express on its own terms. On the other hand, the progression of the terms he uses, particularly the metaphors, suggests that he in fact admires principles quite antipathetic to those upon which the express runs, and that perhaps he can find the express tolerable only by transforming it into something it is not and cannot be.

Poems such as "The Express," "The Landscape near the Aerodrome," and "Pylons" suggest a flight from the material values upon which modern popular culture is founded. In this they can have even greater pertinence now than when they were written. An examination of other early poems suggests a wish, or at least a need, to escape the human element as well. For all of their apparent humanism, they propose a withdrawal from the very society that Spender would help redeem, and confirm the Marxist critique of Romanticism as an elevation of private concerns at the expense of the public good. They bring to mind, too, Hugh MacDiarmid's indictment of the Auden group's ultimate lack of political commitment.

PLATONIC IMAGES

Certainly, it seems no accident that Spender wrote so much about Romanticism and especially about Percy Bysshe Shelley. His discussion of the modern poet's difficulties in reconciling the Romantic ideal of the individual imagination and sensibility with a public, collective age seems almost an abstract of poems such as "Without that one clear aim, the path of flight" or "From all these events, from the slum, from the war, from the boom." In the first of these, a sonnet, Spender complains of being choked and imprisoned by social reality, of needing desperately to escape on the "wings" of poetry. So politically suspect a motive for writing, which he reinforces by other Platonic images suggestive of Shelley, informs the second poem. There Spender expresses a faith, not in reformist action, but in the power of time to obliterate the memory not only of wrongdoing but also of those who would correct it. What might have horrified Thomas Hardy thus consoles Spender. In "Perhaps," he takes comfort in the more escapist position that troubling public events may be only fantasies. Even "I think continually of those who were truly great," so often cited as the epitome of 1930's selflessness, suggests that Spender's characteristic way of coping with social problems is to forget them: to ignore the present by dreaming of the "truly great."

Individual poems and the collective poetry of Spender rarely show him consistent in this regard. His struggle with the irreconcilables of individual and group, private and public, and realism and idealism have their stylistic level, as elegances of metaphor and syntax frequently accompany and undermine his call for action in the present. To an age grown increasingly aware of the limitations, if not the futility, of collective behavior and of the traps into which both leader and follower can fall, Spender poses the dilemma of the morally and socially sensitive individual. For this reason he commands a not inconsiderable place among the poets of the twentieth century.

OTHER MAJOR WORKS

LONG FICTION: *The Backward Son*, 1940; *The Temple*, 1988.

SHORT FICTION: *The Burning Cactus*, 1936; *Engaged in Writing and The Fool and the Princess*, 1958.

PLAYS: *Trial of a Judge*, pr. 1938; *Danton's Death*, pr. 1939 (with Goronwy Rees); *To the Island*, pr. 1951; *Mary Stuart*, pr. 1957; *Lulu*, pr. 1958; *Rasputin's End*, pb. 1963; *Oedipus Trilogy: A Play in Three Acts Based on the Oedipus Plays of Sophocles*, pr. 1983.

NONFICTION: *The Destructive Element: A Study of Modern Writers and Beliefs*, 1935; *Forward from Liberalism*, 1937; *Citizens in War and After*, 1945; *European Witness*, 1946; *Poetry Since 1939*, 1946; *World Within World: The Autobiography of Stephen Spender*, 1951; *Shelley*, 1952; *The Creative Element: A Study of Vision, Despair, and Orthodoxy Among Some Modern Writers*, 1953; *The Making of a Poem*, 1955; *The Struggle of the Modern*, 1963; *Love-Hate Relations: A Study of Anglo-American Sensibilities*, 1974; *Eliot*, 1975; *The Thirties and After*, 1978; *Journals, 1939-1983*, 1985.

BIBLIOGRAPHY

Blamires, Harry. *Twentieth Century English Literature*. Rev. ed. New York: Schocken Books, 1985. This standard account of the development of English literature devotes only four pages to Spender, but it represents the judgment of the last quarter of the century and places the poet well in his generation and cultural context. Includes an index, a useful list for further reading, and a chronology.

Connors, J. J. *Poets and Politics: A Study of the Careers of C. Day Lewis, Stephen Spender, and W. H. Auden in the 1930's*. New Haven, Conn.: Yale University Press, 1967. Connors concentrates on the political activities and influence of these three figures. Politics, however, directly affected their poetry, and Connors points this out accurately and in detail. Supplemented by a complete and easy-to-use index.

Hynes, Samuel. *The Auden Generation: Literature and Politics in the 1930's*. New York: Viking Press, 1976. Like J. J. Connors, Hynes examines the interphase between politics and literature, but he is more concerned with the literature. His broader scope covers the entire spectrum of literature and looks hard at its social functions during a period of intense propaganda. Includes an appendix and full notes.

Leeming, David Adams. *Stephen Spender: A Life in Modernism*. New York: Henry Holt, 1999. Leeming's biography demonstrates that Stephen Spender's life reflected the complexity and flux of the century in which he lived: his sexual ambivalence, his famous friends, the free-love days in Germany between the wars, the CIA-*Encounter* scandal. In David Leeming's capable hands, this comprehensive, unauthorized study of Spender is a meditation on modernity itself.

Maxwell, D. E. S. *Poets of the Thirties*. London: Routledge & Kegan Paul, 1969. Maxwell's work is a classic on the period, re-creating the complex world of that time with clarity and insight. The book, a marvelous cornucopia of anecdotes, clearly underlines Spender's role. The index helps readers connect details.

Sternlicht, Sanford V. *Stephen Spender*. New York: Twayne, 1992. A study of the entire Spender canon that discusses all genres of the author's work. Sternlicht begins by providing the reader with a well researched, biographical sketch of the poet's development over several decades. He also includes a lengthy and insightful discussion of Spender's influential role as literary and political critic.

Thurley, Geoffrey. "A Kind of Scapegoat: A Retrospect on Stephen Spender." In *The Ironic Harvest: English Poetry in the Twentieth Century*. London: Edward Arnold, 1974. Provides a good synthesis of the changing estimate of the enduring value of Spender's poetry. This account is even-handed and comprehensive and places Spender well in the context of the 1930's.

Weatherhead, A. Kingsley. *Stephen Spender and the Thirties*. Lewisburg, Pa.: Bucknell University Press, 1975. Covers most aspects of interest in Spender's work and life and is the most comprehensive single source. Weatherhead knows his subject well and develops it with sympathetic detail. His bibliography is still useful.

Bruce K. Martin;
bibliography updated by the editors

EDMUND SPENSER

Born: London, England; c. 1552
Died: London, England; January 13, 1599

PRINCIPAL POETRY

The Shepheardes Calender, 1579
The Faerie Queene, 1590, 1596
Complaints, 1591
Daphnaïda, 1591
Colin Clouts Come Home Againe, 1595
Astrophel, 1595
Amoretti, 1595
Epithalamion, 1595
Fowre Hymnes, 1596
Prothalamion, 1596
The Poetical Works of Edmund Spenser, 1912 (J. C. Smith and Ernest de Selincourt, editors)

OTHER LITERARY FORMS

Like most Renaissance writers, Edmund Spenser usually prefaced his poems with dedicatory letters that complimented the recipients and also provided helpful interpretations for other readers. Further indications of Spenser's theories about "English versifying" appear in his correspondence with Gabriel Harvey: *Three Proper, and Wittie, Familiar Letters* (1580) and *Foure Letters and Certaine Sonnets* (1586). Although *A View of the Present State of Ireland* was written in 1596, it was not published until 1633, thirty-four years after the author's death. In this treatise, Spenser presented a clear picture of Elizabethan Ireland and its political, economic, and social evils. The serious tone of this work deepens the significance of the Irish allusions and imagery throughout Spenser's poetry.

ACHIEVEMENTS

The inscription on Edmund Spenser's monument hails him as "the Prince of Poets in his time," but his reputation as "poet's poet" continued among his Romantic peers three centuries later. What was praised and imitated changed with time, but the changes themselves suggest the extent of Spenser's achievements. His popularity among his contemporaries was documented not only in commentaries written during his lifetime but also in William Camden's account of Spenser's funeral, during which mourning poets threw into his tomb their elegies and the pens with which they had written these tributes. Among his fellow Elizabethans, Spenser first gained renown as a love poet, a pastoral writer, and a restorer of the native language—all three of these roles already enacted in his early work, *The Shepheardes Calender*, in which he demonstrated the expansiveness of rural dialect and English unadulterated with continental vocabulary. Later, in a more courtly work, *The Faerie Queene*, Spenser still sought variety in language more through native archaisms than through foreign idiom. Despite its simplicity of diction, *The Shepheardes Calender* contained an elaborate academic apparatus that demanded recognition for its author as a serious poet. The fact that Spenser took his work seriously was also manifested in various levels of satire and in metrical experimentation which strengthened what Philip Sidney described as his "poetical sinews."

Seventeenth century imitators echoed Spenser's allegorical and pastoral elements, his sensuous description, and his archaic phrasing. These early Spenserians, however, did not fully comprehend their model. Their servile imitations of surface themes and complex metrical forms temporarily diminished Spenser's reputation and probably stimulated later eighteenth century parodies. The serious side of Spenser, however, gradually received more notice. In *Areopagitica* (1644), for example, John Milton extolled him as "a better teacher than Scotus or Aquinas," and when the neoclassicists praised him, it was primarily for allegorical didacticism. In the nineteenth century, admiration of Spenser's moral allegory yielded to delight in his metrical virtuosity and the beauties of his word-pictures. When such great Romantics as Sir Walter Scott, Lord Byron, and John Keats imitated the Spenserian or "Faerie Queene" stanza form, they demonstrated anew the strength and flexibility of Spenser's metrical inventiveness. Modern holistic criticism continues to find deeper levels of Spenserian inventiveness in structural intricacy, allegorical ingenuity, and both narrative and descriptive aptness.

BIOGRAPHY

If allusions in his own poetry can be read autobiographically, Edmund Spenser was born in London in

1552, apparently into a mercantile family of moderate income. In 1561, the Merchant Taylors' School opened with Richard Mulcaster as its first headmaster, and in that same year or shortly afterward Spenser was enrolled, probably as a scholarship student. From Mulcaster, Spenser learned traditional Latin and Greek, and also an awareness of the intricacies and beauties of the English language unusual among both schoolboys and schoolmasters of that time. Later, Spenser as "Colin Clout" paid tribute to Mulcaser as the "olde Shephearde" who had made him "by art more cunning" in the "song and musicks mirth" that fascinated him in his "looser yeares." Even before Spenser went to Cambridge, fourteen of his schoolboy verse translations had been incorporated into the English version of Jan van der Noot's *Theatre for Worldlings* (1569).

At Pembroke College, Cambridge, Spenser took his B.A. degree in 1573 and his M.A. in 1576; little else is known about his activities during that period except that he made several lifelong friends, among them Gabriel Harvey and Edward Kirke. Both Harvey and Kirke were later among Spenser's prepublication readers and critics, and Kirke today remains the most likely candidate for the role of "E. K.," the commentator whose glosses and arguments interpret enigmatic passages in *The Shepheardes Calender.* The Spenser-Harvey letters reveal young Spenser's theories on poetry and also his hopes for the patronage of Philip Sidney and Sidney's uncle, the earl of Leicester, Queen Elizabeth's favored courtier. Harvey's greetings to a woman, whom he addresses as "Mistress Immerito" and "Lady Colin Clout," also suggest that Spenser was married about 1580; nothing more is known of the first wife, but there are records of a son and a daughter at the time of Spenser's second marriage to Elizabeth Boyle in 1594.

When Spenser found himself unable to gain an appointment as a Fellow at Cambridge, he accepted the post of secretary to John Young, Bishop of Rochester. In 1580, he went to Ireland as secretary for Arthur Lord Grey, the newly appointed Lord Governor. When Grey was recalled from Ireland two years later because his policies did not control the Irish rebellion as the English court desired, Spenser remained behind. For several years he moved into minor offices in different sections of the country; about 1589, he became "undertaker" of Kilcolman, an estate in Cork. As an "undertaker," Spenser received a grant of land previously confiscated from an Irish rebel, agreeing to see to the restoration of the estate and to establish tenant farmers on it. Love for Kilcolman is reflected in his poetry even though his days there were shadowed by litigation with an Irish neighbor who claimed the property and by a new outbreak of rebellion which eventually destroyed the estate and forced him to leave Ireland about a month before his death in 1599.

Edmund Spenser (Library of Congress)

With the exception of *The Shepheardes Calender*, all of Spenser's major poetry was written in Ireland. The landscape and the people of his adopted country are reflected in imagery and allusions; political and economic conditions appear in various guises, perhaps nowhere so strongly and pervasively as in Book V of *The Faerie Queene*, the Book of Justice. Although Spenser lived most of his adult life far from the court of Elizabeth, he maintained constant contact with events and friends there. His strongest bid for court recognition came in *The Faerie Queene*, with its creation of Gloriana, the Fairyland reflection of the living Queen of Britain, who rewarded him for his portrait of her by granting him an annual pension. Two of Queen Elizabeth's favorites played major roles in Spenser's later years: Sir Walter Ralegh and Robert, Earl of Essex. Ralegh, who owned an estate neighboring Spenser's Kilcolman, frequently encouraged the poet's work in a general way and, if there is any validity in Spenser's famous prefatory letter, influenced specific changes in the structure of *The Faerie Queene*. Essex financed the poet's funeral and his burial in the Poet's Corner of Westminster Abbey in 1599.

Analysis

By an eclectic mingling of old traditions, Edmund Spenser created new poetry—new in verse forms, in language, and in genre. From the Middle Ages, Spenser had inherited complex allegorical traditions and a habit of interlacing narrative strands; these traditions were fused with classical myth and generic conventions, some of them transformed by continental imitators before they reached Spenser. This fusion of medievalism and classicism was in turn modified by currents of thought prevalent in Tudor England, especially by the intense nationalism that manifested itself in religion, language, politics, and international affairs.

To some extent, Spenser's poetic development evolved naturally from his deliberate selection of Vergil as his model. Like Vergil, he started his published career with pastoral eclogues; like him, too, he turned, in his last major work, from shepherds to great heroes. Before Spenser evoked classical muses in his epic, however, the tradition of Vergil had picked up romantic coloring and allegorical overtones from continental epics, especially Ludovico Ariosto's highly allegorized *Orlando furioso* (1532). Spenser himself announced the three-way pattern adopted for *The Faerie Queene:* "Fierce wars and faithful loves shall moralize my song." Long after Spenser's death his admirers continued to compare him with Vergil, often to Spenser's advantage. Vergil provided stimulus not only for the pastoral and epic genres in which Spenser wrote his two major works but also for the mythical allusions that permeate most of his work and for the serious use of poetry, especially in political and religious satire and in the reflection of nationalistic pride. Vergil's exaltation of Augustus and the Roman Empire accorded well with the nationalism of Elizabethan England, a nationalism poetically at its zenith in *The Faerie Queene*.

Vergil's sobriquet "Tityrus" became for Spenser a means of double praise when he hailed his fourteenth century predecessor Geoffrey Chaucer as an English Tityrus, the "God of shepheards." Rustic language, interlocked narratives, and experiments in vernacular quantitative verse forms in *The Shepheardes Calender* all reflect Chaucerian influence; in a less direct way, the vogue of courtly love in medieval and Renaissance literature was also channeled partly through Chaucer. During the two centuries between Chaucer and Spenser, love poetry became permeated with a blend of Petrarchan and Neoplatonic elements. Petrarchan lovers taught Spenser's shepherds to lament over their ladies' cruelty, to extol their beauty, and to describe their own pains, anxieties, and ecstasies with conventional images. The more sensuous aspects of love remained central to many of the *Amoretti* sonnets and to several set pieces in *The Faerie Queene*, such as Acrasia's Bower of Bliss and Busiranes' Mask of Cupid, but idealistic Neoplatonic concepts also emerged here. Such Neoplatonic concepts undergird the *Fowre Hymnes*. The first two hymns praise erotic human love and the inspirational force of feminine beauty; the other two deprecate these more earthly powers, elevating in their place the heavenly love and beauty of Christ, the source of all true human love and beauty.

In *The Faerie Queene*, too, idealistic Neoplatonic elements assume more pervasive significance than do Petrarchan motifs. The Platonic identification of the good and the beautiful, for example, is often manifest, especially in Gloriana, Una, and Belphoebe; and the true and false Florimels of Books III to V exemplify true and false beauty, the former inspiring virtuous love and marriage and the second inciting sensuous lust. Although Books III and IV are called the Books of Chastity and Friendship, their linked story dramatically demonstrates variant forms of love. The concept of love as either debilitating or inspiring reflects one of the mythical traditions transmitted from antiquity through the Middle Ages: the double significance of Venus as good and evil love. As the goddess of good, fruitful love, Venus herself frequents the Garden of Adonis, where nature is untouched by deceptive art, where spring and harvest meet, and where love flourishes joyfully. In her own temple, Venus listens to the sound of "lovers piteously complaining" rather than rejoicing.

Renaissance pageantry and Tudor emblem books contributed to the pictorial quality with which Spenser brought myths to life—classical tales, rustic folklore, and his own mythic creations. One of the most picturesque of Spenser's new myths describes the "spousals" of the Thames and Medway rivers, a ceremony attended by such "wat'ry gods" as Neptune and his son Albion; by other rivers, remote ones such as the Nile and the Ganges, Irish neighbors such as the Liffey and the Mulla, and streams that paid tribute to one of the betrothed rivers; and by Arion, accompanied by his dolphin and carrying the harp with which he provided wedding music. Scenes like these exemplify the artistry with which Spenser created new poetry out of old traditions.

The Shepheardes Calender and Colin Clouts Come Home Againe

Classic and contemporary models, rural and courtly milieu, universal and occasional topics—from such a mixture Spenser formed his first major work, the "little booke," which he dedicated to Sidney and which he signed "Immerito," the Unworthy One. *The Shepheardes Calender* went through five editions between 1579 and 1597, none of them bearing Spenser's name. Such anonymity fits common Renaissance practice, but it may also have had additional motivation from Spenser's awareness of sensitive topical allusions with too thin an allegorical veil. Contemporary praise of Spenser indicates that by 1586 the anonymity was technical rather than real. In his twelve eclogues, one for each month of the year, Spenser imitated conventions that Renaissance writers attributed to Vergil and to his Greek predecessors: debates between rustic speakers in a rural setting, varied by a singing match between shepherds, a lament for the death of a beloved companion, praise of the current sovereign, alternating exultation and despair over one's mistress, and veiled references to contemporary situations. A fifteenth century French work, translated as *The Kalender and compost of Shepherds*, probably suggested to Spenser not only his title but also the technique of emblematic illustration, the application of zodiacal signs to everyday life and to the seasons, and the arrangement of instructional commentary according to the months. Barbabe Googe's *The Zodiake of Life* (1565) strengthened the satirical and philosophical undertone of the calendar theme.

Despite the surface simplicity connoted by its nominal concern with shepherds, Spenser's book is a complex work. Not the least of its complexities are the paraphernalia added by "E. K.": the dedicatory epistle, the introductory arguments (for the whole book and for each eclogue), and the glosses. Although the initials themselves make Spenser's Cambridge friend Edward Kirke the most likely person to designate as the mysterious commentator, the Renaissance love for name-games does not exclude other possible solutions of the identity puzzle. Even Spenser himself has been suggested as a candidate for the enigmatic role. Many of E. K.'s annotations supply information essential to an understanding of the poet's cryptic allusions, to the identification of real-life counterparts for the characters, and occasionally to a modernization of archaic diction. Some annotations, however, are either accidentally erroneous or pedantically misleading: for example, several source references and the etymology for "aeglogues." E. K. derives the term "eclogues" from "Goteheardes tales" rather than from "conversations of shepherds," the more usual Renaissance understanding of the term; in actuality, "eclogues" are etymologically short selections which convention came to associate with pastoral settings.

The twelve separate selections could have produced a sense of fragmentation, but instead they create a highly unified whole. The most obvious unifying device is the calendar framework, which gives to the individual poems their titles and their moods. Another source of unity lies in the shepherd characters who appear repeatedly, especially Colin Clout, a character borrowed from the Tudor satirist John Skelton and used by Spenser as his own persona. Colin appears in four of the eclogues and is the topic of conversation in three others; his friendship for Hobbinol (identified by E. K. as Harvey), and his love for Rosalind (unidentified) provide a thread of plot throughout the twelve poems. Moreover, the figure of Colin represents the whole life of "everyman"—or at least every poet—as he passes from the role of "shepherd boy" in "January" to that of the mature "gentle shepherd" in "December."

In his general argument, E. K. establishes three categories for the topics of the eclogues: plaintive, recreative, and moral. The four selections which E. K. classifies as plaintive are those in which Colin's is the main voice. "January" and "June" are laments about his futile love for Rosalind; "December," too, is a conventional love plaint, although it adds the dimension of Colin's approaching death. "November," one of the most highly structured eclogues, is a pastoral elegy for Dido, the daughter of one "greate shepehearde" and the beloved of another "greate shepheard Lobbin." E. K. pleads ignorance of the identity of both shepherds, but most critics identify "Lobbin" as a typical anagram for Robin (Robert Dudley) plus Leicester, thus suggesting a covert allusion to a love interest of Elizabeth's favorite, the Earl of Leicester.

The first of the three recreative selections, "March," is a sprightly, occasionally bawdy, discussion of love by two shepherd boys. "April" starts out with a description of Colin's lovesickness but then moves on to an encomium on "fayre Elissa, Queene of shepheardes all," a transparent allusion to Queen Elizabeth. The singing contest in "August" gives Spenser an opportunity to exploit shifting moods and an intricate variety of metrical patterns.

It is sometimes difficult to interpret the satire in the eclogues which E. K. classes as "moral" because of the ambivalence of the dialogue structure itself and because of the uncertain implications of the fables included in four of the five moral selections. Besides, misperception on the part of the characters or the commentator can be part of the comedy. In "May," "July," and "September," different pairs of shepherds discuss religious "shepherds," making clear allusions to contemporary churchmen. In contrast to the sometimes vehement satire in these religious eclogues, the debate on youth and age in "February" has a light, bantering tone. As a statement of Spenser's views on poetry, "October" is perhaps the most significant "moral" eclogue. When the disillusioned young poet Cuddie complains that his oaten reeds are "rent and wore" without having brought him any reward, the idealistic Piers tries to convince him that glory is better than gain. He encourages Cuddie to leave rustic life, to lift himself "out of the lowly dust," but Cuddie complains that the great worthies that "matter made for Poets on to play" are long dead. The ambivalence of the pastoral debate is particularly evident here because the two voices apparently represent a conflict within Spenser himself. The inner Piers has an almost Platonic vision of poetry and sees potential inspiration in the active life of the court; but the inner Cuddie, fearing the frustrations of the poet's role, resigns himself to the less conspicuous, less stimulating rural life.

In a sequel to the eclogues, *Colin Clouts Come Home Againe*, Colin describes to his friends a trip to London, apparently a reflection of Spenser's trip to make arrangements for the publication of *The Faerie Queene*. The question-and-answer format allows Colin to touch on varied topics: the level of poetic artistry in London, conventional satire of life at court, topographical poetry about the "marriage" of two Irish rivers, and Platonic deification of love. Although this more mature Colin is less critical of court life than the earlier one had been, Ireland rather than England is still "home" to him.

THE FAERIE QUEENE

Any study of *The Faerie Queene* must take into account the explanatory letter to Ralegh printed in all early editions under the heading: "A Letter of the Author's, Expounding his Whole Intention in the course of this Work. . . ." The fact that the letter was printed at the end rather than the beginning of the first edition (Books I-III only) suggests that Spenser was writing with a retrospective glance at what was already in the printer's press, even though he was also looking toward the overall structure of what had not yet been assembled. Ralegh had apparently requested such an explanation, and Spenser here clarified elements which he considered essential to understanding his "continued Allegory of dark conceit." These elements can be summarized as purpose, genre, narrative structure, and allegorical significance.

In carrying out his purpose "to fashion a gentleman or noble person in vertuous and gentle discipline," Spenser imitated other Renaissance conduct books which set out to form representatives of different levels of polite society, such as those peopled by princes, schoolmasters, governors, and courtiers. By coloring his teaching with "historical fiction," Spenser obeyed Horace's precept to make poetry both useful and pleasing; he also followed the example of classic and Renaissance writers of epic by selecting for the center of that fiction a hero whose historicity was overlaid by legend: Arthur. Theoretically, an epic treats a major action of a single great man, while a romance recounts great deeds of many men. Kaleidoscopic visions of the deeds of many great knights and ladies within the separate books superimpose a coloring of romance, but the overall generic designation of *The Faerie Queene* as "epic" is possible because Arthur appears in the six books as a unifying hero. Through Arthur, the poet also paid tribute to his sovereign, whose family, according to the currently popular Tudor myth, claimed descent from Arthur's heirs.

Although the complexity of the poem stems partly from the blending of epic and romance traditions, Spenser's political concern added an even greater complication to his narrative structure. He wanted to create a major role by which he could pay tribute to a female sovereign in a genre that demanded a male hero. From this desire came two interlocked plot lines with Gloriana, the Faerie Queene, as the motivating force of both: The young Arthur "before he was king" was seeking as his bride the beautiful Queen of Fairyland whom he had seen in a vision; meanwhile, this same queen had sent out on quests twelve different knights, one for each book of the epic. At strategic points within these separate books Arthur would interrupt his quest to aid the currently central figure. Since Spenser completed only six of the proposed twelve books, the climatic wedding of Arthur and Gloriana never took place and the dramatic dispersion and reassembling of Gloriana's knights occurred only in the poet's explanation, not in his poem.

Patterns of allegory, like patterns of narrative, intertwine throughout the poem. By describing his allegory as "continued," Spenser did not imply that particular meanings were continuously retained but rather that central allegories recurred. In the letter to Ralegh, for example, Spenser explains that in his "general intention" Gloriana means glory, but in a more "particular" way she is "the glorious person" of Elizabeth. Spenser is not satisfied to "shadow" Elizabeth only as Gloriana. In the letter and in the introduction to Book III, he invites Elizabeth to see herself as both Gloriana and Belphoebe, "In th'one her rule, in th'other her rare chastity." Less pointedly, she is also "shadowed" in Una, the image of true religion (Book I); in Britomart, the beautiful Amazonian warrior (Books III-V); and in Mercilla, the just queen (Book V). The glories of Elizabeth thus appear as a pervasive aspect of the "continued allegory," even though they are represented by different characters. Allegorical continuity also comes from Spenser's plan to have his twelve knights as "patrons" of the "twelve private moral virtues" devised by Aristotle, with Arthur standing forth as the virtue of magnificence, "the perfection of all the rest." The titles of the six completed books indicate the central virtues of their heroes: holiness, temperance, chastity, friendship, justice, and courtesy.

Historical and topical allusions appear frequently. Only when such allusions link references to Arthur and Gloriana, however, do they form a continuous thread of allegory. In the Proem to Book II, "The Legend of Sir Guyon, or of Temperance," Spenser encourages Elizabeth to see her face in the "fair mirror" of Gloriana, her kingdom in the "land of faery," and her "great ancestry" in his poem. In Canto X he inserts a patch of "historical fiction" in which Arthur and Guyon examine the chronicles of Briton kings and elfin emperors, the first ending with the father of Arthur, Uther Pendagron, and the second with Tanaquil, called "Glorian . . . that glorious flower." Spenser prefaces his lengthy account of British history (stanzas 5-69) with a tribute to his own "sovereign queen" whose "realm and race" had been derived from Prince Arthur; he thus identifies the realm of the "renowned prince" of this story as the England of history. The second chronicle describes an idealized land where succession to the crown is peaceful, where the elfin inhabitants can trace their race back to Prometheus, creator of Elf (Adam) and Fay (Eve), and where Elizabeth-Gloriana can find her father and grandfather figured in Oberon and Elficleos. The "continued" historical allegory looks to the wedding of Arthur and Gloriana as blending real and ideal aspects within England itself.

Topical political allegory is most sustained in Book V, "The Legend of Artegall, or of Justice." In this book

Elizabeth appears as Queen Mercilla and as Britomart; Mary Stuart as Duessa (sentenced by Mercilla) and as Radigund (defeated in battle by Britomart); Arthur Lord Grey as the titular hero, Artegall; and the Earl of Leicester as Prince Arthur himself in one segment of the narrative. Several European rulers whom Elizabeth had either opposed or aided also appear in varied forms. Contemporary political problems are reflected in the story of Artegall's rescue of Irena (Ireland) from the giant Grantorto (literally translated as "Great Wrong"), usually allegorically identified as the Pope. Spenser's personal defense of Lord Grey shows through the naïve allegory of Canto XII, where Artegall, on the way back to Faery Court, is attacked by two hags, Envy and Detraction, and by the Blatant Beast (Calumny). Spenser thus suggests the cause of the misunderstandings that led to Elizabeth's recalling Grey from Ireland. Elizabeth's controversy with Mary Stuart, doubly reflected in Book V, also provides a significant level of meaning in Book I, "The Legende of the Knight of the Red Crosse, or of Holinesse."

A closer look at the tightly structured development of Book I shows more clearly Spenser's approach to heroic and allegorical poetry in the epic as a whole. On the literal level of romantic epic, Gloriana assigns to an untrained knight the quest he seeks: the rescue of the parents of a beautiful woman from a dreaded dragon. The plot traces the separation of Red Cross and Una, Red Cross's travels with the deceptive Duessa (duplicity), Una's search for Red Cross, the reunion of Una and her knight, the fulfillment of the quest, and the betrothal of hero and heroine. Vivid epic battles pit Red Cross against the serpentine Error and her swarming brood of lesser monsters, against a trio of evil brothers (Sansfoy, Sansjoy, and Sansloy), against the giant Orgoglio (from whose dungeon he must be rescued by Prince Arthur), and eventually against one of the fiercest, best-described dragons in literature. In Canto X, Red Cross learns his identity as St. George, changeling descendant of human Saxon kings rather than rustic elfin warrior. Red Cross's dragon-fight clearly reflects pictorial representations of St. George as dragon-slayer.

All three levels of allegory recognized by medieval exegetes are fully developed in Book I: typical, anagogical, and moral. Typically, Una is the true Church of England, and Elizabeth is the protector of this Church; Duessa is the Church of Rome and Mary Stuart, its supporter. Red Cross is both abstract holiness defending truth and a figure of Christ himself. Arthur, too, is a figure of Christ or of grace in his rescue of Red Cross—here a kind of Everyman—from Orgoglio, the forces of Antichrist.

Anagogical or apocalyptic elements appear primarily in sections treating Duessa and the dragon and in Red Cross's vision of heaven. Duessa, at her first appearance, reflects the description of the scarlet woman in the Revelation of St. John, and the mount given her later by Orgoglio is modeled on the apocalyptic seven-headed beast. The mouth of the great dragon of Canto XI belches forth flames like those often pictured erupting from the jaws of hell in medieval mystery plays. Red Cross is saved from the dragon by his contacts with the Well of Life and the Tree of Life, both borrowed from Revelation. Before Red Cross confronts the dragon, he has an apocalyptic vision of the New Jerusalem, a city rivaling in beauty even the capital of Fairyland, Cleopolis.

The moral level provides the most "continued" allegory in Book I. Red Cross-Everyman must develop within himself the virtue of holiness if he is eventually to conquer sin and attain the heavenly vision. When holiness is accompanied by truth, Error can be readily conquered. However, when holiness is deceived by hypocrisy (Archimago), it is easily separated from truth and is further deceived by duplicity (Duessa) masquerading as fidelity (Fidessa). Tempted to spiritual sloth, Red Cross removes his armor of faith and falls to pride (Orgoglio). He must then be rescued from the chains of this sin by grace (Prince Arthur), must be rescued from Despair by truth, and must be spiritually strengthened in the House of Holiness, conducted by Dame Caelia (heaven) and her daughters Fidelia, Speranza, and Charissa (faith, hope, and charity). Only then can he repent of his own sins and become holy enough to conquer sin embodied in the dragon.

If Book I best exemplifies self-contained, carefully structured allegorical narrative, Books III and IV exemplify the interweaving common in medieval and early Renaissance narrative poetry. Characters pursue one another throughout the two books; several stories are not completed until Book V. In fact, Braggadochio, the cowardly braggart associated with false Florimell in this section, steals Guyon's horse in Book II and is judged for the crime in Book V. Belphoebe, too, introduced in a comic interlude with Braggadochio in Book II, becomes a central figure in the Book of Chastity. Belphoebe blends the beauty of Venus (Bel) with the chastity of Diana (Phoebe); her twin sister, Amoret, is a more earthly representation of Venus, destined to generate beauty and human love. Britomart, the nominal heroine of Book III, embodies the chastity of Belphoebe in her youth but the generative love of Amoret in maturity. Despite complex and not always consistent allegorical equations applicable to these central characters, Spenser moves them through their adventures with a delicate interlacing of narrative and allegorical threads typical of the romantic epic at its most entertaining level.

Amoretti and Epithalamion

The sonnet sequence *Amoretti* ("little love poems") and the *Epithalamion* (songs "on the marriage bed") together provide a poetic account of courtship and marriage, an account which tradition links to actualities in Spenser's relationship with Elizabeth Boyle, whom he married in 1594. References to seasons suggest that the "plot" of the sonnet sequence extends from New Year's Day in one year (Sonnet 4) through a second New Year's Day (Sonnet 62) to the beginning of a third winter in the closing sonnet (Sonnet 89), a time frame of about two years. Several sonnets contain references which tempt readers to autobiographical interpretations. In Sonnet 60, "one year is spent" since the planet of "the winged god" began to move in the poet; even more significantly, the poet refers to the "sphere of Cupid" as containing the forty years "wasted" before this year. By simple arithmetical calculations, biographers of Spenser have deduced from his assumed age in 1593 his birth in 1552. Two sonnets refer directly to his work on *The Faerie Queene:* Sonnet 33 blames on his "troublous" love his inability to complete the "Queen of Faery" for his "sacred empress" and Sonnet 80 rejoices that having run through six books on Fairyland he can now write praises "low and mean,/ Fit for the handmaid of the Faery Queen."

Collectively and individually the *Amoretti* follow a popular Renaissance tradition established by Petrarch and imitated by numerous English sonneteers. In metrical structure, Spenser's sonnets blended Italian and English forms. The five-rhyme restriction in the Italian octave-plus-sestet pattern (*abbaabba cdecde*) was adapted to fit the English pattern of three quatrains plus couplet; instead of the seven rhymes used in most English sonnets, the interlocked rhymes of the Spenserian quatrains created a more intricate, as well as more restricted, form (*abab bcbc cdcd ee*).

Although Spenser's metrical pattern was innovative, most of his conceits and images were conventional; for example, love is related to a judicial court (Sonnet 10) and to religious worship (Sonnets 22 and 68); the beloved is a cruel causer and observer of his pain (Sonnets 20, 31, 41, 42, and 54) and the Neoplatonic ideal of beauty (Sonnets 3, 9, 45, 61, 79, and 88); love is warfare (Sonnets 11, 12, 14, and 57), a storm (Sonnet 46), sickness (Sonnet 50), and a sea journey (Sonnet 63). The poet at times promises the immortality of fame through his praise (Sonnets 27, 29, 69, 75, and 82); at other times he simply rejoices in the skill which enables him as poet to offer his gift of words (Sonnets 1 and 84). Even the kind of praise offered to his beloved is traditional. In Sonnet 40, "An hundred Graces" sit "on each eyelid" and the lover's "storm-beaten heart" is cheered "when cloudy looks are cleared." Elsewhere, eyes are weapons (Sonnets 7, 16, and 49) and a means of entanglement (Sonnet 37). The beloved is a "gentle deer" (Sonnet 67) and a "gentle bee" caught in a sweet prison woven by the spider-poet (Sonnet 71); but she is also a cruel panther (Sonnet 53) and a tiger (Sonnet 56). Physical beauties are compared to precious metals and gems (Sonnet 15), to sources of light (Sonnet 9), and to the sweet odors of flowers (Sonnet 64). Classical myths color several sonnets, identifying the beloved with Penelope, Pandora, Daphne, and the Golden Apples of Hercules (Sonnets 23, 24, 28, and 77) and the poet-lover with Narcissus, Arion, and Orpheus (Sonnets 35, 38, and 44).

In typical Petrarchan fashion, the lyrical moments in the *Amoretti* fluctuate between joy and pain, between exultation over love returned and anxiety over possible rejection. The sequence ends on a note of anxiety not in keeping with a set of poems conceived as a prelude for the glowing joy of the *Epithalamion*. Despite clear references to the 1592-1594 period of Spenser's life, it seems unlikely that all eighty-nine sonnets were written during this period or that all were originally intended for a sequence in praise of Elizabeth Boyle. The *Epithalamion*, however, is clearly Spenser's celebration of his own wedding at Kilcolman on St. Barnabas' Day (June 11), 1594.

In its basic form and development, this marriage song is as conventional as the sonnets with which it was first published; but it is also original and personal in its variations on tradition. Classical allusions, for example, are countered by the homely invocation to nymphs of the Irish river and lake near Spenser's home (lines 56-66), by the imprecation against the "unpleasant choir of frogs still croaking" in the same lake (line 349), and by some of the attendants: "merchants' daughters," "fresh boys," and childlike angels "peeping in" the face of the bride. Although allusions to classical gods and goddesses heighten the lyric mood, other elements retain a more personal touch.

Structurally, Spenser adapted the *canzone* form. As used by Dante and Petrarch, the *canzone* consisted of a series of long stanzas followed by a short stanza (a *tornata*) responding to the preceding stanzas. Within the stanzas one or more three-foot lines varied the basic five-foot line; the *tornata*, too, had one short line. A. Kent Hieatt has demonstrated in *Short Time's Endless Monument* (1960) the ingenuity with which Spenser varied the basic *canzone* structure to reflect units of time in general and to relate poetic divisions with night/day divisions on the longest day of the year in southern Ireland. Hieatt points out that variations in verse form correspond to days in the year (365 long lines), hours in the day (24 stanzas), spring and fall equinoxes (parallel diction, imagery, and thought in stanzas 1-12 and 13-24), degrees of the sun's daily movement (359 long lines before the *tornata*, corresponding to 359 degrees of the sun's movement as contrasted with 360 degrees of the stars' movement), and the division between waking and sleeping hours (indicated by a change in the refrain at the end of stanza 17). It is variations within stanza 17 that most personalize the time element to make the "bedding" of the bride occur at the point in the poem representing nightfall on the poet's wedding day, the day of the summer solstice in southern Ireland. At the end of the stanza, the refrain, which had for sixteen stanzas been describing the answering echo of the woods, changes to "The woods no more shall answer, nor your echo ring": All is quiet so that the poet-bridegroom can welcome night and the love of his bride.

Complaints

The collection of moralizing, melancholy verse titled *Complaints* reflects an as yet not fully developed artistry in the author. Although published in the aftermath of fame brought by *The Faerie Queene*, most of the nine poems were probably first drafted much earlier. The most significant poem in this volume was probably the satirical beast fable, "Prosopopoia: Or, Mother Hubberd's Tale." Following the tradition of Giovanni Boccaccio and Geoffrey Chaucer, the poet creates a framework of tale-tellers, one of whom is "a good old woman" named Mother Hubberd. In Mother Hubberd's story, a Fox and an Ape gain personal prosperity through the gullibility of farmers, the ignorance and worldliness of clergymen, and the licentiousness of courtiers. About two-thirds of the way through, the satire turns more specifically to the concern of England in 1579 with a possible marriage between the twenty-four-year-old Duc d'Alencon and Queen Elizabeth, then forty-six. The marriage was being engineered by Lord Burleigh (the Fox of the narrative) and by Jean de Simier, whom Elizabeth playfully called her "Ape." This poem, even more than *The Shepheardes Calender*, demonstrates Spenser's artistic simplicity and the Chaucer-like irony of his worldview. Burleigh's later hostility to Spenser gives evidence of the pointedness of the poet's satiric barbs. "Virgil's Gnat" also exemplifies a satiric beast fable, this time with Leicester's marriage as the target, hit so effectively that Spenser himself was wounded by Leicester's lessened patronage. In "Muiopotmos: Or, The Fate of the Butterfly," beast fable is elevated by philosophical overtones, epic machinery, and classical allusions. Some type of personal or political allegory obviously underlies the poem, but critical interpretations vary widely in attempting to identify the chief figures, the Spider and the Butterfly. Despite such uncertainty, however, one message is clear: Life and beauty are mutable.

Mutability permeates *Complaints*; it is even more central to the posthumous fragment known as the "Mutabilitie Cantos." The publisher Matthew Lownes printed these two cantos as "The Legend of Constancy," a fragmentary Book VII of *The Faerie Queene*. Lownes's identification of these two cantos with the unfinished epic was apparently based on similar poetic form, an allusion to the poet's softening his stern style in singing of hills and woods "mongst warres and knights," and a reference to the records of Fairyland as registering mutability's genealogy. There are, however, no knights, human or elf, in these cantos. Instead, Jove and Nature represent allegorically the cosmic principle of Constancy, the permanence that underlies all change. Despite the philosophical victory of Nature, one of the most effective extended passages in the cantos represents change through a processional pageant of the seasons, the months, day and night, the hours, and life and death.

The principle of underlying permanence applies to Spenser's works as well as to the world of which he wrote. In his shepherds and shepherdesses, his knights and ladies, his own personae, and even in the animal figures of his fables, images of Everyman and Everywoman still live. Time has thickened some of the allegorical veils that conceal as well as reveal, language then new has become archaic, and poetic conventions have become freer since Spenser's poetry first charmed his contemporaries. Despite such changes, however, the evocative and creative power that made Spenser "the Prince of Poets in his time" remains constant.

Other major works

NONFICTION: *Three Proper, and Wittie, Familiar Letters*, 1580; *Foure Letters and Certaine Sonnets*, 1586; *A View of the Present State of Ireland*, 1633 (wr. 1596).

MISCELLANEOUS: *The Works of Edmund Spenser: A Variorum Edition*, 1932-1949 (Edwin Greenlaw et al., editors).

Bibliography

Berry, Phillipa. *Of Chastity and Power: Elizabethan Literature and the Unmarried Queen*. London: Routledge & Kegan Paul, 1989. This example of feminist critical theory supplies a fascinating analysis of Elizabeth I and her relationship with the male writers who sought to make her fame immortal. Berry analyzes the works of Edmund Spenser in relation to those of John Lyly, Sir Walter Ralegh, George Chapman, and William Shakespeare.

Bieman, Elizabeth. *Plato Baptized: Towards the Interpretation of Spenser's Mimetic Fictions*. Toronto: University of Toronto Press, 1988. Offers a clear and insightful reading of Spenser in relation to the Christian and Platonic sources that inform his thought. Bieman offers subtle and rich readings of the *Fowre Hymnes* and the "Mutabilitie Cantos."

Hamilton, A. C., et al., eds. *The Spenser Encyclopedia*. Toronto: University of Toronto Press, 1990. This 858-page volume represents the cooperative efforts of Spenserian scholars to compile a series of articles on every aspect of Spenser's life and work. The superbly indexed volume also offers many useful articles on the history of England and on literary theory and practice.

Heale, Elizabeth. *The Faerie Queene: A Reader's Guide*. Cambridge, England: Cambridge University Press, 1987. Offers an up-to-date guide to Spenser's *The Faerie Queene*, the first great epic poem in English. Emphasizes the religious and political context for each episode. One chapter is devoted to each book of *The Faerie Queene*. An index is supplied for characters and episodes.

Heninger, S. K., Jr. *Sidney and Spenser: The Poet as Maker.* University Park: Pennsylvania State University Press, 1989. In this study of mimesis, or imitation, S. K. Heninger considers the transmutation of allegory to fiction. Examines the aesthetic elements in art, music, and literature, analyzes the forms of Spenser's major works and considers the relationship between form and content. This lengthy, 646-page study of Renaissance aesthetics offers an essential background for understanding Spenser's art.

Morrison, Jennifer Klein and Matthew Greenfield Aldershot, eds. *Edmund Spenser: Essays on Culture and Allegory.* Burlington, Vt.: Ashgate, 2000. A collection of critical essays dealing with the works of Spenser. Includes bibliographical references and an index.

Oram, William A. *Edmund Spenser.* New York: Twayne, 1997. An introductory biography and critical study of selected works by Spencer. Includes bibliographic references and an index.

Patterson, Annabel. *Pastoral and Ideology: Virgil to Valery*. Berkeley: University of California Press, 1987. Offers a learned and graceful introduction to the three great types of poems given authority in classical tradition: the pastoral, the georgic, and the epic. Patterson supplies a careful reading of Spenser's *The Shepheardes Calender* that illustrates its political commentary on the church and state.

Wells, Robin Headlam. *Spenser's "Faerie Queene" and the Cult of Elizabeth*. Totawa, N.J.: Barnes & Noble Books, 1983. This study of Spenser concentrates on the ways in which the moral and political allegory in the poem are parts of a continuous pattern of meaning. Wells contends that the idea of praise is fundamental to the poem and that for the first time it gives voice to the national myth.

Marie Michelle Walsh;
bibliography updated by the editors

William Stafford

Born: Hutchinson, Kansas; January 17, 1914
Died: Lake Oswego, Oregon; August 28, 1993

Principal poetry

West of Your City, 1960
Traveling Through the Dark, 1962
The Rescued Year, 1966
Eleven Untitled Poems, 1968
Weather: Poems, 1969
Allegiances, 1970
Temporary Facts, 1970
Poems for Tennessee, 1971 (with Robert Bly and William Matthews)
Someday, Maybe, 1973
That Other Alone, 1973
In the Clock of Reason, 1973
Going Places: Poems, 1974
North by West, 1975 (with John Haines)
Braided Apart, 1976 (with Kim Robert Stafford)
Stories That Could Be True: New and Collected Poems, 1977
The Design in the Oriole, 1977
Two About Music, 1978
All About Light, 1978
Things That Happen Where There Aren't Any People, 1980
Sometimes Like a Legend, 1981
A Glass Face in the Rain: New Poems, 1982
Smoke's Way: Poems from Limited Editions, 1968-1981, 1983
Roving Across Fields: A Conversation and Uncollected Poems, 1942-1982, 1983
Segues: A Correspondence in Poetry, 1983 (with Marvin Bell)
Stories and Storms and Strangers, 1984
Listening Deep, 1984
Wyoming, 1985
Brother Wind, 1986
An Oregon Message, 1987
Fin, Feather, Fur, 1989
A Scripture of Leaves, 1989
How to Hold Your Arms When It Rains: Poems, 1990
Passwords, 1991
My Name Is William Tell, 1992
The Darkness Around Us Is Deep, 1993 (selected by Robert Bly)

Other literary forms

In addition to poetry, William Stafford published an autobiographical account of his conscientious objector service during World War II, *Down in My Heart* (1947), and edited poetry volumes and authored chapters in collections of critical analysis. Stafford's *Writing the Australian Crawl: Views on the Writer's Vocation* (1978) and *You Must Revise Your Life* (1986) contain essays on writing and the teaching of writing, as well as interviews with Stafford that were originally published in literary magazines.

Achievements

William Stafford is considered one of the most prolific of contemporary American poets. Although he was forty-six years old when his first collection of poems was published in 1960, he more than made up for this late start in the next decade. Stafford's second volume, *Traveling Through the Dark*, won the National Book

Award for Poetry in 1963. In 1970, Stafford was named consultant in poetry to the Library of Congress. Throughout his career, he received numerous awards and honors, such as the Shelley Memorial Award, a Yaddo Foundation Fellowship, a National Endowment for the Arts grant, a Guggenheim Fellowship, a Danforth Foundation grant, the Melville Cane Award, and the American Academy and Institute of Arts Award in Literature.

Widely recognized as a spontaneous, natural poet, Stafford greatly influenced the world of literature with his views on the teaching of writing. Equating the act of writing with coming to know the self, Stafford says that writing consists of finding the way as the process unfolds. He can indulge his impulses—knowing that they will bring recurrent patterns and meaning—because in back of his images is the coherence of the self. In his distinguished career as a professor, Stafford put such views into practice in his teaching and made them available to a wider audience through lectures, interviews, and his many published essays on the process of writing.

William Stafford

Biography

On January 17, 1914, William Edgar Stafford was born to Earl Ingersoll and Ruby Mayher Stafford in Hutchinson, Kansas. With his younger brother and sister, Stafford grew up in a series of small Kansas towns—Wichita, Liberal, Garden City, El Dorado—as his father moved the family from place to place in search of work. Earl and Ruby Stafford were nonconformists who held strong moral and spiritual beliefs. They instilled in their children a deep sense of individuality, justice, and tolerance. From long hours with his father in the Midwestern countryside, Stafford developed his love of nature. He credits his mother, and the gossipy stories she loved to tell, with helping him perceive the intricacies of language. Although certainly not scholars, both parents loved books, and the whole family raided the local library each week, vying for their favorites.

As an adolescent during the Depression, Stafford was already helping to support his family: raising vegetables, working as an electrician's helper, and delivering newspapers (at one time their only source of income). After high school, Stafford attended junior college and then enrolled in the University of Kansas, waiting on tables to pay his way. During his undergraduate years, Stafford began his habit of writing daily and began to translate his social and political beliefs into action. He participated in a demonstration against segregation in the university cafeteria and, when World War II broke out, registered as a conscientious objector.

Stafford spent the war incarcerated in conscientious objector camps in Arkansas, California, and Illinois, working on soil-conservation projects and fighting forest fires. These were formative years for him, a time of introspection, for Stafford was acutely aware of his unorthodox position against a generally popular war. He rigorously examined the tensions between the outer life of daily appearances and the inner life of conviction, developing a deep patience and an abiding sense of integrity. In order to write before the day's labor began, Stafford arose before dawn; this habit continued into later life. While at a camp in California, Stafford met, and soon married, Dorothy Frantz, a minister's daughter. When the war ended, the couple returned to the University of Kansas, and Stafford began work on his M.A. degree. He submitted an account of his conscientious objector experiences as his thesis project, which was subsequently published as his first book, *Down in My Heart*.

After graduation, Stafford taught high school briefly, worked in a church relief agency, and kept writing stories and poems. From 1948 to 1950, he was an instructor in English at Lewis and Clark College in Portland, Oregon. He then moved, with his wife and small children, to the University of Iowa, where he studied under Robert Penn Warren, Randall Jarrell, Reed Whittemore, Karl Shapiro, and others.

Stafford considered these years to be his reference point for how others lived the literary life. His own writing habits and perspective on the world of letters, however, had already been clearly established. When Stafford left Iowa in 1952, he took with him firmly held, idiosyncratic attitudes about writing and how it should be taught. In 1954, when he received his Ph.D. from Iowa, Stafford was already teaching English at Manchester College in Indiana. Next, he taught briefly at San Jose State College and then returned to Lewis and Clark College, beginning a teaching career there that lasted for almost twenty-five years.

After his first book of poems, *West of Your City*, Stafford published many collections with his major publisher, Harper & Row; more than twenty-five other books or chapbooks of poetry with small presses; several collections of prose; short pieces of critical analysis; and interviews. He traveled widely, lecturing and reading his work in the United States and abroad. During the Vietnam War, university students in the United States discovered Stafford's pacifist beliefs, and he was in great demand on college campuses. Precisely because of these beliefs, however, Stafford never became the antiwar poet that the students were seeking. In 1980, Stafford retired from teaching to become professor emeritus at Lewis and Clark College, continuing to publish new collections of poems. He died on August 28, 1993, in Lake Oswego, Oregon.

ANALYSIS

William Stafford was a poet of the personal and the particular. With an optimistic outlook, he wrote personally but not confessionally, and his particulars are sometimes regional but not provincial. Stafford wrote most often in the first person, both singular and plural, and his poems are characteristically quite short. They investigate the processes of everyday life, looking through specific situations and happenings to uncover universal connections between humans and nature. Although Stafford celebrates nature in his work, this is not an end in itself; rather, it is a means to transcend surface manifestation and uncover the underlying unboundedness of life. In this sense, Stafford has been called a wisdom poet, one who uses nature in pursuit of a higher truth. His poems present situations, objects, and people that entice the reader to go beyond the towns and settlements of life—where what one knows can be readily seen—and search for what lies at their edges, in the wilderness, to listen to the silence one can come to understand, perhaps, as one's own self.

Although much of Stafford's work grows out of personal memories, a strictly biographical reading can be misleading. His work does not lend itself strictly to chronological investigation, either, for Stafford's key themes and metaphorical language in his first published collection are still characteristic of his later volumes. In addition, the order in which Stafford's poems have been published does not necessarily reflect the order in which they were written. He does not prepare his collections as thematic, structured volumes; rather, he views them as groupings of self-sufficient fragments. It is the incremental progression in individual works, not collections, that interests Stafford, and his focus is on the process of writing rather than on meaning or content. Though criticized for such an internal perspective, Stafford maintains a steadfast unwillingness to analyze his work intellectually. He believes that one should not defend or value what one has written but rather abandon it; others must decide about its significance.

Because Stafford's vision of life has remained essentially stable throughout his literary career, themes, images, and even words recur in his poems and take on specific significance, forming almost a shorthand language in themselves. Stafford's major theme is the spiritual search for the self, represented metaphorically as the search for "home." It is a quest for unity with the Absolute, which he associates with the adjectives "deep," "dark," and "silent." Subthemes are his focus on family and small-town living, much of which can be traced to his Kansas boyhood; the sacredness of nature and of wilderness, often in contrast to war, technology, and human alienation; and the exploration of truth as it unfolds through the common activities of daily life.

Stafford has been criticized for his overt simplicity and for his prose style. On the surface, many of his poems do seem to reflect an idyllic Midwest childhood, a longing for the uncomplicated (and perhaps a bit romanticized) past when people lived in greater harmony with nature. Stafford certainly does write in a conversational style. Yet it is this surface accessibility that invites the reader to enter the poems. Once the reader is in, Stafford hints at deeper levels of reality and may ask his readers to do or be or imagine seemingly impossible things. Many poems have a parablelike quality and present rather didactic messages, often in the last line. After the surface message is delivered, however, the silence resounds. Stafford is a poet who roams far into his own wilderness. He dreams, and he tests his dreams through the process of telling their stories. Because Stafford's clear vision is firmly rooted, he has the flexibility to follow where imagination and the sounds of language take him.

Down in My Heart

Published in 1947, Stafford's first book, *Down in My Heart*, is a spiritual autobiography of his four years in conscientious objector work camps during World War II. Within the context of narratives about firefighting, an altercation with a mob in a small town, and a pacifist wedding, he reveals the concerns of a man alienated from the majority of his countrymen by his social and political beliefs. This volume sows seeds that sprout as major themes in his later poetry. Stafford presents his metaphorical "home" as ultimately free from any particular location in his narrative about building yet another work camp. He also touches on other ideas that will unfold as significant poetic themes, such as the power of storytelling, the nature of the hero, sound and silence, and interactions between the individual and society.

West of Your City

Stafford's first volume of poetry, *West of Your City*, presents a poet of already mature voice, with a strong sense of his material. Running through these poems, arranged in three sections called "Midwest," "Farwest," and "Outside," is the theme of "home." For Stafford, "home" certainly means the security of the Kansas towns of his boyhood, and the persona of many poems in this collection and the poet himself are very similar. Stafford begins "One Home" with the line "Mine was a Midwest home—you keep your world" and moves through references to his personal history. His vision of home also extends, however, beyond the secure Kansas settlements into the adventure of wilderness at their edges. He concludes, "Kicking cottonwood leaves we ran toward storms./ Wherever we looked the land would hold us up." Running toward adventure, the speaker finds home wherever he looks. Venturing into the wilderness, into what is unknown, the individual has the chance to get a glimpse of what is closest to him, what he can ultimately know best because it is what he is—the self.

The well-known poem "Bi-focal" presents the sense of double vision that pervades virtually all Stafford's work as it unfolds his theme of underlying legends. The poem begins, "Sometimes up out of this land/ a legend begins to move." It locates "the surface, a map of roads/ leading wherever go miles" and "the legend under,/ fixed, inexorable,/ deep as the darkest mine." The poem concludes, "So, the world happens twice—/ Once what we see it as;/ second it legends itself/ deep, the way it is." This poem contrasts what is seen—what seems to be real on the surface of life—with the unseen, what is "deep." "Deep" is clearly defined as the way the world is. The speaker in the poem, like the poet, is able to see both levels, but it is the deeper way of seing that Stafford emphasizes in his work. He does so not by denigrating the surface details, but rather by penetrating them and revealing their more profound essence and the silence of legends at their source. The poems in *West of Your City*, written mostly in the first person, draw heavily from Stafford's memories. Yet the personal details expand to include his reader's life. Even the title of the volume demands the reader's attention: not west of "my"—the poet's—city, but west of the reader's.

Traveling Through the Dark

Stafford's second collection, *Traveling Through the Dark*, established his reputation and won the National Book Award in 1963. Themes from the first collection reoccur, the subject matter is again straightforward, and the tone is gently conversational. Stafford's voice here is less tentative, more sure, but still it asks questions, encouraging the reader to travel past the everyday world of light into the dark wilderness where the real journey takes place. His image of darkness is firmly established here, and it is not a negative one. He associates darkness with depth, silence, and intuition, the edges toward which life always progresses, the edges beyond which greater understanding of the self may be found.

In this volume, Stafford transcends the boundaries of time and space, of past and future, and explores what he finds in the gaps. He moves beyond what he can see, to listen for what language has to tell him. The poem that gives the volume its title is one of Stafford's most famous works and has been frequently anthologized. It is characteristic of Stafford in that its form and narrative are simple, yet underneath lies more complexity. While driving a mountain road at night, the speaker in the poem comes upon a dead deer. He stops and gets out, confident that he should roll the animal over the edge of the cliff in order to clear the narrow road for cars that will follow his. As he comes closer and touches the deer, however, he finds that there is an unborn fawn waiting, still alive. The man begins to have doubts about what is the right action. Should he do what might seem to be best on the surface—push the doe over the cliff and avoid further accidents on the road? Or is it possible to save the fawn? If so, would it be the right thing to do? Described with characteristic understatement, the moment of decision is swift: He decides to push her off.

"Traveling Through the Dark" has been read as a poem of conflict between nature and society, symbolized by the car. The speaker clearly sympathizes with the fawn, which "lay there waiting,/ alive, still, never to be born." Yet he accepts the forces of technology that caused the problem and realizes that the safety of the next passersby—in cars again—depends on his clearing the road. It has been noted that the personified car, which "aimed ahead its lowered parking lights" and under whose hood "purred the steady engine," is actually the most alive thing in this poem. This may be the ironic voice of a pragmatist who sees nature as something for human beings to use as they please. A more expanded reading, however, would bridge the nature-society dichotomy somewhat by allowing nature to include the car and, by extension, society as well. From such a perspective, the car is both a symbol of death (a significant theme of subject-object unity in Stafford's poetry) and a symbol of life, a part of "our group" in the road. The poem uses the word "swerve" twice. Once the meaning is literal, the anticipated physical movement of further cars coming upon the carcass in the road. The second time, though, it is the speaker who swerves, and his swerving is internal. Having "thought hard for us all—my only swerving," he makes a decision. Yet what is he swerving toward, or away from?

It may appear that the speaker's dependence on progress is greater than his ability to control it. Even so, for the moment that he considers saving the fawn, he swerves away from society toward nature. Yet perhaps the swerve is in the opposite direction. Perhaps he is swerving from a more simplistic view of nature toward an understanding that encompasses the interests of society within its purview. From his upbringing and especially as a result of his years doing conscientious objector service during World War II, Stafford characteristically considers all sides of his questions. Perhaps the speaker in this poem comes to recognize his own part in the process of the narrative. Is he only the man who finds the dead deer, or does he also bear part of the responsibility for the killing? Underlying the obvious choice to be made—what to do with the deer—may be a suggestion that longing to return to the old ways and escape from society is not really much different from embracing progress without a firm connection with the simplicity and order of nature at its base. There is also the suggestion that Stafford himself may still be making his decisions. When asked about this poem, Stafford responded, "Choices are always Hobson's choices. All you have to do is get a little more alert to see that even your best moves are compromises—and complicated."

Yet, the poem ends on an optimistic note. There is still time to prevent further disaster, the speaker decides, and he pushes the doe "over the edge into the river." It is interesting that the poem ends on the image of the river, which, in Stafford's linguistic shorthand, is consistently used as a metaphor for the changing nature of life.

Stafford's voice has been criticized as being simply his real-life "I" speaking normally but in a privileged position, and "Travelling Through the Dark" has been cited as a representative example of the poet firmly in control of all meaning. In refuting this attack, Dick Barnes agrees that Stafford does speak normally, but suggests that artists such as Stafford speak out of a solitude that others can barely imagine, "where the self is dead and the soul opens inward upon eternity. What makes [the artist's] act complete is that, speaking that way, he listens at the same time, and in listening joins any others who may be hearing in a kind of causal communion." Barnes uses "self" here in a relative sense: With death of the self, the individuality that keeps one localized to time and space is no longer restricting the soul.

Stafford, in his wilderness quest, may be in search of something even greater than mere removal of restriction. His death metaphor represents a creative force, a unity of subjectivity and objectivity. A reading of Stafford's work from the perspective of growth of consciousness might suggest that the death of the "self" is first found in the transcendental experience of unbounded awareness that is beyond the limitations of the relative states of consciousness—waking, dreaming, and sleeping. Repeated direct experience of this state of pure consciousness is the basis for the individual's growth toward higher states of consciousness. The "self" rises to the value of the "Self," providing the stable foundation for the eventual unity of subject and object that Stafford is seeking in his poetry.

The Rescued Year

The Rescued Year was Stafford's second collection with Harper & Row, which—over the years—became his major publisher. It shows a stability of vision, and Stafford has said that he considers this to be his most unified volume. Fourteen of the poems had already appeared in *West of Your City*, and some had been included in Stafford's Ph.D. dissertation, "Winterward." Others were written at the same time as poems in his earlier volumes. The poems reprinted from *West of Your City* reemphasize Stafford's major interests: home, the quest journey, sound and silence, duality of vision, memory and reality, the power of the story. One of these reprinted works, "Listening," defines the nature of the father image in Stafford's poems, which has been associated with the more intuitive, deep, unseen values of the wilderness. "My father could hear a little animal step,/ or a moth in the dark against the screen,/ and every far sound called the listening out/ into places where the rest of us had never been." Listening goes beyond seeing. The father understands more from what he hears in the darkness than the rest of the family could learn from what "came to our porch for us on the wind." The son could watch his father's face change when the understanding came, when "the walls of the world flared, widened." With even this secondary experience of silence, the son was changed. "My father heard so much that we still stand/ inviting the quiet by turning the face." From the father, the son learns to want to hear the sounds of the underlying processes of nature. The son learns patience. In "Listening," the speaker sees little, for little comes to him on the porch, within the familiar. Seeing his father listen, however, he and the other children are inspired to wait "for a time when something in the night/ will touch us too from that other place." They are waiting to be able to hear the silence themselves. This sequence of seeing, touching, listening is reminiscent of "Traveling Through the Dark," as the speaker first sees the doe, then touches her warm side, and then hears the wilderness listening. Learning from his father, as a representative of deeper levels of reality, is a theme in many of Stafford's poems.

Over a third of the poems in *The Rescued Year* deal with Stafford's boyhood and a Kansas setting. "Across Kansas" tells of traveling through the night as his family sleeps. Driving past the town where he was born, the speaker says, "I drove down an aisle of sound," locating his sense of memory and reality within the sense of hearing. Once he has this experience of sound, even what he sees has more meaning. The speaker "owns" his face more, and he sees his self in everything that the light struck. Again, as in many poems, the last line is telling. "My state still dark, my dream too long to tell." The traveling is through a darkness much deeper than the Kansas night.

Stafford's imagination creates the story of his reality in much of this volume. Yet the collection also focuses on more contemporary issues, as in the long poem "Following the Markings of Dag Hammerskjöld: A Gathering of Poems in the Spirit of His Life and Writings." Some critics have objected to this new subject matter. Considering the confusing time in which this collection was published, however, even Stafford's warnings in such poems as "At the Bomb Test Site" seem gentle.

Allegiances

With publication of *Allegiances*, critics and scholars started to ask for more discrimination, for Stafford to publish only his best work. Then as now, however, Stafford preferred to let the reader decide what was good. In this volume, his allegiances are generally to people, places, and objects from the rural plains. Stafford suggests that truth is inherent in the common things, if one goes deep enough. His real hero is the common man. In the poem that gives the volume its title, he says, "It is time for all the heroes to go home/ if they have any, time for all of us common ones/ to locate ourselves by the real things/ we live by." He describes the journey to taste "far streams" where one can touch gold and "come back, changed/ but safe, quiet, grateful." Some have criticized this volume for a sort of blurred perspective that reflects less connection between Stafford's inner and outer lives. Some poems in *Allegiances* do deal with the social and political climate at the time—the assassination of Martin Luther King, Jr., bombings, television news, and the like—but the volume is hardly overtly revolutionary. What it does seem to suggest is that, at a precarious time in the world, Stafford had come to expect moral guidance from himself and other serious writers.

Someday, Maybe

The first poem in *Someday, Maybe*, "An Introduction to Some Poems," suggests that this volume will take a changed direction. It begins, "Look: no one ever promised for sure/ that we would sing. We have decided/ to moan." The speaker—clearly Stafford—expresses disillusionment. He is trying to turn his dreams into stories to give them strength. He suggests that the reader should do that too, "and hold them close at you, close at the/ edge we share, to be right." Many of the stories are based on Indian legends, or legends that Stafford fashions. These, perhaps, may offer some direction from a time when people were more in touch with nature than they were in the early 1970's. Though Stafford does not use poetry directly as a political vehicle, his concerns are underlying, and he searches into language for a way of dispelling his doubts about the world. In "After That Sound, After That Sight," the speaker says that "after that sound, we weren't people anymore," and "we are afraid to listen." This is not the optimistic Stafford one has come to expect. Yet poetry—language—is reliable. In "Report from a Far Place," Stafford says words are "snowshoes" with which he can still step across the world. They "creak, sag, bend, but/ hold," and "in war or city or camp/ they could save your life." He thus invites others to follow their tracks.

Stories That Could Be True

Stories That Could Be True: New and Collected Poems lets critics and scholars see Stafford's work to that date as a whole. The new poems, such as "Song Now," tell the story of the speaker who returns from a far place, from both "Before" and "After," to find a home in the present, where "silence puts a paw/ wherever the music rests." The poem concludes, "Guitar string is:/ it can save this place." Despite growing disillusionment over the changes that are occurring in American society, Stafford continues to seek a reintegration in this volume. With a growing acceptance of death—a significant theme—comes an awareness of the primacy of the present and the desire to live it. The stories are put before the readers not so that they can come to know them in themselves, but so that they can, perhaps, come to know their own stories better. The meaning of the story, for Stafford, is in its telling.

A Glass Face in the Rain

In *A Glass Face in the Rain: New Poems*, Stafford brings the process of storytelling, the process of writing, to the forefront. In his dedication poem, he says that the volume is intended for everyone, but especially for those on a "parallel way." These are the people readers do not see often, he says, or even think of often, "but it is precious to us that they are sharing/ the world." This volume was published after *Things That Happen Where There Aren't Any People*, a collection of more impersonal poems that focus on nature without human presence. Here, once again, however, Stafford's poems are grounded in the world of humanity. In "Glimpses," the speaker is definitely in the present and his presence there matters. "My debt to the world begins again," he says, "that I am part of this permanent dream." Stafford's part of the dream of life is to write poems. This collection continues to develop his acceptance of his own death, considering a future world that he will not be alive to see. Stafford has expanded his desire to be part of the process, and now he wants to communicate. In "Tuned In Late One Night," the speaker begins, "Listen—this is a faint station/ left alive in the vast universe./ I was left here to tell you a message." In "A Message from Space," he is trying to hear a message from the heavens, but when the message comes, it is surprising. "Everything counts," it says. "The message is the world."

An Oregon Message

In 1987, Stafford published a seventh volume with Harper & Row, *An Oregon Message*. By this time the message had become explicit, and Stafford wanted the reader on his side. He precedes the poems with a brief prose explanation of how he writes, "Some Notes on Writing"; it is the first time such a preface has been included in a volume of his poetry. In it, he says that "it is my habit to allow language its own freedom and confidence" even though such poems may bewilder readers who "try to control all emergent elements in discourse for the service of predetermined ends." He continues, "I must be willingly fallible in order to deserve a place in the realm where miracles happen." Stafford is, by extension, inviting the reader, too, to deserve a place in the miracle.

People and places from Stafford's past again figure prominently in this volume. He seems to be taking stock of them in a new way, though, seeking deeper integration than before. He blends the past, present, and future together, and a sense of playfulness emerges. In "Thinking About Being Called Simple by a Critic," Stafford alludes to William Carlos Williams's plum poem in his first line, "I wanted the plums, but I waited." While he waits, he hears the echo of a critic who said "how stupid I was." As Stafford probes the truth of these words, he starts to enjoy them and decides that the critic must be a friend: "Who but a friend/ could give so sternly what the sky/ feels for everyone but few learn to/ cherish?" Stafford feels rightly put in his place—and delights in it. He goes to the refrigerator, opens it, sees that "sure enough the light was on," and reaches in to get the plums.

Yet there is also a didactic tone in this volume. Stafford is ready to tell what he has been hearing in the silence all these years. In "Lie Detector," he says that the heart proclaims "the truth all the time, hidden but always/ there," because it is "acting the self, helplessly true." He concludes the poem in a celebration of the present: "At night, no one else near, you walk/ . . . your heart marching along/ with you, saying, 'Now,' saying, 'Yes,'/ saying, 'Here.'" The last poem in the collection, "Maybe Alone on My Bike," is representative of Stafford's blending of the serious and the playful. As he rides home ("maybe alone"), he says, "I listen," and reflects back at the distance he has traveled, thinking of the splendor and marvels of life as it reveals itself. He intones, "O citizens of our great amnesty:/ we might have died. We live," but then comes back to concrete narrative with his concluding line: "and I hear in the [bicycle] chain a chuckle I like to hear." Stafford is still listening, he is still finding meaning, and what was quiet bliss is now bubbling up to the surface as delight.

Passwords

Delight extends into Stafford's eighth collection with a major publisher, *Passwords*. These poems from the heart invite the reader to continue to make serendipitous discoveries through language, memory, and feeling.

Legacy

Stafford wrote in the same voice all his life. Critics generally consider him to be a poet of place or a poet of myths. Yet he created his own myths, and he was at home everywhere. He said that the crucial parts of writing have to do with what is shared by human beings rather than their superficial differences. By exploring the great diversity the world has to offer, Stafford glimpsed a unified vision of nature at its depths. Resting on an undercurrent of optimism, he unfolded this field of all possibilities, locating playfulness in the serious, imagination in the practical, profundity in the commonplace. In doing so, he took the chance of being misunderstood, but that is part of the way he viewed the process of writing. Though he seemed to be giving messages to his readers, Stafford was simply inviting them to find their own way. He said that he preferred not to assert his poems, but to have them "climb toward the reader without my proclaiming anything." He hoped that "sometimes for every reader a poem would arrive: it would go out for him, and find his life."

Other major works

nonfiction: *Down in My Heart*, 1947; *Friends to This Ground: A Statement for Readers, Teachers, and Writers of Literature*, 1967; *Leftovers, A Care Pack-*

age: Two Lectures, 1973; *Writing the Australian Crawl: Views on the Writer's Vocation*, 1978; *You Must Revise Your Life*, 1986; *Writing the World*, 1988.

EDITED TEXTS: *The Voices of Prose*, 1966 (with Frederick Caudelaria); *The Achievement of Brother Antonius: A Comprehensive Selection of His Poems with a Critical Introduction*, 1967; *Poems and Perspectives*, 1971 (with Robert H. Ross); *Modern Poetry of Western America*, 1975 (with Clinton F. Larson).

BIBLIOGRAPHY

Andrews, Tom, ed. *On William Stafford: The Worth of Local Things*. Ann Arbor: University of Michigan Press, 1993. Presents an assortment of over fifty mostly (but not wholly) complimentary essays on Stafford's poetry and prose. Overall, they rank Stafford among the best American poets. Important historical analogies are proposed, favorably comparing his subject matter, voice, and vision to those of poets such as Whitman and Frost. There is enough hard criticism, especially regarding the occasional flatness of Stafford's style, to allow the reader to share in the debate.

Holden, Jonathan. *The Mark to Turn*. Lawrence: University Press of Kansas, 1976. This volume, the first book-length study of Stafford's work, is a useful overview of his major themes and technique. Holden focuses his close readings on poems from Stafford's first published collection and the four collections with his major publisher that followed. The ninety-one-page study includes a biography.

Kitchen, Judith. *Writing the World: Understanding William Stafford*. Corvallis: Oregon State University Press, 1999. This comprehensive volume is accessible for the student as well as the good nonacademic reader. In addition to a short biography and overview of Stafford's work, it presents detailed analysis of seven of Stafford's major collections and also considers his chapbooks and distinguished small-press editions. This 175-page work concludes with a detailed bibliography of primary and secondary sources.

Lensing, George S., and Ronald Moran. "William Stafford." In *Four Poets and the Emotive Imagination: Robert Bly, James Wright, Louis Simpson, and William Stafford*. Baton Rouge: Louisiana State University Press, 1976. This scholarly volume defines a body of poetry termed "Emotive Imagination" and discusses its emergence within the tradition of American poetry. The chapter on Stafford considers his work from a mythic perspective, both as a reflection of Native American myths and as archetypal poetry that explores the traditional quest theme.

Nordstrom, Lars. "A William Stafford Bibliography." *Studia Neophilologica* 59 (1987): 59-63. Although it is difficult to assemble an exhaustive bibliography because Stafford publishes frequently with small presses, this relatively complete one includes both primary and secondary sources. In addition to prose and poetry collections, it lists critical studies, symposia, interviews, doctoral dissertations, film, and reference materials.

Pinsker, Sanford. "William Stafford: 'The Real Things We Live By.'" In *Three Pacific Northwest Poets*. Boston: Twayne, 1987. This chapter begins with a biographical sketch and then unfolds a book-by-book analysis of six of Stafford's collections, offering close readings of representative poems to support more general conclusions. It includes a selected bibliography.

Stitt, Peter. "William Stafford's Wilderness Quest." In *The World: Hieroglyphic Beauty: Five American Poets*. Athens: University of Georgia Press, 1985. This excellent chapter develops Stafford as a "wisdom poet" and explores his process-rather-than-substance view of writing. It includes an interview with Stafford originally conducted at his home in 1976 and updated in 1981 at the Bread Loaf Writers' Conference.

Jean C. Fulton;
bibliography updated by the editors

GASPARA STAMPA

Born: Padua(?), Italy; c. 1523
Died: Venice, Italy; April 23, 1554

Principal poetry

Rime, 1554
Selected Poems, 1994

Other literary forms

Gaspara Stampa is remembered only for her poetry.

Achievements

Gaspara Stampa produced only one lyric collection during her short life: the *Rime*. Modeled after Petrarch's prototypical *canzoniere*, Stampa's work offers modern readers exceptional insight into the artistic aspirations and literary ideals of the Italian Renaissance, a period which cherished creative imitation. Like many of her contemporaries, Stampa emulated the language, form, and thought of the traditional master. In a period that did not favor radical innovation, the *Rime* kept to the forms favored by Petrarch—the sonnet, madrigal, and sestina—as well as to his basic motifs, rhetorical devices, and conventional images.

In addition, Stampa employed the standardized lyric vocabulary formulated by Petrarch and adopted by his followers. Stampa's borrowings from Petrarch are numerous and acknowledged. The very structure of her opus follows an established format for collections of love poetry in the sixteenth century. Like Petrarch, she presents a love story as it unfolds in a series of inner conflicts in an atmosphere of painful self-awareness; like him, she orders the loose threads of her plot line in a chronological fashion. Nevertheless, both master and disciple transcend the barriers of biographical or realistic experience and enter the realm of universality. Nor was Stampa a mere copier. Her reworking of the Petrarchan model enriches her verse by constantly functioning as a sounding board against which her own words echo forcefully. Like the most successful *Petrarchisti*, she manipulates her borrowings so that the atmosphere of the original is transferred to the new composition. This "translation" is all the more significant because Stampa was forced to operate within the masculine lexicon of the dominant Petrarchan/Neoplatonic code. One of the privileged women who received a solid education in the sixteenth century, she was one of the first poets to express the woman's view of the love experience.

Stampa's feminine sensibility is clearly expressed in her poetry. Even within the confines of her creative imitation, the writer possesses a singular lyric personality, easily recognizable for its sincerity of expression, lack of rhetorical affectation, and emotive power, in contrast to the repetitive monotony of numerous other Petrarchan adherents. These very qualities, justly appreciated today, were the probable cause for her lack of popularity in her own day. Insufficiently erudite and controlled, Stampa's compositions lacked the formal dress and decorum so admired during the late Renaissance. A minor player on the stage of Venetian culture, Stampa had little influence and no resonance. After centuries of critical neglect, however, she is now recognized as one of the great love poets of her tradition. The rich psychological nuances of her sonnets and the extraordinary musicality of her madrigals, joined with the spontaneity of her discourse, separate her from the scores of Petrarchan imitators and make her one of Italy's foremost women writers and one of the best lyric poets of the Renaissance.

Biography

Very little is actually known about the historical Gaspara Stampa. Documentation of her life is scarce, and most data are limited to contemporary letters and occasional poems dedicated to her. Even the exact year and location of her birth are uncertain, as is the social status of her family, although some evidence suggests that her father had been a successful Paduan jeweler whose trade permitted a comfortable bourgeois existence. Some information can be drawn from the *Rime*, although it is not always wise to use the poetry as a biographical source. It appears that sometime after 1530, the three Stampa children were taken to Venice by their widowed mother and were given a good Humanistic education. The daughters, Gaspara and Cassandra, demonstrated exceptional musical aptitude and soon achieved excellent reputations as musicians, while their brother, Baldassare, was becoming greatly admired as a promising young poet before his untimely death in 1544. The siblings, particularly Baldassare, participated actively in the social world of the Venetian *ridotti*, or salons, meeting some of the most prominent artists, musicians, patrons, and intellectuals of the time. It was a sophisticated environment where the nobility freely mingled with dandies, foreigners, students, and courtesans. It was an ambiance generally inaccessible to the maidens and matrons of the city, who lived a sheltered existence. Gaspara and Cassandra had a *ridotto* of their own, where they entertained guests with song and poetry. Sometime in 1548, at such a gathering, Stampa met Count Collatino di Collato, a feudal gentleman-warrior known for his patronage of artists and musicians. The romantic involvement of Stampa and the Count became literary history. For the first time, the young woman seriously devoted herself to poetry, producing hundreds of compositions dedicated to the man and the love which would dominate her life for three years. Collatino was an indifferent lover, however, and, after a series of separations and conflicts, the two ended their affair. Stampa found consolation in her art and in another man, the patrician Bartolomeo Zen, who appears in a limited number of sonnets in the *Rime*. Stampa died in 1554, barely thirty, having published only three of her numerous sonnets in an anthology. Her complete opus was edited posthumously by Cassandra and appeared a few months after the poet's death. Then, for two hundred years, the writer and her work were forgotten.

The fictional Gaspara Stampa first appeared in 1738, in a biographical sketch accompanying the second edition of the *Rime*. A direct descendent of Collatino, Count Antonio Rambaldo, wrote this short profile of Stampa, and thus began the first of her legends. Describing Stampa as a sweet young noblewoman of great talent, the Count accused his ancestor of cruelty and betrayal leading to the unnatural and untimely death (by poison?) of the distraught lady. This version of Stampa's life appealed to the Romantic soul, and a number of fictional renderings followed, including one novel and two plays. Stampa had become a female Werther, an unwary virgin doomed to unhappiness and death.

This mythical Stampa was ravished in 1913 when a literary scholar, Abdelkader Salza, concluded that the poet had not been a young innocent but a high-class prostitute, a courtesan. Given the independence of Stampa's life, her known participation in the Venetian demimonde, and her sexual liberty, such a conclusion remains plausible but unproved; Gaspara may also have been a *virtuosa*, or professional musician, for example. The critical debate concerning the poet's social and moral standing raged for decades, involving some of Italy's major literati. As a result, another legend was born: The eternal *appassionata* emerged to replace the virginal victim. In such a biographical furor, Stampa's *Rime* was interpreted variously as a document, a diary, even an epistolary novel in verse. The historical figure and the fictional protagonist merged, and, in the process, the poet was ignored. It is only during the past fifty years that some literary critics have begun to evaluate the artist and separate her from the woman, discovering that Gaspara Stampa was a serious writer, cognizant of the difficulties of her craft and of the need to develop a personal style that would adequately express what she wished to convey.

Analysis

Rime

Most modern editions of the *Rime* are based on the one prepared in 1913 by Salza, who divided Gaspara Stampa's poetry into two major groupings: the "Rime d'amore" (love poems) and the "Rime varie" (miscellaneous poems). The former includes more than two hundred compositions, preponderantly sonnets, which chronicle the poet's love for Collatino and, later, Zen. The latter contains Stampa's occasional poetry, addressed to friends, acquaintances, and celebrities. Salza's edition concludes with eight religious sonnets, extracted from their original positioning among the love poems, so that the text ends on a morally contrite and uplifting note probably not intended by the author.

The miscellaneous poems are Stampa's most conventional works, often mere exercises in the art of writing. Adhering to shared literary expectations and the collective Petrarchan taste, they are expressions of social courtesy, gallantry, polite exchange, and encomium. Their function was public, in a century which utilized poetry as a tool of communication and flattery. Nevertheless, the "Rima varie" offer clear indications of Stampa's personal attitudes toward poetry, poetics, and her own accomplishments. Most of her addressees were avowed, if occasionally innovative, members of Venice's Petrarchan literary elite. Their relationship to Stampa was primarily artistic, poetry functioning as the common social denominator. In her laudatory verse, Stampa is often concerned with the intellectual and stylistic attainments of those to whom her poems were addressed. By praising them, she is making an express value judgment on conventional Petrarchianism, accepting it as the ideal poetic model and stating that fame can be obtained through successful emulation.

From reading the "Rima varie," it appears that the poet had a well-formulated critical criterion, by which she judged her own work and that of others—a criterion based on the theory of creative imitation. Whereas she praises her fellow poets, Stampa projects an air of artistic insecurity in regard to her own abilities, declaring time and again that her "style" is inadequate, that she lacks sufficient eloquence, that her technique is crude. Often the poet suggests that her artistic failure is a result of her gender. The frailty of women is presented as implying intellectual inferiority as well, in a series of negative qualifiers Stampa uses to describe herself, ranging from "vile" to "humble." Within her cultural environment, these disclaimers and confessions of inadequacy were Stampa's way of defining herself as an unsatisfactory *Petrarchista*, a writer who aspires to great art but fails.

Petrarchanism

The Petrarchan origin of Gaspara Stampa's poetry is undeniable and indeed is clearly acknowledged by the poet herself in the *Rime*'s opening sonnet, which both paraphrases and pays homage to Petrarch's prefatory poem to his *Canzoniere* (1470). Similar paraphrases open many Renaissance collections of love poetry, immediately acknowledging their artistic origins in the medieval master. In Stampa's case, this declared derivation serves two purposes. On the one hand, the poet directly associates her compositions with those of their literary source; on the other, she also contrasts the two works by altering the premises of the sonnets. Thus, Stampa's prefatory sonnet informs the reader that she is about to construct an exemplary love story in the pattern established for *canzonieri*, but it also declares that Petrarch's moral environment is not operative in this Renaissance work. Petrarch had from the outset of his collection emphasized the victory of the soul over earthly *vanitas*; Stampa, the disciple, retains none of her master's religious conflicts.

The first sonnet of the *Canzoniere* had emphasized spiritual repentance; the first sonnet of the *Rime* proposes the unending exaltation of human love, not its moral rejection. From the beginning, Stampa distinguishes her poetic universe from Petrarch's and initiates her subversive interpretation of the model. Here, and throughout her collection, Stampa divests her borrowings of their original moral and religious implications. She uses Petrarchan themes, images, metaphors, poetic devices, forms, vocabulary, and even whole lines but rejects the Christian consciousness that shapes the psychological ambiance of the medieval source. One example is the poem "La vita fugge," which replicates the first line of a famous Petrarchan sonnet. Both poems are concerned with the passage of time and the ensuing emotions of loss and dread, but Stampa purposely distorts the original's premises. Whereas Petrarch had been preoccupied with time wasted in transient pleasures, Stampa regrets the loss of pleasure in the transience of time. What had been a poem of spiritual suffering is transformed into a complaint against the fleeting nature of earthly love. In similar fashion, Stampa's anniversary poems—also derived from the *Canzoniere*—engage in an argument with their model. In contrast to Petrarch's Good Friday, a feast of death, Stampa proposes Christmas, a celebration of birth, as the anniversary of her love.

Stampa's rejection of Petrarch's spiritual battles places her directly in the more naturalistic world of the Renaissance but does not negate her greatest contact with his poetic universe. It is in the act of loving and in psychological self-awareness that Stampa comes closest to her literary mentor. Both are exceptional landscapers of their interior worlds, delving into the deepest recesses of emotion and thought. For both, the principal issue is love. More intense than Petrarch's collection, Stampa's "Rime d'amore" is compactly powerful in its analysis of the states and stages of loving. Nothing deflects the poet from her theme. Love is omnipresent in the *Rime*, an overwhelming force that controls the poetic persona, ranging from feelings of extreme joy to painful masochism.

Equally present is the beloved, principally Collatino, who is never named directly but who is consistently idealized. The beloved is the poet's *signore*, or lord, concurrently feudal master, gentleman, superior, and god. To create such an exceptional figure, Stampa borrowed from both Petrarchianism and Platonism, easily associating him with abstractions such as the true, the beautiful, and the good as well as linking him poetically to the representation of Christ in the anniversary poems. Like an idol, the beloved receives amorous tributes but does not reciprocate, being enamored of his own beautiful self. Stampa deifies her man, rendering him as a Platonic emanation, a translucent reflection, or an immaterial beauty. She compares him to the planets, the elements, and the seasons, attributing mystical qualities to him. He is a celestial Mars, an Apollo, and an Adonis—a figure of myth, not a mere man. In keeping with Stampa's Petrarchan inspiration, however, this idol is also a cruel beloved, a pagan icon who demands immolation as a sacrifice for love. Even the Platonic desire to acquire beauty through union with the loved one becomes a means of torment, for union—understood physically as well as spiritually—is denied through separation, abandonment, and rejection. The glorification of the beloved in Stampa is concurrent with the self-denigration of the lover. The Stampean persona loses self to love, as exemplified by the figure of Echo, the nymph who had wasted away for love of Narcissus (the Count?), retaining only her voice (poetry?). Gaspara also associates love with death, in Platonic terms, for the lover is lost to the beloved. To these standard themes, the poet adds the novel one of jealousy, whose pain survives even as the persona's identity withers.

Language

It is Stampa's language that most clearly separates her from the other imitators of Petrarch and lyric poets of the sixteenth century. Common, everyday speech often intrudes into the courtly diction of emulation. The poet tends toward spoken language, creating an atmosphere of directness and sincerity often lacking in the work of her more polished contemporaries. To achieve such spontaneity, Stampa employs direct and indirect discourse, dialogue, apostrophe, invocation, and direct address. Her verse is also unique for its musicality. Given her instrumental and vocal training, it is not surprising that her poems are often melodious, rhythmic, and aurally suggestive, linking her to the later contributions of the Arcadian school and the melodrama of Pietro Metastasio. Stampa's lyric idiom has a distinct identity, a private language which unites conventional style, colloquialisms, musical cadence, and directness.

Sensuality

Also unique to Stampa is her sensual honesty. Her poetry is not explicitly erotic, but it is sensuous, its sexuality being contained by the generalities of Petrarchan diction. The *carpe diem* theme, the call to the beloved to enjoy pleasure and beauty before they disappear in time, links some of her poetry to that of Christopher Marlowe, Robert Herrick, and Andrew Marvell. The pain and negativity of love found in Stampa is also given rhetorical dress in her unusual use of the hyperbole. Just as the Petrarchan antithesis had served Stampa well in describing the dichotomy of loving, so the conceit serves to express love's pain and imperiousness, as well as the beloved's cruelty. Contradictory feelings, the tensions and extremes of emotion, frustration, passion, anger, and hopelessness are dramatized through language. It is this emotive tension that separates Gaspara Stampa from other lyric poets in her century, justifying her famous line: "Love has made me such that I live in fire."

Bibliography

Bassanese, Fiora A. *Gaspara Stampa*. Boston: Twayne, 1982. Comprehensive and authoritative, this rare full-length critical study of Stampa in English synthesizes the full range of continental scholarship, with sound original conclusions. Annotated bibliography of Italian sources is also useful.

Braden, Gordon. "Gaspara Stampa and the Gender of Petrarchism." *Texas Studies in Literature and Language* 38, no. 2 (Summer, 1996), 115-139. Article reviews the range of Petrarchan poetic conventions and suggests an unorthodox interpretation of Stampa's position within that tradition.

Cesareo, G. A. *Gaspara Stampa donna e poetessa*. Napoli: Perella, 1920. An influential biographical and literary study notable for its defense of Stampa against earlier attacks on her morality and character. In Italian.

Moore, Mary B. *Desiring Voices: Women Sonneteers and Petrarchism*. Carbondale: Southern Illinois University Press, 2000. Places Stampa within a larger European poetic community, providing feminist insights. Devotes a chapter to Stampa, with new translation of several poems.

Philippy, Patricia Berrahou. *Love's Remedies: Recantation and Renaissance Lyric Poetry.* Lewisburg, Pa.: Bucknell University Press, 1995. A chapter on Stampa elucidates her position in Italian literature and her deviation from the established male Petrarchan conventions.

Stortoni, Laura Anna, and Mary Prentice Lillie. *Gaspara Stampa: Selected Poems.* New York: Italica Press, 1994. A bilingual edition, with new translations and notes. The introduction is particularly helpful with its insights into Stampa's life and times. The translations are both lyrical and faithful. A chronology of Stampa's life prefaces the text.

Warnke, Frank J. *Three Women Poets: Renaissance and Baroque.* Lewisburg: Bucknell University Press, 1987. Presents a convincing argument that Stampa is the prime female poet of Italy. Ranks her in skill with Louise Labe and Sor Juanna Ines de la Cruz. Good translations of the poetry of each poet are provided, and the comparisons of the three are particularly enlightening.

Fiora A. Bassanese;
bibliography updated by Allene Phy-Olsen

Statius

Publius Papinius Statius
Born: Neapolis, Italy; c. 45 C.E.
Died: Neapolis, Italy; c. 96 C.E.

Principal poetry

Thebais, c. 90 (*Thebaid*, 1767)
Silvae, c. 91-95 (English translation, 1908)
Achilleid, c. 95-96 (English translation, 1660)

Other literary forms

Statius's reputation, for good or ill, rests upon his poetry, although he did write in other forms. A lost work, "Agave," is mentioned by the satirist Juvenal, who says that Statius wrote it for the mime Paris. More important are the prose prefaces that Statius wrote to begin each of the books of the *Silvae*. Tore Janson, in *Latin Prose Prefaces* (1964), maintains that they are a "new type" of introduction in prose to a collection of poetry. Stephen Thomas Newmyer, in *The "Silvae" of Statius* (1979), says that for Statius the preface is "a useful device for conveying information concerning the circumstances of composition of the individual poems, for indicating the contents of the books, for stating some apologetic remarks about public reaction to the *Silvae*, and, not least, for flattering the recipients of the books."

Achievements

Statius set himself an ambitious goal when he chose to write epic. He lived to see the completed *Thebaid* published about 90 C.E. (a privilege granted neither Vergil nor Lucan); the poem ends with a burst of pride, expectation, and just a little humility:

> Wilt thou endure in the time to come, O my *Thebais*, for twelve years the object of my wakeful toil, wilt thou survive thy master and be read? Of a truth already present Fame hath paved thee a friendly road, and begun to hold thee up, young as thou art, to future ages. Already great-hearted Caesar deigns to know thee, and the youth of Italy eagerly learns and recounts thy verse. O live, I pray! nor rival the divine *Aeneid*, but follow afar and ever venerate its footsteps. Soon, if any envy as yet o'erclouds thee, it shall pass away, and, after I am gone, thy well-won honours shall be duly paid.

Statius's wish for lasting fame was granted—at least until recent years. Neither Valerius Flaccus's *Argonautica* (ninth century C.E.; English translation, 1934) nor Silius Italicus's *Punica* (tenth century C.E.; English translation, 1933), the only other Flavian epics, enjoyed the prominence of Statius through the medieval and Renaissance periods of European literature. In the late fourth century, Claudian used the *Silvae* as models for his own occasional poems, and a little later Sidonius Apollinaris copied more from Statius than from Vergil. In the fifth century, Lactantius Placidus wrote an allegorizing commentary on the *Thebaid*; in the sixth century, Fulgentius saw a Christian psychomachy in both Statius and Vergil. Later, both Petrarch and Desiderius Erasmus listed Statius among their favorite classical poets. Giovanni Boccaccio, too, was indebted to Statius. Because of possible Christian interpretations and because of the romantic, adventuresome nature of his stories, Statius was very popular throughout the medieval period and into the Renaissance, but nowhere is his influence more apparent than in the works of Dante Alighieri and Geoffrey Chaucer.

In *La divina commedia* (c. 1320; *The Divine Comedy*), Dante and his guide, Vergil, meet Statius in Purgatory. Statius, who reveals that he had in life been a secret Christian, has just finished his penance for the sins of sloth and prodigality and becomes Dante's model for the released soul, passing from Purgatory into Heaven. As such, Statius travels with Vergil and Dante, the pilgrim from canto 21, to canto 30, when Vergil disappears and Statius continues with Dante until they cross into Paradise in canto 33. Dante calls the two "the good escorts" and "my poets." C. S. Lewis, noting that every one of Statius's major characters can be found somewhere in *The Divine Comedy*, argues persuasively that as much as Dante loved Vergil, as a medieval Christian he was more comfortable with the worldview implicit in the *Thebaid*. Lewis concludes, "It was not perverse of Dante to save Statius and damn Virgil."

Chaucer, too, found Statius to be a valuable source. Boyd A. Wise, in *The Influence of Statius upon Chaucer* (1911), says that the only Latin authors more familiar to Chaucer were Ovid and Boethius. Wise cites ten works of Chaucer that show evidence of direct borrowings from the *Thebaid*, and there are additional borrowings through Boccaccio. "The Knight's Tale," for example, comes to Chaucer through Boccaccio's *Teseida* (c. 1340-1341; *The Book of Theseus*), and is itself the source for John Fletcher and William Shakespeare's *The Two Noble Kinsmen* (c. 1613) and John Dryden's "Palamon and Arcite." Chaucer mentions Statius by name in *The House of Fame* (1372-1380), where his statue is on an iron pillar, coated with tiger's blood, upholding the fame of Thebes and Achilles. Chaucer mentions Statius by name again in the envoi to *Troilus and Criseyde* (1382), the work influenced more than any other by Statius: "Go, litel bok . . . And kis the steppes, where as thow seest pace/ Virgile, Ovide, Omer, Lucan, and Stace."

Statius has been admired and imitated to a lesser extent by other famous writers (Edmund Spenser, John Milton), and some not so famous (John of Salisbury, Joseph of Exeter, John Gower, John Lydgate). The eighteenth century, however, was the last period in English literature when Statius was uncritically admired. Alexander Pope and Thomas Gray each translated parts of the *Thebaid*, but when J. H. Mozley prepared the Loeb translations of Statius in 1928, he recorded no modern edition of either the *Thebaid* or *Achilleid*. Modern readers have criticized Statius for being artificial, florid, sentimental, bombastic, episodic, trivial, pedantic, heavily mythological, digressive, obscure, and baroque in the worst sense. Even friendly critics have been circumspect. Moses Hadas, in *A History of Latin Literature* (1952), is representative when he says, "Statius' merits are in miniature rather than in total effect; episodes are better than the fabric of which they are part, and flashing phrases better than their context." More recently, scholars have seen structure and purpose where others have found none. In choosing the elements of his story, in expressing them in poetic language, in arranging the parts, in developing the themes, Statius reshapes the style of his great predecessors Vergil, Ovid, and Lucan, within the context of the polished and autocratic age of Domitian. Statius tries to make a virtue of excess, a choice that reflects the time in which he lived and the cultured circle for which he wrote. Statius's style is not Vergil's, but what Statius does, he does better than anyone else.

Biography

Most of what is known about Publius Papinius Statius comes from what he himself chose to tell in the *Silvae*. Statius was born between 40 c.e. and 45 in Neapolis, into a family of modest circumstances and a cultural blend of the Roman and the Hellenic. His father was a schoolmaster who had won poetry contests in both Italy and Greece and had translated Homer into prose. Statius senior had written a poem on the ambitious topic of the civil wars of 69 c.e., and at the time of his death he was contemplating another on the eruption of Vesuvius. Statius gives his father credit for his education and even for guidance in the composition of the *Thebaid*. His father, then, and Vergil, whose tomb he visited, and Lucan, whose birthday he commemorates, were his great mentors.

Statius moved from Neapolis to Rome and earned a living with his writing. Juvenal, the only contemporary to mention him, says that Statius gave recitations of the *Thebaid* to enthusiastic audiences but would have starved had he not sold material to a famous mime named Paris. Nowhere, however, does Statius himself complain about finances. He addresses each of the first four books of the *Silvae* to a different wealthy and influential friend and seems to have enjoyed the patronage of Domitian. Statius and Martial knew many of the same important people, but neither poet mentions the other.

In Rome, Statius married a widow named Claudia. She and Statius were childless, although the poet speaks with affection about Claudia's daughter from a previous marriage and with real grief about his adopted son, a freed slave who died as a child. Statius and Claudia lived together, apparently happily, for many years. It is in the poem addressed to her that Statius says he won Domitian's poetry competition at Alba, but later lost in the Capitoline contest of 94 C.E. In the *Silvae*, he entreats Claudia, who knows, he says, how sick he has recently been and how hard he labored over the *Thebaid*, to return with him to Neapolis. This she apparently did, and the poet is presumed to have died there about 96 C.E. Statius himself saw the *Thebaid* published about 90 C.E. and the first four books of the *Silvae* between 91 C.E. and 95; book 5 of the *Silvae* and the fragment *Achilleid* were published by an anonymous editor after Statius's death.

Analysis

Statius wrote in the middle of what has been called the Silver Age of Latin literature. A contemporary of Valerius Flaccus, Quintilian, and Martial, Statius was heavily influenced by his Neronian predecessors Seneca and Lucan. Statius's poetry was written during the reign of Domitian, a patron who must have been difficult to please, fancying himself (as he did) both a poet and a god. Statius's poetry exemplifies much of what is typical of Silver Age poetry. He was a skilled writer of Vergilian hexameters, heavily influenced by various schools of rhetoric, and fond of mythology, intellectual display, epigram, and description. On these matters, there is consensus. About the other characteristics of Statius's work, there is not. E. M. W. Tillyard, in *The English Epic and Its Background* (1954), sees psychological power as one of Statius's strengths. Mozley, in his introduction to the Loeb edition of Statius's works, says, "Psychologically, he is not conspicuous for remarkable insight." Gordon Williams, in *Change and Decline: Roman Literature in the Early Empire* (1978), sees only a "vague, watery Stoicism." David Vessey, in *Statius and the "Thebaid"* (1973), sees Stoicism as basic to the philosophical foundation of the *Thebaid*. T. M. Greene, in *Descent from Heaven: A Study in Epic Continuity* (1963), sees the "lurid, frenzied, blood-sodden" *Thebaid* as "a series of violent episodes, empty of moral or historical meaning." Vessey sees the *Thebaid* as "an epic not of sin but of redemption, a chronicle not of evil but of triumphant good." In general, however, there seems to be a trend toward a reestimation of Statius that is more favorable than it has been for several centuries.

Silvae

Statius believed the *Thebaid* to be the work through which he would achieve immortality, but a good deal of attention has been paid to the *Silvae*, occasional poems he himself describes as "produced in the heat of the moment and by a kind of joyful glow of improvisation." The *Silvae* comprise thirty-two poems in five books. The first four books were arranged by Statius from a presumably much larger number of light poems and published between 91 C.E. and 95; book 5 is without the same kind of prose preface that begins books 1 through 4 and probably was published posthumously. The *Silvae* were known and admired until the Carolingian Age, after which they were lost. They were rediscovered by the scholar Poggio in 1417.

Donnis Martin, in "Similarities Between the *Silvae* of Statius and the Epigrams of Martial," maintains that there had been nothing exactly like the *Silvae* before in Latin literature. The poems were like earlier lyric and elegiac poems in subject, but they differed from the earlier poems in their meter, their length, and their concern for rhetorical form. The same can be said for a comparison between Statius and his contemporary, Martial. Martial wrote epigrams on the same topics as seven of Statius's poems (for example, the marriage of Stella and Violentilla, the death of Claudius Etruscus's father, a statue of Hercules), but the forms of their works are very different. The poems of the *Silvae* are predominantly written in dactylic hexameter, but four are hendecasyllabic, and there is one each in Sapphics and Alcaics. The length of the poems varies from 19 to 293 lines, with the average a little more than 100 lines. Many of the poems can be identified with a particular rhetorical type. There are multiple examples of the *epicedion* (consolation) and *ecphrasis* (description), and less numerous examples of the *epithalamium* (marriage song), *proempticon* (farewell), *genethliacon* (birthday poem), and others.

This range of rhetorical types alone might make the reader raise an eyebrow at Statius's repeated protests that the *Silvae* are but "trifling pieces." Indeed, later scholarship has found remarkable patterns within and among these "trifling" poems. Newmyer sees in the composition of each book a carefully balanced structure, depending upon a chiastic or recessed-panel organization in which poems are balanced around a central point. The pattern may be determined by the rhetorical type, the meter, the theme, or the length of individual poems. David Bright, in *Elaborate Disarray: The Nature of Statius' "Silvae"* (1980), also sees recessed-panel organization in the books: Bright sees the theme of nature worked and reworked along with other themes, such as art, death, travel, and family ties. In the *Silvae*, nature is for the most part ordered by the hand of man or God. This is interesting in the context of the word *silva*, the basic meaning of which is "forest" and, by extension, "material." Patterns are established only to be broken or left incomplete. Bright concludes that in the *Silvae*, and also in his other works, Statius "cultivated the clash between order and disarray, moderation and wilful excess, simplicity and extravagance."

The poems of the *Silvae* are diverse, and opinion about them varies. Hardest for the modern reader to appreciate are the long and seemingly digressive poems and the poems to or about Domitian. H. E. Butler's comments in *Post-Augustan Poetry from Seneca to Juvenal* (1909) are notorious: Butler says he cannot quote *Silvae* Poem 4, book 3, calling it "one of the most disgusting productions in the whole range of literature." Of Domitian, Butler says: "The emperor who can accept flattery of such a kind has certainly qualified for assassination." It is true that Statius wrote flattery, but in the years before Domitian's death by assassination in 96 C.E., those who did not, did not write. It is strange that Martial, who flattered the tyrant just as much but lived to retract his words, does not suffer, as Statius does, from the charge of sycophancy.

Several of Statius's occasional poems, particularly those in *Silvae*, do have the ability to charm even the modern reader. Poem 3, book 2, a birthday gift to Atedius Melior, tells a myth explaining why a plane tree on Melior's land grows bent over a lake. In comic hendecasyllables, Poem 9, book 4, teases Plotius Grypus for returning a worthless book in exchange for a valuable one. Also in hendecasyllables (Statius says that he will not be so bold as to write in Lucan's own meter) is Poem 7, book 2, a birthday poem praising Lucan, the author of the *Bellum civile* (c. 90-95 C.E.). This birthday poem is atypical because Lucan was already deceased, and so his *genethliacon* has some of the characteristics of an *epicedion*. Other *epicedia* that show real emotion are Statius's laments on the deaths of his father and his adopted son. In a lighter vein is the mock *epicedion* on the death of Melior's parrot. Perhaps the most famous and most admired of all Statius's poems is Poem 4, book 5, the gentle, nineteen-line poem "To Sleep." John W. Mackail, J. Wight Duff, and others see it as almost a sonnet. They mean the comparison as a high compliment, but it is based on fundamental misconceptions, as J. V. Cunningham has demonstrated in his excellent essay, "Classical and Medieval: Statius on Sleep."

The poems of *Silvae* are also read for extraliterary reasons. Here, Statius presents a vivid picture of life in the Flavian Age: Places, people, and events are drawn in bold strokes. The reader becomes acquainted with the men to whom Statius dedicates the first four books of the *Silvae:* L. Arruntius Stella, a patrician poet whose marriage Statius celebrates; Atedius Melior, another of his rich patrons; Pollius Felix, a wealthy Epicurean; and Vitorius Marcellus, an accomplished man of equestrian family who eventually became a praetor. There are also historians, art collectors, imperial secretaries, politicians, orators, the son of a freedman, and a eunuch. Statius describes sumptuous villas, marble baths, a temple of Hercules, and a statue of the same god. He also shows people enduring a death or celebrating a birth, setting out on a journey, beginning or enjoying a happy marriage. He shows both how people—and poets—survive under despotism and, in a more lighthearted vein, what goes on at a Saturnalia celebration. The *Silvae* are as polished and full of artifice as the age they so succinctly describe.

Thebaid

The *Thebaid* is no less polished and full of artifice. Statius says he worked on the epic for twelve years, and on it, he believed, rested his claim to enduring fame. Still, he claims not to rival the "divine *Aeneid*" (c. 29-19 B.C.E.) but only to follow in its footsteps. Statius's debt to Vergil is real, but no less real than his debt to later authors, particularly Lucan. Statius treads a middle ground. He takes from Vergil without seeking to duplicate his classicism; he also takes from Lucan without trying to emulate his new type of epic. Consider the opening lines of the *Thebaid*:

> Fraternal rage, the guilty Thebes alarms,
>
> The alternate reign destroyed by impious arms,
>
> Demand our song. . . .

This has not the classical directness of Vergil's "Arma virumque cano," ("I sing of arms and the man) but Statius tells the reader, as does Vergil, exactly what the topic will be. Echoing Lucan's "cognatasque acies," Statius will write of "Fraternas acies," the action around which all other action revolves. It is easy to sympathize with J. Wight Duff's statement in *A Literary History of Rome in the Silver Age* (1953), which says that Statius makes "a dull start with frigid professions of ignorance as to where in the Theban story he should begin, and with equally frigid flattery of Domitian." Both items, however, are to be expected: the first because such a catalog displays Statius's range of learning, and the second because it was a prudent necessity. The forty-six lines of the proem, despite the two passages to which Duff objects, are carefully arranged. The opening lines tell the reader that this will be a story, not of a single hero, but of "strife of brethren" and "impious hatred" and "the guilty tale of Thebes." After the catalog of associated stories he chooses to eschew, Statius returns to his topic:

> And fix, O Muse! the barrier of thy song,
>
> At Oedipus—from his disasters trace
>
> The long confusion of his guilty race.

Then, after the obligatory obeisance to Domitian, Statius ends the proem with another reiteration of his topic, mentioning again the Theban wars fatal to the two brothers and to many other heroes. The four heroes Statius names are not random choices: Each is an ally of Polynices, killed in a different one of the four books directly preceding the fatal duel between Polynices and Eteocles in book 11.

Just as Achilles' wrath and his great oath in book 1 of the *Iliad* (c. 800 B.C.E.) control the subsequent action of that epic, so do Oedipus's hate and his great curse control the action of the *Thebaid*. A paradoxical situation is presented in which the blind Oedipus hides in physical darkness but is haunted by "the fierce daylight of the mind." He invokes the gods of Tartarus, Styx, and Tisiphone to advance an "unnatural wish." Oedipus, however, builds his case and the suspense for twenty more lines before he explicitly identifies his unnatural wish: namely, to have his two sons destroy each other. Oedipus pronounces this curse even though he realizes that it is evil. Like Achilles, Oedipus lives to regret his oath, which is completed only in book 11 when Polynices and Eteocles kill each other in a duel. Only then, too late, does Oedipus grieve and regret. As he does, he admits that mercy has entered his heart and declares that Nature has conquered him. The mention of mercy is a foreshadowing of the remarkable scene in book 12 of the Altar of Mercy at Athens, to which the Argive women go as suppliants. Tillyard calls the scene of the Altar of Mercy "probably the most famous and the most influential passage in Statius." Oedipus's address to Nature is also remarkable. This is the same *Natura* to whom the Argive women and Theseus appeal in book 12. C. S. Lewis, in *The Allegory of Love* (1936), traces in Statius a tendency to make the old Olympians mere figures of a specific trait (for example, Mars represents war) and to make abstractions, such as *Clementia, Pietas*, or *Virtus*, almost gods. The idea of *Natura*, for example, is both very Stoic and very medieval. It is a short step from here to allegory.

Another example of this tendency occurs directly as a result of Oedipus's curse in book 1. The Fury Tisiphone, who rises to fulfill the curse, while related to Vergil's and Seneca's Furies, is more allegory than snaky goddess. David Vessey says, "She has become a *figura* of violence and madness, a personification of *odium* and *furor*; she is an objectified embodiment of Oedipus's spiritual state." It was for such purposes that Statius reinstated the divine machinery which Lucan had banished from his epic. Tisiphone swoops down upon Thebes and stirs up discord, and the two sons of Oedipus are infected. Neither of the brothers is without guilt, as the short but skillful speech by an anonymous Theban makes clear, but Eteocles has more opportunity to do wrong and so appears more tyrannical.

In contrast to the violence, disorder, and darkness on Earth shines Jupiter's realm in Heaven. Jupiter, the supreme but not capricious ruler, states his conviction that not only Thebes but also Argos must be destroyed because of the misdeeds of their inhabitants. Juno objects, pleading for Argos in a polished rhetorical set piece. Vessey juxtaposes Jupiter's response here to his response to Bacchus in book 7. Vessey sees Jupiter as the administrator of Fate, a just and clement administrator. In the case of Thebes and Argos, however, the crimes of humankind demand retribution. Juno bows to Jupiter's dictates, as she does in the *Iliad*; thus, chaos on Earth is contrasted to the harmony and compliance in Heaven.

In book 1 of the *Iliad*, Homer shows men in council and gods in council; Statius gives an internalized or indirect picture of his two human protagonists, shows the gods in council, and continues the first book of his epic. Thus, the pattern of a debate in the Greek camp contrasted to a debate in Heaven is expanded and complicated. Book 1 of the *Thebaid* has a tripartite construction: Thebes, Heaven, Argos. After Jupiter's reinforcement of Oedipus's curse, the action turns to Polynices and his journey to Argos. This disenfranchised son is really no better than his brother Eteocles. He wishes not so much to excel in his own right as to humiliate his brother. He journeys to Argos through a storm that mirrors, as Tillyard points out, his internal state. Statius probably had in his mind two famous storms (*Aeneid*, book 1; *Bellum civile*, book 5); in turn, his storm probably inspired an episode in Spenser's *The Faerie Queen* (1590, 1596): Britomart's fight to gain entrance to a pigsty during a terrible storm resembles Polynices' fight with Tydeus when both arrive at Argos simultaneously.

Polynices and Tydeus fight before they speak. They are, as King Adrastus of Argos says, full of *furor*. They are in direct contrast to Adrastus, who stops their fight, predicting that a friendship may come from it. His prediction proves true: Polynices gives to Tydeus the affection more naturally owed to his brother. The two intruders, however, will change Adrastus more than he changes them. When they appear, Polynices is wearing a lion's skin, Tydeus a boar's. They are the boar and the lion who Apollo prophesied would wed Adrastus's daughters, and they bring Adrastus from his soft peace to the hardship and loss of war.

Much of the celebration with which book 1 ends is occupied with the praise of Apollo and Adrastus's telling of the myth of Coroebus, who appeases a god's anger by his *pietas* (dutifulness). Duff dismisses this myth as a digression, but Vessey rightly sees it as "symbolically related to the main themes of the whole *Thebais*." The king and his daughter, her disastrous union with a stranger, the Fury-like monster, the abandoned babe, Coroebus and his companion who set out to save their city—all these characters from the myth are types that appear elsewhere in the epic. Coroebus tells Apollo that he killed the god's monster because of his *pietas* and his "consciousness of right." Indeed, Coroebus is a symbol of *pietas*, governed by it as was pious Aeneas in Vergil's epic. Oedipus and his sons are impelled by the opposite emotion. The first word after the proem is *impia*; madness and hate replace *pietas* in Oedipus, Polynices, and Eteocles, and the results are violence and death for all surrounding them. It is a measure of Adrastus's failure that he dismisses the importance of Polynices' parentage. After telling the myth, he says to Polynices, "Cease to lament, or to recount the woes of thy fathers: in our house also hath there been many a fall from duty (*pietas*), but past error (*culpa*) binds not posterity." Here from Adrastus's own lips comes confirmation that Jupiter's damnation of Argos is just; the reader also sees how mistaken Adrastus is about the nature of error.

Book 1 of the *Thebaid* is a masterful beginning of an ambitious work. It sets in motion Oedipus's curse and Jupiter's decree, both of which are finally fulfilled with the deaths of Eteocles and Polynices in book 11. In book 1, the madness of impoverished Thebes is contrasted to the peace of luxurious Argos; later, the failings of both cities are apparent in comparison to Athens, just as the failings of Eteocles and Adrastus are more apparent in comparison to Athens's king, Theseus. Journeys, tyrants, city types, *pietas* or its lack—all these motifs establish parallels and contrasts between the first book of the *Thebaid* and the last, helping to unify the epic. Book 1 establishes the guilt and horror that will be expiated only in book 12. It contains a lengthy mythological digression which, like the later Hypsipyle episode, reinforces important themes. Book 1 also provides contrasting models of behavior, ruled respectively by *pietas* and by *furor*, demonstrating the strength of the one and the destructiveness of the other. With its rhetorical display, skillful descriptive passages, romance, and violence, the first book is representative of the craftsmanship of the whole *Thebaid*.

The most memorable passages of the *Thebaid* are unusual for their variety. Many of the finest passages are dramatic: the storm in book 1 which culminates in the fight between Polynices and Tydeus; the descent of Amphiareus alive into the underworld and his speech to the deities there; the deeds of Argia and Antigone in book 12, culminating in the cremation of Polynices with Eteocles, when even in death a double flame signals their continued hatred. There are critics who believe that some of Statius's dramatic passages are too extreme, going beyond good taste in their attempt to thrill the audience, such as Tydeus in book 8 gnawing on the head of his dead foe as he himself dies (an episode imitated by Dante in the *Inferno*). Other passages have been criticized for carrying realism to the point of absurdity, such as when Tiresias is so horrified by the visions he calls from the underworld that his hair stands on end, carrying his chaplet with it. More often, however, Statius is remembered for his fine descriptions of characters such as Tisiphone in book 1 and of places such as the abode of Mars in book 3. In contrast to the violence and horror of most of the *Thebaid*, two of Statius's most famous descriptions are of the Abode of Sleep in book 10 and the Altar of Mercy in book 12.

As a writer, Statius reflected his age. He borrowed extensively from his predecessors, Homer and Vergil, Ovid and Lucan. Statius was imbued with the rhetorical style and the Stoicism of the time. His *Thebaid* is cruel and violent but ends with *pietas* triumphing over wickedness. His *Silvae* provide a mirror of the people and places of the Flavian era. Statius excels at description, using any number of rhetorical or metrical tricks to achieve his end—often a scene of horror or pathos. Both his style and his stories are extreme, but he was admired from his own time through the medieval period and the Renaissance into the eighteenth century. A poet so admired by Chaucer and Dante well deserves the reconsideration he is beginning to receive.

Bibliography

Dominik, William J. *The Mythic Voice of Statius: Power and Politics in the "Thebaid."* New York: E. J. Brill, 1994. Examines in detail the thematic design of the *Thebaid* and explores the poem's political undercurrents.

_______. *Speech and Rhetoric in Statius's "Thebaid."* New York: Olms-Weidmann, 1994. Presents a critical analysis of the stylistic, narrative, and thematic functions of the characters' speeches in the *Thebaid*.

Geyssen, John W. *Imperial Panegyric in Statius: A Literary Commentary on Silvae*. New York: Peter Lang, 1996. Examines Statius as a panegyrist working within an accepted poetic tradition, focusing on the first of the *Silvae*.

Hardie, Alex. *Statius and the Silvae: Poets, Patrons, and Epideixis in the Graeco-Roman World*. Liverpool, England: Francis Cairns, 1983. Considers Statius's performance as a Latin poet against the context of contemporary social and literary history.

Vessey, David. *Statius and the "Thebaid."* Cambridge, England: Cambridge University Press, 1973. Provides a critical analysis and evaluation of Statius's epic, placing the work in its historical and literary context and surveying its form, style, and content.

_______, ed. *Statius: "Thebaid."* Translated by A. D. Melville. Oxford, England: Clarendon, 1992. Provides a general introduction to the *Thebaid* as well as a summary of the poem and a list of principal characters.

Elizabeth A. Holtze;
bibliography updated by William Nelles

Timothy Steele

Born: Burlington, Vermont; January 22, 1948

Principal poetry

Uncertainties and Rest, 1979
The Prudent Heart, 1983
Nine Poems, 1984
On Harmony, 1984
Short Subjects, 1985
Sapphics Against Anger and Other Poems, 1986
Beatitudes, 1988
The Color Wheel, 1994
Sapphics and Uncertainties: Poems, 1970-1986, 1995

Other literary forms

Although Timothy Steele rarely reviews books, he is one of the leading prosodists of his generation. In *Missing Measures: Modern Poetry and the Revolt Against Meter* (1990) Steele discusses the flawed historical assumptions behind much of the modernist poetry. His knowledge of both classical and romance languages and literature serves him well here. In a quote for the book, X. J. Kennedy writes that "Steele's arguments strike me as so forceful, so well thought through, that anyone who assails them will find the going difficult." This has proven all too true as the critical establishment has found it in its own best interests to ignore Steele's argument rather than attempt its refutation.

Steele has also published a book of prosody, *All the Fun's in How You Say a Thing* (1999), which not only is a good introduction to poetics but also helps dispel many modernist assumptions. He makes an excellent case that, regardless of T. S. Eliot's contentions, the iambic measure is alive because of variations within the meter rather than those caused by the breaking of the meter. In addition, Steele makes a persuasive argument for the near nonexistence of the Pyrrhus and spondee in English language poetry.

Achievements

Timothy Steele is probably the leading poet-scholar of the New Formalist movement, though he is not its best-known exponent. He is a modest man of very little self-promotion, but the learning displayed in *Missing Measures* shows him to be a scholar of the first rank.

Nonetheless, his poetry has received considerable attention. Steele is the recipient of a Guggenheim Fellowship, the Peter I. B. Lavan Younger Poet Award of the Academy of American Poets, the Commonwealth Club of California Medal for Poetry, the Los Angeles PEN Center Literary Award for Poetry, a California Arts Council Grant, and the California State University, Los Angeles, Outstanding Professor Award in 1992 and the school's President's Distinguished Professor Award in 1998-1999.

Biography

Timothy Reid Steele was born in Burlington, Vermont, in 1948 to Edward William Steele, a teacher, and Ruth Reid Steele, a nurse. His New England upbringing is readily apparent in many of his poems, despite the fact that he has spent most of his writing life far removed from the Northeast, though Southern California, where Steele lived for several years, plays a prominent role in his writing.

Steele left Vermont to study at Stanford University, earning his B.A. in 1970. It was at Stanford that Steele came under the influence of Yvor Winters, who reinforced his formalist inclinations. Returning to New England for graduate work at Brandeis, Steele worked with another important Formalist-scholar, J. V. Cunningham. Cunningham's concision and love for the epigram show a real influence on Steele's development, though Steele's dissertation at Brandeis was on the history and conventions of detective fiction. He was awarded his Ph.D. from Brandeis in 1977. He offered to take over *Counter/ Measures*, a magazine published by X. J. and Dorothy Kennedy, which was one of the few periodicals in the country publishing formal verse at the time and was going out of business. Kennedy urged Steele to instead concentrate on his own work.

While working on his dissertation, Steele crossed the country yet again, returning to Stanford as Jones Lecturer in Poetry from 1975 to 1977. Upon completion of his Ph.D., he assumed a lectureship in English at the University of California, Los Angeles (UCLA) until 1983; in 1979, he married Victoria Lee Erpelding, a librarian of rare books at UCLA, and published his first full-length collection, *Uncertainties and Rest* from Louisiana State University Press, which was a strong debut but attracted little attention. In 1986 Steele took a one-year position as lecturer in English at the University of California at Santa Barbara and published his second collection, *Sapphics Against Anger and Other Poems*; this collection received much more attention than the first, partly because it was from a major publisher, Random House. In 1987, he became professor of English at California State University, Los Angeles, eventually becoming one of the school's most distinguished and honored professors.

In 1990, Steele published one of the major critical works of the late twentieth century, *Missing Measures*. Steele examines the critical and historical assumptions of modernism and finds them flawed; classic, medieval, and Renaissance texts were mistakenly conflated, leading to major misunderstandings in scholarship. One particular strand he traces shows how the words "poetry" and "verse" came to be construed as meaning different things; he also traces the dangers inherent in modernism's fascination with poetry as music. Overall, Steele makes a sustained argument that modernism is a failed revolution that has resulted not in new forms but in the formlessness and inwardness plaguing much poetry today, particularly academic poetry. Steele's wide reading and facility in several languages reveal a first-rate critical mind at work.

In 1994 Steele published his next full-length collection, *The Color Wheel*, from the Johns Hopkins University Press; the following year, University of Arkansas Press brought out *Sapphics and Uncertainties: Poems, 1970-1986*, a compilation of Steele's first two books. In 1997, Steele edited *The Poems of J. V. Cunningham*, an impressive work of scholarship whose notes and comments threaten to dwarf the rather slender body of poetry. In 1999 Steele published a book of prosody, *All the Fun's in How You Say a Thing*, the title of which was taken from a poem of Robert Frost.

Analysis

Timothy Steele is the most formal of the major poets associated with New Formalism. While rhyme and meter are common to these poets, Steele works in more ornate stanzaic patterns than most of his contemporaries. Many New Formalists prefer the term Expansive poetry, because a return to storytelling is emphasized as much as a return to traditional forms. Steele, however, seems strictly a lyric poet, more likely to write an epigram than an epic.

Uncertainties and Rest

The wonder of Steele's first collection, *Uncertainties and Rest*, is not how little attention it received at its time of publication despite its quality but the fact that it was published at all. It was the first book of formal verse to be published by a national press for anyone of Steele's generation. By the time other New Formalists were publishing their first books in the mid-1980's, Steele was publishing his second.

The tone of *Uncertainties and Rest*, its title a subtle reference to meter, can be uneven at times, but what comes through clearly is a formally trained voice dealing with matters of the moment. The Kansas in "Over the Rainbow" is not the Kansas of Judy Garland: "At the weigh stations,/ The trucks rev up. All roads and cultures end/ In time and space, and all destinations/ In mere convenience." Then there is the country bar in the Everglades where "At ten of eight, two whores in fine array/ Arrive, and the farmhands start closing in," from "Two for the Road." However, such gritty, slightly tawdry realism does not dominate the volume, and it all but disappears from Steele's subsequent poetry. There are several poems of family and youth here, and from the beginning Steele has displayed a finely tuned eye for the natural world.

There are also some strong love lyrics here, probably representing some of the later work in the collection, an example of which is "Last Night as You Slept":

> The clock's dial a luminous two-ten,
> Its faint glow on pillow and sheet,
> I woke—and the good fatigue and heat
> We'd shared were gone.

Steele also includes epigrams, one of which has been widely anthologized: "Here lies Sir Tact, a diplomatic fellow/ Whose silence was not golden, but just yellow."

Sapphics Against Anger and Other Poems

Choosing "Sapphics Against Anger" as the title poem was appropriate for Steele in at least two ways. For one, the mention of a classical form, of which W. H.

Auden was a master, announces that this is a book of formal concerns. Second, it speaks for the spirit of the poems wherein the voice is restrained and often praiseful; indeed, the title poem ends,

> For what is, after all, the good life save that
> Conducted thoughtfully, and what is passion
> If not the holiest of powers, sustaining
> Only if mastered.

Such might be taken as a good synopsis of Steele's aesthetic. In "The Sheets" the speaker ponders the clean laundry on the line, which leads to biographer Giorgio Vasari's tale of Leonardo's buying caged birds and setting them free and on to a childhood memory. "Near Olympic" describes an ethnically mixed neighborhood in West Los Angeles in great detail through the use of rhymed couplets. Despite the use of a form most prominent in the eighteenth century, there is nothing artificial in Steele's use of the measure, nor is the poem in any way condescending to its subject matter. The poem is composed in such a loving fashion as to say these nameless people matter.

"Timothy" calls attention to the fact that the poet shares a name with the hay he's mowing: "And I took pleasure in the thought/ The fresh hay's name was mine as well." This close identification reaches a moment of epiphany at the end of the poem. Work done,

> . . . the grass, which seemed a thing
> In which the lonely and concealed
> Had risen from its sorrowing
> And flourished in the open field.

There are also poems from a general history as well as a personal one: among others, "The Wartburg, 1521-22," Wartburg being where Martin Luther hid after the Diet of Worms, which marks the role one man played in the formation of the modern religious consciousness. When Luther at last leaves, "His mount's as humble as the mount of Christ" and "above the Schloss,/ A widening band of chimney smoke is curled/ Vaguely downward, toward the modern world."

More and more in *Sapphics Against Anger and Other Poems*, the California landscape starts to demand equal time with that of New England; Steele seems more and more transplanted rather than transported. While still a New Englander, he sees much to praise in the tropical abundance of Southern California.

The Color Wheel

While one could see considerable development between *Uncertainties and Rest* and *Sapphics Against Anger and Other Poems*, the progression from *Sapphics* to *The Color Wheel* (1994) seems much less pronounced. This is, to some extent, to be expected, a matter of a poet hitting his stride in his maturity. Steele has not taken the next step to greatness in this collection, but it does confirm him as one of the best and most skillful contemporary poets.

Mixed in with New England memories of childhood are poems distinctly displaying lives of Southern Californians: Steele's eighty-two-year-old neighbor to whom he brings flowers ("Fae"), the forty-two-year-old punch-drunk failed boxer ("Cory in April"). Civilization as something precious and fragile is a continued theme in Steele's work, notably here in "The Library." The speaker wants a tidy metaphor but rejects its easiness: "I could construct a weighty paradigm,/ The Library as Mind. It's somehow truer/ To recollect details of closing time." After further meditation, the speaker leaves the library and notes how "The squirrel creeps, nosing round, compelled to hoard/ By instinct, habit and necessity." Once again the reader is made aware of the closeness of the human and the natural world in many of Steele's poems.

Few, if any, other poets could write a poem with a title such as "Beatitudes, While Setting Out the Trash" and make it believable. Steele does, partly through the grace of his versification and partly through humor: "A squirrel on the lawn rears and inspects/ A berry in its paws and seems to hold/ The pose of a Tyrannosaurus Rex." The speaker, after putting the trash on the curb, sticks his hands into his sweatshirt pockets and refers to himself as a "mammal cousin of the kangaroo" and closes the poem describing a bird:

> He grooms, by nuzzling, a raised underwing;
> He shakes and sends a shiver through his breast,
> As if, from where he perches, counseling
> That *Blessed are the meek*, for they are blest.

From poems such as this, Timothy Steele has taken his place not only as the craftsman of his generation of poets but also as its chief envoy of sanity and demeanor.

Other major works

nonfiction: *Missing Measures: Modern Poetry and the Revolt Against Meter*, 1990; *All the Fun's in How You Say a Thing*, 1999.

edited texts: *The Music of His History: Poems for Charles Gullens on His Sixtieth Birthday*, 1989; *The Poems of J. V. Cunningham*, 1997.

Bibliography

Crosscurrents: A Quarterly 8, no. 2. Special issue titled "Expansionist Poetry: The New Formalism and the New Narrative." This groundbreaking issue on the Expansive movement includes many essays essential to understanding that movement and Steele. Steele contributes two poems, "Decisions, Decisions" and "Practice," while taking part in the symposium that forms the center of the issue. A good format to sense Steele's interactions with his peers in the movement.

Feirstein, Frederick, ed. *Expansive Poetry: Essays on the New Narrative and the New Formalism*. Ashland, Oreg.: Story Line Press, 1989. Collection includes Steele's essay "Tradition and Revolution: The Modern Movement and Free Verse," which is an excellent telescoping of the larger argument Steele makes in *Missing Measures*. This collection also includes other perspectives on the New Formalist movement, many of which offer insight into poet Dana Gioia's aesthetic.

McPhillips, Robert. "Reading the New Formalists." In *Poetry After Modernism*, edited by Robert McDowell. Ashland, Oreg.: Story Line Press, 1991. McPhillips deals with several New Formalist poets, prominently featuring Steele, and their relationships to each other and to their craft. This volume is also helpful as a general guide to the New Formalist movement, of which Steele is a prominent practitioner.

Steele, Timothy. "Timothy Steele: An Interview." Interview by Kevin Walzer. *Edge City Review* 2, no. 2 (1996). An in-depth interview with Steele covering his career through 1995. Steele comments on his influences, criticisms of *Missing Measures*, and on New Formalism in general.

_______. "Timothy Steele Interview." Interview by Cynthia Haven. *The Cortland Review*, June 15, 2001. http://www.cortlandreview.com/features/00/06/. In an interview, Steele touches on metrical poetry, New Formalism, and Walt Whitman, with an emphasis on his desire to keep the metrical tradition alive and understandable to new readers.

Robert Darling

Gertrude Stein

Born: Allegheny, Pennsylvania; February 3, 1874
Died: Neuilly-sur-Seine, France; July 27, 1946

Principal poetry

Tender Buttons: Objects, Food, Rooms, 1914
Geography and Plays, 1922
Before the Flowers of Friendship Faded Friendship Faded, 1931
Two (Hitherto Unpublished) Poems, 1948
Bee Time Vine and Other Pieces, 1913-1927, 1953
Stanzas in Meditation and Other Poems, 1929-1933, 1956

Other literary forms

Most of Gertrude Stein's works did not appear until much later than the dates of their completion; the plays and theoretical writings in the following partial list bear the dates of composition rather than of publication. Much of her writing, including novelettes, shorter poems, plays, prayers, novels, and several portraits, appeared posthumously, as did the last two books of poetry noted above, in the Yale Edition of the Unpublished Writings of Gertrude Stein, in eight volumes edited by Carl Van Vechten. A few of her plays have been set to music, the operas have been performed, and the later children's books have been illustrated by various artists. No recent complete bibliographical listing of her complete works exists, nor does one of scholarly articles about her, except as appendices to major studies, notably by Richard Bridgman and Michael J. Hoffman.

Achievements

Gertrude Stein did not win tangible recognition for her literary achievements, though she did earn the Medal of French Recognition from the French government for services during World War II. Nevertheless, her contribution to art, and specifically to writing, is as great as that of Ezra Pound or James Joyce. It is, however, diametrically opposed to that of these figures in style, content, and underlying philosophy of literature. She advanced mimetic representation to its ultimate, doing away progressively with memory, narration, plot, the strictures of formalized language, and the distinction among styles and genres. Her view of life was founded upon a sense of the living present that shunned all theorizing about meaning and purpose, making writing a supreme experience unto itself. For the first fifteen years of her artistic life, she worked at her craft with stubborn persistence while carrying on an active social life among the Parisian avant-garde. She became influential as a person of definite taste and idiosyncratic manners rather than as an artist in her own right. Her parlor became legend, and writers as diverse as Ernest Hemingway and Sherwood Anderson profited from her ideas. In the 1920's she was the matron of the American expatriates, and her work, by then known to most writers, was either ferociously derided or enthusiastically applauded.

It was the poetry of *Tender Buttons* that first brought Gertrude Stein to the attention of the public, though after 1926, novels, critical essays, and prose portraits increasingly circulated. She secured a place in American letters with the publication of *The Autobiography of Alice B. Toklas* (1933), which was also a commercial success. She did not receive any official recognition during her lifetime, except as a curiosity in the world of letters.

Literary criticism has traditionally simply skirted the "problem" of Gertrude Stein, limiting itself to broad generalizations. There exists a group of Stein devotees responsible for preserving the texts; this group includes Robert Bartlett Haas, Carl Van Vechten, Donald Gallup, and Leon Katz. Stein's work has been illuminated by two indispensable scholar-critics, Richard Bridgman and Donald Sutherland; and there are useful interpretive suggestions in studies by Rosalind Miller, Allegra Stewart, Norman Weinstein, and Michael J. Hoffman. Stein's major impact has been upon writers of later generations, especially in the late 1950's, through the 1960's, and up to the present time; the poetry of Aram Saroyan, Robert Kelly, Clark Coolidge, Jerome Rothenberg, and Lewis Welch is especially indebted to Stein. New insights into this revolutionary writer in the wake of global revisions of the notion of writing and critical thinking have been offered in short pieces by S. C. Neuman, William H. Gass, and Neil Schmitz. Today, a place of eminence is accorded to Stein's fairy tales and children's stories, the theoretical writings, the major works *The Autobiography of Alice B. Toklas* and *The Making of Americans*, the shorter works *Three Lives* and *Ida, a Novel*, and finally *Tender Buttons*, considered by many to be a masterpiece of twentieth century literature.

Biography

Gertrude Stein was born in Allegheny, Pennsylvania, on February 3, 1874. Her grandfather, Michael Stein, came from Austria in 1841, married Hanna Seliger, and settled in Baltimore. One of his sons, Daniel, Gertrude's father, was in the wholesale wool and clothing industry. Daniel was mildly successful and very temperamental. He married Amelia Keyser in 1864, and had five children, Michael (born in 1865), Simon (1867), Bertha

Gertrude Stein (Library of Congress)

(1870), Leo (1872), and Gertrude (1874). In 1875, the family moved to Vienna, and three years later Daniel returned to the United States, leaving his family for a one-year stay in Paris. In 1879, the family moved back to the United States and spent a year in Baltimore with Amelia Keyser's family. In 1880, Daniel found work in California, and the family relocated again, in Oakland. Memories of these early moves would dot Gertrude's mature works. Leo and Gertrude found that they had much in common, took drawing and music lessons together, frequented the Oakland and San Francisco public libraries, and had time to devote to their intellectual and aesthetic interests. When in 1888 their mother died of cancer, Leo and Gertrude found themselves more and more detached from the rest of the family. In 1892, Daniel Stein died and the eldest son, Michael, took the family back to Baltimore; but the Steins began to scatter. In 1892 Leo entered Harvard, while Gertrude and Bertha stayed with their aunt, Fannie Bachrach. Michael, always patriarchal and the image of stability, married Sarah Samuels and later moved to Paris, where he became a respected member of the intellectual elite, maintaining a Saturday night open house at their apartment in rue Madame. Matisse's portrait of Michael is now in San Francisco.

Gertrude was a cuddled and protected child. At sixteen she weighed 135 pounds and later in college she hired a boy to box with her every day to help her reduce. Her niece, Gertrude Stein Raffel, recalls that her heaviness "was not unbecoming. She was round, roly-poly, and angelic looking." During her adolescent years she became very introspective and critical, and was often depressed and concerned with death. Already emotionally independent, owing to her mother's protracted invalidism and her father's neglect and false representation of authority, Gertrude saw in her brother Leo her only friend. Their bond would not be broken for another twenty years, and she would follow him everywhere, the two delving into matters of mutual interest.

In 1893, Gertrude Stein entered the Harvard Annex, renamed Radcliffe College the following year. She gravitated toward philosophy and psychology, and took courses with such luminaries as George Santayana, Josiah Royce, Herbert Palmer, and William James. In 1894 she worked in the Harvard Psychological Laboratory with Hugo Münsterberg. Her interest in psychology expanded and in 1896 she published, together with Leon Solomons, a paper on "Normal Motor Automatism" which appeared in the *Psychological Review.* A second article "Cultivated Motor Automatism," appeared two years later. In 1897, Gertrude followed her brother to The Johns Hopkins University and began the study of medicine. She specialized in brain research and was encouraged to continue, even though by 1901 her dedication had waned. She attempted four examinations, failed them, and withdrew without a degree.

In 1902 Gertrude traveled, first to Italy, then to London, where she met Bertrand Russell. She spent much time in the British Museum Library studying the Elizabethans, especially William Shakespeare. In the meantime, Leo also abandoned his studies, reverting to an earlier passion for history. A specialist in Renaissance costume, he was drawn to contemporary art, and when, in 1904, he and Gertrude saw a Paul Cézanne exhibit in Florence, they started buying paintings; Leo became a major collector of Henri Matisse. The two settled in the now-famous apartment at 27 rue de Fleurus, where Gertrude Stein's literary career began, though her first sustained effort, *Q.E.D.*, written in 1903, would remain unpublished until 1950 (as *Things as They Are*). In 1905, while working on a translation of Gustave Flaubert's *Trois contes*, she wrote *Three Lives*. During that period she met Pablo Picasso, who would be very influential in her thinking about art, and with whom she would remain friends for decades. The following year he painted the famous portrait now at the Metropolitan Museum. These days of intense work and thinking saw Gertrude Stein fast at work on her first major long novel, *The Making of Americans*, which she completed in 1910.

Her trips abroad and throughout France from the home base in Paris became an essential part of her existence. In 1907 her brother Michael introduced Gertrude to Alice B. Toklas, who soon became her secretary, going to work on the proofs of *Three Lives*. Alice learned to use a typewriter and the following year, in Fiesole, Italy, she began to copy parts of the manuscript of *The Making of Americans*. Leo, intellectually independent, was moving toward his own aesthetic, though he was still busy promoting new American and French talents.

As a painter Leo was not successful, and he came eventually to dislike all contemporary painters except the Cubists. In 1913 he moved from the rue de Fleurus apartment, and with him went all of the Renoirs and most of the Matisses and Cézannes, while Gertrude kept the Picassos. Leo's place had been taken by Alice, who stayed with Gertrude until her death in 1946.

The writer first began to be noticed as a result of Alfred Stieglitz's publication of her "portraits" of Matisse and Picasso in *Camera Work* in 1912. That year she spent the summer in Spain, capturing the sense of her idea of the relationship between object and space, with which she had been struggling. Here she began the prose poem *Tender Buttons*, which brought her to the attention of most of her contemporaries, eliciting varying reactions. She continued to write "portraits" while visiting Mabel Dodge in Florence, at the Villa Curonia. At the Armory Show in New York in 1913, Gertrude was responsible for the presentation of the Pablo Picasso exhibit. When the war broke out, she was in London, where she met the philosopher Alfred North Whitehead. She continued to work intensely, mostly on poetry and plays, and visited Barcelona and Palma de Majorca. In 1916 Gertrude and Alice returned to France and the next year did voluntary war relief work in the South. In 1922 she was awarded a "Medaille de la Reconnaissance Française."

With the appearance of her first collected volume, *Geography and Plays*, in 1922, her fame among the cognoscenti was assured, together with a lively controversy over her truly original style. She was invariably visited by the younger expatriate artists from the United States, and her parlor became a focal point for the exchange of ideas. Sherwood Anderson introduced her to Hemingway in 1922, and the younger writer learned much from her about the craft of writing. Hemingway was influential in securing publication of parts of *The Making of Americans* in Ford Maddox Ford's magazine, *Transatlantic Review.* (The nine-hundred-page work was later abridged to half its size by her translator into French, and the shorter version was published in 1925 by Contact Editions, Paris.) Her relationship with Hemingway, however, because of conflicting temperaments, was short-lived; their friendship soon degenerated into bickering.

Gertrude Stein entered another phase of her life when she was asked to lecture in Oxford and Cambridge in 1926. The text of the conference, titled "Composition as Explanation," constituted her first critical statement on the art of writing; she subsequently returned to a personal exposition of her ideas in *How to Write* (1931), breaking new ground at the stylistic level. This period of major intellectual and thematic upheaval witnessed several transformations in her art. She began to devote more time to the theater, and eventually tackled the difficult task of writing about ideas in the little known *Stanzas in Meditation and Other Poems* (written between 1929 and 1933 but not published until 1956). In 1929 she left Paris and moved to Bilignin. Her *Lucy Church Amiably* (written in 1927) had not pleased her, but *Four Saints in Three Acts* (pr., pb. 1934), with music by Virgil Thomson, was successfully produced in New York. After publication of the well-received *The Autobiography of Alice B. Toklas* (1933), she traveled to America for a lecture tour. Her *Lectures in America* (1935) dealt with her philosophy of composition.

Compelled to close her apartment at rue de Fleurus shortly after her return to France, Gertrude moved with Alice to rue Christine; with the onset of the war in 1939, however, they returned to Bilignin. During the war, the two women lived for a time in Culoz, where they first witnessed the German occupation and then the arrival of the Americans, which would be experiences recounted in *Wars I Have Seen* (1945). In December, 1944, she returned to Paris, only to leave soon afterward to entertain American troops stationed in occupied Germany. Her views on the American soldier and the society that produced him changed considerably during these two years. In October, 1945, she traveled to Brussels to lecture. Weary and tired, she decided to visit her friend Bernard Fay in the country. Her trip was abruptly interrupted by her illness and she entered the American Hospital in Neuilly-sur-Seine, where, after an unsuccessful cancer operation, she died on July 27, 1946.

Analysis

It is customary to refer to Gertrude Stein's poetry—and her work in general—with the qualifiers "abstract," "repetitive," and "nonsensical," terms which, in view of the predominance of multilayered levels of signification in twentieth century art, do little if any justice to a most remarkable literary achievement. The proper evaluation of Stein's work requires a willingness to rethink certain basic notions concerning art, discourse, and life, a task that is perhaps as difficult as the reading of Stein's voluminous production itself. Her work, however, is really not excessively abstract, especially when one considers that her poetic rests upon the fundamental axiom of "immediate existing." Nothing could be more concrete than that. Whatever she may be describing, each unit is sure to be a complete, separate assertion, a reality immediately given—in the present, the only time there is.

Repetition is insistence: A rose is a rose is a rose is a rose. Each time it is new, different, unique, because the experience of the word is unique each time it is uttered. Stylistically, this entails the predominance of parataxis and asyndeton, words being "so nextily" in their unfolding. Repetition of the *same* is often supplanted by repetition of the *different*, where the juxtaposition is in kind and quality. An example of the latter is the following passage from *A Long Gay Book* (1932):

> All the pudding has the same flow and the sauce is painful, the tunes are played, the crinkling paper is burning, the pot has cover and the standard is excellence.

Whether operating at the syntagmatic or at the paradigmatic level, as above, the repetition serves the purpose of emphasizing and isolating *a* thing, not simply *anything*. The break with all previous associations forces one to consider *this* pudding and *this* sauce, allowing a concretization of the experience in *this* particular frame of the present. If the content appears to have no "logical" coherence, it is because it is not meant to, since the experience of the immediate does not warrant ratiocination or understanding of any sort. Art in Gertrude Stein is perception of the immediate, a capturing of the instantaneity of the word as event, sense, or object. The notion is clearly nonreferential in that art does not need a world to know that it exists. Although it occasionally refers to it, it does not *have* to—in fact, the less it does, the better. What is of paramount importance is that this self-contained entity comes alive in the continuous present of one's experience of it, and only then. The influence of Stein's painter friends was unequivocal. Not all discourse that links the work of art to history and other realms of life is, properly speaking, a preoccupation of the artist: It does not constitute an aesthetic experience, remaining just that—criticism, sociology, and philosophy. Meaning is something that comes after the experience, thanks to reflection, to the mediation of reason, and the standardization of logic and grammar; it is never given in the immediacy of the poetic expression. Gertrude Stein's writings attempt to produce the feeling of something happening or being lived—in short, to give things (objects, emotions, ideas, words) a *sense* that is new and unique and momentary, independent and defiant of what an afterthought may claim to be the "true" meaning or sense of an experience or artistic event. From this perspective, can it still be honestly said that Stein's work is "nonsense," with all the negative implications usually associated with the epithet?

Things as They Are

Gertrude Stein had from very early in her career a keen sense of the distance that naturally exists between objects and feelings as perceived, and their transposition into conventional formalized speech. Her first novel, *Q.E.D.* (for the Latin *quod erat demonstrandum*, meaning "which was to be proved"), written in 1903 and known after 1950 as *Things as They Are*, while it dealt with the then taboo topic of lesbianism in a *ménage à trois* of three women, is already shorn of such typical narrative features as symbolism, character development, climax, and descriptions of setting, though it is cast in an intelligible variation of standard prose. At the limits of the Jamesian novel, what happens among the characters and the space of emotional relatedness is more important than the characters as characters. The focal point is the introspection of these human natures, and all elaborations and complications of feelings remain internal, intimate, within the consciousness of the individual being described or, most often, within the dialectic of the relationship. Doing away with all contingent background material meant zooming in on the poetic process itself; but for all practical purposes the author is still struggling within the precincts of the most sophisticated naturalism: She is still representing, in the tradition of Henry James and Gustave Flaubert, two authors whom she admired greatly. The characters are at odds with the author: They are white American college women constantly preoccupied with the propriety of their relationship and therefore demand of the author a polite, cultivated, and literary realization.

Three Lives

The problem of the language to employ in writing is dealt with in the next work, *Three Lives*, where the progressive abandonment of inherited expressive forms is much stronger and can be said to constitute a first milestone in Gertrude Stein's stylistic development, especially in "Melanchta," the last of the three stories. Here Stein describes a love story set among lower-class blacks where she can explore the intensity of "uneducated" speech and where, as Donald Sutherland quite aptly points out, there exists "a direct relationship between feeling and word." Typical of her entire literary career, at the time of publication the printer inquired whether the author really knew English! In *Three Lives*, Stein was "groping for a continuous present and for using everything again and again." This continuous present is immediate and partakes of the human mind as it exists at any given moment when confronted with the object of writing. It is different from the prolonged present of duration, as in Henri Bergson, where aspects of human nature may enter. At the stylistic level, punctuation is rare and the present participle is employed as a substantive for its value in retaining the sense of process, of continuity in a present mode that knows no before and no after. This "subjective time" of writing is paralleled by similar developments in the visual and plastic arts, from which Stein drew copiously. Her admiration and appreciation of what Cézanne had done for painting was matched by the unrelenting support that she bestowed upon the upcoming younger generation of artists, such as Picasso, Matisse, Juan Gris, and Francis Picabia. Cézanne had taught her that there are no less important areas on a canvas *vis à vis* the theme or figure that traditionally dominated representational painting, and he returned to "basics," such as color, tone, distribution, and the underlying abstractions, reaching out for those essentials in the welter of external detail in order to capture a sense without which there would be no painting. Picasso went even further, forsaking three-dimensional composition for the surface purity of plane geometry, ushering in Cubism. For Stein, perception takes place against the tabula rasa of immediate consciousness, and Cubism offered the flatness of an interior time which could be brought to absolute elementalism, simplicity, and finality.

Tender Buttons

Things as They Are and *Three Lives*, for all their stylistic experimentation, are clearly works of prose. In *Tender Buttons*, however, Stein blurs the distinction between prose and poetry. She works with "meaningless" babble, puns, games, rhymes, and repetitions. Much as in Lewis Carroll and Tristam Tzara, the word itself is seen as magic. In a world of pure existence, dialogue disappears, replaced by word lists and one-word utterances. Interactions of characters are no longer tenable, and people give way to objects. The portrait is supplanted by the still life, and the technique of composition is reminiscent of Picasso's collages, *not* of automatic writing. The intention seems to be to give the work its autonomy independent of both writer and reader: One sees and reads what one sees and reads, the rest being reconstruction from memory or projections of the viewer's intellect. The effort is ambitious: to see language being born. Disparate critical ideas have been invoked to "interpret" *Tender Buttons*, and it is likely that Norman Weinstein (*Gertrude Stein and the Literature of Modern Consciousness*, 1970), comes closest when he summons the studies of Jean Piaget, the Sapir-Whorf language hypothesis, R. D. Laing, and the dimension of schizophrenia. On the opposite bank, Allegra Stewart (*Gertrude Stein and the Present*, 1967) reads the work as a Jungian mandala and relates the alchemical correspondences to all of the literary movements of the epoch, such as Dada, Futurism, and so on.

"A jack in kill her, a jack in, makes a meadowed king, makes a to let." The plastic use of language permits the bypassing of the rule where, for example, a substantive is the object of a preposition. The infinitive "to let" appears as the object of a verb and is modified by the indefinite article "a." If analysis emphasizes the dislocation, the derangement, of standard usage, suggesting that alternative modes of expression are possible and even revealing, no matter how unwieldly, it should also note the foregrounding of "events" in an atemporal framework, where even nouns are objects that do not need the passing of ages to be what they are. Sense, if not altogether certain meanings, can be obtained only in the suspended perception of the reading, especially aloud.

This effort to see and write in the "continuous present" requires, Stein said, a passionate identification with the thing to be described: A steady, trance-like concentration upon the object will first of all divest it of all its customary appellations and then permit the issuing forth of words and structures that alone can speak as *that* thing in front of the observer.

"Poetry and Grammar"

In "Poetry and Grammar" (1935), Stein says: "Poetry is concerned with using with abusing, with losing with wanting, with denying with avoiding with adoring with replacing the noun. . . . Poetry is doing nothing but using losing refusing and pleasing and betraying and caressing nouns." In this spirit of reevaluation of the nature and process of naming things she will then go all out in making sure that the things she looks at will by themselves elicit the way they are to be called, never being for a moment worried that such a process may be at odds with the limited range of possibilities offered by conventional reality; she did not only want to rename things, but to "find out how to know that they were there by their names or by replacing their names." As Shakespeare had done in Arden, the goal was to create "a forest without mentioning the things that make a forest."

With this new discovery, for the ensuing twenty years she kept busy revisiting timeworn forms and models of poetic expression, charging them with fresh blood and impetus. The underlying magic would be constant: "looking at anything until something that was not the name of that thing but was in a way that actual thing would come to be written." This process was possible because Stein had arrived at a particular conception of the essence of language: It is not "imitation either of sounds or colors or emotions," but fundamentally an "intellectual recreation." The problem of mimesis and representation was forever behind her, and the idea of *play* became fundamental in her work.

1920's and 1930's

The third stage of Stein's poetry came in the late 1920's and early 1930's, at a time when she was both very happy at receiving some recognition, and much depressed about some new problems of her craft. Of the three materials that she felt art had to deal with, sight, sound, and sense, corresponding to the spatial, the temporal, and the conceptual dimensions of the mind, she had up to then worked intensely on the first two, relegating the third to the background by ignoring it or by simply rejecting it as a response to conventional grammatical and logical sense. At times, she handled the problem of sense by mediating it through her theoretical writings, especially after 1925.

With the ending of the Roaring Twenties, however, much of the spatiality in literature also disappeared. Painting became intellectual, poets became religious or political, and the newer waves did not seem to hold much promise. Stein had also reached a conclusion concerning works of art: that there are no masterpieces containing ideas; in philosophy, there are no masterpieces. Ideas and philosophy require almost by definition a mediated, sequential array of items over time and in history, ideas being *about* something or other. For a poetic of the unique, concrete thing—again, against all claims that Stein's is a poetic of the abstract—the task of dealing with ideas, which are by nature abstract, posed no small problem. Still, owing also to her attention to religious thought and the artistic implications of meditation, communion, trance, and revelation, she felt the need to come to terms with this hitherto untrodden ground.

Stanzas in Meditation

Stein set about writing a poem of ideas without all of the historical and philosophical underpinnings and referents that accompany works such as Ezra Pound's *The Cantos* (1925-1972) and T. S. Eliot's *The Waste Land* (1922). True to the credo that art is immanent and immediate, she wrote *Stanzas in Meditation*, a long poem made up of five parts and running to 163 stanzas, some a line long, others extending over several pages.

Remarkably little has been written about this forgotten but truly major composition, for the difficulty once again is the unpreparedness of criticism to deal with another of Stein's innovations: Instead of writing *about* ideas, she writes *the* ideas: Thinking, in other words, does not occur in the mind *after* reading the words on the page, but the words themselves *are* the ideas, making ideas partake of the human mind instead of human nature. The old reliable technique of stopping the momentous thoughts on the page as consciousness becomes aware of them creates once again the typical situation with Stein's art: One experiences ideas as one reads; one cannot lean back and expect to put together a "coherent" whole. There are in fact no philosophical terms in the traditional sense and no organization as such. Norman Weinstein writes that "The poem is not *about* philosophy, but *is* philosophy set into motion by verbal action." The disembodied, fragmentary, and discontinuous vision of the Cubists is here interweaved with the process-philosophy of William James and Alfred North Whitehead. Stylistically, each line tends to be objective and stable and corresponds to what in prose is the sentence. As the lines build up into a stanza, they swell with tension, and, like the paragraph, constitute a specific unit of attention. The poem will occasionally evidence images and allow symbols, but these are accidental, perhaps because the idea itself can best or only be expressed in that particular fashion. According to Sutherland, the poem can be entered in a tradition that lists Plato, Pindar, the English Metaphysicals, and Gerard Manley Hopkins. The poem can be read by simply beginning at random, which is perhaps the best way for the uninitiated to get a "sense" of it and familiarize themselves with the tone, lyricism, and surprisingly deceiving content. The technique of repetition is still present, revealing new contexts for given words, and Stein coins new expressions for ancient truisms. The text is a gold mine of brilliant aphorisms: "There is no hope or use in all," or "That which they like they knew."

The Autobiography of Alice B. Toklas

Between the time of the appearance of *The Autobiography of Alice B. Toklas* (1933) and the publication, shortly before her death, of *The Gertrude Stein First Reader and Three Plays* (1946), thirteen other books came out, among which were the highly successful and important *The Geographical History of America* (1936) and *Everybody's Autobiography* (1937). During these years Stein's major efforts were directed to the problem of self-presentation and the formal structure of autobiography. She put the writer on the same ground as the reader, ending the privileged position of both biographer and autobiographer. She continued to elaborate the poetic of impersonal, timeless, and spaceless writing, assuring that experience, flow, and place remain within the confines of the continuous present of perception. Her poetry during this period was chiefly written for children, rhymed and chanted and playful, with no pretense at being anything more than a momentary flash in the continuum of life, a diversion, a game. Many of these works were published either as limited editions or posthumously in the Yale Edition of her uncollected writings, where they can now be read in chronological sequence.

Other major works

LONG FICTION: *Three Lives*, 1909; *The Making of Americans*, 1925; *Lucy Church Amiably*, 1930; *A Long Gay Book*, 1932; *Ida, a Novel*, 1941; *Brewsie and Willie*, 1946; *Blood on the Dining-Room Floor*, 1948; *Things as They Are*, 1950 (originally known as *Q.E.D.*); *Mrs. Reynolds and Five Earlier Novelettes, 1931-1942*, 1952; *As Fine as Melanctha*, 1954; *A Novel of Thank You*, 1958.

PLAYS: *Geography and Plays*, pb. 1922; *Operas and Plays*, pb. 1932; *Four Saints in Three Acts*, pr., pb. 1934; *In Savoy: Or, Yes Is for a Very Young Man (A Play of the Resistance in France)*, pr., pb. 1946; *The Mother of Us All*, pr. 1947 (opera); *Last Operas and Plays*, pb. 1949; *In a Garden: An Opera in One Act*, pb. 1951; *Lucretia Borgia*, pb. 1968; *Selected Operas and Plays*, pb. 1970.

NONFICTION: "Composition as Explanation," 1926; *How to Write*, 1931; *The Autobiography of Alice B. Toklas*, 1933; *Matisse, Picasso, and Gertrude Stein, with Two Shorter Stories*, 1933; *Portraits and Prayers*, 1934; *Lectures in America*, 1935; *Narration: Four Lectures*, 1935; *The Geographical History of America*, 1936; *Everybody's Autobiography*, 1937; *Picasso*, 1938; *Paris France*, 1940; *What Are Masterpieces?*, 1940; *Wars I Have Seen*, 1945; *Four in America*, 1947; *Reflections on the Atomic Bomb*, 1973; *How Writing Is Written*, 1974.

CHILDREN'S LITERATURE: *The World Is Round*, 1939.

MISCELLANEOUS: *The Gertrude Stein First Reader and Three Plays*, 1946; *The Yale Edition of the Unpublished Writings of Gertrude Stein*, 1951-1958

(8 vols.; Carl Van Vechten, editor); *Selected Writings of Gertrude Stein*, 1962;

Bibliography

Bloom, Harold, ed. *Modern Critical Views: Gertrude Stein*. New York: Chelsea House, 1986. Bloom's perceptive introduction to this collection of critical essays, as well as chapters from a number of full-length studies of Stein's work, describes her as the greatest master of dissociative rhetoric in modern writing. The essays, written by leading Stein scholars, deal with biographical as well as feminist, intellectual, and physical issues. Concludes with a useful chronology of Stein's life and work.

Bridgman, Richard. *Gertrude Stein in Pieces*. New York: Oxford University Press, 1970. This lengthy work is one of the most valuable assessments of Stein's achievement in modern times. Bridgman's study, essentially a biography, discusses each of Stein's works chronologically and analyzes them in the context of her personal life. Vastly informative, objective, and crucial to any preliminary reading. Includes a bibliography and appendices.

Curnutt, Kirk, ed. *The Critical Response to Gertrude Stein*. Westport, Conn.: Greenwood Press, 2000. While including quintessential pieces on Stein by Carl Van Vechten, William Carlos Williams, and Katherine Anne Porter, this guide to her critical reception also includes previously obscure estimations from contemporaries such as H. L. Mencken, Mina Loy, and Conrad Aiken.

DeKoven, Marianne. *A Different Language: Gertrude Stein's Experimental Writing*. Madison: University of Wisconsin Press, 1983. In this relatively brief work, the author reads Stein's work chronologically through its major periods and devises "genres" such as "lively words," "voices and plays," "melody," and "landscape" to describe her experimental forms. Viewing the incoherence and unrestrictive play in the writing as essentially positive forces, DeKoven argues that Stein's writing successfully overcame conventional expectations of meaning and form. Contains notes and an index.

Dubnick, Randa. *The Structure of Obscurity: Gertrude Stein, Language, and Cubism*. Urbana: University of Illinois Press, 1984. Dubnick's interdisciplinary study deals not only with Gertrude Stein but also with cubism, structuralism, and semiotics. The author distinguishes between Stein's prose (genuine cubism), which exaggerates syntax and minimizes vocabulary, and poetry (synthetic cubism), which abbreviates syntax and extends vocabulary. Includes a bibliography.

Gass, William H. "Gertrude Stein: Her Escape from Protective Language." In *Fiction and the Figures of Life*. New York: Alfred A. Knopf, 1970. In a brilliant assessment of Stein's writing, in particular her use of language, Gass presents a rigorous defense of Stein's intellectual reach. Convincingly examines why she was first wrongly and uncritically admired, then censured by many without reason.

Kellner, Bruce. *A Gertrude Stein Companion: Content with Example*. Westport, Conn.: Greenwood Press, 1988. This lengthy and exhaustive study on Stein's life and work introduces the novice and the somewhat conversant reader to a variety of sources for approaching Stein's work. An insightful introduction titled "How to Read Gertrude Stein," is followed by a series of critical essays on her writing, a bibliography of her published writing, biographical sketches of her most prominent friends and acquaintances, as well as her observations on a variety of subjects. Contains an annotated bibliography and numerous illustrations.

Neuman, Shirley, and Ira B. Nadel, eds. *Gertrude Stein and the Making of Literature*. New York: Macmillan, 1988. These essays by eleven Stein scholars provide new approaches and perspectives on the full range of her work. Includes modernist and postmodernist theory and practice, explications of little-read works, and assessments of the process of composition from notebook to manuscript to printed page. The wide variety in subject matter makes this a valuable addition to Stein's criticism.

Simon, Linda. *Gertrude Stein Remembered*. Lincoln: University of Nebraska Press, 1994. Consists of short memoirs of the modernist writer by her colleagues and contemporaries. Selections include pieces by Daniel-Henri Kahnweiler, Sylvia Beach, Sherwood Anderson, Cecil Beaton, and Eric Sevareid, who offer intimate and often informal views of Stein. She is portrayed not just as an influential avant-garde writer but also as a young student at Radcliffe, visionary art collector, hostess, friend, and photographic subject.

Peter Carravetta;
bibliography updated by the editors

Gerald Stern

Born: Pittsburgh, Pennsylvania; February 22, 1925

Principal poetry

The Pineys, 1969
The Naming of Beasts and Other Poems, 1973
Rejoicings, 1973
Lucky Life, 1977
The Red Coal, 1981
Father Guzman, 1982
Paradise Poems, 1984
Lovesick: Poems, 1987
Learning Another Kingdom: Selected Poems, 1990
Two Long Poems, 1990
Bread Without Sugar, 1992
Odd Mercy, 1995
This Time: New and Selected Poems, 1998
Last Blue: Poems, 2001

Other literary forms

While Gerald Stern is known almost primarily as a poet, he has also written a number of perceptive essays.

Achievements

Stern's poetic achievements have been recognized by four National Endowment for the Arts grants, the Melville Caine Award (for *The Red Coal*), the Bernard F. Conners and Bess Hokin Awards, the Ruth Lilly Prize, and fellowships from the Guggenheim Foundation and the Academy of American Poets. *Lucky Life* was the Lamont Poetry Selection, *Bread Without Sugar* won the Paterson Prize, and *This Time* was honored with the National Book Award.

Biography

Born in 1925 into a second-generation Jewish family, Gerald Stern grew up in Pittsburgh. He earned a B.A. from the University of Pittsburgh, an M.A. from Columbia University, and did additional graduate work at the University of Paris. Stern began his working career as an English teacher and a principal. After spending a number of years in Europe, mainly Paris and London, during the 1950's (though with a stint as an English teacher in Glasgow, Scotland), he returned to the United States and began teaching at Temple University in 1957. He also taught at the University of Pennsylvania, Indiana University of Pennsylvania, Somerset County College in New Jersey, and (beginning in 1982) at the University of Iowa. Until his retirement, Stern would divide his time between his home in eastern Pennsylvania and the Writers' Workshop of the University of Iowa, where he was a professor of English. After retirement, he maintained a hectic schedule of readings and workshops while living in both Easton, Pennsylvania, and New York City. Relocating to Lambertville, New Jersey, Stern was named New Jersey's state poet in 2000.

Analysis

Unlike the poems of many of his contemporaries, those of Gerald Stern explode upon the reader's attention with high and impassioned rhetoric. The poems seem to tumble forward like trees in a flood, snaring, collecting, and finally sweeping subject matter one would have thought only peripherally connected to the main thrust. By using an engaging conversational tone, combined with the frequent use of repetition to sweep together myriad details, Stern's poems display a direct link to the poetics of Walt Whitman. Moreover, a psalmist's zest for parallelism and anaphora discloses a debt to biblical poetry and reinforces the pervasively spiritual, specifically Jewish, sensibility of Stern's work. His frequent use of surrealistic images, meanwhile, reveals a debt to twentieth century Spanish poets, and his love of humble specifics shows him to be a descendant of Ezra Pound and William Carlos Williams. The poems are, among other things, evidence of an immense curiosity about life set against the depersonalizing matrix of twentieth century history.

Eschewing the drift toward, on the one hand, hermeticism, and, on the other, the poetry of confession, Stern's poems, by capitalizing on many of the features of "open" poetry (in various of its historical incarnations), have shown a way for poetry to become equal to the task of transforming both memory and modern history into art. Although it is but one way, Stern's poetic is both stimulating and eminently suitable for representing and interpreting the variety of American life in a way that encompasses both the tragic and the humorous in its fabric.

Gerald Stern

Rejoicings

Rejoicings announces most of the themes and much of the style of Gerald Stern's subsequent, better-known work. Already present are the tutelary spirits who people his later poems and the tension between his love of "high" culture as represented by various philosophers and poets, all heroes of the intellect and art, and his yearning for spontaneity and the "natural," represented by home-grown resources, as in "Immanuel Kant and the Hopi":

> I am going to write twenty poems about my ruined
>   country,
>   Please forgive me, my old friends,
> I am walking in the direction of the Hopi!
> I am walking in the direction of Immanuel Kant!
> I am learning to save my thoughts—like
> one of the Dravidians—so that nothing will
> be lost, nothing I tramp upon, nothing I
> chew, nothing I remember.

While holding most of the Western intellectual tradition in high respect, Stern equally holds its neglect of emotion, intuition, and experience to be responsible for much of the misery to which human beings are taught to accommodate themselves. Thus, many of the poems in the collection have an aspect of unlearning about them, even as they continue to extol the finer mentors of Western tradition. Others look for a "third" way somehow to be negotiated between the mind/body dichotomy, as in "By Coming to New Jersey":

> By coming to New Jersey I have discovered the third
>   world
> that hangs between Woodbridge Avenue and Victory
>   Bridge.
> It is a temporary world,
> full of construction and water holes,
> full of barriers and isolated hydrants . . .

The "third world" of experience is one to which he will return again and again, finding it populated with all the things that are of little consequence to the heave of civilization: birds, flowers, weeds, bugs, and the like, as well as human detritus—the junkyards of America, superseded and yet everywhere visible as testimonials to other dimensions of life.

Lucky Life

Although Stern had been publishing steadily for many years, the publication in 1977 of *Lucky Life* proved to be a watershed in his career. Expansive and ebullient, slyly melodramatic and hyperbolic (whether depicting the tragic, the nostalgic, or the mundane) but always wonderfully readable, the poems appeared during a period when the loose aesthetic of the 1960's had been exhausted, and the predictable return to formalism was just getting under way. The book seemed in some ways to partake of neither, though this is only a partial truth, for the poems are certainly more informed by the openness of the 1960's than by the subsequent swing the other way. By reaching back, through Whitman, to the psalmists, and imbuing the various techniques of poetic repetition with a dizzying parade of disjunctive images, emotional outbursts, jeremiads, and tender soliloquies, *Lucky Life* seemed to point the way to a new kind of democratic poetry, a kind of Whitman modernized and extended: "I am going to carry my bed into New York City tonight/ complete with dangling sheets and ripped blankets;/ I am going to push it across three dark highways/ or coast along under 600,000 faint stars."

Just as Whitman found American possibility teeming in New York, Stern, a century and a half later, locates it in the moral imperative to preserve its authentic and unrepeatable artifacts (as well as the national character that went into making them), as in "Straus Park":

> . . . if you yourself go crazy when you walk through
> the old shell
> on Stout's Valley Road,
> then you must know how I felt when I saw Stanley's
> Cafeteria
> boarded up and the sale sign out . . .

To this he opposes "California," that state of mind "with its big rotting sun": "Don't go to California yet!/ Come with me to Stanley's and spend your life/ weeping in the small park on 106th Street." California is not a state of mind but a fact of life—to some, an ideal (to the poet, the wrong one). Still, it is possible to carry some of Stanley's memories even to California: "Take the iron fence with you/ when you go into the desert./ . . . Do not burn again for nothing./ Do not cry out again in clumsiness and shame."

The feeling for nostalgic way stations, for what, in a more somber locution, is sometimes called tradition, informs the poet's subject matter in a personal but dynamic way that is nevertheless always under threat by the rise of anonymity, conformity, and the pervasiveness of substitutes. These poems, then, are atavistic expressions of grief and longing for the return of the authentic: "What would you give for your dream/ to be as clear and simple as it was then/ in the dark afternoons, at the old scarred tables?" Characteristically, the poet often identifies this longing and grief with his Jewishness, as when he stops to examine road kill in "Behaving Like a Jew": "I am going to be unappeased at the opossum's death./ I am going to behave like a Jew/ and touch his face, and stare into his eyes,/ and pull him off the road." Led by a detour to a dilapidated coffeehouse called (the poem's title) "This Is It" ("the first condemned building in the United States"), the poet talks to its owner, a "coughing lady," and commiserates with her over the collapse of the neighborhood. He listens to the stories of her youth, about her dog "and its monotonous existence," and proclaims, "Everyone is into my myth! The whole countryside/ is studying weeds, collecting sadness, dreaming/ of odd connections."

Sometimes, Stern begins his nostalgia on an ironic note before devolving into seriousness, as in "If You Forget the Germans":

> If you forget the Germans climbing up and down the
> Acropolis,
> then I will forget the poet falling through his rotten
> floor in New Brunswick;
> and if you stop telling me about your civilization in
> 1400 B.C.,
> then I will stop telling you about mine in 1750 and
> 1820 and 1935 . . .

After a list of such playful give-and-take, the poet shifts key: "Here are the thoughts I have had;/ here are the people I have talked to and worn out;/ here are the stops in my throat." The real theme—the search for happiness amid the ubiquity of details and through the murderous lurch of time—is discovered in a journey into the poet's own typically broken past, narrated in a mock travelogue ("If you go by bus . . ."). Yet after a series of perplexing directions, he admonishes, "Do not bury yourself outright in the litter." Instead, he says, in an ending that finds echoes in Christian liturgy:

> Sing and cry and kiss in the ruined dining room
> in front of the mirror, in the plush car seat,
> a 1949 or '50, still clean and perfect
> under the black dust and the newspapers,
> as it was when we cruised back and forth all night
> looking for happiness;
> as it was when we lay down and loved in the old darkness.

Happiness is the subject of the title poem: "Lucky life isn't one long string of horrors/ and there are moments of peace, and pleasure, as I lie in between the blows." With age and the accretions of scars and memories, happiness becomes more problematical: "Each year I go down to the island I add/ one more year to the darkness;/ and though I sit up with my dear friends . . ./ after a while they all get lumped together." Announcing that "This year was a crisis," the poet lumbers through memories of past vacations, through dreams of getting lost on South Main Street in a town in New Jersey, of looking for a particular statue of Christopher Columbus, of sitting at a bar listening to World War II veterans, then dreams of himself sitting on a porch "with a whole new set of friends, mostly old and humorless." There follows a burst of apostrophes: "Dear Waves, what will you do for me this year?/ Will you drown out my scream?/ Will you let me rise through the fog?" The poem ends:

> Lucky life is like this. Lucky there is an ocean to
> come to.
> Lucky you can judge yourself in this water.
> Lucky the waves are cold enough to wash out the
> meanness.
> Lucky you can be purified over and over again.

The Red Coal

With the publication of *The Red Coal* in 1981, some critics believed that Stern had fallen into self-imitation and saw the poems as mannered in their style and sometimes bombastic in their treatment of subject matter. For example, the critic for *The New York Times Book Review* asserted, "In poem after poem he sets up for himself some temptation over which he wins a lyrical triumph. The invariability with which he clears those hurdles makes one suspect that the fences have been lowered." A dissenting view, however, would simply note that, in a poem, all triumphs are "lyrical," for in what sense could they be "actual"? Perhaps the insinuation of repetition is the more damaging. While it is true that Stern's poems offer little in the way of stylistic variation, their range is impressive.

Simply to list the place-names and people who gather to Stern's poems like flocking birds is to suggest the presence of a poet with wide cultural affinities and concerns. While all the figures and places could, with skepticism, be seen as a form of name-dropping, it is more likely that they play a totemic role, suggesting whole ranges of other experience anterior to the specific subject matter. Nicolaus Copernicus, Isaac Stern, Jascha Heifetz, Emma Goldman, Eugene V. Debs, Pablo Picasso, Vincent van Gogh, Casimir Pulaski, Galileo, Albert Einstein, Fyodor Dostoevski, Guillaume Apollinaire, Hart Crane, Ezra Pound, Thomas Jefferson, Gustave Flaubert, Wyndham Lewis, Maurice Ravel, Aleksandr Nikolayevich Scriabin, Antonio Vivaldi, Eugene O'Neill, Johann Wolfgang von Goethe—all these and many more haunt the poems like figures in a pantheon.

As for the kind of mind necessary for the poet's—and, by extrapolation, modern man's—survival, Stern compares a model of Galileo's to one of his own in a poem intriguingly titled "I Remember Galileo": "I remember Galileo describing the mind/ as a piece of paper blown around by the wind,/ and I loved the sight of it sticking to a tree/ or jumping into the back seat of a car." At first, he says he watched paper "for years," as if to test the adequacy of the metaphor, but "yesterday I saw the mind was a squirrel caught crossing/ Route 60 between the wheels of a giant truck." The squirrel escapes, but not before "his life [was] shortened by all that terror." The poet decides that "Paper will do in theory," but the alert, capable squirrel, "his whole soul quivering," finishes his mad scramble across the highway and escapes up his "green ungoverned hillside."

Such seizures and terror, often encountered in retrospect, are usually made over to the poet's advantage, as in "The Red Coal," the title poem, whose central image (most likely derived from the biblical story of the infant Moses, who chose Pharaoh's tray of burning embers over a tray of rubies) presides like a second sun over the poet's difficult but intellectually and spiritually formative years traveling with his friend, the poet Jack Gilbert:

> I didn't live in Paris for nothing and walk
> with Jack Gilbert down the wide sidewalks
> thinking of Hart Crane and Apollinaire
>
> and I didn't save the picture of the two of us
> moving through a crowd of stiff Frenchmen
> and put it beside the one of Pound and Williams
>
> unless I wanted to see what coals had done
> to their lives too . . .

The incandescent coal represents the yearning for knowledge, "as if knowledge is what we needed and now/ we have that knowledge." On the other hand, the coal almost certainly guarantees pain for those who would be its avatars: "The tears are . . . what, all along, the red coal had/ in store for us." Yet the tears are not the result of futility or disappointment; they are the liquid registers of experience as it imposes itself upon time, the baffling sea change of the body and mind that puts even the most familiar past at a strange remove: "Sometimes I sit in my blue chair trying to remember/ what it was like in the spring of 1950/ before the burning coal entered my life."

Many of the poems in *The Red Coal* cast a backward look over the poet's life, coming to terms with the effects of his commitment, "getting rid of baggage,/ finding a way to change, or sweeten, my clumsy life." That clumsiness, that self-estrangement, appropriately finds an equivalence, and hence an inward dialogue, with the lowly and dishonored things of the world, from weeds and animals (including insects and spiders) to Emma Goldman inveighing against the tyranny of property and the injustice toward winos whose lives the bright and aggressive world has cast aside. Such pity and commiseration are particularly strong in Stern and at times take on a marked spiritual coloring. In "The Poem of Liberation," the poet observes a large "vegetable garden planted in the rubble/ of a wrecked apartment house, as if to claim/ the spirit back before it could be buried/ in another investment of glass and cement." In "Dear Mole," the title animal is compared to John Ruskin, "always cramming and ramming, spluttering in disgust/ . . . always starting over,/ his head down, his poor soul warbling and wailing." A monkey appears in "For Night to Come":

> All morning we lie
> on our backs, holding hands, listening to birds,
> and making little ant hills in the sand.
> He shakes a little, maybe from the cold,
> maybe a little from memory,
> maybe from dread.

As the day passes, they "watch the stars together/ like the good souls we are,/ a hairy man and a beast/ hugging each other in the white grass."

FATHER GUZMAN

Between his 1981 collection *The Red Coal* and the 1984 *Paradise Poems*, Stern published a book-length dramatic poem, *Father Guzman*. Cast in the form of a half-demented conversation between a savvy fifteen-year-old street urchin and a Maryknoll priest—both prisoners in a South American jail—the poem is an energetic, if at times prosy, political dialogue that touches on the likes of Christopher Columbus, Simón Bolívar, and Abraham Lincoln, by way of Plato, Ovid, Tommaso Campanella, Johann Wolfgang von Goethe and Dante Alighieri. Father Guzman, whose head has just been cracked by rifle-butts of the National Guard, sits in his cell and confronts the taunts of the Boy, a native; from the initial exchange extends an impassioned conversation of forty pages. Foulmouthed and in-the-know, the Boy begins the poem by extolling his hero (Bolívar) and his affiliation (anarchist). Father Guzman replies that in the room where he was beaten were two American policemen carrying looseleaf notebooks. He compares them with flies and suggests that their incarceration is the result of the same oppression:

> You know the common fly
> has 33 million microorganisms
> flourishing in its gut and a half billion more
> swarming over its body and legs? You know
> that Bolivar left to his vice-presidents
> the tasks of pity?

Father Guzman concludes that Bolívar was "a Caesar" and "that the Mellons plan to betray the universe/ that Nelson Rockefeller was an ichneumon and/ David Rockefeller is a house fly." This makes the Boy sit up, and, weakly suggesting that his admiration of Bolívar results from the fact that both were orphans, changes the subject to "Venus, Bolívar's favorite goddess." Father Guzman understands how the mythology of heroes is such that even tyrants and demagogues can appeal to the masses through the lens of "love," a lens capable of distorting everyone equally:

> but I have seen enough,
> of what you call love to last me a lifetime;
> and I have read de Rougement and Goethe,
> but I prefer to talk about this slum
> and the nature of oil capitalism . . .

The Boy, buoyed on the crest of his own puberty, continues unconcerned, by listing his "favorites": Plato, the Ovid of *Amores*, the author of the *Kama Sutra* ("The section on plural intercourse/ really turns me on"), and other *maestros* of love. Father Guzman responds that he would like the Boy to experience the pornographic trenches of New York ("you would love New York City"). He admits that he, too, "wanted to burn [his] seed . . . to die!": "What Raleigh fought for, what the insane Spaniards/ dreamed of for a lifetime. I saw the/ issue of their violent quest." The Boy shifts again ("There is true love in the universe, you know that!/ Think of Dante! Think of the Duke of Windsor") but demurs and admits, "you I love more than my own flesh and blood."

In the second section, Father Guzman asks the Boy, "Why is life/ a joke to you?" The Boy replies that he would simply like to go for a swim and forget about history. Father Guzman interjects: "Listen to me! Without a dream you'd die!/ This slime of ours would fill/ the whole world!" The Boy says that his dream is to live "without misery and sickness and hunger." Father Guzman turns the talk to Utopias and Campanella's *La cittá del sole* (1602; *The City of the Sun*, 1637), saying that he "worship[s] his spirit," but concedes that he does not like "the Caesar Complex . . ./ and all that control, in industry, education, and art,/ control of the mind, even of the heart." The Boy characteristically focuses on the control of the heart and exclaims, "I hate policemen! I can't stand them/ looking at you as if they knew/ what you already had in your pockets." Father Guzman wonders why, "in the whole history of the world/ there have never been two months of kindness?" and steers the talk to his admiration of Charles Fourier, "one of the true madmen of love/ and one of the great enemies of repression." The Boy asks Father Guzman what he believes in, and Guzman replies, "my heart is still old-fashioned and I want/ people to be happy in a world I recognize . . ./ . . . where souls can manage a little . . ./ without shaming themselves in front of the rats and weasels."

In section 3, the Boy puts on a dress and convincingly impersonates Father Guzman's former lover, who explains that she left him "when I saw your sadness and confusion." Dramatizing the ritual in painful detail, the Boy concludes, "There's nothing sadder than talking to the dress." They then act out an exchange between the American ambassador (Guzman) and the president (the Boy). The talk then turns to El Dorado. "Gomez" admits that there is no El Dorado but asserts that the dream is nevertheless a good one because it is idealistic, a kind of Grail. The "Ambassador" explains that in North America there is no such dream and consequently the jails are "like hotels": " . . . They sit there,/ all those priests and rabbis, weeping/ in the hallways, lecturing the police."

"Gomez" shows his machismo by describing tortures that he has invented and tries to justify the graft and nepotism he has installed in his country when the Boy breaks through: "I can't do it! I quit!" Guzman concurs, "I don't know how we started in the first place." Yet the pair play one more charade, with Father Guzman playing the part of Columbus: "I challenge anyone on horseback or foot/ to deny my rights to take this place by force." "Columbus" tells the Boy that he can bring him more than he has ever dreamed. The Boy claims not to understand the meaning of Columbus and wonders if in his cynicism he has been too hard on his country: "After all,/ we've changed, haven't we?" Exhausted by the heat of their encounter, the Boy begins to think of exile, and Father Guzman recommends New York: "Brooklyn's the place for you! I understand/ Flatbush is having a comeback. You could go/ either to Brooklyn College or N.Y.U." The poem ends with both prisoners looking at a star, and Father Guzman makes the comment, "Campanella is probably washing himself/ in the flames. Dante is probably/ explaining the sweetness to Virgil." The Boy replies, "It is a beautiful night. Life is still good./ And full of pleasure—and hope—"

Despite the unconvincing precocity of the Boy and Father Guzman's pervasive profanity, both in thought and in speech, the poem manages to dramatize most of Stern's previous themes: love of pleasure and exploration (as symbolized by poets and philosophers), the striving for justice, sympathy for the downtrodden, and hatred of exploitation and greed, especially that which is institutionalized by politics. It is a bold essay into history, poetry, and psychology, and though one can hear the poet's private voice coming through at times, it marks a welcome change from the Whitman-like first-person poems that so markedly characterize the earlier work.

PARADISE POEMS

In *Paradise Poems*, Stern works to bring his poems to a higher rhetorical pitch and, frequently, a longer format. A deeper, more elegiac strain runs through the poems, and the most notable poems are formal elegies for poets W. H. Auden ("In Memory of W. H. Auden") and Gil Orlovitz ("At Jane's"), the Yiddish actor Luther Adler ("Adler"), the photographer Alfred Stieglitz ("Kissing Stieglitz Goodbye"), and the poet's father ("The Expulsion"). In the elegy for Auden, the younger Stern plays Caliban to Auden's Prospero, as he waits outside for Auden's "carved face to let me in," hoping, like all young poets, to get the master's nod but realizing "that I would have to wait for ten more years/ or maybe twenty more years for the first riches/ to come my way, and knowing that the stick/ of that old Prospero would never rest/ on my poor head. . . ." Though Auden is "dear . . . with his robes/ and his books of magic," Stern understands that "I had to find my own way back, I had to/ free myself, I had to find my own pleasure/ in my own sweet cave, with my own sweet music."

By contrast, "At Jane's" sets the death of the impoverished and neglected poet Orlovitz against Stern's rising success. Orlovitz's death in a New York City street is portrayed as a stylish exit, adding a note of poignancy to his loss: "He fell in the street/ in front of a doorman; oh his death was superb,/ the doorman blew his whistle, Orlovitz climbed/ into a yellow cab, he'd never disappoint/ a doorman."

Stern, meanwhile, finds himself "brooding a little . . . / saying inside/ one of Orlovitz's poems/ going back again/ into the cave." Later, in a contrapuntal image of American-style safety and success, Stern finds himself among the tea-and-chatter of inconsequential, provincial literary life: "I wore my black suit for the reading, I roared/ and whispered through forty poems, I sat like a lamb/ in a mayor's living room, I sat like a dove/ eating cheese and smiling, talking and smiling . . ."

"The Expulsion" alludes to the expulsion from the Garden into history and memory. The paradise here is the "paradise of two," father and son. The expulsion also means coming to terms with the fact and significance of mortality. Stern's father has lived the exile of countless immigrants: memories of the old country, the myriad adjustments and new fittings needed for life in America, the striving for success, and then death—almost a cliché—in Florida. It is, in many ways, a typical life, yet it is horrifyingly disjunctive, with so many losses trailing after it, that death itself is somewhat anticlimactic: "He had/ fifty-eight suits, and a bronze coffin; he lay/ with his upper body showing, a foot of carpet." Yet this life partakes of a paradise that is only revealed with the father's passing: "My father/ and I are leaving Paradise, an angel/ is shouting, my hand is on my mouth." That paradise will now become a fixture of memory and art, a fertile and yet minatory place:

> Our lives are merging, our shoes
> are not that different. The angel is rushing by,
> her lips are curled, there is a coldness, even
> a madness to her, Adam and Eve are roaring,
> the whole thing takes a minute, a few seconds,
> and we are left on somebody's doorstep . . .

Already this paradise is becoming "the secret rooms, the long and brutal corridor/ down which we sometimes shuffle, and sometimes run."

The universality of exile is the theme of "The Same Moon Above Us," perhaps the most interesting poem in the collection. Here, the figure of Ovid, whose exile from Rome began a literary tradition that modern poets as different as Osip Mandelstam and Derek Walcott have found resonant with significance, is superimposed on the figure of a bum, "a man sleeping over the grilles" of New York. The point is to transform the exile into something triumphant, which these poets, to the greater glory of art, were able to do and which the bum, in his way, must also do: "The truth is he has become his own sad poem." When Stern writes "I think in his fifties he learned a new language/ to go with the freezing rain," one does not know whether this refers to the bum or to Ovid. Yet there is no confusion, for the harder one looks at the bum struggling among the garbage, the more Ovid comes into view, and vice versa. The poem is a haunting meditation on displacement and survival by transformation, no doubt the chief theme of this century's most valued poetry.

Lovesick

While Stern has never been bashful about either his ecstasies or his laments, the 1987 volume *Lovesick* explicitly sustains both categories, as the triple pun in the title suggests: that love brings to our attention the priority of life (that is, prior to all, including poetry); that the full acknowledgment of that life by means of our love of it can become a burden—although a blessed one; and that the poet is not afraid to reiterate the "luck" attendant on these seeming truisms. Stern's poems frequently hint that the difference between truisms and the truth is often a matter of perspective, with our century unfortunately specializing in conversions of the latter into the former. This attention to perspective further suggests the pervasive nostalgia for an Old World sensibility, through which the thought of his poems often loops on its way to the subject.

The volume, indeed, begins with a revisionist point of view toward a familiar subject, a dead dog ("The Dog"). The "speaker" is the dog—a persona unattempted by most contemporary poets, though Philip Levine and Thom Gunn come to mind—who moreover negotiates its soliloquy posthumously. Thus, Stern has set forth a potentially bathetic situation that he neatly escapes by turning the tables on the curiosity seeker, who is both the reader (and, by allusion, the speaker in "Behaving Like a Jew") by exposing anthropomorphism for what it is: an attempted escape from our obligation to love the world by coopting it in our own (linguistic) image. Thus, the dog is both knowing and superior, for it can rely on no such escape:

> I hope the dog's way
> doesn't overtake him, one quick push
> barely that, and the mind freed, something else,
> some other thing, to take its place.

The dog's ploy is to ask for a mutual recognition: "great loving stranger, remember/ the death of dogs . . . give me your pity./ How could there be enough?" In doing so, it questions the sophisticated reader's learned disposition to exclude whole categories of emotion by grossly and obtusely dismissing them as "sentimental." This is not to say that Stern wishes to give sentimentality, as it were, a second chance. Rather, his poems serve as ironic reminders that the objects of rationality have taken more than their share of an intensity originally meant for emotion. This is the "pity" that we "naturally" assign to objects of rationality.

By "pity," with its moral overtones, the reader is also meant to understand *sympathy*—or, in Keatsian terms, "negative capability." As with John Keats, Stern's sympathy extends to the nonhuman kingdoms of plant and animal. In fact, Stern may be said to start there, since it is all the more a matter of sympathy to transcend human limitations to celebrate the virtues of the truly "other." In "Bob Summers' Body," Stern conveys this same feeling toward another kind of otherness, as he watches the corpse of a friend being cremated:

> He turned over twice
> and seemed to hang with one hand to the railing
> as if he had to sit up once and scream
> before he reached the flames.

Seeing death in terms of life has the advantage of emboldening us so that thoughts of it do not "make cowards of us all," as Hamlet imagined. In Stern's revision, "there is such horror/ standing before Persephone with a suit on,/ the name of the manufacturer in the lining." Such horror has its humor, too, for humor often follows from a rearrangement of perspective. In the end, though, the death is a "plush darkness," not only naturalized but humanized as well—one might even argue, "accessorized," thanks to the cozy adjective "plush." A similar fellow-feeling arises in "This Was a Wonderful Night," where the poet appears to indulge in innocent, fanciful conversations and matter-of-fact pastimes, until it is clear that all the principal figures with whom the poet interacts are dead:

> This was a wonderful night. I heard the Brahms
> piano quintet, I read a poem by Schiller,
> I read a story, I listened to Gloomy Sunday.
> No one called me, I studied the birthday poem
> of Alvaros de Campos.

Nevertheless, the poet is happy to be "singing/ one or two songs . . . going east and west/ in the new country, my heart forever pounding."

"Steps"

The motion of *Lovesick*, in spite of the trademark forays into the past and into the dimension of the other, is an ascending one, culminating in one of Stern's best poems, "Steps." This poem serves, as well, as the final entry in *Leaving Another Kingdom*, a volume that brings together substantial portions of each of Stern's first five books. Here the poet remembers, and cites his body as testimony to ("I gasp and pant as if I were pulling a mule"), the fact of steps (as well as actual steps) whose climbing took their toll ("The thing about climbing/ is how you give up") in order to return the fact of elevation:

> I gave up on twenty landings,
> I gave up in Paris once, it was impossible,
> you reach a certain point, it is precise,
> you can't go further; sometimes it's shameful, you're in
> the middle of a pair of stairs, you bow
> your head. . . .

Remembering steps in Pittsburgh, in Greece, West Virginia, and elsewhere, the poet knows that the climb, in spite of its real and allegorical exactions, is the only path to the empyreal:

> Imagine Zeus
> in West Virginia, imagine the temple to Hera
> in Vandergrift, P. A. My heart is resting,
> my back feels good, my breathing is easy. I think
> of all my apartments, all that climbing; I reach
> for a goldenrod, I reach for a poppy. . . .

The image of the poppy (which the poet chews in the poem's final line) confers a feeling of restfulness, and serves as a kind of general benediction for the lovesickness, for "the hands/ that held the books, and the face that froze, and the shoulders/ that fought the wind, and the mouth that struggled for air" ("All I Have Are the Tracks").

BREAD WITHOUT SUGAR

Bread Without Sugar justifiably raised Stern's reputation a few more notches. He assured his place as our greatest poet of sentiment and of a qualified nostalgia. Not traditionally religious, his poems continue to express a schmaltzy humanism even while the central persona remains a devout sensualist. He is a great elaborator who finds a language and cadence for the rhythms of imagination and memory. He is a constant questioner and yet a thinker, too. Grieving and arguing are two sides of the Stern dialectic. In "Brain of My Heart," two voices talk to each other and talk through him: "one is tormented / one is full of sappy wisdom." This kind of cheerful self-deflation is part of the continuing Stern charm.

The volume's title poem is a formal elegy, a remembrance of the poet's father that is reminiscent of Allen Ginsberg's "Kaddish," though it is neither as excessively elaborated nor as self-consciously monumental. It opens out, grandly, from the occasion of the graveyard thoughts to offer personal, familial, and cultural ruminations. Unexpected juxtapositions give the poem energy, tension, and wonder.

LATER POEMS

More recent volumes, including the eerily titled *Last Blue*, continue to revel Stern's marvelous instrument, a bittersweet cantorial voice of blissful suffering and unapologetic appetite. The warm, whimsical complexity of "Hot Dog," Stern's much-applauded long poem from *Odd Mercy*, shows that at seventy and beyond, he is just as vigorous and inventive in his art as ever.

Stern's has been one of the more refreshing voices to emerge in American poetry since the 1960's, a voice neither too refined to proclaim its ecstasies nor too decorous to lament its sorrows. Sorrow and ecstasy are, after all, the two horizons of emotional exchange, but they are all too frequently bred or shouldered out of existence by the daily grind, and Stern, a historian of emotions, has clearly sought, throughout his career, to restore them. Because his poems are impatient with limitation, it is perhaps tempting to regard them as the enemies of restraint—restraint by which many believe the gears of civilized life are oiled. One must consider, however, that the battle between freedom and restraint is an ancient contest, and the struggle will doubtless persist as long as human beings exist. Stern's importance will not be decided on the basis of his beliefs but on the strength of his art. The literary son of Whitman yet his own man, Stern has produced an instrument capable of intimating, as perhaps no other contemporary American has, the sheer fullness of life in the twentieth century. That he has not substantially modulated this instrument may be a valid criticism. On the other hand, the persistence with which he repeats his enormous embrace of the world in poem after poem suggests a loyalty to his means that is equal to his loyalty to his vision.

Bibliography

Hillringhouse, Mark. "Gerald Stern: Ten Poems and an Interview." *The American Poetry Review* 13 (March/April, 1984): 19-30. This extensive interview, which took place in 1982, provides a good first-person summary of the career up to, and including, *Paradise Poems*. Stern speaks to specific thematic and compositional features of his poems and to his concerns with biography, the past, Jewish writing, and his relationship to other contemporary poets.

McCorkle, James. *Conversant Essays: Contemporary Poets on Poetry*. Detroit: Wayne State University Press, 1990. Larry Lewis discusses English poetry's preoccupation with the loss of Eden in his essay, "Eden and My Generation." Here Lewis lists Stern's *Lucky Life* as one of the works he says does *not* reflect a fall from Eden. Instead, he sees Stern's *Lucky Life* as rooted in a sense of home and place.

Pinsker, Sanford. "The Poetry of Constant Renewal and Celebration: An Afternoon's Chat with Gerald Stern." *The Missouri Review* 5 (Winter, 1981/1982): 55-67. Reprinted in Pinsker, *Conversations with Contemporary American Writers*. Amsterdam: Costerus, 1985. In this short but valuable interview, which appeared after the publication of Stern's award-winning *Lucky Life*, the poet responds to questions about his relationship to Whitman, Romanticism, and what Pinsker calls "Jewish" Romanticism.

Somerville, Jane. *Making the Light Come: The Poetry of Gerald Stern*. Detroit: Wayne State University Press, 1990. This, the first full-length study of Stern's poetry, pays particular attention to the function of the "eccentric" speaker of the poems—the controlling principle in a "poetry of performance." While acknowledging the role of biography, artistic predecessors, and philosophical sources, Somerville focuses on the function of biblical materials as central to an understanding of Stern's work. The book follows a thematic organization, beginning with Stern's poetic modes, then turns to his treatment of "nostalgia" and, in successive chapters, three elemental roles enacted by the speaker: gardener, rabbi, and angel. The text is supplemented by a bibliography and an index.

Stern, Gerald. "What Is This Poet?" In *What Is a Poet?*, edited by Hank Lazer. Tuscaloosa: University of Alabama Press, 1987. This document, the product of a symposium on contemporary American poetry held at the University of Alabama in 1984, comes close to being a "testament" of the poet's beliefs and is therefore a valuable document for any serious study of Stern's poetry. The poet addresses a wide spectrum of concerns but emphasizes his education as a poet, including his reading of the Romantics (Keats and Percy Bysshe Shelley) and their American counterparts (Ralph Waldo Emerson and especially Whitman), and the Modernists (T. S. Eliot, Crane, and Pound). This essay is especially recommended for those wishing to see the vitality of tradition in a frequently revolutionary poet.

Stitt, Peter. "Gerald Stern: Weeping and Wailing and Singing for Joy." In his *Uncertainty and Plenitude: Five Contemporary American Poets*. Iowa City: University of Iowa Press, 1997. Stitt finds little thematic progress in Stern's career or in the ordering of poems in his books, but rather a body of work that gains its strength and coherence from the force of Stern's personality. Exploring Stern's Whitmanesque techniques, Stitt argues that Stern is less a prosodist than an orchestrator of images and subjects. Stern's buoyant vision discovers holiness in his world, but also much that is cruel and chaotic.

Vinson, James, and D. L. Kirkpatrick, eds. *Contemporary Poets*. 3d ed. New York: St. Martin's Press, 1980. Part of the entry on Stern, by Gaynor F. Bradish, is a statement by the poet in which he chooses "The One Thing in Life" (from *Lucky Life*) to express his artistic position. Bradish describes Stern's poetry as written in the confessional mode and "deeply felt." Notes Stern makes considerable use of repetition for rhetorical effect.

Wojahn, David. "The Red Coal." *Poetry East* 6 (Fall, 1981): 96-102. Describes these poems as investigating the meaning of memory, which is both their strength and their weakness. Notes that Stern's most successful poems are his long ones, which are all the more compelling because of the momentum gained along the way.

David Rigsbee,
updated by Philip K. Jason

Wallace Stevens

Born: Reading, Pennsylvania; October 2, 1879
Died: Hartford, Connecticut; August 2, 1955

Principal poetry

Harmonium, 1923, expanded 1931
Ideas of Order, 1935
Owl's Clover, 1936
The Man with the Blue Guitar and Other Poems, 1937
Parts of a World, 1942
Notes Toward a Supreme Fiction, 1942
Esthétique du Mal, 1945
Transport to Summer, 1947
The Auroras of Autumn, 1950
Selected Poems, 1953
The Collected Poems of Wallace Stevens, 1954

Other literary forms

Wallace Stevens's significant achievement is in his poetry, but he did write several experimental one-act verse plays, a number of essays on poetry, and numerous letters and journal notes that contain perceptive comments on his work. In 1916 he published in the magazine *Poetry* his first one-act verse play, *Three Travelers Watch a Sunrise*, for which he received a special prize from *Poetry*; in 1920 the play was performed at the Provincetown Playhouse in New York. A second verse play, *Carlos Among the Candles*, was staged in New York in 1917 and later published, again in *Poetry*. A third play, *Bowl, Cat, and Broomstick*, was produced at the Neighborhood Playhouse in New York in the same year but was never published during the poet's life. Between 1942 and 1951 he gave a series of lectures on poetry at Princeton and other universities, and these were collected in *The Necessary Angel: Essays on Reality and the Imagination* (1951). Later essays, as well as a number of uncollected poems and plays, appeared in *Opus Posthumous* (1957). The poet wrote excellent letters, and his daughter, Holly Stevens, collected and edited the best of them in *Letters of Wallace Stevens* (1966). In *Souvenirs and Prophecies: The Young Wallace Stevens* (1977) she presented important entries from the poet's journal (1898-1914). Focusing upon the relationship between the imagination and reality, Stevens's canon is highly unified; the prose and the plays help illuminate the difficult poetry.

Achievements

Although Wallace Stevens never has had as large an audience as that enjoyed by Robert Frost and did not receive substantial recognition until several years before his death, he is usually considered to be one of the best five or six English-language poets of the twentieth century. *Harmonium* reveals a remarkable style—or, to be more precise, a number of remarkable styles. While critics praised, or more often condemned, the early poetry for its gaudiness, colorful imagery, flamboyant rhetoric, whimsicality, and odd points of view, one also finds in this volume spare Imagist poems as well as abstract philosophical poems which anticipate his later work. The purpose of his rhetorical virtuosity in *Harmonium* and in subsequent volumes was not merely to dazzle the reader but to convey the depth of emotion, the subtle complexity of thought, and the associative processes of the mind.

Strongly influenced by early nineteeth century English poets, Stevens became a modern Romantic who transformed and extended the English Romantic tradition as he accommodated it to the twentieth century world. *Harmonium* and subsequent volumes reveal his assimilation of the innovations of avant-garde painting, music, poetry, and philosophy. One finds in his canon, for example, intimations of Pablo Picasso, Henri Matisse, and Henri Bergson, and of cubism, Impressionism, Imagism, and Symbolism. Such influences were always subordinated to the poet's romantic sensibility, however, which struggled with the central Romantic problem—the need to overcome the gulf between the inner, human reality and outer, objective reality. A secular humanist who rejected traditional Christianity, arcane mysticism, and the pessimism of *The Waste Land* (1922) and the *Cantos* (beginning in 1925), he succeeded as a Romantic poet in the modern world. His contribution to poetry was recognized in 1950 with the award of the Bollingen Prize and in 1955 with the National Book Award and the Pulitzer Prize for *The Collected Poems of*

Wallace Stevens. His reputation has continued to grow since his death in 1955.

Biography

On October 2, 1879, in Reading, Pennsylvania, Wallace Stevens was born to Garrett Barcalow Stevens and the former Margaretha Catherine Zeller. Wallace Stevens's father was a successful attorney who occasionally published poetry and prose in the local papers.

In 1897 Stevens was graduated from Reading Boys High School and enrolled at Harvard as a special student with the ambition to become a writer. He published stories and poetry in the *Harvard Advocate* and the *Harvard Monthly* and became acquainted with the poet and philosopher George Santayana, whose books provided support for his belief that in an agnostic age poetry must assume the role of traditional religion. After completing his special three-year course in English at Harvard, he joined the staff of the *New York Tribune*, but failed as a reporter.

Wallace Stevens (© Bettmann/Corbis)

In the fall of 1901 he entered the New York Law School and, after passing the bar three years later, began legal practice. He was not successful as a practicing attorney, however, and in 1908 he joined the New York office of the American Bonding Company. The next year he married Elsie Moll.

In 1916 Stevens joined the Hartford Accident and Indemnity Company and moved to Hartford, Connecticut, which was to be his permanent residence. He now led a double life. During the day he was a successful businessman, while at night and on weekends he was a poet. Few of his associates in the insurance world knew of his second career. Beginning in 1914 his work had begun to be published in *Poetry* and the other little magazines. At this time he became acquainted with an avant-garde group of writers and artists, including William Carlos Williams, Alfred Kreymborg, and Marcel Duchamp. His involvement in the business world, however, permitted only occasional participation in the activities of literary groups.

In 1923, at the age of forty-four, Stevens published his first volume of poetry. *Harmonium* was largely ignored by the critics, however, and he wrote only a few poems in the next five or six years. In 1924 his only child, Holly, was born, and subsequently he devoted his time to his family and to his business career. In 1931 Alfred A. Knopf reissued *Harmonium*, and in 1934 Stevens was promoted to vice-president of his insurance company. With his business career secure and with *Harmonium* receiving some recognition, he began to write and publish again. By the time *The Auroras of Autumn* appeared in 1950, his reputation had been firmly established. Even after the mandatory retirement age of seventy, he continued to work at his insurance company, and rejected an offer to be the Charles Eliot Norton lecturer at Harvard for the 1955-1956 academic year because he felt that if he accepted he might be forced to retire. He died in 1955, two months before his seventy-sixth birthday.

Analysis

Wallace Stevens frequently alludes to or quotes from the English Romantics in his letters and in his essays, and there is little doubt that this twentieth century poet is working within the Romantic tradition. The best evidence for the contention that he is a twentieth century Romantic, however, is his poetry. Repeatedly, one finds in his work the "reality-imagination complex," as he calls it. While one can see the central beliefs of William Wordsworth and John Keats in Stevens's poetry (celebration of nature, acceptance of mutability, rejection of supernatural realms, and belief in the brotherhood of man), the foundation of his Romanticism is his Wordsworthian imagination. The function of this imagination in Stevens's poetry is to make sordid reality, what Wordsworth calls "the dreary intercourse of daily life," palatable without resorting to mysticism. It is a difficult task; failure results in a profound alienation ("dejection" in the language of the Romantics).

Stevens does not merely repeat what Wordsworth and Keats have accomplished in their work but extends the Romantic tradition. He differs from his predecessors in his radical nontranscendentalism. In a May 30, 1910, letter to his wife he quotes from Keats's "Epistle to John Hamilton Reynolds": "It is a flaw/ In happiness, to see beyond our bourn,—/ It forces us in summer skies to mourn,/ It spoils the singing of the Nightingale." This idea is the premise of all Stevens's work. He takes the secular Romanticism of Wordsworth and Keats to its logical conclusion.

"Of Modern Poetry"

Stevens's poem "Of Modern Poetry" provides a good introduction to both his theory and his method. The modern poem whose origin goes back to the discursive odes of Wordsworth and Keats is "the poem of the mind in the act of finding/ What will suffice." This modern meditation shows the process of the mind confronting reality, searching for a secular solution to the individual person's feeling of meaninglessness. Before the Romantic period (1789-1832) this was not a major problem, and thus there was no need for this type of meditation. Or, as Stevens says: "It has not always had/ To find: the scene was set; it repeated what/ Was in the script." Now the poet ("the actor") is "a metaphysician in the dark," the man of vital imagination who seeks to redeem ugly reality and overcome his alienation by secular meditation. It is a meditation which will not descend to negation or ascend to supernaturalism ("below which it cannot descend,/ Beyond which it has no will to rise").

The meditation utilizes conversational speech, "the real language of men," as Wordsworth says in the preface to the *Lyrical Ballads* (1800), or the "speech of the place," as Stevens states here, and seeks its affirmation in everyday reality. Yet this "poem of the act of the mind" may create heightened moments in everyday reality, "spots of time," as Wordsworth calls them in *The Prelude* (1850). It is these "spots of time" that often allow the imagination to redeem reality by ordering it, enchanting it, transforming it, or creating a feeling of stasis, of permanence beyond time. By these heightened moments and by the process of the meditation itself, the imagination strives to rectify the individual's sense of loss.

In short, Stevens expands the Wordsworthian-Keatsian discursive act of the mind in a radical fashion. In a number of his acts of the mind the only unifying element is the solitary mind searching for what will suffice to ease its alienation. In these acts of the mind the imagination can create moments of illumination which help regenerate the poet—and regeneration is the central goal of modern meditations, those "poems of our climate."

"Poems of Our Climate"

"Poems of Our Climate" reveals the function and limitation of a spot of time in a secular Romantic meditation. In the first six lines of the poem the mind seizes a specific, seemingly ordinary moment and freezes it into a timeless moment, reminiscent of the stasis in the beginning of "Ode on a Grecian Urn." Unlike Keats, however, Stevens does not linger over this moment that the imagination has endowed with meaning. He does not wait until the fourth stanza to grow disenchanted but instinctively feels that this cannot be a permanent state—"one desires/ So much more than that." The evanescent and heightened quality of the frozen moment ("The light/ In the room more like a snowy air,/ Reflecting snow") immediately becomes the monotony of "Cold, a cold porcelain, low and round,/ With nothing more than the carnations there."

Stevens must reject this "cold pastoral" because one needs more than purity ("this complete simplicity").

One does not want to be stripped of all his "torments." The vital individual (the "vital I") is "evilly compounded"—an identity forged out of a world of pains and troubles, of good and evil experience.

The spot of time is a temporary relief from the banality or ugliness of reality, but it cannot be a permanent state. The "never-resting mind" always feels the compulsion to return to reality to remeditate and recompose it. "The imperfect is our paradise" might be Stevens's twentieth century reformulation of Keats's essential feeling in "Ode on Melancholy." Like Keats, he is ambivalent—both bitter and delighted over man's existence. Instinctively he desires to escape to an ideal state, but intellectually he realizes the impossibility of doing so. Man finds meaning only in human reality, which is by definition imperfect. Strip life of its torments and it becomes banality; conceal the dark side of existence or the "evil" aspects of one's nature and vitality is erased. Pure stasis untainted by life would be meaningless, and an art that mirrored this would be meaningless too. Stevens believes that art should express pain, struggle, and conflict, and thus he prefers the modern poets of "flawed words and stubborn sounds" to the "bawds of euphony." Stevens's poetry is a continual search; it is a continual oscillation between the depths of depression and heightened moments of affirmation. "[The mind] can never be satisfied, the mind, never" concludes Stevens in "The Well Dressed Man with a Beard."

"Large Red Man Reading" and "Disillusionment of Ten O'Clock"

Stevens sees external reality as the Other outside the self. "Large Red Man Reading" is a poem that reveals the crucial importance of the regenerative capacity of the imagination and the need to embrace the everyday world and reject the supernatural. As he seeks to reconcile himself to an earthly reality devoid of supernatural inclinations, Stevens contrasts the vital man of imagination (the large red man reading) with those who are "dead" to the imagination, "the ghosts." Ghosts as symbolic of those dead to the imaginative life occur elsewhere in his work. In "Disillusionment of Ten O'Clock," for example, Stevens complains that "the houses are haunted/ By white night-gowns" who do not "dream" (that is, imagine) of catching tigers "in red weather," as an old sailor does. In the ghostly realms of the modern world life is colorless—a dreary intercourse of daily life without imagination. In "Large Red Man Reading" the ghosts seem to recognize that a life without the imaginative interaction between the mind and reality is worthless. After leading a dull life on earth, they had hoped to find their paradise in heaven, but they have become dissatisfied with heaven ("the wilderness of stars") and returned to earth. They returned to hear the "large red man reading," for he is the vital individual of the imagination, a true giant in a paltry age. (Reading and study symbolize meditation, or the life of the imagination, in Stevens's poetry.)

In the course of the meditation it becomes clear why the ghosts have returned to earth. Heaven lacked the reality of earthly existence, its joys and its torments. The ghosts want to hear the large red man read from the "poem of life" in all its prosaic beauty and banality—"the pans above the stove, the pots on the table, the tulips among them." In contrast to the mythic abstraction of heaven, the ghosts would eagerly reach out for any sensory knowledge ("They were those that would have wept to step barefoot into reality"), even though this knowledge might mean pain ("run fingers over leaves/ And against the most coiled thorn") as well as pleasure. Stevens has mocked, with good-natured humor, the traditional belief that people desire to go to a paradisiacal heaven after dissatisfaction with the sinful, painful life on earth. The ghosts return to earth for the true paradise of an ever-changing sensuous reality ("being") heightened by the imagination ("reading").

The imagination

The imagination's attempt to redeem reality is, however, not always completely successful—stalemate or even defeat are possibilities. Stevens is a darker poet than the critics have made him out to be—despite the fact that modern criticism has largely overcome the once popular cliché of the insouciant hedonist of impressionistic, pictorial poems. Often his poems of naturalistic celebration end on a tentative note of affirmation, for the ugly side of reality is an able match for the imagination; the mind can never completely transform reality into something purely positive. Furthermore, in a significant number of his acts of the mind, a sense of loss threatens to dominate. It is in these poems of "the whole of Harmonium," as he would have preferred to call his canon, that one finds a profound sense of loss ("the burden of the mystery," as both Wordsworth and Keats called it) as the very genesis of the work. In these works the imagination must grapple with "dejection," ascertain its causes or roots, and seek to resolve it as far as possible. These meditations of Stevens's are different from his others only in degree. Here, however, the imagination does not appear as potent as in his other acts, and spots of time do not seem to have the intensity, or the frequency, that one finds in his other meditations.

Stevens does not have only one attitude toward this sense of loss—and certainly not one type of "dejection" poem. His imagination takes a variety of forms and attitudes. It is probably a mistake to stress a chronological development in his attitude toward the burden of the mystery, although a case might be made for some lessening of humor and flamboyance and a gradual movement toward an autumnal tone during his career. Instead, one should stress the variety and complexity of his responses. To show that his attitude toward the problem is much more complex than is usually thought, one must examine several of his poems, from his earliest to those written just before his death. Finally, it will also become clear that despite the sophistication of his responses to the problem, he was always a secular romantic who rejected the leap into transcendence and refused to submit to existential despair.

"Sunday Morning"

At the heart of "Sunday Morning" (1915) is a profound sense of loss, evoked by abandonment of traditional religious belief. Modern human beings can no longer justify suffering and death with Christian certitudes. This complicated meditative poem struggles with the problem at length, pondering questions that are central to Stevens's work. How does one dispel his anxiety when he realizes that all past mythologies are irrelevant? If there is no afterlife, how does one come to terms with death? Even as Keats did, Stevens overcomes his desire for the supernatural and puts his faith in humanist values.

"In the very Temple of Delight/ Veiled Melancholy has her sovran shrine," Keats had proclaimed in "Ode on Melancholy," and Stevens more vehemently reiterates this idea that life is process and there can be no separation of opposites, no separation of pleasure and pain. "Death is the mother of beauty," Stevens's speaker twice asserts in the course of the meditation. The very transiency of things makes them valuable; paradoxically, it is death that makes things beautiful. Stanza VI, reminiscent of Keats's "Ode on a Grecian Urn," shows that a heaven without mortality is a false paradise devoid of life. "Does ripe fruit never fall?" asks the frustrated speaker. The boughs will always hang heavy with fruit in "that perfect sky," and we can only "pick the strings of our insipid lutes" in this monotonous heaven, just as Keats's boughs will never shed their leaves and his bold lovers will always remain in the frustrating position of being poised over each other in the first stage of their lovemaking, a lovemaking of perpetual anticipation, not consummation.

Stevens believes that death is necessary for a true paradise because life can be enjoyed only when there are cycles of desire and fulfillment or disappointment. Death also has some positive value because it makes man aware of his common humanity, what Stevens significantly calls "heavenly fellowship." Wordsworth, in "Lines Composed a Few Miles Above Tintern Abbey" and "Ode: Intimations of Immortality from Recollections of Early Childhood," had expressed similar sentiments, but Stevens's attitude is more extreme. He supposes that the rejection of God results in a world that is intrinsically meaningless, whereupon one realizes that one must return to man as the only source of value.

"Sunday Morning" presents, in short, a radical humanism that Wordsworth and Keats had anticipated a century earlier. Instead of religion ("the thought of heaven") Stevens offers naturalistic reality, the "beauty of the earth." A person's emotional contact with nature is a substitute for rituals performed before an invisible deity. The only immortality that has any meaning for modern human beings, the poet argues, is the permanence of nature as felt in the seasonal cycle—nothing endures as "April's green endures." Depression and disillusionment are as natural as joy and hope, and memory of these opposite feelings helps form one's "soul" or identity. Echoing Keats, Stevens suggests that "all pleasures and all pains" are involved in one's responses to nature. In short, one's intense responses to external reality are "measures destined" for the "soul."

"A Postcard from the Volcano"

"A Postcard from the Volcano" (1936) is a meditation with a profound sense of loss at its foundation; about the precise nature of this loss, however, there is no critical agreement. The poem is as perplexing and intriguing as its bizarre title; to understand it, one must account for the sense of loss and explain the shift of tone at the end of the work.

"A Postcard from the Volcano" is divided into two parts by the ellipsis. The first part presents the problem: The poet feels dejected because he realizes that after his death the imaginative expression of his life in poetry will seem foreign to the new generation. The poet will have become an irrelevant ghost, such as Stevens has elsewhere mocked as the antithesis of the vital life of the imagination. The world of the past, especially that world interpreted by the poet's imagination, will become meaningless to the children of the present.

They will "pick up our bones" but will never be able to comprehend that these once had vitality and a keen sense of participation in the moment ("that these were once/ As quick as foxes on the hill"). They will not be able to perceive the impact of the past on the present, or realize how one can change his world through the manipulations of language. "We knew for long the mansion's look/ And what we said of it became/ A part of what it is."

Stevens pauses in his meditation. The pause seems to give birth to a new feeling—a change finally occurs when the mind swerves away from its dejection to a reconciling thought in the last two lines. Admittedly, the children ("still weaving budded aureoles") will have an innocent view of reality in which everything is viewed one-dimensionally. They will reiterate the poet's meditations and never comprehend his vision. They will say of his world that it seems "As if he that lived there left behind/ A spirit storming in blank walls,/ A dirty house in a gutted world"—they will see the poet as a mere ghost ranting without an audience. Yet Stevens's meditation shifts in the last two lines to a partial reconciliation. While the poet's vision will seem irrelevant and "run down" to the children, it will also be one with "A tatter of shadows peaked to white,/ Smeared with the gold of the opulent sun." That is, they will feel intuitively some of the vitality of the dead poet's vision. They will not intellectually understand the world of the past (it will be a "shadow" to them), but some of the remnants of the past will seem "smeared with the gold of the opulent sun" and consequently reveal the vitalistic imagination of the dead poet.

"The Course of a Particular"

In "The Course of a Particular" (1951) Stevens presents a bleak winter landscape. The speaker in this matter-of-fact meditation does not appear to be much concerned with the "nothingness of winter." In fact, the speaker seems to be intellectually aware of the sense of loss but to remain emotionally tranquil, as if he had become accustomed to it. While the nothingness of the winter landscape becomes a "little less" because the poet can accept it more each day, he still feels he should try to humanize the sense of loss. He tries and then pauses. The attempt is half-hearted—"there is a resistance involved."

The humanizing metaphor of the crying leaves does not make the scene more human or more real to him. He tries to imagine harshness and the human responses to it, but the attempt does not work. Stevens discovers here that he cannot rewrite Percy Bysshe Shelley's "Ode to the West Wind" in the 1950's. All he feels is a dull monotonous winter scene; he cannot despair over a cold, inanimate universe. In "Sunday Morning" the separation of the self from nature was the cause for alienation, but now Stevens simply takes the separation for granted. He cannot pretend to be part of nature, even for a moment; if he says he is part of nature he immediately feels "resistance." He can no longer make the effort. Instead of attempting ennobling interchange of the imagination and reality, he concentrates on the particulars of reality before him. Winter is merely winter, wind-blown trees, snow, and ice.

In the final two stanzas the poet tries to transform the scene, but the cry of the leaves has no supernatural ("divine") significance, nor mythic ("puffed out heroes") significance, nor human significance. The "crying" leaves are simply leaves being blown by the wind; they do not transcend their phenomenological meaning. To imagine them crying is unsatisfactory. Finally, the poet asserts that the cry is simply the shrill winter wind and concerns no one at all. The poet has accepted the nothingness of modern life; the cry of the leaves does not symbolize a sense of loss but is simply another detail of reality.

"FAREWELL WITHOUT A GUITAR"

The sense of loss in "Farewell Without a Guitar" (1954) is subdued. In lesser hands, this poem would have quickly degenerated into sentimental melancholy or nostalgia. Yet Stevens, with his few spare images, evokes a genuine feeling; like Hemingway, he expresses the most elemental emotions by cutting language to the bone. To do otherwise would be to luxuriate in an excess of emotion.

In "Farewell Without a Guitar," he suggests that things have come to their natural finale. While there is a sense of loss, there is also a sense of completion and fulfillment implicit in the meditation. The poem is so titled because Stevens's farewell is not accompanied by the music of lush poetry. Loss (and acceptance of it) is evoked without gaudy imaginative embellishment.

The paradise of spring yields to the autumnal terminal—youth to death, gaudy exuberance to spare imagism, celebration to farewell. Autumn is described as "The thousand leaved red," suggesting its beauty and naturalness, not the desolation of bare trees and cold, lifeless days. "Thunder of light" in the second stanza presages the storm of the third stanza and suggests that this storm is a virile one, one of power, not enervation. The oxymoronic metaphor might also suggest a heightened consciousness of reality, a consciousness that occurs when one comes to the end of life. The riderless horse is an apt image for the symbolic death of the man of imagination, the end of the poet's career. Stevens had previously symbolized the romantic poet, or the man of imagination, as "a youth, a lover with phosphorescent hair,/ Dressed poorly, arrogant of his streaming forces," who on his horse madly passes by the literal-minded Mrs. Alfred Uruguay ("Her no and no made yes impossible") on her slow donkey.

There will be no more imaginative excursions now. Only memories and past acts of the mind remain. Yet this activity of the mind and the memory of the past sensory contact with reality ("The blows and buffets of fresh senses/ Of the rider that was") now seem to form "a final construction"—a kind of spot of time that serves as the only immortality one can know. Sensuous reality in the present is heightened by this "construction"—a construction created out of the interchange of past sensuous reality ("male reality"), the imagination ("that other"), and the instinct for affirmation of the romantic poet ("her desire").

The autumnal sense of loss, rooted in Stevens's realization that he has come to the end of his career, is really transformed into an acceptance of loss, the celebration of his own farewell; it is reminiscent of Keats's "To Autumn." Reality is viewed in its most sensuous aspects, and affirmed. Reality had also been accepted in "The Course of a Particular," but it hardly appeared positive there. In contrast, in Stevens's final poems, mere existence ("mere being" or a life of process) is accepted and found affirmative.

Stevens differs from most twentieth century poets in his romantic faith in the power of the imagination to affirm mundane reality, or at least to make it palatable. He sees the imagination as the source of man's salvation in a godless world. Tough-minded and skeptical, he is not the kind of Romantic abhorred by T. E. Hulme, Ezra Pound, and the Imagists. He is not a visionary Romantic in pursuit of transcendent realms; he believes that the modern poet can reside only in the everyday world.

In his book of essays *The Necessary Angel* (1951), he states that the poet must avoid "the hieratic" and must "move in the direction of the credible." Without completely immersing himself in a sordid everyday world or escaping to an ideal world, the twentieth century romantic strives for the necessary balance between the imagination and reality. In his Preface to William Carlos Williams's *Collected Poems, 1921-1931*, reprinted in *Opus Posthumous* (1957), Stevens gives the best description of the "romantic poet nowadays": "he is the hermit who dwells alone with the sun and moon, but insists on taking a rotten newspaper."

OTHER MAJOR WORKS

PLAYS: *Three Travelers Watch a Sunrise*, pb. 1916, pr. 1920; *Carlos Among the Candles*, pr. 1917; *Bowl, Cat, and Broomstick*, pr. 1917.

NONFICTION: *The Necessary Angel: Essays on Reality and the Imagination*, 1951; *Letters of Wallace Stevens*, 1966; *Souvenirs and Prophecies: The Young Wallace Stevens*, 1977.

MISCELLANEOUS: *Opus Posthumous*, 1957 (Samuel French Morse, editor).

BIBLIOGRAPHY

Bates, Milton J. *Wallace Stevens: A Mythology of Self.* Berkeley: University of California Press, 1985. A study of Stevens's life and works that attempts to show how he transformed his biography into a "fable of identity." Bates traces several "selves" found in the poems. This readable, biographical approach to studying the poems discusses the familial, philosophical, and aesthetic background of the poet. Family papers and letters are used extensively. The parallels between Stevens's life and poetry are excellent in the account of the poet's growth and development.

Bloom, Harold. *Wallace Stevens: The Poems of Our Climate*. Ithaca, N.Y.: Cornell University Press, 1977. This full commentary on almost all Stevens's poetry refers to his precursors such as William Wordsworth, Percy Bysshe Shelley, John Keats, Ralph Waldo Emerson, and especially Walt Whitman. A chapter on American poetics from Emerson to Stevens explores the prevalent themes of fate, freedom, and power. Includes an index of Stevens's work.

Cleghorn, Angus J. *Wallace Stevens' Poetics: The Neglected Rhetoric*. New York: Palgrave, 2000. A study responding to critical misapprehension about *Owl's Clover*, argues that the poem's rhetorical poetics are crucial to understanding Stevens's complete poetry as an ethical challenge to the destructive and rigidly repetitive routes of history.

Kessler, Edward. *Images of Wallace Stevens*. New Brunswick, N.J.: Rutgers University Press, 1972. A study of the significant images in Stevens's poetry in which each chapter focuses on a particular image or group of images: "North and South," "Sun and Moon," "Music and the Sea," and so on. Good bibliographical references are included in the footnotes and a bibliography is included in notes following the text.

Morse, Samuel F. *Wallace Stevens: Poetry as Life*. New York: Pegasus, 1970. This study relates Stevens's life to his poetry and introduces his poetic ideas, theories, and methods. This is the authorized critical biography commissioned by Stevens's widow and daughter. Supplemented by a short select bibliography.

Rehder, Robert M. *The Poetry of Wallace Stevens*. Basingstoke: Macmillan, 1988. A fifty-page biographical introduction is followed by chapters on each of Stevens's major books. This volume is a good introductory study that gives a broad view of the poet's life. It includes extended readings of several of the major poems and comments on Stevens's style, but few references are made to other works on the poet. Much of the biographical material is taken from Peter Brazeau's *Parts of a World* (1983) and Holly Bright Stevens's *Souvenirs and Prophecies* (1976).

Riddel, Joseph. *The Clairvoyant Eye: The Poetry and Poetics of Wallace Stevens*. Baton Rouge: Louisiana State University Press, 1965. This skillful reading of the major poems sees Stevens's view of a poem as an "act of Mind" and portrays the poet as being able to be looked at from several critical postures—particularly philosophical, historical, and structural. The study includes an account of his theory of imagination and how it relates to the changes and developments in his style. Each chapter begins with a commentary on the context of the particular phase under discussion and ends with a reading of one of the major poems.

Sharpe, Tony. *Wallace Stevens: A Literary Life*. New York: St. Martin's Press, 2000. Sharpe explores the symbiotic and antagonistic relations between Stevens's literary life and his working life as a senior executive, outlining the personal, historical, and publishing contexts which shaped his writing career, and suggesting how awareness of these contexts throws new light on the poems.

Vendler, Helen. *On Extended Wings: Wallace Stevens's Longer Poems*. Cambridge, Mass.: Harvard University Press, 1969. Vendler's study concentrates on the problems defined by the poems themselves and not the social, biographical, or historical contexts. Analyzes the longer poems in chronological order and focuses on style, form, and internal evolution.

Allan Chavkin;
bibliography updated by the editors